CHILDREN AND THE LAW:

CASES AND MATERIALS

Second Edition

Martin R. Gardner
Steinhart Foundation Professor of Law
University of Nebraska College of Law

Anne Proffitt Dupre
J. Alton Hosch Professor of Law
University of Georgia School of Law

ISBN#: 0-8205-6410-9

Library of Congress Cataloging-in-Publication Data

Gardner, Martin R.
   Children and the law : cases and materials / Martin R. Gardner, Anne Profitt
Dupree.--
2nd ed.
      p. cm.
   Includes Index.
   ISBN 0-8205-6410-9 (hardbound)
      1. Children--Legal status, laws, etc.--United States--Cases. 2. Parent and child
(Law)--United States--Cases. 3. Juvenile justice, Administration of--United States--
Cases. I. Dupre, Anne Proffitt. II. Title.
KF479.A7G37 2006
346.7301'35--dc22

                                                                    2005037284

Editorial Offices
744 Broad Street, Newark, NJ 07102 (973) 820-2000
201 Mission St., San Francisco, CA 94105-1831 (415) 908-3200
701 East Water Street, Charlottesville, VA 22902-7587 (434) 972-7600
www.lexis.com

DEDICATION

To my dear wife, Anne

M.R.G.

For my husband, William G. Dupre,
my father, George H. Proffitt,
and in memory of my mother, Elizabeth Gates Proffitt

A.P.D.

ACKNOWLEDGMENTS

I wish to express appreciation for the support provided by the Ross McCollum Research Fund at the University of Nebraska, College of Law; for the research assistance of Sam Randall; and for the secretarial support of Vida Eden.

M.R.G.

Heartfelt thanks to my two research assistants, Danielle Logan and Evelyne Kay ("Katie") White, and to my administrative assistant, Cindy Wentworth.

A.P.D.

The authors also thank the following authors and publishers for permission to reprint portions of the following copyrighted material:

Batey, Robert, *The Rights of Adolescents*, 23 Wm. & Mary L. Rev. 363, 364, 370, 373–74, 376, 378–80, 383–84 (1982). Reprinted with permission.

Coons, John E., *Intellectual Liberty and the Schools*, 1 Notre Dame J.L. Ethics & Pub. Pol'y 495, 501–510 (1985). Copyright © 1985 Notre Dame Journal of Law, Ethics & Public Policy, Volume 1, Issue 4. Thomas J. White Center on Law & Government. Reprinted by permission. Further reproduction is strictly prohibited.

Federle, Katherine Hunt, *The Abolition of the Juvenile Court: A Proposal for the Preservation of Children's Rights*, 16 J. Contemp. L. 23, 24, 49–51 (1990). Reprinted with permission.

Feld, Barry C., *Abolish the Juvenile Court: Youthfulness, Criminal Responsibility, and Sentencing Policy*, 88 J. Crim. L. & Criminology 68, 131–36 (1997). Reprinted by special permission of Northwestern University School of Law, *Journal of Criminal Law and Criminology*.

Feld, Barry C., *The Juvenile Court Meets the Principle of Offense: Note Punishment, Treatment, and the Difference It Makes*, 68 B.U. L. Rev. 821, 822–25 (1988). Reprinted with permission.

Feld, Barry C., *The Transformation of the Juvenile Court*, 75 Minn. L. Rev. 691, 722–25 (1991). Reprinted with permission.

Foster, Henry H. & Doris Jonas Freed, *A Bill of Rights for Children*, 6 Fam. L.Q. 343, 344–47 (1972). Copyright © 1972 ABA Publishing. Reprinted by permission.

Gardner, Martin R., *Punishment and Juvenile Justice: A Conceptual Framework for Assessing Constitutional Rights of Youthful Offenders*, 35 Vand. L. Rev. 791, 792–95, 815–16, 817–18 (1982).

Gardner, Martin R., *Punitive Juvenile Justice: Some Observations on a Recent Trend*, 10 INT'L J.L. & PSYCHIATRY 129, 148–51 (1987). Copyright © 1987. Reprinted with permission from Elsevier.

Gregory, John DeWitt, *Juvenile Court Jurisdiction Over Noncriminal Misbehavior: The Argument Against Abolition*, 39 OHIO ST. L. J. 242, 267–72 (1978). Copyright © 1978 The Ohio State University. Originally published in 39 OHIO ST. L. J. 242 (1978). Reprinted with permission.

Hafen, Bruce C., *Children's Liberation and the New Egalitarianism: Some Reservations About Abandoning Youth to Their "Rights"*, 1976 BYU L. REV. 605, 650–51, 656. Reprinted with permission.

Ketcham, Orman W., *Why Jurisdiction Over Status Offenders Should be Eliminated From Juvenile Courts*, 57 B.U. L. REV. 645, 645–55, 661 (1977). Reprinted with permission.

Melton, Gary B., *Toward "Personhood" for Adolescents: Autonomy and Privacy as Values in Public Policy*, 38 AM. PSYCHOL. 99, 99–102 (1983). Copyright © 1983 by the American Psychological Association. Reprinted (or Adapted) with permission.

Morris, Herbert, PERSONS AND PUNISHMENT IN PHILOSOPHY OF LAW 572, 580–81 (Joel Feinberg & Hyman Gross eds., 1975). Reprinted with permission.

Mosteller, Robert P., *Remaking Confrontation Clause and Hearsay Doctrine Under the Challenge of Child Sexual Abuse Prosecutions*, 1993 U. ILL. L. REV. 691, 691–94. Copyright © 1993 The Board of Trustees of the University of Illinois. Reprinted with permission.

Richards, David A. J., *The Individual, the Family, and the Constitution: A Jurisprudential Perspective*, 55 N.Y.U. L. REV. 1, 8, 11, 19–21, 23–26, 54–57 (1980). Reprinted with permission.

Rosenberg, Irene Merker, *Leaving Bad Enough Alone: A Response to the Juvenile Court Abolitionists*, 1993 WIS. L. REV. 163, 166, 169–71, 173. Copyright © 1993 by The Board of Regents of the University of Wisconsin System. Reprinted by permission of the Wisconsin Law Review.

Scott, Elizabeth S., N. Dickon Reppucci & Jennifer L. Wollard, *Evaluating Adolescent Decisionmaking in Legal Contexts*, 19 LAW & HUM. BEHAV. 221, 224–231, 240 (1995). Copyright © 1995. Reprinted with kind permission from Springer Science and Business Media.

Scott, Elizabeth S. & Laurence Steinberg, *Blaming Youth*, 81 TEX. L. REV. 799, 801–802, 825, 829, 832, 835–39 (2003). Copyright © 2003 Texas Law Review Association. Reprinted with permission.

Smallheer, Randi-Lynn, *Sentence Blending and the Promise of Rehabilitation: Bringing the Juvenile Justice System Full Circle*, 28 HOFSTRA L. REV. 259, 278–79 (1999). Reprinted with permission of the *Hofstra Law Review Association*.

Walkover, Andrew, *The Infancy Defense in the New Juvenile Court*, 31 UCLA L. REV. 503, 503–05, 523–25, 527–31 (1984).

PREFACE

Only a few years ago, courses in children and the law were relatively uncommon in American law schools. Legal issues involving children were routinely considered solely in traditional family law or domestic relations courses.

In recent years, however, separate courses in juvenile law or children and the law have appeared in more and more law school curricula. The courses tend to take two forms: 1) courses focusing solely on the juvenile justice system (delinquency and status offenses); or 2) courses examining the rights of young people in public and private law settings outside, and in addition to, the juvenile justice system.

A few years ago, this casebook's authors, both longtime teachers of juvenile law, concluded that we were not entirely satisfied with the then existing teaching materials. While several casebooks existed, we felt that none adequately covered the range of issues entailed in the second of the above described courses. In particular, we found that no existing casebook effectively covered the issues emerging in the area of school law while providing sufficiently extensive treatment of the juvenile justice system.

To address these concerns, we offer the present casebook. The book presents materials for a general course in children and the law while at the same time providing sufficient attention to the juvenile justice system so as to be utilized as the vehicle for teaching a more narrow course in juvenile delinquency and status offenses. Moreover, these materials are unique among children and the law casebooks in offering extensive coverage of issues involving children and schools. Indeed, Chapter Four, The Child and the School, offers sufficient coverage for a separate course or seminar in education law.

The casebook is divided into five sections:

Chapter One presents a general overview of minority as a legal status. Included is a consideration of contrasting theories of rights of young people. Reference to these theories ("protectionist" and "personhood" rights) is made throughout the materials.

Chapter Two, The Child and the Family, considers issues involving the child, parent, and state. Much of the Chapter centers on issues involving the care of the child. Because some of these topics overlap with family law and domestic law courses they receive relatively light treatment. With this in mind, some instructors may choose to limit coverage of portions of this Chapter because of overlap. On the other hand, the Chapter provides extensive coverage of child abuse, a criminal law matter usually not covered in any other law school course.

Chapter Three, The Child and Society, is a short section treating issues outside the family context but not within the school nor the juvenile justice system, topics treated in Chapters Four and Five respectively.

Chapter Four, The Child and the School, offers extensive treatment of issues encountered by children within the educational system. Such issues are current, significant, and, in our opinion, worthy of more extended coverage than afforded in other children and the law casebooks.

Chapter Five, The Juvenile Justice System, treats juvenile court jurisdiction over matters of delinquency and status offenses. Attention is focused throughout on the question of the extent to which juvenile justice in fact realizes its raison d'etre as a non-punitive alternative to the criminal justice system.

Throughout the book, we occasionally briefly quote, without citation, from one of the present author's previous works, Martin Gardner's UNDERSTANDING JUVENILE LAW. We recommend that source as a possible supplement to this casebook.

Martin R. Gardner
Anne Proffitt Dupre

August 2005

TABLE OF CONTENTS

——————

                                                              Page

DEDICATION iii
ACKNOWLEDGMENTS v
PREFACE ix

Chapter 1 **MINORITY AS A LEGAL STATUS:**
           PROTECTIONISM OR PERSONHOOD?   1

§ 1.01   Overview   1

         [A] Chronological Age Rules   1

              [1] Common Law   1

              [2] Modern Statutes: Different Ages for Different
                   Contexts   1

         [B] Individualized Standards for Assessing
              Maturity   2

§ 1.02   Social Science and the Process of Maturation:
         The Nature of Adolescence   3

         Melton, *Toward "Personhood" for Adolescents: Autonomy
         and Privacy as Values in Public Policy*   3

         Scott, et al., *Evaluating Adolescent Decisionmaking in
         Legal Contexts*   5

         Notes and Questions 10

§ 1.03   The Rights of Juveniles: Contrasting Theories 10

         [A] Overview 10

         [B] The Protectionist Theory 11

              Hafen, *Children's Liberation and the New
              Egalitarianism: Some Reservations About
              Abandoning Youth to Their "Rights"* 11

              Coons, *Intellectual Liberty and the Schools* 13

         [C] The Personhood Theory 18

              Richards, *The Individual, the Family, and the
              Constitution: A Jurisprudential Perspective* 19

              Batey, *The Rights of Adolescents* 22

              Foster & Freed, *A Bill of Rights for Children* 24

         [D] Mixed Theories 26

                                                          Page

          Morris, PERSONS AND PUNISHMENT IN
          PHILOSOPHY OF LAW   26
          Notes and Questions   27

Chapter 2   THE CHILD AND THE FAMILY **29**

§ 2.01   Setting the Framework: The Interests of Parent,
          Child, State   29
          [A]   The Trilogy: *Meyer, Pierce,* and *Prince*   29
                Meyer v. State of Nebraska   29
                Notes and Questions   32
                Pierce v. Society of Sisters   33
                Notes and Questions   36
                Prince v. Massachusetts   37
                Notes and Questions   46
          [B]   Parental Authority and Compulsory Education . . .   46
                Wisconsin v. Yoder   46
                Notes and Questions   60
§ 2.02   Care of the Child   61
          [A]   Custody   62
                [1]   The Best Interest of the Child   62
                      [a]   The Primary Caretaker   63
                            Kennedy v. Kennedy   63
                            Notes and Questions   69
                      [b]   Other Factors in the Best Interest
                            Analysis   71
                            [i]   Child's Preference   71
                            [ii]   Sexual Conduct and Sexual
                                   Orientation of Parent   71
                            [iii] Religion   72
                            [iv]   Physical and Mental Disability . . .   72
                            [v]   Domestic Violence   73
                            [vi]   Child Care Issues   73
                                   Ireland v. Smith   73
                                   Questions   78
                [2]   Joint Custody   78
                      Notes and Questions   80
          [B]   Technology and the New Family   81

Page

In re Baby M. 81

Notes and Questions 105

[C] Family Visitation 107

Uniform Marriage and Divorce Act § 407 —
Visitation 107

Troxel v. Granville 108

Notes and Questions 124

[D] Neglect and Endangerment 124

Michigan Compensation Laws Annotated § 712A.2
Authority and jurisdiction of court 125

In the Interest of D.K. 125

In re Matthew S. 131

L.L. v. Colorado 139

Notes and Questions 146

[E] Termination of Parental Rights 147

Santosky v. Kramer 147

Notes and Questions 162

[F] Foster Care 162

Notes and Questions 166

[G] Adoption 169

Notes and Questions 171

Dewees v. Stevenson 174

Notes and Questions 178

[H] Intrafamily Tort Actions 180

Anderson v. Stream 180

Burnette v. Wahl 185

Notes and Questions 195

[I] Emancipation 196

Accent Service Company, Inc. v. Ebsen 196

Notes and Questions 198

In re Snyder 200

Notes and Questions 204

§ 2.03 Child Abuse 204

[A] Introduction 204

[B] Defining Child Abuse 205

[1] Statutory Provisions 206

                                                    Page

        Maryland Code Annotated, Article 27,
        § 35C   206

        Nebraska Revised Statutes § 28-707   207

        Nevada Revised Statutes § 200.508   207

        Arizona Revised Statutes Annotated
        § 13-3623   208

        Notes and Questions   210

   [2] Constitutional Issues   211

        State v. Sinica   211

        State v. Meinert   214

        Notes and Questions   216

   [3] Scope Issues   218

        [a] What is "Abuse"?   218

             In the Matter of Shane T.   218

             Notes and Questions   221

        [b] Who is a "Child"?   222

             Whitner v. State   222

             Notes and Questions   233

[C] Adjudicating Child Abuse   235

   [1] The Battered Child Syndrome (BCS)   236

        State v. Tanner   236

        Notes and Questions   248

   [2] The Battering Parent Syndrome (BPS)   249

        People v. Walkey   249

        Notes and Questions   254

   [3] Munchausen Syndrome by Proxy (MSP)   255

        People v. Phillips   255

        Notes and Questions   264

   [4] Child Sexual Abuse Accommodation Syndrome
        (CSAAS)   265

        Steward v. State   265

        Notes and Questions   277

   [5] The Child Witness   280

        Mosteller, *Remaking Confrontation Clause and
        Hearsay Doctrine Under the Challenge of Child
        Sexual Abuse Prosecutions*   280

        Maryland v. Craig   281

Page

Notes and Questions   292

Idaho v. Wright   295

White v. Illinois   303

Notes and Questions   307

[D] Child Abuse Reporting Statutes   309

California Penal Code   310

§ 11165.7 — Mandated reporter   310

§ 11166 — Report; duty; time   313

§ 11172 — Liability of person making reports;
reimbursement by state of attorney fees
incurred in defending action   315

Nebraska Revised Statutes   316

§ 28-711 — Child subjected to abuse or neglect;
report; contents; toll-free number   316

§ 28-717 — Violations; penalty   317

Notes and Questions   317

Landeros v. Flood   318

*Deshaney v. Winnebago County Department of Social
Services*   322

Notes and Questions   329

[E] Central Registries   329

Valmonte v. Bane   330

Notes and Questions   338

§ 2.04   Protecting the Health of the Child   339

[A] Physical Health and Religious Practice   339

In re Fetus Brown   339

In the Matter of Cabrera   346

Notes and Questions   354

In the Interest of D.L.E.   355

In re E.G.   357

Notes and Questions   363

[B] Mental Health   364

Parham v. J.R.   364

Notes and Questions   383

Chapter 3   THE CHILD AND SOCIETY **385**

§ 3.01   Introduction   385

Page

§ 3.02   Obscenity and Pornography 385

          Ginsberg v. New York 385

          Notes and Questions 394

§ 3.03   Privacy Rights of Minors: Abortion and
          Birth Control 400

          Ohio v. Akron Center for Reproductive Health 404

          Notes and Questions 422

§ 3.04   Contract Liability 423

          Georgia Code Annotated § 13-3-20 423

          Swalberg v. Hannegan 424

          Dodson v. Shrader 425

          Notes and Questions 429

§ 3.05   Tort Liability 430

          Bailey v. C.S. 430

          Kuhns v. Brugger 432

          Notes and Questions 437

Chapter 4 THE CHILD AND THE SCHOOL 439

§ 4.01   First Amendment Rights of Students 439

          [A] Student Rights of Speech and Expression 440

               *Tinker v. Des Moines Independent Community
               School District* 440

               Notes and Questions 449

               Bethel School District v. Fraser 451

               Notes and Questions 460

          [B] Student Publications 462

               Hazelwood School District v. Kuhlmeier 462

               Notes and Questions 476

          [C] A Long Way from Black Armbands? Issues for the
               Twenty-first Century 480

               [1] Dress Codes and School Uniforms 480

                    [a] Dress Codes 480

                         *Boroff v. Van Wert City Board of
                         Education* 480

                         Notes and Questions 487

                    [b] School Uniforms 490

                         Notes and Questions 490

Page

       [2] Political Speech? 491

       [3] Disrespect and Threats 493

            The Columbine Effect and Zero Tolerance . . . 494

       [4] Internet Speech 496

       [5] Societal Consequences 498

   [D] The Right to Receive Information and Ideas 501

       Board of Education, Island Trees Union Free School District v. Pico 502

       Notes and Questions 529

       The Right to Receive and the Internet 532

§ 4.02 Religion in School: Children Caught in the Controversy 535

   [A] The Establishment Clause 535

       [1] Financial Aid to Religious Institutions 535

            School Vouchers 536

       [2] The Curriculum Controversy 538

            Evolution vs. Creation 538

            Sex Education 539

       [3] Prayer and Religious Expression 541

            Santa Fe Independent School District v. Doe 542

            Notes and Questions 545

   [B] The Free Exercise Clause 548

§ 4.03 School Discipline and the Constitution 550

   [A] Suspension 550

       Goss v. Lopez 550

       Notes and Questions 562

       A Constitutional Right to Education? 566

   [B] Corporal Punishment 567

       [1] Eighth Amendment and Procedural Due Process 567

            Ingraham v. Wright 567

            Notes and Questions 584

       [2] Substantive Due Process 585

            Brown v. Ramsey 585

            Notes and Questions 593

   [C] "Zero Tolerance" Policies 594

Page

Seal v. Morgan 594

Notes and Questions 608

§ 4.04   School Searches and the Fourth Amendment 610

    [A]   Individualized Suspicion 610

        New Jersey v. T.L.O. 610

        Notes and Questions 631

    [B]   Urinalysis Drug Testing 636

        Board of Education of Independent School District No. 92 of Pottawatomie County v. Earls 637

        Notes and Questions 651

    [C]   Dog Sniffs 652

        B.C. v. Plumas Unified School District 652

        Notes and Questions 659

    [D]   Exclusionary Rule 660

        Thompson v. Carthage School District 660

        Notes and Questions 664

    [E]   Locker Searches 665

        State v. Overton 665

        Notes and Questions 667

§ 4.05   Discrimination, Harassment and Bullying 670

    [A]   Sexual Harassment in School 673

        [1]   Teacher Harassing Student 673

            Gebser v. Lago Vista Independent School District 673

            Notes and Questions 686

        [2]   Student Harassing Student 689

            Davis v. Monroe County Board of Education 689

            Notes and Questions 715

        [3]   Same Sex Harassment 718

            Montgomery v. Independent School District No. 709 718

            Notes and Questions 734

    [B]   Bullying 735

        Stevenson v. Martin County Board of Education 735

        Notes and Questions 743

Page

[C] Sexual Harassment Policies Versus Free Expression 746

Saxe v. State College Area School District 746

Notes and Questions 761

§ 4.06 The Disabled Student 765

[A] "Free Appropriate Public Education" 767

Board of Education of the Hendrick Hudson Central School District v. Rowley 767

Notes and Questions 782

[B] Inclusion 786

Oberti v. Board of Education 787

Hartmann v. Loudoun County Board of Education 803

Notes and Questions 812

[C] Discipline 817

§ 4.07 Leaving No Child Behind? 823

Chapter 5 THE JUVENILE JUSTICE SYSTEM 827

§ 5.01 Overview 827

§ 5.02 The Supreme Court and Juvenile Court Procedure 828

[A] Supreme Court Cases 828

Kent v. United States 828

Notes and Questions 836

In re Gault 837

Notes and Questions 855

In re Winship 857

Notes and Questions 862

McKeiver v. Pennsylvania 863

Notes and Questions 870

Breed v. Jones 871

Notes and Questions 878

[B] The Significance of Sanctions: Punishment Versus Therapy 878

Gardner, *Punishment and Juvenile Justice: A Conceptual Framework for Assessing Constitutional Rights of Youthful Offenders* 879

§ 5.03 Jurisdiction 882

Page

[A] Overview 882

[B] Age 882

    [1] Maximum Age 882

        Lamb v. Brown 882

        Notes and Questions 884

    [2] Minimum Age 884

        In re Interest of Dow 885

        Notes and Questions 888

[C] Delinquency 889

    [1] Exclusive Jurisdiction 889

        United States v. Bland 890

        Notes and Questions 898

    [2] Concurrent Jurisdiction 899

        Nebraska Revised Statutes § 43-247 899

        State v. Mohi 900

        Notes and Questions 913

    [3] Waiver 914

        Nevada Revised Satutes § 62.080 914

        California Welfare and Institutions Code
        § 707 915

        Nebraska Revised Statutes 916

            § 43.261 916

            § 43.276 917

        Notes and Questions 921

        Matter of Johnson 921

        Questions 924

        Roper v. Simmons 925

        Notes and Questions 943

[D] Status Offenses 944

    S.S. v. State 945

    Notes and Questions 953

    Schleifer v. Charlottesville 954

    Notes and Questions 967

    Note on Proposals to Abolish Status Offense
    Jurisdiction 968

    Ketcham, *Why Jurisdiction Over Status Offenders
    Should be Eliminated From Juvenile Courts* 968

Page

Gregory, *Juvenile Court Jurisdiction Over Noncriminal Misbehavior: The Argument Against Abolition* 971

§ 5.04 The Pre-Adjudication Process 974

[A] Police Investigation 974

[1] Search and Seizure 974

Lanes v. State 975

Questions 984

State In Interest of J.B. 985

Notes and Questions 989

[B] Interrogation 990

Fare v. Michael C. 990

Notes and Questions 999

Yarborough v. Alvorado 1000

Notes and Questions 1008

Commonwealth v. Williams 1008

Notes and Questions 1014

[C] Detention and Bail 1015

Alabama Code § 12-15-59 1015

Minnesota Statutes Annotated § 260.171 1015

Nebraska Revised Statute § 43-253 1018

Hawaii Revised Statutes § 571-32 1019

Notes and Questions 1019

Schall v. Martin 1020

Notes and Questions 1038

§ 5.05 Adjudication 1038

[A] Delinquency 1038

[1] Procedure 1038

[a] Jury Determinations 1039

In re Felder 1039

Notes and Questions 1045

[b] Closed Proceedings 1046

R.L.R. v. State 1047

In re J.S. 1050

Notes and Questions 1057

[2] Affirmative Defenses 1058

[a] Competency To Be Adjudicated 1059

Page

			Matter of Welfare of D.D.N.	1059
			Notes and Questions	1062
		[b]	The Insanity Defense	1064
			In the Interest of Causey	1064
			Notes and Questions	1067
		[c]	The Infancy Defense	1070
			In re Tyvonne	1070
			Notes and Questions	1076
			Morse, *Immaturity and Irresponsibility*	1077
			Scott & Steinberg, *Blaming Youth*	1080
		[d]	The Battered Child Defense	1081
			Appeal in Maricopa County	1081
			Notes and Questions	1086
		[e]	The Defense of Duress and Gang Activity	1088
	[B]	Status Offenses		1089
		[1]	Procedures	1089
			[a] Constitutional Protections	1089
			In the Matter of Spalding	1089
			Notes and Questions	1103
			[b] Statutory Provisions and Judicial Interpretation	1104
		[2]	Affirmative Defenses	1106
§ 5.06	Dispositions			1107
	[A]	Hearing Procedure		1107
	[B]	Delinquency Cases		1109
		[1]	The Traditional Theory: Promoting the Juvenile's Best Interests	1109
			Feld, *The Juvenile Court Meets the Principle of Offense: Note Punishment, Treatment, and the Difference It Makes*	1109
			South Dakota Codified Laws § 26-8C-7	1110
			Nebraska Revised Statutes § 43-286	1112
			In re Interest of J.A.	1114
			In re Appeal No. 179	1116
			In re Aline D.	1119
			Notes and Questions	1125

Page

[a] Disposition Alternatives 1128

    [i] Probation 1128

        Probation Revocation 1130

    [ii] Restitution 1130

        State in Interest of D.G.W. 1130

        Notes and Questions 1135

    [iii] Community Service 1135

        M.J.W. v. State 1135

        Notes and Questions 1137

    [iv] Confinement 1137

        Nelson v. Heyne 1137

        Notes and Questions 1142

[b] The Right to Rehabilitative
Treatment 1142

    Nelson v. Heyne 1142

    Notes and Questions 1145

[2] Punitive Juvenile Justice 1148

Walkover, *The Infancy Defense in the New
Juvenile Court* 1148

North Carolina General Statutes 1150

    § 7B-2500 — Purpose 1150

    § 7B-2506 — Dispositional Alternatives for
Delinquent Juveniles 1150

    § 7B-2507 — Delinquency History
Levels 1153

    § 7B-2508 — Dispositional Limits for Each
Class of Offense and Delinquency History
Level 1155

    § 7B-2513 — Commitment of Delinquent
Juvenile to Office 1156

California Welfare and Institutions Code
§ 202 1157

In re Eric J. 1158

Notes and Questions 1162

[3] "Blended Sentencing" 1163

In the Matter of S.L.M. 1163

Notes and Questions 1168

[C] Status Offense Cases 1170

Page

      Incarceration as a Secondary Disposition   1173

      Right to Rehabilitative Treatment   1175

§ 5.07   The Future of Juvenile Justice   1176

      Feld, *The Transformation of the Juvenile Court*   1176

      Feld, *Abolish the Juvenile Court: Youthfulness, Criminal Responsibility, and Sentencing Policy*   1178

      Federle, *The Abolition of the Juvenile Court: A Proposal for the Preservation of Children's Rights*   1180

      Rosenberg, *Leaving Bad Enough Alone: A Response to the Juvenile Court Abolitionists*   1182

      Scott & Steinberg, *Blaming Youth*   1185

      Gardner, *Punitive Juvenile Justice: Some Observations on a Recent Trend*   1188

Table of Cases TC-1

Index I-1

Chapter 1

MINORITY AS A LEGAL STATUS: PROTECTIONISM OR PERSONHOOD?

§ 1.01 OVERVIEW

The phenomenon of childhood is not unique to humans. Most other forms of life also embody a process where infants over time become adult members of the species. However, human infants are unique, at least among the primates, in the extent of their vulnerability and dependence on an extended period of socialization and learning in order to achieve maturity. Thus, childhood for humans is a comparatively long period during which young people gradually acquire the competencies and capacities of adulthood.

Because young people are perceived to be vulnerable and dependent upon more competent adults, they are viewed as a distinct class for legal purposes. From Biblical times to the present, the law has imposed disabilities upon, and provided special protections for, young persons.

[A] Chronological Age Rules

[1] Common Law

At common law an "infant" was any person who had not attained the age of majority as prescribed by law. The term "infant" retains current usage, but is often replaced by the more modern terms "minor," "juvenile," or "child."

The common law defined the status of minority in terms of chronological age without regard to individualized characteristics such as physical maturity, mental capacity, education, experience, or accomplishment. While the age of majority varied for different classes of people under the early law, the common law eventually settled upon the age of twenty-one as the age at which persons attained full legal capacity for most purposes. The criminal law, however, designated age fourteen as the age at which offenders were fully responsible for their actions. The common law thus created what at first glance appears to be a puzzling situation: while a fifteen-year-old is too young to enter into a contract, the same person is old enough to be held accountable for her criminal conduct.

[2] Modern Statutes: Different Ages for Different Contexts

With the passage of the Twenty-Sixth Amendment giving eighteen-year-olds the right to vote, most states reduced the age of majority to eighteen. For a time, many states attempted to treat eighteen-year-olds as adults for all legal purposes and thus, among other things, lowered the legal age for alcohol consumption to age eighteen. Attempts at establishing eighteen as the single age of majority were short-lived, however. In response to influences from the federal government to establish age twenty-one as a uniform national minimum age for permissible alcohol consumption, all states as of 1988 had enacted legislation establishing age twenty-one as the minimum legal drinking age. Thus, while eighteen remains the "age of majority" in most states, being of "legal age" does not assure that one will enjoy all the rights and privileges as adults.

Conversely, states routinely establish a general age of majority but choose to permit young people to engage in some governmentally regulated conduct at an earlier age. For example, states generally permit young people to operate motor vehicles at ages younger than the designated age of majority. As another example, Nebraska establishes the age of majority at nineteen, but allows young people who are eighteen or older to use tobacco. Indeed, the laws of virtually every state consist of a complexity of rules granting privileges and imposing prohibitions on the basis of age levels both greater and lesser than the specified "age of majority."

Some of these apparent anomalies, for example granting driving privileges at an age earlier than the age of majority but restricting drinking past that age, can be explained as early extensions of privileges to young people while retaining residual control over their possible abuse of the privilege granted. This explanation suggests that the law permits young people a period of transition to grow to adulthood by enjoying some, but not all, of the rights and privileges inherent in adulthood.

[B] Individualized Standards for Assessing Maturity

Defining legal adulthood solely in terms of chronological age standards is controversial. Arriving at adulthood is a process rather than the occurrence of a particular birthday. While young people grow to adulthood by experiencing increasing degrees of autonomy, not all of them mature and become responsible adults at the same chronological age.

While maturity is clearly a matter of individual variation, some social science data suggests that at the beginning of the period of adolescence (often identified as fourteen years of age) young people routinely employ the same decisionmaking processes as those utilized by most adults. As illustrated later in this Chapter, reliance on such data has led some to advocate treating the considered choices of competent adolescents as having the same legal effect as similar choices of adults. In this view, an adolescent should legally be permitted to contract, marry, choose a religion, or make enforceable decisions to engage in legally permissible conduct opposed by the adolescent's parents. Such choices could be denied legal effect only if the individual adolescent decisionmaker were shown to be incompetent. Proponents of this position reject the traditional method of distinguishing juveniles from adults solely by chronological age standards, and instead favor a system presuming adolescents to be adults in lieu of an individualized showing of incompetence.

In contrast to the prevailing chronological age model, a few manifestations of the individualized approach do exist in current juvenile law. Several such examples will be examined in detail in later Chapters.

§ 1.02   SOCIAL SCIENCE AND THE PROCESS OF MATURATION: THE NATURE OF ADOLESCENCE

Juvenile law is premised on empirical assumptions that young people are vulnerable, dependent, and incompetent. These assumptions are seldom disputed in the context of very young children. However, the assumptions become more controversial when related to adolescents. Indeed, some social science research calls into question basic assumptions of traditional juvenile law as applied to adolescents. Appreciation of the role of the social sciences in shaping policy is thus essential to understanding juvenile law.

The psychological and sociological literature on the subject of adolescence is immense. Even a brief summary of the research is well beyond the scope of this work. The following excerpts are intended to illustrate the significance of social science research and assumptions in shaping juvenile law and theories of juvenile rights.

Gary B. Melton, *Toward "Personhood" for Adolescents: Autonomy and Privacy as Values in Public Policy*

38 AMERICAN PSYCHOLOGIST 99, 99–102 (1983) (citations omitted)

. . . [T]he children's rights movement . . . has been marked by ambivalence. Some who consider themselves "child advocates" seek to "liberate" children and increase their self-determination; others strive to protect children and to increase community responsibilities for their nurturance. Still others view children's interests as almost always coextensive with those of their parents because of what these theorists regard as children's need for authoritative parents.

COMPETENCE AND AUTONOMY

Although varying orientations toward children's rights are not necessarily mutually exclusive, the underlying theory of each of these broad orientations rests, in part, on a variant assumption of minors' *competence* — that is, whether children and adolescents are capable of competent independent decisionmaking. The ambivalence in public policy flows from divergent views of whether minors can be considered, in view of their immaturity in decisionmaking, to be true moral agents who are full and autonomous members of the community. . . .

. . . .

Essentially, the argument is that minors are dependent beings who lack the capacity, at least in some circumstances, for mature, independent choice. Lacking evidence to the contrary, they are presumed to lack autonomy, and therefore to lack independent liberty interests. Moreover, to the extent that privacy is predicated on respect for the boundaries — both physical and psychological — of the person, minors' lack of status as autonomous persons also raises questions of whether they possess justifiable expectations of privacy.

. . . .

. . . The existing literature clearly suggests that, for most purposes, adolescents cannot be distinguished from adults on the ground of competence in decisionmaking alone. Grisso and Vierling, for example, considered the developmental literature on problem-solving activities and vulnerability to social influence and concluded that there was no basis in that literature for distinguishing adolescents aged 15 and older from adults. They suggested further that ages 11 to 14 should be viewed as a transition period in the development of important cognitive and social abilities; youth in this age group might be competent as decisionmakers in some contexts. Some caution about the junior-high-age group is particularly important, given C. C. Lewis' finding that seventh and eighth graders appear to be less likely than older adolescents to consider potential risks and potential future consequences of decisions.

Since Grisso and Vierling's review, a substantial literature on adolescents' decisionmaking in specific legally relevant contexts has developed. In terms of competence to consent to psychotherapy, for example, there is evidence that adolescents have adult-like concepts of psychotherapy, mental health professionals, and mental disorder itself. In perhaps the best-designed study of this sort, Weithorn and Campbell presented hypothetical dilemmas about medical and psychological treatment decisions to 9-, 14-, 18-, and 21-year-olds. The responses of the 14-year-olds could not be differentiated from those of the adult groups according to any of the major standards of competency: evidence of a choice; reasonable outcome of choice; reasonable decisionmaking process; understanding of the facts.

The evidence on specific decisional competencies of adolescents is not limited to treatment decisions. For example, even elementary schoolchildren are frequently competent to consent to research, at least when their reasons for or against participation are evaluated relative to those of adult populations. Similarly, C. C. Lewis found that the reasons given by pregnant minors for or against abortion are similar to the reasons given by pregnant adults. In short, the . . . assumption of adolescents' incompetence as decisionmakers cannot be supported by the available psychological research.

. . . .

I am arguing that adolescents' personhood should be recognized by policy-makers. Insofar as denial of autonomy has been based on assumptions of incompetence, current psychological research does not support such an age-graded distinction. Moreover, recognition of personhood might facilitate adolescents' personal individuation. . . . [T]here seems to be ample basis for reversal of current presumptions in favor of a view of adolescents as autonomous persons possessed of independent interests regarding liberty and privacy. . . .

Such a reversal of presumptions would probably result in substantial changes in the scope of adolescents' liberty and privacy rights. Assuming that compelling state interests to the contrary could not be demonstrated, adolescents' independent interests in decisions relating to such matters as psychotherapy, medical treatment, psychiatric hospitalization, abortion, and contraception would have to be recognized. Indiscriminate searches of high school students could not be upheld on the ground that students have no expectation of privacy.

. . . .

. . . To the extent that the assumption of incompetence has led to the courts' ambivalence about the personhood of adolescents, then this ambivalence may be reduced by the kind of psychological evidence described here.

————

Elizabeth S. Scott, N. Dickon Reppucci & Jennifer L. Woolard, *Evaluating Adolescent Decisionmaking in Legal Contexts*

19 LAW AND HUMAN BEHAVIOR 221, 224–231, 240 (1995)
(citations omitted)

Adolescents pose a dilemma for legal policymakers. Traditionally they have been classified with younger children as minors, and been denied legal rights and privileges accorded to adults. However, most would agree that presumptions of vulnerability, dependence, and incompetence that justify paternalistic legal policies seem less valid when applied to adolescents. Some observers have argued that adolescents' legal treatment is unduly restrictive and that they should be given more of the rights and privileges accorded to adults. Others alarmed by the social costs of juvenile crime, argue that the law protects adolescents excessively from the consequences of their conduct, and that they should be held responsible for the harms that they cause in the same manner as adults.

These critics of paternalistic legal policies are likely to diverge in their political agendas, but their arguments share an important empirical premise — that adolescent decisionmaking is more like that of adults than the law has assumed. Some advocates for adolescent self-determination have been explicit in making this claim. For example, on the issue of abortion, reformers argue that developmental theory and empirical research demonstrate that by midadolescence, minors are indistinguishable from adults in their decisionmaking. Their capacity for reasoning and understanding is similar to that of adults, and thus, they meet adult standards of legal competence under informed consent doctrine. Under this argument, the case of different legal treatment, to the extent that it is based on a presumption of incompetence, is greatly weakened. This argument has been extended to challenge a wide range of restrictive paternalistic policies directed at children and adolescents.

Our purpose is to challenge the usefulness of this approach to evaluating adolescent decisionmaking capacity and to suggest an expanded framework that will allow researchers to contribute more effectively to the development of empirically accurate legal policies. Our challenge is twofold. First, we believe that advocates' claims exaggerate the scientific evidence that no differences distinguish the decisionmaking of adults and minors under informed consent tests. Second, and of greater importance for our purposes, the informed consent model incorporates a narrower range of decisionmaking factors than appear to be relevant to courts and policymakers, and thus its utility is somewhat limited.

Informed consent standards of legal competence, and the model based on these standards, focus on two aspects of cognitive functioning — capacity for reasoning and understanding. Protective legal policies directed toward minors, however, are based not only on the presumption that adolescents differ from adults in these capacities, but also that their choices and behavior are affected, in ways that distinguish them developmentally from adults, by other decisionmaking factors that are not included under an informed consent model. For example: adolescents are presumed to be more susceptible to peer influence; to have a tendency to focus more on immediate rather than long-term consequences; and to be less risk averse and thus more inclined to make risky choices than are adults. Our goal is to propose a model to compare adolescent and adult decisionmaking that incorporates this broader range of factors — peer (and parental) influence, risk preference and perception, and temporal perspective — as well as those included under an informed consent model.

. . . .

. . . [A]dvocates of adolescent self-determination on issues such as abortion have drawn on child development theory and empirical research to argue that no significant differences separate adolescents and adults in their capacity to make informed medical decisions. In our view, although the limited relevant research generally supports their position, these advocates exaggerate the robustness of the scientific evidence. We concur with Gardner, Scherer, and Tester's (1989) careful and persuasive argument that advocates overstep the limits of science in claiming that the research *demonstrates* that no differences distinguish the decisionmaking capability of adolescents and adults. We highlight and expand upon the important points of this critique.

First, the early researchers relied on the principles of Piaget's stage theory of cognitive development that are no longer widely accepted among cognitive psychologists. . . .

Even if the theoretical foundation were more credible, only a handful of studies have compared decisionmaking by adults and adolescents in legally relevant contexts, and most have examined only a small number of subjects. Furthermore, many of the studies provide only indirect evidence that adolescents are competent decisionmakers. . . .

. . . .

The upshot of this brief review of the current empirical picture is that scientific authority is at best tentative for the assertion that adolescents' capacities for reasoning and understanding in making decisions are similar to those of adults. It is clear that research should move beyond the Piagetian stage framework to examine differential capacity in various contexts. Generalizability and external validity would be enhanced by moving studies out of the laboratory to more ecologically valid situations and samples. In short, future research comparing adults and adolescents, using instruments designed to test competence in an informed consent framework, is needed to establish a proposition that has come to be accepted as proven among advocates for adolescent self-determination.

COMPETENCE AND JUDGMENT

Even if further research confirms that adolescents and adults have similar abilities to understand disclosed information, to appreciate its meaning, and to make decisions through a rational process, this conclusion is not likely to resolve, in the minds of policymakers, the issue of whether adolescents should be accorded the same legal treatment as adults. Although the legal presumption that minors are incompetent and need legal protection rests in part on an intuition that their capacity for understanding and reasoning is less developed than is that of adults', it also rests on the belief that their judgment is less mature. In essence, the intuition behind paternalistic policies is that developmentally linked traits and responses systematically affect the decision-making of adolescents in a way that may incline them to make choices that threaten harm to their own and others' health, life, or welfare, to a greater extent than do adults.

. . . .

Two arguments support the claim that the evaluation of adolescent legal capacity appropriately considers judgment as well as reasoning and understanding. The first is that a different response would carry a significant social cost. Informed consent policy reflects a conclusion that the importance of respecting adults' autonomy in the context of health care decisions outweighs the social cost of poor decisions by occasional "outliers", particularly given the substantial costs of any other approach. It is plausible to assume that most people are motivated to make health-promoting medical decisions (*i.e.*, use good judgment), and thus that the social cost of respecting autonomy is tolerable. If adolescents *as a class* have poorer judgment (and choose different outcomes) than adults, then the social cost of according them freedom and of holding them to adult standards of responsibility might be significant. In fact, in many legal contexts, anticipated social cost of poor judgment by adults justifies restriction of freedom (*e.g.*, seat belt and motorcycle helmet laws, product safety regulations) and reduced responsibility (*e.g.*, laws allowing "cooling off periods" before enforcing door-to-door sales contracts). If immature adolescent decisionmaking creates costs that fall primarily on minors themselves, then the societal interest in preventing harm to this group may be particularly acute.

The second argument for considering judgment hinges on an important distinction that can be drawn between the poor choices made by individuals and those that the law presumes are made by minors as a group. The adult's "poor" decision (to refuse recommended treatment, for example) is presumed to reflect the subjective values and preferences of the individual. In the case of the adolescent refusing treatment, the values and preferences are presumed to reflect common age-linked developmental characteristics that predictably will change. It is assumed that with maturity, most individuals will make a different choice. If this is so, then the autonomy claim seems less compelling than is that of adults. Moreover, implicit in the presumption that developmental factors affect judgment is a prediction (or hope, in the case of delinquent behavior) that the adolescent will become an adult with different values and preferences from her youthful self. If this is so, then the case for protecting the opportunities and prospects of that future adult from the costs of her immature youthful judgement and choices seems powerful.

. . . .

DEVELOPMENTAL FACTORS IN ADOLESCENCE

In general, adolescents are presumed to be less independent in their decisionmaking than adults, and to be subject to the influence of both parents and peers. [The authors summarize "tentative evidence" suggest[ing] that adolescents are "more subject to parental influence" than are young adults.]

A more pressing concern for paternalists is that adolescents are believed to have a greater inclination to respond to peer influence than do adults. Peer influence appears to operate through two processes, social comparison and conformity. Through social comparison, adolescents use others' behavior as a measure of their own behavior. Social conformity, which appears to peak around age 15, leads adolescents to adapt their behavior and attitudes to those of their peers. Berndt found that peer conformity varies by age and target behavior. Conformity peaked in the ninth grade for situations involving antisocial behavior, but no age changes in peer influence on prosocial behavior were found. The importance of peer influence to adolescent decisionmaking could be relevant in two ways. In some contexts, adolescents might be more vulnerable to direct peer pressure in making choices. More indirectly, adolescent desire for peer approval may affect decisionmaking without any explicit coercion. For example, an adolescent may reject a particular outcome because she believes that her friends will disapprove. Comparisons to adults are difficult to make, however, because little research simultaneously examines peer influence on adolescents and adults.

Adolescents seem to differ from adults in their perception of and attitude toward risk. Adolescents and young adults take more risks with health and safety than do older adults, by more frequently engaging in activities such as criminal conduct, unprotected sex, and speeding. We are talking about the assessment of and attitude toward risk, not simply a lack of self control or impulsiveness. Different attitudes toward risk might result if adolescents are less risk averse than adults. It is unclear whether attitude toward risk remains constant across decisionmaking domains. In some contexts, adolescent risk preferences may be linked to other developmental factors; for example, adolescents may be *more* averse than adults to risking social ostracism. Elkind suggests that adolescents conceptualize themselves as invulnerable to the potentially negative consequences of risk — a viewpoint consistent with legal paternalism. Findings that low-risk teens', their parents', and high-risk teens' estimates of personal invulnerability were not greater for teens than for adults cast some doubt on Elkind's characterizations. However, their comparison fails to provide data about the accuracy of each group's perception of its own level of vulnerability to particular risks. Thus, even though teenagers may perceive that they are as vulnerable (or more vulnerable) to unwanted pregnancy as are their mothers, this information does not tell us how accurately they perceive the actual level of risk they face.

Some differences have been demonstrated in other components of risk perception and attitudes. In making choices, adolescents appear to focus less on protection against losses than on opportunities for gains in making choices as compared to adults. Adolescents appear to weigh the negative consequences of *not* engaging in risky behaviors more heavily than adults although overall response patterns of adults and adolescents were quite similar. Differences in risk perception have also been observed. Research suggests that perception of risks increases through adolescence (perhaps with increased experience). Adolescents may sometimes be unaware of risks that adults perceive or they may calculate differently the probability or magnitude of a given risk. For example, adolescents may be less willing than adults to risk disfiguring side effects of a medical treatment regimen due to concerns about body image and peer approval, but they may be more willing than adults to engage in behaviors such as bungee jumping.

Attitude toward risk is closely linked to differences in temporal perspective. In general, adolescents seem to discount the future more than adults and to weigh more heavily the short-term consequences of decisions — both risks and benefits — a response that in some settings contributes to risky behavior. Gardner and Herman hypothesize that this tendency may be linked to the greater uncertainty that young people may feel about their own futures, an uncertainty that might make short-term consequences seem more salient to an evaluation of different options. It may also reflect the reality that adolescents have had less experience. It may be harder for an adolescent than for an adult to contemplate the meaning of a consequence that will be realized 10 to 15 years in the future, because such a time span is not easily made relevant to adolescent experience. Nurmi's review of the adolescent future orientation literature confirms that adolescents are most interested in major developmental tasks of late adolescence and early adulthood (*i.e.*, career, education, marriage). Future planning skills grow more efficient with age, but continue to develop at least into the early 20's.

. . . .

THE JUDGMENT FRAMEWORK AND LEGAL POLICY

The task of science is to chart the similarities and differences in adolescent and adult decisionmaking. The task of policymakers is to decide about appropriate legal responses. Currently, the intuitions about adolescent immaturity that have supported paternalistic legal responses are being challenged by critics across the political spectrum. Whether paternalism is appropriate depends, in part, on empirical issues that currently are unsettled. If research findings indicate that the differences between adolescents and adults are less than we supposed, then the burden to justify restrictive policies directed toward minors becomes greater. On the other hand, evidence of youthful immaturity may bolster special protections for minors. . . .

. . . .

It is clear that no simplistic formula defines the relationship between adolescent decisionmaking capability and policies of restriction, protection, and self-determination. Adolescents (or some adolescents) may be indistinguishable from adults in approaching a particular choice, and yet extending legal authority may appear to carry too high a cost in terms of administration, enforcement, or family disruption, with too little benefit to the minor. Moreover, the political cost of extending freedom may be an inclination to withdraw special protections from youth. Policy choices will be driven by distinctive formulas based on many variables of which competence is only one. Nonetheless, to the extent that presumptions about adolescent decisionmaking capability are important in shaping policy, those presumptions are more usefully based on data than on intuition and ideology.

———

NOTES AND QUESTIONS

1. Do the above excerpts provide a basis for justifying traditional legal distinctions between adolescents and adults?

2. For additional social science input, see, *e.g.*, Elizabeth Cauffman & Laurence Steinberg, *The Cognitive and Affective Influences on Adolescent Decision-Making*, 68 TEMPLE L. REV. 1763 (1995); Laurence Steinberg & Elizabeth Cauffman, *Maturity in Judgment in Adolescence: Psychosocial Factors in Adolescent Decision Making*, 20 LAW & HUM. BEHAV. 249 (1996); Jennifer L. Woolard et al., *Theoretical and Methodological Issues in Studying Children's Capacities in Legal Contexts*, 20 LAW & HUM. BEHAV. 219 (1996).

§ 1.03 THE RIGHTS OF JUVENILES: CONTRASTING THEORIES

[A] Overview

Explicating theories of juvenile rights is a complicated matter. The task is particularly difficult given that three sets of interests — the child's, her parents' or guardians', and the government's — routinely coalesce and require accommodation. As will become evident in later chapters of this casebook, no clear design of constitutional rights appears from the caselaw. The courts tend to proceed in a piecemeal fashion in resolving various conflicts arising between the state and the child, sometimes aligning the parent's interests with the child's, but other times with the interests of the state, or as a separate interest against those of the child and the state. As will be shown in later chapters, the United States Supreme Court appears to have recognized full-fledged constitutional rights for young people in some contexts but not in others. Matters are slightly clearer outside the context of constitutional law, but even there anomalies caution against identifying a single coherent theory to rationalize the law.

Much of the difficulty in the theory of juvenile law appears as a consequence of the interplay of two often conflicting theories of rights that are both reflected, to a degree at least, in current law. The first, and more predominant of the two is the protectionist theory which entitles young people to paternalistic care. The second theory, herein designated the personhood theory, affords young people rights guaranteed to autonomous persons.

The tension between these two theories of rights will be discussed throughout this casebook. While it is possible to sketch pure models of protectionism and personhood respectively, the theories often overlap in court opinions and sometimes even in the commentary of theorists. As you study the following excerpts, consider whether it is possible or desirable to explicate juvenile rights theory, particularly as it applies to adolescents, entirely in terms of either protectionism or personhood concepts.

[B] The Protectionist Theory

While democratic traditions recognize rights of autonomy and personhood to each individual, children, like women and some racial minorities, historically were not possessors of the full panoply of legally recognized rights. Although legal distinctions based on gender and race have been diminished, if not eliminated altogether, children continue to be denied full equality under the law. The perception of limited mental capacity, which historically for John Locke and other Enlightenment thinkers eliminated children as autonomous persons under the Social Contract, continues to operate as a barrier to affording juveniles the same rights enjoyed by adults. The perception of vulnerability and dependence, which for John Stuart Mill required the law to protect children "against their own actions as well as against external injury," endures to this day as a basis for paternalistic legal treatment not applied to adults.

To say that young people do not possess the rights afforded autonomous persons is not to say that juveniles are without rights. They possess rights of protection that include rights to receive care, affection, discipline, and guidance enabling development into mature and responsible adulthood. Protection rights also incorporate rights to be supported, maintained, educated, and provided legal remedies consistent with the minor's best interests when obligated caretakers fail to provide the minor the protection to which he is entitled.

Bruce C. Hafen, *Children's Liberation and the New Egalitarianism: Some Reservations About Abandoning Youth to Their "Rights"*

1976 Brigham Young University Law Review 605, 650–51, 656

The term "choice rights" . . . applies to minors' decisions having serious long-term consequences that have traditionally required either legal or parental approval (or both) in order to be enforceable. To suggest that legal rights of this special character should not be given premature approval is, however, not to argue for increased state-supported parental interference with the vast variety of less solemn choices that arise daily in the lives of children. Indeed, the availability of gradually increasing freedom to live with the consequences of one's own decisions is a critical element in the development of mature judgmental capacities. Still, the development of the capacity for responsible choice selection is an educational process in which growth can be smothered and stunted if unlimited freedom and unlimited responsibility are thrust too soon upon the young. Moreover, the lifelong effects of binding, childish choices can create permanent deprivations far more detrimental than the temporary limitations upon freedom inherent in the discipline of educational processes.

The development of the capacity to function as a mature, independent member of society is essential to the meaningful exercise of the full range of choice rights characteristic of the individual tradition. Precisely because of their lack of capacity, minors should enjoy legally protected rights to special treatment (including some protection against their own immaturity) that will optimize their opportunities for the development of mature capabilities that are in their best interest. Children will outgrow their restricted state, but the more important question is whether they will outgrow it with maximized capacities. An assumption that rational and moral capacity exists, when in fact it does not exist, may lead to an abandonment of the protections, processes, and opportunities that can develop these various capacities. In this sense, the concept of restricting certain choice rights is in fact an important form of protection rights. For these reasons, some distinction between rights of protection and rights of choice must be preserved. . . . The existing children's rights decisions of the Supreme Court could reasonably be categorized as cases involving rights of protection only. It would be both inappropriate and contrary to the ultimate interests of children to construe those decisions as encouraging the removal of traditional constraints upon minors' exercise of choice rights.

B. *The Right of a Child Not to be Abandoned to His "Rights": The Most Basic Right?*

The influences of some parental authority and responsibility are inevitable in view of the natural dependence of children. Rather than inhibiting optimal child development, however, this element of the parent-child relationship may be the child's most valuable source of developmental sustenance. Psychological evidence indicates that children "are not adults in miniature, they are beings *per se*, different from their elders in their mental nature, their functioning, their understanding of events, and their reactions to them." Children have many special needs that must be met in their quest for maturity and independence. The most critical of these needs is a satisfactory and permanent psychological relationship with their parents. Thus, even assuming the highest policy priority for fulfilling the actual needs of children, the worst possible results would be visited upon children by "liberating" them from the crucial psychological matrix of true family relationships. That kind of liberation would constitute the most ironic adult treatment of children — "abandoning them to their 'rights.'"

. . . .

For most parents, the "rights" of parenthood leave them no alternative but an assumption of parental responsibility, because that responsibility, both by nature and by law, can be assumed by no one else until the parent has failed. But when state-enforced policies undermine traditional parental rights, those same policies will inevitably undermine the assumption of parental responsibility. To undermine parental initiative would not be wise because our society has found no realistic alternative to it. The encouragement of parental responsibility for children is certainly less detrimental than a pervasive state assumption of child-rearing. Indeed, the development of policies that encourage parental responsibility is probably the best thing we could do for our children. One might even say that children have a right to such policies.

John E. Coons, *Intellectual Liberty and the Schools*

1 NOTRE DAME JOURNAL OF LAW, ETHICS AND PUBLIC POLICY 495, 501–510 (1985)

A. *The Special Problem of Children's Liberty*

A major difficulty . . . is the meaning of liberty in the context of childhood. In school, as in virtually all aspects of life, children remain subject to adult rule to a fairly advanced age, generally eighteen. This does not deny that the child at an early age has a will — and often a reason — as distinct and effective as that of an adult. Most adults agree that children lead a moral life which is significant even if relatively narrow in scope. And, as the child advances in competence and understanding, the justification for limiting his choices becomes progressively problematic. Nevertheless, a general subordination to parents and/or bureaucrats endures. What is its rationale? Confusion and ambivalence on this issue are evident both in the social literature of childhood and in court opinions deciding whether to support the will of the child, the state or the parent regarding such matters as obscenity, curfews, arm bands in the classroom, cosmetic surgery, abortion and the selection of school library books. Why is the autonomy principle so murky in its application even to relatively mature children?

One possible answer is that self-determination for children is necessarily in conflict with the autonomy of supervising adults. It is unlikely that father and junior can both know best; but it is certain that they cannot both rule. Yet, though this is technically correct, it could mislead. In spite of formal subordination, it may be that the child's autonomy can in practice be consistent with the rule of adults; indeed, extending the point, it will be argued here that without an adult regime the younger child's liberty can scarcely be imagined. If the experience of autonomy is to be available to a child, adult authority must be its instrument, for a child's freedom to choose at all depends upon protections and limits.

Analysis here can start with the political reality that children will be formally subject to the discretion of some particular adult or set of adults. This adult regime will be arranged in the name of child protection, children's liberty, parental liberty, or the interests of third persons — or all four. A parent or a public bureaucracy, or some combination of both, will hold the legal authority to direct his comings and goings until some age. If eighteen is the wrong age, make it fifteen — or twenty-one. The principle remains the same. Universal liberation for children in the sense of formal legal autonomy is a non-idea. The only real question here is by what rationale and under what structures should legal authority over the child be parceled out between parent, state, and the child himself if liberty — as opposed to other possible values — is to remain primary?

This inescapable limit on children's freedom is not merely an artifact of politics. It is a fact of nature. Even if one held liberty to be the sole concern, there would remain a practical, insuperable and permanent obstacle to liberation. Children are small, weak, and inexperienced; adults are big, strong and initiated. One may liberate children from the law of man, but the law of nature is beyond repeal. There is no way to send an eight-year-old out of the sovereignty of the family and into a world of liberty. For he will there be introduced to a new sovereignty of one kind or another. It may be a regime of want, ignorance, and general oppression; it may be one of delightful gratification. The ringmaster could be Fagin or Mary Poppins. Whatever the reality, it will be created by people with more power, and by the elements. Children — at least small children — will not be liberated; they will be dominated. . . .

This is true even of mature teenagers who might have a ripened capacity for autonomy or at least for autonomy in regard to specific activities such as driving. Until formal emancipation these persons will be subject to general-purpose adult regimes either of the state, the family or both. And while particular rights of a child to drive, travel or choose a religion could theoretically be recognized by law, the overall adult regime will retain very significant reins through its control of the purse and its other general powers. The state might decide to allow every child of fifteen to choose his school; nevertheless, so long as parents can retaliate by withholding the car, the allowance, new clothes and other privileges, the child's so-called right loses much of its substance.

But consider the other side: Despite this inevitability of adult dominion, a *de facto* liberty for children is not a self-contradiction. The child's strong and important interest in liberty can indeed be a favored object of policy. It can be pursued precisely by securing his legal subordination to the particular adult regime that most respects that interest. A child subject to adult authority will in practice be allowed his own choice in varying doses; these will depend upon what the particular authority thinks appropriate. The relevant question then becomes, which regime is the likelier source of such practical autonomy? There are two candidates: On the one hand stands the parent or parent substitute; on the other, some agency of the state. And, of course, authority may be parceled between them in countless ways. This is an oversimplification, but it is a place to start.

Now let us raise slightly the level of complexity. Obviously the child has not merely a liberty interest, but what can fairly be labeled a "welfare" interest; this is composed of physical safety, normal growth, affection, education and the like. His liberty interest — our special focus here — is related to, but quite different from, the welfare interest. Its core is the religious-philosophic premise that children, like adults, have wills and make choices. In this capacity for choice lies the child's claim to be part of the moral community. Ideally the choices of a child display an advancing rationality and virtue; but, in any case, choice has an absolute value for him just as it has for adults. However, unlike adults, in the case of children the liberty interest often must be subordinated to the welfare interest; otherwise little Lucy will not survive — or at least not develop — so as to exercise her full potential for autonomy. Children can make choices that society deems too costly both to the child's welfare interest and to his expanding capacity for choice. We want the adult free to decide whether to stay up late; hence we curfew the child.

Insofar as one wished to maximize children's liberty, the trick would be to find that special adult regime which would make the daily selections between yea and nay with sensitivity to the child's interest in choice here and now but with equal concern for his growing capacity for self-determination. Employing these criteria an ideal regime would decide when self-direction by the child is desirable and when it is not. It may be beneficial or baneful today for Lucy to be allowed to choose for herself whether to read or go to the movies; it may be wise or foolish to give her the choice to attend either school A or school B. In which adult shall we lodge the authority to decide whether Lucy may decide for herself? And in those cases where choice is to be denied her, who shall then decide the substantive issue?

This last question is not exclusively about liberty; for it does not arise until it has already been determined that the child shall not make the decision. It could be decided, for example, that ten-year-olds shall not be free to consent to surgery; which adult shall then consent or refuse — the state or the parent or both in some combination? The focus here seems to be welfare. Nevertheless, the question remains at least partly about the child's liberty. For, though the child's own preference in the matter cannot be decisive, it may be relevant to the correctness of the decision judged in terms either of liberty or welfare. Thus which regime has the most effective access to his views and can give them proper weight is often an important liberty issue. In truth, decisions about a child's welfare so implicate the child's interest in autonomy that there would be something eccentric about any theory that simply divorced the two. Nevertheless, the primary concern in this essay justifies a somewhat lopsided emphasis upon liberty.

It is now necessary to consider some criteria by which to evaluate the two adult regimes that compete for authority. The questions are who shall determine whether the child is to choose or be chosen for, and, if the latter, who shall decide? On the one hand stands the state operating through its professionalized agencies; on the other hand stands the family composed ambiguously of at least two, and usually more, human wills. Would there be a preferred way to approach the allocation of authority over these issues, if the object were to enhance liberty?

B. *Parental Representation of the Child's Liberty Interest*

Let us begin with a reservation. Since the child's welfare interest must be respected (even in the name of liberty), it is silly to suppose that the state should simply remain inert in the face of grave risk to the child. When the chips are down, few would abandon the child to a sadistic or wholly neglectful parent. The state may not be much good at setting minimum standards of protection, but it is all we have, unless we are to invite vigilante enforcement of child protection. . . .

. . . .

There are at least four reasons to expect parental primacy to be in general the most effective agent of liberty. Three concern promotion of the child's own liberty and will be described briefly in this section. The fourth is grounded in the liberty of the parent and is considered thereafter. At the risk of being tiresome, I shall state now and repeat that these speculations and assertions are based principally upon personal observation through twenty-five years of watching schools and families and raising more than my quota of the world's progeny. There is no social science bearing directly on this issue.

Regarding the liberty of the child, it should be observed *first*, that the normal parent has a selfish interest in the child's becoming independent. Few adults want their children to be permanent moral and economic burdens. Parents suffer when the child's autonomy suffers; what is good for the child's liberty tends to be good for parents and vice versa. This conclusion, of course, is not a logical necessity, nor could it be proved by experiment; without self-contradiction one could imagine that most parents prefer that their offspring remain moral puppets and economic parasites. Doubtless some do want just that for reasons that, long before Freud, the mass of mankind recognized as pathetic and pathological. It is the stuff of sad novels about the high bourgeoisie.

But that is the point; such motivation is not a normality. Emphatically it is not the stuff of ordinary families where adults work for a living and expect their children to do likewise. For them such an attitude constitutes moral and economic insanity. Quite evidently most parents feel that they prosper by making decisions that enhance their child's autonomy, and they suffer from those that create dependency.

Professionally bureaucrats may also in most instances work for the child's autonomy. If so, this is to their credit, for often they have a strong objective interest in maintaining dominance over the child and family; the less the child advances, the more the professional is needed. While one can admire professional restraint where it occurs, the question nonetheless would remain whether the best strategy is to entrust the fostering of the child's liberty to the altruism of experts. Of course, the danger to liberty from professional domination arises chiefly in situations where the client is captive; when, by contrast, the family is free to "exit," economic incentives can help to unite the self-interest of the professional to that of the child. . . .

. . . .

The second argument for parental choice is that parents care most about the child and that caring promotes decisions that advance his autonomy. Caring is cousin to accountability, but there is a real difference. The distinction is one of altruism — or, more properly — love. Caring denotes not self-interest, but disinterest coupled with an affection focused upon a particular child. Such a focus is normal to the family and uncharacteristic, or even improper, to the professions.

There will no doubt be instances in which accountability and caring will conflict. The support of and special care for a retarded or mentally ill child, for example, is seldom in an adult's self-interest; this is especially true when the harassed parent is offered the opportunity to pack the child away in a state institution. Love, of course, may persist where interest fails, and heroism is common in the parental role. But whether or not love prevails over interest, it must in every case be accounted a benefit to the child in the decision process. And the normal case in which both love and self-interest are allied in the deciding parent must be accounted the ideal.

Still there remains the question whether parental love seeks autonomy as a specific good. To the extent that parental love is conceived as a kind of narcissism, one could be led to expect conflict and ambivalence regarding the child's autonomy. On this issue, one consults his encounters with people who are parents and with the central traditions of our culture. At least the latter — and for me the former as well — hold that generally the relation is not only profoundly unselfish but provides the principal, if imperfect, model of selflessness; that we are our own children's keeper is acknowledged even by egotists who regard brotherhood as a canard. And, if one accepts this picture as reality, it is also easy to believe that the autonomy of the child is a primary parental object. For to love selflessly is by definition to love one who is distinctly other; perhaps, indeed, the more distinct the other becomes, the richer the possibility for loving him. It may take Albert Schweizer to love Mankind, but a mere mother could love Lucy. And the more the child becomes Lucy, the more her mother loves her.

But let us lean over backwards: The very intensity of the relation could be thought problematic. Parental fervor could get in the way of good judgment about the proper means to secure autonomy. This too seems plausible and is confirmed intermittently, especially in medical decisionmaking. On rare occasions parents seem misled by their very concern into neurotic and bizarre decisions. Surely, however, these are the exceptions proving the rule that parental caring, on the whole, supports autonomy. Equally important, these aberrations are precisely the kind of behavior which minimum standards of protection are designed to prevent.

The third premise is simply that the parent's knowledge of what will nourish autonomy will in general be superior to that of the bureaucratic decision-maker, at least for purposes of reaching decision in difficult cases. This is probable for two reasons. The first is that the parent has special access to the child's own view of things. For obvious reasons, the child's voice is difficult to hear in large institutions; indeed, outside the home, many youngsters respond to crises in their school or day care experience with a silent passivity that masks the problem and discourages adult inquiry. By contrast, the intimacy of the family maximizes the child's own power to move adults to do his will. In the normal family, even the silence of a child is a strong form of communication. Whatever the family is, it is a debating society, and the child's voice is difficult to exclude.

The parents' knowledge is thereby enhanced in ways closed to an alien professional. Doubtless the professionals' own knowledge is in certain dimensions wholly superior. He "knows" about children in general — the pathologies that sometimes bind them and the therapies that can loose them. There are unfortunately narrow limits to this kind of science and striking dissensus among the professionals. Still no one doubts its potential importance. Insofar as this kind of knowledge is reliable, however, its conclusion can usually be shared effectively with parents in various ways during the decisionmaking process whether the subject be medicine, discipline or education. The parents' knowledge, by contrast, is less subject to communication; it is too immediate, too immanent. It is often literally unspeakable. It follows, curiously, that in an important sense parents can be the more knowledgeable deciders, for they can combine the conclusions of the professional with their own incommunicable insights. This, of course, assumes a relation in which parents not only control the final decision but have access to professionals (of varying opinions).

The import of these first three considerations — self-interest, caring and knowledge — is that the family (almost without regard to its lifestyle) tends to be the right environment for the child's gradual transition from a dependent and dominated infancy to an adolescence marked by an ever increasing practical liberty bestowed by parents. In the run of families the child achieves formal autonomy at eighteen almost without a ripple. Granted, the pilgrimage through adolescence is seldom negotiated without pain; the family, nevertheless, represents the best odds for "breaking away" with one's soul intact. Were it a most miserable institution, the family might in relative terms represent the efficient medium of liberty.

Again, the parental primacy is limited. It cannot preempt the duty of the state, where necessary, to intervene to protect the child's health and safety and, thereby, indirectly, to support his liberty. To that end the state imposes its minimum standards; but their application is triggered only by demonstrated and basic family failure. To justify intervention, government historically has been required to overcome a strong presumption favoring parental authority. Quite plausibly this policy may rest on the conviction that constant or unpredictable intrusion into the family would poison the source of the very liberty of the child that the state is trying to protect.

[C]   The Personhood Theory

In determining the proper balance between the interests of children, parents, and the state, some argue that respect as a person and rights to autonomy available to adults should similarly be afforded to adolescents. As developed in the article by David Richards, excerpted immediately below, the theory of human rights that underlies the Constitution assumes that every person has the capacity for autonomy and the right to equal respect in his pursuit of autonomy. Autonomy is the central aspect of moral personality because of the unique capacity of humans to shape their lives through rational planning. As rational planners, all persons are assumed equally capable of defining the meaning of their own lives. Any individual capable of rational self-rule is entitled to be treated as a person, which in turn entails freedom from paternalistic interventions against his will.

Persons are entitled to exercise their capacity for autonomy and be treated with dignity and respect. Persons also enjoy a right to be protected from unwanted invasions of personal privacy.

Very young children lack the capacity for rationality and thus possess, in Professor Herbert Morris's words, only a "future interest" in personhood and the rights that flow therefrom. Herbert Morris, *Persons and Punishment*, in PHILOSOPHY OF LAW 572, 581 (J. Feinberg & H. Gross eds., 1975). Paternalistic responses are therefore appropriate until such time as the young person develops a capacity for rationality. When that capacity is developed, arguably by adolescence, paternalistic responses are inconsistent with personhood rights.

David A. J. Richards, *The Individual, the Family, and the Constitution: A Jurisprudential Perspective*

55 NEW YORK UNIVERSITY LAW REVIEW 1, 8, 11, 19–21, 23–26, 54–57 (1980)

A. *Rights and Autonomy*

The human rights theory that underlies the Constitution involves, first, the belief that every person has a capacity for autonomy, and, second, the principle that every person has the right to equal concern and respect in his pursuit of autonomy.

. . . .

Recognizing that the notion of human rights requires only a capacity for autonomy clarifies a common intuition. People often speak and think of a denial of human rights as an affront to dignity, a form of disrespect. If human rights rest on equal concern and respect for individual autonomy, then to deny people their rights expresses disrespect or contempt for their capacity for autonomy. Thus, the denial of rights has traditionally been justified on the ground that persons within a given class are akin to permanent infants, a status that allows for forms of paternalistic interference that would otherwise be improper. The apologists for the enslavement of blacks and the subjection of women regularly invoked such arguments. The advance of the idea of human rights has therefore rested on the repudiation of presumptions of incapacity that we now perceive as resting on an unjustified contempt.

. . . .

. . . [T]he imperative of treating persons as equals mandates basic respect for their capacity to take responsibility for their ends and lives. Fundamental to fostering such responsibility is allowing individuals with the essential capacities to take risks and make mistakes — even clearly irrational ones — because responsibility for the sting of one's own mistakes is a crucial part of the kind of independence we associate with autonomy. Paternalistic overprotection degrades its object by encouraging dependency.

. . . .

THE RIGHTS OF CHILDREN AND PARENTS

The principle of equal respect for each person's pursuit of autonomy rests on the idea that all persons have the capacity for autonomy and that principles of political right must express the moral imperative of protecting that capacity. It remains to consider the implications of this conception for broad questions of justice regarding the rights of children and parents. In this section, I shall attempt to formulate these rights. In the following sections, I shall assess the extent to which recent case law has properly applied them.

Children are the beneficiaries of two classes of rights: first, equal opportunity, and second, liberal paternalism. Parents, as such, have rights over their children derived from liberal paternalism. Parents, as men and women, have general rights against one another of fair dealing in child rearing. We may now examine some aspects of these rights.

A. *The Right of Children to Equal Opportunity*

The human infant is born the most vulnerable of the primates and therefore depends on an extended period of socialization and learning. The principle of equal opportunity requires that this period be structured to allow each person an equal chance to develop both his or her own ends in life and the capacity to realize ends that are compatible with like freedom for others. In American society, the fulfillment of this principle implicates both the family and educational institutions.

. . . .

B. *Children and Liberal Paternalism*

Classical liberal theory has, sharply circumscribed the scope of legitimate paternalism. Nonetheless, children, as a class, have traditionally been excepted from this liberal principle. John Stuart Mill expressly exempts children from the scope of his principle of liberty, and John Locke permits "Parental power," albeit within specific limits. How does the principle of liberal paternalism apply to children?

The principle of liberal paternalism, it will be recalled, permits forms of interference in others' conduct only if both of two conditions are satisfied: first, the individual must lack rational capacities or the opportunity to exercise them; and second, the irrational conduct must be likely to lead to severe and permanent impairment of the capacity to achieve one's own ends. Important constraints on the principle are that the operative idea of irrationality must be defined consistently with the moral constraints of a neutral theory of the good and that the incapacity of the individual must, to the extent feasible, be remedied, not perpetuated.

. . . .

. . . Certainly, in early childhood, it might be developmental insanity to expose the child to inconsistent systems of pluralistic values. At this stage, it may suffice that a stable and intelligible system of values is lovingly imparted, including basic metaphysical and normative perspectives on life as well as general interests that the parent desires to share with the child. Parents meet this task in diverse ways, and there is no question that, in consequence, the ends of their children take correspondingly different forms. This is both empirically natural and normatively unobjectionable. But these facts do not justify the inference that parental attitudes may prevail, without qualification, throughout childhood and adolescence. Parents understandably continue to urge their values and interests on their children throughout this period; but, to be consistent with the values of Lockean independence, they must do so in ways that acknowledge and foster the child's critical rationality in making decisions on her or his own. In particular, since the goal is to realize rational independence, education, both at school and home, must take the form of liberal education. Parents may not justly mold their children's interests to conform with their own interests and values, no matter how profound, if they do so in a way that unfairly deprives the children of developing the capacity to assess these matters by rationally weighing arguments and evidence.

Locke, writing in pre-industrial England, could not have anticipated the development of the concept of childhood into adolescence. Yet, as commentators have pointed out, the concept of adolescence suggests that the status of childhood may constitute a constitutionally invalid suspect or semi-suspect classification. Such a hypothesis appears to be premised on liberal constraints on paternalism. First, adolescents cannot be stereotyped as lacking rational capacity. The law's assumption that adulthood occurs suddenly at eighteen or twenty-one obviously contradicts the facts of developmental psychology and historical experience. Rational capacity often ripens well before these ages, and in many areas persons under these ages seem fully competent to make many decisions. . . .

. . . Under the view of privacy espoused by this Article, the rights to use contraceptives and to have abortions are associated with the protection and enhancement of personal autonomy in making strategic life decisions. These considerations apply, as well, to sexually active adolescents, indeed in some respects more strongly to these adolescents than to adults.

Consider, for example, the moralistic arguments against the use of contraceptives or abortion services by minors. If contraception permits adults to regulate the consequences of their sexual lives rationally and humanely, consonant with ethical concerns for population control, it also enables adolescents to achieve these ends. Adolescents, using contraception, can explore their sexuality and the role of sexuality in relationships without fear of procreation for which they, of all age groups, may not be ready. If adolescents' sexual conduct is governed by principles of equal concern and respect, there can be, I believe, no principled ethical objection to it. In contrast, the moralistic condemnation of all forms of sexual activity among adolescents encourages fears and misunderstandings of sexuality instead of facilitating sexual self-esteem and the sense of ethical discriminations that should rule all human relations. Similarly, the moralistic condemnation of abortions performed on minors appears to rest on reasons of no more ethical force than those applied to adults.

The paternalistic arguments against the use of contraceptives or abortion services by minors fare no better; indeed, they appear less persuasive as applied to minors than as applied to adults. Surely, of all sexually active groups, it is most in the interest of minors, whose relationships are usually extra-marital and often experimental, to use contraceptives. Indeed, liberal paternalism requires that educators fully inform adolescents of the availability and uses of contraceptives. . . .

Moreover, the application of the right to privacy to minors in these contexts protects and fosters capacities of rational independence in strategic life choices involving issues of sex, love, and procreation. The shifts in moral judgments that underlie the emergence of the constitutional right to privacy in the areas of contraception and abortion sometimes divide the generations in one household; it is a mark of generational conflicts in post-industrial society that we cannot justly assume that the older generation's moral judgments are sounder than the younger's. The right to privacy, applied to minors, protects their right to autonomous self-definition in those special contexts in which parental moralism and paternalism appear suspect on independent grounds. Furthermore, in the case of abortion, this protection of adolescent women from moralistic parents may be especially needed.

Let us remind ourselves, finally, that the idea of rights respects and fosters the capacity of people to take personal responsibility for their lives; it does not ensure that they will always exercise their rights wisely or well. Indeed, the willingness to allow people to experiment, make their own mistakes, and learn from bearing the consequences is part of the education in self-awareness that rights cultivate. We allow adolescents their rights to privacy because it appears, in the contexts of contraception and abortion, that we thus better respect their potential for dignity. Any mistakes they make in exercising these rights not only do not appear irreparable, but also appear to be of the kind that will better enable them to achieve a rational vision of their own good. At the same time, since these rights fall into the morally ambiguous area of adolescence, adults have a special responsibility for affording the kind of education that will enable children to exercise these rights wisely. It is cruel folly to extend the right to privacy to children and not, concomitantly, to ensure the kind of sexual education that will enable them to use these rights responsibly. If parents will not perform this role reasonably, the task must fall on educators in the schools.

————

Robert Batey, *The Rights of Adolescents*

23 WILLIAM AND MARY LAW REVIEW 363, 364, 370, 373–374, 376, 378–80, 383–84 (1982)

Evidence of the adolescent's capacity for moral reasoning has been a by-product of modern psychology's interest in cognitive development, the process by which a child acquires the intellectual skills of an adult. The attainment of skill at moral reasoning has been one of the primary focuses of the study of cognitive development.

[The author reviews research by Piaget, Kohlberg and others suggesting that the law's "traditional judgment" of incapacity is invalid for most adolescents.]

From the assumption that adolescents lack the capacity to make moral choices affecting their own lives, Anglo-American jurisprudence has drawn the conclusion that the adolescent's parents have the right to make those choices. The conclusion that parents have the right to make the adolescent's moral choices must be rejected, however, because, as studies indicate, the law's underlying assumption that adolescents lack the capacity to make moral choices is incorrect. Because a large majority of adolescents do have the moral reasoning capacities of adults, the law should accord the considered choices of competent adolescents the same treatment it accords similar choices of adults. . . .

. . . .

The thesis of this article can be stated simply: the law should accord the considered choices of competent adolescents the same treatment it accords similar choices of adults. Another way of phrasing the same principle is that in a situation in which the state would defer to the desires of an adult, the state can refuse to defer to the considered desires of an adolescent only upon a showing that the adolescent is not competent to make the decisions.

The principle will change the current legal treatment of adolescents in two ways. First, adoption of this principle as a guideline for legal action will reduce drastically situations in which parents may enlist the assistance of the state in controlling adolescent children. Parent-induced state intervention in the life of an adolescent will be appropriate only if the parents can demonstrate the adolescent's inability to make an adult decision. Second, adhering to this principle will expand greatly circumstances in which an adolescent may obtain state assistance in enforcing his choice over the objections of his parents. If the adolescent can establish competence to make the choice involved, the choice will be effective, regardless of the parents' wishes and regardless of whether the adolescent is seeking to block or force parental action.

. . . .

State intervention in the life of an adolescent solely because his parents disapprove of choices the adolescent has made should be tolerated only if the adolescent is not capable of making mature choices. If the minor is competent to make the decisions, the parents' opposition to his chosen course, no matter how vigorous, should not be a ground for state action.

. . . .

Recognizing the rights of competent adolescents will not only mean that parents can utilize the powers of the state against their children less frequently; this recognition will also mean that adolescent children can use these same powers against their parents more frequently. If parents override the decision of their competent adolescent child, the adolescent should be able to obtain court assistance if effectuating his choice.

. . . .

If parents can force decisions on adolescents, the courts should provide some mechanism to enable competent adolescents to overturn those decisions. Similarly, if parents can veto decisions made by their adolescent children, those children should be able to obtain judicial assistance in overriding such vetoes, unless the parents can demonstrate that the child did not make a mature choice. Thus, if an adolescent desires to pursue a particular education but his parents thwart that desire, the adolescent should be allowed to take his complaint to court. The traditional concept of the parent-child relationship would tolerate such a lawsuit only if the parents' refusal constituted nonsupport, a difficult showing for the adolescent to make. Recognition of the adolescent's capacity for adult moral reasoning, however, requires a different standard: the court should enjoin the parents from interfering unless the parents can establish that the adolescent has made an immature judgment.

As in the other settings discussed, the court proceeding in this situation would focus first on the reasons given by the parents and then on the reasoning of the adolescent. The parents would offer an "adult" explanation for opposing the child's education plan to show that the adolescent's motivations were "childish." The adolescent would then seek to deny this assertion by offering "adult" reasons for his choice. If satisfied that such reasons motivated the adolescent, the court should enjoin the parents' obstructionism.

. . . .

. . . [D]eferring to family privacy makes no sense if the complainant is an adolescent with a demonstrable ability to form and to voice mature opinions. In this latter situation, courts should feel bound to treat the dispute as an argument between adults and to adjudicate the matter accordingly. Anything less constitutes a denial of the adolescent's rights.

Adolescence marks the end of a child's transition to adulthood, to autonomous interaction in society. The law largely has ignored this transitional process, adhering instead to the concept that childhood is a legally disabling condition that vanishes completely on the attainment of a certain birthday. This Article proposes abandonment of this monolithic view of childhood, urging instead a recognition that some children — those properly labeled adolescents — are in most circumstances capable of making choices for themselves. Experimental data support this conclusion regarding adolescent decisionmaking and indicate that the considered choices of competent adolescents are not appreciably inferior to those of adults. Accordingly, the law should treat the choices of both adults and adolescents similarly, honoring the decision of an adolescent absent a showing either of incompetence to decide or of a lack of reflection in the decisionmaking process.

Adoption of this principle would dramatically affect the law's attitude toward the parent-child relationship by partially emancipating the adolescent. Thus, the legal aspects of adolescence would match the psychological aspects of adolescence by denoting the end of the transition to adulthood.

———

Henry H. Foster & Doris Jonas Freed, *A Bill of Rights for Children*

6 FAMILY LAW QUARTERLY 343, 344–47 (1972)

Children are *persons* and the law should recognize that fact, although it will take some doing. The status of minority is the last legal relic of feudalism and the arguments for and against perpetuation of that status have a familiar ring. In good measure they are the same arguments that were advanced over the issues of slavery and the emancipation of married women.

. . . .

Authority carries with it added responsibility and in the case of adults dealing with minors there are obligations of fairness and empathy. The relative helplessness and lack of autonomy of children require self-restraint and legal checks on parental and other authority. Moreover, if children are persons, their points of view should be considered, adult decisions should be reasoned, and their true best interests should always be reckoned with in terms of reality rather than fantasy. In addition to love, children are entitled to respect.

. . . .

. . . With regard to the 10 principles that follow, obviously some pertain with greater force and some with lesser force depending upon the maturation factor. Although marriage is "a basic civil right of man" we would not argue that a child of three has a constitutional right to marry. The child of three, however, should not be treated as an object or thing, and in a custody proceeding between his parents, it is our contention that he should receive legal protection and representation.

. . . .

. . . The generalizations that are made in the following "Bill of Rights for Children" will be particularized seriatim in an attempt to give the basic framework for analysis, rather than a detailed blueprint for decision. The premise behind the following principles is that children are people; they are entitled to assert individual interest in their own right, to have a fair consideration given to their claims, and to have their best interests judged in terms of pragmatic consequences.

A BILL OF RIGHTS FOR CHILDREN

A child has a moral right and should have a legal right:

1. To receive parental love and affection, discipline and guidance, and to grow to maturity in a home environment which enables him to develop into a mature and responsible adult;

2. To be supported, maintained, and educated to the best parental ability, in return for which he has the moral duty to honor his father and mother;

3. To be regarded as a *person*, within the family, at school, and before the law;

4. To receive fair treatment from all in authority;

5. To be heard and listened to;

6. To earn and keep his own earnings;

7. To seek and obtain medical care and treatment and counseling;

8. To emancipation from the parent-child relationship when that relationship has broken down and the child has left home due to abuse,

neglect, serious family conflict, or other sufficient cause, and his best interest would be served by the termination of parental authority;

9. To be free of legal disabilities or incapacities save where such are convincingly shown to be necessary and protective of the actual best interest of the child; and

10. To receive special care, consideration, and protection in the administration of law or justice so that his best interests always are a paramount factor.

[D] Mixed Theories

Some commentators have argued that the rights of adolescents should be founded on neither protection nor personhood rights exclusively but on a combination of the two theories. Franklin Zimring, for example, argues in his book, THE CHANGING WORLD OF ADOLESCENCE, that because the practice of independent decisionmaking is an integral part of the maturation process, adolescents should be permitted freedom to make important choices. Yet, at the same time, because such choices may not be fully mature, some protection against the consequences of ill-advised choices may be desirable. Therefore, Zimring advocates a model of "semi-autonomy" where adolescents are permitted to learn how to make independent choices but are, at the same time, shielded from the full burden of adult responsibilities and consequences that flow from certain of those choices.

Rather than a single "age of majority" for all legal purposes, he advocates that the law adopt one age for "phasing-in" the liberty interests enjoyed by adults and a different age for cutting off special entitlements (e.g., the Job Corps) reserved for minors and for assessing adult responsibility for misdeeds and self-support. Thus, the age of majority for protecting adult liberty interests could be set at eighteen while twenty-one could be the legal age for purposes of denying juvenile entitlements and imposing adult responsibilities.

Such a model treats different categories of adulthood in different ways. It appears to simultaneously embrace aspects of both the protectionist and personhood theories of rights.

The following ideas from Professor Herbert Morris appear to embrace aspects of both protectionism and personhood theories. Is the same thing true of any of the other theorists excerpted above?

Herbert Morris, PERSONS AND PUNISHMENT IN PHILOSOPHY OF LAW

572, 580–81 (Joel Feinberg & Hyman Gross eds., 1975)

[The] right to be treated as a person is a fundamental human right belonging to all human beings by virtue of their being human. It is also a natural, inalienable, and absolute right. I want now to defend these claims so reminiscent of an era of philosophical thinking about rights that many consider to have been seriously confused.

If the right is one that we possess by virtue of being human beings, we are immediately confronted with an apparent dilemma. If, to treat another as a person requires that we provide him with reasons for acting and avoid force or deception, how can we justify the force and deception we exercise with respect to children and the mentally ill? If they, too, have a right to be treated as persons are we not constantly infringing their rights? One way out of this is simply to restrict the right to those who satisfy the conditions of being a person. Infants and the insane, it might be argued, do not meet these conditions, and they would not then have the right. Another approach would be to describe the right they possess as a prima facie right to be treated as a person. This right might then be outweighed by other considerations. This approach generally seems to me, as I shall later argue, inadequate.

I prefer this tack. Children possess the right to be treated as persons, but they possess this right as an individual might be said, in the law of property, to possess a future interest. There are advantages in talking of individuals as having a right though complete enjoyment of it is postponed. Brought to our attention, if we ascribe to them the right, is the legitimacy of their complaint if they are not provided with opportunities and conditions assuring their full enjoyment of the right when they acquire the characteristics of persons? More than this, all persons are charged with the sensitive task of not denying them the right to be a person and to be treated as a person by failing to provide the conditions for their becoming individuals who are able freely and in an informed way to choose and who are prepared themselves to assume responsibility for their choices. There is an obligation imposed upon us all, unlike that we have with respect to animals, to respond to children in such a way as to maximize the chances of their becoming persons. This may well impose upon us the obligation to treat them as persons from a very early age, that is, to respect their choices and to place upon them the responsibility for the choices to be made. There is no need to say that there is a close connection between how we respond to them and what they become. It also imposes upon us all the duty to display constantly the qualities of a person, for what they become, they will largely become because of what they learn from us is acceptable behavior.

NOTES AND QUESTIONS

1. If personhood theorists such as Batey and Melton, § 1.03, *supra*, are correct that policy makers should afford competent adolescents the rights of adults, does it follow that such adolescents should also be held to adult standards of responsibility? Should, for example, competent adolescents be held criminally responsible, even where the death penalty is at stake? If not, does it make sense to grant competent adolescents adult *rights* but not hold them to adult *responsibilities*? Franklin Zimring's book, THE CHANGING WORLD OF LEGAL ADOLESCENCE (1982), briefly described *supra*, is worth examining in detail on this issue. See Chapter 5, *infra* for consideration of the law's response to youthful violators of the criminal law.

2. Does the Foster and Freed "Bill of Rights for Children" express a consistent personhood theory of rights? What about the first two rights, (1) the right to receive "love and affection, discipline and guidance" and (2) the right to be "supported, maintained and educated"? Are these rights not more at home with protectionist theory? If so, does that call into question Foster and Freed's conclusion that "children are persons"?

3. For more theoretical discussion of the fundamental rights of youngsters, see, *e.g.*, Rhonda Gay Hartman, *Adolescent Autonomy: Clarifying an Ageless Conundrum*, 51 HASTINGS L.J. 1265 (2000); Laurence D. Houlgate, *Three Concepts of Children's Constitutional Rights: Reflections on the Enjoyment Theory*, 2 U. PA. J. CONST. L. 77 (1999); Katherine Hunt Federle, *Children's Rights and the Need for Protection*, 34 FAM. L.Q. 421 (2000); Bruce L. Hafen & Jonathan O. Hafen, *Abandoning Children to Their Autonomy: The United Nations Convention on the Rights of the Child*, 37 HARV. INT'L L.J. 449 (1996); Martha Minow, *Whatever Happened to Children's Rights?*, 80 MINN. L. REV. 267 (1995); Lee E. Teitelbaum, *Children's Rights and the Problem of Equal Respect*, 27 HOFSTRA L. REV. 799 (1999).

Chapter 2

THE CHILD AND THE FAMILY

§ 2.01 SETTING THE FRAMEWORK: THE INTERESTS OF PARENT, CHILD, STATE

[A] The Trilogy: *Meyer, Pierce,* and *Prince*

The relationship between parent and child is generally viewed as essential to the framework of society. Until the late 1800s parental control over a child was almost unquestioned, and the state interfered very little in the family unit. In the early part of the twentieth century, state involvement in the lives of children grew with the idea that the state has a responsibility for protecting the welfare of children, who were considered some of society's most vulnerable members. The passage of compulsory school laws, the emergence of agencies that provide health care and other social services for poor children, and the creation of juvenile courts are all examples of growing state involvement in the lives of children. In addition to its interest in protecting children, the state also has an interest in its own preservation that prompts it to protect children so they will be able to participate effectively in economic and democratic institutions as adults. Sometimes parental choices may subvert these state interests, or they may conflict with the interest of the child in his or her own autonomy. Although, as the cases that follow demonstrate, the United States Supreme Court has determined that parental autonomy in the control of their children's upbringing is of a constitutional dimension, the contours of that constitutional interest are not well-defined.

MEYER v. STATE OF NEBRASKA

Supreme Court of the United States
262 U.S. 390 (1923)

Mr. Justice McReynolds *delivered the opinion of the Court.*

Plaintiff in error was tried and convicted in the District Court for Hamilton County, Nebraska, under an information which charged that on May 25, 1920, while an instructor in Zion Parochial School, he unlawfully taught the subject of reading in the German language to Raymond Parpart, a child of ten years, who had not attained and successfully passed the eighth grade. The information is based upon "An act relating to the teaching of foreign languages in the State of Nebraska," approved April 9, 1919, which follows:

> Section 1. No person, individually or as a teacher, shall, in any private, denominational, parochial or public school, teach any subject to any person in any language other than the English language.

29

Sec. 2. Languages, other than the English language, may be taught as languages only after a pupil shall have attained and successfully passed the eighth grade as evidenced by a certificate of graduation issued by the county superintendent of the county in which the child resides.

Sec. 3. Any person who violates any of the provisions of this act shall be deemed guilty of a misdemeanor and upon conviction, shall be subject to a fine of not less than twenty-five dollars ($25), nor more than one hundred dollars ($100) or be confined in the county jail for any period not exceeding thirty days for each offense.

Sec. 4. Whereas, an emergency exists, this act shall be in force from and after its passage and approval.

The Supreme Court of the State affirmed the judgment of conviction. . . . And it held that the statute forbidding this did not conflict with the Fourteenth Amendment, but was a valid exercise of the police power. . . .

The problem for our determination is whether the statute as construed and applied unreasonably infringes the liberty guaranteed to the plaintiff in error by the Fourteenth Amendment. "No State shall . . . deprive any person of life, liberty, or property, without due process of law."

While this Court has not attempted to define with exactness the liberty thus guaranteed, the term has received much consideration and some of the included things have been definitely stated. Without doubt, it denotes not merely freedom from bodily restraint, but also the right of the individual to contract, to engage in any of the common occupations of life, to acquire useful knowledge, to marry, establish a home and bring up children, to worship God according to the dictates of his own conscience, and generally to enjoy those privileges long recognized at common law as essential to the orderly pursuit of happiness by free men. The established doctrine is that this liberty may not be interfered with, under the guise of protecting the public interest, by legislative action which is arbitrary or without reasonable relation to some purpose within the competency of the State to effect. Determination by the legislature of what constitutes proper exercise of police power is not final or conclusive, but is subject to supervision by the courts.

The American people have always regarded education and acquisition of knowledge as matters of supreme importance which should be diligently promoted. The Ordinance of 1787 declares, "Religion, morality, and knowledge being necessary to good government and the happiness of mankind, schools and the means of education shall forever be encouraged." Corresponding to the right of control, it is the natural duty of the parent to give his children education suitable to their station in life; and nearly all the States, including Nebraska, enforce this obligation by compulsory laws.

Practically, education of the young is only possible in schools conducted by especially qualified persons who devote themselves thereto. The calling always has been regarded as useful and honorable, essential, indeed, to the public welfare. Mere knowledge of the German language cannot reasonably be regarded as harmful. Heretofore it has been commonly looked upon as helpful and desirable. Plaintiff in error taught this language in school as part of his occupation. His right thus to teach and the right of parents to engage him so to instruct their children, we think, are within the liberty of the Amendment.

The challenged statute forbids the teaching in school of any subject except in English; also the teaching of any other language until the pupil has attained and successfully passed the eighth grade, which is not usually accomplished before the age of twelve. The Supreme Court of the State has held that "the so-called ancient or dead languages" are not "within the spirit or the purpose of the act." Latin, Greek, Hebrew are not proscribed; but German, French, Spanish, Italian and every other alien speech are within the ban. Evidently the legislature has attempted materially to interfere with the calling of modern language teachers, with the opportunities of pupils to acquire knowledge, and with the power of parents to control the education of their own. It is said the purpose of the legislation was to promote civic development by inhibiting training and education of the immature in foreign tongues and ideals before they could learn English and acquire American ideals; and "that the English language should be and become the mother tongue of all children reared in this State." It is also affirmed that the foreign born population is very large, that certain communities commonly use foreign words, follow foreign leaders, move in a foreign atmosphere, and that the children are thereby hindered from becoming citizens of the most useful type and the public safety is imperiled.

That the State may do much, go very far, indeed, in order to improve the quality of its citizens, physically, mentally and morally, is clear; but the individual has certain fundamental rights which must be respected. The protection of the Constitution extends to all, to those who speak other languages as well as to those born with English on the tongue. Perhaps it would be highly advantageous if all had ready understanding of our ordinary speech, but this cannot be coerced by methods which conflict with the Constitution — a desirable end cannot be promoted by prohibited means.

For the welfare of his Ideal Commonwealth, Plato suggested a law which should provide: "That the wives of our guardians are to be common, and their children are to be common, and no parent is to know his own child, nor any child his parent. . . . The proper officers will take the offspring of the good parents to the pen or fold, and there they will deposit them with certain nurses who dwell in a separate quarter; but the offspring of the inferior, or of the better when they chance to be deformed, will be put away in some mysterious, unknown place, as they should be." In order to submerge the individual and develop ideal citizens, Sparta assembled the males at seven into barracks and intrusted their subsequent education and training to official guardians. Although such measures have been deliberately approved by men of great genius, their ideas touching the relation between individual and State were wholly different from those upon which our institutions rest; and it hardly will be affirmed that any legislature could impose such restrictions upon the people of a State without doing violence to both letter and spirit of the Constitution.

The desire of the legislature to foster a homogeneous people with American ideals prepared readily to understand current discussions of civic matters is easy to appreciate. Unfortunate experiences during the late war and aversion toward every characteristic of truculent adversaries were certainly enough to quicken that aspiration. But the means adopted, we think, exceed the limitations upon the power of the State and conflict with rights assured to plaintiff in error. The interference is plain enough and no adequate reason therefor in time of peace and domestic tranquility has been shown.

The power of the State to compel attendance at some school and to make reasonable regulations for all schools, including a requirement that they shall give instructions in English, is not questioned. Nor has challenge been made of the State's power to prescribe a curriculum for institutions which it supports. Those matters are not within the present controversy. Our concern is with the prohibition approved by the [Nebraska] Supreme Court. . . . No emergency has arisen which renders knowledge by a child of some language other than English so clearly harmful as to justify its inhibition with the consequent infringement of rights long freely enjoyed. We are constrained to conclude that the statute as applied is arbitrary and without reasonable relation to any end within the competency of the State.

As the statute undertakes to interfere only with teaching which involves a modern language, leaving complete freedom as to other matters, there seems no adequate foundation for the suggestion that the purpose was to protect the child's health by limiting his mental activities. It is well known that proficiency in a foreign language seldom comes to one not instructed at an early age, and experience shows that this is not injurious to the health, morals or understanding of the ordinary child.

The judgment of the court below must be reversed and the cause remanded for further proceedings not inconsistent with this opinion.

Reversed.

Mr. Justice Holmes, with Mr. Justice Sutherland, *dissented.*

———

NOTES AND QUESTIONS

1. The following excerpts are from the Nebraska Supreme Court opinion that upheld the statute:

> The salutary purpose of the statute is clear. The legislature had seen the baneful effects of permitting foreigners, who had taken residence in this country, to rear and educate their children in the language of their native land. The result of that condition was found to be inimical to our own safety. To allow the children of foreigners, who had emigrated here, to be taught from early childhood the language of the country of their parents was to rear them with that language as their mother tongue. It was to educate them so that they must always think in that language, and, as a consequence, naturally inculcate in them the ideas and sentiments foreign to the best interests of this country.

The statute, therefore, was intended not only to require that the education of all children be conducted in the English language, but that, until they had grown into that language and until it had become a part of them, they should not in the schools be taught any other language. The obvious purpose of this statute was that the English language should be and become the mother tongue of all children reared in this state. The enactment of such a statute comes reasonably within the police power of the state. *Pohl v. State,* 132 N.E. 20 (Ohio 1921); *State v. Bartels,* 181 N.W. 508 (Iowa 1921).

It is suggested that the law is an unwarranted restriction, in that it applies to all citizens of the state and arbitrarily interferes with the rights of citizens who are not of foreign ancestry, and prevents them, without reason, from having their children taught foreign languages in school. That argument is not well taken, for it assumes that every citizen finds himself restrained by the statute. The hours which a child is able to devote to study in the confinement of school are limited. It must have ample time for exercise or play. Its daily capacity for learning is comparatively small. A selection of subjects for its education, therefore, from among the many that might be taught, is obviously necessary. The legislature no doubt had in mind the practical operation of the law. The law affects few citizens, except those of foreign lineage. Other citizens, in their selection of studies, except perhaps in rare instances, have never deemed it of importance to teach their children foreign languages before such children have reached the eighth grade. In the legislative mind, the salutary effect of the statute no doubt outweighed the restriction upon the citizens generally, which, it appears, was a restriction of no real consequence.

Meyer v. Nebraska, 262 U.S. 390, 397–399 (1923) (quoting Nebraska Supreme Court opinion).

2. Does the state have a legitimate policy objective for the statute that it simply carried too far? Are there social costs if some children grow up speaking entirely in a language that is not English?

3. Whose rights are being vindicated here? Is there constitutional interest in the child to learn German? What if the child wanted to learn German, but the parents disagreed?

PIERCE v. SOCIETY OF SISTERS

Supreme Court of the United States
268 U.S. 510 (1925)

MR. JUSTICE MCREYNOLDS *delivered the opinion of the Court.*

. . . .

The challenged Act, effective September 1, 1926, requires every parent, guardian or other person having control or charge or custody of a child between eight and sixteen years to send him "to a public school for the period of time a public school shall be held during the current year" in the district where the child resides; and failure so to do is declared a misdemeanor. There are exemptions — not specially important here — for children who are not normal, or who have completed the eighth grade, or who reside at considerable distances from any public school, or whose parents or guardians hold special permits from the County Superintendent. The manifest purpose is to compel general attendance at public schools by normal children, between eight and sixteen, who have not completed the eighth grade. And without doubt enforcement of the statute would seriously impair, perhaps destroy, the profitable features of appellees' business and greatly diminish the value of their property.

Appellee, the Society of Sisters, is an Oregon corporation, organized in 1880, with power to care for orphans, educate and instruct the youth, establish and maintain academies or schools, and acquire necessary real and personal property. It has long devoted its property and effort to the secular and religious education and care of children, and has acquired the valuable good will of many parents and guardians. It conducts interdependent primary and high schools and junior colleges, and maintains orphanages for the custody and control of children between eight and sixteen. In its primary schools many children between those ages are taught the subjects usually pursued in Oregon public schools during the first eight years. Systematic religious instruction and moral training according to the tenets of the Roman Catholic Church are also regularly provided. All courses of study, both temporal and religious, contemplate continuity of training under appellee's charge; the primary schools are essential to the system and the most profitable. It owns valuable buildings, especially constructed and equipped for school purposes. The business is remunerative — the annual income from primary schools exceeds thirty thousand dollars — and the successful conduct of this requires long time contracts with teachers and parents. The Compulsory Education Act of 1922 has already caused the withdrawal from its schools of children who would otherwise continue, and their income has steadily declined. The appellants, public officers, have proclaimed their purpose strictly to enforce the statute.

After setting out the above facts the Society's bill alleges that the enactment conflicts with the right of parents to choose schools where their children will receive appropriate mental and religious training, the right of the child to influence the parents' choice of a school, the right of schools and teachers therein to engage in a useful business or profession, and is accordingly repugnant to the Constitution and void. And, further, that unless enforcement of the measure is enjoined the corporation's business and property will suffer irreparable injury.

Appellee, Hill Military Academy, is a private corporation organized in 1908 under the laws of Oregon, engaged in owning, operating and conducting for profit an elementary, college preparatory and military training school for boys between the ages of five and twenty-one years. [The opinion further describes the Hill Military Academy.] By reason of the statute and threat of enforcement appellee's business is being destroyed and its property depreciated; parents and guardians are refusing to make contracts for the future instruction of their sons, and some are being withdrawn.

The Academy's bill states the foregoing facts and then alleges that the challenged Act contravenes the corporation's rights guaranteed by the Fourteenth Amendment and that unless appellants are restrained from proclaiming its validity and threatening to enforce it, irreparable injury will result. The prayer is for an appropriate injunction.

[The lower court granted the injunctions.]

. . . .

No question is raised concerning the power of the State reasonably to regulate all schools, to inspect, supervise and examine them, their teachers and pupils; to require that all children of proper age attend some school, that teachers shall be of good moral character and patriotic disposition, that certain studies plainly essential to good citizenship must be taught, and that nothing be taught which is manifestly inimical to the public welfare.

The inevitable practical result of enforcing the Act under consideration would be destruction of appellees' primary schools, and perhaps all other private primary schools for normal children within the State of Oregon. These parties are engaged in a kind of undertaking not inherently harmful, but long regarded as useful and meritorious. Certainly there is nothing in the present records to indicate that they have failed to discharge their obligations to patrons, students or the State. And there are no peculiar circumstances or present emergencies which demand extraordinary measures relative to primary education.

Under the doctrine of *Meyer v. Nebraska*, we think it entirely plain that the Act of 1922 unreasonably interferes with the liberty of parents and guardians to direct the upbringing and education of children under their control. As often heretofore pointed out, rights guaranteed by the Constitution may not be abridged by legislation which has no reasonable relation to some purpose within the competency of the State. The fundamental theory of liberty upon which all governments in this Union repose excludes any general power of the State to standardize its children by forcing them to accept instruction from public teachers only. The child is not the mere creature of the State; those who nurture him and direct his destiny have the right, coupled with the high duty, to recognize and prepare him for additional obligations.

Appellees are corporations and therefore, it is said, they cannot claim for themselves the liberty which the Fourteenth Amendment guarantees. . . . But they have business and property for which they claim protection. These are threatened with destruction through the unwarranted compulsion which appellants are exercising over present and prospective patrons of their schools. . . .

The injury to appellees was present and very real, not a mere possibility in the remote future. If no relief had been possible prior to the effective date of the Act, the injury would have become irreparable. Prevention of impending injury by unlawful action is a well recognized function of courts of equity. The decrees below are

Affirmed.

———

NOTES AND QUESTIONS

1. The statute in *Meyer* was passed after World War I, a likely result of antipathy towards Germany and all things German. The Oregon statute in *Pierce* reflected concern about the influx of immigrants, many of whom were Roman Catholic. Some of the state's arguments were printed in the Supreme Court opinion syllabus:

> The subject of immigration is one which is exclusively under the control of the Central Government. The States have nothing to say as to the number or class of the immigrants who may be permitted to settle within their limits. It would therefore appear to be both unjust and unreasonable to prevent them from taking the steps which each may deem necessary and proper for Americanizing its new immigrants and developing them into patriotic and law-abiding citizens. At present, the vast majority of the private schools in the country are conducted by members of some particular religious belief. They may be followed, however, by those organized and controlled by believers in certain economic doctrines entirely destructive of the fundamentals of our government. Can it be contended that there is no way in which a State can prevent the entire education of a considerable portion of its future citizens being controlled and conducted by bolshevists, syndicalists and communists?

The issues presented in *Meyer* and *Pierce* are no less relevant in education policy today. What ways do states today attempt to preserve a society of shared values? To what extent does this interfere with the goal of cultural diversity?

2. Whose rights were vindicated in *Pierce*? After *Pierce* and *Meyer*, what is the interest of the parent in controlling the upbringing of the child in the face of state interference? What interest does the child have in his or her education? *See* Barbara Bennett Woodhouse, *Who Owns the Child*, Meyer *and* Pierce *and the Child as Property*, 33 WM. & MARY L. REV. 995 (1992) (arguing that the parental liberty described in the cases essentially was a liberty to control the child as parental property); Paula Abrams, *The Little Red Schoolhouse:* Pierce, *State Monopoly of Education and the Politics of Intolerance*, 20 CONST. COMMENT 61 (2003) (*Pierce* in historical context).

3. What would public schools be like if *Pierce* had come out the other way? If parents did not have the option to send their children to private schools,

would powerful parents demand that public schools improve and provide the funds for them to do so?

Are there any policy arguments that might justify a common public education? What about this argument made by the state in *Pierce*?

> The voters of Oregon might have felt that the mingling together, during a portion of their education, of the children of all races and sects, might be the best safeguard against future internal dissensions and consequent weakening of the community against foreign dangers.

4. *Pierce* guaranteed parents the right to send their child to either sectarian or nonsectarian private schools. Could a state shut down its public schools? The United States Supreme Court has determined that education is not a fundamental right (so as to be entitled to strict scrutiny under the equal protection clause) under the federal constitution, *San Antonio Public School Dist. v. Rodriguez*, 411 U.S. 1 (1973). But every state provides for a free public education by statute, and every state has an education clause in its state constitution. In *Plyler v. Doe*, 457 U.S. 202 (1982), the Supreme Court held unconstitutional a state statute that denied funds for the education of undocumented alien children. Because of the cost to the Nation and to the innocent children who would be victims of the statute, the Court ruled that the discrimination in the statute was not rational.

5. Parents also have the option to educate their child at home. All states allow for some exception from compulsory school attendance requirements for parents who wish to educate their children at home. States vary in the amount of regulation and supervision that they impose on home schooling, but most require some kind of standardized evaluation of the educational progress of the child who is schooled at home. What are some of the pros and cons of a state policy that allows parents to home school their children? How much should the state regulate home schooling? What if it were determined that the manner of schooling that a parent employed was harmful for a child? In the next opinion, the Supreme Court addresses the power of the state to intervene in the decision of a parent (or guardian) if there is a threat of harm to the child or to public welfare.

PRINCE v. MASSACHUSETTS

Supreme Court of the United States
321 U.S. 158 (1944)

Mr. Justice Rutledge *delivered the opinion of the Court.*

The case brings for review another episode in the conflict between Jehovah's Witnesses and state authority. This time Sarah Prince appeals from convictions for violating Massachusetts' child labor laws, by acts said to be a rightful exercise of her religious convictions.

When the offenses were committed she was the aunt and custodian of Betty M. Simmons, a girl nine years of age. Originally there were three separate complaints. They were, shortly, for (1) refusal to disclose Betty's identity and age to a public officer whose duty was to enforce the statutes; (2) furnishing her with magazines, knowing she was to sell them unlawfully, that is, on the street; and (3) as Betty's custodian, permitting her to work contrary to law. . . . [The state Supreme Judicial Court reversed the conviction under the first complaint on state grounds; but sustained the judgments founded on the other two.] They present the only questions for our decision. These are whether §§ 80 and 81 [of Massachusetts' child labor law], as applied, contravene the Fourteenth Amendment by denying or abridging appellant's freedom of religion and by denying to her the equal protection of the laws.

Sections 80 and 81 form parts of Massachusetts' comprehensive child labor law. They provide methods for enforcing the prohibitions of § 69, which is as follows:

> No boy under twelve and no girl under eighteen shall sell, expose or offer for sale any newspapers, magazines, periodicals or any other articles of merchandise of any description, or exercise the trade of bootblack or scavenger, or any other trade, in any street or public place.

Sections 80 and 81, so far as pertinent, read:

> Whoever furnishes or sells to any minor any article of any description with the knowledge that the minor intends to sell such article in violation of any provision of sections sixty-nine to seventy-three, inclusive, or after having received written notice to this effect from any officer charged with the enforcement thereof, or knowingly procures or encourages any minor to violate any provisions of said sections, shall be punished by a fine of not less than ten nor more than two hundred dollars or by imprisonment for not more than two months, or both.

> Any parent, guardian or custodian having a minor under his control who compels or permits such minor to work in violation of any provision of sections sixty to seventy-four, inclusive, . . . shall for a first offense be punished by a fine of not less than two nor more than ten dollars or by imprisonment for not more than five days, or both; . . . .

The story told by the evidence has become familiar. It hardly needs repeating, except to give setting to the variations introduced through the part played by a child of tender years. Mrs. Prince, living in Brockton, is the mother of two young sons. She also has legal custody of Betty Simmons, who lives with them. The children too are Jehovah's Witnesses and both Mrs. Prince and Betty testified they were ordained ministers. The former was accustomed to go each week on the streets of Brockton to distribute "Watchtower" and "Consolation," according to the usual plan. [Typically specified small sums are generally asked and received but the publications may be had without the payment if so desired.] She had permitted the children to engage in this activity previously, and had been warned against doing so by the school attendance officer, Mr. Perkins. But, until December 18, 1941, she generally did not take them with her at night.

That evening, as Mrs. Prince was preparing to leave her home, the children asked to go. She at first refused. Childlike, they resorted to tears; and, motherlike, she yielded. Arriving downtown, Mrs. Prince permitted the children "to engage in the preaching work with her upon the sidewalks." That is, with specific reference to Betty, she and Mrs. Prince took positions about twenty feet apart near a street intersection. Betty held up in her hand, for passers-by to see, copies of "Watch Tower" and "Consolation." From her shoulder hung the usual canvas magazine bag, on which was printed: "Watchtower and Consolation 5 cents per copy." No one accepted a copy from Betty that evening and she received no money. Nor did her aunt. But on other occasions, Betty had received funds and given out copies.

Mrs. Prince and Betty remained until 8:45 p.m. A few minutes before this, Mr. Perkins approached Mrs. Prince. A discussion ensued. He inquired and she refused to give Betty's name. However, she stated the child attended the Shaw School. Mr. Perkins referred to his previous warnings and said he would allow five minutes for them to get off the street. Mrs. Prince admitted she supplied Betty with the magazines and said, "Neither you nor anybody else can stop me. . . . This child is exercising her God-given right and her constitutional right to preach the gospel, and no creature has a right to interfere with God's commands." However, Mrs. Prince and Betty departed. She remarked as she went, "I'm not going through this any more. We've been through it time and time again. I'm going home and put the little girl to bed." It may be added that testimony, by Betty, her aunt and others, was offered at the trials, and was excluded, to show that Betty believed it was her religious duty to perform this work and failure would bring condemnation "to everlasting destruction at Armageddon."

As the case reaches us, the questions are no longer open whether what the child did was a "sale" or an "offer to sell" within § 69 or was "work" within § 81. The state court's decision has foreclosed them adversely to appellant as a matter of state law. The only question remaining therefore is whether, as construed and applied, the statute is valid. Upon this the court said: "We think that freedom of the press and of religion is subject to incidental regulation to the slight degree involved in the prohibition of the selling of religious literature in streets and public places by boys under twelve and girls under eighteen, and in the further statutory provisions herein considered, which have been adopted as means of enforcing that prohibition."

Appellant does not stand on freedom of the press. Regarding it as secular, she concedes it may be restricted as Massachusetts has done.[1] Hence, she rests squarely on freedom of religion under the First Amendment, applied by the Fourteenth to the states. She buttresses this foundation, however, with a claim of parental right as secured by the due process clause of the latter Amendment.[2] Cf. Meyer v. Nebraska. These guaranties, she thinks, guard

---

[1] [7] Appellant's brief says: "The purpose of the legislation is to protect children from economic exploitation and keep them from the evils of such enterprises that contribute to the degradation of children." And at the argument counsel stated the prohibition would be valid as against a claim of freedom of the press as a nonreligious activity.

[2] [8] The due process claim, as made and perhaps necessarily, extends no further than that to freedom of religion, since in the circumstances all that is comprehended in the former is included in the latter.

alike herself and the child in what they have done. Thus, two claimed liberties are at stake. One is the parent's, to bring up the child in the way he should go, which for appellant means to teach him the tenets and the practices of their faith. The other freedom is the child's, to observe these; and among them is "to preach the gospel . . . by public distribution" of "Watchtower" and "Consolation," in conformity with the scripture: "A little child shall lead them."

. . . .

To make accommodation between these freedoms and an exercise of state authority always is delicate. It hardly could be more so than in such a clash as this case presents. On one side is the obviously earnest claim for freedom of conscience and religious practice. With it is allied the parent's claim to authority in her own household and in the rearing of her children. The parent's conflict with the state over control of the child and his training is serious enough when only secular matters are concerned. It becomes the more so when an element of religious conviction enters. Against these sacred private interests, basic in a democracy, stand the interests of society to protect the welfare of children, and the state's assertion of authority to that end, made here in a manner conceded valid if only secular things were involved. The last is no mere corporate concern of official authority. It is the interest of youth itself, and of the whole community, that children be both safeguarded from abuses and given opportunities for growth into free and independent well-developed men and citizens. Between contrary pulls of such weight, the safest and most objective recourse is to the lines already marked out, not precisely but for guides, in narrowing the no man's land where this battle has gone on.

The rights of children to exercise their religion, and of parents to give them religious training and to encourage them in the practice of religious belief, as against preponderant sentiment and assertion of state power voicing it, have had recognition here, most recently in *West Virginia State Board of Education v. Barnette*. Previously in *Pierce v. Society of Sisters*, this Court had sustained the parent's authority to provide religious with secular schooling, and the child's right to receive it, as against the state's requirement of attendance at public schools. And in *Meyer v. Nebraska*, children's rights to receive teaching in languages other than the nation's common tongue were guarded against the state's encroachment. It is cardinal with us that the custody, care and nurture of the child reside first in the parents, whose primary function and freedom include preparation for obligations the state can neither supply nor hinder. *Pierce v. Society of Sisters, supra.* And it is in recognition of this that these decisions have respected the private realm of family life which the state cannot enter.

But the family itself is not beyond regulation in the public interest, as against a claim of religious liberty. And neither rights of religion nor rights of parenthood are beyond limitation. Acting to guard the general interest in youth's well being, the state as *parens patriae* may restrict the parent's control by requiring school attendance, regulating or prohibiting the child's labor and in many other ways. Its authority is not nullified merely because the parent grounds his claim to control the child's course of conduct on religion or conscience. Thus, he cannot claim freedom from compulsory vaccination for the child more than for himself on religious grounds. The right to practice religion freely does not include liberty to expose the community or the child to communicable disease or the latter to ill health or death. The catalogue need not be lengthened. It is sufficient to show what indeed appellant hardly disputes, that the state has a wide range of power for limiting parental freedom and authority in things affecting the child's welfare; and that this includes, to some extent, matters of conscience and religious conviction.

But it is said the state cannot do so here. This, first, because when state action impinges upon a claimed religious freedom, it must fall unless shown to be necessary for or conducive to the child's protection against some clear and present danger, and, it is added, there was no such showing here. The child's presence on the street, with her guardian, distributing or offering to distribute the magazines, it is urged, was in no way harmful to her, nor in any event more so than the presence of many other children at the same time and place, engaged in shopping and other activities not prohibited. Accordingly, in view of the preferred position the freedoms of the First Article occupy, the statute in its present application must fall. It cannot be sustained by any presumption of validity. And, finally, it is said, the statute is, as to children, an absolute prohibition, not merely a reasonable regulation, of the denounced activity.

Concededly a statute or ordinance identical in terms with § 69, except that it is applicable to adults or all persons generally, would be invalid. But the mere fact a state could not wholly prohibit this form of adult activity, whether characterized locally as a "sale" or otherwise, does not mean it cannot do so for children. Such a conclusion granted would mean that a state could impose no greater limitation upon child labor than upon adult labor. Or, if an adult were free to enter dance halls, saloons, and disreputable places generally, in order to discharge his conceived religious duty to admonish or dissuade persons from frequenting such places, so would be a child with similar convictions and objectives, if not alone then in the parent's company, against the state's command.

The state's authority over children's activities is broader than over like actions of adults. This is peculiarly true of public activities and in matters of employment. A democratic society rests, for its continuance, upon the healthy, well-rounded growth of young people into full maturity as citizens, with all that implies. It may secure this against impeding restraints and dangers within a broad range of selection. Among evils most appropriate for such action are the crippling effects of child employment, more especially in public places, and the possible harms arising from other activities subject to all the diverse influences of the street. It is too late now to doubt that legislation appropriately designed to reach such evils is within the state's police power, whether against the parent's claim to control of the child or one that religious scruples dictate contrary action.

It is true children have rights, in common with older people, in the primary use of highways. But even in such use streets afford dangers for them not affecting adults. And in other uses, whether in work or in other things, this difference may be magnified. This is so not only when children are unaccompanied but certainly to some extent when they are with their parents. What may be wholly permissible for adults therefore may not be so for children, either with or without their parents' presence.

Street preaching, whether oral or by handing out literature, is not the primary use of the highway, even for adults. While for them it cannot be wholly prohibited, it can be regulated within reasonable limits in accommodation to the primary and other incidental uses. But, for obvious reasons, notwithstanding appellant's contrary view, the validity of such a prohibition applied to children not accompanied by an older person hardly would seem open to question. The case reduces itself therefore to the question whether the presence of the child's guardian puts a limit to the state's power. That fact may lessen the likelihood that some evils the legislation seeks to avert will occur. But it cannot forestall all of them. The zealous though lawful exercise of the right to engage in propagandizing the community, whether in religious, political or other matters, may and at times does create situations difficult enough for adults to cope with and wholly inappropriate for children, especially of tender years, to face. Other harmful possibilities could be stated, of emotional excitement and psychological or physical injury. Parents may be free to become martyrs themselves. But it does not follow they are free, in identical circumstances, to make martyrs of their children before they have reached the age of full and legal discretion when they can make that choice for themselves. Massachusetts has determined that an absolute prohibition, though one limited to streets and public places and to the incidental uses proscribed, is necessary to accomplish its legitimate objectives. Its power to attain them is broad enough to reach these peripheral instances in which the parent's supervision may reduce but cannot eliminate entirely the ill effects of the prohibited conduct. We think that with reference to the public proclaiming of religion, upon the streets and in other similar public places, the power of the state to control the conduct of children reaches beyond the scope of its authority over adults, as is true in the case of other freedoms, and the rightful boundary of its power has not been crossed in this case.

In so ruling we dispose also of appellant's argument founded upon denial of equal protection. It falls with that based on denial of religious freedom, since in this instance the one is but another phrasing of the other. Shortly, the contention is that the street, for Jehovah's Witnesses and their children, is their church, since their conviction makes it so; and to deny them access to it for religious purposes as was done here has the same effect as excluding altar boys, youthful choristers, and other children from the edifices in which they practice their religious beliefs and worship. The argument hardly needs more than statement, after what has been said, to refute it. However Jehovah's Witnesses may conceive them, the public highways have not become their religious property merely by their assertion. And there is no denial of equal protection in excluding their children from doing there what no other children may do.

Our ruling does not extend beyond the facts the case presents. We neither lay the foundation "for any [that is, every] state intervention in the indoctrination and participation of children in religion" which may be done "in the name of their health and welfare" nor give warrant for "every limitation on their religious training and activities." The religious training and indoctrination of children may be accomplished in many ways, some of which, as we have noted, have received constitutional protection through decisions of this Court. These and all others except the public proclaiming of religion on the streets, if this may be taken as either training or indoctrination of the proclaimer, remain unaffected by the decision.

The judgment is

Affirmed.

[The opinion of MR. JUSTICE JACKSON, *dissenting on the grounds for affirmance*, and who was joined by MR. JUSTICE ROBERTS and MR. JUSTICE FRANKFURTER, *is omitted*.]

MR. JUSTICE MURPHY, *dissenting*:

This attempt by the state of Massachusetts to prohibit a child from exercising her constitutional right to practice her religion on the public streets cannot, in my opinion, be sustained.

The record makes clear the basic fact that Betty Simmons, the nine-year old child in question, was engaged in a genuine religious, rather than commercial, activity. She was a member of Jehovah's Witnesses and had been taught the tenets of that sect by her guardian, the appellant. Such tenets included the duty of publicly distributing religious tracts on the street and from door to door. Pursuant to this religious duty and in the company of the appellant, Betty Simmons on the night of December 18, 1941, was standing on a public street corner and offering to distribute Jehovah's Witness literature to passersby. There was no expectation of pecuniary profit to herself or to appellant. It is undisputed, furthermore, that she did this of her own desire and with appellant's consent. She testified that she was motivated by her love of the Lord and that He commanded her to distribute this literature; this was, she declared, her way of worshiping God. She was occupied, in other words, in "an age-old form of missionary evangelism" with a purpose "as evangelical as the revival meeting."

Religious training and activity, whether performed by adult or child, are protected by the Fourteenth Amendment against interference by state action, except insofar as they violate reasonable regulations adopted for the protection of the public health, morals and welfare. Our problem here is whether a state, under the guise of enforcing its child labor laws, can lawfully prohibit girls under the age of eighteen and boys under the age of twelve from practicing their religious faith insofar as it involves the distribution or sale of religious tracts on the public streets. No question of freedom of speech or freedom of press is present and we are not called upon to determine the permissible restraints on those rights. Nor are any truancy or curfew restrictions in issue. The statutes in question prohibit all children within the specified age limits from selling or offering to sell "any newspapers, magazines, periodicals or any other articles of merchandise of any description . . . in any street or public place." Criminal sanctions are imposed on the parents and guardians who compel or permit minors in their control to engage in the prohibited transactions. The state court has construed these statutes to cover the activities here involved, thereby imposing an indirect restraint through the parents and guardians on the free exercise by minors of their religious beliefs. This indirect restraint is no less effective than a direct one. A square conflict between the constitutional guarantee of religious freedom and the state's legitimate interest in protecting the welfare of its children is thus presented.

As the opinion of the Court demonstrates, the power of the state lawfully to control the religious and other activities of children is greater than its power over similar activities of adults. But that fact is no more decisive of the issue posed by this case than is the obvious fact that the family itself is subject to reasonable regulation in the public interest. We are concerned solely with the reasonableness of this particular prohibition of religious activity by children.

In dealing with the validity of statutes which directly or indirectly infringe religious freedom and the right of parents to encourage their children in the practice of a religious belief, we are not aided by any strong presumption of the constitutionality of such legislation. On the contrary, the human freedoms enumerated in the First Amendment and carried over into the Fourteenth Amendment are to be presumed to be invulnerable and any attempt to sweep away those freedoms is prima facie invalid. It follows that any restriction or prohibition must be justified by those who deny that the freedoms have been unlawfully invaded. The burden was therefore on the state of Massachusetts to prove the reasonableness and necessity of prohibiting children from engaging in religious activity of the type involved in this case.

The burden in this instance, however, is not met by vague references to the reasonableness underlying child labor legislation in general. The great interest of the state in shielding minors from the evil vicissitudes of early life does not warrant every limitation on their religious training and activities. The reasonableness that justifies the prohibition of the ordinary distribution of literature in the public streets by children is not necessarily the reasonableness that justifies such a drastic restriction when the distribution is part of their religious faith. If the right of a child to practice its religion in that manner is to be forbidden by constitutional means, there must be convincing proof that such a practice constitutes a grave and immediate danger to the state or to the health, morals or welfare of the child. The vital freedom of religion, which is "of the very essence of a scheme of ordered liberty," cannot be erased by slender references to the state's power to restrict the more secular activities of children.

The state, in my opinion, has completely failed to sustain its burden of proving the existence of any grave or immediate danger to any interest which it may lawfully protect. There is no proof that Betty Simmons' mode of worship constituted a serious menace to the public. It was carried on in an orderly, lawful manner at a public street corner. And "one who is rightfully on a street which the state has left open to the public carries with him there as elsewhere the constitutional right to express his views in an orderly fashion. This right extends to the communication of ideas by handbills and literature as well as by the spoken word." The sidewalk, no less than the cathedral or the evangelist's tent, is a proper place, under the Constitution, for the orderly worship of God. Such use of the streets is as necessary to the Jehovah's Witnesses, the Salvation Army and others who practice religion without benefit of conventional shelters as is the use of the streets for purposes of passage. It is claimed, however, that such activity was likely to affect adversely the health, morals and welfare of the child. Reference is made in the majority opinion to "the crippling effects of child employment, more especially in public places, and the possible harms arising from other activities subject to all the diverse influences of the street." To the extent that they flow from participation in ordinary commercial activities, these harms are irrelevant to this case. And the bare possibility that such harms might emanate from distribution of religious literature is not, standing alone, sufficient justification for restricting freedom of conscience and religion. Nor can parents or guardians be subjected to criminal liability because of vague possibilities that their religious teachings might cause injury to the child. The evils must be grave, immediate, substantial. Yet there is not the slightest indication in this record, or in sources subject to judicial notice, that children engaged in distributing literature pursuant to their religious beliefs have been or are likely to be subject to any of the harmful "diverse influences of the street." Indeed, if probabilities are to be indulged in, the likelihood is that children engaged in serious religious endeavor are immune from such influences. Gambling, truancy, irregular eating and sleeping habits, and the more serious vices are not consistent with the high moral character ordinarily displayed by children fulfilling religious obligations. Moreover, Jehovah's Witness children invariably make their distributions in groups subject at all times to adult or parental control, as was done in this case. The dangers are thus exceedingly remote, to say the least. And the fact that the zealous exercise of the right to propagandize the community may result in violent or disorderly situations difficult for children to face is no excuse for prohibiting the exercise of that right.

No chapter in human history has been so largely written in terms of persecution and intolerance as the one dealing with religious freedom. From ancient times to the present day, the ingenuity of man has known no limits in its ability to forge weapons of oppression for use against those who dare to express or practice unorthodox religious beliefs. And the Jehovah's Witnesses are living proof of the fact that even in this nation, conceived as it was in the ideals of freedom, the right to practice religion in unconventional ways is still far from secure. Theirs is a militant and unpopular faith, pursued with a fanatical zeal. They have suffered brutal beatings; their property has been destroyed; they have been harassed at every turn by the resurrection and enforcement of little used ordinances and statutes. *See* Mulder and Comisky, *Jehovah's Witnesses Mold Constitutional Law*, 2 Bill of Rights Review, No. 4, p. 262. To them, along with other present-day religious minorities, befalls the burden of testing our devotion to the ideals and constitutional guarantees of religious freedom. We should therefore hesitate before approving the application of a statute that might be used as another instrument of oppression. Religious freedom is too sacred a right to be restricted or prohibited in any degree without convincing proof that a legitimate interest of the state is in grave danger.

———

NOTES AND QUESTIONS

1. What is the state interest in enacting child labor laws? Are the activities that Betty and her aunt were engaged in the kind of activities at which child labor laws generally were aimed? What was the risk of harm to Betty under the facts of this case? What if Betty merely gave witness on the street, that is, merely told others about her faith? The Court states that the law would not be constitutional if applied to adults. Why? Should it make a difference that Betty was accompanied by an adult, especially a parent or guardian?

2. What is the interest that the aunt/guardian claims? Is it different from the parental interest in *Meyer* or *Pierce*? In what way do child labor laws encroach on parental authority? the child's autonomy? Does Betty have an independent interest here, at least with regard to the free exercise of religion? Would she have a greater interest if she were older? How does the Court weigh these conflicting interests in *Prince*? What is the source of the state's power to nullify parental authority?

[B]   Parental Authority and Compulsory Education

WISCONSIN v. YODER

Supreme Court of the United States
406 U.S. 205 (1972)

MR. CHIEF JUSTICE BURGER *delivered the opinion of the Court.*

On petition of the State of Wisconsin, we granted the *writ of certiorari* in this case to review a decision of the Wisconsin Supreme Court holding that respondents' convictions for violating the State's compulsory school-attendance law were invalid under the Free Exercise Clause of the First Amendment to the United States Constitution made applicable to the States by the Fourteenth Amendment. For the reasons hereafter stated we affirm the judgment of the Supreme Court of Wisconsin.

Respondents [are members of the Amish religious community.] They and their families are residents of . . . Wisconsin. Wisconsin's compulsory school-attendance law required them to cause their children to attend public or private school until reaching age 16, but the respondents declined to send their children, ages 14 and 15, to public school after they complete[d] the eighth grade. The children were not enrolled in any private school, or within any recognized exception to the compulsory-attendance law, and they are conceded to be subject to the Wisconsin statute.

On complaint of the school district administrator for the public schools, respondents were charged, tried, and convicted of violating the compulsory-attendance law in Green County Court and were fined the sum of $55 each. Respondents defended on the ground that the application of the compulsory-attendance law violated their rights under the First and Fourteenth Amendments. The trial testimony showed that respondents believed, in accordance with the tenets of Old Order Amish communities generally, that their children's attendance at high school, public or private, was contrary to the Amish religion and way of life. They believed that by sending their children to high school, they would not only expose themselves to the danger of the censure of the church community, but, as found by the county courts, also endanger their own salvation and that of their children. The State stipulated that respondents' religious beliefs were sincere.

In support of their position, respondents presented as expert witnesses scholars on religion and education whose testimony is uncontradicted. They expressed their opinions on the relationship of the Amish belief concerning school attendance to the more general tenets of their religion, and described the impact that compulsory high school attendance could have on the continued survival of Amish communities as they exist in the United States today. The history of the Amish sect was given in some detail. . . . As a result of [the Amish] common heritage, Old Order Amish communities today are characterized by a fundamental belief that salvation requires life in a church community separate and apart from the world and worldly influence. This concept of life aloof from the world and its values is central to their faith.

A related feature of Old Order Amish communities is their devotion to a life in harmony with nature and the soil, as exemplified by the simple life of . . . our early national life. Amish beliefs require members of the community to make their living by farming or closely related activities. . . .

Amish objection to formal education beyond the eighth grade is firmly grounded in these central religious concepts. They object to the high school, and higher education generally, because the values they teach are in marked variance with Amish values and the Amish way of life; they view secondary school education as an impermissible exposure of their children to a "worldly" influence in conflict with their beliefs. The high school tends to emphasize intellectual and scientific accomplishments, self-distinction, competitiveness, worldly success, and social life with other students. Amish society emphasizes informal learning-through-doing; a life of "goodness," rather than a life of intellect; wisdom, rather than technical knowledge, community welfare, rather than competition; and separation from, rather than integration with, contemporary worldly society.

Formal high school education beyond the eighth grade is contrary to Amish beliefs, not only because it places Amish children in an environment hostile to Amish beliefs with increasing emphasis on competition in class work and sports and with pressure to conform to the styles, manners, and ways of the peer group, but also because it takes them away from their community, physically and emotionally, during the crucial and formative adolescent period of life. During this period, the children must acquire Amish attitudes favoring manual work and self-reliance and the specific skills needed to perform the adult role of an Amish farmer or housewife. They must learn to enjoy physical labor. Once a child has learned basic reading, writing, and elementary mathematics, these traits, skills, and attitudes admittedly fall within the category of those best learned through example and "doing" rather than in a classroom. . . . In short, high school attendance with teachers who are not of the Amish faith — and may even be hostile to it — interposes a serious barrier to the integration of the Amish child into the Amish religious community. Dr. John Hostetler, one of the experts on Amish society, testified that the modern high school is not equipped, in curriculum or social environment, to impart the values promoted by Amish society.

The Amish do not object to elementary education through the first eight grades as a general proposition because they agree that their children must have basic skills in the "three R's" in order to read the Bible, to be good farmers and citizens, and to be able to deal with non-Amish people when necessary in the course of daily affairs. They view such a basic education as acceptable because it does not significantly expose their children to worldly values or interfere with their development in the Amish community during the crucial adolescent period. While Amish accept compulsory elementary education generally, wherever possible they have established their own elementary schools in many respects like the small local schools of the past. . . .

On the basis of such considerations, Dr. Hostetler testified that compulsory high school attendance could not only result in great psychological harm to Amish children, because of the conflicts it would produce, but would also, in his opinion, ultimately result in the destruction of the Old Order Amish church community as it exists in the United States today. The testimony of Dr. Donald A. Erickson, an expert witness on education, also showed that the Amish succeed in preparing their high school age children to be productive members of the Amish community. He described their system of learning through doing the skills directly relevant to their adult roles in the Amish community as "ideal" and perhaps superior to ordinary high school education. The evidence also showed that the Amish have an excellent record as law-abiding and generally self-sufficient members of society.

Although the trial court in its careful findings determined that the Wisconsin compulsory school-attendance law "does interfere with the freedom of the Defendants to act in accordance with their sincere religious belief" it also concluded that the requirement of high school attendance until age 16 was a "reasonable and constitutional" exercise of governmental power, and therefore denied the motion to dismiss the charges. The Wisconsin Circuit Court affirmed the convictions. The Wisconsin Supreme Court, however, sustained respondents' claim under the Free Exercise Clause of the First Amendment and reversed the convictions. A majority of the court was of the opinion that the State had failed to make an adequate showing that its interest in "establishing and maintaining an educational system overrides the defendants' right to the free exercise of their religion." . . .

I

There is no doubt as to the power of a State, having a high responsibility for education of its citizens, to impose reasonable regulations for the control and duration of basic education. . . . Thus, a State's interest in universal education, however highly we rank it, is not totally free from a balancing process when it impinges on fundamental rights and interest, such as those specifically protected by the Free Exercise Clause of the First Amendment, and the traditional interest of parents with respect to the religious upbringing of their children so long as they . . . "prepare [them] for additional obligations." . . .

It follows that in order for Wisconsin to compel school attendance beyond the eighth grade against a claim that such attendance interferes with the practice of a legitimate religious belief, it must appear either that the State does not deny the free exercise of religious belief by its requirement, or that there is a state interest of sufficient magnitude to override the interest claiming protection under the Free Exercise Clause. . . .

The essence of all that has been said and written on the subject is that only those interests of the highest order and those not otherwise served can overbalance legitimate claims to the free exercise of religion. We can accept it as settled, therefore, that, however strong the State's interest in universal compulsory education, it is by no means absolute to the exclusion or subordination of all other interests. . . .

II

We come then to the quality of the claims of the respondents concerning the alleged encroachment of Wisconsin's compulsory school-attendance statute on their rights and the rights of their children to the free exercise of the religious beliefs they and their forbears have adhered to for almost three centuries. In evaluating those claims we must be careful to determine whether the Amish religious faith and their mode of life are, as they claim, inseparable and interdependent. . . . [I]f the Amish asserted their claims because of their subjective evaluation and rejection of the contemporary secular values accepted by the majority . . . their claims would not rest on a religious basis. . . . [If the] choice was philosophical and personal rather than religious, . . . such belief does not rise to the demands of the Religion Clauses.

Giving no weight to such secular considerations, however, we see that the record in this case abundantly supports the claim that the traditional way of life of the Amish is not merely a matter of personal preference, but one of deep religious conviction, shared by an organized group, and intimately related to daily living. . . .

. . . .

As the society around the Amish has become more populous, urban, industrialized, and complex, particularly in this century, government regulation of human affairs has correspondingly become more detailed and pervasive. The Amish mode of life has thus come into conflict increasingly with requirements of contemporary society exerting a hydraulic insistence on conformity to majoritarian standards. . . . As the record so strongly shows, the values and programs of the modern secondary school are in sharp conflict with the fundamental mode of life mandated by the Amish religion; modern laws requiring compulsory secondary education have accordingly engendered great concern and conflict. The conclusion is inescapable that secondary schooling, by exposing Amish children to worldly influences . . . and by substantially interfering with the religious development of the Amish child and his integration into the way of life of the Amish faith community at the crucial adolescent stage of development, contravenes the basic religious tenets and practice of the Amish faith, both as to the parent and the child.

In sum, the unchallenged testimony of acknowledged experts in education and religious history, almost 300 years of consistent practice, and strong evidence of a sustained faith pervading and regulating respondents' entire mode of life support the claim that enforcement of the State's requirement of compulsory formal education after the eighth grade would gravely endanger if not destroy the free exercise of respondents' religious beliefs.

III

Neither the findings of the trial court nor the Amish claims as to the nature of their faith are challenged in this Court by the State of Wisconsin. Its position is that the State's interest in universal compulsory formal secondary education to age 16 is so great that it is paramount to the undisputed claims of respondents that their mode of preparing their youth for Amish life, after the traditional elementary education, is an essential part of their religious belief and practice. Nor does the State undertake to meet the claim that the Amish mode of life and education is inseparable from and a part of the basic tenets of their religion — indeed, as much a part of their religious belief and practices as baptism, the confessional, or a Sabbath may be for others.

Wisconsin . . . argues that "actions," even though religiously grounded, are outside the protection of the First Amendment. But our decisions have rejected the idea that religiously grounded conduct is always outside the protection of the Free Exercise Clause. . . .

. . . .

We turn, then, to the State's broader contention that its interest in its system of compulsory education is so compelling that even the established religious practices of the Amish must give way. Where fundamental claims of religious freedom are at stake, however, we cannot accept such a sweeping claim; despite its admitted validity in the generality of cases, we must searchingly examine the interests that the State seeks to promote by its requirement for compulsory education to age 16, and the impediment to those objectives that would flow from recognizing the claimed Amish exemption. . . .

The State advances two primary arguments in support of its system of compulsory education. It notes . . . that some degree of education is necessary to prepare citizens to participate effectively and intelligently in our open political system if we are to preserve freedom and independence. Further, education prepares individuals to be self-reliant and self-sufficient participants in society. We accept these propositions.

However, the evidence adduced by the Amish in this case is persuasively to the effect that an additional one or two years of formal high school for Amish children in place of their long-established program of informal vocational education would do little serve those interests. Respondents' experts testified at trial, without challenge, that the value of all education must be assessed in terms of its capacity to prepare the child for life. It is one thing to say that compulsory education for a year or two beyond the eighth grade may be necessary when its goal is the preparation of the child for life in modern society as the majority live, but it is quite another if the goal of education be viewed as the preparation of the child for life in the separated agrarian community that is the keystone of the Amish faith. . . .

The State attacks respondents' position as one fostering "ignorance" from which the child must be protected by the State. No one can question the State's duty to protect children from ignorance but this argument does not square with the facts disclosed in the record. . . . [T]he Amish community has been a highly successful social unit within our society. . . . Its members are productive and very law-abiding members of society; they reject public welfare in any of its usual modern forms. The Congress itself recognized their self-sufficiency by authorizing exemption of such groups as the Amish from the obligation to pay social security taxes.

It is neither fair nor correct to suggest that the Amish are opposed to education beyond the eighth grade level. What this record shows is that they are opposed to conventional formal education of the type provided by a certified high school because it comes at the child's crucial adolescent period of religious development. Dr. Donald Erickson, for example, testified that their system of learning-by-doing was an "ideal system" of education in terms of preparing Amish children for life as adults in the Amish community. . . .

. . . There can be no assumption that today's majority is "right" and the Amish and others like them are "wrong." A way of life that is odd or even erratic but interferes with no rights or interest of others is not to be condemned because it is different.

The State, however, supports its interest in providing an additional one or two years of compulsory high school education to Amish children because of the possibility that some such children will choose to leave the Amish community, and that if this occurs they will be ill-equipped for life. The State argues that if Amish children leave their church they should not be in the position of making their way in the world without the education available in the one or two additional years the State requires. However, on this record, that argument is highly speculative. There is no specific evidence of the loss of Amish adherents by attrition, nor is there any showing that upon leaving the Amish community Amish children, with their practical agricultural training and habits of industry and self-reliance, would become burdens on society because of educational shortcomings. Indeed, this argument of the State appears to rest primarily on the State's mistaken assumption, already noted, that the Amish do not provide any education for their children beyond the eighth grade, but allow them to grow in "ignorance." To the contrary, not only do the Amish accept the necessity for formal schooling through the eighth grade level, but continue to provide what has been characterized by the undisputed testimony of expert educators as an "ideal" vocational education for their children in the adolescent years.

There is nothing in this record to suggest that the Amish qualities of reliability, self-reliance, and dedication to work would fail to find ready markets in today's society. Absent some contrary evidence supporting the

State's position, we are unwilling to assume that persons possessing such valuable vocational skills and habits are doomed to become burdens on society should they determine to leave the Amish faith, nor is there any basis in the record to warrant a finding that an additional one or two years of formal school education beyond the eighth grade would serve to eliminate any such problem that might exist.

. . . The Amish alternative to formal secondary school education has enabled them to function effectively in their day-to-day life under self-imposed limitations on relations with the world, and to survive and prosper in contemporary society as a separate, sharply identifiable and highly self-sufficient community for more than 200 years in this country. In itself this is strong evidence that they are capable of fulfilling the social and political responsibilities of citizenship without compelled attendance beyond the eighth grade at the price of jeopardizing their free exercise of religious belief.

The requirement for compulsory education beyond the eighth grade is a relatively recent development in our history. Less than 60 years ago, the educational requirements of almost all of the States were satisfied by completion of the elementary grades, at least where the child was regularly and lawfully employed. The independence and successful social functioning of the Amish community for a period approaching almost three centuries and more than 200 years in this country are strong evidence that there is at best a speculative gain, in terms of meeting the duties of citizenship, from an additional one or two years of compulsory formal education. Against this background it would require a more particularized showing from the State on this point to justify the severe interference with religious freedom such additional compulsory attendance would entail.

. . . The origins of the requirement for school attendance to age 16, an age falling after the completion of elementary school but before completion of high school, are not entirely clear. But to some extent such laws reflected the movement to prohibit most child labor under age 16 that culminated in the provisions of the Federal Fair Labor Standards Act of 1938. . . . [T]he 16-year child labor age limit may to some degree derive from a contemporary impression that children should be in school until that age. But at the same time, it cannot be denied that, conversely, the 16-year education limit reflects, in substantial measure, the concern that children under that age not be employed under conditions hazardous to their health, or in work that should be performed by adults.

The requirement of compulsory schooling to age 16 must therefore be viewed as aimed not merely at providing educational opportunities for children, but as an alternative to the equally undesirable consequence of unhealthful child labor displacing adult workers, or, on the other hand, forced idleness. The two kinds of statutes — compulsory school attendance and child labor laws — tend to keep children of certain ages off the labor market and in school; this regimen in turn provides opportunity to prepare for a livelihood of a higher order than that which children could pursue without education and protects their health in adolescence.

In these terms, Wisconsin's interest in compelling the school attendance of Amish children to age 16 emerges as somewhat less substantial than requiring such attendance for children generally. For, while agricultural employment is not totally outside the legitimate concerns of the child labor laws, employment of children under parental guidance and on the family farm from age 14 to age 16 is an ancient tradition that lies at the periphery of the objectives of such laws. There is no intimation that the Amish employment of their children on family farms is in any way deleterious to their health or that Amish parents exploit children at tender years. Any such inference would be contrary to the record before us. Moreover, employment of Amish children on the family farm does not present the undesirable economic aspects of eliminating jobs that might otherwise be held by adults.

IV

Finally, the State, on authority of *Prince v. Massachusetts*, argues that a decision exempting Amish children from the State's requirement fails to recognize the substantive right of the Amish child to a secondary education, and fails to give due regard to the power of the State as *parens patriae* to extend the benefit of secondary education to children regardless of the wishes of their parents. Taken at its broadest sweep, the Court's language in *Prince*, might be read to give support to the State's position. However, the Court was not confronted in *Prince* with a situation comparable to that of the Amish as revealed in this record; this is shown by the Court's severe characterization of the evils that it thought the legislature could legitimately associate with child labor, even when performed in the company of an adult. . . . The court later took great care to confine *Prince* to a narrow scope . . . the conduct or actions so regulated have invariably posed some substantial threat to public safety, peace or order. . . .

This case, of course, is not one in which any harm to the physical or mental health of the child or to the public safety, peace, order, or welfare has been demonstrated or may be properly inferred. The record is to the contrary, and any reliance on that theory would find no support in the evidence.

Contrary to the suggestion of the dissenting opinion of Mr. Justice Douglas, our holding today in no degree depends on the assertion of the religious interest of the child as contrasted with that of the parents. It is the parents who are subject to prosecution here for failing to cause their children to attend school, and it is their right of free exercise, not that of their children, that must determine Wisconsin's power to impose criminal penalties on the parent. The dissent argues that a child who expresses a desire to attend public high school in conflict with the wishes of his parents should not be prevented from doing so. There is no reason for the Court to consider that point since it is not an issue in the case. The children are not parties to this litigation. The State has at no point tried this case on the theory that respondents were preventing their children from attending school against their expressed desires, and indeed the record is to the contrary. The State's position from the outset has been that it is empowered to apply its compulsory-attendance law to Amish parents in the same manner as to other parents — that is, without regard to the wishes of the child. That is the claim we reject today.

Our holding in no way determines the proper resolution of possible competing interests of parents, children, and the State in an appropriate state court proceeding in which the power of the State is asserted on the theory that Amish parents are preventing their minor children from attending high school despite their expressed desires to the contrary. Recognition of the claim of the State in such a proceeding would, of course, call into question traditional concepts of parental control over the religious upbringing and education of their minor children recognized in this Court's past decisions. It is clear that such an intrusion by a State into family decisions in the area of religious training would give rise to grave questions of religious freedom comparable to those raised here and those presented in *Pierce v. Society of Sisters*. On this record we neither reach nor decide those issues.

The State's argument proceeds without reliance on any actual conflict between the wishes of parents and children. It appears to rest on the potential that exemption of Amish parents from the requirements of the compulsory-education law might allow some parents to act contrary to the best interests of their children by foreclosing their opportunity to make an intelligent choice between the Amish way of life and that of the outside world. The same argument could, of course, be made with respect to all church schools short of college. There is nothing in the record or in the ordinary course of human experience to suggest that non-Amish parents generally consult with children of ages 14–16 if they are placed in a church school of the parents' faith.

Indeed it seems clear that if the State is empowered, as *parens patriae*, to "save" a child from himself or his Amish parent by requiring an additional two years of compulsory formal high school education, the State will in large measure influence, if not determine, the religious future of the child. Even more markedly than in *Prince*, therefore, this case involves the fundamental interest of parents, as contrasted with that of the State, to guide the religious future and education of their children. The history and culture of Western civilization reflect a strong tradition of parental concern for the nurture and upbringing of their children. This primary role of the parents in the upbringing of their children is now established beyond debate as an enduring American tradition. If not the first, perhaps the most significant statements of the Court in this area are found in *Pierce v. Society of Sisters*, in which the Court observed:

> Under the doctrine of *Meyer v. Nebraska*, we think it entirely plain that the Act of 1992 unreasonably interferes with the liberty of parents and guardians to direct the upbringing and education of children under their control. As often heretofore pointed out, rights guaranteed by the Constitution may not be abridged by legislation which has no reasonable relation to some purpose with the competency of the State. The fundamental theory of liberty upon which all governments in this Union repose excludes any general power of the State to standardize its children by forcing them to accept instructions from public teachers only. The child is not the mere creature of the State; those who nurture him and direct his destiny have the right, coupled with the high duty, to recognize and prepare him for additional obligations.

The duty to prepare the child for "additional obligations," referred to by the Court, must be read to include the inculcation of moral standards, religious beliefs, and elements of good citizenship. *Pierce*, of course, recognized that where nothing more than the general interest of the parent in the nurture and education of his children is involved, it is beyond dispute that the State acts "reasonably" and constitutionally in requiring education to age 16 in some public or private school meeting the standards prescribed by the State.

However read, the Court's holding in *Pierce* stands as a charter of the rights of parents to direct the religious upbringing of their children. And, when the interests of parenthood are combined with a free exercise claim of the nature revealed by this record, more than merely a "reasonable relation to some purpose within the competency of the State" is required to sustain the validity of the State's requirement under the First Amendment. To be sure, the power of the parent, even when linked to a free exercise claim, may be subject to limitation under *Prince* if it appears that parental decisions will jeopardize the health or safety of the child, or have a potential for significant social burdens. But in this case, the Amish have introduced persuasive evidence undermining the arguments the State has advanced to support its claims in terms of the welfare of the child and society as a whole. The record strongly indicates that accommodating the religious objections of the Amish by forgoing one, or at most two, additional years of compulsory education will not impair the physical or mental health of the child, or result in an inability to be self-supporting or to discharge the duties and responsibilities of citizenship, or in any other way materially detract from the welfare of society.

In the face of our consistent emphasis on the central values underlying the Religion Clauses in our constitutional scheme of government, we cannot accept a *parens patriae* claim of such all-encompassing scope and with such sweeping potential for broad and unforeseeable application as that urged by the State.

V

For the reasons stated we hold, with the Supreme Court of Wisconsin, that the First and Fourteenth Amendments prevent the State from compelling respondents to cause their children to attend formal high school to age 16. Our disposition of this case, however, in no way alters our recognition of the obvious fact that courts are not school boards or legislatures, and are ill-equipped to determine the "necessity" of discrete aspects of a State's program of compulsory education. This should suggest that courts must move with great circumspection in performing the sensitive and delicate task of weighing a State's legitimate social concern when faced with religious claims for exemption from generally applicable education requirements. It cannot be overemphasized that we are not dealing with a way of life and mode of education by a group claiming to have recently discovered some "progressive" or more enlightened process for rearing children for modern life.

Aided by a history of three centuries as an identifiable religious sect and a long history as a successful and self-sufficient segment of American society, the Amish in this case have convincingly demonstrated the sincerity of their religious beliefs, the interrelationship of belief with their mode of life, the vital role that belief and daily conduct play in the continued survival of Old Order Amish communities and their religious organization, and the hazards presented by the State's enforcement of a statute generally valid as to others.

Beyond this, they have carried the even more difficult burden of demonstrating the adequacy of their alternative mode of continuing informal vocational education in terms of precisely those overall interests that the State advances in support of its program of compulsory high school education. In light of this convincing showing, one that probably few other religious groups or sects could make, and weighing the minimal difference between what the State would require and what the Amish already accept, it was incumbent on the State to show with more particularity how its admittedly strong interest in compulsory education would be adversely affected by granting an exemption to the Amish. . . .

Nothing we hold is intended to undermine the general applicability of the State's compulsory school-attendance statutes or to limit the power of the State to promulgate reasonable standards that, while not impairing the free exercise of religion, provide for continuing agricultural vocational education under parental and church guidance by the Old Order Amish or others similarly situated. The States have had a long history of amicable and effective relationships with church-sponsored schools, and there is no basis for assuming that, in this related context, reasonable standards cannot be established concerning the content of the continuing vocational education of Amish children under parental guidance, provided always that state regulations are not inconsistent with what we have said in this opinion.

Affirmed.

MR. JUSTICE POWELL and MR. JUSTICE REHNQUIST *took no part in the consideration or decision of this case.*

MR. JUSTICE STEWART, with whom MR. JUSTICE BRENNAN *joins, concurring.*

This case involves the constitutionality of imposing criminal punishment upon Amish parents for their religiously based refusal to compel their children to attend public high schools. Wisconsin has sought to brand these parents as criminals for following their religious beliefs, and the Court today rightly holds that Wisconsin cannot constitutionally do so.

This case in no way involves any questions regarding the right of the children of Amish parents to attend public high schools, or any other institutions of learning, if they wish to do so. As the Court points out, there is no suggestion whatever in the record that the religious beliefs of the children here concerned differ in any way from those of their parents. Only one of the children testified. The last two questions and answers on her cross-examination accurately sum up her testimony:

> Q. So I take it then, Frieda, the only reason you are not going to school, and did not go to school since last September, is because of your religion?
>
> A. Yes.
>
> Q. That is the only reason?
>
> A. Yes.

It is clear to me, therefore, that this record simply does not present the interesting and important issue discussed in Part II of the dissenting opinion of Mr. Justice Douglas. With this observation, I join the opinion and the judgment of the Court.

MR. JUSTICE WHITE, with whom MR. JUSTICE BRENNAN and MR. JUSTICE STEWART *join, concurring.*

Cases such as this one inevitably call for a delicate balancing of important but conflicting interests. I join the opinion and judgment of the Court because I cannot say that the State's interest in requiring two more years of compulsory education in the ninth and tenth grades outweighs the importance of the concededly sincere Amish religious practice to the survival of that sect.

This would be a very different case for me if respondents' claim were that their religion forbade their children from attending any school at any time and from complying in any way with the educational standards set by the State. Since the Amish children are permitted to acquire the basic tools of literacy to survive in modern society by attending grades one through eight and since the deviation from the State's compulsory-education law is relatively slight, I conclude that respondents' claim must prevail, largely because "religious freedom — the freedom to believe and to practice strange and, it may be, foreign creeds — has classically been one of the highest values of our society." . . .

The importance of the state interest asserted here cannot be denigrated, however: "Today, education is perhaps the most important function of state and local governments. Compulsory school attendance laws and the great expenditures for education both demonstrate our recognition of the importance of education to our democratic society. It is required in the performance of our most basic public responsibilities, even service in the armed forces. It is the very foundation of good citizenship. Today it is a principal instrument in awakening the child to cultural values, in preparing him for later professional training, and in helping him to adjust normally to his environment." . . .

. . . .

In the present case, the State is not concerned with the maintenance of an educational system as an end in itself, it is rather attempting to nurture and develop the human potential of its children, whether Amish or non-Amish: to expand their knowledge, broaden their sensibilities, kindle their imagination, foster a spirit of free inquiry, and increase their human understanding and tolerance. It is possible that most Amish children will wish to continue living the rural life of their parents, in which case their training at home will adequately equip them for their future role. Others, however, may wish to become nuclear physicists, ballet dancers, computer programmers, or historians, and for these occupations, formal training will be necessary. There is evidence in the record that many children desert the Amish faith when they come of age.[3] A State has a legitimate interest not only in seeking to develop

---

[3] [3] Dr. Hostetler testified that though there was a gradual increase in the total number of Old Order Amish in the United States over the past 50 years, "at the same time the Amish have also lost members [of] their church" and that the turnover rate was such that "probably two-thirds [of the present Amish] have been assimilated non-Amish people." Justice Heffernan, dissenting below, opined that "[l]arge numbers of young people voluntarily leave the Amish community each year and are thereafter forced to make their way in the world."

the latent talents of its children but also in seeking to prepare them for the life style that they may later choose, or at least to provide them with an option other than the life they have led in the past. In the circumstances of this case, although the question is close, I am unable to say that the State has demonstrated that Amish children who leave school in the eighth grade will be intellectually stultified or unable to acquire new academic skills later. The statutory minimum school attendance age set by the State is, after all, only 16.

. . . I join the Court because the sincerity of the Amish religious policy here is uncontested, because the potentially adverse impact of the state requirement is great, and because the State's valid interest in education has already been largely satisfied by the eight years the children have already spent in school.

Mr. Justice Douglas, *dissenting in part.*

I agree with the Court that the religious scruples of the Amish are opposed to the education of their children beyond the grade schools, yet I disagree with the Court's conclusion that the matter is within the dispensation of parents alone. The Court's analysis assumes that the only interests at stake in the case are those of the Amish parents on the one hand, and those of the State on the other. The difficulty with this approach is that, despite the Court's claim, the parents are seeking to vindicate not only their own free exercise claims, but also those of their high-school-age children.

It is argued that the right of the Amish children to religious freedom is not presented by the facts of the case, as the issue before the Court involves only the Amish parents' religious freedom to defy a state criminal statute imposing upon them an affirmative duty to cause their children to attend high school.

First, respondents' motion to dismiss in the trial court expressly asserts, not only the religious liberty of the adults, but also that of the children, as a defense to the prosecutions. It is, of course, beyond question that the parents have standing as defendants in a criminal prosecution to assert the religious interests of their children as a defense.[4] Although the lower courts and a majority of this Court assume an identity of interest between parent and child, it is clear that they have treated the religious interest of the child as a factor in the analysis.

Second, it is essential to reach the question to decide the case, not only because the question was squarely raised in the motion to dismiss, but also because no analysis of religious-liberty claims can take place in a vacuum. If the parents in this case are allowed a religious exemption, the inevitable

---

4 [1] Thus, in *Prince v. Massachusetts*, a Jehovah's Witness was convicted for having violated a state child labor law by allowing her nine-year-old niece and ward to circulate religious literature on the public streets. There, as here, the narrow question was the religious liberty of the adult. There, as here, the Court analyzed the problem from the point of view of the State's conflicting interest in the welfare of the child. But, as Mr. Justice Brennan, speaking for the Court, has . . . pointed out, "The Court [in *Prince*] implicitly held that the custodian had standing to assert alleged freedom of religion . . . rights of the child that were threatened in the very litigation before the Court and that the child had no effective way of asserting herself." . . . Here, as in *Prince*, the children have no effective alternate means to vindicate their rights. The question, therefore, is squarely before us.

effect is to impose the parents' notions of religious duty upon their children. Where the child is mature enough to express potentially conflicting desires, it would be an invasion of the child's rights to permit such an imposition without canvassing his views. As in *Prince v. Massachusetts*, it is an imposition resulting from this very litigation. As the child has no other effective forum, it is in this litigation that his rights should be considered. And, if an Amish child desires to attend high school, and is mature enough to have that desire respected, the State may well be able to override the parents' religiously motivated objections.

Religion is an individual experience. It is not necessary, nor even appropriate, for every Amish child to express his views on the subject in a prosecution of a single adult. Crucial, however, are the views of the child whose parent is the subject of the suit. Frieda Yoder has in fact testified that her own religious views are opposed to high-school education. I therefore join the judgment of the Court as to respondent Jonas Yoder. But Frieda Yoder's views may not be those of Vernon Yutzy or Barbara Miller. I must dissent, therefore, as to respondents Adin Yutzy and Wallace Miller as their motion to dismiss also raised the question of their children's religious liberty.

II

This issue has never been squarely presented before today. Our opinions are full of talk about the power of the parents over the child's education. . . . And we have in the past analyzed similar conflicts between parent and State with little regard for the views of the child. *See Prince v. Massachusetts.* Recent cases, however, have clearly held that the children themselves have constitutionally protectible interests.

These children are "persons" within the meaning of the Bill of Rights. We have so held over and over again. . . . In *In re Gault*, we held that "neither the Fourteenth Amendment nor the Bill of Rights is for adults alone." In *In re Winship*, we held that a 12-year-old boy, when charged with an act which would be a crime if committed by an adult, was entitled to procedural safeguards contained in the Sixth Amendment. [The opinion continued to review cases where Justice Douglas supported his position that the Court had recognized children are "persons" within the meaning of the Bill of Rights.]

. . . .

On this important and vital matter of education, I think the children should be entitled to be heard. While the parents, absent dissent, normally speak for the entire family, the education of the child is a matter on which the child will often have decided views. He may want to be a pianist or an astronaut or an oceanographer. To do so he will have to break from the Amish tradition.[5]

It is the future of the student, not the future of the parents, that is imperiled by today's decision. If a parent keeps his child out of school beyond the grade school, then the child will be forever barred from entry into the new and

---

[5] [2] A significant number of Amish children do leave the Old Order. Professor Hostetler notes that "[t]he loss of members is very limited in some Amish districts and considerable in others." . . . In one Pennsylvania church, he observed a defection rate of 30 percent. Rates up to 50 percent have been reported by others. . . .

amazing world of diversity that we have today. The child may decide that that is the preferred course, or he may rebel. It is the student's judgment, not his parents', that is essential if we are to give full meaning to what we have said about the Bill of Rights and of the right of students to be masters of their own destiny.[6] If he is harnessed to the Amish way of life by those in authority over him and if his education is truncated, his entire life may be stunted and deformed. The child, therefore, should be given an opportunity to be heard before the State gives the exemption which we honor today.

The views of the two children in question were not canvassed by the Wisconsin courts. The matter should be explicitly reserved so that new hearings can be held on remand of the case.[7]

III

I think the emphasis of the Court on the "law and order" record of this Amish group of people is quite irrelevant. A religion is a religion irrespective of what the misdemeanor or felony records of its members might be. I am not at all sure how the Catholics, Episcopalians, the Baptists, Jehovah's Witnesses, the Unitarians, and my own Presbyterians would make out if subjected to such a test. . . . [T]he Amish, whether with a high or low criminal record, certainly qualify by all historic standards as a religion within the meaning of the First Amendment.

 . . . .

NOTES AND QUESTIONS

1. Compare how the Court balances the interest of the parents and the interest of the state in *Yoder* and in *Prince*. Is there a difference between the two cases? Is the state's interest in prohibiting child labor more important than the state's interest in ensuring an education of a certain level for its citizens? Or is it that the parental interest in *Yoder* is more important than that of the parent (guardian) in *Prince*? Or is the answer a more insidious reason — that the Amish are simply more appealing than Jehovah's Witnesses?

---

[6] [3] The court below brushed aside the students' interests with the offhand comment that "[w]hen a child reaches the age of judgment, he can choose for himself his religion." . . . But there is nothing in this record to indicate that the moral and intellectual judgment demanded of the student by the question in this case is beyond his capacity. Children far younger than the 14-and 15-year-olds involved here are regularly permitted to testify in custody and other proceedings. Indeed, the failure to call the affected child in a custody hearing is often reversible error. . . . Moreover, there is substantial agreement among child psychologists and sociologists that the moral and intellectual maturity of the 14-year-old approaches that of the adult. . . . The maturity of Amish youth, who identify with and assume adult roles from early childhood . . . is certainly not less than that of children in the general population.

[7] [4] Canvassing the views of all school-age Amish children in the State of Wisconsin would not present insurmountable difficulties. A 1968 survey indicated that there were at that time only 256 such children in the entire State. . . .

2. What if members of another religious sect have sincere religious objections to sending their child to public school and wish to practice the Amish tradition of isolation? What would they have to show to circumvent a state's compulsory education laws? How should a court go about making the assessment of the sincerity of religious beliefs? *See* Stephen G. Gilles, *Liberal Parentalism and Children's Educational Rights*, 26 CAPITAL U. L. REV. 9 (1997) (arguing that *Yoder* ought to stand for the principle that parents have the right to determine the religious upbringing of their children unless their choices cause serious, demonstrable harm to the children).

3. If the state's interest is not important enough to outweigh the parental interest in *Yoder*, what is the justification for compulsory education for non-Amish children?

4. Would an Amish child with an eighth-grade education be able to choose later to move outside the Amish community and have a different life? Would the result have been the same if the Amish wished to permit only a fifth-grade education?

5. Justice Douglas's dissent stated that the views of the Amish children should have been heard before a court makes a decision that will have such a significant effect on their future. Would an Amish child be likely to voice a viewpoint that differs from that of the parent? What would be the likely impact on the child and on the Amish community? Should the court appoint a guardian to ascertain the best interests of the child? Suppose an Amish child stated that she wished to stay in school so that she could attend college and then law school. What weight should the trial court give to this statement? To what extent should the views of the child be protected under the Constitution when they differ from the views of the parent? The section on abortion rights of minor females *infra* addresses this issue in a different context.

6. In *Employment Division v. Smith*, 494 U.S. 872 (1990), the Supreme Court held that a state criminal law that prohibited the use of peyote could be applied to someone who used peyote because of a sincerely held religious belief that the drug should be used in a religious ceremony. Justice Scalia wrote for the majority, stating that the Court had never held that religious beliefs excuse an individual from complying with an otherwise valid state law and that the government's ability to enforce generally applicable prohibitions of socially harmful conduct did not depend on measuring the effects of the governmental action on the spiritual development of a religious objector. The Court attempted to distinguish *Yoder* by noting that it involved the Free Exercise Clause in conjunction with the right of parents to direct the education of their child.

§ 2.02 CARE OF THE CHILD

Who should have the primary responsibility for the custody and care of the child? What is the extent of the obligation to provide such care? The biological parents are the first legal custodians of the child. If the biological parents are married when the child is born, one set of problems arises if the biological parents divorce. A court may award sole legal or sole physical custody (or both) to one parent, with the concomitant right to make certain decisions about the child. The noncustodial parent may retain the right to make certain decisions about the child, as well as the right of visitation, subject to the power of the court. Third persons who have an interest in the child's welfare, like the child's grandparents, may also wish to have visitation rights with the child. Courts may award parents joint custody, where both parents share legal custody (the right to make decisions relating to the health, education and welfare of the child) and/or physical custody (where each parent has significant periods of physical custody). If the biological parents have never been married to each other, special problems arise, especially with the ability to conceive a child now enhanced by technology. The biological parents may give up their rights to their child, and the child may be adopted. The state may terminate the parents' right to the child and the child may be adopted or placed in foster care. This chapter highlights some of the problems that arise when courts attempt to resolve these complex issues.

[A] Custody

[1] The Best Interest of the Child

Under common law, with its roots in the legal rights of property ownership, fathers had the sole right to the custody of their minor children. This rule of paternal custody began to change in the nineteenth century, as courts, and then state legislatures established a new orthodoxy of maternal preference. Until recently, the maternal preference rule greatly enhanced the ability of mothers to gain custody of their children. Under the "tender years" presumption, unless she was unfit, it was presumed that it would be better for children, especially young children, if they were placed with their mother. What is the assumption that underlies the "tender years" doctrine? Is it based on nature or social role?

The maternal presumption has been abandoned in most states, and it has been replaced by the "best interest" standard, a protean concept that gives broad discretion to judges who are making this most significant decision. Some state statutes merely state that the judge must make the custody decision in accordance with the best interest of the child, while other statutes enumerate the factors that a court may consider when making the best interest analysis. The Uniform Marriage and Divorce Act lists the following factors:

§ 402. Best Interest of Child

The court shall determine custody in accordance with the best interest of the child. The court shall consider all relevant factors including:

(1) the wishes of the child's parent or parents as to his custody;

(2) the wishes of the child as to his custodian;

(3) the interaction and interrelationship of the child with his parent or parents, his siblings, and any other person who may significantly affect the child's best interest;

(4) the child's adjustment to his home, school, and community; and

(5) the mental and physical health of all individuals involved.

The court shall not consider conduct of a proposed custodian that does not affect his relationship to the child.

Uniform Marriage and Divorce Act (amended 1973) § 402.

Although this legislative model was enacted by a only small number of states, its provisions have had an influence on the statutes in many jurisdictions, and many states include factors similar to those listed above. Some states include other factors, which may include the length of time the child has lived in a stable environment, the capacity and disposition of the parties to give the child love, affection and guidance, and to continue educating and raising the child in the child's culture, religion or creed, and the effect on the child of any actions of abuse that have occurred between the parents. *See* MINN. STAT. ANN. § 518.17. One factor that may be considered in determining the best interest of the child is the child's "primary caretaker."

[a] The Primary Caretaker

KENNEDY v. KENNEDY

Court of Appeals of Minnesota
403 N.W.2d 892 (1987)

CRIPPEN, J.

This appeal deals with the sufficiency of evidence to support trial court findings that neither parent was the primary caretaker of three children. We sustain the finding and affirm placement of physical custody of the children with their father. We modify the trial court's judgment to provide for joint legal custody of all four children of the parties and to make final the trial court's placement of custody of a fourth child with his mother.

FACTS

The parties were married in 1970. They have four children, daughters born in 1972 and 1980, and sons born in 1978 and 1984. Since 1976, respondent Duane Kennedy has practiced law. Appellant Carole Lindstrom, formerly Carole Kennedy, has a college degree in anthropology. She was actively employed until 1977, when the oldest child of the marriage was 5-years-old and the parties were expecting their second child. Since then, she has done typing at home for a court reporter for two and one-half years, and she was employed for six months in 1983 as a temporary secretary.

During the last five years of their marriage, the couple lived in a rural home near Grand Meadow, Minnesota. Respondent was employed in Rochester. He and the three older children continue to live in the farm home. Appellant, with the youngest child of the parties, resides with her widowed father at Ashland, Wisconsin.

CASE HISTORY

In a November 1984 dissolution judgment, the trial court split custody of the children. The three older children were placed in the sole custody of respondent, their father. The youngest child, now nearly age 3, was placed in the temporary custody of appellant, his mother, pending a further social study and hearing.

In November 1985, this court reviewed the 1984 custody decision, based on standards announced by the Minnesota Supreme Court in *Pikula v. Pikula*, 374 N.W.2d 705 (Minn. 1985) (initially filed in September 1985). *Kennedy v. Kennedy,* 376 N.W.2d 702 (Minn. Ct. App. 1985). We remanded the case for the trial court to determine which party was the primary parent in January 1984, when the proceeding was commenced. This appeal is from the trial court's decision on remand.

1984 TRIAL

At a trial in August 1984, the trial court heard 14 witnesses on the child custody issue, including a veteran court services investigator who had contacted over 30 people in preparing a written report. The trial judge interviewed the three older children. The evidence indicated that both parents cared deeply for their children and enjoyed good relationships with them. The children were healthy and well-adjusted. The court services officer recommended placing custody of the three older children with their father, based partly on interviews with the children. The officer and the other witnesses offered conflicting evidence on the involvement of each parent with the children, the time appellant was away from the home in social activities, and the demonstrations by each parent of unselfish concern for the daily needs of the children. Between 1977 and 1982, appellant had responsibility for child care during more hours than respondent, but she acknowledged that beginning in 1982, marital difficulties arose and respondent became increasingly more involved. Respondent's evidence showed him heavily involved in child care and effective in dealings with the children throughout the couple's parenting years.

TRIAL COURT FINDINGS

In 1986, on remand, the trial court found appellant was the primary caretaker of the youngest child, who had lived with her separately since he was an infant, but that "neither parent was the primary caretaker" of the other three children. This additional finding was stated:

> Responsibility for the performance of child care was shared by both parents, in an essentially equal way. From time to time, the parents assumed different duties, but the quantum of their care for the children was such that neither can be said to have become the primary parent.

In an attached memorandum, the trial court stated that it was confronted by a great deal of conflicting evidence on contributions of each parent, that the court believed it was appropriate to evaluate child care from the vantage point of the children, that visits with the children were particularly helpful to the court, and that the court believed, under *Pikula*, that it was to consider care both in terms of its quantity and quality.

In addition, the trial court found:

> During the course of this marriage, [appellant's] professional and social pursuits took her from the home so that there was more personal contact between [respondent] and his children in their care, and less by [appellant] than would normally be the case, leading me to conclude that [appellant] was not a traditional homemaker.

For the record, at the hearing on February 28, 1986, the trial court likewise commented:

> There was a great deal more personal contact between the father and the children, and a great deal more absence on the part of the mother than is normally the case when you think of a breadwinner that goes to work at seven and gets home at six, and the mother is home all day. So this was a situation which I took into account.
>
> . . . .
>
> Professional and vocational and social pursuits of Mrs. Kennedy [took] her from the home on a good many days and evenings and weekends, during which time the children were frequently and extensively cared for either by their father or in the home of other relatives . . . .

Finally, noting that application of the *Pikula* standard was limited to younger children, the trial court found on remand that the two older children (born in 1972 and 1978) are old enough to express a preference about custody.

The trial court on remand made its findings supplementary to its 1984 findings, which preceded the *Pikula* decision and dwelled on statutory custody standards.[8] Consistent with its 1986 primary care findings, the court found

---

8 [5] The trial court is required to consider the best interests of the child. *See* MINN. STAT. § 518.17, subd. 3 (1986). Subdivision 1 of section 518.17 provides:

"The best interests of the child" means all relevant factors to be considered and evaluated by the court including:

(a) The wishes of the child's parent or parents as to custody;

(b) The reasonable preference of the child, if the court deems the child to be of sufficient age to express preference;

(c) The interaction and interrelationship of the child with a parent or parents, siblings, and any other person who may significantly affect the child's best interests;

(d) The child's adjustment to home, school, and community;

(e) The length of time the child has lived in a stable, satisfactory environment and the desirability of maintaining continuity;

(f) The permanence, as a family unit, of the existing or proposed custodial home;

(g) The mental and physical health of all individuals involved;

(h) The capacity and disposition of the parties to give the child love, affection, and guidance, and to continue educating and raising the child in the child's culture and religion or creed, if any; and

(i) The child's cultural background.

The court shall not consider conduct of a proposed custodian that does not affect the custodian's relationship to the child.

in 1984 that "there is a fairly equal balance between the parties" as to interaction and interrelationship with the children. The court found the parties have an equal capacity and disposition to meet the children's needs.

The court found in 1984 that the three older children were adapted to a stable home and healthy school environment in Grand Meadow, and that the permanence of this environment could be assured in a custodial placement with their father. This finding related to standards found in subsections (d), (e) and (f) of the statute.[9] The court noted in 1984 that it "considered" the uncertainty of appellant's future plans.[10] Finally, the court expressly considered present and future bonding between the children in reaching its custody decision.

1986 CONCLUSIONS

On January 27, 1986, the trial court issued an order for judgment based on its original and supplementary findings. The court provided for joint legal custody of all four children, placed physical custody of the three older children with respondent, and placed physical custody of the youngest child with appellant.

Respondent's motion for amended findings and conclusions was heard on February 28. Because appellant's counsel did not appear at the motion hearing, the hearing occurred without an exchange of conflicting views of the parties on matters addressed in the motion. On March 7, the trial court issued a modified order for judgment granting respondent sole legal custody of the three older children, and providing that the custody placement of the youngest child with appellant was "temporary," with the issue of permanent custody for this child "reserved by the court for further proceedings." . . .

Appellant contends the trial court's findings and conclusions are not supported by the evidence, and that appellant was a traditional homemaker and the primary parent of the children.

ISSUES

1. Were the evidence and trial court findings sufficient to sustain the trial court's placement of custody of three children with respondent?

---

[9] [6] As we observed in 1985, findings on environment cut two ways. Together with the standard on parent interaction (subsection (c)), they constitute the "continuity" standards given special priority in *Pikula*. On the other hand, they relate in part to benefits one parent may contribute solely because of his or her economic advantage. Here respondent has the advantage of an award of the family homestead. When remanding the case, we instructed the trial court to focus on personal interaction of the children and parents. In its 1986 memorandum the trial court observed that it does not base its custody findings on "things" the father could contribute to the children, but that it thought it "worth noting" that there would be trauma for the children if they lost what their father provided for them. In this regard, the trial court referred to the *Pikula* opinion. *Pikula*, 374 N.W.2d at 714 (the supreme court acts on its "understanding of the traumatic impact on children of separation from the primary caretaker parent").

[10] [7] We warned in 1985 that this consideration, together with reliance on the security of respondent's situation, risked discrimination against a traditional homemaker. In its 1986 memorandum, the trial court stated it did not place "any special emphasis" on the uncertainty of appellant's future plans, noting that "it was a factor, but not a compelling or conclusive one."

2. Do the evidence and findings support the court's denial of joint legal custody?

3. Did the trial court abuse its discretion in reserving the right to alter its placement of custody of the youngest child with appellant?

ANALYSIS

1. *Custody with respondent*

Appellate review of a custody determination is "limited to whether the trial court abused its discretion by making findings unsupported by the evidence or by improperly applying the law."

A determination of child custody must be based on the best interests of the child, requiring consideration of "all relevant factors," including those enumerated by statute. The *Pikula* court established the rule that:

> When both parents seek custody of a child too young to express a preference, and one parent has been the primary caretaker of the child, custody should be awarded to the primary caretaker absent a showing that that parent is unfit to be the custodian.

> "Ordinarily," the *Pikula* court noted, "a parent who has performed the traditional role of homemaker" will be able to establish primary parent status. On the other hand, one who works outside the home may be a primary parent.

> The *Pikula* rule applies only where "one parent has been the primary caretaker." The supreme court explained:

> When the facts demonstrate that responsibility for and performance of child care was shared by both parents in an entirely equal way, then no preference arises. . . .

Here the trial court found that caretaking was shared "in an essentially equal way," and that neither parent was the primary parent. In addition, the court found that the circumstances here were not those normally expected for one working parent and a traditional homemaker; the court found the father a great deal more and the mother a great deal less in contact with the children than might normally be expected where only the father worked full-time. Based on these findings, the court did not apply the *Pikula* preference.

Trial court findings of fact will not be set aside unless they are clearly erroneous. Findings based on conflicting evidence will be affirmed unless they are manifestly and palpably contrary to the evidence as a whole. We must view the evidence in the light most favorable to the court's findings.

Here there is sufficient evidence to support the trial court's findings that respondent, while working outside the home, had unusual involvement in child care, including care in the home, medical care, and recreation. The court heard testimony that respondent provided more than half of evening child care. Appellant acknowledged that respondent became progressively more involved in child care during the two years before the couple separated. While appellant was active in child care, some witnesses stated she was also active outside the home and often depended on others, including respondent, to care for the children. Examining the whole record in a light favorable to the trial court's findings, the court did not clearly err in finding that neither parent was the *Pikula* primary parent.

There is also evidence supporting the finding of the trial court that two of the children were old enough to express a preference on child care, so that the primary parent preference was inapplicable, at least as to those children.

When the primary parent preference is inappropriate to the case, the trial court must look to other indicia of the children's best interests. Here the trial court addressed the § 518.17 standards in its 1984 findings. While the court found an "equal balance" between the parents on several standards, the court found that the children would be hurt by a change of their environment, and that respondent could assure them of continuity of care. These findings are supported by competent evidence.

We warned in 1985 that the trial court must not consider continuity of care solely in terms of respondent's economic opportunities to continue caring for the children in their former home. On remand, the trial court has addressed personal interaction of each parent with the children, denying that it bases its custodial care preference on matters of economic ability. The record adequately supports the court's preference for the father's custodial care, based on the quantity and quality of his interaction with the children.

We note our misgivings prompted by the trial court's decision to split custody of the four children. That choice of action is always "unfortunate." *Schultz v. Schultz,* 266 Minn. 205, 208 (1963). We will carefully scrutinize decisions to split custody. On the other hand, the choice to split custody is not conclusively erroneous. Here the trial court expressly considered the bonding among the children and particularly among the three older children. We cannot say the trial court abused its discretion in 1984 or 1986 by choosing not to separate the infant child from his mother, but to find it best for the older children to be together in their father's custody.

Finally, we note that the specificity of the trial court's findings was barely adequate. While the findings here serve to show the trial court properly considered appropriate standards, it would assist the parties and this court if the findings were more highly particularized. . . .

2. *Joint legal custody*

In the form of conclusions drafted by the trial court, dated in January 1986, the court acted on its findings about capable and sharing parents by ordering joint legal custody for all four children. This decision harmonizes with 1986 legislation, effective on August 1, 1986. . . . The statute now mandates use of a rebuttable presumption that requested joint legal custody is in the best interests of the children. In its March order, the trial court rescinded the joint legal custody provision. . . .

Appellant asks for an award of legal and physical custody of all four children, putting before us the question whether our decision to affirm should include the trial court's decision against joint legal custody.

The trial court's January order was supported by the evidence in the case and the court's findings about the parents. . . . The trial court stated no conflict between joint legal custody and the children's best interests, and the record shows none. . . .

[W]e find no basis for denying a provision for joint legal custody of all four children. On the other hand, because the parties have briefed the case solely with reference to appellant's request for reversal of the placement of physical custody, we think that a final decision on legal custody must be made by the trial court. Thus, we vacate the trial court's award of sole legal custody, so that a request for joint legal custody can be put before the trial court free of the requirement for a special showing of changed circumstances.

3. *Temporary placement*

. . . .

This issue has also been neglected in briefing because the parties concentrated on the question of physical custody of the older children. Accordingly, we modify the trial court's decision to require either permanence of the present custodial placement for the youngest child or immediate trial court reconsideration of the placement based on lawfully sufficient evidence and findings.

DECISION

The trial court's March 1986 custody decision is affirmed as modified (1) to permit appellant's request for joint legal custody of the couple's children without a special showing of changed circumstances, and (2) to provide for permanence of the placement of the youngest child's custody placement with appellant, effective 60 days after the date this opinion is filed, save only as that award is altered before that time by a trial court order lawfully supported by competent evidence and particularized findings.

Affirmed as modified.

———

NOTES AND QUESTIONS

1. Additional factors have been added to the Minnesota statute, Minn. Stat. Ann., § 587.17, since the *Kennedy* case:

Subdivision 1. The best interests of the child.

    (a) "The best interests of the child" means all relevant factors to be considered and evaluated by the court including:

        (1) the wishes of the child's parent or parents as to custody;

        (2) the reasonable preference of the child, if the court deems the child to be of sufficient age to express preference;

        (3) the child's primary caretaker;

(4) the intimacy of the relationship between each parent and the child;

(5) the interaction and interrelationship of the child with a parent or parents, siblings, and any other person who may significantly affect the child's best interests;

(6) the child's adjustment to home, school, and community;

(7) the length of time the child has lived in a stable, satisfactory environment and the desirability of maintaining continuity;

(8) the permanence, as a family unit, of the existing or proposed custodial home;

(9) the mental and physical health of all individuals involved; except that a disability, as defined in section 363A.03, of a proposed custodian or the child shall not be determinative of the custody of the child, unless the proposed custodial arrangement is not in the best interest of the child;

(10) the capacity and disposition of the parties to give the child love, affection, and guidance, and to continue educating and raising the child in the child's culture and religion or creed, if any;

(11) the child's cultural background;

(12) the effect on the child of the actions of an abuser, if related to domestic abuse, as defined in section 518B.01, that has occurred between the parents or between a parent and another individual, whether or not the individual alleged to have committed domestic abuse is or ever was a family or household member of the parent; and

(13) except in cases in which a finding of domestic abuse as defined in section 518B.01 has been made, the disposition of each parent to encourage and permit frequent and continuing contact by the other parent with the child.

The court may not use one factor to the exclusion of all others. The primary caretaker factor may not be used as a presumption in determining the best interests of the child. The court must make detailed findings on each of the factors and explain how the factors led to its conclusions and to the determination of what is in the best interests of the child. *See* Thomas J. Walsh, *In the Best Interest of a Child: A Comparative Look at the Treatment of Children under Wisconsin and Minnesota Custody Statutes*, 85 MARQ. L. REV. 929 (2002) (examining child custody and placement statutes in Wisconsin and Minnesota and suggesting that the "custodial factors" listed in statutes can be grouped into four broad categories: "1) factors that analyze the wishes of the parents and child, 2) factors that analyze the stability and consistency of the parents' relationship with the child, 3) factors that focus on the physical and mental health of the parties and the children, and 4) factors that look at the behaviors of each party"); Julie B. Artis, *Judging the Best Interests of the Child: Judges' Accounts of the Tender Years Doctrine*, 38 LAW & SOC'Y REV. 769 (2004) (describing face-to-face interviews with 25 Indiana judges and arguing that while state custody laws are now gender-neutral, over half the judges interviewed continue to employ the tender years doctrine).

2. Does the primary caretaker factor (or presumption) focus too much on homemaking tasks as opposed to other qualities? Might it penalize the mother who works to support a husband with few job prospects? Might there be something special about the bond that develops between the child and the secondary caretaker parent?

3. What factors should the court consider when separating siblings?

[b] Other Factors in the Best Interest Analysis

[i] Child's Preference

One factor that courts may consider in the best interest analysis is "the wishes of the child as to his custodian." What are some of the key issues that judges should consider when weighing this factor?

[ii] Sexual Conduct and Sexual Orientation of Parent

How should the sexual conduct of a parent affect the best interest analysis? A trend in some states had emerged where, absent evidence of direct impact on the child, courts ignore the sexual conduct of a parent, with one court stating that "amorality, immorality, sexual deviation, and what we conveniently consider to be aberrant sexual practices do not *ipso facto* constitute unfitness for custody." *Feldman v. Feldman,* 358 N.Y.S. 2d 507, 510 (N.Y. App. Div. 1974). Yet at least the dissenting judge was outraged when a mother who had an open adulterous affair with a convicted felon was awarded custody instead of the father, who worked 45 to 55 hours per week and would have had to leave the children in the care of a next door neighbor during work hours. *Hanhart v. Hanhart,* 501 N.W.2d 776 (S.D. 1993) (Henderson, J., dissenting) (arguing that the relationship between the mother and the felon boyfriend "affected the children's development of what is right and wrong in this world"). Should the judges in child custody cases place more weight on moral values? *See, e.g., Santmier v. Santmier,* 494 So. 2d 95 (Ala. Civ. App. 1986) ("Given the testimony of several persons regarding the wife's affair [with a man] who was then married to another woman, and the conduct of the wife toward the children and others during the course of the affair, we cannot say that the trial court abused its discretion in awarding custody of the children to the husband.").

The majority of courts do not consider homosexuality per se evidence of unfitness. Yet some courts seem to react strongly to parents involved in homosexual activities. In *Roe v. Roe,* 324 S.E.2d 691 (Va. 1985), the court stated, "Although we decline to hold that every lesbian mother or homosexual father is per se an unfit parent . . . the father's continuous exposure of the child to his immoral and illicit relationship renders him an unfit and improper custodian as a matter of law." In some jurisdictions, the court's analysis focuses on whether the parent's sexual orientation is harming the child. *See*

M.A.B. v. R.B., 510 N.Y.S.2d 960 (Sup. Ct. 1986) (where father's homosexuality had no adverse, deleterious affect on his son, court held it was "impermissible as a matter of law to decide the question of custody on the basis of the father's sexual orientation."); *see also In re Marriage of D.F.D.,* 862 P.2d 368 (Mont. 1993) (father's cross-dressing not grounds to deny joint custody without finding significant risk of harm to two-year-old son). What evidence would be relevant to the inquiry regarding harm to the child? Who should have the burden of proof?

[iii] Religion

To what extent should the religion of the parent be a factor in the best interest analysis? What if one parent is a practicing Jehovah's Witness who will not allow the child to celebrate birthdays and holidays, sing the national anthem, salute the flag, participate in extra-curricular activities in school, socialize with non-Witnesses, or attend college? *See Pater v. Pater,* 588 N.E. 2d 794 (Ohio 1992) (improper inquiry by trial court into religious beliefs and practices of Jehovah's Witness religion was abuse of discretion). What if one parent would keep the child in the Amish Community and the child would leave school (per *Wisconsin v. Yoder*) at age 14? Courts must tread lightly here to avoid interfering with the First Amendment's protection of the free exercise of religion, but where should the line fall?

What if one parent demands that the child be raised in the religion of that parent? Courts must steer clear of favoring one religion over another to avoid First Amendment Establishment Clause problems. Although courts generally avoid judging the merits of a particular religion, some religious practices that would have an effect on the development of the child may be relevant to the custody decision. *See Egelkamp v. Egelkamp,* 524 A.2d 501 (Pa. Super. 1987) ("Although courts may not render value judgments on the merits of a particular religious view or belief, they may properly examine the effect that those views or beliefs have on the development of a child involved in a custody dispute."). What kinds of views or beliefs might be examined to ascertain their effect on a child's development? What if one parent is a member of a religion that would deny medical treatment to its members?

Suppose one parent is religious and the other is an atheist? Could a court weigh religion as a plus-factor, reasoning that a child would be better off raised in a home with religious training than without it?

[iv] Physical and Mental Disability

Should a parent's physical disability be a factor in the best interest analysis? If all else is equal and a parent is a quadriplegic or suffers from epilepsy, or is dealing with a seriously debilitating illness, how should the judge factor that into the custody consideration? *See In re Marriage of Carney,* 598 P.2d 36 (Cal. 1979) (court should carefully determine whether the parent's condition will in fact have a substantial and lasting adverse effect on the best interests of the child). Is it relevant if the parent has a terminal illness?

Mental disability generally does not per se establish unfitness. The inquiry again focuses on the nexus between the disability and the adverse effect on the child. How predictable can mental health practitioners be in predicting the future conduct of their patients? To what extent should the effect of medication on the illness be considered?

[v] Domestic Violence

Many states have made domestic violence a factor for consideration in the best interest analysis. The violence may be against the child in question (which is often a *per se* factor) or a sibling, or a spouse. Abuse of a sibling or spouse is not an enumerated statutory factor in some states. Unfortunately, some parents may use the abuse factor inappropriately by making false allegations of abuse. This may backfire on the parent making the accusation. *See Young v. Young,* 628 N.Y.S.2d 957 (App. Div. 1995) (custody granted to father because mother made false allegations of child abuse).

[vi] Child Care Issues

If one parent is a professional (as you lawyers-to-be will likely find out), he or she may have less time to spend with children than the other parent. Parents who have substantial duties at work may have to use day care facilities or babysitters. The next case received a great deal of attention in the media after the trial court decision.

IRELAND v. SMITH

Supreme Court of Michigan
547 N.W.2d 686 (1996)

Per Curiam

This is a custody dispute. Following a hearing, the circuit court ordered that the defendant father be given custody of the parties' minor child. The Court of Appeals set aside the circuit court order and remanded the case for further proceedings before a different judge. The Court of Appeals retained jurisdiction. We approve the remand ordered by the Court of Appeals, though we modify the accompanying directions.

I

In their mid-teens, plaintiff Jennifer Ireland and defendant Steven Smith conceived a child, Maranda, who was born in 1991. The parties did not marry, but continued living with their respective parents while they completed high school. After initially planning to put the baby up for adoption, Ms. Ireland decided instead to keep her. The child lived with Ms. Ireland and her mother in Mount Clemens.

After a time, Mr. Smith began visiting the child and providing a few items for her care. However, Maranda continued to live with her mother and maternal grandmother, who provided nearly all the necessary support.

In January 1993, Ms. Ireland began an action to obtain child-support payments from Mr. Smith. She also obtained an ex parte order that granted her continuing custody of Maranda.

Ms. Ireland enrolled as a scholarship student at the University of Michigan in Ann Arbor for the fall semester of 1993. She and Maranda lived in the university's family housing unit. On weekdays, Maranda attended a university-approved day-care center.

During this period, Mr. Smith remained at his parents' home. He evidently continues to live with them.

In May and June 1994, the circuit court conducted a trial regarding the issue of custody. It would be difficult to exaggerate the extent to which the parties disagreed with regard to the proper setting for Maranda. Each produced witnesses who spoke very disparagingly of the other, and there was little agreement about the facts of this matter.

Following the hearing, the circuit court issued an opinion in which it discussed each of the statutory factors for determining the best interests of the child.[11] The court found that each of the statutory factors weighed evenly between the parties, except factor e, which concerns:

> The permanence, as a family unit, of the existing or proposed custodial home or homes.

The circuit court found that factor e "heavily" favored Mr. Smith. It contrasted the stability of continued residence with Mr. Smith and his parents with the occasional moves that were likely as Ms. Ireland continued her education. In an extended discussion of this factor, the court also noted the demands

---

[11] [1] As used in this act, "best interests of the child" means the sum total of the following factors to be considered, evaluated, and determined by the court:

(a) The love, affection, and other emotional ties existing between the parties involved and the child.

(b) The capacity and disposition of the parties involved to give the child love, affection, and guidance and to continue the education and raising of the child in his or her religion or creed, if any.

(c) The capacity and disposition of the parties involved to provide the child with food, clothing, medical care or other remedial care recognized and permitted under the laws of this state in place of medical care, and other material needs.

(d) The length of time the child has lived in a stable, satisfactory environment, and the desirability of maintaining continuity.

(e) The permanence, as a family unit, of the existing or proposed custodial home or homes.

(f) The moral fitness of the parties involved.

(g) The mental and physical health of the parties involved.

(h) The home, school, and community record of the child.

(i) The reasonable preference of the child, if the court considers the child to be of sufficient age to express preference.

(j) The willingness and ability of each of the parties to facilitate and encourage a close and continuing parent-child relationship between the child and the other parent or the child and the parents.

(k) Domestic violence, regardless of whether the violence was directed against or witnessed by the child.

(l) Any other factor considered by the court to be relevant to a particular child custody dispute.

that would be imposed on Ms. Ireland as she sought both to raise a child and attend the university.

For those reasons, the circuit court ordered that Mr. Smith be given custody of Maranda. Ms. Ireland appealed, and the Court of Appeals entered a stay. . . .

The Court of Appeals agreed with the circuit court that Ms. Ireland had provided an established custodial environment.[12] However, it found that the circuit court had erred in determining that factor e favored Mr. Smith. The Court of Appeals upheld the circuit court's determination that the other statutory factors favored neither party. . . .

II

In the central portion of its analysis, the Court of Appeals first explained its conclusion that the evidentiary record did not support a factual finding that factor e favored Mr. Smith:

> We find no support in the record for the trial court's speculation that there is "no way that a single parent, attending an academic program at an institution as prestigious as the University of Michigan, can do justice to their studies and to raising of an infant child." The evidence shows that the child has thrived in the university environment. Defendant concedes that he has no complaint about the university day care, and the trial court recognized that the child has had a "meaningful experience" there. The trial court found plaintiff's day-care arrangements "appropriate," but concluded that defendant's plan to have his mother baby-sit was better for the child because she was a "blood relative" rather than a "stranger." Both parties will necessarily need the help of other people to care for their child as they continue their education and employment, and eventually their careers. In light of undisputed evidence that plaintiff's child-care arrangements are appropriate and working well, the evidence does not support the trial court's judgment that defendant's proposed, but untested, plans for the child's care would be better.

The Court of Appeals then explained that the circuit court had committed an error of law in its application of factor e. Observing that the factor concerns "permanence" of the custodial home, not its "acceptability," the Court stated:

> Moreover, an evaluation of each party's arrangements for the child's care while her parents work to go to school is not an appropriate consideration under this factor. We find the trial court committed clear legal error in considering the "acceptability" of the parties' homes and child-care arrangements under this factor, which is directed to the "permanence, as a family unit," of the individual parties. "This factor exclusively concerns whether the family unit will remain intact, not an evaluation about whether one custodial home would be more

---

[12] [2] Where an established custodial environment exists, custody may not be changed unless there is "clear and convincing evidence that [a change] is in the best interest of the child."

acceptable than the other." *See Fletcher v Fletcher*, 504 N.W.2d 684 (1993). . . .

Finally, the Court of Appeals provided direction for the proceedings on remand:

> On remand, the trial court is to consider "up-to-date information" regarding this factor, as well as the fact that the child has "been living with the plaintiff during the appeal and any other changes in circumstances arising *since the trial court's original custody order*." The trial court is not, however, to entertain or revisit further "evidence" concerning events before the trial in May and June 1994.

III

We affirm the decision of the Court of Appeals to remand this case, and we agree that the circuit court erred in finding that factor e heavily favored Mr. Smith. However, we write to clarify the analysis and modify the terms of the remand.

A

First, there is the issue how properly to understand factor e. As the Court of Appeals observed, we discussed this factor in *Fletcher*, where we explained:

> Factor e requires the trial court to consider "the permanence, as a family unit, of the existing or proposed custodial home or homes." In the instant case, the trial court focused on the "*acceptability* of the custodial home," as opposed to its permanence. It stated its findings as follows:

> > The Court is satisfied that either parent would provide permanence, as a family unit, and would offer acceptable custodial homes. It is undisputed that plaintiff as a father is accustomed to and willing to preform [sic] the day to day jobs to maintain a household. The Court feels that some weight should be assigned in favor of plaintiff because the evidence shows that defendant had been out of the home in the evening many times and thus not caring for the family while plaintiff has been present on those occasions.

> Because acceptability of the home is not pertinent to factor e, the panel found that it was legal error for the trial court to consider it. We agree with the Court of Appeals. The facts relied upon and expressed by the judge relate to acceptability, rather than permanence, of the custodial unit. Therefore, the trial court's error seems to go beyond mere word choice. . . .

We adhere to that explanation. . . .

In this instance, we discern no significant difference between the stability of the settings proposed by the two parties. Ms. Ireland likely will continue to spend time both at the University of Michigan and at her mother's home in Mount Clemens (two settings that are now familiar to the child). It is also possible that she will change residences at the university, and that she will move again after completing her education. Such changes, normal for a young adult at this stage of life, do not disqualify Ms. Ireland for custody. Neither are such changes to be ignored, however. While a child can benefit from reasonable mobility and a degree of parental flexibility regarding residence, the Legislature has determined that "permanence, as a family unit, of the existing or proposed custodial home or homes" is a value to be given weight in the custodial determination.

In some respects, Mr. Smith's proposed custodial home appears more stable. However, that stability may be chimerical. He will not live with his parents forever, and until the likely path of his life becomes more apparent, it is difficult to determine accurately how stable a custodial home he can offer. It would be ironic indeed if the uncertainty of Mr. Smith's plans regarding education, employment, and the early years of adulthood worked to his benefit as a court considered factor e.

In all events, however, the best interests of Maranda, not of Ms. Ireland or Mr. Smith, are central. As in every case, the circuit judge is to give careful consideration to the whole situation. When the court turns to factor e, it must weigh all the facts that bear on whether Ms. Ireland or Mr. Smith can best provide Maranda the benefits of a custodial home that is marked by permanence, as a family unit.

B

Second, we need to confirm that actual and proposed child-care arrangements — whether in the custodial home or elsewhere — are a proper consideration in a custody case. Many children spend a significant amount of time in such settings, and no reasonable person would doubt the importance of child-care decisions. While not directly within the scope of factor e, a parent's intentions in this regard are related to several of the statutory factors:

> (b) The capacity and disposition of the parties involved to give the child love, affection, and guidance and to continue the education and raising of the child in his or her religion or creed, if any.

> (c) The capacity and disposition of the parties involved to provide the child with food, clothing, medical care or other remedial care recognized and permitted under the laws of this state in place of medical care, and other material needs.

> . . . .

> (h) The home, school, and community record of the child.

To the extent that these factors fail to capture this aspect of child-rearing, it certainly falls within the final factor:

> (i) Any other factor considered by the court to be relevant to a particular child custody dispute.

Having said that child-care arrangements are a proper consideration, we then encounter the issue that brought sixty-one amici curiae to the Court of Appeals (all in support of Ms. Ireland): *How* are such arrangements to be considered? Does a parent seeking custody lose ground by proposing to place a child in a day-care center while the parent works or goes to school? Is in-home care from parents and other relatives better than day care with other children under the supervision of licensed caregivers? Is day care better?

Such questions are not susceptible of a broad answer. Certainly, placement of a child in a good day-care setting can have many benefits and is in no sense a sign of parental neglect. Both single and married parents have many obligations, and day care generally is an entirely appropriate manner of balancing those obligations.

At the same time, it requires no stretch of imagination to produce hypothetical situations in which a parent's unwise choices in this regard would reflect poorly on the parent's judgment. More fundamentally, every child, every adult, and every custody case is unique. There can be no broad rules that dictate a preference for one manner of child care over another. The circuit court must look at each situation and determine what is in the best interests of the child.

. . . .

QUESTIONS

1. To what extent do you think that the "professional parent" cases have been influenced by gender bias and the notion that women should be at home with children?

2. If one parent gets home every night after 9:00 and spends little time with the child during the week, should that be a factor if the other parent is home every night at 5:30?

[2] Joint Custody

The trend toward joint custody has increased greatly since the last quarter of the twentieth century. Joint physical custody involves both parents sharing the physical care of the child and the child's residence. Joint legal custody refers to the power of the parent to make decisions about the welfare of the child, including decisions involving health care, education and religion. The courts and the legislatures are not always clear about which form of joint custody is being considered. Moreover, deciding the point at which the child spends enough time with one parent so as to constitute joint physical custody is often confusing.

The court in *Taylor v. Taylor*, 508 A.2d 964 (Md. 1986), explains some of the issues:

> This dynamic and emotionally charged field of law is unfortunately afflicted with significant semantical problems, described by one writer as a "frightful lack of linguistic uniformity." [Citing D. Millier, 13 FAM.

L.Q. 345, 376 (1979).] The inability of courts and commentators to agree on what is meant by the term "joint custody" makes difficult the task of distilling principles and guidelines from a rapidly growing body of literature and case law. What one writer sees as an amorphous concept another sees as a structured legal arrangement. While it is clear that both parents in a joint custody arrangement function as "custodians" in the sense that they are actually involved in the overall welfare of their child, a distinction must be made between sharing parental responsibility in major decision-making matters and sharing responsibility for providing a home for the child.

> Embraced within the meaning of "custody" are the concepts of "legal" and "physical" custody. Legal custody carries with it the right and obligation to make long range decisions involving education, religious training, discipline, medical care, and other matters of major significance concerning the child's life and welfare. . . . Joint legal custody means that both parents have an equal voice in making those decisions, and neither parent's rights are superior to the other.

Id. at 967. The *Taylor* court pointed out that the parent who does not have legal custody may still make certain decisions about the child's welfare when that parent has physical custody of the child:

> The parent not granted legal custody will, under ordinary circumstances, retain authority to make necessary day-to-day decisions concerning the child's welfare during the time the child is in that parent's physical custody. Thus, a parent exercising physical custody over a child, whether pursuant to an order of visitation or to an order of shared physical custody, necessarily possesses the authority to control and discipline the child during the period of physical custody. Similarly, that parent has the authority to consent to emergency surgery or emergency major medical care when there is insufficient time to contact the parent having legal custody. We need not here consider the issues that may arise when the parent having legal custody cannot agree with the parent exercising physical custody concerning emergency medical care. This residuum of authority should be exercised so as not to conflict with the long range decisions and policies made by the parent having legal custody.

Id. at n.4. Thus physical custody has its own set of rights and responsibilities:

> Physical custody, on the other hand, means the right and obligation to provide a home for the child and to make the day-to-day decisions required during the time the child is actually with the parent having such custody. Joint physical custody is in reality "shared" or "divided" custody. Shared physical custody may, but need not, be on a 50/50 basis, and in fact most commonly will involve custody by one parent during the school year and by the other during summer vacation months, or division between weekdays and weekends, or between days and nights.

With respect to physical custody, there is no difference between the rights and obligations of a parent having temporary custody of a child pursuant to an order of shared physical custody, and one having temporary custody pursuant to an award of visitation. Thus, a determination to grant legal custody to one parent and to allocate physical custody between the parents may be accomplished either by granting sole custody to one parent and specified rights of visitation to the other, or by granting legal custody to one parent and specified periods of physical custody to each parent. In either instance the effect will be the same.

Proper practice in any case involving joint custody dictates that the parties and the trial judge separately consider the issues involved in both joint legal custody and joint physical custody, and that the trial judge state specifically the decision made as to each.

Id. at 967.

The best interest of the child is paramount in the court's decision on joint custody, but factors that courts consider when determining whether joint custody would be appropriate include (1) the capacity of the parents to communicate and to reach shared decisions affecting the child's welfare; (2) willingness of the parents to share custody; (3) the fitness of the parents; (4) the relationship established between the child and each parent; (5) the preference of the child; (6) the potential disruption of the child's schooling and social life; (7) the geographic proximity of the parental homes; (8) the demands of parental employment; (9) the age and number of children; (10) the sincerity of the parents' request (was one parent asking for joint custody to gain bargaining leverage over the other?); (11) financial status of the parents; (12) the benefit to the parents (their self-image ultimately is likely to benefit the child). *Id.* at 971–75.

For a discussion of how family lawyers approach the joint custody issues, see Gwyneth I. Williams, *Looking at Joint Custody Through the Language and Attitudes of Attorneys*, 26 Just. Sys. J. 1-34 (2005).

NOTES AND QUESTIONS

1. What are the advantages of joint custody? The problems? Might a judge be inclined to opt for joint custody to avoid making the hard decision between two parents?

2. In *Elk Grove Unified School District v. Newdow*, 542 U.S. 1 (2004), the United States Supreme Court ducked a contentious issue regarding the Pledge of Allegiance because of the father's situation regarding the custody of his daughter. The father, an atheist, contended that the words "under God" in the Pledge violated the establishment and free exercise clauses of the first amendment and that the school district's recitation policy was unconstitutional. Pursuant to a state-court order, the child's father and mother had joint legal custody and the father had the right to consult on issues relating to the child's education. The child's mother, who possessed final authority over decisions concerning health, education, and welfare of the daughter, disagreed

with father and had no objection either to the reciting or hearing others recite the Pledge of Allegiance. She believed her daughter would be harmed if litigation were permitted to proceed. State law precluded the father from suing as his daughter's next friend, and the Supreme Court held that the father lacked prudential standing to bring action in federal court.

The Seventh Circuit ruled that a noncustodial divorced father with a child in public school had no federal substantive due process right to receive notices, records and correspondence that the custodial parent receives from school. *Crowley v. McKinney*, 400 F.3d (7th Cir. 2005). The court acknowledged that *Meyer* and *Pierce* addressed the constitutional rights of parents with respect to the education of their children. The court determined, however, that denying the option of private education was a greater intrusion on parental control than limiting parental involvement in the activities of the school their children attend. Moreover, *Meyer* and *Pierce* concerned the rights of parents acting together. In this case, the mother had sole custody and did not join the noncustodial parent's claim.

The issues surrounding child custody are complex and nuanced. The materials in this section present the basic framework surrounding the custody issue. The problems surrounding child custody are covered more deeply in a course on Family Law. For an excellent reference or course book, see ELLMAN, KURTZ & SCOTT, FAMILY LAW 559–679 (2004).

[B] Technology and the New Family

Advances in reproductive technology have allowed for artificial insemination of sperm, "surrogate" motherhood, in vitro fertilization, embryo transfer and embryo storage. The following case made national headlines and made the general public aware of some of the difficult issues surrounding reproductive technology. The case deals with issues surrounding adoption, termination of parental rights, custody and visitation.

IN RE BABY M

Supreme Court of New Jersey
537 A.2d 1227 (1988)

WILENTZ, CHIEF JUSTICE

In this matter the Court is asked to determine the validity of a contract that purports to provide a new way of bringing children into a family. For a fee of $10,000, a woman agrees to be artificially inseminated with the semen of another woman's husband; she is to conceive a child, carry it to term, and after its birth surrender it to the natural father and his wife. The intent of the contract is that the child's natural mother will thereafter be forever separated from her child. The wife is to adopt the child, and she and the natural father are to be regarded as its parents for all purposes. The contract providing for this is called a "surrogacy contract," the natural mother inappropriately called the "surrogate mother."

We invalidate the surrogacy contract because it conflicts with the law and public policy of this State. While we recognize the depth of the yearning of infertile couples to have their own children, we find the payment of money to a "surrogate" mother illegal, perhaps criminal, and potentially degrading to women. Although in this case we grant custody to the natural father, the evidence having clearly proved such custody to be in the best interests of the infant, we void both the termination of the surrogate mother's parental rights and the adoption of the child by the wife/stepparent. We thus restore the "surrogate" as the mother of the child. We remand the issue of the natural mother's visitation rights to the trial court, since that issue was not reached below and the record before us is not sufficient to permit us to decide it *de novo*.

We find no offense to our present laws where a woman voluntarily and without payment agrees to act as a "surrogate" mother, provided that she is not subject to a binding agreement to surrender her child. Moreover, our holding today does not preclude the Legislature from altering the current statutory scheme, within constitutional limits, so as to permit surrogacy contracts. Under current law, however, the surrogacy agreement before us is illegal and invalid.

I

FACTS

In February 1985, William Stern and Mary Beth Whitehead entered into a surrogacy contract. It recited that Stern's wife, Elizabeth, was infertile, that they wanted a child, and that Mrs. Whitehead was willing to provide that child as the mother with Mr. Stern as the father.

The contract provided that through artificial insemination using Mr. Stern's sperm, Mrs. Whitehead would become pregnant, carry the child to term, bear it, deliver it to the Sterns, and thereafter do whatever was necessary to terminate her maternal rights so that Mrs. Stern could thereafter adopt the child. Mrs. Whitehead's husband, Richard,[13] was also a party to the contract; Mrs. Stern was not. Mr. Whitehead promised to do all acts necessary to rebut the presumption of paternity under the Parentage Act. *N.J.S.A.* 9:17-43a(1), -44a. Although Mrs. Stern was not a party to the surrogacy agreement, the contract gave her sole custody of the child in the event of Mr. Stern's death. Mrs. Stern's status as a nonparty to the surrogate parenting agreement presumably was to avoid the application of the baby-selling statute to this arrangement. *N.J.S.A.* 9:3-54.

Mr. Stern, on his part, agreed to attempt the artificial insemination and to pay Mrs. Whitehead $10,000 after the child's birth, on its delivery to him.

---

[13] [4] Subsequent to the trial court proceedings, Mr. and Mrs. Whitehead were divorced, and soon thereafter Mrs. Whitehead remarried. Nevertheless, in the course of this opinion we will make reference almost exclusively to the facts as they existed at the time of trial, the facts on which the decision we now review was reached. We note moreover that Mr. Whitehead remains a party to this dispute. For these reasons, we continue to refer to appellants as Mr. and Mrs. Whitehead.

In a separate contract, Mr. Stern agreed to pay $7,500 to the Infertility Center of New York ("ICNY"). The Center's advertising campaigns solicit surrogate mothers and encourage infertile couples to consider surrogacy. ICNY arranged for the surrogacy contract by bringing the parties together, explaining the process to them, furnishing the contractual form, and providing legal counsel.

The history of the parties' involvement in this arrangement suggests their good faith. William and Elizabeth Stern were married in July 1974, having met at the University of Michigan, where both were Ph.D. candidates. Due to financial considerations and Mrs. Stern's pursuit of a medical degree and residency, they decided to defer starting a family until 1981. Before then, however, Mrs. Stern learned that she might have multiple sclerosis and that the disease in some cases renders pregnancy a serious health risk. Her anxiety appears to have exceeded the actual risk, which current medical authorities assess as minimal. Nonetheless that anxiety was evidently quite real, Mrs. Stern fearing that pregnancy might precipitate blindness, paraplegia, or other forms of debilitation. Based on the perceived risk, the Sterns decided to forego having their own children. The decision had special significance for Mr. Stern. Most of his family had been destroyed in the Holocaust. As the family's only survivor, he very much wanted to continue his bloodline.

Initially the Sterns considered adoption, but were discouraged by the substantial delay apparently involved and by the potential problem they saw arising from their age and their differing religious backgrounds. They were most eager for some other means to start a family.

The paths of Mrs. Whitehead and the Sterns to surrogacy were similar. Both responded to advertising by ICNY. The Sterns' response, following their inquiries into adoption, was the result of their long-standing decision to have a child. Mrs. Whitehead's response apparently resulted from her sympathy with family members and others who could have no children (she stated that she wanted to give another couple the "gift of life"); she also wanted the $10,000 to help her family.

Both parties, undoubtedly because of their own self-interest, were less sensitive to the implications of the transaction than they might otherwise have been. Mrs. Whitehead, for instance, appears not to have been concerned about whether the Sterns would make good parents for her child; the Sterns, on their part, while conscious of the obvious possibility that surrendering the child might cause grief to Mrs. Whitehead, overcame their qualms because of their desire for a child. At any rate, both the Sterns and Mrs. Whitehead were committed to the arrangement; both thought it right and constructive.

Mrs. Whitehead had reached her decision concerning surrogacy before the Sterns, and had actually been involved as a potential surrogate mother with another couple. After numerous unsuccessful artificial inseminations, that effort was abandoned. Thereafter, the Sterns learned of the Infertility Center, the possibilities of surrogacy, and of Mary Beth Whitehead. The two couples met to discuss the surrogacy arrangement and decided to go forward. On February 6, 1985, Mr. Stern and Mr. and Mrs. Whitehead executed the surrogate parenting agreement. After several artificial inseminations over a period of months, Mrs. Whitehead became pregnant. The pregnancy was uneventful and on March 27, 1986, Baby M was born.

Not wishing anyone at the hospital to be aware of the surrogacy arrangement, Mr. and Mrs. Whitehead appeared to all as the proud parents of a healthy female child. Her birth certificate indicated her name to be Sara Elizabeth Whitehead and her father to be Richard Whitehead. In accordance with Mrs. Whitehead's request, the Sterns visited the hospital unobtrusively to see the newborn child.

Mrs. Whitehead realized, almost from the moment of birth, that she could not part with this child. She had felt a bond with it even during pregnancy. Some indication of the attachment was conveyed to the Sterns at the hospital when they told Mrs. Whitehead what they were going to name the baby. She apparently broke into tears and indicated that she did not know if she could give up the child. She talked about how the baby looked like her other daughter, and made it clear that she was experiencing great difficulty with the decision.

Nonetheless, Mrs. Whitehead was, for the moment, true to her word. Despite powerful inclinations to the contrary, she turned her child over to the Sterns on March 30 at the Whiteheads' home.

The Sterns were thrilled with their new child. They had planned extensively for its arrival, far beyond the practical furnishing of a room for her. It was a time of joyful celebration — not just for them but for their friends as well. The Sterns looked forward to raising their daughter, whom they named Melissa. While aware by then that Mrs. Whitehead was undergoing an emotional crisis, they were as yet not cognizant of the depth of that crisis and its implications for their newly-enlarged family.

Later in the evening of March 30, Mrs. Whitehead became deeply disturbed, disconsolate, stricken with unbearable sadness. She had to have her child. She could not eat, sleep, or concentrate on anything other than her need for her baby. The next day she went to the Sterns' home and told them how much she was suffering.

The depth of Mrs. Whitehead's despair surprised and frightened the Sterns. She told them that she could not live without her baby, that she must have her, even if only for one week, that thereafter she would surrender her child. The Sterns, concerned that Mrs. Whitehead might indeed commit suicide, not wanting under any circumstances to risk that, and in any event believing that Mrs. Whitehead would keep her word, turned the child over to her. It was not until four months later, after a series of attempts to regain possession of the child, that Melissa was returned to the Sterns, having been forcibly removed from the home where she was then living with Mr. and Mrs. Whitehead, the home in Florida owned by Mary Beth Whitehead's parents.

The struggle over Baby M began when it became apparent that Mrs. Whitehead could not return the child to Mr. Stern. Due to Mrs. Whitehead's refusal to relinquish the baby, Mr. Stern filed a complaint seeking enforcement of the surrogacy contract. He alleged, accurately, that Mrs. Whitehead had not only refused to comply with the surrogacy contract but had threatened to flee from New Jersey with the child in order to avoid even the possibility of his obtaining custody. The court papers asserted that if Mrs. Whitehead were to be given notice of the application for an order requiring her to relinquish custody, she would, prior to the hearing, leave the state with the baby. And that is precisely what she did. After the order was entered, *ex parte*, the process server, aided by the police, in the presence of the Sterns, entered Mrs. Whitehead's home to execute the order. Mr. Whitehead fled with the child, who had been handed to him through a window while those who came to enforce the order were thrown off balance by a dispute over the child's current name.

The Whiteheads immediately fled to Florida with Baby M. They stayed initially with Mrs. Whitehead's parents, where one of Mrs. Whitehead's children had been living. For the next three months, the Whiteheads and Melissa lived at roughly twenty different hotels, motels, and homes in order to avoid apprehension. From time to time Mrs. Whitehead would call Mr. Stern to discuss the matter; the conversations, recorded by Mr. Stern on advice of counsel, show an escalating dispute about rights, morality, and power, accompanied by threats of Mrs. Whitehead to kill herself, to kill the child, and falsely to accuse Mr. Stern of sexually molesting Mrs. Whitehead's other daughter.

Eventually the Sterns discovered where the Whiteheads were staying, commenced supplementary proceedings in Florida, and obtained an order requiring the Whiteheads to turn over the child. Police in Florida enforced the order, forcibly removing the child from her grandparents' home. She was soon thereafter brought to New Jersey and turned over to the Sterns. The prior order of the court, issued *ex parte*, awarding custody of the child to the Sterns *pendente lite*, was reaffirmed by the trial court after consideration of the certified representations of the parties (both represented by counsel) concerning the unusual sequence of events that had unfolded. Pending final judgment, Mrs. Whitehead was awarded limited visitation with Baby M.

The Sterns' complaint, in addition to seeking possession and ultimately custody of the child, sought enforcement of the surrogacy contract. Pursuant to the contract, it asked that the child be permanently placed in their custody, that Mrs. Whitehead's parental rights be terminated, and that Mrs. Stern be allowed to adopt the child, *i.e.*, that, for all purposes, Melissa become the Sterns' child.

The trial took thirty-two days over a period of more than two months. . . . There were twenty-three witnesses to the facts recited above and fifteen expert witnesses, eleven testifying on the issue of custody and four on the subject of Mrs. Stern's multiple sclerosis; the bulk of the testimony was devoted to determining the parenting arrangement most compatible with the child's best interests. Soon after the conclusion of the trial, the trial court announced its opinion from the bench. It held that the surrogacy contract was valid; ordered that Mrs. Whitehead's parental rights be terminated and that sole custody of the child be granted to Mr. Stern; and, after hearing brief testimony from Mrs. Stern, immediately entered an order allowing the adoption of Melissa by Mrs. Stern, all in accordance with the surrogacy contract. Pending the outcome of the appeal, we granted a continuation of visitation to Mrs. Whitehead, although slightly more limited than the visitation allowed during the trial.

Although clearly expressing its view that the surrogacy contract was valid, the trial court devoted the major portion of its opinion to the question of the baby's best interests. The inconsistency is apparent. The surrogacy contract calls for the surrender of the child to the Sterns, permanent and sole custody in the Sterns, and termination of Mrs. Whitehead's parental rights, all without qualification, all regardless of any evaluation of the best interests of the child. As a matter of fact the contract recites (even before the child was conceived) that it is in the best interests of the child to be placed with Mr. Stern. In effect, the trial court awarded custody to Mr. Stern, the natural father, based on the same kind of evidence and analysis as might be expected had no surrogacy contract existed. Its rationalization, however, was that while the surrogacy contract was valid, specific performance would not be granted unless that remedy was in the best interests of the child. The factual issues confronted and decided by the trial court were the same as if Mr. Stern and Mrs. Whitehead had had the child out of wedlock, intended or unintended, and then disagreed about custody. . . .

On the question of best interests — and we agree, but for different reasons, that custody was the critical issue — the court's analysis of the testimony was perceptive, demonstrating both its understanding of the case and its considerable experience in these matters. We agree substantially with both its analysis and conclusions on the matter of custody.

The court's review and analysis of the surrogacy contract, however, is not at all in accord with ours. The trial court concluded that the various statutes governing this matter, including those concerning adoption, termination of parental rights, and payment of money in connection with adoptions, do not apply to surrogacy contracts. It reasoned that because the Legislature did not have surrogacy contracts in mind when it passed those laws, those laws were therefore irrelevant. Thus, assuming it was writing on a clean slate, the trial court analyzed the interests involved and the power of the court to accommodate them. It then held that surrogacy contracts are valid and should be enforced, *id.* at 388, and furthermore that Mr. Stern's rights under the surrogacy contract were constitutionally protected. . . .

Mrs. Whitehead contends that the surrogacy contract, for a variety of reasons, is invalid. She contends that it conflicts with public policy since it guarantees that the child will not have the nurturing of both natural parents — presumably New Jersey's goal for families. She further argues that it deprives the mother of her constitutional right to the companionship of her child, and that it conflicts with statutes concerning termination of parental rights and adoption. With the contract thus void, Mrs. Whitehead claims primary custody (with visitation rights in Mr. Stern) both on a best interests basis (stressing the "tender years" doctrine) as well as on the policy basis of discouraging surrogacy contracts. She maintains that even if custody would ordinarily go to Mr. Stern, here it should be awarded to Mrs. Whitehead to deter future surrogacy arrangements.

In a brief filed after oral argument, counsel for Mrs. Whitehead suggests that the standard for determining best interests where the infant resulted from a surrogacy contract is that the child should be placed with the mother absent a showing of unfitness. All parties agree that no expert testified that

Mary Beth Whitehead was unfit as a mother; the trial court expressly found that she was *not* "unfit," that, on the contrary, "she is a good mother for and to her older children," and no one now claims anything to the contrary.

One of the repeated themes put forth by Mrs. Whitehead is that the court's initial *ex parte* order granting custody to the Sterns during the trial was a substantial factor in the ultimate "best interests" determination. That initial order, claimed to be erroneous by Mrs. Whitehead, not only established Melissa as part of the Stern family, but brought enormous pressure on Mrs. Whitehead. The order brought the weight of the state behind the Sterns' attempt, ultimately successful, to gain possession of the child. The resulting pressure, Mrs. Whitehead contends, caused her to act in ways that were atypical of her ordinary behavior when not under stress, and to act in ways that were thought to be inimical to the child's best interests in that they demonstrated a failure of character, maturity, and consistency. She claims that any mother who truly loved her child might so respond and that it is doubly unfair to judge her on the basis of her reaction to an extreme situation rarely faced by any mother, where that situation was itself caused by an erroneous order of the court. Therefore, according to Mrs. Whitehead, the erroneous *ex parte* order precipitated a series of events that proved instrumental in the final result.

The Sterns claim that the surrogacy contract is valid and should be enforced, largely for the reasons given by the trial court. They claim a constitutional right of privacy, which includes the right of procreation, and the right of consenting adults to deal with matters of reproduction as they see fit. As for the child's best interests, their position is factual: given all of the circumstances, the child is better off in their custody with no residual parental rights reserved for Mrs. Whitehead.

Of considerable interest in this clash of views is the position of the child's guardian *ad litem*, wisely appointed by the court at the outset of the litigation. As the child's representative, her role in the litigation, as she viewed it, was solely to protect the child's best interests. She therefore took no position on the validity of the surrogacy contract, and instead devoted her energies to obtaining expert testimony uninfluenced by any interest other than the child's. We agree with the guardian's perception of her role in this litigation. She appropriately refrained from taking any position that might have appeared to compromise her role as the child's advocate. She first took the position, based on her experts' testimony, that the Sterns should have primary custody, and that while Mrs. Whitehead's parental rights should not be terminated, no visitation should be allowed for five years. As a result of subsequent developments, mentioned *infra*, her view has changed. She now recommends that no visitation be allowed at least until Baby M reaches maturity.

Although some of the experts' opinions touched on visitation, the major issue they addressed was whether custody should be reposed in the Sterns or in the Whiteheads. The trial court, consistent in this respect with its view that the surrogacy contract was valid, did not deal at all with the question of visitation. Having concluded that the best interests of the child called for custody in the Sterns, the trial court enforced the operative provisions of the surrogacy contract, terminated Mrs. Whitehead's parental rights, and granted an adoption to Mrs. Stern. Explicit in the ruling was the conclusion that the best interests determination removed whatever impediment might have existed in enforcing the surrogacy contract. This Court, therefore, is without guidance from the trial court on the visitation issue, an issue of considerable importance in any event, and especially important in view of our determination that the surrogacy contract is invalid.

II

INVALIDITY AND UNENFORCEABILITY OF SURROGACY CONTRACT

We have concluded that this surrogacy contract is invalid. Our conclusion has two bases: direct conflict with existing statutes and conflict with the public policies of this State, as expressed in its statutory and decisional law.

One of the surrogacy contract's basic purposes, to achieve the adoption of a child through private placement, though permitted in New Jersey "is very much disfavored." Its use of money for this purpose — and we have no doubt whatsoever that the money is being paid to obtain an adoption and not, as the Sterns argue, for the personal services of Mary Beth Whitehead — is illegal and perhaps criminal. In addition to the inducement of money, there is the coercion of contract: the natural mother's irrevocable agreement, prior to birth, even prior to conception, to surrender the child to the adoptive couple. Such an agreement is totally unenforceable in private placement adoption. Even where the adoption is through an approved agency, the formal agreement to surrender occurs only *after* birth and then, by regulation, only after the birth mother has been offered counseling. Integral to these invalid provisions of the surrogacy contract is the related agreement, equally invalid, on the part of the natural mother to cooperate with, and not to contest, proceedings to terminate her parental rights, as well as her contractual concession, in aid of the adoption, that the child's best interests would be served by awarding custody to the natural father and his wife — all of this before she has even conceived, and, in some cases, before she has the slightest idea of what the natural father and adoptive mother are like.

The foregoing provisions not only directly conflict with New Jersey statutes, but also offend long-established State policies. These critical terms, which are at the heart of the contract, are invalid and unenforceable; the conclusion therefore follows, without more, that the entire contract is unenforceable.

A. *Conflict with Statutory Provisions*

The surrogacy contract conflicts with: (1) laws prohibiting the use of money in connection with adoptions; (2) laws requiring proof of parental unfitness or abandonment before termination of parental rights is ordered or an adoption is granted; and (3) laws that make surrender of custody and consent to adoption revocable in private placement adoptions. . . .

(1) [M]oney paid to Mrs. Whitehead was stated to be for her services — not for the adoption; the sole purpose of the contract was stated as being that "of

giving a child to William Stern, its natural and biological father"; the money was purported to be "compensation for services and expenses and in no way . . . a fee for termination of parental rights or a payment in exchange for consent to surrender a child for adoption"; the fee to the Infertility Center ($7,500) was stated to be for legal representation, advice, administrative work, and other "services." Nevertheless, it seems clear that the money was paid and accepted in connection with an adoption. . . .

As for the contention that the Sterns are paying only for services and not for an adoption, we need note only that they would pay nothing in the event the child died before the fourth month of pregnancy, and only $1,000 if the child were stillborn, even though the "services" had been fully rendered. Additionally, one of Mrs. Whitehead's estimated costs, to be assumed by Mr. Stern, was an "Adoption Fee," presumably for Mrs. Whitehead's incidental costs in connection with the adoption.

Mr. Stern knew he was paying for the adoption of a child; Mrs. Whitehead knew she was accepting money so that a child might be adopted; the Infertility Center knew that it was being paid for assisting in the adoption of a child. The actions of all three worked to frustrate the goals of the statute. It strains credulity to claim that these arrangements, touted by those in the surrogacy business as an attractive alternative to the usual route leading to an adoption, really amount to something other than a private placement adoption for money. . . .

The evils inherent in baby-bartering are loathsome for a myriad of reasons. The child is sold without regard for whether the purchasers will be suitable parents. N. Baker, *Baby Selling: The Scandal of Black Market Adoption* (1978). The natural mother does not receive the benefit of counseling and guidance to assist her in making a decision that may affect her for a lifetime. In fact, the monetary incentive to sell her child may, depending on her financial circumstances, make her decision less voluntary. Furthermore, the adoptive parents may not be fully informed of the natural parents' medical history.

Baby-selling potentially results in the exploitation of all parties involved. Conversely, adoption statutes seek to further humanitarian goals, foremost among them the best interests of the child. The negative consequences of baby-buying are potentially present in the surrogacy context, especially the potential for placing and adopting a child without regard to the interest of the child or the natural mother.

(2) The termination of Mrs. Whitehead's parental rights, called for by the surrogacy contract and actually ordered by the court, fails to comply with the stringent requirements of New Jersey law. Our law, recognizing the finality of any termination of parental rights, provides for such termination only where there has been a voluntary surrender of a child to an approved agency or to the Division of Youth and Family Services ("DYFS"), accompanied by a formal document acknowledging termination of parental rights, or where there has been a showing of parental abandonment or unfitness. A termination may ordinarily take one of three forms: an action by an approved agency, an action by DYFS, or an action in connection with a private placement adoption. The three are governed by separate statutes, but the standards for termination

are substantially the same, except that whereas a written surrender is effective when made to an approved agency or to DYFS, there is no provision for it in the private placement context. . . .

Where the parent has not executed a formal consent, termination requires a showing of "forsaken parental obligation," *i.e.*, "willful and continuous neglect or failure to perform the natural and regular obligations of care and support of a child."

Where DYFS is the agency seeking termination, the requirements are similarly stringent, although at first glance they do not appear to be so. DYFS can, as can any approved agency, accept a formal voluntary surrender or writing having the effect of termination and giving DYFS the right to place the child for adoption. Absent such formal written surrender and consent, similar to that given to approved agencies, DYFS can terminate parental rights in an action for guardianship by proving that the best interests of such child require that he be placed under proper guardianship." Despite this "best interests" language, however, this Court has recently held . . . that in order for DYFS to terminate parental rights it must prove, by clear and convincing evidence, that "[t]he child's health and development have been or will be seriously impaired by the parental relationship," that "[t]he parents are unable or unwilling to eliminate the harm and delaying permanent placement will add to the harm," that "[t]he court has considered alternatives to termination," and that "[t]he termination of parental rights will not do more harm than good." This interpretation of the statutory language requires a most substantial showing of harm to the child if the parental relationship were to continue, far exceeding anything that a "best interests" test connotes.

In order to terminate parental rights under the private placement adoption statute, there must be a finding of "intentional abandonment or a very substantial neglect of parental duties without a reasonable expectation of a reversal of that conduct in the future." . . .

In *Sees v. Baber*, 74 N.J. 201 (1977), we . . . established that without proof that parental obligations had been forsaken, there would be no termination in a private placement setting.

As the trial court recognized, without a valid termination there can be no adoption. . . . Our statutes, and the cases interpreting them, leave no doubt that where there has been no written surrender to an approved agency or to DYFS, termination of parental rights will not be granted in this state absent a very strong showing of abandonment or neglect. . . .

In this case a termination of parental rights was obtained, not by proving the statutory prerequisites, but by claiming the benefit of contractual provisions. From all that has been stated above, it is clear that a contractual agreement to abandon one's parental rights, or not to contest a termination action, will not be enforced in our courts. The Legislature would not have so carefully, so consistently, and so substantially restricted termination of parental rights if it had intended to allow termination to be achieved by one short sentence in a contract.

Since the termination was invalid, it follows, as noted above, that adoption of Melissa by Mrs. Stern could not properly be granted.

(3) The provision in the surrogacy contract stating that Mary Beth White-head agrees to "surrender custody . . . and terminate all parental rights" contains no clause giving her a right to rescind. It is intended to be an irrevocable consent to surrender the child for adoption — in other words, an irrevocable commitment by Mrs. Whitehead to turn Baby M over to the Sterns and thereafter to allow termination of her parental rights. The trial court required a "best interests" showing as a condition to granting specific perfor-mance of the surrogacy contract. Having decided the "best interests' issue in favor of the Sterns, that court's order included, among other things, specific performance of this agreement to surrender custody and terminate all paren-tal rights.

Mrs. Whitehead, shortly after the child's birth, had attempted to revoke her consent and surrender by refusing, after the Sterns had allowed her to have the child "just for one week," to return Baby M to them. The trial court's award of specific performance therefore reflects its view that the consent to surrender the child was irrevocable. We accept the trial court's construction of the contract; indeed it appears quite clear that this was the parties' intent. Such a provision, however, making irrevocable the natural mother's consent to surrender custody of her child in a private placement adoption, clearly conflicts with New Jersey law. . . .

It is clear that the Legislature so carefully circumscribed all aspects of a consent to surrender custody — its form and substance, its manner of execution, and the agency or agencies to which it may be made — in order to provide the basis for irrevocability. It seems most unlikely that the Legislature intended that a consent not complying with these requirements would also be irrevocable, especially where, as here, that consent falls radically short of compliance. Not only do the form and substance of the consent in the surrogacy contract fail to meet statutory requirements, but the surrender of custody is made to a private party. It is not made, as the statute requires, either to an approved agency or to DYFS.

These strict prerequisites to irrevocability constitute a recognition of the most serious consequences that flow from such consents: termination of paren-tal rights, the permanent separation of parent from child, and the ultimate adoption of the child. Because of those consequences, the Legislature severely limited the circumstances under which such consent would be irrevoca-ble. . . . There is no doubt that a contractual provision purporting to consti-tute an irrevocable agreement to surrender custody of a child for adoption is invalid. . . .

B. *Public Policy Considerations*

The surrogacy contract's invalidity, resulting from its direct conflict with the above statutory provisions, is further underlined when its goals and means are measured against New Jersey's public policy. The contract's basic premise, that the natural parents can decide in advance of birth which one is to have custody of the child, bears no relationship to the settled law that the child's best interests shall determine custody. . . .

The surrogacy contract guarantees permanent separation of the child from one of its natural parents. Our policy, however, has long been that to the extent possible, children should remain with and be brought up by both of their natural parents. . . . This is not simply some theoretical ideal that in practice has no meaning. The impact of failure to follow that policy is nowhere better shown than in the results of this surrogacy contract. A child, instead of starting off its life with as much peace and security as possible, finds itself immediately in a tug-of-war between contending mother and father. . . .

This is the sale of a child, or, at the very least, the sale of a mother's right to her child, the only mitigating factor being that one of the purchasers is the father. Almost every evil that prompted the prohibition on the payment of money in connection with adoptions exists here.

The differences between an adoption and a surrogacy contract should be noted, since it is asserted that the use of money in connection with surrogacy does not pose the risks found where money buys an adoption. Katz, *Surrogate Motherhood and the Baby-Selling Laws,* 20 COLUM. J. L. & SOC. PROBS. 1 (1986).

First, and perhaps most important, all parties concede that it is unlikely that surrogacy will survive without money. Despite the alleged selfless motivation of surrogate mothers, if there is no payment, there will be no surrogates, or very few. That conclusion contrasts with adoption; for obvious reasons, there remains a steady supply, albeit insufficient, despite the prohibitions against payment. The adoption itself, relieving the natural mother of the financial burden of supporting an infant, is in some sense the equivalent of payment.

Second, the use of money in adoptions does not *produce* the problem — conception occurs, and usually the birth itself, before illicit funds are offered. With surrogacy, the "problem," if one views it as such, consisting of the purchase of a woman's procreative capacity, at the risk of her life, is caused by and originates with the offer of money.

Third, with the law prohibiting the use of money in connection with adoptions, the built-in financial pressure of the unwanted pregnancy and the consequent support obligation do not lead the mother to the highest paying, ill-suited, adoptive parents. She is just as well-off surrendering the child to an approved agency. In surrogacy, the highest bidders will presumably become the adoptive parents regardless of suitability, so long as payment of money is permitted.

Fourth, the mother's consent to surrender her child in adoptions is revocable, even after surrender of the child, unless it be to an approved agency, where by regulation there are protections against an ill-advised surrender. In surrogacy, consent occurs so early that no amount of advice would satisfy the potential mother's need, yet the consent is irrevocable.

The main difference, that the unwanted pregnancy is unintended while the situation of the surrogate mother is voluntary and intended, is really not significant. Initially, it produces stronger reactions of sympathy for the mother whose pregnancy was unwanted than for the surrogate mother, who "went into this with her eyes wide open." On reflection, however, it appears that the essential evil is the same, taking advantage of a woman's circumstances (the unwanted pregnancy or the need for money) in order to take away her child, the difference being one of degree.

In the scheme contemplated by the surrogacy contract in this case, a middle man, propelled by profit, promotes the sale. Whatever idealism may have motivated any of the participants, the profit motive predominates, permeates, and ultimately governs the transaction. The demand for children is great and the supply small. The availability of contraception, abortion, and the greater willingness of single mothers to bring up their children has led to a shortage of babies offered for adoption. The situation is ripe for the entry of the middleman who will bring some equilibrium into the market by increasing the supply through the use of money.

Intimated, but disputed, is the assertion that surrogacy will be used for the benefit of the rich at the expense of the poor. *See, e.g.*, Radin, *Market Inalienability*, 100 HARV. L. REV. 1849, 1930 (1987). In response it is noted that the Sterns are not rich and the Whiteheads not poor. Nevertheless, it is clear to us that it is unlikely that surrogate mothers will be as proportionately numerous among those women in the top twenty percent income bracket as among those in the bottom twenty percent. Put differently, we doubt that infertile couples in the low-income bracket will find upper income surrogates.

In any event, even in this case one should not pretend that disparate wealth does not play a part simply because the contrast is not the dramatic "rich versus poor." At the time of trial, the Whiteheads' net assets were probably negative — Mrs. Whitehead's own sister was foreclosing on a second mortgage. Their income derived from Mr. Whitehead's labors. Mrs. Whitehead is a homemaker, having previously held part-time jobs. The Sterns are both professionals, she a medical doctor, he a biochemist. Their combined income when both were working was about $89,500 a year and their assets sufficient to pay for the surrogacy contract arrangements.

The point is made that Mrs. Whitehead *agreed* to the surrogacy arrangement, supposedly fully understanding the consequences. Putting aside the issue of how compelling her need for money may have been, and how significant her understanding of the consequences, we suggest that her consent is irrelevant. There are, in a civilized society, some things that money cannot buy. In America, we decided long ago that merely because conduct purchased by money was "voluntary" did not mean that it was good or beyond regulation and prohibition. Employers can no longer buy labor at the lowest price they can bargain for, even though that labor is "voluntary,"or buy women's labor for less money than paid to men for the same job, or purchase the agreement of children to perform oppressive labor, or purchase the agreement of workers to subject themselves to unsafe or unhealthful working conditions. There are, in short, values that society deems more important than granting to wealth whatever it can buy, be it labor, love, or life. Whether this principle recommends prohibition of surrogacy, which presumably sometimes results in great satisfaction to all of the parties, is not for us to say. We note here only that, under existing law, the fact that Mrs. Whitehead "agreed" to the arrangement is not dispositive.

The long-term effects of surrogacy contracts are not known, but feared — the impact on the child who learns her life was bought, that she is the offspring of someone who gave birth to her only to obtain money; the impact on the natural mother as the full weight of her isolation is felt along with the full reality of the sale of her body and her child; the impact on the natural father and adoptive mother once they realize the consequences of their conduct. Literature in related areas suggests these are substantial considerations, although, given the newness of surrogacy, there is little information. The surrogacy contract is based on, principles that are directly contrary to the objectives of our laws. It guarantees the separation of a child from its mother; it looks to adoption regardless of suitability; it totally ignores the child; it takes the child from the mother regardless of her wishes and her maternal fitness; and it does all of this, it accomplishes all of its goals, through the use of money.

Beyond that is the potential degradation of some women that may result from this arrangement. In many cases, of course, surrogacy may bring satisfaction, not only to the infertile couple, but to the surrogate mother herself. The fact, however, that many women may not perceive surrogacy negatively, but rather see it as an opportunity, does not diminish its potential for devastation to other women.

In sum, the harmful consequences of this surrogacy arrangement appear to us all too palpable. In New Jersey the surrogate mother's agreement to sell her child is void. Its irrevocability infects the entire contract, as does the money that purports to buy it.[14]

---

14 [11] Michigan courts have also found that these arrangements conflict with various aspects of their law. Most recently, a Michigan trial court in a matter similar to the case at bar held that surrogacy contracts are void as contrary to public policy, and therefore are unenforceable. The court expressed concern for the potential exploitation of children resulting from surrogacy arrangements that involve the payment of money. The court also concluded that insofar as the surrogacy contract may be characterized as one for personal services, the thirteenth amendment should bar specific performance. *Yates v. Keane*, Nos. 9758, 9772, slip op. (Mich. Cir. Ct. Jan. 21, 1988).

The Supreme Court of Kentucky has taken a somewhat different approach to surrogate arrangements. In *Surrogate Parenting Assocs. v. Commonwealth ex. rel. Armstrong*, 704 S.W.2d 209 (Ky.1986), the court held that the "fundamental differences" between surrogate arrangements and baby-selling placed the surrogate parenting agreement beyond the reach of Kentucky's baby-selling statute. *Id.* at 211. The rationale for this determination was that unlike the normal adoption situation, the surrogacy agreement is entered into before conception, and is not directed at avoiding the consequences of an unwanted pregnancy. *Id.* at 211–12.

Concomitant with this pro-surrogacy conclusion, however, the court held that a "surrogate" mother has the right to void the contract if she changes her mind during pregnancy or immediately after birth. *Id.* at 212–13. The court relied on statutes providing that consent to adoption or to the termination of parental rights prior to five days after the birth of the child is invalid, and concluded that consent before conception must also be unenforceable. *Id.* at 212–13.

The adoption phase of an uncontested surrogacy arrangement was analyzed in *Matter of Adoption of Baby Girl, L.J.*, 132 Misc. 2d 972, 505 N.Y.S.2d 813 (Sur.1986). Although the court expressed strong moral and ethical reservations about surrogacy arrangements, it approved the adoption because it was in the best interests of the child. *Id.* at 815. The court went on to find that surrogate parenting agreements are not void, but are voidable if they are not in accordance with the state's adoption statutes. *Id.* at 817. The court then upheld the payment of money in connection with the surrogacy arrangement on the ground that the New York Legislature did not contemplate surrogacy when the baby-selling statute was passed. *Id.* at 818. Despite the court's ethical and moral problems with surrogate arrangements, it concluded that the Legislature was the appropriate forum to address the legality of surrogacy arrangements. *Ibid.*

In contrast to the law in the United States, the law in the United Kingdom concerning surrogate parenting is fairly well-settled. Parliament passed the Surrogacy Arrangements Act, 1985, ch. 49, which made initiating or taking part in any negotiations with a view to making or arranging a surrogacy contract a criminal offense. The criminal sanction, however, does not apply to the

III

TERMINATION

We have already noted that under our laws termination of parental rights cannot be based on contract, but may be granted only on proof of the statutory requirements. That conclusion was one of the bases for invalidating the surrogacy contract. Although excluding the contract as a basis for parental termination, we did not explicitly deal with the question of whether the statutory bases for termination existed. We do so here. As noted before, if termination of Mrs. Whitehead's parental rights is justified, Mrs. Whitehead will have no further claim either to custody or to visitation, and adoption by Mrs. Stern may proceed pursuant to the private placement adoption statute. If termination is not justified, Mrs. Whitehead remains the legal mother, and even if not entitled to custody, she would ordinarily be expected to have some rights of visitation.

Nothing in this record justifies a finding that would allow a court to terminate Mary Beth Whitehead's parental rights under the statutory standard. It is not simply that obviously there was no "intentional abandonment or very substantial neglect of parental duties without a reasonable expectation of reversal of that conduct in the future," quite the contrary, but furthermore that the trial court never found Mrs. Whitehead an unfit mother and indeed affirmatively stated that Mary Beth Whitehead had been a good mother to her other children. Although the question of best interests of the child is dispositive of the custody issue in a dispute between natural parents, it does not govern the question of termination. It has long been decided that the mere fact that a child would be better off with one set of parents than with another is an insufficient basis for terminating the natural parent's rights. . . .

IV

CONSTITUTIONAL ISSUES

Both parties argue that the Constitutions — state and federal — mandate approval of their basic claims. The source of their constitutional arguments is essentially the same: the right of privacy, the right to procreate, the right to the companionship of one's child, those rights flowing either directly from the fourteenth amendment or by its incorporation of the Bill of Rights, or from the ninth amendment, or through the penumbra surrounding all of the Bill of Rights. They are the rights of personal intimacy, of marriage, of sex, of family, of procreation. Whatever their source, it is clear that they are fundamental rights protected by both the federal and state Constitutions. *Lehr v. Robertson,* 463 U.S. 248 (1983); *Santosky v. Kramer,* 455 U.S. 745 (1982);

"surrogate" mother or to the natural father, but rather applies to other persons engaged in arranging surrogacy contracts on a commercial basis. Since 1978, English courts have held surrogacy agreements unenforceable as against public policy, such agreements being deemed arrangements for the purchase and sale of children. It should be noted, however, that certain surrogacy arrangements, *i.e.,* those arranged without brokers and revocable by the natural mother, are not prohibited under current law in the United Kingdom.

Zablocki v. Redhail, 434 U.S. 374 (1978); *Quilloin v. Walcott,* 434 U.S. 246 (1978); *Carey v. Population Servs. Int'l,* 431 U.S. 678 (1977); *Roe v. Wade,* 410 U.S. 113 (1973); *Stanley v. Illinois,* 405 U.S. 645 (1972); *Griswold v. Connecticut,* 381 U.S. 479 (1965); *Skinner v. Oklahoma,* 316 U.S. 535 (1942); *Meyer v. Nebraska,* 262 U.S. 390 (1923). The right asserted by the Sterns is the right of procreation; that asserted by Mary Beth Whitehead is the right to the companionship of her child. We find that the right of procreation does not extend as far as claimed by the Sterns. As for the right asserted by Mrs. Whitehead, since we uphold it on other grounds (*i.e.,* we have restored her as mother and recognized her right, limited by the child's best interests, to her companionship), we need not decide that constitutional issue, and for reasons set forth below, we should not.

The right to procreate, as protected by the Constitution, has been ruled on directly only once by the United States Supreme Court. *See Skinner* (forced sterilization of habitual criminals violates equal protection clause of fourteenth amendment). Although *Griswold* is obviously of a similar class, strictly speaking it involves the right *not* to procreate. The right to procreate very simply is the right to have natural children, whether through sexual intercourse or artificial insemination. It is no more than that. Mr. Stern has not been deprived of that right. Through artificial insemination of Mrs. Whitehead, Baby M is his child. The custody, care, companionship, and nurturing that follow birth are not parts of the right to procreation; they are rights that may also be constitutionally protected, but that involve many considerations other than the right of procreation. To assert that Mr. Stern's right of procreation gives him the right to the custody of Baby M would be to assert that Mrs. Whitehead's right of procreation does *not* give her the right to the custody of Baby M; it would be to assert that the constitutional right of procreation includes within it a constitutionally protected contractual right to destroy someone else's right of procreation.

We conclude that the right of procreation is best understood and protected if confined to its essentials, and that when dealing with rights concerning the resulting child, different interests come into play. There is nothing in our culture or society that even begins to suggest a fundamental right on the part of the father to the custody of the child as part of his right to procreate when opposed by the claim of the mother to the same child. We therefore disagree with the trial court: there is no constitutional basis whatsoever requiring that Mr. Stern's claim to the custody of Baby M be sustained. Our conclusion may thus be understood as illustrating that a person's rights of privacy and self-determination are qualified by the effect on innocent third persons of the exercise of those rights.

   . . . .

Mr. Stern also contends that he has been denied equal protection of the laws by the State's statute granting full parental rights to a husband in relation to the child produced, with his consent, by the union of his wife with a sperm donor. The claim really is that of Mrs. Stern. It is that she is in precisely the same position as the husband in the statute: she is presumably infertile, as is the husband in the statute; her spouse by agreement with a third party procreates with the understanding that the child will be the couple's child.

The alleged unequal protection is that the understanding is honored in the statute when the husband is the infertile party, but no similar understanding is honored when it is the wife who is infertile.

It is quite obvious that the situations are not parallel. A sperm donor simply cannot be equated with a surrogate mother. The State has more than a sufficient basis to distinguish the two situations — even if the only difference is between the time it takes to provide sperm for artificial insemination and the time invested in a nine-month pregnancy — so as to justify automatically divesting the sperm donor of his parental rights without automatically divesting a surrogate mother. Some basis for an equal protection argument might exist if Mary Beth Whitehead had contributed her egg to be implanted, fertilized or otherwise, in Mrs. Stern, resulting in the latter's pregnancy. That is not the case here, however.

Mrs. Whitehead, on the other hand, asserts a claim that falls within the scope of a recognized fundamental interest protected by the Constitution. As a mother, she claims the right to the companionship of her child. This is a fundamental interest, constitutionally protected. Furthermore, it was taken away from her by the action of the court below. Whether that action under these circumstances would constitute a constitutional deprivation, however, we need not and do not decide. By virtue of our decision Mrs. Whitehead's constitutional complaint — that her parental rights have been unconstitutionally terminated — is moot. We have decided that both the statutes and public policy of this state require that that termination be voided and that her parental rights be restored. It therefore becomes unnecessary to decide whether that same result would be required by virtue of the federal or state Constitutions. . . .

V

CUSTODY

Having decided that the surrogacy contract is illegal and unenforceable, we now must decide the custody question without regard to the provisions of the surrogacy contract that would give Mr. Stern sole and permanent custody. (That does not mean that the existence of the contract and the circumstances under which it was entered may not be considered to the extent deemed relevant to the child's best interests.) With the surrogacy contract disposed of, the legal framework becomes a dispute between two couples over the custody of a child produced by the artificial insemination of one couple's wife by the other's husband. Under the Parentage Act the claims of the natural father and the natural mother are entitled to equal weight, *i.e.*, one is not preferred over the other solely because he or she is the father or the mother. The applicable rule given these circumstances is clear: the child's best interests determine custody.

We note again that the trial court's reasons for determining what were the child's best interests were somewhat different from ours. It concluded that the surrogacy contract was valid, but that it could not grant specific performance unless to do so was in the child's best interests. The approach was that of a Chancery judge, unwilling to give extraordinary remedies unless they well served the most important interests, in this case, the interests of the child. While substantively indistinguishable from our approach to the question of best interests, the purpose of the inquiry was not the usual purpose of determining custody, but of determining a contractual remedy.

We are not concerned at this point with the question of termination of parental rights, either those of Mrs. Whitehead or of Mr. Stern. As noted in various places in this opinion, such termination, in the absence of abandonment or a valid surrender, generally depends on a showing that the particular parent is unfit. The question of custody in this case, as in practically all cases, assumes the fitness of both parents, and no serious contention is made in this case that either is unfit. The issue here is which life would be *better* for Baby M, one with primary custody in the Whiteheads or one with primary custody in the Sterns.

The circumstances of this custody dispute are unusual and they have provoked some unusual contentions. The Whiteheads claim that even if the child's best interests would be served by our awarding custody to the Sterns, we should not do so, since that will encourage surrogacy contracts — contracts claimed by the Whiteheads, and we agree, to be violative of important legislatively-stated public policies. Their position is that in order that surrogacy contracts be deterred, custody should remain in the surrogate mother unless she is unfit, regardless of the best interests of the child. We disagree. Our declaration that this surrogacy contract is unenforceable and illegal is sufficient to deter similar agreements. We need not sacrifice the child's interests in order to make that point sharper.

The Whiteheads also contend that the award of custody to the Sterns *pendente lite* was erroneous and that the error should not be allowed to affect the final custody decision. As noted above, at the very commencement of this action the court issued an *ex parte* order requiring Mrs. Whitehead to turn over the baby to the Sterns; Mrs. Whitehead did not comply but rather took the child to Florida. Thereafter, a similar order was enforced by the Florida authorities resulting in the transfer of possession of Baby M to the Sterns. The Sterns retained custody of the child throughout the litigation. The Whiteheads' point, assuming the *pendente* award of custody *was* erroneous, is that most of the factors arguing for awarding permanent custody to the Sterns resulted from that initial *pendente lite* order. Some of Mrs. Whitehead's alleged character failings, as testified to by experts and concurred in by the trial court, were demonstrated by her actions brought on by the custody crisis. For instance, in order to demonstrate her impulsiveness, those experts stressed the Whiteheads' flight to Florida with Baby M; to show her willingness to use her children for her own aims, they noted the telephone threats to kill Baby M and to accuse Mr. Stern of sexual abuse of her daughter; in order to show Mrs. Whitehead's manipulativeness, they pointed to her threat to kill herself; and in order to show her unsettled family life, they noted the innumerable moves from one hotel or motel to another in Florida. Furthermore, the argument continues, one of the most important factors, whether mentioned or not, in favor of custody in the Sterns is their continuing custody during the litigation, now having lasted for one-and-a-half years. The Whiteheads' conclusion is that had the trial court not given initial custody to the

Sterns during the litigation, Mrs. Whitehead not only would have demon-strated her perfectly acceptable personality — the general tenor of the opinion of experts was that her personality problems surfaced primarily in crises — but would also have been able to prove better her parental skills along with an even stronger bond than may now exist between her and Baby M. Had she not been limited to custody for four months, she could have proved all of these things much more persuasively through almost two years of custody.

The argument has considerable force. It is of course possible that the trial court was wrong in its initial award of custody. It is also possible that such error, if that is what it was, may have affected the outcome. We disagree with the premise, however, that in determining custody a court should decide what the child's best interests *would be* if some hypothetical state of facts had existed. Rather, we must look to what those best interests *are, today*, even if some of the facts may have resulted in part from legal error. The child's interests come first: we will not punish it for judicial errors, assuming any were made. The custody decision must be based on all circumstances, on everything that *actually* has occurred, on everything that is relevant to the child's best interests. Those circumstances include the trip to Florida, the telephone calls and threats, the substantial period of successful custody with the Sterns, and all other relevant circumstances. . . .

There were eleven experts who testified concerning the child's best interests, either directly or in connection with matters related to that issue. Our reading of the record persuades us that the trial court's decision awarding custody to the Sterns (technically to Mr. Stern) should be affirmed since "its findings . . . could reasonably have been reached on sufficient credible evidence present in the record." More than that, on this record we find little room for any different conclusion. The trial court's treatment of this issue is both com-prehensive and, in most respects, perceptive. We agree substantially with its analysis with but few exceptions that, although important, do not change our ultimate views.

Our custody conclusion is based on strongly persuasive testimony contrast-ing both the family life of the Whiteheads and the Sterns and the personalities and characters of the individuals. The stability of the Whitehead family life was doubtful at the time of trial. Their finances were in serious trouble (foreclosure by Mrs. Whitehead's sister on a second mortgage was in process). Mr. Whitehead's employment, though relatively steady, was always at risk because of his alcoholism, a condition that he seems not to have been able to confront effectively. Mrs. Whitehead had not worked for quite some time, her last two employments having been part-time. One of the Whiteheads' positive attributes was their ability to bring up two children, and apparently well, even in so vulnerable a household. Yet substantial question was raised even about that aspect of their home life. The expert testimony contained criticism of Mrs. Whitehead's handling of her son's educational difficulties. Certain of the experts noted that Mrs. Whitehead perceived herself as omnipotent and omniscient concerning her children. She knew what they were thinking, what they wanted, and she spoke for them. As to Melissa, Mrs. Whitehead expressed the view that she alone knew what that child's cries and sounds meant. Her inconsistent stories about various things engendered grave doubts about her ability to explain honestly and sensitively to Baby M — and at the right time — the nature of her origin. Although faith in professional counseling is not a *sine qua non* of parenting, several experts believed that Mrs. Whitehead's contempt for professional help, especially professional psychological help, coincided with her feelings of omnipotence in a way that could be devastating to a child who most likely will need such help. In short, while love and affection there would be, Baby M's life with the Whiteheads promised to be too closely controlled by Mrs. Whitehead. The prospects for wholesome, independent psychological growth and development would be at serious risk.

The Sterns have no other children, but all indications are that their household and their personalities promise a much more likely foundation for Melissa to grow and thrive. There *is* a track record of sorts — during the one-and-a-half years of custody Baby M has done very well, and the relationship between both Mr. and Mrs. Stern and the baby has become very strong. The household is stable, and likely to remain so. Their finances are more than adequate, their circle of friends supportive, and their marriage happy. Most important, they are loving, giving, nurturing, and open-minded people. They have demonstrated the wish and ability to nurture and protect Melissa, yet at the same time to encourage her independence. Their lack of experience is more than made up for by a willingness to learn and to listen, a willingness that is enhanced by their professional training, especially Mrs. Stern's experience as a pediatrician. They are honest; they can recognize error, deal with it, and learn from it. They will try to determine rationally the best way to cope with problems in their relationship with Melissa. When the time comes to tell her about her origins, they will probably have found a means of doing so that accords with the best interests of Baby M. All in all, Melissa's future appears solid, happy, and promising with them.

Based on all of this we have concluded, independent of the trial court's identical conclusion, that Melissa's best interests call for custody in the Sterns. Our above-mentioned disagreements with the trial court do not, as we have noted, in any way diminish our concurrence with its conclusions. We feel, however, that those disagreements are important enough to be stated. They are disagreements about the evaluation of conduct. They also may provide some insight about the potential consequences of surrogacy.

It seems to us that given her predicament, Mrs. Whitehead was rather harshly judged — both by the trial court and by some of the experts. She was guilty of a breach of contract, and indeed, she did break a very important promise, but we think it is expecting something well beyond normal human capabilities to suggest that this mother should have parted with her newly born infant without a struggle. Other than survival, what stronger force is there? We do not know of, and cannot conceive of, any other case where a perfectly fit mother was expected to surrender her newly born infant, perhaps forever, and was then told she was a bad mother because she did not. We know of no authority suggesting that the moral quality of her act in those circumstances should be judged by referring to a contract made before she became pregnant. We do not countenance, and would never countenance, violating a court order as Mrs. Whitehead did, even a court order that is wrong; but her resistance to an order that she surrender her infant, possibly forever, merits a measure of understanding. We do not find it so clear that her efforts to keep her infant, when measured against the Sterns' efforts to take her away, make one, rather than the other, the wrongdoer. The Sterns suffered, but so did she. And if we go beyond suffering to an evaluation of the human stakes involved in the struggle, how much weight should be given to her nine months of pregnancy, the labor of childbirth, the risk to her life, compared to the payment of money, the anticipation of a child and the donation of sperm?

There has emerged a portrait of Mrs. Whitehead, exposing her children to the media, engaging in negotiations to sell a book, granting interviews that seemed helpful to her, whether hurtful to Baby M or not, that suggests a selfish, grasping woman ready to sacrifice the interests of Baby M and her other children for fame and wealth. That portrait is a half-truth, for while it may accurately reflect what ultimately occurred, its implication, that this is what Mary Beth Whitehead wanted, is totally inaccurate, at least insofar as the record before us is concerned. There is not one word in that record to support a claim that had she been allowed to continue her possession of her newly born infant, Mrs. Whitehead would have ever been heard of again; not one word in the record suggests that her change of mind and her subsequent fight for her child was motivated by anything other than love — whatever complex underlying psychological motivations may have existed.

We have a further concern regarding the trial court's emphasis on the Sterns' interest in Melissa's education as compared to the Whiteheads'. That this difference is a legitimate factor to be considered we have no doubt. But it should not be overlooked that a best-interests test is designed to create not a new member of the intelligentsia but rather a well-integrated person who might reasonably be expected to be happy with life. "Best interests" does not contain within it any idealized lifestyle; the question boils down to a judgment, consisting of many factors, about the likely future happiness of a human being. Stability, love, family happiness, tolerance, and, ultimately, support of independence — all rank much higher in predicting future happiness than the likelihood of a college education. We do not mean to suggest that the trial court would disagree. We simply want to dispel any possible misunderstanding on the issue.

Even allowing for these differences, the facts, the experts' opinions, and the trial court's analysis of both argue strongly in favor of custody in the Sterns. Mary Beth Whitehead's family life, into which Baby M would be placed, was anything but secure — the quality Melissa needs most. And today it may be even less so.[15] Furthermore, the evidence and expert opinion based on it reveal personality characteristics, mentioned above, that might threaten the child's best development. The Sterns promise a secure home, with an understanding relationship that allows nurturing and independent growth to develop together. Although there is no substitute for reading the entire record,

---

[15] [18] Subsequent to trial, and by the time of oral argument, Mr. and Mrs. Whitehead had separated, and the representation was that there was no likelihood of change. Thereafter Mrs. Whitehead became pregnant by another man, divorced Mr. Whitehead, and remarried the other man. Both children are living with Mrs. Whitehead and her new husband. Both the former and present husband continue to assert the desire to have whatever parental relationship with Melissa that the law allows, with Mrs. Whitehead continuing to maintain her claim for custody.

including the review of every word of each experts' testimony and reports, a summary of their conclusions is revealing. Six experts testified for Mrs. Whitehead: one favored joint custody, clearly unwarranted in this case; one simply rebutted an opposing expert's claim that Mary Beth Whitehead had a recognized personality disorder; one testified to the adverse impact of separation on *Mrs. Whitehead*; one testified about the evils of adoption and, to him, the probable analogous evils of surrogacy; one spoke only on the question of whether Mrs. Whitehead's consent in the surrogacy agreement was "informed consent"; and one spelled out the strong bond between mother and child. None of them unequivocally stated, or even necessarily implied, an opinion that custody in the Whiteheads was in the best interests of Melissa — the ultimate issue. The Sterns' experts, both well qualified — as were the Whiteheads' — concluded that the best interests of Melissa required custody in Mr. Stern. Most convincingly, the three experts chosen by the court-appointed guardian *ad litem* of Baby M, each clearly free of all bias and interest, unanimously and persuasively recommended custody in the Sterns.

Some comment is required on the initial *ex parte* order awarding custody *pendente lite* to the Sterns (and the continuation of that order after a plenary hearing). The issue, although irrelevant to our disposition of this case, may recur; and when it does, it can be of crucial importance. When father and mother are separated and disagree, at birth, on custody, only in an extreme, truly rare, case should the child be taken from its mother *pendente lite, i.e.,* only in the most unusual case should the child be taken from its mother before the dispute is finally determined by the court on its merits. The probable bond between mother and child, and the child's need, not just the mother's, to strengthen that bond, along with the likelihood, in most cases, of a significantly lesser, if any, bond with the father — all counsel against temporary custody in the father. A substantial showing that the mother's continued custody would threaten the child's health or welfare would seem to be required.

In this case, the trial court, believing that the surrogacy contract might be valid, and faced with the probable flight from the jurisdiction by Mrs. Whitehead and the baby if *any* notice were served, ordered, *ex parte*, an immediate transfer of possession of the child, *i.e.*, it ordered that custody be transferred immediately to Mr. Stern, rather than order Mrs. Whitehead not to leave the State. We have ruled, however, that the surrogacy contract is unenforceable and illegal. It provides no basis for either an *ex parte*, a plenary, an interlocutory, or a final order requiring a mother to surrender custody to a father. Any application by the natural father in a surrogacy dispute for custody pending the outcome of the litigation will henceforth require proof of unfitness, of danger to the child, or the like, of so high a quality and persuasiveness as to make it unlikely that such application will succeed. Absent the required showing, all that a court should do is list the matter for argument on notice to the mother. Even her threats to flee should not suffice to warrant any other relief unless her unfitness is clearly shown. At most, it should result in an order enjoining such flight. The erroneous transfer of custody, as we view it, represents a greater risk to the child than removal to a foreign jurisdiction, unless parental unfitness is clearly proved. Furthermore, we deem it likely that, advised of the law and knowing that her custody cannot seriously be challenged at this stage of the litigation, surrogate mothers will obey any court order to remain in the jurisdiction.

VI

VISITATION

The trial court's decision to terminate Mrs. Whitehead's parental rights precluded it from making any determination on visitation. Our reversal of the trial court's order, however, requires delineation of Mrs. Whitehead's rights to visitation. It is apparent to us that this factually sensitive issue, which was never addressed below, should not be determined *de novo* by this Court. We therefore remand the visitation issue to the trial court for an abbreviated hearing and determination as set forth below. . . .

Based on the opinions of her experts, the guardian *ad litem* recommended suspension of Mrs. Whitehead's visitation rights for five years, with a reevaluation at that time. The basis for that recommendation, whether one regards it as the right or the wrong conclusion, was apparently bolstered when it was learned that Mrs. Whitehead had become pregnant, divorced Richard Whitehead, and then married the father of her new child-to-be. Without any further expert testimony, the guardian *ad litem* revised her position. She now argues that instead of five years, visitation should be suspended until Melissa reaches majority. This radical change in the guardian *ad litem*'s position reinforces our belief that further consideration must be given to this issue. . . .

The foregoing does not fully describe the extent to which this record leaves us uninformed on the visitation issue. No one, with one exception, included a word about visitation in the final briefs before the trial court. . . . Only the grandparents dealt with visitation, but with their visitation, not with the issue of Mrs. Whitehead's visitation. . . .

We also note the following for the trial court's consideration: First, this is not a divorce case where visitation is almost invariably granted to the non-custodial spouse. To some extent the facts here resemble cases where the non-custodial spouse has had practically no relationship with the child, but it only "resembles" those cases. In the instant case, Mrs. Whitehead spent the first four months of this child's life as her mother and has regularly visited the child since then. Second, she is not only the natural mother, but also the legal mother, and is not to be penalized one iota because of the surrogacy contract. Mrs. Whitehead, as the mother (indeed, as a mother who nurtured her child for its first four months — unquestionably a relevant consideration), is entitled to have her own interest in visitation considered. Visitation cannot be determined without considering the parents' interests along with those of the child.

In all of this, the trial court should recall the touchstones of visitation: that it is desirable for the child to have contact with both parents; that besides the child's interests, the parents' interests also must be considered; but that when all is said and done, the best interests of the child are paramount.

We have decided that Mrs. Whitehead is entitled to visitation at some point, and that question is not open to the trial court on this remand. The trial court will determine what kind of visitation shall be granted to her, with or without conditions, and when and under what circumstances it should commence. It also should be noted that the guardian's recommendation of a five-year delay is most unusual — one might argue that it begins to border on termination. Nevertheless, if the circumstances as further developed by appropriate proofs or as reconsidered on remand clearly call for that suspension under applicable legal principles of visitation, it should be so ordered. . . .

We would expect that after the visitation issue is determined the trial court, in connection with any other applications in the future, will attempt to assure that this case is treated like any other so that this child may be spared any further damaging publicity.

While probably unlikely, we do not deem it unthinkable that, the major issues having been resolved, the parties' undoubted love for this child might result in a good faith attempt to work out the visitation themselves, in the best interests of their child.

CONCLUSION

This case affords some insight into a new reproductive arrangement: the artificial insemination of a surrogate mother. The unfortunate events that have unfolded illustrate that its unregulated use can bring suffering to all involved. Potential victims include the surrogate mother and her family, the natural father and his wife, and most importantly, the child. Although surrogacy has apparently provided positive results for some infertile couples, it can also, as this case demonstrates, cause suffering to participants, here essentially innocent and well-intended.

We have found that our present laws do not permit the surrogacy contract used in this case. Nowhere, however, do we find any legal prohibition against surrogacy when the surrogate mother volunteers, without any payment, to act as a surrogate and is given the right to change her mind and to assert her parental rights. Moreover, the Legislature remains free to deal with this most sensitive issue as it sees fit, subject only to constitutional constraints.

If the Legislature decides to address surrogacy, consideration of this case will highlight many of its potential harms. We do not underestimate the difficulties of legislating on this subject. In addition to the inevitable confrontation with the ethical and moral issues involved, there is the question of the wisdom and effectiveness of regulating a matter so private, yet of such public interest. Legislative consideration of surrogacy may also provide the opportunity to begin to focus on the overall implications of the new reproductive biotechnology — *in vitro* fertilization, preservation of sperm and eggs, embryo implantation and the like. The problem is how to enjoy the benefits of the technology — especially for infertile couples — while minimizing the risk of abuse. The problem can be addressed only when society decides what its values and objectives are in this troubling, yet promising, area.

The judgment is affirmed in part, reversed in part, and remanded for further proceedings consistent with this opinion.

NOTES AND QUESTIONS

1. The trial court granted Mary Beth Whitehead Gould broad visitation rights on remand, including shared holidays.

2. What are the statutory and constitutional interests of all the parties in the case? What if the sperm donor and his wife had breached the contract because the baby was born with a severe disability? What if the disability was due to the mother's alcohol consumption during pregnancy?

3. Are surrogacy contracts "degrading to women" as the court states in *Baby M*? Or does the court's interference with these contracts reveal an underlying paternalism regarding a woman's right to make decisions and enter into contracts?

4. What are the interests of a sperm donor? Does he have the duty to support or to demand custodial rights? In states following the Uniform Parentage Act, the sperm donor "is treated in law as if he were not the natural father of a child thereby conceived." Uniform Parentage Act, § 5 (1973). Under the Uniform Parentage Act, when a woman is artificially inseminated with semen donated from a man not her husband, her husband is treated in law as if he were the natural father of the child thereby conceived. *Id.* The *Baby M* court was unequivocal, "A sperm donor simply cannot be equated with a surrogate mother." Do you agree? Is there an equal protection problem if a surrogate mother is treated differently from a surrogate father? What if a woman donates her egg to another woman?

5. State legislation takes a varied approach to surrogacy: Some states make the surrogacy contract void, *see, e.g.*, N.Y. Dom Rel Law § 121–24 (void and imposing civil penalty); some states make the surrogacy contract void if it is for compensation, *see, e.g.*, La. Rev. Stat. Ann. § 9:2713; at least one state imposes a criminal penalty for a surrogacy contract, *see, e.g.*, Mich. Comp. Laws. Ann. § 722. 857 ("A person other than an unemancipated minor female or a female diagnosed as being mentally retarded or as having a mental illness or developmental disability who enters into, induces, arranges, procures, or otherwise assists in the formation of a contract described in subsection (1) is guilty of a felony punishable by a fine of not more than $50,000.00 or imprisonment for not more than 5 years, or both"); and some states allow surrogacy contracts, *see, e.g.*, Fla. Stat. Ann. § 742.15 (only if commissioning mother is unable to gestate to term, or gestation will risk the physical health of the commissioning mother or the health of the fetus). Attempts to pass federal legislation that would have imposed criminal penalties on the participants in and the facilitators of a surrogacy contract have failed.

6. The rules that decide who a child's parents are — what Professor Martha Matthews calls "the legal definition of parenting" — have evolved to deal with situations where reproductive technology and changing societal mores meet. *See* Martha Matthews, *Am I My Child's Parent?*, 23 Children's Legal Rts. J. 44 (2003). When Nancy and Michele, living together after a commitment ceremony, wished to have children, Nancy underwent donor insemination. She

gave birth to two children four years apart. Michele was named as the father on the birth certificate, and the children received her last name. After Nancy and Michele separated, they argued over custody arrangements, and Nancy filed an action seeking a declaration that Michele was not the parent of the children. The court determined that Michele was not a parent under the California Parentage Act and that she could not claim de facto parenthood to seek either custody or visitation. *Nancy S. v. Michele G.*, 279 Cal. Rptr. 212 (Cal. Ct. App 1991).

In 2004 the rules had changed . . . perhaps. While Kristine and Lisa were in a long-term lesbian relationship, they arranged for Kristine to conceive a child through artificial insemination. *See Kristine H. v. Lisa R.*, 16 Cal. Rptr. 123 (Cal. App. 2004). One month before the child's birth, the women obtained a prebirth judgment based on their own stipulation in which they declared themselves to be the joint intended legal parents of the unborn child. Lisa never adopted the child, but the two women raised her together for almost two years before they separated. The court held that the prebirth judgment was void, because a determination of parentage could not rest simply on the parties' agreement. The sole basis upon which the family court could determine parentage was under California's version of the Uniform Parentage Act, CAL. FAM. CODE § 7600 *et seq.* When read in a gender-neutral manner, CAL. FAM. CODE § 7611(d) could be applied to establish legal parentage in a partner of the same sex with no biological connection to the child. On remand, the family court had to determine whether the partner had satisfied the statutory requirements to become a presumed parent. The California Supreme Court granted review to hear the case and reversed the court of appeal. The California Supreme Court determined that the mother was estopped from challenging the validity of the stipulated judgment and declined to address the judgment's validity. 37 Cal. 4th 156 (Cal. Sup. Ct. 2005).

Other cases addressing these complicated issues include *In re Parentage of MJ*, 203 Ill. 2d 526 (2003), where a mother brought action against man with whom she had ten-year intimate relationship seeking to establish paternity and impose support obligations for twins conceived through artificial insemination by an anonymous donor. The Illinois Supreme Court held that: (1) failure to obtain written consent of putative father to insemination precluded claim for paternity under the Parentage Act, but (2) the Parentage Act did not prohibit mother's action based on common law theories of oral contract or promissory estoppel.

Professor Emily Buss contends that states should have broad authority to recognize nontraditional caregivers as parents if they wish to do so. But when these caregivers have not been recognized as parents, the Constitution does not allow the state to compel contact with the child. *See* Emily Buss, *"Parental" Rights*, 88 VA. L. REV. 635 (2002); *see also* Vanessa S. Browne-Barbour, *Bartering for Babies: Are Preconception Agreements in the Best Interests of Children?*, 26 WHITTIER L. REV. 429 (2004) (arguing that preconception agreements — surrogacy contracts — even when pre-approved by a court are not based upon a true best-interest-of-the-child analysis because they lack a determination of the individual needs of a particular child); Sara Hoffman Jurand, *State Appeals Courts Focus on Intent in Egg, Sperm Donor Cases*, 40

TRIAL 78 (Aug. 2004) (noting recent appeals courts decisions in California and Washington ruling that "a sperm or egg donor does not have parental rights or obligations unless the parties agreed beforehand that he or she would be a parent"); Cynthia R. Mabry, *"Who Is My Real Father?" The Delicate Task of Identifying a Father and Parenting Children from an In Vitro Mix-Up*, 18 NAT'L BLACK L.J. 1 (2004-2005) (examining British case of a white couple and black couple seeking infertility treatment at the same center whose mix-up resulted in the white couple giving birth to black twins; compares how both British and American laws handle these complex situations); Melanie Jacobs, *Micah Has One Mommy and One Legal Stranger: Adjudicating Maternity for Nonbiological Lesbian Coparents*, 50 BUFF. L. REV. 341 (2002) (arguing that it is preferable for courts to use the Uniform Parentage Act, rather than equitable doctrines, to resolving disputes between lesbian coparents and their former same-sex partners); Richard F. Storrow, *Parenthood by Pure Intention: Assisted Reproduction and the Functional Approach to Parenthood*, 53 HASTINGS L.J. 597 (2002) (arguing that surrogacy and artificial insemination provide courts and legislatures with the opportunity to redefine the concept of family to bolster recognition of parenthood by intention for unwed individuals).

In addition to struggling with difficult issues presented by new reproductive technologies, the *Baby M* court addressed more traditional problems surrounding the visitation right of the non-custodial parent, adoption, and termination of parental rights. The following sections examine these issues.

[C] Family Visitation

UNIFORM MARRIAGE AND DIVORCE ACT (1973)
§ 407 — Visitation

(a) A parent not granted custody of the child is entitled to reasonable visitation rights unless the court finds, after a hearing, that visitation would endanger seriously the child's physical, mental, moral, or emotional health.

(b) The court may modify an order granting or denying visitation rights whenever modification would serve the best interest of the child; but the court shall not restrict a parent's visitation rights unless it finds that the visitation would endanger seriously the child's physical, mental, moral, or emotional health.

———

What kinds of parental behavior might lead a court to refuse to grant visitation rights to a noncustodial parent? Should the nonmarital sexual activity of the parent during overnight visitation restrict that parent's right of visitation? Courts generally permit visitation if a parent is involved in nonmarital heterosexual activity if the children do not appear to be harmed by the overnight visits. *See, e.g., Jones v. Haraway*, 537 So. 2d 946 (Ala. Civ. App. 1988) (indiscreet behavior, such as living with someone of the opposite sex without the benefit of marriage, was only a factor to be considered, and visitation would not be modified absent evidence presented showing that such misconduct was detrimental to the child). Courts in cases involving homosexual activity may sometimes be more willing to restrict visitation:

> Where the *only* evidence before the trial court, in a visitation modification proceeding, is that the minor children of the parties will be harmed by exposure to their noncustodial parent's homosexual lifestyle, the trial court abuses its discretion by failing to impose conditions upon the noncustodial parent's exercise of visitation, which would protect the welfare and best interests of the children. If the court is unable to devise adequate safeguards, its only alternative is to terminate visitation until the children attain such an age as they will not be adversely affected by learning of their parent's lifestyle.

Roberts v. Roberts, 489 N.E.2d 1067 (Ohio Ct. App. 1985) (emphasis in original).

Without a finding of harm to the child, however, a growing number of jurisdictions are refusing to interrupt visitation. In *Blew v. Verta,* 617 A.2d 31 (Pa. Super. 1992), the court reversed an order that prohibited the mother from visiting the child in the presence of her female partner, because the trial court's determination that the child had been harmed by the mother's lesbian relationship was not supported by its own findings of fact, and thus represented a gross abuse of discretion.

Parents may not be the only people involved in a child's life who would like visitation rights with a child. Grandparents, step-parents, and gay or lesbian partners who have helped to raise a child may also have an interest in preserving their relationship with a child. Common law would not recognize the rights of these third parties over the objection of the natural parent. In the last quarter of the twentieth century, however, many states passed statutes that allowed for visitation by third parties. By the year 2000, all fifty states had passed statutes that allowed for grandparent visitation in some form. Parents sometimes claim that these statutes interfere with their constitutional right to raise their child as they see fit. The following case is the United States Supreme Court's first foray into this area of children and the law.

TROXEL v. GRANVILLE

Supreme Court of the United States
530 U.S. 57 (2000)

JUSTICE O'CONNOR announced the judgment of the Court and delivered an opinion, in which THE CHIEF JUSTICE, JUSTICE GINSBURG, and JUSTICE BREYER *join*.

Section 26.10.160(3) of the Revised Code of Washington permits "any person" to petition a superior court for visitation rights "at any time," and authorizes that court to grant such visitation rights whenever "visitation may serve the best interest of the child." Petitioners Jenifer and Gary Troxel petitioned a Washington Superior Court for the right to visit their grandchildren, Isabelle and Natalie Troxel. Respondent Tommie Granville, the mother of Isabelle and Natalie, opposed the petition. The case ultimately reached the Washington Supreme Court, which held that § 26.10.160(3) unconstitutionally interferes with the fundamental right of parents to rear their children.

I

Tommie Granville and Brad Troxel shared a relationship that ended in June 1991. The two never married, but they had two daughters, Isabelle and Natalie. Jenifer and Gary Troxel are Brad's parents, and thus the paternal grandparents of Isabelle and Natalie. After Tommie and Brad separated in 1991, Brad lived with his parents and regularly brought his daughters to his parents' home for weekend visitation. Brad committed suicide in May 1993. Although the Troxels at first continued to see Isabelle and Natalie on a regular basis after their son's death, Tommie Granville informed the Troxels in October 1993 that she wished to limit their visitation with her daughters to one short visit per month.

In December 1993, the Troxels commenced the present action by filing, in the Washington Superior Court for Skagit County, a petition to obtain visitation rights with Isabelle and Natalie. . . . Section 26.10.160(3) provides: "Any person may petition the court for visitation rights at any time including, but not limited to, custody proceedings. The court may order visitation rights for any person when visitation may serve the best interest of the child whether or not there has been any change of circumstances." At trial, the Troxels requested two weekends of overnight visitation per month and two weeks of visitation each summer. Granville did not oppose visitation altogether, but instead asked the court to order one day of visitation per month with no overnight stay. In 1995, the Superior Court issued an oral ruling and entered a visitation decree ordering visitation one weekend per month, one week during the summer, and four hours on both of the petitioning grandparents' birthdays.

Granville appealed, during which time she married Kelly Wynn. Before addressing the merits of Granville's appeal, the Washington Court of Appeals remanded the case to the Superior Court for entry of written findings of fact and conclusions of law. On remand, the Superior Court found that visitation was in Isabelle and Natalie's best interests: "The Petitioners [the Troxels] are part of a large, central, loving family, all located in this area, and the Petitioners can provide opportunities for the children in the areas of cousins and music." . . . The court took into consideration all factors regarding the best interest of the children and considered all the testimony before it. The children would be benefitted from spending quality time with the Petitioners, provided that that time is balanced with time with the childrens' [sic] nuclear family. The court finds that the childrens' [sic] best interests are served by spending time with their mother and stepfather's other six children."

Approximately nine months after the Superior Court entered its order on remand, Granville's husband formally adopted Isabelle and Natalie. The

Washington Court of Appeals reversed the lower court's visitation order and dismissed the Troxels' petition for visitation, holding that nonparents lack standing to seek visitation under § 26.10.160(3) unless a custody action is pending. In the Court of Appeals' view, that limitation on nonparental visitation actions was "consistent with the constitutional restrictions on state interference with parents' fundamental liberty interest in the care, custody, and management of their children." Having resolved the case on the statutory ground, however, the Court of Appeals did not expressly pass on Granville's constitutional challenge to the visitation statute.

The Washington Supreme Court granted the Troxels' petition for review and, after consolidating their case with two other visitation cases, affirmed. The court disagreed with the Court of Appeals' decision on the statutory issue and found that the plain language of § 26.10.160(3) gave the Troxels standing to seek visitation, irrespective of whether a custody action was pending. The Washington Supreme Court nevertheless agreed with the Court of Appeals' ultimate conclusion that the Troxels could not obtain visitation of Isabelle and Natalie pursuant to § 26.10.160(3). The court rested its decision on the Federal Constitution, holding that § 26.10.160(3) unconstitutionally infringes on the fundamental right of parents to rear their children. In the court's view, there were at least two problems with the nonparental visitation statute. First, according to the Washington Supreme Court, the Constitution permits a State to interfere with the right of parents to rear their children only to prevent harm or potential harm to a child. Section 26.10.160(3) fails that standard because it requires no threshold showing of harm. Second, by allowing " 'any person' to petition for forced visitation of a child at 'any time' with the only requirement being that the visitation serve the best interest of the child," the Washington visitation statute sweeps too broadly. "It is not within the province of the state to make significant decisions concerning the custody of children merely because it could make a 'better' decision." The Washington Supreme Court held that "parents have a right to limit visitation of their children with third persons," and that between parents and judges, "the parents should be the ones to choose whether to expose their children to certain people or ideas." Four justices dissented from the Washington Supreme Court's holding on the constitutionality of the statute.

We granted certiorari, and now affirm the judgment.

II

The demographic changes of the past century make it difficult to speak of an average American family. The composition of families varies greatly from household to household. While many children may have two married parents and grandparents who visit regularly, many other children are raised in single-parent households. In 1996, children living with only one parent accounted for 28 percent of all children under age 18 in the United States. Understandably, in these single-parent households, persons outside the nuclear family are called upon with increasing frequency to assist in the everyday tasks of child rearing. In many cases, grandparents play an important role. For example, in 1998, approximately 4 million children — or 5.6

percent of all children under age 18 — lived in the household of their grandparents.

The nationwide enactment of nonparental visitation statutes is assuredly due, in some part, to the States' recognition of these changing realities of the American family. Because grandparents and other relatives undertake duties of a parental nature in many households, States have sought to ensure the welfare of the children therein by protecting the relationships those children form with such third parties. The States' nonparental visitation statutes are further supported by a recognition, which varies from State to State, that children should have the opportunity to benefit from relationships with statutorily specified persons — for example, their grandparents. The extension of statutory rights in this area to persons other than a child's parents, however, comes with an obvious cost. For example, the State's recognition of an independent third-party interest in a child can place a substantial burden on the traditional parent-child relationship. Contrary to Justice STEVENS' accusation, our description of state nonparental visitation statutes in these terms, of course, is not meant to suggest that "children are so much chattel." Rather, our terminology is intended to highlight the fact that these statutes can present questions of constitutional import. In this case, we are presented with just such a question. Specifically, we are asked to decide whether § 26.10.160(3), as applied to Tommie Granville and her family, violates the Federal Constitution.

The Fourteenth Amendment provides that no State shall "deprive any person of life, liberty, or property, without due process of law." We have long recognized that the Amendment's Due Process Clause, like its Fifth Amendment counterpart, "guarantees more than fair process." The Clause also includes a substantive component that "provides heightened protection against government interference with certain fundamental rights and liberty interests."

The liberty interest at issue in this case — the interest of parents in the care, custody, and control of their children — is perhaps the oldest of the fundamental liberty interests recognized by this Court. More than 75 years ago, in *Meyer v. Nebraska*, we held that the "liberty" protected by the Due Process Clause includes the right of parents to "establish a home and bring up children" and "to control the education of their own." Two years later, in *Pierce v. Society of Sisters*, we again held that the "liberty of parents and guardians" includes the right "to direct the upbringing and education of children under their control." We explained in *Pierce* that "the child is not the mere creature of the State; those who nurture him and direct his destiny have the right, coupled with the high duty, to recognize and prepare him for additional obligations." We returned to the subject in *Prince v. Massachusetts*, and again confirmed that there is a constitutional dimension to the right of parents to direct the upbringing of their children. "It is cardinal with us that the custody, care and nurture of the child reside first in the parents, whose primary function and freedom include preparation for obligations the state can neither supply nor hinder."

In subsequent cases also, we have recognized the fundamental right of parents to make decisions concerning the care, custody, and control of their children. *See, e.g., Stanley v. Illinois* ("It is plain that the interest of a parent in the companionship, care, custody, and management of his or her children 'comes to this Court with a momentum for respect lacking when appeal is made to liberties which derive merely from shifting economic arrangements'" (citation omitted)); *Wisconsin v. Yoder* ("The history and culture of Western civilization reflect a strong tradition of parental concern for the nurture and upbringing of their children. This primary role of the parents in the upbringing of their children is now established beyond debate as an enduring American tradition"); *Quilloin v. Walcott* ("We have recognized on numerous occasions that the relationship between parent and child is constitutionally protected"); *Parham v. J. R.* ("Our jurisprudence historically has reflected Western civilization concepts of the family as a unit with broad parental authority over minor children. Our cases have consistently followed that course"); *Santosky v. Kramer* (discussing "the fundamental liberty interest of natural parents in the care, custody, and management of their child").

Section 26.10.160(3), as applied to Granville and her family in this case, unconstitutionally infringes on that fundamental parental right. The Washington nonparental visitation statute is breathtakingly broad. According to the statute's text, "*any person* may petition the court for visitation rights *at any time*," and the court may grant such visitation rights whenever "visitation may serve *the best interest of the child*." That language effectively permits any third party seeking visitation to subject any decision by a parent concerning visitation of the parent's children to state-court review. Once the visitation petition has been filed in court and the matter is placed before a judge, a parent's decision that visitation would not be in the child's best interest is accorded no deference. Section 26.10.160(3) contains no requirement that a court accord the parent's decision any presumption of validity or any weight whatsoever. Instead, the Washington statute places the best-interest determination solely in the hands of the judge. Should the judge disagree with the parent's estimation of the child's best interests, the judge's view necessarily prevails. Thus, in practical effect, in the State of Washington a court can disregard and overturn *any* decision by a fit custodial parent concerning visitation whenever a third party affected by the decision files a visitation petition, based solely on the judge's determination of the child's best interests. The Washington Supreme Court had the opportunity to give § 26.10.160(3) a narrower reading, but it declined to do so.

Turning to the facts of this case, the record reveals that the Superior Court's order was based on precisely the type of mere disagreement we have just described and nothing more. The Superior Court's order was not founded on any special factors that might justify the State's interference with Granville's fundamental right to make decisions concerning the rearing of her two daughters. To be sure, this case involves a visitation petition filed by grandparents soon after the death of their son — the father of Isabelle and Natalie — but the combination of several factors here compels our conclusion that § 26.10.160(3), as applied, exceeded the bounds of the Due Process Clause.

First, the Troxels did not allege, and no court has found, that Granville was an unfit parent. That aspect of the case is important, for there is a presumption that fit parents act in the best interests of their children. As this Court explained in *Parham*:

> Our constitutional system long ago rejected any notion that a child is the mere creature of the State and, on the contrary, asserted that parents generally have the right, coupled with the high duty, to recognize and prepare [their children] for additional obligations. . . . The law's concept of the family rests on a presumption that parents possess what a child lacks in maturity, experience, and capacity for judgment required for making life's difficult decisions. More important, historically it has recognized that natural bonds of affection lead parents to act in the best interests of their children. . . .

Accordingly, so long as a parent adequately cares for his or her children (*i.e.*, is fit), there will normally be no reason for the State to inject itself into the private realm of the family to further question the ability of that parent to make the best decisions concerning the rearing of that parent's children.

The problem here is not that the Washington Superior Court intervened, but that when it did so, it gave no special weight at all to Granville's determination of her daughters' best interests. More importantly, it appears that the Superior Court applied exactly the opposite presumption. In reciting its oral ruling after the conclusion of closing arguments, the Superior Court judge explained:

> The burden is to show that it is in the best interest of the children to have some visitation and some quality time with their grandparents. I think in most situations a commonsensical approach [is that] it is normally in the best interest of the children to spend quality time with the grandparent, unless the grandparent, [*sic*] there are some issues or problems involved wherein the grandparents, their lifestyles are going to impact adversely upon the children. That certainly isn't the case here from what I can tell.

The judge's comments suggest that he presumed the grandparents' request should be granted unless the children would be "impacted adversely." In effect, the judge placed on Granville, the fit custodial parent, the burden of *disproving* that visitation would be in the best interest of her daughters. The judge reiterated moments later: "I think [visitation with the Troxels] would be in the best interest of the children and I haven't been shown it is not in [the] best interest of the children."

The decisional framework employed by the Superior Court directly contravened the traditional presumption that a fit parent will act in the best interest of his or her child. In that respect, the court's presumption failed to provide any protection for Granville's fundamental constitutional right to make decisions concerning the rearing of her own daughters. . . . In an ideal world, parents might always seek to cultivate the bonds between grandparents and their grandchildren. Needless to say, however, our world is far from perfect, and in it the decision whether such an intergenerational relationship would be beneficial in any specific case is for the parent to make in the first instance. And, if a fit parent's decision of the kind at issue here becomes subject to judicial review, the court must accord at least some special weight to the parent's own determination.

Finally, we note that there is no allegation that Granville ever sought to cut off visitation entirely. Rather, the present dispute originated when Granville informed the Troxels that she would prefer to restrict their visitation with Isabelle and Natalie to one short visit per month and special holidays. In the Superior Court proceedings Granville did not oppose visitation but instead asked that the duration of any visitation order be shorter than that requested by the Troxels. While the Troxels requested two weekends per month and two full weeks in the summer, Granville asked the Superior Court to order only one day of visitation per month (with no overnight stay) and participation in the Granville family's holiday celebrations. The Superior Court gave no weight to Granville's having assented to visitation even before the filing of any visitation petition or subsequent court intervention. The court instead rejected Granville's proposal and settled on a middle ground, ordering one weekend of visitation per month, one week in the summer, and time on both of the petitioning grandparents' birthdays. Significantly, many other States expressly provide by statute that courts may not award visitation unless a parent has denied (or unreasonably denied) visitation to the concerned third party. . . .

Considered together with the Superior Court's reasons for awarding visitation to the Troxels, the combination of these factors demonstrates that the visitation order in this case was an unconstitutional infringement on Granville's fundamental right to make decisions concerning the care, custody, and control of her two daughters. The Washington Superior Court failed to accord the determination of Granville, a fit custodial parent, any material weight. In fact, the Superior Court made only two formal findings in support of its visitation order. First, the Troxels "are part of a large, central, loving family, all located in this area, and the [Troxels] can provide opportunities for the children in the areas of cousins and music." Second, "the children would be benefitted from spending quality time with the [Troxels], provided that that time is balanced with time with the childrens' [sic] nuclear family." These slender findings, in combination with the court's announced presumption in favor of grandparent visitation and its failure to accord significant weight to Granville's already having offered meaningful visitation to the Troxels, show that this case involves nothing more than a simple disagreement between the Washington Superior Court and Granville concerning her children's best interests. The Superior Court's announced reason for ordering one week of visitation in the summer demonstrates our conclusion well: "I look back on some personal experiences. . . . We always spent as kids a week with one set of grandparents and another set of grandparents, [and] it happened to work out in our family that [it] turned out to be an enjoyable experience. Maybe that can, in this family, if that is how it works out." As we have explained, the Due Process Clause does not permit a State to infringe on the fundamental right of parents to make childrearing decisions simply because a state judge believes a "better" decision could be made. Neither the Washington nonparental visitation statute generally — which places no limits on either the persons who may petition for visitation or the circumstances in which such a petition may be granted — nor the Superior Court in this specific case required anything more. Accordingly, we hold that § 26.10.160(3), as applied in this case, is unconstitutional.

Because we rest our decision on the sweeping breadth of § 26.10.160(3) and the application of that broad, unlimited power in this case, we do not consider the primary constitutional question passed on by the Washington Supreme Court — whether the Due Process Clause requires all nonparental visitation statutes to include a showing of harm or potential harm to the child as a condition precedent to granting visitation. We do not, and need not, define today the precise scope of the parental due process right in the visitation context. In this respect, we agree with Justice KENNEDY that the constitutionality of any standard for awarding visitation turns on the specific manner in which that standard is applied and that the constitutional protections in this area are best "elaborated with care." Because much state-court adjudication in this context occurs on a case-by-case basis, we would be hesitant to hold that specific nonparental visitation statutes violate the Due Process Clause as a *per se* matter.

. . . .

We therefore hold that the application of § 26.10.160(3) to Granville and her family violated her due process right to make decisions concerning the care, custody, and control of her daughters.

Accordingly, the judgment of the Washington Supreme Court is affirmed.

It is so ordered.

JUSTICE SOUTER, *concurring in the judgment.*

. . . .

Our cases, it is true, have not set out exact metes and bounds to the protected interest of a parent in the relationship with his child, but *Meyer's* repeatedly recognized right of upbringing would be a sham if it failed to encompass the right to be free of judicially compelled visitation by "any party" at "any time" a judge believed he "could make a 'better' decision" than the objecting parent had done. The strength of a parent's interest in controlling a child's associates is as obvious as the influence of personal associations on the development of the child's social and moral character. Whether for good or for ill, adults not only influence but may indoctrinate children, and a choice about a child's social companions is not essentially different from the designation of the adults who will influence the child in school. Even a State's considered judgment about the preferable political and religious character of schoolteachers is not entitled to prevail over a parent's choice of private school. It would be anomalous, then, to subject a parent to any individual judge's choice of a child's associates from out of the general population merely because the judge might think himself more enlightened than the child's parent. To say the least (and as the Court implied in *Pierce*), parental choice in such matters is not merely a default rule in the absence of either governmental choice or the government's designation of an official with the power to choose for whatever reason and in whatever circumstances.

. . . .

I would simply affirm the decision of the Supreme Court of Washington that its statute, authorizing courts to grant visitation rights to any person at any time, is unconstitutional. I therefore respectfully concur in the judgment.

JUSTICE THOMAS, *concurring in the judgment.*

I write separately to note that neither party has argued that our substantive due process cases were wrongly decided and that the original understanding of the Due Process Clause precludes judicial enforcement of unenumerated rights under that constitutional provision. As a result, I express no view on the merits of this matter, and I understand the plurality as well to leave the resolution of that issue for another day.

Consequently, I agree with the plurality that this Court's recognition of a fundamental right of parents to direct the upbringing of their children resolves this case. Our decision in *Pierce v. Society of Sisters*, 268 U.S. 510 (1925), holds that parents have a fundamental constitutional right to rear their children, including the right to determine who shall educate and socialize them. The opinions of the plurality, JUSTICE KENNEDY, and JUSTICE SOUTER recognize such a right, but curiously none of them articulates the appropriate standard of review. I would apply strict scrutiny to infringements of fundamental rights. Here, the State of Washington lacks even a legitimate governmental interest — to say nothing of a compelling one — in second-guessing a fit parent's decision regarding visitation with third parties. On this basis, I would affirm the judgment below.

JUSTICE STEVENS, *dissenting.*

. . . .

II

In my view, the State Supreme Court erred in its federal constitutional analysis because neither the provision granting "any person" the right to petition the court for visitation, nor the absence of a provision requiring a "threshold . . . finding of harm to the child," provides a sufficient basis for holding that the statute is invalid in all its applications. I believe that a facial challenge should fail whenever a statute has "a 'plainly legitimate sweep.'" Under the Washington statute, there are plainly any number of cases — indeed, one suspects, the most common to arise — in which the "person" among "any" seeking visitation is a once-custodial caregiver, an intimate relation, or even a genetic parent. Even the Court would seem to agree that in many circumstances, it would be constitutionally permissible for a court to award some visitation of a child to a parent or previous caregiver in cases of parental separation or divorce, cases of disputed custody, cases involving temporary foster care or guardianship, and so forth. As the statute plainly sweeps in a great deal of the permissible, the State Supreme Court majority incorrectly concluded that a statute authorizing "any person" to file a petition seeking visitation privileges would invariably run afoul of the Fourteenth Amendment.

The second key aspect of the Washington Supreme Court's holding — that the Federal Constitution requires a showing of actual or potential "harm" to the child before a court may order visitation continued over a parent's objections — finds no support in this Court's case law. While, as the Court recognizes, the Federal Constitution certainly protects the parent-child relationship from arbitrary impairment by the State, we have never held that the parent's liberty interest in this relationship is so inflexible as to establish a rigid constitutional shield, protecting every arbitrary parental decision from any challenge absent a threshold finding of harm.[16] The presumption that parental decisions generally serve the best interests of their children is sound, and clearly in the normal case the parent's interest is paramount. But even a fit parent is capable of treating a child like a mere possession.

Cases like this do not present a bipolar struggle between the parents and the State over who has final authority to determine what is in a child's best interests. There is at a minimum a third individual, whose interests are implicated in every case to which the statute applies — the child.

It has become standard practice in our substantive due process jurisprudence to begin our analysis with an identification of the "fundamental" liberty interests implicated by the challenged state action. My colleagues are of course correct to recognize that the right of a parent to maintain a relationship with his or her child is among the interests included most often in the constellation of liberties protected through the Fourteenth Amendment. Our cases leave no doubt that parents have a fundamental liberty interest in caring for and guiding their children, and a corresponding privacy interest — absent exceptional circumstances — in doing so without the undue interference of strangers to them and to their child. Moreover, and critical in this case, our cases applying this principle have explained that with this constitutional liberty comes a presumption (albeit a rebuttable one) that "natural bonds of affection lead parents to act in the best interests of their children." *Parham v. J. R.,* 442 U.S. 584 (1979).

Despite this Court's repeated recognition of these significant parental liberty interests, these interests have never been seen to be without limits. In *Lehr v. Robertson*, 463 U.S. 248 (1983), for example, this Court held that a putative biological father who had never established an actual relationship with his child did not have a constitutional right to notice of his child's adoption by the man who had married the child's mother. As this Court had recognized in an earlier case, a parent's liberty interests "do not spring full-blown from the biological connection between parent and child. They require relationships more enduring." 463 U.S. at 260 (quoting *Caban v. Mohammed,* 441 U.S. 380, 397(1979)).

Conversely, in *Michael H. v. Gerald D.*, 491 U.S. 110 (1989), this Court concluded that despite both biological parenthood and an established relationship with a young child, a father's due process liberty interest in maintaining some connection with that child was not sufficiently powerful to overcome a state statutory presumption that the husband of the child's mother was the child's parent. As a result of the presumption, the biological father could be denied even visitation with the child because, as a matter of state law, he was

---

[16] [7] The suggestion by JUSTICE THOMAS that this case may be resolved solely with reference to our decision in *Pierce v. Society of Sisters*, 268 U.S. 510, 535, 69 L. Ed. 1070, 45 S. Ct. 571 (1925), is unpersuasive. *Pierce* involved a parent's choice whether to send a child to public or private school. While that case is a source of broad language about the scope of parents' due process rights with respect to their children, the constitutional principles and interests involved in the schooling context do not necessarily have parallel implications in this family law visitation context, in which multiple overlapping and competing prerogatives of various plausibly interested parties are at stake.

not a "parent." A plurality of this Court there recognized that the parental liberty interest was a function, not simply of "isolated factors" such as biology and intimate connection, but of the broader and apparently independent interest in family.

A parent's rights with respect to her child have thus never been regarded as absolute, but rather are limited by the existence of an actual, developed relationship with a child, and are tied to the presence or absence of some embodiment of family. These limitations have arisen, not simply out of the definition of parenthood itself, but because of this Court's assumption that a parent's interests in a child must be balanced against the State's long-recognized interests as *parens patriae*, and, critically, the child's own complementary interest in preserving relationships that serve her welfare and protection.

While this Court has not yet had occasion to elucidate the nature of a child's liberty interests in preserving established familial or family-like bonds, it seems to me extremely likely that, to the extent parents and families have fundamental liberty interests in preserving such intimate relationships, so, too, do children have these interests, and so, too, must their interests be balanced in the equation. [17] At a minimum, our prior cases recognizing that children are, generally speaking, constitutionally protected actors require that this Court reject any suggestion that when it comes to parental rights, children are so much chattel. The constitutional protection against arbitrary state interference with parental rights should not be extended to prevent the States from protecting children against the arbitrary exercise of parental authority that is not in fact motivated by an interest in the welfare of the child. This is not, of course, to suggest that a child's liberty interest in maintaining contact with a particular individual is to be treated invariably as on a par with that child's parents' contrary interests. Because our substantive due process case law includes a strong presumption that a parent will act in the best interest of her child, it would be necessary, were the state appellate courts actually to confront a challenge to the statute as applied, to consider whether the trial court's assessment of the "best interest of the child" incorporated that presumption. . . . I think it safe to assume that trial judges usually give great deference to parents' wishes, and I am not persuaded otherwise here.

But presumptions notwithstanding, we should recognize that there may be circumstances in which a child has a stronger interest at stake than mere protection from serious harm caused by the termination of visitation by a "person" other than a parent. The almost infinite variety of family relationships that pervade our ever-changing society strongly counsel against the creation by this Court of a constitutional rule that treats a biological parent's liberty interest in the care and supervision of her child as an isolated right

---

17 [8] This Court has on numerous occasions acknowledged that children are in many circumstances possessed of constitutionally protected rights and liberties. *See Parham v. J. R.*, 442 U.S. 584 (1979) (liberty interest in avoiding involuntary confinement); *Planned Parenthood of Central Mo. v. Danforth*, 428 U.S. 52 (1976) ("Constitutional rights do not mature and come into being magically only when one attains the state-defined age of majority. Minors, as well as adults, are protected by the Constitution and possess constitutional rights"); *Tinker v. Des Moines Independent Community School Dist.*, 393 U.S. 503, 506–507(1969) (First Amendment right to political speech); *In re Gault*, 387 U.S. 1, 13 (1967) (due process rights in criminal proceedings).

that may be exercised arbitrarily. It is indisputably the business of the States, rather than a federal court employing a national standard, to assess in the first instance the relative importance of the conflicting interests that give rise to disputes such as this. Far from guaranteeing that parents' interests will be trammeled in the sweep of cases arising under the statute, the Washington law merely gives an individual — with whom a child may have an established relationship — the procedural right to ask the State to act as arbiter, through the entirely well-known best-interests standard, between the parent's protected interests and the child's. It seems clear to me that the Due Process Clause of the Fourteenth Amendment leaves room for States to consider the impact on a child of possibly arbitrary parental decisions that neither serve nor are motivated by the best interests of the child.

Accordingly, I respectfully dissent.

JUSTICE SCALIA, *dissenting.*

In my view, a right of parents to direct the upbringing of their children is among the "unalienable Rights" with which the Declaration of Independence proclaims "all Men . . . are endowed by their Creator." And in my view that right is also among the "other [rights] retained by the people" which the Ninth Amendment says the Constitution's enumeration of rights "shall not be construed to deny or disparage." The Declaration of Independence, however, is not a legal prescription conferring powers upon the courts; and the Constitution's refusal to "deny or disparage" other rights is far removed from affirming any one of them, and even farther removed from authorizing judges to identify what they might be, and to enforce the judges' list against laws duly enacted by the people. Consequently, while I would think it entirely compatible with the commitment to representative democracy set forth in the founding documents to argue, in legislative chambers or in electoral campaigns, that the state has *no power* to interfere with parents' authority over the rearing of their children, I do not believe that the power which the Constitution confers upon me *as a judge* entitles me to deny legal effect to laws that (in my view) infringe upon what is (in my view) that unenumerated right.

Only three holdings of this Court rest in whole or in part upon a substantive constitutional right of parents to direct the upbringing of their children — two of them from an era rich in substantive due process holdings that have since been repudiated [citing *Meyer v. Nebraska, Pierce v. Society of Sisters* and *Wisconsin v. Yoder*]. The sheer diversity of today's opinions persuades me that the theory of unenumerated parental rights underlying these three cases has small claim to *stare decisis* protection. A legal principle that can be thought to produce such diverse outcomes in the relatively simple case before us here is not a legal principle that has induced substantial reliance. While I would not now overrule those earlier cases (that has not been urged), neither would I extend the theory upon which they rested to this new context.

Judicial vindication of "parental rights" under a Constitution that does not even mention them requires (as JUSTICE KENNEDY's opinion rightly points out) not only a judicially crafted definition of parents, but also — unless, as no one believes, the parental rights are to be absolute — judicially approved assessments of "harm to the child" and judicially defined gradations of other persons (grandparents, extended family, adoptive family in an adoption later found to be invalid, long-term guardians, etc.) who may have some claim against the wishes of the parents. If we embrace this unenumerated right, I think it obvious — whether we affirm or reverse the judgment here, or remand as JUSTICE STEVENS or JUSTICE KENNEDY would do — that we will be ushering in a new regime of judicially prescribed, and federally prescribed, family law. I have no reason to believe that federal judges will be better at this than state legislatures; and state legislatures have the great advantages of doing harm in a more circumscribed area, of being able to correct their mistakes in a flash, and of being removable by the people.[18]

For these reasons, I would reverse the judgment below.

JUSTICE KENNEDY, *dissenting*.

. . . .

The first flaw the State Supreme Court found in the statute is that it allows an award of visitation to a non-parent without a finding that harm to the child would result if visitation were withheld; and the second is that the statute allows any person to seek visitation at any time. In my view the first theory is too broad to be correct, as it appears to contemplate that the best interests of the child standard may not be applied in any visitation case. I acknowledge the distinct possibility that visitation cases may arise where, considering the absence of other protection for the parent under state laws and procedures, the best interests of the child standard would give insufficient protection to the parent's constitutional right to raise the child without undue intervention by the state; but it is quite a different matter to say, as I understand the Supreme Court of Washington to have said, that a harm to the child standard is required in every instance.

Given the error I see in the State Supreme Court's central conclusion that the best interests of the child standard is never appropriate in third-party visitation cases, that court should have the first opportunity to reconsider this case. I would remand the case to the state court for further proceedings. If it then found the statute has been applied in an unconstitutional manner because the best interests of the child standard gives insufficient protection to a parent under the circumstances of this case, or if it again declared the statute a nullity because the statute seems to allow any person at all to seek visitation at any time, the decision would present other issues which may or may not warrant further review in this Court. These include not only the protection the Constitution gives parents against state-ordered visitation but also the extent to which federal rules for facial challenges to statutes control in state courts. These matters, however, should await some further case. The judgment now under review should be vacated and remanded on the sole ground that the harm ruling that was so central to the Supreme Court of Washington's decision was error, given its broad formulation.

---

18 [2] I note that respondent is asserting only, *on her own behalf*, a substantive due process right to direct the upbringing of her own children, and is not asserting, *on behalf of her children*, their First Amendment rights of association or free exercise. I therefore do not have occasion to consider whether, and under what circumstances, the parent could assert the latter enumerated rights.

Turning to the question whether harm to the child must be the controlling standard in every visitation proceeding, there is a beginning point that commands general, perhaps unanimous, agreement in our separate opinions: As our case law has developed, the custodial parent has a constitutional right to determine, without undue interference by the state, how best to raise, nurture, and educate the child. The parental right stems from the liberty protected by the Due Process Clause of the Fourteenth Amendment. *Pierce* and *Meyer*, had they been decided in recent times, may well have been grounded upon First Amendment principles protecting freedom of speech, belief, and religion. Their formulation and subsequent interpretation have been quite different, of course; and they long have been interpreted to have found in Fourteenth Amendment concepts of liberty an independent right of the parent in the "custody, care and nurture of the child," free from state intervention. The principle exists, then, in broad formulation; yet courts must use considerable restraint, including careful adherence to the incremental instruction given by the precise facts of particular cases, as they seek to give further and more precise definition to the right.

The State Supreme Court sought to give content to the parent's right by announcing a categorical rule that third parties who seek visitation must always prove the denial of visitation would harm the child. After reviewing some of the relevant precedents, the Supreme Court of Washington concluded "the requirement of harm is the sole protection that parents have against pervasive state interference in the parenting process." For that reason, "short of preventing harm to the child," the court considered the best interests of the child to be "insufficient to serve as a compelling state interest overruling a parent's fundamental rights."

While it might be argued as an abstract matter that in some sense the child is always harmed if his or her best interests are not considered, the law of domestic relations, as it has evolved to this point, treats as distinct the two standards, one harm to the child and the other the best interests of the child. The judgment of the Supreme Court of Washington rests on that assumption, and I, too, shall assume that there are real and consequential differences between the two standards.

On the question whether one standard must always take precedence over the other in order to protect the right of the parent or parents, "our Nation's history, legal traditions, and practices" do not give us clear or definitive answers. The consensus among courts and commentators is that at least through the 19th century there was no legal right of visitation; court-ordered visitation appears to be a 20th-century phenomenon. . . ." [C]ontemporary state-court decisions acknowledge that "historically, grandparents had no legal right of visitation," and it is safe to assume other third parties would have fared no better in court.

To say that third parties have had no historical right to petition for visitation does not necessarily imply, as the Supreme Court of Washington concluded, that a parent has a constitutional right to prevent visitation in all cases not involving harm. True, this Court has acknowledged that States have the authority to intervene to prevent harm to children, but that is not the same as saying that a heightened harm to the child standard must be satisfied in every case in which a third party seeks a visitation order. It is also true that the law's traditional presumption has been "that natural bonds of affection lead parents to act in the best interests of their children," and "simply because the decision of a parent is not agreeable to a child or because it involves risks does not automatically transfer the power to make that decision from the parents to some agency or officer of the state. The State Supreme Court's conclusion that the Constitution forbids the application of the best interests of the child standard in any visitation proceeding, however, appears to rest upon assumptions the Constitution does not require.

My principal concern is that the holding seems to proceed from the assumption that the parent or parents who resist visitation have always been the child's primary caregivers and that the third parties who seek visitation have no legitimate and established relationship with the child. That idea, in turn, appears influenced by the concept that the conventional nuclear family ought to establish the visitation standard for every domestic relations case. As we all know, this is simply not the structure or prevailing condition in many households. For many boys and girls a traditional family with two or even one permanent and caring parent is simply not the reality of their childhood. This may be so whether their childhood has been marked by tragedy or filled with considerable happiness and fulfillment.

Cases are sure to arise — perhaps a substantial number of cases — in which a third party, by acting in a caregiving role over a significant period of time, has developed a relationship with a child which is not necessarily subject to absolute parental veto. *See Michael H. v. Gerald D.,* 491 U.S. 110 (1989) (putative natural father not entitled to rebut state law presumption that child born in a marriage is a child of the marriage); *Quilloin v. Walcott,* 434 U.S. 246 (1978) (best interests standard sufficient in adoption proceeding to protect interests of natural father who had not legitimated the child); *see also Lehr v. Robertson,* 463 U.S. 248, 261 (1983) ("The importance of the familial relationship, to the individuals involved and to the society, stems from the emotional attachments that derive from the intimacy of daily association, and from the role it plays in 'promoting a way of life' through the instruction of children . . . as well as from the fact of blood relationship."). Some pre-existing relationships, then, serve to identify persons who have a strong attachment to the child with the concomitant motivation to act in a responsible way to ensure the child's welfare. As the State Supreme Court was correct to acknowledge, those relationships can be so enduring that "in certain circumstances where a child has enjoyed a substantial relationship with a third person, arbitrarily depriving the child of the relationship could cause severe psychological harm to the child," and harm to the adult may also ensue. In the design and elaboration of their visitation laws, States may be entitled to consider that certain relationships are such that to avoid the risk of harm, a best interests standard can be employed by their domestic relations courts in some circumstances.

Indeed, contemporary practice should give us some pause before rejecting the best interests of the child standard in all third-party visitation cases, as the Washington court has done. The standard has been recognized for many years as a basic tool of domestic relations law in visitation proceedings. Since

1965 all 50 States have enacted a third-party visitation statute of some sort. Each of these statutes, save one, permits a court order to issue in certain cases if visitation is found to be in the best interests of the child. While it is unnecessary for us to consider the constitutionality of any particular provision in the case now before us, it can be noted that the statutes also include a variety of methods for limiting parents' exposure to third-party visitation petitions and for ensuring parental decisions are given respect. Many States limit the identity of permissible petitioners by restricting visitation petitions to grandparents, or by requiring petitioners to show a substantial relationship with a child, or both. The statutes vary in other respects — for instance, some permit visitation petitions when there has been a change in circumstances such as divorce or death of a parent, and some apply a presumption that parental decisions should control. Georgia's is the sole State Legislature to have adopted a general harm to the child standard, *see* GA. CODE ANN. § 19-7-3(c) (1999), and it did so only after the Georgia Supreme Court held the State's prior visitation statute invalid under the Federal and Georgia Constitutions.

In light of the inconclusive historical record and case law, as well as the almost universal adoption of the best interests standard for visitation disputes, I would be hard pressed to conclude the right to be free of such review in all cases is itself "implicit in the concept of ordered liberty." In my view, it would be more appropriate to conclude that the constitutionality of the application of the best interests standard depends on more specific factors. In short, a fit parent's right vis-a-vis a complete stranger is one thing; her right vis-a-vis another parent or a *de facto* parent may be another. The protection the Constitution requires, then, must be elaborated with care, using the discipline and instruction of the case law system. We must keep in mind that family courts in the 50 States confront these factual variations each day, and are best situated to consider the unpredictable, yet inevitable, issues that arise.

It must be recognized, of course, that a domestic relations proceeding in and of itself can constitute state intervention that is so disruptive of the parent-child relationship that the constitutional right of a custodial parent to make certain basic determinations for the child's welfare becomes implicated. The best interests of the child standard has at times been criticized as indeterminate, leading to unpredictable results. If a single parent who is struggling to raise a child is faced with visitation demands from a third party, the attorney's fees alone might destroy her hopes and plans for the child's future. Our system must confront more often the reality that litigation can itself be so disruptive that constitutional protection may be required; and I do not discount the possibility that in some instances the best interests of the child standard may provide insufficient protection to the parent-child relationship. We owe it to the Nation's domestic relations legal structure, however, to proceed with caution.

It should suffice in this case to reverse the holding of the State Supreme Court that the application of the best interests of the child standard is always unconstitutional in third-party visitation cases. . . . In my view the judgment under review should be vacated and the case remanded for further proceedings.

———

NOTES AND QUESTIONS

1. After *Troxel*, what is the status of third parties, grandparents and others, who wish to establish visitation rights with a child? What standard will courts use to make that determination?

2. Has the *Troxel* plurality reinforced the constitutional dimension of a parent's interest in bringing up his or her child? Or did the fractured opinions dilute it? What is the nature of the parent's constitutional claim? Is it a liberty interest or a fundamental right? Does it make a difference? *See* Sally F. Goldfarb, *Visitation for Nonparents After* Troxel v. Granville: *Where Should States Draw the Line?*, 32 RUTGERS L. REV. 783 (2001); Stephen G. Gilles, *Parental (and Grandparental) Rights After* Troxel v. Granville, 9 SUP. CT. ECON. REV. 69 (2001); Ellen Maurus, *Over the Hills and Through the Woods to Grandparents' House We Go: Or Do We, Post* Troxel?, 43 ARIZ. L. REV. 751 (2001).

The Georgia grandparent visitation statute provides that the court may grant any grandparent of the child reasonable visitation rights if the court finds the health or welfare of the child would be harmed unless the visitation is granted, and if the best interests of the child would be served by the visitation. The court must make specific written findings of fact in support of its rulings. The statute does not authorize an action requesting visitation where the parents of the minor child are not separated and the child is living with both of the parents. *See* OCGA § 19-7-3. In applying this statute, the Georgia Court of Appeals stated "absent clear and convincing evidence that the child will experience actual physical, mental, or emotional harm if visitation was denied, the trial court cannot justify mandating grandparent visitation over the objections of the parent." *Rainey v. Lange*, 261 Ga. App. 491 (2003).

Do siblings have an interest that is of a different constitutional dimension from a grandparent? *See* Paige Ingram Castaneda, *0 Brother (Or Sister) Where Art Thou: Sibling Standing in Texas*, 55 BAYLOR L. REV. 749 (2003); Ellen Maurus, *"Where Have You Been, Fran?" The Right of Siblings to Seek Court Access to Override Parental Denial of Visitation*, 66 TENN. L. REV. 977 (1999) (arguing that siblings should have ability to show whether it is in their best interest to maintain their relationship after being separated).

3. Does the child have an interest that is of constitutional dimension in determining the adults that will be a part of his or her life? If so, how would you articulate that interest and on what is it based?

[D] Neglect and Endangerment

As mentioned above, parents owe a duty of support and care to their children. Failure to adhere to this duty often results in abuse, neglect, and endangerment to the child triggering state intervention. Intervention through the criminal law will be considered *infra* at § 2.03. Issues within the civil child protection system will be considered here.

MICHIGAN COMPILED LAWS ANNOTATED (1993)
§ 712A.2 Authority and jurisdiction of court

Juvenile division of probate court; authority and jurisdiction § 2. The juvenile division of the probate court shall have the following authority and jurisdiction:

. . . .

(b) Jurisdiction in proceedings concerning any child under eighteen years of age found within the county:

(1) Whose parent or other person legally responsible for the care and maintenance of the child, when able to do so, neglects or refuses to provide proper or necessary support, education, medical, surgical, or other care necessary for his or her health or morals, who is subject to a substantial risk or harm to his or her mental well-being, who is abandoned by his or her parents, guardian, or other custodian, or who is without proper custody or guardianship. As used in this subparagraph:

(A) "Education" means learning based on an organized educational program that is appropriate, given the age, intelligence, ability, and any psychological limitations of a child, in the subject areas of reading, spelling, mathematics, science, history, civics, writing, and English grammar.

(B) "Without proper custody or guardianship" does not include the situation where a parent has placed the child with another person who is legally responsible for the care and maintenance of the child and who is able to and does provide the child with proper care and maintenance.

(2) Whose home or environment, by reason of neglect, cruelty, drunkenness, criminality, or depravity on the part of a parent, guardian, or other custodian, is an unfit place for the child to live in.

IN THE INTEREST OF D.K.

Supreme Court of South Dakota
245 N.W.2d 644 (1976)

DUNN, CHIEF JUSTICE.

These appeals arise from an order adjudicating D.K. to be a neglected and dependent child as defined by SDCL 26-8-6 and from a dispositional order which temporarily deprived the mother of the custody of her child based upon that adjudication. Finding the trial court's conclusion supported by a preponderance of the evidence, we affirm.

The difficulties experienced by this infant in his relatively short lifetime can be recounted only with sympathy. D.K. was born August 17, 1974, five weeks prematurely. He was released to his mother two weeks later. His 24-year-old mother receives approximately $200 a month in ADC (Aid to Dependent Children) benefits as her sole support; she also receives food stamps. In addition to D.K., she has a daughter who is approximately eighteen months older than D.K. D.K.'s father does not live with them and provides no support or assistance. As a result, the mother must raise these two small children herself.

On September 24, 1974, D.K. was admitted to the hospital. His mother complained that he was suffering from a cold and that he had been vomiting. The doctor discovered on September 28th that the child had lobar emphysema, a congenital lung disease. D.K. was flown to Denver where he underwent surgery to remove part of the left lung (left upper lobectomy). Late in October, the child was again at home with his mother.

On November 5, 1974, D.K. was brought to the hospital, this time by a public health nurse. He remained in the hospital with an upper respiratory infection until the 14th of November when he was taken into custody by the Division of Social Welfare. A state social worker had filed a report in district county court seeking a preliminary investigation to determine whether D.K. was a dependent or neglected child. The court entered an order placing D.K. in the custody of the Division of Social Welfare on November 14, 1974, but dismissed that order for want of jurisdiction after a hearing on December 4, 1974. D.K. was returned to the custody of his mother on December 5, 1974.

On December 9, 1974, a petition of dependency was filed in district county court by the Pennington County State's Attorney. A hearing was set for December 20, 1974, but was never conducted. The state filed and was granted a motion to dismiss on January 20, 1975.

In the meantime, D.K. was again placed in the hospital, this time with a cold. D.K. was brought in by his mother on December 13, 1974, and remained in the hospital until December 26th with bronchiolitis. To add to this child's problems, it was discovered that he was allergic to certain foods, among them cow's milk. During this stay, the doctor prescribed a special diet of soybean milk formula.

On January 24, 1975, D.K.'s mother brought him to the hospital with a severe case of diaper rash. Shortly after admission, he developed bronchitis. He was released to his mother on January 30th.

On February 14, 1975, D.K. was hospitalized for bronchitis and bronchiolitis after his mother became concerned by his coughing and wheezing. He was discharged on March 10th, but on March 12th he was readmitted because his mother complained that he could not keep his food down. The diagnosis was mild gastritis, although that was not confirmed during the hospitalization. On March 17, 1975, D.K. was released to the custody of the Pennington County Sheriff and a notification of temporary custody was served on the mother at that time. A hearing on the matter of temporary custody was held on March 19, 1975; on March 31st an order was entered *Nunc pro tunc* March 19th, giving temporary custody of D.K. to the Division of Social Welfare.

A petition of dependency was filed on March 25, 1975, and the matter was heard on April 3 and 5, 1975, in the Juvenile Division of the Seventh Judicial

Circuit. On June 11, 1975, an adjudicatory order was entered finding D.K. to be a dependent and neglected child as provided in SDCL 26-8-6. A dispositional order was entered *Nunc pro tunc* September 23, 1975, placing D.K. in the temporary custody of the state.

It is from these orders that the mother appeals. . . .

D.K. was found to be a neglected or dependent child as defined by SDCL 26-8-6:

> In this chapter unless the context otherwise plainly requires neglected or dependent child means a child: whose parent, guardian, or custodian has abandoned him or has subjected him to mistreatment or abuse; who lacks proper parental care through the actions or omissions of the parent, guardian, or custodian; whose environment is injurious to his welfare; whose parent, guardian, or custodian fails or refuses to provide proper or necessary subsistence, education, medical care or any other care necessary for his health, guidance, or well-being; or who is homeless, without proper care, or not domiciled with his parent, guardian, or custodian through no fault of his parent, guardian or custodian. Provided however, notwithstanding any other provision of this chapter, no child who in good faith is under treatment solely by spiritual means through prayer in accordance with the tenets and practices of a recognized church or religious denomination by a duly accredited practitioner thereof shall, for that reason alone, be considered to have been neglected within the purview of this chapter.

A finding that a child is neglected or dependent comes after an adjudicatory hearing to determine if the allegations in the petition are supported by a preponderance of the evidence. Our duty on review is to uphold the trial court's decision unless the findings of fact are "clearly erroneous." One manner used to determine whether clear error has been committed is to determine if the findings are contrary to the clear preponderance of the evidence. Using that standard, we believe the findings of the trial court are supported by a preponderance of the evidence.

The frequency of hospitalization of D.K., although not determinative of parental neglect, does infer that the child was perhaps not receiving adequate care at home. The evidence shows the house was dirty, with food and clothes scattered on the floor and with a strong odor of urine in the air. The odor was emanating not from a diaper pail or pile of dirty diapers but from the bedding of the child's crib where he was lying in a wet diaper under a wet blanket. Upon one admission to the hospital, D.K. was found to be wearing soiled clothes with a bad odor. The lack of cleanliness cannot be justified on the basis of poverty or on the basis of lack of time to properly clean the home and care for the children, as appellant's sole occupation was the care of the children in this small home.

On more than one occasion there was no food for the child, once for more than twenty-four hours, despite the availability of the formula and cereal upon request from the welfare department, and even though appellant used her food stamps to feed her sister and her sister's friend who were staying with appellant while they looked for jobs. There is evidence that on more than one occasion appellant did not follow the prescribed diet. Once she fed D.K. orange juice which the doctor testified might have caused gastritis in March 1975. Upon admission to the hospital on January 24, 1975, a male companion stated that appellant had been "giving him the kind (of liquid) from a carton." D.K.'s older sister drank from his bottle and replaced the bottle in his mouth at least twice, once while a public health nurse was present and once while appellant was alone with her children.

The doctor testified that because of D.K.'s medical problems special care was required. This special care included a limited diet and very careful attention to normal hygiene. He stated that the presence of wet clothing and blankets and failure to feed for twenty-four hours might lower the child's resistance to infection. He also stated that the older child's placing the bottle in her mouth could certainly transmit an infection.

Appellant was repeatedly advised of D.K.'s special needs, including his diet. However, appellant testified that no one ever indicated D.K. needed a special diet or special care. This testimony seems incredible because at the same time appellant testified that she had been giving D.K. the formula and cereal prescribed. On visits by personnel from the public health and welfare departments, the dominant subject of conversation was not D.K.'s care but appellant's problems with her boyfriend and D.K.'s putative father, even though he was providing no support for appellant or the child and even though appellant was not seeking any support from him.

The trial court concluded that D.K. was without the care necessary to his health and welfare, that his mother failed to provide for his special medical needs, and that his mother did not feed him the diet prescribed by his doctor. This, according to the court, constituted lack of proper parental care and a failure to provide proper or necessary subsistence, medical care or any other care necessary to the child's health and well-being.

We have recognized that parents have a fundamental right to their children. However, this right is not absolute and must be balanced against the state's duty to protect children within its borders. Our legislature has recognized this approach, balancing the parent's right with the state's duty as guardian of neglected and dependent children. SDCL 26-7-11:

> Every proceeding under Chapter 26-8 shall be in the interest of the child and the state, but with due regard to the rightful parents and others directly interested; and in any proceeding the child shall be dealt with, protected, and cared for as a ward of the state.

It is for the court to determine this delicate balance, keeping the best interests of the child paramount. . . .

In balancing the interests, there must be a showing of neglect or dependence by a preponderance of the evidence. While SDCL 26-8-6 defines neglect or dependence in terms of parental conduct or home environment, we must also focus our attention on the harm to the child. Absent evidence of potential harm, the state's interest in protecting the child is outweighed by the legitimate parental interest in retaining custody of the child.

Appellant contends that the statute is so vague and broad "as to reach virtually any family in any community," but that poor families are most often singled out because of their frequent contact with welfare workers. While children in many families not receiving welfare assistance may be lacking proper parental care, we believe the problems D.K. experienced in his home were not a result of appellant's poverty. They were instead a result of her inability because of limited intelligence or her unwillingness to provide the proper care. Based upon the evidence discussed above and upon other evidence in the record which supports the latter conclusion, the trial court could properly disturb the parental relation where, as here, it found the well-being of the child plainly requires it.

A reasonably intelligent person should by common understanding and practice "realize that for a child with a special health problem such as D.K.'s proper or necessary medical care or any other care necessary for his health or well-being" requires special attention to diet and personal hygiene. We reiterate . . . that the language of the statute provides adequate standards from which an average intelligent person can regulate his conduct. In this case a higher standard of care must exist to meet the minimum level of proper or necessary subsistence medical care or any other care necessary for his health or well-being.[19] Providing proper medical care for a child not only involves taking him to a doctor when his condition becomes serious or critical, it also involves providing the diet and hygiene necessary for the child's well-being at home.

Admittedly, this is a close case; there is no physical abuse of the child in the usual sense which makes for any easy decision. However, the neglect shown of this unfortunate child who requires special care and attention by a mother who is either incapable or unwilling to care for these special needs escalates this neglect to a case of abuse in this instance. As the doctor testified, "his health and perhaps his life are at risk if he remains at home." The trial court had an opportunity to observe the mother and was in a far better position to determine the best interests of the child. There was substantial evidence produced by the state to sustain the finding that D.K. was a dependent and neglected child.

We think it is of particular importance to note that this is not a permanent termination of parental rights. It is a temporary placement subject to periodic review by the court. Should D.K.'s health improve to the point where he has outgrown his present problems, or the mother's life stabilize so that there would be a reasonable basis for believing she would properly care for him, the court is free to return the child to her.

Affirmed.

---

19 [3] The following states have declared by statute that the failure to provide special care to a child where it is necessary for his physical or mental condition is ground for determination as a neglected or dependent child: Alaska Stat. § 47.10.010(a)(9) (1975); Iowa Code Ann. § 232.2(13)(b) (Supp. 1975); Minn. Stat. § 260.015, subd. 10(d) (Supp. 1975); Okl. Stat. Ann. tit. 10, § 1101(d) (Supp. 1974); and Wis. Stat. Ann. § 48.13(1)(e) (Supp. 1974).

WINANS, JUSTICE (*dissenting*).

I respectfully dissent. The conduct of the mother does not warrant the degree of state intervention pursued in this case. While I recognize that the conditions described reflect a less than ideal environment for this child, the environment provided was not so deficient that it amounted to neglect.

It is the duty of the court to determine the delicate balance between the fundamental right of parents to their children and the legitimate state interest in protecting children within its borders. The best interests of the child must be kept paramount. We are not to decide whether someone other than the parent is better able to care for the child, nor are we to insure that the child has a perfect home. Many homes fall short of perfection. I do not think that the legislature intended that parents be deprived of even temporary custody of their children merely because they are not able to furnish an environment we would wish all children to have. The court's duty is to decide if the environment provided is so imperfect that it amounts to neglect of the child.

The trial court found that D.K. was without the care necessary to his health and welfare; that his mother failed to provide for his special medical needs; and that his mother did not feed him the diet prescribed by the doctor. This, according to the majority, constituted a lack of proper parental care and a failure to provide proper or necessary subsistence, medical care or any other care necessary to the child's health and well-being. Essentially this is a restatement of the broad statutory standards for neglect found in SDCL 26-8-6. Admittedly the statutory standards in this type of case must be broad, but those legislative guidelines must not be so broad that they permit *ad hoc* judicial determinations as to what conduct falls within the statute's purview. To justify judicial intervention into the time-honored parent-child relationship we should require that some minimum threshold level of deficient conduct be established. The conduct reflected by the record, while less than perfect in several regards, does not rise to that minimum level of deficiency.

The evidence showed that on occasion the house was dirty, D.K. was in wet diapers, and there was a smell of urine in the air. The baby was fed several times by propping the bottle. The child has a history of typical childhood diseases — diaper rash, colds, bronchitis, croup. The doctor's testimony was that the congenital lung defect might lower resistance to such viral infections. He expressed the same opinion as to wet diapers. He concluded that the child needed special attention because of this and recommended that the child be kept out of crowds, that his diet be observed, and that he be kept clean.

The record contains no evidence that the mother subjected the child to crowds. The child was placed on a special diet in December, 1974. Assuming that the mother was informed of the diet at this time, a fact that is hardly clear from the record, the evidence shows only one occasion that the child was actually ill because the diet was not followed, that being when the child was fed orange juice. This is certainly not overwhelming support for the finding that the mother failed to follow the prescribed diet.

The record showed that food was a problem for this family; that is certainly not unusual for families forced to subsist on government aid. Although I am deeply troubled by the one instance when the child was without food for 24 hours, the record demonstrates that on other occasions the mother was able to secure food for her family from other sources, including the welfare department. Indeed the doctor's records reflect at several points his observation that the child was well-nourished.

The trial court found that the mother failed to provide for the special medical needs of her child. The record shows that she brought the child to the hospital five of the six times he was there. Surely that indicates some concern for the child's health. In fact the doctor testified that he thought the mother might be oversensitive to the child's health problems.

Even assuming the standards found in SDCL 26-8-6 are not impermissibly broad, I do not feel the preponderance of the evidence supports a finding of neglect. Many of the deficiencies noted exist in many homes across the state. We should exercise great caution before we impose the practical standards of the wealthy and educated on the poor and less educated segments of our society.

The trial court did not consider less intrusive measures as a possible solution. Nor is there any indication that the court considered possible harm to the child brought about by separation from his mother. I would find that these are factors that must be considered before the state can justify interference with family life.

Examination of cases in this area of the law shows that while the conditions relied on by the trial court in this case have been considered by other courts, none has relied solely on similar facts to justify a finding of neglect. Typically factors like a dirty house and wet diapers are accompanied by other circumstances which cause the court to consider whether the situation is one that warrants judicial interference. These cases demonstrate that a minimum threshold of deficient conduct must be crossed before intervention by the long arm of the state is justified. I do not believe there is justification for the degree of interference present in this case and would therefore reverse.

IN RE MATTHEW S.

Second District Court of Appeal of California
49 Cal. Rptr. 2d 139 (1996)

GILBERT, ASSOCIATE JUSTICE.

A mother has delusions about the health of her minor son. Here we hold substantial evidence supports the conclusion that the minor is at risk of suffering serious emotional damage.

Alexandra S. appeals from the jurisdictional and dispositional orders declaring her children, Matthew S. and Sarah S., to be dependents of the juvenile court.

Substantial evidence supports the jurisdictional order as to Matthew S. We affirm.

FACTS

Alexandra S. had these delusions: her son's penis had been mutilated, he was being treated at UCLA while she was on a trip to South America, she murdered the treating physician when she returned to find her son in a "septic state" at the hospital. Acting on these delusions, she took her thirteen-year-old son to a urologist, Doctor Michael deWit Clayton, for an examination on September 2, 1994. He found no evidence of injury whatsoever to her son's penis, and her son stated he had no such injury. Alexandra S. admitted that she needs help with her psychiatric problems, but that she had trouble finding such help at the time. Although Doctor Clayton did not believe that Matthew S. was in danger of mistreatment, he contacted mental health services to investigate the matter. Doctor Clayton expressed concern whether her children were in good condition and what effect her delusions might have on them.

As a result of Doctor Clayton's referral, the Department of Social Services for the County of San Luis Obispo (the Department) interviewed the children and Alexandra S. Matthew S. did not want to discuss the urological examination at the time. He said that his mother makes confusing statements. For example, his mother says she was married to Gregory Harrison (the actor) who was murdered by the Mafia. When Alexandra S. was told that Mr. Harrison is alive, she suggested that his murder and funeral were staged. Sarah S., then sixteen, also reported her mother's delusions regarding Harrison. Sarah S. said that her mother tried to pull Matthew S.'s pants down to make sure his genitals were healthy. Alexandra S. also has an adult daughter, Lana. The previous year, Alexandra S. tried to touch Lana's breasts to show her how to massage them to stay healthy.

Alexandra S. said that Matthew S. complained that his penis was hurting, that she took him into the bathroom, pulled down his pants, saw a plastic bag wrapped around his mutilated penis and took him to UCLA to repair the damage. She disagreed with Doctor Clayton's diagnosis and felt she could disprove him by observing her son's penis.

Alexandra S. and her ex-husband, Wesley S., were divorced years ago due to increasing emotional distance between them. Wesley S. lives and works in Brazil and is erratic about sending child and spousal support of $900 per month. He does not want custody of the children, and he realizes that the children prefer to live with their mother. Until shortly before the instant hearing, Alexandra S. worked as a dietitian at a hospital. She was fired because she refused to undergo therapy when she revealed that she had been molested as a child.

The Department temporarily placed the minor children in protective custody with distant relatives on October 5, 1994. On October 7, 1994, the Department filed dependency petitions on behalf of Matthew S. and his sixteen-year-old sister, Sarah S. The children were permitted to return to their mother's home on October 11, 1994.

The petitions allege that there is a substantial risk that the children will suffer serious physical harm as a result of the mother's failure or inability to adequately supervise or protect them or to provide them with adequate food, clothing, shelter or medical treatment due to their mother's serious emotional problems.

The petitions also alleged that Matthew S. is suffering or is at substantial risk of suffering serious emotional damage as evidenced by severe anxiety, depression or withdrawal which is the result of being included in his mother's delusional discussions about his genitals. The petitions alleged that his mother's emotional problems and behavior placed him at grave risk of sexual abuse.

Lastly, the petitions alleged that the children have been left without any provision for support in that their father is employed in Brazil and Alexandra S. has primary physical custody.

The initial report of the investigating social worker, Lance Hillsinger, concluded there is no reason to remove the children from the mother's home at this time, but he recommended court intervention to monitor whether she might commit "physical acts on her beliefs." Hillsinger, however, did not think that Alexandra S. would be violent in the near future. He saw evidence that the mother's "peculiar beliefs are starting to crumble." Alexandra S. understands that others view her as delusional, and she admits she may be delusional. Alexandra S. is aware that she suffers from multiple personality disorders and she has participated in extensive therapy. Although she used to drink, she no longer does so. She does not feel she is any threat to her children and she believes she should not be permitted to parent them if she were a danger to them.

Sarah S. and Matthew S. "have a good, warm relationship, a close, loving relationship that would be the envy of many mothers with teenage children." Neither Sarah S. nor Matthew S. was afraid of their mother and both recognized that what she says is just talk. The children have had no concerns that she would become violent, and they wanted to remain in their mother's well-kept, three-bedroom home. They were happy to be back in their mother's care and she did not discuss her delusions after they returned home. Matthew S. is a good student who stated that he can concentrate better on his school work when he is home with his mother.

Doctor Beryl Davis conducted psychological evaluations which she submitted to the court on November 22, 1994. Doctor Davis described Sarah S. as an attractive, healthy-appearing young woman who offered information in a helpful manner. Sarah S. discussed her mother's delusions, but said she has never felt that her mother was a threat to her or to Matthew S. She denied saying that her mother tried to pull down Matthew S.'s pants. Sarah S. said she has a close relationship with her mother and can tell her anything. Aside from her mother's delusions, her mother deals with her "in a normal 'mother' way." She is best friends with her brother and is also a good student. She is worried about their reduced financial circumstances, but says that her mother provides meals and helps with her homework. She does not lack food, clothes or shelter.

Doctor Davis concluded that Matthew S. is an attractive, healthy-appearing boy who showed no signs of neglect. He was polite and cooperative, but reticent to discuss his mother's delusions about his genitals. He said his mother never tried to pull his pants down, and he never has felt threatened by her for any reason. He said he felt confused by his mother's delusions, but she has not mentioned them again since they went to the urologist. Discipline in the home consists of "being sent to his room and talking about what has been done wrong." He acknowledged that his grades had briefly dropped during the upheaval brought about by the intervention of the Department with the family, but that his grades are better again and he likes school.

Alexandra S. also was pleasant and neatly dressed. She discussed her delusions with Doctor Davis in a consistent, lucid manner. Her speech was normal, there was no looseness of associations and her eye contact was good. She denied trying to pull down Matthew S.'s pants, and she was satisfied with the urologist's opinion. She takes her children to doctors if any health concerns arise. Alexandra S. stated she was concerned about Matthew S., but agreed that doctors should diagnose him. Alexandra S. told Doctor Davis that Matthew S. had nighttime enuresis in the fourth grade, and the doctor advised her to allow him to bathe himself thereafter. Since that time, she has always honored his privacy. She explained her attempt to massage Lana's breasts by saying she wanted to explain breast self-examination to Lana and that she was concerned about Lana's complaints about numbness in the area.

She admitted that she had been molested as a child and that once she tried to commit suicide as a young teenager. She is neither suicidal nor homicidal now, and when she needs medications she takes them. She recently lost her position as a dietitian at French Hospital because she refused to attend therapy as a condition of employment after she revealed that she had been molested as a child. Her divorce occurred because of religious differences and because "they didn't work hard enough on communicating."

Testing scored by computer revealed that her use of fantasy could result in neglect of people and practical matters. It also showed that she misinterprets and distorts perceptual input more than most people and appears to have a strong need to be dependent. Doctor Davis was concerned about her morbid, violent delusions as expressions of anger, but the children expressed no fear of her and they "appear to be healthy, and reasonably well-adjusted." The children are confused about their mother's delusions, although "[t]hey appear, however, to be able to recognize their mother's delusions and to deal adequately with them." Alexandra S. seeks the help of physicians and follows through with their assistance.

Doctor Davis concluded that Alexandra S. has a rich and complex delusional system which appears to have increased and deepened since her divorce in 1986. She also concluded it would do more harm than good to everyone involved to remove the children from the mother. Nonetheless, she believed the family should be closely supervised to monitor the situation. She recommended that therapy and information sessions be required and that child protective services should remain involved to help them.

Hillsinger's supplemental report dated November 29, 1994, prepared after the Department received Doctor Davis's report, provided a case plan involving such further psychiatric evaluation and therapy, among other things.

Alexandra S. was denied Aid to Families with Dependent Children (AFDC) shortly before the jurisdictional/dispositional hearing of December 28, 1994. On her application she stated she had expensive homes and was married to actor Gregory Harrison.

After the jurisdictional/dispositional hearing, the juvenile court found true by clear and convincing evidence the allegations that Matthew S. is at risk of physical and emotional harm due to his mother's serious emotional problems stemming from her intense delusions with violent themes involving Matthew S. The court struck, however, the allegation that there is great danger that she will act out her violent delusions. The court also found true that Matthew S. is at risk of developing severe emotional problems as a result of being included in his mother's delusional discussions. Lastly, the court found true the allegation there is no provision for support in that Wesley S. is employed in Brazil and the current family order gives primary physical custody to Alexandra S. The court struck the allegation regarding sexual abuse of Matthew S.

The court declared Matthew S. to be a dependent of the court and permitted him to reside with his mother under court-ordered family maintenance. Alexandra S. stated that the involvement of child protective services in her life has created more stress than it has alleviated. She resents the intrusion and does not want to comply with a case plan. This appeal ensued from the jurisdictional and dispositional orders.

DISCUSSION

Alexandra S. asserts that the orders should be reversed because there is no substantial evidence to support them. A juvenile court may order children to be dependents thereof if the Department establishes by a preponderance of the evidence that allegations made pursuant to § 300 are true. The Department has the burden of showing specifically how the minors have been or will be harmed and harm may not be presumed from the mere fact of mental illness of a parent.

Because the Department dismissed the petition as to Sarah S., we are only concerned about whether substantial evidence supports the findings and orders as to Matthew S. The findings and orders concern allegations found true by the court under § 300, subdivisions (b), (c), and (g). We review the findings and orders under the substantial evidence test. We affirm the rulings of the juvenile court if there is reasonable, credible evidence of solid value to support them.

Section 300, subdivision (b)

Under § 300, subdivision (b), the Department had to show *that the minor has suffered, or there is a substantial risk that the minor will suffer, serious physical harm or illness,* as a result of the failure or inability of the parent to adequately supervise or protect the minor, or by the willful or negligent failure of the parent to provide the minor with adequate food, clothing, shelter, or medical treatment, or by the inability of the parent to provide regular care for the minor due to the parent's mental illness or substance abuse.

Here, the court struck the allegation that there is great danger that Alexandra S. will act out her violent delusions. Nonetheless, the court found that Matthew S. is at risk of physical and emotional harm due to Alexandra S.'s emotional problems stemming from her violent delusions. The court also found a failure to provide adequate food, clothing and shelter because Alexandra S. did not properly fill out the AFDC application.

There is no evidence that Matthew S. has suffered, or that there is substantial risk that he will suffer, serious physical harm or illness as a result of Alexandra S.'s supervision and protection of him. Neither is there any showing of such harm from failure to provide food, clothing or shelter. Aside from going to the urologist to make sure her son was not harmed after she had a delusion, she is an excellent mother. Matthew S. consistently expressed no fear of Alexandra S. for any reason. Neither did his siblings. She has a well-kept home, provides meals to her children and has consistently obtained medical treatment for the children. Her children are healthy, well groomed and attractive. She has voluntarily participated in extensive therapy for herself over the years, too. There is no evidence that she drinks or abuses substances. Doctor Davis and Lance Hillsinger saw no evidence of neglect.

Section 300, subdivision (g)

Under § 300, subdivision (g), the Department had the burden to show that "[t]he minor has been left without any provision for support. . . ." The court found true the allegation that Wesley S. is employed in Brazil and that Alexandra S. has primary physical custody. The finding does not state or indicate that Matthew S. has been left without any provision for support, and there is no evidence that this is so. Although Alexandra S.'s financial resources are being strained because she recently lost her job, she has been supporting her children for years and continues to do so. She is seeking new employment. There is no evidence of malnutrition, deprivation of shelter, clothes or medical care for Matthew S.

Section 300, subdivision (c)

Under § 300, subdivision (c), the Department had the burden to show that Matthew S. "is suffering serious emotional damage, or is at substantial risk of suffering serious emotional damage," as evidenced by severe anxiety, depression, withdrawal, or untoward aggressive behavior. Here, the court found that Matthew S. is at risk of developing severe emotional problems as a result of Alexandra S.'s delusions about his health. The court concluded that Alexandra S. is "unable to acknowledge this difficulty or to provide Matthew with a stable and non-threatening environment."

Substantial evidence supports the court's finding even though there are notable positive aspects in the home environment. Neither of the children feels threatened by their mother. Matthew S. likes school and is a good student. His grades have improved since he returned to his mother's home, and he appears to be "reasonably well-adjusted." Matthew S. and Sarah S. appear to have a warm close relationship with their mother. This is why the Department recommends the children not be removed from the home.

Although the children have not as yet suffered harm at their mother's hands, substantial evidence points to potential serious emotional harm. It is problematic that Alexandra S.'s delusions could result in some catastrophic event giving rise to a substantial risk that Matthew S. could suffer serious physical harm or illness as the Department postulates. Substantial evidence does, however, point to a substantial risk of emotional harm.

Alexandra S. brings a foreboding sense of dread, danger and catastrophe to the lives of her children. Although Matthew S. so far has been able to deal with his mother's delusions, he is confused by them. As Hillsinger points out, Matthew S. is forced to shoulder a tremendous burden. He has a close loving relationship with his mother, but he "remains silent. He does not speak up for an apology, not out of a fear of retaliation, but out of a fear he will aggravate his mother's emotional problems. This is a lot of self-control to expect from a thirteen year old." Hillsinger also pointed out that at this time in his life, Matthew S. did not have the capacity "to escape from [his mother's] generalized and overwhelming sense that everybody is in immediate danger from some obscure and threatening force."

As the Department points out, Matthew S. was the most affected by his mother's illness. He suffered the indignity and embarrassment of the medical examination. His reticence to speak about his feelings and his reluctance to obtain assistance is understandable, but it reflects withdrawal and it points to the need for court supervision. Matthew S. has neglected his own emotional needs because of his fear of aggravating his mother's condition. In such a situation there is a substantial risk he could suffer serious emotional damage.

The Department points out that should Alexandra S.'s condition deteriorate, a distinct possibility occasioned by the stress arising from financial pressures, Matthew S. would most likely not seek help.

Despite the doctor's assurance that Matthew S. had not been mutilated, Alexandra S. still believed he had been mutilated and would consequently die. Because of intervention by the court and the Department she has apparently not spoken of these fears to her children since they have been returned to her. The continuing jurisdiction of the court would help ensure that Alexandra S. continue to keep her fears to herself. This in turn would relieve Matthew S. from the burden of his mother's delusions.

Upon our review of the entire record we conclude that substantial evidence supports the juvenile court's finding that Matthew S. is at risk of developing severe emotional problems. Therefore, we affirm the dispositional order of the juvenile court as to Matthew S.

We trust the Department will pursue its case plan in an unobtrusive manner and will cause as little disruption to the family as possible. Of course should matters improve so that there is no longer a substantial risk of emotional damage to Matthew S., dismissal of the petition would be appropriate.

YEGAN, J., *concurs*.

STEVEN J. STONE, PRESIDING JUSTICE, *dissenting*.

I dissent. As my colleagues have pointed out, there is no evidence that Matthew S. has suffered, nor is there a substantial risk that he will suffer, serious physical harm or illness as a result of Alexandra S.'s supervision or protection of him. Neither is there any showing of such harm from willful or negligent failure to provide food, clothing, shelter or medical treatment. The majority further acknowledges there is no evidence that Matthew S. is without any provision for support. Alexandra S. has supported her children in a well-kept three-bedroom home by obtaining various jobs over the ten years since her divorce, despite erratic payments of child and spousal support by her ex-husband. Her children are healthy, well groomed, and she has consistently obtained medical care for them over the years. There is no evidence of neglect or of lack of support for Matthew S.

The majority concludes there is substantial evidence to support the finding of the juvenile court that Matthew S. is at risk of developing severe emotional problems in the future as the result of her inclusion of him in her delusions, under § 300, subdivision (c).

But, as the majority states, there is no evidence that any of the children have yet suffered emotional harm at the hands of Alexandra S. The record does not show that the juvenile court has ever taken jurisdiction over any of these children before. One of the children, Lana S., is an adult. Sarah S. is now over sixteen, and the court dismissed the petition as to her. And Matthew S. was thirteen at the time the San Luis Obispo County Department of Social Services (the Department) petitioned the court for jurisdiction over him. Given the record before us today, we have no evidence to prognosticate a strong potential for future severe emotional damage to Matthew S.

The majority states that Alexandra S. brings a sense of dread, danger and catastrophe to the lives of her children through her delusions. This is speculation only. The evidence does not support that conclusion. Doctor Davis observed that Matthew and Sarah S. "express no fear of their mother and appear to be healthy, and reasonably well-adjusted." Doctor Beryl Davis concluded that although Sarah S. and Matthew S. are confused about their mother's delusional status, they both appear to be "able to recognize their mother's delusions and to deal adequately with them." As the majority points out, Hillsinger found that Sarah S. and Matthew S. "have a good, warm relationship, a close, loving relationship that would be the envy of many mothers with teenage children."

The majority suggests that Matthew S.'s understandable reticence to express his feelings to Lance Hillsinger and to Doctor Davis, and his reluctance to obtain assistance from them, establishes the need for judicial dependency. I disagree. § 300, subdivision (c) requires the Department to prove that a child is at *substantial risk* of suffering *severe emotional damage as evidenced by severe anxiety, depression, withdrawal or untoward aggressive behavior* before the juvenile court may assume jurisdiction.

By its revision of § 300 to include subdivision (c), the Legislature explained that it wanted "to provide more clear-cut guidance to social workers and judges regarding the types of situations which the Legislature considers abusive or neglectful." The new legislation provided definitions which focus on specific harms to a child. "The legislative history thus confirms an unmistakable intention to narrow the grounds on which children may be subjected to juvenile court jurisdiction." That Alexandra S. is delusional does not mean that Matthew S. is likely to suffer severe emotional harm.

Although Doctor Davis found Matthew S. to be shy and uncomfortable in talking to her about his mother's beliefs regarding his genitals, she also stated that he is "polite and cooperative about providing information." We should not conclude that his shyness and protective nature constitute severe anxiety, depression, withdrawal or untoward behavior justifying judicial intervention. Doctor Davis found Matthew S. to be a reasonably well-adjusted teenager.

On this record, it is speculation to predict that some catastrophic event could occur which would create a substantial risk that Matthew S. will suffer serious emotional harm. Where children, as here, do not fall within the descriptions of § 300, the Department may still offer *voluntary* services pursuant to § 300. But, § 300 expressly provides that it is not intended "to disrupt the family unnecessarily or to intrude inappropriately into family life. . . ."

The Department's intervention has disrupted the family already. Although the orders permit the children to remain with their mother, the case plan and the other orders of the court restrict the family and require it to accede to the intervention of the Department. The case plan requires Alexandra S. to cooperate with announced, as well as unannounced home calls. It also requires her and her children to participate in therapy, including in-home counseling. Furthermore, it requires Alexandra S. to facilitate telephone contact between her children and their father, who lives in Brazil. The family feels intruded upon by such involvement of the Department in their lives.

Both Matthew S. and Sarah S. have a good, warm, close relationship with Alexandra S. that would be the envy of many mothers. Matthew S. does not exhibit severe anxiety, depression, withdrawal or untoward aggressive behavior. He is a polite, reasonably well-adjusted teenager. Substantial evidence does not support the finding of jurisdiction over Matthew S. and the concomitant intrusion of the Department into the lives of this family.

I would reverse the jurisdictional and dispositional orders and direct the juvenile court to dismiss the instant petition.

L.L. v. COLORADO

Supreme Court of Colorado
10 P.3d 1271 (2000)

JUSTICE RICE *delivered the Opinion of the Court.*

This court granted certiorari to address whether the court of appeals erred when it affirmed the trial court and held that a parent's due process rights are not violated when the majority of her parental rights, including the right to custody and visitation, are suspended until her children are eighteen years of age, pursuant to findings of fact made under a preponderance of the evidence standard. We affirm the court of appeals and hold that Petitioner's due process rights were not violated when the trial court significantly limited her parental rights in a guardianship hearing based on findings of fact under a preponderance of the evidence standard.

I

FACTS AND PROCEDURAL HISTORY

In 1994, Petitioner was convicted of a drug-related offense and sentenced to a brief period of incarceration. The El Paso County Department of Human

Services ("DHS") issued a Notice of Temporary Custody Hearing and on February 2, 1994, the district court placed Petitioner's two children, R.W. and T.W., in the temporary custody of their maternal grandmother ("Grandmother"). The father of both children ("Father") was incarcerated at the time. R.W. was nine-years-old and T.W. was four.

Upon release from prison, Petitioner sought to end the temporary custody arrangement and DHS recommended that the custody of the children be returned to Petitioner. On January 30, 1995, the court ordered temporary custody to be shared by both Petitioner and Grandmother.

In February 1995, DHS filed a petition in dependency and neglect based on a belief that neither Petitioner nor Grandmother was adequately caring for the children. At a hearing on the petition, DHS presented evidence that Grandmother allegedly permitted Petitioner to take the children to her home while she was under the influence of various illegal drugs. The district court placed the children in the legal and physical custody of DHS, granting Petitioner and Grandmother supervised visitation only.

On April 19, 1995, the court placed custody of the children with Grand-mother, with DHS exercising protective supervision. On June 22, 1995, the court revoked Grandmother's custody due to her failure to follow court orders, and the children were again placed in the legal and physical custody of DHS. The court ordered that the children be placed in foster care, granted Petitioner and Grandmother supervised visitation, and ordered Petitioner and Grand-mother to refrain from disparaging each other or the foster parents to the children, and to refrain from discussing court proceedings with the children. On August 24, 1995, the court adjudicated the children dependent and neglected, adopted a proposed treatment plan, and continued custody of the children with DHS.

On September 10, 1996, DHS petitioned the court to grant permanent guardianship of the children to the foster parents. The court scheduled the permanency planning and guardianship hearings for October 4, 1996, but continued the hearings several times at the request of Petitioner, Father, and Grandmother.

On April 28, 1997, the court held a permanency planning hearing, deter-mined that there was no substantial probability that the children could be returned to Petitioner within six months, and continued foster care placement.

On December 16, 1997, DHS filed a motion to terminate the parent-child legal relationship of Petitioner and Father. On February 18, 1998, the court ordered mediation, but the parties could not reach a resolution. However, DHS subsequently decided to seek only permanent guardianship of the children, rather than termination of the parent-child legal relationship.

On March 4, 1998, the court held a hearing on permanent guardianship. Father consented to permanent guardianship being placed in the foster parents, with no visitation rights, but Petitioner opposed both the entry of permanent guardianship and the proposed no contact order. The court found that the children needed ongoing treatment, that they were being harmed by the continued contact with Petitioner and Grandmother, that they needed stability and permanency, and that it was in the children's best interests to be placed in the permanent guardianship of the foster parents. Accordingly, the court ordered:

That custody of the subject children shall continue with [DHS];

That the foster parents are hereby appointed as permanent legal guardians of the subject children;

That as permanent guardians, said custodians have:

a) The authority to consent to marriage, to enlistment in the armed forces and to medical and surgical treatment;

b) The authority to represent the children in legal actions and to make other decisions of substantial significance concerning said children;

c) The rights and responsibility [sic] of legal and physical custody when such custody has not been vested in another person, agency, or institution;

That [Respondent] and [Grandmother] are to have no contact with the subject children;

That there shall be one termination visit between said parties and the subject children;

That this matter is continued to June 5, 1998, for written review; [and]

That the Court shall retain jurisdiction herein as provided by law. . . .

Petitioner appealed to the court of appeals, asserting that the trial court violated her due process rights when it ordered the functional equivalent of a termination of her parental rights without applying the "clear and convincing evidence" standard of proof. The court of appeals affirmed the district court order. In a divided panel, the court found that the district court order did not act as the functional equivalent of a termination of Petitioner's parental rights.[20] The majority stated that Petitioner still retains various rights, including the right to consent or withhold consent to the children's adoption, the right to determine the children's religious affiliation, the right to reasonable parenting time, except as restricted by a court,[21] and the right to seek a modification of the disposition in order to regain custody and increase parenting time. The court of appeals concluded that the district court order "reflects a careful consideration of the children's present needs while leaving open the possibility of the mother's increased involvement with the children in the future." The dissent disagreed with the majority opinion, arguing that the effect of the district order was "so restrictive of [Petitioner's] parental rights that it cannot pass constitutional muster unless it is premised on facts proved under an enhanced standard."

Petitioner filed a petition for a *writ of certiorari*, arguing that the district court violated her due process rights when it drastically restricted her

---

[20] [4] The majority noted that, although not articulated by the district court, it appeared that the standard of proof applied was a preponderance of the evidence.

[21] [5] In this case, Petitioner has no parenting time due to a no-contact order.

parental rights based on findings obtained under a preponderance of the evidence standard. We granted certiorari to address whether the trial court's order deprived Petitioner of due process by drastically restricting her parental rights based on findings obtained under a preponderance of the evidence standard.

II

DEPENDENCY AND NEGLECT PROCEEDINGS

Article 3 of the Colorado Children's Code, titled "Dependency and Neglect," provides specific provisions whereby the state can intercede to protect the health, safety, and welfare of minors from abuse, neglect, or abandonment. In particular, Article 3 governs child abuse and neglect proceedings, temporary custody and shelter of minors, and termination of the parent-child legal relationship. The Article states in its legislative declaration that "the stability and preservation of the families of this state and the safety and protection of children are matters of statewide concern," and to that end, that the state shall "make a commitment to make 'reasonable efforts' to prevent the placement of abused and neglected children out of the home and to reunify the family whenever appropriate." To that end, the Children's Code encompasses a number of procedures aimed at protecting children from emotional and physical harm while at the same time seeking to repair and maintain family ties.

Often, the process begins with a report of abuse or neglect. The state may file a petition alleging that a child is dependent or neglected. An adjudicatory hearing is then held, where the state must establish by a preponderance of the evidence that a child is dependent or neglected. Once the court determines a child is dependent or neglected, the court has the authority to order a variety of dispositions, including: placement of legal custody in the parents or guardian, with or without protective supervision; placement of legal custody in a relative, with or without protective supervision; placement of legal custody in the county department of social services, a foster home, or other child care facility; and mental and physical examinations of a child. In addition, the court must approve a treatment plan that seeks to resolve family difficulties and preserve the family unit. However, when a court determines that the goal of maintaining the family unit is not feasible . . . the court may order termination of the parent-child relationship after the filing of a motion for termination. [22]

III

CONSTITUTIONAL SIGNIFICANCE

The United States Supreme Court has recognized that parents possess a right to the "companionship, care, custody, and management" of their children,

---

[22] [5] Termination of the parent-child relationship will only be considered after a proper motion for termination has been filed.

Stanley v. Illinois, 405 U.S. 645, 651(1972), and a fundamental right to maintain family relationships free from governmental interference. Very recently, the Court reiterated this position, noting that "the interest of parents in the care, custody, and control of their children — is perhaps the oldest of the fundamental liberty interests recognized by this Court." *Troxel v. Granville,* 530 U.S. 57 (2000). As such, the government must meet certain due process and equal protection standards before these constitutional rights can be extinguished. Logically, the greater the deprivation, the greater the procedural protection provided to parents.

When a permanent termination of parental rights is sought, a parent's rights must be protected "with fundamentally fair procedures." *Santosky v. Kramer,* 455 U.S. 745, 745 (1982). [T]he Supreme Court concluded that due process mandated a higher standard of proof than a preponderance of the evidence standard when parental rights were being permanently terminated. In holding that the minimum standard of proof required in a parental rights termination proceeding is clear and convincing evidence, the Court stated that the private interest affected is commanding, the risk of error from using a preponderance of the evidence standard is substantial, and the countervailing governmental interest favoring that standard is comparatively slight. The court noted that the standard of proof necessary turns in large part on both the nature of the threatened private interest and the permanency of the threatened loss.

This court, in the same year, applied the *Santosky* standard to termination proceedings in Colorado. We held that the clear and convincing evidence standard mandated by *Santosky* was adequate to protect the rights of the natural parent in termination proceedings.

In addition, this court addressed the issue of whether the preponderance of the evidence standard that applies during a dependency or neglect proceeding was sufficient to protect a parent's due process rights even though an adverse finding in that hearing could be the basis of a subsequent termination of parental rights. [W]e concluded that this standard was appropriate and constitutional. The court noted that the governmental interests reflected in the Children's Code are more extensive and weighty than those present in the *Santosky* case. In particular, we noted that prior to filing a petition in dependency or neglect, the state has limited authority to take action to protect a child. In addition, the court pointed out that a dependency or neglect proceeding is remedial in nature and the purpose is to preserve the family unit and assist parents and children in establishing a healthy relationship and home environment. The court stated, "[w]hen a dependency or neglect proceeding is viewed in light of its primary purpose — as helpful and remedial in preserving and mending familial ties — the importance of permitting State intervention on a standard of proof lower than clear and convincing becomes evident." Accordingly, we held that while a standard of clear and convincing evidence is constitutionally mandated in a proceeding for terminating the parent-child relationship, a standard of a preponderance of the evidence is sufficient for dependency and neglect proceedings.

IV

APPLICATION

Petitioner raises the question of what standard of proof is required by due process when a parent is deprived of significant parental rights that do not amount to a permanent termination of the parent-child relationship. Petitioner asserts that the district court order, which granted custody of her children to DHS, appointed the foster parents as "permanent" legal guardians, and ordered that she have no contact with her children until they were over eighteen-years-old, other than one "termination visit," was the functional equivalent of the termination of her parental rights. Accordingly, she argues that the decision should have been governed by a clear and convincing evidence standard.

At a hearing to determine an appropriate disposition in a dependency or neglect proceeding, the state must show that "by a preponderance of the evidence . . . a separation of the child from the parents or guardian is in the best interests of the child. Although the trial court never articulated the burden of proof, the court of appeals found, and we agree, that there is nothing in the record to suggest that the trial court did not employ this standard.

Although DHS did not seek to terminate Petitioner's parental rights, Petitioner is losing the majority of her parenting rights, including the right to the custody, care, and companionship of her children. As the trial court order indicates, the foster parents, as permanent legal guardians, are conferred the authority to consent to marriage, to enlistment in the armed forces, and to medical or surgical treatment. They have the authority to represent the children in legal actions, and they have all the "rights and responsibility [sic] of legal and physical custody."

However, despite the fact that Petitioner is losing many of her parental rights, this custody order differs significantly from a total termination of parental rights. First, the trial court retains jurisdiction over the case until the children are twenty-one-years-old. This means that Petitioner may petition to seek a modification of the disposition to regain custody or increase parenting time. In fact, the trial court, in its order limiting Petitioner's custody and visitation rights, continued the case until June 5, 1998, to reevaluate the case then.

In addition, although she loses many of her rights under this order, Petitioner, as the parent of her minor children, retains the right to consent or withhold consent to adoption, the right to reasonable parenting time except as restricted by the court,[23] and the right to determine the children's religious affiliation.

We recognize that there is some tension between the appearance of finality in such orders and the continuing jurisdiction of the juvenile court to address the mother's right to petition for modification. However, the "permanency" and "finality" of the order herein would yield to any modifications that are

---

[23] [7] Although Petitioner presently has no parenting time due to a no-contact order, she retains the right to petition the court to modify that order.

subsequently made by the court as a result of substantial changes in circumstances. Because guardianship orders are merely a plan for permanency that is subject to change as warranted by the best interests of the children, Petitioner's residual right to petition for modification is sufficient to refute the argument that this guardianship order was the functional equivalent of termination.

Accordingly, we reiterate here that due process of law is accorded to parties when an adjudicatory hearing of a dependency or neglect proceeding is governed by a preponderance of the evidence standard. Although Petitioner is suffering the loss of many of her parental rights, this fact does not change our analysis of the constitutionality of dependency or neglect proceedings. . . . [T]he governmental interest here is significant. The adjudication of dependency or neglect petitions provide the state with the means to intervene to assist parents and children in establishing a home environment that will preserve the family unit. The purpose of dependency or neglect proceedings is not to deprive parents of their rights to raise their children; rather, it is to preserve the family and protect children.

Similarly, we reiterate our concern that "[t]he effect of heightening the standard of proof at the adjudicatory stage could be pernicious." The preponderance of the evidence standard in dependency or neglect proceedings permits the state to take the proper role as an intervenor, a role that corresponds with the legislative intent of the Children's Code "[t]o secure for each child subject to [its] provisions such care and guidance, preferably in his own home, as will best serve his welfare and the interests of society; [and t]o preserve and strengthen family ties whenever possible, including improvement of home environment." Heightening the burden of proof for dependency or neglect proceedings could have the effect of making it more difficult for the state to protect children, lessening the ability of the court and the state to fashion workable solutions, and increasing the risk of an adversarial environment between the state and parents.

Although the trial court order in this case results in the deprivation of many of Petitioner's parental rights, it was a decision reached by the court after more than four years of court and DHS involvement attempting to reconcile the family issues that were contributing to an unsafe and unhealthy environment for these children. Despite many years of effort, neither the court nor DHS believed that the children could be returned safely to Petitioner's custody. However, because DHS sought a permanent custody order, rather than termination of the parent-child relationship, Petitioner retains the right to petition the court for a change in custody status. Because Petitioner is not deprived of all her parental rights, and because the trial court retains jurisdiction to modify its existing order, we hold that the trial court order relating to Petitioner's custody and visitation rights does not violate her constitutional rights to due process.

V

CONCLUSION

Accordingly, we affirm the judgment of the court of appeals and hold that Petitioner's due process rights were not violated when the trial court significantly limited her parental rights at a guardianship hearing, held pursuant to a dependency and neglect proceeding, based on findings of fact under a preponderance of the evidence standard.

———

NOTES AND QUESTIONS

1. In his dissenting opinion in the *D.K.* case, Justice Winans argues that the "conduct of the mother does not warrant the degree of state intervention pursued in this case." To what extent is the "conduct of the mother" the issue?

Do you agree with Justice Winans' comment that "[t]o justify judicial intervention into the time honored parent-child relationship we should require that some minimum threshold level of deficient conduct be established"? Could it be argued that the point of the neglect statute is not so much to define parental conduct that will trigger state intervention but to notify juvenile authorities when they can exercise their discretion to intervene on behalf of children at risk? Along these lines consider, Meir Dan-Cohen, *Decision Rules and Conduct Rules: On Acoustic Separation in Criminal Law*, 97 HARV. L. REV. 625 (1984).

Justice Winans also concedes that statutory neglect standards "must be broad." Why? Could the legislature have defined the neglect standard more precisely?

Consider Carlos Clark, *An Argument for Considering Parental Smoking in Child Abuse and Neglect Proceedings*, 19 J. CONTEMP. HEALTH L. & POL'Y 225 (2002), and Laura A. Kelly, *What Should be the Standards For Intervening Between Parent and Child? The Parental Prosecution For a Young Boy's Obesity*, 9 BUFF. WOMEN'S L.J. 7 (2000). Kelly describes a case in Indiana where parents were charged with criminal neglect for allowing their 4-year-old son to reach 138 pounds — four times the average weight of a 4-year-old. The court placed the child into foster care where he lost more than 50 pounds — and many of his health problems improved — while on a strict starvation diet.

A variety of commentators have argued that broad definitions of neglect invite subjective and arbitrary enforcement. In the words of one observer: "The awesome power of the state is set in motion in its most pernicious form: state officials are authorized to act as they wish, intervening in one family while choosing to leave a second, seminal family alone." Martin Guggenheim, *The Political and Legal Implications of Psychological Parenting Theory*, 12 N.Y.U. REV. L. & SOC. CHANGE 549, 554 (1984).

2. Neglect provisions have been attacked on vagueness grounds in a variety of jurisdictions. As in *D.K.*, the courts routinely uphold the constitutionality of the statutes. *See, e.g.*, Matter of B.K., 429 A.2d 1331 (D.C. 1981) (upholding statute defining neglected children as those "without proper parental care or control, subsistence, education as required by law or other care of control necessary for [their] physical, mental, or emotional health, and the deprivation is not due to the lack of financial means of [their] parent, guardian, or other custodian"). *But see Roe v. Conn,* 417 F. Supp. 769 (M.D. Ala. 1976) (child

neglect statute unconstitutionally vague where trial court removed a child from custody of his mother in part on ground that he was white and she was living with a black man — appellate court enjoined enforcement of statute in absence of a showing of physical or emotional harm to the child).

3. Is there sufficient basis for state intervention in *Matthew S.*? In his dissenting opinion, Justice Stone notes that the California Legislature revised § 300(c) in order to "provide more clear-cut guidance to social workers and judges regarding the types of situations which the legislature considers . . . neglectful." Does the revision provide "clear cut guidance"?

4. The *L.L.* court holds that a standard of "preponderance of the evidence" is sufficient for dependency and neglect proceedings. As a policy matter, is that standard preferable to the more rigorous "clear and convincing" standard required in termination proceedings given the "remedial" nature of neglect proceedings? Considering the *L.L.* facts, how likely is it that the neglect proceeding will "remedy" the family problems and result in "preserving and mending family ties"?

5. Should the emphasis in cases like *L.L.* be on the emotional and psychological well-being of the children involved rather than on the interests of the parents? For an argument that "psychological parent-child relationships," whether or not they involve natural parents, should be given legal protection, see JOSEPH GOLDSTEIN ET AL., BEYOND THE BEST INTERESTS OF THE CHILD (1973). Along these lines, some commentators argue that other things being equal, protecting permanent relationships, particularly for pre-adolescent children, should be the central concern for courts considering the best interests of children. *See, e.g.*, Katherine Bartlett, *Rethinking Parenthood as an Exclusive Status: The Need for Legal Alternatives When the Premise of the Nuclear Family Has Failed*, 70 VA. L. REV. 879, 904–905 (1984).

[E]   Termination of Parental Rights

The *Baby M* case addressed the termination of the natural mother's rights under the applicable state statutes. The next case examined the parent's rights under the federal constitution.

SANTOSKY v. KRAMER

Supreme Court of the United States
455 U.S. 745 (1981)

JUSTICE BLACKMUN *delivered the opinion of the Court.*

Under New York law, the State may terminate, over parental objection, the rights of parents in their natural child upon a finding that the child is "permanently neglected." The New York Family Court Act requires that only a "fair preponderance of the evidence" support that finding. Thus, in New York, the factual certainty required to extinguish the parent-child relationship is no greater than that necessary to award money damages in an ordinary civil action.

Today we hold that the Due Process Clause of the Fourteenth Amendment demands more than this. Before a State may sever completely and irrevocably the rights of parents in their natural child, due process requires that the State support its allegations by at least clear and convincing evidence.

I

A

New York authorizes its officials to remove a child temporarily from his or her home if the child appears "neglected," within the meaning of Art. 10 of the Family Court Act. *See* §§ 1012(f), 1021–1029. Once removed, a child under the age of 18 customarily is placed "in the care of an authorized agency," usually a state institution or a foster home. At that point, "the state's first obligation is to help the family with services to . . . reunite it. . . ." But if convinced that "positive, nurturing parent-child relationships no longer exist," the State may initiate "permanent neglect" proceedings to free the child for adoption.

The State bifurcates its permanent neglect proceeding into "factfinding" and "dispositional" hearings. At the factfinding stage, the State must prove that the child has been "permanently neglected," as defined by FAM. CT. ACT §§ 614.1.(a)-(d) and SOC. SERV. LAW § 384-b.7.(a). The Family Court judge then determines at a subsequent dispositional hearing what placement would serve the child's best interests.

At the factfinding hearing, the State must establish, among other things, that for more than a year after the child entered state custody, the agency "made diligent efforts to encourage and strengthen the parental relationship." The State must further prove that during that same period, the child's natural parents failed "substantially and continuously or repeatedly to maintain contact with or plan for the future of the child although physically and financially able to do so." Should the State support its allegations by "a fair preponderance of the evidence," the child may be declared permanently neglected. Section 611. That declaration empowers the Family Court judge to terminate permanently the natural parents' rights in the child. Termination denies the natural parents physical custody, as well as the rights ever to visit, communicate with, or regain custody of the child.

New York's permanent neglect statute provides natural parents with certain procedural protections.[24] But New York permits its officials to establish "permanent neglect" with less proof than most States require. Thirty-five States, the District of Columbia, and the Virgin Islands currently specify a higher standard of proof, in parental rights termination proceedings, than a "fair preponderance of the evidence." The only analogous federal statute of which we are aware permits termination of parental rights solely upon "evidence beyond a reasonable doubt." Indian Child Welfare Act of 1978, Pub. L. 95-608, § 102(f), 92 Stat. 3072, 25 U. S. C. § 1912(f) (1976 ed., Supp. IV).

---

[24] [2] Most notably, natural parents have a statutory right to the assistance of counsel and of court-appointed counsel if they are indigent. FAM. CT. ACT § 262.(a)(iii).

The question here is whether New York's "fair preponderance of the evidence" standard is constitutionally sufficient.

B

Petitioners John Santosky II and Annie Santosky are the natural parents of Tina and John III. In November 1973, after incidents reflecting parental neglect, respondent Kramer, Commissioner of the Ulster County Department of Social Services, initiated a neglect proceeding under Fam. Ct. Act § 1022 and removed Tina from her natural home. About 10 months later, he removed John III and placed him with foster parents. On the day John was taken, Annie Santosky gave birth to a third child, Jed. When Jed was only three days old, respondent transferred him to a foster home on the ground that immediate removal was necessary to avoid imminent danger to his life or health.

In October 1978, respondent petitioned the Ulster County Family Court to terminate petitioners' parental rights in the three children. Petitioners challenged the constitutionality of the "fair preponderance of the evidence" standard specified in Fam. Ct. Act § 622. The Family Court Judge rejected this constitutional challenge, and weighed the evidence under the statutory standard. While acknowledging that the Santoskys had maintained contact with their children, the judge found those visits "at best superficial and devoid of any real emotional content." After deciding that the agency had made " 'diligent efforts' to encourage and strengthen the parental relationship," he concluded that the Santoskys were incapable, even with public assistance, of planning for the future of their children. The judge later held a dispositional hearing and ruled that the best interests of the three children required permanent termination of the Santoskys' custody.[25]

Petitioners appealed, again contesting the constitutionality of § 622's standard of proof. The New York Supreme Court, Appellate Division, affirmed, holding application of the preponderance-of-the-evidence standard "proper and constitutional." That standard, the court reasoned, "recognizes and seeks to balance rights possessed by the child . . . with those of the natural parents. . . ."

The New York Court of Appeals then dismissed petitioners' appeal to that court "upon the ground that no substantial constitutional question is directly involved." We granted certiorari to consider petitioners' constitutional claim.

II

Last Term, in *Lassiter v. Department of Social Services*, this Court, by a 5-4 vote, held that the Fourteenth Amendment's Due Process Clause does not require the appointment of counsel for indigent parents in every parental status termination proceeding. The case casts light, however, on the two central questions here — whether process is constitutionally due a natural

---

[25] [18] Since respondent Kramer took custody of Tina, John III, and Jed, the Santoskys have had two other children, James and Jeremy. The State has taken no action to remove these younger children. At oral argument, counsel for respondents replied affirmatively when asked whether he was asserting that petitioners were "unfit to handle the three older ones but not unfit to handle the two younger ones."

parent at a State's parental rights termination proceeding, and, if so, what process is due.

In *Lassiter*, it was "not disputed that state intervention to terminate the relationship between [a parent] and [the] child must be accomplished by procedures meeting the requisites of the Due Process Clause." The absence of dispute reflected this Court's historical recognition that freedom of personal choice in matters of family life is a fundamental liberty interest protected by the Fourteenth Amendment.

The fundamental liberty interest of natural parents in the care, custody, and management of their child does not evaporate simply because they have not been model parents or have lost temporary custody of their child to the State. Even when blood relationships are strained, parents retain a vital interest in preventing the irretrievable destruction of their family life. If anything, persons faced with forced dissolution of their parental rights have a more critical need for procedural protections than do those resisting state intervention into ongoing family affairs. When the State moves to destroy weakened familial bonds, it must provide the parents with fundamentally fair procedures.

In *Lassiter*, the Court and three dissenters agreed that the nature of the process due in parental rights termination proceedings turns on a balancing of the "three distinct factors" specified in *Mathews v. Eldridge*: the private interests affected by the proceeding; the risk of error created by the State's chosen procedure; and the countervailing governmental interest supporting use of the challenged procedure. While the respective *Lassiter* opinions disputed whether those factors should be weighed against a presumption disfavoring appointed counsel for one not threatened with loss of physical liberty, that concern is irrelevant here. Unlike the Court's right-to-counsel rulings, its decisions concerning constitutional burdens of proof have not turned on any presumption favoring any particular standard. To the contrary, the Court has engaged in a straightforward consideration of the factors identified in *Eldridge* to determine whether a particular standard of proof in a particular proceeding satisfies due process.

In *Addington v. Texas*, the Court, by a unanimous vote of the participating Justices, declared: "The function of a standard of proof, as that concept is embodied in the Due Process Clause and in the realm of factfinding, is to 'instruct the factfinder concerning the degree of confidence our society thinks he should have in the correctness of factual conclusions for a particular type of adjudication.'" *Addington* teaches that, in any given proceeding, the minimum standard of proof tolerated by the due process requirement reflects not only the weight of the private and public interests affected, but also a societal judgment about how the risk of error should be distributed between the litigants.

Thus, while private parties may be interested intensely in a civil dispute over money damages, application of a "fair preponderance of the evidence" standard indicates both society's "minimal concern with the outcome," and a conclusion that the litigants should "share the risk of error in roughly equal fashion." When the State brings a criminal action to deny a defendant liberty or life, however, "the interests of the defendant are of such magnitude that historically and without any explicit constitutional requirement they have been protected by standards of proof designed to exclude as nearly as possible the likelihood of an erroneous judgment." The stringency of the "beyond a reasonable doubt" standard bespeaks the "weight and gravity" of the private interest affected, society's interest in avoiding erroneous convictions, and a judgment that those interests together require that "society [impose] almost the entire risk of error upon itself."

The "minimum requirements [of procedural due process] being a matter of federal law, they are not diminished by the fact that the State may have specified its own procedures that it may deem adequate for determining the preconditions to adverse official action." Moreover, the degree of proof required in a particular type of proceeding "is the kind of question which has traditionally been left to the judiciary to resolve." "In cases involving individual rights, whether criminal or civil, '[the] standard of proof [at a minimum] reflects the value society places on individual liberty.'"

This Court has mandated an intermediate standard of proof — "clear and convincing evidence" — when the individual interests at stake in a state proceeding are both "particularly important" and "more substantial than mere loss of money." Notwithstanding "the state's 'civil labels and good intentions,'" the Court has deemed this level of certainty necessary to preserve fundamental fairness in a variety of government-initiated proceedings that threaten the individual involved with "a significant deprivation of liberty" or "stigma."

In *Lassiter*, to be sure, the Court held that fundamental fairness may be maintained in parental rights termination proceedings even when some procedures are mandated only on a case-by-case basis, rather than through rules of general application. But this Court never has approved case-by-case determination of the proper *standard of proof* for a given proceeding. Standards of proof, like other "procedural due process rules[,] are shaped by the risk of error inherent in the truth-finding process as applied to the *generality of cases*, not the rare exceptions." Since the litigants and the factfinder must know at the outset of a given proceeding how the risk of error will be allocated, the standard of proof necessarily must be calibrated in advance. Retrospective case-by-case review cannot preserve fundamental fairness when a class of proceedings is governed by a constitutionally defective evidentiary standard.

III

In parental rights termination proceedings, the private interest affected is commanding; the risk of error from using a preponderance standard is substantial; and the countervailing governmental interest favoring that standard is comparatively slight. Evaluation of the three *Eldridge* factors compels the conclusion that use of a "fair preponderance of the evidence" standard in such proceedings is inconsistent with due process.

A

"The extent to which procedural due process must be afforded the recipient is influenced by the extent to which he may be 'condemned to suffer grievous loss.'" Whether the loss threatened by a particular type of proceeding is sufficiently grave to warrant more than average certainty on the part of the factfinder turns on both the nature of the private interest threatened and the permanency of the threatened loss.

Lassiter declared it "plain beyond the need for multiple citation" that a natural parent's "desire for and right to 'the companionship, care, custody, and management of his or her children'" is an interest far more precious than any property right. When the State initiates a parental rights termination proceeding, it seeks not merely to infringe that fundamental liberty interest, but to end it. 'If the State prevails, it will have worked a unique kind of deprivation. . . . A parent's interest in the accuracy and justice of the decision to terminate his or her parental status is, therefore, a commanding one."

In government-initiated proceedings to determine juvenile delinquency, civil commitment, deportation, and denaturalization, this Court has identified losses of individual liberty sufficiently serious to warrant imposition of an elevated burden of proof. Yet juvenile delinquency adjudications, civil commitment, deportation, and denaturalization, at least to a degree, are all *reversible* official actions. Once affirmed on appeal, a New York decision terminating parental rights is *final* and irrevocable. Few forms of state action are both so severe and so irreversible.

Thus, the first *Eldridge* factor — the private interest affected — weighs heavily against use of the preponderance standard at a state-initiated permanent neglect proceeding. We do not deny that the child and his foster parents are also deeply interested in the outcome of that contest. But at the factfinding stage of the New York proceeding, the focus emphatically is not on them.

The factfinding does not purport — and is not intended — to balance the child's interest in a normal family home against the parents' interest in raising the child. Nor does it purport to determine whether the natural parents or the foster parents would provide the better home. Rather, the factfinding hearing pits the State directly against the parents. The State alleges that the natural parents are at fault. The questions disputed and decided are what the State did — "made diligent efforts," — and what the natural parents did not do — "maintain contact with or plan for the future of the child." The State marshals an array of public resources to prove its case and disprove the parents' case. Victory by the State not only makes termination of parental rights possible; it entails a judicial determination that the parents are unfit to raise their own children.

At the factfinding, the State cannot presume that a child and his parents are adversaries. After the State has established parental unfitness at that initial proceeding, the court may assume at the *dispositional* stage that the interests of the child and the natural parents do diverge. But until the State proves parental unfitness, the child and his parents share a vital interest in preventing erroneous termination of their natural relationship.[26] Thus, at the

26 [11] For a child, the consequences of termination of his natural parents' rights may well be far-reaching. In Colorado, for example, it has been noted: "The child loses the right of support and maintenance, for which he may thereafter be dependent upon society; the right to inherit; and all other rights inherent in the legal parent-child relationship, not just for [a limited] period . . . , but forever." *In re K. S.*, 33 Colo. App. 72, 76, 515 P. 2d 130, 133 (1973).

factfinding, the interests of the child and his natural parents coincide to favor use of error-reducing procedures.

However substantial the foster parents' interests may be, they are not implicated directly in the factfinding stage of a state-initiated permanent neglect proceeding against the natural parents. If authorized, the foster parents may pit their interests directly against those of the natural parents by initiating their own permanent neglect proceeding. Alternatively, the foster parents can make their case for custody at the dispositional stage of a state-initiated proceeding, where the judge already has decided the issue of permanent neglect and is focusing on the placement that would serve the child's best interests. For the foster parents, the State's failure to prove permanent neglect may prolong the delay and uncertainty until their foster child is freed for adoption. But for the natural parents, a finding of permanent neglect can cut off forever their rights in their child. Given this disparity of consequence, we have no difficulty finding that the balance of private interests strongly favors heightened procedural protections.

B

Under *Mathews v. Eldridge*, we next must consider both the risk of erroneous deprivation of private interests resulting from use of a "fair preponderance standard and the likelihood that a higher evidentiary standard would reduce that risk. Since the factfinding phase of a permanent neglect proceeding is an adversary contest between the State and the natural parents, the relevant question is whether a preponderance standard fairly allocates the risk of an erroneous factfinding between these two parties.

In New York, the factfinding stage of a state-initiated permanent neglect proceeding bears many of the indicia of a criminal trial. The Commissioner of Social Services charges the parents with permanent neglect. They are served by summons. The factfinding hearing is conducted pursuant to formal rules of evidence. The State, the parents, and the child are all represented by counsel. The State seeks to establish a series of historical facts about the intensity of its agency's efforts to reunite the family, the infrequency and insubstantiality of the parents' contacts with their child, and the parents' inability or unwillingness to formulate a plan for the child's future. The attorneys submit documentary evidence, and call witnesses who are subject to cross-examination. Based on all the evidence, the judge then determines whether the State has proved the statutory elements of permanent neglect by a fair preponderance of the evidence.

At such a proceeding, numerous factors combine to magnify the risk of erroneous factfinding. Permanent neglect proceedings employ imprecise substantive standards that leave determinations unusually open to the subjective values of the judge. In appraising the nature and quality of a complex series of encounters among the agency, the parents, and the child, the court possesses unusual discretion to underweigh probative facts that

---

Some losses cannot be measured. In this case, for example, Jed Santosky was removed from his natural parents' custody when he was only three days old; the judge's finding of permanent neglect effectively foreclosed the possibility that Jed would ever know his natural parents.

might favor the parent. Because parents subject to termination proceedings are often poor, uneducated, or members of minority groups, such proceedings are often vulnerable to judgments based on cultural or class bias.

The State's ability to assemble its case almost inevitably dwarfs the parents' ability to mount a defense. No predetermined limits restrict the sums an agency may spend in prosecuting a given termination proceeding. The State's attorney usually will be expert on the issues contested and the procedures employed at the factfinding hearing, and enjoys full access to all public records concerning the family. The State may call on experts in family relations, psychology, and medicine to bolster its case. Furthermore, the primary witnesses at the hearing will be the agency's own professional caseworkers whom the State has empowered both to investigate the family situation and to testify against the parents. Indeed, because the child is already in agency custody, the State even has the power to shape the historical events that form the basis for termination.

The disparity between the adversaries' litigation resources is matched by a striking asymmetry in their litigation options. Unlike criminal defendants, natural parents have no "double jeopardy" defense against repeated state termination efforts. If the State initially fails to win termination, as New York did here, it always can try once again to cut off the parents' rights after gathering more or better evidence. Yet even when the parents have attained the level of fitness required by the State, they have no similar means by which they can forestall future termination efforts.

Coupled with a "fair preponderance of the evidence" standard, these factors create a significant prospect of erroneous termination. A standard of proof that by its very terms demands consideration of the quantity, rather than the quality, of the evidence may misdirect the factfinder in the marginal case. Given the weight of the private interests at stake, the social cost of even occasional error is sizable.

Raising the standard of proof would have both practical and symbolic consequences. The Court has long considered the heightened standard of proof used in criminal prosecutions to be "a prime instrument for reducing the risk of convictions resting on factual error." An elevated standard of proof in a parental rights termination proceeding would alleviate "the possible risk that a factfinder might decide to [deprive] an individual based solely on a few isolated instances of unusual conduct [or] . . . idiosyncratic behavior." "Increasing the burden of proof is one way to impress the factfinder with the importance of the decision and thereby perhaps to reduce the chances that inappropriate" terminations will be ordered.

The Appellate Division approved New York's preponderance standard on the ground that it properly "balanced rights possessed by the child . . . with those of the natural parents. . . . By so saying, the court suggested that a preponderance standard properly allocates the risk of error *between* the parents and the child. That view is fundamentally mistaken.

The court's theory assumes that termination of the natural parents' rights invariably will benefit the child.[27] Yet we have noted above that the parents and the child share an interest in avoiding erroneous termination. Even accepting the court's assumption, we cannot agree with its conclusion that a preponderance standard fairly distributes the risk of error between parent and child. Use of that standard reflects the judgment that society is nearly neutral between erroneous termination of parental rights and erroneous failure to terminate those rights. For the child, the likely consequence of an erroneous failure to terminate is preservation of an uneasy status quo. For the natural parents, however, the consequence of an erroneous termination is the unnecessary destruction of their natural family. A standard that allocates the risk of error nearly equally between those two outcomes does not reflect properly their relative severity.

C

Two state interests are at stake in parental rights termination proceedings — a *parens patriae* interest in preserving and promoting the welfare of the child and a fiscal and administrative interest in reducing the cost and burden of such proceedings. A standard of proof more strict than preponderance of the evidence is consistent with both interests.

"Since the State has an urgent interest in the welfare of the child, it shares the parent's interest in an accurate and just decision" at the *factfinding* proceeding. As *parens patriae*, the State's goal is to provide the child with a permanent home. Yet while there is still reason to believe that positive, nurturing parent-child relationships exist, the *parens patriae* interest favors preservation, not severance, of natural familial bonds. "[The] State registers no gain towards its declared goals when it separates children from the custody of fit parents." *Stanley v. Illinois,* 405 U.S. at 652.

The State's interest in finding the child an alternative permanent home arises only "when it is *clear* that the natural parent cannot or will not provide a normal family home for the child." Soc. Serv. Law § 384-b.1(a)(iv) (emphasis added). At the factfinding, that goal is served by procedures that promote an accurate determination of whether the natural parents can and will provide a normal home.

Unlike a constitutional requirement of hearings, or court-appointed counsel, a stricter standard of proof would reduce factual error without imposing substantial fiscal burdens upon the State. As we have observed, 35 States

---

[27] [15] This is a hazardous assumption at best. Even when a child's natural home is imperfect, permanent removal from that home will not necessarily improve his welfare. *See, e.g.,* Wald, *State Intervention on Behalf of "Neglected" Children: A Search for Realistic Standards,* 27 Stan. L. Rev. 985, 993 (1975) ("In fact, under current practice, coercive intervention frequently results in placing a child in a more detrimental situation than he would be in without intervention").

Nor does termination of parental rights necessarily ensure adoption. *See* Brief for Community Action for Legal Services, Inc., et al. as *Amici Curiae* 22–23. Even when a child eventually finds an adoptive family, he may spend years moving between state institutions and "temporary" foster placements after his ties to his natural parents have been severed. *See* Smith v. Organization of Foster Families, 431 U.S., at 833–838 (describing the "limbo" of the New York foster care system).

already have adopted a higher standard by statute or court decision without apparent effect on the speed, form, or cost of their factfinding proceedings.

Nor would an elevated standard of proof create any real administrative burdens for the State's factfinders. New York Family Court judges already are familiar with a higher evidentiary standard in other parental rights termination proceedings not involving permanent neglect. New York also demands at least clear and convincing evidence in proceedings of far less moment than parental rights termination proceedings. We cannot believe that it would burden the State unduly to require that its factfinders have the same factual certainty when terminating the parent-child relationship as they must have to suspend a driver's license.

IV

The logical conclusion of this balancing process is that the "fair preponderance of the evidence" standard prescribed by FAM. CT. ACT § 622 violates the Due Process Clause of the Fourteenth Amendment. The Court noted in *Addington*: "The individual should not be asked to share equally with society the risk of error when the possible injury to the individual is significantly greater than any possible harm to the state." Thus, at a parental rights termination proceeding, a near-equal allocation of risk between the parents and the State is constitutionally intolerable. The next question, then, is whether a "beyond a reasonable doubt" or a "clear and convincing" standard is constitutionally mandated.

In *Addington*, the Court concluded that application of a reasonable-doubt standard is inappropriate in civil commitment proceedings for two reasons — because of our hesitation to apply that unique standard "too broadly or casually in non-criminal cases," and because the psychiatric evidence ordinarily adduced at commitment proceedings is rarely susceptible to proof beyond a reasonable doubt.

Like civil commitment hearings, termination proceedings often require the factfinder to evaluate medical and psychiatric testimony, and to decide issues difficult to prove to a level of absolute certainty, such as lack of parental motive, absence of affection between parent and child, and failure of parental foresight and progress. The substantive standards applied vary from State to State. Although Congress found a "beyond a reasonable doubt" standard proper in one type of parental rights termination case, another legislative body might well conclude that a reasonable-doubt standard would erect an unreasonable barrier to state efforts to free permanently neglected children for adoption.

A majority of the States have concluded that a "clear and convincing evidence" standard of proof strikes a fair balance between the rights of the natural parents and the State's legitimate concerns. We hold that such a standard adequately conveys to the factfinder the level of subjective certainty about his factual conclusions necessary to satisfy due process. We further hold that determination of the precise burden equal to or greater than that standard is a matter of state law properly left to state legislatures and state courts.

We, of course, express no view on the merits of petitioners' claims. At a hearing conducted under a constitutionally proper standard, they may or may not prevail. Without deciding the outcome under any of the standards we have approved, we vacate the judgment of the Appellate Division and remand the case for further proceedings not inconsistent with this opinion.

It is so ordered.

JUSTICE REHNQUIST, with whom THE CHIEF JUSTICE, JUSTICE WHITE, and JUSTICE O'CONNOR join, *dissenting.*

I believe that few of us would care to live in a society where every aspect of life was regulated by a single source of law, whether that source be this Court or some other organ of our complex body politic. But today's decision certainly moves us in that direction. By parsing the New York scheme and holding one narrow provision unconstitutional, the majority invites further federal-court intrusion into every facet of state family law. If ever there were an area in which federal courts should heed the admonition of Justice Holmes that "a page of history is worth a volume of logic," it is in the area of domestic relations. This area has been left to the States from time immemorial, and not without good reason.

Equally as troubling is the majority's due process analysis. The Fourteenth Amendment guarantees that a State will treat individuals with "fundamental fairness" whenever its actions infringe their protected liberty or property interests. By adoption of the procedures relevant to this case, New York has created an exhaustive program to assist parents in regaining the custody of their children and to protect parents from the unfair deprivation of their parental rights. And yet the majority's myopic scrutiny of the standard of proof blinds it to the very considerations and procedures which make the New York scheme "fundamentally fair."

I

State intervention in domestic relations has always been an unhappy but necessary feature of life in our organized society. For all of our experience in this area, we have found no fully satisfactory solutions to the painful problem of child abuse and neglect. We have found, however, that leaving the States free to experiment with various remedies has produced novel approaches and promising progress.

Throughout this experience the Court has scrupulously refrained from interfering with state answers to domestic relations questions. "Both theory and the precedents of this Court teach us solicitude for state interests, particularly in the field of family and family-property arrangements." This is not to say that the Court should blink at clear constitutional violations in state statutes, but rather that in this area, of all areas, "substantial weight must be given to the good-faith judgments of the individuals [administering a program] . . . that the procedures they have provided assure fair consideration of the . . . claims of individuals."

This case presents a classic occasion for such solicitude. As will be seen more fully in the next part, New York has enacted a comprehensive plan to *aid* marginal parents in regaining the custody of their child. The central purpose of the New York plan is to reunite divided families. Adoption of the preponderance-of-the-evidence standard represents New York's good-faith effort to balance the interest of parents against the legitimate interests of the child and the State. These earnest efforts by state officials should be given weight in the Court's application of due process principles. "Great constitutional provisions must be administered with caution. Some play must be allowed for the joints of the machine, and it must be remembered that legislatures are ultimate guardians of the liberties and welfare of the people in quite as great a degree as the courts."

The majority may believe that it is adopting a relatively unobtrusive means of ensuring that termination proceedings provide "due process of law." In fact, however, fixing the standard of proof as a matter of federal constitutional law will only lead to further federal-court intervention in state schemes. By holding that due process requires proof by clear and convincing evidence the majority surely cannot mean that any state scheme passes constitutional muster so long as it applies that standard of proof. A state law permitting termination of parental rights upon a showing of neglect by clear and convincing evidence certainly would not be acceptable to the majority if it provided no procedures other than one 30-minute hearing. Similarly, the majority probably would balk at a state scheme that permitted termination of parental rights on a clear and convincing showing merely that such action would be in the best interests of the child.

After fixing the standard of proof, therefore, the majority will be forced to evaluate other aspects of termination proceedings with reference to that point. Having in this case abandoned evaluation of the overall effect of a scheme, and with it the possibility of finding that strict substantive standards or special procedures compensate for a lower burden of proof, the majority's approach will inevitably lead to the federalization of family law. Such a trend will only thwart state searches for better solutions in an area where this Court should encourage state experimentation. "It is one of the happy incidents of the federal system that a single courageous State may, if its citizens choose, serve as a laboratory; and try novel social and economic experiments without risk to the rest of the country. This Court has the power to prevent an experiment." *New State Ice Co. v. Liebmann,* 285 U.S. 262, 311 (1932) (BRANDEIS, J., dissenting). It should not do so in the absence of a clear constitutional violation. As will be seen in the next part, no clear constitutional violation has occurred in this case.

II

. . . .

I do not disagree with the majority's conclusion that the interest of parents in their relationship with their children is sufficiently fundamental to come within the finite class of liberty interests protected by the Fourteenth Amendment. Once it is determined that due process applies, [however,] the question remains what process is due." *Morrissey v. Brewer,* 408 U.S. 471, 481 (1972). It is the majority's answer to this question with which I disagree.

A

. . . .

[I]it is obvious that a proper due process inquiry cannot be made by focusing upon one narrow provision of the challenged statutory scheme. Such a focus threatens to overlook factors which may introduce constitutionally adequate protections into a particular government action. Courts must examine *all* procedural protections offered by the State, and must assess the *cumulative* effect of such safeguards. As we have stated before, courts must consider "the fairness and reliabilitys of the existing . . . procedures" before holding that the Constitution requires more. Only through such a broad inquiry may courts determine whether a challenged governmental action satisfies the due process requirement of "fundamental fairness."

. . . .

[The dissent pointed out that Tina Apel, the oldest of petitioners' five children, was removed from their custody by court order in November 1973 when she was two years old. Removal proceedings were commenced in response to complaints by neighbors and reports from a local hospital that Tina had suffered injuries in petitioners' home including a fractured left femur, treated with a homemade splint; bruises on the upper arms, forehead, flank, and spine; and abrasions of the upper leg. The following summer John Santosky III, petitioners' second oldest child, was also removed from petitioners' custody. John, who was less than one year old at the time, was admitted to the hospital suffering malnutrition, bruises on the eye and forehead, cuts on the foot, blisters on the hand, and multiple pin pricks on the back. Jed Santosky, the third oldest of petitioners' children, was removed from his parents' custody when only three days old as a result of the abusive treatment of the two older children.

The dissent reviewed the New York statutory scheme and argued that when considered as a whole, it meets the requirement of fundamental fairness and comports with the requirements of due process].

As this account demonstrates, the State's extraordinary 4-year effort to reunite petitioners' family was not just unsuccessful, it was altogether rebuffed by parents unwilling to improve their circumstances sufficiently to permit a return of their children. At every step of this protracted process petitioners were accorded those procedures and protections which traditionally have been required by due process of law. Moreover, from the beginning to the end of this sad story all judicial determinations were made by one Family Court Judge. After four and one-half years of involvement with petitioners, more than seven complete hearings, and additional periodic supervision of the State's rehabilitative efforts, the judge no doubt was intimately familiar with this case and the prospects for petitioners' rehabilitation. It is inconceivable to me that these procedures were "fundamentally unfair" to petitioners. Only by its obsessive focus on the standard of proof and its almost complete disregard of the facts of this case does the majority find otherwise. As the discussion above indicates, however, such a focus does not comport with the flexible standard of fundamental fairness embodied in the Due Process Clause of the Fourteenth Amendment.

B

In addition to the basic fairness of the process afforded petitioners, the standard of proof chosen by New York clearly reflects a constitutionally permissible balance of the interests at stake in this case. . . .

On one side is the interest of parents in a continuation of the family unit and the raising of their own children. The importance of this interest cannot easily be overstated. Few consequences of judicial action are so grave as the severance of natural family ties. Even the convict committed to prison and thereby deprived of his physical liberty often retains the love and support of family members. "This Court's decisions have by now made plain beyond the need for multiple citation that a parent's desire for and right to 'the companionship, care, custody, and management of his or her children' is an important interest that 'undeniably warrants deference and, absent a powerful countervailing interest, protection.' " In creating the scheme at issue in this case, the New York Legislature was expressly aware of this right of parents "to bring up their own children."

On the other side of the termination proceeding are the often countervailing interests of the child.[28] A stable, loving homelife is essential to a child's physical, emotional, and spiritual well-being. It requires no citation of authority to assert that children who are abused in their youth generally face extraordinary problems developing into responsible, productive citizens. The same can be said of children who, though not physically or emotionally abused, are passed from one foster home to another with no constancy of love, trust, or discipline. If the Family Court makes an incorrect factual determination resulting in a failure to terminate a parent-child relationship which rightfully should be ended, the child involved must return either to an abusive home[29] or to the often unstable world of foster care.[30] The reality of these risks is

---

[28] [13] . . . The child has an interest in the outcome of the factfinding hearing independent of that of the parent. To be sure, "the child and his parents share a vital interest in preventing *erroneous* termination of their natural relationship." (emphasis added). But the child's interest in a continuation of the family unit exists only to the extent that such a continuation would not be harmful to him. An error *in the factfinding hearing* that results in a failure to terminate a parent-child relationship which rightfully should be terminated may well detrimentally affect the child. . . .

[29] [14] The record in this case illustrates the problems that may arise when a child is returned to an abusive home. Eighteen months after Tina, petitioners' oldest child, was first removed from petitioner's home, she was returned to the home on a trial basis. Katherine Weiss, a supervisor in the Child Protective Unit of the Ulster County Child Welfare Department, later testified in Family Court that "[the] attempt to return Tina to her home just totally blew up." When asked to explain what happened, Mrs. Weiss testified that "there were instances on the record in this court of Mr. Santosky's abuse of his wife, alleged abuse of the children and proven neglect of the children." Tina again was removed from the home, this time along with John and Jed.

[30] [15] . . . "Over fifty percent of the children in foster care have been in this 'temporary' status for more than two years; over thirty percent for more than five years. During this time, many children are placed in a sequence of ill-suited foster homes, denying them the consistent support and nurturing that they so desperately need." Besharov, *State Intervention To Protect Children: New York's Definition of "Child Abuse" and "Child Neglect,"* 26 N. Y. L. S. L. Rev. 723, 770–771 (1981) (footnotes omitted). In this case, petitioners' three children have been in foster care for more than four years, one child since he was only three days old. Failure to terminate petitioners' parental rights will only mean a continuation of this unsatisfactory situation.

magnified by the fact that the only families faced with termination actions are those which have voluntarily surrendered custody of their child to the State, or, as in this case, those from which the child has been removed by judicial action because of threatened irreparable injury through abuse or neglect. Permanent neglect findings also occur only in families where the child has been in foster care for at least one year.

In addition to the child's interest in a normal homelife, "the State has an urgent interest in the welfare of the child." *Lassiter v. Department of Social Services.* Few could doubt that the most valuable resource of a self-governing society is its population of children who will one day become adults and themselves assume the responsibility of self-governance. "A democratic society rests, for its continuance, upon the healthy, well-rounded growth of young people into full maturity as citizens, with all that implies." *Prince v. Massachusetts.* Thus, "the whole community" has an interest "that children be both safeguarded from abuses and given opportunities for growth into free and independent well-developed . . . citizens."

When, in the context of a permanent neglect termination proceeding, the interests of the child and the State in a stable, nurturing homelife are balanced against the interests of the parents in the rearing of their child, it cannot be said that either set of interests is so clearly paramount as to require that the risk of error be allocated to one side or the other. Accordingly, a State constitutionally may conclude that the risk of error should be borne in roughly equal fashion by use of the preponderance-of-the-evidence standard of proof. This is precisely the balance which has been struck by the New York Legislature: "It is the intent of the legislature in enacting this section to provide procedures not only assuring that the rights of the natural parent are protected, but also, where positive, nurturing parent-child relationships no longer exist, furthering the best interests, needs, and rights of the child by terminating the parental rights and freeing the child for adoption."

III

For the reasons heretofore stated, I believe that the Court today errs in concluding that the New York standard of proof in parental-rights termination proceedings violates due process of law. The decision disregards New York's earnest efforts to *aid* parents in regaining the custody of their children and a host of procedural protections placed around parental rights and interests. The Court finds a constitutional violation only by a tunnel-vision application of due process principles that altogether loses sight of the unmistakable fairness of the New York procedure.

Even more worrisome, today's decision cavalierly rejects the considered judgment of the New York Legislature in an area traditionally entrusted to state care. The Court thereby begins, I fear, a trend of federal intervention in state family law matters which surely will stifle creative responses to vexing problems. Accordingly, I dissent.

NOTES AND QUESTIONS

1. *Lassiter v. Department of Social Services*, 452 U.S. 18 (1981), held that due process does not require that indigent parents in termination proceedings have counsel appointed in every case, but only on a case-by-case basis, taking into account the nature of the case and the parent's ability to go forward without counsel. *See also M.L.B. v. S.L.J.*, 519 U.S. 102 (1996) (parent whose rights have been terminated cannot be denied a right to an appeal because she lacks the means to pay for record preparation fees).

2. Did the *Santosky* majority correctly discern and correctly weigh the interest of the child in the termination proceeding? Were the interests of the parent and child in conflict in this case?

3. One factor that courts consider in termination hearings is whether the cause of the deprivation is likely to continue or be remedied. *See* OCGA § 15-11-94 (a)(3). In *In the Interest of S.R.B.*, 614 S.E.2d 150 (Ga. App. 2005), the court stated that it was entitled to discount the mother's promise to obtain stable housing and employment. "The decision as to a child's future must rest on more than positive promises which are contrary to the negative past fact."

[F]   Foster Care

When children are removed from the parental home because of abuse and neglect or because the parent has voluntarily relinquished custody, the state may place the children in the foster care system with foster parents who care for the child with compensation from the state. Although foster care is intended to be an interim placement for the child until they are able to return home to their parents or other relatives or until they are adopted, some children may remain in foster care indefinitely. Some children meet with abuse in foster care that is similar to that which precipitated their removal from the parental home, but other children develop deep emotional ties to their foster parents. Do foster parents have any rights when the state seeks to remove a foster child from the home of the foster parent? In 1977 the Supreme Court heard the claim of a foster parent group that the Due Process Clause requires a hearing before the state can remove a child from a foster home if the child has been in the foster home for a substantial amount of time. *See Smith v. Organization of Foster Families for Equality and Reform*, 431 U.S. 816 (1977). The Court, in an opinion by Justice BRENNAN, discussed the purported interest of the foster parent in the familial relationship with the foster child. The court determined that even if the foster parent had a protected constitutional interest, the state's hearing procedure satisfied the requirements of due process. The following is an excerpt from that opinion:

> Our first inquiry is whether appellees have asserted interests within the Fourteenth Amendment's protection of "liberty" and "property." The appellees have not renewed in this Court their contention, rejected by the District Court, that the realities of the foster-care system in

New York gave them a justified expectation amounting to a "property" interest that their status as foster parents would be continued. Our inquiry is therefore narrowed to the question whether their asserted interests are within the "liberty" protected by the Fourteenth Amendment.

The appellees' basic contention is that when a child has lived in a foster home for a year or more, a psychological tie is created between the child and the foster parents which constitutes the foster family the true "psychological family" of the child. *See* J. GOLDSTEIN, A. FREUD, & A. SOLNIT, BEYOND THE BEST INTERESTS OF THE CHILD (1973). That family, they argue, has a "liberty interest" in its survival as a family protected by the Fourteenth Amendment. Upon this premise they conclude that the foster child cannot be removed without a prior hearing satisfying due process. Appointed counsel for the children, however, disagrees, and has consistently argued that the foster parents have no such liberty interest independent of the interests of the foster children, and that the best interests of the children would not be served by procedural protections beyond those already provided by New York law. The intervening natural parents of children in foster care also oppose the foster parents, arguing that recognition of the procedural right claimed would undercut both the substantive family law of New York, which favors the return of children to their natural parents as expeditiously as possible, and their constitutionally protected right of family privacy, by forcing them to submit to a hearing and defend their rights to their children before the children could be returned to them.

The District Court did not reach appellees' contention "that the foster home is entitled to the same constitutional deference as that long granted to the more traditional biological family." Rather than "reach[ing] out to decide such novel questions," the court based its holding that "the pre-removal procedures presently employed by the state are constitutionally defective," not on the recognized liberty interest in family privacy, but on an independent right of the foster child "to be heard before being condemned to suffer grievous loss."

The court apparently reached this conclusion by weighing the "harmful consequences of a precipitous and perhaps improvident decision to remove a child from his foster family," and concluding that this disruption of the stable relationships needed by the child might constitute "grievous loss." But if this was the reasoning applied by the District Court, it must be rejected. Authority exists that such a finding does not, in and of itself, implicate the due process guarantee. What was said in *Board of Regents v. Roth*, applies equally well here:

> The District Court decided that procedural due process guarantees apply in this case by assessing and balancing the weights of the particular interests involved. . . . [A] weighing process has long been a part of any determination of the *form* of hearing required in particular situations by procedural due process. But, to determine whether due process requirements apply in the first

place, we must look not to the "weight" but to the nature of the interest at stake. . . . We must look to see if the interest is within the Fourteenth Amendment's protection of liberty and property.[31]

We therefore turn to appellees' assertion that they have a constitutionally protected liberty interest — in the words of the District Court, a 'right to familial privacy,' — in the integrity of their family unit. This assertion clearly presents difficulties.

It is, of course, true that 'freedom of personal choice in matters of . . . family life is one of the liberties protected by the Due Process Clause of the Fourteenth Amendment.' *Cleveland Board of Education v. LaFleur.* There does exist a "private realm of family life which the state cannot enter," *Prince v. Massachusetts,* that has been afforded both substantive and procedural protection. But is the relation of foster parent to foster child sufficiently akin to the concept of "family" recognized in our precedents to merit similar protection?[32] Although considerable difficulty has attended the task of defining "family" for purposes of the Due Process Clause, *see Moore v. East Cleveland,* pp. 494 (plurality opinion of POWELL, J.); pp. 531 (STEWART, J., dissenting); pp. 541 (WHITE, J., dissenting), we are not without guides to some of the elements that define the concept of "family" and contribute to its place in our society.

First, the usual understanding of "family" implies biological relationships, and most decisions treating the relation between parent and child have stressed this element. . . .

---

[31] [44] Appellants argue, with the dissenting judge below, that in any event appellee foster parents have no standing to rely upon a supposed right of the foster *children* to avoid "grievous loss," because the foster children are independently represented by court-appointed counsel, who has consistently opposed the relief requested by appellees, and denied that the children have any such right.

This argument misunderstands the peculiar circumstances of this lawsuit. Ordinarily, it is true, a party would not have standing to assert the rights of another, himself a party in the litigation; the third party himself can decide how best to protect his interests. But children usually lack the capacity to make that sort of decision, and thus their interest is ordinarily represented in litigation by parents or guardians. In this case, however, the State, the natural parents, and the foster parents, all of whom share some portion of the responsibility for guardianship of the child, are parties, and all contend that the position they advocate is most in accord with the rights and interests of the children. In this situation, the District Court properly appointed independent counsel to represent the children, so that the court could have the benefit of an independent advocate for the welfare of the children, unprejudiced by the possibly conflicting interests and desires of the other parties. It does not follow, however, that independent counsel, who is not a guardian *ad litem* of the children, is solely authorized to determine the children's best interest.

No party denies, or could deny, that there is an Art. III "case or controversy" between the foster parents and the defendant state officials concerning the validity of the removal procedures. Accordingly, their standing to raise the rights of the children in their attack on those procedures is a prudential question. We believe it would be most imprudent to leave entirely to court-appointed counsel the choices that neither the named foster children nor the class they represent are capable of making for themselves, especially in litigation in which all parties have sufficient attributes of guardianship that their views on the rights of the children should at least be heard.

[32] [48] Of course, recognition of a liberty interest in foster families for purposes of the procedural protections of the Due Process Clause would not necessarily require that foster families be treated as fully equivalent to biological families for purposes of substantive due process review.

A biological relationship is not present in the case of the usual foster family. But biological relationships are not exclusive determination of the existence of a family. The basic foundation of the family in our society, the marriage relationship, is of course not a matter of blood relation. Yet its importance has been strongly emphasized in our cases. . . .

Thus the importance of the familial relationship, to the individuals involved and to the society, stems from the emotional attachments that derive from the intimacy of daily association, and from the role it plays in 'promot[ing] a way of life' through the instruction of children, as well as from the fact of blood relationship. No one would seriously dispute that a deeply loving and interdependent relationship between an adult and a child in his or her care may exist even in the absence of blood relationship.[33] At least where a child has been placed in foster care as an infant, has never known his natural parents, and has remained continuously for several years in the care of the same foster parents, it is natural that the foster family should hold the same place in the emotional life of the foster child, and fulfill the same socializing functions, as a natural family.[34] For this reason, we cannot dismiss the foster family as a mere collection of unrelated individuals.

But there are also important distinctions between the foster family and the natural family. First, unlike the earlier cases recognizing a right to family privacy, the State here seeks to interfere, not with a relationship having its origins entirely apart from the power of the State, but rather with a foster family which has its source in state law and contractual arrangements. The individual's freedom to marry and reproduce is 'older than the Bill of Rights.' Accordingly, unlike the property interests that are also protected by the Fourteenth Amendment, the liberty interest in family privacy has its source, and its contours are ordinarily to be sought, not in state law, but in intrinsic human rights, as they have been understood in 'this Nation's history and tradition.' Here, however, whatever emotional ties may develop between foster parent and foster child have their origins in an arrangement in which the State has been a partner from the outset. While the Court has recognized that liberty interests may in some cases arise from positive-law sources, in such a case, and particularly where, as here, the claimed interest derives from a knowingly assumed contractual relation with the State, it is appropriate to ascertain from state law the expectations and entitlements of the parties. In this case,

---

[33] [51] Adoption, for example, is recognized as the legal equivalent of biological parenthood.

[34] [52] The briefs dispute at some length the validity of the "psychological parent" theory propounded in J. Goldstein, A. Freud, & A. Solnit, BEYOND THE BEST INTERESTS OF THE CHILD (1973). That book, on which appellee foster parents relied to some extent in the District Court, is indeed controversial. *See, e.g.,* Strauss & Strauss, Book Review, 74 COLUM. L. REV. 996 (1974); Kadushin, *Beyond the Best Interests of the Child: An Essay Review*, 48 SOC. SERV. REV. 508, 512 (1974). But this case turns, not on the disputed validity of any particular psychological theory, but on the legal consequences of the undisputed fact that the emotional ties between foster parent and foster child are in many cases quite close, and undoubtedly in some as close as those existing in biological families.

the limited recognition accorded to the foster family by the New York statutes and the contracts executed by the foster parents argue against any but the most limited constitutional "liberty" in the foster family.

A second consideration related to this is that ordinarily procedural protection may be afforded to a liberty interest of one person without derogating from the substantive liberty of another. Here, however, such a tension is virtually unavoidable. Under New York law, the natural parent of a foster child in voluntary placement has an absolute right to the return of his child in the absence of a court order obtainable only upon compliance with rigorous substantive and procedural standards, which reflect the constitutional protection accorded the natural family. Moreover, the natural parent initially gave up his child to the State only on the express understanding that the child would be returned in those circumstances. These rights are difficult to reconcile with the liberty interest in the foster family relationship claimed by appellees. It is one thing to say that individuals may acquire a liberty interest against arbitrary governmental interference in the family-like associations into which they have freely entered, even in the absence of biological connection or state-law recognition of the relationship. It is quite another to say that one may acquire such an interest in the face of another's constitutionally recognized liberty interest that derives from blood relationship, state-law sanction, and basic human right — an interest the foster parent has recognized by contract from the outset. Whatever liberty interest might otherwise exist in the foster family as an institution, that interest must be substantially attenuated where the proposed removal from the foster family is to return the child to his natural parents.

As this discussion suggests, appellees' claim to a constitutionally protected liberty interest raises complex and novel questions. It is unnecessary for us to resolve those questions definitively in this case, however, for, like the District Court, we conclude that 'narrower grounds exist to support' our reversal. We are persuaded that, even on the assumption that appellees have a protected 'liberty interest,' the District Court erred in holding that the preremoval procedures presently employed by the State are constitutionally defective.

Smith v. O.F.F.E.R., 431 U.S. at 838–47.

———

NOTES AND QUESTIONS

1. How should the courts resolve the question whether foster parents have a constitutionally protected interest in the relationship with their foster children? The lower courts generally have not been receptive to the claim. *See, e.g., Kyees v. County Department of Public Welfare,* 600 F.2d 693 (7th Cir. 1979). *But see In re Jonathan G.,* 482 S.E.2d 893 (W. Va. App. 1996) (based

on statutory grounds, foster parents who had custody of an abused child for over two years were entitled to limited participation in parental termination proceedings).

2. Do children have a liberty interest in remaining in a stable, loving home with adults who have acted in a parental capacity for a substantial amount of time? Should children be able to bring parental termination suits in their own right?

3. Because the underlying premise of foster care is that it is to be an interim placement until the child can be returned to his or her parents or put up for adoption, some state agencies traditionally had specific policies that prohibited the foster parents from adopting the children in their care. One asserted reason for this policy was the concern that foster parents, because the arrangement is temporary, must remain somewhat detached so that they will be able and willing to facilitate the child's return to the biological parent. More recently, however, some states have passed statutes that allow foster parents to adopt their foster children, and some courts have been more receptive to the idea than in the past. *See, e.g.,* N.Y. Soc. Services Law § 383 (giving preference to foster parents who have had child in their care for over 12 months). In addition, Congress has enacted the Adoption and Safe Families Act of 1997, 42 U.S.C. § 675(5) (2005) (AFSA), which encourages states to expedite adoption for abused and neglected children. ASFA includes provisions to reduce the numbers of foster care children and to alleviate "foster care drift." It provides incentives for increasing the number of children adopted out of foster care and reduces inter-jurisdictional barriers that delay adoptions across state lines. ASFA also set forth new timelines regulating the amount of time children can remain in foster care before being placed for adoption. Timelines under previous legislation, The Child Welfare Act, required that every child in foster care receive a dispositional hearing within the first eighteen months in state custody. ASFA changed "dispositional" hearings to "permanency" hearings and requires states to hold these hearings within the child's first twelve months in foster care and at least once every twelve months as long as the child remains in state custody. ASFA requires that every child in foster care have a permanent plan within twelve months, and it requires states to petition a court for termination of parental rights once a child has resided in state custody for fifteen of the most recent twenty-two months. 42 U.S.C. § 675(5)(E). A state can be excused from this obligation if: (1) the state has placed the child in the care of a relative; (2) the state can provide a compelling reason for maintaining the parental relationship; or (3) the state has failed to provide reasonable efforts to reunite the family. *Id.*

ASFA attempted to explain the meaning of "reasonable efforts" by amending sections of the Social Security Act. Amended section 671(a)(15) now requires that, in making reasonable efforts to reunite the family and in determining whether reasonable efforts had been made, "the child's health and safety shall be the paramount concern." 42 U.S.C. § 671(a)(15)(A). "Reasonable efforts shall be made to preserve and reunify families: (i) prior to the placement of a child in foster care, to prevent or eliminate the need for removing the child from the child's home; and (ii) to make it possible for a child to safely return to the child's home." 42 U.S.C. § 671(a)(15)(B). The state must make reasonable efforts "to place the child in a timely manner in accordance with the permanency plan, and to complete whatever steps are necessary to finalize the permanent placement of the child." 42 U.S.C. § 671(a)(15)(C). The ASFA regulations require a judicial determination that the state has made reasonable efforts to finalize a permanency plan. 45 C.F.R. § 1356.21(b)(3) (2005).

A parent's current and previous conduct may excuse states from making reasonable efforts. A state does not have to make reasonable efforts where the parent has performed any of several specific acts: (1) subjected the child to aggravated circumstances (as defined by state law); (2) committed murder or voluntary manslaughter of another child of the parent; (3) aided or abetted, attempted, conspired, or solicited to commit such murder or manslaughter; or (4) committed a felony assault that results in serious bodily injury to the child or another child of the parent. 42 U.S.C. § 671(a)(15)(D).

ASFA specifically authorizes states to work on concurrent planning, allowing states to make reasonable efforts toward a permanent out-of-home placement and reasonable efforts toward reunification at the same time. 42 U.S.C. § 671(a)(15)(F). *See* Robert M. Gordon, *Drifting Through Byzantium: The Promise and Failure of the Adoption and Safe Families Act of 1997*, 83 Minn L. Rev 637 (1999).

4. A study of 749 17-year-olds in foster care in Illinois, Iowa and Wisconsin found that over half can read at a seventh-grade level, about one-third had repeated a grade and almost 20 percent had been expelled from school. Many had switched schools five or more times during their time in foster care; nearly two-thirds of the boys and half the girls had been arrested, convicted of a crime or sent to a correctional facility. Julie Blair, *Foster Care Children Are Poorly Educated, 3-State Study Charges*, Educ. Wk., Feb. 25, 2004 (citing Midwest Evaluation of the Adult Functioning of Former Foster Care Youth — Wave 1 from the Chapin Hall Center for Children at the University of Chicago).

5. What obligation should the foster parent have to reinforce the religious or cultural views of the biological parent? *See* Kelsi Brown Corkran, *Free Exercise in Foster Care: Defining the Scope of Religious Rights For Foster Children and Their Families*, 72 U. Chi. L. Rev. 325 (2005) (arguing that while foster parents should attempt to accommodate the religious preferences of the child — or the child's biological parents — they are not required to make any more than reasonable accommodations, especially if doing so infringes on the foster parent's own religious rights); *Bruker v. City of New York*, 337 F. Supp. 2d 539 (S.D.N.Y. 2004) (Jewish mother's religious training of her daughter was afforded some constitutional protection under the First Amendment when her daughter was placed non-Jewish foster care home).

6. In *Kenny A. v. Perdue*, 356 F. Supp. 3d 1353 (N.D. Ga. 2005), the court concluded — in the first ruling of its kind in the nation — that foster children have a right to counsel in deprivation and termination of parental proceedings under the due process clause of the Georgia constitution, Ga. Const. art. I, § I, para. I. The court also determined that plaintiffs had set forth evidence that created a genuine issue of material fact as to whether they were receiving, or faced a substantial risk of receiving, ineffective assistance of counsel. According to the court, filing a complaint with the State Bar was not an adequate legal remedy for this kind of deficiency.

[G] Adoption

The adoption process creates a permanent parent-child relationship whereby persons other than the child's biological parents become the child's legal parents. Every state allows adoption through state agencies or state-licensed agencies. Some states allow "private placement" adoption — sometimes called "gray market" adoption — where the parent releases the child to intermediaries (such as lawyers, physicians, clergy, relatives) or directly to the adopting parents. Other states either prohibit or discourage private placement adoption. Black market adoptions, where a child is bought and sold for a fee, are universally prohibited, but payment of the expenses of the biological parents, including medical expenses, and the professional fees of adoption agencies, lawyers and doctors is generally permissible.

Before any child is eligible to be adopted, the rights of the biological parent must be terminated. Adoption typically begins when the biological parents voluntarily relinquish their parental rights and consent to the adoption of the child. For a discussion of the involuntary termination of parental rights in cases of abuse and neglect. *See* § 2.02[E] *supra*. There are certain exceptions that may come into play when dealing with the consent of an unmarried father. Before the United States Supreme Court decided *Stanley v. Illinois*, 405 U.S. 645 (1972), unwed fathers had little say in the adoption of their biological children. Only the mother's consent was required for adoption, (although some states required the father's consent if the father had legitimated the child) and the father was not even entitled to notice that the child was being adopted. *Stanley* began a line of cases that examined the contours of the rights of unwed fathers.

Stanley v. Illinois involved an unwed father who wished to raise his children after their mother died. Under Illinois law, the children of unwed fathers became wards of the state if the mother died, although married fathers, and mothers (even if unwed) were presumed to be fit to raise their children. The Court held that Stanley was entitled, under the Due Process Clause, to a hearing on his fitness as a parent and that the state's denying a hearing for unwed fathers — while granting a hearing for a married father or mother, a divorced father, or an unwed mother — violated the Equal Protection Clause.

In *Quilloin v. Walcott*, 434 U.S. 246 (1978), the Supreme Court addressed a Georgia statute that provided that only the consent of the mother of an illegitimate child was required before adoption unless the father had legitimated the child. The mother had married, and her husband wished to adopt her child, with whom he had been living for nine years. The boy had stated that he wished to be adopted. The biological father had made some support payments, had visited the child, and he opposed the adoption. After receiving notice of the adoption, he petitioned the court to be named the child's legitimate parent and for visitation rights. The Court stated that a violation of due process would occur if the state attempted to break up a "natural family," but pointed out that the father in this case had never had or sought actual or legal custody of his child. According to the Court, the adoption would give full recognition to a family unit already in existence. Under these circumstances, the Court required that the state find only that the adoption and the denial of legitimation was "in the best interest of the child." The Court also rejected the father's equal protection claim, stating that this father's interests were distinguishable from a separated or divorced father who was no longer living with the child. The father in this case had never exercised actual or legal custody over the child and "had never shouldered any significant responsibility for the daily supervision, education, protection or care of the child." It was permissible for the state to recognize this difference in its commitment to the welfare of the child.

In *Caban v. Mohammed*, 441 U.S. 380 (1979), the Court again focused on the nature of the relationship between the father and his children. The statute in question was a New York law that provided that children born out of wedlock could be adopted with the consent of the mother alone. Unlike the father in *Quillion*, the father in *Caban* had a substantial relationship with his children. He had lived with their mother for five years, fathered two children, saw his children frequently, and had custody of them at one point. When the mother married another man, her husband petitioned to adopt the children. The Supreme Court stated that the statutory distinction between unmarried mothers and unmarried fathers violated the Equal Protection Clause because it did not bear a substantial relationship to the state's interest in providing adoptive homes for illegitimate children. Although it may be difficult to locate some unwed fathers, thus impeding adoption, the Court observed that this problem need not be fixed with inflexible gender-based line-drawing. If the father has never come forward to participate in the rearing of his child, the Equal Protection Clause would not prevent a state from withholding the right to veto an adoption from that father. But in cases where the father has established a substantial relationship with the child, he should be easy to identify and locate. Precluding the involved father from the adoption proceeding does not bear a substantial relationship to the asserted interest of the state in promoting the adoption of illegitimate children.

One question left open after *Caban* was the extent of the constitutional protections afforded an unwed father who has little more than a biological relationship with the child. The father in *Lehr v. Robertson*, 463 U.S. 248 (1983), who had never supported and rarely seen his daughter in the two years since her birth, claimed that he had a right to notice and an opportunity to be heard before the child could be adopted. The Court focused its opinion on whether the New York statutory scheme adequately protected the father's right to form a relationship with his child. Under New York law, a man who filed with the "putative father registry" was deemed to have demonstrated his intent to claim paternity of a child and therefore was entitled to receive notice of adoption proceedings. Notice was also required for fathers who had been adjudicated a child's father; those who were identified as the father on the child's birth certificate; those who live openly with the child and the child's mother and who hold themselves out to be the father of the child; those who have been identified as the father by the child's mother in a sworn written statement; and those who were married to the child's mother before the child was six months old. The father in the *Lehr* case had not entered his name in the putative father registry, and he did not satisfy any of the other requirements provided in the statute. Again, the Court focused on the nature and extent of the relationship between the father and child, stating that "[t]he difference between the developed parent-child relationship in *Stanley* and

Caban, and the potential relationship involved in *Quilloin* and [*Lehr*], is both clear and significant." According to the Court, when an unwed father shows a full commitment to the responsibilities of parenthood by stepping forward to participate in the raising of the child, "his interest in personal contact with his child acquires substantial protection under the due process clause." "[T]he mere existence of a biological link does not merit constitutional protection." The father in *Lehr* fared no better under the Equal Protection Clause. The Court stated, "[I]f one parent has an established custodial relationship with the child and the other parent has either abandoned or never established a relationship, the Equal Protection Clause does not prevent a state from according the two parents different legal rights."

Improved DNA testing has provided men who are uncertain or unaware of this biological fact with the means to prove that they are *not* the father of a child. "Paternity fraud" describes the situation where a man believes he is a child's father and functions as the father; he later learns that he is not the child's biological father. He then seeks to remove the "bonds of parentage" and to disestablish paternity because of the alleged fraud. *See* Melanie Jacobs, *When Daddy Doesn't Want to Be Daddy Anymore: An Argument Against Paternity Fraud Claims*, 16 Yale J.L. & Feminism 194 (2004). Comparing nonpaternity to a wrongful criminal conviction, one website by a "duped dad" has the motto, "If the genes don't fit, you must acquit." Fathers seeking relief from paternity (and from the child support payments that accompany it) have found support in a growing number of state legislatures. *See, e.g.*, Ohio Stat. §§ 3119.961–3119.962 (permitting disestablishment of paternity based upon blood or genetic tests that exclude biological paternity). Commentators have proposed various solutions. *See, e.g.*, Jacobs, *supra*, at 198 (proposing statute of limitations to help to balance the best interest of the child in preserving an intact father-child relationship and the father's interest in challenging an unfair paternity establishment); June Carbone & Naomi Cahn, *Which Tie Binds? Redefining the Parent-Child Relationship in an Age of Genetic Certainty*, 11 Wm. & Mary Bill Rts. J. 1011, 1066-70 (2003) (proposing mandatory paternity tests for all children at birth).

NOTES AND QUESTIONS

1. How would the father of a newborn establish a custodial relationship with his child? Does he have a constitutionally protected right to have an opportunity to establish a relationship with the child? Consider the interests of all the parties involved when you analyze this question.

2. What if a father is unaware of the pregnancy and birth of the child? The Uniform Adoption Act provides:

§ 3-404. Investigation and Notice to Unknown Father

(a) If, at any time in a proceeding for adoption or for termination of a relationship of parent and child under [Part] 5, the court finds that an unknown father of a minor adoptee may not have received notice, the court shall determine whether he can be identified. The determination must be based on evidence that includes inquiry of appropriate persons in an effort to identify an unknown father for the purpose of providing notice.

If the father is identified, the Act provides that notice be served, and if notice cannot be served, the court may order publication or public posting if the court believes that publication or posting is likely to lead to receipt of notice by the father.

3. If an unwed father receives notice and the right to participate in the adoption proceedings, may he veto the adoption by withholding his consent? The Uniform Adoption Act addresses Consent To and Relinquishment For Adoption:

§ 2-401. Persons Whose Consent Required

(a) Unless consent is not required or is dispensed with under § 2-202, in a direct placement of a minor for adoption by a parent or guardian authorized under this [Act] to place the minor, a petition to adopt the minor may be granted only if consent to the adoption has been executed by:

(1) the woman who gave birth to the minor and the man, if any, who

(i) is or has been married to the woman if the minor was born during the marriage or within 300 days after the marriage was terminated or a court issued a decree of separation;

(ii) attempted to marry the woman before the minor's birth by a marriage solemnized in apparent compliance with the law, although the attempted marriage is or could be declared invalid, if the minor was born during the attempted marriage or within 300 days after the attempted marriage was terminated;

(iii) under applicable law, has been judicially determined to be the father of the minor, or has signed a document which has the effect of establishing his parentage of the minor, and:

(A) has provided, in accordance with his financial means, reasonable and consistent payments for the support of the minor and has visited or communicated with the minor; or

(B) after the minor's birth, but before the minor's placement for adoption, has married or attempted to marry the woman who gave birth to the minor by a marriage solemnized in apparent compliance with law, although the attempted marriage is or could be declared invalid; or

(iv) has received the minor into his home and openly held out the minor as his child;

(2) the minor's guardian if expressly authorized by a court to consent to the minor's adoption; or

(3) the current adoptive or other legally recognized mother and father of the minor.

(b) Unless consent is not required under § 2402, in a placement of a minor for adoption by an agency authorized under this [Act] to place the minor, a petition to adopt the minor may be granted only if consent to the adoption has been executed by:

    (1) the agency that placed the minor for adoption; and

    (2) any individuals described in subsection (a) who have not relinquished the minor.

(c) Unless the court dispenses with the minor's consent, a petition to adopt a minor who has attained 12 years of age may be granted only if, in addition to any consent required by subsections (a) and (b), the minor has executed an informed consent to the adoption.

§ 2-402. Persons Whose Consent Not Required

(a) Consent to an adoption of a minor is not required of:

    (1) an individual who has relinquished the minor to an agency for purposes of adoption;

    (2) an individual whose parental relationship to a minor has been terminated or determined not to exist.

    (3) a parent who has been judicially declared incompetent;

    (4) a man who has not been married to the woman who gave birth to the minor and who, after the conception of the minor, executed a verified statement, denying paternity or disclaiming any interest in the minor and acknowledging that his statement shall be irrevocable when executed;

    (5) the personal representative of a deceased parent's estate, or

    (6) a parent or other person who has not executed a consent or a relinquishment and who fails to file an answer or an appearance in a proceeding for adoption or for termination of a parental relationship with the requisite time after service of notice of the proceeding.

(b) The court may dispense with the consent of:

    (1) a guardian or an agency whose consent is otherwise required upon a finding that the consent is being withheld contrary to the best interest of a minor adoptee, or

    (2) a minor adoptee who has attained 12 years of age upon a finding that it is not in the best interest of the minor to require the consent.

    4. What are the necessary qualities of an adoptive parent? To what extent should issues like age or infertility be considered? What about race or ethnicity or religion? The debate about transracial adoptions splits those who believe that transracial adoptions are good for society and good for the child and those who believe that both the minority community and the child will be harmed when children of minority communities are adopted into the majority community.

DEWEES v. STEVENSON

United States District Court for the Eastern District of
Pennsylvania
779 F. Supp. 25 (1991)

WALDMAN, J.

Plaintiffs seek to enjoin defendants from refusing to consider plaintiffs as adoptive parents for their foster child, Dante Kirby, and from taking him from the foster home on November 23, 1991 to participate in a National Adoption Center event to attempt to find prospective adoptive parents. Plaintiffs allege that defendants have refused to consider plaintiffs' request to adopt Dante because of their race and in so doing have violated the equal protection and due process guarantees of the Fourteenth Amendment. Plaintiffs also seek a declaration that defendants alleged refusal to consider plaintiffs as adoptive parents violates these Constitutional guarantees. . . .

From the record adduced on November 20, 1991, the court makes the following findings of fact and conclusions of law.

I

FINDINGS

Plaintiffs are a white couple who have been married for 27 years and who reside in Royersford, Pennsylvania in an almost exclusively white area. Mrs. DeWees is a high school graduate and housewife. Mr. DeWees is the maintenance manager for a trucking company. Plaintiffs have three natural children, ages 26, 23 and 21 years, and five grandchildren for whom they have cared.

Defendants are the Chester County, Pennsylvania Children and Youth Services Agency (CCCYS), its director and its adoption supervisor, Kay Thalheimer. In January of 1988, plaintiffs applied to CCCYS to be foster parents. During the ensuing review and evaluation process, Mrs. DeWees stated that she did not want to take any black foster children because "[she] did not want people to think that [she] or her daughter were sleeping with a black man." According to Mrs. DeWees, she gave this reason because she was reluctant to give her real reason which was her concern that she would not know how to take care of a black child. Plaintiffs requested for placement children under three years of age because they felt they "couldn't deal with children after three years old." CCCYS approved plaintiffs as foster parents and entered into a foster parents agreement with them on May 9, 1988. The agreement provides, inter alia, that CCCYS shall have all responsibility for planning for any foster child.

Pursuant to the agreement, CCCYS variously placed seven foster children with plaintiffs. They were from two to twenty months in age. Three were black and two were bi-racial. Plaintiffs never received any complaints from CCCYS about their care of any foster child. Plaintiffs' attitude about black children changed and they came "to accept them as any other child."

On November 10, 1989, CCCYS placed Dante Kirby, then two months old, with plaintiffs. Since August 20, 1991, Dante is plaintiffs' only remaining foster child. Plaintiffs understood that Dante's placement with them was not permanent. On three different occasions Dante was to be returned to his parents, but it did not work out as planned. Dante's mother is white and his father is black. On November 12, 1991, with their consent, their parental rights were terminated by the Chester County Court of Common Pleas. Plaintiffs have cared well for Dante. They provide him with his own room and interact frequently with him. He plays and interacts well with plaintiffs' grandchildren. They have supplemented the amounts provided by CCCYS for clothing and toys, and have provided Dante with medical care for his respiratory problems. There clearly is a bond of mutual affection between plaintiffs and Dante.

On June 13, 1991, after being advised by Dante's caseworker that Dante's mother and father intended to relinquish their parental rights, plaintiffs wrote to defendant Thalheimer to express an interest in adopting Dante. On July 18, 1991, defendant Thalheimer met with and interviewed plaintiffs for an hour and a half, and then referred them to Dr. Joseph Crumbley for further evaluation of their request to adopt Dante. On August 22, 1991, Dr. Crumbley interviewed plaintiffs at his office in Philadelphia for approximately two hours. Dante was present. In assessing plaintiffs' ability to raise and socialize a bi-racial child, Dr. Crumbley utilized the Workers' Assessment Guide for families Adopting Cross-Racially and Cross-Culturally of the U.S. Department of Health and Human Services. Ms. Thalheimer is a social worker with 20 years of experience in the field of adoption. She has experience with trans-racial adoptions. She has placed bi-racial children with white, black and bi-racial adoptive parents respectively. She is white.

Dr. Crumbley is a family therapist and consultant with a Ph.D. in social work. He is a consultant to three adoption agencies and among his areas of specialization are child abuse, foster care and adoption. He has experience with trans-racial adoptions. He is black.

Dr. Crumbley forwarded an evaluation and recommendation to Ms. Thalheimer on September 11, 1991. He concluded that although Dante was emotionally attached to plaintiffs, they would not be appropriate adoptive parents. That a foster child has bonded with his foster parents is viewed by professionals as strong evidence that he would bond with new adoptive parents as well. Dr. Crumbley was concerned about plaintiffs' responses that race had "no impact" on developing a child's identity and self-esteem, that addressing racial issues was not important in raising a minority child; and, that they would not prepare Dante to deal with racial discrimination but rather would address the problem if and when it occurred. He was also concerned about plaintiffs' lack of friends in and contact with the minority community, and Mrs. DeWees' statement that she would "not manufacture black friends."

Dr. Crumbley concluded that plaintiffs lacked the ability to: be sufficiently sensitive to the needs of a bi-racial child during the critical period of socialization, self-identification and personality development of age two through six years; educate a minority child about prejudice and provide him with the skills effectively to respond to it; and, provide positive bi-racial and minority role models through interaction with the minority community.

Based on her interview and Dr. Crumbley's report, Ms. Thalheimer concluded that plaintiffs lacked the sensitivity to racial issues and inter-racial network of community resources needed properly to raise Dante. She decided not to grant plaintiffs' request to adopt Dante, and so advised them by letter of September 26, 1991.

Since receiving this letter, plaintiffs have a greater realization of the importance of the issues identified by Dr. Crumbley and are willing to undertake any course of action recommended by defendants to prepare to address the needs of a bi-racial child. They are willing to "grow and learn." They have located and are prepared to participate in a support group of trans-racial adoptive families. In Dr. Crumbley's opinion, the only evidence adduced on the point, plaintiffs could learn to address Dante's race-related psychological and social needs with appropriate counseling, education and training but this would take a substantial period of time and Dante is now at a "critical" point.

The court has no expertise in the area of cross-racial adoption. Nevertheless, the court cannot accept Dr. Crumbley's view that generally only whites with extensive specialized training or who have experienced discrimination themselves will be able adequately to address the needs of a minority child in his or her formative years. The court does find that particular sensitivity, awareness and skills are necessary for a successful trans-racial adoption of a young child, and that Dr. Crumbley based his recommendation on his conclusion that plaintiffs had not demonstrated those qualities and could acquire them only over a long period.

Ms. Thalheimer did not refuse to consider plaintiffs as adoptive parents because of race or any other reason. Rather, she did consider plaintiffs' request to adopt Dante and decided not to grant it. Ms. Thalheimer is currently prepared to place Dante for adoption with any suitable couple, regardless of race, who appear to her to have the awareness, sensitivity and skills to address adequately the needs of a bi-racial child in his formative years. Her decision was based on the perceived best interests of the child, and not on the color of plaintiffs' skins.

II

CONCLUSIONS OF LAW

To sustain their due process claim, plaintiffs must show that they are being deprived of a federally secured right by persons acting under color of state law. Defendants are clearly acting under color of state law. Foster parents do not have a cognizable liberty interest in maintaining a relationship with a foster child vis-a-vis prospective adoptive parents, particularly where the relationship is based on a contract under which the state retains responsibility for the child and places him in a foster home on a temporary basis.

The essence of the equal protection clause is a requirement that similarly situated people be treated alike. *City of Cleburne, Texas v. Cleburne Living Center*, 473 U.S. 432, 439 (1985). . . . Racial classifications are inherently suspect and can survive an equal protection challenge only if they are necessary to achieve a compelling state interest. *Loving v. Virginia*, 388 U.S.

1, 11 (1967). . . . The state's responsibility to protect the best interests of a child in its custody is a compelling interest for purposes of the equal protection clause. Because of the potential difficulties inherent in a trans-racial adoption, a state agency may consider race and racial attitudes in assessing prospective adoptive parents.

While the degree of plaintiffs' sensitivity and attitudes about racial issues may be related to their race and experience as whites in a white majority society, defendants refused their request to adopt a minority child because of perceptions about their attitudes and not their race. To the extent that perceived attitudes about race and coping with race-related problems motivated defendants' decision, this was Constitutionally permissible in determining the best interests of a young child eligible for adoption. Plaintiffs have failed to establish on the record adduced and under applicable legal precedent and principles that their due process or equal protection rights have been violated.

III

CONCLUSION

The court has not found that plaintiffs are in any way unfit or could not acquire the knowledge and skills necessary to provide for Dante's future needs. Foster parents play a vital role in our society. They provide a welcome alternative to institutionalization of children without parents able or willing to care for them while the permanent placement process ensues. State agencies have a moral obligation to be sensitive to the position of foster parents who, particularly with extended placements, are likely to develop emotional bonds to the children placed in their homes. Ultimately, however, the state's responsibility to protect and pursue the best interests of children in its custody must take precedence.

This court is not empowered to sit as a super adoption agency review board. The court thus is not passing upon the wisdom of defendants' actions but only on whether they were motivated by Constitutionally impermissible considerations of race. The court has found that defendants made a considered judgment based on professional input and Constitutionally permissible factors. This finding turns on the importance of awareness of and sensitivity to issues of race in the context of a trans-racial adoption. These factors, in turn, are important largely because of the realities of the larger society in which we live. As the court stated at the hearing on November 20, 1991, it is concerned that the very problems which give rise to race-related concerns may unintentionally be exacerbated by overemphasizing them. It is difficult to make race irrelevant, as it should be, if adoption and other social decisions are driven by racial considerations, however benign.

In making adoption decisions, state agencies cannot ignore the realities of the society in which children entrusted to them for placement will be raised, or the affect on children of those realities as documented by professional studies. The court would hope, however, that these agencies also will be mindful of the possibility that an overemphasis on racial issues may retard efforts to achieve a color blind society, and of the need to avoid even the appearance that an adoption decision may have been based on race *per se.*

———

NOTES AND QUESTIONS

1. In *Palmore v. Sidoti*, 466 U.S. 429 (1984), the United States Supreme Court held that it was unconstitutional for a trial court to modify a custody order and to award custody to a child's father because the child's Caucasian mother lived with and then married a black man. The Supreme Court stated, "The core purpose of the Fourteenth Amendment was to do away with all governmentally imposed discrimination based on race." Although a child living with a step-parent of a different race "may be subject to a variety of pressures and stresses" that would not be present if the child were with a parent of the same race, "the reality of private biases and the possible injury they might inflict" were not permissible considerations for a court considering the removal of a child from its natural mother. "Private biases may be outside the reach of the law, but the law cannot, directly or indirectly, give them effect."

Congress passed the Interethnic Provisions of the Small Business Jobs Protection Act in 1996, which provides:

Adoption and foster care rights

(1) Prohibited conduct. A person or government that is involved in adoption or foster care placements may not–

(A) deny to any individual the opportunity to become an adoptive or a foster parent, on the basis of the race, color, or national origin of the individual, or of the child, involved; or

(B) delay or deny the placement of a child for adoption or into foster care, on the basis of the race, color, or national origin of the adoptive or foster parent, or the child, involved.

42 U.S.C. § 1996b. Noncompliance with the Act is a violation of Title VI. How would the *DeWees* case fare under this federal statute?

2. Congress explicitly endorsed race-matching in adoption when it passed the Indian Child Welfare Act of 1978, 25 U.S.C. § 1901 *et seq.* The Act provides that in any adoptive placement of an Indian child under state law, "preference shall be given, in the absence of good cause to the contrary, to a placement with (1) members of the child's extended family; (2) other members of the Indian child's tribe; or other Indian families." 25 U.S.C. § 1915(b). The Interethnic Provisions of the Small Business Jobs Protection Act specifically exempts the Indian Child Welfare Act from its provisions. The Indian Child Welfare Act contains numerous other jurisdictional, procedural and substantive provisions that make it difficult to remove an Indian child from the tribe, including exclusive jurisdiction for tribal courts in adoption proceedings for a child living on a reservation, §1911, and for Indian children not living on a reservation, either the tribe or the Indian parent may petition and have the

case transferred to the tribal court. In termination of parental rights and foster care placement cases, the petitioner must prove beyond a reasonable doubt (for termination) or by clear and convincing evidence (for foster placement) that leaving the child in the home is likely to result in serious emotional or physical damage to the child. Moreover, the petitioner must meet this burden by presenting testimony from an expert in Indian culture and child-raising. When might the tribe's interests conflict with those of the child?

3. International adoptions have increased dramatically in the last decade of the twentieth century with significant numbers from China, South Korea and Eastern Europe. The United Nations General Assembly has passed the Declaration on Social and Legal Principles Relating to Adoption and Foster Placement of Children Nationally and Internationally and the Convention on the Rights of the Child. These declarations attempt to discourage trafficking in children for profit and set forth certain standards for citizenship after adoption. Should there be a preference for adoption or foster care in the child's country of origin? What issues arise for parents who adopt children from other countries?

4. At the same time that the Massachusetts Supreme Court reiterated its view that denying a marriage license to same-sex couples violated that state's constitution, the Eleventh Circuit Court of Appeals determined that a Florida statute that bars sexually active gay and lesbians from adopting children does not violate due process or equal protection rights under the federal constitution. *Lofton v. Secretary of the Dept. of Children and Family Services*, 358 F.3d 804 (11th Cir. 2004). The court stated that the statute was rationally related to the state's interest in securing an optimal home environment for children. It rejected the argument that the United States Supreme Court had recognized a fundamental right to private sexual intimacy that would trigger strict scrutiny in *Lawrence v. Texas*, 539 U.S. 558 (2003). The court also determined that the categorical ban was not an equal protection violation as the legislature could rationally conclude that homosexuals and heterosexual singles are not similarly situated in relevant respects. Unpersuaded by studies that showed no child welfare basis for prohibiting homosexual adoption, the court stated that the studies were in their nascent stage and had yielded inconclusive and conflicting results. According to the court, the legislature had not acted irrationally in proceeding "with deliberate caution" before placing adoptive children in a family unit that was not yet shown to be equivalent to "the marital structure that has established a proven track record spanning centuries." The U.S. Supreme Court refused to grant certiorari in the case.

5. Legal issues surrounding adoption may not end once the adoption is complete. Deciding whether states should allow adult adoptees access to their birth records raises significant concerns that pit the right to know against the right to privacy. Traditionally, courts have refused to allow adopted adults access to their records. As the advocates for adoptee rights became more vocal, some states have passed legislation that allows for voluntary adoption registries and confidential intermediaries. For a detailed history of the issues surrounding adoptee rights, see E. Wayne Carp, ADOPTION POLITICS: BASTARD NATION AND BALLOT INITIATIVE 58 (2004) (explaining how "Bastard Nation," called a "radical adoptee rights organization," began an initiative in Oregon

that was ultimately successful in getting legislation passed that gave adult adoptees the right to access their original birth certificate). *See also Doe v. Sundquist*, 2 S.W.3d 919 (Tenn. 1999) (upholding statute that allowed adult adoptees access to their records but gave biological parents the right to block access). Is this the kind of right that should vary from state to state?

[H]   Intrafamily Tort Actions

ANDERSON v. STREAM

Supreme Court of Minnesota
295 N.W.2d 595 (1980)

SCOTT, JUSTICE.

These two appeals raise similar issues regarding the exceptions to the abrogation of parental immunity as adopted by this court in *Silesky v Kelman*, 161 N.W.2d 631 (1968). In both cases, the trial courts concluded that the exceptions were applicable and thus held that the injured children had no actionable claim against their respective parent[s]. We reverse.

The operative facts of these appeals have been stipulated to by the respective parties:

Anderson v. Stream v. Anderson

Edward and Ruth Anderson are the parents of Breeanna Anderson, who was born on June 16, 1975. Defendants Edna and Martin Stream live in a house next door to the Anderson home, and the two families share a common driveway. The line dividing the two properties runs generally down the center of the driveway. There is no fence between the two houses.

On Sunday morning, May 15, 1977, Breeanna, who was approximately twenty-three months of age, asked her parents if she could go outside and play. Breeanna was allowed to do so, but was told to "stay in the back." While Breeanna played outdoors, Mr. Anderson read the Sunday newspaper and Mrs. Anderson did housework. About 10 or 15 minutes after she began to play, Breeanna was injured when Edna Stream backed her automobile over the child's leg. After the accident occurred, Breeanna was found sitting partially on the Streams' lawn and partially on the portion of the driveway located closest to the Stream home.

Neither Mr. nor Mrs. Anderson saw the accident. However, during the 10–15 minute period Breeanna was playing, Mrs. Anderson saw her daughter twice; once, when Breeanna was playing by the back step, and later, when she was playing in the front yard of the Anderson home. Also, the parties agree that the Andersons had observed Breeanna playing on or about the common driveway on several occasions prior to May 15, 1977.

Edward Anderson, as guardian for his minor daughter, and in an individual capacity, brought an action against the Streams for the damages which resulted from the child's injuries. The Streams later impleaded Mr. Anderson and his wife for contribution and indemnity. Thereafter, the Andersons moved for summary judgment against the Streams on the third-party complaint, claiming no common liability existed because they could not be held liable to their child. The district court granted the motion and dismissed the third-party complaint on the ground that parental immunity was applicable. The Streams now appeal from the judgment entered in the district court.

Nuessle v. Nuessle

On the afternoon of October 4, 1975, Michael Nuessle, who was about three-years-old at the time, accompanied his father, James Nuessle, on an errand to a drugstore located on the northwest corner of the intersection of Victoria Street and Grand Avenue in St. Paul. Defendant entered the drugstore, and after 10 to 15 seconds noticed that his son was not with him. It is unclear whether Michael actually entered the store. After looking briefly in the store for his son, defendant, through the glass door of the store, saw Michael crossing Grand Avenue. Michael was walking alongside an adult male, whom the child may have mistaken for his father. Defendant hurried outside, and without looking for traffic and in an act which defendant described as one of "panic," yelled Michael's nickname, "Micker." The child turned around, saw his father, and took a few steps to the north, recrossing the center line of Grand Avenue, while remaining in the crosswalk. Michael was then struck by the left front part of an automobile driven by a westbound driver who did not see the boy before hitting him. The child sustained serious injuries, including damage to his brain stem.

This action was commenced to recover damages against James Nuessle for Michael's injuries. Defendant subsequently moved for summary judgment on the ground that in this case the parental immunity doctrine operated to bar his son's claim. The trial court agreed, ruling that the first exception to the abolishment of parental immunity was applicable. Plaintiff now seeks review of the district court's decision.

The parties raise a number of issues in these appeals, including: whether the parents' conduct constitutes an "affirmative act of negligence" as recognized by this court in *Romanik v Toro Co.*, 277 N.W.2d 515 (Minn. 1979); whether the parents' alleged wrongdoing involves parental supervision; whether parental supervision qualifies as an exercise of "parental authority" under the first *Silesky* exception, and, if so, whether the conduct in question is "reasonable" within the meaning of *Silesky*; and, solely in regard to the Anderson appeal, whether the parents' alleged negligent act involves an exercise of "parental discretion with respect to the provision . . . of housing" as contemplated by the second *Silesky* exception, and, if so, whether that exercise of parental discretion is "ordinary." An additional issue presented, and the one we find decisive in these cases, is whether the *Silesky* exceptions to the abrogation of parental immunity should be retained. After a careful and painstaking examination of this difficult and important question, we conclude, for the reasons discussed herein, that the exceptions should no longer be followed in this state.

The *Silesky* decision, rendered in 1968, abrogated the long-standing doctrine of parental immunity subject to the following exceptions: "(1) where the alleged negligent act involves an exercise of *reasonable parental authority* over the child; and (2) where the alleged negligent act involves an exercise of ordinary parental discretion with respect to the provision of food, clothing, housing, medical and dental services, and other care. . . ." These exceptions were expressly adopted from the Wisconsin Supreme Court's decision in *Goller v. White*, 122 N.W.2d 193 (1963). The language used in *Silesky* is identical to that set out in *Goller* except for the addition by this court of the term "reasonable" to modify the phrase "parental authority,' in the first exception.

While the *Silesky* court was well-intentioned in continuing the immunity doctrine in regard to certain parental conduct, application of the exceptions has proven to be very difficult because their precise scope is by no means clear. . . . The prospect of applying these vaguely worded, highly subjective standards to the ever-increasing number of parent-child liability cases coming before this court is reason to reflect upon the degree of difficulty in meaningful interpretation of the exceptions and alternative means of providing parents with some leeway in exercising their parental authority and discretion. We believe that since the problems inherent in construing the *Silesky* exceptions present a real danger of arbitrary line-drawing and in light of the fact that instructing the jury on a "reasonable parent" standard adequately protects functions which are parental in nature, the continued existence of the *Silesky* exceptions cannot be justified.

. . . .

Difficulty in application would not, in and of itself, cause us to cast aside the *Silesky* exceptions. The determinative consideration upon which we rest our decision is that the areas of parental authority and discretion, for which the *Silesky* exceptions were designed to provide safeguards, can be effectively protected by use of a "reasonable parent" standard, as adopted by the court in *Gibson v Gibson*, 479 P.2d 648 (1971). In that case, the California Supreme Court completely abolished the doctrine of parental immunity. While recognizing that "traditional concepts of negligence cannot be blindly applied to" acts involving parental authority and discretion, the court refused to adopt the *Goller* exceptions by reasoning, in part, that "[t]he *Goller* view will inevitably result in the drawing of arbitrary distinctions about when particular parental conduct falls within or without the immunity guidelines." . . . Instead, the *Gibson* opinion held that the better approach is to have the jury take into consideration the parental function when determining whether the parent acted negligently. As stated by the *Gibson* court:

> The standard to be applied is the traditional one of reasonableness, but viewed in light of the parental role. Thus, we think the proper test of a parent's conduct is this: What would an ordinarily reasonable and prudent parent have done in similar circumstances?

. . . .

. . . [O]ur preference for the *Gibson* approach recognizes the practical advantages offered by utilization of a "reasonable parent" standard. It attains the *Silesky* goal of according parents some flexibility in their exercise of parental functions, but the interpretive pitfalls associated with the *Silesky* exceptions are avoided. In reaching this conclusion, we reject the contention that juries are incapable of rationally and equitably deciding whether a parent has acted negligently in exercising his parental control and discretion. Our system of justice places great faith in juries, and we see no compelling reason to distrust their effectiveness in the parent-child context. Nor do the arguments relating to family discord and collusion require a different result than that reached herein. These claims, which were found to be unpersuasive in the initial decision abrogating intrafamilial immunity . . . are no more convincing today.

It should also be observed that our decision to abolish the *Silesky* exceptions in favor of a "reasonable parent" standard is supported by basic principles of public policy. A fundamental concept of our legal system and a right guaranteed by our state constitution, is that a remedy be afforded to those who have been injured due to the conduct of another. . . . Related thereto is the equitable doctrine of contribution, which requires that those who contribute to an injury bear liability in direct proportion to their relative culpability. . . . These considerations are promoted by today's holding.

Finally, the prevalence of liability insurance is a pertinent and important factor in subjecting parents to suit by their children. . . .

After all, our paramount objective is to compensate the child for his or her injuries, and the widespread existence of homeowner's and renter's liability insurance will help effectuate this goal. To deny the injured child this source of funds on the ground that prosecution of the claim would in some way disrupt the family unit is an anomaly this court will not tolerate. . . . "[W]here a child is protected by liability insurance there is more likelihood of friction, resentment, and discord by a parent's failure to assert a claim than by instituting suit." . . .

In summary, by this decision we totally abolish the doctrine of parental immunity[35] and consequently overrule *Silesky* to the extent it retained parental immunity in the form of the aforementioned exceptions. In so doing, we adopt the approach of the California Supreme Court in *Gibson* of charging the jury on a "reasonable parent" standard.

Reversed and remanded for trial.

ROGOSHESKE, JUSTICE (*dissenting*).

I disagree with the majority's complete abrogation of parent-child tort immunity in negligence cases. I am not persuaded that the parent-child relationship, long preserved from legal interference on public policy grounds, has so declined in importance that considerations of insurance and simplified judicial administration under a jury standard warrant application of general tort principles to family interactions. In my view, the *Silesky* exceptions to abrogation of parental immunity should be retained and, on these facts, the first exception should be applied to immunize negligent parental supervision.

---

[35] [9] We note that our complete abrogation of parental immunity will not subject parents to suit for negligent child rearing. Such claims of improper parenting are not actionable on public policy grounds. . . .

. . . .

The parent-child relationship is legally unique in at least two principal respects. First, a parent is required to provide his child with such necessaries as food, clothing and shelter. Second, a parent has the authority to impose the supervision, discipline and control of his child that is essential to his exercise of the socially conferred responsibility and privilege of training the child. The *Silesky* exceptions, which embrace these two special aspects of the parent-child relationship, encourage performance of parental obligations by preserving the integrity of family decisionmaking and fostering a family atmosphere of respect and trust. The exceptions implicitly acknowledge that the varied economic, educational, cultural, religious and ethnic backgrounds of parents, and the individual personalities and development paces of children result in such a multitude of permutations of parent-child relationships that no objective standard of proper child rearing is possible. While the exceptions recognize that discharge of parental functions depends on natural instinct, love and morality rather than legal sanctions, they do not assume too much by permitting parents to act negligently toward their children with impunity. Each exception contains language of limitation, *i.e.*, the exercise of parental authority must be "reasonable," the exercise of parental discretion "ordinary." Thus I remain convinced that the parent-child relationship is a special one which the law ought to protect so long as the protection is of conduct tending to fulfill the duties and objectives of the relationship.

In my view, the *Silesky* exceptions possess major advantages over the "reasonable parent" approach. First, the objective standard encourages parents to disparage the favored American principle of freedom of choice in family matters by holding out the possibility of an insurance recovery if a parent is willing to expose his conduct and judgment to public scrutiny. Second, jury verdicts based on a reasonable parent standard in this value-laden area do not inspire public confidence, since they would necessarily substitute parental judgments based upon the individual juror's views of proper or ideal child-rearing practices. The tendency toward arbitrary and intrusive standards of good parenting, which stems from the fact that most jurors have strong views in this area due to their personal experiences as parents and children, cannot be alleviated by precise instructions. The reasonable parent standard thus invites a recovery-oriented parent to gamble that a jury will find him negligent. Moreover, since the jury must consider the family context and the parent is the best, and perhaps only, witness capable of expressing the personal, cultural and socio-economic principles by which he raises his children, the danger of collusion is significant. These are not the types of claims our adversary system of factfinding is equipped to impartially resolve, and the parent's incentive for an opportunity to influence the result is so great as to further undermine the process.

Moreover, abolition of immunity is not restricted to parents who voluntarily put their conduct in issue. An estranged or divorced parent may sue on the child's behalf, thereby compelling the other parent to have his actions publicly aired and judged, adding to the acrimony normally incident to the breakup of the family unit. Such suits could be used as tools to manipulate the child's affections and to destroy loyalty to the sued parent. Also, parents who value family privacy may decline to sue negligent third parties because our third-party procedural rules invite, if not require, their being impleaded on claims that they negligently supervised their child. To the extent that parents cannot control when they will be sued, the reasonable parent standard discourages novel child-rearing practices. In addition, it creates potential for judgments discriminating against parents whose conduct does not conform to prevailing community standards.

. . . .

In both of these cases the alleged negligence consists of the failure of parents to supervise their children. I am persuaded that negligent supervision is the type of parental act contemplated by the first *Silesky* exception which provides immunity for an exercise of parental authority. . . . A parent's exercise of authority over his or her child involves more than discipline. It includes the providing of instruction and education so that a child may be aware of dangers to his or her well being. We find it impossible to separate such general phenomena as authority and supervision. In order to adequately supervise a child, every parent knows that some amount of discipline is inextricably involved. The right to exercise authority over a child certainly includes the responsibility to supervise that child's behavior. Each parent has unique and inimitable methods and attitudes on how children should be supervised. Likewise, each child requires individualized guidance depending on intuitive concerns which only a parent can understand. Also, different cultural, educational and financial conditions affect the manner in which different parents supervise their children. Allowing a cause of action for negligent supervision would enable others, ignorant of a case's peculiar familial distinctions and bereft of any standards, to second-guess a parent's management of family affairs considerably beyond these statutory protections. . . . I would hold that where the alleged negligent conduct is a parent's failure to supervise his child the parent is immune under the "parental authority" exception if as here, the omission is not outrageous.

BURNETTE v. WAHL

Supreme Court of Oregon (en banc)
588 P.2d 1105 (1978)

HOLMAN, JUSTICE.

Three identical cases have been consolidated for appeal. Plaintiffs are five minor children aged two to eight who, through their guardian, are bringing actions against their mothers for emotional and psychological injury caused by failure of defendant-mothers to perform their parental duties to plaintiffs. Plaintiffs' appeal from orders of dismissal entered after demurrers were sustained to the complaints. . . .

[Plaintiffs are in the custody and are wards of the state.]

. . . Among these counts are strewn various allegations of parental failure upon which the causes of action rest. They are:

"1. Since (date), defendant intentionally, wilfully maliciously and with cruel disregard of the consequences failed to provide plaintiff with care, custody, parental nurturance, affection, comfort, companionship, support, regular contact and visitation.

"2. She has failed in violation of ORS 109.010 [36] to maintain plaintiff, who, due to . . . age and indigency, is poor and unable to work to maintain . . . self.

"3. She has abandoned plaintiff by deserting the child with intent to abandon . . . and with intent to abdicate all responsibility for . . . care and raising, in violation of ORS 163.535. [37]

"4. She has neglected the plaintiff by negligently leaving . . . unattended in or at a place for such period of time as would have been likely to endanger the health or welfare of the plaintiff, in violation of ORS 163.545. [38]

"5. She has refused or neglected without lawful excuse to provide support for plaintiff, in violation of ORS 163.555. [39]

"6. Defendant has maliciously, intentionally, and with cruel disregard of the consequences, deserted and abandoned her child.

"7. Defendant has alienated the affections of the plaintiff in that she has intentionally, wilfully and maliciously abandoned, deserted, neglected and failed to maintain regular contact or visitation, or to provide for the plaintiff and has deprived plaintiff of the love, care, affection and comfort to which plaintiff is entitled."

It is apparent that the first allegation is general in nature and is intended to be all-encompassing. The second, third, fourth and fifth allege violation of statutory duties in which abandonment and desertion comprise the central theme. The sixth allegation is one of abandonment and desertion purportedly based on common law.

The seventh allegation is an attempt to allege alienation of affections. Although these allegations of parental failure allege lack of support and physical care along with affectional neglect, from the allegations of injury in

---

[36] [1] "ORS 109.010 Duty of Support. Parents are bound to maintain their children who are poor and unable to work to maintain themselves, and children are bound to maintain their parents in like circumstances."

[37] [2] "ORS 163.535 Abandonment of a Child. (1) A person commits the crime of abandonment of a child if, being a parent, lawful guardian or other person lawfully charged with the care or custody of a child under 15 years of age, he deserts the child in any place with intent to abandon it. "(2) Abandonment of a child is a Class C felony."

[38] [3] "ORS 163.545 Child Neglect. (l) A person having custody or control of a child under 10 years of age commits the crime of child neglect if, with criminal negligence, he leaves the child unattended in or at any place for such period of time as may be likely to endanger the health or welfare of such child. "(2) Child neglect is a Class A misdemeanor."

[39] [4] "ORS 163.555 Criminal Nonsupport. (1) A person commits the crime of criminal nonsupport if, being the parent, lawful guardian or other person lawfully charged with the support of a child under 18 years of age, born in or out of wedlock, he refuses or neglects without lawful excuse to provide support for such child." . . . "(3) Criminal nonsupport is a Class C felony."

the complaint and the statements made in plaintiffs' brief, it appears that the injuries claimed are solely emotional and psychological.

Preliminary to a more detailed discussion, it should be noted that these claims of parental failure are different from those tort claims usually made upon behalf of children against parents. The adjudicated cases concern physical or emotional injuries resulting from physical acts inflicted upon children such as beatings and rapes and from automobile accidents. Plaintiffs admit they can cite no cases permitting them to recover from their parents for solely emotional or psychological damage resulting from failure to support, nurture and care for them.

The legislature, recognizing the necessity of parental nurture, support and physical care for children, has enacted a vast array of laws for the purpose of protecting or vindicating those rights. These are much more extensive and all-inclusive than are those statutes alleged to have been violated in plaintiffs' allegations of tortuous conduct.

ORS ch. 418 establishes extensive provisions for aid to dependent children, and it is under the provisions of this chapter and as wards of the juvenile court that plaintiffs are presently attempting to have their needs met. Most of the statutes cited in [the footnotes] deal with meeting children's physical needs, but plaintiffs' protection is not afforded solely by these laws. ORS 418.015 provides:

> "(1) The Children's Services Division may, in its discretion, accept custody of children and may provide care, support and protective services for children who are dependent, neglected, mentally or physically disabled or who for other reasons are in need of public service.

> "(2) The Children's Services Division shall accept any child placed in its custody by a court under, but not limited to ORS chapter 419, and shall provide such services for the child as the division finds to be necessary." "Care" "protective services" and "such services for the child as the division finds to be necessary" are all terms which include emotional nurturing as well as physical care. This reading of the statute is reflected in the Children's Services Division's publication entitled, "Permanent Planning for Children in Substitute Care" (1977).

We recognize that this is not a proceeding to secure parental nurturing, support and physical care for plaintiffs, but rather an action for psychological injury claimed to have been caused by the absence of these services. However, the statutory enactments demonstrate that the legislature has put its mind to the deprivations of which plaintiff children are alleged to be victims and has attempted to remedy such situations by enacting a vast panoply of procedures, both civil and criminal, to insure that children receive proper nurturing, support and physical care. It has never undertaken to establish, however, a cause of action for damages for any emotional injury to the child which may have been caused by a parent's refusal to provide these services. This failure of the legislature to act is significant because this is not a field of recovery which has heretofore been recognized by courts and it would therefore be natural for it to have provided such a remedy if it thought it was wise in view of the social problem it attempts to solve and the statutory provisions it has enacted for that purpose. It has had no difficulty in the past in creating new causes of action for persons aggrieved by conditions which it is attempting to rectify. . . .

The establishment by courts of a civil cause of action based on a criminal or regulatory statute is not premised upon legislative intent to create such an action. It is obvious that had the legislature intended a civil action it would have provided for one, as legislatures many times do. Therefore, the underlying assumption is that it was not intended that the statute create any civil obligation or afford civil protection against the injuries which it was designed to prevent. When neither the statute nor the common law authorizes an action and the statute does not expressly deny it, the court should recognize that it is being asked to bring into existence a new type of tort liability on the basis of its own appraisal of the policy considerations involved. If a court decides to create a cause of action for the act or omission which violates the statute, the interest which is invaded derives its protection solely from the court although the legislative action in branding the act or omission as culpable is taken into consideration by the court in deciding whether a common law action should be established. If a civil cause of action based upon a statute is established by a court, it is because the court, not the legislature, believes it is necessary and desirable to further vindicate the right or to further enforce the duty created by statute.

Because it is plain to the legislature that it could have created the civil liability and it has not, courts must look carefully not only at the particular statute establishing the right or duty but at all statutes which might bear either directly or indirectly on the legislative purpose. If there is any chance that invasion into the field by the court's establishment of a civil cause of action might interfere with the total legislative scheme, courts should err on the side of non-intrusion because it is always possible for the legislature to establish such a civil cause of action if it desires. Courts have no omnipotence in the field of planning, particularly social planning of the kind involved here. Courts should exercise restraint in fields in which the legislature has attempted fairly comprehensive social regulation.

There is no doubt but that the statutory provisions previously cited show a strong state policy of requiring the kind of parental nurturing, support and physical care of children which the defendants here are alleged to have denied their children. As previously indicated, it does not follow as a matter of course that it would be wise or judicious to vindicate that policy by a tort action for damages by children against their mothers. The state also has other policies within its statutory plan of which such a cause of action might well be destructive, particularly the policy of reuniting abandoned children with their parents, if possible. This policy is demonstrated by ORS 418.485, which states that "it is the policy of the State of Oregon to strengthen family life and to insure the protection of all children either in their own homes or in other appropriate care. . . ." This same policy is even evident in ORS 418.745, in such a serious matter as physical child abuse, which states it to be "facilitating the use of protective social services to prevent further abuse, safeguard and enhance the welfare of abused children, and preserve family life when consistent with the protection of the child by stabilizing the family and improving parental capacity. . . ." Also, as part of the Oregon Juvenile Code, we find ORS 419.474(2), which states that the provisions of the Act "shall be liberally construed to the end that a child coming within the jurisdiction of the court may receive such care, guidance and control, preferably in his own home, as will lead to the child's welfare. . . ."

It is recognized by the statutory scheme that in some instances the reestablishment of a biological family is impossible and it therefore provides for a proceeding to terminate parental rights in order that a new family unit for the child may be formed. The section providing for parental termination, ORS 419.523, contains the following language in subsection (2) which demonstrates the importance which the legislature puts upon the establishment of the child in the home with its natural parents: "The rights of the parent or parents may be terminated as provided in subsection (1) of this section if the court finds that the parent or parents are unfit by reason of conduct or condition seriously detrimental to the child *and integration of the child into the home of the parent or parents is improbable in the foreseeable future* due to conduct or conditions not likely to change. . . ." (Emphasis added.)

The statute further provides that the court shall, among other things, consider the following in determining whether to terminate the parents' rights: "(e) Lack of effort of the parent to adjust his circumstances, conduct, or conditions to make the return of the child possible or failure of the parent to effect a lasting adjustment after reasonable efforts by available social agencies for such extended duration of time that it appears reasonable that no lasting adjustment can be effected." What emerges is a comprehensive plan to furnish children in the position of these plaintiffs with parental nurturing and physical care, preferably in family units with their parents. If this is not possible, it provides for means of divesting parental rights so that a new family unit may be created for the child.

It could be contended that the criminal statutes are inconsistent with such a plan. However, no plan established by the legislature over a period of years can ever have perfect symmetry. Also, the legislature is undoubtedly aware that, for obvious reasons, parents of dependent children are not prosecuted criminally if there is hope of establishing the family unit.

It is significant that plaintiffs' complaints do not allege that proceedings for the termination of the defendants' parental rights have taken place. In such circumstances, it would be exceedingly unwise for this court to step in and to initiate a new and heretofore unrecognized cause of action in a field of social planning to which the legislature has devoted a great deal of time and effort in evolving what appears to be an all-encompassing plan. Those persons designated by statute for aiding the plaintiffs in these cases have not yet taken the step for which the plan provides when there is no longer any hope of reestablishing these children in a family unit with their mothers. Tort actions such as the present ones might well be destructive of any plans the social agencies and the juvenile court might have for these children. It is inappropriate for this court to insert a new cause of action into the picture.

. . . . Plaintiffs are unable to point to any literature in the field of child care or family planning which advocates an action for money damages to vindicate a right of the kind asserted here.

In addition, there is a limitation to the extent to which use may be made of tort actions for the purpose of accomplishing social aims. If there is ever a field in which juries and general trial courts are ill equipped to do social engineering, it is in the realm of the emotional relationship between mother and child. It is best we leave such matters to other fields of endeavor. There are certain kinds of relationships which are not proper fodder for tort litigation, and we believe this to be one of them. . . . A tort action for damages by emotionally deprived persons against their parents is, in our opinion, not going to solve the social problem in the same manner in which the legislature is attempting to solve it.

In addition to the contention that defendants should be liable for civil damages because of their violation of criminal and regulatory statutes, plaintiffs also contend that defendants are responsible because of the infliction of severe emotional distress by intentional acts. Plaintiffs allege that defendants intentionally deserted and abandoned them; however, they do not contend that defendants deserted them for the purpose of inflicting emotional harm upon them. We recognize that this tort usually also encompasses the infliction of emotional harm under circumstances from which a reasonable person would conclude that harm was almost certain to result. We believe this latter rationale is inapplicable as between parents and children. If it were otherwise, the children of divorced parents would almost always have an action for emotional damage against their parents. Divorce has become a way of life with almost certain emotional trauma of a greater or lesser degree to the children from the legal dissolution of the family and the resultant absence of at least one of the parents and sometimes both.

In addition, plaintiffs contend that the common law tort of alienation of affections is applicable. They argue that because such a cause of action is intended to compensate one spouse for the intentional alienation of another spouse's affections by a third party, and . . . [that] this cause of action has been extended to the children, it should exist against the parent himself. The statement of the argument is its refutation. Also, the tort of alienation of affections has recently been abolished by the legislature. . . .

Plaintiffs generally contend that without respect to previously recognized theories of recovery, we should recognize a new tort of parental desertion. For all the reasons previously given in declining to use recognized theories of recovery, we also decline this invitation.

The judgment of the trial court is affirmed.

. . . .

LENT, JUSTICE, *concurring in part; dissenting in part.*

I agree with the majority that the asserted cause of action for alienation of affections must fall. I further agree with the majority that from a technical, pleading standpoint plaintiff (I shall speak of the plaintiffs and defendants in the singular) has failed to state a cause of action for "outrageous conduct" for failure to state that defendant intended to cause the severe emotional distress described in the complaint.

. . . .

The majority seems to take the position that what it finds to be a comprehensive legislative scheme is sufficient unto the evil of the day. I do not agree with that position and the limited condemnation of the defendant's conduct found in that legislative scheme.

The community has still other interests in condemning defendant's conduct and compensating plaintiff's injuries. At present there are over one-third of a million children in the United States who are dependent upon the community for their parental care.[40] In Oregon [in] 1976-77 the number of dependent children was over 6,000. The future is bleak for the vast majority of these children, at least those in the position of the plaintiff, whose parents have abandoned them permanently.[41] Only approximately five percent of such children are ever adopted and placed in a permanent parental situation. The costs in dollars and cents of taking care of these children is staggering. In 1972, the total cost at all levels of government was 712.5 million dollars. The present cost may be estimated at approximately 800 million dollars. In Oregon the Children's Services Division budget for the 1977-1979 biennium to provide "family services" for dependent children is over 43 million dollars.

It is estimated that the total direct cost to the community of foster care in 1972 for a child from the age of one to eighteen was $122,500. This is about five times the cost of raising a child in a low-budget family situation. In Oregon the cost of foster care is approximately $200 per month per child. Other types of dependent child care cost as much as $978.57 per child per month.

. . . Indirect costs are those which result from the effects of prolonged foster care delinquency, economic dependency, crimes and corrections. Possibly the greatest costs are those which cannot be measured by dollars and cents at all the loss in human potential. This latter cost to the community can best be stated in the words of those who have done the pioneering research on this subject.

All researchers report the psychological phenomenon known as "separation trauma," the trauma produced by the initial separation from the mother regardless of the circumstances of the case. A second element noted by researchers is the development of ambiguous relationships by the dependent child, with a concomitant loss of self-identity. A third general phenomenon found by the researchers stems from the instability of the foster care system itself, where multiple placements are the norm. This instability in relationships fosters personality disturbance.

---

[40] [1] . . . As of 1971, there were 330,373 children in foster care. This figure includes 260,430 in foster families, 5,640 in group homes, and 64,303 in institutions. . . .

[41] [3] [I]t was reported that approximately 42 percent of dependencies resulted from the voluntary act of the mother. These include:

Unwillingness of mother to assume parental duties — 9.1%

Abandonment and desertion — 12.5%

Neglect and abuse — 17.4%

Unwillingness of mother to continue parental duties — 2.9%

The authors of *Beyond The Best Interests of The Child* amply summarize the effects of parentless dependency on different age-group children and relate them to the costs to society: "When *infants and young children* find themselves abandoned by the parent, they not only suffer separation distress and anxiety but also setbacks in the quality of their next attachments, which will be less trustful.

"Resentment toward the adults who have disappointed them in the past makes (school age children) adopt the attitude of not caring for anybody; or of making the new parent the scapegoat for the shortcomings of the former one. In any case, multiple placement at these ages puts many children beyond the reach of educational influences, and becomes the direct cause of behavior which the schools experience as disrupting and the courts label as dissocial, delinquent, or even criminal.

"*Adults* who as children suffered from disruptions of continuity may themselves, in 'identifying' with their many 'parents,' treat their children as they themselves were treated continuing a cycle costly for both a new generation of children as well as for society itself." (emphasis added)

The sum of the cost to the community direct and indirect, monetary and intangible cannot be computed with complete accuracy; however. . . .

"Adequate care of children is not inexpensive. It is just as costly to mend a child emotionally crippled by disorganized family life as it is to cure the crippled leg of a child stricken with polio. For children in need of parents the community will pay the price sooner or later. The high incidence of mental disorders, criminality, or at best economic dependency among adults who as children had lived in the limbo of foster care, is clear evidence of this."

In view of the costs, both tangible and intangible to society of caring for these dependent children who have well been termed the "orphans of the living" and the character of defendant's conduct as admitted by the demurrer, I believe defendant should shoulder so much of the financial burden as her resources permit. Further, I would hold that the emotional harm which the demurrer admits plaintiff has suffered is such as the community should conclude is monetarily compensable. . . . [P]laintiff has alleged a cause of action.

LINDE, JUSTICE, *dissenting*.

. . . .

The simple issue before us is whether a young child who allegedly has suffered severe mental and emotional injuries as a result of being deserted and abandoned by a parent acting "maliciously, intentionally, and with cruel disregard of the consequences" conduct which the legislature has declared to be a crime may upon proper proof hold the parent responsible in damages for these severe mental and emotional injuries. Contrary to the majority opinion, I believe that these allegations, which plead a violation of ORS 163.535, state a claim on which a child so injured may go to trial.

In reaching this conclusion, I differ with the majority's treatment of its two crucial premises: (1) the source of civil liability for violation of criminal laws, and (2) the significance to be accorded to Oregon's child protection laws.

. . . It should be noted at the outset that awarding civil damages for violations of prohibitory laws is not an uncommon or radical theory of recovery. The question when the victim of criminal or otherwise prohibited conduct may recover damages from the wrongdoer is increasingly important in many areas of law. . . .

. . . The American Law Institute's Restatement (Second) of Torts, Tentative Draft No. 23, 1977, lists a number of other illustrations in its discussion of proscriptive or prescriptive statutes as sources of civil liability.

Sometimes a common law court will assimilate the statutory duty into an existing principle of liability, . . . but that is not always so. [42]

Of course, the question of civil recovery for breach of a statutory duty can be an issue only when the legislation itself is silent on the point. If the legislature either provides for a civil remedy or clearly indicates that it means other provisions for enforcement to be complete and exclusive, there is nothing for a court to decide. It would help to clarify not only private rights, but also the particular public policy if the legislative assembly as a routine step in the drafting of penal legislation faced the question of its civil consequences, or alternatively, if it were to enact a general formula for determining these consequences when a statute is otherwise silent.

Unfortunately legislatures do neither, but nothing can be inferred from that fact, given the existing practice of recognizing such consequences when the nature of the protective statute appears to imply them. The majority overstates the case when it equates legislative silence with an "underlying assumption . . . that it was not intended that the statute create any civil obligation or afford civil protection against the injuries which it was designed to prevent." Nor does it follow, when a court finds that the duty created or defined by the statute does imply a civil cause of action, that the court is engaged in pronouncing common law. The difference between a new common law theory of recovery in tort or otherwise and a civil claim based on a statute is obvious: The latter claim stands and falls with the statute from which it is implied, and it will disappear as soon as the amendment or repeal of the statute indicates a reconsideration of the previous public policy. Thus, while a court is often left at large to divine the implications of a statutory policy, it is equally an overstatement to say that the court simply makes its own judgment whether to "create a cause of action" deriving "solely" from the court's own appraisal whether additional protection for the claimed interest is "necessary and desirable."

---

[42] [3] . . . The violation of a legislative enactment by doing a prohibited act, or by failing to do a required act, makes the actor liable for an invasion of an interest of another if:

(a) the intuit of the enactment is exclusively or in part to protect an interest of the other as an individual; and

(b) the interest invaded is one which the enactment is intended to protect; and,

(c) where the enactment is intended to protect an interest from a particular hazard, the invasion of the interests results from that hazard; and,

(d) the violation is a legal cause of the invasion, and the other has not so conducted himself as to disable himself from maintaining an action.

[Restatement of Torts § 286.]

The relevance of criminal or regulatory laws to civil liability is more complex than merely being an element "taken into consideration by the court in deciding whether a common law action should be established," as the majority puts it. Such laws express distinct kinds of policies. First, the most familiar criminal laws are redefinitions of common-law crimes against private persons or property. They have equally familiar civil analogues in common-law torts. Only "victimless crimes" and crimes deemed to endanger the public as a collectivity, such as bribery, counterfeiting, or tax evasion, are likely to lack a corresponding civil liability. Violations of game laws or environmental protection laws may be other examples. Second, regulatory laws specify standards of socially responsible conduct for the protection of persons endangered by the conduct. While the tort standard may go further, we have recognized the force of the criminal or regulatory standard in negligence cases even when it was set by agencies or local governments that presumably could not themselves create civil liability whether or not they had such an intent. . . . Third, governmental sanctions, penal or otherwise, may be enacted to add governmental enforcement to the recognized obligations of a relationship existing apart from the legislation. In such a situation the "underlying assumption," to use the majority's phrase, is hardly that the penal sanction makes the civil obligation unnecessary. Rather, the statute shows that the obligation is considered of such importance that it deserves enforcement by public prosecution.

. . . It can hardly be questioned that a statute like 163.535, which makes it a crime intentionally to desert and abandon a child, is of the third kind. It and the related sections did not enact a novel prohibition against parental neglect for the convenience of the general public or the protection of taxpayers. They enacted a legislative definition and public enforcement of certain minimal obligations of an existing relationship. Jurisprudentially it might be said that parents have a duty not to abandon and desert their young children because ORS 163.535 makes it a crime to do so, but a legislator would surely think ORS 163.535 should make it a crime to abandon and desert a child because the parent's existing duty to the child, not to the state deserved governmental reenforcement. It is the parent's duty thus recognized under Oregon law that plaintiffs invoke in these cases.

The majority does not really deny that ORS 163.535 constitutes such a legislative recognition and reenforcement of the parent's private obligation to the child, not of some socially convenient behavior. Rather, the majority would deny a remedy for the intentional breach of this obligation on the ground that other public policies militate against such a remedy. Upon examination, the majority's statutory citations refer to the single policy of maintaining and preserving the position of the child within a functioning family as long as this is possible. Without in any way questioning that this is indeed the state's public policy, I do not agree that it supports the conclusion that the legislature meant to deny the child a remedy for injuries from a parent's unlawful acts.

First, it must be kept in mind what conduct violates ORS 163.535. The statute makes it a felony to desert one's child with intent to abandon it. Of course, we have no evidence of the actual facts in these cases, but the allegations are that defendants did desert and abandon their children "maliciously, intentionally, and with cruel disregard of the consequences." If that is true, the parents have in fact ended the family unit, so that solicitude about not impairing it by litigation may sacrifice the children's legal rights to a pious hope. Contrary to the majority, I do not believe it is this court's own judgment of the possible effects of litigation on family relations that matters (a question on which counsel was unable to enlighten us and that, if taken seriously, is hardly within judicial notice) but rather what view of these effects may be attributed to the legislature. More important for interpreting the legislative policy, however, the statute means that a district attorney or grand jury on the alleged facts could prosecute the parents for a felony. It is incongruous to hold that the legislature provided for a felony prosecution of parents who egregiously violate a duty toward their children, but that it meant to exclude civil actions on behalf of the maliciously abandoned children for fear of impairing the family unit. To hold that the plaintiffs cannot invoke this duty, one must assume a legislative policy that a deserted and abandoned child (or a guardian on its behalf) should ask a district attorney to seek the criminal punishment of the parent for this desertion, but that the child should have no claim that would be of any benefit to itself. That seems too unlikely a policy to attribute to the legislature without some showing that it was intended.

Moreover, the majority's premise proves too much. . . . Perhaps the explanation for the majority's unwillingness to follow these assumptions to their conclusion is that the injuries alleged are psychological and emotional rather than physical. But if a civil remedy is denied on the majority's premise that it is precluded by a state policy of preserving family unity, that premise would apply equally to bar recovery of damages by a child crippled by physical abuse. And despite the majority's reference to statutory proceedings for the termination of parental rights, it is at least questionable that a termination proceeding would create rights to a financial recovery to compensate for such very real and costly harm caused before the termination proceeding.

Although the majority does not say so, its premise is the equivalent of the doctrine of intrafamily tort immunity which Oregon has abandoned at least with respect to intentional torts, . . . though attributed here to a supposed legislative policy subordinating legal claims of children against their parents to reliance on "protective social services." I perceive no such prescribed reliance on social services when parents who have deliberately mistreated their children in a manner made criminal by statute have the assets to be responsible for the harm caused thereby. In my view, plaintiffs have alleged at least one triable cause of action arising from an alleged intentional violation of duties recognized in ORS 163.535. Therefore, the demurrers should have been overruled.

NOTES AND QUESTIONS

1. *Anderson* represents a trend towards abolishing the parent-child tort immunity doctrine. Some states permit actions by children against parents only where the alleged breach of duty consists of one owed to the world at

large rather one occurring in the exercise of parental discretion and authority. *See, e.g.,* *Holodook v. Spencer,* 324 N.E.2d 338 (N.Y. 1974) (action by child against parent permitted where mother negligently operated car resulting in injuring to her child who was a passenger therein). Other states continue to adhere to the immunity doctrine. *See, e.g.,* *Mitchell v. Mitchell,* 598 So. 2d 801 (Ala. 1992).

2. Is there a significant distinction in *Anderson,* which permits tort actions by children against their parents, and *Burnette* which does not?

[I] Emancipation

ACCENT SERVICE COMPANY, INC. v. EBSEN

Supreme Court of Nebraska
306 N.W.2d 575 (1981)

Van Pelt, District Judge.

This is an appeal from a $2,555.01 judgment of the District Court of Knox County, Nebraska, entered in favor of the plaintiff-appellee, as assignee, against the defendant-appellant for hospital expenses incurred by defendant's son. The District Court, in affirming the judgment of the county court, found that the evidence was insufficient to establish emancipation by the minor, and that the evidence did establish a contractual liability on the part of the defendant to pay for her son's medical services.

Appellant's first assignment of error is that the trial court erred in finding that there was insufficient evidence of a complete emancipation. Violet Ebsen, a widow, and her eighteen-year-old son, Dwaine, lived together until approximately December 1976. Dwaine then began associating and staying overnight with people his mother did not like and of whom she did not approve. Arguments over his associations and conduct took place in December of 1976 and in January of 1977. As a result of one such argument, on February 1, 1977, Dwaine took his personal belongings and moved from his mother's home in Verdigre, Nebraska, to Orchard, Nebraska. Both the mother and son agreed that he should move out and support himself. After moving out, Dwaine received no further support from his mother. On February 24, 1977, while still living in Orchard, Dwaine was shot and taken to a hospital in Norfolk, Nebraska. There, the hospital expenses were incurred that are the subject of this litigation. After being hospitalized for two weeks, Dwaine returned to his mother's home for three days and then left. He had been self-supporting and has not returned to his mother's home since leaving.

Whether Dwaine Ebsen was emancipated at the time of his hospitalization is relevant, since the complete emancipation of a child relieves the parent from liability to those who furnish necessaries of life to that child. . . .

The emancipation of a child by a parent may be proved by circumstantial evidence or by an express agreement, or implied from the conduct of the parties. . . . Although this court has not had an occasion to discuss the factors to be considered in determining whether a minor has become emancipated, they were recently analyzed:

> In general, even in the absence of statute, parents are under a legal as well as a moral obligation to support, maintain, and care for their children, the basis of such a duty resting not only upon the fact of the parent-child relationship, but also upon the interest of the state as *parens patriae* of children and of the community at large in preventing them from becoming a public burden. However, various voluntary acts of a child, such as marriage or enlistment in military service, have been held to terminate the parent's obligation of support, the issue generally being considered by the courts in terms of whether an emancipation of the child has been effectuated. In those cases involving the issue of whether a parent is obligated to support an unmarried minor child who has voluntarily left home without the consent of the parent, the courts, in actions to compel support from the parent, have uniformly held that such conduct on the part of the child terminated the support obligation.
>
> Correlative to a parent's obligation of support and maintenance of a minor child is the liability of a parent to others who have performed the support obligation for the parent by furnishing the child with necessaries. Generally, a parent's liability for necessaries furnished a minor child will depend on a variety of circumstances, but it appears clear that no liability exists where the parent has been ready and willing at all times to supply necessaries to himself and to otherwise fulfill his obligation to support the child. Thus, it has been held that a parent was not liable to a third person furnishing necessaries to an unmarried minor child while voluntarily living apart from the parent with consent, the courts concluding that in such a case the parent was under no obligation to support the child and that the child carried with him no authority to bind the parent for the necessaries furnished. However, a parent has been held liable for necessaries furnished his unmarried minor child by a third person while the child was living apart from the parent without consent, where there was evidence that the parent authorized the sale of the goods to the child.

Where a child departed from the family home and the parent consented to the departure, the child was found to be emancipated. . . .

In the instant case, after several months of arguing and the defendant in effect telling her son to either change his behavior or move out, he left his mother's home with her consent. From that time until the hospital expense was incurred, he furnished his own support and received nothing from his mother. Under these facts, Dwaine Ebsen became emancipated, and his mother became relieved of liability to those furnishing him necessaries.

Appellant's second assignment of error is that the trial court erred in finding that there was evidence of a contractual agreement by the defendant to pay her son's hospital expenses. If such an agreement existed, defendant would be liable, regardless of her son's emancipation, under general principles of contract law.

The county court was unable to make a finding that there was or was not a contractual agreement, but entered judgment for the plaintiff on the basis that Dwaine Ebsen was not emancipated. The District court affirmed the judgment of the county court, with the following additional finding: "3. That Defendant authorized Plaintiff's assignor to furnish medical service of an emergency nature to her minor son, Dwaine Ebsen, orally and by the execution of Exhibit '3' in writing, immediately prior to the furnishing of the first part of said services."

Exhibit 3 . . . is a consent to operation, anesthetics, and other medical services. This document contains no language of a promise, express or implied, to pay for services. Lucille Loberg, the hospital employee who was present when the defendant signed Exhibit 3, testified that normally the hospital uses another document which specifies how the bill is to be paid. However, no such document signed by the defendant was ever produced or received in evidence.

Nor does the record reveal any oral promise to pay the hospital expenses. The closest testimony to such a promise was in the county court, where the defendant, under examination by the plaintiff's attorney, stated that by signing Exhibit 3 she wanted her son attended to and wanted him to stay alive. Under examination by her own attorney, she testified that at no time did she say anything to anyone at the hospital that she could or would pay the bill. Plaintiff has the burden of proving any oral or written agreement by a preponderance of the evidence. There is no such evidence in the record.

. . . For the reasons set forth above, the order and judgment of the District Court are reversed, and the cause is remanded with directions to dismiss plaintiff's petition and cause of action, at plaintiff's costs.

———

NOTES AND QUESTIONS

1. *Accent Services* represents the common law approach to emancipation. What is the purpose of the emancipation doctrine? Do those purposes continue to be relevant in light of the nearly ubiquitous lowering of the age of majority to 18?

For discussion of the history of emancipation, see Francis C. Cady, *Emancipation of Minors*, 12 CONN. L. REV. 62 (1979).

2. Some states have enacted statutes providing grounds for judicial emancipation. For example, CAL. FAMILY CODE §§ 7002, 7120–22 (West 1994) provides:

Emancipated minor; description

A person under the age of eighteen years is an emancipated minor if any of the following conditions is satisfied:

(a) The person has entered into a valid marriage, whether or not the marriage has been dissolved.

(b) The person is on active duty with the armed forces of the United States.

(c) The person has received a declaration of emancipation pursuant to § 7122.

. . . .

Petitions for declaration of emancipation; contents:

(a) A minor may petition the superior court of the county in which the minor resides or is temporarily domiciled for a declaration of emancipation.

(b) The petition shall set forth with specificity all of the following facts:

(1) The minor is at least fourteen years of age.

(2) The minor willingly lives separate and apart from the minor's parents or guardian with the consent or acquiescence of the minor's parents or guardian.

(3) The minor is managing his or her own financial affairs. As evidence of this, the minor shall complete and attach a declaration of income and expenses as provided in § 1285.50 of the California Rules of Court.

(4) The source of the minor's income is not derived from any activity declared to be a crime by the laws of this state or the laws of the United States.

Notice of declaration proceedings:

(a) Before the petition for a declaration of emancipation is heard, notice the court determines is reasonable shall be given to the minor's parents, guardian, or other person entitled to the custody of the minor, or proof shall be made to the court that their addresses are unknown or that for other reasons the notice cannot be given.

(b) The clerk of the court shall also notify the district attorney of the county where matter is to be heard of the proceeding. If the minor is a ward or dependent child of the court, notice shall be given to the probation department.

(c) The notice shall include a form whereby the minor's parents, guardian, or other person entitled to the custody of the minor may give their written consent to the petitioner's emancipation. The notice shall include a warning that a court may void or rescind the declaration of emancipation and the parents may become liable for support and medical insurance coverage pursuant to Chapter 2 (commencing with § 4000) of Part 2 of Division 9 of this code and §§ 11350, 11350.1, 11475.1, and 11490 of the Welfare and Institutions Code.

Findings of court; issuance of declaration of emancipation:

(a) The court shall sustain the petition if it finds that the minor is a person described by § 7120 and that emancipation would not be contrary to the minor's best interest.

(b) If the petition is sustained, the clerk shall forthwith issue a declaration of emancipation, which shall be filed by the county clerk.

(c) A declaration is conclusive evidence that the minor is emancipated.

3. Does emancipation have any effect other than freeing parents from support obligations to the emancipated child? Does emancipation enhance the contractual capacity of the emancipated minor? While common law emancipation generally does not change the minor's contractual capacity, 1 DONALD T. KRAMER, LEGAL RIGHTS OF CHILDREN 669 (2d ed. 1994), statutes in some states provide that certain disabilities of minority (such as incapacity to contract or to convey real property) may be removed by emancipation decrees under the statute. *Id.*

4. The *Accent Services* court emphasized several times that the minor left his mother's home *with her consent.* Is parental consent necessary for common law emancipation? Suppose the mother had not consented? Should a minor have a right to "emancipate himself" contrary to his parent's wishes. Consider the following case:

IN RE SNYDER

Supreme Court of Washington (en banc)
532 P.2d 278 (1975)

HUNTER, ASSOCIATE JUSTICE.

Paul Snyder and Nell Snyder, petitioners, seek review of the King County Juvenile Court's finding that their daughter, Cynthia Nell Snyder, respondent, was an incorrigible child as defined Under RCW 13.04.010(7). The issue before this court is whether the juvenile court's determination is supported by substantial evidence.

Cynthia Nell Snyder is sixteen-years-old, attends high school, and has consistently received above average grades. Prior to the occurrences which led to this action, she resided with her parents in their North Seattle home. The record shows that as Cynthia entered her teen years, a hostility began to develop between herself and her parents. This environment within the family home worsened due to a total breakdown in the lines of communication between Cynthia and her parents. Cynthia's parents, being strict disciplinarians, placed numerous limitations on their daughter's activities, such as restricting her choice of friends, and refusing to let her smoke, date, or participate in certain extracurricular activities within the school, all of which caused Cynthia to rebel against their authority. These hostilities culminated in a total collapse of the parent-child relationship. This atmosphere resulted in extreme mental abuse to all parties concerned.

On June 18, 1973, Mr. Snyder, having concluded that the juvenile court might be able to assist him in controlling his daughter, removed Cynthia from the family home and delivered her to the Youth Service Center. As a result, Cynthia was placed in a receiving home. On July 19, 1973, in an attempt to avoid returning home, Cynthia filed a petition in the Juvenile Department of the Superior Court for King County, alleging that she was a dependent child as defined by RCW 13.04.010(2) and (3), which provide:

> This chapter shall be known as the "Juvenile Court Law" and shall
> apply to all minor children under the age of eighteen years who are
> delinquent or dependent; and to any person or persons who are
> responsible for or contribute to, the delinquency or dependency of such
> children. For the purpose of this chapter the words "dependent child"
> shall mean any child under the age of eighteen years: (2) Who has
> no parent, guardian or other responsible person; or who has no parent
> or guardian willing to exercise, or capable of exercising, proper
> parental control; or (3) Whose home by reason of neglect, cruelty or
> depravity of his parents or either of them, or on the part of his
> guardian, or on the part of the person in whose custody or care he
> may be, or for any other reason, is an unfit place for such child; . . . .

On July 23, 1973, Cynthia was placed in the temporary custody of the
Department of Social and Health Services and an attorney was appointed to
be her guardian *ad litem*. On October 12, 1973, the juvenile court held that
the allegations attacking the fitness of Cynthia's parents were incorrect, at
least to the extent that they alleged dependency, and that Cynthia should be
returned to the custody of her parents. Cynthia did return to the family
residence, where she remained until November 16, 1973. At that time,
following additional confrontations in her home, Cynthia went to Youth
Advocates, a group which assists troubled juveniles, who in turn directed her
to the Youth Service Center. On November 21, 1973, Margaret Rozmyn, who
was in charge of the intake program at the center, filed a petition alleging
that Cynthia was incorrigible as defined under RCW 13.04.010(7), which
provides: "For the purpose of this chapter the words 'dependent child' shall
mean any child under the age of eighteen years: (7) Who is incorrigible; that
is, who is beyond the control and power of his parents, guardian, or custodian
by reason of the conduct or nature of said child; . . . ."

A hearing was held on December 3, 1973, to determine temporary custody.
The court . . . ultimately decided that Cynthia should be placed in a foster
home pending the outcome of the factfinding hearing. . . . At that time,
Commissioner Quinn found that Cynthia was incorrigible and continued the
matter for one week in order for the entire family to meet with a counselor.
Originally, the commissioner indicated that he was inclined to have Cynthia
return home, while at the same time being placed under supervised probation.
However, on December 18, 1973, Commissioner Quinn, upon hearing the comments and conclusions of the counseling psychiatrists chosen by the parents,
decided that Cynthia was to be placed in a foster home, under the supervision
of the probation department of the juvenile court, and that she and her parents
were to continue counseling, subject to subsequent review by the court. The
parents immediately filed a motion for revision of the commissioner's decision,
which was denied by the Superior Court for King County in August of 1974.

This court assumed jurisdiction of the case upon our issuance of the
requested *writ of certiorari*.

The sole issue presented by these facts is whether there is substantial
evidence in the record, taken as a whole, to support the juvenile court's
determination that Cynthia Nell Snyder is incorrigible. Her parents contend

that Cynthia is not incorrigible, as a matter of law, since the only evidence to support such a finding is their daughter's own statements. We disagree.

A child is incorrigible when she is beyond the power and control of her parents by reason of her own conduct. RCW 13.04.010(7). In reviewing the record in search of substantial evidence, we must find "evidence in sufficient quantum to persuade a fair-minded, rational person of the truth of a declared premise." . . . In applying this criteria for review, we are mindful that our paramount consideration, irrespective of the natural emotions in cases of this nature, must be the welfare of the child. . . . When the questions of dependency and incorrigibility arise, "we have often noted what we think is a realistic and rational appellate policy of placing very strong reliance on trial court determinations of what course of action will be in the best interest of the child." . . . In reviewing the record, we find no evidence which would indicate that Commissioner Quinn acted unfairly, irrationally, or in a prejudicial manner in reaching his conclusion. Therefore, we must give "very strong" credence to his determinations. We feel it is imperative to recognize that the issue of who is actually responsible for the breakdown in the parent-child relationship is irrelevant to our disposition of this case. The issue is whether there is substantial evidence to support a finding that the parent-child relationship has dissipated to the point where parental control is lost and, therefore, Cynthia is incorrigible. It is for this reason that Cynthia's conduct, her state of mind, and the opinion of Doctor Gallagher, the psychiatrist chosen by Mr. and Mrs. Snyder, are of such paramount importance. This child has established a pattern of refusing to obey her parents and, on two occasions, has, in effect, fled her home by filing petitions in the juvenile court in order that she might be made a ward of the court. Cynthia's adamant state of mind can be best understood by considering her Clear and Unambiguous testimony in response to her attorney's direct examination.

Q. Your petition alleges that you absolutely refuse to go home and obey your parents, is that correct?

A. Yes.

Q. You are under oath today, of course, and is that the statement you would make to the Court today?

A. Yes.

Q. Cindy, do you understand the consequences of filing a petition of this nature?

A. Yes.

Q. Did we discuss this matter?

A. Yes.

Q. Have we discussed this on several occasions?

A. Yes.

Q. What is your understanding of what might be the consequences of this type of petition?

A. I could be put in the Youth Center or I could be put into another institution of some kind or I could go into the custody of the Department of Social and Health Services.

Q. So you understand it is conceivable that you might not be able to go back home even if you want to go back home, is that correct?

A. Yes.

Q. In spite of all that, is it still your statement today that at the time of the petition anyway you refused to go back home?

A. Yes.

Q. Is that your position right now?

A. Yes.

Q. The position then, why don't you state that for the Court?

A. I refuse to go back there. I just won't do it.

MR. SANDERS (Attorney for parents): I object to the whole line of testimony. I think it is irrelevant whether she refuses to go back home. That is not an issue in the case.

THE COURT: Overruled.

A. I just absolutely refuse to go back there. I can't live with them.

In addition, the parents and the older sister, by their testimony, admitted that a difficult situation existed in the home. The court also considered the testimony of the intake officer from the Youth Service Center as to the attitude of Cynthia. Finally, the court considered the opinion of Dr. Gallagher, who met with Cynthia and her parents, and reported that counseling would not be beneficial until all of the individuals concerned backed away from the hard and fast positions they now held in regard to this matter which, in his opinion, was the cause of the tension which resulted in overt hostility. In other words, the finding of incorrigibility is not supported solely by Cynthia's testimony and her refusal to return home. But in addition thereto, the commissioner's opinion finds support in the testimony of other individuals who are familiar with the situation, either from a personal or a professional standpoint. The fact that the commissioner gave serious consideration to the testimony of Cynthia, an interested party, is inconsequential since it only goes to the weight to be given to her statements as a witness. . . .

Having found the juvenile court's finding of incorrigibility, as defined in RCW 13.04.010(7), to be supported by substantial evidence within the entire record, we are constitutionally bound to affirm the juvenile court's decision. . . .

  . . . .

It is implicit in the record that the petitioner parents believe the juvenile court has given sympathy and support to Cynthia's problems in disregard of their rights as parents, and that the juvenile court has failed to assume its responsibility to assist in the resolution of the parents' problems with their minor child. We find this presumption of the petitioners to be unsupported by the evidence.

The record clearly shows that numerous attempts were made by the juvenile court commissioner to reconcile the family differences, as evidenced by its unsuccessful attempt at sending Cynthia home subsequent to the disposition of the first petition, the attempt to gain assistance through professional counseling, and the numerous and extensive exchanges between Commissioner Quinn and the Snyder family during the proceeding. The avenues for counseling were to remain open and counseling of both parties was to continue, which was interrupted by the interposition of the application by the parents for our review. In view of our disposition of this case, we are satisfied that the juvenile court, in exercising its continuing jurisdiction, will continue to review the progress of the parties to the end of a hoped for reconciliation.

The decision of the juvenile court for King County is affirmed.

STAFFORD, C.J. and FINLEY, ROSELLINI, HAMILTON, WRIGHT, UTTER and BRACHTENBACH, J.J., *concur.*

———

NOTES AND QUESTIONS

1. Should the state have intervened in *Snyder* contrary to the wishes of the parents? Is the case explainable in terms of protectionist theory? Should adolescents be allowed personhood rights to decide with whom they will live?

2. Does *Snyder* grant a right to minors to "divorce" their parents if they so desire? At least one commentator has so read the case and criticized it on such grounds. *See* Bruce Hafin, *Children's Liberation and the New Egalitoriansim: Some Reservations About Abandoning Youth to Their Rights*, 1976 B.Y.U. L. REV. 605, 608–9. Apparently no court has recognized such a right subsequent to *Snyder*.

§ 2.03 CHILD ABUSE

[A] Introduction

The U.S. Department of Health and Human Services, Administration for Children and Families (http://www.acf.hhs.gov) releases its most current child abuse statistics, as reported by the states, in April of each year. The following includes statistics released in April 2005, which analyzed data for calendar year 2003.

In 2003, an estimated 1,500 children died of abuse and neglect — an average of more than 4 children per day. More than three-quarters (78.7 percent) of the children who die are younger than four years of age. Of these fatalities, 89 percent were under the age of eight; 43.6 percent of the children were under the age of one; 48.3 percent of child victims were male; 51.7 percent of victims were female; 83.9 percent of victims were abused by a parent; 40.8 percent of child victims were maltreated by their mothers acting alone; another 18.8 percent were maltreated by their fathers acting alone; and 16.9 percent were abused by both parents.

Types of maltreatment included:

Neglect (including medical neglect)	61%
Physical Abuse	19%
Sexual Abuse	10%
Psychological Maltreatment	5%
Medical Maltreatment	2%
Other	17%

Percentages total more than 100% because children may have been victims of more than one type of abuse.

The above statistics paint a horrible picture of child victimization. In fact, the situation may be even worse given the fact that child abuse usually occurs outside the public eye with victims often incapable of reporting its occurrence making it difficult to document the incidence and extent of the problem.

The widespread occurrence of child abuse was not brought to public consciousness until fairly recently. In the mid 1950's, the medical profession identified the "battered child syndrome," a diagnostic vehicle for distinguishing accidental injuries common to children from injuries inflicted by human agents. With this development, policy makers became aware of the widespread problem of child abuse. In response, legislatures nationwide enacted criminal statutes specifically aimed at curbing this insidious evil. Moreover, regarding evidentiary issues unique to child victims, courts and legislatures have generated a body of law sensitized to the problem of adjudicating child abuse. Similar to situations of neglect, child abuse may trigger a variety of state responses. This section of these materials, however, focuses primarily on criminal law matters.

[B] Defining Child Abuse

Child abuse is universally punished as a crime under state laws. In addition, all states have enacted child abuse reporting statutes that impose criminal penalties in certain circumstances for failure to report abuse. These materials will consider reporting statutes later and will presently attend to issues dealing with the proscription of conduct of those directly abusing children.

While all states punish child abuse, many do so under long-standing crimes such as assault, battering, and homicide. Some states, however, have enacted statutes defining a distinct crime of child abuse or cruelty to children. As you study the following provisions, note that the definition of abuse regarding the direct abuser is sometimes different from that adopted in the reporting statutes considered later.

[1] Statutory Provisions

MARYLAND CODE ANNOTATED
Article 27, § 35C (2000 Supp.)

Causing abuse to child.

(a) *Definitions.* — (1) In this section the following words have the meanings indicated.

(2) "Abuse" means:

(i) The sustaining of physical injury by a child as a result of cruel or inhumane treatment or as a result of a malicious act by any parent or other person who has permanent or temporary care or custody or responsibility for supervision of a child, or by any household or family member, under circumstances that indicate that the child's health or welfare is harmed or threatened thereby; or

(ii) Sexual abuse of a child, whether physical injuries are sustained or not.

(3) "Child" means any individual under the age of 18 years.

(4) "Family member" means a relative of a child by blood, adoption, or marriage.

(5) "Household member" means a person who lives with or is a regular presence in a home of a child at the time of the alleged abuse.

(6) (i) "Sexual abuse" means any act that involves sexual molestation or exploitation of a child by a parent or other person who has permanent or temporary care or custody or responsibility for supervision of a child, or by any household or family member.

(ii) "Sexual abuse" includes, but is not limited to:

1. Incest, rape, or sexual offense in any degree;

2. Sodomy; and

3. Unnatural or perverted sexual practices.

(b) *Violation constitutes felony; penalty; sentencing.* — (1) A parent or other person who has permanent or temporary care or custody or responsibility for the supervision of a child or a household or family member who causes abuse to the child is guilty of a felony and on conviction is subject to imprisonment in the penitentiary for not more than 15 years.

(2) If the violation results in the death of the victim, the person is guilty of a felony and upon conviction is subject to imprisonment for not more than 30 years.

(3) The sentence imposed under this section may be imposed separate from and consecutive to or concurrent with a sentence for any offense based upon the act or acts establishing the abuse.

Nebraska Revised Statutes
§ 28-707 (2005 Supp.)

Child Abuse; Privileges Not Available; Penalties.

(1) A person commits child abuse if he or she knowingly, intentionally, or negligently causes or permits a minor child to be:

(a) Placed in a situation that endangers his or her life or physical or mental health;

(b) Cruelly confined or cruelly punished;

(c) Deprived of necessary food, clothing, shelter, or care;

(d) Placed in a situation to be sexually exploited by allowing, encouraging, or forcing such minor child to solicit for or engage in prostitution, debauchery, public indecency, or obscene or pornographic photography, films, or depictions; or

(e) Placed in a situation to be sexually abused as defined in § 28-319 or 28-320.01.

(2) The statutory privilege between patient and physician, between client and professional counselor, and between husband and wife shall not be available for excluding or refusing testimony in any prosecution for a violation of this section.

(3) Child abuse is a Class I misdemeanor if the offense is committed negligently.

(4) Child abuse is a Class IIIA felony if the offense is committed knowingly and intentionally and does not result in serious bodily injury as defined in § 28-109.

(5) Child abuse is a Class III felony if the offense is committed knowingly and intentionally and results in serious bodily injury as defined in such section.

(6) Child abuse is a Class IB felony if the offense is committed knowingly and intentionally and results in the death of such child.

Nevada Revised Statutes
§ 200.508 (2005)

Abuse, Neglect or Endangerment of Child: Penalties; Definitions.

1. A person who:

(a) Willfully causes a child who is less than 18 years of age to suffer unjustifiable physical pain or mental suffering as a result of abuse or neglect or to be placed in a situation where the child may suffer physical pain or mental suffering as the result of abuse or neglect; or

(b) Is responsible for the safety or welfare of a child and who permits or allows that child to suffer unjustifiable physical pain or mental suffering as a result of abuse or neglect or to be placed in a situation where the child may suffer physical pain or mental suffering as the result of abuse or neglect, is guilty of a gross misdemeanor unless a more severe penalty is prescribed by law for an act or omission which brings about the abuse, neglect or danger.

2. A person who violates any provision of subsection 1, if substantial bodily or mental harm results to the child:

(a) If the child is less than 14 years of age and the harm is the result of sexual abuse or exploitation, is guilty of a category A felony and shall be punished by imprisonment in the state prison for life with the possibility of parole, with eligibility for parole beginning when a minimum of 10 years has been served; or

(b) In all other such cases to which paragraph (a) does not apply, is guilty of a category B felony and shall be punished by imprisonment in the state prison for a minimum term of not less than 2 years and a maximum term of not more than 20 years.

3. As used in this section:

(a) "Abuse or neglect" means physical or mental injury of a non-accidental nature, sexual abuse, sexual exploitation, negligent treatment or maltreatment of a child under the age of 18 years, as set forth in paragraph (d) and NRS 432B.070, 432B.100, 432B.110, 432B.140 and 432B.150, under circumstances which indicate that the child's health or welfare is harmed or threatened with harm.

(b) "Allow" means to do nothing to prevent or stop the abuse or neglect of a child in circumstances where the person knows or has reason to know that the child is abused or neglected.

(c) "Permit" means permission that a reasonable person would not grant and which amounts to a neglect of responsibility attending the care, custody and control of a minor child.

(d) "Physical injury" means:

(1) Permanent or temporary disfigurement; or

(2) Impairment of any bodily function or organ of the body.

(e) "Substantial mental harm" means an injury to the intellectual or psychological capacity or the emotional condition of a child as evidenced by an observable and substantial impairment of the ability of the child to function within his normal range of performance or behavior.

ARIZONA REVISED STATUTES ANNOTATED
§ 13-3623 (2005)

Child . . . Abuse; Emotional Abuse; Classification; Exception; Definitions

A. Under circumstances likely to produce death or serious physical injury, any person who causes a child . . . to suffer physical injury or, having the care or custody of a child . . . , who causes or permits the person or health of the child . . . to be injured or who causes or permits a child . . . to be placed in a situation where the person or health of the child . . . is endangered is guilty of an offense as follows:

1. If done intentionally or knowingly, the offense is a class 2 felony and if the victim is under fifteen years of age it is punishable pursuant to § 13-604.

2. If done recklessly, the offense is a class 3 felony.

3. If done with criminal negligence, the offense is a class 4 felony.

B. Under circumstances other than those likely to produce death or serious physical injury to a child . . . any person who causes a child . . . to suffer physical injury or abuse or, having the care or custody of a child . . . who causes or permits the person or health of the child . . . to be injured or who causes or permits a child . . . to be placed in a situation where the person or health of the child . . . is endangered is guilty of an offense as follows:

1. If done intentionally or knowingly, the offense is a class 4 felony.

2. If done recklessly, the offense is a class 5 felony.

3. If done with criminal negligence, the offense is a class 6 felony.

C. For the purposes of subsections A and B of this section, the terms endangered and abuse include but are not limited to circumstances in which a child . . . is permitted to enter or remain in any structure or vehicle in which volatile, toxic or flammable chemicals are found or equipment is possessed by any person for the purpose of manufacturing a dangerous drug in violation of § 13-3407, subsection A, paragraph 4.

. . . .

F. For the purposes of this section:

1. "Abuse," when used in reference to a child, means abuse as defined in § 8-201, [Defined as follows: "Abuse means the infliction or allowing of physical injury, impairment of bodily function or disfigurement or the infliction of or allowing another person to cause serious emotional damage as evidenced by severe anxiety, depression, withdrawal or untoward aggressive behavior and which emotional damage is diagnosed by a medical doctor or psychologist pursuant to § 8-821 and which is caused by the acts or omissions of an individual having care, custody and control of a child. Abuse shall include inflicting or allowing sexual abuse pursuant to § 13-1404, sexual conduct with a minor pursuant to § 13-1405, sexual assault pursuant to § 13-1406, molestation of a child pursuant to § 13-3552, sexual exploitation of a minor pursuant to § 13-3553, incest pursuant to § 13-3608 or child prostitution pursuant to § 13-3212] except for those acts in the definition that are declared unlawful by another statute of this title. . . .

2. "Child" means an individual who is under eighteen years of age.

. . . .

4. "Physical injury" means the impairment of physical condition and includes any skin bruising, pressure sores, bleeding, failure to thrive, malnutrition, dehydration, burns, fracture of any bone, subdural hematoma, soft tissue swelling, injury to any internal organ or any physical condition that imperils health or welfare.

5. "Serious physical injury" means physical injury that creates a reasonable risk of death or that causes serious or permanent disfigurement,

serious impairment of health or loss or protracted impairment of the function of any bodily organ or limb.

———

NOTES AND QUESTIONS

1. Are statutes defining a distinct crime of child abuse a good idea? Are there advantages to having distinct child abuse statutes that would not be available if prosecution for child abuse were brought under traditional assault, battery, or homicide statutes? Note that the Maryland statute (subsection (b)(3)) specifically permits cumulative punishment under the child abuse provision and other criminal statutes proscribing the same misconduct. Is this a desirable approach?

2. The Maryland statute appears to limit liability to situations resulting in "physical injury" (subsection (2)(i)) while the Nebraska, Nevada, and Arizona provisions extend liability to harm, or even risk of harm, to mental or psychological health. Is one or the other of these statutory approaches preferable?

3. For other examples of statutory provisions defining a distinct crime of child abuse including protections against emotional as well as physical harm, see CAL. PENAL CODE § 273(a) (West 2005) (infliction of "unjustifiable physical pain or mental suffering"); COLO. REV. STAT. § 18-6-401 (2005) (injury or threat thereof to child's "life or health"); 720 ILL. COMP. STAT. ANN. 5/12 — 21.6 (West Supp. 2005) (endangering "life or health" of child); IOWA CODE ANN. § 726.6 (West Supp. 2005) (creating a "substantial risk to a child's physical, mental or emotional health or safety"); MO. ANN. STAT. § 568.045 —.060 (West 2005) (creating "substantial risk to the life, body, or health" of a child).

Delaware includes harm to the child's "moral welfare":

Endangering the Welfare of a Child; Class E or G Felony.

(a) A person is guilty of endangering the welfare of a child when:

(1) Being a parent, guardian or other person legally charged with the care or custody of a child less than 18-years-old the person:

a. Knowingly acts in a manner likely to be injurious to the physical, mental or moral welfare of the child; . . . .

DEL. CODE ANN. tit. 11, § 1102 (Supp. 2005).

[2] Constitutional Issues

STATE v. SINICA

Supreme Court of Nebraska
372 N.W.2d 445 (1985)

WHITE, JUSTICE.

This is an appeal from a decision of the district court for Lancaster County, Nebraska, in a criminal case.

Pursuant to NEB. REV. STAT. § 29-2315.01 (Cum. Supp. 1984), the State filed an application for leave to docket an appeal to this court, taking exceptions to the ruling of the lower court. We sustain one of the exceptions.

Appellee, Peter M. Sinica, was arrested and charged with child abuse, specifically that he "did knowingly or intentionally cause or permit Peter M. Sinica, Jr., a minor child, to be cruelly punished." Appellee was bound over to the district court after a preliminary hearing. Appellee raised the question of the constitutionality of the statute in both the county court and the district court. The trial court sustained a motion to quash the information, holding that NEB. REV. STAT. § 28-707(1) (Cum. Supp. 1984) is "so vague that it violates due process of law."

. . . .

The appellee is the father of the alleged victim. The incident which gave rise to the complaint was called to the attention of the nine-year-old child's teacher, who questioned the child about a cut on his face. On questioning, the child revealed that his father had struck him on the face and beaten him with a belt on his buttocks and back. The police were summoned and the child was treated at a local hospital. Photographs taken by the police show the child's buttocks to be severely bruised. The entire surface of the child's backside was a deep purple color. Strap and bruise marks also appear about the child's back and shoulders. The child testified that the punishment was inflicted because the child had disobeyed an order from the appellee. The child was to have brought home notes from his teachers showing that all his schoolwork had been completed before leaving on a family vacation.

The State's exceptions are twofold: (1) That the appellee lacked standing to attack the constitutionality of the statute . . . and (2) Even on a facial challenge the relevant statutory language, "cruelly punished," is not vague or uncertain.

The State's first exception is overruled. Regardless of whether an individual may have standing to challenge a statute for vagueness . . . the appellee may have standing to assert that a statute is overbroad because it reaches a substantial amount of constitutionally protected conduct.

The right to privacy, a fundamental right within the penumbras of the guarantees of the Bill of Rights, includes a right to freedom of choice in marriage and family decisions. The Supreme Court has further recognized the fundamental liberty interest of parents in the care, custody, and management of their children. Thus, the liberty to engage in these parental activities is protected by the due process guarantees of the fourteenth amendment to the U.S. Constitution.

. . . When a statute is facially challenged as to overbreadth and vagueness, "our first task is to determine whether the enactment reaches a substantial amount of constitutionally protected conduct." If the overbreadth challenge fails, "[w]e are to then examine the facial vagueness. . . ." Vagueness is a constitutional vice conceptually distinct from overbreadth, in that an overbroad law need lack neither clarity nor precision and a vague law need not reach constitutionally protected activity. However, . . . the Supreme Court recognized that in making an overbreadth determination

> a court should evaluate the ambiguous as well as the unambiguous scope of the enactment. To this extent, the vagueness of a law affects overbreadth analysis. The Court has long recognized that ambiguous meanings cause citizens to 'steer far wider of the unlawful zone' . . . than if the boundaries of the forbidden areas were clearly marked.

Under the facts of this case we find that it would be impossible to determine whether § 28-707(1) is overbroad and impinges on the constitutional right of a parent to reasonably correct and discipline a child without examining the statutory language for clarity and precision in proscribing the offense of child abuse.

Section 28-707(1) reads as follows:

> (1) A person commits child abuse if he or she knowingly, intentionally, or negligently causes or permits a minor child to be: (a) Placed in a situation that endangers his or her life or health; or (b) Cruelly confined or cruelly punished; or (c) Deprived of necessary food, clothing, shelter, or care.

We focus in particular on subsection (b). Is the term "cruelly punish" defined with sufficient definiteness, and are there ascertainable standards of guilt to inform someone of common intelligence what course is lawful to pursue? . . . The term "cruelly punished" is not defined in a separate section of the statute. However, "cruel" is defined by Webster's Ninth New Collegiate Dictionary 311 (1985) as "1: disposed to inflict pain or suffering: devoid of humane feelings 2 a: causing or conducive to injury, grief, or pain b: unrelieved by leniency." "Punish" is defined by the same source as "1 a: to impose a penalty on for a fault, offense, or violation b: to inflict a penalty for the commission of (an offense) in retribution or retaliation 2 a: to deal with roughly or harshly b: to inflict injury on."

In *People v. Jennings*, 641 P.2d 276 (Colo.1982), the defendant, Jennings, was charged with child abuse under a statute similar to § 28-707, which provided that a person was guilty of child abuse if he " 'knowingly, intentionally, or negligently, and without justifiable excuse,' caus[ed] or permitt[ed] a child to be 'abandoned, tortured, cruelly confined or cruelly punished.' " After a jury trial and a judgment of conviction, the trial court found the words "cruelly punished" to be unconstitutionally vague because of the subjective nature of the words. On appeal the Colorado Supreme Court reversed. The court held that the term "cruelly punished" is one capable of definition and applies to clearly proscribed conduct.

That a distinction can be made between permissible punishment and 'cruel' punishment is supported by the traditional common law rule concerning parental discipline of children. At common law the parent of a minor child or one standing in loco parentis was privileged in using a reasonable amount of force upon a child for purposes of safeguarding or promoting the child's welfare. While at common law the precise test of what constituted permissible force varied from jurisdiction to jurisdiction, as a general proposition, so long as the chastisement was moderate and reasonable in light of the child's age and condition, the misconduct being punished, the kind of punishment inflicted, the degree of harm done to the child and other relevant circumstances, the parent or custodian would incur neither civil nor criminal liability, even though identical behavior against a stranger would be grounds for an action in tort or prosecution for assault and battery or a similar offense.

. . . The Colorado Supreme Court observed: "Since the contours of the common law privilege have been subject for centuries to definition and refinement through careful and constant judicial decisionmaking, terms like 'cruel' or 'inhumane' and 'malicious' have acquired a relatively widely accepted connotation in the law." . . .

Given sufficient definition by the common law, the term "cruelly punished" would not meet the further evil of a vague statute, that of arbitrary and discriminatory application on an *ad hoc* and subjective basis by policemen, judges, and juries. . . .

A number of other jurisdictions have examined the phrases "cruel punishment" and "inhumane punishment," "unnecessary punishment or infliction of pain," "cruel mistreatment" and "cruel maltreatment," and have found that such phrases do not violate the due process clause of the Fourteenth Amendment to the U.S. Constitution nor the similar provisions in their own state Constitutions.

The appellee urged before the trial court and in his brief to this court that "cruelly punished" could encompass a broad range of disciplinary techniques. "Many people operate under the philosophy that any physical discipline is cruel, while just as many others believe that spanking is a necessary part of child rearing."

While this assertion may be true, we believe the term "cruelly punished" is capable of an easily understood meaning as distinguished from the reasonable discipline of a child allowed by the common law and protected by the Constitution. It is a mark of statutory interpretation that in construing a statute the Supreme Court will presume that the Legislature intended a sensible rather than an absurd result. Further, when a statute is constitutionally suspect, we endeavor to interpret it in a manner consistent with the Constitution.

Since the term "cruelly punished" has been sufficiently defined by the common law and does not include reasonable disciplinary measures, the appellee's overbreadth challenge to § 28-707(1) must fail. Child abuse is not a constitutionally protected activity.

Under our analysis appellee's contention that § 28-707 as applied to his conduct is vague would also fail.

As to the alleged facial vagueness of § 28-707(1) as asserted in appellee's brief, the appellee will not be heard to challenge the statute. Since his conduct would be clearly proscribed by the statute, he cannot complain of its application as to the conduct of others.

Exception sustained, and cause remanded for further proceedings.

STATE v. MEINERT

Supreme Court of Kansas
594 P.2d 232 (1979)

HOLMES, JUSTICE:

This is an appeal by the State from an order of the district court dismissing a criminal complaint against Wayne Meinert on the ground that K.S.A. 21-3608(1) (A) is unconstitutionally vague. Defendant was charged under the statute with the offense of endangering a child. While the facts are not necessary in determining the question before this court, they will be recited briefly.

Defendant and Charlene Meinert were baby-sitting with three-year-old Jeanette Lowery. Defendant admitted having spanked Jeanette for urinating on the floor and not in the proper receptacle. The parents had not given the Meinerts permission to spank Jeanette. Ron Lowery, Jeanette's father, filed a complaint against Wayne Meinert alleging a violation of K.S.A. 21-3608(1)(A), stating in his affidavit supporting the complaint that red marks were still visible on the child's buttocks four hours after the spanking took place.

K.S.A. 21-3608 provides in pertinent parts:

Endangering a child. (1) Endangering a child is willfully:

(A) Causing or permitting a child under the age of eighteen (18) years to suffer unjustifiable physical pain or mental distress; or

(B) Unreasonably causing or permitting a child under the age of eighteen (18) years to be placed in a situation in which its life, body or health may be injured or endangered.

Defendant contended that the words "unjustifiable physical pain" as used in the statute are unconstitutional and fail to sufficiently identify the prohibited conduct as required by § 10 of the Kansas Bill of Rights and the Fifth and Fourteenth Amendments to the United States Constitution. The trial court so held and we agree with the trial court.

When statutes are challenged as unconstitutional, certain principles guide this court's consideration.

Long-standing and well-established rules of this court are that the constitutionality of a statute is presumed, that all doubts must be resolved in favor of its validity, and before the statute may be stricken down, it must clearly appear the statute violates the constitution. Moreover, it is the court's duty to uphold the statute under attack, if possible, rather than defeat it, and if there is any reasonable way to construe the statute as constitutionally valid, that should be done. . . .

The vagueness test applicable to criminal statutes was iterated in *State v. Kirby*, 563 P.2d 408 (Kan. 1977):

The test to determine whether a criminal statute is unconstitutionally void by reason of being vague and indefinite is whether its language conveys a sufficiently definite warning as to the conduct proscribed when measured by common understanding and practice. If a statute conveys this warning it is not void for vagueness. Conversely, a statute which either requires or forbids the doing of an act in terms so vague that persons of common intelligence must necessarily guess at its meaning and differ as to its application is violative of due process. At its heart the test for vagueness is a commonsense determination of fundamental fairness. . . .

In *State v. Hill*, we stated:

It is well recognized that in order to satisfy the constitutional requirements of due process, a state statute must be sufficiently explicit in its description of the acts, conduct or conditions required or forbidden, to prescribe the elements of the offense with reasonable certainty. The standards of certainty in a statute punishing for criminal offenses is higher than in those depending primarily upon civil sanction for enforcement. The offenses must be defined with appropriate definiteness. There must be ascertainable standards of guilt, but impossible standards of specificity are not required. Men of common intelligence cannot be required to guess at the meaning of the statute. The vagueness may be for uncertainty with respect to persons within the scope of the statute or in regard to applicable tests to ascertain guilt. The test is whether the language conveys a sufficient definite warning as to the proscribed conduct when measured by common understanding and practice.

With the foregoing in mind, we now turn to the issue of whether K.S.A. 21-3608(1)(A) is unconstitutionally vague on its face.

. . . .

Nowhere in our criminal code is there any definition of "unjustifiable physical pain or mental suffering." In *State v. Kirby*, 563 P.2d 408 (Kan. 1977), we held K.S.A. 21-3431 unconstitutional and said:

In our judgment the phrase 'endangering of life' is vague and ambiguous. 21-3431 does not define 'endangering of life,' nor is the term defined in the definition, § 21-3110, or anywhere else in the criminal code. . . . Counsel for the state points out that on the one hand, the language could be construed to proscribe any act which possibly could imperil human life, no matter how remote that possibility might be. On the other hand, it could be construed to proscribe only those acts which are immediately and inherently life threatening. The difficulty with this argument is that, assuming the state is correct in its position, it would from a practical standpoint be impossible for a person of common intelligence in every factual situation to draw a clear line between acts which are and which are not immediately and inherently life threatening.

It is to be noted that the title of the statute before us is "endangering a child" and in *Kirby* this court found the language "endangering of life" to be too indefinite to pass constitutional muster. Where is the line to be drawn in determining if discipline or other treatment of a child is justified or unjustified? How does one decide whether or not a spanking is due a child and, if so, should it be administered with the hands, a fly swatter, or a belt? Is one slap, two slaps, or five slaps too many? Are two hard slaps a violation of the statute, but five very light slaps not? Do red marks lasting only one hour relieve one from prosecution? Some persons do not believe in any form of corporal punishment and to them any such treatment would be unjustified. On the other hand, others may believe any correction, however severe, which produces temporary pain only, and no lasting injury or disfigurement, is justified. The statute could conceivably cover anything from a minor spanking or slapping to severe beating depending upon the personal beliefs of the individual.

. . . .

. . . We are of the opinion that K.S.A. 21-3608(1)(A) is so vague and uncertain that it fails to establish the reasonably definite standards of guilt required by due process of law.

The judgment is affirmed.

NOTES AND QUESTIONS

1. As *Sinica* and *Meinert* make clear, parents, and those standing *in loco parentis*, are entitled at common law to employ reasonable force, including corporal punishment in disciplining children in their charge. For an extensive discussion of parental rights to inflict corporal punishment as a defense in child abuse cases, see Kandice K. Johnson, *Crime or Punishment: The Parental Corporal Punishment Defense — Reasonable and Necessary, or Excused Abuse?*, 1998 U. ILL. L. REV. 413. The Johnson article proposes a statutory approach that would deny justifiable disciplinary force to situations resulting in "physical injury," defined as "any damage to or impairment of tissue or organ" not including "transient red marks or temporary pain." *Id.* at 471-72.

Moreover, permissible disciplinary force is excluded in situations where the child is placed in "substantial risk of either death, serious physical or emotional injury (defined, as a 'medically diagnosable mental condition, trauma, or illness'), or gross degradation." *Id.* Do you find the proposed statute preferable to the common law approach that assesses whether parental force was "reasonable" under the circumstances of the particular case?

For codifications of the common law defense as well as other statutory approaches to defining permissible parental disciplinary force, see *Id.* at 484–87 (Appendix).

For a discussion of a variety of issues surrounding corporal punishment, see Susan H. Bitensky, *Spare the Rod, Embrace Human Rights: International Law's Mandate Against All Corporal Punishment of Children*, 21 WHITTIER L. REV. 147 (1999); Joel R. Brandes, *"A Good Spank Never Hurt Anybody"*, 225 N.Y. L.J. 3 (2001); David Orentlicher, *Spanking and other Corporal Punishment of Children by Parents: Overvaluing Pain, Undervaluing Children*, 35 HOUS. L. REV. 147 (1998); James Podgers, *When does Punishment Go Too Far? Courts Struggle to Find the Line Between Parental Discipline and Child Abuse*, 82 A.B.A. J. 40 (1996); Jane M. Spinak, *Reflections on a Case (of Motherhood)*, 95 COLUM. L. REV. 1990 (1995); Murray A. Straus & Carrie L. Yodanis, *Corporal Punishment by Parents: Implications for Primary Prevention of Assaults on Spouses and Children*, 2 U. CHI. L. SCH. ROUNDTABLE 35 (1995).

2. In response to the *Meinert* case, the Kansas Legislature amended the child endangerment statute, removing the unconstitutional "unjustifiable physical pain" provision. The Kansas statute currently defines "endangering a child" as follows:

(a) Endangering a child is intentionally and unreasonably causing or permitting a child under the age of 18 years to be placed in a situation in which the child's life, body or health may be injured or endangered.

(b) Nothing in this section shall be construed to mean a child is endangered for the sole reason the child's parent or guardian, in good faith, selects and depends upon spiritual means alone through prayer, in accordance with the tenets and practice of a recognized church or religious denomination, for the treatment or cure of disease or remedial care of such child.

(c) Endangering a child is a class A person misdemeanor.

KAN. STAT. ANN. § 21-3608 (1995). The amended statute has been judicially upheld. *See State v. Wilson*, 987 P.2d 1060 (Kan. 1999).

3. For further discussion of cases addressing alleged vagueness of child abuse statutes, see Milton Roberts, Annotation, *Validity and Construction of Penal Statute Prohibiting Child Abuse*, 1 A.L.R. 4th 38, 49-61 (1980).

[3] Scope Issues

[a] What is "Abuse"?

IN THE MATTER OF SHANE T.

Family Court, Richmond County
453 N.Y.S.2d 590 (1982)

DANIEL D. LEDDY, JR., JUDGE.

Today, this Court finds that fourteen-year-old Shane T. is an abused child in that he has been repeatedly called a "fag," "faggot," and "queer" by his natural father, a respondent herein. His father also taunted him continually by saying that he should have been a girl. In holding that Shane is an abused child, the Court concludes that the phrase "physical injury" as contemplated by § 1012(e)(i) of the Family Court Act need not be inflicted by physical force and that it encompasses the stomach pain experienced by Shane when his father challenged the boy's sexual identity.

The instant proceeding arose from petitions filed by the Commissioner of Social Services on February 8, 1982 against the natural parents seeking an adjudication that Shane and his two sisters are abused children.[43] After carefully considering all of the testimony adduced and evaluating the demeanor of the respective witnesses, the Court finds that the following facts have been established beyond a reasonable doubt.[44]

Shane is the natural child of the respondents and presently resides with his mother and two sisters. His father is a construction worker who has been separated from his wife for some time, although they continue to see each other.

Over the course of the last several years, Shane has been subjected to an unrelenting torrent of verbal abuse by his father directed at his sexual identity. Specifically, he has been regularly called a "fag," "faggot," and "queer". In desperation, the boy pleaded with his mother to intervene on his behalf and prevail upon his father to cease making these accusations. However, the mother's efforts were abortive, resulting only in a repetition of the taunts by the father with the added assertion that they were true.

Nor were these accusations limited to the home. On one particular occasion, the respondent's father humiliated the boy by calling him a "fag" while they were shopping in a store.

Section 1012(e)(i) defines an "abused child" as one

> Less than eighteen years of age whose parent or other person legally responsible for his care inflicts or allows to be inflicted upon such child physical injury by other than accidental means which causes or creates

---

[43] [2] By short form order, issued simultaneously herewith, the Court finds that Shane's sisters are neglected children as defined in FCA Sec. 1012(f)(i)(B).

[44] [3] The Court is aware, of course, that a mere preponderance of the credible evidence would suffice under the statute (FCA § 1046(b)).

a substantial risk of death, or serious or protracted disfigurement, or protracted impairment of physical or emotional health or protracted loss or impairment of the function of any bodily organ.

The wording of this section is similar to that contained in § 10.00(10) of the Penal Law, from which it was derived.

As defined in the Penal Law, "physical injury means impairment of physical condition or substantial pain."

Whether "substantial pain" has been established is ordinarily a question for the trier of fact. In reaching a determination, the subjective reaction of the injured party is a proper factor to be considered although there is an objective level below which the question is one of law. Thus, such things as petty slaps, shoves, kicks and the like delivered out of hostility, meanness and similar motives, are not within the contemplation of assault as defined in the Penal Law.

In deciding whether Shane has experienced "substantial pain," the Court initially considers the observation of Chief Judge Cooke:

> Pain is, by definition, a subjective concept and cannot be quantified or expressed with precision. Knowledge of the circumstances and the description of the sensation accompanying the use of force, however, provide a ready basis for measuring, within one's own experience, the degree of pain felt by another.

It must be immediately observed that there is no specific requirement of the use of force in the definition of an abused child. Thus, Judge Cooke's statement relating to "the use of force" is specifically referenced to the assault. . . . In fact, while § 1012(e)(i) of the Family Court Act is derived from § 10.00(10) of the Penal Law, there are substantial differences between the statutes. Thus, it is sufficient for a finding of abuse that there be protracted impairment of emotional health or a substantial risk thereof. It is clear, therefore, that it is the actual or potential impact on the child, as opposed to the *per se* seriousness of the injury, that forms the predicate for abuse. In this regard, the Family Court Act provision differs markedly from the Penal Law definition of "serious physical injury." Furthermore, while § 1012(e)(i) of the Family Court Act makes specific reference to "emotional health," § 10.00(10) of the Penal Law refers merely to "health."

The foregoing is consistent with the fact that Article 10 of the Family Court Act is a civil proceeding "designed to establish procedures to help protect children from injury or mistreatment and to help safeguard their physical, mental and *emotional well-being*." Therefore, this Court concludes that the "physical injury" referred to in § 1012(e)(i) of the Family Court Act need not be inflicted by physical force. Rather, to constitute abuse, mere words are sufficient provided that their effect on the child falls within the language of the statute. To hold otherwise would constitute an unjustifiably narrow interpretation of the statute that would frustrate the legislature's intent.

As he testified, Shane repeatedly tried to forestall tears, but they besieged his eyes, nonetheless. He told the Court how he would cry and his stomach would twist when his father called him a "fag." At one point, he was asked whether he was beginning to believe that he was a homosexual. He clenched his hands, sat forward, and cried out "No!". His demeanor strongly suggested, however, that he would like someone, anyone, to reassure him.

It should be noted that, in addition to the verbal indignities to which he was subjected, Shane was frequently forced to remove his father's shoes and massage his feet.[45] The boy complied without protest since he was constantly in fear of his father. This fear was well-founded since the father has a history of assaultive behavior in the home.[46] Against this background, it is hardly surprising that Shane is now in therapy. This sensitive, handsome little boy has been trapped in an emotional roller coaster that seemingly plunges only downward, at a terrifying speed, toward an end that seems never to come.

To fail to acknowledge this boy's plight would be an affront to the clear legislative intent of Article 10 of the Family Court Act; to fail to label the father's actions as child abuse would strip the phrase of all meaning; to fail to warn other parents against this insidious type of abuse would perpetuate the suffering of countless other defenseless children.

The respondent father seeks to justify his verbal abuse of Shane as a form of legitimate parental discipline designed to cure the child of certain unspecified "girlie" behavior. He stated that it would be embarrassing [sic] to him if Shane were "queer." It is very sad and even shocking that, at this late date in our constitutional development, many parents continue to view their home as a kingdom where they reign as king and queen and their children are relegated to the role of indentured servants.

While a parent's right to raise his or her child remains fundamental, it is equally fundamental that children have constitutional rights which must be respected by all, including their parents. . . . [T]he bill of rights is not for adults alone. Time and again, courts have reiterated the validity of state interference in the parental-child relationship when necessary to protect the child's health and welfare. Cases such as these and the principles that underline them form the constitutional predicate for child protective statutes such as Article 10 of the Family Court Act. Accordingly, the father's defense is not only legally insufficient but, rather, it is singularly ludicrous.

The behavior of this respondent father is as serious a form of abuse as if he had plunged a knife into the stomach of this child. In fact, it's probably worse since the agony and heartache suffered by Shane has already assailed him for several years and constitutes a grave and imminent threat to his future psychological development.

The respondent mother testified that she tried to keep peace in the marital home. And the Court does find that she attempted to dissuade her husband

---

[45] [4] In holding that Shane's sisters are neglected children, the Court made a finding that the respondent father frequently forced them to massage his scalp.

[46] [5] The testimony revealed that on Easter of 1981, the respondent father beat the respondent mother so severely that she had to flee to the roof of their home to escape him. On this occasion, Shane hid under his bed to avoid his father. Similarly, on Thanksgiving of 1981, the boy hid in a tree for two hours when his father visited the home. In addition, the respondent father constantly threatened to break his children's legs.

from continuing his verbal abuse of Shane. Despite this, the fact remains that she failed to protect her son from an ongoing, serious abuse.

She hardly discharged her parental duty to Shane by, in effect, keeping peace at his expense. When her husband persisted in his abuse of the child, she had an obligation to act meaningfully to protect the boy. And, in this regard, no action is meaningful unless and until it results in a cessation of the abuse and protection of the child. To uphold any lesser standard would seriously undercut legislative efforts to halt the senseless abuse and neglect of children.

It is also significant that the respondent mother continues to speak of a reconciliation with her husband despite the absence of any indication that he recognizes the seriousness of his actions toward Shane or the need to involve himself in therapy.

Accordingly, the Court finds that the respondent mother allowed physical injury to be inflicted upon Shane which created a substantial risk of protracted impairment of his emotional health. FCA § 1012(e)(i).

Therefore, on the entire record it is

ORDERED that Shane T. be, and he hereby is, declared to be an abused child by both respondents, and it is further

ORDERED that he be, and he so is, remanded to the Commissioner of Social Services, and it is further

ORDERED that the Family Court Clinic be, and it hereby is, directed to perform an immediate psychiatric and psychological evaluation of Shane on an emergency basis, and it is further

ORDERED that the Probation Department be, and it hereby is, directed to conduct an investigation and prepare a report in aid of disposition, and it is further

ORDERED that the adjourned date of August 18, 1982 be, and the same hereby is, vacated and the matter is adjourned to September 15, 1982 for a dispositional hearing, and it is further

ORDERED, that the Clerk be and he hereby is directed to supply two copies of the decision to the Department of Probation.

NOTES AND QUESTIONS

1. *Shane T.* is a civil case but the conduct involved would appear to be criminal under some state provisions. For example, the Nebraska provision noted earlier, § 2.03[B][1] *supra*, defines criminal child abuse as, *inter alia*, "endanger[ing] [a child's] mental health." Would not the father in *Shane T.* be guilty of felonious child abuse under NEB. REV. STAT., § 28-707 (1)(a), (4) or (5)? Should he be?

What if the father had merely urged his son "to be a man" rather than calling him derogatory epithets with the result that the son experienced the same anxiety and stomach pain as Shane T.?

Note that under the Nebraska statute no actual harm need be caused the child, actions "endangering" the child's "mental health" are sufficient. Under this definition would a parent abuse his child if he "merely" insults the child, yells at the child, or swears at the child?

2. In the *Sinica* case, § 2.03[B][2] *supra*, the Nebraska Supreme Court upheld the "cruel punishment" provision of the Nebraska statute against a vagueness attack. In light of the considerations discussed in Note 1 immediately above, are there more significant vagueness problems pertaining to the "endangering mental health" provision of the Nebraska Statute? Is that provision unconstitutionally vague particularly in light of the parent's right to subject his child to reasonable measures of discipline? *See* Francis A. Allen, *The Erosion of Legality in American Justice: Some Latter-Day Adventures of the Nulla Poena Principle*, 29 ARIZ. L. REV. 385 (1987); John Calvin Jeffries, Jr., *Legality, Vagueness and the Construction of Penal Statutes,* 71 VA. L. REV. 189 (1985).

3. Would the conduct of the father in *Shane T.* be child abuse under the Maryland Statute, § 2.03[B][1] *supra*, which limits child abuse to "physical injury"? Do you agree with the court in *Shane T.* that the "behavior of [Shane's] father] is as serious a form of abuse as if he had plunged a knife into [Shane's] stomach"?

4. What about the "passive parent"? This parent is not the actual abuser but nonetheless fails to intervene to protect the child from harm. Failure to protect legislation codifies a parent's duty to protect their children. *See, e.g.*, MINN. STAT. § 609.378 (2005) (parent or guardian may be sentenced to prison for up to one year or fined up to $3000 or both). Most of the reported cases are prosecutions of mothers who fail to intervene when their child is being abused. Domestic violence may also be a part of the picture. Should a mother be able to defend against the "passive parent" charge be attributing her inaction to her own abuse?

[b]　Who is a "Child"?

WHITNER v. STATE

Supreme Court of South Carolina
492 S.E.2d 777 (1997)

TOAL, JUSTICE.

This case concerns the scope of the child abuse and endangerment statute in the South Carolina Children's Code (the Code), S.C. CODE ANN. § 20-7-50 (1985). We hold the word "child" as used in that statute includes viable fetuses.

FACTS

On April 20, 1992, Cornelia Whitner (Whitner) pled guilty to criminal child neglect, S.C. CODE ANN. § 20-7-50 (1985), for causing her baby to be born with cocaine metabolites in its system by reason of Whitner's ingestion of crack cocaine during the third trimester of her pregnancy. The circuit court judge sentenced Whitner to eight years in prison. Whitner did not appeal her conviction.

Thereafter, Whitner filed a petition for Post Conviction Relief (PCR), pleading the circuit court's lack of subject matter jurisdiction to accept her guilty plea as well as ineffective assistance of counsel. Her claim of ineffective assistance of counsel was based upon her lawyer's failure to advise her the statute under which she was being prosecuted might not apply to prenatal drug use. The petition was granted on both grounds. The State appeals.

LAW/ANALYSIS

A. Subject Matter Jurisdiction

The State first argues the PCR court erred in finding the sentencing circuit court lacked subject matter jurisdiction to accept Whitner's guilty plea. We agree.

Under South Carolina law, a circuit court lacks subject matter jurisdiction to accept a guilty plea to a nonexistent offense. For the sentencing court to have had subject matter jurisdiction to accept Whitner's plea, criminal child neglect under § 20-7-50 would have to include an expectant mother's use of crack cocaine after the fetus is viable.[47] All other issues are ancillary to this jurisdictional issue.

S.C. CODE ANN. § 20-7-50 (1985) provides:

> Any person having the legal custody of any *child* or helpless person, who shall, without lawful excuse, refuse or neglect to provide, as defined in § 20-7-490, the proper care and attention for such *child* or helpless person, so that the life, health or comfort of such *child* or helpless person is endangered or is likely to be endangered, shall be guilty of a misdemeanor and shall be punished within the discretion of the circuit court. (emphasis added).

The State contends this section encompasses maternal acts endangering or likely to endanger the life, comfort, or health of a *viable fetus*.

Under the Children's Code, "child" means a "person under the age of eighteen." S.C. CODE ANN. § 20-7-30(1) (1985). The question for this Court, therefore, is whether a viable fetus is a "person" for purposes of the Children's Code.

In interpreting a statute, this Court's primary function is to ascertain the intent of the legislature. Of course, where a statute is complete, plain, and

---

[47] [2] The State argues we need not reach the issue of the applicability of § 20-7-50 to viable fetuses, because the indictment alleged a violation on the date of the child's birth. We disagree. The basis for the indictment was the presence of cocaine after the child's birth, which no one has alleged, the behavior giving rise to the abuse and neglect charge necessarily occurred before the child was born. Morever, the record of Whitner's original hearing and the hearing on her petition for Post Conviction Relief make clear the conviction was for her neglecting her child by ingesting crack cocaine during pregnancy. For that reason, we must determine whether § 20-7-50 applies to such behavior.

unambiguous, legislative intent must be determined from the language of the statute itself. We should consider, however, not merely the language of the particular clause being construed, but the word and its meaning in conjunction with the purpose of the whole statute and the policy of the law. Finally, there is a basic presumption that the legislature has knowledge of previous legislation as well as of judicial decisions construing that legislation when later statutes are enacted concerning related subjects.

South Carolina law has long recognized that viable fetuses are persons holding certain legal rights and privileges. In 1960, this Court decided *Hall v. Murphy*, 113 S.E.2d 790 (S.C. 1960). That case concerned the application of South Carolina's wrongful death statute to an infant who died four hours after her birth as a result of injuries sustained prenatally during viability. The Appellants argued that a viable fetus was not a person within the purview of the wrongful death statute, because, *inter alia*, a fetus is thought to have no separate being apart from the mother.

We found such a reason for exclusion from recovery "unsound, illogical and unjust," and concluded there was "no medical or other basis" for the "assumed identity" of mother and viable unborn child. In light of that conclusion, this Court unanimously held: "We have no difficulty in concluding that a fetus having reached that period of prenatal maturity where it is capable of independent life apart from its mother is a person."

Four years later, in *Fowler v. Woodward*, 138 S.E.2d 42 (S.C. 1964), we interpreted *Hall* as supporting a finding that a viable fetus injured while still in the womb need not be born alive for another to maintain an action for the wrongful death of the fetus. . . .

. . . .

More recently, we held the word "person" as used in a criminal statute includes viable fetuses. *State v. Horne*, 319 S.E.2d 703 (S.C. 1984), concerned South Carolina's murder statute, S.C. CODE ANN. § 16-3-10 (1976). The defendant in that case stabbed his wife, who was nine months' pregnant, in the neck, arms, and abdomen. Although doctors performed an emergency caesarean section to deliver the child, the child died while still in the womb. The defendant was convicted of voluntary manslaughter and appealed his conviction on the ground South Carolina did not recognize the crime of feticide.

This Court disagreed. In a unanimous decision, we held it would be "grossly inconsistent . . . to construe a viable fetus as a 'person' for the purposes of imposing civil liability while refusing to give it a similar classification in the criminal context." Accordingly, the Court recognized the crime of feticide with respect to viable fetuses.

Similarly, we do not see any rational basis for finding a viable fetus is not a "person" in the present context. Indeed, it would be absurd to recognize the viable fetus as a person for purposes of homicide laws and wrongful death statutes but not for purposes of statutes proscribing child abuse. Our holding in *Hall* that a viable fetus is a person rested primarily on the plain meaning of the word "person" in light of existing medical knowledge concerning fetal development. We do not believe that the plain and ordinary meaning of the word "person" has changed in any way that would now deny viable fetuses status as persons.

The policies enunciated in the Children's Code also support our plain meaning reading of "person." S.C. CODE ANN. § 20-7-20(C) (1985), which describes South Carolina's policy concerning children, expressly states: "It shall be the policy of this State to concentrate on the *prevention of children's problems* as the most important strategy which can be planned and implemented on behalf of children and their families." (emphasis added). The abuse or neglect of a child at *any* time during childhood can exact a profound toll on the child herself as well as on society as a whole. However, the consequences of abuse or neglect which takes place after birth often pale in comparison to those resulting from abuse suffered by the viable fetus before birth. This policy of prevention supports a reading of the word "person" to include viable fetuses. Furthermore, the scope of the Children's Code is quite broad. It applies "to all children who have need of services." When coupled with the comprehensive remedial purposes of the Code, this language supports the inference that the legislature intended to include viable fetuses within the scope of the Code's protection.

Whitner advances several arguments against an interpretation of "person" as used in the Children's Code to include viable fetuses. We shall address each of Whitner's major arguments in turn.

Whitner's first argument concerns the number of bills introduced in the South Carolina General Assembly in the past five years addressing substance abuse by pregnant women. Some of these bills would have criminalized substance abuse by pregnant women; others would have addressed the issue through mandatory reporting, treatment, or intervention by social service agencies. Whitner suggests that the introduction of several bills touching the specific issue at hand evinces a belief by legislators that prior legislation had not addressed the issue. Whitner argues the introduction of the bills proves that § 20-7-50 was not intended to encompass abuse or neglect of a viable fetus.

We disagree with Whitner's conclusion about the significance of the proposed legislation. Generally, the legislature's subsequent acts "cast no light on the intent of the legislature which enacted the statute being construed." Rather, this Court will look first to the language of the statute to discern legislative intent, because the language itself is the best guide to legislative intent. Here, we see no reason to look beyond the statutory language. Additionally, our existing case law strongly supports our conclusion about the meaning of the statute's language.

Whitner also argues an interpretation of the statute that includes viable fetuses would lead to absurd results obviously not intended by the legislature. Specifically, she claims if we interpret "child" to include viable fetuses, every action by a pregnant woman that endangers or is likely to endanger a fetus, whether otherwise legal or illegal, would constitute unlawful neglect under the statute. For example, a woman might be prosecuted under § 20-7-50 for smoking or drinking during pregnancy. Whitner asserts these "absurd" results could not have been intended by the legislature and, therefore, the statute should not be construed to include viable fetuses.

We disagree for a number of reasons. First, the same arguments against the statute can be made whether or not the child has been born. After the birth of a child, a parent can be prosecuted under § 20-7-50 for an action that is likely to endanger the child without regard to whether the action is illegal in itself. For example, a parent who drinks excessively could, under certain circumstances, be guilty of child neglect or endangerment even though the underlying act — consuming alcoholic beverages — is itself legal. Obviously, the legislature did not think it "absurd" to allow prosecution of parents for such otherwise legal acts when the acts actually or potentially endanger the "life, health or comfort" of the parents' born children. We see no reason such a result should be rendered absurd by the mere fact the child at issue is a viable fetus.

Moreover, we need not address this potential parade of horribles advanced by Whitner. In this case, which is the only case we are called upon to decide here, certain facts are clear. Whitner admits to having ingested crack cocaine during the third trimester of her pregnancy, which caused her child to be born with cocaine in its system. Although the precise effects of maternal crack use during pregnancy are somewhat unclear, it is well documented and within the realm of public knowledge that such use can cause serious harm to the viable unborn child. *See, e.g.*, Joseph J. Volpe, M.D., *Effect of Cocaine Use on the Fetus*, 327 NEW ENG. J. MED. 399 (1992); Ira J. Chasnoff, M.D., et al., *Cocaine Use in Pregnancy*, 313 NEW ENG. J. MED. 666 (1985). There can be no question here Whitner endangered the life, health, and comfort of her child. We need not decide any cases other than the one before us.

We are well aware of the many decisions from other states' courts throughout the country holding maternal conduct before the birth of the child does not give rise to criminal prosecution under state child abuse/endangerment or drug distribution statutes. *See, e.g., Johnson v. State,* 602 So. 2d 1288 (Fla. 1992); *Commonwealth v. Welch,* 864 S.W.2d 280 (Ky. 1993); *State v. Gray,* 584 N.E.2d 710 (Ohio 1992); *Reyes v. Superior Court,* 75 Cal. App. 3d 214, 141 Cal. Rptr. 912 (1977); *State v. Carter,* 602 So. 2d 995 (Fla. Ct. App. 1992); *State v. Gethers,* 585 So. 2d 1140 (Fla. Ct. App. 1991); *State v. Luster,* 419 S.E.2d 32 (Ga. 1992), *cert. denied* (Ga.1992); *Commonwealth v. Mellegrini,* No. 87970, slip op. (Mass. Super. Ct. Oct. 15, 1990); *People v. Hardy,* 469 N.W.2d 50, app. denied, 437 Mich. 1046, 471 N.W.2d 619 (1991); *Commonwealth v. Kemp,* 643 A.2d 705 (Pa. 1994). Many of these cases were prosecuted under statutes forbidding delivery or distribution of illicit substances and depended on statutory construction of the terms "delivery" and "distribution." Obviously, such cases are inapplicable to the present situation. The cases concerning child endangerment statutes or construing the terms "child" and "person" are also distinguishable, because the states in which these cases were decided have entirely different bodies of case law from South Carolina. For example, in *Commonwealth v. Welch*, the Kentucky Supreme Court specifically noted Kentucky law has not construed the word "person" in the criminal homicide statute to include a fetus (viable or not). In *Reyes v. Superior Court*, the California Court of Appeals noted California law did not recognize a fetus as a "human being" within the purview of the state murder and manslaughter statutes, and that it was thus improper to find the fetus was a "child" for purposes of the felonious child endangerment statute.

Massachusetts, however, has a body of case law substantially similar to South Carolina's, yet a Massachusetts trial court has held that a mother pregnant with a viable fetus is not criminally liable for transmission of cocaine to the fetus. *See Commonwealth v. Pellegrini,* No. 87970, slip op. (Mass. Super. Ct. Oct. 15, 1990).[48] Specifically, Massachusetts law allows wrongful death actions on behalf of viable fetuses injured in utero who are not subsequently born alive. Similarly, Massachusetts law permits homicide prosecutions of third parties who kill viable fetuses. *See Commonwealth v. Cass,* 467 N.E.2d 1324 (Mass. 1984) (ruling a viable fetus is a person for purposes of vehicular homicide statute); *Commonwealth v. Lawrence,* 536 N.E.2d 571 (Mass. 1989) (viable fetus is a person for purposes of common law crime of murder). Because of the similarity of the case law in Massachusetts to ours, the *Pellegrini* decision merits examination.

In *Pellegrini,* the Massachusetts Superior Court found that state's distribution statute does not apply to the distribution of an illegal substance to a viable fetus. The statute at issue forbade distribution of cocaine to persons under the age of eighteen. Rather than construing the word "distribution," however, the superior court found that a viable fetus is not a "person under the age of eighteen" within the meaning of the statute. In so finding, the court had to distinguish *Lawrence* and *Cass, supra,* both of which held viable fetuses are "persons" for purposes of criminal laws in Massachusetts.

The Massachusetts trial court found *Lawrence* and *Cass* "accord legal rights to the unborn only where the mother's or parents' interest in the potentiality of life, not the state's interest, are sought to be vindicated." In other words, a viable fetus should only be accorded the rights of a person for the sake of its mother or both its parents. Under this rationale, the viable fetus lacks rights of its own that deserve vindication. Whitner suggests we should interpret our decisions in *Hall, Fowler,* and *Horne* to accord rights to the viable fetus only when doing so protects the special parent-child relationship rather than any individual rights of the fetus or any State interest in potential life. We do not think *Hall, Fowler,* and *Horne* can be interpreted so narrowly.

If the *Pellegrini* decision accurately characterizes the rationale underlying *Lawrence* and *Cass,* then the reasoning of those cases differs substantially from our reasoning in *Hall, Fowler,* and *Horne, supra.* First, *Hall, Fowler,* and *Horne* were decided primarily on the basis of the meaning of "person" as understood in the light of existing medical knowledge, rather than based on any policy of protecting the relationship between mother and child. As a homicide case, *Horne* also rested on the State's — not the mother's — interest in vindicating the life of the viable fetus. Moreover, the United States Supreme Court has repeatedly held that the states have a compelling interest in the life of a viable fetus. *See Roe v. Wade,* 410 U.S. 113 (1973); *see also Planned Parenthood v. Casey,* 505 U.S. 833 (1992); *Webster v. Reproductive Health Servs.,* 492 U.S. 490 (1989). If, as Whitner suggests we should, we read *Horne* only as a vindication of the mother's interest in the life of her unborn child, there would be no basis for prosecuting a mother who kills her viable fetus by stabbing it, by shooting it, or by other such means, yet a third party could be prosecuted for the very same acts. We decline to read *Horne* in a way that insulates the mother from all culpability for harm to her viable child. Because

---

48 [5] We note that *Pellegrini* was decided by a Massachusetts superior court. To date, no appellate court in Massachusetts has addressed the issue directly.

the rationale underlying our body of law — protection of the viable fetus — is radically different from that underlying the law of Massachusetts, we decline to follow the decision of the Massachusetts Superior Court in *Pellegrini*.

The dissent contends that our holding in this case is inconsistent with *Doe v. Clark*, 457 S.E.2d 336 (S.C. 1995). Specifically, it suggests that *Doe v. Clark*, in which we construed another provision of the Children's Code, stands for the proposition that the definition of "child" in S.C. CODE ANN. § 20-7-50 (1 985) means a "child in being and not a fetus." Contrary to the dissent's characterization of that case, *Doe* turned on the specific language in the consent provisions of the Adoption Act, S.C. CODE ANN. §§ 20-7-1690 and -1700 (Law Co-op Supp.1994).

In *Doe*, Wylanda Clark, who was pregnant, signed a consent form allowing the Does to adopt the child upon its birth. After the child was born, Clark decided she wanted to keep the baby and attempted to argue that the consent she executed was void because it did not contain certain information required by statute. The trial judge held Clark's consent was valid. Clark appealed.

On appeal, we reversed the trial court. However, the basis for our reversal was not that "child" as defined in the Children's Code only includes born children, but that the adoption statutes contemplate that the natural mother's consent to the adoption must be given after the birth of the child to be adopted. Specifically, § 20-7-1700(A)(3) requires the consent form to contain the race, sex, and *date of birth* of the adoptee, as well as any names by which the adoptee has been known. Clearly, the date of birth requirement could not be fulfilled until after the birth of the child. Furthermore, § 20-7-1690, which specifies who must consent to an adoption, provides that consent is required of "the mother of a child born when the mother was not married." Citing these sections as well as the Children's Code's definition of child, we concluded that a natural mother cannot consent to adoption until after the birth of her child. We did not hold that the term "child" excludes viable fetuses, nor do we think our holding in *Doe* can be read so broadly.

Finally, the dissent implies that we have ignored the rule of lenity requiring us to resolve any ambiguities in a criminal statute in favor of the defendant. The dissent argues that "[a]t most, the majority only suggests that the term 'child' as used in § 20-7-50 is ambiguous," and that the ambiguity "is created not by reference to our decisions under the Children's Code or by reference to the statutory language and applicable rules of statutory construction, but by reliance on decisions in two different fields of the law, civil wrongful death and common law feticide."

Plainly, the dissent misunderstands our opinion. First, we do not believe the statute is ambiguous and, therefore, the rule of lenity does not apply. Furthermore, our interpretation of the statute is based primarily on the plain meaning of the word "person" as contained *in the statute*. We need not go beyond that language. However, because our prior decisions in *Murphy*, *Fowler*, and *Horne* support our reading of the statute, we have discussed the rationale underlying those holdings. We conclude that both statutory language and case law compel the conclusion we reach. We see no ambiguity.

. . . .

Constitutional Issues

1. Fair Notice/Vagueness

Whitner argues that § 20-7-50 does not give her fair notice that her behavior is proscribed.[49] We disagree.

The statute forbids any person having legal custody of a child from refusing or neglecting to provide proper care and attention to the child so that the life, health, or comfort of the child is endangered or is likely to be endangered. As we have found above, the plain meaning of "child" as used in this statute includes a viable fetus. Furthermore, it is common knowledge that use of cocaine during pregnancy can harm the viable unborn child. Given these facts, we do not see how Whitner can claim she lacked fair notice that her behavior constituted child endangerment as proscribed in § 20-7-50. Whitner had all the notice the Constitution requires.

2. Right to Privacy

Whitner argues that prosecuting her for using crack cocaine after her fetus attains viability unconstitutionally burdens her right of privacy, or, more specifically, her right to carry her pregnancy to term. We disagree.

Whitner argues that § 20-7-50 burdens her right of privacy, a right long recognized by the United States Supreme Court. She cites *Cleveland Board of Education v. LaFleur*, 414 U.S. 632 (1974), as standing for the proposition that the Constitution protects women from measures penalizing them for choosing to carry their pregnancies to term.

In *LaFleur*, two junior high school teachers challenged their school systems' maternity leave policies. The policies required "every pregnant school teacher to take maternity leave without pay, beginning [four or] five months before the expected birth of her child." A teacher on maternity leave could not return to work "until the beginning of the next regular school semester which follows the date when her child attains the age of three months." The two teachers, both of whom had become pregnant and were required against their wills to comply with the school systems' policies, argued that the policies were unconstitutional.

The United States Supreme Court agreed. It found that "[b]y acting to penalize the pregnant teacher for deciding to bear a child, overly restrictive maternity leave regulations can constitute a heavy burden on the exercise of these protected freedoms." The Court then scrutinized[50] the policies to determine whether "the interests advanced in support of" the policy could "justify the particular procedures [the School Boards] ha[d] adopted." Although it found that the purported justification for the policy — continuity of instruction — was a "significant and legitimate educational goal," the Court concluded that the "absolute requirement[] of termination at the end of the

---

[49] [6] In a related argument, Whitner suggests § 20-7-50 is void for vagueness. This argument lacks merit. As we noted in our interpretation of § 20-7-50, *supra*, the same argument could be made about the statute as applied to a child who has already been born.

[50] [7] The Court applied a rational relationship test, the least rigorous form of scrutiny.

fourth or fifth month of pregnancy" was not a rational means for achieving continuity of instruction and that such a requirement "may serve to hinder attainment of the very continuity objectives that they are purportedly designed to promote." Finding no rational relationship between the purpose of the maternity leave policy and the means crafted to achieve that end, the Court concluded the policy violated the Due Process Clause of the Fourteenth Amendment.

Whitner argues that the alleged violation here is far more egregious than that in *LaFleur*. She first suggests that imprisonment is a far greater burden on her exercise of her freedom to carry the fetus to term than was the unpaid maternity leave in *LaFleur*. Although she is, of course, correct that imprisonment is more severe than unpaid maternity leave, Whitner misapprehends the fundamentally different nature of her own interests and those of the government in this case as compared to those at issue in *LaFleur*.

First, the State's interest in protecting the life and health of the viable fetus is not merely legitimate. It is compelling. *See, e.g., Roe v. Wade,* 410 U.S. 113 (1973); *Planned Parenthood v. Casey,* 505 U.S. 833 (1992). The United States Supreme Court in *Casey* recognized that the State possesses a profound interest in the potential life of the fetus, not only after the fetus is viable, but throughout the expectant mother's pregnancy. *See Casey*, 505 U.S. at 877 (plurality opinion).

Even more importantly, however, we do not think any fundamental right of Whitner's — or any right at all, for that matter — is implicated under the present scenario. It strains belief for Whitner to argue that using crack cocaine during pregnancy is encompassed within the constitutionally recognized right of privacy. Use of crack cocaine is illegal, period. No one here argues that laws criminalizing the use of crack cocaine are themselves unconstitutional. If the State wishes to impose additional criminal penalties on pregnant women who engage in this already illegal conduct because of the effect the conduct has on the viable fetus, it may do so. We do not see how the fact of pregnancy elevates the use of crack cocaine to the lofty status of a fundamental right.

Moreover, as a practical matter, we do not see how our interpretation of § 20-7-50 imposes a burden on Whitner's right to carry her child to term. In *LaFleur*, the Supreme Court found that the mandatory maternity leave policies burdened women's rights to carry their pregnancies to term because the policies prevented pregnant teachers from exercising a freedom they would have enjoyed but for their pregnancies. In contrast, during her pregnancy after the fetus attained viability, Whitner enjoyed the same freedom to use cocaine that she enjoyed earlier in and predating her pregnancy — none whatsoever. Simply put, South Carolina's child abuse and endangerment statute as applied to this case does not restrict Whitner's freedom in any way that it was not already restricted. The State's imposition of an additional penalty when a pregnant woman with a viable fetus engages in the already proscribed behavior does not burden a woman's right to carry her pregnancy to term; rather, the additional penalty simply recognizes that a third party (the viable fetus or newborn child) is harmed by the behavior.

Section 20-7-50 does not burden Whitner's right to carry her pregnancy to term or any other privacy right. Accordingly, we find no violation of the Due Process Clause of the Fourteenth Amendment.

CONCLUSION

For the foregoing reasons, the decision of the PCR Court is reversed.

FINNEY, CHIEF JUSTICE:

I respectfully dissent, and would affirm the grant of post-conviction relief to respondent Whitner.

The issue before the Court is whether a fetus is a "child" within the meaning of S.C. CODE ANN. § 20-7-50 (1985), a statute which makes it a misdemeanor[51] for a "person having legal custody of any child or helpless person" to unlawfully neglect that child or helpless person. Since this is a penal statute, it is strictly construed against the State and in favor of respondent.

The term child for purposes of § 20-7-50 is defined as a "person under the age of eighteen" unless a different meaning is required by the circumstances. S.C. CODE ANN. § 20-7-30(1) (1985). We have already held that this same definition found in another part of the Children's Code means a child in being and not a fetus. *Doe v. Clark*, 457 S.E.2d 336 (S.C. 1995). It would be incongruous at best to hold the definition of "child" in the civil context of *Doe* is more restrictive than it is in the criminal context we consider today.

More importantly, it is apparent from a reading of the entire statute that the word child in § 20-7-50 means a child in being and not a fetus. A plain reading of the entire child neglect statute demonstrates the intent to criminalize only acts directed at children, and not those which may harm fetuses. First, § 20-7-50 does not impose criminal liability on every person who neglects a child, but only on a person having legal custody of that child. The statutory requirement of legal custody is evidence of intent to extend the statute's reach only to children, because the concept of legal custody is simply inapplicable to a fetus. Second, § 20-7-50 refers to S.C. CODE ANN. § 20-7-490 (1985 and Supp.1994) for the definition of neglect. Section 20-7-490 defines a neglected child as one harmed or threatened with harm, and further defines harm. § 20-7-490(B), (C), and (D). The vast majority of acts which constitute statutory harm under § 20-7-490 are acts which can only be directed against a child, and not towards a fetus.[52] The reliance upon § 20-7-490 in § 20-7-50 is further evidence that the term child as used in the child neglect statute does not encompass a fetus. Read in context, and in light of the statutory purpose of protecting persons of tender years, it is clear that "child" as used in § 20-7-50 means a child in being.

At most, the majority only suggests that the term "child" as used in § 20-7-50 is ambiguous. This suggestion of ambiguity is created not by reference to our decisions under the Children's Code or by reference to the statutory language and applicable rules of statutory construction, but by reliance on decisions in two different fields of the law, civil wrongful death and common law feticide. Here, we deal with the Children's Code, and the meaning of

---

[51] [1] After this case arose, the statute was amended to change the classification from misdemeanor to felony. 1993 Act No. 184, § 55 (effective January 1, 1994).

[52] [2] Examples include condoning delinquency, using excessive corporal punishment, committing sexual offenses against the child, and depriving her of adequate food, clothing, shelter or education.

language used in a criminal statute under that Code. We have already indicated that a child within the meaning of § 20-7-90(A) (1985), which criminalizes non-support, must be one already born. Even if these wrongful death, common law, and Children's Code decisions are sufficient to render the term child in § 20-7-50 ambiguous, it is axiomatic that the ambiguity must be resolved in respondent's favor.

I would affirm.

MOORE, JUSTICE:

I concur with the dissent in this case but write separately to express my concerns with today's decision.

In my view, the repeated failure of the legislature to pass proposed bills addressing the problem of drug use during pregnancy is evidence the child abuse and neglect statute is not intended to apply in this instance. This Court should not invade what is clearly the sole province of the legislative branch. At the very least, the legislature's failed attempts to enact a statute regulating a pregnant woman's conduct indicate the complexity of this issue. While the majority opinion is perhaps an argument for what the law should be, it is for the General Assembly, and not this Court, to make that determination by means of a clearly drawn statute. With today's decision, the majority not only ignores legislative intent but embarks on a course of judicial activism rejected by every other court to address the issue.

As discussed in the Chief Justice's dissent, we are bound by the rules of statutory construction to strictly construe a criminal statute in favor of the defendant and resolve any ambiguity in her favor. I cannot accept the majority's assertion that the child abuse and neglect statute unambiguously includes a "viable fetus." If that is the case, then why is the majority compelled to go to such great lengths to ascertain that a "viable fetus" is a "child"?

Contrary to the majority's strained analysis in this case, one need look no further than the language of § 20-7-50 to clearly discern legislative intent that the statute apply only to children in being. "Legal custody" is not a qualification applicable to a viable fetus. I simply disagree the legislature intended a statute entitled "Unlawful neglect of child or helpless person by legal custodian" to render a pregnant woman criminally liable for any type of conduct potentially harmful to the unborn fetus.

In construing this statute to include conduct not contemplated by the legislature, the majority has rendered the statute vague and set for itself the task of determining what conduct is unlawful. Is a pregnant woman's failure to obtain prenatal care unlawful? Failure to quit smoking or drinking? Although the majority dismisses this issue as not before it, the impact of today's decision is to render a pregnant woman potentially criminally liable for myriad acts which the legislature has not seen fit to criminalize. To ignore this "down-the-road" consequence in a case of this import is unrealistic. The majority insists that parents may already be held liable for drinking after a child is born. This is untrue, however, without some further act on the part of the parent. A parent who drinks and then hits her child or fails to come home may be guilty of criminal neglect. The mere fact of drinking, however, does not constitute neglect of a child in being.

The majority attempts to support an over inclusive construction of the child abuse and neglect statute by citing other legal protections extended equally to a viable fetus and a child in being. The only law, however, that specifically regulates the conduct of a mother toward her unborn child is our abortion statute under which a viable fetus is in fact treated differently from a child in being.[53]

The majority argues for equal treatment of viable fetuses and children, yet its construction of the statute results in even greater inequities. If the statute applies only when a fetus is "viable," a pregnant woman can use cocaine for the first twenty-four weeks[54] of her pregnancy, the most dangerous period for the fetus, and be immune from prosecution under the statute so long as she quits drug use before the fetus becomes viable. Further, a pregnant woman now faces up to ten years in prison for ingesting drugs during pregnancy but can have an illegal abortion and receive only a two-year sentence for killing her viable fetus.[55]

Because I disagree with the conclusion § 20-7-50 includes a viable fetus, I would affirm the grant of post-conviction relief.

NOTES AND QUESTIONS

1. As mentioned in the *Whitner* opinion, a number of states have rejected arguments to extend child abuse and drug distribution statutes to the conduct of pregnant mothers. In *Arkansas Dept. of Human Services (DHS) v. Collier*, 351 Ark. 506 (2003), a lower court judge, who had terminated the parental rights of a woman's 13-month-old child, learned that the mother was again pregnant and had violated the court's order to remain drug free. The judge held the mother in contempt of court for violating that order and found that the unborn child was in imminent danger of severe maltreatment and was dependent-neglected, as defined by the Arkansas Juvenile Code. The court ordered that the child be placed in the custody of DHS and further ordered DHS to ensure that the woman receive adequate prenatal care and that she be examined by a doctor as soon as possible. The Arkansas Supreme Court held that the state code clearly defines "juvenile" as an individual from "birth to age eighteen." An unborn fetus obviously does not fall within this definition as there has been no birth. Thus, the unborn fetus could not be declared dependent-neglected and placed in state custody.

Policy reasons for not extending protection to unborn children are summarized by the Florida Supreme Court in *Johnson v. State*, 602 So. 2d 1288 (Fla. 1992), as follows:

---

53 [1] A woman may have a legal abortion of a viable fetus if necessary to preserve her health, S.C. CODE ANN. § 44-41-20(c) (1985), while of course, she may not justify the death of a child in being on this ground.

54 [2] Viability is presumed to occur no sooner than the twenty-fourth week of pregnancy. S.C. CODE ANN. § 44-41-10(1) (1985).

55 [3] S.C. CODE ANN. § 44-41-80(b) (1985).

It is well-established that the effects of cocaine use by a pregnant woman on her fetus and later on her newborn can be severe. On average, cocaine-exposed babies have lower birth weights, shorter body lengths at birth, and smaller head circumferences than normal infants. Cocaine use may also result in sudden infant death syndrome, neural-behavioral deficiencies as well as other medical problems and long-term developmental abnormalities. American Public Health Association 1990 Policy Statement. The basic problem of damaging the fetus by drug use during pregnancy should not be addressed piece-meal, however, by prosecuting users who deliver their babies close in time to use of drugs and ignoring those who simply use drugs during their pregnancy.

. . . .

However, prosecuting women for using drugs and "delivering" them to their newborns appears to be the least effective response to this crises. Rather than face the possibility of prosecution, pregnant women who are substance abusers may simply avoid prenatal or medical care for fear of being detected. Yet the newborns of these women are, as a group, the most fragile and sick, and most in need of hospital neonatal care. A decision to deliver these babies "at home" will have tragic and serious consequences. . . .

[C]riminal penalties may exacerbate the harm done to fetal health by deterring pregnant substance abusers from obtaining help or care from either the health or public welfare professions, the very people who are best able to prevent future abuse. The California Medical Association has noted:

> While unhealthy behavior cannot be condoned, to bring criminal charges against a pregnant woman for activities which may be harmful to her fetus is inappropriate. Such prosecution is counter-productive to the public interest as it may discourage a woman from seeking prenatal care or dissuade her from providing accurate information to health care providers out of fear of self-incrimination. This failure to seek proper care or to withhold vital information concerning her health could increase the risks to herself and her baby. Florida's Secretary of Health and Rehabilitative Services has also observed that potential prosecution under existing child abuse or drug use statutes already "makes many potential reporters reluctant to identify women as substance abusers." . . .

Prosecution of pregnant women for engaging in activities harmful to their fetuses or newborns may also unwittingly increase the incidence of abortion.

Id. at 1295–96.

Do you find these considerations persuasive?

2. In 2002, Regina McKnight became the first woman in the United States ever to be convicted for giving birth to a stillborn baby. *State v. McKnight*, 576 S.E.2d 168 (S.C. 2003). Women had been convicted of child abuse and

involuntary manslaughter under child neglect and child abuse statutes, but no one before McKnight had been convicted of murder under a "homicide by child abuse" statute. *See* Shalini Bhargava, *Challenging Punishment and Privatization: A Response to the Conviction of Regina McKnight*, 39 HARV. C.R.-C.L. L. REV. 513, n.1 (2004). McKnight gave birth to a nearly full-term stillborn child. An autopsy showed a substance metabolized by cocaine in the infant. She was convicted of homicide by child abuse, and the South Carolina Supreme Court upheld the conviction. *McKnight*, 576 S.E. 2d 168. The court held that the state sufficiently demonstrated that the cocaine caused the stillbirth and that her act of using cocaine, knowing that she was pregnant, was sufficient to go to the jury on whether she acted with extreme indifference. The legislature intended the child abuse provision to apply to the stillbirth of a fetus given the legislature's inaction after the supreme court previously held that the term "child" included a viable fetus. McKnight had ample notice that her conduct was proscribed and therefore there was no due process violation. Her use of cocaine while pregnant did not trigger a right to privacy. There was no Eighth Amendment violation because the gravity of the offense was severe and the penalty was proportionate to other murder offenses.

In *Ferguson v. City of Charleston*, 532 U.S. 67 (2001), the United States Supreme Court invalidated a South Carolina policy where a state hospital turned over positive drug tests of pregnant women to the police for criminal prosecution if the women did not enroll in or remain in a substance abuse treatment program. Given the primary purpose of the program, which was to use the threat of arrest and prosecution in order to force women into treatment, and given the extensive involvement of law enforcement officials at every stage of the policy, the Court held that the case simply did not fit within the closely guarded category of fourth amendment "special needs." Thus, the general prohibition against nonconsensual, warrantless, and suspicionless searches applied to the policy.

After five years of wrangling, Congress passed the Unborn Victims of Violence Act in 2004. *See* Pub. L. 108-212. The Act makes it a crime to harm an unborn child during an assault on a pregnant woman. The law defines unborn child as a child in utero at any stage of development that is carried in the womb. Although the law bars prosecution for conduct relating to an abortion performed with the consent of the mother or out of medical necessity, abortion opponents hailed the act as a measure that protects the unborn. Abortion rights advocates raised concerns over this first recognition in federal law of an embryo or fetus as a person separate from the woman.

[C] Adjudicating Child Abuse

The prosecution of child abuse offenders raises a variety of unique procedural and evidentiary issues. Because child abuse routinely occurs in the privacy of the home, the crime is often proved solely on the basis of circumstantial evidence enriched by expert testimony, as well as through a variety of presumptions and relaxation of some ordinary rules of evidence.

Expert testimony is often essential in proving child abuse. As the following materials illustrate, the fact of abuse is often not provable without expert testimony describing the "battered child syndrome." The materials also show that expert testimony of other "syndromes," arguably relevant in adjudicating child abuse, may or may not be legally admissible. Moreover, this section will discuss special evidentiary rules aimed at protecting the child victim from being traumatized by the judicial process supposedly without denying the defendant's constitutional rights.

[1] The Battered Child Syndrome (BCS)

STATE v. TANNER

Supreme Court of Utah
675 P.2d 539 (1983)

DURHAM, JUSTICE:

The defendant and appellant, Kathy Tanner, appeals from her conviction for manslaughter in the death of her three-year-old daughter. The defendant was tried before the court and sentenced to an indeterminate term of not less than one or more than fifteen years in prison. The defendant here argues that there was insufficient evidence to support the verdict, that some evidence was erroneously admitted, and that some evidence was erroneously excluded.

The key evidence in this case is the mute testimony of the body of three-year-old Tawnya Tanner. There is no question that she died on March 21, 1980, of "subdural hematoma associated with multiple contusions of the body," as stated in the autopsy report. That report, the contents of which were stipulated to by the defendant, enumerated the many contusions scattered over the child's body literally from head to foot. The contusions are clearly visible in the photographs admitted in evidence, as are the bulges of the scalp where the severely bruised brain protruded through the craniotomy sites. At trial the court permitted the prosecution's medical experts to testify regarding the condition of the child's body, the nature of the injuries and the cause of death. This testimony included the witnesses' observations regarding the "battered child syndrome." The defendant claims error in the admission of this battered child syndrome testimony and the admission of instances of prior bad acts that she alleges were presented "to establish that Tawnya was a victim of the Battered Child Syndrome."

The issue of the admissibility of "battered child syndrome" testimony has not previously been presented to this Court. The development of the medical-social concept of the battered child syndrome is traced in McCoid, "The Battered Child & Other Assaults Upon the Family: Part One," 50 MINN. L. REV. 1 (1965). The author points out that the "development of the concept of the battered child syndrome has moved from an initial identification of physical phenomenon [sic] to concern with the causative factors outside of the body of the child." Early publications concentrated on the identification of the pattern of injuries observed, but in the 1950s, articles began to address the origins of the trauma, including the role of the parents. Increasingly, as attention and research focused on the problem and statistics were assembled, the medical profession became aware of the abusive character of the injuries and the grave danger to the helpless child in the custody of an abusive caretaker. McCoid summarizes:

> From this review, it appears that by early 1965, there had come a recognition of a distinctive phenomenon called "the battered child syndrome" which, though it begins with a pattern of injuries to the child, is really descriptive of a pattern of conduct on the part of the parents or others who are to guard the welfare of the child. The medical description can perhaps best be summarized as multiple injuries in various stages of healing, primarily to the long bones and soft tissues and frequently coupled with poor hygiene and malnutrition, but peculiarly identified by the marked discrepancy between the clinical or physical findings and the historical data provided by the parents. Described in terms of the conduct of the parents or their characteristics, the studies seem to confirm that the abuser is likely to be an emotionally immature individual from almost any walk or stratum of society, a person who probably suffers from the pressures of marital difficulties or economic circumstances or other emotional pressures not directly related to the child himself, so that the child becomes merely a focus for generalized frustration or anger and an outlet for the poorly controlled aggressiveness of the parent.

Over the past fifteen years, cases discussing the use of battered child syndrome evidence have appeared with increasing frequency in the state reporters. The battered child syndrome has become a well-recognized medical diagnosis, which must be testified to by an expert witness:

> The diagnosis is dependent on inferences, not a matter of common knowledge, but within the area of expertise of physicians whose familiarity with numerous instances of injuries accidentally caused qualifies them to express with reasonable probability that a particular injury or group of injuries to a child is not accidental or is not consistent with the explanation offered therefor but is instead the result of physical abuse by a person of mature strength.

In *People v. Jackson*, 18 Cal.App.3d 504, 95 Cal.Rptr. 919 (1971), the court pointed out that "[a]n expert medical witness may give his opinion as to the means used to inflict a particular injury, based on his deduction from the appearance of the injury itself." Such testimony is not accusatory, but only indicates the cause of death. Similarly, when an expert testifies as to the existence of the "battered child syndrome," he expresses no opinion regarding a defendant's culpability, but rather testifies that, as the witness in *Jackson* stated:

> [I]t would take thousands of children to have the severity and number and degree of injuries that this child had over the span of time that we had by accidental means. In other words, the "battered child syndrome" simply indicates that a child found with the type of injuries outlined above has not suffered those injuries by accidental means. This conclusion is based upon an extensive study of the subject by medical science.

Id. [56] In *Bludsworth v. State*, Nev., 646 P.2d 558 (1982), the defendants argued that evidence of bruises and a bite mark on the body of the child was incompetent because there was no prior establishment that either defendant was responsible for the injuries. The court affirmed the admission of the evidence, stating:

> Admissibility of the bite mark and other bruise evidence does not depend on connecting either defendant to the infliction of the injury. It is independent, relevant circumstantial evidence tending to show that the child was intentionally, rather than accidentally, injured on the day in question.

Id. at 559. In *People v. DeJesus*, 389 N.E.2d 260 (Ill. 1979), the defendant claimed error in the use of battered child syndrome evidence, arguing that it suggested to the jury that the defendant was guilty of prior offenses. The court held that the expert's diagnosis and explanation of medical terms of art do not indicate wrongdoing on the part of a particular defendant, but merely describe the nature of the injuries.

The defendants in these cases frequently argue that evidence of injuries other than that which is the immediate cause of death, *i.e.*, any evidence of the battered child syndrome, is incompetent or is more prejudicial than probative. Again, we emphasize that evidence regarding the child's physical condition does not directly indicate the culpability of any particular defendant. In *Ashford v. State,* Okl. Crim., 603 P.2d 1162 (Okla. 1979), an eight-month-old baby was found to have injuries from five days to two weeks old and partially healed fractures from four to eight weeks old, in addition to a fatal subdural hemorrhage. The court held that "[i]n a case of this nature, the past injuries are admissible to counter any claim that the latest injury happened through accident or simple negligence. *The pattern of abuse* is relevant to show the intent of the act." *Id.* at 1164 (emphasis added). In other words, the pattern of abuse is relevant to show that *someone* injured the child intentionally, rather than accidentally.

Battered child syndrome evidence is most frequently cited as admissible to show absence of accident. It is relevant to claims of accidents by the child, *e.g.,* "She was clumsy and fell a lot," as well as accidents by the adult, "I tripped while I was carrying him." Expert testimony as to types of injuries, their size, location and severity, together with evidence of their varying age and progress in healing, allows the lifeless or preverbal victim to testify in the only way possible. We are satisfied that the concept of the battered child syndrome is grounded in scientific research and is widely accepted in the

---

56 [2] The *Jackson* opinion continues:

The additional finding that the injuries were probably occasioned by someone who is ostensibly caring for the child is simply a conclusion based on logic and reason. Only someone regularly "caring" for the child has the continuing opportunity to inflict these types of injuries; an isolated contact with a vicious stranger would not result in this pattern of successive injuries stretching through several months. That these inferences may be made from evidence of the battered child's condition does not militate against the use of the evidence. The finder of fact is entitled to make reasonable inferences from the evidence, as discussed *infra.*

medical community. Our research shows that all courts which have addressed the question have affirmed the admission of expert medical testimony regarding the presence of the battered child syndrome. We, therefore, conclude that in appropriate factual circumstances, testimony regarding the battered child syndrome is admissible when given by a properly qualified expert witness. We caution trial courts to weigh carefully the probative value against the potential for undue prejudice that may be created by the use of the term "battered child syndrome." The term should not be applied broadly or as a generalization. The expert should be able to testify in detail regarding the nature of the child's injuries and whether the explanation given for the injuries is reasonable. Any deficiencies in the testimony, however, go to its weight rather than to its admissibility. . . .

In the instant case, the testimony of four medical experts was presented by the State. The doctor on duty in the emergency room described Tawnya's condition as "moribund," in other words, a dying condition. He testified that the defendant told him that Tawnya fell, but that the explanation did not seem consistent with the severity of the child's condition. A neurosurgeon was the next to examine Tawnya. He testified that he found no spontaneous respiration, that Tawnya had dilated pupils with hemorrhages in the right eye indicating intercranial pressure, and that he observed one acute "relative fresh" bruise just ahead of the right ear, several new and old bruises on the face and an old bruise on the inner thigh. He further testified that he performed a bilateral craniotomy to relieve the pressure on the brain and that he found a very large subdural hematoma or blood clot with bruised brain tissue. He stated that the severity of the swelling and the hematoma indicated that a significant amount of force had been applied. Tawnya died the next morning, never having regained consciousness.

As already mentioned, the autopsy report stating that Tawnya died of "subdural hematoma associated with multiple contusions of the body" was stipulated to at trial. The medical examiner's expert opinion was that the multiple bruises on Tawnya's chin were not consistent with a single fall. The State's fourth expert, Dr. Palmer, based his opinion on his review of the police records, the autopsy report, the neurosurgeon's report, and his extensive experience as a pediatrician specializing in the study of child abuse. Dr. Palmer testified regarding the phenomena that alert a physician to the possibility of the battered child syndrome, such as: too many bruises and bruises in atypical locations considering the child's age; fractures, such as spiral fractures, of a type and severity not otherwise explained; severe head injuries not otherwise explained; and in general, a history of the trauma given by a caretaker that is inconsistent with the child's injuries. The doctor also testified that abusive disciplinary methods are frequently part of the battered child syndrome, that the parents of such children are typically very young or inexperienced and that they are likely to have a history of prior abusive conduct. Dr. Palmer went on to identify in Tawnya the characteristics of the battered child, emphasizing in particular the inadequate explanation given by the defendant for Tawnya's injuries. Counsel for the defendant took full advantage of the opportunity to challenge Dr. Palmer's opinions and the bases for his conclusions.

All four of the State's experts were properly qualified and testified within their areas of expertise. The term "battered child syndrome" was not used broadly, but was defined and applied to Tawnya with particularity. We, therefore, find that the trial court did not err by admitting testimony regarding the battered child syndrome.

The defendant also alleges error in the admission of testimony regarding specific instances of prior bad acts. She refers to Rule 47 of the Utah Rules of Evidence, which prohibits the use of evidence of specific conduct which tends to prove that a trait of the defendant's character is bad. She also cites Rule 55 of the Utah Rules of Evidence, which makes inadmissible evidence that the defendant committed a crime or civil wrong on a particular occasion for the purpose of inferring that the defendant committed a crime or wrong on another occasion. She alleges that evidence of prior bad acts was offered to establish the existence of the battered child syndrome. In this she is mistaken. The testimony regarding the battered child syndrome was based on the experts' observations of Tawnya's damaged body and was independent of evidence of the defendant's conduct.

The defendant also relies on Rules 47 and 55 of the Utah Rules of Evidence to contest the admission in evidence of specific instances of her prior conduct. This same allegation of error is raised in nearly all of the cases of a similar nature that we have reviewed. For example, in *State v. Tucker*, 435 A.2d 986 (Conn. 1980), witnesses testified that they had seen the defendant abuse the sixteen-month-old victim, such as dropping the child from his bicycle, shaking him violently, causing him to fall out of his stroller and to hit his head, and slapping and hitting him. The defendant challenged the admission of the testimony as lacking probative value with regard to the intent to commit murder, and further argued that, even if probative, the evidence should have been excluded as prejudicial. The court held that the evidence was relevant to establish "a pattern of behavior and an attitude toward the child that is indicative of the defendant's state of mind." The court also found the evidence admissible to show that the child's death was the result of an intentional act rather than an accidental act. In *People v. Henson*, 304 N.E.2d 358 (N.Y. 1973), the court held that evidence of the defendant parents' prior abusive acts was admissible to show absence of accident or mistake. The court stated that evidence of the battered child syndrome, together with other evidence such as the injuries having been caused while the child was in the parents' sole custody, permits the jury to infer that the child's injuries were not accidental and that the injuries were caused by the parents.

In the case before us, the defendant objects to the testimony regarding her treatment of Tawnya, alleging that its admission violated Rule 47 by attempting to prove a bad character trait with specific instances of conduct other than a conviction of a crime. She argues further that such evidence is not admissible as one of the exceptions under Rule 55, such as admissibility to show absence of mistake or accident, motive, opportunity, intent, plan, etc., because she did not raise the defense of accident or mistake. We agree with the courts in the *Tucker* and *Henson* decisions, *supra*, that such instances do tend to show that the crime charged was the result of intentional rather than accidental acts, but we find it unnecessary to base the admissibility of this evidence on whether or not the defendant has raised the defense of accident or mistake, or indeed, on any of the exceptions listed in Rule 55. . . . Rule 55 of the Utah Rules of Evidence . . . is inclusionary: evidence of other crimes or civil wrongs that is competent and relevant to prove some material fact, *other than to show merely the general disposition of the defendant,* is admissible. The determination of relevancy is within the discretion of the trial judge.

In cases of child abuse, such as the one before us, evidence of specific instances of the defendant's treatment of the child is relevant to establish not merely a general disposition for violence or ill-will towards all children, but to establish a specific pattern of behavior by the defendant toward one particular child, the victim. We distinguish this evidence of the defendant's conduct, relevant to establishing a pattern of behavior by the defendant, from evidence of the battered child syndrome given by experts that is relevant to establishing the nature of the injuries to the child and that is nonaccusatory and independently admissible, as discussed, *supra.* The two categories of evidence should, of course, be corroborative in order to support a conviction. This pattern of behavior by the defendant is relevant to establishing absence of accident or mistake (as held by numerous courts),[57] opportunity, knowledge or the identity of the defendant as the person responsible for the crime charged.

. . . Evidence of other violence or anger as, for example, abuse of other adults or inanimate objects, is too general to be relevant to the specific emotional propensity to abuse a child. While recognizing the relevance of specific instances of prior abuse, however, we refrain from specifying "specific emotional propensity" as a special category or exception to be added to the list contained in Rule 55. Such exceptions are subject to arbitrary and rigid use, as discussed above. The same danger exists in attempting to avoid Rule 55 by categorizing specific instances of prior abuse as habit or custom, under Rule 50. Although evidence of habit is far more specific than evidence of character and therefore less likely to be unduly prejudicial, complete avoidance of Rule 55 may lead to avoidance of the central consideration, *i.e.,* relevance. There is no substitute for a case-by-case inquiry into relevance.

Even when admissible as relevant, evidence of other crimes or civil wrongs may be excluded if the trial judge finds that the probative value is substantially outweighed by the risk that its admission will consume unnecessary time, cause undue prejudice, or unfairly surprise a party. In order to preserve the policy underlying Rule 55 (conviction for commission of the crime charged and not for a criminal disposition), the judge must weigh not only the probative value of the evidence but also the *need* for the evidence and the *necessity* for a "full inquiry into the facts relating to the issues" against the potential for undue prejudice to the defendant. Where there is child abuse, there will invariably be secrecy. The great disparity of power and control between the abuser and the child assures that there will be little, if any, direct evidence. Even in cases where the victim survives, the child's age and vulnerability make it unlikely that he or she could be expected to testify competently. In these cases, it is probable that evidence of prior abusive conduct by a caretaker may be the only available link between the specific nature

---

57 [5] In *McMichael v. State,* 577 P.2d 398 (Nev. 1978), a sex crime case, the court held that intent and lack of mistake were put in issue by the defendant's plea of not guilty.

of the child's injuries and the caretaker who has offered either no explanation or an inadequate explanation for those injuries. . . .

In the instant case, the defendant told the doctors who treated Tawnya that the three-year-old had fallen off a slide at the park. She called her cousin while Tawnya was in surgery and related the same story, which she also told to two police officers. The defendant claimed that Tawnya was unconscious when she arrived home from work and that Leland Foote, with whom the defendant was living, told her that Tawnya had fallen from a slide earlier that day when Tawnya and her five-year-old brother, Brian, played there. Indeed, Foote originally told police officers that when the two children returned from the park, Tawnya had a minor nosebleed and said that she had fallen. He claimed that she ate her lunch normally and watched television and that he later found her unconscious on the floor. Foote subsequently pled guilty to manslaughter and testified against the defendant,[58] relating that she disciplined Tawnya harshly, especially when Tawnya wet herself. He stated that on March 20, he and the defendant's two small children walked to the defendant's place of work to meet her and walk home with her, that Tawnya was lively and well, that after returning to their apartment, he went into the bathroom where he heard two loud thumps as if something heavy had been thrown against the wall in the next room and that when he left the bathroom, he saw the defendant watching TV and he saw Tawnya lying unconscious on the floor. Foote related specific instances of the defendant's treatment of Tawnya, such as throwing her against a wall or the floor, kicking her, making her sit in a tub of cold water until the child could not stand, whipping her with a belt and rubbing the child's face in her messy pants. Additional witnesses — Foote's relatives, the defendant's relatives and the defendant's co-workers — corroborated this testimony by relating instances in which they personally saw the defendant abuse Tawnya or heard the defendant talk about disciplining Tawnya in ways they considered harsh. All of the incidents were personally observed by the witnesses, who were extensively cross-examined. The testimony was relevant not only to the absence of accident or mistake, as we noted above, but also to the defendant's pattern of behavior toward the victim. Where the presence of the battered child syndrome is shown in the child and the defendant is the child's caretaker, logic and the interests of justice demand as complete a story as possible concerning the crime and the surrounding circumstances. Medical testimony indicated that Tawnya's fatal injury was part of a pattern of abusive injuries. Evidence of the defendant's conduct during substantially all of Tawnya's life establishes an explanation for the many nonfatal injuries found on Tawnya's body. . . . This evidence, together

---

58 [6] The defendant argues that Foote's guilty plea and his contradictory explanations of Tawnya's injury together cast such doubt upon his veracity as to make his testimony wholly incredible. The reasons for Foote's guilty plea are not found in the record before us. However, the court was made aware of the guilty plea and the possibility of bias in Foote's testimony during cross-examination by the defendant. The court was also aware of Foote's differing versions of the events on March 20, since both counsel questioned Foote regarding his reasons for changing his testimony. It is the duty of the finder of fact to weigh the testimony and determine its credibility. We assume that the court believed at least that portion of Foote's testimony which is corroborated by other witnesses. We will not interfere in the factfinder's determination regarding the credibility of the evidence.

with the defendant's lack of reasonable explanation for the injuries, is relevant to establish the identity of the one responsible for the fatal injury.

The defendant also objected to the admission of expert testimony regarding Tawnya's physical condition as an infant. Dr. Palmer's testimony was based on a report made by a physician who treated Tawnya at the Oregon Medical Center when Tawnya was three months old. Tawnya was admitted because of "failure to thrive," a condition that may be caused by a variety of physiological problems or by neglect or abuse. After her admission, a routine x-ray revealed that Tawnya had sustained fractures of the right clavicle, the right eleventh rib, the right tibia, and that she had an abnormality of the left humerus. He observed that two of the fractures were spiral fractures and stated that a self-inflicted spiral or torsion fracture is inconsistent with the degree of mobility possible for a three-month-old infant. He also noted that the parents' explanation of a fall from a couch was not sufficient to account for the injuries. Separate and apart from any evidence pertaining to the defendant's conduct, he testified that these physical symptoms were all indicators that would alert a physician to the possibility of the battered child syndrome. Although Dr. Palmer's testimony dealt only with Tawnya's physical condition and contained no accusatory statements regarding the defendant, this evidence is not relevant to Tawnya's condition at the time of her death, but rather is relevant to establishing a pattern of conduct by the defendant. The defendant points out that, although Tawnya was temporarily removed from her home as a result of this medical report, neither she nor Tawnya's father was ever prosecuted or convicted for any abuse of Tawnya. . . . Medical records of the child's current or past condition that indicate either the presence or absence of abusive injuries must always be relevant to the issues at trial where, as here, expert testimony has established the presence of the battered child syndrome in the victim.

The question remains as to whether the trial court abused its discretion by admitting the evidence of the defendant's prior conduct under the standards set forth in Rule 45 of the Utah Rules of Evidence. As we have discussed above, child abuse is most likely to occur in the privacy of the home under circumstances that make the existence of direct evidence rare. In this case, the victim could not testify, and there were no competent witnesses to the crime. Under such circumstances, the admission of highly relevant evidence regarding the defendant's conduct toward the victim was justified by necessity and by the very specific nature of the evidence.

. . . .

The defendant's conviction is affirmed.

HALL, C.J., and OAKS and HOWE, J.J., *concur.*

STEWART, JUSTICE (*dissenting*):

I dissent. The trial of this case was, I submit, tainted by the admission of prejudicial child syndrome evidence that lacked an adequate foundation, and by the testimony of the prosecution's chief witness that on its face was at least partly perjurious, if not entirely so. I would reverse and remand for a new trial.

There is no real issue as to the cause of Tawnya Tanner's death. The unrebutted evidence established that the cause of death was a blow to the head. The defendant made no claim that she had accidentally or mistakenly caused the death. Her claim was that she had not caused the death in any way. The only real issue is who killed Tawnya Tanner. There are only two realistic possibilities: either Kathy Tanner, the defendant, or Leland Foote, her live-in boyfriend.

The brutal killing of a three-year-old child naturally evokes deep and powerful feelings of revulsion and abhorrence which are common to all. Yet such cases are precisely those in which it is most important to adhere to those rules of evidence which are designed to sift truth from error and to prevent the insinuation of prejudice into the truth-finding processes of the courts. Compliance with those rules is essential to prevent abhorrence for the crime committed from tainting the crucial determination of who committed the crime.

Without even defining what battered child syndrome evidence is, the majority holds that it is admissible even though there is no evidence that the defendant was the sole caretaker of the child when the various injuries, including the fatal blow, were inflicted. . . . The Court's theory of the admissibility of the battered child syndrome evidence is that it established a "pattern of conduct" by the defendant. Thus, under the Court's rationale, it appears that the explosive battered child syndrome evidence may be admitted in virtually all cases in which a parent is accused of killing his or her child and the child has been battered, even though, as here, there is another person who may have been responsible for the fatal injury, and perhaps some of the abuse. On the facts of this case, the Court's ruling represents, I submit, a departure from basic rules of evidence.

The majority opinion states that the "key evidence in this case is the mute testimony of the body of three-year-old Tawnya Tanner." I disagree. That evidence surely does tend to establish that Tawnya was badly abused; indeed, there was other evidence that the defendant herself had on occasion abused the child. But the key evidence in the trial of the case was the highly inconsistent, and at least partially, but undeniably, perjurious testimony of the State's key witness, Leland Foote, the defendant's live-in boyfriend. And truly the key question is whether the defendant or Leland Foote committed the crime. *Foote had earlier pleaded guilty to a manslaughter charge for the exact same crime pursuant to a plea bargain, after having been first charged with second degree murder.*

Battered child syndrome evidence is circumstantial evidence that the caretaker of a child may be responsible for the fatal injury of a child. However, in this case, Foote was also a caretaker. His testimony pointed the finger of guilt solely at the defendant. It is at best strange that notwithstanding Foote's plea of guilty to the charge of killing Tawnya, his trial testimony placed the entire blame for the death of Tawnya on the defendant and in no way inculpated him in the crime in the slightest degree. That testimony must have been contrary to the evidence which the prosecution had against Foote, or it would never have filed the second degree murder charge against Foote, nor would Foote have pleaded guilty. Into these extraordinary circumstances, the "battered child syndrome" evidence was interjected along with other evidence of defendant's prior misconduct.

. . . .

The breadth of the majority's holding, however, opens the door to virtually any child abuse evidence when an infant is killed, without regard for those rules of evidence designed to insure a verdict based on the allegations of the crime charged and not the character of the defendant. In essence, the majority ignores the long-standing rules that restrict the use of prior crime evidence by establishing a high threshold of relevancy and allows the battered child syndrome evidence on the same test of relevancy used for run-of-the-mill evidence. If that were the established law in determining admissibility of prior crime evidence, there would be no need for Rule 55, which serves to insure fairness and reliability in the truth-seeking function of a trial.

I

The majority's definition of battered child syndrome evidence and its explanation of why it is admissible is both confusing and inconsistent. In its own language, and sometimes quoting with approval from other courts, the majority states that the evidence is admissible because it states "no opinion regarding a defendant's culpability," "does not directly indicate the culpability of any particular defendant," "only indicates the cause of death," and "merely describes the nature of the injuries." Furthermore, the majority states that "[m]edical testimony indicated that Tawnya's fatal injury was part of a pattern of abusive injuries."

In justifying the evidence admitted in this case, the majority cites experts who state that the diagnosis is "really descriptive of a pattern of conduct on the part of the parents," is "concern[ed] with the causative factors outside of the body of the child," includes a description of the parents' conduct and characteristics, *and allows for an inference that the parent or guardian inflicted the injuries.* Thus, on the one hand, the majority asserts that the battered child syndrome evidence is not accusatory and only describes the cause of death (which in fact it does not do), and on the other hand admits that such evidence incriminates the parents. The majority cannot have it both ways.

In the instant case, the testimony included reference to the defendant's culpability. The expert testified regarding the typical profile of an abusing parent and the inadequate explanation for Tawnya's injuries. The majority states:

> The doctor also testified that abusive disciplinary methods are frequently part of the battered child syndrome, that the parents of such children are typically very young or inexperienced and that they are likely to have a history of prior abusive conduct. Dr. Palmer went on to identify in Tawnya the characteristics of the battered child, emphasizing in particular the inadequate explanation given by the defendant for Tawnya's injuries.

That testimony goes beyond battered child syndrome evidence which describes the child's injuries, and falls into the category of battering parent syndrome evidence, which includes a profile of the typical battering parent.

Those courts which have considered the admissibility of battering parent syndrome evidence have warned against the improper use of such evidence. . . .

In the present case, the only direct evidence probative of the defendant's guilt came from a perjured witness — the defendant's live-in boyfriend — who had already pleaded guilty to having killed the child after striking a bargain with the prosecutor to obtain a reduction in the charge against him from second degree murder to manslaughter. Under the circumstances, that evidence is highly suspect. In *State v. Mulder*, 629 P.2d 462 (Wash. 1981), the court allowed child abuse syndrome evidence but stated that other *"[e]vidence must still be produced to establish that it was the defendant who caused the injuries in question."* That is not only lacking in this case, but there is evidence quite to the contrary.

One commentator, who favors admissibility of battered child syndrome evidence, agrees that the evidence may be used too broadly: "[I]f the 'battered child syndrome' diagnosis were used indiscriminately, a parent might be convicted for a beating administered by another person." . . . This comment is particularly appropriate in the instant case. It is not unusual for the male companion of a female who has a child whom he has not fathered to engage in acts of child abuse that may kill a child or result in a battered child syndrome. Even babysitters have been convicted of homicides which could be attributed to a parent or parents who have abused a child.

In my view, the analysis of whether battered child syndrome evidence is admissible must begin with the long-established proposition that a person under our system of law may be tried only for a specific act and not for his character. . . . Rule 55 of the Utah Rules of Evidence strikes a balance between this proposition and the rules of evidence by limiting the admissibility of prior acts to instances where they are especially probative.

. . . .

It is not enough that a person of the defendant's particular character is more likely to have committed the crime than someone else — although that proposition may be empirically true and therefore meet the general test of relevance. Thus, a charge of driving under the influence of alcohol may not be proved by showing that the defendant is an alcoholic; a crime of larceny may not be proved by showing that the defendant is a cleptomaniac or has a sociopathic personality; perjury may not be proved by showing that the defendant is a pathological liar.

Thus, for reasons wholly apart from relevancy, the courts generally bar evidence of other wrongs, with few exceptions, for reasons based upon fundamental principles of justice and the concept that man is an autonomous agent invested with free will whose actions are not governed by forces beyond his control.

The purpose behind not allowing evidence of past wrongs is not to exclude relevant evidence, although that may occur, but to protect defendants from irrational decisions. Dean Wigmore has explained this policy in a discussion of admissibility of past crimes to prove character:

> It is objectionable, not because it has no appreciable probative value, but because it has too much. The natural and inevitable tendency of the tribunal — whether judge or jury — is to give excessive weight to the vicious record of crime thus exhibited, and either to allow it to bear too strongly on the present charge, or to take the proof of it as justifying a condemnation irrespective of guilt of the present charge. . . .

Dean Wigmore enumerates three reasons why evidence of past crimes should not be admitted absent special circumstances:

(1) The over-strong tendency to believe the defendant guilty of the charge merely because he is a likely person to do such acts; (2) the tendency to condemn, not because he is believed guilty of the present charge, but because he has escaped unpunished from other offences; . . . (3) The injustice of attacking one necessarily unprepared to demonstrate that the attacking evidence is fabricated.

> All these reasons apply to battered child syndrome evidence, and the rules of evidence should be applied to prevent the defendant from being found guilty because he or she had previously committed numerous wrongs. Even if a parent has abused a child, the parent should not be subjected to the risk of conviction of homicide solely on the basis of his or her prior acts. . . .

. . . .

II

The majority also sustains the admission of additional evidence of past criminal acts other than that evidence admitted under the battered child syndrome theory. The majority indicates that the evidence of past bad acts should be admitted under Rule 55 if the evidence is corroborated by battered child syndrome evidence.

. . . .

For Rule 55 to protect the fundamental philosophical values upon which our criminal justice system is based, it must be interpreted to exclude evidence of past acts unless the evidence is highly and specifically relevant to a particular issue that is contested in the case. It is not sufficient that it merely have some relevance.

Even though the evidence need not fall into one of the specific categories listed in the rule, the language of the rule still requires that the evidence prove some material fact other than the disposition to commit a wrong. The majority seeks to justify the admissibility of evidence of past bad acts on the ground that it was relevant to establish the cause of death, even though the evidence of past bad acts added nothing to the unrebutted medical testimony which established the cause of death. That justification is simply not adequate.

The majority also justifies the admissibility of defendant's prior bad acts and the battered child syndrome evidence on the ground that they show "*a specific pattern of behavior by the defendant.*" But that is precisely what Rule 55 is aimed at preventing — character evidence that shows a propensity to commit a crime. . . .

The evidence might, however, have been admissible, in my view, on other theories, such as identity, intent, or to rebut a claim of accident. But the evidence of battered child syndrome would have no probative value on any issue, except that which was really not in controversy unless the defendant was shown to have been the sole caretaker at the time of the abusive acts and of the homicide. The prosecution failed to prove that critical point in this case, and without that foundation the evidence should not have been admitted.

III

I think this case should be remanded to the trial court for a hearing as to what evidence the prosecutors had which provoked them to file a second degree murder charge against Leland Foote. It is clear beyond question that he perjured himself during his testimony at the trial in this matter and that the testimony he gave which inculpated the defendant was exculpatory as to him. In fact, his testimony was so glaringly untrustworthy that the trial judge specifically admonished the defendant as to the potential consequences of perjury and discontinued taking evidence until Foote could be represented by independent counsel because of the risk he was running in telling different stories.

It may be true that both Foote and the defendant were mutually guilty in causing the death of the deceased, but there is nothing in this record which would support a conviction of Foote even as an accomplice. On the other hand, there was polygraph evidence submitted by the defendant, confirmed by a polygraph expert from the police department, and admitted by the trial court which indicated that the defendant was not guilty of the crime.

. . . I cannot avoid the conclusion that the defendant did not receive a fair trial. I think the case should be reversed and retried.

NOTES AND QUESTIONS

1. As noted by the *Tanner* court, "all courts which have addressed the question have affirmed the admission of expert medical testimony regarding the presence of the battered child syndrome." The court also points out that BCS evidence "is most frequently cited as admissible to show absence of accident." Was the BCS evidence in *Tanner* limited to that purpose? Should it have been?

The McCoid article quoted by the *Tanner* court describes BCS in terms of a typical pattern of injuries suffered by abused children but also in reference to the "origins of the trauma," *i.e.*, an abusive caretaker. In *State v. Wilkerson*, 247 S.E.2d 905 (N.C. 1978), the court permitted a medical expert called by the state to testify not only that the injuries of the child victim fit the typical BCS pattern but also that battered children typically suffer their injuries at the hands of "over-zealous disciplinarians or caretakers." The doctor added that "the syndrome usually occurs in a disciplinary situation involving the child and some guardian or custodian, a parent . . . someone who has physical custody of the child at that time." *Id.* at 909. To what extent is evidence of *who caused the harm*, rather than the nature of the harm itself, a *medical* matter within the expertise of the medical expert? Does such evidence give an opinion as to the "ultimate issue" of guilt and thus invade the province of the jury?

2. One of the medical experts in *Tanner* was permitted to testify that parents of children fitting the BCS profile are "typically very young or inexperienced and . . . are likely to have a history of prior abusive conduct." Is such testimony speaking to the battered child or to the battering parent? Consider this question in light of the discussion of the "battering parent syndrome" in the next section *infra*. Is the admission of the "prior bad act" evidence in *Tanner* logically linked to the BCS evidence?

3. Some courts may disagree with *Tanner*'s admission of "prior bad act" evidence of abuse. *See, e.g., Harvey v. State,* 604 P.2d 586 (Alaska 1979) (where there was no defense of accident and the central issue was causation, not intent, it was reversible error for the trial court to admit defendant's prior acts of child abuse).

4. Juveniles charged with killing or assaulting their caretakers sometimes seek to admit BCS evidence as a defense. For consideration of defensive use of BCS evidence, see § 5.05[A][2][d], *infra*.

5. For commentary on BCS in addition to the McCoid article cited in *Tanner*, see Barbara R. Grumet, *The Plaintive Plaintiffs: Victims of the Battered Child Syndrome*, 4 FAM. L.Q. 296 (1970); Note, *Evidence — Child Abuse — Expert Medical Testimony Concerning "Battered Child Syndrome" Held Admissible*, 42 FORDHAM L. REV. 935 (1974); Comment, *Evidentiary Problems in Criminal Child Abuse Prosecutions*, 63 GEO. L.J. 257 (1974). *See also* Milton Roberts, Annotation, *Admissibility of Expert Medical Testimony on Battered Child Syndrome*, 98 A.L.R. 3d 306 (1980).

[2] The Battering Parent Syndrome (BPS)

PEOPLE v. WALKEY

Court of Appeal of California, Fourth District, Division 1
223 Cal. Rptr. 132 (1986)

LOVETT, ASSOCIATE JUSTICE

A jury convicted Frederick Bruce Walkey, Jr. of first degree murder (PEN. CODE, § 187) and child endangerment (§ 273a, subd. (1)). The court sentenced Walkey to prison for 25 years to life for the murder. The court also imposed but stayed a three-year term for the child endangerment. Walkey appeals.

FACTS

Walkey and his wife Alicia lived in Oceanside with Ellen Cosby and her two-year-old son Nathanel. Walkey was intimate with Cosby and acted as a substitute father for Nathanel, including physically punishing him. At about 1:00 p.m. on February 17, 1983, Walkey, Cosby and Nathanel went to K-Mart where they had lunch. Nathanel ate and was playful and cheerful. They returned home about 3:00 p.m. Nathanel was in the backyard with Walkey and then took a nap on the living room couch. At about 5:30 p.m., Cosby left to go shopping while Walkey and his wife stayed with Nathanel.

Vickie Helmstadter went to Cosby's house at about 6:30 p.m. and found Cosby was not home. Helmstadter saw Walkey coming up the stairs from the cellar carrying Nathanel. When Helmstadter called Nathanel's name, he did not respond. She noticed there was no movement of his legs and his arms were hanging relaxed. She also noticed Walkey looked scared. He told her to go in the house and wait for him.

Walkey put Nathanel in another room and came out to see Helmstadter. She paid Walkey $10 she owed him and left. As she was leaving, Howard Miller and Glenn Faulkner were coming in, looking for Cosby. Walkey told them Cosby was not at home and to come back later. They did not leave. Walkey then said he was going to check on Nathanel. He returned carrying Nathanel, who was motionless, wrapped in blankets. Walkey said Nathanel had defecated in his bed and Walkey was going to clean him up. Miller heard water running in the bathroom. Walkey came out carrying some bed sheets. At Walkey's suggestion, he and Miller and Faulkner went outside to play horseshoes. About 20 minutes later, Walkey's wife called out for them to come in because Nathanel was not breathing.

A paramedic arrived within five minutes and saw Nathanel was not breathing and had no pulse. He also noticed Nathanel looked like he had been severely beaten. Nathanel was covered with bruises and his abdomen was distended. Walkey said he had taken Nathanel out of the bathtub and also said Nathanel had earlier fallen and hit his head.

Nathanel was taken to Tri-City Hospital where resuscitation efforts were unsuccessful. The examining physician pronounced Nathanel dead at 7:29 p.m. The doctor saw bite marks on Nathanel's neck and arms and also saw old and new bruises. An X-ray showed Nathanel had a fractured rib.

An autopsy revealed 17 different bruises, abrasions and lacerations. The fresh bruises probably occurred within two hours of Nathanel's death. Nathanel's facial injuries were most likely the result of a blunt object impacting with relatively severe force. Nathanel's upper body had various abrasions and bruises, including two bite marks inflicted two hours or less before his death. His abdomen was tense and distended due to a large hemorrhage. Nathanel had received a severe penetrating blow, crushing and tearing open the intestines. The cause of death was related to this blow. Nathanel's injuries were nonaccidental and occurred between 5:00 and 6:30 p.m.

The pathologist who performed the autopsy testified at trial Nathanel's abdominal injuries were caused by a blow from a blunt object delivered with extreme force such that an average size female would not be able to inflict the injury. The pathologist testified Nathanel would have experienced extreme pain. Shock would set in either immediately or within one-half hour so that Nathanel would be unconscious or in a depressed state.

Nathanel had additional injuries, including a partially healed fractured rib (about two months old), a hemorrhaged spleen and a partially healed torn liver. These injuries indicated Nathanel had received a previous severe abdominal blow at least two weeks before he died. Nathanel also had two large deep bruises on the back of his head causing life-threatening injury to the brain and surrounding tissue.

Dr. Sperber, a forensic dentist, testified at trial. He had taken photographs and impressions of the bite marks on Nathanel's body. Dr. Sperber also had taken dental impressions of Cosby, Walkey and Mrs. Walkey. Comparing the teeth marks of Nathanel with these dental impressions, Dr. Sperber testified neither Cosby nor Mrs. Walkey could have caused Nathanel's bite marks and he had no doubt Walkey caused them.

Dr. Chadwick, the physician who reviewed the photographs taken of Nathanel at the hospital and during the autopsy, testified Nathanel was a battered child. The number of bruises on Nathanel's body were inconsistent with accidental injuries. He also testified about the various factors that make up the profile of a child abuser.

Walkey testified in his own defense, claiming Nathanel was with him in the cellar for about ten minutes the day he died. Walkey left the house about 4:30 p.m. and returned about 6:10 p.m. Nathanel was sleeping on the living room couch. Walkey went back to the cellar. Hearing Nathanel cry, Walkey left the cellar and saw Nathanel lying on his face at the bottom of the back door stairway with Nathanel's dog jumping around him. Nathanel's lip was bleeding so Walkey carried him into the house, cleaned his lip and gave him a bath. While bathing Nathanel, Walkey bit him on the forearm because Nathanel had bitten him. Walkey then put Nathanel down on the waterbed in the bedroom. When Walkey returned ten minutes later to check on Nathanel, he found Nathanel had vomited and was not breathing.

Walkey testified he never struck Nathanel in the abdomen or anywhere else. He testified he loved Nathanel very much.

. . . .

III

Walkey contends the court erred in allowing Dr. Chadwick to testify about the "battering parent syndrome." We agree with Walkey's assertion this testimony was impermissible character evidence.

A

Dr. Chadwick was the physician who had reviewed the photographs taken of Nathanel at the hospital and during the autopsy. Based on the number and types of bruises on Nathanel's body, Dr. Chadwick concluded Nathanel was a battered child. He also explained to the jury the various factors constituting the profile of a child abuser, stating the most important single factor is "having been abused oneself in infancy or childhood." Other factors, he explained, were social isolation, unreasonable expectations of young children (including toilet training at a very early age), and stress.

After Walkey testified on direct examination, a juror sent the court a note asking whether Walkey was an abused child. Walkey objected, under Evidence Code § 352, to the prosecution questioning him on this matter. The court overruled the objection, finding the probative value of this line of questioning outweighed its prejudicial effect.

The prosecutor was allowed to elicit from Walkey on cross-examination that when Walkey was a child, he was disciplined by being bitten and hit with a board. The prosecutor also asked Walkey whether remembered telling Ellen Cosby that Walkey's stepfather used to take him out to the garage to beat him. Walkey denied telling this to Cosby. Following this testimony, the court refused Walkey's request to reopen the defense's case to have Walkey's stepfather testify he never took Walkey out to the garage to beat him. During closing argument, the prosecutor argued Walkey fit Dr. Chadwick's profile of a battering parent.[59]

---

59 [6] The prosecutor argued the following:

"We also know that Mr. Walkey was at least to some extent battered. Whether it was a board or a cord, we know that that was the sort of treatment that he received as he was growing up.

"Now, why is that important? Why is that something which is singled out and said, 'Uh-huh, look at this.' Remember the testimony of Dr. Chadwick? I asked him, 'Dr. Chadwick, is there a profile that helps us to identify people who are likely to abuse or who abuse children?'

"He said that is not a very good word for it. He said there are a number of factors that the experts in this field see again and again, and recognize as being factors. What were they?

"Maybe some of you wrote them down, something that will be of value to you, not just in this case, but in your life after this case.

"He said, and I quote, 'The most important single one is the fact of having been abused oneself in infancy or childhood.'

"Oh, we know that did not happen to Ellen Cosby. We know that did happen to Fred Walkey, and there were other factors not just that one. That is the single most important, but what are the others?

"Social isolation from the presence of others who are around to prevent it.

"Well, I suggest what that means is you have parents coming to visit, you have grandparents coming to visit, you are going here for Thanksgiving, here for Christmas, and you don't dare take that grandchild home with a bruise on its cheek to grandmother. That is a social pressure, that keeps people who might abuse from doing it.

"I suggest that you don't take him to the base hospital at Camp Pendleton like Ellen Cosby did if you are the person who does the abusing.

"Unreasonable expectation was a factor that Dr. Chadwick mentioned, and specifically one of the unreasonable expectations, that this child at 25 months is going to learn to say, 'I have to go to the bathroom, take me now,' and not have any accidents. It is what this killing is all about, ladies and gentlemen.

"A child who had a toilet training accident, and the defendant decided that he was going to teach him that that was not something that he should do, and he didn't fly off the handle and just do it like that.

"He did it, he set out with a purpose of doing it, and he did it intentionally, premeditated, willful, deliberate. " 'You are not going to do this again, and I am going to teach you not to do it.' Then that is what happened.

No California court has considered the issue of the admissibility of "battering parent syndrome" evidence.[60] Other courts that have addressed the issue have disallowed evidence to show the defendant fit within the battering parent profile, reasoning character evidence in criminal cases may not be used to prove a defendant acted in conformity with such character. (*See, e.g.*, *State v. Loebach* (Minn. 1981) 310 N.W.2d 58, 64; *Sanders v. State* (1983) 251 Ga. 70, 303 S.E.2d 13, 18; *Duley v. State* (1983) 56 MD. APP. 275, 467 A.2d 776, 780.)

"Such evidence invites a jury to conclude that because the defendant has been identified by an expert with experience in child abuse cases as a member of a group having a higher incidence of child . . . abuse, it is more likely the defendant committed the crime."

Thus, the nature and extent of the potential prejudice to a defendant generated by character evidence renders it inadmissible. We agree with those courts holding the prosecution may not introduce character evidence of a defendant to show the defendant has the characteristics of a typical battering parent.

C

Evidence Code § 1102 precludes evidence of specific acts of the defendant to prove character as circumstantial evidence of his disposition to commit the crime with which he is charged. The prosecution may not cross-examine the defendant as to specific matters in an attempt to prove bad character until and unless the defendant first puts in evidence of his good character. Here, Walkey did not put his character in evidence. The prosecution's obvious purpose in introducing battering parent evidence was to show Walkey fit within that profile. Although Dr. Chadwick never expressly concluded Walkey fit the profile, his testimony clearly implicated Walkey's character. Dr. Chadwick's testimony tended to associate Walkey with a group of persons who, in Dr. Chadwick's opinion, are often child abusers. This, coupled with Walkey's

"What are the other factors that Dr. Chadwick talked about? He said a lot of other things going on that are impinging on one's life that causes frustration and anger. "Did Mr. Walkey have a lot of other things going on in his life that caused frustration and anger?

"Yeah, he was U.A., unauthorized absence from the Marine Corps. They had declared him a deserter. He didn't think that was fair, but he knew they had done that. That was some pressure. That was some frustration. That was some anger.

"He is living under the same roof with his wife, sleeping with somebody else, yet his wife is there. Did that cause a little frustration? Caused a little anger? Were there disagreements about that?

"Miller told you about one. He said, 'I woke up in the middle of the night, and I heard this argument going on, and the next morning Alicia Walkey came down and asked me to take her to the hospital, and I said, "Did Fred do that," and she said, "No, I tripped over a toy."

"Do you think she tripped over a toy? Fred Walkey fits the profile that Dr. Chadwick testified about."

[60] [7] Battering parent syndrome represents a distinctly different concept from battered child syndrome. The latter has become an accepted medical diagnosis and expert testimony on the subject is admissible in child abuse prosecutions. An expert testifying as to the existence of the battered child syndrome expresses no opinion on a defendant's culpability; rather, such evidence is most often used by the prosecution to preclude an inference of accident.

admission he was physically disciplined as a child and other testimony Walkey had certain characteristics typical of a battering parent,[61] impermissibly allowed the jury to infer Walkey was a battering parent and therefore must have caused Nathanel's injuries. Accordingly, the court erred in admitting that part of Dr. Chadwick's testimony used to prove Walkey fit the diagnosis of a battering parent.

D

The error in admitting battering parent testimony was, however, harmless. The prosecution's case against Walkey was strong. Nathanel's injuries were established as being non-accidental. Walkey's testimony Nathanel received his injuries as a result of falling down the stairs or being knocked down by his dog is entirely inconsistent with the medical experts' testimony Nathanel's fatal injuries were caused by a severe blow to the abdomen with a blunt object. Walkey was with Nathanel during the hours these injuries were inflicted. Several witnesses saw Walkey carrying Nathanel, unconscious. Walkey admitted disciplining Nathanel by biting him and the bite marks on Nathanel's body were consistent with the dental impressions taken of Walkey. Thus, it is not reasonably probable a result more favorable to Walkey would have resulted absent the improper testimony.

DISPOSITION

The judgment is modified by reducing the degree of Walkey's murder conviction to second degree murder, and as so modified, is affirmed. . . .

―――――

NOTES AND QUESTIONS

1. In footnote 7 of *Walkey*, the court distinguishes admissible BCS evidence from inadmissible BPS evidence. Is this distinction convincing in explaining why the BCS evidence was admissible in the *Tanner* case *supra* but the BPS evidence in *Walkey* was inadmissible?

2. In *Loebach v. State*, discussed in *Walkey*, the Court held BPS evidence to be inadmissible character evidence. The *Loebach* court noted three basic reasons for the exclusion of character evidence used to prove that a criminal defendant acted in conformity with such character:

> First, there is the possibility that the jury will convict a defendant in order to penalize him for his past misdeeds or simply because he is an undesirable person. Second, there is the danger that a jury will overvalue the character evidence in assessing the guilt for the crime

---

[61] [8] The prosecution introduced evidence that a soiled diaper was found on the bathroom floor the day Nathanel died, implying Nathanel's beating was a result of a toilet training accident. Evidence of stress in Walkey's life was also presented, such as his unauthorized absence from the military and his living arrangement with both his wife and Cosby. Also, Cosby testified she was never abused as a child, thereby ruling her out as a typical battering parent.

charged. Finally, it is unfair to require an accused to be prepared not only to defend against immediate charges, but also to disprove or explain his personality or prior actions.

310 N.W.2d at 63. Do these reasons support the *Walkey* court's refusal to permit BPS evidence?

In addition, the *Loebach* court expressed the possibility that BPS evidence may eventually be admissible in the state's case-in-chief:

We now hold that in future cases the prosecution will not be permitted to introduce evidence of "battering parent" syndrome or to establish the character of the defendant as a "battering parent" unless the defendant first raises that issue. We feel this finding is required until further evidence of the scientific accuracy and reliability of syndrome or profile diagnoses can be established.

310 N.W.2d at 64. Suppose eventually it is established that 100 percent of child abusers fit the BPS profile. Should the state then be allowed to admit evidence in its case-in-chief that the defendant fit the profile?

3. For commentary on BPS, see Thomas N. Bulleit, Jr., Note, *The Battering Parent Syndrome: Inexpert Testimony as Character Evidence*, 17 U. MICH. J. L. REFORM 653 (1984); Gregory G. Sarno, Annotation, *Admissibility at Criminal Prosecution of Expert Testimony on Battering Parent Syndrome*, 43 A.L.R. 4th 1203 (1986).

[3] Munchausen Syndrome by Proxy (MSP)

PEOPLE v. PHILLIPS

Court of Appeal of California, First District, Division 1
175 Cal. Rptr. 703 (1981)

GRODIN, ASSOCIATE JUSTICE.

Following a lengthy jury trial, appellant was convicted of murdering one of her two adopted children, and of willfully endangering the life or health of the other, by deliberately administering a sodium compound into the food of each of them. As grounds for reversal she asserts . . . the erroneous admission of certain psychiatric testimony into evidence. . . . We find no reversible error and therefore affirm, for reasons which follow.

SUMMARY OF THE EVIDENCE

By nearly all accounts, Priscilla Phillips was a kind, helpful and loving person, a dutiful wife to her husband and a devoted mother to their two sons, who at the time of trial were nine and six years of age. Highly educated, with a master's degree in social work, she was employed in the Marin County Health and Human Services Department. After the birth of her sons, she turned her attention increasingly to religious and civil volunteer work, and became active in a variety of community organizations. Among the many organizations to which she volunteered time and energy was the Child Protective Services Unit of the Marin County child abuse agency.

After the birth of her second son in 1973, appellant developed physical symptoms which led to a hysterectomy in 1975. Deeply upset that she could not have another child, especially a daughter, appellant and her husband decided to adopt a Korean infant who had been found abandoned on the streets of Seoul. They called her Tia.

Tia arrived at the Phillips' household in November 1975. Appellant promptly took her to Dr. Aimy Taniguchi, a pediatrician at the Kaiser clinic in San Rafael, for examination. Dr. Taniguchi found Tia to be in good health except for a diaper rash and an ear infection, and prescribed treatment for both. By late November the rash and the infection appeared to have been successfully treated.

On January 26, 1976, appellant brought Tia into the clinic and informed Dr. Taniguchi that Tia had a low-grade fever. A urine specimen revealed a urinary tract infection for which Dr. Taniguchi prescribed first a sulfur-based antibiotic, which did not appear to help, and then a different antibiotic, which worked successfully. Tia's ear infection recurred, however, and was twice treated in February.

On February 27, 1976, appellant brought Tia into the clinic and told Dr. Taniguchi that Tia had a fever and had vomited violently in the morning. The source of the fever could not be determined.

On March 2, 1976, appellant brought Tia to the clinic again and reported that she had been vomiting off and on since the last visit. The doctor believed that the ear infection might be persisting, and added another antibiotic. Later that day, appellant brought Tia into the Kaiser Hospital at San Rafael and told the doctor on call that Tia was having brief "staring spells," and Tia was admitted for observation.

Dr. William Leider, a pediatric neurologist from San Francisco Kaiser, was called in to evaluate Tia's condition, and a variety of tests were performed, including blood sugar and blood calcium tests, a urine culture, a lumbar puncture, X-rays, and an intravenous pyleogram, but the tests revealed no abnormalities. Dr. Al Baumann, an ear, nose and throat specialist, examined Tia, found evidence of a low-grade infection, and because of her previous ear infection recommended an operation called a myringotomy, which entails removal of fluid from the ear drums. The operation was performed on March 5. On March 6, Dr. Taniguchi informed appellant that all of the diagnostic tests were complete, that the results were normal, that the ear operation was successful, and that she planned to discharge Tia within 48 hours.

During the evening of March 6, however, while Tia was still in the hospital, she began to cry and was unable to be comforted. The next day she began to vomit and have diarrhea. Her diet was changed from regular baby formula to clear liquid, but she did not improve. By March 9 feeding by mouth was discontinued and Tia was given intravenous fluids. She improved and was given clear fluids by mouth, but on the evening of March 10 the diarrhea attacks recurred. Feeding by mouth was again discontinued, and the diarrhea stopped abruptly.

Tia remained hospitalized, and the pattern continued. Further diagnostic tests revealed no abnormality, and the doctors were baffled. In April 1976 she was transferred to Kaiser Hospital in San Francisco, where a central venous hyperalimentation device was implanted through a catheter to permit introduction of nutritious fluids. She remained in San Francisco until June 8, 1976, and was then returned to Kaiser San Rafael to monitor her progress on nasogastric feeding. On July 7, 1976, she was taken to Stanford Medical Center for an intestinal biopsy. Although playful and alert when admitted, by the evening of July 8 she had developed cramps, acute diarrhea, and projectile vomiting. The diarrhea stopped abruptly the next morning. On July 10 Tia was transferred to a San Francisco hospital for the performance of a laparotomy to explore for tumors. Two days later, while at that hospital, Tia had another bout of diarrhea. Her doctors found this "inexplicable." On July 14 or 15, while still at the San Francisco hospital, appellant suggested that Tia be given solid foods. The doctors agreed to try her suggestion, and it appeared to work. Tia "really did very well" and had normal body functions. On July 28 she was discharged. The laparotomy was not performed.

On August 6 appellant called Dr. Taniguchi and told her that Tia's illness had recurred, that she was very sick with vomiting and diarrhea. Upon examination at the hospital, Tia was found to be severely dehydrated, lethargic, and unresponsive to stimulation. Tests revealed she was suffering from an extreme level of sodium in her blood. This finding coincided with prior readings, taken during periods when Tia was having attacks of diarrhea and vomiting; these findings also showed abnormally high levels of blood serum sodium, and of bicarbonate. The doctors had no explanation for this phenomenon.

Tia was admitted to the hospital, improved rapidly, and was released on August 9. On August 23, however, she was again hospitalized with the same symptoms. Abdominal X-rays showed no obstruction of the intestinal tract. She was discharged on August 28 but the symptoms reappeared and she was hospitalized twice in September and twice in October. Electrolyte readings continued to fluctuate, but again, all diagnostic tests were normal. In November 1976 a laparotomy was performed at Kaiser Hospital in San Francisco, but it revealed no abnormalities. Tia was discharged on November 26.

On December 3, 1976, Tia was examined by her pediatrician and was found to be doing well. Three days later she was back in the emergency room in shock, vomiting convulsively, and displaying elevated sodium and bicarbonate levels. On December 11, having improved to the point that she could take formula, she was discharged. Less than three hours later she was back with the same symptoms, and was discharged again on December 22. A similar episode occurred in January 1977.

On February 2, 1977, appellant brought Tia to the emergency room for the last time. The child was in critical condition. She was having generalized seizures. She had an extreme level of sodium in her blood. An X-ray showed aspiration of vomit into her right lung. She was unable to eliminate carbon dioxide from her body, and she began to demonstrate abnormal posturings which indicated damage to her central nervous system. She died on February 3.

Several months after Tia's death, appellant and her husband adopted another Korean infant whom they named Mindy. On February 3, 1979 the anniversary of Tia's death appellant brought Mindy to the hospital. The child had been vomiting, and she had diarrhea. Mindy was admitted to the hospital; her symptoms eventually subsided; and she was discharged on February 10. On February 16 Mindy was hospitalized again with the same symptoms. Her sodium level was elevated. Dr. Taniguchi began to note similarities between Mindy's case and Tia's case: "[T]hinking about it as objectively as possible, I realized that these two girls were not related in any way and . . . it just seemed incredible that they could even possibly have the same type of problem. . . ." At a pediatric staff conference on February 22, all doctors present agreed that "it was important to consider the possibility that this child was being poisoned."

The following day Dr. Arnhold, a pediatrician at Kaiser, gave Dr. Taniguchi a copy of an article from the Journal of the American Medical Association concerning a form of child abuse which had been reported in the British Medical Journal, Lancet, by a physician named Meadow. The article noted Meadow's observations of a case in which one little girl underwent innumerable manipulative, anesthetic, radiologic and surgical procedures during the six years of her life because her parents provided false information about her symptoms, tampered with her urine specimens, and otherwise interfered with observation by physicians and nurses; and of a second case in which a 14-month-old infant died of hypernatremia after repeated hospital admissions for vomiting and drowsiness that were precipitated by ingestion of large quantities of salt given to her surreptitiously by her mother. Both mothers appeared to be loving, cooperative, and appreciative of the care given to their children. Dr. Meadow had denominated the phenomena "Munchausen syndrome by proxy," after the so-called "Munchausen syndrome" in which a patient beguiles a physician into performing unnecessary diagnostic and surgical procedures on the basis of false reports of symptoms.

Dr. Taniguchi proceeded with a series of tests to determine a medical cause for Mindy's symptoms: "Again, I was faced with the puzzling finding of an elevated sodium; and for the first time [I] began to look at it in terms of what was going into the patient and what was coming out of the patient. And, it did not add up. There was much more coming out than was going in." Mindy continued to have diarrhea. Sodium levels were abnormally high.

On February 24, around 2:45 p. m., Leslie McCarcy, a pediatric nurse at the hospital, arrived on duty and received a report from Cathy Place, the outgoing nurse. The question of Mindy's formula came up. Appellant was in Mindy's hospital room at the time. According to Nurse McCarcy, "Mrs. Phillips came out to the desk and Cathy asked her if she had made up the formula and Mrs. Phillips said yes, she had. It was in the refrigerator."

The next morning, February 25, the pediatrician on duty checked Mindy's intake and output charts. "I found that indeed, there was a large amount of unaccountable sodium in Mindy's stool and urine. . . . She was losing about five times the amount of sodium she was receiving." The doctor then went to the nurse on duty and asked her where Mindy's formula was kept. He took a sample of the formula and had it analyzed. The sodium content was 448 milliequivalents per liter. According to the manufacturer's specification, the sodium content should have been only 15 milliequivalents per liter. The doctor had Mindy's formula replaced and transferred her to the intensive care unit.

Appellant was forbidden to feed Mindy, and was forbidden to visit the child except in the presence of a nurse. She was told that sodium appeared to be the cause of Mindy's illness, and that some sort of laxative salt might be a cause of the diarrhea. Appellant said, "I don't know anything about things like that," and asked what the doctor was going to do. When he told her that under the circumstances it was his obligation to call the Child Protective Services, appellant became downcast and said, "Then I'll be a suspect."

Once Mindy was placed in the ICU unit, she recovered quickly. She "seemed fine. . . . She did not have any more diarrhea at all. . . . She ate well, she was happy. . . ."

Dr. Boyd Stephens, Coroner of the City and County of San Francisco, testified on the basis of his observations that the cause of Tia's death was sodium poisoning, and that the amount of the sodium was so high that it had to have been administered into the gastrointestinal tract. Dr. Malcolm Holliday, Professor of Pediatrics at the University of California, concurred, and concluded that since Tia's chloride levels were normal, and her bicarbonate level was high, that the form of the salt was sodium bicarbonate. He testified that two to three teaspoons of sodium bicarbonate, dissolved in liquid, would have been sufficient to produce the symptoms which Tia and Mindy displayed.

At each of the hospitals to which Tia was admitted, parents were encouraged to participate in the care of their infants and young children; and mothers were permitted to remain overnight and to feed their babies. Throughout Tia's hospitalizations, appellant visited frequently and for prolonged periods of time. Because of her dedication, she won the admiration, sympathy, and respect of hospital staff members. Because of her obvious intelligence, her frequent presence, and her willingness to help, she was allowed to perform "minor nursing chores," including administration of formula through the nasogastric tube. The pediatric facility at each hospital had a small room or kitchen area, not visible from the nursing station, which contained an unlocked refrigerator for formulas and other foods. Appellant had access to those areas.

In order to suggest a motive for appellant's alleged conduct, the prosecution, over the objections of defense counsel, presented evidence relating to the so-called "Munchausen's syndrome by proxy" through the testimony of Dr. Martin Blinder, a psychiatrist. Dr. Blinder had not examined appellant, nor had he treated patients who displayed the syndrome which was the subject of his testimony. Rather, his testimony was based upon various reports in professional journals, copies of which were made available to the jury.

In response to a hypothetical question, Dr. Blinder theorized that a mother who repeatedly and surreptitiously administered a cathartic sodium compound to her adopted children, under circumstances identical to those presented by this case, displayed symptoms consistent with Munchausen's syndrome by proxy. He testified that the syndrome "is one in which an individual either directly or through the vehicle of a child feigns, simulates, or actually fabricates a physical illness. . . . Typically, the illness is a dramatic one." "And 'by proxy' simply means instead of the person making themselves ill, they go through the psychodynamic process in another. It's usually the mother. . . . She's outwardly devoted to the child and invariably, the child is very small, less than two years of age. . . . The mothers who perpetrate a child abuse or Munchausen's form of child abuse typically will transfer their own unmet parental needs . . . onto pediatricians, nurses, spouses, maybe even the community and get from these people through their child's illness the attention and sympathy they never got from their own parents."

Describing the syndrome, Dr. Blinder continued: "The mother will flourish on the ward. She seems to almost to blossom in the medical drama of the hospital. . . . The concern, competence and intelligence of these mothers . . . makes it hard for the doctors to suspect them as the possible cause of their child's illness. . . . When the mother is confronted with evidence that she in fact is responsible for the illness, [she] cannot accept responsibility, even when the evidence is incontrovertible. . . . The literature describes some mothers who are frankly psychotic. . . . But a great number of the mothers who do this to their children are not overtly mentally ill." Asked about appellant herself — as opposed to a hypothetical mother — Dr. Blinder testified, "Without a clinical examination of this defendant herself, I cannot say with the necessary degree of certainty that she indeed is reflecting a Munchausen Syndrome."

Appellant testified in her own behalf. She denied that she had ever given Tia or Mindy sodium bicarbonate or any other sodium compound, and she denied that she had ever done anything to harm either child. She admitted that she had, on "some occasions," prepared Mindy's hospital formula herself. Friends, acquaintances, and hospital nurses testified concerning appellant's reputation for truthfulness and her care and deep concern for Tia and Mindy. Defense psychiatrists testified, based on their examinations of appellant, that her mental condition was "essentially normal" with "none of the distortions in thinking or emotion that have been described in the articles on Munchausen Syndrome by proxy or that one might expect if Mrs. Phillips had committed (the) alleged acts." According to defense experts, appellant was "not suffering from any significant mental disease or illness."

. . . .

2. *Admission of Dr. Blinder's testimony was not error.*

Appellant argues, "The trial court abused its discretion and committed prejudicial error in permitting expert opinion testimony, in answer to a hypothetical question, on Munchausen syndrome by proxy, where the facts of the question related specifically to appellant and the named victims, where appellant's mental condition was not at issue, and where illness attributed to appellant was not recognized by medical profession." This composite argument contains several components, which we proceed to analyze.

a. The form of the hypothetical question.

Dr. Blinder first testified as to his qualifications and his familiarity with medicine, psychiatry, family therapy, child abuse, and a group of symptoms called "Munchausen syndrome by proxy." He was then asked for a description of the Munchausen syndrome. The court requested that the prosecution proceed by means of a hypothetical question and then elicit a description of the syndrome. The prosecutor began: "I'll ask . . . that you assume the following facts: Number one, that the defendant, Priscilla E. Phillips, did repeatedly and surreptitiously administer doses of a cathartic sodium-type compound over a period of approximately 12 months to first one adopted Korean orphan, Tia Phillips, . . . and then engaged in similar conduct with a second adopted Korean orphan, Mindy Phillips, over a period of approximately one month until this poisoning was discovered by hospital officials." At that point, the defense objected: "It's assuming the guilt of the defendant which is totally inadmissible in a criminal proceeding. . . ." The objection was overruled, and the prosecutor continued with his question. The defense then objected that the question was argumentative, complex, and assumed facts not in evidence. The objection was overruled, and the prosecutor continued with his question. The defense then objected to the prosecutor's use of appellant's name. The court thereupon instructed the jury to disregard the prosecutor's mention of appellant: "Strike Mrs. Phillips and just say the defendant involved in this hypothetical case, because it's entirely a hypothetical case presented to the doctor and you're to consider it as such." The prosecutor continued with his question, substituting "the defendant" for "Mrs. Phillips." Further defense objections were overruled, and Dr. Blinder was permitted to testify, "I have an opinion. . . . [Y]our hypothetical person evinces symptoms consistent with . . . Munchausen's Syndrome by proxy."

Dr. Blinder then proceeded to describe the syndrome. He said that he could not render an opinion concerning appellant herself, because he had never examined her. Dr. Blinder's testimony continued until the afternoon recess. Immediately following the recess, the court *sua sponte* and without objection read to the jury CALJIC No. 2.82 concerning hypothetical questions. The court read the entire instruction twice, including the following sentence: "It is for you, the jury, to determine from all the evidence whether or not the facts assumed in a hypothetical question have been proved." This instruction was given again at the conclusion of the case, along with CALJIC No. 2.80, concerning expert testimony generally.

Appellant argues that the hypothetical question was phrased improperly in that the names of Mrs. Phillips and the alleged victims were repeatedly used, and that this impropriety was prejudicial because it may have led the jury to believe that Dr. Blinder was expressing an opinion about Mrs. Phillips' mental condition when, in fact, he had never met her, much less examined her.

We do not agree. That Dr. Blinder had never met or examined appellant was made clear to the jury repeatedly. Thus, any impropriety in the form of the question could not have misled the jurors. Dr. Blinder was saying, in effect, that the conduct ascribed to appellant was explicable in terms of the syndrome which had been reported in the literature. Whether that testimony was properly admitted is the key question, to which we now turn.

b. Admissibility of psychiatric evidence by the prosecution where defendant has not made her mental state an issue.

Appellant suggests this may be the "first time in the history of California criminal jurisprudence in which the prosecution was permitted to put into evidence, as part of its case in chief, the mental condition of the defendant without the issue first being raised either by plea or by the introduction of the defendant's state of mind as part of the defense." That may be true, but it is hardly persuasive as to the admissibility of such testimony. The rules of evidence do not preclude innovation.

While a prosecutor ordinarily need not prove motive as an element of a crime, the absence of apparent motive may make proof of the essential elements less persuasive. Clearly that was the principal problem confronting the prosecutor here. In the absence of a motivational hypothesis, and in the light of other information which the jury had concerning her personality and character, the conduct ascribed to appellant was incongruous and apparently inexplicable. As both parties recognize, Dr. Blinder's testimony was designed to fill that gap.

The evidence was thus relevant, and therefore admissible "[e]xcept as otherwise provided by statute." Appellant points to no statutory provision which would preclude the prosecutor from introducing otherwise admissible psychiatric testimony relevant to motivation on the ground that the defendant had not placed his or her mental state in issue.

. . . .

c. Reliability of the evidence.

Evidence Code § 801 describes the boundaries of expert testimony: "If a witness is testifying as an expert, his testimony in the form of an opinion is limited to such an opinion as is: (a) Related to a subject that is sufficiently beyond common experience that the opinion of an expert would assist the trier of fact; and (b) Based on matter (including his special knowledge, skill, experience, training, and education) perceived by or personally known to the witness or made known to him at or before the hearing, whether or not admissible, that is of a type that reasonably may be relied upon by an expert in forming an opinion upon the subject to which his testimony relates, unless an expert is precluded by law from using such matter as a basis for his opinion." Testimony outside these boundaries, *i.e.*, "testimony in the form of an opinion that is based in whole or in significant part on matter that is not a proper basis for such an opinion," is subject to exclusion upon objection.

The existence, nature, validity, and applicability to these facts of the phenomenon characterized as "Munchausen syndrome by proxy" are all matters sufficiently beyond common experience that expert opinion would assist the trier of fact, and appellant does not argue otherwise. Thus, the requirements of subdivision (a) of § 801 are satisfied. It is the provisions of subdivision (b) that form the focus of appellant's attack.

Under the provisions of subdivision (b), the fact that Dr. Blinder's testimony was based in large measure upon reports by others rather than upon his personal observations of the defendant or of other persons displaying that syndrome may affect the weight of his testimony but does not render that testimony inadmissible if those reports meet the standard of reasonable reliability.

All of the studies cited by Dr. Blinder appeared in professional technical journals and were written by medical specialists on the basis of personal observations.[62] "While a layman may not testify to a fact which he has learned only by reading a medical book, there is no question that a professional physician may rely upon medical texts as the basis for his testimony.

Appellant does not question Dr. Blinder's qualifications to appraise the reliability of these studies, nor does she suggest that information contained in them could feasibly have been presented except through the reported data.

---

[62] [1] Dr. Blinder in the course of his testimony on direct examination, listed six authorities upon which he relied. Two of these, the report by Dr. Meadow published in Lancet and the summary of that report which appeared in the Journal of the American Medical Association, have previously been described. We here briefly summarize the other four.

In the November 1965 issue of Pediatrics there appeared a report by Dr. Mark S. Dine concerning a mother who fed her 19 month-old son perpehenazine tranquilizer that had been prescribed for her own use. When confronted with the evidence that she had been poisoning her son, the mother's reaction was one of dismay and denial. Dr. Dine suggested that "the poisoning of children by the deliberated administration of medications or other toxic substances" be regarded as a form of child abuse along with the previously recognized phenomena of the "battered child" syndrome, sexual molestation, and gross neglect; and he cautioned that "physicians who are responsible for the care of children must be alert to the possibility not only of physical trauma inflicted by parents, but also of deliberate drug intoxication as a cause of illness even when the history excludes this factor."

In the British Medical Journal for April 1976 there appeared an article by Rogers, et. al., entitled *Non-accidental Poisoning: An Extended Syndrome of Child Abuse.* The authors, physician, psychiatrists and researchers at the Hospital for Sick Children and poisons unit at Guy's Hospital in London, reported in detail six cases of non-accidental poisoning of children by their parents. One of these involved a trained children's nurse who had administered small doses of salt to her two-month-old infant in her daily feeds. Referring to earlier studies involving such phenomena, the authors cautioned: "This manifestation of child abuse may be commoner than previously supposed."

In the September 1977 issue of the American Journal, Clinical Pediatrics, Drs. Fleisher and Ament from the Departments of Pediatric and Medicine of the UCLA Center for the Health Sciences reported their finding in three cases of children administered phenolphthalein in the form of laxatives by emotionally disturbed mothers. Based on their studies, they advanced the opinion that the mothers in these cases were using their babies' illnesses to elicit sympathetic interest and involvement when they felt such a need, and to inflict grief or frustation when they felt angry or retaliatory.

The same journal in June of the following year carried an article entitled *Intentional Poisoning of Two Siblings by Prescription Drugs: An Unusual Form of Child Abuse.* The authors, Drs. Hvizdala and Gellady of the Department of Pediatrics, University of Florida College of Medicine, cited a study in 1975 by Kempe and Schmitt calling attention to intentional poisoning by prescription drugs as a form of child abuse. Their own report involved two instances of deliberate poisoning of children by parents. One of these was a mother who appeared concerned and anxious to help the physicians in determining the cause of her children's problems and who, when first evaluated by the Division of Family Services, was described as "a very responsible and capable parent." The authors noted the similarity to Munchausen's syndrome, and referred to the study by Meadow in Lancet. They concluded that "[t]he scarcity of reports may reflect the difficulty of recognizing this form of deliberate poisoning of children."

Indeed, she does not directly question the trustworthiness of these studies at all, or the accuracy of Dr. Blinder's interpretation of them to the jury. Rather, she rests upon the proposition that Munchausen's syndrome by proxy is an "unrecognized illness not generally accepted by the medical profession," and points to the fact that the syndrome is not listed or discussed as a form of mental illness in the American Psychiatric Association's Diagnostic and Statistical Manual of Mental Disorders.

We are aware of no such requirement. We are not confronted here with the admissibility of evidence developed by some new scientific technique such as voiceprint identification, nor with conflict within the scientific community. In *People v. Jackson* (1971) 18 Cal.App.3d 504, 507, 95 Cal.Rptr. 919, the court referred to the "battered child syndrome" as an "accepted medical diagnosis" on the basis of medical literature not unlike that presented here. The studies here show intentional poisoning of infants by their mothers to be another form of child abuse. In the absence of some reason to doubt their validity, we find no abuse of discretion in the trial court's decision to allow expert testimony based thereon.

In her brief on appeal, appellant makes general reference to Evidence Code § 352 as a basis for excluding Dr. Blinder's testimony. We acknowledge that the probative value of Dr. Blinder's testimony was somewhat speculative, and that it posed some risk of both confusion and prejudice: while it purported to attribute symptoms of mental illness to the defendant, it at the same time invited the jury to speculate that she was suffering from Munchausen's syndrome by proxy. Both risks were minimized somewhat, however, by the trial court's instructions and by the defendant's own witnesses. Were it within our function to determine independently whether the probative value of his testimony outweighed those risks we might have reached a different conclusion than the trial court did in this case, but under applicable principles that is not the question. The trial court has a wide range of discretion under § 352, and we cannot say that it abused that discretion by admitting Dr. Blinder's testimony into evidence.

. . . .

The judgment is affirmed.

NOTES AND QUESTIONS

1. The *Phillips* court permits prosecutorial employment of MSP evidence in part to show a possible motive for the crime, specifically that the defendant might have been a person who craved attention and made her children sick in order to receive sympathy herself. Is this in effect calling the defendant's character into question? If so, is *Phillips* consistent with *Walkey* which forbids the prosecution from introducing evidence of the defendant's character. For an indication that some courts may see prosecutorial use of MSP evidence as inadmissible character evidence, see *Commonwealth v. Robinson*, 565 N.E.2d

1229, 1237–38 (Mass. App. Ct. 1991) (discussing trial court's exclusion of state's expert evidence of MSP where mother was charged with causing her hospitalized child's death by poisoning with massive doses of salt). For a discussion of *Phillips* in terms of character evidence, see Martin R. Gardner, *The* Mens Rea *Enigma: Observations on the Role of Motive in the Criminal Law Past and Present*, 1993 UTAH L. REV. 635, 728–32.

2. For an account of a mother who may have suffocated five of her children while suffering from MSP, claiming the children died of sudden infant death syndrome, see David Bjerkie et al., *When is Crib Death a Cover for Murder?*, TIME, April 11, 1994 at 63. Because many MSP cases are believed to be undetected, reliable statistics are lacking. Estimates suggest that 1,000 cases of child abuse per year are related to MSP. *See* www.clevelandclinic.org.

3. For other reported cases involving mothers with MSP, see *Reid v. Texas*, 964 S.W.2d 723 (Tex. Ct. App. 1998); *In re Jessica Z.*, 515 N.Y.S.2d 370 (N.Y. Fam. Ct. 1987); *In re Colin B.*, 493 A.2d 1083 (Md. Ct. Spec. App. 1985). One response to the attention given to MSP is the formation of the group Mothers Against Munchausen Syndrome by Proxy Allegations (MAMA). MAMA expresses concern about a growing number of accusations it claims are false. The group questions whether MSP actually exists and contends that the MSP diagnosis is made to dodge medical malpractice claims.

4. For a view of MSP from a victim's perspective, see JULIE GREGORY, SICKENED (2003). For commentary on evidentiary use of MSP, see Marie M. Brady, *Munchausen Syndrome by Proxy: How Should We Weigh Our Options?*, 18 L. & PSYCHOL. REV. 361 (1994); Michael T. Flannery, *First, Do No Harm: The Use of Covered Video Surveillance to Detect Munchausen Syndrome by Proxy — An Unethical Means of "Preventing" Child Abuse*, 32 U. MICH. J. L. REFORM 105 (1998); Michael T. Flannery, *Munchausen Syndrome by Proxy: Broadening the Scope of Child Abuse*, 28 U. RICH. L. REV. 1175 (1994); Lynn Holland Goldman, *Mommie Dearest? Prosecuting Cases of Munchausen Syndrome by Proxy*, 13 CRIM. JUST. 26 (Wtr. 1999); Suzanne Painter Mochow, *Munchausen Syndrome by Proxy: A Subtle Form of Child Abuse and a Potential Due Process Nightmare*, 18 J. JUV. L. 167 (1997).

[4]   Child Sexual Abuse Accommodation Syndrome (CSAAS)

STEWARD v. STATE

Supreme Court of Indiana
652 N.E.2d 490 (1995)

DICKSON, JUSTICE.

In prosecutions for child molesting, is child sexual abuse syndrome, profile, or pattern evidence admissible to prove that child abuse occurred? To address this important question, we grant transfer.

Defendant Bobby Joe Steward was convicted of two counts of child molesting, one involving victim S.M. and the other involving victim A.M. In his appeal from the convictions, the defendant presented multiple issues. Our Court of Appeals affirmed the defendant's conviction for molesting A.M. but reversed the conviction relating to S.M. because the trial court unconstitutionally excluded evidence of allegations claimed to have been made by S.M. that she had been molested by others, proffered by the defendant to offer an alternative explanation for the State's evidence that her behavior was consistent with that of a victim of sexual abuse. As to those issues addressed by the Court of Appeals, we summarily affirm pursuant to Indiana Appellate Rule 11(B)(3).

In his briefs to this Court and the Court of Appeals, the defendant argues that expert testimony regarding the child sexual abuse syndrome is unreliable and unscientific and thus inadmissible, citing, inter alia, Indiana Evidence Rule 702; *Daubert v. Merrell Dow Pharmaceuticals, Inc.* (1993), 509 U.S. 579; *Commonwealth v. Dunkle* (Pa. 1992), 602 A.2d 830. In his transfer petition, the defendant asserts that the Court of Appeals failed to address this argument.

The Court of Appeals discussed the possible problems with the use of such syndrome evidence for the purpose of vouching for a victim's credibility, correctly noting that a witness may not testify that another is or is not telling the truth but finding that the defendant waived this claim of error by failing to make a timely objection. We grant transfer solely to address the defendant's further argument that, regardless of the resolution of the vouching issue, such syndrome testimony is scientifically unreliable evidence and is thus inadmissible. This is an important question likely to arise in future cases, including the retrial of this defendant.[63]

The defendant, a 52-year-old police officer and family friend of the alleged victims, was convicted of one count of child molesting, a class C felony, for performing sexual intercourse with S.M. when she was 15 years of age; acquitted of three other counts of child molesting as to S.M.; and convicted of child molesting, a class D felony, for touching and/or fondling S.M.'s 13-year-old sister, A.M., with the intent to arouse sexual desires.

As noted by the Court of Appeals, the State presented evidence at trial that S.M.'s behavior was consistent with that of other victims of child sexual abuse in order to prove that sexual contact occurred. The State called Betty Watson, Ph.D., a licensed clinical psychologist with considerable professional experience who had provided treatment for S.M. After stating that common traits or behavioral symptoms are found in teenagers who have experienced sexual abuse, Dr. Watson testified that S.M. exhibited such symptoms, identifying poor self-esteem, "family problems," association with an older peer group, depression, leaving home without permission, and problems with school behavior and performance.

---

[63] [1] In support of this transfer petition, the defendant further contends that his conviction for the child molesting of A.M. should be reversed because the child sexual abuse syndrome evidence, although directly relating only to S.M., generally prejudiced the defendant by bolstering the credibility of the State's witnesses, impliedly bolstering S.M.'s testimony, and strengthening the State's portrayal of the defendant as a sexual deviant. As to his conviction for molesting A.M., we agree with the Court of Appeal's finding that by failing to object to the testimony, the defendant waived his claim, and we find that no fundamental error occurred.

The State also presented testimony from Michael S. Girton, a minister and executive director of a licensed group residential treatment facility, and his wife, Katherine R. Girton, a caseworker at the facility. After establishing that Rev. Girton had taken courses in "sexual abuse work," including "being able to identify sexual abuse," the State asked him whether, based upon his personal experience, "kids who have known incidents of sexual abuse exhibit certain traits or characteristics or behavior patterns." Rev. Girton answered, "Yes," and described the following types of behavior that he looks for "in the characterization of sexual abuse":

> Anything for medical reasons, from bladder infections to abnormal medical problems, and more of the characteristics, the girls can be anything from promiscuous, they can be very timid, they can come in with extremely low esteem. Almost exclusively, that is going to be a major characteristic. Some of the different cues can range in areas from being really over timid to different kind of touches and approaches, where you would approach them in different directions or from different manners or methods. You might even put your hand on their shoulder and that might freak them out or something. There is a lot of different areas where just working with them it becomes really quite evident. You can see that behavior demonstrated quite plainly.

Both Rev. and Mrs. Girton testified that there was a marked change in S.M.'s behavior immediately after S.M. disclosed to them and to Dr. Watson that she had had a sexual relationship with the defendant. The defendant argues that testimony concerning similarities between S.M.'s behaviors and those of known child abuse victims is not scientifically reliable evidence to prove S.M. was sexually abused and is therefore inadmissible.

THE PROBLEM

The admissibility of expert testimony regarding child sexual abuse syndrome evidence is controversial and has received substantial criticism. Recognition of the prevalence of child sexual abuse and intensive study of the problem by behavioral scientists did not begin until the mid-1970s. David McCord, *Expert Psychological Testimony About Child Complainants in Sexual Abuse Prosecutions: A Foray Into the Admissibility of Novel Psychological Evidence*, 77 J. CRIM. L. & CRIMINOLOGY 1, 2-3 (1986). The Child Sexual Abuse Accommodation Syndrome (CSAAS) was first identified by Dr. Roland Summit in a 1983 article in which he described five experiences typically occurring in sexually abused children: (1) secrecy about the sexual abuse, often ensured by threats of negative consequences of disclosure; (2) emotional helplessness to resist or complain; (3) entrapment and accommodation, where the child sees no way to escape ongoing abuse and thus learns to adapt; (4) delayed, conflicted, and unconvincing disclosure of the abuse; and (5) retraction of the child's allegations in an attempt to restore order to the family structure when the disclosure threatens to destroy it. Roland C. Summit, *The Child Sexual Abuse Accommodation Syndrome,* 7 Child Abuse & Neglect 177, 181–88 (1983). [hereinafter Summit, *The CSAAS*]. Summit has noted that, since his original identification and description of CSAAS, which he refers to as "a clinical observation," it "has become both elevated as gospel and denounced as dangerous pseudo-science." Roland C. Summit, *Abuse of the Child Sexual Abuse Accommodation Syndrome,* 1 J. of Child Sexual Abuse 153, 153 (1992) [hereinafter Summit, *Abuse of the CSAAS*]. The syndrome was not intended as a diagnostic device and does not detect sexual abuse. John E.B. Myers et al.,[64] *Expert Testimony in Child Sexual Abuse Litigation,* 68 NEB.L. REV. 1, 67 (1989). Rather, the syndrome was designed for purposes of treating child victims and offering them more effective assistance "within the family and within the systems of child protection and criminal justice," and helps to explain reactions — such as recanting or delayed reporting — of children assumed to have experienced abuse.

Because children's responses to sexual abuse vary widely, and because many of the characteristics identified by CSAAS, or by similar victim behavior groupings, may result from causes unrelated to abuse, diagnostic use of syndrome evidence in courtrooms poses serious accuracy problems. . . . The syndrome's discoverer has noted, "Adversarial rivals seem determined to enhance it or to destroy it according to their designated role." Summit, *Abuse of the CSAAS, supra,* at 156. Summit explains that:

> Some criticism has been a legitimate defense against improper use by prosecutors and expert witnesses called by prosecution. There has been some tendency to use the CSAAS as an offer of proof that a child has been abused. A child may be said to be *suffering from* or *displaying* the CSAAS, as if it is a malady that proves the alleged abuse. Or a child's conspicuous helplessness or silence might be said to be *consistent with* the CSAAS, as if not complaining proves the complaint. Some have contended that a child who retracts is a more believable victim than one who has maintained a consistent complaint.

Summit, *Abuse of the CSAAS, supra,* at 159–60. Our discussion today encompasses not only CSAAS but also similar descriptions of "typical" behavior profiles or patterns, whether or not termed "syndromes," all of which we shall refer to generally as "child sexual abuse syndrome," or "syndrome evidence."[65]

---

[64] [4] Meyers is listed as a Professor of Law at the McGeorge School of Law, University of Pacific, in Sacramento, California. The expertise of his co-authors is widespread and varied. At the time of publication, their credentials included: Jan Bays, M.D. and F.A.A.P., Medical Director of Child Abuse Programs at Emmanuel Hospital and Health Center, Portland, Oregon; Judith Becker, Ph.D., Professor of Clinical Psychology at Columbia University's College of Physicians and Surgeons and Director of the Sexual Behavior Clinic, New York Psychiatric Institute; Lucy Berliner, M.S.W., Assistant Clinical Professor of Social Work at the University of Washington's College of Social Work, and Research Director of Harborview Sexual Assault Center in Seattle, Washington; David L. Corwin, M.D., psychiatric consultant to the Hospital, Oakland, California, and a child psychiatrist in private practice; and Karen J. Saywitz, Ph.D., Assistant Professor of Psychiatry at UCLA School of Medicine and the Director of Child and Adolescent Psychology Services in the Division of Child and Adolescent Psychiatry, Harbor/UCLA Medical Center, Los Angeles.

[65] [5] The Pennsylvania Supreme Court, for instance, grouped together the CSAAS syndrome phenomena known as "Sexually Abused Child Syndrome" and "the Child Abuse Syndrome." It should be noted that our analysis today is not applicable to battered child syndrome, which identifies signs — including various physical symptoms and their inconsistency with a story about accidental injury — of physical child abuse and is generally considered a sound diagnostic tool.

Courts have witnessed the presentation of child sexual abuse syndrome evidence for three major purposes: (1) to prove directly — through either implication or explicit testimony of the expert's conclusion — the fact that abuse actually occurred; (2) to counter claims that the testimony or behavior of alleged victims is inconsistent with abuse or otherwise not credible; and (3) to opine that, because the behavioral characteristics of the child comport with the syndrome profile, the child is likely to be telling the truth. In this opinion we explore the first and second of these applications and summarily affirm the Court of Appeals decision as to the third.

Trial and appellate courts face the challenge of determining under what circumstances, if any, such evidence is admissible, acutely aware of the potentially severe consequences of error in either direction. This challenge is heightened by the distinctive evidentiary problems posed by prosecutions for child sexual abuse: Often these cases pit the word of a traumatized child against that of an adult. Child sexual abuse typically occurs in private, when the abuser is confident that there will be no witnesses. Therefore, the child victim is usually the only eyewitness. The prosecution's case is severely hampered if the court finds the child to be too young to be a witness or incompetent to testify. Even if the child does testify, several factors often limit the effectiveness of this testimony. The child's cognitive and verbal abilities may not enable her to give consistent, spontaneous, and detailed reports of her sexual abuse. A child who must testify against a trusted adult, such as a parent or relative, may experience feelings of fear and ambivalence, and may retract her story because of family pressures or insensitivities in the legal process. Prosecutors face another dilemma when offering the child victim as a witness if the child has delayed reporting the abuse. Jurors may interpret delayed disclosure as evidence of fabrication, especially if defense counsel suggests this conclusion during cross-examination of the child. Further, jurors may hold misconceptions that the child has memory deficits, is suggestible, cannot distinguish between fact or fantasy, or is likely to fabricate sexual experiences with adults. These problems are compounded by the lack of corroborative physical or mental evidence in many child sexual abuse cases.

The utilization of innovative methodologies to address these problems must be balanced with "the preservation of the constitutional right to presumption of innocence in a criminal case." . . .

. . . The Delaware Supreme Court has observed:

> a sexual abuse charge by itself imposes a stigma on the accused and conviction provides a serious penalty. In interpreting our rules of evidence, we must be aware not only of the needs of society in general but also the defendant's right to a fair trial.

Wheat v. State, 527 A.2d 269 (Del. 1987). The particular dilemma expert testimony poses in these emotionally charged cases has been aptly described by the Supreme Court of Michigan:

> Given the nature of the offense and the terrible consequences of a miscalculation — the consequences when an individual, on many occasions a family member, is falsely accused of one of society's most

heinous offenses, or, conversely, when one who commits such a crime would go unpunished and a possible reoccurrence of the act would go unprevented — appropriate safeguards are necessary. To a jury recognizing the awesome dilemma of whom to believe, an expert will often represent the only seemingly objective source, offering it a much sought-after hook on which to hang its hat.

People v. Beckley, 456 N.W.2d 391 (Mich. 1990).

OTHER STATES' APPROACHES

A few decisions from other states have held child sexual abuse syndrome evidence inadmissible for any purpose,[66] and some cases have permitted expert testimony opining that, because of the correlation between a child's behavior and the syndrome, the child has been sexually abused.[67] Most jurisdictions, however, have settled somewhere between these two extremes.

A significant number of state courts have recognized as a misuse of the syndrome the admission of child sexual abuse syndrome testimony as substantive proof that abuse has been detected in a particular case. Wisconsin courts, for instance, have rejected the use of testimony that the defendant's daughter was "a typical case of intrafamilial sexual abuse" and thus an incest victim, and have held to be error the admission of expert testimony that a complainant's behavior following an alleged sexual assault was proof that the assault occurred. . . . The Arkansas Supreme Court held that a trial court erred in permitting an expert to testify that, in part because the victim's history was consistent with the doctor's experiences dealing with child abuse, he believed that abuse had occurred.

. . . .

Additional disagreement exists on the issue of the admissibility of syndrome evidence where the expert merely describes certain behavioral characteristics as being consistent with sexual abuse, thereby offering direct proof through implication, rather than where the expert explicitly draws the conclusion for the jury. Numerous cases have ruled such implication evidence inadmissible as proof that an assault occurred. In contrast, other jurisdictions have ruled in favor of admissibility where the expert presents evidence of abuse through implication but refrains from giving an explicit opinion on whether abuse occurred.

It is important to recognize that syndrome evidence is not similarly problematic in all situations. The reliability of syndrome evidence, although highly questionable for purposes of affirmatively proving sexual abuse, is generally

---

[66] [6] *See* Hester v. Commonwealth, 734 S.W.2d 457 (Ky. 1987), *cert denied* 484 U.S. 989; Mitchell v. Commonwealth, 777 S.W.2d 930 (Ky. 1989); *Dunkle,* 602 A.2d 830.

[67] [7] *See* Broderick C. Kings's Way Assembly of God Church, 808 P.2d 1211 (Alaska 1991); Matter of Cheryl H., 153 Cal. App. 3d 1098, 200 Cal.Rptr. 789 (1984), *overruled in part by* People v. Brown, 883 P.2d 949 (Cal. 1994); Glendening v. State, 536 So. 2d 212 (Fla. 1988), *cert. denied* 492 U.S. 907 (1989); State v. Hester, 760 P.2d 27 (Idaho 1988); State v. Geyman, 729 P.2d 475 (Mont. 1986); Townsend v. State, 734 P.2d 705 (Nev. 1987); State v. Timperio, 528 N.E.2d 594 (Ohio 1987); State v. Edward C.L., 398 S.E.2d 123 (W. Va. 1990).

accepted for purposes of helping the jury to understand that a complainant's reactions are not atypical of a young sexual assault victim. As the Myers article notes:

> The accommodation syndrome has a place in the courtroom. The syndrome helps explain why many sexually abused children delay reporting their abuse, and why many children recant allegations of abuse and deny that anything occurred. If use of the syndrome is confined to these rehabilitative functions, the confusion clears, and the accommodation syndrome serves a useful forensic purpose.

Myers et al., *supra,* at 67-68. Thus, behavioral characteristics of child abuse victims, even where inadmissible to prove abuse, are far less controversial when offered to rebut a claim by the defense that a child complainant's behavior — such as delayed reporting or retracting allegations — is inconsistent with her claim of abuse. This more limited, but nonetheless important, purpose is in harmony with the syndrome's original mission. Indeed, "[a] myriad of expert writings in the psychology field have countenanced" such use of the evidence, which has "received nearly universal judicial approval."

. . . .

The following cases, for example, have allowed expert testimony to explain failures to report or delays in reporting incidents of abuse or sexual assault. . . . Several state decisions have allowed such expert testimony to explain recantations or other apparent inconsistencies in children's reports or behavior. . . .

Many of these courts have differentiated between admitting such evidence to explain the victim's seemingly suspicious behaviors and admitting it to prove that abuse occurred. . . .

The use of syndrome evidence for rehabilitative purposes has not met with universal approval. In *Dunkle,* the Pennsylvania Supreme Court prohibited from admission in child sexual abuse cases essentially all expert testimony concerning behavior patterns. Dunkle's approach is noteworthy because much of the expert testimony excluded seems to have been offered for rehabilitative, not diagnostic, purposes. The evidence sought to explain in general terms, without reference to the alleged victim, "why a victim would delay reporting an offense, why a victim might be unable to recall exact dates and times of an alleged offense, and why victims of sexual abuse omitted details of the incident when they first told their stor [ies]." Permitting such evidence, the *Dunkle* court believed, "would infringe upon the jury's right to determine credibility," because the reasons for delay, inconsistencies, and omissions in victims' allegations "are easily understood by lay people and do not require expert analysis." Such a complete exclusion of child sexual abuse syndrome evidence for any purpose is generally not favored. *See* Myers et al., *supra,* at 89, 92–93 (recognizing need for expert testimony to counteract jurors' commonly held misconceptions about sexual abuse and to explain emotional reactions that cause children's seemingly self-impeaching behavior).

A contrasting approach has been taken by the Michigan Supreme Court. While finding syndrome evidence admissible when a victim's behavior becomes an issue in a case, it noted that:

the evidence has a very limited use and should be admitted cautiously because of the danger of permitting an inference that as a result of certain behavior sexual abuse in fact occurred, when evidence of the syndrome is not a conclusive finding of abuse. Although syndrome evidence may be appropriate as a tool for purposes of treatment, we hold that it is unreliable as an indicator of sexual abuse.

Beckley, 456 N.W.2d at 406. The Michigan court allowed the testimony "to give the jury a framework of possible alternatives for the behaviors of the victim at issue," and to assist the jury in "dispelling any popular misconception commonly associated with the demonstrated reaction." *Id.* The court cautioned that:

> to assist the jury in understanding the unique reactions of victims of sexual assault, the testimony should be limited to whether the behavior of this particular victim is common to the class of reported child abuse victims. The expert's evaluation of the individual behavior traits at issue is not centered on what was observed in this victim, but rather whether the behavioral sciences recognize this behavior as being a common reaction to a unique criminal act.

Id. at 406–07. The *Beckley* court warned:

> Given the abhorrence of the crime, it is inevitable that those who treat a child victim will have an emotional inclination toward protecting the child victim. The expert who treats a child victim may lose some objectivity concerning a particular case. Therefore to avoid the pitfall of the treating professional being inclined to give an opinion regarding whether the complaining witness had been sexually abused, we caution the trial court to carefully scrutinize the treating professional's ability to aid the trier of fact when exercising discretion and qualifying such an expert witness.

Beckley, 456 N.W.2d at 408. The Michigan Supreme Court concluded that it was unwilling to have "the so-called child sexual abuse syndrome . . . introduced as a scientific tool, standing on its own merits as a doctrine or benchmark for determining causality in child sexual abuse cases." *Id.* at 409. However, it also held that:

> persons otherwise properly qualified as experts in dealing with sexually abused children should be permitted to rely on their own experience and their knowledge of the experience of others to rebut an inference that specific behavioral patterns attributed to the victim are not [sic] uncharacteristic of the class of child sexual abuse victims. Such witnesses should be permitted to testify regarding characteristics of sexually abused children so long as it is without reference to a fixed set of behaviors constituting a "syndrome."

Id.

Commentators have embraced judicial decisions rejecting the use of CSAAS to prove abuse and advocating limiting its use to explaining victim behaviors that are seemingly inconsistent with their allegations. *See, e.g.,* Marian D. Hall, *The Role of Psychologists as Experts in Cases Involving Allegations of Child Sexual Abuse*, 23 FAM. L.Q. 451, 463 (1989) (noting that behavioral science research does not demonstrate the existence of an accurate method of identifying an individual child as having been sexually abused); McCord, *supra,* at 67 (advocating that the admissibility of expert opinion testimony be limited to explaining the complainant's unusual actions); Myers et al., *supra,* at 68 (identifying the utility of expert testimony on child sexual abuse syndrome to rehabilitate the credibility of victims whose behavior may appear self-impeaching).

CONCLUSION

The admissibility of child sexual abuse syndrome evidence will be primarily determined in the courts of this state in accordance with the provisions in the Indiana Rules of Evidence defining "relevant evidence," EVID. R. 401; declaring its general admissibility, EVID. R. 402; permitting exclusion due to the danger of unfair prejudice, EVID. R. 403; prohibiting opinions concerning witness truthfulness, EVID. R. 704(b); and, most particularly, prescribing the requirements for expert scientific testimony, EVID. R. 702.

Federal Rule of Evidence 702 was adopted as subsection (a) of the Indiana rule. Subsection (b) of the Indiana rule is unique in its express requirement that expert testimony must be based upon reliable scientific principles.

> (a) If scientific, technical, or other specialized knowledge will assist the trier of fact to understand the evidence or to determine a fact in issue, a witness qualified as an expert by knowledge, skill, experience, training, or education, may testify thereto in the form of an opinion or otherwise.

> (b) Expert scientific testimony is admissible only if the court is satisfied that the scientific principles upon which the expert testimony rests are reliable.

EVID. R. 702.

The United States Supreme Court's *Daubert* decision, coincidentally handed down just weeks after Indiana's Rule 702(b) was adopted, interpreted Federal Rule of Evidence 702 as requiring that expert testimony "be supported by appropriate validation — *i.e.,* 'good grounds,' based on what is known," and as "establish[ing] a standard of evidentiary reliability." The concerns driving *Daubert* coincide with the express requirement of Indiana Rule of Evidence 702(b) that the trial court be satisfied of the reliability of the scientific principles involved. Thus, although not binding upon the determination of state evidentiary law issues, the federal evidence law of *Daubert* and its progeny is helpful to the bench and bar in applying Indiana Rule of Evidence 702(b). Of particular relevance to our inquiry here are *Daubert*'s statements that "scientific validity for one purpose is not necessarily scientific validity for other, unrelated purposes," and that Federal Rule of Evidence 702 "requires a valid scientific connection to the pertinent inquiry as a precondition to admissibility." Child sexual abuse syndrome evidence must satisfy the reliability requirement of Rule 702(b) as well as the Rule 403 balancing test.

> Although relevant, evidence may be excluded if its probative value is substantially outweighed by the danger of unfair prejudice, confusion of the issues, misleading the jury, or by considerations of undue delay or needless presentation of cumulative evidence.

EVID. R. 403. If determined to be sufficiently reliable to be eligible for admission into evidence as expert testimony, its probative value must also outweigh the danger that it will unfairly prejudice the defendant. As the U.S. Supreme Court pointed out in *Daubert*,

> Conjectures that are probably wrong are of little use . . . in the project of reaching a quick, final, and binding legal judgment — often of great consequence — about a particular set of events in the past. We recognize that in practice, a gatekeeping role for the judge, no matter how flexible, inevitably on occasion will prevent the jury from learning of authentic insights and innovations. That, nevertheless, is the balance that is struck by Rules of Evidence designed not for the exhaustive search for cosmic understanding but for the particularized resolution of legal disputes.

Under Indiana Evidence Rule 702(b), expert scientific testimony is admissible only if reliability is demonstrated to the trial court. We agree . . . that reliability may be established either by judicial notice or, in its absence, by the proponent of the scientific testimony providing sufficient foundation to convince the trial court that the relevant scientific principles are reliable. This sort of inquiry is generally more appropriate for trial courts than for appellate resolution. While we, like the Utah Supreme Court, "do not mean to imply that [syndrome] testimony is unreliable as a matter of law," the reliability of such evidence for the purpose of proving abuse is at present extremely doubtful and the subject of substantial and widespread repudiation by courts and scientists.

It is possible that foundational support may be discovered in the future which will expand the purposes for which such expert testimony may be deemed reliable. . . .

Furthermore, we decline to distinguish between expert testimony which offers an unreserved conclusion that the child in question has been abused and that which merely uses syndrome evidence to imply the occurrence of abuse. Where a jury is confronted with evidence of an alleged child victim's behaviors, paired with expert testimony concerning similar syndrome behaviors, the invited inference — that the child was sexually abused because he or she fits the syndrome profile — will be as potentially misleading and equally as unreliable as expert testimony applying the syndrome to the facts of the case and stating outright the conclusion that a given child was abused. The danger of the jury misapplying syndrome evidence thus remains the same whether an expert expresses an explicit opinion that abuse has occurred or merely allows the jury to draw the final conclusion of abuse. Exclusion of such evidence is authorized by Indiana Rule of Evidence 403.

However, we recognize that, once a child's credibility is called into question, proper expert testimony may be appropriate. *Daubert* notes the importance of "a valid scientific connection *to the pertinent inquiry* as a precondition to admissibility." Because research generally accepted as scientifically reliable recognizes that child victims of sexual abuse may exhibit unexpected behavior patterns seemingly inconsistent with the claim of abuse, such evidence may be permissible under Indiana Evidence Rule 702(a)'s authorization of "specialized knowledge [which] will assist the trier of fact to understand the evidence." Therefore, if the defense discusses or presents evidence of such unexpected behavior by the child, or if during trial testimony the child recants a prior allegation of abuse, a trial court may consider permitting expert testimony, if based upon reliable scientific principles, regarding the prevalence of the specific unexpected behavior within the general class of reported child abuse victims. To be admissible, such scientific evidence must assist the finder of fact in understanding a child's responses to abuse and satisfy the requirements of both Rule 702(b) and the Rule 403 balancing test.

We agree . . . that when the relevant inquiry is the syndrome's reliability and probative value for rehabilitative and related purposes, "[s]uch evidence may harm defendant's interests, but we cannot say it is *unfairly* prejudicial; it merely informs jurors that commonly held assumptions are not necessarily accurate and allows them to fairly judge credibility." . . .

Transfer is granted. As to the issues addressed therein, the opinion of the Court of Appeals is summarily affirmed. We affirm, as did the Court of Appeals, the defendant's conviction for Child Molesting, a class D felony, and reverse his conviction for Child Molesting, a class C felony, and remand this cause for a new trial on the latter charge consistent with this opinion.

SULLIVAN, JUSTICE, *dissenting*.

Cases of alleged child abuse provide a particular challenge for the criminal justice system. . . . Expert testimony has proved to be helpful in meeting this challenge. . . .

I believe our rules of evidence provide a fair yet flexible regime for determining whether any particular expert testimony proffered on the subject of sexual abuse is admissible. Assuming that the proffered testimony is relevant and will assist the jury in understanding the evidence or a fact at issue, and that the witness is properly qualified as an expert (issues not implicated by this case or by the majority opinion), the trial court must determine whether the scientific principles upon which the expert testimony rests are reliable. As to the reliability of expert testimony concerning child sexual abuse accommodation syndrome and similar evidence, the majority sets general rules for the following three situations:

(1) Child sexual abuse accommodation syndrome evidence is presently[68] not scientifically reliable enough to permit an expert to offer "an unreserved conclusion that the child in question has been abused."

---

[68] [13] While the majority says that such evidence is not "unreliable as a matter of law," the majority would permit trial courts to consider admitting the evidence only if *future* empirical research and scientific investigation resolves present doubts about reliability.

(2) Child sexual abuse accommodation syndrome is also presently not scientifically reliable enough to permit the use of expert testimony "merely . . . to imply the occurrence of abuse."

(3) However, child sexual abuse accommodation syndrome is presently scientifically reliable enough to permit the use of expert testimony to assist the factfinder in understanding a child's response to abuse when, but only when, the defense asserts or implies that the alleged child victim's conduct was inconsistent with the claim of abuse, or if the child recanted a prior allegation of abuse.

As to situation (1), I certainly agree that an expert may not comment directly on whether the child has been sexually abused or whether the child has testified truthfully. But as to situation (2), the Court of Appeals correctly pointed out that our rule has been that expert testimony that a putative rape victim's behavior was consistent with that of one who had in fact been raped merely tended to show that the victim had been raped and was not a direct opinion that the victim was telling the truth. I see no basis for having different rules for child sexual abuse and for rape. And I also think that banning expert testimony because the "danger of the jury misapplying [the evidence] remains the same whether an expert expresses an explicit opinion . . . or merely allows the jury to draw the final conclusion" has very restrictive implications for expert testimony generally.

I acknowledge the majority's citation of *Daubert*'s observation that scientific evidence can be reliable for one purpose but not another. It seems clear to me, however, that the purposes of the testimony in situations (2) and (3) are the same — to aid the jury in assessing the credibility of the child witness. While the former may be more prejudicial than the latter, that does not make the scientific principles upon which the former is based less reliable than the latter's.

I do not think we can say that the scientific principles upon which child sexual abuse accommodation syndrome is based are not reliable as direct evidence but are reliable as rebuttal evidence. In logic, either those principles are reliable for purposes of aiding the jury in assessing the child victim's credibility or they are not. The majority cites dozens of opinions where such evidence was found to be reliable, at least for rebuttal purposes, and I would hold that to the extent that that authority establishes its reliability for rebuttal evidence, it establishes it for direct evidence as well.

Once the trial court determines that expert testimony is admissible under Evidence Rule 702(b), the proffered testimony is still subject to challenge under Indiana Evidence Rule 403 which, as the majority points out, provides:

> Although relevant, evidence may be excluded if its probative value is substantially outweighed by the danger of unfair prejudice, confusion of the issues, misleading the jury, or by consideration of undue delay or needless presentation of cumulative evidence.

It is here, rather than under the rubric of scientific or expert testimony, that I think the real battle over the admissibility of child sexual abuse accommodation syndrome should be fought in most cases. We recently observed that scientific evidence is subject to particular scrutiny under Evidence Rule 403. But whether any particular evidence violates Evidence Rule 403 is a matter first and foremost for the trial court to decide: we review only for an abuse of discretion. While *Daubert*'s progeny suggest some heightened scrutiny of such determinations is appropriate when scientific evidence is involved, I agree with the analysis given this evidence in this case by Judge Najam and concur in his view that it was not erroneous for the trial court to admit Dr. Watson's testimony.[69] More generally, I would hold that, while Evidence rule 704 prohibits the use of child sexual abuse accommodation syndrome evidence in situation (1), the reliability test of Evidence Rule 702(b) applies in the same way to such evidence in both situations (2) and (3), and that the admissibility of such evidence under Evidence Rule 403 is committed to the sound discretion of the trial court.

I would make one final observation. In *Henson v. State, supra,* this court reversed the conviction of an appellant convicted of rape on grounds that he was denied due process of law when the trial court refused to permit him to introduce evidence that the putative victim's conduct was not consistent with that which would have been predicted were she suffering from rape trauma syndrome. I cannot avoid the conclusion that today's opinion prohibits a defendant from offering child sexual abuse accommodation syndrome evidence in his own defense.

———

NOTES AND QUESTIONS

1. As *Steward* points out, use of CSAAS evidence is controversial, especially when used to prove that abuse occurred in a particular case. Some courts question the scientific reliability of CSAAS. *See, e.g., Newkirk v. Commonwealth,* 937 S.W.2d 690 (Ky. 1997) (rejecting use of CSAAS evidence even for purposes of rebuttal where prosecution sought to rehabilitate child victim witness who had recanted out of court accusations against defendant prior to testifying against him at trial). For a summary of the admissibility of CSAAS in the various states, see Elizabeth Trainor, *Admissibility of Expert Testimony on Child Sexual Abuse Syndrome (CSAAS) in Criminal Cases,* 85 A.L.R. 5th 595 (2001).

2. For commentary on the admissibility of CSAAS evidence, see Gail Ezra Carey, Casenote, Evidence — *Expert Testimony — The Admissibility of Child Sexual Abuse Accommodation Syndrome in Child Sexual Abuse Prosecutions,* 26 RUTGERS L.J. 251 (1994); Rosemary L. Flint, Note, *Child Sexual Abuse Accommodation Syndrome: Admissibility Requirements.,* 23 AM. J. CRIM. L. 171 (1995); Patrick Larson, *The Admissibility of Expert Testimony on Child Sexual Abuse Accommodation Syndrome as Indicia of Abuser: Aiding the Prosecution in Meeting its Burden of Proof,* 16 OHIO N.U. L. REV. 81 (1989).

---

[69] [14] The majority does not explicitly conclude that Dr. Watson's testimony was erroneously admitted but that is the only inference I can draw from its opinion.

3. Convicted rape and sexual assault offenders serving time in state prisons report that two-thirds of their victims were under the age of 18. One of every seven victims of sexual assault reported to law enforcement agencies was under the age of six. Among rape victims less than 12 years of age, 90 percent of the children knew the offender. The person who sexually molests a child may also be a child. Forty percent of the offenders who sexually assaulted children under the age of 6 were juveniles (under the age of 18).

The term *paedophilia erotica* was coined in 1896 by the Vienna psychiatrist Richard von Krafft-Ebing in his writing PSYCHOPATHIA SEXUALIS, giving the following characteristics:

- the sexual interest is toward children, either prepubescent or at the beginning of puberty

- the sexual interest is the primary one, *i.e.*, exclusively or mainly toward children

- the sexual interest remains over time

Some other definitions of pedophilia require an age difference of at least five years. A person may not necessarily be a pedophile simply because he or she is sexually aroused by children; rather, a pedophile is someone whose primary sexual attraction is toward children. Pedophilia is often used more generally to describe anyone who is sexually aroused by children and who may have fantasies or sexual urges even if they may not necessarily consummate sexual acts with children. There is evidence that at least a quarter of all adult men may have feelings of sexual arousal from children.

Pedophiles often refer to themselves as boylovers or girllovers (many are not attracted to both); they may also be known as "childlovers." Those who are attracted to adolescents, or to girls and boys undergoing puberty may not like the term "childlover" and prefer the term "minor attracted adult."

A person committing child sexual abuse is often assumed to be a pedophile. In the same way that adult rape may occur for non-sexual reasons, there may be other motivations for the abuse. Most who sexually abuse children are not primarily interested in children. These perpetrators are referred to as situational offenders, whereas pedophiles who are primarily attracted toward children are called structured pedophiles or fixated pedophiles, as their orientation is fixed by the structure of their personality. *See* en.wikipedia.org; *see also* DOUGLAS W. PRYOR, UNSPEAKABLE ACTS: WHY MEN SEXUALLY ABUSE CHILDREN (1996) (detailing interviews with 27 adult men who had sexually abused children where the offender was part of the victim's family circle).

4. The priest abuse scandal presents an opportunity to study the response of institutions when child sexual abuse occurs. Researchers at the John Jay College or Criminal Justice (part of the City University of New York), in a study entitled *The Nature and Scope of Sexual Abuse of Minors by Catholic Priests and Deacons in the United States, 1952-2002*, report that accusations of child molestation have been made against 4,392 priests (4 percent of those serving in those years). Over ten thousand people reported they had been abused by priests as children during that time. Scholars have raised concerns that the stated numbers, based solely on self-reporting by the Catholic church, does not present the full extent of the problem. Another troubling issue is that

while some dioceses reported no cases of abuse, one large diocese reported a proportion that reached as high as 24 percent of priests in the diocese. Critics claim that this indicates that some dioceses were more forthcoming than others with data. *See* Burton Bollag, *Pulling Back the Veil*, CHRON. HIGHER EDUC., Mar. 19, 2004. In defending lawsuits by victims of priest abuse, some Catholic dioceses have claimed first amendment protection from state scrutiny of how priests are supervised or have argued that confidentiality between a priest and a bishop is crucial to the free exercise of religion. *See generally* Michael S. Winters, *The Betrayal*, THE NEW REPUBLIC, May 6, 2002, at 24; MARCI A. HAMILTON, GOD VS. THE GAVEL: RELIGION AND THE RULE OF LAW (2005).

5. The ease of international travel has encouraged "sex tourism," where persons visit another country, typically one where poverty and unemployment rates are devastating, for the purpose of having sex with children. Congress has passed legislation to attack this problem. Under the Child Abuse Prevention Act, a "person who travels in interstate commerce or travels into the United States, or a United States citizen or an alien admitted for permanent residence in the United States who travels in foreign commerce, for the purpose of engaging in any illicit sexual conduct with another person shall be fined under this title or imprisoned not more than 30 years, or both." Moreover, any United States citizen or alien admitted for permanent residence who travels in foreign commerce, and engages in any illicit sexual conduct with another person shall be fined under this title or imprisoned not more than 30 years, or both. The term "illicit sexual conduct" is defined as a sexual act with a person under 18 years of age that would be in violation U.S. law if the sexual act occurred in the territorial jurisdiction of the United States; or any commercial sex act with a person under 18 years of age.

6. The Seventh Circuit Court of Appeals made headlines in 2004 in *Doe v. City of Lafayette*, 377 F.3d 757 (7th Cir. 2004) (en banc). After learning that a convicted sex offender had been cruising city parks and watching young children, the city sent him a letter banning him from all public parks under the city's jurisdiction. The banned person sued the city, contending that the ban violated his constitutional rights. The Seventh Circuit held that the city was properly granted summary judgment on the convicted sex offender's first amendment claim because he did not go to the park to engage in any expression, but rather he went cruising for children to satisfy his sexual urges. By subjecting him to the ban, the city was not punishing him for pure thought, for having sexual fantasies about children. The city was also properly granted summary judgment on the convicted sex offender's substantive due process claim because his right to enter the parks to loiter or for other innocent purposes was not fundamental. The city's interest in protecting children was compelling, and the ban of the convicted sex offender from the city's parks was rationally related to that end.

7. The issue of children and sexual conduct can have many layers. A professor at the University of Missouri–Kansas City caused a furor in his state over an essay that he published comparing the "moral panic" over pedophilia with the outrage in previous generations over feminism and homosexuality. The Missouri legislature voted to cut $100,000 from the university's budget,

whereupon the American Association of University Professors, citing concerns of academic freedom, issued a strong statement on behalf of the professor. The essay, published in the JOURNAL OF HOMOSEXUALITY, argued that the notion of the innocent child was a social construct and that intergenerational sex had been permissible or obligatory in many cultures and periods of history. *See* Jodi Wilgoren, *Scholar's Pedophilia Essay Stirs Outrage and Revenge*, N.Y. TIMES, April 29, 2002.

[5] The Child Witness

Robert P. Mosteller, *Remaking Confrontation Clause and Hearsay Doctrine Under the Challenge of Child Sexual Abuse Prosecutions*

1993 UNIVERSITY OF ILLINOIS LAW REVIEW 691, 691–94

Child sexual abuse is a major and growing problem in the United States. Recognizing the significance and emotional power of the problem, state legislatures have responded with an impressive array of legislative innovations that admit out-of-court statements of child victims and attempt to shield children from emotional and psychological trauma resulting from participation in judicial proceedings. . . .

The frequent association of *reform* with children's issues is easily understood. First, we as a society care intensely about the treatment of children, and as a result, child welfare has been a paramount concern of state legislatures throughout this century. Mistreatment of children, particularly sexual abuse, is especially horrendous. All agree that action is required and perpetrators must be apprehended and punished. Second, because children obviously differ from adults, society is willing to rethink procedures and evidentiary rules. We begin almost with a presumption that the ground rules should be different. Thus, the initial inquiry is what changes to make in the process rather than whether it should be altered at all. . . . Third, proof in child cases is often problematic. Children frequently have difficulty testifying effectively as a result of their different and somewhat limited abilities to remember, conceptualize, and communicate, and because of fear and the obstacles presented by the courtroom setting.

States have experimented with new hearsay exceptions[70] that admit out-of-court statements by children and with new procedures for receiving testimony from children in court. In the area of hearsay, one approach has been to identify specific crimes — principally sexual abuse — and, regarding those crimes, to admit the hearsay statements of children below a specified age if the statements are deemed generally trustworthy. This approach authorizes the admission of a broad array of statements of a child victim of sexual abuse, limited solely by the Confrontation Clause.

---

[70] [2] Rule 801(c) of the *Federal Rules of Evidence* provides a simple and widely used definition of hearsay: "A statement, other than one made by the declarant while testifying at the trial or hearing, offered in evidence to prove the truth of the matter asserted." FED. R. EVID. (801(c). Conceptually, hearsay is not admissible, *see* FED. R. EVID. 802, unless it falls within one of the many hearsay exceptions. *See* FED. R. EVID. 803 & 804.

To shield children from trauma, statutes and the case law have treated the trauma that would result from testifying as bases for finding a child unavailable to be called as a witness. In these situations, hearsay statements under this new exception may constitute the only evidence from the child, and the defense may be prohibited from questioning the child, who is physically available and could provide some information to the jury if cross-examined. . . .

A number of states have experimented with a second much more controversial hearsay exception. This exception permits the prosecution to produce ex parte videotaped statements by the child before trial and admit them as an alternative to the child's direct examination. This procedure has some potential for shielding children from trauma, but its chief purpose is to enhance the effectiveness of the state's proof.

. . . .

Legislatures have authorized new methods of presenting testimony to shield children from the trauma of testifying. First, through videotaped recordings, children testify in the presence of the defendant but do so by way of a deposition taken in a less formal and more comfortable environment than the typical courtroom. Second, using either videotaped recording or live closed circuit television, children testify outside the courtroom *and* outside the presence of the defendant upon a specified showing that trauma would otherwise interfere with effective testimony.

Adding complication, all of the above techniques can be "mixed and matched" as desired. For example, where a statute specifies that the child victim must testify for her hearsay statement to be admitted, it may permit such testimony to be received through an electronic medium and/or outside the defendant's physical presence.

Child abuse hearsay provides a major testing ground for both hearsay rules and the Confrontation Clause. . . . Similarly, the innovation of ex parte videotaped statements challenges the core concepts of the Confrontation Clause. If the clause imposes no restraint on such statutory innovations, the meagerness of its basic protection will be starkly established. On the other hand, if there is anything of significance remaining to the confrontation right, the answers worked out in the conflict between our intense interest in effective prosecution of child abusers and the fundamental prerequisites of confrontation may establish the analysis in other problematic areas.

MARYLAND v. CRAIG

Supreme Court of the United States
497 U.S. 836 (1990)

Justice O'Connor *delivered the opinion of the Court.*

This case requires us to decide whether the Confrontation Clause of the Sixth Amendment categorically prohibits a child witness in a child abuse case from testifying against a defendant at trial, outside the defendant's physical presence, by one-way closed circuit television.

I

In October 1986, a Howard County grand jury charged respondent, Sandra Ann Craig, with child abuse, first and second degree sexual offenses, perverted sexual practice, assault, and battery. The named victim in each count was a 6-year-old girl who, from August 1984 to June 1986, had attended a kindergarten and prekindergarten center owned and operated by Craig.

In March 1987, before the case went to trial, the State sought to invoke a Maryland statutory procedure that permits a judge to receive, by one-way closed circuit television, the testimony of a child witness who is alleged to be a victim of child abuse.[71] To invoke the procedure, the trial judge must first "determin[e] that testimony by the child victim in the courtroom will result in the child suffering serious emotional distress such that the child cannot reasonably communicate." Once the procedure is invoked, the child witness, prosecutor, and defense counsel withdraw to a separate room; the judge, jury, and defendant remain in the courtroom. The child witness is then examined and cross-examined in the separate room, while a video monitor records and displays the witness' testimony to those in the courtroom. During this time the witness cannot see the defendant. The defendant remains in electronic communication with defense counsel, and objections may be made and ruled on as if the witness were testifying in the courtroom.

---

[71] [1] Maryland Cts. & Jud. Proc. Code Ann. § 9-102 of the Courts and Judicial Proceedings Article of the Annotated Code of Maryland (1989) provides in full:

(a)(1) In a case of abuse of a child as defined in § 5-701 of the Family Law Article or Article 27, § 35A of the Code, a court may order that the testimony of a child victim be taken outside the courtroom and shown in the courtroom by means of a closed circuit television if:

(i) The testimony is taken during the proceeding; and

(ii) The judge determines that testimony by the child victim in the courtroom will result in the child suffering serious emotional distress such that the child cannot reasonably communicate.

(2) Only the prosecuting attorney, the attorney for the defendant, and the judge may question the child. "(3) The operators of the closed circuit television shall make every effort to be unobtrusive.

(b)(1) Only the following persons may be in the room with the child when the child testifies by closed circuit television:

(i) The prosecuting attorney;

(ii) The attorney for the defendant;

(iii) The operators of the closed circuit television equipment; and

(iv) Unless the defendant objects, any person whose presence, in the opinion of the court, contributes to the well-being of the child, including a person who has dealt with the child in a therapeutic setting concerning the abuse.

(2) During the child's testimony by closed circuit television, the judge and the defendant shall be in the courtroom.

(3) The judge and the defendant shall be allowed to communicate with the persons in the room where the child is testifying by any appropriate electronic method.

(c) The provisions of this section do not apply if the defendant is an attorney pro se.

(d) This section may not be interpreted to preclude, for purposes of identification of a defendant, the presence of both the victim and the defendant in the courtroom at the same time.

In support of its motion invoking the one-way closed circuit television procedure, the State presented expert testimony that the named victim as well as a number of other children who were alleged to have been sexually abused by Craig, would suffer "serious emotional distress such that [they could not] reasonably communicate," if required to testify in the courtroom. The Maryland Court of Appeals characterized the evidence as follows:

> The expert testimony in each case suggested that each child would have some or considerable difficulty in testifying in Craig's presence. For example, as to one child, the expert said that what "would cause him the most anxiety would be to testify in front of Mrs. Craig. . . ." The child "wouldn't be able to communicate effectively." As to another, an expert said she "would probably stop talking and she would withdraw and curl up." With respect to two others, the testimony was that one would "become highly agitated, that he may refuse to talk or if he did talk, that he would choose his subject regardless of the questions" while the other would "become extremely timid and unwilling to talk."

Craig objected to the use of the procedure on Confrontation Clause grounds, but the trial court rejected that contention, concluding that although the statute "take[s] away the right of the defendant to be face to face with his or her accuser," the defendant retains the "essence of the right of confrontation," including the right to observe, cross-examine, and have the jury view the demeanor of the witness. The trial court further found that, "based upon the evidence presented . . . the testimony of each of these children in a courtroom will result in each child suffering serious emotional distress . . . such that each of these children cannot reasonably communicate." The trial court then found the named victim and three other children competent to testify and accordingly permitted them to testify against Craig via the one-way closed circuit television procedure. The jury convicted Craig on all counts, and the Maryland Court of Special Appeals affirmed the convictions.

The Court of Appeals of Maryland reversed and remanded for a new trial. The Court of Appeals rejected Craig's argument that the Confrontation Clause requires in all cases a face-to-face courtroom encounter between the accused and his accusers, but concluded:

> [U]nder § 9-102(a)(1)(ii), the operative "serious emotional distress" which renders a child victim unable to "reasonably communicate" must be determined to arise, at least primarily, from face-to-face confrontation with the defendant. Thus, we construe the phrase "in the courtroom" as meaning, for sixth amendment and [state constitution] confrontation purposes, "in the courtroom in the presence of the defendant." Unless prevention of "eyeball-to-eyeball" confrontation is necessary to obtain the trial testimony of the child, the defendant cannot be denied that right.

Reviewing the trial court's finding and the evidence presented in support of the § 9-102 procedure, the Court of Appeals held that, "as [it] read *Coy* [v.

Iowa, 487 U.S. 1012,(1988)], the showing made by the State was insufficient to reach the high threshold required by that case before § 9-102 may be invoked."

We granted certiorari to resolve the important Confrontation Clause issues raised by this case.

II

The Confrontation Clause of the Sixth Amendment, made applicable to the States through the Fourteenth Amendment, provides: "In all criminal prosecutions, the accused shall enjoy the right . . . to be confronted with the witnesses against him."

We observed in *Coy v. Iowa* that "the Confrontation Clause guarantees the defendant a face-to-face meeting with witnesses appearing before the trier of fact." This interpretation derives not only from the literal text of the Clause, but also from our understanding of its historical roots.

We have never held, however, that the Confrontation Clause guarantees criminal defendants the *absolute* right to a face-to-face meeting with witnesses against them at trial. Indeed, in *Coy v. Iowa,* we expressly "le[ft] for another day . . . the question whether any exceptions exist" to the "irreducible literal meaning of the Clause: 'a right to *meet face to face* all those who appear and give evidence *at trial.*' The procedure challenged in *Coy* involved the placement of a screen that prevented two child witnesses in a child abuse case from seeing the defendant as they testified against him at trial. In holding that the use of this procedure violated the defendant's right to confront witnesses against him, we suggested that any exception to the right "would surely be allowed only when necessary to further an important public policy" — *i.e.,* only upon a showing of something more than the generalized, "legislatively imposed presumption of trauma" underlying the statute at issue in that case. We concluded that "[s]ince there ha[d] been no individualized findings that these particular witnesses needed special protection, the judgment [in the case before us] could not be sustained by any conceivable exception." Because the trial court in this case made individualized findings that each of the child witnesses needed special protection, this case requires us to decide the question reserved in *Coy.*

The central concern of the Confrontation Clause is to ensure the reliability of the evidence against a criminal defendant by subjecting it to rigorous testing in the context of an adversary proceeding before the trier of fact. The word "confront," after all, also means a clashing of forces or ideas, thus carrying with it the notion of adversariness. As we noted in our earliest case interpreting the Clause:

> The primary object of the constitutional provision in question was to prevent depositions or *ex parte* affidavits, such as were sometimes admitted in civil cases, being used against the prisoner in lieu of a personal examination and cross-examination of the witness in which the accused has an opportunity, not only of testing the recollection and sifting the conscience of the witness, but of compelling him to stand face to face with the jury in order that they may look at him, and judge

by his demeanor upon the stand and the manner in which he gives his testimony whether he is worthy of belief.

As this description indicates, the right guaranteed by the Confrontation Clause includes not only a "personal examination," but also "(1) insures that the witness will give his statements under oath — thus impressing him with the seriousness of the matter and guarding against the lie by the possibility of a penalty for perjury; (2) forces the witness to submit to cross-examination, the 'greatest legal engine ever invented for the discovery of truth'; [and] (3) permits the jury that is to decide the defendant's fate to observe the demeanor of the witness in making his statement, thus aiding the jury in assessing his credibility."

The combined effect of these elements of confrontation — physical presence, oath, cross-examination, and observation of demeanor by the trier of fact — serves the purposes of the Confrontation Clause by ensuring that evidence admitted against an accused is reliable and subject to the rigorous adversarial testing that is the norm of Anglo-American criminal proceedings. . . .

We have recognized, for example, that face-to-face confrontation enhances the accuracy of factfinding by reducing the risk that a witness will wrongfully implicate an innocent person. ("It is always more difficult to tell a lie about a person 'to his face' than 'behind his back.' . . .That face-to-face presence may, unfortunately, upset the truthful rape victim or abused child; but by the same token it may confound and undo the false accuser, or reveal the child coached by a malevolent adult"). We have also noted the strong symbolic purpose served by requiring adverse witnesses at trial to testify in the accused's presence. ("[T]here is something deep in human nature that regards face-to-face confrontation between accused and accuser as 'essential to a fair trial in a criminal prosecution' ").

Although face-to-face confrontation forms "the core of the values furthered by the Confrontation Clause," we have nevertheless recognized that it is not the *sine qua non* of the confrontation right. . . .

For this reason, we have never insisted on an actual face-to-face encounter at trial in *every* instance in which testimony is admitted against a defendant. Instead, we have repeatedly held that the Clause permits, where necessary, the admission of certain hearsay statements against a defendant despite the defendant's inability to confront the declarant at trial.

. . . .

In sum, our precedents establish that "the Confrontation Clause reflects a *preference* for face-to-face confrontation at trial," a preference that "must occasionally give way to considerations of public policy and the necessities of the case." "[W]e have attempted to harmonize the goal of the Clause — placing limits on the kind of evidence that may be received against a defendant — with a societal interest in accurate factfinding, which may require consideration of out-of-court statements." . . .

. . . .

That the face-to-face confrontation requirement is not absolute does not, of course, mean that it may easily be dispensed with. As we suggested in *Coy,* our precedents confirm that a defendant's right to confront accusatory witnesses may be satisfied absent a physical, face-to-face confrontation at trial only where denial of such confrontation is necessary to further an important public policy and only where the reliability of the testimony is otherwise assured.

III

Maryland's statutory procedure, when invoked, prevents a child witness from seeing the defendant as he or she testifies against the defendant at trial. We find it significant, however, that Maryland's procedure preserves all of the other elements of the confrontation right: The child witness must be competent to testify and must testify under oath; the defendant retains full opportunity for contemporaneous cross-examination; and the judge, jury, and defendant are able to view (albeit by video monitor) the demeanor (and body) of the witness as he or she testifies. Although we are mindful of the many subtle effects face-to-face confrontation may have on an adversary criminal proceeding, the presence of these other elements of confrontation — oath, cross-examination, and observation of the witness' demeanor — adequately ensures that the testimony is both reliable and subject to rigorous adversarial testing in a manner functionally equivalent to that accorded live, in-person testimony. These safeguards of reliability and adversariness render the use of such a procedure a far cry from the undisputed prohibition of the Confrontation Clause: trial by *ex parte* affidavit or inquisition. Rather, we think these elements of effective confrontation not only permit a defendant to "confound and undo the false accuser, or reveal the child coached by a malevolent adult," but may well aid a defendant in eliciting favorable testimony from the child witness. Indeed, to the extent the child witness' testimony may be said to be technically given out of court (though we do not so hold), these assurances of reliability and adversariness are far greater than those required for admission of hearsay testimony under the Confrontation Clause. We are therefore confident that use of the one-way closed circuit television procedure, where necessary to further an important state interest, does not impinge upon the truth-seeking or symbolic purposes of the Confrontation Clause.

The critical inquiry in this case, therefore, is whether use of the procedure is necessary to further an important state interest. The State contends that it has a substantial interest in protecting children who are allegedly victims of child abuse from the trauma of testifying against the alleged perpetrator and that its statutory procedure for receiving testimony from such witnesses is necessary to further that interest.

We have of course recognized that a State's interest in "the protection of minor victims of sex crimes from further trauma and embarrassment" is a "compelling" one. . . .

We likewise conclude today that a State's interest in the physical and psychological well-being of child abuse victims may be sufficiently important to outweigh, at least in some cases, a defendant's right to face his or her accusers in court. That a significant majority of States have enacted statutes to protect child witnesses from the trauma of giving testimony in child abuse cases attests to the widespread belief in the importance of such a public policy. . . . Thirty-seven States, for example, permit the use of videotaped testimony of sexually abused children; 24 States have authorized the use of one-way closed circuit television testimony in child abuse cases; and 8 States authorize the use of a two-way system in which the child witness is permitted to see the courtroom and the defendant on a video monitor and in which the jury and judge are permitted to view the child during the testimony.

The statute at issue in this case, for example, was specifically intended "to safeguard the physical and psychological well-being of child victims by avoiding, or at least minimizing, the emotional trauma produced by testifying."

Given the State's traditional and "transcendent interest in protecting the welfare of children," and buttressed by the growing body of academic literature documenting the psychological trauma suffered by child abuse victims who must testify in court, see Brief for American Psychological Association as *Amicus Curiae* 7-13; G. Goodman et al., *Emotional Effects of Criminal Court Testimony on Child Sexual Assault Victims, Final Report to the National Institute of Justice* (presented as conference paper at annual convention of American Psychological Assn., Aug. 1989), we will not second-guess the considered judgment of the Maryland Legislature regarding the importance of its interest in protecting child abuse victims from the emotional trauma of testifying. Accordingly, we hold that, if the State makes an adequate showing of necessity, the state interest in protecting child witnesses from the trauma of testifying in a child abuse case is sufficiently important to justify the use of a special procedure that permits a child witness in such cases to testify at trial against a defendant in the absence of face-to-face confrontation with the defendant.

The requisite finding of necessity must of course be a case-specific one: The trial court must hear evidence and determine whether use of the one-way closed circuit television procedure is necessary to protect the welfare of the particular child witness who seeks to testify. The trial court must also find that the child witness would be traumatized, not by the courtroom generally, but by the presence of the defendant. Denial of face-to-face confrontation is not needed to further the state interest in protecting the child witness from trauma unless it is the presence of the defendant that causes the trauma. In other words, if the state interest were merely the interest in protecting child witnesses from courtroom trauma generally, denial of face-to-face confrontation would be unnecessary because the child could be permitted to testify in less intimidating surroundings, albeit with the defendant present. Finally, the trial court must find that the emotional distress suffered by the child witness in the presence of the defendant is more than *de minimis, i.e.,* more than "mere nervousness or excitement or some reluctance to testify." We need not decide the minimum showing of emotional trauma required for use of the special procedure, however, because the Maryland statute, which requires a determination that the child witness will suffer "serious emotional distress such that the child cannot reasonably communicate," § 9-102(a)(1)(ii), clearly suffices to meet constitutional standards.

To be sure, face-to-face confrontation may be said to cause trauma for the very purpose of eliciting truth, but we think that the use of Maryland's special procedure, where necessary to further the important state interest in preventing trauma to child witnesses in child abuse cases, adequately ensures the accuracy of the testimony and preserves the adversary nature of the trial. Indeed, where face-to-face confrontation causes significant emotional distress in a child witness, there is evidence that such confrontation would in fact *disserve* the Confrontation Clause's truth-seeking goal.

. . . .

IV

The Maryland Court of Appeals held, as we do today, that although face-to-face confrontation is not an absolute constitutional requirement, it may be abridged only where there is a "case-specific finding of necessity." Given this latter requirement, the Court of Appeals reasoned that "[t]he question of whether a child is unavailable to testify . . . should not be asked in terms of inability to testify in the ordinary courtroom setting, but in the much narrower terms of the witness's inability to testify in the presence of the accused." . . .

In addition, however, the Court of Appeals interpreted our decision in *Coy* to impose two subsidiary requirements. First, the court held that "§ 9-102 ordinarily cannot be invoked unless the child witness initially is questioned (either in or outside the courtroom) in the defendant's presence." Second, the court asserted that, before using the one-way television procedure, a trial judge must determine whether a child would suffer "severe emotional distress" if he or she were to testify by *two*-way closed circuit television.

Reviewing the evidence presented to the trial court in support of the finding required under § 9-102(a)(1)(ii), the Court of Appeals determined that "the finding of necessity required to limit the defendant's right of confrontation through invocation of § 9-102 . . . was not made here." . . . The Court of Appeals appears to have rested its conclusion at least in part on the trial court's failure to observe the children's behavior in the defendant's presence and its failure to explore less restrictive alternatives to the use of the one-way closed circuit television procedure. Although we think such evidentiary requirements could strengthen the grounds for use of protective measures, we decline to establish, as a matter of federal constitutional law, any such categorical evidentiary prerequisites for the use of the one-way television procedure. The trial court in this case, for example, could well have found, on the basis of the expert testimony before it, that testimony by the child witnesses in the courtroom in the defendant's presence "will result in [each] child suffering serious emotional distress such that the child cannot reasonably communicate," § 9-102(a)(1)(ii). So long as a trial court makes such a case-specific finding of necessity, the Confrontation Clause does not prohibit a State from using a one-way closed circuit television procedure for the receipt of testimony by a child witness in a child abuse case. Because the Court of Appeals held that the trial court had not made the requisite finding of necessity under its interpretation of "the high threshold required by [*Coy*] before § 9-102 may be invoked," we cannot be certain whether the Court of Appeals would reach the same conclusion in light of the legal standard we establish today. We therefore vacate the judgment of the Court of Appeals of Maryland and remand the case for further proceedings not inconsistent with this opinion.

It is so ordered.

JUSTICE SCALIA, with whom JUSTICE BRENNAN, JUSTICE MARSHALL, and JUSTICE STEVENS join, *dissenting*.

Seldom has this Court failed so conspicuously to sustain a categorical guarantee of the Constitution against the tide of prevailing current opinion. The Sixth Amendment provides, with unmistakable clarity, that "[i]n all criminal prosecutions, the accused shall enjoy the right . . . to be confronted with the witnesses against him." The purpose of enshrining this protection in the Constitution was to assure that none of the many policy interests from time to time pursued by statutory law could overcome a defendant's right to face his or her accusers in court. . . .

Because of this subordination of explicit constitutional text to currently favored public policy, the following scene can be played out in an American courtroom for the first time in two centuries: A father whose young daughter has been given over to the exclusive custody of his estranged wife, or a mother whose young son has been taken into custody by the State's child welfare department, is sentenced to prison for sexual abuse on the basis of testimony by a child the parent has not seen or spoken to for many months; and the guilty verdict is rendered without giving the parent so much as the opportunity to sit in the presence of the child, and to ask, personally or through counsel, "it is really not true, is it, that I — your father (or mother) whom you see before you — did these terrible things?" Perhaps that is a procedure today's society desires; perhaps (though I doubt it) it is even a fair procedure; but it is assuredly not a procedure permitted by the Constitution.

. . . .

I

According to the Court, "we cannot say that [face-to-face] confrontation [with witnesses appearing at trial] is an indispensable element of the Sixth Amendment's guarantee of the right to confront one's accusers." That is rather like saying "we cannot say that being tried before a jury is an indispensable element of the Sixth Amendment's guarantee of the right to jury trial." The Court makes the impossible plausible by recharacterizing the Confrontation Clause, so that confrontation (redesignated "face-to-face confrontation") becomes only one of many "elements of confrontation." The reasoning is as follows: The Confrontation Clause guarantees not only what it explicitly provides for — "face-to-face" confrontation — but also implied and collateral rights such as cross-examination, oath, and observation of demeanor (TRUE); the purpose of this entire cluster of rights is to ensure the reliability of evidence (TRUE); the Maryland procedure preserves the implied and collateral rights (TRUE), which adequately ensure the reliability of evidence (perhaps TRUE); therefore the Confrontation Clause is not violated by denying what it explicitly provides for — "face-to-face" confrontation (unquestionably FALSE). This reasoning abstracts from the right to its purposes, and then eliminates the right. It is wrong because the Confrontation Clause does not guarantee reliable evidence; it guarantees specific trial procedures that were thought to *assure* reliable evidence, undeniably among which was "face-to-face" confrontation. Whatever else it may mean in addition, the defendant's constitutional right "to be confronted with the witnesses against him" means, always and everywhere, at least what it explicitly says: the "right to meet face to face all those who appear and give evidence at trial."

. . . .

III

The Court characterizes the State's interest which "outweigh[s]" the explicit text of the Constitution as an "interest in the physical and psychological well-being of child abuse victims," an "interest in protecting" such victims "from the emotional trauma of testifying,". That is not so. A child who meets the Maryland statute's requirement of suffering such "serious emotional distress" from confrontation that he "cannot reasonably communicate" would seem entirely safe. Why would a prosecutor want to call a witness who cannot reasonably communicate? And if he did, it would be the State's own fault. Protection of the child's interest — as far as the Confrontation Clause is concerned [72] — is entirely within Maryland's control. The State's interest here is in fact no more and no less than what the State's interest always is when it seeks to get a class of evidence admitted in criminal proceedings: more convictions of guilty defendants. That is not an unworthy interest, but it should not be dressed up as a humanitarian one.

And the interest on the other side is also what it usually is when the State seeks to get a new class of evidence admitted: fewer convictions of innocent defendants — specifically, in the present context, innocent defendants accused of particularly heinous crimes. The "special" reasons that exist for suspending one of the usual guarantees of reliability in the case of children's testimony are perhaps matched by "special" reasons for being particularly insistent upon it in the case of children's testimony. Some studies show that children are substantially more vulnerable to suggestion than adults, and often unable to separate recollected fantasy (or suggestion) from reality. *See* Lindsay & Johnson, *Reality Monitoring and Suggestibility: Children's Ability to Discriminate Among Memories From Different Sources, in Children's Eyewitness Memory* 92 (S. Ceci, M. Toglia, & D. Ross eds. 1987); Feher, *The Alleged Molestation Victim, The Rules of Evidence, and the Constitution: Should Children Really Be Seen and Not Heard?*, 14 AM. J. CRIM. L. 227, 230–233 (1987); Christiansen, *The Testimony of Child Witnesses: Fact, Fantasy, and the Influence of Pretrial Interviews*, 62 WASH. L. REV. 705, 708–711 (1987). The injustice their erroneous testimony can produce is evidenced by the tragic Scott County investigations of 1983-1984, which disrupted the lives of many (as far as we know)

---

72 [2] A different situation would be presented if the defendant sought to call the child. In that event, the State's refusal to compel the child to appear, or its insistence upon a procedure such as that set forth in the Maryland statute as a condition of its compelling him to do so, would call into question — initially, at least, and perhaps exclusively — the scope of the defendant's Sixth Amendment right "to have compulsory process for obtaining witnesses in his favor."

innocent people in the small town of Jordan, Minnesota. At one stage those investigations were pursuing allegations by at least eight children of multiple murders, but the prosecutions actually initiated charged only sexual abuse. Specifically, 24 adults were charged with molesting 37 children. In the course of the investigations, 25 children were placed in foster homes. Of the 24 indicted defendants, one pleaded guilty, two were acquitted at trial, and the charges against the remaining 21 were voluntarily dismissed. There is no doubt that some sexual abuse took place in Jordan; but there is no reason to believe it was as widespread as charged. A report by the Minnesota attorney general's office, based on inquiries conducted by the Minnesota Bureau of Criminal Apprehension and the Federal Bureau of Investigation, concluded that there was an "absence of credible testimony and [a] lack of significant corroboration" to support reinstitution of sex-abuse charges, and "no credible evidence of murders." The report describes an investigation full of well-intentioned techniques employed by the prosecution team, police, child protection workers, and foster parents, that distorted and in some cases even coerced the children's recollection. Children were interrogated repeatedly, in some cases as many as 50 times; answers were suggested by telling the children what other witnesses had said; and children (even some who did not at first complain of abuse) were separated from their parents for months. The report describes the consequences as follows:

> As children continued to be interviewed the list of accused citizens grew. In a number of cases, it was only after weeks or months of questioning that children would 'admit' their parents abused them.
>
> . . . .
>
> In some instances, over a period of time, the allegations of sexual abuse turned to stories of mutilations, and eventually homicide.

The value of the confrontation right in guarding against a child's distorted or coerced recollections is dramatically evident with respect to one of the misguided investigative techniques the report cited: some children were told by their foster parents that reunion with their real parents would be hastened by "admission" of their parents' abuse. Is it difficult to imagine how unconvincing such a testimonial admission might be to a jury that witnessed the child's delight at seeing his parents in the courtroom? Or how devastating it might be if, pursuant to a psychiatric evaluation that "trauma would impair the child's ability to communicate" in front of his parents, the child were permitted to tell his story to the jury on closed-circuit television?

In the last analysis, however, this debate is not an appropriate one. I have no need to defend the value of confrontation, because the Court has no authority to question it. It is not within our charge to speculate that, "where face-to-face confrontation causes significant emotional distress in a child witness," confrontation might "in fact *disserve* the Confrontation Clause's truth-seeking goal." If so, that is a defect in the Constitution — which should be amended by the procedures provided for such an eventuality, but cannot be corrected by judicial pronouncement that it is archaic, contrary to "widespread belief," and thus null and void. For good or bad, the Sixth Amendment requires confrontation, and we are not at liberty to ignore it. To quote the document one last time (for it plainly says all that need be said): "In *all* criminal prosecutions, the accused shall enjoy the right . . . to be confronted with the witnesses against him" (emphasis added).

The Court today has applied "interest-balancing" analysis where the text of the Constitution simply does not permit it. We are not free to conduct a cost-benefit analysis of clear and explicit constitutional guarantees, and then to adjust their meaning to comport with our findings. The Court has convincingly proved that the Maryland procedure serves a valid interest, and gives the defendant virtually everything the Confrontation Clause guarantees (everything, that is, except confrontation). I am persuaded, therefore, that the Maryland procedure is virtually constitutional. Since it is not, however, actually constitutional I would affirm the judgment of the Maryland Court of Appeals reversing the judgment of conviction.

————

NOTES AND QUESTIONS

1. To address the perceived problem of child victim witness trauma created by testifying in formalized courtroom settings and/or by testimony in the physical presence of the accused abuser, some states have enacted statutes similar to the Maryland provision examined in *Craig* that permit closed circuit or videotaped testimony outside the presence of the defendant. For example, the Kansas statute provides:

Videotape of testimony of child victim admissible in certain cases; limitations; standard of proof; objections, restrictions.

(a) On motion of the attorney for any party to a criminal proceeding in which a child less than 13 years of age is alleged to be a victim of the crime, subject to the conditions of subsection (b), the court may order that the testimony of the child be taken:

(1) In a room other than the courtroom and be televised by closed-circuit equipment in the courtroom to be viewed by the court and the finder of fact in the proceeding; or

(2) outside the courtroom and be recorded for showing in the courtroom before the court and the finder of fact in the proceeding if:

(A) The recording is both visual and aural and is recorded on film or videotape or by other electronic means;

(B) the recording equipment is capable of making an accurate recording, the operator of the equipment is competent and the recording is accurate and has not been altered;

(C) every voice on the recording is identified; and

(D) each party to the proceeding is afforded an opportunity to view the recording before it is shown in the courtroom, and a copy of a written transcript is provided to the parties.

(b) The state must establish by clear and convincing evidence that to require the child who is the alleged victim to testify in open court will so traumatize the child as to prevent the child from reasonably communicating to the jury or render the child unavailable to testify. The court shall make such an individualized finding before the state is permitted to proceed under this section.

(c) At the taking of testimony under this section:

(1) Only the attorneys for the defendant, the state and the child, any person whose presence would contribute to the welfare and well-being of the child and persons necessary to operate the recording or closed-circuit equipment may be present in the room with the child during the child's testimony;

(2) only the attorneys may question the child;

(3) the persons operating the recording or closed-circuit equipment shall be confined to an adjacent room or behind a screen or mirror that permits them to see and hear the child during the child's testimony but does not permit the child to see or hear them; and

(4) the court shall permit the defendant to observe and hear the testimony of the child in person, but shall ensure that the child cannot hear or see the defendant.

KAN. STAT. ANN. § 22-3434 (2005).

Other states address the child trauma problem by permitting use of out of court depositions by the child victim in the presence of the defendant, at least sometimes. For example, Florida statutory law provides:

Videotaping of testimony of victim or witness under age 16 or person with mental retardation

(1) On motion and hearing in camera and a finding that there is a substantial likelihood that a victim or witness who is under the age of 16 or who is a person with mental retardation as defined in § 393.063(42) would suffer at least moderate emotional or mental harm due to the presence of the defendant if the child or person with mental retardation is required to testify in open court, or that such victim or witness is otherwise unavailable as defined in § 90.804(1), the trial court may order the videotaping of the testimony of the victim or witness in a case, whether civil or criminal in nature, in which videotaped testimony is to be utilized at trial in lieu of trial testimony in open court.

(2) The motion may be filed by:

(a) The victim or witness, or the victim's or witness's attorney, parent, legal guardian, or guardian ad litem;

(b) A trial judge on his or her own motion;

(c) Any party in a civil proceeding; or

(d) The prosecuting attorney or the defendant, or the defendant's counsel.

(3) The judge shall preside, or shall appoint a special master to preside, at the videotaping unless the following conditions are met:

(a) The child or person with mental retardation is represented by a guardian ad litem or counsel;

(b) The representative of the victim or witness and the counsel for each party stipulate that the requirement for the presence of the judge or special master may be waived; and

(c) The court finds at a hearing on the motion that the presence of a judge or special master is not necessary to protect the victim or witness.

(4) The defendant and the defendant's counsel shall be present at the videotaping, unless the defendant has waived this right. The court may require the defendant to view the testimony from outside the presence of the child or person with mental retardation by means of a two-way mirror or another similar method that will ensure the defendant can observe and hear the testimony of the victim or witness in person, but that the victim or witness cannot hear or see the defendant. The defendant and the attorney for the defendant may communicate by any appropriate private method.

. . . .

(6) The motion referred to in subsection (1) may be at any time with reasonable notice to each party to the cause, and videotaping of testimony may be made any time after the court grants the motion. The videotaped testimony shall be admissible as evidence in the trial of the cause; however, such testimony shall not be admissible in any trial or proceeding in which such witness testifies by use of closed circuit television pursuant to § 92.54.

(7) The court shall make specific findings of fact, on the record, as to the basis for its ruling under this section.

FLA. STAT. ANN. § 92.53 (West Supp. 2005).

2. Is there a risk that in a majority of cases testimony of child victim witnesses will be received outside the courtroom and/or the presence of the defendant? Under the above Florida statute, for example, is it not arguable that in virtually every case it could be shown that there exists a "substantial likelihood" that a child victim witness might "suffer moderate emotional or mental harm" if required to testify in the formalized setting of the courtroom and/or in the physical presence of the defendant? If so have the confrontation rights of defendants been unduly compromised?

3. The widespread belief that child witnesses are especially vulnerable to trauma if required to testify in court in the defendant's presence may merely be an article of faith. As of 1993 two commentators observed: "While ample anecdotal evidence exists to suggest that children are traumatized by giving testimony in court, good empirical research on this topic is sparse." Nancy Walker Perry & Bradley D. McAuliff, *The Use of Videotaped Child Testimony: Public Policy Implications*, 7 NOTRE DAME J. L. ETHICS & PUB. POL'Y 387, 417 (1993). For discussion of the competence and credibility of children as witnesses, see generally NANCY WALKER PERRY & LAWRENCE S. WRIGHTSMAN,

THE CHILD WITNESS (1991); John E. B. Myers et al., *Psychological Research on Children as Witnesses: Practical Implications for Forensic Interviews and Courtroom Testimony*, 28 PAC. L.J. 3 (1996).

IDAHO v. WRIGHT

Supreme Court of the United States
497 U.S. 805 (1990)

JUSTICE O'CONNOR *delivered the opinion of the Court.*

This case requires us to decide whether the admission at trial of certain hearsay statements made by a child declarant to an examining pediatrician violates a defendant's rights under the Confrontation Clause of the Sixth Amendment.

I

Respondent Laura Lee Wright was jointly charged with Robert L. Giles of two counts of lewd conduct with a minor under 16, in violation of Idaho Code § 18-1508 (1987). The alleged victims were respondent's two daughters, one of whom was 5-1/2 and the other 2-1/2-years-old at the time the crimes were charged.

Respondent and her ex-husband, Louis Wright, the father of the older daughter, had reached an informal agreement whereby each parent would have custody of the older daughter for six consecutive months. The allegations surfaced in November 1986 when the older daughter told Cynthia Goodman, Louis Wright's female companion, that Giles had had sexual intercourse with her while respondent held her down and covered her mouth, and that she had seen respondent and Giles do the same thing to respondent's younger daughter. The younger daughter was living with her parents — respondent and Giles — at the time of the alleged offenses.

Goodman reported the older daughter's disclosures to the police the next day and took the older daughter to the hospital. A medical examination of the older daughter revealed evidence of sexual abuse. One of the examining physicians was Dr. John Jambura, a pediatrician with extensive experience in child abuse cases. Police and welfare officials took the younger daughter into custody that day for protection and investigation. Dr. Jambura examined her the following day and found conditions "strongly suggestive of sexual abuse with vaginal contact," occurring approximately two to three days prior to the examination.

At the joint trial of respondent and Giles, the trial court conducted a *voir dire* examination of the younger daughter, who was three-years-old at the time of trial, to determine whether she was capable of testifying. The court concluded, and the parties agreed, that the younger daughter was "not capable of communicating to the jury."

At issue in this case is the admission at trial of certain statements made by the younger daughter to Dr. Jambura in response to questions he asked regarding the alleged abuse. Over objection by respondent and Giles, the trial court permitted Dr. Jambura to testify before the jury as follows: . . .

"A. When I asked her 'Does daddy touch you with his pee-pee,' she did admit to that. When I asked, 'Do you touch his pee-pee,' she did not have any response.

"Q. Excuse me. Did you notice any change in her affect or attitude in that line of questioning?

"A. Yes.

"Q. What did you observe?

"A. She would not — oh, she did not talk any further about that. She would not elucidate what exactly — what kind of touching was taking place, or how it was happening. She did, however, say that daddy does do this with me, but he does it a lot more with my sister than with me.

"Q. And how did she offer that last statement? Was that in response to a question or was that just a volunteered statement?

"A. That was a volunteered statement as I sat and waited for her to respond, again after she sort of clammed-up, and that was the next statement that she made after just allowing some silence to occur."

On cross-examination, Dr. Jambura acknowledged that a picture that he drew during his questioning of the younger daughter had been discarded. Dr. Jambura also stated that although he had dictated notes to summarize the conversation, his notes were not detailed and did not record any changes in the child's affect or attitude.

The trial court admitted these statements under Idaho's residual hearsay exception, which provides in relevant part:

"Rule 803. Hearsay exceptions; availability of declarant immaterial. — The following are not excluded by the hearsay rule, even though the declarant is available as a witness.

. . . .

"(24) Other exceptions. A statement not specifically covered by any of the foregoing exceptions but having equivalent circumstantial guarantees of trustworthiness, if the court determines that (A) the statement is offered as evidence of a material fact; (B) the statement is more probative on the point for which it is offered than any other evidence which the proponent can procure through reasonable efforts; and (C) the general purposes of these rules and the interests of justice will best be served by admission of the statement into evidence."

Respondent and Giles were each convicted of two counts of lewd conduct with a minor under 16 and sentenced to 20 years' imprisonment. Each appealed. . . .

The Supreme Court of Idaho held that the admission of the inculpatory hearsay testimony violated respondent's federal constitutional right to confrontation because the testimony did not fall within a traditional hearsay exception and was based on an interview that lacked procedural safeguards. The court found Dr. Jambura's interview technique inadequate because "the questions and answers were not recorded on videotape for preservation and perusal by the defense at or before trial; and, blatantly leading questions were used in the interrogation." The statements also lacked trustworthiness, according to the court, because "this interrogation was performed by someone with a preconceived idea of what the child should be disclosing." Noting that expert testimony and child psychology texts indicated that children are susceptible to suggestion and are therefore likely to be misled by leading questions, the court found that "[t]he circumstances surrounding this interview demonstrate dangers of unreliability which, because the interview was not [audio or video] recorded, can never be fully assessed." The court concluded that the younger daughter's statements lacked the particularized guarantees of trustworthiness necessary to satisfy the requirements of the Confrontation Clause and that therefore the trial court erred in admitting them. Because the court was not convinced, beyond a reasonable doubt, that the jury would have reached the same result had the error not occurred, the court reversed respondent's conviction on the count involving the younger daughter and remanded for a new trial.

We granted certiorari, and now affirm.

II

. . . .

Although we have recognized that hearsay rules and the Confrontation Clause are generally designed to protect similar values, we have also been careful not to equate the Confrontation Clause's prohibitions with the general rule prohibiting the admission of hearsay statements. The Confrontation Clause, in other words, bars the admission of some evidence that would otherwise be admissible under an exception to the hearsay rule.

In *Ohio v. Roberts,* [448 U.S. 56 (1980),] we set forth "a general approach" for determining when incriminating statements admissible under an exception to the hearsay rule also meet the requirements of the Confrontation Clause. We noted that the Confrontation Clause "operates in two separate ways to restrict the range of admissible hearsay." "First, in conformance with the Framers' preference for face-to-face accusation, the Sixth Amendment establishes a rule of necessity. In the usual case . . . , the prosecution must either produce, or demonstrate the unavailability of, the declarant whose statement it wishes to use against the defendant." Second, once a witness is shown to be unavailable, "his statement is admissible only if it bears adequate 'indicia of reliability.' Reliability can be inferred without more in a case where the evidence falls within a firmly rooted hearsay exception. In other cases, the evidence must be excluded, at least absent a showing of particularized guarantees of trustworthiness."

. . . .

Applying the *Roberts* approach to this case, we first note that this case does not raise the question whether, before a child's out-of-court statements are admitted, the Confrontation Clause requires the prosecution to show that a child witness is unavailable at trial — and, if so, what that showing requires. The trial court in this case found that respondent's younger daughter was incapable of communicating with the jury, and defense counsel agreed. The court below neither questioned this finding nor discussed the general requirement of unavailability. For purposes of deciding this case, we assume without deciding that, to the extent the unavailability requirement applies in this case, the younger daughter was an unavailable witness within the meaning of the Confrontation Clause.

The crux of the question presented is therefore whether the State, as the proponent of evidence presumptively barred by the hearsay rule and the Confrontation Clause, has carried its burden of proving that the younger daughter's incriminating statements to Dr. Jambura bore sufficient indicia of reliability to withstand scrutiny under the Clause. . . .

In *Roberts,* we suggested that the "indicia of reliability" requirement could be met in either of two circumstances: where the hearsay statement "falls within a firmly rooted hearsay exception," or where it is supported by "a showing of particularized guarantees of trustworthiness." . . .

We note at the outset that Idaho's residual hearsay exception, Idaho Rule Evid. 803(24), under which the challenged statements were admitted, is not a firmly rooted hearsay exception for Confrontation Clause purposes. Admission under a firmly rooted hearsay exception satisfies the constitutional requirement of reliability because of the weight accorded longstanding judicial and legislative experience in assessing the trustworthiness of certain types of out-of-court statements. The residual hearsay exception, by contrast, accommodates ad hoc instances in which statements not otherwise falling within a recognized hearsay exception might nevertheless be sufficiently reliable to be admissible at trial. Hearsay statements admitted under the residual exception, almost by definition, therefore do not share the same tradition of reliability that supports the admissibility of statements under a firmly rooted hearsay exception. Moreover, were we to agree that the admission of hearsay statements under the residual exception automatically passed Confrontation Clause scrutiny, virtually every codified hearsay exception would assume constitutional stature, a step this Court has repeatedly declined to take.

The State in any event does not press the matter strongly and recognizes that, because the younger daughter's hearsay statements do not fall within a firmly rooted hearsay exception, they are "presumptively unreliable and inadmissible for Confrontation Clause purposes," and "must be excluded, at least absent a showing of particularized guarantees of trustworthiness." The court below concluded that the State had not made such a showing, in large measure because the statements resulted from an interview lacking certain procedural safeguards. The court below specifically noted that Dr. Jambura failed to record the interview on videotape, asked leading questions, and questioned the child with a preconceived idea of what she should be disclosing.

Although we agree with the court below that the Confrontation Clause bars the admission of the younger daughter's hearsay statements, we reject the apparently dispositive weight placed by that court on the lack of procedural safeguards at the interview. Out-of-court statements made by children regarding sexual abuse arise in a wide variety of circumstances, and we do not believe the Constitution imposes a fixed set of procedural prerequisites to the admission of such statements at trial. The procedural requirements identified by the court below, to the extent regarded as conditions precedent to the admission of child hearsay statements in child sexual abuse cases, may in many instances be inappropriate or unnecessary to a determination whether a given statement is sufficiently trustworthy for Confrontation Clause purposes. . . .

The State responds that a finding of "particularized guarantees of trustworthiness" should instead be based on a consideration of the totality of the circumstances, including not only the circumstances surrounding the making of the statement, but also other evidence at trial that corroborates the truth of the statement. We agree that "particularized guarantees of trustworthiness" must be shown from the totality of the circumstances, but we think the relevant circumstances include only those that surround the making of the statement and that render the declarant particularly worthy of belief. This conclusion derives from the rationale for permitting exceptions to the general rule against hearsay:

> The theory of the hearsay rule . . . is that the many possible sources of inaccuracy and untrustworthiness which may lie underneath the bare untested assertion of a witness can best be brought to light and exposed, if they exist, by the test of cross-examination. But this test or security may in a given instance be superfluous; it may be sufficiently clear, in that instance, that the statement offered is free enough from the risk of inaccuracy and untrustworthiness, so that the test of cross-examination would be a work of supererogation.

. . . .

We think the "particularized guarantees of trustworthiness" required for admission under the Confrontation Clause must likewise be drawn from the totality of circumstances that surround the making of the statement and that render the declarant particularly worthy of belief. Our precedents have recognized that statements admitted under a "firmly rooted" hearsay exception are so trustworthy that adversarial testing would add little to their reliability. . . . Because evidence possessing "particularized guarantees of trustworthiness" must be at least as reliable as evidence admitted under a firmly rooted hearsay exception, we think that evidence admitted under the former requirement must similarly be so trustworthy that adversarial testing would add little to its reliability. . . . Thus, unless an affirmative reason, arising from the circumstances in which the statement was made, provides a basis for rebutting the presumption that a hearsay statement is not worthy of reliance at trial, the Confrontation Clause requires exclusion of the out-of-court statement.

The state and federal courts have identified a number of factors that we think properly relate to whether hearsay statements made by a child witness in child sexual abuse cases are reliable. . . . [1](spontaneity and consistent repetition), [2](mental state of the declarant), [3](use of terminology unexpected of a child of similar age), [4](lack of motive to fabricate). Although these cases (which we cite for the factors they discuss and not necessarily to approve the results that they reach) involve the application of various hearsay exceptions to statements of child declarants, we think the factors identified also apply to whether such statements bear "particularized guarantees of trustworthiness" under the Confrontation Clause. These factors are, of course, not exclusive, and courts have considerable leeway in their consideration of appropriate factors. We, therefore, decline to endorse a mechanical test for determining "particularized guarantees of trustworthiness" under the Clause. Rather, the unifying principle is that these factors relate to whether the child declarant was particularly likely to be telling the truth when the statement was made.

As our discussion above suggests, we are unpersuaded by the State's contention that evidence corroborating the truth of a hearsay statement may properly support a finding that the statement bears "particularized guarantees of trustworthiness." To be admissible under the Confrontation Clause, hearsay evidence used to convict a defendant must possess indicia of reliability by virtue of its inherent trustworthiness, not by reference to other evidence at trial. . . .

In short, the use of corroborating evidence to support a hearsay statement's "particularized guarantees of trustworthiness" would permit admission of a presumptively unreliable statement by bootstrapping on the trustworthiness of other evidence at trial, a result we think at odds with the requirement that hearsay evidence admitted under the Confrontation Clause be so trustworthy that cross-examination of the declarant would be of marginal utility.

. . . .

. . . Corroboration of a child's allegations of sexual abuse by medical evidence of abuse, for example, sheds no light on the reliability of the child's allegations regarding the identity of the abuser. There is a very real danger that a jury will rely on partial corroboration to mistakenly infer the trustworthiness of the entire statement. . . .

Finally, we reject respondent's contention that the younger daughter's out-of-court statements in this case are *per se* unreliable, or at least presumptively unreliable, on the ground that the trial court found the younger daughter incompetent to testify at trial. First, respondent's contention rests upon a questionable reading of the record in this case. The trial court found only that the younger daughter was "not capable of communicating to the jury." Although Idaho law provides that a child witness may not testify if he "appear[s] incapable of receiving just impressions of the facts respecting which they are examined, or of relating them truly," the trial court in this case made no such findings. Indeed, the more reasonable inference is that, by ruling that the statements were admissible under Idaho's residual hearsay exception, the trial court implicitly found that the younger daughter, at the time she made the statements, was capable of receiving just impressions of the facts and of relating them truly. In addition, we have in any event held that the Confrontation Clause does not erect a *per se* rule barring the admission of prior statements of a declarant who is unable to communicate to the jury at the time of trial. Although such inability might be relevant to whether the earlier hearsay statement possessed particularized guarantees of trustworthiness, a *per se* rule of exclusion would not only frustrate the truth-seeking purpose of the Confrontation Clause, but would also hinder States in their own "enlightened development in the law of evidence."

III

The trial court in this case, in ruling that the Confrontation Clause did not prohibit admission of the younger daughter's hearsay statements, relied on the following factors:

> In this case, of course, there is physical evidence to corroborate that sexual abuse occurred. It also would seem to be the case that there is no motive to make up a story of this nature in a child of these years. We're not talking about a pubescent youth who may fantasize. The nature of the statements themselves as to sexual abuse are such that they fall outside the general believability that a child could make them up or would make them up. This is simply not the type of statement, I believe, that one would expect a child to fabricate.

> We come then to the identification itself. Are there any indicia of reliability as to identification? From the doctor's testimony it appears that the injuries testified to occurred at the time that the victim was in the custody of the Defendants. The [older daughter] has testified as to identification of [the] perpetrators. Those — the identification of the perpetrators in this case are persons well known to the [younger daughter]. This is not a case in which a child is called upon to identify a stranger or a person with whom they would have no knowledge of their identity or ability to recollect and recall. Those factors are sufficient indicia of reliability to permit the admission of the statements.

Of the factors the trial court found relevant, only two relate to circumstances surrounding the making of the statements: whether the child had a motive to "make up a story of this nature," and whether, given the child's age, the statements are of the type "that one would expect a child to fabricate." The other factors on which the trial court relied, however, such as the presence of physical evidence of abuse, the opportunity of respondent to commit the offense, and the older daughter's corroborating identification, relate instead to whether other evidence existed to corroborate the truth of the statement. These factors, as we have discussed, are irrelevant to a showing of the "particularized guarantees of trustworthiness" necessary for admission of hearsay statements under the Confrontation Clause.

. . . Given the presumption of inadmissibility accorded accusatory hearsay statements not admitted pursuant to a firmly rooted hearsay exception, we agree with the court below that the State has failed to show that the younger daughter's incriminating statements to the pediatrician possessed sufficient "particularized guarantees of trustworthiness" under the Confrontation

Clause to overcome that presumption. . . . Accordingly, the judgment of the Supreme Court of Idaho is affirmed.

JUSTICE KENNEDY, with whom THE CHIEF JUSTICE, JUSTICE WHITE, and JUSTICE BLACKMUN join, *dissenting.*

. . . The Court today holds that it is not, provided that the child's statements bear "particularized guarantees of trustworthiness." I agree. My disagreement is with the rule the Court invents to control this inquiry and with the Court's ultimate determination that the statements in question here must be inadmissible as violative of the Confrontation Clause.

Given the principle, for cases involving hearsay statements that do not come within one of the traditional hearsay exceptions, that admissibility depends upon finding particular guarantees of trustworthiness in each case, it is difficult to state rules of general application. I believe the Court recognizes this. The majority errs, in my view, by adopting a rule that corroboration of the statement by other evidence is an impermissible part of the trustworthiness inquiry. The Court's apparent ruling is that corroborating evidence may not be considered in whole or in part for this purpose. This limitation, at least on a facial interpretation of the Court's analytic categories, is a new creation by the Court; it likely will prove unworkable and does not even square with the examples of reliability indicators the Court itself invokes; and it is contrary to our own precedents.

. . . .

The short of the matter is that both the circumstances existing at the time the child makes the statements and the existence of corroborating evidence indicate, to a greater or lesser degree, whether the statements are reliable. If the Court means to suggest that the circumstances surrounding the making of a statement are the best indicators of reliability, I doubt this is so in every instance. And, if it were true in a particular case, that does not warrant ignoring other indicators of reliability such as corroborating evidence, absent some other reason for excluding it. If anything, I should think that corroborating evidence in the form of testimony or physical evidence, apart from the narrow circumstances in which the statement was made, would be a preferred means of determining a statement's reliability for purposes of the Confrontation Clause, for the simple reason that, unlike other indicators of trustworthiness, corroborating evidence can be addressed by the defendant and assessed by the trial court in an objective and critical way.

In this case, the younger daughter's statements are corroborated in at least four respects: (1) physical evidence that she was the victim of sexual abuse; (2) evidence that she had been in the custody of the suspect at the time the injuries occurred; (3) testimony of the older daughter that their father abused the younger daughter, thus corroborating the younger daughter's statement; and (4) the testimony of the older daughter that she herself was abused by their father, thus corroborating the younger daughter's statement that her sister had also been abused. These facts, coupled with the circumstances surrounding the making of the statements acknowledged by the Court as suggesting that the statements are reliable, give rise to a legitimate argument that admission of the statements did not violate the Confrontation Clause.

Because the Idaho Supreme Court did not consider these factors, I would vacate its judgment reversing respondent's conviction and remand for it to consider in the first instance whether the child's statements bore "particularized guarantees of trustworthiness" under the analysis set forth in this separate opinion.

For these reasons, I respectfully dissent.

WHITE v. ILLINOIS

Supreme Court of the United States
502 U.S. 346 (1992)

CHIEF JUSTICE REHNQUIST *delivered the opinion of the Court.*

In this case we consider whether the Confrontation Clause of the Sixth Amendment requires that, before a trial court admits testimony under the "spontaneous declaration" and "medical examination" exceptions to the hearsay rule, the prosecution must either produce the declarant at trial or the trial court must find that the declarant is unavailable. The Illinois Appellate Court concluded that such procedures are not constitutionally required. We agree with that conclusion.

Petitioner was convicted by a jury of aggravated criminal sexual assault, residential burglary, and unlawful restraint. The events giving rise to the charges related to the sexual assault of S.G., then four-years-old. Testimony at the trial established that in the early morning hours of April 16, 1988, S.G.'s babysitter, Tony DeVore, was awakened by S.G.'s scream. DeVore went to S.G.'s bedroom and witnessed petitioner leaving the room, and petitioner then left the house. DeVore knew petitioner because petitioner was a friend of S.G.'s mother, Tammy Grigsby. DeVore asked S.G. what had happened. According to DeVore's trial testimony, S.G. stated that petitioner had put his hand over her mouth, choked her, threatened to whip her if she screamed and had "touch[ed] her in the wrong places." Asked by DeVore to point to where she had been touched, S.G. identified the vaginal area.

Tammy Grigsby, S.G.'s mother, returned home about 30 minutes later. Grigsby testified that her daughter appeared "scared" and a "little hyper." Grigsby proceeded to question her daughter about what had happened. At trial, Grigsby testified that S.G. repeated her claims that petitioner had choked and threatened her. Grigsby also testified that S.G. stated that petitioner had "put his mouth on her front part." Grigsby also noticed that S.G. had bruises and red marks on her neck that had not been there previously. Grigsby called the police.

Officer Terry Lewis arrived a few minutes later, roughly 45 minutes after S.G.'s scream had first awakened DeVore. Lewis questioned S.G. alone in the kitchen. At trial, Lewis' summary of S.G.'s statement indicated that she had offered essentially the same story as she had first reported to DeVore and to Grigsby, including a statement that petitioner had "used his tongue on her in her private parts."

After Lewis concluded his investigation, and approximately four hours after DeVore first heard S.G.'s scream, S.G. was taken to the hospital. She was examined first by Cheryl Reents, an emergency room nurse, and then by Dr. Michael Meinzen. Each testified at trial, and their testimony indicated that, in response to questioning, S.G. again provided an account of events that was essentially identical to the one she had given to DeVore, Grigsby, and Lewis.

S.G. never testified at petitioner's trial. The State attempted on two occasions to call her as a witness, but she apparently experienced emotional difficulty on being brought to the courtroom and in each instance left without testifying. The defense made no attempt to call S.G. as a witness, and the trial court neither made, nor was asked to make, a finding that S.G. was unavailable to testify.

Petitioner objected on hearsay grounds to DeVore, Grigsby, Lewis, Reents, and Meinzen being permitted to testify regarding S.G.'s statements describing the assault. The trial court overruled each objection. With respect to DeVore, Grigsby, and Lewis the trial court concluded that the testimony could be permitted pursuant to an Illinois hearsay exception for spontaneous declarations. Petitioner's objections to Reents' and Meinzen's testimony was similarly overruled, based on both the spontaneous declaration exception and an exception for statements made in the course of securing medical treatment. . . .

Petitioner was found guilty by a jury, and the Illinois Appellate Court affirmed his conviction. . . . The Illinois Supreme Court denied discretionary review, and we granted certiorari.

. . . .

In [*Ohio v.*] *Roberts*, [448 U.S. 56 (1980),] we considered a Confrontation Clause challenge to the introduction at trial of a transcript containing testimony from a probable-cause hearing, where the transcript included testimony from a witness not produced at trial but who had been subject to examination by defendant's counsel at the probable-cause hearing. In the course of rejecting the Confrontation Clause claim in that case, we used language that might suggest that the Confrontation Clause generally requires that a declarant either be produced at trial or be found unavailable before his out-of-court statement may be admitted into evidence. However, we think such an expansive reading of the Clause is negated by our subsequent decision in [*United States v.*] *Inadi*, [475 U.S. 387 (1986)].

In *Inadi* we considered the admission of out-of-court statements made by a co-conspirator in the course of the conspiracy. As an initial matter, we rejected the proposition that Roberts established a rule that "no out-of-court statement would be admissible without a showing of unavailability." To the contrary, rather than establishing "a wholesale revision of the law of evidence" under the guise of the Confrontation Clause, we concluded that "*Roberts* must be read consistently with the question it answered, the authority it cited, and its own facts." So understood, *Roberts* stands for the proposition that unavailability analysis is a necessary part of the Confrontation Clause inquiry only when the challenged out-of-court statements were made in the course of a prior judicial proceeding.

Having clarified the scope of *Roberts*, the Court in *Inadi* then went on to reject the Confrontation Clause challenge presented there. In particular, we refused to extend the unavailability requirement established in *Roberts* to all out-of-court statements. Our decision rested on two factors. First, unlike former in-court testimony, co-conspirator statements "provide evidence of the conspiracy's context that cannot be replicated, even if the declarant testifies to the same matters in court." Also, given a declarant's likely change in status by the time the trial occurs, simply calling the declarant in the hope of having him repeat his prior out-of-court statements is a poor substitute for the full evidentiary significance that flows from statements made when the conspiracy is operating in full force.

Second, we observed that there is little benefit, if any, to be accomplished by imposing an "unavailability rule." Such a rule will not work to bar absolutely the introduction of the out-of-court statements; if the declarant either is unavailable, or is available and produced for trial, the statements can be introduced. . . . Many declarants will be subpoenaed by the prosecution or defense, regardless of any Confrontation Clause requirement, while the Compulsory Process Clause and evidentiary rules permitting a defendant to treat witnesses as hostile will aid defendants in obtaining a declarant's live testimony. And . . . an unavailability rule would . . . likely . . . impose substantial . . . burdens on the factfinding process. The prosecution would be required to repeatedly locate and keep continuously available each declarant, even when neither the prosecution nor the defense has any interest in calling the witness to the stand. An additional inquiry would be injected into the question of admissibility of evidence, to be litigated both at trial and on appeal.

These observations, although expressed in the context of evaluating co-conspirator statements, apply with full force to the case at hand. We note first that the evidentiary rationale for permitting hearsay testimony regarding spontaneous declarations and statements made in the course of receiving medical care is that such out-of-court declarations are made in contexts that provide substantial guarantees of their trustworthiness.[73] But those same factors that contribute to the statements' reliability cannot be recaptured even by later in-court testimony. A statement that has been offered in a moment of excitement — without the opportunity to reflect on the consequences of one's exclamation — may justifiably carry more weight with a trier of fact than a similar statement offered in the relative calm of the courtroom. Similarly, a statement made in the course of procuring medical services, where the declarant knows that a false statement may cause misdiagnosis or mistreatment, carries special guarantees of credibility that a trier of fact may not think replicated by courtroom testimony. They are thus materially different from the statements at issue in *Roberts*, where the out-of-court statements sought to be introduced were themselves made in the course of a judicial proceeding,

---

[73] [8] Indeed, it is this factor that has led us to conclude that "firmly rooted" exceptions carry sufficient indicia of reliability to satisfy the reliability requirement posed by the Confrontation Clause. *See* Idaho v. Wright, 497 U.S. 805, 817, 820–821 (1990). There can be no doubt that the two exceptions we consider in this case are "firmly rooted." The exception for spontaneous declarations is at least two centuries old, and may date to the late 17th century. It is currently recognized under Federal Rule of Evidence 803(2), and in nearly four-fifths of the States. The exception for statements made for purposes of medical diagnosis or treatment is similarly recognized in Federal Rule of Evidence 803(4), and is equally widely accepted among the States.

and where there was consequently no threat of lost evidentiary value if the out-of-court statements were replaced with live testimony.

The preference for live testimony in the case of statements like those offered in *Roberts* is because of the importance of cross-examination, "the greatest legal engine ever invented for the discovery of truth." Thus courts have adopted the general rule prohibiting the receipt of hearsay evidence. But where proffered hearsay has sufficient guarantees of reliability to come within a firmly rooted exception to the hearsay rule, the Confrontation Clause is satisfied.

We therefore think it clear that the out-of-court statements admitted in this case had substantial probative value, value that could not be duplicated simply by the declarant later testifying in court. To exclude such probative statements under the strictures of the Confrontation Clause would be the height of wrongheadedness, given that the Confrontation Clause has a basic purpose the promotion of the "integrity of the factfinding process." And as we have also noted, a statement that qualifies for admission under a "firmly rooted" hearsay exception is so trustworthy that adversarial testing can be expected to add little to its reliability. Given the evidentiary value of such statements, their reliability, and that establishing a generally applicable unavailability rule would have few practical benefits while imposing pointless litigation costs, we see no reason to treat the out-of-court statements in this case differently from those we found admissible in *Inadi*. . . .

As a second line of argument, petitioner presses upon us two recent decisions involving child testimony in child-sexual-assault cases, *Coy v. Iowa*, and *Maryland v. Craig*. Both *Coy* and *Craig* required us to consider the constitutionality of courtroom procedures designed to prevent a child witness from having to face across an open courtroom a defendant charged with sexually assaulting the child. In *Coy* we vacated a conviction that resulted from a trial in which a child witness testified from behind a screen, and in which there had been no particularized showing that such a procedure was necessary to avert a risk of harm to the child. In *Craig* we upheld a conviction that resulted from a trial in which a child witness testified via closed circuit television after such a showing of necessity. Petitioner draws from these two cases a general rule that hearsay testimony offered by a child should be permitted only upon a showing of necessity — *i.e.*, in cases where necessary to protect the child's physical and psychological well-being.

Petitioner's reliance is misplaced. *Coy* and *Craig* involved only the question of what in-court procedures are constitutionally required to guarantee a defendant's confrontation right once a witness is testifying. Such a question is quite separate from that of what requirements the Confrontation Clause imposes as a predicate for the introduction of out-of-court declarations. *Coy* and *Craig* did not speak to the latter question. As we recognized in *Coy*, the admissibility of hearsay statements raises concerns lying at the periphery of those that the Confrontation Clause is designed to address. There is thus no basis for importing the "necessity requirement" announced in those cases into the much different context of out-of-court declarations admitted under established exceptions to the hearsay rule.

Affirmed.

[The concurring opinion of JUSTICES THOMAS and SCALIA is omitted.]

————

NOTES AND QUESTIONS

1. The continued vitality of *White v. Illinois* was cast into doubt by the United States Supreme Court's decision in *Crawford v. Washington*, 541 U.S. 36 (2004). The Court in *Crawford*, explicitly abrogating *Ohio v. Roberts*' "indicia of reliability," held that the Confrontation Clause of the Sixth Amendment protects the criminally accused against the admission of out-of-court statements that are "testimonial" in nature, unless the declarant is unavailable and the defendant has had a prior opportunity for cross-examination, regardless of whether such statements are deemed reliable by the court. *Id.* at 68-69. The Court, while expressly declining to define "testimonial," did provide a non-exclusive list of examples of testimonial hearsay that included at a minimum "prior testimony at a preliminary hearing, before a grand jury, or at a former trial, and to police interrogations." *Id.* at 68. The *Crawford* Court hinted that nontestimonial hearsay might be outside the scope of the Confrontation Clause altogether, a possibility that *White* had rejected. *See* The Supreme Court, *2003 Term Leading Cases*, 118 HARV. L. REV. 316, 322 (2004).

While *Crawford* may call into question the *White* decision, the Court declined to expressly overrule it: "Although our analysis in [*Crawford*] casts doubt on [*White*], we need not definitively resolve whether it survives [*Crawford*]." 541 U.S. at 61. Nevertheless, the Court did cite *White* as "[o]ne case arguably in tension with the rule requiring a prior opportunity for cross-examination when the proffered statement is testimonial." *Id.* at 58, n8. Because *White* was not expressly overruled, "it is arguably still good law. . . . Furthermore, based on the Court's [footnote 8] it appears that *Crawford* represents a scaling-back of the use of excited utterances rather than an outright prohibition; *Crawford* recognizes the 'tension' between its cross-examination requirement and the past use of excited utterances." Celeste E. Byrom, Note, *The Use of the Excited Utterance Hearsay Exception in the Prosecution of Domestic Violence Cases After* Crawford v. Washington, 24 REV. LITIG. 409, 424 (2005).

Commentators disagree as to what extent, if any, *Crawford* may have overruled *White*. *See* Miguel A. Mendez, Essay, Crawford v. Washington: *A Critique*, 57 STAN. L. REV. 569, 580 (2004) (noting that *Crawford* "might overrule" *White*); Alexandra A. E. Shapiro & Noreen A. Kelly-Najah, Commentary, *Supreme Court Breathes New Life into the Confrontation Clause in* Crawford v. Washington, 14 ANDREWS' PROF. LIAB. LITIG. REP. 15, Oct. 2004, at 2 n3 (stating that although *Crawford* "clearly overrules *Roberts*, the court merely distinguishes subsequent cases such as *White*, *Lilly* and *Lee*, reasoning that the results of these cases have generally been faithful to the original meaning of the Confrontation Clause, even if their rationales were not"); Andrew King-Ries, Crawford v. Washington: *The End of Victimless Prosecution?*, 28 SEATTLE

U.L. Rev. 301, 317 & n121 (2005) (noting that the Court suggested that *White* is still good law while distinguishing *White* "by finding that *White* never reached the issue of whether spontaneous declarations were testimonial"); John F. Yetter, *Wrestling With* Crawford v. Washington *and the New Constitutional Law of Confrontation*, Fla. B.J., Oct. 2004, at 29 n27 (stating that "if the hearsay in *White* in fact contained a testimonial statement, then the result would have been directly in conflict with *Crawford*, and *White* should have been overruled. Nonetheless, these comments do comprehend that the excited utterance made to the police officer in *White* might have been a 'testimonial' statement and the Court certainly did not foreclose that result"); Tom Lininger, *Prosecuting Batterers After* Crawford, 91 Va. L. Rev. 747, 765, 777 (2005) (noting that dictum in *Crawford* "suggested that the Supreme Court had doubts about the continued vitality of *White*" and stating that "Justice Scalia's majority opinion went so far as to suggest, in dictum, that *White* may have been wrongly decided"); Maj. Robert Wm. Best, *Developments in the Sixth Amendment: Black Cats on Strolls*, Army Law., July 2004, at 55, 63 (noting that the Court "sought to downplay the *Crawford* decision's impact on such cases as *White*"); Byrom, *supra*, 24 Rev. Litig. at 419 (noting that the rule announced in *Crawford* "signals a surprising departure from the holdings of *Ohio v. Roberts* and *White* and yet the Court has left us with little guidance as to the implementation of the rule").

2. It is a widely held view among policy makers that children's statements about sexual abuse are generally trustworthy and that the circumstances of most abuse make admission of out-of-court statements necessary. Acting on these beliefs, many legislatures have enacted special statutory hearsay exceptions for statements of children alleging sexual abuse. For example, Minnesota law provides:

> Certain out-of-court statements admissible. An out-of-court statement made by a child under the age of ten years or a person who is mentally impaired as defined in § 609.341, subdivision 6, alleging, explaining, denying, or describing any act of sexual contact or penetration performed with or on the child or any act of physical abuse of the child or the person who is mentally impaired by another, not otherwise admissible by statute or rule of evidence, is admissible as substantive evidence if:
>
>> (a) the court or person authorized to receive evidence finds, in a hearing conducted outside of the presence of the jury, that the time, content, and circumstances of the statement and the reliability of the person to whom the statement is made provide sufficient indicia of reliability; and
>>
>> (b) the child or person mentally impaired as defined in § 609.341, subdivision 6, either:
>>
>>> (i) testifies at the proceedings; or
>>>
>>> (ii) is unavailable as a witness and there is corroborative evidence of the act: and
>>
>> (c) the proponent of the statement notifies the adverse party of the proponent's intention to offer the statement and the particulars

of the statement sufficiently in advance of the proceeding at which the proponent intends to offer the statement into evidence to provide the adverse party with a fair opportunity to prepare to meet the statement.

For purposes of this subdivision, an out-of-court statement includes video, audio, or other recorded statements. An unavailable witness includes an incompetent witness.

MINN. CODE ANN. § 595.02(3) (West 2005).

Are such statutes necessary after the Supreme Court decision in *Wright*? Should courts and policy makers pay more attention to Justice Scalia's observations in his *Craig* dissent:

> The "special" reasons that exist for suspending . . . the usual guarantees of reliability in the case of children's testimony are perhaps matched by "special" reasons for being particularly insistent upon [them] in the case of children's testimony. Some studies show that children are substantially more vulnerable to suggestion than adults, and often unable to separate recollected fantasy (or suggestion) from reality.

497 U.S. at 868 (Scalia J., dissenting).

For a discussion of the problem of interviewing child witnesses without creating undue suggestion, see Nancy E. Walker & Matthew Nguyen, *Interviewing the Child Witness: The Do's and the Don't's, the How's and the Why's*, 29 CREIGHTON L. REV. 1587 (1996). *See also* Nancy W. Perry et al., *When Lawyers Question Children Is Justice Served?* 19 LAW & HUM. BEHAV. 609 (1995).

3. For a thorough evaluation of the constitutionality of accommodations for child witnesses, see Robert P. Mosteller, *Remaking Confrontation Clause and Hearsay Doctrine Under the Challenge of Child Sexual Abuse Prosecutions*, 1993 U. ILL. L. REV. 691. *See also* Robert P. Mosteller, *Child Sexual Abuse and Statements for the Purpose of Medical Diagnosis or Treatment*, 67 N.C. L. REV. 257 (1989); Note, *The Testimony of Child Victims in Sex Abuse Prosecutions: Two Legislative Innovations*, 98 HARV. L. REV. 806 (1985). For a discussion of the Federal Child Victim's and Child Witness' Rights Statute, 18 U.S.C. § 3509 (1994), see Scott M. Smith, *Validity, Construction, and Application of Child Victims' and Child Witnesses' Rights Statute*, 121 A.L.R. FED. 631 (1994).

[D]   Child Abuse Reporting Statutes

As a feature of the heightened concern about child abuse, legislatures in all states have enacted statutes that impose duties upon certain persons or entities to report any abuse of which they know, suspect, or have reason to believe is occurring. The statutes typically require that reports be made to specified child protection agencies which must maintain central registries of abusers. Moreover, the statutes abrogate certain privileged communications and preclude tort actions against persons who in good faith make false accusations of abuse.

Statutorily obligated reporters who fail to report known or suspected abuse are themselves subject to criminal liability, although such failure is seldom prosecuted. Breach of the duty to report may also result in loss of employment or other non-criminal consequences for persons who deal with children on an on-going basis.

The first generation of statutes, initiated in the 1960's, applied reporting obligations only to physicians who came in contact with abused children. Legislators saw the medical profession, with its new-found ability to diagnose battered child syndrome, as uniquely privy to an awareness of the incidence of child abuse. After the initial wave of legislation, the categories of persons obligated to report have been expanded in all jurisdictions to include other persons who routinely have contact with children such as mental health professionals, nurses, dentists, teachers and other school personnel, social workers, law enforcement officials and day care providers. Approximately half the state statutes now extend the duty to report to *any* person.

CALIFORNIA PENAL CODE (2005)

§ 11165.7. Mandated reporter

(a) As used in this article, "mandated reporter" is defined as any of the following:

(1) A teacher.

(2) An instructional aide.

(3) A teacher's aide or teacher's assistant employed by any public or private school.

(4) A classified employee of any public school.

(5) An administrative officer or supervisor of child welfare and attendance, or a certificated pupil personnel employee of any public or private school.

(6) An administrator of a public or private day camp.

(7) An administrator or employee of a public or private youth center, youth recreation program, or youth organization.

(8) An administrator or employee of a public or private organization whose duties require direct contact and supervision of children.

(9) Any employee of a county office of education or the California Department of Education, whose duties bring the employee into contact with children on a regular basis.

(10) A licensee, an administrator, or an employee of a licensed community care or child day care facility.

(11) A Head Start program teacher.

(12) A licensing worker or licensing evaluator employed by a licensing agency as defined in § 11165.11.

(13) A public assistance worker.

(14) An employee of a child care institution, including, but not limited to, foster parents, group home personnel, and personnel of residential care facilities.

(15) A social worker, probation officer, or parole officer.

(16) An employee of a school district police or security department.

(17) Any person who is an administrator or presenter of, or a counselor in, a child abuse prevention program in any public or private school.

(18) A district attorney investigator, inspector, or family support officer unless the investigator, inspector, or officer is working with an attorney appointed . . . to . . . represent a minor.

(19) A peace officer, as defined in Chapter 4.5 . . . who is not otherwise described in this section.

(20) A firefighter, except for voluntary firefighters.

(21) A physician, surgeon, psychiatrist, psychologist, dentist, resident, intern, podiatrist, chiropractor, licensed nurse, dental hygienist, optometrist, marriage, family and child counselor, clinical social worker, or any other person who is currently licensed under Division 2 (commencing with § 500) of the Business and Professions Code.

(22) Any emergency medical technician I or II, paramedic, or other person certified pursuant to Division 2.5 (commencing with § 1798) of the Health and Safety Code.

(23) A psychological assistant registered pursuant to § 2913 of the Business and Professions Code.

(24) A marriage, family and child therapist trainee, as defined in subdivision (c) of § 4980.03 or the Business and Professions Code.

(25) An unlicenced marriage, family, and child therapist intern registered under § 4980.44 of the Business and Professions Code.

(26) A state or county public health employee who treats a minor for venereal disease or any other condition.

(27) A coroner.

(28) A medical examiner, or any other person who performs autopsies.

(29) A commercial film and photographic print processor, as specified in subdivision (e) of § 11166. As used in this article, "commercial film and photographic print processor" means any person who develops exposed photographic film into negatives, slides, or prints, or who makes prints from negatives or slides, for compensation. The term includes any employee of such a person; it does not include a person who develops film or makes prints for a public agency.

(30) A child visitation monitor. As used in this article, "child visitation monitor" means any person who, for financial compensation, acts as monitor of a visit between a child and any other person when the monitoring of that visit has been ordered by a court of law.

(31) An animal control officer or humane society officer. For the purposes of this article, the following terms have the following meanings.

(A) "Animal control officer" means any person employed by a city, county, or city and county for the purpose of enforcing animal control laws or regulations.

(B) "Humane society officer" means any person appointed or employed by a public or private entity as a humane officer who is qualified pursuant to § 14502 or 14503 or the Corporations Code.

(32) A clergy member, as specified in subdivision (c) of § 11166. As used in this article, "clergy member" means a priest, minister, rabbi, religious practitioner, or similar functionary of a church, temple, or recognized denomination or organization.

(33) Any custodian of records of a clergy member.

(34) Any employee of any police department, county sheriff's department, county probation department, or county welfare department.

(35) An employee or volunteer of a Court Appointed Special Advocate program, as defined [in the California Rules of Court].

(36) A custodial officer as defined in § 831.5.

(37) Any person providing services to a minor child under § 12300 or 12300.1 of the Welfare and Institutions Code.

(b) Except as provided in paragraph (35) of subdivision (a), volunteers of public or private organizations whose duties require direct contact with and supervision of children are not mandated reporters but are encouraged to obtain training in the identification and reporting of child abuse and neglect and are further encouraged to report known or suspected instances of child abuse or neglect to an agency specified in § 11165.9.

(c) Employers are strongly encouraged to provide their employees who are mandated reporters with training in the duties imposed by this article. This training shall include training in child abuse and neglect identification and training in child abuse and neglect reporting. Whether or not employers provide their employees with training in child abuse and neglect identification and reporting, the employers shall provide their employees who are mandated reporters with the statement required pursuant to subdivision (a) of § 11166.5.

(d) School districts that do not train their employees specified in subdivision (a) in the duties of mandated reporters under the child abuse reporting laws shall report to the State Department of Education the reasons why this training is not provided.

(e) Unless otherwise specifically provided, the absence of training shall not excuse a mandated reporter from the duties imposed by this article.

(f) Public and private organizations are encouraged to provide their volunteers whose duties require direct contact with and supervision of children with training in the identification and reporting of child abuse and neglect.

In *Cardwell,* the Tennessee court held that a minor 17 years, 7 months old was mature enough to consent to medical treatment. We note that in other jurisdictions, courts have ordered health care for minors over the objections of the minors' parents. These cases, however, involve minors who were younger than E.G. or the minor in *Cardwell.* Moreover, the issue in the above cases was not whether a minor could assert a right to control medical treatment decisions, but whether the minor's parents could refuse treatment on behalf of their child. Here, E.G. contends she was mature enough to have controlled her own health care. We find that she may have done so if indeed she would have been adjudged mature.

The trial judge must determine whether a minor is mature enough to make health care choices on her own. An exception to this, of course, is if the legislature has provided otherwise, as in the Consent by Minors to Medical Operations Act. We feel the intervention of a judge is appropriate for two reasons.

First, Illinois public policy values the sanctity of life. When a minor's health and life are at stake, this policy becomes a critical consideration. A minor may have a long and fruitful life ahead that an immature, foolish decision could jeopardize. Consequently, when the trial judge weighs the evidence in making a determination of whether a minor is mature enough to handle a health care decision, he must find proof of this maturity by clear and convincing evidence.

Second, the State has a *parens patriae* power to protect those incompetent to protect themselves. "[I]t is well-settled that the State as *parens patriae* has a special duty to protect minors and, if necessary, make vital decisions as to whether to submit a minor to necessary treatment where the condition is life threatening, as wrenching and distasteful as such actions may be." The State's *parens patriae* power pertaining to minors is strongest when the minor is immature and thus incompetent (lacking in capacity) to make these decisions on her own. The *parens patriae* authority fades, however, as the minor gets older and disappears upon her reaching adulthood. The State interest in protecting a mature minor in these situations will vary depending upon the nature of the medical treatment involved. Where the health care issues are potentially life threatening, the State's *parens patriae* interest is greater than if the health care matter is less consequential.

Therefore, the trial judge must weigh these two principles against the evidence he receives of a minor's maturity. If the evidence is clear and convincing that the minor is mature enough to appreciate the consequences of her actions, and that the minor is mature enough to exercise the judgment of an adult, then the mature minor doctrine affords her the common law right to consent to or refuse medical treatment. This common law right is not absolute. The right must be balanced against four State interests: (1) the preservation of life; (2) protecting the interests of third parties; (3) prevention of suicide; and (4) maintaining the ethical integrity of the medical profession. Of these four concerns, protecting the interests of third parties is clearly the most significant here. The principal third parties in these cases would be parents, guardians, adult siblings, and other relatives. If a parent or guardian opposes an unemancipated mature minor's refusal to consent to treatment for a life-threatening health problem, this opposition would weigh heavily against the minor's right to refuse. In this case, for example, had E.G. refused the transfusions *against* the wishes of her mother, then the court would have given serious consideration to her mother's desires.

Nevertheless, in this case both E.G. and her mother agreed that E.G. should turn down the blood transfusions. They based this refusal primarily on religious grounds, contending that the first amendment free exercise clause entitles a mature minor to decline medical care when it contravenes sincerely held religious beliefs. Because we find that a mature minor may exercise a common law right to consent to or refuse medical care, we decline to address the constitutional issue.

The final issue we must address is whether the finding of neglect entered against Rosie Denton, E.G.'s mother, should stand. If the trial judge had ruled that E.G. was a mature minor, then no finding of neglect would be proper. Although the trial judge was impressed with E.G.'s maturity and sincerity, the judge did not explicitly hold that E.G. was a mature minor. The trial judge, guided only by the law as it existed prior to this opinion, rightly felt that he must protect the minor's health and well-being. This case is one of first impression with this court. Therefore, the trial judge had no precedent upon which to base a mature minor finding. Because E.G. is no longer a minor, nothing would be gained by remanding this case back to the trial court for an explicit determination of E.G.'s maturity. Nevertheless, since the trial judge did not have any clear guidance on the mature minor doctrine, we believe that the finding of neglect should not stand. Accordingly, we affirm the appellate court in part and reverse in part, and remand this case to the circuit court of Cook County for the sole purpose of expunging the finding of neglect against Denton.

Appellate court affirmed in part and reversed in part;
circuit court reversed; case remanded with directions.

JUSTICE WARD, *dissenting*:

I must respectfully dissent. I consider the majority has made an unfortunate choice of situations to announce, in what it calls a case of first impression, that a minor may with judicial approval reject medical treatment, even if the minor's death will be a medically certain consequence. The majority cites decisions where a minor was permitted to exercise what was called a common law right to consent to medical treatment. The safeguarding of health and the preservation of life are obviously different conditions from one in which a minor will be held to have a common law right, as the majority puts it, to refuse medical treatment and sometimes in effect take his own life. That violates the ancient responsibility of the State as *parens patriae* to protect minors and to decide for them, as the majority describes, vital questions, including whether to consent to or refuse necessary medical treatment. . . .

Unless the legislature for specific purposes provides for a different age, a minor is one who has not attained legal age. It is not disputed that E.G. has not attained legal age. It is fundamental that where language is clear there is no need to seek to interpret or depart from the plain language and meaning and read into what is clear exceptions or limitations. The majority nevertheless would in effect define a minor in these grave situations to be one who has not attained legal age unless it is a "mature" minor who is involved. If so this protection that the law gives minors has been lost and the child may make his own decision even at the cost of his life. The majority acknowledges that this is a case of first impression. It may now be critically described by some as a holding without precedent. I point out again that this is not a holding where consent to treatment is the question but rather a unique one where a minor's injury or very self-destruction may be involved.

I am sure that in a host of matters of far lesser importance it would not be held that a minor however mature could satisfy a requirement of being of legal age. It would not be held that a minor was eligible to vote, to obtain a driver's or a pilot's license, or to enlist in one of the armed services before attaining enlistment age.

The trial court appointed a guardian to consent to transfusions for the minor. The appellate court reversed as to this, stating the minor was a mature minor. This court affirms the appellate court in this regard but does not attempt to state a standard by which "mature" is to be measured by judges in making these important findings.

. . . .

NOTES AND QUESTIONS

1. The *D.L.E.* court interpreted a statute exempting "spiritual treatment" as a sufficient ground for neglect where a child might benefit from medical care. What position would (should?) the court take if the child's life was in "imminent danger" for want of medical care rejected by guardians administering "spiritual" healing?

2. Is a statutory exemption for faith healing in neglect provisions necessary in light of First Amendment protections for religious freedom? Is such an exemption wise as a policy matter? For a case interpreting a statute similar to the Colorado statute in *D.L.E.*, see *Newmark v. Williams*, 588 A.2d 1108 (Del. 1991).

3. The *E.G.* case considers the issue whether "mature minors" should be permitted to refuse necessary medical treatment. In a dissenting opinion in *E.G.* omitted by the authors, Justice Clark observed:

> The majority states that '[t]he paramount issue raised by this appeal is whether [an allegedly mature] minor like E.G. has a right to refuse medical treatment.' The majority recognizes that the issue in '[t]his cases is one of first impression with this court. In fact, this case is almost one of first impression in this *country*. Neither the majority opinion nor the parties to this appeal cite any case which has addressed the issue of a minor's right to refuse treatment. The only case that I am aware of that has addressed a comparable issue is *In re D.P.* (Santa Clara County (Cal.) Juv. Ct. July 3, 1986), No. 91950, a California juvenile court proceeding that is cited in the *amicus curiae*

brief filed in this case by the Watchtower Bible and Tract Society of New York, Inc.

549 N.E.2d at 329–30 (Clark, J., dissenting). Given such paucity of existing authority, is the *E.G.* majority on firm ground in recognizing a right to refuse treatment?

Note, however, that at the time of *E.G.*, some case authority did exist for the (analogous?) proposition that "mature minors" could validly consent to non-necessary medical treatment. *See, e.g., Younts v. St. Francis Hosp. & School of Nursing, Inc.,* 469 P.2d 330 (Kan. 1970) (seventeen-year-old minor "was mature enough" to consent to a skin graft from her forearm to repair an injured finger); *Lacy v. Laird,* 139 N.E.2d 25, 34 (Ohio 1956) (trial court erred in finding that an eighteen-year-old could not consent to a "simple" surgical procedure to reshape her nose).

4. The *E.G.* majority refers to United States Supreme Court case law granting a variety of constitutional rights to minors. Do such cases compel recognition of a "mature minor's" right to refuse treatment? Consider the following observation of the Court in the case immediately following: "Most children, even in adolescence, simply are not able to make sound judgments concerning many decisions, including their need for medical care or treatment. Parents can and must make those judgments." *Parham v. J.R.,* 442 U.S. 584, 603 (1979).

[B] Mental Health

PARHAM v. J.R.

Supreme Court of the United States
442 U.S. 584 (1979)

Mr. Chief Justice Burger *delivered the opinion of the Court.*

The question presented in this appeal is what process is constitutionally due a minor child whose parents or guardian seek state administered institutional mental health care for the child and specifically whether an adversary proceeding is required prior to or after the commitment.

I

(a) Appellee J.R., a child being treated in a Georgia state mental hospital, was a plaintiff in this class action based on 42 U.S.C. § 1983, in the District Court for the Middle District of Georgia. Appellants are the State's Commissioner of the Department of Human Resources, the Director of the Mental Health Division of the Department of Human Resources, and the Chief Medical Officer at the hospital where appellee was being treated. Appellee sought a declaratory judgment that Georgia's voluntary commitment procedures for children under the age of 18, Ga. Code §§ 88-503.1, 88-503.2 (1975),[86] violated the Due Process Clause of the Fourteenth Amendment and requested an injunction against their future enforcement.

. . . [T]he District Court held that Georgia's statutory scheme was unconstitutional because it failed to protect adequately the appellees' due process rights. . . .

To remedy this violation, the court enjoined future commitments based on the procedures in the Georgia statute. It also commanded Georgia to appropriate and expend whatever amount was "reasonably necessary" to provide nonhospital facilities deemed by the appellant state officials to be the most appropriate for the treatment of those members of plaintiffs' class who could be treated in a less drastic, nonhospital environment. . . .

. . . .

(b) J.L., a plaintiff before the District Court who is now deceased, was admitted in 1970 at the age of six years to Central State Regional Hospital in Milledgeville, GA. Prior to this admission, J.L. had received out-patient treatment at the hospital for over two months. J. L.'s mother then requested the hospital to admit him indefinitely.

The admitting physician interviewed J.L. and his parents. He learned that J.L.'s natural parents had divorced and his mother had remarried. He also learned that J.L. had been expelled from school because he was uncontrollable. He accepted the parents' representation that the boy had been extremely aggressive and diagnosed the child as having a "hyperkinetic reaction of childhood."

J.L.'s mother and stepfather agreed to participate in family therapy during the time their son was hospitalized. Under this program, J.L. was permitted to go home for short stays. Apparently his behavior during these visits was erratic. After several months, the parents requested discontinuance of the program.

In 1972, the child was returned to his mother and stepfather on a furlough basis, *i.e.*, he would live at home but go to school at the hospital. The parents found they were unable to control J.L. to their satisfaction, and this created family stress. Within two months, they requested his readmission to Central State. J.L.'s parents relinquished their parental rights to the county in 1974.

Although several hospital employees recommended that J.L. should be placed in a special foster home with "a warm, supported, truly involved

---

[86] [3] Section 88-503.1 provides:

> The superintendent of any facility may receive for observation and diagnosis . . . any individual under 18 years of age for whom such application is made by his parent or guardian. . . . If found to show evidence of mental illness and to be suitable for treatment, such person may be given care and treatment at such facility and such person may be detained by such facility for such period and under such conditions as may be authorized by law.

Section 88-503.2 provides:

> The superintendent of the facility shall discharge any voluntary patient who has recovered from his mental illness or who has sufficiently improved that the superintendent that hospitalization of the patient is no longer desireable.

couple," the Department of Family and Children Services was unable to place him in such a setting. On October 24, 1975, J.L. (with J.R.) filed this suit requesting an order of the court placing him in a less drastic environment suitable to his needs.

(c) Appellee J.R. was declared a neglected child by the county and removed from his natural parents when he was three months old. He was placed in seven different foster homes in succession prior to his admission to Central State Hospital at the age of seven.

Immediately preceding his hospitalization, J.R. received outpatient treatment at a county mental health center for several months. He then began attending school where he was so disruptive and incorrigible that he could not conform to normal behavior patterns. Because of his abnormal behavior, J.R.'s seventh set of foster parents requested his removal from their home. The Department of Family and Children Services then sought his admission at Central State. The agency provided the hospital with a complete sociomedical history at the time of his admission. In addition, three separate interviews were conducted with J.R. by the admission team of the hospital.

It was determined that he was borderline retarded, and suffered an "unsocialized, aggressive reaction of childhood." It was recommended unanimously that he would "benefit from the structured environment" of the hospital and would "enjoy living and playing with boys of the same age."

J.R.'s progress was re-examined periodically. In addition, unsuccessful efforts were made by the Department of Family and Children Services during his stay at the hospital to place J.R. in various foster homes. On October 24, 1975, J. R. (with J.L.) filed this suit requesting an order of the court placing him in a less drastic environment suitable to his needs.

(d) GEORGIA CODE § 88-503.1 (1975) provides for the voluntary admission to a state regional hospital of children such as J.L. and J.R. Under that provision, admission begins with an application for hospitalization signed by a "parent or guardian." Upon application, the superintendent of each hospital is given the power to admit temporarily any child for "observation and diagnosis." If, after observation, the superintendent finds "evidence of mental illness" and that the child is "suitable for treatment" in the hospital, then the child may be admitted "for such period and under such conditions as may be authorized by law."

Georgia's mental health statute also provides for the discharge of voluntary patients. Any child who has been hospitalized for more than five days may be discharged at the request of a parent or guardian. Section 88-503.3(a) (1975). Even without a request for discharge, however, the superintendent of each regional hospital has an affirmative duty to release any child "who has sufficiently improved that the superintendent determines that hospitalization of the patient is no longer desirable." Section 88-503.2 (1975).

Georgia's Mental Health Director has not published any statewide regulations defining what specific procedures each superintendent must employ when admitting a child under eighteen. Instead, each regional hospital's superintendent is responsible for the procedures in his or her facility. There is substantial variation among the institutions with regard to their admission procedures and their procedures for review of patients after they have been admitted. [The Court proceeded to provide a brief description of the different hospitals' procedures.]

. . . .

Although most of the focus of the District Court was on the State's mental hospitals, it is relevant to note that Georgia presently funds over fifty community mental health clinics and thirteen specialized foster care homes. The State has built seven new regional hospitals within the past fifteen years, and it has added a new children's unit to its oldest hospital. The state budget in fiscal year 1976 was almost $150 million for mental health care. Georgia ranks 22nd among the states in per capita expenditures for mental health and 15th in total expenditures.

The District Court nonetheless rejected the State's entire system of providing mental health care on both procedural and substantive grounds. The District Court found that forty-six children could be "optimally cared for in another, less restrictive, non-hospital setting if it were available." . . . These "optimal" settings included group homes, therapeutic camps, and home-care services. [The testimony of state officials] expressed confidence in the Georgia program and informed the court that the State could not justify enlarging its budget during fiscal year 1977 to provide the specialized treatment settings urged by appellees in addition to those then available.

. . . .

II

In holding unconstitutional Georgia's statutory procedure for voluntary commitment of juveniles, the District Court first determined that commitment to any of the eight regional hospitals constitutes a severe deprivation of a child's liberty. The court defined this liberty interest in terms of both freedom from bodily restraint and freedom from the "emotional and psychic harm" caused by the institutionalization.[87] Having determined that a liberty interest is implicated by a child's admission to a mental hospital, the court considered what process is required to protect that interest. It held that the process due "includes at least the right after notice to be heard before an impartial tribunal." . . .

In requiring the prescribed hearing, the court rejected Georgia's argument that no adversary-type hearing was required since the State was merely assisting parents who could not afford private care by making available treatment similar to that offered in private hospitals and by private physicians. The court acknowledged that most parents who seek to have their children admitted to a state mental hospital do so in good faith. It, however, relied on one of appellees' witnesses who expressed an opinion that "some still

---

[87] [7] In both respects, the District Court found strong support for its holding in this Court's decision in In re Gault, 387 U.S. 1 (1967). In that decision, we held that a state cannot institutionalize a juvenile delinquent without first providing certain due process protections.

look upon mental hospitals as a 'dumping ground.' " . . .[88] No specific evidence of such "dumping," however, can be found in the record.

The District Court also rejected the argument that review by the superintendents of the hospitals and their staffs was sufficient to protect the child's liberty interest. The court held that the inexactness of psychiatry, coupled with the possibility that the sources of information used to make the commitment decision may not always be reliable, made the superintendent's decision too arbitrary to satisfy due process. The court then shifted its focus drastically from what was clearly a procedural due process analysis to what appears to be a substantive due process analysis and condemned Georgia's "officialdom" for its failure, in the face of a state-funded 1973 report outlining the "need" for additional resources to be spent on nonhospital treatment, to provide more resources for noninstitutional mental health care. The court concluded that there was a causal relationship between this intransigence and the State's ability to provide any "inflexible due process" to the appellees. The District Court therefore ordered the State to appropriate and expend such resources as would be necessary to provide nonhospital treatment to those members of appellees' class who would benefit from it.

III

In an earlier day, the problems inherent in coping with children afflicted with mental or emotional abnormalities were dealt with largely within the family. . . . Increasingly, [parents] turned for assistance to local, public sources or private charities. Until recently, most of the states did little more than provide custodial institutions for the confinement of persons who were considered dangerous. . . .

. . . Ironically, as most states have expanded their efforts to assist the mentally ill, their actions have been subjected to increasing litigation and heightened constitutional scrutiny. Courts have been required to resolve the thorny constitutional attacks on state programs and procedures with limited precedential guidance. . . .

The parties agree that our prior holdings have set out a general approach for testing challenged state procedures under a due process claim. Assuming the existence of a protectible property or liberty interest, the Court has required a balancing of a number of factors:

> First, the private interest that will be affected by the official action; second, the risk of an erroneous deprivation of such interest through the procedures used, and the probable value, if any, of additional or substitute procedural safeguards; and finally, the Government's interest, including the function involved and the fiscal and administrative burdens that the additional or substitute procedural requirement would entail. . . .

---

[88] [8] In light of the District Court's holding that a judicial or quasi-judicial body should review voluntary commitment decisions, it is at least interesting to note that the witness who made the statement quoted in the text was not referring to parents as the people who "dump" children into hospitals. This witness opined that some juvenile court judges and child welfare agencies misused the hospitals. . . .

In applying these criteria, we must consider first the child's interest in not being committed. Normally, however, since this interest is inextricably linked with the parents' interest in and obligation for the welfare and health of the child, the private interest at stake is a combination of the child's and parents' concerns. Next, we must examine the State's interest in the procedures it has adopted for commitment and treatment of children. Finally, we must consider how well Georgia's procedures protect against arbitrariness in the decision to commit a child to a state mental hospital.

(a) It is not disputed that a child, in common with adults, has a substantial liberty interest in not being confined unnecessarily for medical treatment and that the state's involvement in the commitment decision constitutes state action under the Fourteenth Amendment. . . . We also recognize that commitment sometimes produces adverse social consequences for the child because of the reaction of some to the discovery that the child has received psychiatric care. . . .

This reaction, however, need not be equated with the community response resulting from being labeled by the state as delinquent, criminal, or mentally ill and possibly dangerous. . . . The state through its voluntary commitment procedures does not "label" the child; it provides a diagnosis and treatment that medical specialists conclude the child requires. In terms of public reaction, the child who exhibits abnormal behavior may be seriously injured by an erroneous decision not to commit. Appellees overlook a significant source of the public reaction to the mentally ill, for what is truly "stigmatizing" is the symptomatology of a mental or emotional illness. . . . The pattern of untreated, abnormal behavior — even if nondangerous — arouses at least as much negative reaction as treatment that becomes public knowledge. A person needing, but not receiving, appropriate medical care may well face even greater social ostracism resulting from the observable symptoms of an untreated disorder.

However, we need not decide what effect these factors might have in a different case. For purposes of this decision, we assume that a child has a protectible interest not only in being free of unnecessary bodily restraints but also in not being labeled erroneously by some persons because of an improper decision by the state hospital superintendent.

(b) We next deal with the interests of the parents who have decided, on the basis of their observations and independent professional recommendations, that their child needs institutional care. Appellees argue that the constitutional rights of the child are of such magnitude and the likelihood of parental abuse is so great that the parents' traditional interests in and responsibility for the upbringing of their child must be subordinated at least to the extent of providing a formal adversary hearing prior to a voluntary commitment.

Our jurisprudence historically has reflected Western civilization concepts of the family as a unit with broad parental authority over minor children. Our cases have consistently followed that course; our constitutional system long ago rejected any notion that a child is "the mere creature of the State" and, on the contrary, asserted that parents generally "have the right, coupled with the high duty, to recognize and prepare [their children] for additional obligations." *Pierce v. Society of Sisters,* 268 U.S. 510, 535 (1925). *See also, Wisconsin v. Yoder,* 406 U.S. 205 (1972); *Prince v. Massachusetts,* 321 U.S. 158 (1944); *Meyer v. Nebraska,* 262 U.S. 390 (1923). Surely, this includes a "high duty" to recognize symptoms of illness and to seek and follow medical advice. The law's concept of the family rests on a presumption that parents possess what a child lacks in maturity, experience, and capacity for judgment required for making life's difficult decisions. More important, historically it has recognized that natural bonds of affection lead parents to act in the best interests of their children. . . .

As with so many other legal presumptions, experience and reality may rebut what the law accepts as a starting point; the incidence of child neglect and abuse cases attests to this. . . . [S]ome parents "may at times be acting against the interests of their children". . . . [This] creates a basis for caution, but is hardly a reason to discard wholesale those pages of human experience that teach that parents generally do act in the child's best interests. . . . The statist notion that governmental power should supersede parental authority in all cases because some parents abuse and neglect children is repugnant to American tradition.

Nonetheless, we have recognized that a state is not without constitutional control over parental discretion in dealing with children when their physical or mental health is jeopardized. *See Wisconsin v. Yoder,* 406 U.S., at 230; *Prince v. Massachusetts,* 321 U.S., at 166. Moreover, the Court recently declared unconstitutional a state statute that granted parents an absolute veto over a minor child's decision to have an abortion. *Planned Parenthood of Central Missouri v. Danforth,* 428 U.S. 52 (1976). Appellees urge that these precedents limiting the traditional rights of parents, if viewed in the context of the liberty interest of the child and the likelihood of parental abuse, require us to hold that the parents' decision to have a child admitted to a mental hospital must be subjected to an exacting constitutional scrutiny, including a formal, adversary, pre-admission hearing.

Appellees' argument, however, sweeps too broadly. Simply because the decision of a parent is not agreeable to a child or because it involves risks does not automatically transfer the power to make that decision from the parents to some agency or officer of the state. The same characterizations can be made for a tonsillectomy, appendectomy, or other medical procedure. Most children, even in adolescence, simply are not able to make sound judgments concerning many decisions, including their need for medical care or treatment. Parents can and must make those judgments. Here, there is no finding by the District Court of even a single instance of bad faith by any parent of any member of appellees' class. We cannot assume that the result in *Meyer v. Nebraska*, and *Pierce v. Society of Sisters*, would have been different if the children there had announced a preference to learn only English or a prefer-ence to go to a public, rather than a church, school. The fact that a child may balk at hospitalization or complain about a parental refusal to provide cosmetic surgery does not diminish the parents' authority to decide what is best for the child. . . . Neither state officials nor federal courts are equipped to review such parental decisions.

Appellees place particular reliance on *Planned Parenthood*, arguing that its holding indicates how little deference to parents is appropriate when the child is exercising a constitutional right. The basic situation in that case, however, was very different; *Planned Parenthood* involved an absolute parental veto over the child's ability to obtain an abortion. Parents in Georgia in no sense have an absolute right to commit their children to state mental hospitals; the statute requires the superintendent of each regional hospital to exercise independent judgment as to the child's need for confinement. . . .

In defining the respective rights and prerogatives of the child and parent in the voluntary commitment setting, we conclude that our precedents permit the parents to retain a substantial, if not the dominant, role in the decision, absent a finding of neglect or abuse, and that the traditional presumption that the parents act in the best interests of their child should apply. We also conclude, however, that the child's rights and the nature of the commitment decision are such that parents cannot always have absolute and unreviewable discretion to decide whether to have a child institutionalized. They, of course, retain plenary authority to seek such care for their children, subject to a physician's independent examination and medical judgment.

(c) The State obviously has a significant interest in confining the use of its costly mental health facilities to cases of genuine need. The Georgia program seeks first to determine whether the patient seeking admission has an illness that calls for inpatient treatment. To accomplish this purpose, the State has charged the superintendents of each regional hospital with the responsibility for determining, before authorizing an admission, whether a prospective patient is mentally ill and whether the patient will likely benefit from hospital care. In addition, the State has imposed a continuing duty on hospital superintendents to release any patient who has recovered to the point where hospitalization is no longer needed.

The State is performing its voluntarily assumed mission also has a significant interest in not imposing unnecessary procedural obstacles that may discourage the mentally ill or their families from seeking needed psychiatric assistance. The *parens patriae* interest in helping parents care for the mental health of their children cannot be fulfilled if the parents are unwilling to take advantage of the opportunities because the admission process is too onerous, too embarrassing, or too contentious. It is surely not idle to speculate as to how many parents who believe they are acting in good faith would forgo state-provided hospital care if such care is contingent on participation in an adversary proceeding designed to probe their motives and other private family matters in seeking the voluntary admission.

The State also has a genuine interest in allocating priority to the diagnosis and treatment of patients as soon as they are admitted to a hospital rather than to time-consuming procedural minutes before the admission. One factor that must be considered is the utilization of the time of psychiatrists, psychologists, and other behavioral specialists in preparing for and participating in hearings rather than performing the task for which their special training has fitted them. Behavioral experts in courtrooms and hearings are of little help to patients.

The amici brief of the American Psychiatric Association points out . . . that the average staff psychiatrist in a hospital presently is able to devote only 47 percent of his time to direct patient care. One consequence of increasing the procedures the state must provide prior to a child's voluntary admission will be that mental health professionals will be diverted even more from the treatment of patients in order to travel to and participate in — and wait for — what could be hundreds — or even thousands — of hearings each year. Obviously the cost of these procedures would come from the public moneys the legislature intended for mental health care. . . .

(d) We now turn to consideration of what process protects adequately the child's constitutional rights by reducing risks of error without unduly trenching on traditional parental authority without undercutting "efforts to further the legitimate interest of both the state and the patient that are served by" voluntary commitments. . . . We conclude that the risk of error inherent in the parental decision to have a child institutionalized for mental health care is sufficiently great that some kind of inquiry should be made by a "neutral factfinder" to determine whether the statutory requirements for admission are satisfied. . . . That inquiry must carefully probe the child's background using all available sources, including, but not limited to, parents, schools, and other social agencies. Of course, the review must also include an interview with the child. It is necessary that the decisionmaker have the authority to refuse to admit any child who does not satisfy the medical standards for admission. Finally, it is necessary that the child's continuing need for commitment be reviewed periodically by a similarly independent procedure.

We are satisfied that such procedures will protect the child from an erroneous admission decision in a way that neither unduly burdens the states nor inhibits parental decisions to seek state help.

Due process has never been thought to require that the neutral and detached trier of fact be law trained or a judicial or administrative officer. . . . Surely, this is the case as to medical decisions, for "neither judges nor administrative hearing officers are better qualified than psychiatrists to render psychiatric judgments." . . . Thus, a staff physician will suffice, so long as he or she is free to evaluate independently the child's mental and emotional condition and need for treatment.

It is not necessary that the deciding physician conduct a formal or quasiformal, hearing. A state is free to require such a hearing, but due process is not violated by use of informal traditional medical investigative techniques. Since well-established medical procedures already exist, we do not undertake to outline with specificity precisely what this investigation must involve. The mode and procedure of medical diagnostic procedures is not the business of judges. What is best for a child is an individual medical decision that must be left to the judgment of physicians in each case. We do no more than emphasize that the decision would represent an independent judgment of what the child requires and that all sources of information that are traditionally relied on by physicians and behavioral specialists should be consulted.

What process in constitutionally due cannot be divorced from the nature of the ultimate decision that is being made. Not every determination by state officers can be made most effectively by use of "the procedural tools of judicial or administrative decisionmaking." . . .

Here, the questions are essentially medical in character: whether the child is mentally or emotionally ill and whether he can benefit from the treatment that is provided by the state. While facts are plainly necessary for a proper resolution of those questions, they are only a first step in the process. . . . [T]he determination of "whether [a person] is mentally ill turns on the meaning of the facts which must be interpreted by expert psychiatrists and psychologists."

Although we acknowledge the fallibility of medical and psychiatric diagnosis, . . . we do not accept the notion that the shortcomings of specialists can always be avoided by shifting the decision from a trained specialist using the traditional tools of medical science to an untrained judge or administrative hearing officer after a judicial-type hearing. Even after a hearing, the nonspecialist decisionmaker must make a medical-psychiatric decision. Common human experience and scholarly opinions suggest that the supposed protections of an adversary proceeding to determine the appropriateness of medical decisions for the commitment and treatment of mental and emotional illness may well be more illusory than real. . . .

Another problem with requiring a formalized, factfinding hearings lies in the danger it poses for significant intrusion into the parent-child relationship. Pitting the parents and child as adversaries often will be at odds with the presumption that parents act in the best interest of their child. It is one thing to require a neutral physician to make a careful review of the parents' decision in order to make sure it is proper from a medical standpoint; it is a wholly different matter to employ an adversary contest to ascertain whether the parents' motivation is consistent with the child's interests.

Moreover, it is appropriate to inquire into how such a hearing would contribute to the successful long-range treatment of the patient. Surely, there is a risk that it would exacerbate whatever tensions already exist between the child and the parents. Since the parents can and usually do play a significant role in the treatment while the child is hospitalized and even more so after release, there is a serious risk that an adversary confrontation will adversely affect the ability of the parents to assist the child while in the hospital. Moreover, it will make this subsequent return home more difficult. These unfortunate results are especially critical with an emotionally disturbed child; they seem likely to occur in the context of an adversary hearing in which the parents testify. A confrontation over such intimate family relationships would distress the normal adult parents and the impact on a disturbed child almost would be significantly greater.[89]

---

[89] [18] While not altogether clear, the District Court opinion apparently contemplated a hearing preceded by a written notice of the proposed commitment. At the hearing the child presumably would be given an opportunity to be heard and present evidence, and the right to cross-examine witnesses, including, of course, the parents. The court also required an impartial trier of fact who would render a written decision reciting the reasons for accepting or rejecting the parental application.

Since the parents in this situation are seeking the child's admission to the state institution, the procedure contemplated by the District Court presumably would call for some other person to be designated as a guardian *ad litem* to act for the child. The guardian, in turn, if not a lawyer, would be empowered to retain counsel to act as an advocate of the child's interest.

Of course, a state may elect to provide such adversary hearings in situations where it perceives that parents and a child may be at odds, but nothing in the Constitution compels such procedures.

It has been suggested that a hearing conducted by someone other than the admitting physician is necessary in order to detect instances where parents are "guilty of railroading their children into asylums" or are using "voluntary commitment procedures in order to sanction behavior of which they disapprov-[e]." . . . Curiously, it seems to be taken for granted that parents who seek to "dump" their children on the state will inevitably be able to conceal their motives and thus deceive the admitting psychiatrists and the other mental health professionals who make and review the admission decision. It is elementary that one early diagnostic inquiry into the cause of an emotional disturbance of a child is an examination into the environment of the child. It is unlikely, if not inconceivable, that a decision to abandon an emotionally normal, heathy child and thrust him into an institution will be a discrete act leaving no trail of circumstances. Evidence of such conflicts will emerge either in the interviews or from secondary sources. It is unrealistic to believe that trained psychiatrists, skilled in eliciting responses, sorting medically relevant facts, and sensing motivational nuances will often be deceived about the family situation surrounding a child's emotional disturbance.[90] Surely a lay, or even law-trained, factfinder would be no more skilled in this process than the professional.

By expressing some confidence in the medical decisionmaking process, we are by no means suggesting it is error free. On occasion, parents may initially mislead an admitting physician or a physician may erroneously diagnose the child as needing institutional care either because of negligence or an over-abundance of caution. That there may be risks of error in the process affords no rational predicate for holding unconstitutional an entire statutory and administrative scheme that is generally followed in more than 30 states.

"[P]rocedural due process rules are shaped by the risk of error inherent in the truth-finding process as applied to the generality of cases, not the rare exceptions." . . . In general, we are satisfied that an independent medical decisionmaking process, which includes the thorough psychiatric investigation described earlier, followed by additional periodic review of a child's condition, will protect children who should not be admitted; we do not believe the risks of error in that process would be significantly reduced by a more formal, judicial-type hearing. The issue remains whether the Georgia practices, as described in the record before us, comport with these minimum due process requirements.

(e) Georgia's statute envisions a careful diagnostic medical inquiry to be conducted by the admitting physician at each regional hospital. The amicus brief for the United States explains: "[I]n every instance the decision whether or not to accept the child for treatment is made by a physician employed by the State. . . . "That decision is based on interviews and recommendations by hospital or community health center staff. The staff interviews the child

---

[90] [19] In evaluating the problem of detecting "dumping" by parents, it is important to keep in mind that each of the regional hospitals has a continuing relationship with the Department of Family and Children Services. The staffs at those hospitals refer cases to the Department when they suspect a child is being mistreated and thus are sensitive to this problem. In fact, J.L.'s situation is in point. The family conflicts and problems were well documented in the hospital records. Equally well documented, however, were the child's severe emotional disturbances and his need for treatment.

and the parent or guardian who brings the child to the facility . . . [and] attempts are made to communicate with other possible sources of information about the child. . . ." Focusing primarily on what it saw as the absence of any formal mechanism for review of the physician's initial decision, the District Court unaccountably saw the medical decision as an exercise of "unbridled discretion." . . . But extravagant characterizations are no substitute for careful analysis, and we must examine the Georgia process in its setting to determine if, indeed, any one person exercises such discretion.

In the typical case, the parents of a child initially conclude from the child's behavior that there is some emotional problem — in short, that "something is wrong." They may respond to the problem in various ways, but generally the first contact with the State occurs when they bring the child to be examined by a psychologist or psychiatrist at a community mental health clinic.

Most often, the examination is followed by outpatient treatment at the community clinic. In addition, the child's parents are encouraged, and sometimes required, to participate in a family therapy program to obtain a better insight into the problem. In most instances, this is all the care a child requires. However, if, after a period of outpatient care, the child's abnormal emotional condition persists, he may be referred by the local clinic staff to an affiliated regional mental hospital.

At the regional hospital an admissions team composed of a psychiatrist and at least one other mental health professional examines and interviews the child — privately in most instances. This team then examines the medical records provided by the clinic staff and interviews the parents. Based on this information, and any additional background that can be obtained, the admissions team makes a diagnosis and determines whether the child will likely benefit from institutionalized care. If the team finds either condition not met, admission is refused.

If the team admits a child as suited for hospitalization, the child's condition and continuing need for hospital care are reviewed periodically by at least one independent, medical review group. For the most part, the reviews are as frequent as weekly, but none are less often than once every two months.

Moreover, as we noted earlier, the superintendent of each hospital is charged with an affirmative statutory duty to discharge any child who is no longer mentally ill or in need of therapy.

As with most medical procedures, Georgia's are not totally free from risk of error in the sense that they give total or absolute assurance that every child admitted to a hospital has a mental illness optimally suitable for institutionalized treatment. But it bears repeating that "procedural due process rules are shaped by the risk of error inherent in the truth-finding process as applied to the generality of cases, not the rare exceptions." . . .

Georgia's procedures are not "arbitrary" in the sense that a single physician or other professional has the "unbridled discretion" the District Court saw to commit a child to a regional hospital. To so find on this record would require us to assume that the physicians, psychologists, and mental health professionals who participate in the admission decision and who review each other's conclusions as to the continuing validity of the initial decision are either oblivious or indifferent to the child's welfare — or that they are incompetent. We note, however, the District Court found to the contrary; it was "impressed by the conscientious, dedicated state employed psychiatrists who, with the help of equally conscientious, dedicated state employed psychologists and social workers, faithfully care for the plaintiff children. . . ."

This finding of the District Court also effectively rebuts the suggestion made in some of the briefs amici that hospital administrators may not actually be "neutral and detached" because of institutional pressure to admit a child who has no need for hospital care. That such a practice may take place in some institutions in some places affords no basis for a finding as to Georgia's program; the evidence in the record provides no support whatever for that charge against the staffs at any of the State's eight regional hospitals. Such cases, if they are found, can be dealt with individually; they do not lend themselves to class-action remedies.

We are satisfied that the voluminous record as a whole supports the conclusion that the admissions staffs of the hospitals have acted in a neutral and detached fashion in making medical judgments in the best interests of the children. The State, through its mental health programs, provides the authority for trained professionals to assist parents in examining, diagnosing, and treating emotionally disturbed children. Through its hiring practices, it provides well-staffed and well-equipped hospitals and — as the District Court found — conscientious public employees to implement the State's beneficent purposes.

Although our review of the record in this case satisfies us that Georgia's general administrative and statutory scheme for the voluntary commitment of children is not *per se* unconstitutional, we cannot decide on this record, whether every child in appellees' class received an adequate, independent diagnosis of his emotional condition and need for confinement under the standards announced earlier in this opinion. On remand, the District Court is free to and should consider any individual claims that initial admissions did not meet the standards we have described in this opinion.

IV

. . . Some members of appellees' class, including J.R., were wards of the State of Georgia at the time of their admission. Obviously their situation differs from those members of the class who have natural parents. While the determination of what process is due varies somewhat when the state, rather than a natural parent, makes the request for commitment, we conclude that the differences in the two situations do not justify requiring different procedures at the time of the child's initial admission to the hospital.

For a ward of the state, there may well be no adult who knows him thoroughly and who cares for him deeply. Unlike with natural parents where there is a presumed natural affection to guide their action, . . . the presumption that the state will protect a child's general welfare stems from a specific state statute. . . . Contrary to the suggestion of the dissent, however, we cannot assume that when the State of Georgia has custody of a child it acts so differently from a natural parent in seeking medical assistance for the child. No one has questioned the validity of the statutory presumption that the State acts in the child's best interest. Nor could such a challenge be mounted on the record before us. There is no evidence that the State, acting as guardian, attempted to admit any child for reasons unrelated to the child's need for treatment. Indeed, neither the District Court nor the appellees have suggested that wards of the State should receive any constitutional treatment different from children with natural parents.

Once we accept that the State's application for a child's admission to a hospital is made in good faith, then the question is whether the medical decisionmaking approach of the admitting physician is adequate to satisfy due process. We have already recognized that an independent medical judgment made from the perspective of the best interests of the child after a careful investigation is an acceptable means of justifying a voluntary commitment. We do not believe that the soundness of this decisionmaking is any the less reasonable in this setting.

. . . .

(b) It is possible that the procedures required in reviewing a ward's need for continuing care should be different from those used to review the need of a child with natural parents. . . .

The absence of an adult who cares deeply for a child has little effect on the reliability of the initial admission decision, but it may have some effect on how long a child will remain in the hospital. . . . "[T]he concern of family and friends generally will provide continuous opportunities for an erroneous commitment to be corrected." For a child without natural parents, we must acknowledge the risk of being "lost in the shuffle." Moreover, there is at least some indication that J.R.'s commitment was prolonged because the Department of Family and Children Services had difficulty finding a foster home for him. Whether wards of the State generally have received less protection than children with natural parents, and, if so, what should be done about it, however, are matters that must be decided in the first instance by the District Court on remand, if the court concludes the issue is still alive.

V

It is important that we remember the purpose of Georgia's comprehensive mental health program. It seeks substantively and at great cost to provide care for those who cannot afford to obtain private treatment and procedurally to screen carefully all applicants to assure that institutional care is suited to the particular patient. The State resists the complex of procedures ordered by the District Court because in its view they are unnecessary to protect the child's rights, they divert public resources from the central objective of administering health care, they risk aggravating the tensions inherent in the family situation, and they erect barriers that may discourage parents from seeking medical aid for a disturbed child.

On this record, we are satisfied that Georgia's medical factfinding processes are reasonable and consistent with constitutional guarantees. Accordingly, it was error to hold unconstitutional the State's procedures for admitting a child for treatment to a state mental hospital. The judgment is therefore reversed, and the case is remanded to the District Court for further proceedings consistent with this opinion.

Reversed and remanded.

MR. JUSTICE STEWART, *concurring in the judgment.*

For centuries it has been a canon of the common law that parents speak for their minor children. So deeply imbedded in our traditions is this principle of law that the Constitution itself may compel a State to respect it. *Meyer v. Nebraska,* 262 U.S. 390. In ironic contrast, the District Court in this case has said that the Constitution requires the State of Georgia to disregard this established principle. I cannot agree.

There can be no doubt that commitment to a mental institution results in a "massive curtailment of liberty". . . . In addition to the physical confinement involved, . . . a person's liberty is also substantially affected by the stigma attached to treatment in a mental hospital. But not every loss of liberty is governmental deprivation of liberty, and it is only the latter that invokes the Due Process Clause of the Fourteenth Amendment.

. . . Clearly, if the appellees in this case were adults who had voluntarily chosen to commit themselves to a state mental hospital, they could not claim that the State had thereby deprived them of liberty in violation of the Fourteenth Amendment. Just as clearly, I think, children on whose behalf their parents have invoked these voluntary procedures can make no such claim.

. . . .

Thus, the basic question in this case is whether the Constitution requires Georgia to ignore basic principles so long accepted by our society. For only if the State in this setting is constitutionally compelled always to intervene between parent and child can there be any question as to the constitutionally required extent of that intervention. I believe this basic question must be answered in the negative.

Under our law, parents constantly make decisions for their minor children that deprive the children of liberty, and sometimes even of life itself. Yet surely the Fourteenth Amendment is not invoked when an informed parent decides upon major surgery for this child, even in a state hospital. I can perceive no basic constitutional differences between commitment to a mental hospital and other parental decisions that result in a child's loss of liberty.

I realize, of course, that a parent's decision to commit his child to a state mental institution results in a far greater loss of liberty than does his decision to have an appendectomy performed upon the child in a state hospital. But if, contrary to my belief, this factual difference rises to the level of a constitutional difference, then I believe that the objective checks upon the parents' commitment decision, embodied in Georgia law . . . are more than constitutionally sufficient.

. . . .

. . . Issues involving the family and issues concerning mental illness are among the most difficult that courts have to face, involving as they often do serious problems of policy disguised as questions of constitutional law. But when a state legislature makes a reasonable definition of the age of minority, and creates a rebuttable presumption that in invoking the statutory procedures for voluntary commitment a parent is acting in the best interests of his minor child, I cannot believe that the Fourteenth Amendment is violated.

For these reasons I concur in the judgment.

MR. JUSTICE BRENNAN, with whom MR. JUSTICE MARSHALL and MR. JUSTICE STEVENS join, *concurring in part and dissenting in part.*

. . . I disagree . . . with the Court's decision to pretermit questions concerning the postadmission procedures due Georgia's institutionalized juveniles. While the question of the frequency of postadmission review hearings may properly be deferred, the right to at least one postadmission hearing can and should be affirmed now. I also disagree with the Court's conclusion concerning the procedures due juvenile wards of the State of Georgia. I believe that the Georgia statute is unconstitutional in that it fails to accord preconfinement hearings to juvenile wards of the State committed by the State acting *in loco parentis.*

I

RIGHTS OF CHILDREN COMMITTED TO MENTAL INSTITUTIONS

Commitment to a mental institution necessarily entails a "massive curtailment of liberty," . . . and inevitably affects "fundamental rights." . . . Persons incarcerated in mental hospitals are not only deprived of their physical liberty, they are also deprived of friends, family, and community. Institutionalized mental patients must live in unnatural surroundings under the continuous and detailed control of strangers. . . . Furthermore . . . persons confined in mental institutions are stigmatized as sick and abnormal during confinement and, in some cases, even after release.

Because of these considerations, our cases have made clear that commitment to a mental hospital "is a deprivation of liberty which the State cannot accomplish without due process of law." . . . In the absence of a voluntary, knowing, and intelligent waiver, adults facing commitment to mental institutions are entitled to full and fair adversary hearings in which the necessity for their commitment is established to the satisfaction of a neutral tribunal. At such hearings they must be accorded the right to "be present with counsel, have an opportunity to be heard, be confronted with witnesses against [them], have the right to cross-examine, and to offer evidence of [their] own." . . .

These principles also govern the commitment of children. "Constitutional rights do not mature and come into being magically only when one attains the state-defined age of majority. Minors as well as adults are protected by the Constitution and possess constitutional rights. *See, e.g., Breed v. Jones,*

421 U.S. 519 (1975); *Goss v. Lopez,* 419 U.S. 565 (1975); *Tinker v. Des Moines School Dist.,* 393 U.S. 503 (1969); *In re Gault,* 387 U.S. 1 (1967)." *Planned Parenthood of Central Missouri v. Danforth,* 428 U.S. 52 (1976).

Indeed, it may well be argued that children are entitled to more protection than are adults. The consequences of an erroneous commitment decision are more tragic where children are involved. Children, on the average, are confined for longer periods than are adults. Moreover, childhood is a particularly vulnerable time of life and children erroneously institutionalized during their formative years may bear the scars for the rest of their lives. Furthermore, the provision of satisfactory institutionalized mental care for children generally requires a substantial financial commitment that too often has not been forthcoming. Decisions of the lower courts have chronicled the inadequacies of existing mental health facilities for children. . . .

In addition, the chances of an erroneous commitment decision are particularly great where children are involved. Even under the best of circumstances psychiatric diagnosis and therapy decisions are fraught with uncertainties. . . . These uncertainties are aggravated when, as under the Georgia practice, the psychiatrist interviews the child during a period of abnormal stress in connection with the commitment, and without adequate time or opportunity to become acquainted with the patient. These uncertainties may be further aggravated when economic and social class separate doctor and child, thereby frustrating the accurate diagnosis of pathology.

These compounded uncertainties often lead to erroneous commitment since psychiatrists tend to err on the side of medical caution and therefore hospitalize patients for whom other dispositions would be more beneficial. . . . Of particular relevance to this case, a Georgia study Commission on Mental Health Services for Children and Youth concluded that more than half of the State's institutionalized children were not in need of confinement if other forms of care were made available or used. . . .

II

RIGHTS OF CHILDREN COMMITTED BY THEIR PARENTS

A

Notwithstanding all this, Georgia denies hearings to juveniles institutionalized at the behest of their parents. Georgia rationalizes this practice on the theory that parents act in their children's best interests and therefore may waive their children's due process rights. Children incarcerated because their parents wish them confined, Georgia contends, are really voluntary patients. I cannot accept this argument.

In our society, parental rights are limited by the legitimate rights and interests of their children. "Parents may be free to be become martyrs themselves. But it does not follow they are free, in identical circumstances, to make martyrs of their children before they have reached the age of full and legal discretion when they can make that choice for themselves." *Prince v. Massachusetts,* 321 U.S. 158 (1944).

. . . .

Additional considerations counsel against allowing parent unfettered power to institutionalize their children without cause or without any hearing to ascertain that cause. The presumption that parents act in their children's best interest, while applicable to most child-rearing decisions, is not applicable in the commitment context. Numerous studies reveal that parental decisions to institutionalize their children often are the results of dislocation in the family unrelated to the children's mental condition. Moreover, even well-meaning parents lack the expertise necessary to evaluate the relative advantages and disadvantages of inpatient as opposed to outpatient psychiatric treatment. Parental decisions to waive hearings in which such questions could be explored, therefore, cannot be conclusively deemed either informed or intelligent. In these circumstances, I respectfully suggest, it ignores reality to assume blindly that parents act in their children's best interests when making commitment decisions and when waiving their children's due process rights.

B

This does not mean States are obliged to treat children who are committed at the behest of their parents in precisely the same manner as other persons who are involuntarily committed. . . . [W]hen parents seek to hospitalize their children special considerations militate in favor of postponement of formal commitment proceedings and against mandatory adversary preconfinement commitment hearings.

First, the prospect of an adversary hearing prior to admission might deter parents from seeking needed medical attention for their children. Second, the hearings themselves might delay treatment of children whose home life has become impossible and who require some form of immediate state care. Furthermore, because adversary hearings at this juncture would necessarily involve direct challenges to parental authority, judgment, or veracity, preadmission hearings may well result in pitting the child and his advocate against the parents. This, in turn, might traumatize both parent and child and make the child's eventual return to his family more difficult.

Because of these special considerations, I believe that States may legitimately postpone formal commitment proceedings when parents seek impatient psychiatric treatment for their children. Such children may be admitted, for a limited period, without prior hearing, so long as the admitting psychiatrist first interviews parent and child and concludes that short-term inpatient treatment would be appropriate.

Georgia's present admission procedures are reasonably consistent with these principles.

C

I do not believe, however, that the present, Georgia juvenile commitment scheme is constitutional in its entirety. Although Georgia may postpone formal commitment hearings, when parents seek to commit their children, the State cannot dispense with such hearings altogether. . . . Whenever prior hearings are impracticable, States must provide reasonably prompt postdeprivation hearings. . . .

The formal postadmission procedures that Georgia now follows are simply not enough to qualify as hearings — let alone reasonably prompt hearings. The procedures lack all the traditional due process safeguards. Commitment decisions are made *ex parte*. Georgia's institutionalized juveniles are not informed of the reasons for their commitment; nor do they enjoy the right to be present at the commitment determination, the right to representation, the right to be heard, the right to be confronted with adverse witnesses, the right to cross-examine, or the right to offer evidence of their own. By any standard of due process, these procedures are deficient. . . . I cannot understand why the court pretermits condemnation of these *ex parte* procedures which operate to deny Georgia's institutionalized juveniles even "some form of hearing," before they are condemned to suffer the rigors of long-term institutional confinement.

The special considerations that militate against preadmission commitment hearings when parents seek to hospitalize their children do not militate against reasonably prompt postadmission commitment hearings. In the first place, postadmission hearings would not delay the commencement of needed treatment. Children could be cared for by the State pending the disposition decision.

Second, the interest in avoiding family discord would be less significant at this stage since the family autonomy already will have been fractured by the institutionalization of the child. In any event, postadmission hearings are unlikely to disrupt family relationships. At later hearings, the case for and against commitment would be based upon the observations of the hospital staff and the judgments of the staff psychiatrists, rather than upon parental observations and recommendations. The doctors urging commitment, and not the parents, would stand as the child's adversaries. As a consequence, postadmission commitment hearings are unlikely to involve direct challenges to parental authority, judgment, or veracity. To defend the child, the child's advocate need not dispute the parents' original decision to seek medical treatment for their child, or even, for that matter, their observations concerning the child's behavior. The advocate need only argue, for example, that the child had sufficiently improved during his hospital stay to warrant outpatient treatment or outright discharge. Conflict between doctor and advocate on this question is unlikely to lead to family discord.

As a consequence, the prospect of a postadmission hearing is unlikely to deter parents from seeking medical attention for their children and the hearing itself is unlikely so to traumatize parent and child as to make the child's eventual return to the family impracticable.

Nor would postadmission hearings defeat the primary purpose of the state juvenile mental heath enterprise. Under the present juvenile commitment scheme, Georgia parents do not enjoy absolute discretion to commit their children to public mental hospitals. Superintendents of state facilities may not accept children for long-term treatment unless they first determine that the children are mentally ill and will likely benefit from long-term hospital care. If the superintendent determines either condition is unmet, the child must be released or refused admission, regardless of the parents' desires. No legitimate state interest would suffer if the superintendent's determinations were reached through fair proceedings with due consideration of fairly presented opposing viewpoints rather than through the present practice of secret, *ex parte* deliberations.

. . . .

IV

Children incarcerated in public mental institutions are constitutionally entitled to a fair opportunity to contest the legitimacy of their confinement. They are entitled to some champion who can speak on their behalf and who stands ready to oppose a wrongful commitment. Georgia should not be permitted to deny that opportunity and that champion simply because the children's parents or guardians wish them to be confined without a hearing. The risk of erroneous commitment is simply too great unless there is some form of adversary review. And fairness demands that children abandoned by their supposed protectors to the rigors of institutional confinement be given the help of some separate voice.

―――――

NOTES AND QUESTIONS

1. In discussing the issue of "labeling," Chief Justice Burger makes the following observation in his opinion for the *Parham* court:

> We . . . recognize that commitment sometimes produces adverse social consequences for the child because of the reaction of some to the discovery that the child has received psychiatric care.

> This reaction, however, need not be equated with the community response resulting from being labeled by the state as delinquent, criminal, or mentally ill and possibly dangerous. The state through its voluntary commitment procedures does not 'label' the child; it provides a diagnosis and treatment that medical specialists conclude the child requires. In terms of public reaction, the child who exhibits abnormal behavior may be seriously injured by an erroneous decision not to commit. Appellees overlook a significant source of the public reaction to the mentally ill, for what is truly "stigmatizing" is the symptomatology of a mental or emotional illness. The pattern of untreated, abnormal behavior — even if nondangerous — arouses at least as much negative reaction as treatment that becomes public knowledge. A person needing, but not receiving, appropriate medical care may well face even greater social ostracism resulting from the observable symptoms of an untreated disorder.

Do you agree with this observation? Could the same thing be said about adults facing the prospect of involuntary hospitalization? If so, why has the Court required a variety of procedural protections in adult commitment proceedings including proof of the statutory grounds for commitment by "clear and convincing evidence." *Addington v. Texas,* 441 U.S. 418 (1979).

2. The *Parham* Court concludes that there exists little evidence to believe that mental hospitals provide "dumping grounds" for troubled youth who do not require hospitalization. The Court assumes that mental health professionals will act as an adequate check against guardians seeking to use hospitals as dumping grounds. Some commentators question the Court's assumption. *See, e.g.,* Lee E. Teitelbaum & James W. Ellis, *The Liberty Interest of Children: Due Process Rights and Their Application*, 12 FAM. L.Q. 153, 196 (1978) ("the results of [a] study indicate that physicians cannot systematically be relied upon to act as a check upon parental desire to institutionalize a child"). Moreover, researchers point out that psychiatric diagnoses of young people in mental hospitals are generally different from adults, with fewer than one-third of juveniles admitted for inpatient psychiatric care suffering from acute mental disorders generally associated with such admissions such as psychotic, serious depressive, or organic disorders. *See* Lois Weithorn, *Mental Hospitalization of Troublesome Youth: An Analysis of Skyrocketing Admission Rates*, 40 STAN. L. REV. 773, 788–91 (1988) (majority of juveniles hospitalized for "conduct disorder, personality or childhood disorder, or transitional disorder," situations of "children with relatively mild psychological problems and children who do not appear to suffer from anything more serious than normal developmental changes").

Chapter 3

THE CHILD AND SOCIETY

§ 3.01 INTRODUCTION

Chapter 2 considered legal issues of children within the family. Chapters 3 through 5 address contexts outside the family. In a sense, the title of this Chapter describes the remainder of these materials. Chapters 4 and 5 treat specific areas of the Child and Society, the school and the juvenile justice system respectively. The present Chapter considers issues of the Child and Society outside the areas covered in Chapters 4 and 5.

§ 3.02 OBSCENITY AND PORNOGRAPHY

GINSBERG v. NEW YORK

Supreme Court of the United States
390 U.S. 629 (1968)

JUSTICE BRENNAN *delivered the opinion of the Court.*

This case presents the question of the constitutionality on its face of a New York criminal obscenity statute which prohibits the sale to minors under 17 years of age of material defined to be obscene on the basis of its appeal to them whether or not it would be obscene to adults.

Appellant and his wife operate "Sam's Stationery and Luncheonette" in Bellmore, Long Island. They have a lunch counter, and, among other things, also sell magazines including some so-called "girlie" magazines. Appellant was prosecuted under two informations, each in two counts, which charged that he personally sold a 16-year-old boy two "girlie" magazines on each of two dates in October 1965, in violation of § 484-h of the New York Penal Law. He was tried before a judge without a jury in Nassau County District Court and was found guilty on both counts. The judge found (1) that the magazines contained pictures which depicted female "nudity" in a manner defined in subsection 1 (b), that is "the showing of . . . female . . . buttocks with less than a full opaque covering, or the showing of the female breast with less than a fully opaque covering of any portion thereof below the top of the nipple . . . ," and (2) that the pictures were "harmful to minors" in that they had, within the meaning of subsection 1 (f) "that quality of . . . representation . . . of nudity . . . [which] . . . (i) predominantly appeals to the prurient, shameful or morbid interest of minors, and (ii) is patently offensive to prevailing standards in the adult community as a whole with respect to what is suitable material for minors, and (iii) is utterly without redeeming social importance for minors." He held that both sales to the 16-year-old boy therefore constituted the violation under § 484-h of "knowingly to sell . . . to a minor" under

385

17 of "(a) any picture . . . which depicts nudity . . . and which is harmful to minors," and "(b) any . . . magazine . . . which contains . . . [such pictures] . . . and which, taken as a whole, is harmful to minors." The conviction was affirmed without opinion by the Appellate Term, Second Department, of the Supreme Court. Appellant was denied leave to appeal to the New York Court of Appeals and then appealed to this Court. We noted probable jurisdiction. Section 388 U.S. 904. We affirm.

I

The "girlie" picture magazines involved in the sales here are not obscene for adults. But § 484-h does not bar the appellant from stocking the magazines and selling them to persons 17 years of age or older.

Obscenity is not within the area of protected speech or press. *Roth v. United States*, 354 U.S. 476, 485. The three-pronged test of subsection 1 (f) for judging the obscenity of material sold to minors under 17 is a variable from the formulation for determining obscenity under *Roth* stated in the plurality opinion in *Memoirs v. Massachusetts*, 383 U.S. 413, 418. Appellant's primary attack upon § 484-h is leveled at the power of the State to adapt this *Memoirs* formulation to define the material's obscenity on the basis of its appeal to minors, and thus exclude material so defined from the area of protected expression. He makes no argument that the magazines are not "harmful to minors" within the definition in subsection 1 (f). Thus "no issue is presented . . . concerning the obscenity of the material involved."

The New York Court of Appeals "upheld the Legislature's power to employ variable concepts of obscenity."[1] In sustaining state power to enact the law, the Court of Appeals said, *Bookcase, Inc. v. Broderick,* at 75, 218 N. E. 2d, at 671:

Material which is protected for distribution to adults is not necessarily constitutionally protected from restriction upon its dissemination to children. In other words, the concept of obscenity or of unprotected matter may vary according to the group to whom the questionable material is directed or from whom it is quarantined. Because of the State's exigent interest in preventing distribution to children of objectionable material, it can exercise its power to protect the health, safety, welfare and morals of its community by barring the distribution to children of books recognized to be suitable for adults.

Appellant's attack is not that New York was without power to draw the line at age 17. Rather, his contention is the broad proposition that the scope of the constitutional freedom of expression secured to a citizen to read or see material concerned with sex cannot be made to depend upon whether the

---

[1] [4] *People v. Tannenbaum*, 18 N. Y. 2d 268, 270, 220 N.E.2d 783, 785, dismissed as moot, 388 U.S. 439. The concept of variable obscenity is developed in Lockhart & McClure, *Censorship of Obscenity: The Developing Constitutional Standards*, 45 Minn. L. Rev. 5 (1960). At 85 the authors state:

Variable obscenity . . . furnishes a useful analytical tool for dealing with the problem of denying adolescents access to material aimed at a primary audience of sexually mature adults. For variable obscenity focuses attention upon the make-up of primary and peripheral audiences in varying circumstances, and provides a reasonably satisfactory means for delineating the obscene in each circumstance.

citizen is an adult or a minor. He accordingly insists that the denial to minors under 17 of access to material condemned by § 484-h, insofar as that material is not obscene for persons 17 years of age or older, constitutes an unconstitutional deprivation of protected liberty.

We have no occasion in this case to consider the impact of the guarantees of freedom of expression upon the totality of the relationship of the minor and the State. It is enough for the purposes of this case that we inquire whether it was constitutionally impermissible for New York, insofar as § 484-h does so, to accord minors under 17 a more restricted right than that assured to adults to judge and determine for themselves what sex material they may read or see. We conclude that we cannot say that the statute invades the area of freedom of expression constitutionally secured to minors.

Appellant argues that there is an invasion of protected rights under § 484-h constitutionally indistinguishable from the invasions under the Nebraska statute forbidding children to study German, which was struck down in *Meyer v. Nebraska*; the Oregon statute interfering with children's attendance at private and parochial schools, which was struck down in *Pierce v. Society of Sisters*; and the statute compelling children against their religious scruples to give the flag salute, which was struck down in *West Virginia State Board of Education v. Barnette*. We reject that argument. We do not regard New York's regulation in defining obscenity on the basis of its appeal to minors under 17 as involving an invasion of such minors' constitutionally protected freedoms. Rather § 484-h simply adjusts the definition of obscenity "to social realities by permitting the appeal of this type of material to be assessed in terms of the sexual interests . . ." of such minors. That the State has power to make that adjustment seems clear, for we have recognized that even where there is an invasion of protected freedoms "the power of the state to control the conduct of children reaches beyond the scope of its authority over adults . . . ." *Prince v. Massachusetts*.[2] In *Prince* we sustained the conviction of the guardian of a nine-year-old girl, both members of the sect of Jehovah's Witnesses, for violating the Massachusetts Child Labor Law by permitting the girl to sell the sect's religious tracts on the streets of Boston.

---

2 [4] Many commentators, including many committed to the proposition that "no general restriction on expression in terms of 'obscenity' can . . .be reconciled with the first amendment," recognize that "the power of the state to control the conduct of children reaches beyond the scope of its authority over adults," and accordingly acknowledge a supervening state interest in the regulation of literature sold to children, Emerson, *Toward a General Theory of the First Amendment*, 72 YALE L.J. 877, 938, 939 (1963):

> Different factors come into play, also, where the interest at stake is the effect of erotic expression upon children. The world of children is not strictly part of the adult realm of free expression. The factor of immaturity, and perhaps other considerations, impose different rules. Without attempting here to formulate the principles relevant to freedom of expression for children, it suffices to say that regulations of communication addressed to them need not conform to the requirements of the first amendment in the same way as those applicable to adults.

Prince v. Massachusetts is urged to be constitutional authority for such regulation. *See, e. g.*, Kuh, *supra*, at 258–260; Comment, *Exclusion of Children from Violent Movies*, 67 COL. L. REV. 1149, 1159–1160 (1967); Note, *Constitutional Problems in Obscenity Legislation Protecting Children*, 54 GEO. L.J. 1379 (1966).

The well-being of its children is of course a subject within the State's constitutional power to regulate, and, in our view, two interests justify the limitations in § 484-h upon the availability of sex material to minors under 17, at least if it was rational for the legislature to find that the minors' exposure to such material might be harmful. First of all, constitutional interpretation has consistently recognized that the parents' claim to authority in their own household to direct the rearing of their children is basic in the structure of our society. "It is cardinal with us that the custody, care and nurture of the child reside first in the parents, whose primary function and freedom include preparation for obligations the state can neither supply nor hinder." *Prince v. Massachusetts.* The legislature could properly conclude that parents and others, teachers for example, who have this primary responsibility for children's well-being are entitled to the support of laws designed to aid discharge of that responsibility. Indeed, subsection 1 (f)(ii) of § 484-h expressly recognizes the parental role in assessing sex-related material harmful to minors according "to prevailing standards in the adult community as a whole with respect to what is suitable material for minors." Moreover, the prohibition against sales to minors does not bar parents who so desire from purchasing the magazines for their children.[3]

The State also has an independent interest in the well-being of its youth. . . .

> While the supervision of children's reading may best be left to their parents, the knowledge that parental control or guidance cannot always be provided and society's transcendent interest in protecting the welfare of children justify reasonable regulation of the sale of material to them. It is, therefore, altogether fitting and proper for a state to include in a statute designed to regulate the sale of pornography to children special standards, broader than those embodied in legislation aimed at controlling dissemination of such material to adults.

In *Prince v. Massachusetts*, this Court, too, recognized that the State has an interest "to protect the welfare of children" and to see that they are "safeguarded from abuses" which might prevent their "growth into free and independent well-developed men and citizens." The only question remaining, therefore, is whether the New York Legislature might rationally conclude, as it has, that exposure to the materials proscribed by § 484-h constitutes such an "abuse."

---

[3] [7] One commentator who argues that obscenity legislation might be constitutionally defective as an imposition of a single standard of public morality would give effect to the parental role and accept laws relating only to minors. Henkin, *Morals and the Constitution: The Sin of Obscenity*, 63 COL. L. REV. 391, 413, n. 68 (1963):

> One must consider also how much difference it makes if laws are designed to protect only the morals of a child. While many of the constitutional arguments against morals legislation apply equally to legislation protecting the morals of children, one can well distinguish laws which do not impose a morality on children, but which support the right of parents to deal with the morals of their children as they see fit.

See also Elias, *Sex Publications and Moral Corruption: The Supreme Court Dilemma*, 9 WM. & MARY L. REV. 302, 320–321 (1967).

Section 484-e of the law states a legislative finding that the material condemned by § 484-h is "a basic factor in impairing the ethical and moral development of our youth and a clear and present danger to the people of the state." It is very doubtful that this finding expresses an accepted scientific fact. But obscenity is not protected expression and may be suppressed without a showing of the circumstances which lie behind the phrase "clear and present danger" in its application to protected speech. To sustain state power to exclude material defined as obscenity by § 484-h requires only that we be able to say that it was not irrational for the legislature to find that exposure to material condemned by the statute is harmful to minors. In *Meyer v. Nebraska*, we were able to say that children's knowledge of the German language "cannot reasonably be regarded as harmful." That cannot be said by us of minors' reading and seeing sex material. To be sure, there is no lack of "studies" which purport to demonstrate that obscenity is or is not "a basic factor in impairing the ethical and moral development of . . . youth and a clear and present danger to the people of the state." But the growing consensus of commentators is that "while these studies all agree that a causal link has not been demonstrated, they are equally agreed that a causal link has not been disproved either."[4] We do not demand of legislatures "scientifically certain criteria of legislation." We therefore cannot say that § 484-h, in defining the obscenity of material on the basis of its appeal to minors under 17, has no rational relation to the objective of safeguarding such minors from harm.

---

4 [10] Magrath, *supra*, at 52. *See, e.g., id.*, at 49–56; Dibble, *Obscenity: A State Quarantine to Protect Children*, 39 So. CAL. L. REV. 345 (1966); Wall, *Obscenity and Youth: The Problem and a Possible Solution*, CRIM. L. BULL., Vol. 1, No. 8, pp. 28, 30 (1965); Note, 55 CAL. L. REV. 926, 934 (1967); Comment, 34 FORDHAM L. REV. 692, 694 (1966). *See also* J. Paul & M. Schwartz, FEDERAL CENSORSHIP: OBSCENITY IN THE MAIL, 191–192; Blakey, Book Review, 41 NOTRE DAME LAW. 1055, 1060, n. 46 (1966); Green, Obscenity, Censorship, and Juvenile Delinquency, 14 U. TORONTO L. REV. 229, 249 (1962); Lockhart & McClure, *Literature, The Law of Obscenity, and the Constitution*, 38 MINN. L. REV. 295, 373–385 (1954); Note, 52 KY. L.J. 429, 447 (1964). But despite the vigor of the ongoing controversy whether obscene material will perceptibly create a danger of antisocial conduct, or will probably induce its recipients to such conduct, a medical practitioner recently suggested that the possibility of harmful effects to youth cannot be dismissed as frivolous. Dr. Gaylin of the Columbia University Psychoanalytic Clinic, reporting on the views of some psychiatrists in 77 YALE L.J., at 592–593, said:

> "It is in the period of growth [of youth] when these patterns of behavior are laid down, when environmental stimuli of all sorts must be integrated into a workable sense of self, when sensuality is being defined and fears elaborated, when pleasure confronts security and impulse encounters control — it is in this period, undramatically and with time, that legalized pornography may conceivably be damaging."

Dr. Gaylin emphasizes that a child might not be as well prepared as an adult to make an intelligent choice as to the material he chooses to read:

> "Psychiatrists . . .made a distinction between the reading of pornography, as unlikely to be per se harmful, and the permitting of the reading of pornography, which was conceived as potentially destructive. The child is protected in his reading of pornography by the knowledge that it is pornographic, *i.e.*, disapproved. It is outside of parental standards and not a part of his identification processes. To openly permit implies parental approval and even suggests seductive encouragement. If this is so of parental approval, it is equally so of societal approval — another potent influence on the developing ego."

II

[The Court analyzed the appellant's claim that parts of the statute were void for vagueness and determined that the statute met the requirements of due process.]

Affirmed.

APPENDIX A TO OPINION OF THE COURT.

New York Penal Law § 484-h as enacted by L. 1965, c. 327, provides:

§ 484-h. Exposing minors to harmful materials

1. Definitions. As used in this section:

(a) "Minor" means any person under the age of seventeen years.

(b) "Nudity" means the showing of the human male or female genitals, pubic area or buttocks with less than a full opaque covering, or the showing of the female breast with less than a fully opaque covering of any portion thereof below the top of the nipple, or the depiction of covered male genitals in a discernibly turgid state.

(c) "Sexual conduct" means acts of masturbation, homosexuality, sexual intercourse, or physical contact with a person's clothed or unclothed genitals, pubic area, buttocks or, if such person be a female, breast.

(d) "Sexual excitement" means the condition of human male or female genitals when in a state of sexual stimulation or arousal.

(e) "Sado-masochistic abuse" means flagellation or torture by or upon a person clad in undergarments, a mask or bizarre costume, or the condition of being fettered, bound or otherwise physically restrained on the part of one so clothed.

(f) "Harmful to minors" means that quality of any description or representation, in whatever form, of nudity, sexual conduct, sexual excitement, or sado-masochistic abuse, when it:

(i) predominantly appeals to the prurient, shameful or morbid interest of minors, and

(ii) is patently offensive to prevailing standards in the adult community as a whole with respect to what is suitable material for minors, and

(iii) is utterly without redeeming social importance for minors.

(g) "Knowingly" means having general knowledge of, or reason to know, or a belief or ground for belief which warrants further inspection or inquiry of both:

(i) the character and content of any material described herein which is reasonably susceptible of examination by the defendant, and

(ii) the age of the minor, provided however, that an honest mistake shall constitute an excuse from liability hereunder if the defendant made a reasonable bona fide attempt to ascertain the true age of such minor.

2. It shall be unlawful for any person knowingly to sell or loan for monetary consideration to a minor:

(a) any picture, photograph, drawing, sculpture, motion picture film, or similar visual representation or image of a person or portion of the human body which depicts nudity, sexual conduct or sado-masochistic abuse and which is harmful to minors, or

(b) any book, pamphlet, magazine, printed matter however reproduced, or sound recording which contains any matter enumerated in paragraph (a) of subdivision two hereof, or explicit and detailed verbal descriptions or narrative accounts of sexual excitement, sexual conduct or sado-masochistic abuse and which, taken as a whole, is harmful to minors.

3. It shall be unlawful for any person knowingly to exhibit for a monetary consideration to a minor or knowingly to sell to a minor an admission ticket or pass or knowingly to admit a minor for a monetary consideration to premises whereon there is exhibited, a motion picture, show or other presentation which, in whole or in part, depicts nudity, sexual conduct or sado-masochistic abuse and which is harmful to minors.

4. A violation of any provision hereof shall constitute a misdemeanor.

JUSTICE STEWART, *concurring in the result.*

A doctrinaire, knee-jerk application of the First Amendment would, of course, dictate the nullification of this New York statute. But that result is not required, I think, if we bear in mind what it is that the First Amendment protects.

The First Amendment guarantees liberty of human expression in order to preserve in our Nation what Mr. Justice Holmes called a "free trade in ideas." To that end, the Constitution protects more than just a man's freedom to say or write or publish what he wants. It secures as well the liberty of each man to decide for himself what he will read and to what he will listen. The Constitution guarantees, in short, a society of free choice. Such a society presupposes the capacity of its members to choose.

When expression occurs in a setting where the capacity to make a choice is absent, government regulation of that expression may co-exist with and even implement First Amendment guarantees. So it was that this Court sustained a city ordinance prohibiting people from imposing their opinions on others "by way of sound trucks with loud and raucous noises on city streets." And so it was that my Brothers BLACK and DOUGLAS thought that the First Amendment itself prohibits a person from foisting his uninvited views upon the members of a captive audience.

I think a State may permissibly determine that, at least in some precisely delineated areas, a child — like someone in a captive audience — is not possessed of that full capacity for individual choice which is the presupposition of First Amendment guarantees. It is only upon such a premise, I should suppose, that a State may deprive children of other rights — the right to marry, for example, or the right to vote — deprivations that would be constitutionally intolerable for adults.

I cannot hold that this state law, on its face,[5] violates the First and Fourteenth Amendments.

JUSTICE DOUGLAS, with whom JUSTICE BLACK *concurs, dissenting.*

. . . .

Today this Court sits as the Nation's board of censors. With all respect, I do not know of any group in the country less qualified first, to know what obscenity is when they see it, and second, to have any considered judgment as to what the deleterious or beneficial impact of a particular publication may be on minds either young or old.

[APPENDICES I, II and III to the opinion of MR. JUSTICE DOUGLAS, *dissenting*, are omitted].

MR. JUSTICE FORTAS, *dissenting.*

This is a criminal prosecution. Sam Ginsberg and his wife operate a luncheonette at which magazines are offered for sale. A 16-year-old boy was enlisted by his mother to go to the luncheonette and buy some "girlie" magazines so that Ginsberg could be prosecuted. He went there, picked two magazines from a display case, paid for them, and walked out. Ginsberg's offense was duly reported to the authorities. The power of the State of New York was invoked. Ginsberg was prosecuted and convicted. The court imposed only a suspended sentence. But as the majority here points out, under New York law this conviction may mean that Ginsberg will lose the license necessary to operate his luncheonette.

The two magazines that the 16-year-old boy selected are vulgar "girlie" periodicals. However tasteless and tawdry they may be, we have ruled (as the Court acknowledges) that magazines indistinguishable from them in content and offensiveness are not "obscene" within the constitutional standards heretofore applied. These rulings have been in cases involving adults.

The Court avoids facing the problem whether the magazines in the present case are "obscene" when viewed by a 16-year-old boy, although not "obscene" when viewed by someone 17 years of age or older. It says that Ginsberg's lawyer did not choose to challenge the conviction on the ground that the magazines are not "obscene." He chose only to attack the statute on its face. Therefore, the Court reasons, we need not look at the magazines and determine whether they may be excluded from the ambit of the First Amendment as "obscene" for purposes of this case. . . .

In my judgment, the Court cannot properly avoid its fundamental duty to define "obscenity" for purposes of censorship of material sold to youths, merely because of counsel's position. By so doing the Court avoids the essence of the problem; for if the State's power to censor freed from the prohibitions of the First Amendment depends upon obscenity, and if obscenity turns on the specific content of the publication, how can we sustain the conviction here without deciding whether the particular magazines in question are obscene?

---

[5] [7] As the Court notes, the appellant makes no argument that the material in this case was not "harmful to minors" within the statutory definition, or that the statute was unconstitutionally applied.

The Court certainly cannot mean that the States and cities and counties and villages have unlimited power to withhold anything and everything that is written or pictorial from younger people. But it here justifies the conviction of Sam Ginsberg because the impact of the Constitution, it says, is variable, and what is not obscene for an adult may be obscene for a child. This it calls "variable obscenity." I do not disagree with this, but I insist that to assess the principle — certainly to apply it — the Court must define it. We must know the extent to which literature or pictures may be less offensive than *Roth* requires in order to be "obscene" for purposes of a statute confined to youth. *See Roth* v. *United States*, 354 U.S. 476 (1957).

I agree that the State in the exercise of its police power — even in the First Amendment domain — may make proper and careful differentiation between adults and children. But I do not agree that this power may be used on an arbitrary, free-wheeling basis. This is not a case where, on any standard enunciated by the Court, the magazines are obscene, nor one where the seller is at fault. Petitioner is being prosecuted for the sale of magazines which he had a right under the decisions of this Court to offer for sale, and he is being prosecuted without proof of "fault" — without even a claim that he deliberately, calculatedly sought to induce children to buy "obscene" material. Bookselling should not be a hazardous profession.

The conviction of Ginsberg on the present facts is a serious invasion of freedom. To sustain the conviction without inquiry as to whether the material is "obscene" and without any evidence of pushing or pandering, in face of this Court's asserted solicitude for First Amendment values, is to give the State a role in the rearing of children which is contrary to our traditions and to our conception of family responsibility. It begs the question to present this undefined, unlimited censorship as an aid to parents in the rearing of their children. This decision does not merely protect children from activities which all sensible parents would condemn. Rather, its undefined and unlimited approval of state censorship in this area denies to children free access to books and works of art to which many parents may wish their children to have uninhibited access. For denial of access to these magazines, without any standard or definition of their allegedly distinguishing characteristics, is also denial of access to great works of art and literature.

If this statute were confined to the punishment of pushers or panderers of vulgar literature I would not be so concerned by the Court's failure to circumscribe state power by defining its limits in terms of the meaning of "obscenity" in this field. The State's police power may, within very broad limits, protect the parents and their children from public aggression of panderers and pushers. This is defensible on the theory that they cannot protect themselves from such assaults. But it does not follow that the State may convict a passive luncheonette operator of a crime because a 16-year-old boy maliciously and designedly picks up and pays for two girlie magazines which are presumably *not* obscene.

NOTES AND QUESTIONS

1. Should there be a different obscenity standard for children? Why or why not? What is the standard, after *Ginsberg*, for determining if a state has gone too far in its definition of "children's obscenity"? Does a minor have some First Amendment right that would restrain the state's ability to limit the minor's access to certain written or pictorial materials? In *Erznoznik v. Jacksonville*, 422 U.S. 205, 213-14 (1975), the Court struck down a Florida statute that made it illegal for drive-in movies to show films containing nudity. The Court said:

> Speech that is neither obscene as to youths nor subject to some other legitimate proscription cannot be suppressed solely to protect the young from ideas and images that a legislative body thinks is unsuitable for them. In most circumstances, the values protected by the First Amendment are no less applicable when government seeks to control the flow of information to minors.

2. What about materials that are not sexually explicit but may be extremely violent? Are violent materials distinguishable from sexual materials with respect to their potential harm to the child? In *American Amusement Machine Assoc. v. Kendrick*, 244 F.3d 572 (7th Cir. 2001), the appeals court ordered the district court to issue a preliminary injunction against an ordinance that restricted minors' access to video games containing graphic violence. The district court had found that the city had a reasonable basis for believing that the ordinance would protect the children from harm. The district court based this determination on a pair of empirical studies which found that playing a violent video game tended to make young persons more aggressive in their attitudes and behavior. The court of appeals found no indication that the games used in the studies were similar to those in the record or to other games likely to be marketed in game arcades in the city. Thus, according to the court of appeals, the benefits of the ordinance were "entirely conjectural." *Cf.* Emily R. Caron, *Blood, Guts & the First Amendment: Regulating Violence in the Entertainment Media,* 11 KAN. J.L. & PUB. POL'Y 89 (2001).

In *Interactive Digital Software Assoc. v. St. Louis County*, 329 F.3d 954 (8th Cir. 2003), a county ordinance made it unlawful for any person knowingly to sell, rent, or make available graphically violent video games to minors, or to "permit the free play of" graphically violent video games by minors, without parent or guardian's consent. The Eighth Circuit held that the ordinance violated first amendment right to free speech under a strict scrutiny standard. The county's conclusion that there was a strong likelihood that minors who played violent video games would suffer a deleterious effect on their psychological health was unsupported in the record and the county could not constitutionally limit first amendment rights as means of aiding parental authority.

Similarly, a district court held that a Washington State statute that imposed criminal penalties for distribution of video games with violent content to minors violated the first amendment under a strict scrutiny test. *Video Software Dealers Assoc. v. Maleng*, 325 F. Supp. 3d 1180 (W.D. Wash. 2004). The state has a compelling interest in protecting its youth and stemming the increase in hostile and antisocial behavior (including violence against law enforcement officers). Although some evidence tends to show a connection between exposure to depictions of violence and the development of aggressive tendencies in minors, the state did not show that the statute was likely to curb such anti-social aggression in minors in a direct and material way.

Does the fact that video games are interactive — thus requiring the players to be participants in the violence — mean that they should receive less protection? *See* Elizabeth A. Previte, *Insert Coins to Slay! Regulating Children's Access to Violent Arcade Games*, 10 VILL. SPORTS & ENT. L.J. 69 (2003) (arguing that courts overlook the danger to children and the weak claim to a speech component of video games). Does it make a difference if it can be demonstrated that consistent long-term exposure to violent video games is harmful to children? Some psychologists claim that violent video games contribute to juvenile violence by training children to equate violence with rewards, creating a stimulus addiction, teaching children that violence resolves conflicts, and desensitizing children to killing, death and violence. *See id.* at 73 (explaining psychologist's beliefs about video game violence). Researchers at Emory University reported in the March 2005 issue of the American Journal of Public Health that a study of 522 teenage girls from poor neighborhoods showed that girls who watched the most rap videos (more than the average of 14 hours a week), were three times as likely as the other girls to have hit a teacher (7.1 percent versus 2.4 percent). They were also 2.5 times more likely to have been arrested (17.3 percent versus 7.2 percent), and nearly two times more likely to have had sex with multiple partners (19.3 percent versus 11 percent). *See also* Anne Proffitt Dupre, *Violence, Depravity and the Movies: The Lure of Deviancy*, 127 USA TODAY 54 (1999) (noting that if the first amendment protects sadistic violence, there is no constitutional protection against empty theaters and discussing why the American public is aroused and titillated by violence).

What about other materials that some adults find offensive? In *F.C.C. v. Pacifica Foundation*, 438 U.S. 726 (1978), an afternoon radio program broadcast a monologue called "Filthy Words" by George Carlin. The Supreme Court determined that broadcasting speech receives less protection under the First Amendment because it intrudes into the home, may be hard to avoid and is uniquely accessible to children, even those too young to read.

3. In addition to preventing minors' access to sexually explicit material, states have also prevented minors' access to other material that is legal for adults. Protecting minors from cigarettes and tobacco products has gained much attention in recent years. Massachusetts passed a regulation that prohibited the advertising of tobacco products within 1000 feet of a public playground, park or school. The Supreme Court determined that the regulation was preempted by the Federal Cigarette Labeling and Advertising Act with respect to cigarettes and that it violated the First Amendment with regard to smokeless tobacco and cigars. *Lorillard Tobacco Co. v. Reilly,* 533 U.S. 525 (2001). In its First Amendment analysis, the Court applied its test

for restrictions on commercial speech from *Central Hudson Gas and Electric Corp. v. Public Service Commission of N.Y.*, 447 U.S. 557 (1980). According to Justice O'Connor, who wrote for at least five Justices throughout the opinion, the regulations were more extensive than necessary to serve the governmental interest in addressing the underage use of smokeless tobacco and cigars. The sweep of the geographical limitation (in some metropolitan areas it would constitute nearly a complete ban) and the range of advertisements restricted (advertisements were restricted inside a store if visible from the outside, outdoor advertisements of any size were restricted, as were oral statements) was so broad that it would impinge on the right of the tobacco retailers to convey truthful information about their products to adults and the corresponding right of adults to receive truthful information about tobacco products. Justice O'Connor referred to the Court's opinion in *Reno v. American Civil Liberties Union*, 521 U.S. 844, 875 (1997), a case involving indecent speech on the internet, which stated, "[T]he governmental interests in protecting children from harmful materials . . . does not justify an unnecessarily broad suppression of speech addressed to adults."

4. In *Reno*, the Court was addressing the Community Decency Act, part of Title V of the Telecommuncations Act of 1966, which made it a crime to transmit any obscene or indecent communication if the party transmitting knew the recipient was under the age of eighteen. 47 U.S.C. § 223(a)(1)(B). The statute also made it a crime to use a computer to transmit to a minor communication that depicted or described sexual or excretory functions that are patently offensive to contemporary community standards or to transmit the communication in such a way that it would be accessible to anyone under 18 years old. § 223(d)(1)(A), (B). The United States Supreme Court struck down § 223(a) and § 223(d) in *Reno v. ACLU*, 521 U.S. 844 (1997), determining that the provisions lacked the precision required of statutes that regulate the content of speech. The Court held that the provisions were overbroad (because there was no feasible way for adults to engage in constitutionally protected indecent speech) and vague (because the failure to define terms like "indecent" and "patently offensive" left speakers uncertain as to what the terms meant).

In December 2001, the Court heard argument over another statute that attempted to shield children from harmful material over the internet. The Child Online Protection Act (COPA), 47 U.S.C. § 231, passed in 1998, makes it a crime knowingly to make "any communication for commercial purposes that is available to any minor and . . . [to] include[ ] any material that is harmful to minors." 47 U.S.C. § 231(a)(1). Unlike the CDA, COPA applies only to commercial web sites. Material that is "harmful to minors" includes material that "the average person, applying contemporary community standards, would find, taking the material as a whole and with respect to minors, is designed to appeal to or is designed to pander to, the prurient interest," and "taken as a whole lack[s] serious literary, artistic, political, or scientific value for minors." 47 U.S.C. § 231(e)(6)(A) (1998) (the quoted material is the first of three provisions that attempt to define "harmful to minors"). *Cf. Miller v. California,* 413 US 15 (1973). Affirmative defenses to liability include requiring a credit card, debit card, or a digital certificate that verifies age. 47 USC § 231(c)(1)(b). In *ACLU v. Reno,* 217 F.3d 162 (3d Cir. 2000), the Third

Circuit affirmed the order of the Eastern District of Pennsylvania, which had temporarily enjoined the enforcement of COPA, because requiring Web publishers to abide by the most restrictive community standards to avoid liability impermissibly burdened speech. The United States Supreme Court held that COPA's use of "community standards" to identify "material that is harmful to minors," did not render the statute facially unconstitutional. The Court remanded the case to the Third Circuit to address whether the statute suffers from overbreadth for other reasons, whether the statute is uncontitutionally vague, whether the statute is unconstitutionally vague, or whether the statute survives strict scrutiny. *Aschroft v. ACLU*, 535 U.S. 564 (2002). In 2004, the Supreme Court affirmed a preliminary injunction against enforcement of COPA, stating that the government had failed to meet its burden of showing that the statute is a less restrictive means of protecting children than filtering software. *Ashcroft v. American Civil Liberties Union*, 542 U.S. 656 (2004).

The Prosecutorial Remedies and Other Tools to End the Exploitation of Children Today Act of 2003 (The PROTECT Act) created a national Amber alert system, and provided for enhanced penalties for child sexual abuse, sexual exploitation, and child pornography. Pub. L. No. 108.21, 117 Stat. 650 (Apr. 30, 2003). *See also* Susan H. Kosse, *Try, Try Again: Will Congress Ever Get It Right? A Summary of Internet Pornography Laws Protecting Children and Possible Solutions*, 38 U. Rich. L. Rev. 721 (2004) (describing how the statute was passed and pointing out that the ACLU stated in letters to senators that PROTECT was an improvement over previous efforts by Congress, but nonetheless claimed that PROTECT is unconstitutional).

5. What if the parents of the boy in *Ginsberg* had bought the magazines for him? What if the magazines contained hard core pornography? What if the parents bought hard core pornography for themselves, but they left material depicting explicit and violent sex lying around the house? Does a parent have a claim that they have the right to raise their child as they see fit, and that they want their child to be exposed to all kinds of sexual material because they believe it is healthier for him than restricting such material? Is there a limit to parental power with regard to the material to which their children can be exposed?

In *Chesebrough v. State*, 255 So. 2d 675, 676 (Fla. 1971), defendant was convicted of violating the following statute:

> Any person who shall handle, fondle or make an assault upon any male or female child under the age of fourteen years in a lewd, lascivious or indecent manner, or *who shall knowingly commit any lewd or lascivious act in the presence of such child*, without intent to commit rape where such child is female, shall be deemed guilty of a felony and punished by imprisonment in the state prison or county jail for not more than ten years.

The circumstances of the offense were as follows:

> Upon inquiry by her son (who was under fourteen years of age) as to how babies are made, the defendant and her husband (stepfather of the child) took him in the bedroom and showed him.

Id.

The Florida Supreme Court upheld defendant's conviction and rejected her claims that the statute was unconstitutionally vague and overbroad. The separate opinion of Justice Ervin concludes:

> I am in agreement with Justice Adkins' excellent opinion insofar as he holds F.S. section 800.04, F.S.A., to be constitutional on its face. However, it appears to me it is being unconstitutionally misapplied to the facts of this case. I don't believe the statute was intended to invade the privacy of a family and a private home, as here, and criminalize the acts of the mother and father. *Compare Griswold v. Connecticut,* 1965, 381 U.S. 479, 497; *see also* 25 MIAMI L. REV. 395 (1971). As defined by Justice Adkins, "lewd and lascivious behavior" is synonymous with wicked, lustful, licentious, and grossly indecent sexual relations. True, what they did is shockingly disagreeable and reprehensible to most of us under current societal conventions; but I am willing to give them the benefit of the doubt that they believed (although perhaps mistakenly) they could give their own son mature understanding and instruction in the biological facts of procreation in the privacy of their home. Engaging in sexual intercourse for such a reason does not seem to fall within the definition of "lewd and lascivious behavior." Had the act not been committed "all in the family" but out in the open, public view, I would agree it violated the statute.

Id. at 679.

Does the dissenting judge's view have merit? Does the intent of the mother in allowing her son to watch matter? What if the reason the mother allowed the boy to watch sexual intercourse was because it increased her husband's sexual enjoyment?

6. Instead of allowing her son to watch sexual intercourse, suppose the mother allowed her son to pose nude for pictures that he posted on the internet? Child pornography comes in many forms, from children posing nude in the bath to child rape involving children as young as toddlers and infants. Rod Nordland & Jeffrey Bartholet, *The Web's Dark Secret,* NEWSWEEK, March 19, 2001, at 46. In *New York v. Ferber,* 458 U.S. 747 (1982), the U.S. Supreme Court held that child pornography was not entitled to first amendment protection. Although law enforcement had made great headway in eradicating child pornography in the United States during the 1980s when pedophiles were using overland mail and neighborhood photo labs, with the advent of the internet, child pornography has "exploded." *Id.* Men can now make instant copies from an overseas website (from film-free digital cameras that allow the user to avoid being found out at a photo store), and they find communities of online clubs and chat rooms. Authorities worry that this connection to other pedophiles will somehow make the pedophile believe that his own impulses are legitimate, because they are shared by so many others In addition, sexual predators can form relationships with kids through the internet and attempt to lure them into relationships.

The appetite for child photos of sexually exploited children is huge. The 200 members of the Wonderland Internet Chat Group each had to provide 10,000 images of child pornography to join, and when police broke up the ring, they found computer disks with over three quarters of a million images of children in Britain alone. Many of the images found showed children as young as three months subjected to explicit sex acts. *Id.* at 47. In one month (only three months after its inception), one sting operation recorded 147,776 hits from individual users and the download of 3.2 million images.

What are the harms that are present in the possession of child pornography? One harm surely is the harm to the child that occurs as the photograph is being taken. Are there additional harms to the child that occur as the photograph is disseminated? What if the photograph is not of a real child, but is made through computer imagery? It is unknown what percentage of the fans of child pornography will go on to molest a child. Without more research, should the possession of child pornography that is wholly created with computer imagery be outlawed? Is the harm to children from child pornography limited to live children?

Congress passed the Child Pornography Prevention Act (CPPA) of 1996, 18 U.S.C. §§ 225b, to address "virtual" child pornography. The statute bans the production, possession or distribution of child pornography, defined as a visual depiction that "conveys the impression" or that "is, or appears to be of a minor engaging in sexually explicit conduct." *Id.* The First, Fourth, Fifth, and Eleventh Circuits upheld CPPA as constitutional, but the Ninth Circuit, in a 2-1 decision, determined that "appears to be a minor" and "conveys the impression" were vague and overbroad, and the United States Supreme Court granted certiorari on the issue. The Supreme Court, in an opinion written by Justice Kennedy, struck down the statute as overbroad. *Ashcroft v. Free Speech Coalition,* 535 U.S. 234 (2002). According to the standard for obscenity in *Miller v. California,* 413 U.S. 15 (1973), the government must prove that the material, taken as a whole, appeals to the prurient interest, is patently offensive in light of community standards, and lacks serious literary, artistic, political or scientific value. Under the CPPA, materials need not appeal to the prurient interest or be patently offensive, and CPPA does not consider the work as a whole. The Court has held that child pornography can be banned even if it does not meet the *Miller* standard. *New York v. Ferber,* 458 U.S. 747 (1982). But unlike *Ferber,* which distinguished child pornography from other sexually explicit speech because of the State's interest in protecting children exploited by the production process, CPPA prohibits speech that records no crime and creates no victims by its production. Justice Thomas filed an opinion concurring in the judgement. Justice O'Connor filed an opinion concurring in the judgment in part and dissenting in part. Chief Justice Rehnquist and Justice Scalia dissented.

What if a person has written diaries explicitly describing the kidnapping, rape and torture of fictitious children? In Columbus, Ohio, Brian Dalton's parents found his diaries with such writings and alerted his probation officer. (He was on probation for downloading child pornography from the Internet). Ohio law allows for conviction for possession of any obscene material that has a minor as a participant or observer. Dalton pleaded guilty but later, after the intervention of the ACLU, moved to withdraw his guilty plea. David Rovella, *"Virtual Kid" Porn Ban Reaches High Court*, NAT'L L.J., August 20, 2001, at A12. The motion was denied, Editorial Comment, *Punishing Thoughts?*, COLUMB. DISPATCH, Sept. 10, 2001, at 10A, but the First Amendment issues remain. How should they be resolved?

If it is wrong to "sexualize" children, what does the media contribute to the view that children are sex objects? Movies, television, magazines and stars — Brooke Shields in one era and Britney Spears more recently — all project images of young girls dressed and posed in sexually provocative scenes. "It sends a message of acceptability." Sharon Begley, *What is a Pedophile?*, NEWSWEEK, March 19, 2001, at 48 (quoting William O'Donohue of the University of Nevada at Reno). Considering the images that the media continually sends forth about children, is child pornography really so far out of the mainstream?

§ 3.03 PRIVACY RIGHTS OF MINORS: ABORTION AND BIRTH CONTROL

In *Roe v. Wade*, 410 U.S. 113, 153 (1973), the United States Supreme Court decided that the right to privacy, "whether it be founded in the Fourteenth Amendment's concept of personal liberty . . . as we feel it is, or . . . in the Ninth Amendment's reservation of rights to the people, is broad enough to encompass a woman's decision whether or not to terminate her pregnancy." Perhaps even more controversial than the issue of the abortion rights of adult women, is the issue of the abortion rights of young women who have not yet reached the age of majority.

The Supreme Court has addressed several state statutes that have restricted a minor's access to abortion. In *Planned Parenthood v. Danforth*, 428 U.S. 52 (1976), the United States Supreme Court considered a Missouri statute that required an unmarried woman under age eighteen to obtain consent of either of her parents or spouse before having an abortion. The *Danforth* Court cited *Tinker v. Des Moines Public School Dist*, 393 U.S. 503 (1969), and stated that "Constitutional rights do not mature and come into being magically only when one attains the state-defined age of majority. Minors, as well as adults, are protected by the Constitution and possess constitutional rights." But the fact that minors have constitutional rights does not necessarily mean that those rights correspond equally to those of adults. As the *Danforth* Court pointed out, "The Court . . . long has recognized that the State has somewhat broader authority to regulate the activities of children than of adults." The issue is a most interesting one: how should the courts balance the conflict between the privacy interest of the minor (which is protected for adults under *Roe v. Wade* and its progeny) and the parental interest in raising their child as they see fit (which is protected by *Pierce v. Society of Sisters* and its progeny)?

In *Danforth* the Court held that the State of Missouri could not constitutionally impose a blanket parental consent requirement as a condition for an unmarried minor's abortion during the first 12 weeks of her pregnancy. According to the Court, there were no significant state interests, whether to safeguard the family unit and parental authority or otherwise, in conditioning an abortion on the consent of a parent with respect to the under-18-year-old pregnant minor. As stressed in *Roe*, "the abortion decision and its effectuation must be left to the medical judgment of the pregnant woman's attending physician." *Id.* at 72–75 (quoting 410 U.S., at 164). The Court first addressed the statutory provision that required the consent of woman's spouse before she could have an abortion. The Court ruled that the state cannot "delegate to a spouse a veto power which the state itself is absolutely and totally prohibited from exercising during the first trimester of pregnancy." Then, when addressing the parental consent provision, the Court emphasized again that "the State does not have the constitutional authority to give a third party an absolute, and possibly arbitrary, veto over the decision of the physician and his patient to terminate the patient's pregnancy, regardless of the reason for withholding the consent." *Id.* at 74. The Court discussed whether there was any significant state interest in conditioning an abortion on the consent of a parent or person in loco parentis that is not present in the case of an adult. The Court determined,

> It is difficult, however, to conclude that providing a parent with absolute power to overrule a determination, made by the physician and his minor patient, to terminate the patient's pregnancy will serve to strengthen the family unit. Neither is it likely that such veto power will enhance parental authority or control where the minor and the nonconsenting parent are so fundamentally in conflict and the very existence of the pregnancy already has fractured the family structure. Any independent interest the parent may have in the termination of the minor daughter's pregnancy is no more weighty than the right of privacy of the competent minor mature enough to have become pregnant.

Id. at 75. The Court pointed out that its holding that the parental consent statute was invalid "does not suggest that every minor, regardless of age or maturity, may give effective consent for termination of her pregnancy." *Id.*

Not long after *Danforth*, the Court struck down a statute that prohibited the distribution of contraceptives to persons under sixteen years old. *Carey v. Population Services International,* 431 U.S. 678 (1977). The Court determined that minors possess liberty interests in privacy under the due process clause to make decisions involving procreation and contraception. State restrictions inhibiting privacy rights of minors are valid only if they serve "any significant state interest. . . . that is not present in the case of an adult." The opinion pointed out that this standard was lower than the "compelling state interest" test applied to restrictions on the privacy rights of adults. *Id.* at n15. This less rigorous standard is "appropriate both because of the States' greater latitude to regulate the conduct of children, . . . and because the right of privacy implicated here is 'the interest in independence in making certain kinds of important decisions,' *Whalen v. Roe,* 429 U.S. 589, 599–600 (1977), and the law has generally regarded minors as having a lesser capability for making important decisions."

The plurality opinion analyzed the state interest in preventing teenage sexual activity:

The argument is that minors' sexual activity may be deterred by increasing the hazards attendant on it. The same argument, however, would support a ban on abortions for minors, or indeed support a prohibition on abortions, or access to contraceptives, for the unmarried, whose sexual activity is also against the public policy of many States. Yet, in each of these areas, the Court has rejected the argument, noting in *Roe v. Wade*, that "no court or commentator has taken the argument seriously." 410 U.S., at 148. The reason for this unanimous rejection was stated in *Eisenstadt v. Baird*: "It would be plainly unreasonable to assume that [the State] has prescribed pregnancy and the birth of an unwanted child [or the physical and psychological dangers of an abortion] as punishment for fornication." We remain reluctant to attribute any such "scheme of values" to the State.

Id. at 695. Moreover, the Court expressed doubt that limiting access to contraceptives would discourage early sexual behavior.

The Court, in a plurality opinion written by Justice Powell, further elaborated on the kind of minor abortion statute that would pass constitutional muster in *Bellotti v. Baird*, 443 U.S. 622 (1979). The Massachusetts statute in that case allowed minors to have abortions only if they obtained the consent of both their parents or satisfied a court that an abortion would be in their best interests. The opinion pointed to "three reasons justifying the conclusion that the constitutional rights of children cannot be equated with those of adults: the peculiar vulnerability of children; their inability to make critical decisions in an informed, mature manner; and the importance of the parental role in child rearing." After discussing the central role that parents hold "in assisting their children on their way to responsible adulthood," the opinion addressed the "unique nature of the abortion decision, especially when made by a minor," that requires the state "to act with particular sensitivity" when it legislates to foster parental involvement in this matter.

The pregnant minor's options are much different from those facing a minor in other situations, such as deciding whether to marry. A minor not permitted to marry before the age of majority is required simply to postpone her decision. She and her intended spouse may preserve the opportunity for later marriage should they continue to desire it. A pregnant adolescent, however, cannot preserve for long the possibility of aborting, which effectively expires in a matter of weeks from the onset of pregnancy.

Moreover, the potentially severe detriment facing a pregnant woman, is not mitigated by her minority. Indeed, considering her probable education, employment skills, financial resources, and emotional maturity, unwanted motherhood may be exceptionally burdensome for a minor. In addition, the fact of having a child brings with it adult legal responsibility, for parenthood, like attainment of the age of majority, is one of the traditional criteria for the termination of the legal disabilities of minority. In sum, there are few situations in which denying a minor the right to make an important decision will have consequences so grave and indelible.

> Yet, an abortion may not be the best choice for the minor. The circumstances in which this issue arises will vary widely. In a given case, alternatives to abortion, such as marriage to the father of the child, arranging for its adoption, or assuming the responsibilities of motherhood with the assured support of family, may be feasible and relevant to the minor's best interests. Nonetheless, the abortion decision is one that simply cannot be postponed, or it will be made by default with far-reaching consequences.

Id. at 642–43.

The plurality opinion reaffirmed the Court's holding in *Danforth* that the state may not impose a blanket provision requiring parental consent for an abortion. The *Bellotti* plurality required the state to provide the minor with an alternative procedure [now known as a judical bypass] "to show either: (1) that she is mature enough and well enough informed to make her abortion decision, in consultation with her physician, independently of her parents' wishes; or (2) that even if she is not able to make this decision independently, the desired abortion would be in her best interests." *Id.* at 643–44.

What kinds of questions would help a judge determine if a minor is mature enough to make the abortion decision for herself? To what extent might the judge's own views about abortion influence this determination? Is there something incongruous about the mature minor doctrine as applied to the abortion decision?

The Supreme Court's most recent foray into the minor abortion arena occurred in two cases that were heard on the same day during October Term 1989. In *Hodgson v. Minnesota*, 497 U.S. 417 (1990), the Court addressed the issue of parental notification, as opposed to parental consent. A majority of five Justices held that the state requirement that both parents be notified of the minor's abortion decision did not reasonably further any state interest and thus was an unconstitutional burden on the minor's right to obtain an abortion. But a different majority of five determined that the constitutional problem with the notice requirement was overcome, because the statute allowed the minor to avoid notifying her parents through a judicial bypass provision.

The *Hodgson* opinion allowed a judicial bypass provision to save what would otherwise be an unconstitutional statute. The Court left open the question as to how onerous the notification provision could be and still be saved by a judicial bypass. At the same time, the Court considered the burdens that could be placed on a minor in a judicial bypass provision in *Ohio v. Akron Center for Reproductive Health*, 497 U.S. 502 (1990). After reading the opinion in that case, draft the most restrictive state statute that you think would pass constitutional muster.

OHIO v. AKRON CENTER FOR REPRODUCTIVE HEALTH

Supreme Court of the United States
497 U.S. 502 (1990)

JUSTICE KENNEDY announced the judgment of the Court and delivered the opinion of the Court with respect to Parts I, II, III, and IV,[6] and an opinion with respect to Part V, in which THE CHIEF JUSTICE, JUSTICE WHITE, and JUSTICE SCALIA join.

The Court of Appeals held invalid an Ohio statute that, with certain exceptions, prohibits any person from performing an abortion on an unmarried, unemancipated, minor woman absent notice to one of the woman's parents or a court order of approval. We reverse, for we determine that the statute accords with our precedents on parental notice and consent in the abortion context and does not violate the Fourteenth Amendment.

I

A

The Ohio Legislature, in November 1985, enacted Amended Substitute House Bill 319 (H. B. 319) and created Ohio Rev. Code Ann. §§ 2151.85 and 2505.073 (Supp. 1988). Section 2919.12(B), the cornerstone of this legislation, makes it a criminal offense, except in four specified circumstances, for a physician or other person to perform an abortion on an unmarried and unemancipated woman under 18 years of age.

The first and second circumstances in which a physician may perform an abortion relate to parental notice and consent. First, a physician may perform an abortion if he provides "at least twenty-four hours actual notice, in person or by telephone," to one of the woman's parents (or her guardian or custodian) of his intention to perform the abortion. § 2919.12(B)(1)(a)(i). The physician, as an alternative, may notify a minor's adult brother, sister, stepparent, or grand-parent, if the minor and the other relative each file an affidavit in the juvenile court stating that the minor fears physical, sexual, or severe emotional abuse from one of her parents. See §§ 2919.12(B)(1)(a)(i), 2919.12(B)(1)(b), 2919.12(B)(1)(c). If the physician cannot give the notice "after a reasonable effort," he may perform the abortion after "at least forty-eight hours constructive notice" by both ordinary and certified mail. § 2919.12(B)(2). Second, a physician may perform an abortion on the minor if one of her parents (or her guardian or custodian) has consented to the abortion in writing. See § 2919.12(B)(1)(a)(ii).

The third and fourth circumstances depend on a judicial procedure that allows a minor to bypass the notice and consent provisions just described. The statute allows a physician to perform an abortion without notifying one of the minor's parents or receiving the parent's consent if a juvenile court issues an order authorizing the minor to consent, or if a juvenile court or court of

---

6 [+] JUSTICE STEVENS and JUSTICE O'CONNOR join only Parts I, II, III, and IV of the opinion.

appeals, by its inaction, provides constructive authorization for the minor to consent.

The bypass procedure requires the minor to file a complaint in the juvenile court, stating (1) that she is pregnant; (2) that she is unmarried, under 18 years of age, and unemancipated; (3) that she desires to have an abortion without notifying one of her parents; (4) that she has sufficient maturity and information to make an intelligent decision whether to have an abortion without such notice, *or* that one of her parents has engaged in a pattern of physical, sexual, or emotional abuse against her, *or* that notice is not in her best interests; and (5) that she has or has not retained an attorney. The Ohio Supreme Court, as discussed below, has prescribed pleading forms for the minor to use.

The juvenile court must hold a hearing at the earliest possible time, but not later than the fifth business day after the minor files the complaint. The court must render its decision immediately after the conclusion of the hearing. Failure to hold the hearing within this time results in constructive authorization for the minor to consent to the abortion. At the hearing the court must appoint a guardian ad litem and an attorney to represent the minor if she has not retained her own counsel. The minor must prove her allegation of maturity, pattern of abuse, or best interests by clear and convincing evidence, and the juvenile court must conduct the hearing to preserve the anonymity of the complainant, keeping all papers confidential.

The minor has the right to expedited review. [The opinion described the review provisions].

B

Appellees in this action include the Akron Center for Reproductive Health, a facility that provides abortions; Max Pierre Gaujean, M.D., a physician who performs abortions at the Akron Center; and Rachael Roe, an unmarried, unemancipated, minor woman, who sought an abortion at the facility. In March 1986, days before the effective date of H. B. 319, appellees and others brought a facial challenge to the constitutionality of the statute in the United States District Court for the Northern District of Ohio. The District Court, after various proceedings, issued a preliminary injunction and later a permanent injunction preventing the State of Ohio from enforcing the statute.

The Court of Appeals for the Sixth Circuit affirmed, concluding that H. B. 319 had six constitutional defects. These points, discussed below, related to the sufficiency of the expedited procedures, the guarantee of anonymity, the constructive authorization provisions, the clear and convincing evidence standard, the pleading requirements, and the physician's personal obligation to give notice to one of the minor's parents. *Akron Center for Reproductive Health v. Slaby*, 854 F.2d 852 (1988). The State of Ohio challenges the Court of Appeals' decision in its entirety. Appellees seek affirmance on the grounds adopted by the Court of Appeals and on other grounds.

II

We have decided five cases addressing the constitutionality of parental notice or parental consent statutes in the abortion context. See *Planned*

Parenthood of Central Mo. v. Danforth, 428 U.S. 52 (1976); *Bellotti v. Baird*, 443 U.S. 622(1979); *H. L. v. Matheson*, 450 U.S. 398 (1981); *Planned Parenthood Assn. of Kansas City, Mo., Inc. v. Ashcroft*, 462 U.S. 476 (1983); *Akron v. Akron Center for Reproductive Health, Inc.*, 462 U.S. 416 (1983). We do not need to determine whether a statute that does not accord with these cases would violate the Constitution, for we conclude that H. B. 319 is consistent with them.

A

This dispute turns, to a large extent, on the adequacy of H. B. 319's judicial bypass procedure. In analyzing this aspect of the dispute, we note that, although our cases have required bypass procedures for parental consent statutes, we have not decided whether parental notice statutes must contain such procedures. See *Matheson*, 450 U.S. at 413, and n.25 (upholding a notice statute without a bypass procedure as applied to immature, dependent minors). We leave the question open, because, whether or not the Fourteenth Amendment requires notice statutes to contain bypass procedures, H. B. 319's bypass procedure meets the requirements identified for parental consent statutes in *Danforth, Bellotti, Ashcroft,* and *Akron. Danforth* established that, in order to prevent another person from having an absolute veto power over a minor's decision to have an abortion, a State must provide some sort of bypass procedure if it elects to require parental consent. As we hold today in *Hodgson v. Minnesota*, 497 U.S. 417, it is a corollary to the greater intrusiveness of consent statutes that a bypass procedure that will suffice for a consent statute will suffice also for a notice statute. *See also Matheson*, 450 U.S. at 411, n.17 (notice statutes are not equivalent to consent statutes because they do not give anyone a veto power of over a minor's abortion decision).

The principal opinion in *Bellotti* stated four criteria that a bypass procedure in a consent statute must satisfy. Appellees contend that the bypass procedure does not satisfy these criteria. We disagree. First, the *Bellotti* principal opinion indicated that the procedure must allow the minor to show that she possesses the maturity and information to make her abortion decision, in consultation with her physician, without regard to her parents' wishes. The Court reaffirmed this requirement in *Akron* by holding that a State cannot presume the immaturity of girls under the age of 15. In the case now before us, we have no difficulty concluding that H. B. 319 allows a minor to show maturity in conformity with the principal opinion in *Bellotti*. The statute permits the minor to show that she "is sufficiently mature and well enough informed to decide intelligently whether to have an abortion."

Second, the *Bellotti* principal opinion indicated that the procedure must allow the minor to show that, even if she cannot make the abortion decision by herself, "the desired abortion would be in her best interests." We believe that H. B. 319 satisfies the *Bellotti* language as quoted. The statute requires the juvenile court to authorize the minor's consent where the court determines that the abortion is in the minor's best interest and in cases where the minor has shown a pattern of physical, sexual, or emotional abuse.

Third, the *Bellotti* principal opinion indicated that the procedure must insure the minor's anonymity. *See* 443 U.S. at 644. H. B. 319 satisfies this standard. Section 2151.85 (D) provides that "the [juvenile] court shall not notify the parents, guardian, or custodian of the complainant that she is pregnant or that she wants to have an abortion." Section 2151.85(F) further states:

> Each hearing under this section shall be conducted in a manner that will preserve the anonymity of the complainant. The complaint and all other papers and records that pertain to an action commenced under this section shall be kept confidential and are not public records.

Section 2505.073(B), in a similar fashion, requires the court of appeals to preserve the minor's anonymity and confidentiality of all papers on appeal. The State, in addition, makes it a criminal offense for an employee to disclose documents not designated as public records.

Appellees argue that the complaint forms prescribed by the Ohio Supreme Court will require the minor to disclose her identity. Unless the minor has counsel, she must sign a complaint form to initiate the bypass procedure and, even if she has counsel, she must supply the name of one of her parents at four different places. Appellees would prefer protections similar to those included in the statutes that we reviewed in *Bellotti* and *Ashcroft*. The statute in *Bellotti* protected anonymity by permitting use of a pseudonym. Appellees also maintain that the Ohio laws requiring court employees not to disclose public documents are irrelevant because the right to anonymity is broader than the right not to have officials reveal one's identity to the public at large.

Confidentiality differs from anonymity, but we do not believe that the distinction has constitutional significance in the present context. The distinction has not played a part in our previous decisions, and, even if the *Bellotti* principal opinion is taken as setting the standard, we do not find complete anonymity critical. H. B. 319, like the statutes in *Bellotti* and *Ashcroft*, takes reasonable steps to prevent the public from learning of the minor's identity. We refuse to base a decision on the facial validity of a statute on the mere possibility of unauthorized, illegal disclosure by state employees. H. B. 319, like many sophisticated judicial procedures, requires participants to provide identifying information for administrative purposes, not for public disclosure.

Fourth, the *Bellotti* principal opinion indicated that courts must conduct a bypass procedure with expedition to allow the minor an effective opportunity to obtain the abortion. H. B. 319, as noted above, requires the trial court to make its decision within five "business day[s]" after the minor files her complaint, requires the court of appeals to docket an appeal within four "days" after the minor files a notice of appeal, and requires the court of appeals to render a decision within five "days" after docketing the appeal.

The District Court and the Court of Appeals assumed that all of the references to days in §§ 2151.85(B)(1) and 2505.073(A) meant business days as opposed to calendar days. They calculated, as a result, that the procedure could take up to 22 calendar days because the minor could file at a time during the year in which the 14 business days needed for the bypass procedure would encompass 3 Saturdays, 3 Sundays, and 2 legal holidays. Appellees maintain, on the basis of an affidavit included in the record, that a 3-week delay could increase by a substantial measure both the costs and the medical risks of an abortion. They conclude, as did those courts, that H. B. 319 does not satisfy the *Bellotti* principal opinion's expedition requirement.

As a preliminary matter, the 22-day calculation conflicts with two well-known rules of construction discussed in our abortion cases and elsewhere. "Where fairly possible, courts should construe a statute to avoid a danger of unconstitutionality." Although we recognize that the other federal courts " 'are better schooled in and more able to interpret the laws of their respective States' " than are we, the Court of Appeals' decision strikes us as dubious. Interpreting the term "days" in § 2505.073(A) to mean business days instead of calendar days seems inappropriate and unnecessary because of the express and contrasting use of "business day[s]" in § 2151.85(B)(1). In addition, because appellees are making a facial challenge to a statute, they must show that "no set of circumstances exists under which the Act would be valid." *Webster v. Reproductive Health Services*, 492 U.S. 490, 524 (1989) (O'CONNOR, J., concurring). The Court of Appeals should not have invalidated the Ohio statute on a facial challenge based upon a worst-case analysis that may never occur. Moreover, under our precedents, the mere possibility that the procedure may require up to 22 days in a rare case is plainly insufficient to invalidate the statute on its face. *Ashcroft*, for example, upheld a Missouri statute that contained a bypass procedure that could require 17 calendar days plus a sufficient time for deliberation and decisionmaking at both the trial and appellate levels.

B

Appellees ask us, in effect, to extend the criteria used by some Members of the Court in *Bellotti* and the cases following it by imposing three additional requirements on bypass procedures. First, they challenge the constructive authorization provisions in H. B. 319, which enable a minor to obtain an abortion without notifying one of her parents if either the juvenile court or the court of appeals fails to act within the prescribed time limits. They speculate that the absence of an affirmative order when a court fails to process the minor's complaint will deter the physician from acting.

We discern no constitutional defect in the statute. Absent a demonstrated pattern of abuse or defiance, a State may expect that its judges will follow mandated procedural requirements. There is no showing that the time limitations imposed by H. B. 319 will be ignored. With an abundance of caution, and concern for the minor's interests, Ohio added the constructive authorization provisions in H. B. 319 to ensure expedition of the bypass procedures even if these time limits are not met. The State represents that a physician can obtain certified documentation from the juvenile or appellate court that constructive authorization has occurred. We did not require a similar safety net in the bypass procedures in *Ashcroft*, and find no defect in the procedures that Ohio has provided.

Second, appellees ask us to rule that a bypass procedure cannot require a minor to prove maturity or best interests by a standard of clear and convincing evidence. They maintain that, when a State seeks to deprive an individual of liberty interests, it must take upon itself the risk of error. *See Santosky v. Kramer*, 455 U.S. 745, 755 (1982). House Bill 319 violates this standard, in their opinion, not only by placing the burden of proof upon the minor, but also by imposing a heightened standard of proof.

This contention lacks merit. A State does not have to bear the burden of proof on the issues of maturity or best interests. The principal opinion in *Bellotti* indicates that a State may require the minor to prove these facts in a bypass procedure. A State, moreover, may require a heightened standard of proof when, as here, the bypass procedure contemplates an *ex parte* proceeding at which no one opposes the minor's testimony. We find the clear and convincing standard used in H. B. 319 acceptable. The Ohio Supreme Court has stated:

> Clear and convincing evidence is that measure or degree of proof which will produce in the mind of the trier of facts a firm belief or conviction as to the allegations sought to be established. It is intermediate, being more than a mere preponderance, but not to the extent of such certainty as is required beyond a reasonable doubt as in criminal cases. It does not mean clear and unequivocal.

Our precedents do not require the State to set a lower standard. Given that the minor is assisted in the courtroom by an attorney as well as a guardian ad litem, this aspect of H. B. 319 is not infirm under the Constitution.

Third, appellees contend that the pleading requirements in H. B. 319 create a trap for the unwary. The minor, under the statutory scheme and the requirements prescribed by the Ohio Supreme Court, must choose among three pleading forms. *See* OHIO REV. CODE ANN. § 2151.85(C) (Supp. 1988). The first alleges only maturity and the second alleges only best interests. She may not attempt to prove both maturity and best interests unless she chooses the third form, which alleges both of these facts. Appellees contend that the complications imposed by this scheme deny a minor the opportunity, required by the principal opinion in *Bellotti*, to prove either maturity or best interests or both.

Even on the assumption that the pleading scheme could produce some initial confusion because few minors would have counsel when pleading, the simple and straightforward procedure does not deprive the minor of an opportunity to prove her case. It seems unlikely that the Ohio courts will treat a minor's choice of complaint form without due care and understanding for her unrepresented status. In addition, we note that the minor does not make a binding election by the initial choice of pleading form. The minor, under H. B. 319, receives appointed counsel after filing the complaint and may move for leave to amend the pleadings. Regardless of whether Ohio could have written a simpler statute, H. B. 319 survives a facial challenge.

III

Appellees contend our inquiry does not end even if we decide that H. B. 319 conforms to *Danforth, Bellotti, Matheson, Ashcroft,* and *Akron.* They maintain that H. B. 319 gives a minor a state-law substantive right "to avoid unnecessary or hostile parental involvement" if she can demonstrate that her maturity or best interests favor abortion without notifying one of her parents. They argue that H. B. 319 deprives the minor of this right without due process because the pleading requirements, the alleged lack of expedition and anonymity, and the clear and convincing evidence standard make the bypass procedure unfair. We find no merit in this argument.

The confidentiality provisions, the expedited procedures, and the pleading form requirements, on their face, satisfy the dictates of minimal due process. We see little risk of erroneous deprivation under these provisions and no need to require additional procedural safeguards. The clear and convincing evidence standard, for reasons we have described, does not place an unconstitutional burden on the types of proof to be presented. The minor is assisted by an attorney and a guardian ad litem and the proceeding is *ex parte*. The standard ensures that the judge will take special care in deciding whether the minor's consent to an abortion should proceed without parental notification. As a final matter, given that the statute provides definite and reasonable deadlines, the constructive authorization provision, also comports with due process on its face.

IV

Appellees, as a final matter, contend that we should invalidate H. B. 319 in its entirety because the statute requires the parental notice to be given by the physician who is to perform the abortion. In *Akron*, the Court found unconstitutional a requirement that the attending physician provide the information and counseling relevant to informed consent. Although the Court did not disapprove of informing a woman of the health risks of an abortion, it explained that "the State's interest is in ensuring that the woman's consent is informed and unpressured; the critical factor is whether she obtains the necessary information and counseling from a qualified person, not the identity of the person from whom she obtains it." Appellees maintain, in a similar fashion, that Ohio has no reason for requiring the minor's physician, rather than some other qualified person, to notify one of the minor's parents.

Appellees, however, have failed to consider our precedent on this matter. We upheld, in *Matheson*, a statute that required a physician to notify the minor's parents. The distinction between notifying a minor's parents and informing a woman of the routine risks of an abortion has ample justification; although counselors may provide information about general risks as in *Akron*, appellees do not contest the superior ability of a physician to garner and use information supplied by a minor's parents upon receiving notice. We continue to believe that a State may require the physician himself or herself to take reasonable steps to notify a minor's parent because the parent often will provide important medical data to the physician. As we explained in *Matheson:*

> The medical, emotional, and psychological consequences of an abortion are serious and can be lasting; this is particularly so when the patient is immature. An adequate medical and psychological case

history is important to the physician. Parents can provide medical and psychological data, refer the physician to other sources of medical history, such as family physicians, and authorize family physicians to give relevant data.

The conversation with the physician, in addition, may enable a parent to provide better advice to the minor. The parent who must respond to an event with complex philosophical and emotional dimensions is given some access to an experienced and, in an ideal case, detached physician who can assist the parent in approaching the problem in a mature and balanced way. This access may benefit both the parent and child in a manner not possible through notice by less qualified persons.

Any imposition on a physician's schedule, by requiring him or her to give notice when the minor does not have consent from one of her parents or court authorization, must be evaluated in light of the complete statutory scheme. The statute allows the physician to send notice by mail if he or she cannot reach the minor's parent "after a reasonable effort," and also allows him or her to forgo notice in the event of certain emergencies. These provisions are an adequate recognition of the physician's professional status. On this facial challenge, we find the physician notification requirement unobjectionable.

V

The Ohio statute, in sum, does not impose an undue, or otherwise unconstitutional, burden on a minor seeking an abortion. We believe, in addition, that the legislature acted in a rational manner in enacting H. B. 319. A free and enlightened society may decide that each of its members should attain a clearer, more tolerant understanding of the profound philosophic choices confronted by a woman who is considering whether to seek an abortion. Her decision will embrace her own destiny and personal dignity, and the origins of the other human life that lie within the embryo. The State is entitled to assume that, for most of its people, the beginnings of that understanding will be within the family, society's most intimate association. It is both rational and fair for the State to conclude that, in most instances, the family will strive to give a lonely or even terrified minor advice that is both compassionate and mature. The statute in issue here is a rational way to further those ends. It would deny all dignity to the family to say that the State cannot take this reasonable step in regulating its health professions to ensure that, in most cases, a young woman will receive guidance and understanding from a parent. We uphold H. B. 319 on its face and reverse the judgment of the Court of Appeals.

It is so ordered.

JUSTICE SCALIA, *concurring.*

[JUSTICE SCALIA reiterated his opinion that the Constitution contains no right to abortion.]

JUSTICE STEVENS, *concurring in part and concurring in the judgment.*

As the Court emphasizes, appellees have challenged the Ohio statute only on its face. The State may presume that, in most of its applications, the statute will reasonably further its legitimate interest in protecting the welfare of its minor citizens. In some of its applications, however, the one-parent notice requirement will not reasonably further that interest. There will be exceptional situations in which notice will cause a realistic risk of physical harm to the pregnant woman, will cause trauma to an ill parent, or will enable the parent to prevent the abortion for reasons that are unrelated to the best interests of the minor. The Ohio statute recognizes that possibility by providing a judicial bypass. The question in this case is whether that statutory protection for the exceptional case is so obviously inadequate that the entire statute should be invalidated. I am not willing to reach that conclusion before the statute has been implemented and the significance of its restrictions evaluated in the light of its administration. I therefore agree that the Court of Appeals' judgment must be reversed, and I join Parts I-IV of the Court's opinion.[7]

. . . .

JUSTICE BLACKMUN, with whom JUSTICE BRENNAN and JUSTICE MARSHALL join, *dissenting.*

I

The constitutional right to "control the quintessentially intimate, personal, and life-directing decision whether to carry a fetus to term," *Webster v. Reproductive Health Services,* 492 U.S. 490, 538 (1989) (opinion concurring in part and dissenting in part), does "not mature and come into being magically only when one attains the state-defined age of majority. Minors, as well as adults, are protected by the Constitution and possess constitutional rights." *Planned Parenthood of Central Mo. v. Danforth; Hodgson v. Minnesota* ("The constitutional protection against unjustified state intrusion into the process of deciding whether or not to bear a child extends to pregnant minors as well as adult women"). Although the Court "has recognized that the State has somewhat broader authority to regulate the activities of children than of adults," in doing so, the State nevertheless must demonstrate that there is a *"significant state interest* in conditioning an abortion . . . that is not present in the case of an adult." *Danforth,* 428 U.S. at 74–75 (emphasis added). "Any independent interest the parent may have in the termination of the minor daughter's pregnancy is no more weighty than the right of privacy of the competent minor mature enough to have become pregnant." *Id.,* at 75.

"The abortion decision differs in important ways from other decisions that may be made during minority. The need to preserve the constitutional right

---

[7] [1] It is perhaps trite for a judge to reiterate the familiar proposition that an opinion about the facial constitutionality of a statute says nothing about the judge's views concerning the wisdom or unwisdom of the measure. I have made this observation before, and am moved by JUSTICE BLACKMUN's eloquent dissent to do so again. It would indeed be difficult to contend that each of the challenged provisions of the Ohio statute — or the entire mosaic — represents wise legislation.

and the unique nature of the abortion decision, especially when made by a minor, require a State to act with *particular sensitivity* when it legislates to foster parental involvement in this matter." *Bellotti v. Baird*, 443 U.S. 622, 642 (1979) (opinion of Powell, J.) (emphasis added) "Particular sensitivity" is mandated because "there are few situations in which denying a minor the right to make an important decision will have consequences so grave and indelible." It should be obvious that "considering her probable education, employment skills, financial resources, and emotional maturity, unwanted motherhood may be exceptionally burdensome for a minor."

The State of Ohio has acted with particular *in*sensitivity in enacting the statute the Court today upholds. Rather than create a judicial-bypass system that reflects the sensitivity necessary when dealing with a minor making this deeply intimate decision, Ohio has created a tortuous maze. Moreover, the State has failed utterly to show that it has any significant state interest in deliberately placing its pattern of obstacles in the path of the pregnant minor seeking to exercise her constitutional right to terminate a pregnancy. The challenged provisions of the Ohio statute are merely "poorly disguised elements of discouragement for the abortion decision." *Thornburgh v. American College of Obstetricians and Gynecologists*, 476 U.S. 747, 763 (1986).

II

The majority does not decide whether the Ohio parental-notice statute must contain a judicial-bypass procedure because the majority concludes that the bypass procedure in the statute "meets the requirements identified for parental consent statutes in *Danforth, Bellotti, Ashcroft*, and *Akron*." I conclude, however, that, because of the minor's emotional vulnerability and financial dependency on her parents, and because of the "unique nature of the abortion decision," and its consequences, a parental-notice statute is tantamount to a parental-consent statute. As a practical matter, a notification requirement will have the same deterrent effect on a pregnant minor seeking to exercise her constitutional right as does a consent statute. *See Akron v. Akron Center for Reproductive Health, Inc.*, 462 U.S. 416, 441, n.31 (1983); *H. L. v. Matheson*, 450 U.S. 398, 420, n.9 (1981) (concurring opinion). Thus a notice statute, like a consent statute, must contain a bypass procedure that comports with the standards set forth in *Bellotti II*. Because I disagree with the Court's conclusion that the Ohio bypass procedure complies with the dictates of *Bellotti II* and its progeny, I would strike down Ohio Amended Substitute House Bill 319.

The *Bellotti II* principal opinion stated:

A pregnant minor is entitled in such a [judicial-bypass] proceeding to show either: (1) that she is mature enough and well enough informed to make her abortion decision, in consultation with her physician, independently of her parents' wishes; or (2) that even if she is not able to make this decision independently, the desired abortion would be in her best interests.

The language of the Ohio statute purports to follow the standards for a bypass procedure that are set forth in *Bellotti II*, but at each stage along the way, the statute deliberately places "substantial state-created obstacles in the pregnant [minor's] path to an abortion," *Maher v. Roe*, 432 U.S. 464, 477, n.10 (1977), in the legislative hope that she will stumble, perhaps fall, and at least ensuring that she "conquer a multi-faceted obstacle course" before she is able to exercise her constitutional right to an abortion. Dellinger & Sperling, *Abortion and the Supreme Court: Retreat from* Roe v. Wade, 138 U. PA. L. REV. 83, 100 (1989). The majority considers each provision in a piecemeal fashion, never acknowledging or assessing the "degree of burden that the entire regime of abortion regulations places" on the minor.

A

The obstacle course begins when the minor first enters the courthouse to fill out the complaint forms. The " 'procedural trap,' " as it appropriately was described by the Court of Appeals, requires the minor to choose among three forms. The first alleges *only* maturity; the second alleges *only* that the abortion is in her best interest. Only if the minor chooses the third form, which alleges both, may the minor attempt to prove both maturity *and* best interest as is her right under *Bellotti II*. The majority makes light of what it acknowledges might be "some initial confusion" of the unsophisticated minor who is trying to deal with an unfamiliar and mystifying court system on an intensely intimate matter. The Court points out that the minor, with counsel appointed after she filed the complaint, "may move for leave to amend the pleadings" and avers that it "seems unlikely that the Ohio courts will treat a minor's choice of complaint form without due care." I would take the Ohio Legislature's word, however, that its pleading requirement was intended to be meaningful. The constitutionality of a procedural provision cannot be analyzed on the basis that it may have no effect. If the pleading requirement prevents some minors from showing either that they are mature or that an abortion would be in their best interests, it plainly is unconstitutional.

The majority fails to elucidate *any* state interest in setting up this barricade for the young pregnant woman — a barricade that will "serve only to confuse . . . her and to heighten her anxiety." *Thornburgh*, 476 U.S. at 762. The justification the State put forward before the Court of Appeals was the "absurd contention that 'any minor claiming to be mature and well enough informed to independently make such an important decision as an abortion should also be mature enough to file her complaint under [the appropriate subsection].' " This proffered "justification" is even more harsh than the Court of Appeals noted. It excludes the mature minor who may not have the intellectual capacity to understand these tangled forms, and it spurns the immature minor who is abused or who contends for some other reason that an abortion without parental involvement would be in her best interest. Surely, the goal of the court proceeding is to assist, not to entrap, the young pregnant woman.

The State's interest in "streamlining" the claims, belatedly asserted for the first time before this Court, is no less absurd. It is ludicrous to confound the pregnant minor, forced to go to court at this time of crisis in her life, with alternative complaint forms that must later be rescinded by appointed counsel and replaced by the only form that is constitutionally valid. Moreover, this ridiculous pleading scheme leaves to the judge's discretion whether the minor may amend her pleading and attempt to prove both her maturity and best interest. To allow the resolution of this vital issue to turn on a judge's discretion does not comport with *Bellotti II*'s declaration that the minor who "fails to satisfy the court that she is competent to make this decision independently . . . *must* be permitted to show that an abortion nevertheless would be in her best interests." (Emphasis added.)

B

As the pregnant minor attempts to find her way through the labyrinth set up by the State of Ohio, she encounters yet another obstruction even before she has completed the complaint form. In *Bellotti II*, the principal opinion insisted that the judicial-bypass procedure "must assure that a resolution of the issue, and any appeals that may follow, will be completed with *anonymity*. . . ." That statement was not some idle procedural requirement, but stems from the proposition that the Due Process Clause protects the woman's right to make her decision "independently and privately." *Hodgson*. The zone of privacy long has been held to encompass an "individual interest in avoiding disclosure of personal matters." *Whalen v. Roe.* The Ohio statute does not safeguard that right. Far from keeping the identity of the minor anonymous, the statute requires the minor to sign her full name and the name of one of her parents on the complaint form. Acknowledging that "confidentiality differs from anonymity," the majority simply asserts that "complete anonymity" is not "critical." That easy conclusion is irreconcilable with *Bellotti*'s anonymity requirement. The definition of "anonymous" is "not named or identified." WEBSTER'S NINTH NEW COLLEGIATE DICTIONARY 88 (1983). Complete anonymity, then, appears to be the only kind of anonymity that a person could possibly have. The majority admits that case law regarding the anonymity requirement has permitted no less. *See ante*, at 512, citing *Planned Parenthood League of Massachusetts v. Bellotti*, 641 F.2d 1006, 1025 (CA1 1981) (pseudonym); *Planned Parenthood Assn. of Kansas City, Mo., Inc. v. Ashcroft*, 462 U.S. 476, 491, n.16 (1983) (initials). *See also Thornburgh*, 476 U.S. at 766 ("The decision to terminate a pregnancy is an intensely private one that must be protected in a way that assures anonymity").

The majority points to Ohio laws requiring court employees not to disclose public documents, blithely assuming that the "mere possibility of unauthorized, illegal disclosure by state employees" is insufficient to establish that the confidentiality of the proceeding is not protected. In fact, the provisions regarding the duty of court employees not to disclose public documents amount to no more than "generally stated principles of . . . confidentiality." *American College of Obstetricians and Gynecologists v. Thornburgh*, 737 F.2d 283, 297 (CA3 1984), *aff'd on other grounds*, 476 U.S. 747(1986). As the District Court pointed out, there are no indications of how a clerk's office, large or small, is to ensure that the records of abortion cases will be distinguished from the records of all other cases that are available to the public. *Cf. Planned Parenthood League of Massachusetts v. Bellotti*, 641 F.2d at 1025 (minor proceeds under pseudonym and affidavit containing her identity is kept in separate, sealed file). Nor are there measures for sealing the record after the case is closed to prevent its public availability; *Planned Parenthood Assn. of the Atlanta Area, Inc. v. Harris,* 670 F. Supp. 971, 991 (ND Ga. 1987) (noting with disapproval that Georgia statute made no provision for court documents to be sealed). This Court is well aware that, unless special care is taken, court documents of an intimate nature will find their way to the press and public. *See The Florida Star v. B. J. F.,* 491 U.S. 524, (1989) (reporter in police room copied police report and published article with rape victim's full name). The State has offered no justification for its failure to provide specific guidelines to be followed by the juvenile court to ensure anonymity for the pregnant minor — even though it has in place a procedure to assure the anonymity of juveniles who have been adjudicated delinquent or unruly. *See* OHIO REV. CODE ANN. § 2151.358 (1976) (detailed provision for sealing record and for expungement of record).

"A woman and her physician will necessarily be more reluctant to choose an abortion if there exists a possibility that her decision and her identity will become known publicly." *Thornburgh,* 476 U.S. at 766. A minor, whose very purpose in going through a judicial-bypass proceeding is to avoid notifying a hostile or abusive parent, would be most alarmed at signing her name and the name of her parent on the complaint form. Generalized statements concerning the confidentiality of records would be of small comfort, even if she were aware of them. True anonymity is essential to an effective, meaningful bypass. In the face of the forms that the minor must actually deal with, the State's assurances that the minor's privacy will be protected ring very hollow. I would not permit the State of Ohio to force a minor to forgo her anonymity in order to obtain a waiver of the parental-notification requirement.

C

Because a "pregnant adolescent . . . cannot preserve for long the possibility of aborting, which effectively expires in a matter of weeks from the onset of pregnancy," this Court has required that the State "must assure" that the "resolution of the issue, and any appeals that may follow, will be completed with . . . sufficient expedition to provide an effective opportunity for an abortion to be obtained." Ohio's judicial-bypass procedure can consume up to three weeks of a young woman's pregnancy. I would join the Sixth Circuit, the District Court, and the other federal courts that have held that a time span of this length fails to guarantee a sufficiently expedited procedure.

The majority is unconcerned that "the procedure may require up to 22 days in a rare case." I doubt the "rarity" of such cases. In any event, the Court of Appeals appropriately pointed out that, because a minor often does not learn of her pregnancy until a late stage in the first trimester, time lost during that trimester is especially critical. The Court ignores the fact that the medical risks surrounding abortion increase as pregnancy advances and that such delay may push a woman into her second trimester, where the medical risks, economic costs, and state regulation increase dramatically. *See Roe v. Wade,* 410 U.S. 113 (1973); *H. L. v. Matheson,* 450 U.S. at 439, and n.25 (dissenting opinion). Minors, who are more likely to seek later abortions than adult women, and who usually are not financially independent, will suffer acutely from any delay. *See Ashcroft*, 462 U.S. at 497–498 (opinion concurring in part and dissenting in part) (an increased cost factor "may seem insignificant from the Court's comfortable perspective," but is not "equally insignificant" to "the unemployed teenager" for whom this additional cost may well put an abortion beyond reach). Because a delay of up to 22 days may limit significantly a woman's ability to obtain an abortion, I agree with the conclusions of the District Court and the Court of Appeals that the statute violates this Court's command that a judicial-bypass proceeding be conducted with sufficient speed to maintain "an effective opportunity for an abortion to be obtained." *Bellotti II*, 443 U.S. at 644 (opinion of POWELL, J.).

D

The Ohio statute provides that if the juvenile or appellate courts fail to act within the statutory time frame, an abortion without parental notification is "constructively" authorized. Although Ohio's Legislature may have intended this provision to expedite the bypass procedure, the confusion that will result from the constructive-authorization provision will add further delay to the judicial-bypass proceeding, and is yet one more obstruction in the path of the pregnant minor. The physician risks civil damages, criminal penalties, including imprisonment, as well as revocation of his license for disobeying the statute's commands, but the statute provides for no formal court order or other relief to safeguard the physician from these penalties. The State argues that a combination of a date-stamped copy of the minor's complaint and a "docket sheet showing no entry" would inform the physician that the abortion could proceed. Yet, the mere absence of an entry on a court's docket sheet hardly would be reassuring to a physician facing such dire consequences, and the State offers no reason why a formal order or some kind of actual notification from the clerk of court would not be possible. There is no doubt that the nebulous authorization envisioned by this statute "in conjunction with a statute imposing strict civil and criminal liability . . . could have a profound chilling effect on the willingness of physicians to perform abortions. . . ." *Colautti v. Franklin*, 439 U.S. 379, 396 (1979). I agree with the Court of Appeals that the "practical effect" of the " 'pocket approval' " provision is to frustrate the minor's right to an expedient disposition of her petition.

E

If the minor is able to wend her way through the intricate course of pre-liminaries Ohio has set up for her and at last reaches the court proceeding, the State shackles her even more tightly with still another "extra layer and burden of regulation on the abortion decision." *Danforth*, 428 U.S. at 66. The minor must demonstrate by "clear and convincing evidence" either (1) her maturity; (2) or that one of her parents has engaged in a pattern of physical, sexual, or emotional abuse against her; or (3) that notice to a parent is not in her best interest. The imposition of this heightened standard of proof unduly burdens the minor's right to seek an abortion and demonstrates a fundamental misunderstanding of the real nature of a court-bypass proceeding.

The function of a standard of proof is to "instruct the factfinder concerning the degree of confidence our society thinks he should have in the correctness of factual conclusions," *Addington v. Texas,* 441 U.S. 418, 423 (1979), quoting *In re Winship,* 397 U.S. 358, 370 (1970) (concurring opinion), and is "a societal judgment about how the risk of error should be distributed between the litigants." *Santosky v. Kramer,* 455 U.S. 745, 755 (1982). By imposing such a stringent standard of proof, this Ohio statute improperly places the risk of an erroneous decision on the minor, the very person whose fundamental right is at stake. *Cf. id.,* at 756 (clear and convincing standard of proof usually has been employed to preserve fundamental fairness in a variety of *government-initiated* proceedings that threaten to deprive the *individual* involved with a significant deprivation of liberty). Even if the judge is satisfied that the minor is mature or that an abortion is in her best interest, the court may not authorize the procedure unless it additionally finds that the evidence meets a "clear and convincing" standard of proof.

The majority asserts that a State may require a heightened standard of proof because the procedure is *ex parte.* According to the majority, the only alternative to the "clear and convincing" standard is a preponderance of the evidence standard, which would require proof by the greater weight of the evidence. The majority reasons that the preponderance standard is unsuited to a *Bellotti II* bypass because, if the minor presents any evidence at all, and no evidence is put forth in opposition, the minor always will present the greater weight of the evidence. Yet, as the State explained at argument, the bypass procedure is inquisitorial in nature, where the judge questions the minor to discover if she meets the requirements set down in *Bellotti II.* The judge will be making this determination after a hearing that resembles an interview, not an evidentiary proceeding. The District Court observed, "the judge's decision will necessarily be based largely on subjective standards without the benefit of any evidence other then a woman's testimony." 633 F. Supp. at 1137. Thus, unlike the procedure the majority seems to envision, it is not the quantity of the evidence presented that is crucial in the bypass proceeding; rather, the crucial factors are the nature of the minor's statements to the judge and her demeanor. Contrary to the majority's theory, if the minor presents evidence that she is mature, she still must *satisfy* the judge that this is so, even without this heightened standard of proof. The use of a heightened standard in the very special context of *Bellotti*'s court-bypass procedure does little to facilitate a fair and reliable result and imports an element from the adversarial process into this unique inquiry where it has no rightful place.

Although I think the provision is constitutionally infirm for all minors, I am particularly concerned about the effect it will have on sexually or physically abused minors. I agree that parental interest in the welfare of their children is "particularly strong where a *normal* family relationship exists." *Bellotti II,* 443 U.S. at 648 (opinion of Powell, J.) (emphasis added). A minor needs no statute to seek the support of loving parents. Where trust and confidence exist within the family structure, it is likely that communication already exists. If that compassionate support is lacking, an unwanted pregnancy is a poor way to generate it.

Sadly, not all children in our country are fortunate enough to be members of loving families. For too many young pregnant women, parental involvement in this most intimate decision threatens harm, rather than promises comfort.[8] The Court's selective blindness to this stark social reality is bewildering and distressing. Lacking the protection that young people typically find in their intimate family associations, these minors are desperately in need of constitutional protection. The sexually or physically abused minor may indeed be "lonely or even terrified," not of the abortion procedure, but of an abusive family member.[9] The Court's placid reference to the "compassionate and mature" advice the minor will receive from within the family must seem an unbelievable and cruel irony to those children trapped in violent families.[10]

Under the system Ohio has set up, a sexually abused minor must go to court and demonstrate to a complete stranger by clear and convincing evidence that she has been the victim of a pattern of sexual abuse. When asked at argument what kind of evidence a minor would be required to adduce at her bypass hearing, the State answered that the minor would tell her side to the judge and the judge would consider how well "the minor is able to articulate what her particular concerns are." The court procedure alone, in many cases, is extremely traumatic. The State and the Court are impervious to the additional burden imposed on the abused minor who, as any experienced social worker or counselor knows, is often afraid and ashamed to reveal what has happened to her to anyone outside the home. The Ohio statute forces that minor, despite her very real fears, to experience yet one more hardship. She must attempt, in public, and before strangers, to "articulate what her particular concerns are" with sufficient clarity to meet the State's "clear and convincing evidence" standard. The upshot is that for the abused minor the risk of error entails a risk of violence.

I would affirm the judgments below on the grounds of the several constitutional defects identified by the District Court and the Court of Appeals. The pleading requirements, the so-called and fragile guarantee of anonymity, the insufficiency of the expedited procedures, the constructive-authorization provision, and the "clear and convincing evidence" requirement singly and collectively cross the limit of constitutional acceptance.

III

Even if the Ohio statute complied with the *Bellotti II* requirements for a constitutional court bypass, I would conclude that the Ohio procedure is

---

[8] [5] In 1986, more than 1 million children and adolescents suffered harm from parental abuse or neglect, including sexual abuse. *See* Brief for American Psychological Association et al. as *Amici Curiae* 9–10, and sources cited therein. This figure is considered to be a minimum estimate because the incidence of abuse is substantially underreported. Pregnancy does not deter, and may even precipitate, physical attacks on women. *Ibid.*

[9] [6] "Pregnant minors may attempt to self-abort or to obtain an illegal abortion rather than risk parental notification." *H. L. v. Matheson*, 450 U.S. at 439, and n.26 (dissenting opinion).

[10] [7] The majority and the State of Ohio piously fail to mention what happens to these unwanted babies, born to mothers who are little more than children themselves, who have little opportunity, education, or life skills. Too often, the unwanted child becomes trapped in a cycle of poverty, despair, and violence. This Court, by experience, knows all too well that the States are unable adequately to supervise and protect these vulnerable citizens. *See Baltimore City Dept. of Social Services v. Bouknight*, 493 U.S. 549 (1990); *DeShaney v. Winnebago County Dept. of Social Services*, 489 U.S. 189 (1989).

unconstitutional because it requires the physician's personal and nondelegable obligation to give the required statutory notice. Particularly when viewed in context with the other impediments this statute places in the minor's path, there is more than a "possibility" that the physician-notification provision "was motivated more by a legislative interest in placing obstacles in the woman's path to an abortion, *see Maher v. Roe,* 432 U.S. 464, 474 (1977), than by a genuine interest in fostering informed decisionmaking." 497 U.S. at 524 (STEVENS, J., concurring in judgment). Most telling in this regard is the fact that, according to the Court of Appeals and the District Court, the State has never claimed that personal notice by the physician was required to effectuate an interest in the minor's health until the matter reached this Court. In fact, the State has taken three different positions as to its justification for this provision. *See* 854 F.2d at 862 ("The state's interest is in insuring that immature, unemancipated minors or minors whose best interests require notification have an adequate opportunity for parental intervention. The state has made no showing that this interest is advanced by requiring the attending physician, as opposed to another qualified, responsible person, to effectuate notification"); 633 F. Supp. at 1135 ("The state's attempt to characterize this duty as 'merely ministerial' does not advance its case at all, but rather suggests that its interest in having the physician perform this function is even less weighty than having him or her perform counseling to obtain informed consent [that was struck down in *Akron v. Akron Center for Reproductive Health, Inc.,* 462 U.S. 416(1983)]." If these chimerical health concerns now asserted in fact were the true motivation behind this provision, I seriously doubt that the State would have taken so long to say so.

Even if the State's interest in the health of the minor were the motivation behind the provision, the State never explains why it is that a physician interested in obtaining information, or a parent interested in providing information to a physician, cannot do so following the actual notification by some other competent professional, such as a nurse or counselor. And the State and the majority never explain why, if the physician's ability to garner information from the parents is of such paramount importance that only the physician may notify the parent, the statute allows the physician to send notice by mail if he or she cannot reach the minor's parent "after a reasonable effort."

The State's asserted interest in the minor's health care is especially ironic in light of the statute's interference with her physician's experienced professional judgment.[11] "If a physician is licensed by the State, he is recognized by the State as capable of exercising acceptable clinical judgment," *Doe v. Bolton,* 410 U.S. 179, 199 (1973), and he should be permitted to exercise that judgment as to whether he or another professional should be the person who will notify a minor's parents of her decision to terminate her pregnancy. I have no doubt that the attending physician, better than the Ohio Legislature, will know when a consultation with the parent is necessary. "If he fails in this,

---

[11] [8] In light of its asserted interest, I find it odd that Ohio allows minors to consent to treatment for sexually transmitted diseases, OHIO REV. CODE ANN. § 3709.241 (1988), and drug and alcohol abuse, § 3719.012(A). In each of these sensitive areas of health care, the State apparently trusts the physician to use his informed medical judgment as to whether he should question or inform the parent about the minor's medical and psychological condition.

professional censure and deprivation of his license are available remedies" already in place. The strictures of this Ohio law not only unduly burden the minor's right to an abortion, but impinge on the physician's professional discretion in the practice of medicine.

IV

The Ohio Legislature, in its wisdom, in 1985 enacted its antiabortion statute. That statute, when subjected to facial challenge, has been held unconstitutional by the United States District Court for the Northern District of Ohio and by the Court of Appeals for the Sixth Circuit. It is now, however, upheld on that challenge by a majority of this Court. The majority opinion takes up each challenged provision in turn; concludes, with brief comment, that it is within the bounds of the principal opinion in *Bellotti II;* and moves on routinely and in the same fashion to the succeeding provisions, one by one. A plurality then concludes, in Part V of the primary opinion, with hyperbole that can have but one result: to further incite an American press, public, and pulpit already inflamed by the pronouncement made by a plurality of this Court last Term in *Webster v. Reproductive Health Services*, 492 U.S. 490 (1989). The plurality indulges in paternalistic comments about "profound philosophic choices"; the "[woman's] own destiny and personal dignity"; the "origins of the other human life that lie within the embryo"; the family as "society's most intimate association"; the striving of the family to give to the minor "advice that is both compassionate and mature"; and the desired assumption that "in most cases" the woman will receive "guidance and understanding from a parent."

Some of this may be so "in most cases" and, it is to be hoped, in judges' own and other warm and protected, nurturing family environments. But those "most cases" need not rely on constitutional protections that are so vital for others. I have cautioned before that there is "another world 'out there'" that the Court "either chooses to ignore or fears to recognize." *Beal v. Doe,* 432 U.S. 438, 463 (1977). It is the unfortunate denizens of that world, often frightened and forlorn, lacking the comfort of loving parental guidance and mature advice, who most need the constitutional protection that the Ohio Legislature set out to make as difficult as possible to obtain.

That that legislature set forth with just such a goal is evident from the statute it spawned. The underlying nature of the Ohio statute is proclaimed by its strident and offensively restrictive provisions. It is as though the legislature said: "If the courts of the United States insist on upholding a limited right to an abortion, let us make that abortion as difficult as possible to obtain" because, basically, whether on professed moral or religious grounds or whatever, "we believe that is the way it must be." This often may be the way legislation is enacted, but few are the instances where the injustice is so evident and the impediments so gross as those inflicted by the Ohio Legislature on these vulnerable and powerless young women.

———

NOTES AND QUESTIONS

What kind of factors will courts consider in making the decision whether the minor is mature enough to make the abortion decision without parental input? Consider the following analysis from *In re B.S.*, 74 P. 3d 285 (Ariz. Ct. App. 2003):

> The court stated that maturity might be measured by examining the minor's experience, perspective, and judgment. "Experience" refers to all that has happened to the minor during her lifetime, including things she has seen or done. To assess the minor's experience level, the court will consider such things as the minor's age and experiences working outside the home, living away from home, traveling on her own, handling personal finances, and making other significant decisions.

> "Perspective" refers to the minor's ability to appreciate and understand the relative gravity and possible detrimental impact of available options, as well as the potential consequences of each. When evaluating the minor's perspective on her decision, the court will examine the steps she took to explore her options and the extent to which she considered and weighed the potential consequences of each option.

> "Judgment" refers to the minor's intellectual and emotional ability to make the abortion decision without the consent of her parents or guardian. To assess judgment, the court will consider the minor's conduct since learning of her pregnancy and her intellectual ability to understand her options and make an informed decision.

> At the hearing before the court, attended by B.S., her boyfriend, and her attorney, B.S. presented forms prepared by Planned Parenthood of Central and Northern Arizona. One form, titled "Counselor/ Clinician Certification — Mature Decision," reflects that a counseling intern counseled B.S. three days before B.S. filed her petition with the court. Preprinted language in the form states that the intern discussed with B.S. the availability and "pros and cons" of "choices the woman has regarding the pregnancy; parenting, adoption or abortion." Further, the intern related "the risks involved in the various types of medical procedures" for abortions. At the bottom of the form, the intern signed a statement that "B.S. is sufficiently mature to make her own decision in her own best interest based on a rational and thought-out analysis of the factors involved and the options available." According to the court, the Planned Parenthood forms were conclusory and provided no foundation for the counseling intern's opinion about B.S.'s level of maturity. In the absence of other documentary evidence or testimony, the forms did not allow the court to assess B.S.'s ability to understand and appreciate either her options or the potential risks and consequences associated with her decision.

B.S. also presented the court with a two-sentence, handwritten letter, purportedly from a high school teacher, who stated that B.S. was a good student in class and, to the teacher's knowledge, had not been disciplined at school. There was no evidence that B.S.'s teacher authored the letter. The letter was not written on school or personal letterhead and was not witnessed. Consequently, the court could not determine its authenticity. Additionally, although the letter provided some evidence of B.S.'s intellect, standing alone, it did not establish that B.S. is sufficiently mature to give informed consent.

Other evidence presented by B.S. was similarly insufficient. B.S. informed the court that a physician had not yet examined her, although she had confirmed her pregnancy through a test. The record does not reflect whether the counseling intern who met with B.S. possessed sufficient knowledge to adequately discuss with B.S. the medical risks associated with any option. Therefore, the court could not know whether B.S. had received and understood accurate medical information about the consequences and risks of both pregnancy and abortion. Without such information, B.S. lacked sufficient perspective to give informed consent to an abortion.

In response to the court's questioning, B.S. explained she desired an abortion because she could not afford to raise a child, and she did not want to be responsible for the child having a bad life. She also related why she had not asked her parents to consent to an abortion. Although this evidence was competent and relevant to the maturity determination, it did not establish that B.S. possessed sufficient maturity to give informed consent. The questions and answers on these topics lasted just over one minute. Additionally, the juvenile court was in the best position to judge B.S.'s demeanor and credibility during this exchange and then decide the impact of her answers on the issue of maturity. In summary, because reasonable evidence supported the juvenile court's finding that B.S. did not present competent evidence that she is sufficiently mature to give informed consent to an abortion, the appeals court determined that the finding was not clearly erroneous.

Id. at 616–18.

§ 3.04　CONTRACT LIABILITY

GEORGIA CODE ANNOTATED
§ 13-3-20 (1982)

Minors — Contracts for property or valuable consideration; contracts for necessaries.

(a) Generally the contract of a minor is voidable. If in a contractual transaction a minor receives property or other valuable consideration and, after arrival at the age of majority, retains possession of such property or continues to enjoy the benefit of such other valuable consideration, he shall have thereby ratified or affirmed the contract and it shall be binding on him.

(b) The contract of a minor for necessaries shall be binding on him as if he were of legal majority except that the party furnishing them to him must prove that the parent or guardian of such minor had failed or refused to supply sufficient necessaries for him.

SWALBERG v. HANNEGAN

Court of Appeals of Utah
883 P.2d 931 (1994)

BENCH, JUDGE:

Defendant minor challenges the trial court's grant of summary judgment ordering him to restore plaintiff adult to his precontractual status, although defendant had disaffirmed his contract with plaintiff. We reverse and remand.

FACTS

. . . .

In 1990, defendant contracted with plaintiff to purchase plaintiff's 1974 Ford truck for $2,500. Defendant's minority was apparently not discussed when the parties entered into the contract and there is no allegation that defendant made any misrepresentation as to his age. Defendant paid plaintiff $640 on the date of sale and agreed to pay the balance of $1,860 three months later. Rather than paying the balance, however, defendant disaffirmed the contract on the basis of his minority. Plaintiff filed a complaint asking that the contract be enforced or, in the alternative, that the truck be returned and that defendant be held responsible for the reasonable value of his use of the truck or for the amount it depreciated while in defendant's possession. Thereafter, while defendant was still a minor, plaintiff obtained possession of the truck.

Both defendant and plaintiff filed motions for summary judgment. Plaintiff argued that when defendant disaffirmed the contract, defendant did not properly "restore" the truck since he purchased it for $2,500 and returned it in a condition worth only $700. The court granted plaintiff's motion and awarded him $1,160, which was the remaining balance minus the value placed upon the truck in its returned condition. Defendant now appeals the trial court's order granting summary judgment in favor of plaintiff.

ANALYSIS

The dispositive issue on appeal is whether a minor who disaffirms a contract is required to restore the full value of the property received under the contract. Defendant argues that Utah law does not require a disaffirming minor to restore the other party to his or her precontractual status. We agree.

UTAH CODE ANN. § 15-2-2 (1986) provides:

> A minor is bound not only for the reasonable value of necessities but also for his contracts, unless he disaffirms them before or within a reasonable time after he obtains his majority and *restores to the other party all money or property received by him by virtue of said contracts and remaining within his control at any time after attaining his majority.*

This statute requires only that the property remaining within the minor's control be returned to the other party. The trial court held, however, that defendant was required to return the property in its original condition or be liable for the difference in value. This holding is clearly contrary to the provisions of this unamended nineteenth century statute, as interpreted by controlling Utah case law.

. . . .

[T]he trial court erred in requiring defendant to restore plaintiff to his precontractual status.

CONCLUSION

Section 15-2-2 requires that a disaffirming minor must only return the property remaining within his or her control. The Utah Supreme Court has interpreted this statute to allow a minor to effectively disaffirm the underlying contract without restoring the full value of the property received under the contract. Although we do not necessarily believe in the wisdom of this approach, we are not in a position to hold contrary to controlling case law under the doctrine of *stare decisis*. If a contracting and disaffirming minor is to be held responsible for waste of property received under a contract, it is for the legislature to so provide.

We reverse the trial court's grant of summary judgment in favor of plaintiff, and remand the case for further proceedings.

DODSON v. SHRADER

Supreme Court of Tennessee
824 S.W.2d 545 (1992)

O'Brien, Justice.

This is an action to disaffirm the contract of a minor for the purchase of a pick-up truck and for a refund of the purchase price. The issue is whether the minor is entitled to a full refund of the money he paid or whether the seller is entitled to a setoff for the decrease in value of the pick-up truck while it was in the possession of the minor.

In early April of 1987, Joseph Eugene Dodson, then sixteen years of age, purchased a used 1984 pick-up truck from Burns and Mary Shrader. The Shraders owned and operated Shrader's Auto Sales in Columbia, Tennessee. Dodson paid $4,900 in cash for the truck, using money he borrowed from his girlfriend's grandmother. At the time of the purchase there was no inquiry by the Shraders, and no misrepresentation by Mr. Dodson, concerning his minority. However, Mr. Shrader did testify that at the time he believed Mr. Dodson to be 18 or 19 years of age.

In December 1987, nine (9) months after the date of purchase, the truck began to develop mechanical problems. A mechanic diagnosed the problem as a burnt valve, but could not be certain without inspecting the valves inside the engine. Mr. Dodson did not want, or did not have the money, to effect these repairs. He continued to drive the truck despite the mechanical problems. One month later, in January, the truck's engine "blew up" and the truck became inoperable.

Mr. Dodson parked the vehicle in the front yard at his parents home where he lived. He contacted the Shraders to rescind the purchase of the truck and requested a full refund. The Shraders refused to accept the tender of the truck or to give Mr. Dodson the refund requested.

Mr. Dodson then filed an action in general sessions court seeking to rescind the contract and recover the amount paid for the truck. The general sessions court dismissed the warrant and Mr. Dodson perfected a *de novo* appeal to the circuit court. At the time the appeal was filed in the circuit court Mr. Shrader, through counsel, declined to accept the tender of the truck without compensation for its depreciation. Before the circuit court could hear the case, the truck, while parked in Dodson's front yard, was struck on the left front fender by a hit-and-run driver. At the time of the circuit court trial, according to Shrader, the truck was worth only $500 due to the damage to the engine and the left front fender.

The case was heard in the circuit court in November 1988. The trial judge, based on previous common-law decisions and, under the doctrine of *stare decisis* reluctantly granted the rescission. The Shraders were ordered, upon tender and delivery of the truck, to reimburse the $4,900 purchase price to Mr. Dodson. The Shraders appealed.

The Court of Appeals, per TODD, J., *affirmed*; CANTRELL, J., *concurring separately*, KOCH, J., *dissenting*.

The earliest recorded case in this State, on the issue involved, appears to be in *Wheaton v. East,* 13 Tenn. 35 (5 Yeager 41) (1833). In pronouncing the rule to apply governing infant's contracts, the court said:

> We do not perceive that any general rule, as to contracts which are void and voidable, can be stated with more precision that is done by Lord Ch. J. Eyre in *Keane v. Boycott,* 2 H. Black, 511, and quoted with approbation by Judge Story, 1 Mason's Rep. 82, and by Chancellor Kent, 2 Com. 193, which is this: 'that when the court can pronounce the contract to be to the infant's prejudice, it is void, and when to his benefit, as for necessaries, it is good; and when the contract is of any uncertain nature, as to benefit or prejudice, it is voidable only, at the election of the infant. . . .

. . . .

As noted by the Court of Appeals, the rule in Tennessee, as modified, is in accord with the majority rule on the issue among our sister states. This rule is based upon the underlying purpose of the "infancy doctrine" which is to protect minors from their lack of judgment and "from squandering their wealth through improvident contracts with crafty adults who would take advantage of them in the marketplace." *Halbman v. Lemke,* 298 N.W.2d 562, 564 (Wis. 1980).

There is, however, a modern trend among the states, either by judicial action or by statute, in the approach to the problem of balancing the rights of minors against those of innocent merchants. As a result, two (2) minority rules have developed which allow the other party to a contract with a minor to refund less than the full consideration paid in the event of rescission.

The first of these minority rules is called the "Benefit Rule." *Hall v. Butterfield,* 59 N.H. 354 (1894). The rule holds that, upon rescission, recovery of the full purchase price is subject to a deduction for the minor's use of the merchandise. This rule recognizes that the traditional rule in regard to necessaries has been extended so far as to hold an infant bound by his contracts, where he failed to restore what he has received under them to the extent of the benefit actually derived by him from what he has received from the other party to the transaction.

The other minority rule holds that the minor's recovery of the full purchase price is subject to a deduction for the minor's "use" of the consideration he or she received under the contract, or for the "depreciation" or "deterioration" of the consideration in his or her possession. *Carter v. Jays Motors,* 65 A.2d 628 (N.J. S. Ct., App. Div. 1949). . . .

We are impressed by the [following] statement:

> At a time when we see young persons between 18 and 21 years of age demanding and assuming more responsibilities in their daily lives; when we see such persons emancipated, married, and raising families; when we see such persons charged with the responsibility for committing crimes; when we see such persons being sued in tort claims for acts of negligence; when we see such persons subject to military service; when we see such persons engaged in business and acting in almost all other respects as an adult, it seems timely to re-examine the case law pertaining to contractual rights and responsibilities of infants to see if the law as pronounced and applied by the courts should be redefined. *Haydocy Pontiac Inc. v. Lee,* 250 N.E. 2d 898, 900 (1969).

. . . .

Upon serious reflection we are convinced that a [new] rule should be adopted in this State concerning the rights and responsibilities of minors in their business dealings.

. . . .

We state the rule to be followed hereafter, in reference to a contract of a minor, to be where the minor has not been overreached in any way, and there has been no undue influence, and the contract is a fair and reasonable one, and the minor has actually paid money on the purchase price, and taken and used the article purchased, that he ought not to be permitted to recover the amount actually paid, without allowing the vender of the goods reasonable compensation for the use of, depreciation, and willful or negligent damage to the article purchased, while in his hands. If there has been any fraud or imposition on the part of the seller or if the contract is unfair, or any unfair advantage has been taken of the minor inducing him to make the purchase, then the rule does not apply. Whether there has been such an overreaching on the part of the seller, and the fair market value of the property returned, would always, in any case, be a question for the trier of fact. This rule will fully and fairly protect the minor against injustice or imposition, and at the same time it will be fair to a business person who has dealt with such minor in good faith.

This rule is best adapted to modern conditions under which minors are permitted to, and do in fact, transact a great deal of business for themselves, long before they have reached the age of legal majority. Many young people work and earn money and collect it and spend it oftentimes without any oversight or restriction. The law does not question their right to buy if they have the money to pay for their purchases. It seems intolerably burdensome for everyone concerned if merchants and business people cannot deal with them safely, in a fair and reasonable way. Further, it does not appear consistent with practice of proper moral influence upon young people, tend to encourage honesty and integrity, or lead them to a good and useful business future, if they are taught that they can make purchases with their own money, for their own benefit, and after paying for them, and using them until they are worn out and destroyed, go back and compel the vendor to return to them what they have paid upon the purchase price. Such a doctrine can only lead to the corruption of principles and encourage young people in habits of trickery and dishonesty.

. . . .

We note that in this case, some nine (9) months after the date of purchase, the truck purchased by the plaintiff began to develop mechanical problems. Plaintiff was informed of the probable nature of the difficulty which apparently involved internal problems in the engine. He continued to drive the vehicle until the engine "blew up" and the truck became inoperable. Whether or not this involved gross negligence or intentional conduct on his part is a matter for determination at the trial level. It is not possible to determine from this record whether a counterclaim for tortious damage to the vehicle was asserted. After the first tender of the vehicle was made by plaintiff, and refused by the defendant, the truck was damaged by a hit-and-run driver while parked on plaintiff's property. The amount of that damage and the liability for that amount between the purchaser and the vendor, as well as the fair market value of the vehicle at the time of tender, is also an issue for the trier of fact.

The case is remanded to the trial court for further proceedings in accordance with this judgment. The costs on appellate review are assessed equally between the parties.

———

NOTES AND QUESTIONS

1. The Georgia statute and the *Swalberg* case represent the traditional common law infancy doctrine. Although generally not contractually liable, minors are bound for the reasonable value of necessaries on the theory that "unless an infant can get credit for necessaries he may starve." *Turner v. Gaither*, 83 N.C. 357, 361 (1880).

2. The *Dodson* case illustrates an approach in some jurisdictions to modify the traditional infancy doctrine. The *Halbman* case, cited in *Dodson*, represents the common law position which, on facts virtually identical to those in *Dodson*, holds that the minor is entitled to rescind the contract and recover the full amount paid even though the adult seller could recover only a severely depreciated automobile. Is the *Dodson* approach preferable to that of *Halbman*? Does the *Dodson* approach embody a personhood view of juvenile rights or can the case be explained on protectionist grounds as well?

3. Some states provide statutes making enforceable contracts entered into by young performers. For example KAN. STAT. ANN. §§ 38-618 and 38-619 (2000) provide:

> Same; contracts affected. This section applies to the following contracts entered into on or after January 1, 2001, between a minor child and any third-party or parties:
>
> > (a) A contract pursuant to which a person is employed or agrees to render artistic or creative services, either directly or though a third party, including, but not limited to, a personal services corporation.
> >
> > (b) A contract pursuant to which a person agrees to: (1) Purchase or otherwise secure, sell, lease, license or otherwise dispose of literary, musical or dramatic properties, or use of a person's likeness, voice recording, performance or story of or incidents in such person's life, either tangible or intangible or any rights therein to use in motion pictures, television, the production of sound recordings in any format now known or hereafter devised, the legitimate or living stage, or otherwise in the entertainment field.
> >
> > (c) A contract pursuant to which a person is employed or agrees to render services as a participant or player in a sport.
> >
> > (d) Where a minor child renders services as an extra, background performer or in a similar capacity, through a casting agency, the casting agency or service shall be considered the minor child's employer for the purposes of this act.
>
> Same; disaffirmance precluded upon judicial approval of contract; approval procedure.
>
> > (a) A contract, otherwise valid, of a type described in K.S.A. 38-618, and amendments thereto, entered into during one's minority,

cannot be disaffirmed on that ground, either during the minority of the person entering into the contract or at any time thereafter, if the contract has been approved by the district court in any county in which the minor resides or is employed or in which any party to the contract has its principal office in this state for the transaction of business.

(b) Approval of the district court may be given upon petition of any party to the contract, after such reasonable notice to all other parties to the contract as is fixed by the district court, with opportunity for such other parties to appear and be heard.

(c) Approval of the district court given under this section extends to the whole of the contract and all of its terms and provisions, including, but not limited to, any optional or conditional provisions contained in the contract for extension, prolongation or termination of the term of the contract.

(d) For the purposes of any proceeding under this act, a parent or legal guardian entitled to the physical custody, care and control of the minor child at the time of the proceeding shall be considered the minor child's guardian *ad litem* for the proceeding, unless the district court shall determine that appointment of a different individual as guardian *ad litem* is required in the best interests of the minor child.

For an evaluation of such statutes, see Erika Munro, *Underage, Under Contract, and Under Protected: An Overview of the Administration and Regulation of Contracts with Minors in the Entertainment Industry in New York and California*, 20 COLUM. J. L. & ARTS 553 (1996).

§ 3.05 TORT LIABILITY

BAILEY v. C.S.

Court of Appeals of Texas
12 S.W.3d 159 (2000)

Opinion by JUSTICE OVARD.

In this personal injury suit, Erica Bailey appeals from a summary judgment granted in favor of C.S. In four points of error, appellant contends the trial court erred in rendering summary judgment because: (1) issues of intent were involved which could not be readily controverted; (2) minors in Texas can be held civilly liable for their intentional torts; (3) regarding intent to commit a battery, C.S. failed to meet his summary judgment burden and failed to controvert appellant's summary judgment evidence; and (4) appellant presented evidence sufficient to create a fact issue on her damages. . . .

FACTUAL AND PROCEDURAL BACKGROUND

On April 16, 1994, appellant was babysitting the two minor children of T.S. and M.S. in their Carrollton home. That evening, appellant was approached by C.S., then four-years-old, about playing a game. Appellant told him she would play with him soon. Shortly thereafter, as appellant helped the other child with his dinner, C.S. became angry, ran up behind appellant, and unexpectedly struck her in the throat. Appellant sustained injuries including loss/impairment of her voice for a period of three to four months as well as a crushed larynx which required speech therapy.

Appellant filed suit against T.S., M.S., and C.S. alleging C.S.'s actions were intentional and constituted a battery. The defendants moved for summary judgment on the claims against C.S. on the grounds that C.S., at age four, was incapable of negligent [12] or intentional conduct as a matter of law and that appellant failed to prove she suffered any damages. The trial court, without specifying a ground, granted the summary judgment on all claims made against C.S. [13]

. . . .

LIABILITY OF MINORS

In appellant's third point of error, she claims C.S. failed to establish he lacked intent to commit a battery as a matter of law. A person commits a battery if he intentionally or knowingly causes physical contact with another when he knows or should reasonably believe the other person will regard the contact as offensive or provocative. C.S. argues he was incapable of the required intent because he was only four-years-old at the time of the incident, but appellant contends minority alone is insufficient to establish C.S. lacked intent as a matter of law. We agree with appellant.

C.S.'s only evidence to support his claim that he was incapable of the intent required for battery is his age. However, several jurisdictions have held minors liable for intentional torts. In addition, two Texas cases hold that minors of "tender years" can be civilly liable for their torts. [A]s a general rule, minors are civilly liable for their own torts. Therefore, C.S.'s minority, standing alone, is insufficient to establish as a matter of law that he lacked the requisite intent to commit a battery.

C.S. relies heavily on *Williams v. Lavender,* 797 S.W.2d 410 (Tex.App.-Fort Worth 1990, no writ), to support his argument that he cannot be liable for intentional torts. In *Williams,* the Fort Worth court stated that to be liable for willful and malicious conduct, a child must be at least twelve years old. From this case, C.S. reasons that a child under twelve years of age is not capable as a matter of law of intentional or knowing conduct; therefore, C.S., at age four, could not be liable for an intentional tort. We conclude this is not the correct interpretation of *Williams.*

Williams addressed whether a minor could form the malicious intent to sustain an award of exemplary damages. As *Williams* recognizes, the legislature set a minimum age limit for willful and malicious conduct only, not intentional torts. We conclude there is currently no specific age at which

---

12 [1] Appellant claims her only cause of action was battery. Therefore, we do not address whether C.S. was capable of negligence.

13 [2] A take-nothing judgment was later rendered against appellant on her claims against T.S. and M..S.

minors are immune from liability for intentional torts as a matter of law. C.S. failed to meet his burden of proof, and the trial court erred in rendering summary judgment. We sustain appellant's third point of error.

. . . .

We reverse the trial court's judgment and remand for further proceedings.

KUHNS v. BRUGGER

Supreme Court of Pennsylvania
135 A.2d 395 (1957)

BENJAMIN R. JONES, JUSTICE.

On July 23, 1953 a tragic and unfortunate event occurred which has resulted in this litigation. Albert G. Kunns, 12-years-old, was wounded by a bullet from a pistol discharged by his cousin, George A. Brugger, also 12-years-old, while in the cottage of their common grandfather, George W. Bach, located at Manchester Beach, Erie County, and, as a result thereof, Kuhns sustained serious physical injuries.

Through a guardian, Kuhns instituted a trespass action, joined in by his parents, against George Brugger; later, by permission of court, the executor of the George W. Bach Estate was joined as an additional party defendant.[14] A motion for severance of the actions having been refused, the suit against both defendants proceeded to trial. The jury returned a verdict against both defendants in the amount of $182,096; the Court below later reduced this amount to $116,604.60 and this reduction was accepted by plaintiffs. From a judgment entered on the verdict these appeals were perfected.

Bach, an elderly man, owned and occupied — at least part of each year — a one-story cottage at Manchester Beach on the shore of Lake Erie. This cottage was located in a somewhat isolated area in the immediate vicinity of which were several commercial fisheries. A hunting devotee, Bach owned various guns and other firearms including the Colt Woodsman .22 calibre automatic pistol which constitutes the focal point of this incident. When this pistol was not in use Bach kept it in a *loaded* condition in an unlocked dresser drawer in his unlocked bedroom.

At approximately noon on July 23, 1953, Bach's two young grandsons, Kuhns and Brugger, went fishing; upon their return at approximately 3:30 P.M. and during Bach's absence, the boys entered their grandfather's bedroom. Katrina Brugger — Brugger's 2-year-old sister — was then playing in the bedroom. In a spirit of play Brugger picked up a so-called "under and over" gun — a combination shotgun and rifle — and pointed it at Kuhns. As he did this, Miss Fries, a great aunt of the boys, entered the bedroom and ordered Brugger to put away the gun which he did. A few minutes later Brugger went to his grandfather's dresser and found in the top left drawer thereof the Colt automatic pistol, previously mentioned, which was then loaded with a clip of cartridges resting in its handle. In order to prepare this pistol for firing one

---

14 [1] George W. Bach, the grandfather, died subsequent to the shooting incident but prior to the time suit was instituted.

draws back an upper slide forcing a cartridge into the firing chamber and the cartridge is then exploded by pulling the trigger. There was some testimony that this pistol at the time was mechanically defective and that, on occasion, if one held his finger on the trigger as he pulled back the slide, the pistol would discharge, without the added requirement of squeezing the trigger — a one-step, rather than a two-step procedure.

According to Brugger the shooting occurred in the following manner: "And I took it [the pistol] out, took it out of the holster, took it in my hand. I believe I had my finger on the trigger. And I pulled the slide back, and then the shot occurred." The bullet, thus ejected, penetrated Kuhn's body and perforated the spinal cord, paralyzing the entire lower portion of his body and destroying all voluntary control of his organs in that part of his body. His condition, as portrayed at trial, is such that he can no longer walk, requires constant care and medication and can never be gainfully employed.

The defendant Brugger takes the dual position that the evidence was insufficient as a matter of law to establish any negligence on his part and that the Court below, in submitting the question of his negligence to the jury, not only held him, a minor, to the standard of conduct required of an adult, but, in effect, charged the jury that he was guilty of negligence *per se* in that he had violated a criminal statute. We shall first concern ourselves with Brugger's appeals.

Brugger's contention that he is entitled to judgment n. o. v. because of the lack of sufficient evidence of negligence on his part is clearly untenable. This Court set forth the required rule of conduct when dealing with *any* dangerous agency: "A higher degree of care is required in dealing with a dangerous agency than in the ordinary affairs of life or business, every reasonable precaution suggested by experience and the known danger ought to be taken." Any loaded firearm, including a pistol, is a highly dangerous instrumentality and, since its possession or use is attended by extraordinary danger, any person having it in his possession or using it is bound to exercise extraordinary care. A person handling or carrying a loaded firearm in the immediate vicinity of others is liable for its discharge, even though the discharge is accidental and unintentional, provided it is not unavoidable.[15] When a person picks up a firearm, points it at another and operates the firing mechanism, with or without the knowledge that the firearm is loaded, and the firearm is discharged, and the evidence so indicates, then a *prima facie* case of negligence is established.

Brugger submits, however, that, because of his age, he was presumptively incapable of negligent conduct and therefore his conduct did not render him liable for the injury which followed the discharge of the firearm. In short, Brugger relies upon his age to absolve him of *any* culpability for his actions

---

[15] [5] Our legislature has recognized that a young child and a firearm constitute a dangerous combination. The Criminal Code declares that any person who knowingly and wilfully sells or causes to be sold a deadly weapon to a person under 16 years of age is guilty of a misdemeanor. It is also unlawful for a person between 12 and 14 years of age to use firearms for hunting unless accompanied by a parent, guardian or adult member of his family. The Uniform Firearms Act prohibits the delivery of a firearm — a pistol or revolver with less than a 12' barrel, a shotgun with less than a 24' barrel or a rifle with less than a 15' barrel — to any person under the age of 18 years.

and the manner in which the Court below instructed the jury to secure a new trial.

Even though the standard of care applicable to a minor differs from that applicable to an adult,[16] nevertheless a minor may be guilty of actionable negligence. Both an adult and a minor are under an obligation to exercise reasonable care; however, the "reasonable care" required of a minor is measured by a different yardstick — it is that measure of care which other minors of like age, experience, capacity and development would ordinarily exercise under similar circumstances. In applying that yardstick, we place minors in three categories based on their age: minors under the age of seven years are conclusively presumed incapable of negligence; minors over the age of fourteen years are presumptively capable of negligence, the burden being placed on such minors to prove their incapacity; minors between the ages of seven and fourteen years are presumed incapable of negligence, but such presumption is rebuttable and grows weaker with each year until the fourteenth year is reached. . . .

Brugger at the age of 12 years was not to be judged by adult standards; on the contrary, it was necessary to inquire whether his conduct was such as should reasonably have been expected of a child of like age, intelligence and experience. Brugger's culpability or exculpability of actionable negligence depended upon a measurement of his conduct based on variable factors — his capacity and understanding based upon his age, intelligence, experience, etc.: a measurement properly to be made by a jury with the opportunity to evaluate his individual capacity to perceive danger. Concerning the capability of negligent conduct of a child between the ages of seven and fourteen it has been said: "Generally their conduct has been determined by a jury. This has been because the ascertainment of the capacity to perceive danger involves the determination of judgment factors, *i.e.*, knowledge, intelligence, experience, character of the danger, which are often associated with questions of fact and hardly ever beyond reasonable doubt." Whether Brugger at his age and under the circumstances had the capacity to understand, comprehend and perceive the danger and risk inherent in handling this pistol was most suitably a question for determination by a jury.

We have carefully examined the trial judge's instructions to the jury on the law applicable to the determination of Brugger's negligence and find such instructions free from error. The trial judge was singularly cautious in explaining to the jury the requisite standard of conduct of a 12-year-old boy, the presumption in his favor and the yardstick to be applied in measuring his conduct. Appellant's complaint concerning that portion of the instructions

---

[16] [7] The Restatement of the Law of Torts, § 283, provides: "Unless the actor is a child, the standard of conduct to which he must conform to avoid being negligent is that of a reasonable man under like circumstances." Comment (e) thereunder states:

A child of tender years is not required to conform to the standard of behavior which it is reasonable to expect of an adult, but his conduct is to be judged by the standard of behavior to be expected from a child of like age, intelligence and experience. The standard of conduct required of such a child is that which it is reasonable to expect of children of like age, intelligence and experience. In so far as concerns the child's capacity to realize the existence of a risk, the individual qualities of the child are taken into account.

which referred to the possibility that Brugger might have violated a criminal statute in pointing the pistol at Kuhns is without merit. Whoever wantonly or playfully points a pistol at another offends against our criminal code and the violation of a statute may be regarded as negligence per se even though the violator be a minor. The trial judge, referring to the statute, said: "Now, I can't instruct you, as a matter of law, that that [the statute] applies in this case and therefore makes George Brugger negligent *per se*, or because of that statute, because the question as to pointing is in dispute. George Brugger says he doesn't think he pointed it. The plaintiff said he did point it. Actually, the gun was pointed but it is a question of intention. *If George Brugger was mature enough to know better, and therefore negligent, then you may use that statute as evidence of negligence per se, and hold him for it. If he did not point it intentionally, then your determination of his guilt will be based upon carelessness, as we have described it for you, if it existed.*" (Emphasis supplied). At the close of the charge the trial judge reiterated the standard of conduct required of a minor. We fail to find any error of commission or omission at the trial which in any manner prejudiced or harmed the defendant Brugger. The verdict of the jury against Brugger was fully warranted by the evidence and a new trial was properly refused.

In considering the defendant Bach Estate's motion for judgment n. o. v. . . . .

[T]he record reveals that the pistol was owned by Bach, that it was kept in an unlocked dresser drawer in his unlocked bedroom with a clip of cartridges in its handle, that young Brugger not only was aware of the existence of the pistol — having been shown it on several occasions by Bach — but also its place of containment in the bedroom, that the unlocked bedroom was open to members of the family, including young grandchildren, that Brugger and Kuhns were accustomed to enter the bedroom, that Kuhns was injured in the bedroom by a shot from a firearm and the pistol was on the top of the dresser immediately after the shooting, that Mrs. Bach related a conversation with Kuhns after the shooting in which he expressed no hard feelings toward Brugger in connection with his injury — this evidence, with other testimony, was sufficient to establish *prima facie* negligence upon Bach's part.

The possession of this loaded Colt pistol did not constitute Bach an insurer against liability for injuries arising from its use nor render him liable without fault; it did, however, impose upon him a very serious and grave responsibility. Its possession placed upon him the duty of exercising not simply ordinary, but extraordinary care so that no harm might be visited upon others. . . .

The duty imposed upon Bach encompassed all those persons who might suffer harm or injury from the pistol's discharge and included the pistol's use not only by Bach but its use by a third person if Bach knew or had reason to know that such person was likely to use the pistol in such a manner as to create "an unreasonable risk of harm to others".

Over many years Bach's grandchildren were visitors and guests at the cottage. Not only were the general living quarters of the cottage unrestricted to them but so also was his bedroom; in this respect the presence of little Katrina Brugger in the bedroom immediately before the shooting incident is highly significant. The grandchildren had the "run of the house" and Bach's bedroom was not "out of bounds".

In that bedroom were kept not only fishing equipment but, at least, two firearms — all attractive to interested boys. Not only was Brugger aware of the fact that his grandfather possessed this pistol but he knew that it was kept in the bedroom; of these facts the grandfather was cognizant. Despite knowledge that the grandchildren frequented the unlocked bedroom Bach not only kept the pistol in an unlocked drawer but also in a loaded condition, *i.e.*, the clip of cartridges was in the pistol handle.

It is contrary to every human experience to expect that children, particularly boys, would not want to touch and handle a pistol. . . . Bach knew or should have known that any 12-year-old boy, such as either of his two grandsons, might rummage around his bedroom and, finding the pistol, handle it. Applying either the "foresight" or the "hindsight" test, it is evident that Bach could have anticipated and foreseen the likelihood of harm resulting from leaving the loaded pistol in an unlocked drawer in a bedroom frequented by children.

. . . .

Under the circumstances Bach was under a duty to keep this pistol away from his young grandchildren. . . . We are not confronted with the question of a grandparent's liability for the tortious conduct of a minor grandchild; on the contrary, we are determining whether the grandparent by his own conduct was guilty of negligence, and whether, if negligent, his negligence was the proximate cause of Kuhn's injury. Bach's liability depends on the nature of the instrumentality involved, the place, the time and the persons likely to be brought in contact with the instrumentality. The gist of the liability sought to be imposed is that Bach was negligent in permitting a highly dangerous instrumentality to be in a place where the incautious hands of a child might come in contact with it and the handling and discharge of this instrumentality by the child was the natural and probable consequence of Bach's negligence and such a consequence as might and ought to have been foreseen by Bach as likely to flow from his act.[17] Bach's act in permitting this weapon, with its deadly potentialities, to remain in a place frequented by young children constituted negligence on his part; the intervention of his young grandchild did not break the chain of causation between his negligence and the injury which occurred and was a natural and probable result to be anticipated from the original negligence.

---

[17] [14] In *Condel v. Savo*, 350 Pa. 350, 352, 39 A.2d 51, 52, 155 A.L.R. 81, it was stated:

At common law the mere relation of parent and child imposes upon the parent no liability for the torts of the child, but the parents may be liable where the act of the child is done as the agent of the parents or where the negligence of the parents makes the injury possible. The injury committed by the child must have been the natural and probable consequence of the parents' negligent act, that is, a consequence which, under the surrounding circumstances, might and ought reasonably to have been foreseen as likely to flow from such negligent act. "In determining what is the proximate cause, the true rule is, that the injury must be the natural and probable consequence of the negligence — such a consequence as, under the surrounding circumstances of the case, might and ought to have been foreseen by the wrongdoer as likely to flow from his act."

. . . .

Under the circumstances herein presented the question of Bach's liability was clearly for the jury to determine. The jury having found that he was negligent, and the evidence being sufficient to sustain such finding, judgment n. o. v. was properly refused.

We find no error which would justify a retrial of this case, and the judgment is accordingly affirmed.

———

NOTES AND QUESTIONS

1. The *Bailey* case holds that a four-year-old might be liable for intentional torts. Do you agree with this conclusion? Can a child of such tender years "intend" harmful actions? The *Williams* case, cited in *Bailey*, limits liability for "malicious" conduct to children over age twelve where exemplary (punitive) damages are at stake. Why the distinction in compensatory and exemplary damages?

2. *Kuhns* addresses negligence issues. In considering the possible liability of the twelve-year-old defendant, the court applied a three-category approach based on age that corresponds to the criminal law infancy defense. Are these categories necessary or even relevant in determining a minor's negligence? Consider footnote 7 of *Kuhns*. Are the age categories necessary only in the context of considering issues of negligence *per se* premised on violations of criminal statutes? If no negligence *per se* issues were at stake in *Kuhns*, would (should?) the court have applied the infancy defense categories?

3. The *Kuhns* court reflects the common law view that parents (in this case the grandfather) are not vicariously liable for harmful acts committed by children in their charge. Do you agree with this common law view?

The view rejecting vicarious parental liability has been statutorily rejected in many jurisdictions. State statutes hold parents liable in varying degrees. Most statutes require willful, intentional, or reckless conduct on the part of the child. Monetary liability limits are common and range from $1,000 to $25,000. *See, e.g.,* CAL. CIV. CODE § 1714.1 (West 1998) (requiring willful misconduct by the minor, which causes damage to person or property up to $25,000 per incident); IND. CODE § 34-31-4-1 (1998) (parents liable for no more than $5,000 of damage caused knowingly, intentionally, or recklessly by the child; *id.* at § 34-31-4-2 (additional liability (no liability limit) on parents whose child is a member of a criminal gang); NEB. REV. STAT. § 43-801 (1998) (parents liable for willful or intentional damage to persons or property with a $1,000 cap on personal injury damages); S.D. CODIFIED LAWS § 25-5-15 (Michie) (parents liable for up to $1500 of damage caused by the willful or malicious conduct of their children).

Chapter 4

THE CHILD AND THE SCHOOL

§ 4.01 FIRST AMENDMENT RIGHTS OF STUDENTS

To what extent does education involve some form of indoctrination? For a democratic society to continue, is it necessary for its young people to learn certain fundamental principles so that they will adhere to those principles when they become adults? How should the common school fulfill its mission to educate for good citizenship?

In *West Virginia v. Barnette*, 319 U.S. 624 (1943), the Court addressed a state's requirement that all students salute the American flag and pledge allegiances to the flag as a regular part of school activities. Jehovah's Witness parents, on behalf of themselves and their children brought suit, requesting an injunction to restrain the law's enforcement. Overruling an 8-1 decision, it had handed down only three years before, *Minersville School District v. Gobitis*, 310 U.S. 586 (1940), the Court determined that "the action of the local authorities in compelling the flag salute and pledge transcends constitutional limitations on their power and invades the sphere of intellect and spirit which it is the purpose of the First Amendment to our Constitution to reserve from all official control." Perhaps the most famous quotation from *Barnette* is Justice Jackson's statement, "If there is any fixed star in our constitutional constellation, it is that no official, high or petty, can prescribe what shall be orthodox in politics, nationalism, religion, or other matters of opinion or force citizens to confess by word or act their faith therein. If there are any circumstances which permit an exception, they do not now occur to us." It was not clear from the opinion, however, if the constitutional rights were held by the parents, the children, or both.

After *Barnette*, Congress, in 1954, added the words "under God" to the Pledge of Allegiance. The Ninth Circuit, in *Newdow v. United States Congress*, 292 F.3d 597 (2002), in an opinion that precipitated a national uproar, held that the addition of the words "under God" and a school district's policy of teacher-led recitation of the pledge violated the First Amendment's Establishment Clause. The day after the opinion was issued, the panel stayed the mandate, pending resolution of petitions for rehearing en banc. The U.S. Supreme Court rejected the challenge by the student's noncustodial parent for lack of "prudential standing." Chief Justice Rehnquist, Justice O'Connor and Justice Thomas would have reached the merits and held the Pledge recitation policy constitutional. *Elk Grove Unified School Dist. v. Newdow*, 542 U.S. 1 (2004).

[A] Student Rights of Speech and Expression

TINKER v. DES MOINES INDEPENDENT COMMUNITY SCHOOL DISTRICT

Supreme Court of the United States
393 U.S. 503 (1969)

Mr. Justice Fortas *delivered the opinion of the Court.*

Petitioner John F. Tinker, 15 years old, and petitioner Christopher Eckhardt, 16 years old, attended high schools in Des Moines, Iowa. Petitioner Mary Beth Tinker, John's sister, was a 13-year-old student in junior high school.

In December 1965, a group of adults and students in Des Moines held a meeting at the Eckhardt home. The group determined to publicize their objections to the hostilities in Vietnam and their support for a truce by wearing black armbands during the holiday season and by fasting on December 16 and New Year's Eve. Petitioners and their parents had previously engaged in similar activities, and they decided to participate in the program.

The principals of the Des Moines schools became aware of the plan to wear armbands. On December 14, 1965, they met and adopted a policy that any student wearing an armband to school would be asked to remove it, and if he refused he would be suspended until he returned without the armband. Petitioners were aware of the regulation that the school authorities adopted.

On December 16, Mary Beth and Christopher wore black armbands to their schools. John Tinker wore his armband the next day. They were all sent home and suspended from school until they would come back without their armbands. They did not return to school until after the planned period for wearing armbands had expired — that is, until after New Year's Day.

This complaint was filed in the United States District Court by petitioners, through their fathers, under § 1983 of Title 42 of the United States Code. It prayed for an injunction restraining the respondent school officials and the respondent members of the board of directors of the school district from disciplining the petitioners, and it sought nominal damages. . . . [T]he District Court dismissed the complaint [because the school authorities' action] was reasonable in order to prevent disturbance of school discipline. The court referred to but expressly declined to follow the Fifth Circuit's holding in a similar case that the wearing of symbols like the armbands cannot be prohibited unless it "materially and substantially interfere[s] with the requirements of appropriate discipline in the operation of the school." *Burnside v. Byars,* 363 F.2d 744, 749 (1966).[1]

---

[1] [1] In *Burnside,* the Fifth Circuit ordered that high school authorities be enjoined from enforcing a regulation forbidding students to wear "freedom buttons." It is instructive that in *Blackwell v. Issaquena County Board of Education,* 363 F.2d 749 (1966), the same panel on the same day reached the opposite result on different facts. It declined to enjoin enforcement of such a regulation in another high school where the students wearing freedom buttons harassed students who did not wear them and created much disturbance.

On appeal, the Court of Appeals for the Eighth Circuit considered the case *en banc*. The court was equally divided, and the District Court's decision was accordingly affirmed, without opinion.

. . . .

I

The District Court recognized that the wearing of an armband for the purpose of expressing certain views is the type of symbolic act that is within the Free Speech Clause of the First Amendment. *See West Virginia v. Barnette,* 319 U.S. 624 (1943). As we shall discuss, the wearing of armbands in the circumstances of this case was entirely divorced from actually or potentially disruptive conduct by those participating in it. It was closely akin to "pure speech" which, we have repeatedly held, is entitled to comprehensive protection under the First Amendment.

First Amendment rights, applied in light of the special characteristics of the school environment, are available to teachers and students. It can hardly be argued that either students or teachers shed their constitutional rights to freedom of speech or expression at the schoolhouse gate. This has been the unmistakable holding of this Court for almost 50 years. In *Meyer v. Nebraska,* 262 U.S. 390 (1923), and *Bartels v. Iowa,* 262 U.S. 404 (1923), this Court, in opinions by Mr. Justice McReynolds, held that the Due Process Clause of the Fourteenth Amendment prevents States from forbidding the teaching of a foreign language to young students. Statutes to this effect, the Court held, unconstitutionally interfere with the liberty of teacher, student, and parent. *See also Pierce v. Society of Sisters,* 268 U.S. 510 (1925); *West Virginia v. Barnette,* 319 U.S. 624 (1943).

In *West Virginia v. Barnette,* this Court held that under the First Amendment, the student in public school may not be compelled to salute the flag. Speaking through Mr. Justice Jackson, the Court said:

> The Fourteenth Amendment, as now applied to the States, protects the citizen against the State itself and all of its creatures — Boards of Education not excepted. These have, of course, important, delicate, and highly discretionary functions, but none that they may not perform within the limits of the Bill of Rights. That they are educating the young for citizenship is reason for scrupulous protection of Constitutional freedoms of the individual, if we are not to strangle the free mind at its source and teach youth to discount important principles of our government as mere platitudes.

319 U.S., at 637.

On the other hand, the Court has repeatedly emphasized the need for affirming the comprehensive authority of the States and of school officials, consistent with fundamental constitutional safeguards, to prescribe and control conduct in the schools. Our problem lies in the area where students in the exercise of First Amendment rights collide with the rules of the school authorities.

II

The problem posed by the present case does not relate to regulation of the length of skirts or the type of clothing, to hair style, or deportment. It does not concern aggressive, disruptive action or even group demonstrations. Our problem involves direct, primary First Amendment rights akin to "pure speech."

The school officials banned and sought to punish petitioners for a silent, passive expression of opinion, unaccompanied by any disorder or disturbance on the part of petitioners. There is here no evidence whatever of petitioners' interference, actual or nascent, with the schools' work or of collision with the rights of other students to be secure and to be let alone. Accordingly, this case does not concern speech or action that intrudes upon the work of the schools or the rights of other students.

Only a few of the 18,000 students in the school system wore the black armbands. Only five students were suspended for wearing them. There is no indication that the work of the schools or any class was disrupted. Outside the classrooms, a few students made hostile remarks to the children wearing armbands, but there were no threats or acts of violence on school premises.

The District Court concluded that the action of the school authorities was reasonable because it was based upon their fear of a disturbance from the wearing of the armbands. But, in our system, undifferentiated fear or apprehension of disturbance is not enough to overcome the right to freedom of expression. Any departure from absolute regimentation may cause trouble. Any variation from the majority's opinion may inspire fear. Any word spoken, in class, in the lunchroom, or on the campus, that deviates from the views of another person may start an argument or cause a disturbance. But our Constitution says we must take this risk, and our history says that it is this sort of hazardous freedom — this kind of openness — that is the basis of our national strength and of the independence and vigor of Americans who grow up and live in this relatively permissive, often disputatious, society.

In order for the State in the person of school officials to justify prohibition of a particular expression of opinion, it must be able to show that its action was caused by something more than a mere desire to avoid the discomfort and unpleasantness that always accompany an unpopular viewpoint. Certainly where there is no finding and no showing that engaging in the forbidden conduct would "materially and substantially interfere with the requirements of appropriate discipline in the operation of the school," the prohibition cannot be sustained.

In the present case, the District Court made no such finding, and our independent examination of the record fails to yield evidence that the school authorities had reason to anticipate that the wearing of the armbands would substantially interfere with the work of the school or impinge upon the rights of other students. Even an official memorandum prepared after the suspension that listed the reasons for the ban on wearing the armbands made no reference to the anticipation of such disruption.[2]

On the contrary, the action of the school authorities appears to have been based upon an urgent wish to avoid the controversy which might result from the expression, even by the silent symbol of armbands, of opposition to this Nation's part in the conflagration in Vietnam.[3] It is revealing, in this respect, that the meeting at which the school principals decided to issue the contested regulation was called in response to a student's statement to the journalism teacher in one of the schools that he wanted to write an article on Vietnam and have it published in the school paper. (The student was dissuaded.)

It is also relevant that the school authorities did not purport to prohibit the wearing of all symbols of political or controversial significance. The record shows that students in some of the schools wore buttons relating to national political campaigns, and some even wore the Iron Cross, traditionally a symbol of Nazism. The order prohibiting the wearing of armbands did not extend to these. Instead, a particular symbol — black armbands worn to exhibit opposition to this Nation's involvement in Vietnam — was singled out for prohibition. Clearly, the prohibition of expression of one particular opinion, at least without evidence that it is necessary to avoid material and substantial interference with schoolwork or discipline, is not constitutionally permissible.

In our system, state-operated schools may not be enclaves of totalitarianism. School officials do not possess absolute authority over their students. Students in school as well as out of school are "persons" under our Constitution. They are possessed of fundamental rights which the State must respect, just as they themselves must respect their obligations to the State. In our system, students may not be regarded as closed-circuit recipients of only that which the State chooses to communicate. They may not be confined to the expression of those sentiments that are officially approved. In the absence of a specific showing

---

[2] [3] The only suggestions of fear of disorder in the report are these:

"A former student of one of our high schools was killed in Viet Nam. Some of his friends are still in school and it was felt that if any kind of a demonstration existed, it might evolve into something which would be difficult to control."

"Students at one of the high schools were heard to say they would wear arm bands of other colors if the black bands prevailed."

Moreover, the testimony of school authorities at trial indicates that it was not fear of disruption that motivated the regulation prohibiting the armbands; the regulation was directed against "the principle of the demonstration" itself. School authorities simply felt that "the schools are no place for demonstrations," and if the students "didn't like the way our elected officials were handling things, it should be handled with the ballot box and not in the halls of our public schools."

[3] [4] The District Court found that the school authorities, in prohibiting black armbands, were influenced by the fact that

the Viet Nam war and the involvement of the United States therein has been the subject of a major controversy for some time. When the arm band regulation involved herein was promulgated, debate over the Viet Nam war had become vehement in many localities. A protest march against the war had been recently held in Washington, D.C. A wave of draft card burning incidents protesting the war had swept the country. At that time two highly publicized draft card burning cases were pending in this Court. Both individuals supporting the war and those opposing it were quite vocal in expressing their views.

of constitutionally valid reasons to regulate their speech, students are entitled to freedom of expression of their views. . . .

In *Keyishian v. Board of Regents,* 385 U.S. 589, 603, Mr. Justice Brennan, speaking for the Court, said:

> "The vigilant protection of constitutional freedoms is nowhere more vital than in the community of American schools." The classroom is peculiarly the "marketplace of ideas." The Nation's future depends upon leaders trained through wide exposure to that robust exchange of ideas which discovers truth 'out of a multitude of tongues, [rather] than through any kind of authoritative selection.

The principle of these cases is not confined to the supervised and ordained discussion which takes place in the classroom. The principal use to which the schools are dedicated is to accommodate students during prescribed hours for the purpose of certain types of activities. Among those activities is personal intercommunication among the students. This is not only an inevitable part of the process of attending school; it is also an important part of the educational process. A student's rights, therefore, do not embrace merely the classroom hours. When he is in the cafeteria, or on the playing field, or on the campus during the authorized hours, he may express his opinions, even on controversial subjects like the conflict in Vietnam, if he does so without "materially and substantially interfer[ing] with the requirements of appropriate discipline in the operation of the school" and without colliding with the rights of others. But conduct by the student, in class or out of it, which for any reason — whether it stems from time, place, or type of behavior — materially disrupts classwork or involves substantial disorder or invasion of the rights of others is, of course, not immunized by the constitutional guarantee of freedom of speech. . . .

If a regulation were adopted by school officials forbidding discussion of the Vietnam conflict, or the expression by any student of opposition to it anywhere on school property except as part of a prescribed classroom exercise, it would be obvious that the regulation would violate the constitutional rights of students, at least if it could not be justified by a showing that the students' activities would materially and substantially disrupt the work and discipline of the school. In the circumstances of the present case, the prohibition of the silent, passive "witness of the armbands," as one of the children called it, is no less offensive to the Constitution's guarantees.

As we have discussed, the record does not demonstrate any facts which might reasonably have led school authorities to forecast substantial disruption of or material interference with school activities, and no disturbances or disorders on the school premises in fact occurred. These petitioners merely went about their ordained rounds in school. Their deviation consisted only in wearing on their sleeve a band of black cloth, not more than two inches wide. They wore it to exhibit their disapproval of the Vietnam hostilities and their advocacy of a truce, to make their views known, and, by their example, to influence others to adopt them. They neither interrupted school activities nor sought to intrude in the school affairs or the lives of others. They caused discussion outside of the classrooms, but no interference with work and no disorder. In the circumstances, our Constitution does not permit officials of the State to deny their form of expression.

We express no opinion as to the form of relief which should be granted, this being a matter for the lower courts to determine. We reverse and remand for further proceedings consistent with this opinion.

Reversed and remanded.

MR. JUSTICE STEWART, *concurring.*

Although I agree with much of what is said in the Court's opinion, and with its judgment in this case, I cannot share the Court's uncritical assumption that, school discipline aside, the First Amendment rights of children are co-extensive with those of adults. Indeed, I had thought the Court decided otherwise just last Term in *Ginsberg v. New York,* 390 U.S. 629. I continue to hold the view I expressed in that case: "[A] State may permissibly determine that, at least in some precisely delineated areas, a child — like someone in a captive audience — is not possessed of that full capacity for individual choice which is the presupposition of First Amendment guarantees." *Cf. Prince v. Massachusetts,* 321 U.S. 158.

[Concurring opinion by MR. JUSTICE WHITE omitted.]

MR. JUSTICE BLACK, *dissenting.*

The Court's holding in this case ushers in what I deem to be an entirely new era in which the power to control pupils by the elected "officials of state supported public schools . . ." in the United States is in ultimate effect transferred to the Supreme Court. The Court brought this particular case here on a petition for certiorari urging that the First and Fourteenth Amendments protect the right of school pupils to express their political views all the way "from kindergarten through high school." Here the constitutional right to "political expression" asserted was a right to wear black armbands during school hours and at classes in order to demonstrate to the other students that the petitioners were mourning because of the death of United States soldiers in Vietnam and to protest that war which they were against. Ordered to refrain from wearing the armbands in school by the elected school officials and the teachers vested with state authority to do so, apparently only seven out of the school system's 18,000 pupils deliberately refused to obey the order. One defying pupil was Paul Tinker, 8 years old, who was in the second grade; another, Hope Tinker, was 11 years old and in the fifth grade; a third member of the Tinker family was 13, in the eighth grade; and a fourth member of the same family was John Tinker, 15 years old, an 11th grade high school pupil. Their father, a Methodist minister without a church, is paid a salary by the American Friends Service Committee. Another student who defied the school order and insisted on wearing an armband in school was Christopher Eckhardt, an 11th grade pupil and a petitioner in this case. His mother is an official in the Women's International League for Peace and Freedom.

As I read the Court's opinion it relies upon the following grounds for holding unconstitutional the judgment of the Des Moines school officials and the two courts below. First, the Court concludes that the wearing of armbands is "symbolic speech" which is "akin to 'pure speech' " and therefore protected by the First and Fourteenth Amendments. Secondly, the Court decides that the public schools are an appropriate place to exercise "symbolic speech" as long as normal school functions are not "unreasonably" disrupted. Finally, the Court arrogates to itself, rather than to the State's elected officials charged with running the schools, the decision as to which school disciplinary regulations are "reasonable."

Assuming that the Court is correct in holding that the conduct of wearing armbands for the purpose of conveying political ideas is protected by the First Amendment, the crucial remaining questions are whether students and teachers may use the schools at their whim as a platform for the exercise of free speech — "symbolic" or "pure" — and whether the courts will allocate to themselves the function of deciding how the pupils' school day will be spent. While I have always believed that under the First and Fourteenth Amendments neither the State nor the Federal Government has any authority to regulate or censor the content of speech, I have never believed that any person has a right to give speeches or engage in demonstrations where he pleases and when he pleases. This Court has already rejected such a notion. In *Cox v. Louisiana,* 379 U.S. 536, 554 (1965), for example, the Court clearly stated that the rights of free speech and assembly "do not mean that everyone with opinions or beliefs to express may address a group at any public place and at any time."

While the record does not show that any of these armband students shouted, used profane language, or were violent in any manner, detailed testimony by some of them shows their armbands caused comments, warnings by other students, the poking of fun at them, and a warning by an older football player that other, nonprotesting students had better let them alone. There is also evidence that a teacher of mathematics had his lesson period practically "wrecked" chiefly by disputes with Mary Beth Tinker, who wore her armband for her "demonstration." Even a casual reading of the record shows that this armband did divert students' minds from their regular lessons, and that talk, comments, etc., made John Tinker "self-conscious" in attending school with his armband. While the absence of obscene remarks or boisterous and loud disorder perhaps justifies the Court's statement that the few armband students did not actually "disrupt" the classwork, I think the record overwhelmingly shows that the armbands did exactly what the elected school officials and principals foresaw they would, that is, took the students' minds off their classwork and diverted them to thoughts about the highly emotional subject of the Vietnam war. And I repeat that if the time has come when pupils of state-supported schools, kindergartens, grammar schools, or high schools, can defy and flout orders of school officials to keep their minds on their own schoolwork, it is the beginning of a new revolutionary era of permissiveness in this country fostered by the judiciary. . . .

I deny, therefore, that it has been the "unmistakable holding of this Court for almost 50 years" that "students" and "teachers" take with them into the "schoolhouse gate" constitutional rights to "freedom of speech or expression." Even *Meyer* did not hold that. It makes no reference to "symbolic speech" at all; what it did was to strike down as "unreasonable" and therefore unconstitutional a Nebraska law barring the teaching of the German language before the children reached the eighth grade. One can well agree with Mr. Justice Holmes and Mr. Justice Sutherland, as I do, that such a law was no more unreasonable than it would be to bar the teaching of Latin and Greek to pupils who have not reached the eighth grade. In fact, I think the majority's reason for invalidating the Nebraska law was that it did not like it or in legal jargon that it "shocked the Court's conscience," "offended its sense of justice," or was "contrary to fundamental concepts of the English-speaking world," as the Court has sometimes said. The truth is that a teacher of kindergarten, grammar school, or high school pupils no more carries into a school with him a complete right to freedom of speech and expression than an anti-Catholic or anti-Semite carries with him a complete freedom of speech and religion into a Catholic church or Jewish synagogue. Nor does a person carry with him into the United States Senate or House, or into the Supreme Court, or any other court, a complete constitutional right to go into those places contrary to their rules and speak his mind on any subject he pleases. It is a myth to say that any person has a constitutional right to say what he pleases, where he pleases, and when he pleases. Our Court has decided precisely the opposite.

In my view, teachers in state-controlled public schools are hired to teach there. Although Mr. Justice McReynolds may have intimated to the contrary in *Meyer v. Nebraska,* certainly a teacher is not paid to go into school and teach subjects the State does not hire him to teach as a part of its selected curriculum. Nor are public school students sent to the schools at public expense to broadcast political or any other views to educate and inform the public. The original idea of schools, which I do not believe is yet abandoned as worthless or out of date, was that children had not yet reached the point of experience and wisdom which enabled them to teach all of their elders. It may be that the Nation has outworn the old-fashioned slogan that "children are to be seen not heard," but one may, I hope, be permitted to harbor the thought that taxpayers send children to school on the premise that at their age they need to learn, not teach. . . .

Iowa's public schools . . . are operated to give students an opportunity to learn, not to talk politics by actual speech, or by "symbolic" speech. And, as I have pointed out before, the record amply shows that public protest in the school classes against the Vietnam war "distracted from that singleness of purpose which the State [here Iowa] desired to exist in its public educational institutions." Here the Court should accord Iowa educational institutions [the right to determine for themselves to what extent free expression should be allowed in its schools]. But even if the record were silent as to protests against the Vietnam war distracting students from their assigned class work, members of this Court, like all other citizens, know, without being told, that the disputes over the wisdom of the Vietnam war have disrupted and divided this country as few other issues ever have. Of course students, like other people, cannot concentrate on lesser issues when black armbands are being ostentatiously displayed in their presence to call attention to the wounded and dead of the war, some of the wounded and the dead being their friends and neighbors. It was, of course, to distract the attention of other students that some students insisted up to the very point of their own suspension from school that they were determined to sit in school with their symbolic armbands.

Change has been said to be truly the law of life but sometimes the old and the tried and true are worth holding. The schools of this Nation have undoubtedly contributed to giving us tranquility and to making us a more law-abiding people. Uncontrolled and uncontrollable liberty is an enemy to domestic peace. We cannot close our eyes to the fact that some of the country's greatest problems are crimes committed by the youth, too many of school age. School discipline, like parental discipline, is an integral and important part of training our children to be good citizens — to be better citizens. Here a very small number of students have crisply and summarily refused to obey a school order designed to give pupils who want to learn the opportunity to do so. One does not need to be a prophet or the son of a prophet to know that after the Court's holding today some students in Iowa schools and indeed in all schools will be ready, able, and willing to defy their teachers on practically all orders. This is the more unfortunate for the schools since groups of students all over the land are already running loose, conducting break-ins, sit-ins, lie-ins, and smash-ins. Many of these student groups, as is all too familiar to all who read the newspapers and watch the television news programs, have already engaged in rioting, property seizures, and destruction. They have picketed schools to force students not to cross their picket lines and have too often violently attacked earnest but frightened students who wanted an education that the pickets did not want them to get. Students engaged in such activities are apparently confident that they know far more about how to operate public school systems than do their parents, teachers, and elected school officials. It is no answer to say that the particular students here have not yet reached such high points in their demands to attend classes in order to exercise their political pressures. Turned loose with lawsuits for damages and injunctions against their teachers as they are here, it is nothing but wishful thinking to imagine that young, immature students will not soon believe it is their right to control the schools rather than the right of the States that collect the taxes to hire the teachers for the benefit of the pupils. This case, therefore, wholly without constitutional reasons in my judgment, subjects all the public schools in the country to the whims and caprices of their loudest-mouthed, but maybe not their brightest, students. I, for one, am not fully persuaded that school pupils are wise enough, even with this Court's expert help from Washington, to run the 23,390 public school systems in our 50 States. I wish, therefore, wholly to disclaim any purpose on my part to hold that the Federal Constitution compels the teachers, parents, and elected school officials to surrender control of the American public school system to public school students. I dissent.

MR. JUSTICE HARLAN, *dissenting*.

I certainly agree that state public school authorities in the discharge of their responsibilities are not wholly exempt from the requirements of the Fourteenth Amendment respecting the freedoms of expression and association. At the same time I am reluctant to believe that there is any disagreement between the majority and myself on the proposition that school officials should be accorded the widest authority in maintaining discipline and good order in their institutions. To translate that proposition into a workable constitutional rule, I would, in cases like this, cast upon those complaining the burden of showing that a particular school measure was motivated by other than legitimate school concerns — for example, a desire to prohibit the expression of an unpopular point of view, while permitting expression of the dominant opinion.

Finding nothing in this record which impugns the good faith of respondents in promulgating the armband regulation, I would affirm the judgment below.

NOTES AND QUESTIONS

1. The *Tinker* case signaled a major change in the power structure of the public schools. The power of school officials before *Tinker* stemmed from the common law doctrine of *in loco parentis*. According to Blackstone's description, a parent "may . . . delegate part of his parental authority, during his life, to the tutor or schoolmaster of his child; who is then *in loco parentis,* and has such a portion of the power of the parent committed to his charge, viz. that of restraint and correction, as may be necessary to answer the purposes for which he is employed." 1 W. BLACKSTONE, COMMENTARIES ON THE LAWS OF ENGLAND 441 (1769). *See Hobbs v. Germany,* 49 So. 515, 517 (Miss. 1909) ("When the schoolroom is entered by the pupil, the authority of the parent ceases, and that of the teacher begins"). Before *Tinker*, the power of school officials to proscribe the attire of students in school under the *in loco parentis* doctrine would not have been questioned.

2. Consider the standard that the Supreme Court set up in *Tinker* for school officials who wish to restrain student expression: "showing that engaging in the forbidden conduct would materially and substantially interfere with the requirements of appropriate discipline in the operation of the school . . ."; whether students can express opinions without "materially and substantially interfering with appropriate discipline" or "colliding with the rights of others"; whether behavior "materially disrupts classwork or involves substantial disorder or invasion of the rights of others . . ."; whether the students' activities "would materially and substantially disrupt the work and discipline of the school"; and whether there were "facts that might reasonably have led school authorities to forecast substantial disruption or material interference with school activities."

Were there any facts that might reasonably have led school authorities to forecast at least some disruption or interference with school activities? How are school officials to determine if interference and disruption would be material or substantial enough to meet the *Tinker* standard? *See* David A. Diamond, *The First Amendment and the Public Schools: The Case Against Judicial Intervention,* 59 TEX. L. REV. 447, 485 (1981) (pointing out that there are different forms of educational disruption); *see also* Anne P. Dupre, *Should Students Have Constitutional Rights? Keeping Order in the Public School,* 65 GEO. WASH. L. REV. 49, 98 (1996) (stating that substantial interference and material disruption standard will allow distractions to occur that will impair the process of learning). After *Tinker*, principals and teachers who are concerned about a student's expression must assess whether the expression in question will be the kind of distraction that will have a sufficient enough impact — material disruption or substantial disorder — on the educational process. This assessment cannot be made in the abstract, as it will vary from school to school, class to class and even from day to day.

What happens if school officials make a mistake? What if the school officials had known about the protest, made the assessment noted above, and determined that although it was likely that there would be some disruption, it would not necessarily meet the higher "material" and "substantial" standard? What if there had been a violent disturbance where a student was injured? In many states, parents of that injured child could sue the school or school officials for negligent failure to supervise. *See e.g., Payne v. North Carolina Dept. of Human Resources,* 382 S.E.2d 449, 451 (N.C. Ct. App. 1989) (asking what degree of care a person of ordinary prudence, charged with a teacher's duties, would exercise under the circumstances). Do you think the school would have a clear victory in the courts if the parents of the injured child argued that reasonable school officials should have seen the potential for harm, given all the intense feeling that surrounded the Vietnam War at the time?

How much learning is lost when a teacher must wait until a student's expression "materially disrupts classwork?" *See* Diane Felmlee et al., *Peer Influence on Classroom Attention*, 48 SOC. PSYCHOL. Q. 215, 223 (1985) ("Our quantitative analysis suggests that a distracting comment or action does indeed have a statistically significant effect on the probability an individual becomes inattentive at a later point in the lesson, even when controlling for a number of individual and group characteristics").

What if there were facts that would "reasonably [lead] school authorities to forecast substantial disruption or material interference with school activities," *Tinker*, by students other than the student speaker? The *Tinker* opinion was not clear about the effect of the "heckler's veto" — whether the standard is met if the expression merely causes others to be disruptive or whether the expression must be disruptive in and of itself. Would it be fair to restrain the speech of the *Tinker* children because other students threaten violence?

3. Unpopular wars remain a source of contention in the classroom. In February 2003, a high school junior in Dearborn, Michigan wore a tee shirt with an image of President Bush and the words "International Terrorist" written beneath it. The student said that he was protesting the President's foreign policy and the imminent war in Iraq. Dearborn has the largest concentration of Arabs outside the Middle East, and the Dearborn school district has a student population that is over 30 per cent Arab. Many of the students are from Iraqi families who left Iraq because of the regime of former president Saddam Hussein. The school administrators stated that they were concerned that Iraqi students would see the shirt as a personal attack. The principal cited violence that had occurred at a nearby high school when Yemenese students had worn tee shirts and carried pictures depicting Saddam Hussein during the Desert Storm war. That particular violent episode was subdued only after police were called in to the school. Based on his concern that the shirt might cause a similar reaction, the principal asked that the student remove his shirt, whereupon the student threatened to call the ACLU and sue the school. The student ultimately moved for a preliminary injunction to restrain the school district from prohibiting the shirt.

The district court held that the student had a substantial likelihood of succeeding on the merits of his claim because his shirt was the type of symbolic act protected by the First Amendment. The principal failed to show that the student's shirt had caused a substantial disruption of or material interference with school activities or created more than an unsubstantiated fear or apprehension of such a disruption or interference. There was no evidence of a substantial disruption of school activities, and no evidence that Arab students might respond to the shirt in a way that would disrupt or interfere with the school environment. The court further held that the school's absolute prohibition on the student wearing the shirt to school would constitute irreparable harm and that the public interest was best served by protecting the student's free expression. *Barber v. Dearborn Public Schools*, 286 F. Supp. 2d 847 (E.D. Mich. 2003).

Was the shirt in *Barber* distinguishable from what the *Tinker* Court called the "silent, passive witness of the armbands"? Review this case again after you read § 4.01[C][2], *infra*, regarding students who wish to display the Confederate flag at school.

BETHEL SCHOOL DISTRICT v. FRASER

Supreme Court of the United States
478 U.S. 675 (1986)

CHIEF JUSTICE BURGER *delivered the opinion of the Court.*

We granted certiorari to decide whether the First Amendment prevents a school district from disciplining a high school student for giving a lewd speech at a school assembly.

I.

A.

On April 26, 1983, respondent Matthew N. Fraser, a student at Bethel High School in Pierce County, Washington, delivered a speech nominating a fellow student for student elective office. Approximately 600 high school students, many of whom were 14-year-olds, attended the assembly. Students were required to attend the assembly or to report to the study hall. The assembly was part of a school-sponsored educational program in self-government. Students who elected not to attend the assembly were required to report to study hall. During the entire speech, Fraser referred to his candidate in terms of an elaborate, graphic, and explicit sexual metaphor.

Two of Fraser's teachers, with whom he discussed the contents of his speech in advance, informed him that the speech was "inappropriate and that he probably should not deliver it," . . . and that his delivery of the speech might have "severe consequences." . . .

During Fraser's delivery of the speech, a school counselor observed the reaction of students to the speech. Some students hooted and yelled; some by gestures graphically simulated the sexual activities pointedly alluded to in respondent's speech. Other students appeared to be bewildered and embarrassed by the speech. One teacher reported that on the day following the speech, she found it necessary to forgo a portion of the scheduled class lesson in order to discuss the speech with the class . . . .

A Bethel High School disciplinary rule prohibiting the use of obscene language in the school provides:

> "Conduct which materially and substantially interferes with the educational process is prohibited, including the use of obscene, profane language or gestures."

The morning after the assembly, the Assistant Principal called Fraser into her office and notified him that the school considered his speech to have been a violation of this rule. Fraser was presented with copies of five letters submitted by teachers, describing his conduct at the assembly; he was given a chance to explain his conduct, and he admitted to having given the speech described and that he deliberately used sexual innuendo in the speech. Fraser was then informed that he would be suspended for three days, and that his name would be removed from the list of candidates for graduation speaker at the school's commencement exercises.

Fraser sought review of this disciplinary action through the School District's grievance procedures. The hearing officer determined that the speech given by respondent was "indecent, lewd, and offensive to the modesty and decency of many of the students and faculty in attendance at the assembly." The examiner determined that the speech fell within the ordinary meaning of "obscene," as used in the disruptive-conduct rule, and affirmed the discipline in its entirety. Fraser served two days of his suspension, and was allowed to return to school on the third day.

B

Respondent, by his father as guardian ad litem, then brought this action. . . . Respondent alleged a violation of his First Amendment right to freedom of speech and sought both injunctive relief and monetary damages under 42 U. S. C. § 1983. The District Court held that the school's sanctions violated respondent's right to freedom of speech under the First Amendment to the United States Constitution, that the school's disruptive-conduct rule is unconstitutionally vague and overbroad, and that the removal of respondent's name from the graduation speaker's list violated the Due Process Clause of the Fourteenth Amendment because the disciplinary rule makes no mention of such removal as a possible sanction. The District Court awarded respondent $278 in damages, $12,750 in litigation costs and attorney's fees, and enjoined the School District from preventing respondent from speaking at the commencement ceremonies. Respondent, who had been elected graduation speaker by a write-in vote of his classmates, delivered a speech at the commencement ceremonies on June 8, 1983.

The Court of Appeals for the Ninth Circuit affirmed the judgment of the District Court, holding that respondent's speech was indistinguishable from the protest armband in *Tinker v. Des Moines Independent Community School*

Dist. The court explicitly rejected the School District's argument that the speech, unlike the passive conduct of wearing a black armband, had a disruptive effect on the educational process. The Court of Appeals also rejected the School District's argument that it had an interest in protecting an essentially captive audience of minors from lewd and indecent language in a setting sponsored by the school, reasoning that the School District's "unbridled discretion" to determine what discourse is "decent" would "increase the risk of cementing white, middle-class standards for determining what is acceptable and proper speech and behavior in our public schools." Finally, the Court of Appeals rejected the School District's argument that, incident to its responsibility for the school curriculum, it had the power to control the language used to express ideas during a school-sponsored activity.

We granted certiorari. We reverse.

II

This Court acknowledged in *Tinker* that students do not "shed their constitutional rights to freedom of speech or expression at the schoolhouse gate." The Court of Appeals read that case as precluding any discipline of Fraser for indecent speech and lewd conduct in the school assembly. That court appears to have proceeded on the theory that the use of lewd and obscene speech in order to make what the speaker considered to be a point in a nominating speech for a fellow student was essentially the same as the wearing of an armband in *Tinker* as a form of protest or the expression of a political position.

The marked distinction between the political "message" of the armbands in *Tinker* and the sexual content of respondent's speech in this case seems to have been given little weight by the Court of Appeals. In upholding the students' right to engage in a nondisruptive, passive expression of a political viewpoint in *Tinker*, this Court was careful to note that the case did "not concern speech or action that intrudes upon the work of the schools or the rights of other students."

It is against this background that we turn to consider the level of First Amendment protection accorded to Fraser's utterances and actions before an official high school assembly attended by 600 students.

III

The role and purpose of the American public school system were well described by two historians, who stated: "[Public] education must prepare pupils for citizenship in the Republic. . . . It must inculcate the habits and manners of civility as values in themselves conducive to happiness and as indispensable to the practice of self-government in the community and the nation." C. BEARD & M. BEARD, NEW BASIC HISTORY OF THE UNITED STATES 228 (1968). In *Ambach v. Norwick*, 441 U.S. 68, 76–77 (1979), we echoed the essence of this statement of the objectives of public education as the "[inculcation of] fundamental values necessary to the maintenance of a democratic political system."

These fundamental values of "habits and manners of civility" essential to a democratic society must, of course, include tolerance of divergent political and religious views, even when the views expressed may be unpopular. But these "fundamental values" must also take into account consideration of the sensibilities of others, and, in the case of a school, the sensibilities of fellow students. The undoubted freedom to advocate unpopular and controversial views in schools and classrooms must be balanced against the society's countervailing interest in teaching students the boundaries of socially appropriate behavior. Even the most heated political discourse in a democratic society requires consideration for the personal sensibilities of the other participants and audiences.

. . . .

The First Amendment guarantees wide freedom in matters of adult public discourse. A sharply divided Court upheld the right to express an antidraft viewpoint in a public place, albeit in terms highly offensive to most citizens. *See Cohen v. California,* 403 U.S. 15 (1971). It does not follow, however, that simply because the use of an offensive form of expression may not be prohibited to adults making what the speaker considers a political point, the same latitude must be permitted to children in a public school. In *New Jersey v. T. L. O.,* 469 U.S. 325, 340–342 (1985), we reaffirmed that the constitutional rights of students in public school are not automatically coextensive with the rights of adults in other settings. As cogently expressed by Judge Newman, "the First Amendment gives a high school student the classroom right to wear Tinker's armband, but not Cohen's jacket." *Thomas v. Board of Education, Granville Central School Dist.,* 607 F.2d 1043, 1057 (CA2 1979) (opinion concurring in result).

Surely it is a highly appropriate function of public school education to prohibit the use of vulgar and offensive terms in public discourse. Indeed, the "fundamental values necessary to the maintenance of a democratic political system" disfavor the use of terms of debate highly offensive or highly threatening to others. Nothing in the Constitution prohibits the states from insisting that certain modes of expression are inappropriate and subject to sanctions. The inculcation of these values is truly the "work of the schools." *Tinker, supra.* The determination of what manner of speech in the classroom or in school assembly is inappropriate properly rests with the school board.

The process of educating our youth for citizenship in public schools is not confined to books, the curriculum, and the civics class; schools must teach by example the shared values of a civilized social order. Consciously or otherwise, teachers — and indeed the older students — demonstrate the appropriate form of civil discourse and political expression by their conduct and deportment in and out of class. Inescapably, like parents, they are role models. The schools, as instruments of the state, may determine that the essential lessons of civil, mature conduct cannot be conveyed in a school that tolerates lewd, indecent, or offensive speech and conduct such as that indulged in by this confused boy.

The pervasive sexual innuendo in Fraser's speech was plainly offensive to both teachers and students — indeed to any mature person. By glorifying male sexuality, and in its verbal content, the speech was acutely insulting to teenage girl students . . . . The speech could well be seriously damaging to its less mature audience, many of whom were only 14 years old and on the threshold of awareness of human sexuality. Some students were reported as bewildered by the speech and the reaction of mimicry it provoked.

This Court's First Amendment jurisprudence has acknowledged limitations on the otherwise absolute interest of the speaker in reaching an unlimited audience where the speech is sexually explicit and the audience may include children. In *Ginsberg v. New York*, this Court upheld a New York statute banning the sale of sexually oriented material to minors, even though the material in question was entitled to First Amendment protection with respect to adults. And in addressing the question whether the First Amendment places any limit on the authority of public schools to remove books from a public school library, all Members of the Court, otherwise sharply divided, acknowledged that the school board has the authority to remove books that are vulgar. *Board of Education v. Pico,* 457 U.S. 853, 871–872 (1982) (plurality opinion). These cases recognize the obvious concern on the part of parents, and school authorities acting *in loco parentis*, to protect children — especially in a captive audience — from exposure to sexually explicit, indecent, or lewd speech.

. . . .

We hold that petitioner School District acted entirely within its permissible authority in imposing sanctions upon Fraser in response to his offensively lewd and indecent speech. Unlike the sanctions imposed on the students wearing armbands in *Tinker*, the penalties imposed in this case were unrelated to any political viewpoint. The First Amendment does not prevent the school officials from determining that to permit a vulgar and lewd speech such as respondent's would undermine the school's basic educational mission. A high school assembly or classroom is no place for a sexually explicit monologue directed towards an unsuspecting audience of teenage students. Accordingly, it was perfectly appropriate for the school to disassociate itself to make the point to the pupils that vulgar speech and lewd conduct is wholly inconsistent with the "fundamental values" of public school education. Justice Black, dissenting in *Tinker*, made a point that is especially relevant in this case:

> I wish therefore, . . . to disclaim any purpose . . . to hold that the Federal Constitution compels the teachers, parents, and elected school officials to surrender control of the American public school system to public school students. 393 U.S., at 526.

IV

Respondent contends that the circumstances of his suspension violated due process because he had no way of knowing that the delivery of the speech in question would subject him to disciplinary sanctions. This argument is wholly without merit. We have recognized that "maintaining security and order in the schools requires a certain degree of flexibility in school disciplinary procedures, and we have respected the value of preserving the informality of the student-teacher relationship." *New Jersey v. T. L. O.* Given the school's need to be able to impose disciplinary sanctions for a wide range of unantici-pated conduct disruptive of the educational process, the school disciplinary rules need not be as detailed as a criminal code which imposes criminal sanctions. Two days' suspension from school does not rise to the level of a penal sanction calling for the full panoply of procedural due process protections applicable to a criminal prosecution. The school disciplinary rule proscribing "obscene" language and the prespeech admonitions of teachers gave adequate warning to Fraser that his lewd speech could subject him to sanctions.

The judgment of the Court of Appeals for the Ninth Circuit is reversed.

JUSTICE BLACKMUN concurs in the result.

JUSTICE BRENNAN, *concurring in the judgment.*

Respondent gave the following speech at a high school assembly in support of a candidate for student government office:

> I know a man who is firm — he's firm in his pants, he's firm in his shirt, his character is firm — but most . . . of all, his belief in you, the students of Bethel, is firm.

> Jeff Kuhlman is a man who takes his point and pounds it in. If necessary, he'll take an issue and nail it to the wall. He doesn't attack things in spurts — he drives hard, pushing and pushing until finally — he succeeds.

> Jeff is a man who will go to the very end — even the climax, for each and every one of you.

> So vote for Jeff for A. S. B. vice-president — he'll never come between you and the best our high school can be. . . .

The Court, referring to these remarks as "obscene," "vulgar," "lewd," and "offensively lewd," concludes that school officials properly punished respondent for uttering the speech. Having read the full text of respondent's remarks, I find it difficult to believe that it is the same speech the Court describes. To my mind, the most that can be said about respondent's speech — and all that need be said — is that in light of the discretion school officials have to teach high school students how to conduct civil and effective public discourse, and to prevent disruption of school educational activities, it was not unconstitutional for school officials to conclude, under the circumstances of this case, that respondent's remarks exceeded permissible limits. Thus, while I concur in the Court's judgment, I write separately to express my understanding of the breadth of the Court's holding.

The Court today reaffirms the unimpeachable proposition that students do not " 'shed their constitutional rights to freedom of speech or expression at the schoolhouse gate.' " If respondent had given the same speech outside of the school environment, he could not have been penalized simply because government officials considered his language to be inappropriate; the Court's opinion does not suggest otherwise. Moreover, despite the Court's characterizations, the language respondent used is far removed from the very narrow class of "obscene" speech which the Court has held is not protected by the First Amendment. It is true, however, that the State has interests in teaching high school students how to conduct civil and effective public discourse and in avoiding disruption of educational school activities. Thus, the Court holds that under certain circumstances, high school students may properly be reprimanded for giving a speech at a high school assembly which school officials conclude disrupted the school's educational mission.[4] Respondent's speech may well have been protected had he given it in school but under different circumstances, where the school's legitimate interests in teaching and maintaining civil public discourse were less weighty.

In the present case, school officials sought only to ensure that a high school assembly proceed in an orderly manner. There is no suggestion that school officials attempted to regulate respondent's speech because they disagreed with the views he sought to express. Nor does this case involve an attempt by school officials to ban written materials they consider "inappropriate" for high school students, or to limit what students should hear, read, or learn about. Thus, the Court's holding concerns only the authority that school officials have to restrict a high school student's use of disruptive language in a speech given to a high school assembly.

The authority school officials have to regulate such speech by high school students is not limitless. Under the circumstances of this case, however, I believe that school officials did not violate the First Amendment in determining that respondent should be disciplined for the disruptive language he used while addressing a high school assembly.[5] Thus, I concur in the judgment reversing the decision of the Court of Appeals.

JUSTICE MARSHALL, *dissenting*.

I agree with the principles that JUSTICE BRENNAN sets out in his opinion concurring in the judgment. I dissent from the Court's decision, however, because in my view the School District failed to demonstrate that respondent's remarks were indeed disruptive. The District Court and Court of Appeals conscientiously applied *Tinker* and concluded that the School District had not demonstrated any disruption of the educational process. I recognize that the school administration must be given wide latitude to determine what forms of conduct are inconsistent with the school's educational mission; nevertheless, where speech is involved, we may not unquestioningly accept a teacher's or administrator's assertion that certain pure speech interfered with education. Here the School District, despite a clear opportunity to do so, failed to bring in evidence sufficient to convince either of the two lower courts that education

---

4 [2] The Court speculates that the speech was "insulting" to female students, and "seriously damaging" to 14-year-olds, so that school officials could legitimately suppress such expression in order to protect these groups. There is no evidence in the record that any students, male or female, found the speech "insulting." And while it was not unreasonable for school officials to conclude that respondent's remarks were inappropriate for a school-sponsored assembly, the language respondent used does not even approach the sexually explicit speech regulated in *Ginsberg v. New York*, 390 U.S. 629 (1968), or the indecent speech banned in *FCC v. Pacifica Foundation*, 438 U.S. 726 (1978). Indeed, to my mind, respondent's speech was no more "obscene," "lewd," or "sexually explicit" than the bulk of programs currently appearing on prime time television or in the local cinema. Thus, I disagree with the Court's suggestion that school officials could punish respondent's speech out of a need to protect younger students.

5 [3] Respondent served two days' suspension and had his name removed from the list of candidates for graduation speaker at the school's commencement exercises, although he was eventually permitted to speak at the graduation. While I find this punishment somewhat severe in light of the nature of respondent's transgression, I cannot conclude that school officials exceeded the bounds of their disciplinary authority.

at Bethel School was disrupted by respondent's speech. I therefore see no reason to disturb the Court of Appeals' judgment.

JUSTICE STEVENS, *dissenting*.

"Frankly, my dear, I don't give a damn."

When I was a high school student, the use of those words in a public forum shocked the Nation. Today Clark Gable's four-letter expletive is less offensive than it was then. Nevertheless, I assume that high school administrators may prohibit the use of that word in classroom discussion and even in extracurricular activities that are sponsored by the school and held on school premises. For I believe a school faculty must regulate the content as well as the style of student speech in carrying out its educational mission.[6] It does seem to me, however, that if a student is to be punished for using offensive speech, he is entitled to fair notice of the scope of the prohibition and the consequences of its violation. The interest in free speech protected by the First Amendment and the interest in fair procedure protected by the Due Process Clause of the Fourteenth Amendment combine to require this conclusion.

This respondent was an outstanding young man with a fine academic record. The fact that he was chosen by the student body to speak at the school's commencement exercises demonstrates that he was respected by his peers. This fact is relevant for two reasons. It confirms the conclusion that the discipline imposed on him — a 3-day suspension and ineligibility to speak at the school's graduation exercises — was sufficiently serious to justify invocation of the School District's grievance procedures. *See Goss v. Lopez,* 419 U.S. 565, 574–575 (1975). More importantly, it indicates that he was probably in a better position to determine whether an audience composed of 600 of his contemporaries would be offended by the use of a four-letter word — or a sexual metaphor — than is a group of judges who are at least two generations and 3,000 miles away from the scene of the crime.

The fact that the speech may not have been offensive to his audience — or that he honestly believed that it would be inoffensive — does not mean that he had a constitutional right to deliver it. For the school — not the student — must prescribe the rules of conduct in an educational institution. But it does mean that he should not be disciplined for speaking frankly in a school assembly if he had no reason to anticipate punitive consequences.

One might conclude that respondent should have known that he would be punished for giving this speech on three quite different theories: (1) It violated the "Disruptive Conduct" rule published in the student handbook; (2) he was specifically warned by his teachers; or (3) the impropriety is so obvious that no specific notice was required. I discuss each theory in turn.

The Disciplinary Rule

At the time the discipline was imposed, as well as in its defense of this lawsuit, the school took the position that respondent violated the following published rule:

---

[6] [1] . . . "Any student of history who has been reprimanded for talking about the World Series during a class discussion of the First Amendment knows that it is incorrect to state that a 'time, place, or manner restriction may not be based upon either the content or subject matter of speech.'"

In addition to the criminal acts defined above, the commission of, or participation in certain noncriminal activities or acts may lead to disciplinary action. Generally, these are acts which disrupt and interfere with the educational process. . . .

Disruptive Conduct. Conduct which materially and substantially interferes with the educational process is prohibited, including the use of obscene, profane language or gestures.

Based on the findings of fact made by the District Court, the Court of Appeals concluded that the evidence did not show "that the speech had a materially disruptive effect on the educational process." The Court of Appeals explained the basis for this conclusion:

> [The] record now before us yields no evidence that Fraser's use of a sexual innuendo in his speech materially interfered with activities at Bethel High School. While the students' reaction to Fraser's speech may fairly be characterized as boisterous, it was hardly disruptive of the educational process. In the words of Mr. McCutcheon, the school counselor whose testimony the District relies upon, the reaction of the student body "was not atypical to a high school auditorium assembly." In our view, a noisy response to the speech and sexually suggestive movements by three students in a crowd of 600 fail to rise to the level of a material interference with the educational process that justifies impinging upon Fraser's First Amendment right to express himself freely.
>
> We find it significant that although four teachers delivered written statements to an assistant principal commenting on Fraser's speech, none of them suggested that the speech disrupted the assembly or otherwise interfered with school activities. *See*, Finding of Fact No. 8. Nor can a finding of material disruption be based upon the evidence that the speech proved to be a lively topic of conversation among students the following day.

Thus, the evidence in the record, as interpreted by the District Court and the Court of Appeals, makes it perfectly clear that respondent's speech was not "conduct" prohibited by the disciplinary rule. Indeed, even if the language of the rule could be stretched to encompass the nondisruptive use of obscene or profane language, there is no such language in respondent's speech. What the speech does contain is a sexual metaphor that may unquestionably be offensive to some listeners in some settings. But if an impartial judge puts his or her own views about the metaphor to one side, I simply cannot understand how he or she could conclude that it is embraced by the above-quoted rule. At best, the rule is sufficiently ambiguous that without a further explanation or construction it could not advise the reader of the student handbook that the speech would be forbidden.

The Specific Warning by the Teachers

Respondent read his speech to three different teachers before he gave it. Mrs. Irene Hicks told him that she thought the speech "was inappropriate and that he probably should not deliver it." Steven DeHart told respondent "that this would indeed cause problems in that it would raise eyebrows." The third teacher, Shawn Madden, did not testify. None of the three suggested that the speech might violate a school rule.

The fact that respondent reviewed the text of his speech with three different teachers before he gave it does indicate that he must have been aware of the possibility that it would provoke an adverse reaction, but the teachers' responses certainly did not give him any better notice of the likelihood of discipline than did the student handbook itself. In my opinion, therefore, the most difficult question is whether the speech was so obviously offensive that an intelligent high school student must be presumed to have realized that he would be punished for giving it.

Obvious Impropriety

Justice Sutherland taught us that a "nuisance may be merely a right thing in the wrong place, — like a pig in the parlor instead of the barnyard." Vulgar language, like vulgar animals, may be acceptable in some contexts and intolerable in others. *See FCC v. Pacifica Foundation.* Indeed, even ordinary, inoffensive speech may be wholly unacceptable in some settings.

It seems fairly obvious that respondent's speech would be inappropriate in certain classroom and formal social settings. On the other hand, in a locker room or perhaps in a school corridor the metaphor in the speech might be regarded as rather routine comment. If this be true, and if respondent's audience consisted almost entirely of young people with whom he conversed on a daily basis, can we — at this distance — confidently assert that he must have known that the school administration would punish him for delivering it?

For three reasons, I think not. First, it seems highly unlikely that he would have decided to deliver the speech if he had known that it would result in his suspension and disqualification from delivering the school commencement address. Second, I believe a strong presumption in favor of free expression should apply whenever an issue of this kind is arguable. Third, because the Court has adopted the policy of applying contemporary community standards in evaluating expression with sexual connotations, this Court should defer to the views of the district and circuit judges who are in a much better position to evaluate this speech than we are.

I would affirm the judgment of the Court of Appeals.

———

NOTES AND QUESTIONS

1. The majority opinion in *Fraser*, written some seventeen years after *Tinker* and in the aftermath of the turbulent sixties, changed the course for student right of expression. After all, Matt Fraser had prevailed in both the district court and the court of appeals under the *Tinker* standard. Indeed, although the Supreme Court majority opinion quotes the *Tinker* majority opinion, it

also quotes — with approval — Justice Black's famous dissent. Had *Tinker* given students in public schools too much power to challenge the authority of teachers and principals? The *Fraser* majority seemed less concerned that schools would become "enclaves of totalitarianism" and more concerned that teachers, parents, and elected school officials should not "surrender control of the American public school system to public school students." *Fraser*, 478 U.S., at 686 (quoting *Tinker*, 393 U.S. at 526, Black, J. dissenting).

2. Consider whether the *Fraser* opinion set forth a new standard that displaces *Tinker* or whether it merely adds to the standard set by *Tinker*. The *Fraser* Court allows school officials to discipline students for "vulgar," "lewd," or "offensive speech." How does the Court define these terms? Think about whether the location (region of the country, rural, city) and type of school (elementary, middle, high school) will effect the scope of what would be considered vulgar or lewd. At least in the obscenity context, the Supreme Court has stated that structuring state obscenity proceedings around a national community standard would be an exercise in futility, as people in different states vary in their tastes and attitudes. *Miller v. California,* 413 U.S. 15, 30, 33 (1973).

3. The *Fraser* Court's divergence from the *Tinker* standard is driven in part by a difference in views about the mission of the public schools. The *Tinker* Court stated that schools exist to "accommodate students," *Tinker v. Des Moines Indep. School Dist.,* 393 U.S. 503, 512 (1969) ("The principal use to which the schools are dedicated is to accommodate students during prescribed hours . . ."). The *Fraser* Court focused more on the school's role in preserving self-government. The *Fraser* opinion emphasized that the mission of the school is to maintain our democratic society by "inculcat[ing] the habits and manners of civility." *Bethel School Dist. v. Fraser,* 478 U.S. 675, 681 (1986) (quoting C. BEARD & M. BEARD, NEW BASIC HISTORY OF THE UNITED STATES 228 (1968)). Because these values — the habits and manners of civility — are "indispensable to the practice of self-government in the community and the nation" they are thus essential for the preservation of a democratic political system. *Id.*

Professor Joseph Tussman states that the tutelary power of the state — the "teaching power" — is more fundamental than even the war power. J. TUSSMAN, GOVERNMENT AND THE MIND 54 (1977). This "teaching power" is the "inherent constitutional power" of the state to establish and direct the institutions that are necessary to ensure its continuity. "The teaching power is a peer to the legislative, the executive, and the judicial powers, if it is not, indeed, the first among them."

4. Justice Brennan states in his concurrence that "in light of the discretion school officials have to teach high school students how to conduct civil and effective public discourse, and to prevent disruption of school educational activities, it was not unconstitutional for school officials to conclude, under the circumstances of this case, that respondent's remarks exceeded permissible limits." 478 U.S. 675, 687–88 (1986) (Brennan, J. concurring). Yet Fraser's speech "may well have been protected had he given it in school but under different circumstances, where the school's legitimate interests in teaching and maintaining civil public discourse were less weighty." *Id.* at 689. How

might a school principal distinguish between the circumstances where she is allowed to curtail certain speech and those in which the school's interests are "less weighty"? Would it make a difference if Fraser gave the speech in the hallway between classes without the knowledge or approval of school officials?

The school lost at the district court and court of appeals under the *Tinker* standard alone, and Justice Marshall, in his dissent, stated that this determination should not be disturbed. Were there any facts presented that could have led the lower courts to determine that the *Tinker* standard had been met? There was some disturbance at the school, both at the assembly and afterwards. The key to the argument depends on how much disruption is needed before a judge decides that the disruption is material (or how much interference with the educational process is needed before a judge decides that the interference is substantial). Who is in the best position to make the determination about interference with the educational process — teachers and principals who work with students in that particular school every day, or federal judges?

You may wish to refer again to Justice Stevens's discussion of the due process issue in his dissent after you read *Goss v. Lopez, infra.*

5. PROBLEM: Suppose you are an attorney for the local school district, which is drafting a student handbook. Your client has asked for your advice about drafting rules for student expression based on these two cases. How would you advise your client?

[B]   Student Publications

HAZELWOOD SCHOOL DISTRICT v. KUHLMEIER

Supreme Court of the United States
484 U.S. 260 (1988)

JUSTICE WHITE *delivered the opinion of the Court.*

This case concerns the extent to which educators may exercise editorial control over the contents of a high school newspaper produced as part of the school's journalism curriculum.

I

Petitioners are the Hazelwood School District in St. Louis County, Missouri; various school officials; Robert Eugene Reynolds, the principal of Hazelwood East High School; and Howard Emerson, a teacher in the school district. Respondents are three former Hazelwood East students who were staff members of *Spectrum*, the school newspaper. They contend that school officials violated their First Amendment rights by deleting two pages of articles from the May 13, 1983, issue of *Spectrum*.

Spectrum was written and edited by the Journalism II class at Hazelwood East. The newspaper was published every three weeks or so during the 1982-1983 school year. More than 4,500 copies of the newspaper were distributed during that year to students, school personnel, and members of the community.

The Board of Education allocated funds from its annual budget for the printing of *Spectrum*. These funds were supplemented by proceeds from sales of the newspaper.

The printing expenses during the 1982-1983 school year totaled $ 4,668.50; revenue from sales was $1,166.84. The other costs associated with the newspaper — such as supplies, textbooks, and a portion of the journalism teacher's salary — were borne entirely by the Board.

The Journalism II course was taught by Robert Stergos for most of the 1982-1983 academic year. Stergos left Hazelwood East to take a job in private industry on April 29, 1983, when the May 13 edition of *Spectrum* was nearing completion, and petitioner Emerson took his place as newspaper adviser for the remaining weeks of the term.

The practice at Hazelwood East during the spring 1983 semester was for the journalism teacher to submit page proofs of each *Spectrum* issue to Principal Reynolds for his review prior to publication. On May 10, Emerson delivered the proofs of the May 13 edition to Reynolds, who objected to two of the articles scheduled to appear in that edition. One of the stories described three Hazelwood East students' experiences with pregnancy; the other discussed the impact of divorce on students at the school.

Reynolds was concerned that, although the pregnancy story used false names "to keep the identity of these girls a secret," the pregnant students still might be identifiable from the text. He also believed that the article's references to sexual activity and birth control were inappropriate for some of the younger students at the school. In addition, Reynolds was concerned that a student identified by name in the divorce story had complained that her father "wasn't spending enough time with my mom, my sister and I" prior to the divorce, "was always out of town on business or out late playing cards with the guys," and "always argued about everything" with her mother. . . . Reynolds believed that the student's parents should have been given an opportunity to respond to these remarks or to consent to their publication. He was unaware that Emerson had deleted the student's name from the final version of the article.

Reynolds believed that there was no time to make the necessary changes in the stories before the scheduled press run and that the newspaper would not appear before the end of the school year if printing were delayed to any significant extent. He concluded that his only options under the circumstances were to publish a four-page newspaper instead of the planned six-page newspaper, eliminating the two pages on which the offending stories appeared, or to publish no newspaper at all. Accordingly, he directed Emerson to withhold from publication the two pages containing the stories on pregnancy and divorce[7] . . . .

Respondents subsequently commenced this action in the United States District Court for the Eastern District of Missouri seeking a declaration that

---

[7] [1] The two pages deleted from the newspaper also contained articles on teenage marriage, runaways, and juvenile delinquents, as well as a general article on teenage pregnancy. Reynolds testified that he had no objection to these articles and that they were deleted only because they appeared on the same pages as the two objectionable articles.

their First Amendment rights had been violated, injunctive relief, and monetary damages. After a bench trial, the District Court denied an injunction, holding that no First Amendment violation had occurred.

The District Court concluded that school officials may impose restraints on students' speech in activities that are " 'an integral part of the school's educational function' " — including the publication of a school-sponsored newspaper by a journalism class — so long as their decision has " 'a substantial and reasonable basis.' " The court found that Principal Reynolds' concern that the pregnant students' anonymity would be lost and their privacy invaded was "legitimate and reasonable," given "the small number of pregnant students at Hazelwood East and several identifying characteristics that were disclosed in the article." The court held that Reynolds' action was also justified "to avoid the impression that [the school] endorses the sexual norms of the subjects" and to shield younger students from exposure to unsuitable material. The deletion of the article on divorce was seen by the court as a reasonable response to the invasion of privacy concerns raised by the named student's remarks. Because the article did not indicate that the student's parents had been offered an opportunity to respond to her allegations, said the court, there was cause for "serious doubt that the article complied with the rules of fairness which are standard in the field of journalism and which were covered in the textbook used in the Journalism II class." . . .

The Court of Appeals for the Eighth Circuit reversed. The court held at the outset that Spectrum was not only "a part of the school adopted curriculum," but also a public forum, because the newspaper was "intended to be and operated as a conduit for student viewpoint." The court then concluded that Spectrum's status as a public forum precluded school officials from censoring its contents except when " 'necessary to avoid material and substantial interference with school work or discipline . . . or the rights of others.' "

The Court of Appeals found "no evidence in the record that the principal could have reasonably forecast that the censored articles or any materials in the censored articles would have materially disrupted classwork or given rise to substantial disorder in the school." School officials were entitled to censor the articles on the ground that they invaded the rights of others, according to the court, only if publication of the articles could have resulted in tort liability to the school. The court concluded that no tort action for libel or invasion of privacy could have been maintained against the school by the subjects of the two articles or by their families. Accordingly, the court held that school officials had violated respondents' First Amendment rights by deleting the two pages of the newspaper.

We granted certiorari, and we now reverse.

II

Students in the public schools do not "shed their constitutional rights to freedom of speech or expression at the schoolhouse gate." *Tinker*. They cannot be punished merely for expressing their personal views on the school premises — whether "in the cafeteria, or on the playing field, or on the campus during the authorized hours," — unless school authorities have reason to believe that such expression will "substantially interfere with the work of the school or impinge upon the rights of other students."

We have nonetheless recognized that the First Amendment rights of students in the public schools "are not automatically coextensive with the rights of adults in other settings," *Bethel School District No. 403 v. Fraser,* and must be "applied in light of the special characteristics of the school environment." A school need not tolerate student speech that is inconsistent with its "basic educational mission," *Fraser,* even though the government could not censor similar speech outside the school. Accordingly, we held in *Fraser* that a student could be disciplined for having delivered a speech that was "sexually explicit" but not legally obscene at an official school assembly, because the school was entitled to "disassociate itself" from the speech in a manner that would demonstrate to others that such vulgarity is "wholly inconsistent with the 'fundamental values' of public school education." We thus recognized that "[t]he determination of what manner of speech in the classroom or in school assembly is inappropriate properly rests with the school board," rather than with the federal courts. It is in this context that respondents' First Amendment claims must be considered.

A

We deal first with the question whether *Spectrum* may appropriately be characterized as a forum for public expression. The public schools do not possess all of the attributes of streets, parks, and other traditional public forums that "time out of mind, have been used for purposes of assembly, communicating thoughts between citizens, and discussing public questions." Hence, school facilities may be deemed to be public forums only if school authorities have "by policy or by practice" opened those facilities "for indiscriminate use by the general public," *Perry Education Assn. v. Perry Local Educators' Assn.,* 460 U.S. 37, 47 (1983), or by some segment of the public, such as student organizations. If the facilities have instead been reserved for other intended purposes, "communicative or otherwise," then no public forum has been created, and school officials may impose reasonable restrictions on the speech of students, teachers, and other members of the school community. "The government does not create a public forum by inaction or by permitting limited discourse, but only by intentionally opening a nontraditional forum for public discourse."

The policy of school officials toward *Spectrum* was reflected in Hazelwood School Board Policy 348.51 and the Hazelwood East Curriculum Guide. Board Policy 348.51 provided that "[s]chool sponsored publications are developed within the adopted curriculum and its educational implications in regular classroom activities." . . . The Hazelwood East Curriculum Guide described the Journalism II course as a "laboratory situation in which the students publish the school newspaper applying skills they have learned in Journalism I." The lessons that were to be learned from the Journalism II course, according to the Curriculum Guide, included development of journalistic skills under deadline pressure, "the legal, moral, and ethical restrictions imposed upon journalists within the school community," and "responsibility and acceptance of criticism for articles of opinion." Journalism II was taught by a faculty member during regular class hours. Students received grades and academic credit for their performance in the course.

School officials did not deviate in practice from their policy that production of *Spectrum* was to be part of the educational curriculum and a "regular classroom activit[y]." The District Court found that Robert Stergos, the journalism teacher during most of the 1982-1983 school year, "both had the authority to exercise and in fact exercised a great deal of control over *Spectrum*." For example, Stergos selected the editors of the newspaper, scheduled publication dates, decided the number of pages for each issue, assigned story ideas to class members, advised students on the development of their stories, reviewed the use of quotations, edited stories, selected and edited the letters to the editor, and dealt with the printing company. Many of these decisions were made without consultation with the Journalism II students. The District Court thus found it "clear that Mr. Stergos was the final authority with respect to almost every aspect of the production and publication of *Spectrum*, including its content." Moreover, after each *Spectrum* issue had been finally approved by Stergos or his successor, the issue still had to be reviewed by Principal Reynolds prior to publication. Respondents' assertion that they had believed that they could publish "practically anything" in *Spectrum* was therefore dismissed by the District Court as simply "not credible." These factual findings are amply supported by the record, and were not rejected as clearly erroneous by the Court of Appeals.

The evidence relied upon by the Court of Appeals in finding *Spectrum* to be a public forum is equivocal at best. For example, Board Policy 348.51, which stated in part that "[s]chool sponsored student publications will not restrict free expression or diverse viewpoints within the rules of responsible journalism," also stated that such publications were "developed within the adopted curriculum and its educational implications." . . . One might reasonably infer from the full text of Policy 348.51 that school officials retained ultimate control over what constituted "responsible journalism" in a school-sponsored newspaper. Although the Statement of Policy published in the September 14, 1982, issue of *Spectrum* declared that "*Spectrum*, as a student-press publication, accepts all rights implied by the First Amendment," this statement, understood in the context of the paper's role in the school's curriculum, suggests at most that the administration will not interfere with the students' exercise of those First Amendment rights that attend the publication of a school-sponsored newspaper. It does not reflect an intent to expand those rights by converting a curricular newspaper into a public forum.[8] Finally, that students were permitted to exercise some authority over the contents of *Spectrum* was

---

8 [2] The Statement also cited *Tinker v. Des Moines Independent Community School Dist.*, 393 U.S. 503 (1969), for the proposition that "[o]nly speech that 'materially and substantially interferes with the requirements of appropriate discipline' can be found unacceptable and therefore be prohibited." This portion of the Statement does not, of course, even accurately reflect our holding in *Tinker*. Furthermore, the Statement nowhere expressly extended the *Tinker* standard to the news and feature articles contained in a school-sponsored newspaper. The dissent apparently finds as a fact that the Statement was published annually in *Spectrum*; however, the District Court was unable to conclude that the Statement appeared on more than one occasion. In any event, even if the Statement says what the dissent believes that it says, the evidence that school officials never intended to designate *Spectrum* as a public forum remains overwhelming.

fully consistent with the Curriculum Guide objective of teaching the Journalism II students "leadership responsibilities as issue and page editors." . . . A decision to teach leadership skills in the context of a classroom activity hardly implies a decision to relinquish school control over that activity. In sum, the evidence relied upon by the Court of Appeals fails to demonstrate the "clear intent to create a public forum" that existed in cases in which we found public forums to have been created. School officials did not evince either "by policy or by practice," any intent to open the pages of *Spectrum* to "indiscriminate use," by its student reporters and editors, or by the student body generally. Instead, they "reserve[d] the forum for its intended purpos[e]," as a supervised learning experience for journalism students. Accordingly, school officials were entitled to regulate the contents of *Spectrum* in any reasonable manner. It is this standard, rather than our decision in *Tinker*, that governs this case.

The question whether the First Amendment requires a school to tolerate particular student speech — the question that we addressed in *Tinker* — is different from the question whether the First Amendment requires a school affirmatively to promote particular student speech. The former question addresses educators' ability to silence a student's personal expression that happens to occur on the school premises. The latter question concerns educators' authority over school-sponsored publications, theatrical productions, and other expressive activities that students, parents, and members of the public might reasonably perceive to bear the imprimatur of the school. These activities may fairly be characterized as part of the school curriculum, whether or not they occur in a traditional classroom setting, so long as they are supervised by faculty members and designed to impart particular knowledge or skills to student participants and audiences.

Educators are entitled to exercise greater control over this second form of student expression to assure that participants learn whatever lessons the activity is designed to teach, that readers or listeners are not exposed to material that may be inappropriate for their level of maturity, and that the views of the individual speaker are not erroneously attributed to the school. Hence, a school may in its capacity as publisher of a school newspaper or producer of a school play "disassociate itself," not only from speech that would "substantially interfere with [its] work . . . or impinge upon the rights of other students," but also from speech that is, for example, ungrammatical, poorly written, inadequately researched, biased or prejudiced, vulgar or profane, or unsuitable for immature audiences.[9] A school must be able to set high standards for the student speech that is disseminated under its auspices — standards that may be higher than those demanded by some newspaper

---

[9] [4] The dissent perceives no difference between the First Amendment analysis applied in *Tinker* and that applied in *Fraser*. We disagree. The decision in *Fraser* rested on the "vulgar," "lewd," and "plainly offensive" character of a speech delivered at an official school assembly rather than on any propensity of the speech to "materially disrup[t] classwork or involv[e] substantial disorder or invasion of the rights of others." Indeed, the *Fraser* Court cited as "especially relevant" a portion of Justice Black's dissenting opinion in *Tinker* " 'disclaim[ing] any purpose . . . to hold that the Federal Constitution compels the teachers, parents, and elected school officials to surrender control of the American public school system to public school students.' " Of course, Justice Black's observations are equally relevant to the instant case.

publishers or theatrical producers in the "real" world — and may refuse to disseminate student speech that does not meet those standards. In addition, a school must be able to take into account the emotional maturity of the intended audience in determining whether to disseminate student speech on potentially sensitive topics, which might range from the existence of Santa Claus in an elementary school setting to the particulars of teenage sexual activity in a high school setting. A school must also retain the authority to refuse to sponsor student speech that might reasonably be perceived to advocate drug or alcohol use, irresponsible sex, or conduct otherwise inconsistent with "the shared values of a civilized social order," or to associate the school with any position other than neutrality on matters of political controversy. Otherwise, the schools would be unduly constrained from fulfilling their role as "a principal instrument in awakening the child to cultural values, in preparing him for later professional training, and in helping him to adjust normally to his environment." *Brown v. Board of Education,* 347 U.S. 483, 493 (1954).

Accordingly, we conclude that the standard articulated in *Tinker* for determining when a school may punish student expression need not also be the standard for determining when a school may refuse to lend its name and resources to the dissemination of student expression. Instead, we hold that educators do not offend the First Amendment by exercising editorial control over the style and content of student speech in school-sponsored expressive activities so long as their actions are reasonably related to legitimate pedagogical concerns.

This standard is consistent with our oft-expressed view that the education of the Nation's youth is primarily the responsibility of parents, teachers, and state and local school officials, and not of federal judges. It is only when the decision to censor a school-sponsored publication, theatrical production, or other vehicle of student expression has no valid educational purpose that the First Amendment is so "directly and sharply implicate[d]" as to require judicial intervention to protect students' constitutional rights.[10]

III

We also conclude that Principal Reynolds acted reasonably in requiring the deletion from the May 13 issue of *Spectrum* of the pregnancy article, the divorce article, and the remaining articles that were to appear on the same pages of the newspaper.

The initial paragraph of the pregnancy article declared that "[a]ll names have been changed to keep the identity of these girls a secret." The principal concluded that the students' anonymity was not adequately protected, however, given the other identifying information in the article and the small number of pregnant students at the school. Indeed, a teacher at the school credibly testified that she could positively identify at least one of the girls and

---

[10] [7] A number of lower federal courts have similarly recognized that educators' decisions with regard to the content of school-sponsored newspapers, dramatic productions, and other expressive activities are entitled to substantial deference. We need not now decide whether the same degree of deference is appropriate with respect to school-sponsored expressive activities at the college and university level.

possibly all three. It is likely that many students at Hazelwood East would have been at least as successful in identifying the girls. Reynolds therefore could reasonably have feared that the article violated whatever pledge of anonymity had been given to the pregnant students. In addition, he could reasonably have been concerned that the article was not sufficiently sensitive to the privacy interests of the students' boyfriends and parents, who were discussed in the article but who were given no opportunity to consent to its publication or to offer a response. The article did not contain graphic accounts of sexual activity. The girls did comment in the article, however, concerning their sexual histories and their use or nonuse of birth control. It was not unreasonable for the principal to have concluded that such frank talk was inappropriate in a school-sponsored publication distributed to 14-year-old freshmen and presumably taken home to be read by students' even younger brothers and sisters.

The student who was quoted by name in the version of the divorce article seen by Principal Reynolds made comments sharply critical of her father. The principal could reasonably have concluded that an individual publicly identified as an inattentive parent — indeed, as one who chose "playing cards with the guys" over home and family — was entitled to an opportunity to defend himself as a matter of journalistic fairness. These concerns were shared by both of Spectrum's faculty advisers for the 1982-1983 school year, who testified that they would not have allowed the article to be printed without deletion of the student's name.[11]

Principal Reynolds testified credibly at trial that, at the time that he reviewed the proofs of the May 13 issue during an extended telephone conversation with Emerson, he believed that there was no time to make any changes in the articles, and that the newspaper had to be printed immediately or not at all. . . .

In sum, we cannot reject as unreasonable Principal Reynolds' conclusion that neither the pregnancy article nor the divorce article was suitable for publication in *Spectrum*. Reynolds could reasonably have concluded that the students who had written and edited these articles had not sufficiently mastered those portions of the Journalism II curriculum that pertained to the treatment of controversial issues and personal attacks, the need to protect the privacy of individuals whose most intimate concerns are to be revealed in the newspaper, and "the legal, moral, and ethical restrictions imposed upon journalists within [a] school community" that includes adolescent subjects and readers. Finally, we conclude that the principal's decision to delete two pages of *Spectrum*, rather than to delete only the offending articles or to require

---

[11] [8] The reasonableness of Principal Reynolds' concerns about the two articles was further substantiated by the trial testimony of Martin Duggan, a former editorial page editor of the St. Louis Globe Democrat and a former college journalism instructor and newspaper adviser. Duggan testified that the divorce story did not meet journalistic standards of fairness and balance because the father was not given an opportunity to respond, and that the pregnancy story was not appropriate for publication in a high school newspaper because it was unduly intrusive into the privacy of the girls, their parents, and their boyfriends. The District Court found Duggan to be "an objective and independent witness" whose testimony was entitled to significant weight.

that they be modified, was reasonable under the circumstances as he understood them. Accordingly, no violation of First Amendment rights occurred.[12]

The judgment of the Court of Appeals for the Eighth Circuit is therefore Reversed.

JUSTICE BRENNAN, with whom JUSTICE MARSHALL and JUSTICE BLACKMUN join, *dissenting*.

When the young men and women of Hazelwood East High School registered for Journalism II, they expected a civics lesson. *Spectrum*, the newspaper they were to publish, "was not just a class exercise in which students learned to prepare papers and hone writing skills, it was a . . . forum established to give students an opportunity to express their views while gaining an appreciation of their rights and responsibilities under the First Amendment to the United States Constitution . . . ." "[A]t the beginning of each school year," the student journalists published a Statement of Policy — tacitly approved each year by school authorities — announcing their expectation that "*Spectrum*, as a student-press publication, accepts all rights implied by the First Amendment . . . . Only speech that 'materially and substantially interferes with the requirements of appropriate discipline' can be found unacceptable and therefore prohibited."[13] The school board itself affirmatively guaranteed the students of Journalism II an atmosphere conducive to fostering such an appreciation and exercising the full panoply of rights associated with a free student press. "School sponsored student publications," it vowed, "will not restrict free expression or diverse viewpoints within the rules of responsible journalism."

This case arose when the Hazelwood East administration breached its own promise, dashing its students' expectations. The school principal, without prior consultation or explanation, excised six articles — comprising two full pages — of the May 13, 1983, issue of *Spectrum*. He did so not because any of the articles would "materially and substantially interfere with the requirements of appropriate discipline," but simply because he considered two of the six "inappropriate, personal, sensitive, and unsuitable" for student consumption.

In my view the principal broke more than just a promise. He violated the First Amendment's prohibitions against censorship of any student expression that neither disrupts classwork nor invades the rights of others, and against any censorship that is not narrowly tailored to serve its purpose.

---

[12] [9] It is likely that the approach urged by the dissent would as a practical matter have far more deleterious consequences for the student press than does the approach that we adopt today. The dissent correctly acknowledges "[t]he State's prerogative to dissolve the student newspaper entirely." . . . It is likely that many public schools would do just that rather than open their newspapers to all student expression that does not threaten "materia[l] disrup[tion of] classwork" or violation of "rights that are protected by law," . . . regardless of how sexually explicit, racially intemperate, or personally insulting that expression otherwise might be.

[13] [1] The Court suggests that the passage quoted in the text did not "exten[d] the *Tinker* standard to the news and feature articles contained in a school-sponsored newspaper" because the passage did not expressly mention them. n.2. It is hard to imagine why the Court (or anyone else) might expect a passage that applies categorically to "a student-press publication," composed almost exclusively of "news and feature articles," to mention those categories expressly. Understandably, neither court below so limited the passage.

I

Public education serves vital national interests in preparing the Nation's youth for life in our increasingly complex society and for the duties of citizenship in our democratic Republic. *See Brown v. Board of Education.* The public school conveys to our young the information and tools required not merely to survive in, but to contribute to, civilized society. It also inculcates in tomorrow's leaders the "fundamental values necessary to the maintenance of a democratic political system . . . ." *Ambach v. Norwick.* All the while, the public educator nurtures students' social and moral development by transmitting to them an official dogma of " 'community values.' "

The public educator's task is weighty and delicate indeed. It demands particularized and supremely subjective choices among diverse curricula, moral values, and political stances to teach or inculcate in students, and among various methodologies for doing so. Accordingly, we have traditionally reserved the "daily operation of school systems" to the States and their local school boards. We have not, however, hesitated to intervene where their decisions run afoul of the Constitution.

Free student expression undoubtedly sometimes interferes with the effectiveness of the school's pedagogical functions. Some brands of student expression do so by directly preventing the school from pursuing its pedagogical mission: The young polemic who stands on a soapbox during calculus class to deliver an eloquent political diatribe interferes with the legitimate teaching of calculus. And the student who delivers a lewd endorsement of a student-government candidate might so extremely distract an impressionable high school audience as to interfere with the orderly operation of the school. *See Bethel School Dist. No. 403 v. Fraser.* Other student speech, however, frustrates the school's legitimate pedagogical purposes merely by expressing a message that conflicts with the school's, without directly interfering with the school's expression of its message: A student who responds to a political science teacher's question with the retort, "socialism is good," subverts the school's inculcation of the message that capitalism is better. Even the maverick who sits in class passively sporting a symbol of protest against a government policy, *cf. Tinker,* or the gossip who sits in the student commons swapping stories of sexual escapade could readily muddle a clear official message condoning the government policy or condemning teenage sex. Likewise, the student newspaper that, like *Spectrum,* conveys a moral position at odds with the school's official stance might subvert the administration's legitimate inculcation of its own perception of community values.

If mere incompatibility with the school's pedagogical message were a constitutionally sufficient justification for the suppression of student speech, school officials could censor each of the students or student organizations in the foregoing hypotheticals, converting our public schools into "enclaves of totalitarianism" that "strangle the free mind at its source." The First Amendment permits no such blanket censorship authority. While the "constitutional rights of students in public school are not automatically coextensive with the rights of adults in other settings," *Fraser,* students in the public schools do not "shed their constitutional rights to freedom of speech or expression at the schoolhouse gate." Just as the public on the street corner must, in the interest of fostering "enlightened opinion," tolerate speech that "tempt[s] [the listener] to throw [the speaker] off the street," public educators must accommodate some student expression even if it offends them or offers views or values that contradict those the school wishes to inculcate.

In *Tinker*, this Court struck the balance. We held that official censorship of student expression — there the suspension of several students until they removed their armbands protesting the Vietnam war — is unconstitutional unless the speech "materially disrupts classwork or involves substantial disorder or invasion of the rights of others . . . ." School officials may not suppress "silent, passive expression of opinion, unaccompanied by any disorder or disturbance on the part of" the speaker. The "mere desire to avoid the discomfort and unpleasantness that always accompany an unpopular viewpoint," or an unsavory subject, does not justify official suppression of student speech in the high school.

This Court applied the *Tinker* test just a Term ago in *Fraser,* upholding an official decision to discipline a student for delivering a lewd speech in support of a student-government candidate. The Court today casts no doubt on *Tinker*'s vitality. Instead it erects a taxonomy of school censorship, concluding that *Tinker* applies to one category and not another. On the one hand is censorship "to silence a student's personal expression that happens to occur on the school premises." On the other hand is censorship of expression that arises in the context of "school-sponsored . . . expressive activities that students, parents, and members of the public might reasonably perceive to bear the imprimatur of the school."

The Court does not, for it cannot, purport to discern from our precedents the distinction it creates. One could, I suppose, readily characterize the students' symbolic speech in *Tinker* as "personal expression that happens to [have] occur[red] on school premises," although *Tinker* did not even hint that the personal nature of the speech was of any (much less dispositive) relevance. But that same description could not by any stretch of the imagination fit Fraser's speech. He did not just "happen" to deliver his lewd speech to an ad hoc gathering on the playground. As the second paragraph of *Fraser* evinces, if ever a forum for student expression was "school-sponsored," Fraser's was. . . . "The assembly was part of a *school-sponsored* educational program in self-government." Yet, from the first sentence of its analysis, *Fraser* faithfully applied *Tinker*. . . .

II

Even if we were writing on a clean slate, I would reject the Court's rationale for abandoning *Tinker* in this case. The Court offers no more than an obscure tangle of three excuses to afford educators "greater control" over school-sponsored speech than the *Tinker* test would permit: the public educator's prerogative to control curriculum; the pedagogical interest in shielding the high school audience from objectionable viewpoints and sensitive topics; and the school's need to dissociate itself from student expression. . . . None of the excuses, once disentangled, supports the distinction that the Court draws. *Tinker* fully addresses the first concern; the second is illegitimate; and the third is readily achievable through less oppressive means.

A

The Court is certainly correct that the First Amendment permits educators "to assure that participants learn whatever lessons the activity is designed to teach. . . ." That is, however, the essence of the *Tinker* test, not an excuse to abandon it. Under *Tinker*, school officials may censor only such student speech as would "materially disrup[t]" a legitimate curricular function. Manifestly, student speech is more likely to disrupt a curricular function when it arises in the context of a curricular activity — one that "is designed to teach" something — than when it arises in the context of a noncurricular activity. Thus, under *Tinker*, the school may constitutionally punish the budding political orator if he disrupts calculus class but not if he holds his tongue for the cafeteria. That is not because some more stringent standard applies in the curricular context. (After all, this Court applied the same standard whether the students in *Tinker* wore their armbands to the "classroom" or the "cafeteria.") It is because student speech in the noncurricular context is less likely to disrupt materially any legitimate pedagogical purpose.

I fully agree with the Court that the First Amendment should afford an educator the prerogative not to sponsor the publication of a newspaper article that is "ungrammatical, poorly written, inadequately researched, biased or prejudiced," or that falls short of the "high standards for . . . student speech that is disseminated under [the school's] auspices. . . ." But we need not abandon *Tinker* to reach that conclusion; we need only apply it. The enumerated criteria reflect the skills that the curricular newspaper "is designed to teach." The educator may, under *Tinker*, constitutionally "censor" poor grammar, writing, or research because to reward such expression would "materially disrup[t]" the newspaper's curricular purpose.

The same cannot be said of official censorship designed to shield the *audience* or dissociate the *sponsor* from the expression. Censorship so motivated might well serve (although, as I demonstrate *infra*, cannot legitimately serve) some other school purpose. But it in no way furthers the curricular purposes of a student *newspaper*, unless one believes that the purpose of the school newspaper is to teach students that the press ought never report bad news, express unpopular views, or print a thought that might upset its sponsors. Unsurprisingly, Hazelwood East claims no such pedagogical purpose.

The Court relies on bits of testimony to portray the principal's conduct as a pedagogical lesson to Journalism II students who "had not sufficiently mastered those portions of the . . . curriculum that pertained to the treatment of controversial issues and personal attacks, the need to protect the privacy of individuals . . . , and 'the legal, moral, and ethical restrictions imposed upon journalists.' ". . . "In that regard, the Court attempts to justify censorship of the article on teenage pregnancy on the basis of the principal's judgment that (1) "the [pregnant] students' anonymity was not adequately protected," despite the article's use of aliases; and (2) the judgment that "the article was not sufficiently sensitive to the privacy interests of the students' boyfriends and parents . . . ." Similarly, the Court finds in the principal's decision to censor the divorce article a journalistic lesson that the author should have given the father of one student an "opportunity to defend himself" against her charge that (in the Court's words) he "chose 'playing cards with the guys' over home and family . . . .'"

But the principal never consulted the students before censoring their work. "[T]hey learned of the deletions when the paper was released . . . ." Further, he explained the deletions only in the broadest of generalities. In one meeting called at the behest of seven protesting Spectrum staff members (presumably a fraction of the full class), he characterized the articles as " 'too sensitive' for 'our immature audience of readers,' " and in a later meeting he deemed them simply "inappropriate, personal, sensitive and unsuitable for the newspaper." The Court's supposition that the principal intended (or the protesters understood) those generalities as a lesson on the nuances of journalistic responsibility is utterly incredible. If he did, a fact that neither the District Court nor the Court of Appeals found, the lesson was lost on all but the psychic Spectrum staffer.

B

The Court's second excuse for deviating from precedent is the school's interest in shielding an impressionable high school audience from material whose substance is "unsuitable for immature audiences." Specifically, the majority decrees that we must afford educators authority to shield high school students from exposure to "potentially sensitive topics" (like "the particulars of teen-age sexual activity") or unacceptable social viewpoints (like the advocacy of "irresponsible se[x] or conduct otherwise inconsistent with 'the shared values of a civilized social order' ") through school-sponsored student activities.

Tinker teaches us that the state educator's undeniable, and undeniably vital, mandate to inculcate moral and political values is not a general warrant to act as "thought police" stifling discussion of all but state-approved topics and advocacy of all but the official position. Otherwise educators could transform students into "closed-circuit recipients of only that which the State chooses to communicate," and cast a perverse and impermissible "pall of orthodoxy over the classroom." Thus, the State cannot constitutionally prohibit its high school students from recounting in the locker room "the particulars of [their] teen-age sexual activity," nor even from advocating "irresponsible se[x]" or other presumed abominations of "the shared values of a civilized social order." Even in its capacity as educator the State may not assume an Orwellian "guardianship of the public mind," *Thomas v. Collins* (JACKSON, J., concurring).

The mere fact of school sponsorship does not, as the Court suggests, license such thought control in the high school, whether through school suppression of disfavored viewpoints or through official assessment of topic sensitivity. The former would constitute unabashed and unconstitutional viewpoint discrimination, as well as an impermissible infringement of the students' "right to receive information and ideas." Just as a school board may not purge its state-funded library of all books that "offen[d] [its] social, political and moral tastes," school officials may not, out of like motivation, discriminatorily excise objectionable ideas from a student publication. The State's prerogative to dissolve the student newspaper entirely (or to limit its subject matter) no more entitles it to dictate which viewpoints students may express on its pages, than the State's prerogative to close down the schoolhouse entitles it to prohibit the nondisruptive expression of antiwar sentiment within its gates.

Official censorship of student speech on the ground that it addresses "potentially sensitive topics" is, for related reasons, equally impermissible. I would not begrudge an educator the authority to limit the substantive scope of a school-sponsored publication to a certain, objectively definable topic, such as literary criticism, school sports, or an overview of the school year. Unlike those determinate limitations, "potential topic sensitivity" is a vaporous non-standard — like "public welfare, peace, safety, health, decency, good order, morals or convenience" or "general welfare of citizens" — that invites manipulation to achieve ends that cannot permissibly be achieved through blatant viewpoint discrimination and chills student speech to which school officials might not object. . . .

C

The sole concomitant of school sponsorship that might conceivably justify the distinction that the Court draws between sponsored and nonsponsored student expression is the risk "that the views of the individual speaker [might be] erroneously attributed to the school." Of course, the risk of erroneous attribution inheres in any student expression, including "personal expression" that, like the armbands in *Tinker*, "happens to occur on the school premises." Nevertheless, the majority is certainly correct that indicia of school sponsorship increase the likelihood of such attribution, and that state educators may therefore have a legitimate interest in dissociating themselves from student speech.

But " '[e]ven though the governmental purpose be legitimate and substantial, that purpose cannot be pursued by means that broadly stifle fundamental personal liberties when the end can be more narrowly achieved.' " Dissociative means short of censorship are available to the school. It could, for example, require the student activity to publish a disclaimer, such as the "Statement of Policy" that Spectrum published each school year announcing that "[a]ll . . . editorials appearing in this newspaper reflect the opinions of the *Spectrum* staff, which are not necessarily shared by the administrators or faculty of Hazelwood East," or it could simply issue its own response clarifying the official position on the matter and explaining why the student position is wrong. Yet, without so much as acknowledging the less oppressive alternatives, the Court approves of brutal censorship.

III

Since the censorship served no legitimate pedagogical purpose, it cannot by any stretch of the imagination have been designed to prevent "materia[l] disrup[tion of] classwork." Nor did the censorship fall within the category that *Tinker* described as necessary to prevent student expression from "inva[ding] the rights of others." If that term is to have any content, it must be limited to rights that are protected by law. "Any yardstick less exacting than [that] could result in school officials curtailing speech at the slightest fear of disturbance," a prospect that would be completely at odds with this Court's pronouncement that the "undifferentiated fear or apprehension of disturbance is not enough [even in the public school context] to overcome the right to freedom of expression." And, as the Court of Appeals correctly reasoned, whatever journalistic impropriety these articles may have contained, they could not conceivably be tortious, much less criminal.

Finally, even if the majority were correct that the principal could constitutionally have censored the objectionable material, I would emphatically object to the brutal manner in which he did so. Where "[t]he separation of legitimate from illegitimate speech calls for more sensitive tools" [citations omitted], the principal used a paper shredder. He objected to some material in two articles, but excised six entire articles. He did not so much as inquire into obvious alternatives, such as precise deletions or additions (one of which had already been made), rearranging the layout, or delaying publication. Such unthinking contempt for individual rights is intolerable from any state official. It is particularly insidious from one to whom the public entrusts the task of inculcating in its youth an appreciation for the cherished democratic liberties that our Constitution guarantees.

IV

The Court opens its analysis in this case by purporting to reaffirm *Tinker*'s time-tested proposition that public school students "do not 'shed their constitutional rights to freedom of speech or expression at the schoolhouse gate.'" That is an ironic introduction to an opinion that denudes high school students of much of the First Amendment protection that *Tinker* itself prescribed. Instead of "teach[ing] children to respect the diversity of ideas that is fundamental to the American system," *Board of Education v. Pico,* and "that our Constitution is a living reality, not parchment preserved under glass," the Court today "teach[es] youth to discount important principles of our government as mere platitudes." *West Virginia Board of Education v. Barnette.* The young men and women of Hazelwood East expected a civics lesson, but not the one the Court teaches them today.

I dissent.

———

NOTES AND QUESTIONS

1. Consider the standard that the Court sets in *Hazelwood* for curtailing student speech in a school-sponsored expressive activity. If educators can exercise editorial control over the style and content of student speech in school-sponsored expressive activities whenever their actions are reasonably related to legitimate pedagogical concerns, can you conceive of a set of circumstances where an educator's decision would not pass this test? *Compare Desilets v. Clearview Regional Board of Education,* 266 N.J. Super. 531 (Superior Ct. N.J. App. Div. 1993) (school refusing to allow student movie reviews of R-rated

movies in school newspaper was not justified by the asserted pedagogical concern — not wanting to be perceived as promoting R-rated movies to middle school students — as the decision whether a child will see an R-rated movie is a parental decision, not an educational decision), *with Poling v. Murphy,* 872 F.2d 757 (6th Cir. 1989) ("Civility is a legitimate pedagogical concern."). Read again the proposed standard that Justice Harlan set forth in his dissent in *Tinker,* and note the comparisons between his dissent and the *Hazelwood* standard.

2. Would a disclaimer really have immunized the school from any responsibility regarding the student articles, as Justice Brennan suggested in his dissent? Even if a disclaimer could absolve the school of any civil liability, does the school have other responsibilities — either to the journalism students or to the school community — that would not be affected by a disclaimer?

Justice Brennan states in his *Hazelwood* dissent that the students in this journalism class expected a civics lesson, but the focus of the class was to understand journalism. When teaching a class in journalism, what responsibility does the educator have in promoting proper journalistic standards of fairness, balance, and privacy? See footnote 8 in the majority opinion. In addition, part of the educational experience of a journalism class might be to understand how the process works in the real world. Do editors in city newspapers ever decide to edit or simply not to print stories?

3. At least six states —Arkansas, California, Colorado, Iowa, Kansas, and Massachusetts — have passed statutes that give students more rights of expression than those allowed by the federal constitution under *Hazelwood. See* A.C.A. § 6-18-1201; CAL. EDUC. CODE § 48907; C.R.S.A. § 22-1-120; I.C.A. § 280.22; K.S.A. § 72-1506; M.G.L.A. 71 § 82. For instance, in California, "there shall be no prior restraint of material prepared for official school publications" unless the content is obscene, libelous, slanderous, likely to present a clear and present danger by inciting students to commit unlawful acts on school premises or violate school regulations, or likely to cause a substantial disruption in a school day. CAL. EDUC. CODE § 48907. Advocates for more free speech for students have observed that they are unsure how to convince legislators or the public to promote student rights in the post-Columbine world. *Sad State of Affairs*, STUDENT PRESS LAW CENTER REPORT 27 (Spring 2003) (noting that the last state student free-expression bill passed in 1995).

4. *Higher Education.* In September 1999 the Sixth Circuit applied the *Hazelwood* standard to a case where a college official (Kentucky State University) had confiscated all copies of a yearbook published in 1994. *Kincaid v. Gibson,* 191 F.3d 719 (6th Cir. 1999). The court determined that the yearbook was a nonpublic forum and that the decision of university officials to refuse to distribute the yearbook because it was "not of proper quality" was reasonable. This marked the first time that a federal appeals court had used the *Hazelwood* standard in a college case. The Sixth Circuit heard the case en banc and reversed. The en banc court held that the yearbook was a limited public forum and stated that *Hazelwood* had little application to the case. The en banc court further decided that the university's actions were not reasonable time, place, and manner restrictions on expressive activity in a limited public forum. *Kincaid v. Gibson,* 236 F.3d 342 (6th Cir. 2001) (en banc).

5. *Underground Newspapers.* The United States Supreme Court has addressed the underground newspaper question only at the higher education level. In *Papish v. Board of Curators of University of Missouri,* 410 U.S. 667 (1973), the Court determined that it was unconstitutional for the university to dismiss a graduate student who had distributed a newspaper on campus that featured, among other things, a political cartoon of a policeman raping the Statue of Liberty and the Goddess of Justice, with a caption that read "With Liberty and Justice for All." The Court, citing *Tinker,* stated that universities were not immune from the sweep of the First Amendment. Moreover, the Court noted, "[T]he mere dissemination of ideas — no matter how offensive to good taste — on a state university campus may not be shut off in the name alone of 'conventions of decency.' . . . [T]he facts set forth in the opinions below show clearly that petitioner was expelled because of the disapproved *content* of the newspaper rather than the time, place, or manner of its distribution." *Id.* at 670 (emphasis in original).

The courts examining the underground newspaper issue in lower education have used the framework set by *Tinker, Fraser,* and *Hazelwood.* Because underground newspapers are not school-sponsored, many courts have focused on *Tinker's* disruption test.

Addressing a school policy that required students to submit student-written material to school officials for approval before distributing the material on school grounds, the Ninth Circuit determined that under *Tinker* and *Hazelwood,* communications like underground newspapers are 'in no sense school-sponsored" and cannot be regulated under a blanket policy on the basis of undifferentiated fears of possible disturbances or embarrassment to school officials. *Burch v. Barker,* 861 F.2d 1149 (9th Cir. 1987).

But student freedom to distribute underground newspapers may be limited because of its content. As noted above, some states have granted more freedom to the student press than that allowed in *Hazelwood.* "Section 48907 of the Education Code and California decisional authority clearly confer editorial control of official student publications on the student editors alone, with very limited exceptions." *Leeb v. DeLong,* 198 Cal. App. 3d 47, 54 (Cal. Ct. App. 1988). Nonetheless, the *Leeb* court determined that the school had the right to censor actionable defamatory material from official student publications. What incentives do students have to suppress defamatory material on their own? Will they be able to respond in damages? Does suspension or expulsion do much to restore the reputation of the defamed party? *See Kuhlmeier v. Hazelwood,* 795 F.2d 1368–79 (8th Cir. 1987) (Wollman, J., dissenting) ("The majority opinion consigns officials to chart a course between the Scylla of a student-led first amendment suit and the Charybdis of a tort action by those claiming to have been injured by the publication of student-written material. Although the commercial press can well afford to retain counsel to advise them daily on questions of possible liability, not many school districts possess similar resources.").

Students who write articles that could result in damage to property or that insult others in the school may lose First Amendment protection if the court determines that school officials reasonably could forecast sufficient disruption from the dissemination of the article. These cases often arise in the context of the student's reaction to the discipline that the school has imposed for the distribution of the underground publication. In an appeal from a grant of a preliminary injunction preventing the expulsion of a student, the Seventh Circuit determined that the school board was justified in determining that an article entitled *So You Want to be a Hacker* (outlining procedures for accessing restricted information) could lead to tampering with that information and could damage the school's computer network. *Boucher v. School Board of the School District of Greenfield,* 134 F.3d 821, 828 (7th Cir. 1998) (citing language from *Tinker* regarding "facts which might reasonably lead school authorities to forecast substantial disruption . . . or material interference with school activities").

The Oregon Court of Appeals upheld the suspension of a high school junior for publishing and distributing an underground newspaper that included an article that discussed the "top ten things [he] would most like to see happen at school." These included feeding snake bite antidote or Visine to someone to make them vomit; depositing disgusting smelling liquid on school grounds; using epoxy glue on locks to "cause a lot of Kaos among the teachers;" exploding a toilet (including what ingredients are needed and how to attain them); bomb threats; and using teacher phone number and addresses to take out or reply to pornographic advertisements (listing teachers' names, addresses and telephone numbers). *Pangle v. Bend-Lapine School Dist.,* 10 P.3d 275 (Or. Ct. App. 2000). The majority opinion stated that Pangle's articles advocated methods for causing personal injury, property damage, and the disruption of school activities, as well as describing where to obtain materials. Thus, the school officials could reasonably forecast substantial interference with the academic operation of the school, "particularly in light of the trend of increasing school violence in this country and the specific actions urged by [the student]." The dissent stated that there was no evidence that the student actually planned to engage in the suggested conduct. Moreover, although portions of the articles could be disconcerting to some readers, "people who believe strongly in what they say do not always speak in dulcet tone . . . . That is the nature of the open society that the First Amendment protects; under *Tinker*, schools are part of that open society." *Id.* at 404 (Armstrong, J., dissenting). Did *Tinker* hold that the "openness" in schools was equivalent to that of the rest of society? Consider the extent to which the underground newspaper cases should apply to cases where students create a website from their home computer. These cases are discussed in § 4.01[C][4], *infra*.

6. *Other Creative Activities in School.* Can student speech be constrained in creative writing class? In *Lacks v. Ferguson School Dist.,* 147 F.3d 718 (8th Cir. 1998), the Eighth Circuit determined that a school district did not violate the First Amendment when it disciplined a teacher who allowed students to use profanity repetitiously and egregiously in their written work in violation of the school written policy against profanity. The teacher had divided her junior English class into small groups and directed them to write short plays that were to be performed for other students in the class and videotaped. The plays written by the students contained repeated uses of the words "fuck," "shit," "ass," "bitch," and "nigger." The court held as a matter of law that the school had a "legitimate academic interest in prohibiting profanity by students in their creative writing." *Id.* at 724. The court noted that the Supreme Court

had stated that schools must "teach by example the shared values of a civilized social order." *Id.* (citing *Fraser*). Thus, it was "too plain for argument" that the speech (allowing one student to call another a "fucking bitch" and a "whore" in front of the class and allowing another to read a poem describing sexual encounters in graphic detail) did not promote these shared social standards.

[C] A Long Way from Black Armbands? Issues for the Twenty-first Century

[1] Dress Codes and School Uniforms

[a] Dress Codes

BOROFF v. VAN WERT CITY BOARD OF EDUCATION

United States Court of Appeal for the Sixth Circuit
220 F.3d 465 (2000)

HARRY W. WELLFORD, CIRCUIT JUDGE.

After Van Wert (Ohio) High School administrators told Nicholas Boroff that he was not allowed to wear "Marilyn Manson" T-shirts to school, Boroff's mother initiated this action on his behalf pursuant to 42 U.S.C. § 1983, alleging that the administrators' refusal to let him wear the T-shirts violated his rights under the First and Fourteenth Amendments. The district court entered summary judgment in favor of the Van Wert City Board of Education and each of the school administrators who were named as defendants. We affirm the decision of the district court.

I. BACKGROUND

This dispute arises out of a high school student's desire to wear "Marilyn Manson" T-shirts to school, and the school's opposing desire to prohibit those T-shirts. Marilyn Manson is the stage name of "goth" rock performer Brian Warner, and also the name of the band in which he is the lead singer. *See* ENCARTA WORLD ENGLISH DICTIONARY (2000) (defining "goth" as "a style of popular music that combines elements of heavy metal with punk" and also "a style of fashion . . . characterized by black clothes, heavy silver jewelry, black eye make-up and lipstick, and often pale face make-up"). Band members take the first part of their stage names from a famous model or celebrity, such as Marilyn Monroe, Madonna, or Twiggy, and the second part from a notorious serial killer, such as Charles Manson, John Wayne Gacy, or Richard Ramirez. Marilyn Manson (the individual) is popularly regarded as a worshiper of Satan, which he has denied. *See* Neil Strauss, *Stage Fright*, ROLLING STONE, June 26 1997, at 20. He is also widely regarded as a user of illegal drugs, which he has not denied. In fact, one of his songs is titled "I Don't Like the Drugs (But the Drugs Like Me)." *See* David Brown, *1998: The Best and Worst / Music*, ENTERTAINMENT WEEKLY, Dec. 25, 1998, at 140; *see also* Gina

Vivinetto, *Marilyn Manson, Not Kinder, Not Gentler*, ST. PETERSBURG TIMES, Mar. 26 1999, at 23 (reporting that Manson no longer stores his drugs and drug paraphernalia in lunch boxes because "everyone . . . is carrying their paraphernalia that way. Too trendy").

On August 29, 1997, Boroff, then a senior at Van Wert High School, went to school wearing a "Marilyn Manson" T-shirt. The front of the T-shirt depicted a three-faced Jesus, accompanied by the words "See No Truth. Hear No Truth. Speak No Truth." On the back of the shirt, the word "BELIEVE" was spelled out in capital letters, with the letters "LIE" highlighted. Marilyn Manson's name (although not his picture) was displayed prominently on the front of the shirt.[14] At the time, Van Wert High School had in effect a "Dress and Grooming" policy that provided that "clothing with offensive illustrations, drug, alcohol, or tobacco slogans . . . are not acceptable." Chief Principal's Aide David Froelich told Boroff that his shirt was offensive and gave him the choice of turning the shirt inside-out, going home and changing, or leaving and being considered truant. Boroff left school.

On September 4, 1997, which was the next school day, Boroff wore another Marilyn Manson T-shirt to school. Boroff and his mother met that day with Froelich, Principal William Clifton, and Superintendent John Basinger. Basinger told the Boroffs that students would not be permitted to wear Marilyn Manson T-shirts on school grounds. Undaunted, Boroff wore different Marilyn Manson T-shirts on each of the next three school days, September 5, 8, and 9, 1997. The shirts featured pictures of Marilyn Manson, whose appearance can fairly be described as ghoulish and creepy. Each day, Boroff was told that he would not be permitted to attend school while wearing the T-shirts.

Boroff did not attend school for the next four days following September 9, 1997. . . . In a memorandum and order dated July 6, 1998, the district court entered summary judgment in favor of the School. This appeal followed.

. . . .

B. *First Amendment Claim*

"It is a highly appropriate function of public school education to prohibit the use of vulgar and offensive terms in public discourse." *Bethel School District No. 403 v. Fraser*. While students do not "shed their constitutional rights to freedom of speech or expression at the schoolhouse gate," *Tinker,* the First Amendment rights of students in the public schools must be "applied in light of the special characteristics of the school environment." *Hazelwood School District v. Kuhlmeier* With those precepts in mind, we apply the *Tinker-Fraser-Kuhlmeier* trilogy to the facts of this case. . . .

The district court below determined that the rule in *Fraser* applied to this case, concluding that "[a] school may prohibit a student from wearing a T-shirt that is offensive, but not obscene, on school grounds, even if the T-shirt has not been shown to cause a substantial disruption of the academic program." The court then held that the School did not act in a manifestly unreasonable manner in finding the T-shirts offensive and in enforcing its dress code.

---

14 [1] Although the origin of the T-shirt is unknown, the distorted portrayal of Jesus seems to have been created in an effort to illustrate the band's hit album "AntiChrist Superstar."

In this appeal, Boroff argues that the district court erred in granting summary judgment to the School. In his appellate brief he maintains "[that] [t]he way to analyze this is to first determine whether the speech is 'vulgar or offensive'. If it is, then *Fraser* allows banning it, and the analysis is complete. Otherwise, apply *Tinker* and examine if there is a threat of substantial disruption such that would allow the school to ban the speech."

Boroff claims that the administrators' decision that the T-shirts are offensive was manifestly unreasonable and unsupported by the evidence. Boroff relies to a great extent on evidence that similar T-shirts promoting other bands, such as Slayer and Megadeth, were not prohibited, and also on evidence that one other student was not prohibited from carrying a backpack that donned three "Marilyn Manson" patches. Because the T-shirts were not "offensive," Boroff reasons, and because there is no evidence that a substantial disruption would arise from his wearing the T-shirts, then the School violated his First Amendment rights. We disagree.

The standard for reviewing the suppression of vulgar or plainly offensive speech is governed by *Fraser.* The School in this case, according to the affidavit of Principal Clifton, found the Marilyn Manson T-shirts to be offensive because the band promotes destructive conduct and demoralizing values that are contrary to the educational mission of the school. Specifically, Clifton found the "three-headed Jesus" T-shirt to be offensive because of the "See No Truth. Hear No Truth. Speak No Truth." mantra on the front, and because of the obvious implication of the word "BELIEVE" with "LIE" highlighted on the back. The principal specifically stated that the distorted Jesus figure was offensive, because "mocking any religious figure is contrary to our educational mission which is to be respectful of others and others' beliefs." The other T-shirts were treated with equal disapproval. Clifton went on to explain the reasoning behind the School's prohibition of the T-shirts generally:

> Although I do not know if [Boroff] intends to communicate anything when wearing the Marilyn Manson t-shirts, I believe that the Marilyn Manson t-shirts can reasonably be considered a communication agreeing with or approving of the views espoused by Marilyn Manson in its lyrics and those views which have been associated to Marilyn Manson through articles in the press. I find some of the Marilyn Manson lyrics and some of the views associated with Marilyn Manson as reported in articles in the news and entertainment press offensive to our basic educational mission at Van Wert High School. Therefore, I believe that all of the Marilyn Manson t-shirts . . . are offensive to and inconsistent with our educational mission at Van Wert High School.

Furthermore, Clifton quotes some of the lyrics from Marilyn Manson songs that the School finds offensive, which include (but certainly are not limited to) lines such as, "you can kill yourself now because you're dead in my mind," "let's jump upon the sharp swords/and cut away our smiles/without the threat of death/there's no reason to live at all," and "Let's just kill everyone and let your god sort them out/Fuck it/Everybody's someone else's nigger/I know you are so am I/I wasn't born with enough middle fingers." The principal attested that those types of lyrics were contrary to the school mission and goal of establishing "a common core of values that include . . . human dignity and worth . . . self respect, and responsibility," and also the goal of instilling "into the students, an understanding and appreciation of the ideals of democracy and help them to be diligent and competent in the performance of their obligations as citizens."

Clifton also submitted to the district court magazine articles that portray Marilyn Manson as having a "pro-drug persona" and articles wherein Marilyn Manson himself admits that he is a drug user and promotes drug use. Clifton concludes from his fourteen years of experience that children are genuinely influenced by the rock group and such propaganda.

Affidavits of other School officials support the administration's position that the Marilyn Manson T-shirts, generally speaking, were prohibited because they were "counter-productive and go against the educational mission of the Van Wert City School District community." The record is devoid of any evidence that the T-shirts, the "three-headed Jesus" T-shirt particularly, were perceived to express any particular political or religious viewpoint.

Under these circumstances, we find that the district court was correct in finding that the School did not act in a manifestly unreasonable manner in prohibiting the Marilyn Manson T-shirts pursuant to its dress code. The Supreme Court has held that the school board has the authority to determine "what manner of speech in the classroom or in school is inappropriate." *Fraser*. The Court has determined that "[a] school need not tolerate student speech that is inconsistent with its 'basic educational mission . . . even though the government could not censor similar speech outside the school.'" *Kuhlmeier*. In this case, where Boroff's T-shirts contain symbols and words that promote values that are so patently contrary to the school's educational mission, the School has the authority, under the circumstances of this case, to prohibit those T-shirts.

The dissent would find that the evidence was sufficient for a reasonable jury to infer that the School has engaged in "viewpoint discrimination" by prohibiting the T-shirts, similar to the armband prohibition in *Tinker*. The dissent primarily relies on one sentence in Principal Clifton's affidavit, in which Clifton stated that he found the "three-headed Jesus" T-shirt to be offensive because "it mocks a major religious figure." Under that reasoning, if a jury finds that the School has prohibited the T-shirts because of any viewpoint expressed on the shirts, then the School must show that it reasonably predicted that allowing the T-shirts would have caused a substantial disruption of, or material interference with, school activities. *See Tinker*.

In our view, however, the evidence does not support an inference that the School intended to suppress the expression of Boroff's viewpoint, because of its religious implications. Rather, the record demonstrates that the School prohibited Boroff's Marilyn Manson T-shirts generally because this particular rock group promotes disruptive and demoralizing values which are inconsistent with and counter-productive to education. The dissenting judge agrees that "if the only T-shirts at issue in this case were the ones that simply displayed illustrations of Marilyn Manson largely unadorned by text, the judgment of the district court might be sustainable." He reasons, however, that the one T-shirt featuring the distorted Jesus figure may have been prohibited because of the School's disagreement with its religious message. In our view, the School's treatment of the "three-headed Jesus" T-shirt and the others is not distinguishable. The record establishes that all of the T-shirts were banned in the same manner for the same reasons — they were determined to be vulgar, offensive, and contrary to the educational mission of the school.

In sum, we are of the view that the School has the authority to prohibit Marilyn Manson T-shirts under these circumstances.

[The court next addressed Boroff's Fourteenth Amendment due process claim and held that it had not been preserved on appeal.]

For the foregoing reasons and for the reasons stated in its opinion, we affirm the decision of the district court.

RONALD LEE GILMAN, CIRCUIT JUDGE, *dissenting*.

. . . Unlike the majority, I believe that a jury could reasonably find that the reason why School officials declared Boroff's Marilyn Manson T-shirts "offensive" was because the first Marilyn Manson T-shirt he wore contained a message about religion that they considered obnoxious. Accordingly, I believe that summary judgment in favor of the Board on Boroff's First Amendment claim was inappropriate, and therefore respectfully dissent.

I

I have little doubt that school administrators may reasonably decide that certain rock performers are so closely identified with illegal drug use or other unlawful activities that T-shirts bearing their images are unacceptable for high school students to wear in school. In fact, after the Supreme Court's decisions in *Fraser* and *Kuhlmeier*, I suspect that forbidding a student from wearing a T-shirt simply because it makes a statement with which school administrators disagree is one of a very few decisions about student dress that school administrators are *not* allowed to make. Nevertheless, from the record presented, a reasonable jury could easily conclude that this was exactly what the School did.

I believe that the School in this case came perilously close to admitting that its decision to prohibit Boroff from wearing the three-headed Jesus T-shirt was made precisely because the School found the T-shirt's viewpoint repugnant. Principal Clifton explained in an affidavit that

> I found the t-shirt which contains the three-faced Jesus to be offensive. . . . This t-shirt is offensive because it mocks a major religious figure. Mocking any religious figure is contrary to our educational missions which is to be respectful of others and others' beliefs. Second, mocking this particular religious figure is particularly offensive to a significant portion of our school community, including students, teachers, staff members and parents.

In view of this explanation, I am at a loss to understand how the majority can say that "the record is devoid of any evidence that the T-shirts, the 'three-headed Jesus' T-shirt particularly, were perceived to express any particular political or religious viewpoint." Of course the three-headed Jesus T-shirt was perceived to express a political or religious viewpoint. Principal Clifton said so himself. It appears unmistakable that the reason why the three-headed Jesus T-shirt was deemed "offensive" was because it said something about a venerated religious figure, and because many people in Van Wert (presumably including Principal Clifton) happen to disagree vehemently with what they perceived the T-shirt as saying. Indeed, from Principal Clifton's explanation, it would not be unreasonable to presume that if the T-shirt had depicted Jesus in a positive light, it would not have been considered "offensive."

Consistent with the Supreme Court's First Amendment jurisprudence, taking sides in that manner would be considered viewpoint discrimination, which is accompanied by an all-but-irrebuttable presumption of unconstitutionality. *See, e.g., Rosenberger v. Rector & Visitors of Univ. of Virginia,* 515 U.S. 819, 828–29, (1995) (describing viewpoint discrimination as "an egregious form of content discrimination" and observing that "when the government targets not subject matter, but particular views taken by speakers on a subject, the violation of the First Amendment is all the more blatant."); *West Virginia State Bd. of Educ. v. Barnette,* 319 U.S. 624, 642, (1943) ("If there is any fixed star in our constitutional constellation, it is that no official, high or petty, can prescribe what shall be orthodox in politics, nationalism, religion, or other matters of opinion . . . .").

II

I also believe that the majority misapprehends the meaning of the terms "vulgar" and "offensive." In First Amendment cases, those terms refer to words and phrases that are themselves coarse and crude, regardless of whether one disagrees with the overall message that the speaker is trying to convey. Roughly speaking, they are the words and phrases that might have appeared on comedian George Carlin's list of words that one cannot say on the radio. . . . *See generally FCC v. Pacifica Foundation,* 438 U.S. 726, 751–55 (reprinting Carlin's "Filthy Words" monologue). That is why the high school administrators in *Pyle v. South Hadley School Committee,* 861 F. Supp. 157, 159 (D. Mass. 1994), were allowed to prohibit a student from wearing a T-shirt proclaiming "See Dick Drink. See Dick die. Don't Be a Dick.", because "unlike *Tinker,* this is not a case about whether a particular viewpoint may be expressed."). The school administrators in *Pyle* were obviously not objecting to the message that drunk driving is bad and should be discouraged.

If Boroff had worn a T-shirt featuring Marilyn Manson's name and the song lyrics contained in the majority's opinion, this would be a very easy case. A number of those words are vulgar, regardless of whether one likes or dislikes Marilyn Manson's music or agrees or disagrees with whatever message Boroff would be trying to convey by wearing the shirt. But that sort of vulgarity is absent from the three-headed Jesus T-shirt that Boroff wore. This particular T-shirt was found "offensive" because it expresses a viewpoint that many people personally find repellent, not because it is vulgar.

Censorship on that basis is simply not permitted in the absence of a reasonable prediction by school officials of substantial disruption of, or material interference with, school activities. Indeed, that was the holding of *Tinker*.

The majority asserts that "the School prohibited the Marilyn Manson T-shirts," including the three-headed Jesus T-shirt that precipitated this case, "because this particular rock group promotes disruptive and demoralizing values which are inconsistent with and counter-productive to education." It is not clear, however, what "disruptive and demoralizing values" the majority is referring to. If the majority is suggesting that the School could have concluded that Marilyn Manson's apparent endorsement of, say, illegal drug use, makes his picture an unacceptable image for students to wear in high school, I would agree. A fair reading of the record, however, suggests that the "disruptive and demoralizing values" that the School was really concerned about was disrespect for a specific venerated religious figure.

Or so a reasonable jury could have found. As noted above, however, school officials are not free to decide that only one side of a topic is open for discussion because the other side is too repugnant or demoralizing to listen to.

I also believe that the majority dropped its guard much too quickly at the School's conclusory invocation of "disruptive and demoralizing values." I am quite confident that the school officials in *Tinker* thought it would be highly disruptive and demoralizing — not to mention downright unpatriotic — for students to wear black armbands in order to protest a war in which thousands of American soldiers were fighting and dying. The Supreme Court nevertheless concluded that the officials could not prohibit the students from wearing the armbands in the absence of evidence that a ban would be necessary to prevent "material and substantial interference with schoolwork or discipline."

III

This brings me to the last, but certainly not least important, matter on which I disagree with the majority. The majority apparently reads the Supreme Court's opinions in *Fraser* and *Kuhlmeier* as essentially overruling *Tinker*, concluding that after *Fraser* and *Kuhlmeier*, school officials can forbid whatever student speech they consider "offensive" (in the sense of promoting "disruptive and demoralizing values"), as long as their decision does not appear "manifestly unreasonable."

That, however, is not what the Supreme Court held in either *Fraser* or *Kuhlmeier*. Fraser concluded that school officials could temporarily suspend a high school student who persisted in giving a speech permeated with obvious sexual metaphors during a school assembly, despite being warned that the speech was "inappropriate" and that delivering it might result in "severe consequences." *Kuhlmeier* concluded that high school administrators do not offend the First Amendment by exercising editorial control over the style and content of school-sponsored publications as long as their actions are reasonably related to legitimate pedagogical concerns.

Because nothing in either *Fraser* or *Kuhlmeier* purports to overrule *Tinker* (indeed, *Tinker* was recently cited with approval by the Supreme Court in *United States v. Playboy Entertainment Group, Inc.,* 529 U.S. 803 (2000)), I believe that it should be left to the Supreme Court to determine whether and when *Tinker* should be cast by the wayside.

Instead, in both *Fraser* and *Kuhlmeier*, the Supreme Court distinguished *Tinker* by noting that the school officials in the latter cases might reasonably have been thought to be endorsing or condoning the student expression at issue had they taken no action. . . . In contrast, I do not believe that school officials can reasonably be thought to endorse or condone a message worn on a student's T-shirt simply because they do not prohibit the student from wearing the T-shirt to school.

————

NOTES AND QUESTIONS

1. When vulgarity is not an issue, sometimes the focus on the *Tinker* standard is clearer. In *Jeglin v. San Jacinto Unified Sch. Dist*, 827 F. Supp. 1459 (C.D. Cal. 1993), the court addressed a policy that prohibited clothing with insignia from college or professional sports teams in elementary, middle and high school as there was evidence showing a correlation between sports apparel and gang colors. Because the school district failed to show any actual or threatened disruptions in elementary or middle school, the policy was struck down. *Cf. Isaacs v. Board of Educ.*, 40 F. Supp. 2d 335 (D. Md. 1999) (assuming an African head-wrap is speech, school's interest of providing a safe, respectful school environment still outweighs student's free speech claim).

Some courts, instead of focusing on disruption, consider whether the student intended to convey a specific message by his or her attire, *see Stephenson v. Davenport Community Sch. Dist.,* 110 F.3d 1303 (8th Cir. 1997) (student admitted cross tattoo was not intended to convey any particularized message and thus did not qualify for First Amendment protection), and the reasonable likelihood that the message would be understood by those who see it. In *Bivens v. Albuquerque Public Schls.,* 899 F. Supp. 556 (D.N.M. 1995), the court addressed a dress code policy that prohibited sagging pants. The court pointed out that "not every defiant act by a high school student is constitutionally protected speech." *Id.* at 560. Under *Texas v. Johnson,* 491 U.S. 397 (1989), the flag burning case, non-verbal conduct must meet a two-part test to be "expressive conduct" that is protected by the First Amendment. "First, the actor must intend to convey a particularized message, and, second, there must be a great likelihood that the message would be understood by those who observe the conduct." *Bivens,* 899 F. Supp. at 561 (citing *Texas v. Johnson,* 491 U.S. at 404). The district court determined that the student intended to convey a message by wearing sagging pants (to express his link with his black identity), but the court found no evidence that his message would be understood by others, as there were many interpretations for the reason a student wears sagging pants. The court also noted that "not all constraints on protected expressive speech by school children are unconstitutional." The school district had made a "strong showing that the dress code was a reasonable response to a perceived threat of gangs in the school." Moreover, the dress code, with other measures, may have been responsible for the perception of an improved climate and learning environment, which are "laudable educational goals that federal courts should be hesitant to impede."

2. Courts have also considered Equal Protection Clause claims respecting dress code policies restricting the wearing of certain clothing by one gender and not the other. *See, e.g., Olesen v. Bd. of Educ.*, 676 F. Supp. 820, 821 (N.D. Ill. 1987) (upholding prohibition on the wearing of earrings by males to discourage gang membership because student was unable to show that the gender-based classification did not substantially relate to a legitimate government objective, since the wearing of earrings by males "generally connote[s] gang membership"). Students may also challenge punishment for a dress codes infraction as violating their Fourteenth Amendment procedural due process rights. For a discussion of the student's right to notice and hearing before being suspended, see § 4.03, *infra.*

3. Do students have a protected right to wear clothes that they feel they "look good in" to school? A middle school student in Fort Thomas, Kentucky, argued that a school dress code restricted her right to look and feel good in her clothes and infringed on her father's right to raise his daughter as he saw fit. The middle school council — under Kentucky law, each school has a site-based decision making council consisting of two parents, three teachers and the school's principal — stated its objective as an effort to provide an appropriate educational environment while allowing students to dress comfortably within limits to facilitate learning. The policy noted, "Students' attire can have a positive or negative effect on the learning process, contribute to students' success, and generate a safe and positive learning environment. We expect students to maintain the type of appearance that is not distracting to students, teachers, or the educational process of the school. Parents and children are equally responsible for the appearance of the child. There is appropriate and inappropriate attire for all of life's activities."

The dress code restricted the following:

— clothing that is too tight, revealing or baggy as well as tops and bottoms that do not overlap;

— hats, caps, scarves, or sweatbands except on special event days such as "spirit" or "reward" days;

— non-jewelry chains and chain wallets;

— clothing that is "distressed" or has "holes in it";

— visible body piercing (other than ears);

— unnaturally colored hair that is "distracting to the educational process," including blue, green, red, purple, [or] orange hair;

— clothing that is too long;

— flip-flop sandals, or high platform shoes;

— pants, shorts or skirts that are not of a solid color of navy blue, black, any shade of khaki, or white; shorts, skirts, or skorts that do not reach mid-thigh or longer;

— bottoms made with stretch knits, flannel, or fleece such as sweatpants, jogging pants, or any type of athletic clothing as well as baggy, sagging, or form-fitting pants;

— tops that are not a solid color and are not crew neck [style], polo style with buttons, oxford style, or turtleneck;

— tops with writing on them and logos larger than the size of a quarter . . . except Highlands logos or other Highlands Spirit Wear;

— tops that are not of an appropriate size and fit; and

— form-fitting or baggy shirts or any material that is sheer or lightweight enough to be seen through.

While the lawsuit was pending, the school district modified the dress code, loosening it in some respects (pants, shorts or skirts may be any solid color, and striped and patterned tops are permitted) and tightened it in others (blue jeans are prohibited, as well as clothing that promotes drugs, alcohol, tobacco, sex, or is offensive or degrading and tops with low, scoop, plunging or revealing necklines).

Attorney Robert Blau sued on his behalf and on the behalf of his daughter Amanda, asking for injunctive relief and monetary damages. The Sixth Circuit held that a mere desire to wear clothes plaintiff "looks good in" does not trigger First Amendment protection since Amanda was not attempting to portray any particularized message. *Blau v. Fort Thomas Pub. Sch. Dist.*, 401 F.3d 381 (6th Cir. 2005). The court determined that the policy was not overbroad because students can wear t-shirts expressing interests in music, art, politics, etc. in the evenings and on the weekends and students can express themselves through extracurriculars, the school newspaper, and buttons. The dress code also furthered important government interests — improvements that had been reported from other school districts that had a dress code. These include bridging socio-economic gaps between families within the school district, focusing attention on learning, increasing school unity and pride, enhancing school safety, promoting good behavior, reducing discipline problems, improving test scores, improving children's self-respect and self-esteem, helping to eliminate stereotypes and producing a cost savings for families.

The court further determined that the policy did not infringe on Mr. Blau's parental rights. Although parents may have a "fundamental right to decide whether to send their child to a public school, they do not have a fundamental right generally to direct how a public school teaches their child." Moreover, the plaintiff's substantive due process claim failed regarding the blue jeans restriction because, according to the court of appeals, the wearing of blue jeans is not on the Supreme Court's short list of fundamental rights.[Ed. !].

Should the court have taken more heed of the fact that — at least for some students — style and taste in clothing is one way in which children engage in self-expression? Is choice in clothing a way that children start to challenge authority? Might this be why some parents desire a school dress code? What kind of particularized message in clothing might pass the *Blau* test but not fail the *Boroff* test? For a discussion of dress codes for teachers, see W. Jay Hughes, *What Not to Wear*, 1 EDUC. L. & POL'Y FORUM, *available at* www.educationlawconsortium.org.

[b]   School Uniforms

NOTES AND QUESTIONS

1. In *Canady v. Bossier Parish School Bd.*, 240 F.3d 437 (5th Cir. 2001), the Fifth Circuit addressed a mandatory school uniform policy that consisted of a choice of two colors of polo or oxford shirts and navy or khaki pants. Parents and students filed suit, claiming that the policy violated the students' First Amendment free speech rights. The school district presented affidavits from school teachers and principals and presented statistics that showed a drastic reduction in disciplinary actions and increased test scores after the school district implemented the uniform policy.

The Court of Appeals determined that choice of clothing is personal expression that happens to occur on school grounds (as opposed to being school-sponsored) and because the uniform policy was unrelated to any viewpoint, the level of scrutiny that should be applied in assessing its constitutionality is higher than the *Hazelwood* standard, but lower than the *Tinker* standard. The court used the traditional time, place, and manner analysis, together with the test for expressive conduct first set forth in *United States v. O'Brien*, 391 U.S. 367 (1968): The uniform policy will pass constitutional muster if "it furthers an important or substantial governmental interest; if the interest is unrelated to the suppression of student expression; and if the incidental restrictions on First Amendment activities are no more than is necessary to facilitate that interest." In applying that standard, the court stated that improving the educational process was an important governmental interest and that this interest — decreasing discipline problems and increasing test scores — is unrelated to suppression of student speech. Moreover, students have other ways to express their views during the school day and they may wear whatever they wish after school hours.

Parents also claimed that the uniform requirement was too big a financial burden, but the court noted that evidence was presented that clothing was donated to the less fortunate. Moreover, the court stated that the clothing was available at inexpensive retail stores, and it was hard to imagine how purchasing a certain color shirt or pants could be any more expensive than the normal cost of a student's school clothes. *See also Littlefield v. Forney Indep. Sch. Dist.,* 108 F. Supp. 2d 681 (N.D. Tex. 2000) (student action of wearing clothing of their choice rather than school uniforms would not be likely to be understood by others as communicating a specific message; even if expressive conduct was implicated, school had a rational basis for instituting the policy — furthering the goal of improving the learning climate). *But see Hicks v. Halifax County Bd. of Educ.,* 93 F. Supp. 2d 649 (E.D.N.C. 1999) (refusing to grant summary judgment in challenge of school uniform policy with no exception, where plaintiffs claimed both free exercise of religion and parental right to direct child's religious upbringing).

"A person's choice of clothing is infused with intentional expression on many levels." *Canady*, 240 F.3d at 440. When does attire function as pure speech? What else might clothing symbolize? The *Canady* court noted that it was making no judgment regarding the extent or type of clothing that would be necessary to communicate a discrete message so as to be afforded first amendment protection. What kind of clothing might the court be alluding to here?

2. Do school uniforms make a difference? Many educators are convinced that they do. One middle school principal discussing the switch to uniforms — khaki pants with polo shirts in white, burgundy, or navy blue — claimed that the difference is "like night and day." "We have 'dress down' days, and the kids' behavior is just completely different on those days." A teacher in the same school noted that test scores have been going up and in-school suspensions have been going down ever since her middle school made the switch. Once targeted for "reconstitution" because of its low scores under the state's former testing program, the school has been improving every year and meets most of its state assessment achievement targets. The teacher believed that the policy has also cut down on the teasing to which middle school children subject one another.

On the other hand, research David Brunsma has written a book, THE SCHOOL UNIFORM MOVEMENT AND WHAT IT TELLS US ABOUT AMERICAN EDUCATION (2004), that disputes the notion that school uniforms have a positive effect on the school environment. After analyzing two massive databases, Brunsma concluded that there was little evidence that school uniforms are effective. A study of one school district at the forefront of the school uniform movement claims otherwise. In 1994, Long Beach, California, a 97,200-student urban district, became the first public school district in the nation to institute a school uniform policy for all students in grades K–8. A two-year evaluation of the program effort showed a 28 percent drop in suspension rates at the elementary level, a 36 percent decline in middle school suspensions, a 51 percent decrease in fights, and a 34 percent drop in assault and battery. Brunsma claims that this study involved only one district and failed to account for changes like demographic shifts that could also explain the results. Brunsma discounts other case studies that point to positive results in Baltimore, Denver, and Aldine, Texas because a manufacturer of school uniforms sponsored the studies.

School uniform policies are often the result of parental demand, and schools with uniform policies tend to be in areas where children are disadvantaged or members of minority groups. Parents state that like the fact that they do not have pressure to purchase designer clothes for school and children cannot change to less appropriate clothing in the school restroom. Administrators point out that uniforms help in ways that may not be measurable, such as the ability to spot strangers who enter school grounds and the ability to spot students who cut class and leave school. *See* Debra Viedero, *Uniform Effects?*, EDUC. WK., Jan. 12, 2005, at 27-29.

[2] Political Speech?

In some schools, the Confederate flag, like the Tinkers' armbands, may be offensive to some students. The flag, however, has not always met with the same fate as the black armbands worn by the Tinker children. In *West v. Derby Unified Sch. Dist.*, 206 F.3d 1358, 136 (10th Cir. 2000), the court determined that "school district officials had reason to believe that a student's display of

Confederate flag might cause disruption and interfere with the right of other students to be secure and let alone." Moreover "the fact that a full-fledged brawl had not yet broken out over the Confederate flag does not mean that the district was required to sit and wait for one." *See also Castorina v. Madison County Sch. Bd.*, 246 F.3d 536 (6th Cir. 2001) (remanding case to district court to resolve plaintiff's factual assertions that students were not disciplined for wearing Malcolm X–inspired shirts and that there were no prior disruptions as a result of Confederate flags).

In *Denno v. Sch. Bd. of Volusia County*, 218 F.3d 1267 (11th Cir. 2000), a student was suspended for displaying a Confederate flag to friends during an outdoor lunch break. He claimed that he was quietly discussing his hobby as a Civil War reenactor and that he was telling others about the historical issues of Southern heritage. He sued school officials under 42 U.S.C. § 1983, claiming his free speech rights were violated by the suspension. Citing *Derby*, the court determined that school officials enjoyed qualified immunity on the damages claim, as no clearly established constitutional rights were violated by the student's suspension. Many people are offended when the Confederate flag is worn on a tee shirt or otherwise displayed, the court observed. Therefore, school officials were not plainly incompetent when they decided that the incident implicated school functions relating to civility. This would make the school subject to the "more flexible" *Fraser* standard, rather than the *Tinker* standard, and would allow school officials to balance a student's freedom to advocate unpopular and controversial views at school versus the school's countervailing interest in teaching students the boundaries of appropriate behavior. *Id.* at 1274–75. Given that there had been no past incidents of racial unrest related to the display of the Confederate flag, how should the case come out under a pure *Tinker* analysis?

The Eleventh Circuit faced another flag case in *Scott v. School Board of Alachua County*, 324 F.3d 1246 (11th Cir. 2003), when the principal suspended a student who wore the Confederate flag in violation of school policy. The court stated that courts may apply the *Fraser* standard "even if such speech does not result in a reasonable fear of immediate disruption" because school officials are "charged with the duty to inculcate habits and manners of civility." The school had presented evidence of racial tension and "one needs only to consult the evening news to understand the concern school administrators had regarding the disruption, hurt feelings, emotional trauma and outright violence which the display of the [Confederate flag] could provoke." The student's brief, however, claimed that the only evidence of racial violence at the school had occurred two years earlier when a white student and a black student had a dispute about a seat on the bus that had nothing to due with the Confederate flag.

In *Sypniewski v. Warren Hills Board of Educ.*, 307 F.3d 243 (3d Cir. 2002), the court of appeals addressed the suspension of a student wearing a shirt with redneck jokes. The court stated that the school must point to a concrete basis for concluding that the association between the speech in question and similar speech that had caused disruption in the past "is strong enough to give rise to well-founded fear of general disruption." "[I]t is not enough that speech is generally similar to speech involved in past incidents of disruption, it must be similar in the right way." *See* James M. Dedman, *At Daggers Drawn: The Confederate Flag and the School Classroom: A Case Study of a Broken First Amendment Formula*, 53 BAYLOR L. REV. 877, 895 (2001) (arguing that under the *Fraser* standard, "school officials can justifiably censor non-disruptive speech so long as the speech is somewhat controversial or marginally unpopular"); Michael J. Henry, *Student Display of the Confederate Flag in Public Schools*, 33 J.L. & EDUC. 573 (2004); C. Knox Withers, *An Uncertain Heritage:* Tinker, Fraser *and the Confederate Flag*, 1 EDUC. L. & POL'Y FORUM, *available at* www.educationlawconsortium.org (2005).

Courts have protected student speech that could be termed political speech in other contexts, even though it was apparently intended to be offensive to teachers. In *Chandler v. McMinnville Sch. Dist.*, 978 F.2d 524 (9th Cir. 1992), teachers went on strike and the school board hired replacement teachers. Children of striking teachers arrived at school with buttons and stickers that read, "I'm Not Listening, Scab" and "Do Scabs Bleed?" The district court had granted the school district's motion to dismiss because it determined the slogans were "offensive" and "inherently disruptive," but the court of appeals reversed. The Ninth Circuit stated that the buttons were not "plainly offensive within the meaning of *Fraser*." *Id.* at 530. The court also decided that the district court erred in its determination that the buttons were inherently disruptive and remanded for a consideration of whether the school district could meet *Tinker's* "reasonable forecast" test.

[3] Disrespect and Threats

Can schools punish students for expression that shows disrespect for a teacher, or is the student's speech protected? In *Rutherford v. Cypress-Fairbanks Ind. Sch. Dist.*, 1998 WL 330527 (S.D. Tex. 1998), a senior made some comments about the high school baseball coaching staff in his yearbook that the coaches thought were unsportsmanlike and disrespectful. The coach decided to remove the student from the starting lineup. The district court granted summary judgment for the school, because schools may punish speech they consider inappropriate to make a point to pupils that such conduct is wholly inconsistent with the fundamental habits and manners of civility. But in *D.G. v. Independent Sch. Dist*, 2000 U.S. Dist. LEXIS 12197 (N.D. Okla. Aug. 21, 2000), the court issued a permanent injunction reinstating a high school junior who had been suspended after school officials found a poem she had written about killing her teacher. Lines in the poem included, "My yearning gets stronger/ To kill the bitcher/" and "And people will ask why / I'll say because the bitch has to die!" The school district argued that although the poem was not seen as a genuine threat, it was blatantly disrespectful and thus disruptive of the school environment. The court rejected the notion that disrespect that goes unpunished is substantially disruptive because it undermines the school's authority to discipline students. "[T]hat argument simply cannot hold water against the right found in the First Amendment." *See also Shoemaker v. State,* 343 Ark. 727 (Ark. Sup. Ct. 2001) (statute that provided that it is a misdemeanor for any person to abuse or insult a public school teacher who is performing regular assigned school responsibilities was unconstitutionally vague). To what extent should speech that is disrespectful of teachers be protected? Which case should control, *Tinker* or *Fraser*?

What about speech with violent overtones? In *Demers v. Leominster School Dep't*, 263 F. Supp. 2d 195 (D. Mass. 2003), a district court determined that suspension was justified where the student drew a picture of the school being surrounded by explosives (together with the superintendent holding a gun to his head with explosives at his feet), and the student refused to attend a psychiatric evaluation. Yet another student's suspension was lifted and erased from her record after nationwide headlines and a public outcry. School officials had found her journal with a story about a student who dreams of killing her math teacher. Paul Donsky & Jen Sansbury, *Teen Writer's Expulsion Lifted*, ATLANTA J.-CONST., Nov. 12, 2003, at C3. Courts may analyze these cases using the "true threat" standard — derived from *Watts v. United States*, 394 U.S. 705, 707 (1969) — to determine the legitimacy of the threat. Factors may include: how the recipient and other listeners reacted to the alleged threat; whether the threat was conditional; whether the threat was communicated directly to the victim; whether the maker of the threat had made similar statements to the victim in the past; and whether the victim had reason to believe that the maker of the threat had a propensity to engage in violence. *J.S. v. Bethlehem Area School Dist.*, 807 A.2d 847, 858 (Pa. 2002); *see also Demers*, 263 F. Supp. 2d at 201 (reasonable students would have viewed plaintiff's drawings as a threat). When a student's expression alludes to violence at the school but does not target specific individuals, how likely is it to be restrained under either the true threat analysis or the *Tinker* material disruption test? *See* Erik S. Johnson & Robert L. Fortson, Tinker's *Material World: How the Supreme Court's First Amendment Student Speech Precedent Fails to Confront Indiscriminate Acts of Violence*, 1 EDUC. L. & POL'Y FORUM, *available at* www.educationlawconsortium.org (arguing that the *Tinker* standard does not adequately address today's climate of school-based violence).

THE COLUMBINE EFFECT AND ZERO TOLERANCE

After an outbreak of highly publicized school shootings across the United States, many schools are not taking lightly any student expression that might be perceived as a threat. In addition to concerns about harm to students and staff if violence erupts, school officials also are aware that their actions may be scrutinized in a civil suit. In some instances, "school killings have become a wellspring for suits by grief-stricken parents," *Looking for Closure and Cash Parents Divert Grief Into Lawsuits*, PROV. J., at B7 (July 26, 2000). Parents of victims of the shootings at Columbine High School in Littleton, Colorado sued the sheriff's office and school officials, including the school principal for not taking action to forestall the tragedy. *Id.* In fact, a 2001 report by the Columbine Review Commission, a panel named to examine the issue by the governor of Colorado, stated that school officials failed to heed warning signs of the violent tendencies of Dylan Klebold and Eric Harris and cited a violent essay written by Klebold as one of the missed signs. *Columbine Report Faults Schools*, EDUC. WK., May 23, 2001, at 4. A spokesperson for the school district said that a teacher reported her concerns about the essay to a school counselor, but that school officials could not have predicted the rampage that he carried out. *Id.*

Courts explicitly take into account the fact the school officials are making decisions in a post-Columbine world. In *Porter v. Ascension Parish Sch. Bd.*,

301 F. Supp. 2d 576, 589 (M.D. La. 2004) the plaintiff argued that the court should not consider Columbine and other incidents when deciding the reasonableness of school officials' behavior. The court disagreed, noting that "school officials cannot operate in a vacuum or in a fantasy world and must be aware of the events occurring at other schools to properly protect their students and faculty." *See also Doe v. Pulaski County Special School District*, 306 F.3d 616, 626 (8th Cir. 2002) ("We find it untenable in the wake of Columbine and Jonesboro that any reasonable school official who came into possession of J.M.'s letter [describing how he wanted to rape, sodomize, and murder a female classmate] would not have taken some action based on its violent and disturbing content"). Some commentators have argued that the wake of Columbine has allowed school officials too much discretion. They contend that "disputes that once would have been settled by a phone call home to parents now end up in court due to overzealous school officials who have exploited the tragedy at Columbine to squelch speech they find disagreeable." Robert D. Richards & Clay Calvert, *Columbine Fallout: The Long-Term Effects on Free Expression Take Hold in Public Schools*, 83 B.U. L. REV. 1089, 1139 (2003). To what extent might school officials agree with the first part of this statement — that disputes that might have once been settled by a phone call to parents now end up in court? How might school officials or their lawyer change the last part of the Richards/Calvert statement? Which side has the better argument?

Pushed by concerned parents who demand that school boards have strict policies to deal with students who carry weapons or threaten harm, school districts have implemented so-called "Zero Tolerance" policies. Margaret Tebo, *Zero Tolerance, Zero Sense*, ABA J. 40 (Apr. 2000). Zero Tolerance policies regarding guns and weapons will be discussed in more detail *infra*, but the policies may also address student speech, both spoken and written. A student who says, "I like you. Don't come to school tomorrow," to another student (the same words uttered by one of the Columbine shooters) may find that he is in serious trouble with both school officials and the police, even if the student later claims that the comment was made in jest. Margaret Tebo, *Comment Backfires in Climate of Fear*, ABA J. 46 (Apr. 2000).

Student journals also come under scrutiny. A high school student, Antonius Brown, who wrote a story in his journal about a deranged student who went on a rampage at Brown's high school was suspended from school, later expelled, and then charged by police with making terrorist threats. John Cloud, *The Columbine Effect*, TIME, Dec. 6, 1999, at 51. Schools have been roundly criticized for overreacting to student speech. *See id.* (calling the crackdown on speech "subzero tolerance"). Other critics argue that although zero tolerance policies stress equal treatment for all offenders, they are merely a "convenient catch phrase for schools unable or unwilling to prevent school violence by identifying and counseling at-risk students before they turn violent." *Zero Tolerance, Zero Sense, supra* at 41, 44. Is identification and counseling the answer? *See Looking for Closure and Cash, supra* (noting that if trained psychiatrists cannot predict unusual behavior by their patients, it is unfair to expect school officials to pick out future problems).

Zero tolerance rules are not unknown in American society. Airline passengers are met with signs as they check into an airport that state that jokes about bombs or guns will be taken seriously:

Not a Joking Matter: furnishing false information about hijacking, bombing, or carrying a concealed weapon aboard aircraft is a violation of Federal law. This includes statements made in jest and we are required to take all seriously. The FBI investigates these and other aircraft crimes.

Federal Security Inspection Rules: False Statements — It is a Federal crime to make false statements concerning: Hijacking, Firearms or other weapons, or Explosives aboard aircraft. Any person making such statements will be subject to arrest and prosecution by the Federal Authorities.

Security Signs at Ben Epps Airport, Athens, GA Aug. 1, 2001.

Especially in the wake of the attacks of September 11, 2001, most travelers understand the reasons why airlines have this "zero tolerance" rule and abide by the warnings without complaint. Should schools be different in this regard?

[4] Internet Speech

The Internet has vastly increased the ease and the opportunity with which students can express themselves. *See* Lisa Guernsey, *Telling Tales Out Of School*, N.Y. TIMES, May 8, 2003, at G1 (teenage gossip has moved from bathroom walls and hallway chatter to the Internet; "today, the Web is the medium for the prolific and sometimes outright nasty rumors of the middle school and high school years"). The Internet allows students to speak from their own personal website that they create at home. To what extent is this different from the underground newspaper cases discussed in § 4.01[C][4], *supra*? As the cases below demonstrate, courts are struggling with the contours of the First Amendment as it applies to students' home web pages and the school's authority to punish students for their off-campus behavior.

In *Beussink v. Woodland R-IV School Dist.*, 30 F. Supp. 2d 1175 (E.D. Mo. 1998), a high school student created a homepage that he posted on the Internet that the court described as highly critical of the school administration using vulgar language. Another student accessed the page while at school and showed it to a teacher. In assessing the propriety of granting the student a preliminary injunction the court relied on *Tinker*. Failing to even mention *Fraser*, the court held that the student had demonstrated the likelihood of success on the merits because the school principal's testimony did not indicate that he disciplined the student based on a reasonable fear of disruption or interference with school discipline. See also *Killion v. Franklin Regional Sch. Dist.,*136 F. Supp. 2d 446 (W.D. Pa. 2001), where the court held that school suspension for email ridiculing the school athletic director violated the student's First Amendment rights. The court decided that the school presented no evidence "of actual disruption." Even though the principal, assistant principal, and athletic director found the list to be rude, abusive and demeaning, and even though the student had written other lists that upset teachers and nearly reduced one to tears, the court determined that "the mere desire to avoid 'discomfort' or 'unpleasantness' is not enough to justify restricting student speech under *Tinker*."

Two years later the Commonwealth Court of Pennsylvania cited *Beussink* for the proposition that schools could discipline students for conduct occurring off school premises if the conduct materially and substantially interferes with the educational process. *J.S. v. Bethlehem Area Sch. Dist.,* 757 A.2d 412 (Pa. Commw. Ct. 2000). The court concluded that the trial court was correct in determining that, despite the student's contention that the speech was mere hyperbole, the web site, entitled "Teacher Sux," hindered the educational process. Noting the effect that the web site had on one of the teachers, the court stated that a reasonable person could be both physically and emotionally disturbed after viewing a web site that contained a picture of her severed head dripping with blood, a picture of her face morphing into Adolf Hitler and a solicitation (whether serious or otherwise) for funds to cover the cost of a hit man.[15]

In a civil action in which she won a $500,000 award, *see* § 4.01[C][5], *infra,* the teacher in *J.S.* testified that she was unable to finish the school year after seeing the web site, fearing for her safety after school shootings around the country. *Student Web Site Invaded Teacher's Privacy,* PENN. L. WKLY. 8 (Nov. 13, 2000). The teacher stated that she suffered from anxiety, loss of appetite, loss of sleep, loss of weight and and other stress-related problems, and that she was taking an anti-anxiety/anti-depressant for her health problems. *J.S.,* 757 A.2d at 416. The teacher returned to teaching the following fall but, harassed by students as the "Web teacher," she quit teaching after a 28-year career. *Student Web Site Invaded Teacher's Privacy, supra.*

In the student's case against the school, the court cited and quoted *Fraser's* statement that "schools must teach by example the shared values of a civilized social order." *J.S.* 757 A.2d at 422. It further noted that "in this day and age where school violence is becoming more commonplace, school officials are justified in taking very seriously threats against faculty and other students." When should the courts use the *Fraser* standard instead of the *Tinker* standard to address internet speech?

According to the dissent in *J.S.,* even if the teacher was affected personally, this is not evidence that the web site materially disrupted classwork or involved substantial disorder. Does the fact that the teacher was unable to teach and to complete the academic year disrupt classwork? What if a substitute teacher can take over? The dissent in *J.S.* also argued that the school district did not perceive the web site as a "true threat," because school officials did not attempt to warn others about the web site and did not punish the student until months after it was discovered.

The Pennsylvania Supreme Court affirmed the lower court's decision, determining that although the speech was not a true threat, the speech still caused a substantial and material disruption. *J.S. v. Bethlehem Area Sch. Dist.,* 807 A.2d 847 (Pa. 2002). Yet the following year a federal district court in Pennsylvania held that a school handbook provision that prohibited "inappropriate, harassing, offensive or abusive" speech was unconstitutionally

---

[15] The web site also discussed "Why Mrs. Fulmer [the teacher] Should be Fired." The list included, "She shows off her fat fucking legs." "The fat fuck smokes." "She's a bitch." The web site went on to state, "Fuck you, Mrs. Fulmer. You are a Bitch. You are a Stupid Bitch." (listed 136 times).

vague and overbroad because the provisions were not (1) defined, (2) limited to geographic boundaries at school or school-sponsored events or (3) limited to speech that caused a material and substantial disruption to the school day. *Flaherty v. Keystone Oaks Sch. Dist.*, 247 F. Supp. 2d 698 (W.D. Pa. 2003).

Compare *Emmett v. Kent Sch. Dist.*, 92 F. Supp. 2d 1088 (W.D. Wash. 2000), where the school district, upon learning that a student posted a web site with mock obituaries and allowed visitors to vote on who would "die" next immediately placed the student on an emergency expulsion. In *Emmett*, although the school modified the suspension to five days, the district court enjoined the school district from enforcing the short-term suspension, as the web site was entirely out of the school's control and the school did not show that the student intended to or actually threatened anyone. *See also* Alexander G. Tuneski, *Online, Not On Grounds: Protecting Student Internet Speech*, 89 VA. L. REV. 139, 178 (2003) (summarizing Supreme Court precedent and recent lower court decisions; and arguing that to protect First Amendment rights, *Tinker's* substantial disruption test must be applied to off-campus speech unless the author takes proactive steps to have his material read or disseminated on school grounds). How quickly should a school act to remove a student for expression in a web site that is posted from the student's home?

Do courts overreact to imagery in teen popular culture? *See* Richards & Calvert, *Columbine Fallout: The Long-Term Effects on Free Expression Take Hold in Public Schools*, 83 B.U. L. REV. 1089, 1110-12 (2003) (suggesting that courts take into account teen popular culture — with all its "violent imagery and profane language" — when deciding cases; and arguing that teen culture "provides a mitigating factor to counteract the context of Columbine on which so many judges seem so obsessed").

Is there a way for school officials or for courts to determine which students are merely mirroring parts of teen culture and which are going to harm others? Should school officials and judges accept the profanity that may accompany teen culture in the schoolhouse or should the schoolhouse be a place for higher pursuits? Courts will be struggling in the upcoming decade to define where the boundary lies between protected student speech and school authority to prohibit student expression. The landscape has certainly changed since the United States Supreme Court's opinion in *Tinker*, and "[t]he Internet marks that landscape change as dramatically as the Front Range marks the end of the Great Plain." *Beidler v. North Thurston Sch. Dist., No 99-2-00236-6* (Thurston Cty. Super. Ct. July 18, 2000) quoted in SPLC REP. (Fall 2000) (case upholding student expression rights, citing *Tinker*).

[5] Societal Consequences

Numerous reports state that a severe teacher shortage is looming. *See generally Shortage of Teachers an Impending Crisis* (Aug. 2004), *available at* www.nccppr.org; *Teachers Wanted*, NEWSWEEK Oct. 2, 2000, at 37 (Dept. of Educ. predicts that the nation will need more than a million new teachers by 2010, nearly half the current force of 2.6 million in elementary and secondary school). Up to forty percent of new teachers leave the profession within five years, often citing lack of financial reward for their effort as a factor. ". . . Add to this the number of teachers eligible for retirement in the next ten years, creating vacancies that cannot be filled, and the result is a teacher shortage." G.D. Litke, *You Get What You Pay For,* TECHNIQUES: CONNECTING EDUCATION AND CAREERS, May 2001, Vol. 76, Issue 5, at 62. Many young teachers leave the profession because they feel overworked and underprepared to cope with the difficulties they face in their particular schools. Jessica Flaxman, *Watch the Back Door: Young Teachers Are Fleeing,* NEWSDAY (N.Y.), March 11, 2001, at B08.

One difficulty that faces many teachers and principals is being subjected to nasty attacks, profanity and ridicule from students. Timothy Dawson, a high school principal in Florida, said he feared for his life after reading lines in a student underground newspaper that stated, "I often wonder what would happen if I shot Dawson in the head and other teachers who have pissed me off." *See ACLU Files Suit on Behalf of One of the "Killian Nine,"* STUDENT PRESS LAW CENTER REPORT 9 (Spring 1999). (Teachers in Florida may continue to be wary of student threats after a middle school teacher was shot and killed by a student who was upset because he had been punished for throwing water balloons. *Teacher Shot to Death Inside Florida School,* CHIC. TRIB. May 27, 2000, at 3.) The student publication in Dawson's case portrayed a picture of Dawson's head with a dart in his forehead and another revealed a cartoon character resembling Dawson engaged in a sex act. *Id.*

Male high school seniors published a paper in which they called a female teacher by name a "stupid bitch ass bitch who has a black skin and is a fucking gigaboo" and "the most fucked up teacher" on campus. They also threatened to rape the teacher and all of her children and to "kill you you fucking whore ass faget maggot burger . . . you stupid mother fucking bitch die nigger." *Nims v. Harrison,* 768 So. 2d 1198 (Fla. App. 1 Dist. 2000). *See also Wilson v. Hinsdale Elementary Sch. Dist. 181,* 810 N.E.2d 637 (Ill. Ct. App. 2004) (upholding expulsion of sixth grader who wrote and produced song "Gonna Kill Mrs. Cox's Baby," and gave copies to two students, one of whom shared the copy with other students who played it on a school computer; Mrs. Cox was one of the student's teachers and was in fact pregnant).

These are merely examples of some of the reported cases. For many teachers, dealing with the stress this kind of expression engenders has become a condition of employment. To what extent might student expression that demeans, ridicules, and threatens teachers contribute to the idea that teaching is no longer a desirable profession? Is this behavior something that teachers must learn to accept as one of the consequences of constitutional freedom? Or has this expression ventured too far beyond the black armbands worn by Mary Beth Tinker?

Some teachers and principals are filing civil charges against students who publish threatening statements or statements impugning professional competency. A jury awarded Justin Swidler's teacher and her husband $500,000 after deciding that the teacher's privacy had been violated by Swidlers' website that contained "obscene and violent images directed mostly at her." *Student Web Site Invaded Teacher's Privacy,* PENN. L. WKLY. 8 (Nov. 13, 2000). Jurors found that Justin's parents were negligent in their supervision of the boy. *Id.* Three teachers in Carmel High School in Indiana settled a defamation suit against a student whose web site referred to eleven teachers as devil worshipers. Teachers discovered the site, which contained an email address that included the phrase "tyme 2-dye," one day after the Columbine shootings. *Libel Lessons*, STUDENT PRESS LAW CENTER REPORT, 16, 17 (Winter 2000-01). A Florida appeals court held that the teacher in *Nims v. Harrison,* 768 So. 2d 1198, discussed *supra*, stated a claim for intentional infliction of emotional distress, as the conduct alleged went "beyond all possible bounds of decency." *See also* Mel Melendez & Pat Kossan, *Colleagues Applaud Teacher Who Took Unruly Kid to Court*, THE ARIZ. REPUB., Apr. 19, 2004, at A1 (teacher filed an injunction against a sophomore who allegedly sexually harassed and abused her with vulgar language; suit sparked response from others identifying with teacher's frustration and hailing her decision to go public).

In Utah one student, Ian Lake, was charged under the state's *criminal* libel statute for statements he made on his personal web site stating that the school principal was the "town drunk," naming girls at his high school as "sluts," and making derogatory remarks about the intelligence of several teachers. *High School Student Faces Criminal Libel Charges for Web Site Remarks*, STUDENT PRESS LAW CENTER REPORT, 34 (Fall 2000).

Ian Lake's father stated that his son was upset by what he perceived as a double standard at his school and that Ian spent a lot of time researching libel laws before constructing his web site. The father stated that students get frustrated when they try to address issues and they are ignored: "I'm getting to the point where I can really understand why some of these 14- and 15-year-old kids are choosing just to go in and shoot people." Mr. Lake noted that Ian "was smart enough to see there was another way to go after them."

The criminal charges against Ian Lake were dropped after the Utah Supreme Court found the criminal libel statute to be overbroad and facially unconstitutional. *I.M.L. v. State*, 61 P.3d 1038 (Utah 2002). After the Supreme Court decision, Utah prosecutors charged Ian with a criminal defamation law. The county attorney, however, was not re-elected and the new county attorney dismissed charges against him in January 2003. Mark Haynes, *Ex-Milford Student's Father to Sue*, THE SALT LAKE TRIB., Jan. 15, 2003, at B2 (father is planning to sue; Ian is working on a new "tell-all" website with a chronology of the case).

When should school officials press criminal charges for student speech or conduct? The Massachusetts Supreme Court upheld a school suspension and a juvenile court sentence of more than five years probation (under the state threatening statute). The student's teacher had confiscated a drawing by the student that depicted the student pointing a gun at the teacher's head as she knelt in prayer pleading, "Please don't shoot me." Given the number of school shootings across the country, the court believed that the teacher was reasonable in interpreting the drawing as a threat. Jessica Portner, *Violent Drawing Was a Real Threat, Mass. Court Rules*, EDUC. WK., Jan 17, 2001, at 3. *See also In the Matter of H.J. v. State of Indiana*, 746 N.E.2d 400 (Ind. Ct. App. 2001) (female juvenile adjudicated a delinquent child for making threats to classmates that would constitute Intimidation, a Class A misdemeanor if committed by an adult); John Cloud, *The Columbine Effect*, TIME, Dec. 6, 1999, at 51 (two 10-year-olds were charged with felonies for trying to kill or injure their teacher when one of them squirted soap gel into the teacher's water bottle). For a law review symposium issue relating largely to the issue of school safety, see *Symposium: School Violence, School Safety, and the Juvenile Justice System*, 37 HOUSTON L. REV. 1 (2000).

Will lawsuits by teachers and principals and juvenile court convictions unduly chill student speech? Or is learning about defamation and threats part of a "civics lesson," *Hazelwood School District v. Kuhlmeier*, 484 U.S. 260, 277 (Brennan, J., dissenting), the lesson that words can harm others and that along with the right of expression go certain responsibilities?

[D] The Right to Receive Information and Ideas

Does the First Amendment encompass the right to hear as well as the right to speak? To what extent can the government curtail a child's exposure to speech? This issue has arisen in areas outside the school context, as well as inside the school. As made clear earlier in *Ginsberg v. New York*, 390 U.S. 629 (1968), the Supreme Court upheld a criminal statute that prohibited the sale to minors of any material (in this case, magazines) that depicted nudity or sexual conduct that "(i) predominantly appeals to the prurient, shameful or morbid interest of minors, and (ii) is patently offensive to prevailing standards in the adult community as a whole with respect to what is suitable material for minors, and (iii) is utterly without redeeming social importance for minors." 390 U.S. at 633. *See also FCC v Pacifica*, 438 U.S. 726 (1978) (radio broadcast of George Carlin's monologue "Filthy Words" not protected, concluding that broadcast speech received less protection than other media because it intrudes into the home, may be hard for the recipient to avoid, and is uniquely accessible to children, even those too young to read). The material in both *Ginsberg* and *Pacifica* was not obscene for adults. Justice Brennan's opinion for the *Ginsberg* Court, cited *Prince v. Commonwealth of Massachusetts*, 321 U.S. 158, 170 (1944), for the proposition that "the power of the state to control the conduct of children reaches beyond the scope of its power over adults . . . ." and required "only that we be able to say that it was not irrational for the legislature to find that exposure to material condemned by the statute to be harmful to minors."

Although the Court noted that there was no definitive study showing that exposure to sex material was harmful to minors, Justice Brennan pointed out that commentators agreed that a causal link had not been disproved either. The Court quoted from one report that noted a distinction between minors looking at pornography, on the one hand, and minors looking at pornography with adult approval, on the other hand. *Id.* at n.10 (quoting William M. Gaylin, M.D., *The Prickly Problem of Pornography*, 77 YALE L.J. 579, 592–93 (1967)). According to psychiatrists, the child is protected in his reading pornography in the first scenario by the knowledge that it is disapproved, that it is outside of parental standards, and thus it does not become a part of his identification process. Openly permitting minors to view pornography implies parental approval and even suggests seductive encouragement. If this is true of parental approval, it is equally true of societal approval — another potent influence on the developing ego. *Id.* Refer again to this report after you read the next case and the notes following it. If this report Justice Brennan quoted is correct, consider whether he should have come out differently in *Pico*, which is set forth below.

The multiple opinions in the next case address whether a child (a student in elementary, middle, or high school) possesses a constitutional right to receive information in the context of the school board's removal of some books from the school library. Seven Justices (all but Marshall and Stevens) wrote opinions in *Pico*. As you read the opinions note how the Justices' views about the extent to which students possess a right to receive information are intertwined with their views about the role of courts and the political process in a constitutional democracy.

BOARD OF EDUCATION, ISLAND TREES UNION FREE SCHOOL DISTRICT v. PICO

Supreme Court of the United States
457 U.S. 853 (1982)

JUSTICE BRENNAN announced the judgment of the Court and delivered an opinion, in which JUSTICE MARSHALL and JUSTICE STEVENS joined, and in which JUSTICE BLACKMUN joined except for Part II-A-(1).

The principal question presented is whether the First Amendment imposes limitations upon the exercise by a local school board of its discretion to remove library books from high school and junior high school libraries.

I

Petitioners are the Board of Education of the Island Trees Union Free School District No. 26. . . . Respondents are [students at the high school and junior high school].

In September 1975, petitioners Ahrens, Martin, and Hughes attended a conference sponsored by Parents of New York United (PONYU), a politically conservative organization of parents concerned about education legislation in the State of New York. At the conference these petitioners obtained lists of books described by Ahrens as "objectionable," and by Martin as "improper fare for school students."[16] It was later determined that the High School library contained nine of the listed books, and that another listed book was in the Junior High School library.[17] In February 1976, at a meeting with the Superintendent of Schools and the Principals of the High School and Junior High School, the Board gave an "unofficial direction" that the listed books be

---

[16] [2] The District Court noted, however, that petitioners "concede that the books are not obscene."

[17] [3] The nine books in the High School library were: Slaughter House Five, by Kurt Vonnegut, Jr.; The Naked Ape, by Desmond Morris; Down These Mean Streets, by Piri Thomas; Best Short Stories of Negro Writers, edited by Langston Hughes; Go Ask Alice, of anonymous authorship; Laughing Boy, by Oliver LaFarge; Black Boy, by Richard Wright; A Hero Ain't Nothin' But A Sandwich, by Alice Childress; and Soul On Ice, by Eldridge Cleaver. The book in the Junior High School library was A Reader for Writers, edited by Jerome Archer. Still another listed book, The Fixer, by Bernard Malamud, was found to be included in the curriculum of a 12th-grade literature course.

removed from the library shelves and delivered to the Board's offices, so that Board members could read them.[18] When this directive was carried out, it became publicized, and the Board issued a press release justifying its action. It characterized the removed books as "anti-American, anti-Christian, anti-[Semitic], and just plain filthy," and concluded that "[it] is our duty, our moral obligation, to protect the children in our schools from this moral danger as surely as from physical and medical dangers."

A short time later, the Board appointed a "Book Review Committee," consisting of four Island Trees parents and four members of the Island Trees schools staff, to read the listed books and to recommend to the Board whether the books should be retained, taking into account the books' "educational suitability," "good taste," "relevance," and "appropriateness to age and grade level." In July, the Committee made its final report to the Board, recommending that five of the listed books be retained and that two others be removed from the school libraries. As for the remaining four books, the Committee could not agree on two, took no position on one, and recommended that the last book be made available to students only with parental approval. The Board substantially rejected the Committee's report later that month, deciding that only one book should be returned to the High School library without restriction,[19] that another should be made available subject to parental approval,[20] but that the remaining nine books should "be removed from elementary and secondary libraries and [from] use in the curriculum." The Board gave no reasons for rejecting the recommendations of the Committee that it had appointed.

Respondents reacted to the Board's decision by bringing the present action . . . [alleging that] petitioners had "ordered the removal of the books from school libraries and proscribed their use in the curriculum because particular passages in the books offended their social, political and moral tastes and not because the books, taken as a whole, were lacking in educational value."

Respondents claimed that the Board's actions denied them their rights under the First Amendment. They asked the court for a declaration that the Board's actions were unconstitutional, and for preliminary and permanent injunctive relief ordering the Board to return the nine books to the school libraries and to refrain from interfering with the use of those books in the schools' curricula.

The District Court granted summary judgment in favor of petitioners. In the court's view, "the parties substantially [agreed] about the motivation

---

[18] [4] The Superintendent of Schools objected to the Board's informal directive, noting:

> "[We] already have a policy . . . designed expressly to handle such problems. It calls for the Superintendent, upon receiving an objection to a book or books, to appoint a committee to study them and make recommendations. I feel it is a good policy — and it is Board policy — and that it should be followed in this instance. Furthermore, I think it can be followed quietly and in such a way as to reduce, perhaps avoid, the public furor which has always attended such issues in the past."

The Board responded to the Superintendent's objection by repeating its directive "that *all copies* of the library books in question be removed from the libraries to the Board's office."

[19] [10] Laughing Boy.

[20] [11] Black Boy.

behind the board's actions," — namely, that "the board acted not on religious principles but on its conservative educational philosophy, and on its belief that the nine books removed from the school library and curriculum were irrelevant, vulgar, immoral, and in bad taste, making them educationally unsuitable for the district's junior and senior high school students."

With this factual premise as its background, the court rejected respondents' contention that their First Amendment rights had been infringed by the Board's actions. Noting that statutes, history, and precedent had vested local school boards with a broad discretion to formulate educational policy, the court concluded that it should not intervene in "the daily operations of school systems" unless "basic constitutional values" were "sharply [implicated]," and determined that the conditions for such intervention did not exist in the present case. . . .

A three-judge panel of the United States Court of Appeals for the Second Circuit reversed the judgment of the District Court, and remanded the action for a trial on respondents' allegations. Each judge on the panel filed a separate opinion. Delivering the judgment of the court, Judge Sifton . . . determined that, at least at the summary judgment stage, petitioners had not offered sufficient justification for their action. . . . Judge Newman . . . viewed the case as turning on the contested factual issue of whether petitioners' removal decision was motivated by a justifiable desire to remove books containing vulgarities and sexual explicitness, or rather by an impermissible desire to suppress ideas.[21] We granted certiorari.

II

We emphasize at the outset the limited nature of the substantive question presented by the case before us. Our precedents have long recognized certain constitutional limits upon the power of the State to control even the curriculum and classroom. For example, *Meyer v. Nebraska*, 262 U.S. 390 (1923), struck down a state law that forbade the teaching of modern foreign languages in public and private schools, and *Epperson v. Arkansas*, 393 U.S. 97 (1968), declared unconstitutional a state law that prohibited the teaching of the Darwinian theory of evolution in any state-supported school. But the current action does not require us to re-enter this difficult terrain, which *Meyer* and *Epperson* traversed without apparent misgiving. For as this case is presented to us, it does not involve textbooks, or indeed any books that Island Trees students would be required to read. Respondents do not seek in this Court to impose limitations upon their school Board's discretion to prescribe the curricula of the Island Trees schools. On the contrary, the only books at issue in this case are *library* books, books that by their nature are optional rather

[21] [17] Judge Mansfield dissented, based upon a distinctly different reading of the record developed in the District Court. According to Judge Mansfield, "the undisputed evidence of the motivation for the Board's action was the perfectly permissible ground that the books were indecent, in bad taste, and unsuitable for educational purposes." He also asserted that in reaching its decision "the Board [had] acted carefully, conscientiously and responsibly after according due process to all parties concerned." Judge Mansfield concluded that "the First Amendment entitles students to reasonable freedom of expression but not to freedom from what some may consider to be excessively moralistic or conservative selection by school authorities of library books to be used as educational tools."

than required reading. Our adjudication of the present case thus does not intrude into the classroom, or into the compulsory courses taught there. Furthermore, even as to library books, the action before us does not involve the *acquisition* of books. Respondents have not sought to compel their school Board to add to the school library shelves any books that students desire to read. Rather, the only action challenged in this case is the *removal* from school libraries of books originally placed there by the school authorities, or without objection from them.

The substantive question before us is still further constrained by the procedural posture of this case. [Justice BRENNAN noted that Petitioners were granted summary judgment by the District Court, and the Court of Appeals reversed that judgment, remanding the action for a trial on the merits of respondents' claims. The U. S. Supreme Court can reverse that judgment and grant petitioners' request for reinstatement of the summary judgment in their favor, only if it determines that "there is no genuine issue as to any material fact," and that petitioners are "entitled to a judgment as a matter of law." In making this determination, any doubt as to the existence of a genuine issue of material fact must be resolved against petitioners as the moving party and the inferences to be drawn from the underlying facts must be viewed in the light most favorable to the party opposing the motion.]

In sum, the issue before us in this case is a narrow one, both substantively and procedurally. It may best be restated as two distinct questions. First, does the First Amendment impose *any* limitations upon the discretion of petitioners to remove library books from the Island Trees High School and Junior High School? Second, if so, do the affidavits and other evidentiary materials before the District Court, construed most favorably to respondents, raise a genuine issue of fact whether petitioners might have exceeded those limitations?

. . . .

A

(1)

The Court has long recognized that local school boards have broad discretion in the management of school affairs. [Citing *Meyer v. Nebraska* and *Pierce v. Society of Sisters.*] *Epperson v. Arkansas* reaffirmed that, by and large, "public education in our Nation is committed to the control of state and local authorities," and that federal courts should not ordinarily "intervene in the resolution of conflicts which arise in the daily operation of school systems." *Tinker v. Des Moines School Dist.,* noted that we have "repeatedly emphasized . . . the comprehensive authority of the States and of school officials . . . to prescribe and control conduct in the schools." We have also acknowledged that public schools are vitally important "in the preparation of individuals for participation as citizens," and as vehicles for "inculcating fundamental values necessary to the maintenance of a democratic political system." *Ambach v. Norwick.* We are therefore in full agreement with petitioners that local school boards must be permitted "to establish and apply their curriculum in such a way as to transmit community values," and that "there is a legitimate and substantial community interest in promoting respect for authority and traditional values be they social, moral, or political."

At the same time, however, we have necessarily recognized that the discretion of the States and local school boards in matters of education must be exercised in a manner that comports with the transcendent imperatives of the First Amendment . . . .

Of course, courts should not "intervene in the resolution of conflicts which arise in the daily operation of school systems" unless "basic constitutional values" are "directly and sharply [implicated]" in those conflicts. *Epperson v. Arkansas*. But we think that the First Amendment rights of students may be directly and sharply implicated by the removal of books from the shelves of a school library. Our precedents have focused "not only on the role of the First Amendment in fostering individual self-expression but also on its role in affording the public access to discussion, debate, and the dissemination of information and ideas." *First National Bank of Boston v. Bellotti*. And we have recognized that "the State may not, consistently with the spirit of the First Amendment, contract the spectrum of available knowledge." *Griswold v. Connecticut,* 381 U.S. 479, 482 (1965). In keeping with this principle, we have held that in a variety of contexts "the Constitution protects the right to receive information and ideas." *Stanley v. Georgia,* 394 U.S. 557, 564 (1969); *see Kleindienst v. Mandel,* 408 U.S. 753, 762–763 (1972) (citing cases). This right is an inherent corollary of the rights of free speech and press that are explicitly guaranteed by the Constitution, in two senses. First, the right to receive ideas follows ineluctably from the *sender's* First Amendment right to send them: "The right of freedom of speech and press . . . embraces the right to distribute literature, and necessarily protects the right to receive it." *Martin v. Struthers,* 319 U.S. 141, 143 (1943) (citation omitted). "The dissemination of ideas can accomplish nothing if otherwise willing addressees are not free to receive and consider them. It would be a barren marketplace of ideas that had only sellers and no buyers." *Lamont v. Postmaster General,* 381 U.S. 301, 308 (1965) (BRENNAN, J., concurring).

More importantly, the right to receive ideas is a necessary predicate to the *recipient's* meaningful exercise of his own rights of speech, press, and political freedom. Madison admonished us:

> A popular Government, without popular information, or the means of acquiring it, is but a Prologue to a Farce or a Tragedy; or, perhaps both. Knowledge will forever govern ignorance: And a people who mean to be their own Governors, must arm themselves with the power which knowledge gives. 9 WRITINGS OF JAMES MADISON 103 (G. Hunt ed. 1910).

As we recognized in *Tinker*, students too are beneficiaries of this principle:

> "In our system, students may not be regarded as closed-circuit recipients of only that which the State chooses to communicate. . . . [School] officials cannot suppress 'expressions of feeling with which they do not wish to contend.'"

In sum, just as access to ideas makes it possible for citizens generally to exercise their rights of free speech and press in a meaningful manner, such access prepares students for active and effective participation in the pluralistic, often contentious society in which they will soon be adult members. Of course all First Amendment rights accorded to students must be construed "in light of the special characteristics of the school environment." But the special characteristics of the school *library* make that environment especially appropriate for the recognition of the First Amendment rights of students.

A school library, no less than any other public library, is "a place dedicated to quiet, to knowledge, and to beauty." *Keyishian v. Board of Regents* observed that "students must always remain free to inquire, to study and to evaluate, to gain new maturity and understanding." The school library is the principal locus of such freedom. As one District Court has well put it, in the school library "a student can literally explore the unknown, and discover areas of interest and thought not covered by the prescribed curriculum. . . . [The] student learns that a library is a place to test or expand upon ideas presented to him, in or out of the classroom."

Petitioners emphasize the inculcative function of secondary education, and argue that they must be allowed *unfettered* discretion to "transmit community values" through the Island Trees schools. But that sweeping claim overlooks the unique role of the school library. It appears from the record that use of the Island Trees school libraries is completely voluntary on the part of students. Their selection of books from these libraries is entirely a matter of free choice; the libraries afford them an opportunity at self-education and individual enrichment that is wholly optional. Petitioners might well defend their claim of absolute discretion in matters of *curriculum* by reliance upon their duty to inculcate community values. But we think that petitioners' reliance upon that duty is misplaced where, as here, they attempt to extend their claim of absolute discretion beyond the compulsory environment of the classroom, into the school library and the regime of voluntary inquiry that there holds sway.

(2)

In rejecting petitioners' claim of absolute discretion to remove books from their school libraries, we do not deny that local school boards have a substantial legitimate role to play in the determination of school library content. We thus must turn to the question of the extent to which the First Amendment places limitations upon the discretion of petitioners to remove books from their libraries. In this inquiry we enjoy the guidance of several precedents. "If there is any fixed star in our constitutional constellation, it is that no official, high or petty, can prescribe what shall be orthodox in politics, nationalism, religion, or other matters of opinion . . . . If there are any circumstances which permit an exception, they do not now occur to us." This doctrine has been reaffirmed in later cases involving education . . . [describing and citing cases].

With respect to the present case, the message of these precedents is clear. Petitioners rightly possess significant discretion to determine the content of their school libraries. But that discretion may not be exercised in a narrowly partisan or political manner. If a Democratic school board, motivated by party affiliation, ordered the removal of all books written by or in favor of Republicans, few would doubt that the order violated the constitutional rights of the students denied access to those books. The same conclusion would surely apply if an all-white school board, motivated by racial animus, decided to remove all books authored by blacks or advocating racial equality and integration. Our Constitution does not permit the official suppression of *ideas*. Thus whether petitioners' removal of books from their school libraries denied respondents their First Amendment rights depends upon the motivation behind petitioners' actions. If petitioners *intended* by their removal decision to deny respondents access to ideas with which petitioners disagreed, and if this intent was the decisive factor in petitioners' decision, then petitioners have exercised their discretion in violation of the Constitution. To permit such intentions to control official actions would be to encourage the precise sort of officially prescribed orthodoxy unequivocally condemned in [our case law]. On the other hand, respondents implicitly concede that an unconstitutional motivation would *not* be demonstrated if it were shown that petitioners had decided to remove the books at issue because those books were pervasively vulgar. And again, respondents concede that if it were demonstrated that the removal decision was based solely upon the "educational suitability" of the books in question, then their removal would be "perfectly permissible." In other words, in respondents' view such motivations, if decisive of petitioners' actions, would not carry the danger of an official suppression of ideas, and thus would not violate respondents' First Amendment rights.

As noted earlier, nothing in our decision today affects in any way the discretion of a local school board to choose books to *add* to the libraries of their schools. Because we are concerned in this case with the suppression of ideas, our holding today affects only the discretion to *remove* books. In brief, we hold that local school boards may not remove books from school library shelves simply because they dislike the ideas contained in those books and seek by their removal to "prescribe what shall be orthodox in politics, nationalism, religion, or other matters of opinion." *West Virginia Board of Education v. Barnette.* Such purposes stand inescapably condemned by our precedents.

B

We now turn to the remaining question presented by this case: Do the evidentiary materials that were before the District Court, when construed most favorably to respondents, raise a genuine issue of material fact whether petitioners exceeded constitutional limitations in exercising their discretion to remove the books from the school libraries? We conclude that the materials do raise such a question, which forecloses summary judgment in favor of petitioners.

Before the District Court, respondents claimed that petitioners' decision to remove the books "was based on [their] personal values, morals and tastes." Respondents also claimed that petitioners objected to the books in part because excerpts from them were "anti-American." The accuracy of these claims was partially conceded by petitioners, and petitioners' own affidavits lent further support to respondents' claims.[22] In addition, the record developed in the District Court shows that when petitioners offered their first public explanation for the removal of the books, they relied in part on the assertion that the removed books were "anti-American," and "offensive to . . . Americans in general."[23] . . .

Standing alone, this evidence respecting the substantive motivations behind petitioners' removal decision would not be decisive. This would be a very different case if the record demonstrated that petitioners had employed established, regular, and facially unbiased procedures for the review of controversial materials. But the actual record in the case before us suggests the exact opposite. Petitioners' removal procedures were vigorously challenged below by respondents, and the evidence on this issue sheds further light on the issue of petitioners' motivations. . . . [R]espondents' allegations and some of the evidentiary materials presented below do not rule out the possibility that petitioners' removal procedures were highly irregular and ad hoc — the antithesis of those procedures that might tend to allay suspicions regarding petitioners' motvations. . . .

The evidence plainly does not foreclose the possibility that petitioners' decision to remove the books rested decisively upon disagreement with constitutionally protected ideas in those books, or upon a desire on petitioners' part to impose upon the students of the Island Trees High School and Junior High School a political orthodoxy to which petitioners and their constituents adhered. Of course, some of the evidence before the District Court might lead a finder of fact to accept petitioners' claim that their removal decision was based upon constitutionally valid concerns. But that evidence at most creates a genuine issue of material fact on the critical question of the credibility of petitioners' justifications for their decision: On that issue, it simply cannot be said that there is no genuine issue as to any material fact.

The mandate shall issue forthwith.

Affirmed.

---

22 [24] For example, petitioner Ahrens stated:

> "I am basically a conservative in my general philosophy and feel that the community I represent as a school board member shares that philosophy. . . . I feel that it is my duty to apply my conservative principles to the decision making process in which I am involved as a board member and I have done so with regard to . . . curriculum formation and content and other educational matters."

> "We are representing the community which first elected us and re-elected us and our actions have reflected its intrinsic values and desires."

Petitioners Fasulo, Hughes, Melchers, Michaels, and Nessim made a similar statement that they had "represented the basic values of the community in [their] actions."

23 [28] When asked to give an example of "anti-Americanism" in the removed books, petitioners Ahrens and Martin both adverted to A Hero Ain't Nothin' But A Sandwich, which notes at one point that George Washington was a slaveholder. *See* A. CHILDRESS, A HERO AIN'T NOTHIN' BUT A SANDWICH 43 (1973); Deposition of Petitioner Ahrens 89; Deposition of Petitioner Martin 20–22. Petitioner Martin stated: "I believe it is anti-American to present one of the nation's heroes, the first President, . . . in such a negative and obviously one-sided life. That is one example of what I would consider anti-American." Deposition of Petitioner Martin 22.

JUSTICE BLACKMUN, concurring in part and concurring in the judgment.

While I agree with much in today's plurality opinion, and while I accept the standard laid down by the plurality to guide proceedings on remand, I write separately because I have a somewhat different perspective on the nature of the First Amendment right involved.

I

To my mind, this case presents a particularly complex problem because it involves two competing principles of constitutional stature. On the one hand, as the dissenting opinions demonstrate, and as we all can agree, the Court has acknowledged the importance of the public schools "in the preparation of individuals for participation as citizens, and in the preservation of the values on which our society rests." *Ambach v. Norwick*. . . . Because of the essential socializing function of schools, local education officials may attempt "to promote civic virtues," *Ambach v. Norwick,* and to "[awaken] the child to cultural values." *Brown v. Board of Education*. Indeed, the Constitution presupposes the existence of an informed citizenry prepared to participate in governmental affairs, and these democratic principles obviously are constitutionally incorporated into the structure of our government. It therefore seems entirely appropriate that the State use "public schools [to] . . . [inculcate] fundamental values necessary to the maintenance of a democratic political system." *Ambach v. Norwick*.

On the other hand, as the plurality demonstrates, it is beyond dispute that schools and school boards must operate within the confines of the First Amendment. In a variety of academic settings the Court therefore has acknowledged the force of the principle that schools, like other enterprises operated by the State, may not be run in such a manner as to "prescribe what shall be orthodox in politics, nationalism, religion, or other matters of opinion." *West Virginia Board of Education v. Barnette*. While none of these cases define the limits of a school board's authority to choose a curriculum and academic materials, they are based on the general proposition that "state-operated schools may not be enclaves of totalitarianism. . . . In our system, students may not be regarded as closed-circuit recipients of only that which the State chooses to communicate." *Tinker v. Des Moines School Dist.*

The Court in *Tinker* thus rejected the view that "a State might so conduct its schools as to 'foster a homogeneous people.'" . . . [Q]uoting *Meyer v. Nebraska*. Similarly, *Keyishian v. Board of Regents* — a case that involved the State's attempt to remove "subversives" from academic positions at its universities, but that addressed itself more broadly to public education in general — held that "[the] classroom is peculiarly the 'marketplace of ideas'"; the First Amendment therefore "does not tolerate laws that cast a pall of orthodoxy over the classroom." "[Free] public education, if faithful to the ideal of secular instruction and political neutrality, will not be partisan or enemy of any class, creed, party, or faction." The Court therefore made it clear that imposition of "ideological discipline" was not a proper undertaking for school authorities.

In combination with more generally applicable First Amendment rules, most particularly the central proscription of content-based regulations of speech, . . . the cases outlined above yield a general principle: the State may not suppress exposure to ideas — for the sole *purpose* of suppressing exposure to those ideas — absent sufficiently compelling reasons. Because the school board must perform all its functions "within the limits of the Bill of Rights," this principle necessarily applies in at least a limited way to public education. Surely this is true in an extreme case: as the plurality notes, it is difficult to see how a school board, consistent with the First Amendment, could refuse for political reasons to buy books written by Democrats or by Negroes, or books that are "anti-American" in the broadest sense of that term. Indeed, Justice Rehnquist appears "cheerfully [to] concede" this point.

In my view, then, the principle involved here is both narrower and more basic than the "right to receive information" identified by the plurality. I do not suggest that the State has any affirmative obligation to provide students with information or ideas, something that may well be associated with a "right to receive." . . . And I do not believe, as the plurality suggests, that the right at issue here is somehow associated with the peculiar nature of the school library; . . . if schools may be used to inculcate ideas, surely libraries may play a role in that process.[24] Instead, I suggest that certain forms of state discrimination *between* ideas are improper. In particular, our precedents command the conclusion that the State may not act to deny access to an idea simply because state officials disapprove of that idea for partisan or political reasons.[25] . . .

As I see it, then, the question in this case is how to make the delicate accommodation between the limited constitutional restriction that I think is imposed by the First Amendment, and the necessarily broad state authority to regulate education. In starker terms, we must reconcile the schools' "inculcative" function with the First Amendment's bar on "prescriptions of orthodoxy."

---

[24] [1] As a practical matter, however, it is difficult to see the First Amendment right that I believe is at work here playing a role in a school's choice of curriculum. The school's finite resources — as well as the limited number of hours in the day — require that education officials make sensitive choices between subjects to be offered and competing areas of academic emphasis; subjects generally are excluded simply because school officials have chosen to devote their resources to one rather than to another subject. As is explained below, a choice of this nature does not run afoul of the First Amendment. In any event, the Court has recognized that students' First Amendment rights in most cases must give way if they interfere "with the schools' work or [with] the rights of other students to be secure and to be let alone," and such interference will rise to intolerable levels if public participation in the management of the curriculum becomes commonplace. In contrast, library books on a shelf intrude not at all on the daily operation of a school.

I also have some doubt that there is a theoretical distinction between removal of a book and failure to acquire a book. But as Judge Newman observed, there is a profound practical and evidentiary distinction between the two actions: "removal, more than failure to acquire, is likely to suggest that an impermissible political motivation may be present. There are many reasons why a book is not acquired, the most obvious being limited resources, but there are few legitimate reasons why a book, once acquired, should be removed from a library not filled to capacity." 638 F.2d 404, 436 (CA2 1980) (Newman, J., concurring in result).

[25] [2] In effect, my view presents the obverse of the plurality's analysis: while the plurality focuses on the failure to provide information, I find crucial the State's decision to single out an idea for disapproval and then deny access to it.

II

In my view, we strike a proper balance here by holding that school officials may not remove books for the *purpose* of restricting access to the political ideas or social perspectives discussed in them, when that action is motivated simply by the officials' disapproval of the ideas involved. It does not seem radical to suggest that state action calculated to suppress novel ideas or concepts is fundamentally antithetical to the values of the First Amendment. At a minimum, allowing a school board to engage in such conduct hardly teaches children to respect the diversity of ideas that is fundamental to the American system. In this context, then, the school board must "be able to show that its action was caused by something more than a mere desire to avoid the discomfort and unpleasantness that always accompany an unpopular view-point," and that the board had something in mind in addition to the suppression of partisan or political views it did not share.

As I view it, this is a narrow principle. School officials must be able to choose one book over another, without outside interference, when the first book is deemed more relevant to the curriculum, or better written, or when one of a host of other politically neutral reasons is present. . . . And, of course, school officials may choose one book over another because they believe that one subject is more important, or is more deserving of emphasis. . . .

Most people would recognize that refusing to allow discussion of current events in Latin class is a policy designed to "inculcate" Latin, not to suppress ideas. Similarly, removing a learned treatise criticizing American foreign policy from an elementary school library because the students would not understand it is an action unrelated to the *purpose* of suppressing ideas. In my view, however, removing the same treatise because it is "anti-American" raises a far more difficult issue.

Concededly, a tension exists between the properly inculcative purposes of public education and any limitation on the school board's absolute discretion to choose academic materials. But that tension demonstrates only that the problem here is a difficult one, not that the problem should be resolved by choosing one principle over another. . . .

Because I believe that the plurality has derived a standard similar to the one compelled by my analysis, I join all but Part II-A(1) of the plurality opinion.

JUSTICE WHITE, *concurring in the judgment.*

[Opinion omitted.]

CHIEF JUSTICE BURGER, with whom JUSTICE POWELL, JUSTICE REHNQUIST, and JUSTICE O'CONNOR join, *dissenting.*

The First Amendment, as with other parts of the Constitution, must deal with new problems in a changing world. In an attempt to deal with a problem in an area traditionally left to the states, a plurality of the Court, in a lavish expansion going beyond any prior holding under the First Amendment, expresses its view that a school board's decision concerning what books are to be in the school library is subject to federal-court review.[26] Were this to become the law, this Court would come perilously close to becoming a "super censor" of school board library decisions. Stripped to its essentials, the issue comes down to two important propositions: *first*, whether local schools are to be administered by elected school boards, or by federal judges and teenage pupils; and *second*, whether the values of morality, good taste, and relevance to education are valid reasons for school board decisions concerning the contents of a school library. In an attempt to place this case within the protection of the First Amendment, the plurality suggests a new "right" that, when shorn of the plurality's rhetoric, allows this Court to impose its own views about what books must be made available to students.

A

I agree with the fundamental proposition that "students do not 'shed their constitutional rights to freedom of speech or expression at the schoolhouse gate.' " . . . Here, however, no restraints of any kind are placed on the students. They are free to read the books in question, which are available at public libraries and bookstores; they are free to discuss them in the classroom or elsewhere. Despite this absence of any direct external control on the students' ability to express themselves, the plurality suggests that there is a new First Amendment "entitlement" to have access to particular books in a school library.

The plurality cites *Meyer v. Nebraska*, which struck down a state law that restricted the teaching of modern foreign languages in public and private schools, and *Epperson v. Arkansas*, which declared unconstitutional under the Establishment Clause a law banning the teaching of Darwinian evolution, to establish the validity of federal-court interference with the functioning of schools. The plurality finds it unnecessary "to re-enter this difficult terrain," yet in the next breath relies on these very cases and others to establish the previously unheard of "right" of access to particular books in the public school library.[27] The apparent underlying basis of the plurality's view seems to be that students have an enforceable "right" to receive the information and ideas that are contained in junior and senior high school library books. This "right" purportedly follows "ineluctably" from the sender's First Amendment right to freedom of speech and as a "necessary predicate" to the recipient's meaningful exercise of his own rights of speech, press, and political freedom. No such right, however, has previously been recognized.

---

26 [1] . . . What the plurality apparently finds objectionable is that the inquiry as to the challenged books was initially stimulated by what is characterized as "a politically conservative organization of parents concerned about education," which had concluded that the books in question were "improper fare for school students." As noted by the District Court, however, and in the plurality opinion, both parties substantially agreed about the motivation of the school board in removing the books:

> "[The] board acted not on religious principles but on its conservative educational philosophy, and on its belief that the nine books removed from the school library and curriculum were irrelevant, vulgar, immoral, and in bad taste, making them educationally unsuitable for the district's junior and senior high school students."

27 [3] Of course, it is perfectly clear that, unwise as it would be, the board could wholly dispense with the school library, so far as the First Amendment is concerned.

It is true that where there is a willing distributor of materials, the government may not impose unreasonable obstacles to dissemination by the third party. And where the speaker desires to express certain ideas, the government may not impose unreasonable restraints. It does not follow, however, that a school board must affirmatively aid the speaker in his communication with the recipient. In short the plurality suggests today that if a writer has something to say, the government through its schools must be the courier. None of the cases cited by the plurality establish this broad-based proposition.

. . . [T]he plurality concludes that "the right to receive ideas is a necessary predicate to the *recipient's* meaningful exercise of his own rights of speech, press, and political freedom." However, the "right to receive information and ideas," *Stanley v. Georgia,* 394 U.S. 557, 564 (1969), does not carry with it the concomitant right to have those ideas affirmatively provided at a particular place by the government. The plurality cites James Madison to emphasize the importance of having an informed citizenry. We all agree with Madison, of course, that knowledge is necessary for effective government. Madison's view, however, does not establish a *right* to have particular books retained on the school library shelves if the school board decides that they are inappropriate or irrelevant to the school's mission. Indeed, if the need to have an informed citizenry creates a "right," why is the government not also required to provide ready access to a variety of information? This same need would support a constitutional "right" of the people to have public libraries as part of a new constitutional "right" to continuing adult education.

The plurality also cites *Tinker,* to establish that the recipient's right to free speech encompasses a right to have particular books retained on the school library shelf. But the cited passage of *Tinker* notes only that school officials may not *prohibit* a student from expressing his or her view on a subject unless that expression interferes with the legitimate operations of the school. The government does not "contract the spectrum of available knowledge" by choosing not to retain certain books on the school library shelf; it simply chooses not to be the conduit for that particular information. In short, even assuming the desirability of the policy expressed by the plurality, there is not a hint in the First Amendment, or in any holding of this Court, of a "right" to have the government provide continuing access to certain books.

B

. . . The plurality pays homage to the ancient verity that in the administration of the public schools " 'there is a legitimate and substantial community interest in promoting respect for authority and traditional values be they social, moral, or political.' " If, as we have held, schools may legitimately be used as vehicles for "inculcating fundamental values necessary to the maintenance of a democratic political system," school authorities must have broad discretion to fulfill that obligation. Presumably all activity within a primary or secondary school involves the conveyance of information and at least an implied approval of the worth of that information. How are "fundamental values" to be inculcated except by having school boards make content-based decisions about the appropriateness of retaining materials in the school library and curriculum. In order to fulfill its function, an elected school board *must* express its views on the subjects which are taught to its students. In doing so those elected officials express the views of their community; they may err, of course, and the voters may remove them. It is a startling erosion of the very idea of democratic government to have this Court arrogate to itself the power the plurality asserts today.

The plurality concludes that under the Constitution school boards cannot choose to retain or dispense with books if their discretion is exercised in a "narrowly partisan or political manner." The plurality concedes that permissible factors are whether the books are "pervasively vulgar" or educationally unsuitable. "Educational suitability," however, is a standardless phrase. This conclusion will undoubtedly be drawn in many — if not most — instances because of the decisionmaker's content-based judgment that the ideas contained in the book or the idea expressed from the author's method of communication are inappropriate for teenage pupils.

The plurality also tells us that a book may be removed from a school library if it is "pervasively vulgar." But why must the vulgarity be "pervasive" to be offensive? Vulgarity might be concentrated in a single poem or a single chapter or a single page, yet still be inappropriate. Or a school board might reasonably conclude that even "random" vulgarity is inappropriate for teenage school students. A school board might also reasonably conclude that the school board's retention of such books gives those volumes an implicit endorsement.

Further, there is no guidance whatsoever as to what constitutes "political" factors. This Court has previously recognized that public education involves an area of broad public policy and "[goes] to the heart of representative government." . . . As such, virtually all educational decisions necessarily involve "political" determinations.

What the plurality views as valid reasons for removing a book at their core involve partisan judgments. Ultimately the federal courts will be the judge of whether the motivation for book removal was "valid" or "reasonable." Undoubtedly the validity of many book removals will ultimately turn on a judge's evaluation of the books. Discretion must be used, and the appropriate body to exercise that discretion is the local elected school board, not judges.

We can all agree that as a matter of *educational policy* students should have wide access to information and ideas. But the people elect school boards, who in turn select administrators, who select the teachers, and these are the individuals best able to determine the substance of that policy. The plurality fails to recognize the fact that local control of education involves democracy in a microcosm. In most public schools in the United States the *parents* have a large voice in running the school. Through participation in the election of school board members, the parents influence, if not control, the direction of their children's education. A school board is not a giant bureaucracy far removed from accountability for its actions; it is truly "of the people and by the people." A school board reflects its constituency in a very real sense and thus could not long exercise unchecked discretion in its choice to acquire or remove books. If the parents disagree with the educational decisions of the school board, they can take steps to remove the board members from office. Finally, even if parents and students cannot convince the school board that book removal is inappropriate, they have alternative sources to the same end. Books may be acquired from bookstores, public libraries, or other alternative sources unconnected with the unique environment of the local public schools.

II

No amount of "limiting" language could rein in the sweeping "right" the plurality would create. The plurality distinguishes library books from textbooks because library books "by their nature are optional rather than required reading." It is not clear, however, why this distinction requires *greater* scrutiny before "optional" reading materials may be removed. It would appear that required reading and textbooks have a greater likelihood of imposing a "pall of orthodoxy" over the educational process than do optional reading. In essence, the plurality's view transforms the availability of this "optional" reading into a "right" to have this "optional" reading maintained at the demand of teenagers.

The plurality also limits the new right by finding it applicable only to the *removal* of books once acquired. Yet if the First Amendment commands that certain books cannot be *removed*, does it not equally require that the same books be *acquired*? Why does the coincidence of timing become the basis of a constitutional holding? According to the plurality, the evil to be avoided is the "official suppression of ideas.". It does not follow that the decision to *remove* a book is less "official suppression" than the decision not to acquire a book desired by someone.[28] Similarly, a decision to eliminate certain material from the curriculum, history for example, would carry an equal — probably greater — prospect of "official suppression." Would the decision be subject to our review?

III

Through use of bits and pieces of prior opinions unrelated to the issue of this case, the plurality demeans our function of constitutional adjudication. Today the plurality suggests that the *Constitution* distinguishes between school libraries and school classrooms, between *removing* unwanted books and *acquiring* books. Even more extreme, the plurality concludes that the Constitution *requires* school boards to justify to its teenage pupils the decision to remove a particular book from a school library. I categorically reject this notion that the Constitution dictates that judges, rather than parents, teachers, and local school boards, must determine how the standards of morality and vulgarity are to be treated in the classroom.

---

28 [8] The formless nature of the "right" found by the plurality in this case is exemplified by this purported distinction. Presumably a school board could, for any reason, choose not to purchase a book for its library. Once it purchases that book, however, it is "locked in" to retaining it on the school shelf until it can justify a reason for its removal. This anomalous result of "book tenure" was pointed out by the District Court in this case. Under the plurality view, if a school board wants to be assured that it maintains control over the education of its students, every page of every book sought to be acquired must be read before a purchase decision is made.

Justice Powell, *dissenting*.

The plurality opinion today rejects a basic concept of public school education in our country: that the States and locally elected school boards should have the responsibility for determining the educational policy of the public schools. After today's decision any junior high school student, by instituting a suit against a school board or teacher, may invite a judge to overrule an educational decision by the official body designated by the people to operate the schools.

I

School boards are uniquely local and democratic institutions. Unlike the governing bodies of cities and counties, school boards have only one responsibility: the education of the youth of our country during their most formative and impressionable years. Apart from health, no subject is closer to the hearts of parents than their children's education during those years. For these reasons, the governance of elementary and secondary education traditionally has been placed in the hands of a local board, responsible locally to the parents and citizens of school districts. Through parent-teacher associations (PTA's), and even less formal arrangements that vary with schools, parents are informed and often may influence decisions of the board. Frequently, parents know the teachers and visit classes. It is fair to say that no single agency of government at any level is closer to the people whom it serves than the typical school board.

I therefore view today's decision with genuine dismay. Whatever the final outcome of this suit and suits like it, the resolution of educational policy decisions through litigation, and the exposure of school board members to liability for such decisions, can be expected to corrode the school board's authority and effectiveness. As is evident from the generality of the plurality's "standard" for judicial review, the decision as to the educational worth of a book is a highly subjective one. Judges rarely are as competent as school authorities to make this decision; nor are judges responsive to the parents and people of the school district.[29]

The new constitutional right, announced by the plurality, is described as a "right to receive ideas" in a school. . . . [T]his newfound right finds no support in the First Amendment precedents of this Court. And even apart from the inappropriateness of judicial oversight of educational policy, the new constitutional right is framed in terms that approach a meaningless generalization. It affords little guidance to courts, if they — as the plurality now authorizes them — are to oversee the inculcation of ideas. The plurality does announce the following standard: A school board's "discretion may not be exercised in a narrowly partisan or political manner." But this is a standardless standard that affords no more than subjective guidance to school boards, their counsel, and to courts that now will be required to decide whether a

---

[29] [1] The plurality speaks of the need for "sensitive" decisionmaking, pursuant to "regular" procedures. One wonders what indeed does this mean. In this case, for example, the board did not act precipitously. It simply did not agree with the recommendations of a committee it had appointed. Would the plurality require — as a constitutional matter — that the board delegate unreviewable authority to such a committee?

particular decision was made in a "narrowly partisan or political manner." Even the "chancellor's foot" standard in ancient equity jurisdiction was never this fuzzy.

How does one limit — on a principled basis — today's new constitutional right? If a 14-year-old child may challenge a school board's decision to remove a book from the library, upon what theory is a court to prevent a like challenge to a school board's decision not to purchase that identical book? And at the even more "sensitive" level of "receiving ideas," does today's decision entitle student oversight of which courses may be added or removed from the curriculum, or even of what a particular teacher elects to teach or not teach in the classroom? Is not the "right to receive ideas" as much — or indeed even more — implicated in these educational questions?[30]

II

. . . .

Just this Term the Court held, in an opinion I joined, that the children of illegal aliens must be permitted to attend the public schools. [*See Plyler v. Doe*]. Quoting from earlier opinions, the Court noted that the "public [school is] a most vital civic institution for the preservation of democratic system of government" and that the public schools are "the primary vehicle for transmitting 'the values on which our society rests.'" By denying to illegal aliens the opportunity "to absorb the values and skills upon which our social order rests" the law under review placed a lifelong disability upon these illegal alien children.

Today the plurality drains much of the content from these apt phrases. A school board's attempt to instill in its students the ideas and values on which a democratic system depends is viewed as an impermissible suppression of other ideas and values on which other systems of government and other societies thrive. Books may not be removed because they are indecent; extol violence, intolerance, and racism; or degrade the dignity of the individual. Human history, not the least that of the 20th century, records the power and political life of these very ideas. But they are not our ideas or values. Although I would leave this educational decision to the duly constituted board, I certainly would not *require* a school board to promote ideas and values repugnant to a democratic society or to teach such values to *children*.

In different contexts and in different times, the destruction of written materials has been the symbol of despotism and intolerance. But the removal of nine vulgar or racist books from a high school library by a concerned local school board does not raise this specter. For me, today's decision symbolizes a debilitating encroachment upon the institutions of a free people.

---

[30] [2] The plurality suggests that the books in a school library derive special protection under the Constitution because the school library is a place in which students exercise unlimited choice. This suggestion is without support in law or fact. It is contradicted by this very case. The school board in this case does not view the school library as a place in which students pick from an unlimited range of books — some of which may be inappropriate for young people. Rather, the school library is analogous to an assigned reading list within which students may exercise a degree of choice.

Attached as an Appendix hereto is Judge Mansfield's summary of excerpts from the books at issue in this case.

Appendix to Opinion of POWELL, J., dissenting

"The excerpts which led the Board to look into the educational suitability of the books in question are set out (with minor corrections after comparison with the text of the books themselves) below. The pagination and the underlinings are retained from the original report used by the board. In newer editions of some of the books, the quotes appear at different pages.

"1) *SOUL ON ICE* by Eldridge Cleaver

PAGE QUOTE

157–158 '. . . There are white men who will pay you to fuck their wives. They approach you and say, "How would you like to fuck a white woman?" "What is this?" you ask. "On the up-and-up," he assures you. "It's all right. She's my wife. She needs black rod, is all. She has to have it. It's like a medicine or drug to her. She has to have it. I'll pay you. It's all on the level, no trick involved. Interested?" You go with him and he drives you to their home. The three of you go into the bedroom. There is a certain type who will leave you and his wife alone and tell you to pile her real good. After it is all over, he will pay you and drive you to wherever you want to go. Then there are some who like to peep at you through a keyhole and watch you have his woman, or peep at you through a window, or lie under the bed and listen to the creaking of the bed as you work out. There is another type who likes to masturbate while he stands beside the bed and watches you pile her. There is the type who likes to eat his woman up after you get through piling her. And there is the type who only wants you to pile her for a little while, just long enough to thaw her out and kick her motor over and arouse her to heat, then he wants you to jump off real quick and he will jump onto her and together they can make it from there by themselves.'

"2) *A HERO AIN'T NOTHING BUT A SANDWICH* by Alice Childress

PAGE QUOTE

10 'Hell, no! *Fuck the society.*'

64–65 'The hell with the junkie, the wino, the capitalist, the welfare checks, the world . . . yeah, and *fuck* you too!'

75–76 'They can have back the spread and curtains, I'm too old for them *fuckin* bunnies anyway.'

"3) *THE FIXER* by Bernard Malamud

PAGE QUOTE

52 'What do you think goes on in the wagon at night: Are the drivers on their knees *fucking their mothers?*'

90 '*Fuck yourself*, said the blinker, etc.'

92 'Who else would do anything like that but a *mother-fucking* Zhid?'

146 'No more noise out of you or I'll shoot your *Jew cock off.*'

189 'Also there's a lot of *fucking in the Old Testament*, so how is that religious?'

192 'You better go *fuck yourself*, Bok, said Kogin, I'm onto your Jew tricks.'

215 'Ding-dong giddyap. A *Jew's cock's* in the devil's hock.'

216 'You *cocksucker* Zhid, I ought make you lick it up off the floor.'

"4) *GO ASK ALICE* by Anonymous

PAGE QUOTE

31 'I wonder if sex without acid could be so exciting, so wonderful, so inde-scribable. I always thought it just took a minute, or that it would be like dogs mating.'

47 'Chris and I walked into Richie and Ted's apartment to find the bastards stoned and making love to each other . . . low class queer.'

81 'shitty, goddamned, pissing, ass, goddamned beJesus, screwing life's, ass, shit. Doris was ten and had *humped* with who knows how many men in between . . . her current stepfather started having sex with her but good . . . *sonofabitch balling her*'.

83 'but now when I face a girl its like facing a boy. I get all excited and turned on. *I want to screw with the girl. . . .*'

84 'I'd rather screw with a guy . . . sometimes I want one of the girls to kiss me. I want her to touch me, to have her sleep under me.'

84 'Another day, another *blow job* . . . If I don't give *Big Ass a blow* he'll cut off my supply . . . and LittleJacon is yelling, "Mama, *Daddy can't come now. He's humping Carla*."

85 'Shit, goddamn, goddamn prick, son-of-a-bitch, ass, pissed, bastard, goddamn, bullshit.

94 'I hope you have a *nice orgasm with your dog tonight.*'

110 'You *fucking* Miss Polly pure.'

117 'Then he said that all I needed was a good *fuck.*'

146 'It might be great because I'm practically a virgin in the sense that I've never had sex except when I've been stoned. . . .'

"5) *SLAUGHTERHOUSE FIVE* by Kurt Vonnegut, Jr.

PAGE QUOTE

29 'Get out of the road, you dumb *motherfucker.*' The last word was still a novelty in the speech of white people in 1944. It was fresh and astonishing to Billy, who had never *fucked* anybody . . . .'

32 'You stake a guy out on an anthill in the desert — see? He's facing upward, and you put *honey* all over his *balls and pecker*, and you cut off his eyelids so he has to stare at the sun till he dies.'

34 'He had a prophylactic kit containing two tough condoms 'For the preven-tion of disease only!' . . . He had a dirty picture of a *woman* attempting *sexual intercourse with a shetland pony.*'

94 & 95 'But the Gospels actually taught this: Before you kill somebody, make absolutely sure he isn't well connected . . . The flaw in the Christ stories, said the visitor from outer space, was that Christ who didn't look

like much, was actually the son of the Most Powerful Being in the Universe. Readers understood that, so, when they came to the crucifixion, they naturally thought . . . Oh boy — they sure picked the wrong guy to lynch this time! And that thought had a brother: There are right people to lynch. People not well connected . . . . The visitor from outer space made a gift to Earth of a new Gospel. In it, Jesus really WAS a nobody, and a pain in the neck to a lot of people with better connections then he had . . . . So the people amused themselves one day by nailing him to a cross and planting the cross in the ground. There couldn't possibly be any repercussions, the lynchers thought . . . since the new Gospel hammered home again and again what a nobody Jesus was. And then just before the nobody died . . . . The voice of God came crashing down. He told the people that he was adopting the bum as his son . . . God said this: *From this moment on, He will punish horribly anybody who torments a bum who has no connections.'*

99 'They told him that there could be no Earthling babies without male homosexuals. There could be babies without female homosexuals.'

120 'Why don't you go *fuck* yourself? Don't think I haven't tried . . . he was going to have revenge, and that revenge was sweet . . . It's the sweetest thing there is, said Lazzaro. People *fuck* with me, he said, and *Jesus Christ* are they ever fucking sorry.'

122 'And he'll pull out a gun and *shoot his pecker off*. The stranger'll let him think a couple of seconds about who Paul Lazzaro is and what life's gonna be like without a *pecker*. Then he'll shoot him once in the guts and walk away. . . . He died on account of this silly *cocksucker* here. So I promised him I'd have this silly *cocksucker* shot after the war.'

134 'In my prison cell I sit . . . With my *britches full of shit*, And my *balls are bouncing* gently on the floor. And I see the bloody snag when she bit me in the bag . . . Oh, I'll never fuck *a Polack* any more.'

173 'And the peckers of the young men would still be *semierect*, and their *muscles* would be *bulging like cannonballs*.'

175 'They didn't have *hard-ons* . . . Everybody else did.'

177 'The magazine, which was published for *lonesome men to jerk off to*.'

178 'and one critic said. . . . 'To describe *blow-jobs* artistically.''

"6) *THE BEST SHORT STORIES BY NEGRO WRITERS* Ed. *by Langston Hughes*

PAGE QUOTE

176 'like bat's shit and camel piss,' . . .

228 'that no-count bitch of a daughter of yours is up there up North making a whore of herself.'

237 'they made her get out and stand in front of the headlights of the car and pull down her pants and raise her dress — they said that was the only way they could be sure. And you can imagine what they said and what they did — .'

303 'You need some pussy. Come on, let's go up to the whore house on the hill.'

'Oh, these bastards, these bastards, this God damned Army and the bastards in it. The sons of bitches!'

436 'he produced a brown rag doll, looked at her again, then grabbed the doll by its legs and tore it part way up the middle. Then he jammed his finger into the rip between the doll's legs. The other men laughed. . . .'

444 'The pimps, hustlers, lesbians, and others trying to misuse me.'

462 'But she had straight firm legs and her breasts were small and upright. No doubt if she'd had children her breasts would be hanging like little empty purses.'

464 'She first became aware of the warm tense nipples on her breasts. Her hands went up gently to clam them.' 'In profile, his penis hung like a stout tassle. She could even tell that he was circumcised.'

406 'Cadillac Bill was busy following Luheaster around, rubbing her stomach and saying, "Magic Stomach, Magic Stomach, bring me a little baby cadillac.' " 'One of the girls went upstairs with Red Top and stayed for about forty-five minutes.'

"7) *BLACK BOY* by Richard Wright

PAGE QUOTE

70–71 'We black children — seven or eight or nine years of age — used to run to the Jew's store and shout:

   . . . Bloody Christ Killers

Never trust a Jew

Bloody Christ Killers

What won't a Jew do . . .

Red, white and blue

Your pa was a Jew

Your ma a dirty dago

What the hell is you?'

265 'Crush that nigger's nuts, nigger!' 'Hit that nigger!'

'Aw, fight, you goddam niggers!' 'Sock 'im, in his f-k-g-piece!' 'Make 'im bleed!'

"8) *LAUGHING BOY* by Oliver LaFarge

PAGE QUOTE

38 'I'll tell you, she is all bad; for two bits she will do the worst thing.'

258–9 'I was frightened when he wanted me to lie with him, but he made me feel all right. He knew all about how to make women forget themselves, that man.'

"9) *THE NAKED APE* by Desmond Morris

PAGE QUOTE

73–74 'Also, the frontal approach provides the maximum possibility for stimulation of the female's clitoris during the pelvic thrusting of the male.

It is true that it will be passively, stimulated by the pulling effect of the male's thrusts, regardless of his body position in relation to the female, but in a face-to-face mating there will in addition be the direct rhythmic pressure of the male's pubic region on to the clitoral area, and this will considerably heighten the stimulation . . .' 'So it seems plausible to consider that face-to-face copulation is basic to our species. There are, of course, a number of variations that do not eliminate the frontal element: male above, female above, side by side, squatting, standing, and so on, but the most efficient and commonly used one is with both partners horizontal, the male above the female. . . .'

80 '. . . This broadening of the penis results in the female's external genitals being subjected to much more pulling and pushing during the performance of pelvic thrusts. With each inward thrust of the penis, the clitoral region is pulled downwards and then with each withdrawal, it moves up again. Add to this the rhythmic pressure being exerted on the clitoris region by the pubic region of the frontally copulating male, and you have a repeated massaging of the clitoris that — were she a male — would virtually be masturbatory.'

94–99 '. . . If either males or females cannot for some reason obtain sexual access to their opposite numbers, they will find sexual outlets in other ways. They may use other members of their own sex, or they may even use members of other species, or they may masturbate. . . .'

"10) *READER FOR WRITERS* . . ."

638 F.2d 404, 419–422, n. 1 (CA2 1980) (Mansfield, J., dissenting).

JUSTICE REHNQUIST, with whom the CHIEF JUSTICE and JUSTICE POWELL join, *dissenting.*

. . . .

A

. . . .

In the course of his discussion, Justice BRENNAN states:

> Petitioners rightly possess significant discretion to determine the content of their school libraries. But that discretion may not be exercised in a narrowly partisan or political manner. If a Democratic school board, motivated by party affiliation, ordered the removal of all books written by or in favor of Republicans, few would doubt that the order violated the constitutional rights of the students . . . . The same conclusion would surely apply if an all-white school board, motivated by racial animus, decided to remove all books authored by blacks or advocating racial equality and integration. Our Constitution does not permit the official suppression of *ideas.*

I can cheerfully concede all of this, but as in so many other cases the extreme examples are seldom the ones that arise in the real world of constitutional litigation. In *this case* the facts taken most favorably to respondents suggest that nothing of this sort happened. The nine books removed undoubtedly did contain "ideas," but in the light of the excerpts from them found in the dissenting opinion of Judge Mansfield in the Court of Appeals, it is apparent that eight of them contained demonstrable amounts of vulgarity and profanity, . . . and the ninth contained nothing that could be considered partisan or political. . . . As already demonstrated, respondents admitted as much. Petitioners did not, for the reasons stated hereafter, run afoul of the First and Fourteenth Amendments by removing these particular books from the library in the manner in which they did. I would save for another day — feeling quite confident that that day will not arrive — the extreme examples posed in Justice Brennan's opinion.

B

Considerable light is shed on the correct resolution of the constitutional question in this case by examining the role played by petitioners. Had petitioners been the members of a town council, I suppose all would agree that, absent a good deal more than is present in this record, they could not have prohibited the sale of these books by private booksellers within the municipality. But we have also recognized that the government may act in other capacities than as sovereign, and when it does the First Amendment may speak with a different voice:

> "[It] cannot be gainsaid that the State has interests as an employer in regulating the speech of its employees that differ significantly from those it possesses in connection with regulation of the speech of the citizenry in general. The problem in any case is to arrive at a balance between the interests of the teacher, as a citizen, in commenting upon matters of concern and the interest of the State, as an employer, in promoting the efficiency of the public services it performs through its employees."

By the same token, expressive conduct which may not be prohibited by the State as sovereign may be proscribed by the State as property owner: "The State, no less than a private owner of property, has power to preserve the property under its control for the use to which it is lawfully dedicated."

With these differentiated roles of government in mind, it is helpful to assess the role of government as educator, as compared with the role of government as sovereign. When it acts as an educator, at least at the elementary and secondary school level, the government is engaged in inculcating social values and knowledge in relatively impressionable young people. Obviously there are innumerable decisions to be made as to what courses should be taught, what books should be purchased, or what teachers should be employed. In every one of these areas the members of a school board will act on the basis of their own personal or moral values, will attempt to mirror those of the community, or will abdicate the making of such decisions to so-called "experts." In this connection I find myself entirely in agreement with the observation of the Court of Appeals for the Seventh Circuit in *Zykan v. Warsaw Community School Corp.*, 631 F.2d 1300, 1305 (1980), that it is "permissible and appropriate for local boards to make educational decisions based upon their personal social, political and moral views." In the very course of administering the many-faceted operations of a school district, the mere decision to purchase some books will necessarily preclude the possibility of purchasing others. The decision to teach a particular subject may preclude the possibility of teaching another subject. A decision to replace a teacher because of ineffectiveness may by implication be seen as a disparagement of the subject matter taught. In each of these instances, however, the book or the exposure to the subject matter may be acquired elsewhere. The managers of the school district are not proscribing it as to the citizenry in general, but are simply determining that it will not be included in the curriculum or school library. In short, actions by the government as educator do not raise the same First Amendment concerns as actions by the government as sovereign.

II

Justice BRENNAN would hold that the First Amendment gives high school and junior high school students a "right to receive ideas" in the school. This right is a curious entitlement. It exists only in the library of the school, and only if the idea previously has been acquired by the school in book form. It provides no protection against a school board's decision not to acquire a particular book, even though that decision denies access to ideas as fully as removal of the book from the library, and it prohibits removal of previously acquired books only if the remover "[dislikes] the ideas contained in those books," even though removal for any other reason also denies the students access to the books.

But it is not the limitations which Justice BRENNAN places on the right with which I disagree; they simply demonstrate his discomfort with the new doctrine which he fashions out of whole cloth. It is the very existence of a right to receive information, in the junior high school and high school setting, which I find wholly unsupported by our past decisions and inconsistent with the necessarily selective process of elementary and secondary education.

A

The right described by Justice BRENNAN has never been recognized in the decisions of this Court and is not supported by their rationale. Justice BRENNAN correctly observes that students do not "shed their constitutional rights to freedom of speech or expression at the schoolhouse gate." But, as this language from *Tinker* suggests, our past decisions in this area have concerned freedom of speech and expression, not the right of access to particular ideas. . . . Neither the District Court nor the Court of Appeals found that petitioners' removal of books from the school libraries infringed respondents' right to speak or otherwise express themselves.

Despite Justice BRENNAN's suggestion to the contrary, this Court has never held that the First Amendment grants junior high school and high school students a right of access to certain information in school. It is true that the Court has recognized a limited version of that right in other settings, and Justice BRENNAN quotes language from five such decisions and one of his own concurring opinions in order to demonstrate the viability of the right-to-receive doctrine. But not one of these cases concerned or even purported to discuss elementary or secondary educational institutions. Justice BRENNAN brushes over this significant omission in First Amendment law by citing for the proposition that "students too are beneficiaries of this [right-to-receive] principle." But *Tinker* held no such thing. One may read *Tinker* in vain to find any recognition of a First Amendment right to receive information. . . .

Nor does the right-to-receive doctrine recognized in our past decisions apply to schools by analogy. Justice BRENNAN correctly characterizes the right of access to ideas as "an inherent corollary of the rights of free speech and press" which "follows ineluctably from the *sender's* First Amendment right to send them." But he then fails to recognize the predicate right to speak from which the students' right to receive must follow. It would be ludicrous, of course, to contend that all authors have a constitutional right to have their books placed in junior high school and high school libraries. . . . Justice BRENNAN . . . fails to explain the constitutional or logical underpinnings of a right to hear ideas in a place where no speaker has the right to express them. . . .

Our past decisions are thus unlike this case where the removed books are readily available to students and nonstudents alike at the corner bookstore or the public library.

B

There are even greater reasons for rejecting Justice BRENNAN's analysis, however, than the significant fact that we have never adopted it in the past. "The importance of public schools in the preparation of individuals for participation as citizens, and in the preservation of the values on which our society rests, has long been recognized by our decisions." Public schools fulfill the vital role of teaching students the basic skills necessary to function in our society, and of "inculcating fundamental values necessary to the maintenance of a democratic political system." The idea that such students have a right of access, *in the school,* to information other than that thought by their educators to be necessary is contrary to the very nature of an inculcative education.

Education consists of the selective presentation and explanation of ideas. The effective acquisition of knowledge depends upon an orderly exposure to relevant information. Nowhere is this more true than in elementary and secondary schools, where, unlike the broad-ranging inquiry available to university students, the courses taught are those thought most relevant to the young students' individual development. Of necessity, elementary and secondary educators must separate the relevant from the irrelevant, the appropriate from the inappropriate. Determining what information *not* to present to the students is often as important as identifying relevant material. This winnowing process necessarily leaves much information to be discovered by students at another time or in another place, and is fundamentally inconsistent with any constitutionally required eclecticism in public education. . . .

As already mentioned, elementary and secondary schools are inculcative in nature. The libraries of such schools serve as supplements to this inculcative role. Unlike university or public libraries, elementary and secondary school libraries are not designed for freewheeling inquiry; they are tailored, as the public school curriculum is tailored, to the teaching of basic skills and ideas. Thus, Justice BRENNAN cannot rely upon the nature of school libraries to escape the fact that the First Amendment right to receive information simply has no application to the one public institution which, by its very nature, is a place for the selective conveyance of ideas.

After all else is said, however, the most obvious reason that petitioners' removal of the books did not violate respondents' right to receive information is the ready availability of the books elsewhere. Students are not denied books by their removal from a school library. The books may be borrowed from a public library, read at a university library, purchased at a bookstore, or loaned by a friend. The government as educator does not seek to reach beyond the confines of the school. Indeed, following the removal from the school library of the books at issue in this case, the local public library put all nine books on display for public inspection. Their contents were fully accessible to any inquisitive student.

C

Justice BRENNAN's own discomfort with the idea that students have a right to receive information from their elementary or secondary schools is demonstrated by the artificial limitations which he places upon the right — limitations which are supported neither by logic nor authority and which are inconsistent with the right itself. The attempt to confine the right to the library is one such limitation, the fallacies of which have already been demonstrated.

As a second limitation, Justice BRENNANn distinguishes the act of removing a previously acquired book from the act of refusing to acquire the book in the first place . . . . If Justice BRENNAN truly has found a "right to receive ideas," however, this distinction between acquisition and removal makes little sense. The failure of a library to acquire a book denies access to its contents just as effectively as does the removal of the book from the library's shelf.

* * *

The justification for this limiting distinction is said by Justice BRENNAN to be his concern in this case with "the suppression of ideas." Whatever may be the analytical usefulness of this appealing sounding phrase, the suppression of ideas surely is not the identical twin of the denial of access to information. Not every official act which denies access to an idea can be characterized as a suppression of the idea. Thus unless the "right to receive information" and the prohibition against "suppression of ideas" are each a kind of Mother-Hubbard catch phrase for whatever First Amendment doctrines one wishes to cover, they would not appear to be interchangeable.

* * *

The final limitation placed by Justice BRENNAN upon his newly discovered right is a motive requirement: the First Amendment is violated only "[if] petitioners *intended* by their removal decision to deny respondents access to ideas with which petitioners disagreed." (emphasis in original). But bad motives and good motives alike deny access to the books removed. If Justice Brennan truly recognizes a constitutional right to receive information, it is difficult to see why the reason for the denial makes any difference. Of course Justice BRENNAN's view is that intent matters because the First Amendment does not tolerate an officially prescribed orthodoxy. But this reasoning mixes First Amendment apples and oranges. The right to receive information differs from the right to be free from an officially prescribed orthodoxy. Not every educational denial of access to information casts a pall of orthodoxy over the classroom.

It is difficult to tell from Justice BRENNAN's opinion just what motives he would consider constitutionally impermissible. I had thought that the First Amendment proscribes content-based restrictions on the marketplace of ideas. Justice BRENNAN concludes, however, that a removal decision based solely upon the "educational suitability" of a book or upon its perceived vulgarity is "perfectly permissible." But such determinations are based as much on the content of the book as determinations that the book espouses pernicious political views.

Moreover, Justice BRENNAN's motive test is difficult to square with his distinction between acquisition and removal. If a school board's removal of books might be motivated by a desire to promote favored political or religious views, there is no reason that its acquisition policy might not also be so motivated. And yet the "pall of orthodoxy" cast by a carefully executed book-acquisition program apparently would not violate the First Amendment under Justice BRENNAN's view.

D

Intertwined as a basis for Justice BRENNAN's opinion, along with the "right to receive information," is the statement that "[our] Constitution does not permit the official suppression of *ideas*." There would be few champions, I suppose, of the idea that our Constitution *does* permit the official suppression of ideas; my difficulty is not with the admittedly appealing catchiness of the phrase, but with my doubt that it is really a useful analytical tool in solving difficult First Amendment problems. . . . A school board which publicly adopts a policy forbidding the criticism of United States foreign policy by any student, any teacher, or any book on the library shelves is indulging in one kind of "suppression of ideas." A school board which adopts a policy that there shall be no discussion of current events in a class for high school sophomores devoted to second-year Latin "suppresses ideas" in quite a different context. A teacher who had a lesson plan consisting of 14 weeks of study of United States history from 1607 to the present time, but who because of a week's illness is forced to forgo the most recent 20 years of American history, may "suppress ideas" in still another way. . . .

In the case before us the petitioners may in one sense be said to have "suppressed" the "ideas" of vulgarity and profanity, but that is hardly an apt description of what was done. They ordered the removal of books containing vulgarity and profanity, but they did not attempt to preclude discussion about the themes of the books or the books themselves. Such a decision, on respondents' version of the facts in this case, is sufficiently related to "educational suitability" to pass muster under the First Amendment.

E

[T]he criticism of Justice BRENNAN's newly found prohibition against the "suppression of ideas" is by no means intended to suggest that the Constitution permits the suppression of ideas; it is rather to suggest that such a vague and imprecise phrase, while perhaps wholly consistent with the First Amendment, is simply too diaphanous to assist careful decision of cases such as this one.

I think the Court will far better serve the cause of First Amendment jurisprudence by candidly recognizing that the role of government as sovereign is subject to more stringent limitations than is the role of government as employer, property owner, or educator. It must also be recognized that the government as educator is subject to fewer strictures when operating an elementary and secondary school system than when operating an institution of higher learning. . . . With respect to the education of children in elementary and secondary schools, the school board may properly determine in many cases that a particular book, a particular course, or even a particular area of knowledge is not educationally suitable for inclusion within the body of knowledge which the school seeks to impart. Without more, this is not a condemnation of the book or the course; it is only a determination akin to that referred to by the Court in *Village of Euclid v. Ambler Realty Co.*, 272 U.S. 365, 388 (1926): "A nuisance may be merely a right thing in the wrong place, — like a pig in the parlor instead of the barnyard."

*   *   *

JUSTICE O'CONNOR, *dissenting*.

If the school board can set the curriculum, select teachers, and determine initially what books to purchase for the school library, it surely can decide which books to discontinue or remove from the school library so long as it does not also interfere with the right of students to read the material and to discuss it. . . .

I do not personally agree with the Board's action with respect to some of the books in question here, but it is not the function of the courts to make the decisions that have been properly relegated to the elected members of school boards. It is the school board that must determine educational suitability, and it has done so in this case. I therefore join the Chief Justice's dissent.

————

NOTES AND QUESTIONS

1. Justice Brennan's opinion in *Pico* was a plurality opinion. Part II-A-(1), which claimed the Constitution's protection of a student's right to receive

information and ideas, was joined by only Justice Marshall and Justice Stevens. Nevertheless, courts cite *Pico* for that very proposition. *See, e.g., Student Press Law Center v. Alexander,* 778 F. Supp. 1227 (D.D.C. 1991) ("The Supreme Court has noted in a variety of contexts that the First Amendment 'protects the right to receive information and ideas' " (quoting *Pico*)); *Schuloff v. Fields,* 950 F. Supp. 66 (E.D.N.Y. 1997) ("The First Amendment protects 'the right to receive information and ideas.' " (citing *Pico*)); *U.S. v. Miami Univ.,* 91 F. Supp. 2d 1132 (S.D. Ohio 2000) ("It is well settled that the right to receive information 'is an inherent corollary of the rights of free speech and press that are explicitly guaranteed by the Constitution. . . .' " (quoting *Pico*); *Ruiz v. Hull,* 957 P.2d 984 (Ariz. 1998) ("In *Board of Education v. Pico,* 457 U.S. 853, 867, the Court recognized that 'the right to receive ideas is a necessary predicate to the recipient's meaningful exercise of his own rights of speech, press and political freedom.' "); *Rossignol v. Voorhaar,* 316 F.3d 516, 522 (4th Cir. 2003) (The First Amendment "protects both a speaker's right to communicate information and ideas to a broad audience and the intended recipients' right to receive that information and those ideas" (citing *Pico*)); *Counts v. Cedarville Sch. Dist.,* 295 F. Supp. 2d 996, 999 (W.D. Ark. 2003) ("the right to read a book is an aspect of the right to receive information and ideas," an "inherent corollary of the rights of free speech and press that are explicitly guaranteed by the Constitution" (citing *Pico*)); *Student Members of SAME v. Rumsfeld,* 321 F. Supp. 2d 388, 394 (D. Conn. 2004) (stating "the Supreme Court has called the right to receive information 'an inherent corollary of the rights of free speech and press that are explicitly guaranteed by the Constitution' " (citing *Pico*)).

2. Did Justice Brennan's opinion go too far in setting forth a constitutional right of students to receive information and ideas? Or — by failing to extend the right to the acquisition decision — did his opinion not go far enough? What is the basis in the Constitution for recognizing a right to receive information? Do students in elementary, middle, or high school gain this right to receive speech as a necessary corollary of their First Amendment right to expression?

3. Consider the criticisms levied by the dissents. Based on the *Pico* decision, is a student likely to prevail in a lawsuit claiming that the school board refused to acquire a book that she wished to read? If the "right to receive" does not include the decision to acquire books, why should it include the decision to remove books?

Does Justice Brennan mean that a school cannot remove a book once it has been acquired? As school board counsel, how would you advise the school board to proceed if it needed to cull books from the school libraries because of space constraints?

Why should the motivation of the school board be a part of the analysis? If students have the "right to receive" ideas, why should the reason for a book's removal be relevant? If a book is removed because of space concerns and/or financial reasons (rather than because the school board does not like its content) is the student still deprived of access to these ideas?

4. How should "mixed motive" cases be handled? School board members may believe that a book should be removed because it is pervasively vulgar or based on its "educational suitablity" (reasons that would pass muster according to

Justice Brennan); yet they may also strongly disagree with the political content in the book. What if the vulgarity is merely contained on one page in a 200-page book? What makes a book educationally unsuitable? How can a court review a school board decision that was made based on a standard like "educational suitability?" Will school board members be tempted to fabricate motives that pass muster to camouflage the real reason they are removing a book?

5. What is the difference between a decision that is legitimately based on "inculcating fundamental values necessary to the maintenance of a democratic political system" and a decision that is illegitimately based on a school official "prescrib [ing] what shall be orthodox in politics, nationalism, religion, or other matters of opinion." If students can be deprived of books that are pervasively vulgar or that advocate drug use, sexual promiscuity, racism or sexism, this would seem to allow school officials the power to close students' minds and to prescribe what shall be orthodox in these matters.

6. Consider the function of the school library and how it connects with the right to receive information and ideas. Does the school library perform the same function throughout lower education? Is it up to the courts or the local school boards to decide what that function will be?

7. One theme running through the dissents is the criticism that Justice Brennan's opinion is anti-democratic. Explain how the dissenters' view of the role of the school board in a democracy differs from that of Justice Brennan and the other Justices who joined his opinion.

8. For more on book removal, see *Counts v. Cedarville Sch. Dist.*, 295 F. Supp. 2d 996 (W.D. Ark. 2003) (finding violation of First Amendment where school board removed Harry Potter series from general circulation in the library and required parental consent to check the books out; policy imposed a burden on student's right to access the book and stigmatized both the books and the students who read them); *Case v. Unified Sch. Dist. No. 233*, 908 F. Supp. 864 (D. Kan. 1995) (removal of *Annie on My Mind*, an award-winning novel with a lesbian story line, was unconstitutional; board members removed book because they disagreed with the book's ideas); *Monteiro v. Tempe Union High Sch. Dist.*, 158 F.3d 1022, 1030 (9th Cir. 1998) (finding that even if the accused works (*Huckleberry Finn, A Rose for Emily*) are racist, a court cannot ban books based on their content; "permitting lawsuits against school districts on the content of literary works . . . could have a chilling effect on a school district's willingness to assign books with themes, characters, snippets of dialogue, or words that might offend the sensibilities of any member of persons or groups"); *Maryland Schools Remove 2 Black-Authored Books*, L.A. TIMES, Jan. 11, 1998, at A6 (discussing removal of Toni Morrison's *Song of Solomon* and Maya Angelou's *I Know Why the Caged Bird Sings* due to parental complaints that they were "trash" and "anti-white"); Jaime Marernee, *Board to Take "Bird" Off List*, ST. PETERSBURG TIMES, June 2, 1998, at 1 (reporting on parent effort to remove Angelou work from eighth-grade reading list); Rebecca Sausner, *Burlington Board Removes Book on Apartheid*, HARTFORD COURANT, Jan. 14, 1997, at A8 (*Kaffir Boy* by Mark Mathabane).

THE RIGHT TO RECEIVE AND THE INTERNET

Consider how the Gaylin report, cited by Justice Brennan in *Ginsberg* and described at the beginning of this section, should influence the issue of internet filtering. Passed in December 2000, the Children's Internet Protection Act (CIPA, 20 U.S.C. § 9134 and 47 U.S.C. § 254(h)) requires schools and libraries to install filters to block patrons from accessing certain "visual depictions" or lose federal funding for technology, including federal E-rate discounts for telecommunication services. To be "certified" with respect to its internet service to minors, a library must install filters that block access to obscenity, child pornography and depictions that are "harmful to minors." The filter may be disengaged for an adult who is doing "bona fide" research. § 254(h)(5)(D). The ACLU led a challenge to the law regarding public libraries, claiming because the technology is unable to block only unlawful speech, the filters will suppress ideas and viewpoints that are constitutionally protected. It is alleged that the statute suffers from the same First Amendment flaws that were problems in *United States v. Reno,* 521 U.S. 844 (1997) (discussed in greater detail below), where the U. S. Supreme Court determined that the statute, although designed to protect children, unconstitutionally prevented adult internet users from accessing constitutionally protected material. The three-judge panel (convened pursuant to CIPA) held in a 195-page decision that two sections of CIPA were facially invalid, because any public library that adhered to CIPA's conditions would necessarily restrict patron's access to a substantial amount of protected speech. *American Library Ass'n, Inc. v. U.S.,* 201 F. Supp. 2d 401 (E.D. Pa. 2002). A divided U. S. Supreme Court reversed. *United States v. American Library Ass'n,* 539 U.S. 194 (2003). Chief Justice Rehnquist delivered the opinion of the Court, and was joined by Justices O'Connor, Scalia and Thomas. The opinion stated that filtering was a "collection decision," not a restraint on private speech. According to the Chief Justice's opinion, this merely fulfills the traditional role of libraries to identify suitable and worthwhile material. The opinion pointed out that since a library's decision to exclude pornography from its print collection is not subject to heightened scrutiny, a library's decision to block online pornography should not have to meet a higher standard. If a public library's use of Internet filtering software would not violate a patron's First Amendment rights, CIPA does not induce libraries to violate the U.S. Constitution. Justice Kennedy and Justice Breyer each wrote separate opinions concurring in the judgment. Justice Stevens and Justice Souter each wrote separate dissenting opinions. Justice Ginsberg joined with Justice Souter.

Other attempts by Congress to protect minors from internet speech have met with skepticism by the courts. Title V of the Telecommunications Act of 1996 included the Community Decency Act, which made it a crime to use a computer to transmit any "obscene, lewd, lascivious, filthy, or indecent [communications] with intent to annoy, abuse, threaten or harass another person." 47 U.S.C. § 223(a)(1)(A) (Supp. 1996). It made it a crime to transmit any obscene or indecent communication if the party transmitting knew the recipient was under the age of eighteen. § 223(a)(1)(B). In addition, the CDA made it a crime to use a computer to transmit to a minor communication that depicted or described sexual or excretory functions that are patently offensive to contemporary community standards or to transmit the communication in

such a way that it would be accessible to anyone under 18 years old.
§ 223(d)(1)(A) & (B). The United States Supreme Court struck down § 223(a)
and § 223(d) in *Reno v. ACLU,* 521 U.S. 844 (1997), determining that the
provisions lacked the precision required of statutes that regulate the content
of speech. The Court held that the provisions were overbroad (because there
was no feasible way for adults to engage in constitutionally protected indecent
speech) and vague (because the failure to define terms like "indecent" and
"patently offensive" left speakers uncertain as to what the terms meant).

Undaunted, Congress passed the Child Online Protection Act (COPA),
which President Clinton signed into law in 1998. COPA makes it a crime
knowingly to make "any communication for commercial purposes that is
available to any minor and that includes any material that is harmful to
minors." 47 U.S.C.§ 231(a)(1). Unlike CDA, COPA applies only to commercial
web sites. Material that is "harmful to minors" includes material that "the
average person, applying contemporary community standards, would find,
taking the material as a whole and with respect to minors, is designed to
appeal to or is designed to pander to, the prurient interest." 47 U.S.C.
§ 231(e)(6)(A) (1998) (the quoted material is the first of three provisions that
attempt to define "harmful to minors"). *Cf. Miller v. California,* 413 U.S. 15
(1973). Affirmative defenses to liability include requiring a credit card, debit
card, or a digital certificate that verifies age. 47 USC § 231(c)(1)(b). In *ACLU
v. Reno,* 217 F.3d 162 (3d Cir. 2000), the Third Circuit affirmed the order of the
Eastern District of Pennsylvania, which had temporarily enjoined the enforcement of COPA, because requiring Web publishers to abide by the most restrictive
community standards to avoid liability impermissibly burdened speech. The
United States Supreme Court granted certiorari, and held that COPA's reliance
on "community standards" did not render the statute overbroad for the purposes
of the First Amendment. The Court remanded the case to the district court to
detrmine if COPA suffers from any other constitutional infirmity. *Ashcroft v.
ACLU,* 535 U.S. 564 (2002). On remand, the Third Circuit determined that
COPA was not narrowly tailored to serve a compelling Government interest, was
overbroad, and was not the least restrictive means to serve the interest of
preventing minors from using the Internet to gain access to harmful materials.
322 F.3d 240 (3d Cir. 2003). The Supreme Court affirmed the preliminary
injunction and remanded once again for trial, allowing the parties to update and
supplement the factual record to reflect current technology. 542 U.S. 656 (2004).

Could a parent successfully claim that school libraries or public libraries
harmed her child by allowing the child to access pornography? *See Kathleen
R. v. City of Livermore,* 104 Cal. Rptr. 2d 772 (Cal. Ct. App. 2001). Kathleen
R. filed a lawsuit against the City of Livermore, California, setting forth both
state and federal claims. She claimed that the City was wasting public funds
on computers that provide access to obscenity and matter harmful to minors;
that it was a public nuisance for respondent knowingly to allow its computers
to be used to access obscenity and matter harmful to minors; and that the
library was unsafe for minors because the computers provide them with access
to harmful matter. The substantive due process section 1983 claim alleged
the following: minors were expected to go to the library to complete public
school assignments; the library encouraged minors to use its computers; the
library had a policy of allowing minors to view and download obscenity and

pornography on the computers; minors exposed to obscenity and pornography suffered emotional and psychological damage and damage to their nervous systems; the city knew its actions and policies placed minors at grave risk of harm; and the city tried to keep parents ignorant of that risk.

The *Kathleen R.* court noted, "A public library is in a "damned if you do, damned if you don't" situation in deciding whether to restrict access to the Internet from its computers to prevent harm to minors. As the court pointed out, *Mainstream Loudoun v. Bd. of Trustees of Loudoun,* 24 F. Supp. 2d 552 (E.D.Va. 1998), showed that a library can be sued if it limits internet access, and the *Kathleen R.* case shows that a library can be sued if it does not limit internet access.

In *Mainstream Loudoun,* county policy requiring use of filtering software on all library computers to filter out child pornography and obscene material (hard core pornography) as well as material deemed harmful to juveniles (soft core pornography) was found to violate the First Amendment. The court determined that internet filtering was analogous to removing books from library shelves, citing *Pico,* and held that the library must satisfy strict scrutiny before regulating exposure to speech based on content. *See Mainstream Loudoun v. Bd. of Trustees,* 2 F. Supp. 2d 783 (E.D. Va. 1998) (denying defendant's summary judgment motion). Later, when granting the plaintiff's motion for summary judgment, the court observed that neither obscenity nor child pornography was protected speech, but that material that came under the definition of "harmful to juveniles" was protected for adults. 24 F. Supp. 552 (E.D. Va. 1998). Thus, this particular regulation was in contravention of the Supreme Court's statement in *Reno v. ACLU* that "the government may not reduce the adult population . . . to . . . only what is fit for children."

The *Kathleen R.* court determined that the state law claims were preempted by federal law, and that the substantive due process claim also failed. Although the government has an interest in protecting minors from harmful materials on the Internet, *Reno v. ACLU,* 521 U.S. at 875, it does not have a constitutional duty to do so. 104 Cal. Rptr. 2d 772, 781.

How should the *Pico* analysis apply to libraries and internet filters, whether by a public or school library? Is the court in *Mainstream Loudoun* correct that the decision to implement filters is a removal decision? If the library provides access only to certain websites, is that more analogous to selecting books? Is the filtering process analogous to book removal because the library or a third-party organization is selecting material to remove? Or by choosing a filtering mechanism is a library selecting the information to be made available? Could a library promulgate a filtering policy that would operate as a valid time, place and manner restriction, (which would not require strict scrutiny)? *See Ward v. Rock Against Racism,* 491 U.S. 781 (1989) (reasonable time, place and manner restrictions on speech are constitutional if they are justified without reference to the content of the speech, are narrowly tailored to serve a significant government interest and leave open ample alternative channels for communication). For an interesting discussion of these issues, see Junichi Semitsu, *Burning Cyberbooks in Public Libraries: Internet Filtering Software vs. The First Amendment,* 52 STAN. L. REV. 509, 526–529 (2000).

§ 4.02   RELIGION IN SCHOOL: CHILDREN CAUGHT IN THE CONTROVERSY

Schools and the children who attend them are often at the center of the contentious national debate surrounding the Constitution's religion clauses. Issues surrounding school vouchers and school prayer have proved to be particularly troublesome — both for courts and policymakers. When tax dollars are meted out to sectarian schools (whether in the form of a voucher or with other types of financial aid), the program must not violate the Establishment Clause. In dealing with issues surrounding prayer and other religious activity in school, courts must be careful that a student's right to exercise her religion freely under the Free Exercise Clause is maintained, but at the same time the court must uphold the principles of the Establishment Clause.

All of the more controversial issues surrounding religion in schools — vouchers, curriculum, prayer — have some effect on how children will learn. Many of these issues arise in the context of lawsuits by parents or taxpayers who object to a local city or school board policy. Some issues, however, like prayer and religious expression, may have a more direct effect on an individual child. The next section sets forth some of the issues surrounding financial aid to children who attend religious schools and school curriculum. The section thereafter examines student religious expression and prayer and sets forth some discussion questions for your own examination of this complicated issue. The courts' analysis of religion in the schools is complex and often confusing. A broad and deep inquiry into this matter could constitute a law school course unto itself. Those who wish to delve deeper into this subject may wish to read Michael M. McConnell, *Commentary: On School Vouchers and the Establishment Clause,* 31 CONN. L. REV. 847 (1999); Don Welch, *The State as a Purveyor of Morality*, 56 WASH. L. REV. 540 (1988); CHARLES GLENN, THE AMBIGUOUS EMBRACE: GOVERNMENT AND FAITH BASED SCHOOLS AND SOCIAL AGENCIES (2000); THOMAS C. HUNT & JAMES C. CARPER, RELIGION AND SCHOOLING IN CONTEMPORARY AMERICA: CONFRONTING OUR CULTURAL PLURALISM (1997); L. LEVY, THE ESTABLISHMENT CLAUSE: RELIGION AND THE FIRST AMENDMENT (1986); and Marci Hamilton, *The Belief/Conduct Paradigm in the Supreme Court's Free Exercise Jurisprudence: A Theological Account of the Failure to Protect Religious Conduct*, 54 OHIO ST. L.J. 713 (1993).

[A]   The Establishment Clause

[1]   Financial Aid to Religious Institutions

In dealing with the question whether a law that gives financial aid to religious schools violates the Establishment Clause, courts generally apply the "*Lemon* test," which requires that (1) the law has a secular purpose; (2) its primary effect may neither advance nor inhibit religion; and (3) it may not excessively entangle church and state. *Lemon v. Kurtzman,* 403 U.S. 602 (1971). The *Lemon* test has come under intense criticism. *See, e.g., Lamb's Chapel v. Center Moriches Union Free School Dist.,* 508 U.S. 384, 398–400 (1993) (Scalia, J., joined by Thomas, J., concurring in the judgment). Nonetheless, the Supreme Court has not overruled *Lemon* and has cited it with approval in *Santa Fe Independent School Dist. v. Doe,* 530 U.S. 290, 314 (2000). *See Freedom From Religion Foundation v. Bugher,* 249 F.3d 606, 611 (7th Cir. 2001) (noting that the entanglement prong has become a part of the primary effect inquiry and that the effect inquiry has been distilled into three criteria: whether the program results in government indoctrination, defines its recipients by reference to religion, or creates excessive entanglement.)

Programs giving financial aid to religious schools have included:

(1) providing salary supplements to parochial school teachers for teaching secular subjects. *Lemon v. Kurtzman,* 403 U.S. 602 (1971) (unconstitutional under entanglement prong);

(2) allowing taxpayers to deduct from state income tax the expenses incurred in providing "tuition, textbooks and transportation" for attending any public or private elementary or secondary school. (96% of students in the state (Minnesota) who were in private schools were in sectarian schools). *Mueller v. Allen,* 463 U.S. 388 (1983) (constitutional under *Lemon* test as program is religiously neutral and confers only the most "attenuated financial benefit" on religious schools);

(3) providing supplemental remedial instruction to disadvantaged children on the premises of sectarian schools by government employees. *Agostini v. Felton,* 521 U.S. 203 (1997) (New York City program where public school teachers were sent into parochial schools during regular school hours to provide remedial education held valid as the aid is allocated on the basis of neutral, secular criteria that neither favor nor disfavor religion and is made available to both religious and secular beneficiaries on a nondiscriminatory basis; thus, aid is less likely to advance religion).

In 2000, a four-justice plurality of the United States Supreme Court determined that a Louisiana school district's program under Chapter 2 of Title I of the 1965 Elementary and Secondary Education Act (now Title VI of the Improving America's Schools Act) did not violate the Establishment Clause because it used federal funds to purchase computers, software and library books for sectarian (nonpublic parochial) schools. The plurality stated that even if direct aid to schools was neutrally available and, before reaching or benefitting any religious school, first passes through the hands (literally or figuratively) of numerous private citizens who are free to direct the aid elsewhere, the government has not provided any "support of religion." *Mitchell v. Helms,* 530 U.S. 793 (2000). Justice O'Connor's concurrence, however, warned that neutrality alone is not sufficient to qualify the aid as being constitutional. 530 U.S. at 836 (O'Connor, J., concurring).

SCHOOL VOUCHERS

Legal commentators combed over the language in *Agostini* and *Mitchell* in an attempt to discern how the Court would vote on the school voucher issue, which has been on the front burner in several states. In *Simmons-Harris v. Zelman,* 234 F.3d 945 (6th Cir. 2000), the Sixth Circuit Court of Appeals held that Ohio's school voucher program violated the Establishment Clause. At issue in the case was a program in Cleveland that gave scholarships to children — with preference to low-income children — so that the children could attend private schools or public schools in adjacent school districts. Scholarship checks were sent to parents, who then signed the checks over to the schools. To participate, the schools were required to meet the state's educational standards and could not discriminate on the basis of race, religion, or ethnic background, or teach hatred of any person on the basis of those characteristics. Further, the participating schools were required to limit the amount they charged for tuition. During the 1999-2000 school year, no public schools participated in the program, and eighty-two percent of the participating schools were religiously affiliated.

Relying heavily on *Committee for Public Education v. Nyquist*, 413 U.S. 756 (1973), the Court of Appeals noted that "the Ohio program contains no effective means of guaranteeing that the state aid derived from public funds will be used exclusively for secular, neutral, and nonideological purposes." 234 F.3d at 958 (quoting *Nyquist*, 413 U.S. at 780). Furthermore, the court reasoned, sectarian schools were better able to participate in the program than nonsectarian schools, because sectarian schools had supplemental income from private donations. Looking at the actual effect of the program, the court stated that ninety-six percent of participating students attended sectarian schools, and no adjacent public schools participated. Thus, the court concluded that the practical effect of the program was to impermissibly promote sectarian schools.

The U.S. Supreme Court reversed the Sixth Circuit in a 5–4 decision. The Court held that because the program was neutral towards religion and provides assistance directly to a broad class of citizens who direct government aid to religious schools wholly as a result of their independent and private choice, the program did not violate the Establishment Clause. *Zelman v. Simmons-Harris*, 536 U.S. 639 (2002).

The constitutions in at least 37 states have provisions that specifically restrict government aid to religious schools. For example, Georgia's constitution states: "No money shall ever be taken from the public treasury, directly or indirectly, in aid of any church, sect, cult, or religious denomination or of any sectarian institution." GA. CONST., art I, sec. II, para. VII. Often called "state Blaine amendments," many of these provisions were added to state constitutions after a failed attempt to amend the federal constitution sponsored by House Speaker James G. Blaine. The failed attempt to pass the Blaine amendment in the mid-1870s and the "state Blaines" that followed have a history steeped in hostility to Catholicism, as their purpose was to impede the growth of Catholic schools.

Several challenges have arisen under these provisions as states look to the *Zelman* decision and create their own voucher programs. The U.S. Supreme Court disappointed voucher proponents when it upheld a scholarship program in the State of Washington that excluded students training for the ministry. The state argued, and the majority of the Court agreed, that it was entitled to ban the financing of religious instruction under its state constitution. *Locke v. Davey*, 540 U.S. 712 (2004); *see also Bush v. Holmes*, 886 So. 2d 340 (Fla. App. 1 Dist. 2004) (program violates the state constitution's no-aid provision by allowing state revenues to be used for sectarian schools, but certifying the question to the Florida Supreme Court); *Owens v. Colorado Congress of*

Parents, Teachers and Students, 92 P.3d 933 (Colo. 2004) (Colorado's constitution requires that "local school districts must retain control over any instruction paid for with locally-raised funds," and the program violates this requirement by "requiring the school districts to pay funds — including those derived from locally-raised tax revenues — to parents, who in turn are required to pay those funds to non-public schools"). *See* Ashley Alderman & Kathleen Hart, *Vouchers and Vespers: The Need for an Uncertain Change in School Voucher Programs*, 1 EDUC. L. & POL'Y FORUM *available at* www.educationlawconsortium.org (setting forth the most likely constitutional grounds for invalidating state Blaine amendments).

[2] The Curriculum Controversy

EVOLUTION VS. CREATION

To what extent can the school curriculum have religious content without violating the Establishment Clause? Do school children have a "right to receive" knowledge about religion at school? The Scopes trial in 1925 did not put an end to the debate about the teaching of evolution to schoolchildren. The United States Supreme Court has addressed two cases regarding the issue. In *Epperson v. Arkansas*, 393 U.S. 97 (1968), the Court examined a statute that made it unlawful for a teacher in a state-supported institution to teach science from an evolutionary perspective. Striking down the statute as unconstitutional under the Establishment Clause, the Court observed that the statute "selects from the body of knowledge a particular segment which it proscribes for the sole reason that it is deemed to conflict with a particular religious doctrine." Again in 1987, the Court addressed the issue in Louisiana's Creationism Act, which prohibited the teaching of the theory of evolution in public schools unless accompanied by instruction in creation science. *Edwards v. Aguillard,* 482 U.S. 578 (1987). The Court struck down that statute, stating that it failed the first prong of *Lemon.* "The preeminent purpose of the Louisiana Legislature was clearly to advance the religious viewpoint that a supernatural being created humankind." But the Court left open the possibility that views questioning evolution might be taught in some circumstances: "We do not imply that a legislature could never require that scientific critiques of prevailing scientific theories be taught . . . teaching a variety of scientific theories about the origins of humankind to schoolchildren might be validly done with the clear secular intent of enhancing the effectiveness of scientific instruction."

The evolution controversy shows no signs of abating. The School Board in Cobb County, Georgia, wished to use the following sticker in science texts: "This textbook contains material on evolution. Evolution is a theory, not a fact, regarding the origin of living things. This material should be approached with an open mind, studied carefully, and critically considered." *Selman v. Cobb County Sch. Dist.*, 2005 U.S. Dist. LEXIS 432, *58 (N.D. Ga. Jan. 13, 2005). Incorporating Justice O'Connor's endorsement test into the *Lemon* analysis, the court determined that an "informed, reasonable observer would interpret the Sticker to convey a message of endorsement of religion." "The Sticker sends a message to those who oppose evolution for religious reasons that they are favored members of the political community, while the Sticker sends a message to those who believe in evolution that they are political outsiders." *See also* Sean Cavanagh, *Pa. School Officials, Science Groups Split Over New Biology Curriculum*, EDUC. WK., Dec. 1, 2004 (furor followed a school district's decision to include the following statement in its revised curriculum: "Students will be made aware of gaps/problems in Darwin's theory and of other theories of evolution including, but not limited to intelligent design"). Michelle Galley, *Evolution Theory Prevails In Most Western Curricula*, EDUC. WK., Jan. 28, 2004, at 8 (noting that in other countries, teachers are often allowed to discuss creationism in conjunction with evolution but many teachers choose not to).

To what extent may students assert their own religious beliefs during classroom discussions? Would failure to allow this kind of discussion violate the student's free exercise rights? Consider this question again after reading the section on religious expression below.

SEX EDUCATION

The teaching of evolution is not the only area of the curriculum that may be subject to lawsuits, and the Establishment Clause is not the only constitutional provision that may form the basis of a claim. *See, e.g., Mozert v. Hawkins County Bd. of Educ.*, 827 F.2d 1058 (6th Cir. 1987) (rejecting parental claim that exposure to material in basic reading series that offended religious beliefs created an unconstitutional burden on the free exercise of religion as children were not required to act (or refrain from acting) in a way forbidden by one's religion or to affirm or disavow a belief forbidden or required by one's religion.)

In *Brown v. Hot, Sexy, and Safer Products, Inc.*, 68 F.3d 525 (1st Cir 1995), the parents' complaint alleged that their children, both fifteen years old, attended a mandatory, school-wide "assembly" at their high school that was designated as a 90-minute AIDS awareness program. According to the complaint, the program facilitator gave sexually explicit monologues and participated in sexually suggestive skits with several minors chosen from the audience. Specifically, the complaint alleges that facilitator: 1) told the students that they were going to have a "group sexual experience, with audience participation"; 2) used profane, lewd, and lascivious language to describe body parts and excretory functions; 3) advocated and approved oral sex, masturbation, homosexual sexual activity, and condom use during promiscuous premarital sex; 4) simulated masturbation; 5) characterized the loose pants worn by one minor as "erection wear"; 6) referred to being in "deep sh—" after anal sex; 7) had a male minor lick an oversized condom with her, after which she had a female minor pull it over the male minor's entire head and blow it up; 8) encouraged a male minor to display his "orgasm face" with her for the camera; 9) informed a male minor that he was not having enough orgasms; 10) closely inspected a minor and told him he had a "nice butt"; and 11) made eighteen references to orgasms, six references to male genitals, and eight references to female genitals. The First Circuit affirmed the district court's grant of the defendant's motion to dismiss, determining that the program did not violate the parent's due process right to direct the upbringing of their children or their free exercise rights — their sincerely held religious values regarding chastity and morality:

> The Supreme Court has explained that a "law that is neutral and of general applicability need not be justified by a compelling governmental interest even if the law has the incidental effect of burdening a particular religious practice." *Church of the Lukumi Babalu Aye, Inc. v. City of Hialeah.*

> The plaintiffs do not allege . . . that the compulsory attendance at the Program was anything but a neutral requirement that applied generally to all students. *Cf. id.* (where city ordinance violated Free Exercise clause because it targeted the ritual slaughter of animals only by religious groups).

> Rather, plaintiffs allege that their case falls within the "hybrid" exception recognized by *Smith* for cases that involve "the Free Exercise Clause in conjunction with other constitutional protections." *Smith,* 494 U.S. at 881 & n.1. The most relevant of the so-called hybrid cases is *Wisconsin v. Yoder*, 406 U.S. 205, 232–33, (1972), in which the Court invalidated a compulsory school attendance law as applied to Amish parents who refused on religious grounds to send their children to school. In so holding, the Court explained that

>> *Pierce* stands as a charter of the rights of parents to direct the religious upbringing of their children. And, when combined with a free exercise claim of the nature revealed by this record, more than merely a "reasonable relation to some purpose within the competency of the State" is required to sustain the validity of the State's requirement under the First Amendment.

> We find that the plaintiffs allegations do not bring them within the sweep of *Yoder* for two distinct reasons.

> First, [the plaintiffs failed to state a due process claim]. Their free exercise challenge is thus not conjoined with an independently protected constitutional protection. Second, their free exercise claim is qualitatively distinguishable from that alleged in *Yoder*.

> Here, the plaintiffs do not allege that the one-time compulsory attendance at the Program threatened their entire way of life. Accordingly, the plaintiffs' free exercise claim for damages was properly dismissed.

Id. at 538–39.

Review the speech by Matthew Fraser for which he was punished in *Bethel v. Fraser. See Bethel Sch. Dist. No. 403 v. Fraser,* 478 U.S. 675, 685, (1986) ("[a] high school assembly or classroom is no place for a sexually explicit monologue directed towards an unsuspecting audience of teenage students"); *see also FCC v. Pacifica Found.,* 438 U.S. 726 (1978). Could the minors at the assembly claim that the school violated their right to be free from offensive speech? The *Brown* court acknowledged these cases, but stated that they did not create a private cause of action against state officials for exposure to patently offensive language. In *Leebaert v. Harrington,* 332 F.3d 134 (2d Cir.

2003), a father challenged the required health course for his seventh-grader. The court refused to use a strict scrutiny analysis because it "would make it difficult or impossible for any public school authority to administer curricula responsive to the overall educational needs of the community and its children." *Id.* at 141. The court also stated that it would not use a stricter legal standard to evaluate hybrid claims as it could "think of no good reason for the standard of review to vary simply with the number of constitutional rights that the plaintiff asserts have been violated." *Id.* at 144. *But see Alfonso v. Fernandez,* 606 N.Y.S.2d 259 (1993) (New York City program that would dispense condoms to minors without prior consent of parents and without parental opt-out provision does not violate Free Exercise Clause, but it does violate parent's due process rights to direct the upbringing of their children)

On what constitutional principle can the parents in these curriculum cases be distinguished from the parents in *Wisconsin v. Yoder,* discussed in § 2.01[B], *supra?*

[3] Prayer and Religious Expression

"Nothing in the United States Constitution as interpreted by this Court . . . prohibits public school students from voluntarily praying at a time before, during, or after the school day." *Wallace v. Jaffree,* 472 U.S. 38, 67 (1985) (O'Connor, J. concurring in the judgment of the Court, which struck down an Alabama statute that authorized a period of silence for "meditation or voluntary prayer" as failing the purpose prong of *Lemon*). *Cf. Brown v. Gilmore,* 258 F.3d 265 (4th Cir. 2001) (state statute requiring public school boards to establish daily minute of silence where students may "meditate, pray, or engage in any other silent activity" does not violate the Establishment Clause as legislature purpose had a number of secular purposes (*e.g.,* to reduce school violence), and the statute did nothing to advance or inhibit religion or foster "excessive entanglement" between state and religion); *Bown v. Gwinnett County Sch. Dist.,* 895 F. Supp. 1564 (N.D. Ga. 1995) (upholding Georgia moment of silence statute). One question that is now at the center of the school prayer debate is where the line is drawn regarding when a student prayer is voluntary and when it is sponsored by the school.

In 1962 the Supreme Court caused an uproar when it held that a twenty-two word invocation used daily in the classrooms in New York was an unconstitutional establishment of religion, stating that it was no part of the business of government to compose official prayers for any group to recite as part of an official program carried on by the government. *Engel v. Vitale,* 370 U.S. 421 (1962). A year later the Court declared that Bible reading and recitation of the Lord's Prayer was unconstitutional. *Abington School District v. Schempp,* 374 U.S. 203 (1963). "The wholesome neutrality of which this Court's [Establishment Clause] cases speak . . . stems from the recognition of the teachings of history that powerful sects or groups might bring about a fusion of governmental and religious functions . . . . This the Establishment Clause prohibits. . . ." Moreover, the Free Exercise Clause guarantees to every person the right "to freely choose his own course [regarding religious training, teaching and observance] free of any compulsion by the state." The Court then set forth a standard for evaluation that foreshadowed the *Lemon* test by asking whether the legislative enactment had a secular purpose and whether its primary effect was to advance or inhibit religion.

In *Lee v. Weisman*, 505 U.S. 577 (1992), the Court addressed the practice of having clergy give nonsectarian prayers — invocations and benedictions — at middle and high school graduation. The Court stated that where the school principal decided that the invocation should be given, chose the religious participant, and directed the content of the prayer, this choice is attributable to the state. This degree of school involvement made it clear that the graduation prayer bore the imprint of the State. This kind of prayer exercise at an event as important as a graduation ceremony presents an unacceptable coercive pressure on students to participate in the prayer, even if only by standing in respectful silence.

What if it is not the school principal, but the students themselves who decide to pray at a school event? In attempt to find a safe harbor from the *Lee* decision, some schools initiated policies whereby students made the choice of the content and delivered it at school functions. The Supreme Court addressed one such policy in *Santa Fe Indep. Sch. Dist. v. Doe*, 530 U.S. 290 (2000). The school district adopted a policy authorizing two student elections, the first to determine whether invocations should be given at football games and the second to select the student who would deliver them. The school district argued that *Lee v. Weisman* was inapposite as the messages at the football games were private student speech that was protected by the Free Exercise Clause, not state-sponsored speech that was prohibited by the Establishment Clause. The Court disagreed.[31] *Sante Fe* is currently the last chapter in the school prayer line of cases.

SANTA FE INDEPENDENT SCHOOL DISTRICT v. DOE

Supreme Court of the United States
530 U.S. 290 (2000)

JUSTICE STEVENS *delivered the opinion of the Court.*

*   *   *

These invocations are authorized by a government policy and take place on government property at government-sponsored school-related events. Of course, not every message delivered under such circumstances is the government's own. We have held, for example, that an individual's contribution to a government-created forum was not government speech. See *Rosenberger v. Rector and Visitors of Univ. of Va.*, 515 U.S. 819 (1995). Although the District relies heavily on *Rosenberger* and similar cases involving such forums. . . , the Santa Fe school officials simply do not "evince either 'by policy or by practice,' any intent to open the [pregame ceremony] to 'indiscriminate use,' . . . by the student body generally." *Hazelwood School Dist. v. Kuhlmeier*, 484

---

[31] The majority relied primarily on *Lee v. Weisman*, but also pointed out that it was proper to use the *Lemon* test to assess facial challenges on Establishment Clause grounds. *Santa Fe Indep. Sch. Dist.*, 530 U.S. at 314.

U.S. 260, 270 (1988) (quoting *Perry Ed. Assn. v. Perry Local Educators' Assn.,* 460 U.S. 37, 47 (1983). Rather, the school allows only one student, the same student for the entire season, to give the invocation. The statement or invocation, moreover, is subject to particular regulations that confine the content and topic of the student's message. . . .

Granting only one student access to the stage at a time does not, of course, necessarily preclude a finding that a school has created a limited public forum. Here, however, Santa Fe's student election system ensures that only those messages deemed "appropriate" under the District's policy may be delivered. That is, the majoritarian process implemented by the District guarantees, by definition, that minority candidates will never prevail and that their views will be effectively silenced. . . . [T]his student election does nothing to protect minority views but rather places the students who hold such views at the mercy of the majority. Because "fundamental rights may not be submitted to vote; they depend on the outcome of no elections," *West Virginia Bd. of Ed. v. Barnette,* 319 U.S. 624 (1943), the District's elections are insufficient safeguards of diverse student speech.

In *Lee,* the school district made the related argument that its policy of endorsing only "civic or nonsectarian" prayer was acceptable because it minimized the intrusion on the audience as a whole. We rejected that claim by explaining that such a majoritarian policy "does not lessen the offense or isolation to the objectors. At best it narrows their number, at worst increases their sense of isolation and affront." Similarly, while Santa Fe's majoritarian election might ensure that *most* of the students are represented, it does nothing to protect the minority; indeed, it likely serves to intensify their offense.

Moreover, the District has failed to divorce itself from the religious content in the invocations. It has not succeeded in doing so, either by claiming that its policy is " 'one of neutrality rather than endorsement' " or by characterizing the individual student as the "circuit-breaker" [footnote omitted] in the process. Contrary to the District's repeated assertions that it has adopted a "hands-off" approach to the pregame invocation, the realities of the situation plainly reveal that its policy involves both perceived and actual endorsement of religion. In this case, as we found in *Lee,* the "degree of school involvement" makes it clear that the pregame prayers bear "the imprint of the State and thus put school-age children who objected in an untenable position."

Once the student speaker is selected and the message composed, the invocation is then delivered to a large audience assembled as part of a regularly scheduled, school-sponsored function conducted on school property. The message is broadcast over the school's public address system, which remains subject to the control of school officials. It is fair to assume that the pregame ceremony is clothed in the traditional indicia of school sporting events, which generally include not just the team, but also cheerleaders and band members dressed in uniforms sporting the school name and mascot. The school's name is likely written in large print across the field and on banners and flags. The crowd will certainly include many who display the school colors and insignia on their school T-shirts, jackets, or hats and who may also be waving signs displaying the school name. It is in a setting such as this that "the board has chosen to permit" the elected student to rise and give the "statement or invocation."

In this context the members of the listening audience must perceive the pregame message as a public expression of the views of the majority of the student body delivered with the approval of the school administration. In cases involving state participation in a religious activity, one of the relevant questions is "whether an objective observer, acquainted with the text, legislative history, and implementation of the statute, would perceive it as a state endorsement of prayer in public schools." *Wallace,* 472 U.S. 38, 73, 76 (O'CONNOR, J., concurring in judgment). Regardless of the listener's support for, or objection to, the message, an objective Santa Fe High School student will unquestionably perceive the inevitable pregame prayer as stamped with her school's seal of approval.

[The Court stated that although the school policy stated that its purpose was to "foster free expression of private persons . . . as well [as to] solemnize sporting events, promote good sportsmanship and student safety, and establish an appropriate environment for competition," the policy's approval of only one specific kind of message, an "invocation," is not necessary to further any of these purposes. Additionally, the fact that only one student is permitted to give a content-limited message suggests that this policy does little to "foster free expression" and the use of an invocation to foster solemnity is impermissible when, in actuality, it constitutes prayer sponsored by the school.

The Court next addressed the School District's argument that there was no impermissible coercion under its policy because the pregame message was by student choice and attendance at football games, and unlike the graduation ceremony in *Lee,* was voluntary.]

The reasons just discussed explaining why the alleged "circuit-breaker" mechanism of the dual elections and student speaker do not turn public speech into private speech also demonstrate why these mechanisms do not insulate the school from the coercive element of the final message. . . . Although it is true that the ultimate choice of student speaker is "attributable to the students," the District's decision to hold the constitutionally problematic election is clearly "a choice attributable to the State," *Lee,* 505 U.S. at 587. . . .

Attendance at a high school football game, unlike showing up for class, is certainly not required in order to receive a diploma. Moreover, we may assume that the District is correct in arguing that the informal pressure to attend an athletic event is not as strong as a senior's desire to attend her own graduation ceremony. There are some students, however, such as cheerleaders, members of the band, and, of course, the team members themselves, for whom seasonal commitments mandate their attendance, sometimes for class credit. The [School] District also minimizes the importance to many students of attending and participating in extracurricular activities as part of a complete educational experience. . . . To assert that high school students do not feel immense social pressure, or have a truly genuine desire, to be involved in the extracurricular event that is American high school football is "formalistic in the extreme." . . . High school home football games are traditional gatherings of a school community; they bring together students and faculty as well as friends and family from years present and past to root for a common cause. Undoubtedly, the games are not important to some students, and they voluntarily choose not to attend. For many others, however, the choice between whether to attend these games or to risk facing a personally offensive religious ritual is in no practical sense an easy one. The Constitution, moreover, demands that the school may not force this difficult choice upon these students for "it is a tenet of the First Amendment that the State cannot require one of its citizens to forfeit his or her rights and benefits as the price of resisting conformance to state-sponsored religious practice." *Lee*, at 596.

Even if we regard every high school student's decision to attend a home football game as purely voluntary, we are nevertheless persuaded that the delivery of a pregame prayer has the improper effect of coercing those present to participate in an act of religious worship. For "the government may no more use social pressure to enforce orthodoxy than it may use more direct means.". . . The constitutional command will not permit the District "to exact religious conformity from a student as the price" of joining her classmates at a varsity football game.

. . .

[N]othing in the Constitution as interpreted by this Court prohibits any public school student from voluntarily praying at any time before, during, or after the schoolday. But the religious liberty protected by the Constitution is abridged when the State affirmatively sponsors the particular religious practice of prayer.

. . . .

[CHIEF JUSTICE REHNQUIST wrote a dissent, which was joined by JUSTICES SCALIA and THOMAS, claiming that the speech under this policy, which would have been selected or created by a student, would be protected private speech.]

———

NOTES AND QUESTIONS

1. Many religious groups were bitterly disappointed with the decision. *See e.g.*, U.S. NEWSWIRE, June 19, 2000 (National Clergy Council, representing religious leaders from Catholic, Evangelical, Orthodox and Protestant traditions stating the opinion is a "bad decision for students, a bad decision for schools and communities, and a bad decision for America"). Grassroots efforts were initiated to circumvent the decision. In the Fall after the decision some students and parents started saying the Lord's Prayer spontaneously at football games. *See* David Firestone, *Action at School Games Seeks to Skirt Court's Church-State Ruling*, N.Y. TIMES, Aug. 26, 2000. For example, at one school in Mississippi a Christian ministry distributed handbills urging people to pray before the game, students held hands and started the prayer, and most of the crowd of 4500 stood and joined in. The scene was repeated at scores of high school football games around the South. If the school does not let the students use the intercom or give official permission for the prayer, does this

practice pass Establishment Clause standards? What if the students in the Youth Nazi party started chanting racist poems before a football game without school permission? If school officials did not stop the "spontaneous" prayer, are they able to step in and stop the racist chanting?

2. What if a school district were to have a policy whereby (1) the discretion whether to have a graduation message was up to the senior class and (2) an election was held where the students in the graduation class chose a student to give a graduation message that would not be monitored or reviewed by school officials? The Eleventh Circuit upheld such a policy, even after the *Santa Fe* decision, declaring that the speech was not state-sponsored. The court of appeals distinguished the policy in *Santa Fe*, pointing out that the *Santa Fe* policy was subject to particular regulations that confined the content and topic of the student's message and that the policy by its terms invited and encouraged religious messages. *Adler v. Duval County*, 250 F.3d 1330 (11th Cir. 2001) (8-4 en banc) Moreover, the Duval policy, unlike *Santa Fe*, does not subject the issue of *prayer* or invocation to an up-or-down vote; the students vote on whether to have a "message." If a student chooses on his or her own to deliver a prayer, this is not reflecting a majority vote to impose religion on unwilling listeners. "The Court in *Santa Fe* had every opportunity to declare that all religious expression permitted at a public school graduation ceremony violates the Establishment Clause; it did not do so." Four dissenters to the en banc opinion argued that the few distinctions between the Santa Fe policy and the Duval policy were insignificant. The circuits have not agreed about the issue raised in *Adler*. *See Lassonde v. Pleasanton Unified School District,* 320 F.3d 979, 984 (9th Cir. 2003) (even with a disclaimer or hands-off approach to the valedictorian speech, there would still be the "coerced participation of dissenters attending their graduation ceremony"); *see also Doe v. School District of Norfolk*, 340 F.3d 605 (8th Cir. 2003) (when a school board member asked the audience to join him in reciting the Lord's Prayer, the court found the speech was not state-sponsored and therefore not a constitutional violation). South Carolina's legislature appears to have based legislation on the *Adler* opinion. *See* S.C. CODE ANN. §§ 59-1-441 & 59-1-442 (2003) ("Policy to permit student to deliver message" and "Policy to permit opening or closing message at school-sponsored athletic events," respectively). For some commentary on this issue, see Danielle Logan, *Prayer in Our Public Schools: Is There Room at the Inn?*, 1 EDUC. L. & POL'Y FORUM, *available at* www.educationlawconsortium.org; Christopher Ramsey, *The Devout Valedictorian and* Lee v. Weisman: *Where the Court Should Go Next*, 1 EDUC. L. & POL'Y FORUM *available at* www.educationlawconsortium.org.

3. What about student expression that is totally private? Can school official restrain private speech because of its religious content? In *C.H. v. Oliva*, 226 F.3d 198 (3d Cir. 2000) (en banc) the plaintiff (a mother acting as guardian ad litem for her son) filed a lawsuit complaining about two incidents that occurred when the boy was in kindergarten and first grade. The kindergarten issue occurred when, in the spirit of the Thanksgiving holiday, the boy's teacher asked the students to make posters depicting what they were "thankful for." The boy produced a poster indicating that he was thankful for Jesus. According to the complaint filed on his behalf by his mother, his poster was placed

on display with others in the hallway of the school. Subsequently, [unidentified] school employees removed his poster because of its religious theme. His teacher, not a named defendant, replaced the poster, although at a less prominent location. "Both [the boy] and [his mother] were made aware of the removal of the poster because of its religious theme."

Because none of the defendants in the case is alleged to have participated in, or been aware of, the decision to remove the poster or to restore it to a "less prominent location," the court of appeals stated that "the fair inference from the facts alleged is that the defendants did not play any role in the challenged decisions and there is no allegation, even conclusory, to the contrary." Thus, the issue was a purely hypothetical one as far as these parties were concerned. Moreover, it was not alleged that the removal occurred as a result of any school policy against the exhibition of religious material. The case was remanded to give plaintiff the opportunity to amend.

The boy had a similar incident in the first grade. His teacher maintained a policy in her class which rewarded students reaching a certain level of reading proficiency by allowing them to read a book of their own choosing to the rest of the class. *C.H. v. Oliva,* 990 F. Supp. 341 (D. N.J. 1997). The boy chose to read a story called "A Big Family," an adaptation of chapters 29–33 of the Book of Genesis, from a book entitled "The Beginner's Bible."[32] Because of its religious content, his teacher did not allow the boy to read the story to the class. Instead, although the other students were allowed to read their non-religious stories to the class, he was only allowed to read the story to his teacher. Using the Supreme Court's *Hazelwood* analysis to address the plaintiff's free speech claim, the district court (which was affirmed by an equally divided en banc appeals court) determined that the class was not a public forum and that the teacher's decision not to allow the boy to read the story was reasonably related to legitimate pedagogical concerns — the school could have been seen as endorsing religion and run afoul of the Establishment Clause. Even though the story had no religious theme, "the speech was the book [the Bible] itself." 990 F. Supp. at 354.

The plaintiff also made an Establishment Clause claim, alleging that the conduct toward the boy amounted to "religious cleansing." The district court applied the *Lemon* test and held that the actions neither advanced nor inhibited religion, nor created an excessive entanglement with religion:

> The boy's teacher properly exercised her editorial control over the students' reading selections to ensure the material was appropriate for their educational level. This obviously concerns more than just determining whether or not the selection was grammatically correct

---

[32] The story "A Big Family" reads:

Jacob traveled far away to his uncle's house. He worked for his uncle, taking care of sheep. While he was there, Jacob got married. He had twelve sons. Jacob's big family lived on his uncle's land for many years. But Jacob wanted to go back home. One day, Jacob packed up all his animals and his family and everything he had. They traveled all the way back to where Esau lived. Now Jacob was afraid that Esau might still be angry at him. So he sent presents to Esau. He sent servants who said, "Please don't be angry anymore." But Esau wasn't angry. He ran to Jacob. He hugged and kissed him. He was happy to see his brother again.

or lewd, but deciding whether or not the themes the selection presented were suitable for a first-grade class. At this age, it is quite reasonable to assume that these children could have been easily confused whether or not [the boy's] teacher merely let the boy read his book, or if she approved of its message. . . . Moreover, the plaintiffs have not shown how [the boy's] teacher's actions advanced or inhibited religion in any sense. She never did or said anything regarding his faith. On the contrary, she let him read the "Bible" to himself during his free periods. [He] was merely forbidden from reading the book to his classmates during school hours, and this did not affect the practice of a tenant of his religion or his religion in general.

Id. at 355.

Would the plaintiff in this case have been better off making a Free Exercise claim?

4. Should students who wish to distribute religious materials at school be constrained by the Establishment Clause? *Compare Westfield High Sch. L.I.F.E. Club v. City of Westfield*, 249 F. Supp. 2d 98 (D. Mass. 2003) (student allowed to distribute candy canes with a religious message attached since the distribution occurred during non-instructional time and amounted to private, school-tolerated speech) *with Walz v. Egg Harbor Township Bd. of Educ.*, 342 F.3d 271 (3d Cir. 2003) (when the distribution takes place during a class's holiday party, the school can restrict such activities because such actions were reasonably directed toward an educational goal of not endorsing religion).

[B] The Free Exercise Clause

"Congress shall make no law . . . prohibiting the free exercise of [religion]." U.S. Const. amend I. Suppose a Fundamentalist Christian student objects in biology class when the teacher begins to discuss evolution. The student claims she is forced to learn something that contradicts her religion in violation of the Free Exercise Clause. Determining where the Establishment Clause prohibition ends and Free Exercise protection begins has proved to be a vexing issue.

The Second Circuit addressed whether Earth Day activities at school violated the Establishment Clause or the Free Exercise Clause. *See Altman v. Bedford Central Sch. Dist,* 245 F.3d 49 (2d Cir. 2001) The district court had found that the celebration of Earth Day constituted a religious ceremony in violation of the Establishment Clause because (a) "the worship of the Earth is a recognized religion (Gaia), which has been and is now current throughout the world," 45 F. Supp. 2d at 393, (b) the proceedings "took on much of the attributes of the ceremonies of worship by organized religions," and (c) the faculty advisor's statements paralleled one statement in Genesis (and hence was found to constitute "clearly religious teaching," at 394), and contradicted another in a way that plaintiffs viewed as an endorsement of birth control, contrary to principles of Catholicism. The court of appeals disagreed, stating that the School District's sponsorship of Earth Day ceremonies had a secular purpose, were not coercive and did not have the effect of endorsing the Gaia religion. *Altman*, 245 F.3d at 77, 79. With regard to the Free Exercise claim, the court of appeals stated:

> [The Free Exercise] Clause has a double aspect. On the one hand, it forestalls compulsion by law of the acceptance of any creed or the practice of any form of worship. Freedom of conscience and freedom to adhere to such religious organization or form of worship as the individual may choose cannot be restricted by law. On the other hand, it safeguards the free exercise of the chosen form of religion. Thus the Amendment embraces two concepts, — freedom to believe and freedom to act. The first is absolute but, in the nature of things, the second cannot be. Where there is no indication that a restriction of a plaintiff's religious activities was the defendant's actual objective, but only that its actions, neutral on their face, had a restrictive effect, the proper inquiry is "whether government has placed a substantial burden on the observation of a central religious belief or practice and, if so, whether a compelling governmental interest justifies the burden." *Jimmy Swaggart Ministries v. Board of Equalization,* 493 U.S. 378, 384–85 (1990) (quoting *Hernandez v. Commissioner,* 490 U.S. 680, 699 (1989)); *see Wisconsin v. Yoder,* 406 U.S. 205, 220–221 (1972).
>
> . . .
>
> Thus, the principal question was whether the Earth Day ceremonies had a religion-burdening effect. The district court focused principally on the faculty advisor's criticism of overpopulation of the Earth, which the court stated was contrary to the teaching of Genesis, and on Father Pacwa's interpretation of that remark as advocacy of birth control. The mere evidence that plaintiffs found that remark and perhaps some other aspects of the ceremonies offensive to their beliefs, however, did not suffice to prove a free exercise violation, for the court made no finding that students were required to participate in the Earth Day ceremonies. The principal of Fox Lane High testified that attendance was not compulsory, and we see no indication that the district court discredited that testimony. Absent a finding that students were required to attend or participate in the Earth Day ceremonies, we conclude that there was no interference with plaintiffs' free exercise of their chosen religion.

Id. at 80.

What if students wear religious attire in violation of the school dress code? In *Chalifoux v. New Caney Sch. Dist.*, 976 F. Supp. 659 (S.D. Tex. 1997), the court recognized the student's right under the Free Exercise Clause to wear a rosary around his neck at school. The court stated that the rosary was deeply rooted in orthodox Catholic beliefs and that the student had not randomly adopted an object as a religious talisman. Because this was a hybrid case where a student speech claim was combined with a free exercise claim, the court adopted a heightened level of scrutiny. Citing *Wisconsin v. Yoder*, 406 U.S. 205 (1972), the court performed a balancing test to determine whether the school's regulation places an "undue burden" on the student's religious exercise and whether the regulation bears more than a "reasonable relation" to the school district's stated objective.

> After considering the burden placed on Plaintiffs' religious exercise and [the school district's] stated objective of regulating gang activity on campus, the Court finds that the prohibition on wearing rosaries violates Plaintiffs' First Amendment rights. This Court does not doubt that a dress code can be one means of restricting gang activity on campus. However, while this Court will not endeavor to make a comprehensive list, surely there are a number of more effective means available to [the school district], other than a blanket ban on wearing rosaries, to control gang activity and ensure the safety of its schools. This is particularly true where, as here, the evidence showed only three instances of alleged gang members wearing rosaries as gang identifiers, with only one of those incidents occurring on campus. Therefore, the Court finds that [the school district's] restriction on rosaries does not "bear more than a reasonable relation" to regulating gang activity in the District. *Yoder*, 406 U.S. at 233. Moreover, the regulation places an undue burden on Plaintiffs, who seek to display the rosary not to identify themselves with a gang, but as a sincere expression of their religious beliefs.

Id. at 671.

§ 4.03 SCHOOL DISCIPLINE AND THE CONSTITUTION

[A] Suspension

After the United States Supreme Court determined in *Tinker v. Des Moines School District*, 393 U.S. 503, 506 (1969), that students did not "shed their constitutional rights at the schoolhouse gate," the question became the extent to which other constitutional rights would enter the schoolhouse. The Court addressed procedural due process rights of students in the following case.

GOSS v. LOPEZ

Supreme Court of the United States
419 U.S. 565 (1975)

MR. JUSTICE WHITE *delivered the opinion of the Court.*

This appeal by various administrators of the Columbus, Ohio, Public School System (CPSS) challenges the judgment of a three-judge federal court, declaring that appellees — various high school students in the CPSS — were denied due process of law contrary to the command of the Fourteenth Amendment in that they were temporarily suspended from their high schools without a hearing either prior to suspension or within a reasonable time thereafter, and enjoining the administrators to remove all references to such suspensions from the students' records.

I

OHIO LAW, REV. CODE ANN. § 3313.64 (1972), provides for free education to all children between the ages of six and 21. Section 3313.66 of the Code empowers the principal of an Ohio public school to suspend a pupil for misconduct for up to 10 days or to expel him. In either case, he must notify the student's parents within 24 hours and state the reasons for his action. A pupil who is expelled, or his parents, may appeal the decision to the Board of Education and in connection therewith shall be permitted to be heard at the board meeting. The Board may reinstate the pupil following the hearing. No similar procedure is provided in § 3313.66 or any other provision of state law for a suspended student. Aside from a regulation tracking the statute, at the time of the imposition of the suspensions in this case the CPSS itself had not issued any written procedure applicable to suspensions. . . .

The nine named appellees, each of whom alleged that he or she had been suspended from public high school in Columbus for up to 10 days without a hearing pursuant to § 3313.66, filed an action under 42 U. S. C. § 1983 against the Columbus Board of Education and various administrators of the CPSS. The complaint sought a declaration that § 3313.66 was unconstitutional in that it permitted public school administrators to deprive plaintiffs of their rights to an education without a hearing of any kind, in violation of the procedural due process component of the Fourteenth Amendment. It also sought to enjoin the public school officials from issuing future suspensions pursuant to § 3313.66 and to require them to remove references to the past suspensions from the records of the students in question.

The proof below established that the suspensions arose out of a period of widespread student unrest in the CPSS during February and March 1971. Six of the named plaintiffs, Rudolph Sutton, Tyrone Washington, Susan Cooper, Deborah Fox, Clarence Byars, and Bruce Harris, were students at the Marion-Franklin High School and were each suspended for 10 days on account of disruptive or disobedient conduct committed in the presence of the school administrator who ordered the suspension. One of these, Tyrone Washington, was among a group of students demonstrating in the school auditorium while a class was being conducted there. He was ordered by the school principal to leave, refused to do so, and was suspended. Rudolph Sutton, in the presence of the principal, physically attacked a police officer who was attempting to remove Tyrone Washington from the auditorium. He was immediately suspended. The other four Marion-Franklin students were suspended for similar conduct. None was given a hearing to determine the operative facts underlying the suspension, but each, together with his or her parents, was offered the opportunity to attend a conference, subsequent to the effective date of the suspension, to discuss the student's future.

Two named plaintiffs, Dwight Lopez and Betty Crome, were students at the Central High School and McGuffey Junior High School, respectively. The former was suspended in connection with a disturbance in the lunchroom which involved some physical damage to school property. Lopez testified that at least 75 other students were suspended from his school on the same day. He also testified below that he was not a party to the destructive conduct but was instead an innocent bystander. Because no one from the school testified with regard to this incident, there is no evidence in the record indicating the official basis for concluding otherwise. Lopez never had a hearing.

Betty Crome was present at a demonstration at a high school other than the one she was attending. There she was arrested together with others, taken to the police station, and released without being formally charged. Before she went to school on the following day, she was notified that she had been suspended for a 10-day period. Because no one from the school testified with respect to this incident, the record does not disclose how the McGuffey Junior High School principal went about making the decision to suspend Crome, nor does it disclose on what information the decision was based. It is clear from the record that no hearing was ever held.

There was no testimony with respect to the suspension of the ninth named plaintiff, Carl Smith. The school files were also silent as to his suspension, although as to some, but not all, of the other named plaintiffs the files contained either direct references to their suspensions or copies of letters sent to their parents advising them of the suspension.

On the basis of this evidence, the three-judge court declared that plaintiffs were denied due process of law because they were "suspended without hearing prior to suspension or within a reasonable time thereafter," and that [the Ohio statute] and regulations issued pursuant thereto were unconstitutional in permitting such suspensions. It was ordered that all references to plaintiffs' suspensions be removed from school files. . . . We affirm.

II

At the outset, appellants contend that because there is no constitutional right to an education at public expense, the Due Process Clause does not protect against expulsions from the public school system. This position misconceives the nature of the issue and is refuted by prior decisions. The Fourteenth Amendment forbids the State to deprive any person of life, liberty, or property without due process of law. Protected interests in property are normally "not created by the Constitution. Rather, they are created and their dimensions are defined" by an independent source such as state statutes or rules entitling the citizen to certain benefits.

. . . .

Here, on the basis of state law, appellees plainly had legitimate claims of entitlement to a public education. OHIO REV. CODE ANN. §§ 3313.48 and 3313.64 (1972 & Supp. 1973) direct local authorities to provide a free education to all residents between five and 21 years of age, and a compulsory-attendance law requires attendance for a school year of not less than 32 weeks. It is true that § 3313.66 of the Code permits school principals to suspend students for up to 10 days; but suspensions may not be imposed without any grounds whatsoever. All of the schools had their own rules specifying the grounds for expulsion or suspension. Having chosen to extend the right to an education to people of appellees' class generally, Ohio may not withdraw that right on grounds of misconduct, absent fundamentally fair procedures to determine whether the misconduct has occurred.

Although Ohio may not be constitutionally obligated to establish and maintain a public school system, it has nevertheless done so and has required its children to attend. Those young people do not "shed their constitutional rights" at the schoolhouse door. *Tinker v. Des Moines School Dist.,* 393 U.S. 503, 506 (1969). "The Fourteenth Amendment, as now applied to the States, protects the citizen against the State itself and all of its creatures — Boards of Education not excepted." *West Virginia Board of Education v. Barnette,* 319 U.S. 624, 637 (1943). The authority possessed by the State to prescribe and enforce standards of conduct in its schools although concededly very broad, must be exercised consistently with constitutional safeguards. Among other things, the State is constrained to recognize a student's legitimate entitlement to a public education as a property interest which is protected by the Due Process Clause and which may not be taken away for misconduct without adherence to the minimum procedures required by that Clause.

The Due Process Clause also forbids arbitrary deprivations of liberty. "Where a person's good name, reputation, honor, or integrity is at stake because of what the government is doing to him," the minimal requirements of the Clause must be satisfied. . . . School authorities here suspended appellees from school for periods of up to 10 days based on charges of misconduct. If sustained and recorded, those charges could seriously damage the students' standing with their fellow pupils and their teachers as well as interfere with later opportunities for higher education and employment. It is apparent that the claimed right of the State to determine unilaterally and without process whether that misconduct has occurred immediately collides with the requirements of the Constitution. [Authors' note: The following year in *Paul v. Davis,* 424 U.S. 693 (1976), the Supreme Court held that there is no liberty interest in reputation alone].

Appellants proceed to argue that even if there is a right to a public education protected by the Due Process Clause generally, the Clause comes into play only when the State subjects a student to a "severe detriment or grievous loss." The loss of 10 days, it is said, is neither severe nor grievous and the Due Process Clause is therefore of no relevance. Appellants' argument is again refuted by our prior decisions; for in determining "whether due process requirements apply in the first place, we must look not to the "weight" but to the *nature* of the interest at stake. Appellees were excluded from school only temporarily, it is true, but the length and consequent severity of a deprivation, while another factor to weigh in determining the appropriate form of hearing, "is not decisive of the basic right" to a hearing of some kind. The Court's view has been that as long as a property deprivation is not *de minimis,* its gravity is irrelevant to the question whether account must be taken of the Due Process Clause. A 10-day suspension from school is not *de minimis* in our view and may not be imposed in complete disregard of the Due Process Clause.

A short suspension is, of course, a far milder deprivation than expulsion. But, "education is perhaps the most important function of state and local governments," *Brown v. Board of Education,* 347 U.S. 483, 493 (1954), and the total exclusion from the educational process for more than a trivial period, and certainly if the suspension is for 10 days, is a serious event in the life of the suspended child. Neither the property interest in educational benefits temporarily denied nor the liberty interest in reputation, which is also implicated, is so insubstantial that suspensions may constitutionally be imposed by any procedure the school chooses, no matter how arbitrary.

III

"Once it is determined that due process applies, the question remains what process is due." We turn to that question, fully realizing as our cases regularly do that the interpretation and application of the Due Process Clause are intensely practical matters and that "[the] very nature of due process negates any concept of inflexible procedures universally applicable to every imaginable situation." We are also mindful of our own admonition:

"Judicial interposition in the operation of the public school system of the Nation raises problems requiring care and restraint. . . . By and large, public education in our Nation is committed to the control of state and local authorities." *Epperson v. Arkansas,* 393 U.S. 97, 104 (1968).

There are certain bench marks to guide us, however. *Mullane v. Central Hanover Trust Co.,* 339 U.S. 306 (1950), a case often invoked by later opinions, said that "[many] controversies have raged about the cryptic and abstract words of the Due Process Clause but there can be no doubt that at a minimum they require that deprivation of life, liberty or property by adjudication be preceded by notice and opportunity for hearing appropriate to the nature of the case." "The fundamental requisite of due process of law is the opportunity to be heard," a right that "has little reality or worth unless one is informed that the matter is pending and can choose for himself whether to . . . contest." At the very minimum, therefore, students facing suspension and the consequent interference with a protected property interest must be given *some* kind of notice and afforded *some* kind of hearing. "Parties whose rights are to be affected are entitled to be heard; and in order that they may enjoy that right they must first be notified."

[T]he timing and content of the notice and the nature of the hearing will depend on appropriate accommodation of the competing interests involved. The student's interest is to avoid unfair or mistaken exclusion from the educational process, with all of its unfortunate consequences. The Due Process Clause will not shield him from suspensions properly imposed, but it disserves both his interest and the interest of the State if his suspension is in fact unwarranted. The concern would be mostly academic if the disciplinary process were a totally accurate, unerring process, never mistaken and never unfair. Unfortunately, that is not the case, and no one suggests that it is. Disciplinarians, although proceeding in utmost good faith, frequently act on the reports and advice of others; and the controlling facts and the nature of the conduct under challenge are often disputed. The risk of error is not at all trivial, and it should be guarded against if that may be done without prohibitive cost or interference with the educational process.

The difficulty is that our schools are vast and complex. Some modicum of discipline and order is essential if the educational function is to be performed. Events calling for discipline are frequent occurrences and sometimes require immediate, effective action. Suspension is considered not only to be a necessary tool to maintain order but a valuable educational device. The prospect of imposing elaborate hearing requirements in every suspension case is viewed with great concern, and many school authorities may well prefer the untrammeled power to act unilaterally, unhampered by rules about notice and hearing. But it would be a strange disciplinary system in an educational institution if no communication was sought by the disciplinarian with the student in an effort to inform him of his dereliction and to let him tell his side of the story in order to make sure that an injustice is not done. . . .[33]

We do not believe that school authorities must be totally free from notice and hearing requirements if their schools are to operate with acceptable efficiency. Students facing temporary suspension have interests qualifying for protection of the Due Process Clause, and due process requires, in connection with a suspension of 10 days or less, that the student be given oral or written notice of the charges against him and, if he denies them, an explanation of the evidence the authorities have and an opportunity to present his side of the story. The Clause requires at least these rudimentary precautions against unfair or mistaken findings of misconduct and arbitrary exclusion from school.

There need be no delay between the time "notice" is given and the time of the hearing. In the great majority of cases the disciplinarian may informally discuss the alleged misconduct with the student minutes after it has occurred. We hold only that, in being given an opportunity to explain his version of the facts at this discussion, the student first be told what he is accused of doing and what the basis of the accusation is. . . . Since the hearing may occur almost immediately following the misconduct, it follows that as a general rule notice and hearing should precede removal of the student from school. We agree with the District Court, however, that there are recurring situations in which prior notice and hearing cannot be insisted upon. Students whose presence poses a continuing danger to persons or property or an ongoing threat of disrupting the academic process may be immediately removed from school. In such cases, the necessary notice and rudimentary hearing should follow as soon as practicable, as the District Court indicated.

In holding as we do, we do not believe that we have imposed procedures on school disciplinarians which are inappropriate in a classroom setting.

---

[33] [9] The facts involved in this case illustrate the point. Betty Crome was suspended for conduct which did not occur on school grounds, and for which mass arrests were made — hardly guaranteeing careful individualized factfinding by the police or by the school principal. She claims to have been involved in no misconduct. However, she was suspended for 10 days without ever being told what she was accused of doing or being given an opportunity to explain her presence among those arrested. Similarly, Dwight Lopez was suspended, along with many others, in connection with a disturbance in the lunchroom. Lopez says he was not one of those in the lunchroom who was involved. However, he was never told the basis for the principal's belief that he was involved, nor was he ever given an opportunity to explain his presence in the lunchroom. The school principals who suspended Crome and Lopez may have been correct on the merits, but it is inconsistent with the Due Process Clause to have made the decision that misconduct had occurred without at some meaningful time giving Crome or Lopez an opportunity to persuade the principals otherwise.

We recognize that both suspensions were imposed during a time of great difficulty for the school administrations involved. At least in Lopez' case there may have been an immediate need to send home everyone in the lunchroom in order to preserve school order and property; and the administrative burden of providing 75 "hearings" of any kind is considerable. However, neither factor justifies a disciplinary suspension without *at any time* gathering facts relating to Lopez specifically, confronting him with them, and giving him an opportunity to explain.

Instead we have imposed requirements which are, if anything, less than a fair-minded school principal would impose upon himself in order to avoid unfair suspensions. Indeed, according to the testimony of the principal of Marion-Franklin High School, that school had an informal procedure, remarkably similar to that which we now require, applicable to suspensions generally but which was not followed in this case. . . .

We stop short of construing the Due Process Clause to require, countrywide, that hearings in connection with short suspensions must afford the student the opportunity to secure counsel, to confront and cross-examine witnesses supporting the charge, or to call his own witnesses to verify his version of the incident. Brief disciplinary suspensions are almost countless. To impose in each such case even truncated trial-type procedures might well overwhelm administrative facilities in many places and, by diverting resources, cost more than it would save in educational effectiveness. Moreover, further formalizing the suspension process and escalating its formality and adversary nature may not only make it too costly as a regular disciplinary tool but also destroy its effectiveness as part of the teaching process.

On the other hand, requiring effective notice and informal hearing permitting the student to give his version of the events will provide a meaningful hedge against erroneous action. At least the disciplinarian will be alerted to the existence of disputes about facts and arguments about cause and effect. He may then determine himself to summon the accuser, permit cross-examination, and allow the student to present his own witnesses. In more difficult cases, he may permit counsel. In any event, his discretion will be more informed and we think the risk of error substantially reduced.

Requiring that there be at least an informal give-and-take between student and disciplinarian, preferably prior to the suspension, will add little to the factfinding function where the disciplinarian himself has witnessed the conduct forming the basis for the charge. But things are not always as they seem to be, and the student will at least have the opportunity to characterize his conduct and put it in what he deems the proper context.

We should also make it clear that we have addressed ourselves solely to the short suspension, not exceeding 10 days. Longer suspensions or expulsions for the remainder of the school term, or permanently, may require more formal procedures. Nor do we put aside the possibility that in unusual situations, although involving only a short suspension, something more than the rudimentary procedures will be required.

. . . .

Affirmed.

MR. JUSTICE POWELL, with whom THE CHIEF JUSTICE, MR. JUSTICE BLACK-MUN, and MR. JUSTICE REHNQUIST join, *dissenting.*

The Court today invalidates an Ohio statute that permits student suspensions from school without a hearing "for not more than ten days." The decision unnecessarily opens avenues for judicial intervention in the operation of our public schools that may affect adversely the quality of education. The Court holds for the first time that the federal courts, rather than educational officials and state legislatures, have the authority to determine the rules applicable to routine classroom discipline of children and teenagers in the public schools. It justifies this unprecedented intrusion into the process of elementary and secondary education by identifying a new constitutional right: the right of a student not to be suspended for as much as a single day without notice and a due process hearing either before or promptly following the suspension.[34]

The Court's decision rests on the premise that, under Ohio law, education is a property interest protected by the Fourteenth Amendment's Due Process Clause and therefore that any suspension requires notice and a hearing. In my view, a student's interest in education is not infringed by a suspension within the limited period prescribed by Ohio law. Moreover, to the extent that there may be some arguable infringement, it is too speculative, transitory, and insubstantial to justify imposition of a *constitutional* rule.

I

Although we held in *San Antonio Independent School Dist. v. Rodriguez*, 411 U.S. 1, 35 (1973), that education is not a right protected by the Constitution, Ohio has elected by statute to provide free education for all youths age six to 21, OHIO REV. CCODE ANN. §§ 3313.48, 3313.64 (1972 & Supp. 1973), with children under 18 years of age being compelled to attend school. § 3321.01 *et seq*. State law, therefore, extends the right of free public school education to Ohio students in accordance with the education laws of that State. The right or entitlement to education so created is protected in a proper case by the Due Process Clause. In my view, this is not such a case.

In identifying property interests subject to due process protections, the Court's past opinions make clear that these interests "are created and their *dimensions are defined* by existing rules or understandings that stem from an independent source such as state law." The Ohio statute that creates the right to a "free" education also explicitly authorizes a principal to suspend a student for as much as 10 days. OHIO REV. CODE ANN. §§ 3313.48, 3313.64, 3313.66 (1972 and Supp. 1973). Thus the very legislation which "defines" the "dimension" of the student's entitlement, while providing a right to education generally, does not establish this right free of discipline imposed in accord with Ohio law. Rather, the right is encompassed in the entire package of statutory provisions governing education in Ohio — of which the power to suspend is one.

The Court thus disregards the basic structure of Ohio law in posturing this case as if Ohio had conferred an unqualified right to education, thereby compelling the school authorities to conform to due process procedures in imposing the most routine discipline.

---

[34] [2] Section 3313.66 also provides authority for the expulsion of pupils, but requires a hearing thereon by the school board upon request of a parent or guardian. The rights of pupils expelled are not involved in this case, which concerns only the limited discretion of school authorities to suspend for not more than 10 days. Expulsion, usually resulting at least in loss of a school year or semester, is an incomparably more serious matter than the brief suspension, traditionally used as the principal sanction for enforcing routine discipline. The Ohio statute recognizes this distinction.

But however one may define the entitlement to education provided by Ohio law, I would conclude that a deprivation of not more than 10 days' suspension from school, imposed as a routine disciplinary measure, does not assume constitutional dimensions. Contrary to the Court's assertion, our cases support rather than "refute" appellants' argument that "the Due Process Clause . . . comes into play only when the State subjects a student to a 'severe detriment or grievous loss.'" Recently, the Court reiterated precisely this standard for analyzing due process claims:

"Whether *any* procedural protections are due depends on the extent to which an individual will be 'condemned to suffer grievous loss.'"

. . . .

The Ohio suspension statute allows no serious or significant infringement of education. It authorizes only a maximum suspension of eight school days, less than 5% of the normal 180-day school year. Absences of such limited duration will rarely affect a pupil's opportunity to learn or his scholastic performance. Indeed, the record in this case reflects no educational injury to appellees. Each completed the semester in which the suspension occurred and performed at least as well as he or she had in previous years. Despite the Court's unsupported speculation that a suspended student could be "seriously [damaged]," there is no factual showing of any such damage to appellees.

. . . .

II

In prior decisions, this Court has explicitly recognized that school authorities must have broad discretionary authority in the daily operation of public schools. This includes wide latitude with respect to maintaining discipline and good order. [The Court quoted relevant passages from *Tinker v. Des Moines School Dist.*, 393 U.S. 503, 507 (1969) and *Epperson v. Arkansas*, 393 U.S. 97, 104 (1968)].

The Court today turns its back on these precedents. It can hardly seriously be claimed that a school principal's decision to suspend a pupil for a single day would "directly and sharply implicate basic constitutional values."

Moreover, the Court ignores the experience of mankind, as well as the long history of our law, recognizing that there *are* differences which must be accommodated in determining the rights and duties of children as compared with those of adults. Examples of this distinction abound in our law: in contracts, in torts, in criminal law and procedure, in criminal sanctions and rehabilitation, and in the right to vote and to hold office. Until today, and except in the special context of the First Amendment issue in *Tinker*, the educational rights of children and teenagers in the elementary and secondary schools have not been analogized to the rights of adults or to those accorded college students. Even with respect to the First Amendment, the rights of children have not been regarded as "co-extensive with those of adults." *Tinker, supra,* at 515 (STEWART, J., concurring).

A

I turn now to some of the considerations which support the Court's former view regarding the comprehensive authority of the States and school officials "to prescribe and control conduct in the schools." Unlike the divergent and even sharp conflict of interests usually present where due process rights are asserted, the interests here implicated — of the State through its schools and of the pupils — are essentially congruent.

The State's interest, broadly put, is in the proper functioning of its public school system for the benefit of *all* pupils and the public generally. Few rulings would interfere more extensively in the daily functioning of schools than subjecting routine discipline to the formalities and judicial oversight of due process. Suspensions are one of the traditional means — ranging from keeping a student after class to permanent expulsion — used to maintain discipline in the schools. It is common knowledge that maintaining order and reasonable decorum in school buildings and classrooms is a major educational problem, and one which has increased significantly in magnitude in recent years.[35] Often the teacher, in protecting the rights of other children to an education (if not his or their safety), is compelled to rely on the power to suspend. . . .

B

The State's generalized interest in maintaining an orderly school system is not incompatible with the individual interest of the student. Education in any meaningful sense includes the inculcation of an understanding in each pupil of the necessity of rules and obedience thereto. This understanding is no less important than learning to read and write. One who does not comprehend the meaning and necessity of discipline is handicapped not merely in his education but throughout his subsequent life. In an age when the home and church play a diminishing role in shaping the character and value judgments of the young, a heavier responsibility falls upon the schools. When an immature student merits censure for his conduct, he is rendered a disservice if appropriate sanctions are not applied or if procedures for their application are so formalized as to invite a challenge to the teacher's authority — an invitation which rebellious or even merely spirited teenagers are likely to accept.

The lesson of discipline is not merely a matter of the student's self-interest in the shaping of his own character and personality; it provides an early understanding of the relevance to the social compact of respect for the rights of others. The classroom is the laboratory in which this lesson of life is best learned. Mr. Justice Black summed it up:

"School discipline, like parental discipline, is an integral and important part of training our children to be good citizens — to be better citizens."

In assessing in constitutional terms the need to protect pupils from unfair minor discipline by school authorities, the Court ignores the commonality of

---

[35] [9] *See generally* S. Bailey, Disruption in Urban Secondary Schools (1970), which summarizes some of the recent surveys on school disruption. A Syracuse University study, for example, found that 85% of the schools responding reported some type of significant disruption in the years 1967-1970.

interest of the State and pupils in the public school system. Rather, it thinks in traditional judicial terms of an adversary situation. To be sure, there will be the occasional pupil innocent of any rule infringement who is mistakenly suspended or whose infraction is too minor to justify suspension. But, while there is no evidence indicating the frequency of unjust suspensions, common sense suggests that they will not be numerous in relation to the total number, and that mistakes or injustices will usually be righted by informal means.

C

One of the more disturbing aspects of today's decision is its indiscriminate reliance upon the judiciary, and the adversary process, as the means of resolving many of the most routine problems arising in the classroom. In mandating due process procedures the Court misapprehends the reality of the normal teacher-pupil relationship. There is an ongoing relationship, one in which the teacher must occupy many roles — educator, adviser, friend, and, at times, parent-substitute.[36] It is rarely adversary in nature except with respect to the chronically disruptive or insubordinate pupil whom the teacher must be free to discipline without frustrating formalities.

The Ohio statute, providing as it does for due notice both to parents and the Board, is compatible with the teacher-pupil relationship and the informal resolution of mistaken disciplinary action. We have relied for generations upon the experience, good faith and dedication of those who staff our public schools, and the nonadversary means of airing grievances that always have been available to pupils and their parents. One would have thought before today's opinion that this informal method of resolving differences was more compatible with the interests of all concerned than resort to any constitutionalized procedure, however blandly it may be defined by the Court.

D

In my view, the constitutionalizing of routine classroom decisions not only represents a significant and unwise extension of the Due Process Clause, but it also was quite unnecessary in view of the safeguards prescribed by the Ohio statute. . . .

In its rush to mandate a constitutional rule, the Court appears to give no weight to the practical manner in which suspension problems normally would be worked out under Ohio law. One must doubt, then, whether the constitutionalization of the student-teacher relationship, with all of its attendant doctrinal and practical difficulties, will assure in any meaningful sense greater protection than that already afforded under Ohio law.

III

No one can foresee the ultimate frontiers of the new "thicket" the Court now enters. Today's ruling appears to sweep within the protected interest in

---

[36] [12] The role of the teacher in our society historically has been an honored and respected one, rooted in the experience of decades that has left for most of us warm memories of our teachers, especially those of the formative years of primary and secondary education.

education a multitude of discretionary decisions in the educational process. Teachers and other school authorities are required to make many decisions that may have serious consequences for the pupil. They must decide, for example, how to grade the student's work, whether a student passes or fails a course, whether he is to be promoted, whether he is required to take certain subjects, whether he may be excluded from interscholastic athletics or other extracurricular activities, whether he may be removed from one school and sent to another, whether he may be bused long distances when available schools are nearby, and whether he should be placed in a "general," "vocational," or "college-preparatory" track.

In these and many similar situations claims of impairment of one's educational entitlement identical in principle to those before the Court today can be asserted with equal or greater justification. Likewise, in many of these situations, the pupil can advance the same types of speculative and subjective injury given critical weight in this case. The District Court, relying upon generalized opinion evidence, concluded that a suspended student may suffer psychological injury in one or more . . . ways . . . . It hardly need be said that if a student, as a result of a day's suspension, suffers "a blow" to his "self esteem," "feels powerless," views "teachers with resentment," or feels "stigmatized by his teachers," identical psychological harms will flow from many other routine and necessary school decisions. The student who is given a failing grade, who is not promoted, who is excluded from certain extracurricular activities, who is assigned to a school reserved for children of less than average ability, or who is placed in the "vocational" rather than the "college preparatory" track, is unlikely to suffer any less psychological injury than if he were suspended for a day for a relatively minor infraction. [37]

If, as seems apparent, the Court will now require due process procedures whenever such routine school decisions are challenged, the impact upon public education will be serious indeed. The discretion and judgment of federal courts across the land often will be substituted for that of the 50 state legislatures, the 14,000 school boards, and the 2,000,000 teachers who heretofore have been responsible for the administration of the American public school system. If the Court perceives a rational and analytically sound distinction between the discretionary decision by school authorities to suspend a pupil for a brief period, and the types of discretionary school decisions described above, it would be prudent to articulate it in today's opinion. Otherwise, the federal courts should prepare themselves for a vast new role in society.

---

[37] [19] There is, no doubt, a school of modern psychological or psychiatric persuasion that maintains that *any* discipline of the young is detrimental. Whatever one may think of the wisdom of this unproved theory, it hardly affords dependable support for a *constitutional* decision. Moreover, even the theory's proponents would concede that the magnitude of injury depends primarily upon the individual child or teenager. A classroom reprimand by the teacher may be more traumatic to the shy, timid introvert than expulsion would be to the aggressive, rebellious extrovert. In my view we tend to lose our sense of perspective and proportion in a case of this kind. For average, normal children — the vast majority — suspension for a few days is simply not a detriment; it is a commonplace occurrence, with some 10% of all students being suspended; it leaves no scars; affects no reputations; indeed, it often may be viewed by the young as a badge of some distinction and a welcome holiday.

IV

Not so long ago, state deprivations of the most significant forms of state largesse were not thought to require due process protection on the ground that the deprivation resulted only in the loss of a state-provided "benefit." *E.g., Bailey v. Richardson,* 86 U.S. App. D.C. 248, 182 F.2d 46 (1950), aff'd by an equally divided Court, 341 U.S. 918 (1951). In recent years the Court, wisely in my view, has rejected the "wooden distinction between 'rights' and 'privileges,'" *Bd. of Regents v. Roth,* 408 U.S., at 571, and looked instead to the significance of the state-created or state-enforced right and to the substantiality of the alleged deprivation. Today's opinion appears to abandon this reasonable approach by holding in effect that government infringement of any interest to which a person is entitled, no matter what the interest or how inconsequential the infringement, requires *constitutional* protection. As it is difficult to think of any less consequential infringement than suspension of a junior high school student for a single day, it is equally difficult to perceive any principled limit to the new reach of procedural due process. [38]

NOTES AND QUESTIONS

1. "In short, the *Goss* majority elevate[d] to constitutional status a particular view of how public school officials should relate to their students." David L. Kirp, *Proceduralism and Bureaucracy: Due Process in the School Setting,* 29 STAN. L. REV. 841, 851 (1976). *See also* Anne P. Dupre, *Should Students Have Constitutional Rights? Keeping Order in the Public Schools,* 65 GEO. WASH. L. REV. 49, 76 (1996) (the *Goss* Court viewed teachers and principals as adversaries of the students, consistent with the social reconstruction model of school power). One commentator, who later became a judge in the Fourth Circuit Court of Appeals, observed that the Supreme Court had done damage to the public schools that would not be "easily repaired or reversed." J. Harvie Wilkinson, III, Goss v. Lopez, *The Supreme Court As School Superintendent,* 1975 SUP. CT. REV. 25, 63.

2. What process is due? In *Mathews v. Eldridge,* 424 U.S. 319, 335 (1976), the Court summarized these factors to be considered: "First, the private interest that will be affected by the official action; second, the risk of an erroneous deprivation of such interest through the procedures used, and the

---

[38] [22] Some half dozen years ago, the Court extended First Amendment rights under limited circumstances to public school pupils. Mr. Justice Black, dissenting, viewed the decision as ushering in "an entirely new era in which the power to control pupils by the elected 'officials of state supported public schools'. . . . is in ultimate effect transferred to the Supreme Court." *Tinker v. Des Moines School Dist.,* 393 U.S. 503, 515 (1969). There were some who thought Mr. Justice Black was unduly concerned. But his prophecy is now being fulfilled. In the few years since *Tinker* there have been literally hundreds of cases by schoolchildren alleging violation of their constitutional rights. This flood of litigation, between pupils and school authorities, was triggered by a narrowly written First Amendment opinion which I could well have joined on its facts. One can only speculate as to the extent to which public education will be disrupted by giving every schoolchild the power to contest *in court* any decision made by his teacher which arguably infringes the state-conferred right to education.

probable value, if any, of additional substitute procedural safeguards, and finally, the Government's interest, including the function involved and the fiscal and administrative burdens that the additional or substitute procedural requirements would entail." How well did the *Goss* Court apply this formula to the context before it?

3. The *Goss* Court held that "students facing suspension and the consequent interference with a protected property interest must be given *some* kind of notice and afforded *some* kind of hearing." What exactly did the Court require regarding notice and hearing for the students in the *Goss* case?

Does the notice component have more than one aspect? Do the school rules have to be clear enough so that the student knows that his or her conduct will result in punishment? Reread Justice Stevens dissent in *Bethel School District. v. Fraser.* If a school rule does not give students proper notice that their conduct is prohibited, it may be void for vagueness. *See Stephenson v. Davenport Community School District,* 110 F.3d 1303 (8th Cir. 1997) (pointing out that void for vagueness doctrine is embodied in the due process clause).

A vague school rule may be constitutionally infirm in two significant respects. First, the doctrine of vagueness incorporates notions of fair notice or warning, and a regulation violates the first essential of due process of law by failing to provide adequate notice of prohibited conduct. In short, a regulation is void-for-vagueness if it forbids or requires the doing of an act in terms so vague that persons of common intelligence must necessarily guess at its meaning and differ as to its application. *Id.* at 1308. Second, the void-for-vagueness doctrine prevents arbitrary and discriminatory enforcement. A vague law impermissibly delegates basic policy matters to policemen, judges, and juries for resolution on an ad hoc and subjective basis. *Id.* (determining that school district's regulation prohibiting gang symbols without providing any definition of gang was void for vagueness).

Schools generally give students notice about what conduct will result in punishment through the use of student handbooks. Many school districts require both student and parents to sign that they have read the rules set forth in the handbook. What if the rules are not clear? The rules must "define the prohibited conduct with sufficient definiteness such that an ordinary individual understands just what conduct is prohibited and must define the prohibited conduct in a manner discouraging arbitrary and discriminatory enforcement." *Weimerslage v. Maine Township High School,* 824 F. Supp. 136, 140 (N.D. Ill. 1993). But school disciplinary regulations need not be drawn with the same precision as a criminal statute, as "the special needs of the school system warrant a broader sweep in school regulations than might be permissible in a criminal code." The *Wiemerslage* court determined that although the language of the school loitering rule was flexible and broad, it nonetheless delineated with sufficient clarity the conduct that was prohibited and thus gave fair notice to the students. *But see Sherpell v. Humnoke Sch. Dist.,* 619 F. Supp. 670 (E.D. Ark. 1985) (*Sherpell I*) (vague school rules may give school officials too much discretion resulting in African-American students being disciplined more than white students).

4. What process is due? Do the notice and hearing always have to occur before a student is removed from school? In *C.B. v. Driscoll,* 82 F. 3d 383 (11th

Cir. 1996), the court determined that the student was properly removed from school before she was given an opportunity to explain herself because she posed a danger to persons or property and was disruptive. The principal spoke to the student and her mother by telephone later that day, but the principal could not remember whether she made the decision to suspend the student before or after that conversation. The court stated that this telephone conversation met the due process hearing requirement because the decision to suspend could have been reversed based on the telephone conversation.

What if the suspension were for a longer time than ten days? Are more formal procedures required? *See, e.g., Donovan v. Ritchie,* 68 F.3d 14 (1st Cir. 1995) (no additional formal procedure necessary where additional punishment — exclusion from school social events and interscholastic athletics — was added to ten-day suspension). What about removal from the general education program to an alternative school? Students do not have "procedural due process rights to notice and an opportunity to be heard when the sanction imposed is attendance at an alternative school absent some showing that the education received at the alternative school is significantly different from or inferior to that received at his regular public school." *Fortune v. City of Detroit Public Schools,* 2004 Mich. App. LEXIS 2660 (Ct. App. Oct. 12, 2004).

For recent cases addressing the quantity and quality of process that is due, see *Schneider v. Board of Sch. Trustees,* 255 F. Supp. 2d 891 (N.D. Ind. 2003) (no due process violation when student — expelled for engaging in oral sex — was not allowed to cross-examine the female classmate involved in the incident); *Camlin v. Beecher Community Sch. Dist.,* 791 N.E.2d 127 (Ill. App. 2003) (opportunity to be heard was insufficient where the school district did not provide specific information about the nature of the charges or the identity of the accuser before the hearing); *Wagner-Garay v. Fort Wayne Cmty. Sch.,* 255 F. Supp. 2d 915 (N.D. Ind. 2003) (no due violation when student was not allowed to cross-examine witnesses or know their identities, because school's interest in avoiding administrative burdens associated with such proceedings greatly outweighed the little value student would have from cross-examination or learning the accusers' names); *Murphy v. Fort Worth Indep. Sch. Dist.,* 258 F. Supp. 2d 569 (N.D. Tex. 2003) (after high school honor student received a reduced punishment for reciting a rap poem in class that a fellow classmate found threatening, the parents of the threatened student contacted the school and the punishment was increased; due process violation occurred since the ex parte communications deprived plaintiff of notice and opportunity to respond) (decision was vacated for mootness since plaintiff graduated. 334 F.3d 470 (5th Cir. 2003)); *Nichols v. DeStefano,* 70 P.3d 505 (Col. App. 2002) (student did not receive a fair hearing when school would not allow her to present character evidence and elicit testimony from teachers because such testimony would have been relevant to the issue of whether expulsion was appropriate).

5. Do Zero Tolerance policies in schools raise procedural due process issues? Will students get the notice and hearing to which they are entitled if the school principal has no choice of punishment once it is determined that the student committed the offense? Or does allowing some kind of discretion give school officials the power to discriminate? *See Sherpell v. Humnoke Sch. Dist.,* 619

F. Supp. 670 (E.D. Ark. 1985) (school rules may give school officials too much discretion in punishment resulting in African-American students being disciplined more than white students). Zero tolerance policies became more prevalent in the late 1990s after the passage of the Gun Free Schools Act of 1994, 20 U.S.C. § 8921 which mandates yearlong suspension for students caught possessing firearms on school grounds. The federal statute provides that the chief administrative officer for a local school district may modify the expulsion requirement on a case-by-case basis. For a discussion of zero tolerance policies and their application in the First Amendment context, see § 4.01, *supra.* For a case and discussion of zero tolerance and substantive due process, see § 4.03[C], *infra.*

6. Justice Powell expressed concern that *Goss* would give "the student who is given a failing grade, who is not promoted, who is excluded from certain extracurricular activities, who is assigned to a school reserved for children of less than average ability, or who is placed in the 'vocational' rather than the 'college preparatory' track" a due process claim. The Supreme Court has been less than enthusiastic in addressing student due process challenges to academic dismissals at the higher education level. *See Board of Curators v. Horowitz,* 435 U.S. 78 (1978) (review of dismissal from medical school by seven outside physicians was more than what due process required); *Regents of the Univ. of Mich. v. Ewing,* 474 U.S. 214 (1985) (stating that federal courts are not the appropriate forum in which to evaluate academic decisions made by educators and should be overridden only when a substantial departure from academic norms). For commentary on how courts analyze academic decisions, see John Dayton & Anne Profitt Dupre, *Grades: Achievement, Attendance or Attitude?,* 199 EDUC. L. REP. 569 (2005).

In K–12 education, courts have been asked to address student due process claims in various contexts. For example, one student claimed that temporary placement in a "timeout" area that was segregated from other students violated due process. *Dickens v. Johnson County School Board of Educ.,* 661 F. Supp. 155, 156–57 (E.D. Tenn. 1987) (rejecting procedural and substantive due process claims where "timeout" did not preclude student from attending classes and was not unduly harsh). Other challenges include due process claims for removal from a varsity cheering squad, *Havercamp v. Unified School District.,* 689 F. Supp. 1055 (D. Kan. 1986); exclusion from a gifted class, *Doe v. Pennsylvania,* 593 F. Supp. 54, 56 (E.D. Pa. 1984); and dismissal from a high school band and a softball team, *Bernstein v. Menard,* 557 F. Supp. 90 (E.D. Va. 1982); *Wooten v. Pleasant Hope R-VI School District.,* 139 F. Supp. 2d 835 (W.D. Mich. 2000) (no property interest in participation on softball team absent explicit language in the school handbook to the contrary).

Students have also challenged their exclusion from the National Honor Society (NHS) on due process grounds. For a law review article that summarizes the cases challenging exclusion from NHS membership, see Thomas A. Schweitzer, *"A" Students Go to Court: Is Membership in the National Honor Society a Cognizable Legal Right?",* 50 SYR. L. REV. 63 (2000). Although one district court decided that a student who was excluded from NHS because of drinking was deprived of a liberty interest in his good name, reputation, honor, and integrity, *Warren v. National Ass'n of Secondary School Principals,* 375

F. Supp. 1043 (N.D. Tex. 1974), the case was decided before *Paul v. Davis*, 424 U.S. 693 (1976), where the Supreme Court held that there is no liberty interest in reputation alone. Since the *Warren* decision, students with due process claims have fared less well. *See, e.g., Karnstein v. Pewaukee Sch. Bd.,* 557 F. Supp. 565 (E.D. Wis. 1983); *Price v. Young,* 580 F. Supp 1 (E.D. Ark. 1983) (both saying no property or liberty interest in NHS membership); *Dangler v. Yorktown Central Sch.,* 771 F. Supp. 625, 628 (S.D.N.Y 1991) (citing *Price* and *Karnstein,* "unanimously courts have concluded that membership in the National Honor Society does not give rise to a property interest which entitles one to due process of law").

For a discussion of cases where students have made successful claims under Title IX for wrongful exclusion from the National Honor Society, see § 4.05, *infra.*

7. How does the *Goss* majority's view of the role of the school and the function of teachers and principals differ from that of Justice Powell and the dissenters?

8. If a student is expelled with due process, is there any obligation to continue to provide him with an education? A court in New Jersey held that the state had an obligation under that state's constitution to provide an alternative school program for an expelled student until he attained his high school diploma or his nineteenth birthday. *State of N.J. In the Interest of G.S.,* 749 A.2d 902 (N.J. Super. Ch. 2000). The court focused on the text of the New Jersey constitution, which states: "The legislature shall provide for the maintenance and support of a thorough and efficient system of free public schools for the instruction of all the children in the State between the ages of five and eighteen years." N.J. CONST. ART. 8, § 4, para. 1.

A CONSTITUTIONAL RIGHT TO EDUCATION?

The United States Constitution never mentions education. In perhaps its most significant education case since *Brown v. Board of Education*, the Supreme Court, in *San Antonio Independent School District v. Rodriguez*, 411 U.S. 1 (1973), held that education was not a fundamental right. This holding dashed the hopes of litigants who hoped to use the federal constitution to address disparities in school funding among school districts.

In *Plyler v. Doe*, 457 U.S. 202 (1982), however, the Supreme Court addressed whether a state could deny access to education to children who were illegal aliens. Although reaffirming that education was not a fundamental right, the Court rejected the state's argument that aliens were not persons within the jurisdiction of the United States and held that the state statute that denied these children access violated the equal protection clause of the U.S. Constitution. Applying the intermediate standard of review — whether the classification in the statute has a substantial relationship to an important government interest — the Court stated that denying children educational benefits imposes a lifetime hardship based on circumstances that the children can not control.

Plyer was the high water mark for school finance litigants seeking help from the federal constitution. In *Kadrmas v. Dickinson Public Schools*, 487 U.S.

450 (1988), the U.S. Supreme Court ruled that denying school bus transportation to an indigent student for failure to pay school bus fees did not violate the child's equal protection rights. Affirming once again that education is not a fundamental right subject to strict scrutiny, the court ruled that the North Dakota statute authorizing school bus user fees for unreorganized school districts satisfied the rational basis test.

Left with little hope of success in federal court, litigants seeking equity in school funding turned to the state courts. The constitutions of all fifty states contain an education clause, although the wording may change from state to state. *See, e.g.*, CAL. CONST. ART. IX, § 1 ("A general diffusion of knowledge and intelligence being essential to the preservation of the rights and liberties of the people, the Legislature shall encourage by all suitable means the promotion of intellectual, scientific, moral, and agricultural improvement."); GA. CONST. ART VIII, § 1, ¶ 1 ("The provision of an adequate public education for the citizens shall be a primary obligation of the State of Georgia."); N.Y. CONST. ART. XI, § 1 ("The legislature shall provide for the maintenance and support of a system of free common schools, wherein all the children of this state may be educated."); VA. CONST. ART. VIII, § 1 ("The General Assembly shall provide for a system of free public elementary and secondary schools for all children of school age throughout the Commonwealth, and shall seek to ensure that an educational program of high quality is established and continually maintained."). The highest courts in at least thirty-six states have issued opinions on the merits of funding litigation suits, with about half upholding state funding systems and half declaring the systems unconstitutional. Some states have experienced protracted serial litigation that has extended for decades. Litigation has been filed and is still pending in many more states. *See* John Dayton & Anne Proffitt Dupre, *School Funding Litigation: Who's Winning the War?*, 57 VAND. L. REV. 2351 (2004).

For a discussion of the continuing obligation of school districts to provide education services to expelled disabled children under federal statute — the Individuals With Disabilities Education Act — see § 4.06, *infra*.

[B] Corporal Punishment

[1] Eighth Amendment and Procedural Due Process

INGRAHAM v. WRIGHT

Supreme Court of the United States
430 U.S. 651 (1977)

MR. JUSTICE POWELL *delivered the opinion of the Court.*

This case presents questions concerning the use of corporal punishment in public schools: First, whether the paddling of students as a means of maintaining school discipline constitutes cruel and unusual punishment in violation of the Eighth Amendment; and, second, to the extent that paddling is constitutionally permissible, whether the Due Process Clause of the Fourteenth Amendment requires prior notice and an opportunity to be heard.

I

Petitioners James Ingraham and Roosevelt Andrews filed the complaint in this case on January 7, 1971, in the United States District Court for the Southern District of Florida. At the time both were enrolled in the Charles R. Drew Junior High School in Dade County, Fla., Ingraham in the eighth grade and Andrews in the ninth. The complaint contained three counts, each alleging a separate cause of action for deprivation of constitutional rights. . . .

Petitioners' evidence may be summarized briefly. In the 1970-1971 school year many of the 237 schools in Dade County used corporal punishment as a means of maintaining discipline pursuant to Florida legislation and a local School Board regulation. The statute then in effect authorized limited corporal punishment by negative inference, proscribing punishment which was "degrading or unduly severe" or which was inflicted without prior consultation with the principal or the teacher in charge of the school. FLA. STAT. ANN. § 232.27 (1961). The regulation contained explicit directions and limitations. The authorized punishment consisted of paddling the recalcitrant student on the buttocks with a flat wooden paddle measuring less than two feet long, three to four inches wide, and about one-half inch thick. The normal punishment was limited to one to five "licks" or blows with the paddle and resulted in no apparent physical injury to the student. School authorities viewed corporal punishment as a less drastic means of discipline than suspension or expulsion. Contrary to the procedural requirements of the statute and regulation, teachers often paddled students on their own authority without first consulting the principal.

Petitioners focused on Drew Junior High School, the school in which both Ingraham and Andrews were enrolled in the fall of 1970. In an apparent reference to Drew, the District Court found that "[t]he instances of punishment which could be characterized as severe, accepting the students' testimony as credible, took place in one junior high school." The evidence, consisting mainly of the testimony of 16 students, suggests that the regime at Drew was exceptionally harsh. The testimony of Ingraham and Andrews, in support of their individual claims for damages, is illustrative. Because he was slow to respond to his teacher's instructions, Ingraham was subjected to more than 20 licks with a paddle while being held over a table in the principal's office. The paddling was so severe that he suffered a hematoma.[39]

. . . .

The District Court made no findings on the credibility of the students' testimony. Rather, assuming their testimony to be credible, the court found no constitutional basis for relief. The court concluded that the punishment authorized and practiced generally in the county schools violated no constitutional right.

---

[39] [9] Stedman's Medical Dictionary (23d ed. 1976) defines "hematoma" as

"[a] localized mass of extravasated blood that is relatively or completely confined within an organ or tissue. . .; the blood is usually clotted (or partly clotted), and, depending on how long it has been there, may manifest various degrees of organization and decolorization."

A panel of the Court of Appeals voted to reverse. The panel concluded that the punishment was so severe and oppressive as to violate the Eighth and Fourteenth Amendments, and that the procedures failed to satisfy the requirements of the Due Process Clause. Upon rehearing, the en banc court rejected these conclusions and affirmed the judgment of the District Court. . . .

We granted certiorari, limited to the questions of cruel and unusual punishment and procedural due process.

II

In addressing the scope of the Eighth Amendment's prohibition on cruel and unusual punishment, this Court has found it useful to refer to "[t]raditional common-law concepts," and to the ["attitudes] which our society has traditionally taken." So, too, in defining the requirements of procedural due process under the Fifth and Fourteenth Amendments, the Court has been attuned to what "has always been the law of the land," and to "traditional ideas of fair procedure." We, therefore, begin by examining the way in which our traditions and our laws have responded to the use of corporal punishment in public schools.

The use of corporal punishment in this country as a means of disciplining schoolchildren dates back to the colonial period. It has survived the transformation of primary and secondary education from the colonials' reliance on optional private arrangements to our present system of compulsory education and dependence on public schools. Despite the general abandonment of corporal punishment as a means of punishing criminal offenders, the practice continues to play a role in the public education of schoolchildren in most parts of the country. Professional and public opinion is sharply divided on the practice, and has been for more than a century. Yet we can discern no trend toward its elimination.

At common law a single principle has governed the use of corporal punishment since before the American Revolution: Teachers may impose reasonable but not excessive force to discipline a child. Blackstone catalogued among the "absolute rights of individuals" the right "to security from the corporal insults of menaces, assaults, beating, and wounding," 1 W. Blackstone, Commentaries *134, but he did not regard it a "corporal insult" for a teacher to inflict "moderate correction" on a child in his care. To the extent that force was "necessary to answer the purposes for which [the teacher] is employed," Blackstone viewed it as "justifiable or lawful." The basic doctrine has not changed. The prevalent rule in this country today privileges such force as a teacher or administrator "reasonably believes to be necessary for [the child's] proper control, training, or education." RESTATEMENT (SECOND) OF TORTS § 147 (2) (1965); see id., § 153 (2). To the extent that the force is excessive or unreasonable, the educator in virtually all States is subject to possible civil and criminal liability.

Although the early cases viewed the authority of the teacher as deriving from the parents, the concept of parental delegation has been replaced by the view — more consonant with compulsory education laws — that the State itself may impose such corporal punishment as is reasonably necessary "for the proper education of the child and for the maintenance of group discipline." 1 F. HARPER & F. JAMES, LAW OF TORTS § 3.20, p. 292 (1956).[40] All of the circumstances are to be taken into account in determining whether the punishment is reasonable in a particular case. Among the most important considerations are the seriousness of the offense, the attitude and past behavior of the child, the nature and severity of the punishment, the age and strength of the child, and the availability of less severe but equally effective means of discipline.

Of the 23 States that have addressed the problem through legislation, 21 have authorized the moderate use of corporal punishment in public schools. Of these States only a few have elaborated on the common-law test of reasonableness, typically providing for approval or notification of the child's parents, or for infliction of punishment only by the principal or in the presence of an adult witness. Only two States, Massachusetts and New Jersey, have prohibited all corporal punishment in their public schools. Where the legislatures have not acted, the state courts have uniformly preserved the common-law rule permitting teachers to use reasonable force in disciplining children in their charge.

Against this background of historical and contemporary approval of reasonable corporal punishment, we turn to the constitutional questions before us.

III

The Eighth Amendment provides: "Excessive bail shall not be required, nor excessive fines imposed, nor cruel and unusual punishments inflicted." Bail, fines, and punishment traditionally have been associated with the criminal process, and by subjecting the three to parallel limitations the text of the Amendment suggests an intention to limit the power of those entrusted with the criminal-law function of government. An examination of the history of the Amendment and the decisions of this Court construing the proscription against cruel and unusual punishment confirms that it was designed to protect those convicted of crimes. We adhere to this longstanding limitation and hold that the Eighth Amendment does not apply to the paddling of children as a means of maintaining discipline in public schools.

A

The history of the Eighth Amendment is well known. The text was taken, almost verbatim, from a provision of the Virginia Declaration of Rights of 1776, which in turn derived from the English Bill of Rights of 1689. The English version, adopted after the accession of William and Mary, was intended to curb the excesses of English judges under the reign of James II. Historians have viewed the English provision as a reaction either to the "Bloody Assize," the treason trials conducted by Chief Justice Jeffreys in 1685 after

---

40 [22] Today, corporal punishment in school is conditioned on parental approval only in California. CAL. EDUC. CODE § 49001 (West Supp. 1977). This Court has held in a summary affirmance that parental approval of corporal punishment is not constitutionally required. Baker v. Owen, 423 U.S. 907 (1975), *aff'g* 395 F. Supp. 294 (M.D.N.C).

the abortive rebellion of the Duke of Monmouth, or to the perjury prosecution of Titus Oates in the same year. In either case, the exclusive concern of the English version was the conduct of judges in enforcing the criminal law. The original draft introduced in the House of Commons provided:

> "The requiring excessive bail of persons committed in criminal cases and imposing excessive fines, and illegal punishments, to be prevented."

Although the reference to "criminal cases" was eliminated from the final draft, the preservation of a similar reference in the preamble indicates that the deletion was without substantive significance. Thus, Blackstone treated each of the provision's three prohibitions as bearing only on criminal proceedings and judgments.

The Americans who adopted the language of this part of the English Bill of Rights in framing their own State and Federal Constitutions 100 years later feared the imposition of torture and other cruel punishments not only by judges acting beyond their lawful authority, but also by legislatures engaged in making the laws by which judicial authority would be measured. Indeed, the principal concern of the American Framers appears to have been with the legislative definition of crimes and punishments. But if the American provision was intended to restrain government more broadly than its English model, the subject to which it was intended to apply — the criminal process — was the same.

At the time of its ratification, the original Constitution was criticized in the Massachusetts and Virginia Conventions for its failure to provide any protection for persons convicted of crimes. This criticism provided the impetus for inclusion of the Eighth Amendment in the Bill of Rights. When the Eighth Amendment was debated in the First Congress, it was met by the objection that the Cruel and Unusual Punishments Clause might have the effect of outlawing what were then the common criminal punishments of hanging, whipping, and earcropping. 1 Annals of Cong. 754 (1789). The objection was not heeded, "precisely because the legislature would otherwise have had the unfettered power to prescribe punishments for crimes."

B

In light of this history, it is not surprising to find that every decision of this Court considering whether a punishment is "cruel and unusual" within the meaning of the Eighth and Fourteenth Amendments has dealt with a criminal punishment. *See Estelle v. Gamble,* 429 U.S. 97 (1976) (incarceration without medical care); *Gregg v. Georgia,* 428 U.S. 153 (1976) (execution for murder); *Furman v. Georgia, supra* (execution for murder); *Powell v. Texas,* 392 U.S. 514 (1968) (plurality opinion) ($ 20 fine for public drunkenness); *Robinson v. California,* 370 U.S. 660 (1962) (incarceration as a criminal for addiction to narcotics); *Trop v. Dulles,* 356 U.S. 86 (1958) (plurality opinion) (expatriation for desertion); *Louisiana ex rel. Francis v. Resweber,* 329 U.S. 459 (1947) (execution by electrocution after a failed first attempt); *Weems v. United States, supra* (15 years' imprisonment and other penalties for falsifying an official document); *Howard v. Fleming,* 191 U.S. 126 (1903) (10 years' imprisonment for conspiracy to defraud); *In re Kemmler, supra* (execution by electrocution); *Wilkerson v. Utah,* 99 U.S. 130 (1879) (execution by firing squad); *Pervear v. Commonwealth,* 5 Wall. 475 (1867) (fine and imprisonment at hard labor for bootlegging).

These decisions recognize that the Cruel and Unusual Punishments Clause circumscribes the criminal process in three ways: First, it limits the kinds of punishment that can be imposed on those convicted of crimes, second, it proscribes punishment grossly disproportionate to the severity of the crime, and third, it imposes substantive limits on what can be made criminal and punished as such. We have recognized the last limitation as one to be applied sparingly. "The primary purpose of [the Cruel and Unusual Punishments Clause] has always been considered, and properly so, to be directed at the method or kind of punishment imposed for the violation of criminal statutes. . . ."

C

Petitioners acknowledge that the original design of the Cruel and Unusual Punishments Clause was to limit criminal punishments, but urge nonetheless that the prohibition should be extended to ban the paddling of schoolchildren. Observing that the Framers of the Eighth Amendment could not have envisioned our present system of public and compulsory education, with its opportunities for noncriminal punishments, petitioners contend that extension of the prohibition against cruel punishments is necessary lest we afford greater protection to criminals than to schoolchildren. It would be anomalous, they say, if schoolchildren could be beaten without constitutional redress, while hardened criminals suffering the same beatings at the hands of their jailers might have a valid claim under the Eighth Amendment. Whatever force this logic may have in other settings, we find it an inadequate basis for wrenching the Eighth Amendment from its historical context and extending it to traditional disciplinary practices in the public schools.

The prisoner and the schoolchild stand in wholly different circumstances, separated by the harsh facts of criminal conviction and incarceration. The prisoner's conviction entitles the State to classify him as a "criminal," and his incarceration deprives him of the freedom "to be with family and friends and to form the other enduring attachments of normal life." Prison brutality, as the Court of Appeals observed in this case, is "part of the total punishment to which the individual is being subjected for his crime and, as such, is a proper subject for Eighth Amendment scrutiny." Even so, the protection afforded by the Eighth Amendment is limited. After incarceration, only the "unnecessary and wanton infliction of pain" constitutes cruel and unusual punishment forbidden by the Eighth Amendment.

The schoolchild has little need for the protection of the Eighth Amendment. Though attendance may not always be voluntary, the public school remains an open institution. Except perhaps when very young, the child is not physically restrained from leaving school during school hours; and at the end of the school day, the child is invariably free to return home. Even while at school, the child brings with him the support of family and friends and is rarely apart from teachers and other pupils who may witness and protest any instances of mistreatment.

The openness of the public school and its supervision by the community afford significant safeguards against the kinds of abuses from which the Eighth Amendment protects the prisoner. In virtually every community where corporal punishment is permitted in the schools, these safeguards are reinforced by the legal constraints of the common law. Public school teachers and administrators are privileged at common law to inflict only such corporal punishment as is reasonably necessary for the proper education and discipline of the child; any punishment going beyond the privilege may result in both civil and criminal liability. As long as the schools are open to public scrutiny, there is no reason to believe that the common-law constraints will not effectively remedy and deter excesses such as those alleged in this case.[41]

We conclude that when public school teachers or administrators impose disciplinary corporal punishment, the Eighth Amendment is inapplicable. The pertinent constitutional question is whether the imposition is consonant with the requirements of due process.

The Fourteenth Amendment prohibits any state deprivation of life, liberty, or property without due process of law. Application of this prohibition requires the familiar two-stage analysis: We must first ask whether the asserted individual interests are encompassed within the Fourteenth Amendment's protection of "life, liberty or property"; if protected interests are implicated, we then must decide what procedures constitute "due process of law." Following that analysis here, we find that corporal punishment in public schools implicates a constitutionally protected liberty interest, but we hold that the traditional common-law remedies are fully adequate to afford due process.

A

"[The] range of interests protected by procedural due process is not infinite." We have repeatedly rejected "the notion that any grievous loss visited upon

---

[41] [39] Putting history aside as irrelevant, the dissenting opinion of MR. JUSTICE WHITE argues that a "purposive analysis" should control the reach of the Eighth Amendment. There is no support whatever for this approach in the decisions of this Court. Although an imposition must be "punishment" for the Cruel and Unusual Punishments Clause to apply, the Court has never held that all punishments are subject to Eighth Amendment scrutiny. The applicability of the Eighth Amendment always has turned on its original meaning, as demonstrated by its historical derivation.

The dissenting opinion warns that as a consequence of our decision today, teachers may "cut off a child's ear for being late to class." This rhetoric bears no relation to reality or to the issues presented in this case. The laws of virtually every State forbid the excessive physical punishment of schoolchildren. Yet the logic of the dissent would make the judgment of which disciplinary punishments are reasonable and which are excessive a matter of constitutional principle in every case, to be decided ultimately by this Court. The hazards of such a broad reading of the Eighth Amendment are clear. "It is always time to say that this Nation is too large, too complex and composed of too great a diversity of peoples for any one of us to have the wisdom to establish the rules by which local Americans must govern their local affairs. The constitutional rule we are urged to adopt is not merely revolutionary — it departs from the ancient faith based on the premise that experience in making local laws by local people themselves is by far the safest guide for a nation like ours to follow."

a person by the State is sufficient to invoke the procedural protections of the Due Process Clause." Due process is required only when a decision of the State implicates an interest within the protection of the Fourteenth Amendment. And "to determine whether due process requirements apply in the first place, we must look not to the 'weight' but to the nature of the interest at stake."

The Due Process Clause of the Fifth Amendment, later incorporated into the Fourteenth, was intended to give Americans at least the protection against governmental power that they had enjoyed as Englishmen against the power of the Crown. The liberty preserved from deprivation without due process included the right "generally to enjoy those privileges long recognized at common law as essential to the orderly pursuit of happiness by free men." *Meyer v. Nebraska.* Among the historic liberties so protected was a right to be free from, and to obtain judicial relief for, unjustified intrusions on personal security.

While the contours of this historic liberty interest in the context of our federal system of government have not been defined precisely, they always have been thought to encompass freedom from bodily restraint and punishment. It is fundamental that the state cannot hold and physically punish an individual except in accordance with due process of law.

This constitutionally protected liberty interest is at stake in this case. There is, of course, a de minimis level of imposition with which the Constitution is not concerned. But at least where school authorities, acting under color of state law, deliberately decide to punish a child for misconduct by restraining the child and inflicting appreciable physical pain, we hold that Fourteenth Amendment liberty interests are implicated.[42]

B

"[The] question remains what process is due." Were it not for the common-law privilege permitting teachers to inflict reasonable corporal punishment on children in their care, and the availability of the traditional remedies for abuse, the case for requiring advance procedural safeguards would be strong indeed.[43] But here we deal with a punishment — paddling — within that tradition, and the question is whether the common-law remedies are adequate to afford due process.

" '[D]ue process,' unlike some legal rules, is not a technical conception with a fixed content unrelated to time, place and circumstances. . . . Representing a profound attitude of fairness . . . 'due process' is compounded of history,

---

[42] [43] Unlike *Goss v. Lopez*, 419 U.S. 565 (1975), this case does not involve the state-created property interest in public education. The purpose of corporal punishment is to correct a child's behavior without interrupting his education. That corporal punishment may, in a rare case, have the unintended effect of temporarily removing a child from school affords no basis for concluding that the practice itself deprives students of property protected by the Fourteenth Amendment. Nor does this case involve any state-created interest in liberty going beyond the Fourteenth Amendment's protection of freedom from bodily restraint and corporal punishment.

[43] [44] If the common-law privilege to inflict reasonable corporal punishment in school were inapplicable, it is doubtful whether any procedure short of a trial in a criminal or juvenile court could satisfy the requirements of procedural due process for the imposition of such punishment.

reason, the past course of decisions, and stout confidence in the strength of the democratic faith which we profess. . . ."

Whether in this case the common-law remedies for excessive corporal punishment constitute due process of law must turn on an analysis of the competing interests at stake, viewed against the background of "history, reason, [and] the past course of decisions." The analysis requires consideration of three distinct factors: "First, the private interest that will be affected. . . ; second, the risk of an erroneous deprivation of such interest . . . and the probable value, if any, of additional or substitute procedural safeguards; and finally, the [state] interest, including the function involved and the fiscal and administrative burdens that the additional or substitute procedural requirement would entail." *Mathews v. Eldridge,* 424 U.S. 319, 335 (1976).

1

Because it is rooted in history, the child's liberty interest in avoiding corporal punishment while in the care of public school authorities is subject to historical limitations. Under the common law, an invasion of personal security gave rise to a right to recover damages in a subsequent judicial proceeding. But the right of recovery was qualified by the concept of justification. Thus, there could be no recovery against a teacher who gave only "moderate correction" to a child. To the extent that the force used was reasonable in light of its purpose, it was not wrongful, but rather "justifiable or lawful."

The concept that reasonable corporal punishment in school is justifiable continues to be recognized in the laws of most States. It represents "the balance struck by this country," between the child's interest in personal security and the traditional view that some limited corporal punishment may be necessary in the course of a child's education. Under that longstanding accommodation of interests, there can be no deprivation of substantive rights as long as disciplinary corporal punishment is within the limits of the common-law privilege.

This is not to say that the child's interest in procedural safeguards is insubstantial. The school disciplinary process is not "a totally accurate, unerring process, never mistaken and never unfair. . . ." *Goss v. Lopez,* 419 U.S. 565, 579–580 (1975). In any deliberate infliction of corporal punishment on a child who is restrained for that purpose, there is some risk that the intrusion on the child's liberty will be unjustified and therefore unlawful. In these circumstances the child has a strong interest in procedural safeguards that minimize the risk of wrongful punishment and provide for the resolution of disputed questions of justification.

We turn now to a consideration of the safeguards that are available under applicable Florida law.

2

Florida has continued to recognize, and indeed has strengthened by statute, the common-law right of a child not to be subjected to excessive corporal punishment in school. Under Florida law the teacher and principal of the school decide in the first instance whether corporal punishment is reasonably necessary under the circumstances in order to discipline a child who has misbehaved. But they must exercise prudence and restraint. For Florida has preserved the traditional judicial proceedings for determining whether the punishment was justified. If the punishment inflicted is later found to have been excessive — not reasonably believed at the time to be necessary for the child's discipline or training — the school authorities inflicting it may be held liable in damages to the child and, if malice is shown, they may be subject to criminal penalties.

Although students have testified in this case to specific instances of abuse, there is every reason to believe that such mistreatment is an aberration. The uncontradicted evidence suggests that corporal punishment in the Dade County schools was, "[w]ith the exception of a few cases, . . . unremarkable in physical severity." Moreover, because paddlings are usually inflicted in response to conduct directly observed by teachers in their presence, the risk that a child will be paddled without cause is typically insignificant. In the ordinary case, a disciplinary paddling neither threatens seriously to violate any substantive rights nor condemns the child "to suffer grievous loss of any kind."

In those cases where severe punishment is contemplated, the available civil and criminal sanctions for abuse — considered in light of the openness of the school environment — afford significant protection against unjustified corporal punishment. Teachers and school authorities are unlikely to inflict corporal punishment unnecessarily or excessively when a possible consequence of doing so is the institution of civil or criminal proceedings against them.

It still may be argued, of course, that the child's liberty interest would be better protected if the common-law remedies were supplemented by the administrative safeguards of prior notice and a hearing. We have found frequently that some kind of prior hearing is necessary to guard against arbitrary impositions on interests protected by the Fourteenth Amendment. But where the State has preserved what "has always been the law of the land," the case for administrative safeguards is significantly less compelling.

3

But even if the need for advance procedural safeguards were clear, the question would remain whether the incremental benefit could justify the cost. Acceptance of petitioners' claims would work a transformation in the law governing corporal punishment in Florida and most other States. Given the impracticability of formulating a rule of procedural due process that varies with the severity of the particular imposition, the prior hearing petitioners seek would have to precede any paddling, however moderate or trivial.

Such a universal constitutional requirement would significantly burden the use of corporal punishment as a disciplinary measure. Hearings — even informal hearings — require time, personnel, and a diversion of attention from normal school pursuits. School authorities may well choose to abandon corporal punishment rather than incur the burdens of complying with the procedural requirements. Teachers, properly concerned with maintaining authority in the classroom, may well prefer to rely on other disciplinary measures — which they may view as less effective — rather than confront the possible disruption that prior notice and a hearing may entail. Paradoxically, such an alteration of disciplinary policy is most likely to occur in the ordinary case where the contemplated punishment is well within the common-law privilege.

Elimination or curtailment of corporal punishment would be welcomed by many as a societal advance. But when such a policy choice may result from this Court's determination of an asserted right to due process, rather than from the normal processes of community debate and legislative action, the societal costs cannot be dismissed as insubstantial.[44] We are reviewing here a legislative judgment, rooted in history and reaffirmed in the laws of many States, that corporal punishment serves important educational interests. This judgment must be viewed in light of the disciplinary problems commonplace in the schools. As noted in *Goss v. Lopez*: "Events calling for discipline are frequent occurrences and sometimes require immediate, effective action." Assessment of the need for, and the appropriate means of maintaining, school discipline is committed generally to the discretion of school authorities subject to state law. "[T]he Court has repeatedly emphasized the need for affirming the comprehensive authority of the States and of school officials, consistent with fundamental constitutional safeguards, to prescribe and control conduct in the schools." *Tinker v. Des Moines School Dist.*, 393 U.S. 503, 507 (1969).[45]

"At some point the benefit of an additional safeguard to the individual affected . . . and to society in terms of increased assurance that the action is just, may be outweighed by the cost." We think that point has been reached in this case. In view of the low incidence of abuse, the openness of our schools, and the common-law safeguards that already exist, the risk of error that may result in violation of a schoolchild's substantive rights can only be regarded as minimal. Imposing additional administrative safeguards as a constitutional requirement might reduce that risk marginally, but would also entail a significant intrusion into an area of primary educational responsibility. We conclude that the Due Process Clause does not require notice and a hearing prior to the imposition of corporal punishment in the public schools, as that practice is authorized and limited by the common law.[46]

---

44 [52] "It may be true that procedural regularity in disciplinary proceedings promotes a sense of institutional rapport and open communication, a perception of fair treatment, and provides the offender and his fellow students a showcase of democracy at work. But . . . [r]espect for democratic institutions will equally dissipate if they are thought too ineffectual to provide their students an environment of order in which the educational process may go forward. . . ." Wilkinson, Goss v. Lopez: *The Supreme Court as School Superintendent*, 1975 Sup. Ct. Rev. 25, 71–72.

45 [54] The need to maintain order in a trial courtroom raises similar problems. In that context, this Court has recognized the power of the trial judge "to punish summarily and without notice or hearing contemptuous conduct committed in his presence and observed by him." *Taylor v. Hayes*, 418 U.S. 488, 497 (1974), citing *Ex parte Terry*, 128 U.S. 289 (1888). The punishment so imposed may be as severe as six months in prison. *See Codispoti v. Pennsylvania*, 418 U.S. 506, 513–515 (1974); *cf. Muniz v. Hoffman*, 422 U.S. 454, 475–476 (1975).

46 [55] Mr. Justice White's dissenting opinion offers no manageable standards for determining what process is due in any particular case. The dissent apparently would require, as a general rule, only "an informal give-and-take between student and disciplinarian." But the dissent would depart from these "minimal procedures" — requiring even witnesses, counsel, and cross-examination — in cases where the punishment reaches some undefined level of severity. School

V

Petitioners cannot prevail on either of the theories before us in this case. The Eighth Amendment's prohibition against cruel and unusual punishment is inapplicable to school paddlings, and the Fourteenth Amendment's requirement of procedural due process is satisfied by Florida's preservation of common-law constraints and remedies. We therefore agree with the Court of Appeals that petitioners' evidence affords no basis for injunctive relief, and that petitioners cannot recover damages on the basis of any Eighth Amendment or procedural due process violation.

Affirmed.

Mr. Justice White, with whom Mr. Justice Brennan, Mr. Justice Marshall, and Mr. Justice Stevens join, *dissenting*.

Today the Court holds that corporal punishment in public schools, no matter how severe, can never be the subject of the protections afforded by the Eighth Amendment. It also holds that students in the public school systems are not constitutionally entitled to a hearing of any sort before beatings can be inflicted on them. Because I believe that these holdings are inconsistent with the prior decisions of this Court and are contrary to a reasoned analysis of the constitutional provisions involved, I respectfully dissent.

I

A

The Eighth Amendment places a flat prohibition against the infliction of "cruel and unusual punishments." This reflects a societal judgment that there are some punishments that are so barbaric and inhumane that we will not permit them to be imposed on anyone, no matter how opprobrious the offense. If there are some punishments that are so barbaric that they may not be imposed for the commission of crimes, designated by our social system as the most thoroughly reprehensible acts an individual can commit, then, a fortiori, similar punishments may not be imposed on persons for less culpable acts, such as breaches of school discipline. Thus, if it is constitutionally impermissible to cut off someone's ear for the commission of murder, it must be unconstitutional to cut off a child's ear for being late to class.[47] Although there

---

authorities are left to guess at the degree of punishment that will require more than an "informal give-and-take" and at the additional process that may be constitutionally required. The impracticality of such an approach is self-evident, and illustrates the hazards of ignoring the traditional solution of the common law. We agree with the dissent that the *Goss* procedures will often be, "if anything, less than a fair-minded school principal would impose upon himself." But before this Court invokes the Constitution to impose a procedural requirement, it should be reasonably certain that the effect will be to afford protection appropriate to the constitutional interests at stake. The dissenting opinion's reading of the Constitution suggests no such beneficial result and, indeed, invites a lowering of existing constitutional standards.

47 [1] There is little reason to fear that if the Eighth Amendment is held to apply at all to corporal punishment of schoolchildren, all paddlings, however moderate, would be prohibited. *Jackson v. Bishop*, 404 F. 2d 571 (CA8 1968), held that any paddling or flogging of prisoners, convicted of crime and serving prison terms, violated the cruel and unusual punishment ban of the Eighth Amendment. But aside from the fact that *Bishop* has never been embraced by this

were no ears cut off in this case, the record reveals beatings so severe that if they were inflicted on a hardened criminal for the commission of a serious crime, they might not pass constitutional muster.

Nevertheless, the majority holds that the Eighth Amendment "was designed to protect [only] those convicted of crimes," relying on a vague and inconclusive recitation of the history of the Amendment. Yet the constitutional prohibition is against cruel and unusual punishments; nowhere is that prohibition limited or modified by the language of the Constitution. Certainly, the fact that the Framers did not choose to insert the word "criminal" into the language of the Eighth Amendment is strong evidence that the Amendment was designed to prohibit all inhumane or barbaric punishments, no matter what the nature of the offense for which the punishment is imposed.

No one can deny that spanking of schoolchildren is "punishment" under any reasonable reading of the word, for the similarities between spanking in public schools and other forms of punishment are too obvious to ignore. Like other forms of punishment, spanking of schoolchildren involves an institutionalized response to the violation of some official rule or regulation proscribing certain conduct and is imposed for the purpose of rehabilitating the offender, deterring the offender and others like him from committing the violation in the future, and inflicting some measure of social retribution for the harm that has been done.

B

We are fortunate that in our society punishments that are severe enough to raise a doubt as to their constitutional validity are ordinarily not imposed without first affording the accused the full panoply of procedural safeguards provided by the criminal process. The effect has been that "every decision of this Court considering whether a punishment is 'cruel and unusual' within the meaning of the Eighth and Fourteenth Amendments has dealt with a criminal punishment." The Court would have us believe from this fact that there is a recognized distinction between criminal and noncriminal punishment for purposes of the Eighth Amendment. This is plainly wrong. "[E]ven a clear legislative classification of a statute as 'non-penal' would not alter the fundamental nature of a plainly penal statute." The relevant inquiry is not

---

Court, the theory of that case was not that bodily punishments are intrinsically barbaric or excessively severe but that paddling of prisoners is "degrading to the punisher and to the punished alike." That approach may be acceptable in the criminal justice system, but it has little if any relevance to corporal punishment in the schools, for it can hardly be said that the use of moderate paddlings in the discipline of children is inconsistent with the country's evolving standards of decency.

On the other hand, when punishment involves a cruel, severe beating or chopping off an ear, something more than merely the dignity of the individual is involved. Whenever a given criminal punishment is "cruel and unusual" because it is inhumane or barbaric, I can think of no reason why it would be any less inhumane or barbaric when inflicted on a schoolchild, as punishment for classroom misconduct.

The issue in this case is whether spankings inflicted on public school-children for breaking school rules is "punishment," not whether such punishment is "cruel and unusual." If the Eighth Amendment does not bar moderate spanking in public schools, it is because moderate spanking is not "cruel and unusual," not because it is not "punishment" as the majority suggests.

whether the offense for which a punishment is inflicted has been labeled as criminal, but whether the purpose of the deprivation is among those ordinarily associated with punishment, such as retribution, rehabilitation, or deterrence.

If this purposive approach were followed in the present case, it would be clear that spanking in the Florida public schools is punishment within the meaning of the Eighth Amendment. The District Court found that "[c]orporal punishment is one of a variety of measures employed in the school system for the correction of pupil behavior and the preservation of order." Behavior correction and preservation of order are purposes ordinarily associated with punishment.

Without even mentioning the purposive analysis applied in the prior decisions of this Court, the majority adopts a rule that turns on the label given to the offense for which the punishment is inflicted. Thus, the record in this case reveals that one student at Drew Junior High School received 50 licks with a paddle for allegedly making an obscene telephone call. The majority holds that the Eighth Amendment does not prohibit such punishment since it was only inflicted for a breach of school discipline. However, that same conduct is punishable as a misdemeanor under Florida law, and there can be little doubt that if that same "punishment" had been inflicted by an officer of the state courts for [that conduct] it would have had to satisfy the requirements of the Eighth Amendment.

C

In fact, as the Court recognizes, the Eighth Amendment has never been confined to criminal punishments.[48] Nevertheless, the majority adheres to its view that any protections afforded by the Eighth Amendment must have something to do with criminals, and it would therefore confine any exceptions to its general rule that only criminal punishments are covered by the Eighth Amendment to abuses inflicted on prisoners. Thus, if a prisoner is beaten mercilessly for a breach of discipline, he is entitled to the protection of the Eighth Amendment, while a schoolchild who commits the same breach of discipline and is similarly beaten is simply not covered.

The purported explanation of this anomaly is the assertion that schoolchildren have no need for the Eighth Amendment. We are told that schools are open institutions, subject to constant public scrutiny; that school children have adequate remedies under state law; and that prisoners suffer the social stigma of being labeled as criminals. How any of these policy considerations got into the Constitution is difficult to discern, for the Court has never considered any of these factors in determining the scope of the Eighth Amendment.

---

48 [4] In *Estelle v. Gamble*, 429 U.S. 97 (1976), a case decided this Term, the Court held that "deliberate indifference to the medical needs of prisoners" by prison officials constitutes cruel and unusual punishment prohibited by the Eighth Amendment. Such deliberate indifference to a prisoner's medical needs clearly is not punishment inflicted for the commission of a crime; it is merely misconduct by a prison official. Similarly, the Eighth Circuit has held that whipping a prisoner with a strap in order to maintain discipline is prohibited by the Eighth Amendment. *Jackson v. Bishop*, 404 F. 2d 571 (1968) (BLACKMUN, J.).

The essence of the majority's argument is that schoolchildren do not need Eighth Amendment protection because corporal punishment is less subject to abuse in the public schools than it is in the prison system. However, it cannot be reasonably suggested that just because cruel and unusual punishments may occur less frequently under public scrutiny, they will not occur at all. The mere fact that a public flogging or a public execution would be available for all to see would not render the punishment constitutional if it were otherwise impermissible. Similarly, the majority would not suggest that a prisoner who is placed in a minimum-security prison and permitted to go home to his family on the weekends should be any less entitled to Eighth Amendment protections than his counterpart in a maximum-security prison. In short, if a punishment is so barbaric and inhumane that it goes beyond the tolerance of a civilized society, its openness to public scrutiny should have nothing to do with its constitutional validity.

Nor is it an adequate answer that schoolchildren may have other state and constitutional remedies available to them. Even assuming that the remedies available to public school students are adequate under Florida law, the availability of state remedies has never been determinative of the coverage or of the protections afforded by the Eighth Amendment. The reason is obvious. The fact that a person may have a state-law cause of action against a public official who tortures him with a thumbscrew for the commission of an antisocial act has nothing to do with the fact that such official conduct is cruel and unusual punishment prohibited by the Eighth Amendment. Indeed, the majority's view was implicitly rejected this Term in *Estelle v. Gamble*, 429 U.S. 97 (1976), when the Court held that failure to provide for the medical needs of prisoners could constitute cruel and unusual punishment even though a medical malpractice remedy in tort was available to prisoners under state law.

D

. . . .

The issue presented in this phase of the case is limited to whether corporal punishment in public schools can ever be prohibited by the Eighth Amendment. I am therefore not suggesting that spanking in the public schools is in every instance prohibited by the Eighth Amendment. My own view is that it is not. I only take issue with the extreme view of the majority that corporal punishment in public schools, no matter how barbaric, inhumane, or severe, is never limited by the Eighth Amendment. Where corporal punishment becomes so severe as to be unacceptable in a civilized society, I can see no reason that it should become any more acceptable just because it is inflicted on children in the public schools.

II

The majority concedes that corporal punishment in the public schools implicates an interest protected by the Due Process Clause — the liberty interest of the student to be free from "bodily restraint and punishment" involving "appreciable physical pain" inflicted by persons acting under color of state law. The question remaining, as the majority recognizes, is what process is due.

The reason that the Constitution requires a State to provide "due process of law" when it punishes an individual for misconduct is to protect the individual from erroneous or mistaken punishment that the State would not have inflicted had it found the facts in a more reliable way. In *Goss v. Lopez*, the Court applied this principle to the school disciplinary process, holding that a student must be given an informal opportunity to be heard before he is finally suspended from public school.

"Disciplinarians, although proceeding in utmost good faith, frequently act on the reports and advice of others; and the controlling facts and the nature of the conduct under challenge are often disputed. *The risk of error is not at all trivial*, and it should be guarded against if that may be done without prohibitive cost or interference with the educational process."

To guard against this risk of punishing an innocent child, the Due Process Clause requires, not an "elaborate hearing" before a neutral party, but simply "an informal give-and-take between student and disciplinarian" which gives the student "an opportunity to explain his version of the facts."

The Court now holds that these "rudimentary precautions against unfair or mistaken findings of misconduct" are not required if the student is punished with "appreciable physical pain" rather than with a suspension, even though both punishments deprive the student of a constitutionally protected interest. Although the respondent school authorities provide absolutely no process to the student before the punishment is finally inflicted, the majority concludes that the student is nonetheless given due process because he can later sue the teacher and recover damages if the punishment was "excessive."

This tort action is utterly inadequate to protect against erroneous infliction of punishment for two reasons. First, under Florida law, a student punished for an act he did not commit cannot recover damages from a teacher "proceeding in utmost good faith . . . on the reports and advice of others"; the student has no remedy at all for punishment imposed on the basis of mistaken facts, at least as long as the punishment was reasonable from the point of view of the disciplinarian, uninformed by any prior hearing.[49] The "traditional

---

49 [11] The majority's assurances to the contrary, it is unclear to me whether and to what extent Florida law provides a damages action against school officials for excessive corporal punishment. Giving the majority the benefit of every doubt, I think it is fair to say that the most a student punished on the basis of mistaken allegations of misconduct can hope for in Florida is a recovery for unreasonable or bad-faith error. But I strongly suspect that even this remedy is not available.

Although the majority does not cite a single case decided under Florida law that recognizes a student's right to sue a school official to recover damages for excessive punishment, I am willing to assume that such a tort action does exist in Florida. I nevertheless have serious doubts about whether it would ever provide a recovery to a student simply because he was punished for an offense he did not commit. All the cases in other jurisdictions cited by the majority involved allegations of punishment disproportionate to the misconduct with which the student was charged; none of the decisions even suggest that a student could recover by showing that the teacher incorrectly imposed punishment for something the student had not done. The majority appears to agree that the damages remedy is available only in cases of punishment unreasonable in light of the misconduct charged. It states: "*In those cases where severe punishment is contemplated,* the available civil and criminal sanctions for abuse . . . afford significant protection against unjustified corporal punishment."

common-law remedies" on which the majority relies thus do nothing to protect the student from the danger that concerned the Court in *Goss* — the risk of reasonable, good-faith mistake in the school disciplinary process.

Second, and more important, even if the student could sue for good-faith error in the infliction of punishment, the lawsuit occurs after the punishment has been finally imposed. The infliction of physical pain is final and irreparable; it cannot be undone in a subsequent proceeding. There is every reason to require, as the Court did in *Goss*, a few minutes of "informal give-and-take between student and disciplinarian" as a "meaningful hedge" against the erroneous infliction of irreparable injury.

The majority's conclusion that a damages remedy for excessive corporal punishment affords adequate process rests on the novel theory that the State may punish an individual without giving him any opportunity to present his side of the story, as long as he can later recover damages from a state official if he is innocent. . . . There is no authority for this theory, nor does the majority purport to find any, in the procedural due process decisions of this Court. Those cases have "consistently held that *some kind of hearing is required at some time before a person is finally deprived* of his property interests . . . [and that] a person's liberty is equally protected. . . ."

. . . .

The majority emphasizes, as did the dissenters in *Goss*, that even the "rudimentary precautions" required by that decision would impose some burden on the school disciplinary process. But those costs are no greater if the student is paddled rather than suspended; the risk of error in the punishment is no smaller; and the fear of "a significant intrusion" into the disciplinary process, is just as exaggerated. The disciplinarian need only take a few minutes to give the student "notice of the charges against him and, if he denies them, an explanation of the evidence the authorities have and an opportunity to present his side of the story." In this context the Constitution requires, "if anything, less than a fair-minded school principal would impose upon himself" in order to avoid injustice.[50]

Even if the common-law remedy for excessive punishment extends to punishment that is "excessive" only in the sense that it is imposed on the basis of mistaken facts, the school authorities are still protected from personal liability by common-law immunity. (They are protected by statutory immunity for liability for enforcing disciplinary rules "[e]xcept in the case of excessive force or cruel and unusual punishment." FLA. STAT. ANN. § 232.275 (1976).) At a minimum, this immunity would protect school officials from damages liability for reasonable mistakes made in good faith. "Although there have been differing emphases and formulations of the common-law immunity of public school officials in cases of student expulsion or suspension, state courts have generally recognized that such officers should be protected from tort liability under state law for all good-faith, nonmalicious action taken to fulfill their official duties." *Wood v. Strickland*, 420 U.S. 308, 318 (1975) (adopting this rule for § 1983 suits involving school discipline).

A final limitation on the student's damages remedy under Florida law is that the student can recover only from the personal assets of the official; the school board's treasury is absolutely protected by sovereign immunity from damages for the torts of its agents. A teacher's limited resources may deter the jury from awarding, or prevent the student from collecting, the full amount of damages to which he is entitled.

50 [18] My view here expressed that the minimal procedures of *Goss* are required for any corporal punishment implicating the student's liberty interest is, of course, not meant to imply that this minimum would be constitutionally sufficient no matter how severe the punishment inflicted.

I would reverse the judgment below.

———

NOTES AND QUESTIONS

1. Observe how certain facts may be used for both sides of the argument. The dissent stresses the fact that no Florida court has ever "recognized" a damages remedy for unreasonable corporal punishment. Does the absence of reported Florida decisions mean that no remedy is available? Or does it suggest that excessive corporal punishment is rare in the public schools? For commentary on Justice Powell's influence on education law, see Victoria J. Dodd, *The Education Justice: The Honorable Lewis Frank Powell, Jr.*, 29 FORDHAM URB. L.J. 683 (2001).

2. If parents object to corporal punishment being used on their child, must school officials refrain from administering corporal punishment? In 1975, the U.S. Supreme Court affirmed, without opinion, a three-judge district court panel ruling that the state's interest in maintaining order was sufficient to sustain the right of teachers and school officials to administer reasonable corporal punishment for disciplinary purposes despite parental objection. *See Baker v. Owen,* 423 U.S. 907 (1975), *aff'g* 395 F. Supp. 294, 301 (M.D.N.C. 1975).

3. The issue of corporal punishment in schools continues to be controversial. *See* Jodi Wilgoren, *Lawsuits Touch Off Debate Over Paddling in Schools*, N.Y. TIMES, May 3, 2001. The New York Times reported that in 2001 corporal punishment was banned in 27 states, an increase from five states in 1984. According to the reported numbers from the U.S. Education Department, 365,000 children were paddled in 1997-98, a figure that has dropped consistently, from 1.4 million in the 1979-80 school year to 613,000 in 1989-90 to 470,000 in 1993-94. *See also* Tawnell D. Hobbs, *DISD Trustees Spar Over Paddling Policy*, THE DALLAS MORNING NEWS, Dec. 9, 2004, at 1B (school board instituted a policy requiring parents to make request in writing if they want their children to be disciplined by paddling; written requests dropped 86 percent in one year, from 3,335 to 453, and board considering total ban); Ellen Barry, *In Memphis, A Battle Won, The Paddle Lost*, L.A. TIMES, Nov. 24, 2004, at A14 (reporting that the Memphis City School Board, one of the last big-city school systems still allowing corporal punishment, voted to ban it; noting that responses to corporal punishment "broke down by race, with black parents most likely to see paddling as a healthy aspect of child rearing"); Theodore Kim, *IPS Board Votes To End Paddling*, THE INDIANAPOLIS NEWS, May 26, 2004, at A1 ("The Indianapolis Public School Board moved to eliminate corporal punishment . . . bringing an end to a decades-old policy and galvanizing the efforts of advocates seeking a statewide ban").

An example of legal commentary about corporal punishment includes Andre R. Imbrogno, *Corporal Punishment in America's Public Schools and the U.N.*

The Court made this reservation explicit in *Goss* by suggesting that more elaborate procedures such as witnesses, counsel, and cross-examination might well be required for suspensions longer than the 10-day maximum involved in that case. A similar caveat is appropriate here.

Convention on the Rights of the Child: A Case for Nonratification, 29 J.L. & EDUC. 125 (April 2000) (rejecting international law as appropriate forum for abolishing corporal punishment in U.S. schools); Kathryn R. Urbonya, *Public School Officials' Use of Physical Force as a Fourth Amendment Seizure: Protecting Students From the Constitutional Chasm Between the Fourth and Fourteenth Amendments*, 69 Geo. WASH. L. REV. 1 (2000) (advocating use of Fourth Amendment to evaluate corporal punishment in schools); John Dayton, *Commentary, Corporal Punishment in Public Schools: The Legal and Political Battle Continues*, 89 ED. LAW REP. 729 (May 1994) (suggesting legality of corporal punishment turns more on elected officials' decisions than court opinions); Jerry R. Parkinson, *Federal Court Treatment of Corporal Punishment in Public Schools: Jurisprudence That is Literally Shocking to the Conscience*, 39 S.D. L. REV. 276 (1994) (criticizing inconsistent results in lower courts following *Ingraham* and arguing that federal courts should take stronger stance toward abolishing corporal punishment in schools); Irene Merker Rosenberg, *A Study in Irrationality: Refusal to Grant Substantive Due Process Protection Against Excessive Corporal Punishment in the Public Schools,* 27 HOUS. L. REV. 399 (1990) (criticizing Fifth Circuit's approach of precluding section 1983 actions for excessive corporal punishment where state remedies exist).

[2]   Substantive Due Process

The *Ingraham* Court did not address whether a student could make a substantive due process claim based on excessive corporal punishment. The following case describes how the lower courts have dealt with the issue.

BROWN v. RAMSEY

U.S. District Court for the Eastern District of Virginia
121 F. Supp. 2d 911 (2000)

ROBERT G. DOUMAR, UNITED STATES DISTRICT JUDGE.

[Daniel, a first-grade student suffering from Asperger's Syndrome, a neurological disorder similar to autism, claimed that his special education teacher and her assistant used a restraint known as a "basket hold" on him, claiming that it made him feel suffocated and choked. (The hold is taught to teachers as a part of a nonviolent intervention strategy and consists of holding the student's wrists and crossing their hands in front of their chests.). The student claimed that while doing this the teacher or assistant would push his head down; the teacher and assistant denied the severity of the hold and the number of times alleged and stated that it was used when the student threatened violence to himself or others.]

A. *Establishing a Substantive Due Process Violation and the Fourth Circuit's* Hall *Decision*

Daniel can establish a § 1983 violation only by demonstrating that Defendants Ramsey and Hart violated his federal constitutional rights. Although the Supreme Court, it [sic] its seminal decision on school corporal punishment, left open the issue of whether public school students have a right under the Substantive Due Process Clause of the Fourteenth Amendment to remain free from excessive corporal punishment, see *Ingraham v. Wright*, the Fourth Circuit has made clear in the wake of *Ingraham* that there may be instances where excessive corporal punishment may indeed give rise to a substantive due process claim. *See Hall v. Tawney,* 621 F.2d 607, 611 (4th Cir. 1980).

Mindful of the doctrine that "not every state law tort becomes a federally cognizable 'constitutional tort' under § 1983 simply because it is committed by a state official," the Fourth Circuit in *Hall*, borrowing heavily from precedent developed in excessive force claims arising in the law enforcement area, enunciated an exacting standard for analyzing substantive due process/corporal punishment claims. Under this standard,

> the substantive due process inquiry in school corporal punishment cases must be whether the force applied caused injury so severe, was so disproportionate to the need presented, and was so inspired by malice or sadism or unwise excess of zeal that it amounted to a brutal and inhumane abuse of official power literally shocking to the conscience.

Thus, the test that both parties concede as controlling the Court's disposition of this case involves four elements: (1) an application of force; (2) causing severe injury; (3) the force applied was disproportionate to the need presented; and (4) the force applied was so inspired by malice or sadism or unwise excess of zeal that it amounted to a brutal and inhumane abuse of official power literally shocking to the conscience. The *Hall* decision has become a seminal case in the area of corporal punishment, and this test, or something very close to it, has been applied in all of the federal circuits to have considered the issue with the exception of the Fifth Circuit.[51]

B. *Precedent Developed under the* Hall *Standard*

The caselaw that has developed under *Hall* and its progeny is very helpful in fleshing out the paramaters [sic] of public school students' substantive due process right [sic] not to be subjected to excessive corporal punishment, and this body of precedent makes clear that plaintiffs have a difficult burden to meet in order to survive a summary judgment motion. As substantive due process claims must necessarily be resolved on a case-by-case basis, the Court reviews the decisions made under the *Hall* analysis for guidance with the application of that analysis to the facts of the instant case.

---

[51] [3] The Fifth Circuit's analysis differs. The Fifth Circuit agrees that "corporal punishment in public schools is a deprivation of substantive due process when it is arbitrary, capricious, or wholly unrelated to the legitimate state goal of maintaining an atmosphere conducive to learning." *Fee v. Herndon*, 900 F.2d 804, 808 (5th Cir. 1990). Nevertheless, the Fifth Circuit refuses to recognize a cause of action when there are adequate state remedies. No other court has adopted this reasoning.

1. *Decisions Where Plaintiffs Survived a Summary Judgment Motion Under the* Hall *Analysis All Involve Severe Physical Injuries*

In *Hall*, the Fourth Circuit held that beating a student so severely that he or she requires hospitalization plainly exceeds the threshold necessary to establish a constitutional violation. The student alleged that she had been subjected to punishment for no apparent reason and had been struck repeatedly and violently with a rubber paddle. After the beating, the student was taken to the emergency room of a nearby hospital "where she was admitted and kept for a period of ten (10) days for the treatment of traumatic injury to the soft tissue of the left hip and thigh, trauma to the skin and soft tissue of the left thigh, and trauma to the soft tissue with ecchyniosis of the left buttock." The district court granted the teacher's motion to dismiss for failure to state a claim. On these facts, however, the Fourth Circuit held that the student's allegations, if proven, stated a claim for relief under § 1983 and remanded the case.

The teacher's conduct in *Garcia by Garcia v. Miera*, 817 F.2d 650 (10th Cir. 1987), also rose to the level of a constitutional violation. The student was severely paddled on two separate occasions. On the first occasion, she was struck until her legs were bleeding. The second time, she was pushed against a desk and hit with a paddle until a welt formed. The district court agreed with defendants' assertion of qualified immunity and granted summary judgment in their favor. The Tenth Circuit reversed, stating:

> [The allegations that] this nine-year-old girl was held up by her ankles and hit several times with a split board of substantial size on the front of her legs until they bled — supported by evidence of a permanent scar — are sufficient [to survive a motion for summary judgment]. The allegations with respect to the second beating, that the punishment was severe enough to cause pain for three weeks — supported by pictures of the injured buttocks, an affidavit from an examining doctor that in his long experience he had not seen bruises like that from routine spankings, and an affidavit from an examining nurse that if a child had received this type of injury at home she would have reported it as child abuse — are also sufficient. These claims may not survive the crucible of trial, but they overcome defendants' motion for summary judgment.

In *Webb v. McCullough*, 828 F.2d 1151, 1158 (6th Cir. 1987), a student alleged that while she was on a trip to Hawaii with the school band, the school principal knocked down her locked bathroom door, hitting her twice with the door in the process, grabbed her, threw her against the wall, and slapped her. The student had locked herself in the bathroom after being told that she and her roommates were being sent home because a teenage boy had been discovered in their room and because school officials had found alcoholic beverages in an adjoining, unoccupied room. The principal became quite angry with the student when she refused to come out of the bathroom, and he tried to jimmy the door lock. When that did not work, he slammed the door three or four times with his shoulder. When the door gave way, it struck the student. The principal then allegedly picked Webb up off of the floor, threw her against the wall, and slapped her. The Sixth Circuit held that because McCullough acted out of malice or anger, not out of an effort to discipline the student or restore order, constitutional liability could attach to his conduct. The court held:

> Because [the principal] was in loco parentis to Webb and because it is possible that the blows were not disciplinary in nature, a trier of fact could find that under the circumstances, McCullough's need to strike Webb was so minimal or non-existent that the alleged blows were a brutal and inhumane abuse of McCullough's official power, literally shocking to the conscience. This makes summary judgment inappropriate.

Most recently, in *Metzger by Metzger v. Osbeck*, 841 F.2d 518, 521 (3d Cir. 1998), a physical education teacher overheard a male student in his swimming class use foul language in the course of a conversation with a female student about baseball cards. The teacher walked up behind the male student and placed his arms around the student's neck and shoulders. While holding the student by the neck, the teacher questioned the student about his use of foul language. During the course of the questioning, the teacher moved his arm up slightly to a position just beneath the student's chin, forcing the student to stand on his toes to avoid being choked. When finally released from the hold, the student lost consciousness and fell to a pool deck, suffering lacerations to his lower lip, a broken nose, fractured teeth and other injuries requiring hospitalization. Applying the *Hall* analysis to these facts, a split panel of the Third Circuit reversed the district court's grant of summary judgment in favor of the teacher and remanded the case for trial.

2. Decisions Granting Summary Judgment to Defendants Under the Hall Analysis, Even Though Plaintiff Sustained Actual Physical Injury

On the other side of the coin, the courts have dismissed claims for conduct below the threshold of a constitutional violation under the *Hall* analysis, even where seemingly harsh or unfair punishment resulting in actual physical injury occurred.

This Court held in *Brooks v. School Board of Richmond*, 569 F. Supp. 1534, 1535 (E.D. Va. 1983) (WARRINER, J.), that pricking a student in the arm with a straight pin does not rise to the level of a constitutional violation. There, Judge Warriner stated:

> Regardless of how much a trial fleshes out the bare bones skeleton, this incident, in and of itself, simply cannot descend to the level of a brutal and inhumane, conscience-shocking, episode that the Fourth Circuit requires[.] As the defendant aptly notes in her reply memorandum, allegations of twenty licks with a two-foot-long paddle causing a severe hematoma and loss of the use of a arm for a week did not shock the conscience of the United States Supreme Court in *Ingraham*.

In *Darden v. Watkins*, 845 F.2d 325, 1988 WL 40083 (6th Cir. 1988) (unpublished table decision), the Sixth Circuit, in an unreported decision, affirmed the district court's grant of summary judgment in favor of a fourth-grade teacher who gave a student three "licks" with a paddle for failure to complete a homework assignment. When the child came home from school, his mother took him to an emergency room where he was examined by a physician "who observed a three-to four-inch area of reddish-blue discoloration over the fleshy part of the plaintiff's left buttock." Nonetheless, applying the Hall analysis, the Sixth Circuit held that while the teacher's actions may have been unwise, they were not "inspired by malice or sadism" so as to establish a substantive due process violation. *See id.* at *5; *see also Saylor v. Board of Education,* 118 F.3d 507, 514–15 (6th Cir. 1997) (affirming grant of summary judgment in favor of teacher and school officials under Hall analysis and holding as a matter of law in a corporal punishment case that bruises caused by five licks of a teacher's paddle did not "shock the conscience"); *Archey v. Hyche,* 1991 U.S. App. LEXIS 12657, 1991 WL 100586, *2 (6th Cir. 1991) (holding no substantive due process violation where a fifth grader suffered severe bruises on being paddled five times for humming in the boys' bathroom); *Wise v. Pea Ridge School District,* 855 F.2d 560, 562 (8th Cir. 1988) (affirming grant of summary judgment and holding that teacher's paddling of sixth-grade student that caused bruising did not shock the conscience); *Hale v. Pringle,* 562 F. Supp. 598, 601 (M.D. Ala. 1983) (holding that infliction of corporal punishment upon student, who was hit on the buttocks 3 to 5 times with a paddle causing minor bruising, did not violate student's substantive due process rights).

In *Brown v. Johnson*, 710 F. Supp. 183 (E.D.Ky. 1989), a nine-year old student alleged that she had been spanked seven times with a paddle on three separate occasions over a thirty minute period. The student was severely bruised from the spanking. Nevertheless, the district court granted the defendants' motion for summary judgment, finding that neither the punishment inflicted nor the injuries sustained shocked the conscience of the court.

In *Jones v. Witinski*, 931 F. Supp. 364 (M.D. Pa. 1996), a teacher became angry at a disruptive student in his seventh-grade math class and, after first asking the student to leave the class, the teacher grabbed the student by the arm and pulled him across a desk before the student fell against a bulletin board and ended up on the floor. The student allegedly suffered physical injuries — including bruises — as well as "continuing psychological trauma." Nonetheless, applying the *Hall* analysis, the district court granted the teacher's motion for summary judgement, stating that "pulling a student by the arm is not 'a brutal and inhumane abuse of official power literally shocking to the conscience.'" According to the court,

> the fact that [the student] may have sustained serious injury as a result [of the fall is extremely unfortunate, but does not alter the character of [the teacher's] acts. It appears from all the evidence before us that [the teacher] never intended to harm [the student] nor cause him to fall against the bulletin board. There is no evidence which suggests otherwise. . . . There is absolutely no evidence in this case from which a reasonable trier of fact could find intent to harm.

Most recently, in *Kurilla v. Callahan*, 68 F. Supp. 2d 556 (M.D. Pa. 1999), an eighth-grade student brought a § 1983 action against a teacher who punched him in the chest while breaking up a fight, causing the student to suffer from a bruise on his chest and a red mark on his neck. The incident also caused the student to "suffer[ ] from anxiety." The teacher was subsequently tried and convicted of harassment under Pennsylvania state law. Nonetheless, applying the *Hall* analysis, the district court granted the teacher's summary judgment motion. Central to the court's holding in *Kurilla* was its decision that the injuries suffered by the student were not "severe" under the *Hall* analysis:

> In this case, [the teacher's] punching of [the student] in the chest caused a bruise and some red marks. While [the student] sought medical care, there is no evidence that medical attention was reasonably necessary. [The student's] injuries did not even warrant x-ray examination or prescription of any medicine. Thus, [the student's] injuries could hardly be described as "severe."

Accordingly, while the court noted that the teacher's actions could be characterized as overzealous, they did not amount "to a brutal and inhumane abuse of official power literally shocking to the conscience."

3. *Decisions Where Student Suffered No Physical Injury and Thus Could Not Withstand Summary Judgment Under the* Hall *Analysis*

In *Lillard v. Shelby County Board of Education*, 76 F.3d 716 (6th Cir. 1996), the Sixth Circuit held that a single slap, which did not result in physical injury, even if given for no legitimate purpose, does not rise to the level of a constitutional violation. The court stated: "It is simply inconceivable that a single slap could shock the conscience. We do not quarrel with a suggestion that [the teacher's] actions were careless and unwise; but they fall far short of 'brutal,' or 'inhumane,' or any of the other adjectives employed to describe an act so vicious as to constitute a violation of substantive due process." The court went on to stress that while it certainly did not condone or excuse the teacher's conduct, it could not find that one slap, "even if made for no legitimate purpose, rises to the level of a constitutional violation. While [the teacher] should reasonably expect to face serious consequences for his treatment of [the student], those consequences should not be found in a federal court through the mechanism of a section 1983 action."

Fewer cases have addressed the issue of alleged psychological abuse, which is the only injury that Daniel clams to have suffered in the instant case. Nonphysical cases of harassment, or abuse, other than sexual abuse, have applied the same "shocks the conscience" standard.

In *Abeyta v. Chama Valley Independent School District*, 77 F.3d 1253, 1258 (10th Cir. 1996), the twelve-year-old plaintiff alleged that her teacher had repeatedly called her a prostitute in front of the class over a month-and-a-half period, and instigated her classmates into calling her the same. The Tenth Circuit analyzed the girl's claim as a substantive due process claim for psychological abuse. While finding the teacher's conduct reprehensible, the Tenth Circuit also found his conduct below the constitutional threshold established by *Hall* and its progeny. The court stated:

> A teacher who calls a student a prostitute engages in a complete abuse of his authority. To do so repeatedly, and turn a deaf ear as other students follow the teacher's example, is flagrant misconduct. But we must leave plaintiff to whatever relief statutory or state tort law may afford her.

> . . . We hold that taking plaintiffs claims as true they do not state an actionable § 1983 claim . . . .

4. *Summary*

To summarize, conduct that might give rise to a state law tort claim does not necessarily give rise to a constitutional claim. The threshold for establishing a constitutional tort for excessive corporal punishment is a high one. The plaintiff must allege more than the commission of an ordinary common-law tort. The Sixth Circuit explained the distinction between the two in *Webb* stating:

> In the context of disciplinary corporal punishment in the public schools . . . the substantive due process claim is quite different than a claim of assault and battery under state tort law. In resolving a state tort claim, decision may well turn on whether ten licks rather than five were excessive . . . so that line-drawing this refined may be required. But substantive due process is concerned with violations of personal rights of privacy and bodily security of so different an order of magnitude that inquiry in a particular case simply need not start at the level of concern those distinctions imply. As in the cognate police brutality cases, the substantive due process inquiry in school corporal punishment cases must be whether the force applied caused injury so severe, was so disproportionate to the need presented, and was so inspired by malice or sadism rather than a merely careless or unwise excess of zeal that it amounted to a brutal and inhumane abuse of official power literally shocking to the conscience . . . . *Not every violation of state tort and criminal assault laws will be a violation of this constitutional right, but some of course may.*

As Judge Friendly stated in *Johnson v. Glick*, 481 F.2d 1028 (2d Cir. 1973),

> in determining whether the constitutional line has been crossed, a court must look to such factors as the need for the application of force, the relationship between the need and the amount of force that was used, the extent of injury inflicted, and whether force was applied in a good faith effort to maintain or restore discipline or maliciously and sadistically for the very purpose of causing harm.

C. *Application of the* Hall *Test to the Instant Case*

Applying this body of precedent and the test enunciated by the Fourth Circuit in Hall to the facts of the instant case, the Court finds that *Hall's* exacting analysis has not been met and therefore Defendants' Motion for Summary Judgement must be granted.

First, as the caselaw discussed above makes clear, *Hall* requires a "severe" injury; Daniel's only injury appears to be that he experienced some pain and suffering at the time of the alleged abuse (for which he never sought medical attention) and that he either currently suffers or has suffered from Post-Traumatic Stress Disorder. The alleged incidents of abuse never manifested any physical injury in Daniel, and he was never taken to or treated by a medical doctor in connection with these alleged incidents. The lack of any physical injury in this case contrasts sharply with the severe physical injuries sustained in school excessive force cases where summary judgment was denied. [Summary cases discussed previously.]

Second, *Hall* requires that the Plaintiffs show that the actions of Ramsey and Hart were disproportionate to the need presented. Plaintiffs cannot carry this burden, as Daniel's own testimony indicates that he [sic] the alleged abuse was not administered arbitrarily but instead only occurred in connection with his being placed in time-out. When asked why he was placed in time-out, Daniel responded that he was given time-out for various reasons, including bad behavior, and that the physical restraint that accompanied his placement in time-out would end when he would "stop crying and be quiet." Moreover, Daniel's [Individual Education Plan that was developed for him to address his disability,] and the laws of the Commonwealth of Virginia, explicitly authorize the use of physical restraint in certain situations. Considering these facts in a light most favorable to Plaintiffs, the Court finds that no reasonable jury could conclude that the force applied by Ramsey and Hart was disproportionate to the need presented under the test enunciated in *Hall* and its progeny.

Third, and finally, *Hall* requires that Ramsey's and Hart's actions be "so inspired by malice or sadism rather than a merely careless or unwise excess of zeal that it amounted to a brutal and inhumane abuse of official power literally shocking to the conscience." As motivating factors for the alleged abuse of Daniel, Mr. and Mrs. Brown state that Ramsey [the teacher] (1) resented having Daniel in her classroom, due to the Browns' active role in the education of their son and the increased administrative supervision over Ramsey that came with Daniel's placement in her classroom; and (2) Ramsey, who is Caucasian, resented racial slurs that Daniel (who is also Caucasian) allegedly muttered about Hart [Ramsey's assistant] as well as his fellow classmates who were "dark-skinned." The Plaintiffs have not set forth or pointed to any such motivating factors with regard to the conduct of Hart that suggest she may have acted with "malice or sadism."

As the cases discussed in this Opinion make clear, even taken as true, the motivating factors Plaintiffs' attribute to Ramsey's conduct do not rise to the level of "malice or sadism" required by *Hall* and its progeny. No reasonable jury could find, on these facts, that Ramsey and Hart possessed such a malevolent state of mind. And even if the motivating factors of Ramsey and Hart, as stated by Mr. and Mrs. Brown, would support such an inference, the nature of the injury and the manner in which it was inflicted still do not support an inference of brutal or inhumane conduct shocking to the conscience.

While the Court appreciates the sincerity with which the Browns have pursued a remedy for the alleged abuse suffered by Daniel, like other courts that have considered these issues, there is nothing before the Court to suggest that the alleged actions of Ramsey and Hart were anything other than a disciplinary measure within the sound discretion of the teacher. . . . While the Plaintiffs may under some stretch of the imagination bring a cause-of-action under some state-law tort theory unknown to the undersigned, the standards for establishing a constitutional injury are far higher and Plaintiffs have failed to meet the exacting standards as stated by the Fourth Circuit in *Hall*. Again, evidence that may give rise to a tort claim will not necessarily establish a substantive due process violation under § 1983; the mere fact that a state official may have committed a tort will not suffice to support a cause of action for constitutional harm. As aptly stated by our Supreme Court, "Our Constitution deals with the large concerns of the governors and the governed, but it does not purport to supplant traditional tort law in laying down rules of conduct to regulate liability for injuries that attend to living in society." Schools and school teachers not only have a duty not to employ unconscionable restraints against individual students, but they also have a duty to educate other students within a class setting and to cure disruptive behavior that would deny the educational opportunities of other students. Otherwise, schools cannot function at all.

NOTES AND QUESTIONS

1. Courts and litigants continue to wrangle over student disciplinary measures that involve physical punishment. *See Doe v. Hawaii Dept. of Educ.*, 334 F.3d 906 (9th Cir. 2003) (rejecting vice-principal's claim of qualified immunity for taping a student's head to a tree after he refused to stop fidgeting; student's right to be free from excessive physical punishment was clearly established at the time the taping took place); *Kirkland v. Greene Co. Bd. of Educ.*, 347 F.3d 903 (11th Cir. 2003) (rejecting principal's claim of qualified immunity when he repeatedly struck a student with a metal cane); *Balch v. Anders*, 324 F.3d 650, 655 (8th Cir. 2003) (student violently kicked a school vending machine, principal grabbed his neck, threw him on a bench — student landed on his shoulder — and held him down by neck and collar. Student suffered a pulled nerve and wore a neck brace for two weeks. Court stated that principal's response was appropriate due to student's violent behavior and that student's injury "falls well short of those sustained by students whose substantive due-process claims have withstood summary judgment"); *Gonzales v. Passino*, 222 F. Supp. 2d 1277 (D.N.M. 2002) (teacher thought student called him a "faggot" and responded by hitting the student's arm with a plastic bat; court found no substantive due process violation since the conduct did not cause serious harm to the student, noting that it does not "condone in the slightest a teacher's gratuitous imposition of pain on a student, no matter how temporary the pain might be") .

2. With many students becoming more and more violent and disrespectful, what should school districts and teachers do to ensure that the response of

school officials is appropriate to the situation? *See* Christopher Anderson, *The Dangerous Lives of Teachers*, 1 EDUC. L. & POL'Y FORUM *available at* www.educationlawconsortium.org (noting increase in violence directed against teachers and students).

[C] "Zero Tolerance" Policies

SEAL v. MORGAN

Court of Appeals for the Sixth Circuit
229 F.3d 567 (2000)

RONALD LEE GILMAN, CIRCUIT JUDGE.

In this action brought pursuant to 42 U.S.C. § 1983, Dustin Wayne Seal seeks monetary damages to compensate him for the Knox County Board of Education's 1996 decision to expel him from high school after a friend's knife was found in the glove compartment of Seal's car. Seal, who denied any knowledge of the knife's presence in the car while it was on school property, argues that the Board's action was irrational and violated his right to due process of law.

. . . .

I. FACTUAL BACKGROUND

In the fall of 1996, Seal was a junior at Powell High School in Knox County, Tennessee. On October 30, 1996, a friend of Seal's named Ray Pritchert, who was also a student at Powell High, became embroiled in an out-of-school dispute with another Powell High student who had begun dating Pritchert's ex-girlfriend. As a result, Pritchert started carrying around a hunting knife. The knife had a three-and-one-half inch blade and bore the inscription "Ray loves Jennie" (apparently Pritchert's ex-girlfriend). Seal knew that Pritchert had the knife, because Pritchert showed it to him that day. The next night, Seal went to pick up his girlfriend at her house, accompanied by Pritchert and another friend, David Richardson. Seal was driving his mother's car, because his own was not working. Pritchert, still carrying the knife, placed it on the floorboard of the car behind the driver's seat where Seal was sitting. When they arrived at the girlfriend's house, Seal went in to get her. Richardson, still in the car, placed the knife in the car's glove compartment. Whether Seal actually saw the knife when it was on the car's floorboard, or at any other point when the knife was in his mother's car, is not entirely clear from the record. It is, however, uncontroverted that Seal knew that Pritchert had been carrying a knife around, and that Pritchert had the knife on his person when he was in the car on October 31, 1996.

The following night was Friday, November 1, 1996. Seal, again driving his mother's car, drove his girlfriend and Pritchert to Powell High. All three were members of the Powell High band, and the Powell High football team had a game scheduled that night. The three had worn their band uniforms, but were informed after entering the school that they would not be required to wear their uniforms that night. They then returned to the car, which Seal had parked in the Powell High parking lot, so that they could put on the clothes they had planned to wear after changing out of their band uniforms. After changing, Seal and Pritchert went back into the school building. There, the band director, Gregory Roach, pulled Pritchert aside and asked him if he and Seal had been drinking. Pritchert said that they had not. Roach let Seal and Pritchert enter the band room, because he did not smell alcohol on Pritchert's breath.

About fifteen minutes later, Roach summoned Seal and Pritchert to his office. There they were joined by Charles Mashburn, the vice-principal of Powell High. Mashburn announced that four students had reported seeing the two of them drinking alcohol. Although Mashburn searched both Seal's and Pritchert's coats and instrument cases, he found no evidence to suggest that either student had been drinking or possessed alcoholic beverages. Mashburn then announced that he needed to search Seal's car for a flask, because one of the assistant band directors said he saw either Seal or Pritchert with a flask, with both students chewing gum and checking the other's breath. Seal consented to the search. Mashburn did not find a flask. He did, however, find two cigarettes in a crumpled pack in the back of the car, a bottle of amoxicillin pills (an antibiotic for which Seal had a prescription) in the console, and Pritchert's knife in the glove compartment.

Mashburn subsequently had Seal accompany him to his office, where he directed Seal to write out a statement about what had just occurred. Seal asked Mashburn what he should write in the statement, and Mashburn replied that Seal should explain why the knife was in the glove compartment. Seal's entire statement reads as follows:

> Went to Roach's office because he thought or had been told that we had a flask and had been drinking, so we went and Mr. Mashburn searched the car. He found a knife and 2 cigs. The knife was there because Ray's ex-girlfriend's boyfriend had been following us around with a few of his friends so we were a little uneasy.

Mashburn then prepared a form Notice of Disciplinary Hearing for Long-Term Suspension From School, charging Seal with possession of a knife, possession of tobacco, and possession of "pills." On November 6, 1996, Powell High's principal, Vicki Dunaway, conducted a disciplinary hearing. After hearing from both Seal and Mashburn, she suspended Seal pending expulsion for possession of a knife. It does not appear from the record that she took any action against Seal for his possession of the two cigarettes or the antibiotic pills. Seal appealed, and on November 14, 1996, Jimmie Thacker, Jr., the Board of Education's disciplinary hearing authority, conducted an appeal hearing.

Seal attended this hearing, as did his parents, his girlfriend, Principal Dunaway, and David Richardson (the student who had placed the knife in the glove compartment of the car belonging to Seal's mother). At the hearing, Seal testified that he knew that Pritchert had had the knife on his person on October 31, 1996, at a time when Seal was driving Pritchert around in his mother's car, but that he had no idea that the knife was in his car on November

1, or at any other time when the car was on school property. Richardson testified that Seal had not been in his mother's car when Richardson put Pritchert's knife in the glove compartment, and that as far as Richardson could tell, Seal did not know that the knife was there. Seal's girlfriend also testified that as far as she knew, Seal did not know the knife was in the glove compartment of his mother's car.

On November 18, 1996, Thacker notified Seal's mother by letter that he had decided to uphold Principal Dunaway's decision to suspend Seal pending expulsion by the Board. In pertinent part, the letter read as follows:

> Testimony and written statements presented during the hearing place the knife in the glove compartment of the car your son was driving and which he parked on the campus of Powell High School. Possession of a weapon on school property is a violation of Knox County Policy JCCC; therefore, I am upholding the principal's decision to suspend Dustin pending expulsion by the board of education.

The next day, Seal's mother telephoned school authorities to indicate that she and Seal wanted to appeal Thacker's decision to the Board. On November 22, 1996, Thacker notified Seal's mother by certified mail that the Board would consider the appeal of Seal's discipline for "possession of a weapon on school campus" at its next meeting.

The Board heard Seal's appeal on December 4, 1996. Seal was represented by counsel, who forcefully argued that Seal had no idea that the knife was in his mother's car either on November 1, 1996, or at any other time that the car was on school property. Board member Sam Anderson responded:

> My concern was because the . . . in our record it shows possession of a knife, possession of tobacco, possession of pills. You know, it doesn't just signify a weapon. And . . . you know . . . and either [sic] of the three are justification . . . .

Anderson then asked Seal whether he had ever seen the knife in his car. Seal said that he had not. He admitted that he knew that Pritchert had the knife the day before November 1, 1996 — off school property — but insisted that he thought Pritchert had simply taken it with him, and that it had not been left in his mother's car. Anderson then explained that

> the problem I see is that we always have to be consistent in sending a clear message to students. Two or three years ago we were dealing with guns, guns, guns. Now, it's down to knives, knives, knives and I don't want to send a confusing message. Justin [sic], you are responsible for what's in your car and that's where I'm torn but I would have to say that you have to be held responsible as a driver for what's in your car. And that's a problem that you're going to have to deal with.

At another Board member's suggestion, the Board then voted unanimously to rule on the appeal based on the record from the hearings conducted before

Principal Dunaway and Disciplinary Hearing Authority Thacker. Anderson then made a motion to uphold Thacker's recommendation to expel Seal, which was approved unanimously. The entire transcript of the Board's proceedings as it relates to Seal spans three pages. In contrast, the transcript of the hearing conducted by Thacker is over fifty pages long.

In pertinent part, the Knox County Board of Education policy pursuant to which Seal was expelled provides that students may not "possess, handle, transmit, use or attempt to use any dangerous weapon [including knives] in school buildings or on school grounds at any time" and that students who are found to have violated the policy "shall be subject to suspension and/or expulsion of not less than one . . . year." The policy also provides that the Superintendent "shall have the authority to modify this suspension requirement on a case-by-case basis," although Superintendent Morgan has argued that it is "not clear" whether he has the power to modify a suspension or expulsion once it has been finally approved by the Board.

Generally, Tennessee law delegates to its local boards of education broad authority to formulate rules for student conduct and to prescribe appropriate remedies for the violation of those rules. Before the 1996-97 school year, however, the Tennessee legislature directed each of its local school boards to develop and adopt, and to file annually with the state commissioner of education, written policies and procedures that would "impose swift, certain and severe disciplinary sanctions on any student" who, among other things, "brings a . . . dangerous weapon" onto school property, or "possesses a dangerous weapon" on school property. Specifically, the legislature encouraged "each local and county board of education . . . to include within such policies and procedures a zero-tolerance policy toward any student who engages in such misconduct."

II. PROCEDURAL BACKGROUND

In April of 1997, Seal's father initiated an action on Seal's behalf in the United States District Court for the Eastern District of Tennessee pursuant to 42 U.S.C. § 1983. After he reached the age of eighteen, Seal was substituted for his father as the plaintiff. Seal claimed that his expulsion violated his rights under the Equal Protection and Due Process clauses of the Fourteenth Amendment, and that the search of his mother's car by Vice-Principal Mashburn violated the Fourth Amendment. Initially, Seal named as defendants the principal, the hearing officer, and every member of the Knox County Board of Education. The district court, however, dismissed on its own motion Seal's claims against all of these defendants, concluding that the only proper party defendants were Allen Morgan, the school district's superintendent, and the Board of Education itself. None of these dismissals are at issue in these appeals.

. . . .

The district court concluded that both Superintendent Morgan and the Board were entitled to summary judgment on Seal's Fourth Amendment claim and Fourteenth Amendment equal protection claim, but that the Board was not entitled to summary judgment on Seal's Fourteenth Amendment due process claim. In addition, the district court concluded that Superintendent Morgan was not entitled to summary judgment on the basis of qualified immunity. The district court then set the case for trial on the issue of damages only, effectively deciding that Seal was entitled to summary judgment on his due process claim. Superintendent Morgan appealed as of right from the denial of his motion for summary judgment on the basis of qualified immunity, and the Board sought and received permission from the district court and this court to take an interlocutory appeal pursuant to 28 U.S.C. § 1292(b).

III. ANALYSIS

A. *The Board*

There is no abstract federal constitutional right to process for process's sake. Rather, the Fourteenth Amendment provides that one may not be deprived of life, liberty, or property without due process of law. State law determines what constitutes "property" for due process purposes. It is undisputed that Seal enjoyed a property interest in his public high school education under Tennessee law.

Due process has two components. The first, procedural due process (often summarized as "notice and an opportunity to be heard"), is a right to a fair procedure or set of procedures before one can be deprived of property by the state. Even when it is clear that one is entitled to due process, "the question remains what process is due." The answer to the question of what process is due "depends on appropriate accommodation of the competing interests involved." In the context of disciplining public school students, the student's interest is "to avoid unfair or mistaken exclusion from the educational process, with all of its unfortunate consequences." Schools, of course, have an unquestionably powerful interest in maintaining the safety of their campuses and preserving their ability to pursue their educational mission. ("Some modicum of discipline and order is essential if the educational function is to be performed. Events calling for discipline are frequent occurrences and sometimes require immediate, effective action.").

The district court rejected Seal's claim that he was denied procedural due process, concluding that he had received all of the process that he was due. Even though Seal, in his brief on appeal, asserts that he was "owed both the substantive and procedural components of the due process law and was denied such," he does not really argue that the Board used unfair procedures before expelling him. Rather, his complaint is with the substantive result — the ultimate decision to expel him. His argument is thus one of substantive due process, the other component of due process. In essence, Seal argues that the Board's ultimate decision was irrational in light of the facts uncovered by the procedures afforded him.

The Due Process Clause provides "heightened protection against government interference with certain fundamental rights and liberty interests." Government actions that burden the exercise of those fundamental rights or liberty interests are subject to strict scrutiny, and will be upheld only when they are narrowly tailored to a compelling governmental interest. The list of fundamental rights and liberty interests — which includes the rights to marry, to have children, to direct the education and upbringing of one's children, to marital privacy, to use contraception, to bodily integrity, to terminate one's pregnancy, and possibly the right to refuse unwanted lifesaving medical treatment, however, is short, and the Supreme Court has expressed very little interest in expanding it. In fact, the Supreme Court has held explicitly that the right to attend public school is not a fundamental right for the purposes of due process analysis.

The Supreme Court has also recognized the uniquely destructive potential of overextending substantive due process protection. Indeed, the Court has specifically cautioned that "judicial interposition in the operation of the public school system of the Nation raises problems requiring care and restraint," and that "by and large, public education in our nation is committed to the control of state and local authorities."

Government actions that do not affect fundamental rights or liberty interests and do not involve suspect classifications will be upheld if it they are rationally related to a legitimate state interest. In the context of school discipline, a substantive due process claim will succeed only in the "rare case" when there is "no 'rational relationship between the punishment and the offense.' "

That said, suspending or expelling a student for weapons possession, even if the student did not knowingly possess any weapon, would not be rationally related to any legitimate state interest. No student can use a weapon to injure another person, to disrupt school operations, or, for that matter, any other purpose if the student is totally unaware of its presence. Indeed, the entire concept of possession — in the sense of possession for which the state can legitimately prescribe and mete out punishment — ordinarily implies knowing or conscious possession.

We would have thought this principle so obvious that it would go without saying. The Board, however, devotes a great deal of the discussion in its briefs to arguing that "scienter" is not required by its "Zero Tolerance Policy," and that the criminal law requirement that possession of a forbidden object be knowing or conscious possession is a "technicality" that should not be "transported into school suspension cases." Frankly, we find it difficult to understand how one can argue that the requirement of conscious possession is a "technicality."

We asked counsel at oral argument whether the Board was seriously arguing that it could expel a student for unconsciously possessing a dangerous weapon, posing a hypothetical example involving a high-school valedictorian who has a knife planted in his backpack without his knowledge by a vindictive student. The question was whether the valedictorian would still be subject to mandatory expulsion under the Board's Zero Tolerance Policy, even if the school administrators and the Board members uniformly believed the valedictorian's explanation that the knife had been planted. Counsel for the Board answered yes. After all, counsel argued, the Board's policy requires "Zero Tolerance," and the policy does not explicitly *say* that the student must know he is carrying a weapon. Only after the Board's counsel sensed — correctly — that this answer was very difficult to accept did counsel backtrack, suggesting that perhaps an exception could be made for our unfortunate hypothetical valedictorian. We find it impossible to take this suggestion seriously, however, and not simply because counsel had just finished arguing the opposite. The suggestion is totally inconsistent with the Board's position in this case, which is that the Zero Tolerance Policy uniformly requires expulsion whenever its terms are violated.

Contrary to the Board's assertion, the criminal law requirement that possession of contraband must be conscious or knowing is neither arcane nor unsettled. . . .

The Board is, of course, correct when it observes that this is not a criminal case, and that its decision to expel Seal is not vulnerable to a substantive due process attack unless it is irrational. We believe, however, that the Board's Zero Tolerance Policy would surely be irrational if it subjects to punishment students who did not knowingly or consciously possess a weapon. The hypothetical case involving the planted knife is but one illustration of why.

Another example would be a student who surreptitiously spikes the punch bowl at a school dance with grain alcohol, with several students, none of whom having any reason to know that alcohol has been added to the punch, taking a drink. Suppose that the school has a code of conduct that mandates suspension or expulsion for any student who possesses or consumes alcohol on school property, but does not specifically provide that the alcohol must be knowingly possessed or consumed. Under the Board's reasoning, the student who spiked the punch bowl would of course be subject to suspension or expulsion, but so would any of the students who innocently drank from the punch bowl, even if the school board was completely convinced that the students had no idea that alcohol had been added to the punch. Suspending the students who drank from the punch bowl, not realizing that alcohol had been added, would not rationally advance the school's legitimate interest in preventing underage students from drinking alcohol on school premises any more than suspending a handful of students chosen at random from the school's directory.

A student who knowingly possesses a weapon and is caught with it can, of course, be lying when he or she claims not to have known of its existence. Simply because a student may lie about what he knew, however, does not mean that it is unnecessary to address the question of what he knew before meting out punishment. The Board, for its part, freely concedes that "the record does not reflect what the Board did or did not consider with respect to [Seal's] knowledge," but argues that "in the absence of findings of fact [by the Board], it ought not be concluded that the Board failed to consider [Seal's] knowledge."

Well, why not? The Board's attorney has insisted that Seal's knowledge was completely irrelevant, and that the Board's Zero Tolerance Policy required Seal's expulsion regardless of whether he knew the knife was in his car. At the Board meeting during which the Board voted to expel Seal, Board Member Sam Anderson, who as far can be determined from the record is the only person having anything to do with the decision to expel Seal who even considered the question of what Seal did or did not know, suggested that it would send a "confusing message" to do anything besides expel Seal, regardless of whether Seal had any idea that the knife was in his car. Then again, he also apparently thought that Seal could have been expelled just as easily for having a prescription antibiotic in his car.

In the case before us, we must remember that it was the Board, not Seal, that moved for summary judgment. As the non-moving party, Seal was entitled to have all reasonable inferences drawn in his favor. The absence of any evidence about what the Board concluded regarding Seal's knowledge is exactly why the Board is *not* entitled to summary judgment. In this regard, we disagree with the dissent's characterization that "Seal admittedly knew that the knife had been placed in his car on October 31, 1996 for use as a weapon" and that "Seal's attorney conceded during oral argument that Seal had no reason to believe the knife had been removed from his car." What Seal's attorney said was that Seal did not specifically see anyone pick the knife up off the floor of the car and remove it. Seal himself testified that he assumed that when Pritchert left Seal's car, Pritchert took his knife with him.

Similarly, the record provides no clue as to how the Board viewed Seal's written statement to Vice-Principal Mashburn on the night in question. Was it a confession (as characterized by the dissenting opinion), or was it an after-the-fact deduction (as Seal insists) by Seal about how and when the knife must have gotten into the glove compartment. The dissent apparently concludes that the Board could rationally have decided that the statement was a confession, even though there is absolutely no indication in the record that this is what the Board actually decided.

* * *

A school board can, of course, disbelieve the student's explanation and conclude that the student knowingly violated school policies. If that occurs, due process would be satisfied as long as the procedures afforded the student were constitutionally adequate and the conclusion was rational. The Board argues that the district court "erred by substituting its own view of the facts for that of the Hearing Officer and the Board of Education." Again, this begs the question — which nothing in the record answers — of what the views of the hearing officer and the Board were. Did the Board expel him because it disbelieved Seal's explanation, did it expel him despite believing his explanation completely, or did it expel him without deciding the issue, in the belief that Seal's knowledge was simply irrelevant to the decision? Of these possibilities, the first one would have been permissible if rationally supported by the record, but the other two would not have been.

. . . .

On the basis of the record presented, a reasonable trier of fact could conclude that Seal was expelled for a reason that would have to be considered irrational. We therefore conclude that the district court correctly denied the Board's motion for summary judgment.

The district court, however, did more than deny the Board's motion for summary judgment. By ordering that the case "proceed to trial by jury . . . only to determine the amount of damages to be awarded" to Seal, the district court effectively entered summary judgment *against* the Board on the issue of liability. It did this even though Seal had not moved for summary judgment. . . .

In the present case, however, we do not believe that this disposition was appropriate. As noted above, one cannot determine conclusively from the record in its present state why Seal was expelled. We do not believe that a reasonable factfinder would be compelled to find that the Board expelled him for an irrational reason, *i.e.,* without making any determination of whether Seal consciously possessed the knife, or despite believing Seal's explanation that he did not. The Board might conceivably be able to show that it expelled Seal for a reason that would have to be accepted as rational. Accordingly, we will affirm the judgment of the district court to the extent that it denied the Board's motion for summary judgment, reverse the judgment of the district court to the extent that it entered summary judgment against the Board on the issue of liability, and remand the case for further proceedings.

On remand, the district court could, as an exercise of its discretion, permit discovery and allow the Board to renew its motion for summary judgment, supplemented by appropriate affidavits or other evidence. . . . The district court's other option would be to conduct a trial on the issues of liability and damages. At trial, the determination of whether the Board's action was rationally related to a legitimate state interest is one of law and would be made by the court. The questions of what the Board did, and why, would be questions of fact for the jury. . . .

B. *Superintendent Morgan*

The doctrine of qualified immunity generally shields government officials from civil liability for performing discretionary functions "insofar as their conduct does not violate clearly established statutory or constitutional rights of which a reasonable person would have known."

As an abstract matter, the right of public school students not to be expelled arbitrarily or irrationally has been clearly established since at least the Supreme Court's decision in *Goss v. Lopez,* 419 U.S. 565 (1975), which held that long-term suspensions and expulsions must comport with minimal standards of due process. More concretely, however, we do not believe that the contours of that right were sufficiently clear to put a reasonable school superintendent on notice in 1996 that a school disciplinary policy's lack of a conscious-possession requirement could produce irrational expulsions and thus violate the legal rights of students expelled under the policy. For this reason, we will reverse the judgment of the district court to the extent that it denied Superintendent Morgan's motion for summary judgment, and remand with instructions to enter summary judgment in his favor.

For the future, however, we expect that our opinion today will clarify the contours of a student's right not to be expelled for truly unknowing or unconscious possession of a forbidden object. . . .

IV. CONCLUSION

We would not for a minute minimize the Board's obligation to maintain the safety of its campuses, and its right to mete out appropriate discipline (including expulsion) to students who commit serious violations of its rules. But we cannot accept the Board's argument that because safety is important, and because it is often difficult to determine a student's state of mind, that it need not make any attempt to ascertain whether a student accused of carrying a weapon knew that he was in possession of the weapon before expelling him.

The decision to expel a student from school is a weighty one, carrying with it serious consequences for the student. We understand full well that the decision not to expel a potentially dangerous student also carries very serious potential consequences for other students and teachers. Nevertheless, the Board may not absolve itself of its obligation, legal and moral, to determine whether students intentionally committed the acts for which their expulsions are sought by hiding behind a Zero Tolerance Policy that purports to make the students' knowledge a non-issue. We are also not impressed by the Board's argument that if it did not apply its Zero Tolerance Policy ruthlessly, and without regard for whether students accused of possessing a forbidden object knowingly possessed the object, this would send an inconsistent message to its students. Consistency is not a substitute for rationality.

For the reasons set forth above, we affirm the judgment of the district court to the extent that it denied the Board's motion for summary judgment, reverse the judgment of the district court to the extent that it entered summary judgment in Seal's favor on the issue of liability, and remand this case for further proceedings consistent with this opinion. With regard to Superintendent Morgan's appeal, we reverse the judgment of the district court and remand with instructions to enter summary judgment in his favor.

SUHRHEINRICH, CIRCUIT JUDGE, *dissenting in part.*

As the majority acknowledges, the right to attend a public school is not a fundamental right for purposes of a due process analysis. A school's disciplinary decision will therefore survive a constitutional substantive due process challenge if it is rationally related to a legitimate government purpose. Furthermore, as the majority notes, the Supreme Court has specifically cautioned that "judicial interposition in the operation of the public school system of the Nation raises problems requiring care and restraint," and that "by and large, public education in our nation is committed to the control of state and local authorities." Thus, it is not the role of the federal courts to set aside decisions of school administrators which the court may view as lacking a basis in wisdom or compassion. Public high school students do have substantive and procedural rights while at school. But § 1983 does not extend the right to relitigate in federal court evidentiary questions arising in school disciplinary proceedings or the proper construction of school regulations. The system of public education that has evolved in this Nation relies necessarily upon the discretion and judgment of school administrators and school board members, and § 1983 was not intended to be a vehicle for federal-court corrections of errors in the exercise of that discretion which do not rise to the level of violations of specific constitutional guarantees. The majority ignores these principles in holding that the Board acted irrationally in expelling Seal.

I.

First of all, the Board's decision was rational because the zero tolerance policy does not contain an express scienter requirement. By holding that "suspending or expelling a student for possessing a weapon, even if that student did not knowingly possess the weapon, would not be rationally related to any state interest," the majority has improperly substituted its interpretation of the regulation for the School Board's. The Board's construction of its regulations is entitled to deference.

Nor is it irrational to interpret the zero tolerance policy as the Board did. In addition to their duty to educate, schools act *in loco parentis*. Given this enormous responsibility, and the potentially devastating consequences of weapons on campus, a strict weapons policy is rationally related to a legitimate government interest — protecting our children from the very real threat of violence. The Columbine High School massacre and other school shootings have, unfortunately, become part of the national consciousness. The Knox County schools themselves are not immune from the threat of violence. Their disciplinary records show twenty injuries as a result of knives and sharp weapons in the three years preceding Seal's expulsion. Given this national and local landscape of violence, it is perfectly rational to establish a strict zero tolerance policy to ensure students' safety.

The Supreme Court has recognized the growing concern over school violence and the "substantial interest" of schools in maintaining discipline on campus. *See New Jersey v. T.L.O.,* 469 U.S. 325, 339 (1985) ("Maintaining order in the classroom has never been easy, but in recent years, school disorder often has taken a particularly ugly form: drug use and violent crime in the schools have become major social problems."); *see also Knox Cty. Educ. Ass'n v. Knox Cty. Bd. of Educ.,* 158 F.3d 361, 378–79 n.23 (6th Cir. 1998) ("Indeed, we do not have to search beyond recent local and national media headlines to understand that schools are, unfortunately, too often turned into places in which children are subjected to grave and even life-threatening dangers. . . ."). The court system should not further hamstring the process of education by substituting its judgment on matters relating to the safety of students for that of school administrators and school board members.[52]

. . . .

Let us remember that we are talking about dangerous weapons here, which the zero tolerance policy defined to include, inter alia, "any firearm, explosive, explosive weapon, Bowie knife, hawk bill knife, ice pick dagger, slingshot, switchblade knife, black jack knuckles . . . ." All the defined weapons, including the weapon possessed by Seal, have the potential to kill or seriously injure a fellow student. In fact, Seal admitted that the knife was placed in

---

[52] [1] The majority argues that "no student can use a weapon to injure another person, to disrupt school operations, or, for that matter, any other purpose if the student is totally unaware of its presence." Aside from the fact that the majority is again improperly substituting its assessments for those of the Board's, I disagree with this proposition. Even if the student who brought the weapon onto school property was unaware of its presence, another student could find the weapon and use it to cause injury. For example, even if the Board believed that Seal did not know the weapon was in the car on November 1, 1996, Pritchert knew it was there and presumably would have used it to injure another student had he felt threatened.

his automobile for use in a fight. As the General Assembly itself has recognized, children are entitled to a safe learning environment. Given the alarming increase in school violence nationwide, the Board's zero tolerance policy, enacted as part of a comprehensive network of state and local control over the schools, is not only rational but prudent.

The majority attempts to bolster its position with the hypothetical of the high-school valedictorian who, unknowingly, has a knife planted in his backpack by a vindictive student. The Board indicated at oral argument that an exception could be made to the zero tolerance policy in that situation. The majority seizes upon this statement as being "totally inconsistent with the Board's position in this case," which is that the Zero Tolerance Policy uniformly requires expulsion whenever its terms are violated.

The majority's hypothetical assumes that the zero tolerance policy affords no discretion to the school administrators. Ironically, the majority would read a scienter requirement into the policy and read discretion out of the policy. Certainly, if at any stage of the proceedings, Seal or the mythical valedictorian provided a reasonable, believable, explanation for the weapon's presence that would end the matter. Furthermore, the analogy is inapt.[53] Here, unlike the unwitting valedictorian, Seal admittedly knew that the knife had been placed in his car on October 31, 1996 for use as a weapon.[54] The Board, as part of its discretionary authority, was therefore free to infer from the facts of the case sub judice that Seal also knew that the knife was in his car the next night, because Seal knew that Pritchert began carrying a hunting knife as a result of a dispute with another PHS student and Seal drove Pritchert to PHS. In light of the evidence and the Board's legitimate interest in preventing school violence, it was not irrational for the Board to expel Seal for possessing a knife in his car because it is undisputed that the knife was there on November 1, 1996.

The majority's ruling, in effect, means that there can be no such thing as zero tolerance. School boards in this circuit will, from today forward, have to include scienter a requirement in any such policy, even if the state does not impose such a condition on the enforcement of a weapons or drug policy.

II.

Even if we assume that scienter is required, the majority's criticism of the Board's ruling is faulty because scienter can be imputed from the fact of possession. Because Seal undisputedly possessed the knife, the Board could reasonably presume that Seal knew it was in his car. At this point, the burden

---

[53] [2] A more apt comparison would be: "Friend hands knife to valedictorian to carry for protection. Valedictorian puts knife in his pocket. Unbeknownst to valedictorian, friend later moves knife to valedictorian's backpack, which valedictorian carries to school." Like Seal, this valedictorian knew at some point that he had the knife on his person. The majority's comparison of Seal to the completely clueless valedictorian is a false analogy.

[54] [3] The majority disagrees with this characterization. Yet, the majority does not, and cannot, dispute that Seal knew the knife was in the car on October 31, 1996 or that Seal explicitly stated that the knife was there because he and Pritchert felt "uneasy." What other possible conclusion can be drawn but that they brought the knife to protect themselves should a fight with Pritcher's [sic] ex-girlfriend's boyfriend materialize?

of persuasion shifted to Seal to explain why he did not know the knife was there. Seal, and the hypothetical valedictorian were, after all, in the best position to explain the situation. The administrative due process hearings gave him the opportunity to rebut the presumption of scienter. Seal failed to meet that burden here. Seal offered no facts to show that he knew the knife had been removed from his car after it was placed there on October 31, 1996. Thus, the Board's decision was rational because there was proof of scienter and a lack of evidence to rebut that presumption. Furthermore, this burden of persuasion makes the policy itself rationally related to the goal of preventing school violence because it affords the student an opportunity to rebut the presumption of scienter, thereby guaranteeing that the zero tolerance policy is reasonably applied. For this reason, there was no substantive due process violation.

III.

The Board's decision is also rational because there is ample proof of scienter here. There is no question that the knife was in Seal's car when it was parked on the PHS parking lot on November 1, 1996. Seal admitted to the Board, and his attorney conceded at oral argument, that he knew the knife was in the car a few days prior to its discovery. He acquiesced to its presence in the car at that time. Seal also knew on October 31, 1996, that Pritchert intended to use the knife if threatened by his ex-girlfriend's boyfriend. Seal's attorney conceded during oral argument that Seal had no reason to believe the knife had been removed from the car.[55] Seal also admitted in his confession that he knew the knife had been in the car for protection because he and Pritchert felt "uneasy." It was certainly plausible that the knife would be needed for protection at PHS on November 1, 1996, as well since the conflict that made them feel uneasy involved a fellow PHS student.

. . .

---

[55] [4] The majority also disagrees with this characterization. This characterization was drawn from the following statements and colloquy at oral argument:

> [Seal's Attorney]: The record has shown that Mr. Seal did know on October 30th [sic] that there was a knife in his mother's car. The knife belonged to Ray Pritchert, was placed in the car by Mr. Pritchert because of what had been going on with some other individuals at the school over this girl [indecipherable].
>
> [Judge Suhrheinrich]: So he knew the knife was in his car. What difference did it matter that he didn't know the exact location of the knife?
>
> [Seal's Attorney]: Well your Honor, I don't think he is saying that he knew the knife was in his car. It was not his knife.
>
> [Judge Suhrheinrich]: No, I appreciate — but I think there is certainly enough in there that he knew that knife was there and he never saw anybody take it out.
>
> [Seal's Attorney]: *He didn't see anybody take it out*, but I think that what he would say was that he assumed it was taken out because it was not his knife.
>
> . . . .
>
> [Judge Suhrheinrich]: But what bothers me in that he knew it was in the car and he never saw it being taken out.
>
> [Seal's Attorney]: Yes your Honor.

(Emphasis added.)

Most significantly, in his signed confession[56] taken on November 1, 1996, Seal did *not* state that he was unaware of the knife's presence. Rather, he stated that "the knife was there because [deleted] ex girlfriend's boyfriend had been following us around with a few of his friends so we were a little uneasy." From this statement, with its significant omission, made on the night in question and not after the fact, the Board could easily have concluded that Seal knew the knife was in the car on November 1, 1996. Given record evidence to support the Board's ruling, it is improper for this court to second-guess the Board's decision. The only statement to the contrary is Seal's statement made after he obtained an attorney. Seal offered no evidence to support that statement, however. This is an insufficient basis to overturn the Board's decision.

<h2 style="text-align:center">IV.</h2>

The real problem here is that the majority does not approve of the manner in which the Board made its decision. Presumably the majority would be satisfied if the Board had explicitly stated that it did not believe Seal's after-the-fact denial, because: (1) Seal knew as of October 30, 1996, that his friend Pritchert was carrying a knife for protection because of a dispute with another PHS student; (2) Seal acquiesced to the presence of the knife in his car on October 31, 1996; (3) Seal drove Pritchert in his car to PHS on November 1, 1996; (4) Seal admitted in his signed confession taken that night that the knife was in the car because Seal and Pritchert felt "uneasy"; (5) it is entirely plausible that Seal and Pritchert would continue to feel uneasy on November 1, 1996, while attending a PHS function; (6) Seal did not state until after the fact that he did not know the knife was in the car on November 1, 1996; (7) there are no facts to support Seal's statement of lack of knowledge; and (8) because there are no facts to back his conclusion, the Board does not believe his statement. Had the Board's ruling followed this blueprint, we would not be remanding the matter to the district court for further proceedings. However, since the majority plans to remand for further proceedings, I think the only proper recourse in this case is to refer the matter back to the Board for more express fact findings on the issue of scienter or to simply allow the Board to present an affidavit concerning its findings. If the Board states that it disbelieved Seal, then there can be no trial, and judgment must be entered for the Board.

This case has far-reaching implications for school boards. School boards in this circuit should be on notice that, in attempting to implement weapons or drug policies, they must find scienter, and articulate those findings in a way that resembles the rulings of a federal district judge.

In any event, I am not prepared to hold school boards to the same standards as federal district courts. The majority has ignored the Supreme Court's

---

[56] [5] The majority rejects this characterization as well, preferring to refer to the November 1 statement as an "after-the-fact deduction." "After-the-fact" to what? The statement was given as an explanation for the knife's presence on school property on November 1, 1996. It was certainly not an "after-the-fact" deduction of the November 1 event, since Seal provided the statement that very evening at vice-principal Mashburn's behest. It is by no means a stretch to characterize the statement as a confession, because Seal acknowledged the weapon's presence.

admonitions in *Goss* and *Wood* that federal courts play a very limited role in public education, which is most properly left in the competent hands of state and local authorities.

For all of the foregoing reasons, I respectfully dissent as to III.A.

————

NOTES AND QUESTIONS

1. One year after the school paid $30,000 in settlement, Dustin Seal committed suicide. Randy Kenner, *Family Sues School Board; Says Zero-Tolerance Expulsion Triggered Son's Suicide*, KNOXVILLE NEWS-SENTINEL, Aug. 8, 2002, at B3.

2. The *Seal* court utilized traditional criminal law concepts to impose a knowledge requirement on the zero tolerance policy. What level of knowledge does the court require? Is the criminal law analogy apt? What policies are served by requiring a student to know that he possesses a weapon before he may be punished?

3. Some criminal laws do not have any mens rea requirement, and impose strict liability on those who commit an unlawful act. *See United States v. U.S. Gypsum Co.*, 438 U.S. 422, 443 n.17 (1978) ("The possibility that those subjected to strict liability will take extraordinary care in their dealings is frequently regarded as one advantage of a rule of strict liability."). Could the *Seal* court have just as easily used the strict liability analogy to find that Seal's suspension was permissible, regardless of his knowledge of the knife?

4. If zero tolerance policies are enacted with the purpose of deterring students from engaging in dangerous behavior, it makes sense that a student who did not know he possessed a weapon would not be deterred from accidentally bringing that weapon on school grounds. But were those really the facts in Dustin Seal's case? As the dissent points out, Seal knew that there was a knife in his car. Didn't Seal have the opportunity to ask Pritchert to leave the knife at home — and shouldn't Seal's failure to do so have been enough to warrant punishment?

5. How should Seal's November 1 statement have been characterized? As an "after-the-fact deduction," as the majority suggests, or as a confession, as the dissent insists? Recall *Goss v. Lopez*: "Nor do we put aside the possibility that in unusual situations, although involving only a short suspension, something more than the rudimentary procedures will be required." 419 U.S. 565, 584. Might a possible confession, combined with a zero tolerance policy, meet the "unusual situation" *Goss* suggests? Could this possibility help explain the outcome in *Seal*?

6. Look again at the Knox County Board of Education policy. Is it written clearly enough for students to know what they may or may not bring to school? Consider the case of Ashley Smith, an eleven-year-old sixth grader who received a ten-day suspension for bringing a Tweety Bird key chain to school. Mary MacDonald, *Chain Reaction: Cobb Lifting Girl's Suspension*, ATLANTA J.-CONST., Sept. 30, 2000, at A1. The school policy forbade students from

bringing weapons, including chains, to school. The school board believed that the 9 3/4-inches-long Tweety Bird chain fell within the school's prohibition, and that it had no choice under the zero tolerance policy but to suspend Ashley. Later, under national media pressure, the school board reduced Ashley's suspension and then lifted it altogether.

Should the school board have lifted Ashley's suspension? Reread Judge Suhrheinrich's dissent. As he noted, "[t]he Columbine High School massacre and other school shootings, have, unfortunately, become part of the national consciousness. . . . Given this national and local landscape of violence, it is perfectly rational to establish a strict zero tolerance policy to ensure students' safety." 229 F.3d at 582–83.

7. In contrast to *Seal*, some circuits have upheld zero tolerance policies. In *Ratner v. Loudoun Cty. Pub. Sch.*, 16 Fed. Appx. 140, 142 (4th Cir. 2001), a student took a knife from a peer who told him she had suicidal thoughts the night before and placed it in his locker. After finding the knife school officials suspended him for the term for violating the zero tolerance policy. The student's mother, suing on his behalf, claimed the suspension amounted to violations of her son's rights to due process and equal protection, as well as his right to be free from cruel and unusual punishment. The Fourth Circuit confirmed the district court's conclusion that no violation had occurred.

> However harsh the result in this case, the federal courts are not properly called upon to judge the wisdom of a zero tolerance policy of the sort alleged to be in place at Blue Ridge Middle School or of its application to Ratner. Instead, our inquiry here is limited to whether Ratner's complaint alleges sufficient facts which if proved would show that the implementation of the school's policy in this case failed to comport with the United States Constitution. We conclude that the facts alleged in this case do not so demonstrate.

8. What other options besides corporal punishment and suspension should be used for school discipline? *See* Eric Blumenson & Eva S. Nilsen, *One Strike and You're Out? Constitutional Constraints on Zero Tolerance in Public Education*, 81 WASH. U.L.Q. 65, 81-82 (2003) (noting that students suspended or expelled under zero tolerance policies "do not simply disappear. . . . They embark on an inauspicious trajectory that is more likely to endanger themselves and others when compared with students who continue to attend their schools." This trajectory starts by breaking the bonds between students and the teachers and counselors who can help, and ends with "greatly increased changes of permanently dropping out of school and of joblessness"); Kimberly Miller & Shannon Colavecchio, *Schools Throw the Checkbook at Discipline*, PALM BEACH POST, Apr. 15, 2002, at A1 (reporting that ten years ago, teachers perceived the biggest discipline problems to be tardiness and excessive socializing; presently, the school district spends $18.3 million/year on alternative education programs for troublesome students).

§ 4.04 SCHOOL SEARCHES AND THE FOURTH AMENDMENT

[A] Individualized Suspicion

NEW JERSEY v. T.L.O.

Supreme Court of the United States
469 U.S. 325 (1985)

JUSTICE WHITE delivered the opinion of the Court.

We granted certiorari in this case to examine the appropriateness of the exclusionary rule as a remedy for searches carried out in violation of the Fourth Amendment by public school authorities. Our consideration of the proper application of the Fourth Amendment to the public schools, however, has led us to conclude that the search that gave rise to the case now before us did not violate the Fourth Amendment. Accordingly, we here address only the questions of the proper standard for assessing the legality of searches conducted by public school officials and the application of that standard to the facts of this case.

I

On March 7, 1980, a teacher at Piscataway High School in Middlesex County, N. J., discovered two girls smoking in a lavatory. One of the two girls was the respondent T.L.O., who at that time was a 14-year-old high school freshman. Because smoking in the lavatory was a violation of a school rule, the teacher took the two girls to the Principal's office, where they met with Assistant Vice Principal Theodore Choplick. In response to questioning by Mr. Choplick, T.L.O.'s companion admitted that she had violated the rule. T.L.O., however, denied that she had been smoking in the lavatory and claimed that she did not smoke at all.

Mr. Choplick asked T.L.O. to come into his private office and demanded to see her purse. Opening the purse, he found a pack of cigarettes, which he removed from the purse and held before T.L.O. as he accused her of having lied to him. As he reached into the purse for the cigarettes, Mr. Choplick also noticed a package of cigarette rolling papers. In his experience, possession of rolling papers by high school students was closely associated with the use of marihuana. Suspecting that a closer examination of the purse might yield further evidence of drug use, Mr. Choplick proceeded to search the purse thoroughly. The search revealed a small amount of marihuana, a pipe, a number of empty plastic bags, a substantial quantity of money in one-dollar bills, an index card that appeared to be a list of students who owed T.L.O. money, and two letters that implicated T.L.O. in marihuana dealing.

Mr. Choplick notified T.L.O.'s mother and the police, and turned the evidence of drug dealing over to the police. At the request of the police, T.L.O.'s mother took her daughter to police headquarters, where T.L.O. confessed that she had been selling marihuana at the high school. On the basis of the confession and the evidence seized by Mr. Choplick, the State brought delinquency charges against T.L.O. in the Juvenile and Domestic Relations Court of Middlesex County.[57] Contending that Mr. Choplick's search of her purse violated the Fourth Amendment, T.L.O. moved to suppress the evidence found in her purse as well as her confession, which, she argued, was tainted by the allegedly unlawful search. The Juvenile Court denied the motion to suppress. . . . Although the court concluded that the Fourth Amendment did apply to searches carried out by school officials, it held that

> a school official may properly conduct a search of a student's person if the official has a reasonable suspicion that a crime has been or is in the process of being committed, *or* reasonable cause to believe that the search is necessary to maintain school discipline or enforce school policies.

. . . .

Applying this standard, the court concluded that the search conducted by Mr. Choplick was a reasonable one. The initial decision to open the purse was justified by Mr. Choplick's well-founded suspicion that T.L.O. had violated the rule forbidding smoking in the lavatory. Once the purse was open, evidence of marihuana violations was in plain view, and Mr. Choplick was entitled to conduct a thorough search to determine the nature and extent of T.L.O.'s drug-related activities. . . . Having denied the motion to suppress, the court on March 23, 1981, found T.L.O. to be a delinquent and on January 8, 1982, sentenced her to a year's probation.

On appeal from the final judgment of the Juvenile Court, a divided Appellate Division affirmed the trial court's finding that there had been no Fourth Amendment violation, but vacated the adjudication of delinquency and remanded for a determination whether T.L.O. had knowingly and voluntarily waived her Fifth Amendment rights before confessing. . . . T.L.O. appealed the Fourth Amendment ruling, and the Supreme Court of New Jersey reversed the judgment of the Appellate Division and ordered the suppression of the evidence found in T.L.O.'s purse.

The New Jersey Supreme Court agreed with the lower courts that the Fourth Amendment applies to searches conducted by school officials. The court also rejected the State of New Jersey's argument that the exclusionary rule should not be employed to prevent the use in juvenile proceedings of evidence unlawfully seized by school officials. . . . With respect to the question of the legality of the search before it, the court agreed with the Juvenile Court that a warrantless search by a school official does not violate the Fourth Amendment so long as the official "has reasonable grounds to believe that a student possesses evidence of illegal activity or activity that would interfere with school discipline and order." However, the court, with two justices dissenting,

---

[57] [1] T.L.O. also received a 3-day suspension from school for smoking cigarettes in a nonsmoking area and a 7-day suspension for possession of marihuana. On T.L.O.'s motion, the Superior Court of New Jersey, Chancery Division, set aside the 7-day suspension on the ground that it was based on evidence seized in violation of the Fourth Amendment.

sharply disagreed with the Juvenile Court's conclusion that the search of the purse was reasonable. According to the majority, the contents of T.L.O.'s purse had no bearing on the accusation against T.L.O., for possession of cigarettes (as opposed to smoking them in the lavatory) did not violate school rules, and a mere desire for evidence that would impeach T.L.O.'s claim that she did not smoke cigarettes could not justify the search. Moreover, even if a reasonable suspicion that T.L.O. had cigarettes in her purse would justify a search, Mr. Choplick had no such suspicion, as no one had furnished him with any specific information that there were cigarettes in the purse. Finally, leaving aside the question whether Mr. Choplick was justified in opening the purse, the court held that the evidence of drug use that he saw inside did not justify the extensive "rummaging" through T.L.O.'s papers and effects that followed.

We granted the State of New Jersey's petition for certiorari. Although the State had argued in the Supreme Court of New Jersey that the search of T.L.O.'s purse did not violate the Fourth Amendment, the petition for certiorari raised only the question whether the exclusionary rule should operate to bar consideration in juvenile delinquency proceedings of evidence unlawfully seized by a school official without the involvement of law enforcement officers. When this case was first argued last Term, the State conceded for the purpose of argument that the standard devised by the New Jersey Supreme Court for determining the legality of school searches was appropriate and that the court had correctly applied that standard; the State contended only that the remedial purposes of the exclusionary rule were not well served by applying it to searches conducted by public authorities not primarily engaged in law enforcement.

Although we originally granted certiorari to decide the issue of the appropriate remedy in juvenile court proceedings for unlawful school searches, our doubts regarding the wisdom of deciding that question in isolation from the broader question of what limits, if any, the Fourth Amendment places on the activities of school authorities prompted us to order reargument on that question.[58] Having heard argument on the legality of the search of T.L.O.'s

---

58 [2] State and federal courts considering these questions have struggled to accommodate the interests protected by the Fourth Amendment and the interest of the States in providing a safe environment conducive to education in the public schools. Some courts have resolved the tension between these interests by giving full force to one or the other side of the balance. Thus, in a number of cases courts have held that school officials conducting in-school searches of students are private parties acting *in loco parentis* and are therefore not subject to the constraints of the Fourth Amendment. At least one court has held, on the other hand, that the Fourth Amendment applies in full to in-school searches by school officials and that a search conducted without probable cause is unreasonable; others have held or suggested that the probable-cause standard is applicable at least where the police are involved in a search; or where the search is highly intrusive. The majority of courts that have addressed the issue of the Fourth Amendment in the schools have, like the Supreme Court of New Jersey in this case, reached a middle position: the Fourth Amendment applies to searches conducted by school authorities, but the special needs of the school environment require assessment of the legality of such searches against a standard less exacting than that of probable cause. These courts have, by and large, upheld warrantless searches by school authorities provided that they are supported by a reasonable suspicion that the search will uncover evidence of an infraction of school disciplinary rules or a violation of the law.

Although few have considered the matter, courts have also split over whether the exclusionary rule is an appropriate remedy for Fourth Amendment violations committed by school authorities.

purse, we are satisfied that the search did not violate the Fourth Amendment.[59]

II

In determining whether the search at issue in this case violated the Fourth Amendment, we are faced initially with the question whether that Amendment's prohibition on unreasonable searches and seizures applies to searches conducted by public school officials. We hold that it does.

It is now beyond dispute that "the Federal Constitution, by virtue of the Fourteenth Amendment, prohibits unreasonable searches and seizures by state officers." Equally indisputable is the proposition that the Fourteenth Amendment protects the rights of students against encroachment by public school officials:

> The Fourteenth Amendment, as now applied to the States, protects the citizen against the State itself and all of its creatures — Boards of Education not excepted. These have, of course, important, delicate, and highly discretionary functions, but none that they may not perform within the limits of the Bill of Rights. That they are educating the young for citizenship is reason for scrupulous protection of Constitutional freedoms of the individual, if we are not to strangle the free mind at its source and teach youth to discount important principles of our government as mere platitudes.

West Virginia State Bd. of Ed. v. Barnette, 319 U.S. 624, 637 (1943).

. . . .

Notwithstanding the general applicability of the Fourth Amendment to the activities of civil authorities, a few courts have concluded that school officials are exempt from the dictates of the Fourth Amendment by virtue of the special nature of their authority over schoolchildren. Teachers and school administrators, it is said, act *in loco parentis* in their dealings with students: their authority is that of the parent, not the State, and is therefore not subject to the limits of the Fourth Amendment.

Such reasoning is in tension with contemporary reality and the teachings of this Court. We have held school officials subject to the commands of the First Amendment, see *Tinker v. Des Moines Independent Community School*

The Georgia courts have held that although the Fourth Amendment applies to the schools, the exclusionary rule does not. Other jurisdictions have applied the rule to exclude the fruits of unlawful school searches from criminal trials and delinquency proceedings.

59 [3] In holding that the search of T.L.O.'s purse did not violate the Fourth Amendment, we do not implicitly determine that the exclusionary rule applies to the fruits of unlawful searches conducted by school authorities. The question whether evidence should be excluded from a criminal proceeding involves two discrete inquiries: whether the evidence was seized in violation of the Fourth Amendment, and whether the exclusionary rule is the appropriate remedy for the violation. Neither question is logically antecedent to the other, for a negative answer to either question is sufficient to dispose of the case. Thus, our determination that the search at issue in this case did not violate the Fourth Amendment implies no particular resolution of the question of the applicability of the exclusionary rule.

District, 393 U.S. 503 (1969), and the Due Process Clause of the Fourteenth Amendment, *see Goss v. Lopez*, 419 U.S. 565 (1975). If school authorities are state actors for purposes of the constitutional guarantees of freedom of expression and due process, it is difficult to understand why they should be deemed to be exercising parental rather than public authority when conducting searches of their students. More generally, the Court has recognized that "the concept of parental delegation" as a source of school authority is not entirely "consonant with compulsory education laws." *Ingraham v. Wright*, 430 U.S. 651, 662 (1977). Today's public school officials do not merely exercise authority voluntarily conferred on them by individual parents; rather, they act in furtherance of publicly mandated educational and disciplinary policies. In carrying out searches and other disciplinary functions pursuant to such policies, school officials act as representatives of the State, not merely as surrogates for the parents, and they cannot claim the parents' immunity from the strictures of the Fourth Amendment.

III

To hold that the Fourth Amendment applies to searches conducted by school authorities is only to begin the inquiry into the standards governing such searches. Although the underlying command of the Fourth Amendment is always that searches and seizures be reasonable, what is reasonable depends on the context within which a search takes place. The determination of the standard of reasonableness governing any specific class of searches requires "balancing the need to search against the invasion which the search entails." On one side of the balance are arrayed the individual's legitimate expectations of privacy and personal security; on the other, the government's need for effective methods to deal with breaches of public order.

We have recognized that even a limited search of the person is a substantial invasion of privacy. *Terry v. Ohio*, 392 U.S. 1, 24–25 (1967). We have also recognized that searches of closed items of personal luggage are intrusions on protected privacy interests, for "the Fourth Amendment provides protection to the owner of every container that conceals its contents from plain view." *United States v. Ross*, 456 U.S. 798, 822–823 (1982). A search of a child's person or of a closed purse or other bag carried on her person,[60] no less than a similar search carried out on an adult, is undoubtedly a severe violation of subjective expectations of privacy.

Of course, the Fourth Amendment does not protect subjective expectations of privacy that are unreasonable or otherwise "illegitimate." To receive the

---

[60] [5] We do not address the question, not presented by this case, whether a schoolchild has a legitimate expectation of privacy in lockers, desks, or other school property provided for the storage of school supplies. Nor do we express any opinion on the standards (if any) governing searches of such areas by school officials or by other public authorities acting at the request of school officials. *Compare Zamora v. Pomeroy*, 639 F.2d 662, 670 (CA10 1981) ("Inasmuch as the school had assumed joint control of the locker it cannot be successfully maintained that the school did not have a right to inspect it"), and *People v. Overton*, 24 N.Y.2d 522 (1969) (school administrators have power to consent to search of a student's locker), *with State v. Engerud*, 94 N.J. 331, 348 (1983) ("We are satisfied that in the context of this case the student had an expectation of privacy in the contents of his locker. . . . For the four years of high school, the school locker is a home away from home. In it the student stores the kind of personal 'effects' protected by the Fourth Amendment").

protection of the Fourth Amendment, an expectation of privacy must be one that society is "prepared to recognize as legitimate." The State of New Jersey has argued that because of the pervasive supervision to which children in the schools are necessarily subject, a child has virtually no legitimate expectation of privacy in articles of personal property "unnecessarily" carried into a school. This argument has two factual premises: (1) the fundamental incompatibility of expectations of privacy with the maintenance of a sound educational environment; and (2) the minimal interest of the child in bringing any items of personal property into the school. Both premises are severely flawed.

Although this Court may take notice of the difficulty of maintaining discipline in the public schools today, the situation is not so dire that students in the schools may claim no legitimate expectations of privacy. We have recently recognized that the need to maintain order in a prison is such that prisoners retain no legitimate expectations of privacy in their cells, but it goes almost without saying that "[the] prisoner and the schoolchild stand in wholly different circumstances, separated by the harsh facts of criminal conviction and incarceration." We are not yet ready to hold that the schools and the prisons need be equated for purposes of the Fourth Amendment.

Nor does the State's suggestion that children have no legitimate need to bring personal property into the schools seem well anchored in reality. Students at a minimum must bring to school not only the supplies needed for their studies, but also keys, money, and the necessaries of personal hygiene and grooming. In addition, students may carry on their persons or in purses or wallets such nondisruptive yet highly personal items as photographs, letters, and diaries. Finally, students may have perfectly legitimate reasons to carry with them articles of property needed in connection with extracurricular or recreational activities. In short, schoolchildren may find it necessary to carry with them a variety of legitimate, noncontraband items, and there is no reason to conclude that they have necessarily waived all rights to privacy in such items merely by bringing them onto school grounds.

Against the child's interest in privacy must be set the substantial interest of teachers and administrators in maintaining discipline in the classroom and on school grounds. Maintaining order in the classroom has never been easy, but in recent years, school disorder has often taken particularly ugly forms: drug use and violent crime in the schools have become major social problems. *See generally* 1 NIE, U.S. Dept. of Health, Education and Welfare, Violent Schools — Safe Schools: The Safe School Study Report to the Congress (1978). Even in schools that have been spared the most severe disciplinary problems, the preservation of order and a proper educational environment requires close supervision of schoolchildren, as well as the enforcement of rules against conduct that would be perfectly permissible if undertaken by an adult. "Events calling for discipline are frequent occurrences and sometimes require immediate, effective action." *Goss v. Lopez,* 419 U.S., at 580. Accordingly, we have recognized that maintaining security and order in the schools requires a certain degree of flexibility in school disciplinary procedures, and we have respected the value of preserving the informality of the student-teacher relationship.

How, then, should we strike the balance between the schoolchild's legitimate expectations of privacy and the school's equally legitimate need to maintain an environment in which learning can take place? It is evident that the school setting requires some easing of the restrictions to which searches by public authorities are ordinarily subject. The warrant requirement, in particular, is unsuited to the school environment: requiring a teacher to obtain a warrant before searching a child suspected of an infraction of school rules (or of the criminal law) would unduly interfere with the maintenance of the swift and informal disciplinary procedures needed in the schools. Just as we have in other cases dispensed with the warrant requirement when "the burden of obtaining a warrant is likely to frustrate the governmental purpose behind the search," we hold today that school officials need not obtain a warrant before searching a student who is under their authority.

The school setting also requires some modification of the level of suspicion of illicit activity needed to justify a search. Ordinarily, a search — even one that may permissibly be carried out without a warrant — must be based upon "probable cause" to believe that a violation of the law has occurred. However, "probable cause" is not an irreducible requirement of a valid search. The fundamental command of the Fourth Amendment is that searches and seizures be reasonable, and although "both the concept of probable cause and the requirement of a warrant bear on the reasonableness of a search, . . . in certain limited circumstances neither is required." Thus, we have in a number of cases recognized the legality of searches and seizures based on suspicions that, although "reasonable," do not rise to the level of probable cause. Where a careful balancing of governmental and private interests suggests that the public interest is best served by a Fourth Amendment standard of reasonableness that stops short of probable cause, we have not hesitated to adopt such a standard.

We join the majority of courts that have examined this issue in concluding that the accommodation of the privacy interests of schoolchildren with the substantial need of teachers and administrators for freedom to maintain order in the schools does not require strict adherence to the requirement that searches be based on probable cause to believe that the subject of the search has violated or is violating the law. Rather, the legality of a search of a student should depend simply on the reasonableness, under all the circumstances, of the search. Determining the reasonableness of any search involves a twofold inquiry: first, one must consider "whether the . . . action was justified at its inception"; second, one must determine whether the search as actually conducted "was reasonably related in scope to the circumstances which justified the interference in the first place." Under ordinary circumstances, a search of a student by a teacher or other school official[61] will be "justified at its inception" when there are reasonable grounds for suspecting that the

---

[61] [7] We here consider only searches carried out by school authorities acting alone and on their own authority. This case does not present the question of the appropriate standard for assessing the legality of searches conducted by school officials in conjunction with or at the behest of law enforcement agencies, and we express no opinion on that question.

search will turn up evidence that the student has violated or is violating either the law or the rules of the school.[62]

Such a search will be permissible in its scope when the measures adopted are reasonably related to the objectives of the search and not excessively intrusive in light of the age and sex of the student and the nature of the infraction.[63]

This standard will, we trust, neither unduly burden the efforts of school authorities to maintain order in their schools nor authorize unrestrained intrusions upon the privacy of schoolchildren. By focusing attention on the question of reasonableness, the standard will spare teachers and school administrators the necessity of schooling themselves in the niceties of probable cause and permit them to regulate their conduct according to the dictates of reason and common sense. At the same time, the reasonableness standard should ensure that the interests of students will be invaded no more than is necessary to achieve the legitimate end of preserving order in the schools.

IV

There remains the question of the legality of the search in this case. We recognize that the "reasonable grounds" standard applied by the New Jersey Supreme Court in its consideration of this question is not substantially different from the standard that we have adopted today. Nonetheless, we believe that the New Jersey court's application of that standard to strike down the search of T.L.O.'s purse reflects a somewhat crabbed notion of reasonableness. Our review of the facts surrounding the search leads us to conclude that the search was in no sense unreasonable for Fourth Amendment purposes.

---

[62] [8] We do not decide whether individualized suspicion is an essential element of the reasonableness standard we adopt for searches by school authorities. In other contexts, however, we have held that although "some quantum of individualized suspicion is usually a prerequisite to a constitutional search or seizure[,] . . . the Fourth Amendment imposes no irreducible requirement of such suspicion." Exceptions to the requirement of individualized suspicion are generally appropriate only where the privacy interests implicated by a search are minimal and where "other safeguards" are available "to assure that the individual's reasonable expectation of privacy is not 'subject to the discretion of the official in the field.'" Because the search of T.L.O.'s purse was based upon an individualized suspicion that she had violated school rules, we need not consider the circumstances that might justify school authorities in conducting searches unsupported by individualized suspicion.

[63] [9] Our reference to the nature of the infraction is not intended as an endorsement of JUSTICE STEVENS' suggestion that some rules regarding student conduct are by nature too "trivial" to justify a search based upon reasonable suspicion. We are unwilling to adopt a standard under which the legality of a search is dependent upon a judge's evaluation of the relative importance of various school rules. The maintenance of discipline in the schools requires not only that students be restrained from assaulting one another, abusing drugs and alcohol, and committing other crimes, but also that students conform themselves to the standards of conduct prescribed by school authorities. We have "repeatedly emphasized the need for affirming the comprehensive authority of the States and of school officials, consistent with fundamental constitutional safeguards, to prescribe and control conduct in the schools." The promulgation of a rule forbidding specified conduct presumably reflects a judgment on the part of school officials that such conduct is destructive of school order or of a proper educational environment. Absent any suggestion that the rule violates some substantive constitutional guarantee, the courts should, as a general matter, defer to that judgment and refrain from attempting to distinguish between rules that are important to the preservation of order in the schools and rules that are not.

The incident that gave rise to this case actually involved two separate searches, with the first — the search for cigarettes — providing the suspicion that gave rise to the second — the search for marihuana. Although it is the fruits of the second search that are at issue here, the validity of the search for marihuana must depend on the reasonableness of the initial search for cigarettes, as there would have been no reason to suspect that T.L.O. possessed marihuana had the first search not taken place. Accordingly, it is to the search for cigarettes that we first turn our attention.

The New Jersey Supreme Court pointed to two grounds for its holding that the search for cigarettes was unreasonable. First, the court observed that possession of cigarettes was not in itself illegal or a violation of school rules. Because the contents of T.L.O.'s purse would therefore have "no direct bearing on the infraction" of which she was accused (smoking in a lavatory where smoking was prohibited), there was no reason to search her purse. Second, even assuming that a search of T.L.O.'s purse might under some circumstances be reasonable in light of the accusation made against T.L.O., the New Jersey court concluded that Mr. Choplick in this particular case had no reasonable grounds to suspect that T.L.O. had cigarettes in her purse. At best, according to the court, Mr. Choplick had "a good hunch." . . .

Both these conclusions are implausible. T.L.O. had been accused of smoking, and had denied the accusation in the strongest possible terms when she stated that she did not smoke at all. Surely it cannot be said that under these circumstances, T.L.O.'s possession of cigarettes would be irrelevant to the charges against her or to her response to those charges. T.L.O.'s possession of cigarettes, once it was discovered, would both corroborate the report that she had been smoking and undermine the credibility of her defense to the charge of smoking. To be sure, the discovery of the cigarettes would not prove that T.L.O. had been smoking in the lavatory; nor would it, strictly speaking, necessarily be inconsistent with her claim that she did not smoke at all. But it is universally recognized that evidence, to be relevant to an inquiry, need not conclusively prove the ultimate fact in issue, but only have "any tendency to make the existence of any fact that is of consequence to the determination of the action more probable or less probable than it would be without the evidence." The relevance of T.L.O.'s possession of cigarettes to the question whether she had been smoking and to the credibility of her denial that she smoked supplied the necessary "nexus" between the item searched for and the infraction under investigation. Thus, if Mr. Choplick in fact had a reasonable suspicion that T.L.O. had cigarettes in her purse, the search was justified despite the fact that the cigarettes, if found, would constitute "mere evidence" of a violation.

Of course, the New Jersey Supreme Court also held that Mr. Choplick had no reasonable suspicion that the purse would contain cigarettes. This conclusion is puzzling. A teacher had reported that T.L.O. was smoking in the lavatory. Certainly this report gave Mr. Choplick reason to suspect that T.L.O. was carrying cigarettes with her; and if she did have cigarettes, her purse was the obvious place in which to find them. Mr. Choplick's suspicion that there were cigarettes in the purse was not an "inchoate and unparticularized suspicion or 'hunch,'" rather, it was the sort of "common-sense [conclusion]

about human behavior" upon which "practical people" — including government officials — are entitled to rely. Of course, even if the teacher's report
were true, T.L.O. *might* not have had a pack of cigarettes with her; she might
have borrowed a cigarette from someone else or have been sharing a cigarette
with another student. But the requirement of reasonable suspicion is not a
requirement of absolute certainty: "sufficient probability, not certainty, is the
touchstone of reasonableness under the Fourth Amendment. . . ." Because
the hypothesis that T.L.O. was carrying cigarettes in her purse was not itself
not unreasonable, it is irrelevant that other hypotheses were also consistent
with the teacher's accusation. Accordingly, it cannot be said that Mr. Choplick
acted unreasonably when he examined T.L.O.'s purse to see if it contained
cigarettes. [64]

Our conclusion that Mr. Choplick's decision to open T.L.O.'s purse was
reasonable brings us to the question of the further search for marihuana once
the pack of cigarettes was located. The suspicion upon which the search for
marihuana was founded was provided when Mr. Choplick observed a package
of rolling papers in the purse as he removed the pack of cigarettes. Although
T.L.O. does not dispute the reasonableness of Mr. Choplick's belief that the
rolling papers indicated the presence of marihuana, she does contend that the
scope of the search Mr. Choplick conducted exceeded permissible bounds when
he seized and read certain letters that implicated T.L.O. in drug dealing. This
argument, too, is unpersuasive. The discovery of the rolling papers concededly
gave rise to a reasonable suspicion that T.L.O. was carrying marihuana as
well as cigarettes in her purse. This suspicion justified further exploration
of T.L.O.'s purse, which turned up more evidence of drug-related activities:
a pipe, a number of plastic bags of the type commonly used to store marihuana,
a small quantity of marihuana, and a fairly substantial amount of money.
Under these circumstances, it was not unreasonable to extend the search to
a separate zippered compartment of the purse; and when a search of that
compartment revealed an index card containing a list of "people who owe me
money" as well as two letters, the inference that T.L.O. was involved in marihuana trafficking was substantial enough to justify Mr. Choplick in examining
the letters to determine whether they contained any further evidence. In short,
we cannot conclude that the search for marihuana was unreasonable in any
respect.

Because the search resulting in the discovery of the evidence of marihuana
dealing by T.L.O. was reasonable, the New Jersey Supreme Court's decision

---

[64] [12] T.L.O. contends that even if it was reasonable for Mr. Choplick to open her purse to
look for cigarettes, it was not reasonable for him to reach in and take the cigarettes out of her
purse once he found them. Had he not removed the cigarettes from the purse, she asserts, he
would not have observed the rolling papers that suggested the presence of marihuana, and the
search for marihuana could not have taken place. T.L.O.'s argument is based on the fact that
the cigarettes were not "contraband," as no school rule forbade her to have them. Thus, according
to T.L.O., the cigarettes were not subject to seizure or confiscation by school authorities, and Mr.
Choplick was not entitled to take them out of T.L.O.'s purse regardless of whether he was entitled
to peer into the purse to see if they were there. Such hairsplitting argumentation has no place
in an inquiry addressed to the issue of reasonableness. If Mr. Choplick could permissibly search
T.L.O.'s purse for cigarettes, it hardly seems reasonable to suggest that his natural reaction to
finding them — picking them up — could be a constitutional violation. We find that neither in
opening the purse nor in reaching into it to remove the cigarettes did Mr. Choplick violate the
Fourth Amendment.

to exclude that evidence from T.L.O.'s juvenile delinquency proceedings on Fourth Amendment grounds was erroneous. Accordingly, the judgment of the Supreme Court of New Jersey is . . .

Reversed.

JUSTICE POWELL, with whom JUSTICE O'CONNOR joins, *concurring.*

I agree with the Court's decision, and generally with its opinion. I would place greater emphasis, however, on the special characteristics of elementary and secondary schools that make it unnecessary to afford students the same constitutional protections granted adults and juveniles in a nonschool setting.

In any realistic sense, students within the school environment have a lesser expectation of privacy than members of the population generally. They spend the school hours in close association with each other, both in the classroom and during recreation periods. The students in a particular class often know each other and their teachers quite well. Of necessity, teachers have a degree of familiarity with, and authority over, their students that is unparalleled except perhaps in the relationship between parent and child. It is simply unrealistic to think that students have the same subjective expectation of privacy as the population generally. But for purposes of deciding this case, I can assume that children in school — no less than adults — have privacy interests that society is prepared to recognize as legitimate.

However one may characterize their privacy expectations, students properly are afforded some constitutional protections. In an often quoted statement, the Court said that students do not "shed their constitutional rights . . . at the schoolhouse gate." The Court also has "emphasized the need for affirming the comprehensive authority of the states and of school officials . . . to prescribe and control conduct in the schools." The Court has balanced the interests of the student against the school officials' need to maintain discipline by recognizing qualitative differences between the constitutional remedies to which students and adults are entitled.

In *Goss v. Lopez*, the Court recognized a constitutional right to due process, and yet was careful to limit the exercise of this right by a student who challenged a disciplinary suspension. The only process found to be "due" was notice and a hearing described as "rudimentary"; it amounted to no more than "the disciplinarian . . . informally [discussing] the alleged misconduct with the student minutes after it has occurred." In *Ingraham v. Wright*, we declined to extend the Eighth Amendment to prohibit the use of corporal punishment of schoolchildren as authorized by Florida law. We emphasized in that opinion that familiar constraints in the school, and also in the community, provide substantial protection against the violation of constitutional rights by school authorities. . . . The *Ingraham* Court further pointed out that the "openness of the public school and its supervision by the community afford significant safeguards" against the violation of constitutional rights.

The special relationship between teacher and student also distinguishes the setting within which schoolchildren operate. Law enforcement officers function as adversaries of criminal suspects. These officers have the responsibility to investigate criminal activity, to locate and arrest those who violate our laws, and to facilitate the charging and bringing of such persons to trial. Rarely does this type of adversarial relationship exist between school authorities and pupils.[65] Instead, there is a commonality of interests between teachers and their pupils. The attitude of the typical teacher is one of personal responsibility for the student's welfare as well as for his education.

The primary duty of school officials and teachers, as the Court states, is the education and training of young people. A State has a compelling interest in assuring that the schools meet this responsibility. Without first establishing discipline and maintaining order, teachers cannot begin to educate their students. And apart from education, the school has the obligation to protect pupils from mistreatment by other children, and also to protect teachers themselves from violence by the few students whose conduct in recent years has prompted national concern. For me, it would be unreasonable and at odds with history to argue that the full panoply of constitutional rules applies with the same force and effect in the schoolhouse as it does in the enforcement of criminal laws.[66]

In sum, although I join the Court's opinion and its holding, my emphasis is somewhat different.

JUSTICE BLACKMUN, *concurring in the judgment.*

I join the judgment of the Court and agree with much that is said in its opinion. I write separately, however, because I believe the Court omits a crucial step in its analysis of whether a school search must be based upon probable cause. The Court correctly states that we have recognized limited exceptions to the probable-cause requirement "[where] a careful balancing of governmental and private interests suggests that the public interest is best served" by a lesser standard. I believe that we have used such a balancing test, rather than strictly applying the Fourth Amendment's Warrant and Probable-Cause Clause, only when we were confronted with "a special law enforcement need for greater flexibility." . . .

Only in those exceptional circumstances in which special needs, beyond the normal need for law enforcement, make the warrant and probable-cause requirement impracticable, is a court entitled to substitute its balancing of interests for that of the Framers. . . .

The Court's implication that the balancing test is the rule rather than the exception is troubling for me because it is unnecessary in this case. The elementary and secondary school setting presents a special need for flexibility justifying a departure from the balance struck by the Framers. As Justice Powell notes, "[without] first establishing discipline and maintaining order, teachers cannot begin to educate their students." Maintaining order in the classroom can be a difficult task. A single teacher often must watch over a

---

65 [1] Unlike police officers, school authorities have no law enforcement responsibility or indeed any obligation to be familiar with the criminal laws. Of course, as illustrated by this case, school authorities have a layman's familiarity with the types of crimes that occur frequently in our schools: the distribution and use of drugs, theft, and even violence against teachers as well as fellow students.

66 [2] As noted above, decisions of this Court have never held to the contrary. The law recognizes a host of distinctions between the rights and duties of children and those of adults. *See Goss v. Lopez*, 419 U.S. 565, 591 (1975) (POWELL, J., dissenting.)

large number of students, and, as any parent knows, children at certain ages are inclined to test the outer boundaries of acceptable conduct and to imitate the misbehavior of a peer if that misbehavior is not dealt with quickly. Every adult remembers from his own schooldays the havoc a water pistol or peashooter can wreak until it is taken away. Thus, the Court has recognized that "[events] calling for discipline are frequent occurrences and sometimes require immediate, effective action." *Goss v. Lopez*, 419 U.S. 565, 580 (1975). Indeed, because drug use and possession of weapons have become increasingly common among young people, an immediate response frequently is required not just to maintain an environment conducive to learning, but to protect the very safety of students and school personnel.

Such immediate action obviously would not be possible if a teacher were required to secure a warrant before searching a student. Nor would it be possible if a teacher could not conduct a necessary search until the teacher thought there was probable cause for the search. A teacher has neither the training nor the day-to-day experience in the complexities of probable cause that a law enforcement officer possesses, and is ill-equipped to make a quick judgment about the existence of probable cause. The time required for a teacher to ask the questions or make the observations that are necessary to turn reasonable grounds into probable cause is time during which the teacher, and other students, are diverted from the essential task of education. A teacher's focus is, and should be, on teaching and helping students, rather than on developing evidence against a particular troublemaker.

Education "is perhaps the most important function" of government, *Brown v. Board of Education*, 347 U.S. 483, 493 (1954), and government has a heightened obligation to safeguard students whom it compels to attend school. The special need for an immediate response to behavior that threatens either the safety of schoolchildren and teachers or the educational process itself justifies the Court in excepting school searches from the warrant and proba-ble-cause requirement, and in applying a standard determined by balancing the relevant interests. I agree with the standard the Court has announced, and with its application of the standard to the facts of this case. I therefore concur in its judgment.

JUSTICE BRENNAN, with whom JUSTICE MARSHALL joins, *concurring in part and dissenting in part*.

I fully agree with Part II of the Court's opinion. Teachers, like all other government officials, must conform their conduct to the Fourth Amendment's protections of personal privacy and personal security. As Justice Stevens points out, this principle is of particular importance when applied to school-teachers, for children learn as much by example as by exposition. It would be incongruous and futile to charge teachers with the task of embuing their students with an understanding of our system of constitutional democracy, while at the same time immunizing those same teachers from the need to respect constitutional protections.

I do not, however, otherwise join the Court's opinion. Today's decision sanctions school officials to conduct full-scale searches on a "reasonableness" standard whose only definite content is that it is *not* the same test as the "probable cause" standard found in the text of the Fourth Amendment. In adopting this unclear, unprecedented, and unnecessary departure from generally applicable Fourth Amendment standards, the Court carves out a broad exception to standards that this Court has developed over years of considering Fourth Amendment problems. Its decision is supported neither by precedent nor even by a fair application of the "balancing test" it proclaims in this very opinion.

I

Three basic principles underly this Court's Fourth Amendment jurisprudence. First, warrantless searches are *per se* unreasonable, subject only to a few specifically delineated and well-recognized exceptions. Second, full-scale searches — whether conducted in accordance with the warrant requirement or pursuant to one of its exceptions — are "reasonable" in Fourth Amendment terms only on a showing of probable cause to believe that a crime has been committed and that evidence of the crime will be found in the place to be searched. Third, categories of intrusions that are substantially less intrusive than full-scale searches or seizures may be justifiable in accordance with a balancing test even absent a warrant or probable cause, provided that the balancing test used gives sufficient weight to the privacy interests that will be infringed.

Assistant Vice Principal Choplick's thorough excavation of T.L.O.'s purse was undoubtedly a serious intrusion on her privacy. [T]he search at issue here encompassed a detailed and minute examination of respondent's pocketbook, in which the contents of private papers and letters were thoroughly scrutinized.[67] Wisely, neither petitioner nor the Court today attempts to justify the search of T.L.O.'s pocketbook as a minimally intrusive search in the *Terry* line. To be faithful to the Court's settled doctrine, the inquiry therefore must focus on the warrant and probable-cause requirements.

. . . .

A

The Warrant Clause is something more than an exhortation to this Court to maximize social welfare as *we* see fit. It requires that the authorities must obtain a warrant before conducting a full-scale search. The undifferentiated governmental interest in law enforcement is insufficient to justify an exception to the warrant requirement. Rather, some *special* governmental interest beyond the need merely to apprehend lawbreakers is necessary to justify a categorical exception to the warrant requirement. For the most part, special governmental needs sufficient to override the warrant requirement flow from "exigency" — that is, from the press of time that makes obtaining a warrant either impossible or hopelessly infeasible. Only after finding an extraordinary governmental interest of this kind do we — or ought we — engage in a balancing test to determine if a warrant should nonetheless be required. . . .

---

67 [1] A purse typically contains items of highly personal nature. Especially for shy or sensitive adolescents, it could prove extremely embarrassing for a teacher or principal to rummage through its contents, which could include notes from friends, fragments of love poems, caricatures of school authorities, and items of personal hygiene.

In this case, such extraordinary governmental interests do exist and are sufficient to justify an exception to the warrant requirement. Students are necessarily confined for most of the schoolday in close proximity to each other and to the school staff. I agree with the Court that we can take judicial notice of the serious problems of drugs and violence that plague our schools. As Justice Blackmun notes, teachers must not merely "maintain an environment conducive to learning" among children who "are inclined to test the outer boundaries of acceptable conduct," but must also "protect the very safety of students and school personnel." A teacher or principal could neither carry out essential teaching functions nor adequately protect students' safety if required to wait for a warrant before conducting a necessary search.

B

I emphatically disagree with the Court's decision to cast aside the constitutional probable-cause standard when assessing the constitutional validity of a schoolhouse search. The Court's decision jettisons the probable-cause standard — the only standard that finds support in the text of the Fourth Amendment — on the basis of its Rohrschach-like "balancing test." Use of such a "balancing test" to determine the standard for evaluating the validity of a full-scale search represents a sizable innovation in Fourth Amendment analysis. This innovation finds support neither in precedent nor policy and portends a dangerous weakening of the purpose of the Fourth Amendment to protect the privacy and security of our citizens. Moreover, even if this Court's historic understanding of the Fourth Amendment were mistaken and a balancing test of some kind were appropriate, any such test that gave adequate weight to the privacy and security interests protected by the Fourth Amendment would not reach the preordained result the Court's conclusory analysis reaches today. Therefore, because I believe that the balancing test used by the Court today is flawed both in its inception and in its execution, I respectfully dissent.

. . . .

The Court begins to articulate its "balancing test" by observing that "the government's need for effective methods to deal with breaches of public order" is to be weighed on one side of the balance. Of course, this is not correct. It is not the government's need for effective enforcement methods that should weigh in the balance, for ordinary Fourth Amendment standards — including probable cause — may well permit methods for maintaining the public order that are perfectly effective. If that were the case, the governmental interest in having effective standards would carry no weight at all as a justification for *departing* from the probable-cause standard. Rather, it is the costs of applying probable cause as opposed to applying some lesser standard that should be weighed on the government's side.

. . . .

In order to tote up the costs of applying the probable-cause standard, it is thus necessary first to take into account the nature and content of that standard, and the likelihood that it would hamper achievement of the goal — vital not just to "teachers and administrators," — of maintaining an effective educational setting in the public schools. . . .

A consideration of the likely operation of the probable-cause standard reinforces this conclusion. Discussing the issue of school searches, Professor LaFave has noted that the cases that have reached the appellate courts "strongly suggest that in most instances the evidence of wrongdoing prompting teachers or principals to conduct searches is sufficiently detailed and specific to meet the traditional probable cause test." The problems that have caused this Court difficulty in interpreting the probable-cause standard have largely involved informants. . . . However, three factors make it likely that problems involving informants will not make it difficult for teachers and school administrators to make probable-cause decisions. This Court's decision in [*Illinois v. Gates,* 462 U.S. 213 (1983),] applying a "totality of the circumstances" test to determine whether an informant's tip can constitute probable cause renders the test easy for teachers to apply. The fact that students and teachers interact daily in the school building makes it more likely that teachers will get to know students who supply information; the problem of informants who remain anonymous even to the teachers — and who are therefore unavailable for verification or further questioning — is unlikely to arise. Finally, teachers can observe the behavior of students under suspicion to corroborate any doubtful tips they do receive.

As compared with the relative ease with which teachers can apply the probable-cause standard, the amorphous "reasonableness under all the circumstances" standard freshly coined by the Court today will likely spawn increased litigation and greater uncertainty among teachers and administrators. Of course, as this Court should know, an essential purpose of developing and articulating legal norms is to enable individuals to conform their conduct to those norms. A school system conscientiously attempting to obey the Fourth Amendment's dictates under a probable-cause standard could, for example, consult decisions and other legal materials and prepare a booklet expounding the rough outlines of the concept. Such a booklet could be distributed to teachers to provide them with guidance as to when a search may be lawfully conducted. I cannot but believe that the same school system faced with interpreting what is permitted under the Court's new "reasonableness" standard would be hopelessly adrift as to when a search may be permissible. The sad result of this uncertainty may well be that some teachers will be reluctant to conduct searches that are fully permissible and even necessary under the constitutional probable-cause standard, while others may intrude arbitrarily and unjustifiably on the privacy of students.[68] . . .

---

68 [7] A comparison of the language of the standard ("reasonableness under all the circumstances") with the traditional language of probable cause ("facts sufficient to warrant a person of reasonable caution in believing that a crime had been committed and the evidence would be found in the designated place") suggests that the Court's new standard may turn out to be probable cause under a new guise. If so, the additional uncertainty caused by this Court's innovation is surely unjustifiable; it would be naive to expect that the addition of this extra dose of uncertainty would do anything other than "burden the efforts of school authorities to maintain order in their schools." If, on the other hand, the new standard permits searches of students in instances when probable cause is absent — instances, according to this Court's consistent formulations, when a person of reasonable caution would not think it likely that a violation existed or that evidence of that violation would be found — the new standard is genuinely objectionable and impossible to square with the premise that our citizens have the right to be free from arbitrary intrusions on their privacy.

II

Applying the constitutional probable-cause standard to the facts of this case, I would find that Mr. Choplick's search violated T.L.O.'s Fourth Amendment rights. After escorting T.L.O. into his private office, Mr. Choplick demanded to see her purse. He then opened the purse to find evidence of whether she had been smoking in the bathroom. When he opened the purse, he discovered the pack of cigarettes. At this point, his search for evidence of the smoking violation was complete.

Mr. Choplick then noticed, below the cigarettes, a pack of cigarette rolling papers. Believing that such papers were "associated," with the use of marihuana, he proceeded to conduct a detailed examination of the contents of her purse, in which he found some marihuana, a pipe, some money, an index card, and some private letters indicating that T.L.O. had sold marihuana to other students. The State sought to introduce this latter material in evidence at a criminal proceeding, and the issue before the Court is whether it should have been suppressed.

On my view of the case, we need not decide whether the initial search conducted by Mr. Choplick — the search for evidence of the smoking violation that was completed when Mr. Choplick found the pack of cigarettes — was valid. For Mr. Choplick at that point did not have probable cause to continue to rummage through T.L.O.'s purse. Mr. Choplick's suspicion of marihuana possession at this time was based *solely* on the presence of the package of cigarette papers. The mere presence without more of such a staple item of commerce is insufficient to warrant a person of reasonable caution in inferring both that T.L.O. had violated the law by possessing marihuana and that evidence of that violation would be found in her purse. Just as a police officer could not obtain a warrant to search a home based solely on his claim that he had seen a package of cigarette papers in that home, Mr. Choplick was not entitled to search possibly the most private possessions of T.L.O. based on the mere presence of a package of cigarette papers. Therefore, the fruits of this illegal search must be excluded and the judgment of the New Jersey Supreme Court affirmed.

* * *

JUSTICE STEVENS, with whom JUSTICE MARSHALL joins, and with whom JUSTICE BRENNAN joins as to Part I, *concurring in part and dissenting in part.*

Assistant Vice Principal Choplick searched T.L.O.'s purse for evidence that she was smoking in the girls' restroom. Because T.L.O.'s suspected misconduct was not illegal and did not pose a serious threat to school discipline, the New Jersey Supreme Court held that Choplick's search of her purse was an unreasonable invasion of her privacy and that the evidence which he seized could not be used against her in criminal proceedings. The New Jersey court's holding was a careful response to the case it was required to decide.

The State of New Jersey sought review in this Court, first arguing that the exclusionary rule is wholly inapplicable to searches conducted by school officials, and then contending that the Fourth Amendment itself provides no protection at all to the student's privacy. The Court has accepted neither of these frontal assaults on the Fourth Amendment. It has, however, seized upon this "no smoking" case to announce "the proper standard" that should govern searches by school officials who are confronted with disciplinary problems far more severe than smoking in the restroom. Although I join Part II of the Court's opinion, I continue to believe that the Court has unnecessarily and inappropriately reached out to decide a constitutional question. More importantly, I fear that the concerns that motivated the Court's activism have produced a holding that will permit school administrators to search students suspected of violating only the most trivial school regulations and guidelines for behavior.

I

The question the Court decides today — whether Mr. Choplick's search of T.L.O.'s purse violated the Fourth Amendment — was not raised by the State's petition for writ of certiorari. That petition only raised one question: "Whether the Fourth Amendment's exclusionary rule applies to searches made by public school officials and teachers in school." The State quite properly declined to submit the former question because "[it] did not wish to present what might appear to be solely a factual dispute to this Court." Since this Court has twice had the threshold question argued, I believe that it should expressly consider the merits of the New Jersey Supreme Court's ruling that the exclusionary rule applies.

The New Jersey Supreme Court's holding on this question is plainly correct. As the state court noted, this case does not involve the use of evidence in a school disciplinary proceeding; the juvenile proceedings brought against T.L.O. involved a charge that would have been a criminal offense if committed by an adult. . . .

Having confined the issue to the law enforcement context, the New Jersey court then reasoned that this Court's cases have made it quite clear that the exclusionary rule is equally applicable "whether the public official who illegally obtained the evidence was a municipal inspector, or a school administrator or law enforcement official." It correctly concluded "that if an official search violates constitutional rights, the evidence is not admissible in criminal proceedings." . . .

The practical basis for this principle is, in part, its deterrent effect, and as a general matter it is tolerably clear to me, as it has been to the Court, that the existence of an exclusionary remedy does deter the authorities from violating the Fourth Amendment by sharply reducing their incentive to do so. In the case of evidence obtained in school searches, the "overall educative effect" of the exclusionary rule adds important symbolic force to this utilitarian judgment.

Justice Brandeis was both a great student and a great teacher. It was he who wrote:

> "Our Government is the potent, the omnipresent teacher. For good or for ill, it teaches the whole people by its example. Crime is contagious. If the Government becomes a lawbreaker, it breeds contempt for law; it invites every man to become a law unto himself; it invites anarchy."

Olmstead v. United States, 277 U.S. 438, 485 (1928) (dissenting opinion).

Those of us who revere the flag and the ideals for which it stands believe in the power of symbols. We cannot ignore that rules of law also have a symbolic power that may vastly exceed their utility.

Schools are places where we inculcate the values essential to the meaningful exercise of rights and responsibilities by a self-governing citizenry. If the Nation's students can be convicted through the use of arbitrary methods destructive of personal liberty, they cannot help but feel that they have been dealt with unfairly. The application of the exclusionary rule in criminal proceedings arising from illegal school searches makes an important statement to young people that "our society attaches serious consequences to a violation of constitutional rights," and that this is a principle of "liberty and justice for all."

Thus, the simple and correct answer to the question presented by the State's petition for certiorari would have required affirmance of a state court's judgment suppressing evidence. That result would have been dramatically out of character for a Court that not only grants prosecutors relief from suppression orders with distressing regularity, but also is prone to rely on grounds not advanced by the parties in order to protect evidence from exclusion. In characteristic disregard of the doctrine of judicial restraint, the Court avoided that result in this case by ordering reargument and directing the parties to address a constitutional question that the parties, with good reason, had not asked the Court to decide. Because judicial activism undermines the Court's power to perform its central mission in a legitimate way, I dissented from the reargument order. I have not modified the views expressed in that dissent, but since the majority has brought the question before us, I shall explain why I believe the Court has misapplied the standard of reasonableness embodied in the Fourth Amendment.

II

The search of a young woman's purse by a school administrator is a serious invasion of her legitimate expectations of privacy. A purse "is a common repository for one's personal effects and therefore is inevitably associated with the expectation of privacy." Although such expectations must sometimes yield to the legitimate requirements of government, in assessing the constitutionality of a warrantless search, our decision must be guided by the language of the Fourth Amendment: "The right of the people to be secure in their persons, houses, papers and effects, against *unreasonable* searches and seizures, shall not be violated. . . ." In order to evaluate the reasonableness of such searches, "it is necessary 'first to focus upon the governmental interest which allegedly justifies official intrusion upon the constitutionally protected interests of the private citizen,' for there is 'no ready test for determining reasonableness other than by balancing the need to search [or seize] against the invasion which the search [or seizure] entails.' "

The "limited search for weapons" in *Terry* was justified by the "immediate interest of the police officer in taking steps to assure himself that the person with whom he is dealing is not armed with a weapon that could unexpectedly and fatally be used against him." When viewed from the institutional perspective, "the substantial need of teachers and administrators for freedom to maintain order in the schools," is no less acute. Violent, unlawful, or seriously disruptive conduct is fundamentally inconsistent with the principal function of teaching institutions which is to educate young people and prepare them for citizenship. When such conduct occurs amidst a sizable group of impressionable young people, it creates an explosive atmosphere that requires a prompt and effective response.

Thus, warrantless searches of students by school administrators are reasonable when undertaken for those purposes. But the majority's statement of the standard for evaluating the reasonableness of such searches is not suitably adapted to that end. The majority holds that "a search of a student by a teacher or other school official will be 'justified at its inception' when there are reasonable grounds for suspecting that the search will turn up evidence that the student has violated or is violating either the law or the rules of the school." This standard will permit teachers and school administrators to search students when they suspect that the search will reveal evidence of even the most trivial school regulation or precatory guideline for student behavior. The Court's standard for deciding whether a search is justified "at its inception" treats all violations of the rules of the school as though they were fungible. For the Court, a search for curlers and sunglasses in order to enforce the school dress code[69] is apparently just as important as a search for evidence of heroin addiction or violent gang activity.

The majority, however, does not contend that school administrators have a compelling need to search students in order to achieve optimum enforcement of minor school regulations. To the contrary, when minor violations are involved, there is every indication that the informal school disciplinary process, with only minimum requirements of due process, can function effectively without the power to search for enough evidence to prove a criminal case. In arguing that teachers and school administrators need the power to search students based on a lessened standard, the United States as *amicus*

---

69 [16] Parent-Student Handbook of Piscataway [N.J.] H. S. (1979), Record Doc. S-1, p. 7. A brief survey of school rule books reveals that, under the majority's approach, teachers and school administrators may also search students to enforce school rules regulating:

    (i) secret societies;

    (ii) students driving to school;

    (iii) parking and use of parking lots during school hours;

    (iv) smoking on campus;

    (v) the direction of traffic in the hallways;

    (vi) student presence in the hallways during class hours without a pass;

    (vii) profanity;

    (viii) school attendance of interscholastic athletes on the day of a game, meet or match;

    (ix) cafeteria use and cleanup;

    (x) eating lunch off-campus; and

    (xi) unauthorized absence.

See id., at 7–18; Student Handbook of South Windsor [Conn.] H. S. (1984); Fairfax County [Va.] Public Schools, Student Responsibilities and Rights (1980); Student Handbook of Chantilly [Va.] H. S. (1984).

curiae relies heavily on empirical evidence of a contemporary crisis of violence and unlawful behavior that is seriously undermining the process of education in American schools.[70] A standard better attuned to this concern would permit teachers and school administrators to search a student when they have reason to believe that the search will uncover *evidence that the student is violating the law or engaging in conduct that is seriously disruptive of school order, or the educational process.*

This standard is properly directed at "[the] sole justification for the [warrantless] search." In addition, a standard that varies the extent of the permissible intrusion with the gravity of the suspected offense is also more consistent with common-law experience and this Court's precedent. . . .

. . . .

The majority offers weak deference to these principles of balance and decency by announcing that school searches will only be reasonable in scope "when the measures adopted are reasonably related to the objectives of the search and not excessively intrusive in light of the age and sex of the student and the nature of the infraction." The majority offers no explanation why a two-part standard is necessary to evaluate the reasonableness of the ordinary school search. Significantly, in the balance of its opinion the Court pretermits any discussion of the nature of T.L.O.'s infraction of the "no smoking" rule.

The "rider" to the Court's standard for evaluating the reasonableness of the initial intrusion apparently is the Court's perception that its standard is overly generous and does not, by itself, achieve a fair balance between the administrator's right to search and the student's reasonable expectations of privacy. The Court's standard for evaluating the "scope" of reasonable school searches is obviously designed to prohibit physically intrusive searches of students by persons of the opposite sex for relatively minor offenses. The Court's effort to establish a standard that is, at once, clear enough to allow searches to be upheld in nearly every case, and flexible enough to prohibit obviously unreasonable intrusions of young adults' privacy only creates uncertainty in the extent of its resolve to prohibit the latter. Moreover, the majority's application of its standard in this case — to permit a male administrator to rummage through the purse of a female high school student in order to obtain evidence that she was smoking in a bathroom — raises grave doubts in my mind whether its effort will be effective. Unlike the Court, I believe the nature of the suspected infraction is a matter of first importance in deciding whether *any* invasion of privacy is permissible.

III

The Court embraces the standard applied by the New Jersey Supreme Court as equivalent to its own, and then deprecates the state court's application of the standard as reflecting "a somewhat crabbed notion of reasonableness." . . .

---

[70] [19] "The sad truth is that many classrooms across the country are not temples of learning teaching the lessons of good will, civility, and wisdom that are central to the fabric of American life. To the contrary, many schools are in such a state of disorder that not only is the educational atmosphere polluted, but the very safety of students and teachers is imperiled." Brief for United States as *Amicus Curiae* 23. *See also* Brief for National Education Association as *Amicus Curiae* 21 ("If a suspected violation of a rule threatens to disrupt the school or threatens to harm students, school officials should be free to search for evidence of it").

In the view of the state court, there is a quite obvious and material difference between a search for evidence relating to violent or disruptive activity, and a search for evidence of a smoking rule violation. This distinction does not imply that a no-smoking rule is a matter of minor importance. Rather, like a rule that prohibits a student from being tardy, its occasional violation in a context that poses no threat of disrupting school order and discipline offers no reason to believe that an immediate search is necessary to avoid unlawful conduct, violence, or a serious impairment of the educational process.

. . . .

Like the New Jersey Supreme Court, I would view this case differently if the Assistant Vice Principal had reason to believe T.L.O.'s purse contained evidence of criminal activity, or of an activity that would seriously disrupt school discipline. There was, however, absolutely no basis for any such assumption — not even a "hunch."

In this case, Mr. Choplick overreacted to what appeared to be nothing more than a minor infraction — a rule prohibiting smoking in the bathroom of the freshmen's and sophomores' building. It is, of course, true that he actually found evidence of serious wrongdoing by T.L.O., but no one claims that the prior search may be justified by his unexpected discovery. As far as the smoking infraction is concerned, the search for cigarettes merely tended to corroborate a teacher's eyewitness account of T.L.O.'s violation of a minor regulation designed to channel student smoking behavior into designated locations. Because this conduct was neither unlawful nor significantly disruptive of school order or the educational process, the invasion of privacy associated with the forcible opening of T.L.O.'s purse was entirely unjustified at its inception.

. . . .

IV

The schoolroom is the first opportunity most citizens have to experience the power of government. Through it passes every citizen and public official, from schoolteachers to policemen and prison guards. The values they learn there, they take with them in life. One of our most cherished ideals is the one contained in the Fourth Amendment: that the government may not intrude on the personal privacy of its citizens without a warrant or compelling circumstance. The Court's decision today is a curious moral for the Nation's youth. Although the search of T.L.O.'s purse does not trouble today's majority, I submit that we are not dealing with "matters relatively trivial to the welfare of the Nation. There are village tyrants as well as village Hampdens, but none who acts under color of law is beyond reach of the Constitution."

I respectfully dissent.

NOTES AND QUESTIONS

1. What is the two-part test that the Court sets forth for school searches? How will a school official be able to tell if there are reasonable grounds for

suspecting that the search will turn up evidence that the student has violated or is violating either the law or the rules of the school? Critics of *T.L.O.* claim that the Court set up a "sliding scale" approach to student search and seizure cases that opens the door "for wholesale abandonment of rules-oriented jurisprudence in favor of case-by-case assessments of reasonableness in which the government usually prevails and privacy takes a back seat." Martin R. Gardner, *The Fourth Amendment and the Public School: Observations on an Unsettled State of Search and Seizure Law*, 36 CRIM. LAW BULL., 373, 378 (2000) (citing Irene M. Rosenberg, New Jersey v. T.L.O.: *Of Children and Smokescreens*, 19 FAM. L.Q. 311, 313–29 (1985)). The reasonable suspicion standard is less rigorous than the probable cause test with respect to the amount of factual information required before a search is permissible. Does this make it less rule-oriented than probable cause? Is it easier to orient rules around the words "probable cause" as opposed to "reasonable suspicion"? Or does the probable cause standard also require a case-by-case assessment of whether probable cause existed?

What about the second prong of the Court's test — the scope of the search? What effort does the Court make to analyze whether the measures adopted by Mr. Choplick were reasonably related to the objectives of the search? Were they? What would make a search excessively intrusive in light of the age and sex of the student and the nature of the infraction? Does a younger student have more or less expectation of privacy? Does a male student have less interest in privacy than a female student? Does the gender of the person who is searching matter? What kinds of infractions would justify a more intrusive search than the search in *T.L.O.*? If the nature of the infraction is concealment of a dangerous weapon, would that justify a more intrusive search? How much more intrusive? Would such an infraction ever justify a strip search? A body cavity search?

2. Cases analyzing the reasonable suspicion standard include *R.C. v. State*, 852 So. 2d 311 (Fla. Dist. Ct. App. 2003) (search based on reasonable suspicion where a principal — questioning a student involved in an altercation — noticed a bulge in the student's pocket; the student was convicted of possessing a knife on school grounds); *Briseno v. State*, 2003 Tex. App. LEXIS 7364 (Ct. App. Aug. 28, 2003) (principal justified in searching backpack for contraband when student was evasive about what class he was late to, allowed the principal to lead him to the wrong room, lied about having to go to his locker for class materials, and dropped his backpack under a library table by another student rather than carrying it to his own seat).

In *Watkins v. Millennium School*, 290 F. Supp. 2d 890 (S.D. Ohio 2003), a third-grade student was visiting in another classroom and was one of three students present when ten dollars (brought in by another student for a field trip) was removed from the teacher's desk. The teacher questioned all three students and asked all three to pull open the waistband of their pants to see if the money was hidden there. Two of the students began to cry, and the teacher took the third to the supply closet to search her further, where she asked the student to pull open her pants so that she could look further. (The court stated that the evidence established that the teacher looked into the pants, not under the student's underwear into the student's most private parts). The court denied summary judgment for defendants because they failed to show that the teacher had evidence of individualized suspicion. The court granted summary judgment for defendants on claims of assault and intentional infliction of emotional distress.

3. In a *T.L.O.* footnote the majority stated, "We here consider only searches carried out by school authorities acting alone and on their own authority. This case does not present the question of the appropriate standard for assessing the legality of searches conducted by school officials in conjunction with or at the behest of law enforcement agencies, and we express no opinion on that question." What if the search is conducted in conjunction with or at the behest of law enforcement agencies? Should the more stringent probable cause standard apply? How much law enforcement involvement would need to occur before a search would be considered to be conducted in conjunction with or at the behest of law enforcement agencies? What about school liaison police officers? *Compare A.J.M. v. State,* 617 So. 2d 1137 (Fla. Dist. Ct. App. 1993) (school resource officer must have probable cause to conduct a search), *with State v. N.G.B.,* 806 So. 2d 567, 568-569 (Fla. Dist. Ct. App. 2002) (reasonable suspicion standard is appropriate when search is initiated by an assistant principal and later assisted by school resource officer), *and People v. Dilworth,* 661 N.E. 2d 310 (Ill. 1996) (applying reasonable suspicion standard to search by police liaison officer "conducting search on his own initiative and authority"); *State v. Angelia D.B.,* 211 Wis. 2d 140 (1997) (reasonable suspicion standard applied to search of student suspected of carrying dangerous weapon on school grounds that was conducted by school liaison officer at request of and in conjunction with school officials). Is there a likelihood that school officials making searches might act as a conduit for law enforcement ? In *State v. Heirtzler,* 789 A.2d 634 (N.H. 2001), the New Hampshire Supreme Court determined that the record supported the trial court's finding that although the police officer (assigned as school resource officer) was responsible for investigating more serious crimes — such as possession of a dangerous weapon — the school accepted responsibility for investigating less serious ones. The officer also conceded that a "silent understanding" existed between him and school officials that passing information to the school when he could not act was a technique used to gather evidence otherwise inaccessible to him due to constitutional restraints. The school, by "a mere wink or nod" or something more concrete, agreed to investigate certain potential criminal matters on the State's behalf or for its benefit. *See* Michael Pinard, *From the Classroom to the Courtroom: Reassessing Fourth Amendment Standards in Public School Searches Involving Law Enforcement Authorities,* 45 ARIZ. L. REV. 1067 (2003) (arguing that the current standards which govern the Fourth Amendment's application in public school searches need to be revamped in light of the increased interdependency between school officials and law enforcement authorities in the years following *New Jersey v. T.L.O.*).

4. What about the exclusionary rule — the issue on which the Court originally granted certiorari? If a school search is deemed to violate the fourth amendment because it did not pass the two-pronged test set forth in *T.L.O.,* should the evidence be excluded in any later criminal proceedings? What are the policy reasons for the exclusionary rule? Do the policies behind the exclusionary rule in the pure criminal context apply equally when school

officials are conducting a search in school? *See Thompson v. Carthage Sch. Dist.*, 87 F.3d 979 (8th Cir. 1996), § 4.04[D], *infra*.

5. *Anonymous Tips.* Justice Brennan states that "The fact that students and teachers interact daily in the school building makes it more likely that teachers will get to know students who supply information; the problem of informants who remain anonymous even to the teachers — and who are therefore unavailable for verification or further questioning — is unlikely to arise." Do you think that Justice Brennan's assessment is correct? Does he cite any authority for this assertion? If school officials do receive an anonymous tip, how should the situation be handled? Does it make a difference if the anonymous tip reports a student who has drugs versus a student who has a weapon? *See* Taylor Hanson, *Psst! Janie's Got a Gun: Anonymous Tips and Fourth Amendment Search and Seizure Rights in Schools*, 37 GA. L. REV 267 (2002).

Does an anonymous tip ever meet the "reasonable suspicion" standard? In *Terry v. Ohio*, 392 U.S. 1 (1968), the Court held that police in the traditional non-school context needed only reasonable suspicion, rather than probable cause, to "stop and frisk" a suspect that the officer reasonably believes may be armed and dangerous. In *Alabama v. White*, 496 U.S. 325, 329 (1990), the Supreme Court noted that "an anonymous tip alone seldom demonstrates the informant's basis of knowledge or veracity," but stated that anonymous tips could meet the reasonable suspicion standard, and then set a framework to analyze when anonymous tips would be enough to give rise to reasonable suspicion. The Court focused on the reliability of the tipster, and stated that this could be established by police officers' corroboration of the tipster's predictions about the suspect's future conduct.

Some courts established a "firearms exception" that allowed police to stop and frisk persons described in anonymous tips, even if the tip did not meet the corroboration standard set forth in *White*. In *Florida v. J.L.*, 529 U.S. 266 (2000), the Supreme Court, in a unanimous opinion, refused to recognize the firearms exception. The Court first determined that the search in question did not meet the *White* standard, a case that the Court stated presented a "close case" on the "borderline" of reasonable suspicion. The Court pointed out that knowledge of the suspect's location, appearance, and future movements does not necessarily mean that the tipster knows about concealed criminal activity. "The reasonable suspicion here at issue requires that a tip be reliable in its assertion of illegality, not just in its tendency to identify a determinate person."

In rejecting the firearms exception, the Court expressed concern that any person seeking to harass another could set in motion an intrusive, embarrassing search by police by placing an anonymous call falsely accusing that person of carrying a gun. Moreover, the Court feared that the firearms exception could easily be stretched to cover drugs, as the argument might be made that there is a strong connection between firearms and drugs. But the Court pointed out that its opinion did "not require us to speculate about the circumstances under which the danger alleged in an anonymous tip might be so great as to justify a search even without a showing of reliability. We do not say, for example, that a report of a person carrying a bomb need bear the same indicia of reliability we demand for a report of a person carrying a firearm before the police can constitutionally conduct a search."

Justice Kennedy stated in a concurring opinion joined by Chief Justice Rehnquist that there are different levels of anonymity. He noted that a tip from someone who placed his credibility at risk by reporting activity on an official line that was equipped with a caller identification feature may be deemed sufficiently reliable.

How should these cases be applied in the school search context? *In re K.C.B.*, 141 S.W.3d 303, 308-309 (Tex. Ct. App. 2004) (while a search for weapons might be justified when triggered by an anonymous tip, immediacy of action is not as necessary for a tip regarding drugs and does not tilt the balance far enough for the search to be deemed justified at its inception); *In re Doe*, 91 P.3d 485, 493 (Haw. 2004) (an anonymous Crime Stoppers' tip that student had marijuana and was selling it at school did not bear any indicia of reliability since school officials did not know "the identity or status (student as opposed to adult citizen) of the informant, the time the tip came in, or the basis, if any, for the informant's knowledge"). Note: *In re Doe* was later overruled for lack of appellate jurisdiction. 100 P.3d 75 (Haw. 2004).

6. Justice Brennan states, "Mr. Choplick's suspicion of marihuana possession at this time was based *solely* on the presence of the package of cigarette papers. The mere presence without more of such a staple item of commerce is insufficient to warrant a person of reasonable caution in inferring both that T.L.O. had violated the law by possessing marihuana and that evidence of that violation would be found in her purse." (emphasis in original). Do you agree that a high school principal in the 1980s seeing cigarette rolling papers is unreasonable in suspecting that this was evidence of marijuana possession?

More importantly, according to the majority opinion, T.L.O. had conceded this issue. ("Although T.L.O. does not dispute the reasonableness of Mr. Choplick's belief that the rolling papers indicated the presence of marihuana, she does contend that the scope of the search Mr. Choplick conducted exceeded permissible bounds when he seized and read certain letters that implicated T.L.O. in drug dealing. This argument, too, is unpersuasive. The discovery of the rolling papers concededly gave rise to a reasonable suspicion that T.L.O. was carrying marihuana as well as cigarettes in her purse. This suspicion justified further exploration of T.L.O.'s purse, which turned up more evidence of drug-related activities: a pipe, a number of plastic bags of the type commonly used to store marihuana, a small quantity of marihuana, and a fairly substantial amount of money."). Why would Justice Brennan raise this particular issue in his dissent?

7. What does the *T.L.O.* majority say about the doctrine of *in loco parentis*? What is left of the *in loco parentis* doctrine after *T.L.O.*? *See* Anne P. Dupre, *Should Students Have Consitutional Rights? Keeping Order in the Public Schools,* 65 GEO. WASH. L. REV. 49, 80 n. 234 (1996) (quoting numerous commentators who wrote that the *T.L.O.* Court had repudiated *in loco parentis*). Review your analysis again after you read the next case.

The *T.L.O.* Court left open the question whether the Fourth Amendment requires individualized suspicion to conduct a school search. The Court addressed that question in the context of a school district that had promulgated a policy for drug-testing in the following case.

[B] Urinalysis Drug Testing

Ten years after *T.L.O.*, the Supreme Court again addressed school searches — this time in the context of random urinalysis drug testing of students who participate in school athletic programs. In *Vernonia School District 47J v. Acton*, 515 U.S. 646 (1995), the Court determined that the drug testing program was reasonable and constitutional. The Court discussed the *in loco parentis* doctrine in its opinion:

> Traditionally at common law, and still today, unemancipated minors lack some of the most fundamental rights of self-determination — including even the right of liberty in its narrow sense, *i.e.*, the right to come and go at will. They are subject, even as to their physical freedom, to the control of their parents or guardians. When parents place minor children in private schools for their education, the teachers and administrators of those schools stand *in loco parentis* over the children entrusted to them. In fact, the tutor or schoolmaster is the very prototype of that status. As Blackstone describes it, a parent "may . . . delegate part of his parental authority, during his life, to the tutor or schoolmaster of his child; who is then *in loco parentis*, and has such a portion of the power of the parent committed to his charge, viz. that of restraint and correction, as may be necessary to answer the purposes for which he is employed." 1 W. Blackstone, Commentaries on the Laws of England 441 (1769).

> In *T.L.O.* we rejected the notion that public schools, like private schools, exercise only parental power over their students, which of course is not subject to constitutional constraints. Such a view of things, we said, "is not entirely 'consonant with compulsory education laws,'" and is inconsistent with our prior decisions treating school officials as state actors for purposes of the Due Process and Free Speech Clauses. But while denying that the State's power over schoolchildren is formally no more than the delegated power of their parents, *T.L.O.* did not deny, but indeed emphasized, that the nature of that power is custodial and tutelary, permitting a degree of supervision and control that could not be exercised over free adults. "A proper educational environment requires close supervision of schoolchildren, as well as the enforcement of rules against conduct that would be perfectly permissible if undertaken by an adult." While we do not, of course, suggest that public schools as a general matter have such a degree of control over children as to give rise to a constitutional "duty to protect," *see DeShaney v. Winnebago County Dept. of Social Servs.*, 489 U.S. 189, 200 (1989), we have acknowledged that for many purposes "school authorities act *in loco parentis*," *Bethel School Dist. No. 403 v. Fraser*, 478 U.S. 675, 684 (1986), with the power and indeed the duty to "inculcate the habits and manners of civility," *id.*, at 681 (internal quotation marks omitted). Thus, while children assuredly do not "shed their constitutional rights . . . at the schoolhouse gate,"

Tinker, the nature of those rights is what is appropriate for children in school [citing *Goss*, *Fraser*, *Hazelwood*, and *Ingraham*].

Id. at 654–56.

Seven years after *Acton*, the Supreme Court addressed a drug testing policy that required all students who participate in extracurricular activities to submit to drug testing.

BOARD OF EDUCATION OF INDEPENDENT SCHOOL DISTRICT NO. 92 OF POTTAWATOMIE COUNTY v. EARLS

Supreme Court of the United States
536 U.S. 822 (2002)

JUSTICE THOMAS *delivered the opinion of the Court.*

The Student Activities Drug Testing Policy implemented by the Board of Education of Independent School District No. 92 of Pottawatomie County (School District) requires all students who participate in competitive extracurricular activities to submit to drug testing. Because this Policy reasonably serves the School District's important interest in detecting and preventing drug use among its students, we hold that it is constitutional.

I

The city of Tecumseh, Oklahoma, is a rural community located approximately 40 miles southeast of Oklahoma City. The School District administers all Tecumseh public schools. In the fall of 1998, the School District adopted the Student Activities Drug Testing Policy (Policy), which requires all middle and high school students to consent to drug testing in order to participate in any extracurricular activity. In practice, the Policy has been applied only to competitive extracurricular activities sanctioned by the Oklahoma Secondary Schools Activities Association, such as the Academic Team, Future Farmers of America, Future Homemakers of America, band, choir, pom-pom, cheerleading, and athletics. Under the Policy, students are required to take a drug test before participating in an extracurricular activity, must submit to random drug testing while participating in that activity, and must agree to be tested at any time upon reasonable suspicion. The urinalysis tests are designed to detect only the use of illegal drugs, including amphetamines, marijuana, cocaine, opiates, and barbituates, not medical conditions or the presence of authorized prescription medications.

At the time of their suit, both respondents attended Tecumseh High School. Respondent Lindsay Earls was a member of the show choir, the marching band, the Academic Team, and the National Honor Society. Respondent Daniel James sought to participate in the Academic Team. Together with their parents, Earls and James brought a Rev. Stat. § 1979, 42 U.S.C. § 1983, action against the School District, challenging the Policy both on its face and as applied to their participation in extracurricular activities. They alleged that the Policy violates the Fourth Amendment as incorporated by the Fourteenth

Amendment and requested injunctive and declarative relief. They also argued that the School District failed to identify a special need for testing students who participate in extracurricular activities, and that the "Drug Testing Policy neither addresses a proven problem nor promises to bring any benefit to students or the school."

Applying the principles articulated in *Vernonia School Dist. 47J v. Acton*, 515 U.S. 646 (1995), in which we upheld the suspicionless drug testing of school athletes, the United States District Court for the Western District of Oklahoma rejected respondents' claim that the Policy was unconstitutional and granted summary judgment to the School District. . . .

The United States Court of Appeals for the Tenth Circuit reversed, holding that the Policy violated the Fourth Amendment. . . . We granted certiorari and now reverse.

II

The Fourth Amendment to the United States Constitution protects "[t]he right of the people to be secure in their persons, houses, papers, and effects, against unreasonable searches and seizures." Searches by public school officials, such as the collection of urine samples, implicate Fourth Amendment interests. *See Vernonia; cf. New Jersey v. T.L.O.*, 469 U.S. 325, 334 (1985). We must therefore review the School District's Policy for "reasonableness," which is the touchstone of the constitutionality of a governmental search.

In the criminal context, reasonableness usually requires a showing of probable cause. The probable-cause standard, however, "is peculiarly related to criminal investigations" and may be unsuited to determining the reasonableness of administrative searches where the "Government seeks to prevent the development of hazardous conditions." The Court has also held that a warrant and finding of probable cause are unnecessary in the public school context because such requirements " 'would unduly interfere with the maintenance of the swift and informal disciplinary procedures [that are] needed.' "

Given that the School District's Policy is not in any way related to the conduct of criminal investigations, respondents do not contend that the School District requires probable cause before testing students for drug use. Respondents instead argue that drug testing must be based at least on some level of individualized suspicion. It is true that we generally determine the reasonableness of a search by balancing the nature of the intrusion on the individual's privacy against the promotion of legitimate governmental interests. But we have long held that "the Fourth Amendment imposes no irreducible requirement of [individualized] suspicion." "[I]n certain limited circumstances, the Government's need to discover such latent or hidden conditions, or to prevent their development, is sufficiently compelling to justify the intrusion on privacy entailed by conducting such searches without any measure of individualized suspicion." Therefore, in the context of safety and administrative regulations, a search unsupported by probable cause may be reasonable "when 'special needs, beyond the normal need for law enforcement, make the warrant and probable-cause requirement impracticable.' "

Significantly, this Court has previously held that "special needs" inhere in the public school context. While schoolchildren do not shed their constitutional rights when they enter the schoolhouse, "Fourth Amendment rights . . . are different in public schools than elsewhere; the 'reasonableness' inquiry cannot disregard the schools' custodial and tutelary responsibility for children." *Vernonia*. In particular, a finding of individualized suspicion may not be necessary when a school conducts drug testing.

In *Vernonia*, this Court held that the suspicionless drug testing of athletes was constitutional. The Court, however, did not simply authorize all school drug testing, but rather conducted a fact-specific balancing of the intrusion on the children's Fourth Amendment rights against the promotion of legitimate governmental interests. Applying the principles of *Vernonia* to the somewhat different facts of this case, we conclude that Tecumseh's Policy is also constitutional.

A

We first consider the nature of the privacy interest allegedly compromised by the drug testing. As in *Vernonia*, the context of the public school environment serves as the backdrop for the analysis of the privacy interest at stake and the reasonableness of the drug testing policy in general. ("Central is the fact that the subjects of the Policy are (1) children, who (2) have been committed to the temporary custody of the State as schoolmaster"); ("The most significant element in this case is the first we discussed: that the Policy was undertaken in furtherance of the government's responsibilities, under a public school system, as guardian and tutor of children entrusted to its care"); ("[W]hen the government acts as guardian and tutor the relevant question is whether the search is one that a reasonable guardian and tutor might undertake").

A student's privacy interest is limited in a public school environment where the State is responsible for maintaining discipline, health, and safety. Schoolchildren are routinely required to submit to physical examinations and vaccinations against disease. Securing order in the school environment sometimes requires that students be subjected to greater controls than those appropriate for adults. *See T.L.O.* (Powell, J., concurring) ("Without first establishing discipline and maintaining order, teachers cannot begin to educate their students. And apart from education, the school has the obligation to protect pupils from mistreatment by other children, and also to protect teachers themselves from violence by the few students whose conduct in recent years has prompted national concern").

Respondents argue that because children participating in nonathletic extracurricular activities are not subject to regular physicals and communal undress, they have a stronger expectation of privacy than the athletes tested in *Vernonia*. This distinction, however, was not essential to our decision in *Vernonia*, which depended primarily upon the school's custodial responsibility and authority.[71]

---

[71] [3] Justice Ginsburg argues that *Vernonia* depended on the fact that the drug testing program applied only to student athletes. But even the passage cited by the dissent manifests

In any event, students who participate in competitive extracurricular activities voluntarily subject themselves to many of the same intrusions on their privacy as do athletes. Some of these clubs and activities require occasional off-campus travel and communal undress. All of them have their own rules and requirements for participating students that do not apply to the student body as a whole. For example, each of the competitive extracurricular activities governed by the Policy must abide by the rules of the Oklahoma Secondary Schools Activities Association, and a faculty sponsor monitors the students for compliance with the various rules dictated by the clubs and activities. This regulation of extracurricular activities further diminishes the expectation of privacy among schoolchildren. *Cf. Vernonia* ("Somewhat like adults who choose to participate in a closely regulated industry, students who voluntarily participate in school athletics have reason to expect intrusions upon normal rights and privileges, including privacy"). We therefore conclude that the students affected by this Policy have a limited expectation of privacy.

B

Next, we consider the character of the intrusion imposed by the Policy. Urination is "an excretory function traditionally shielded by great privacy." But the "degree of intrusion" on one's privacy caused by collecting a urine sample "depends upon the manner in which production of the urine sample is monitored." *Vernonia.*

Under the Policy, a faculty monitor waits outside the closed restroom stall for the student to produce a sample and must "listen for the normal sounds of urination in order to guard against tampered specimens and to insure an accurate chain of custody." The monitor then pours the sample into two bottles that are sealed and placed into a mailing pouch along with a consent form signed by the student. This procedure is virtually identical to that reviewed in *Vernonia* except that it additionally protects privacy by allowing male students to produce their samples behind a closed stall. Given that we considered the method of collection in *Vernonia* a "negligible" intrusion, the method here is even less problematic.

In addition, the Policy clearly requires that the test results be kept in confidential files separate from a student's other educational records and released to school personnel only on a "need to know" basis. Respondents nonetheless contend that the intrusion on students' privacy is significant because the Policy fails to protect effectively against the disclosure of confidential information and, specifically, that the school "has been careless in protecting that information: for example, the Choir teacher looked at students' prescription drug lists and left them where other students could see them." But the choir teacher is someone with a "need to know," because during off-campus trips she needs to know what medications are taken by her students. Even before the Policy was enacted the choir teacher had access to this

---

the supplemental nature of this factor, as the Court in *Vernonia* stated that "[l]egitimate privacy expectations are even less with regard to student athletes." In upholding the drug testing program in *Vernonia*, we considered the school context "[c]entral" and "[t]he most significant element." This hefty weight on the side of the school's balance applies with similar force in this case even though we undertake a separate balancing with regard to this particular program.

information. In any event, there is no allegation that any other student did see such information. This one example of alleged carelessness hardly increases the character of the intrusion.

Moreover, the test results are not turned over to any law enforcement authority. Nor do the test results here lead to the imposition of discipline or have any academic consequences. Rather, the only consequence of a failed drug test is to limit the student's privilege of participating in extracurricular activities. Indeed, a student may test positive for drugs twice and still be allowed to participate in extracurricular activities. After the first positive test, the school contacts the student's parent or guardian for a meeting. The student may continue to participate in the activity if within five days of the meeting the student shows proof of receiving drug counseling and submits to a second drug test in two weeks. For the second positive test, the student is suspended from participation in all extracurricular activities for 14 days, must complete four hours of substance abuse counseling, and must submit to monthly drug tests. Only after a third positive test will the student be suspended from participating in any extracurricular activity for the remainder of the school year, or 88 school days, whichever is longer.

Given the minimally intrusive nature of the sample collection and the limited uses to which the test results are put, we conclude that the invasion of students' privacy is not significant.

C

Finally, this Court must consider the nature and immediacy of the government's concerns and the efficacy of the Policy in meeting them. *See Vernonia.* This Court has already articulated in detail the importance of the governmental concern in preventing drug use by schoolchildren. The drug abuse problem among our Nation's youth has hardly abated since *Vernonia* was decided in 1995. In fact, evidence suggests that it has only grown worse. As in *Vernonia*, "the necessity for the State to act is magnified by the fact that this evil is being visited not just upon individuals at large, but upon children for whom it has undertaken a special responsibility of care and direction." The health and safety risks identified in *Vernonia* apply with equal force to Tecumseh's children. Indeed, the nationwide drug epidemic makes the war against drugs a pressing concern in every school.

Additionally, the School District in this case has presented specific evidence of drug use at Tecumseh schools. Teachers testified that they had seen students who appeared to be under the influence of drugs and that they had heard students speaking openly about using drugs. A drug dog found marijuana cigarettes near the school parking lot. Police officers once found drugs or drug paraphernalia in a car driven by a Future Farmers of America member. And the school board president reported that people in the community were calling the board to discuss the "drug situation." We decline to second-guess the finding of the District Court that "[v]iewing the evidence as a whole, it cannot be reasonably disputed that the [School District] was faced with a 'drug problem' when it adopted the Policy."

Respondents consider the proffered evidence insufficient and argue that there is no "real and immediate interest" to justify a policy of drug testing nonathletes. We have recognized, however, that "[a] demonstrated problem of drug abuse [is] not in all cases necessary to the validity of a testing regime," but that some showing does "shore up an assertion of special need for a suspicionless general search program." The School District has provided sufficient evidence to shore up the need for its drug testing program.

Furthermore, this Court has not required a particularized or pervasive drug problem before allowing the government to conduct suspicionless drug testing. [T]he need to prevent and deter the substantial harm of childhood drug use provides the necessary immediacy for a school testing policy. Indeed, it would make little sense to require a school district to wait for a substantial portion of its students to begin using drugs before it was allowed to institute a drug testing program designed to deter drug use.

Given the nationwide epidemic of drug use, and the evidence of increased drug use in Tecumseh schools, it was entirely reasonable for the School District to enact this particular drug testing policy. We reject the Court of Appeals' novel test that "any district seeking to impose a random suspicionless drug testing policy as a condition to participation in a school activity must demonstrate that there is some identifiable drug abuse problem among a sufficient number of those subject to the testing, such that testing that group of students will actually redress its drug problem." Among other problems, it would be difficult to administer such a test. As we cannot articulate a threshold level of drug use that would suffice to justify a drug testing program for schoolchildren, we refuse to fashion what would in effect be a constitutional quantum of drug use necessary to show a "drug problem."

Respondents also argue that the testing of nonathletes does not implicate any safety concerns, and that safety is a "crucial factor" in applying the special needs framework. They contend that there must be "surpassing safety interests," or "extraordinary safety and national security hazards," in order to override the usual protections of the Fourth Amendment. Respondents are correct that safety factors into the special needs analysis, but the safety interest furthered by drug testing is undoubtedly substantial for all children, athletes and nonathletes alike. We know all too well that drug use carries a variety of health risks for children, including death from overdose.

We also reject respondents' argument that drug testing must presumptively be based upon an individualized reasonable suspicion of wrongdoing because such a testing regime would be less intrusive. In this context, the Fourth Amendment does not require a finding of individualized suspicion, and we decline to impose such a requirement on schools attempting to prevent and detect drug use by students. Moreover, we question whether testing based on individualized suspicion in fact would be less intrusive. Such a regime would place an additional burden on public school teachers who are already tasked with the difficult job of maintaining order and discipline. A program of individualized suspicion might unfairly target members of unpopular groups. The fear of lawsuits resulting from such targeted searches may chill enforcement of the program, rendering it ineffective in combating drug use. *See Vernonia* (offering similar reasons for why "testing based on 'suspicion' of drug use would not be better, but worse"). In any case, this Court has repeatedly stated that reasonableness under the Fourth Amendment does not require employing the least intrusive means, because "[t]he logic of such elaborate less-restrictive-alternative arguments could raise insuperable barriers to the exercise of virtually all search-and-seizure powers."

Finally, we find that testing students who participate in extracurricular activities is a reasonably effective means of addressing the School District's legitimate concerns in preventing, deterring, and detecting drug use. While in *Vernonia* there might have been a closer fit between the testing of athletes and the trial court's finding that the drug problem was "fueled by the 'role model' effect of athletes' drug use," such a finding was not essential to the holding. *Vernonia* did not require the school to test the group of students most likely to use drugs, but rather considered the constitutionality of the program in the context of the public school's custodial responsibilities. Evaluating the Policy in this context, we conclude that the drug testing of Tecumseh students who participate in extracurricular activities effectively serves the School District's interest in protecting the safety and health of its students.

III

Within the limits of the Fourth Amendment, local school boards must assess the desirability of drug testing schoolchildren. In upholding the constitutionality of the Policy, we express no opinion as to its wisdom. Rather, we hold only that Tecumseh's Policy is a reasonable means of furthering the School District's important interest in preventing and deterring drug use among its schoolchildren. Accordingly, we reverse the judgment of the Court of Appeals.

It is so ordered.

JUSTICE BREYER, *concurring.*

I agree with the Court that *Vernonia School Dist. 47J v. Acton*, 515 U.S. 646 (1995), governs this case and requires reversal of the Tenth Circuit's decision. The school's drug testing program addresses a serious national problem by focusing upon demand, avoiding the use of criminal or disciplinary sanctions, and relying upon professional counseling and treatment. In my view, this program does not violate the Fourth Amendment's prohibition of "unreasonable searches and seizures." I reach this conclusion primarily for the reasons given by the Court, but I would emphasize several underlying considerations, which I understand to be consistent with the Court's opinion.

I

In respect to the school's need for the drug testing program, I would emphasize the following: First, the drug problem in our Nation's schools is serious in terms of size, the kinds of drugs being used, and the consequences of that use both for our children and the rest of us. . . .

Second, the government's emphasis upon supply side interdiction apparently has not reduced teenage use in recent years. . . .

Third, public school systems must find effective ways to deal with this problem. Today's public expects its schools not simply to teach the fundamentals, but "to shoulder the burden of feeding students breakfast and lunch, offering before and after school child care services, and providing medical and psychological services," all in a school environment that is safe and encourages learning. The law itself recognizes these responsibilities with the phrase *in loco parentis* — a phrase that draws its legal force primarily from the needs of younger students (who here are necessarily grouped together with older high school students) and which reflects, not that a child or adolescent lacks an interest in privacy, but that a child's or adolescent's school-related privacy interest, when compared to the privacy interests of an adult, has different dimensions. A public school system that fails adequately to carry out its responsibilities may well see parents send their children to private or parochial school instead — with help from the State.

Fourth, the program at issue here seeks to discourage demand for drugs by changing the school's environment in order to combat the single most important factor leading schoolchildren to take drugs, namely, peer pressure. Malignant Neglect 4 (students "whose friends use illicit drugs are more than 10 times likelier to use illicit drugs than those whose friends do not"). It offers the adolescent a nonthreatening reason to decline his friend's drug-use invitations, namely, that he intends to play baseball, participate in debate, join the band, or engage in any one of half a dozen useful, interesting, and important activities.

II

In respect to the privacy-related burden that the drug testing program imposes upon students, I would emphasize the following: First, not everyone would agree with this Court's characterization of the privacy-related significance of urine sampling as " 'negligible.' " Some find the procedure no more intrusive than a routine medical examination, but others are seriously embarrassed by the need to provide a urine sample with someone listening "outside the closed restroom stall." When trying to resolve this kind of close question involving the interpretation of constitutional values, I believe it important that the school board provided an opportunity for the airing of these differences at public meetings designed to give the entire community "the opportunity to be able to participate" in developing the drug policy. The board used this democratic, participatory process to uncover and to resolve differences, giving weight to the fact that the process, in this instance, revealed little, if any, objection to the proposed testing program.

Second, the testing program avoids subjecting the entire school to testing. And it preserves an option for a conscientious objector. He can refuse testing while paying a price (nonparticipation) that is serious, but less severe than expulsion from the school.

Third, a contrary reading of the Constitution, as requiring "individualized suspicion" in this public school context, could well lead schools to push the boundaries of "individualized suspicion" to its outer limits, using subjective criteria that may "unfairly target members of unpopular groups," or leave those whose behavior is slightly abnormal stigmatized in the minds of others. If so, direct application of the Fourth Amendment's prohibition against "unreasonable searches and seizures" will further that Amendment's liberty-protecting objectives at least to the same extent as application of the mediating "individualized suspicion" test, where, as here, the testing program is neither criminal nor disciplinary in nature. . . .

I conclude that the school's drug testing program, constitutionally speaking, is not "unreasonable."

And I join the Court's opinion.

JUSTICE GINSBURG, with whom JUSTICE STEVENS, JUSTICE O'CONNOR, and JUSTICE SOUTER join, *dissenting.*

Seven years ago, in *Vernonia School Dist. 47J v. Acton*, 515 U.S. 646 (1995), this Court determined that a school district's policy of randomly testing the urine of its student athletes for illicit drugs did not violate the Fourth Amendment. In so ruling, the Court emphasized that drug use "increase[d] the risk of sports-related injury" and that Vernonia's athletes were the "leaders" of an aggressive local "drug culture" that had reached " 'epidemic proportions.' " Today, the Court relies upon *Vernonia* to permit a school district with a drug problem its superintendent repeatedly described as "not . . . major," to test the urine of an academic team member solely by reason of her participation in a nonathletic, competitive extracurricular activity — participation associated with neither special dangers from, nor particular predilections for, drug use.

"[T]he legality of a search of a student," this Court has instructed, "should depend simply on the reasonableness, under all the circumstances, of the search." Although " 'special needs' inhere in the public school context," those needs are not so expansive or malleable as to render reasonable any program of student drug testing a school district elects to install. The particular testing program upheld today is not reasonable; it is capricious, even perverse: Petitioners' policy targets for testing a student population least likely to be at risk from illicit drugs and their damaging effects. I therefore dissent.

I

A

A search unsupported by probable cause nevertheless may be consistent with the Fourth Amendment "when special needs, beyond the normal need for law enforcement, make the warrant and probable-cause requirement impracticable." In *Vernonia*, this Court made clear that "such 'special needs' exist in the public school context." The Court observed:

> [W]hile children assuredly do not "shed their constitutional rights at the schoolhouse gate," the nature of those rights is what is appropriate for children in school. Fourth Amendment rights, no less than First and Fourteenth Amendment rights, are different in public schools than elsewhere; the "reasonableness" inquiry cannot disregard the schools' custodial and tutelary responsibility for children.

The *Vernonia* Court concluded that a public school district facing a disruptive and explosive drug abuse problem sparked by members of its athletic teams had "special needs" that justified suspicionless testing of district athletes as a condition of their athletic participation.

This case presents circumstances dispositively different from those of *Vernonia*. True, as the Court stresses, Tecumseh students participating in competitive extracurricular activities other than athletics share two relevant characteristics with the athletes of *Vernonia*. First, both groups attend public schools. "[O]ur decision in *Vernonia*" the Court states, "depended primarily upon the school's custodial responsibility and authority." Concern for student health and safety is basic to the school's caretaking, and it is undeniable that "drug use carries a variety of health risks for children, including death from overdose."

Those risks, however, are present for all schoolchildren. *Vernonia* cannot be read to endorse invasive and suspicionless drug testing of all students upon any evidence of drug use, solely because drugs jeopardize the life and health of those who use them. Many children, like many adults, engage in dangerous activities on their own time; that the children are enrolled in school scarcely allows government to monitor all such activities. If a student has a reasonable subjective expectation of privacy in the personal items she brings to school, *see T.L.O.*, surely she has a similar expectation regarding the chemical composition of her urine. Had the *Vernonia* Court agreed that public school attendance, in and of itself, permitted the State to test each student's blood or urine for drugs, the opinion in *Vernonia* could have saved many words. ("[I]t must not be lost sight of that [the Vernonia School District] program is directed to drug use by school athletes, where the risk of immediate physical harm to the drug user or those with whom he is playing his sport is particularly high.").

The second commonality to which the Court points is the voluntary character of both interscholastic athletics and other competitive extracurricular activities. "By choosing to 'go out for the team,' [school athletes] voluntarily subject themselves to a degree of regulation even higher than that imposed on students generally." Comparably, the Court today observes, "students who participate in competitive extracurricular activities voluntarily subject themselves to" additional rules not applicable to other students.

The comparison is enlightening. While extracurricular activities are "voluntary" in the sense that they are not required for graduation, they are part of the school's educational program; for that reason, the petitioner (hereinafter School District) is justified in expending public resources to make them available. Participation in such activities is a key component of school life, essential in reality for students applying to college, and, for all participants, a significant contributor to the breadth and quality of the educational experience. Students "volunteer" for extracurricular pursuits in the same way they might volunteer for honors classes: They subject themselves to additional requirements, but they do so in order to take full advantage of the education offered them.

Voluntary participation in athletics has a distinctly different dimension: Schools regulate student athletes discretely because competitive school sports by their nature require communal undress and, more important, expose students to physical risks that schools have a duty to mitigate. For the very reason that schools cannot offer a program of competitive athletics without intimately affecting the privacy of students, *Vernonia* reasonably analogized school athletes to "adults who choose to participate in a closely regulated industry." Industries fall within the closely regulated category when the nature of their activities requires substantial government oversight. Interscholastic athletics similarly require close safety and health regulation; a school's choir, band, and academic team do not.

In short, *Vernonia* applied, it did not repudiate, the principle that "the legality of a search of a student should depend simply on the reasonableness, under all the circumstances, of the search." *T.L.O.* Enrollment in a public school, and election to participate in school activities beyond the bare minimum that the curriculum requires, are indeed factors relevant to reasonableness, but they do not on their own justify intrusive, suspicionless searches. *Vernonia* accordingly, did not rest upon these factors; instead, the Court performed what today's majority aptly describes as a "fact-specific balancing." Balancing of that order, applied to the facts now before the Court, should yield a result other than the one the Court announces today.

B

Vernonia initially considered "the nature of the privacy interest upon which the search [there] at issue intruded]." The Court emphasized that student athletes' expectations of privacy are necessarily attenuated:

> Legitimate privacy expectations are even less with regard to student athletes. School sports are not for the bashful. They require 'suiting up' before each practice or event, and showering and changing afterwards. Public school locker rooms, the usual sites for these activities, are not notable for the privacy they afford. The locker rooms in *Vernonia* are typical: No individual dressing rooms are provided; shower heads are lined up along a wall, unseparated by any sort of partition or curtain; not even all the toilet stalls have doors. [T]here is an element of communal undress inherent in athletic participation.

Competitive extracurricular activities other than athletics, however, serve students of all manner: the modest and shy along with the bold and uninhibited. Activities of the kind plaintiff-respondent Lindsay Earls pursued — choir, show choir, marching band, and academic team — afford opportunities to gain self-assurance, to "come to know faculty members in a less formal setting than the typical classroom," and to acquire "positive social supports and networks [that] play a critical role in periods of heightened stress."

On "occasional out-of-town trips," students like Lindsay Earls "must sleep together in communal settings and use communal bathrooms." But those situations are hardly equivalent to the routine communal undress associated with athletics; the School District itself admits that when such trips occur, "public-like restroom facilities," which presumably include enclosed stalls, are ordinarily available for changing, and that "more modest students" find other ways to maintain their privacy.[72]

After describing school athletes' reduced expectation of privacy, the *Vernonia* Court turned to "the character of the intrusion . . . complained of." Observing that students produce urine samples in a bathroom stall with a coach or teacher outside, *Vernonia* typed the privacy interests compromised by the process of obtaining samples "negligible." As to the required pretest disclosure of prescription medications taken, the Court assumed that "the School District would have permitted [a student] to provide the requested information in a confidential manner — for example, in a sealed envelope delivered to the testing lab." On that assumption, the Court concluded that *Vernonia*'s athletes faced no significant invasion of privacy.

In this case, however, Lindsay Earls and her parents allege that the School District handled personal information collected under the policy carelessly, with little regard for its confidentiality. Information about students' prescription drug use, they assert, was routinely viewed by Lindsay's choir teacher, who left files containing the information unlocked and unsealed, where others, including students, could see them; and test results were given out to all activity sponsors whether or not they had a clear "need to know."

In granting summary judgment to the School District, the District Court observed that the District's "[p]olicy expressly provides for confidentiality of test results, and the Court must assume that the confidentiality provisions will be honored." The assumption is unwarranted. Unlike *Vernonia* where the District Court held a bench trial before ruling in the School District's favor, this case was decided by the District Court on summary judgment. At that stage, doubtful matters should not have been resolved in favor of the judgment seeker. Finally, the "nature and immediacy of the governmental concern," *Vernonia*, faced by the Vernonia School District dwarfed that confronting Tecumseh administrators. *Vernonia* initiated its drug testing policy in response to an alarming situation: "[A] large segment of the student body, particularly those involved in interscholastic athletics, was in a state of rebellion . . . fueled by alcohol and drug abuse as well as the student[s'] misperceptions about the drug culture." Tecumseh, by contrast, repeatedly reported to the Federal Government during the period leading up to the adoption of the policy that "types of drugs [other than alcohol and tobacco] including controlled dangerous substances, are present [in the schools] but have not identified themselves as major problems at this time." As the Tenth Circuit observed, "without a demonstrated drug abuse problem among the group being tested, the efficacy of the District's solution to its perceived problem is . . . greatly diminished."[73]

---

[72] [1] According to Tecumseh's choir teacher, choir participants who chose not to wear their choir uniforms to school on the days of competitions could change either in "a rest room in a building" or on the bus, where "[m]any of them have figured out how to [change] without having [anyone] see anything."

[73] [2] The Court finds it sufficient that there be evidence of some drug use in Tecumseh's schools: "As we cannot articulate a threshold level of drug use that would suffice to justify a drug testing program for schoolchildren, we refuse to fashion what would in effect be a constitutional quantum of drug use necessary to show a 'drug problem.'" One need not establish a bright-line "constitutional quantum of drug use" to recognize the relevance of the superintendent's reports characterizing drug use among Tecumseh's students as "not [a] major proble[m]."

. . . .

Not only did the Vernonia and Tecumseh districts confront drug problems of distinctly different magnitudes, they also chose different solutions: Vernonia limited its policy to athletes; Tecumseh indiscriminately subjected to testing all participants in competitive extracurricular activities. Urging that "the safety interest furthered by drug testing is undoubtedly substantial for all children, athletes and nonathletes alike," the Court cuts out an element essential to the *Vernonia* judgment. Citing medical literature on the effects of combining illicit drug use with physical exertion, the *Vernonia* Court emphasized that "the particular drugs screened by [Vernonia's] Policy have been demonstrated to pose substantial physical risks to athletes."

At the margins, of course, no policy of random drug testing is perfectly tailored to the harms it seeks to address. The School District cites the dangers faced by members of the band, who must "perform extremely precise routines with heavy equipment and instruments in close proximity to other students," and by Future Farmers of America, who "are required to individually control and restrain animals as large as 1500 pounds." For its part, the United States acknowledges that "the linebacker faces a greater risk of serious injury if he takes the field under the influence of drugs than the drummer in the halftime band," but parries that "the risk of injury to a student who is under the influence of drugs while playing golf, cross country, or volleyball (sports covered by the policy in *Vernonia*) is scarcely any greater than the risk of injury to a student handling a 1500-pound steer (as [Future Farmers of America] members do) or working with cutlery or other sharp instruments (as [Future Homemakers of America] members do)." One can demur to the Government's view of the risks drug use poses to golfers, for golfers were surely as marginal among the linebackers, sprinters, and basketball players targeted for testing in Vernonia as steer-handlers are among the choristers, musicians, and academic-team members subject to urinalysis in Tecumseh. Notwithstanding nightmarish images of out-of-control flatware, livestock run amok, and colliding tubas disturbing the peace and quiet of Tecumseh, the great majority of students the School District seeks to test in truth are engaged in activities that are not safety sensitive to an unusual degree. There is a difference between imperfect tailoring and no tailoring at all.

The Vernonia district, in sum, had two good reasons for testing athletes: Sports team members faced special health risks and they "were the leaders of the drug culture." No similar reason, and no other tenable justification, explains Tecumseh's decision to target for testing all participants in every competitive extracurricular activity.

Nationwide, students who participate in extracurricular activities are significantly less likely to develop substance abuse problems than are their less-involved peers. Even if students might be deterred from drug use in order to preserve their extracurricular eligibility, it is at least as likely that other students might forgo their extracurricular involvement in order to avoid detection of their drug use. Tecumseh's policy thus falls short doubly if deterrence is its aim: It invades the privacy of students who need deterrence least, and risks steering students at greatest risk for substance abuse away from extracurricular involvement that potentially may palliate drug problems.[74]

To summarize, this case resembles *Vernonia* only in that the School Districts in both cases conditioned engagement in activities outside the obligatory curriculum on random subjection to urinalysis. The defining characteristics of the two programs, however, are entirely dissimilar. The Vernonia district sought to test a subpopulation of students distinguished by their reduced expectation of privacy, their special susceptibility to drug-related injury, and their heavy involvement with drug use. The Tecumseh district seeks to test a much larger population associated with none of these factors. It does so, moreover, without carefully safeguarding student confidentiality and without regard to the program's untoward effects. A program so sweeping is not sheltered by *Vernonia;* its unreasonable reach renders it impermissible under the Fourth Amendment.

II

. . . .

Close review of Tecumseh's policy [establishes that the policy does not] advance the " 'special needs' [existing] in the public school context [to maintain] swift and informal disciplinary procedures [and] order in the schools," *Vernonia*. What is left is the School District's undoubted purpose to heighten awareness of its abhorrence of, and strong stand against, drug abuse. But the desire to augment communication of this message does not trump the right of persons — even of children within the schoolhouse gate — to be "secure in their persons against unreasonable searches and seizures."

. . . "Justice Brandeis recognized the importance of teaching by example: 'Our Government is the potent, the omnipresent teacher. For good or for ill, it teaches the whole people by its example.'" That wisdom should guide decisionmakers in the instant case: The government is nowhere more a teacher than when it runs a public school.

It is a sad irony that the petitioning School District seeks to justify its edict here by trumpeting "the schools' custodial and tutelary responsibility for children." *Vernonia*. In regulating an athletic program or endeavoring to combat an exploding drug epidemic, a school's custodial obligations may permit searches that would otherwise unacceptably abridge students' rights. When custodial duties are not ascendant, however, schools' tutelary obligations to their students require them to "teach by example" by avoiding symbolic measures that diminish constitutional protections. "That [schools] are educating the young for citizenship is reason for scrupulous protection of Constitutional freedoms of the individual, if we are not to strangle the free mind at its source and teach youth to discount important principles of our government as mere platitudes." *West Virginia Bd. of Ed. v. Barnette*, 319 U.S. 624 (1943).

---

[74] [4] The Court notes that programs of individualized suspicion, unlike those using random testing, "might unfairly target members of unpopular groups." Assuming, arguendo, that this is so, the School District here has not exchanged individualized suspicion for random testing. It has installed random testing in addition to, rather than in lieu of, testing "at any time when there is reasonable suspicion."

For the reasons stated, I would affirm the judgment of the Tenth Circuit declaring the testing policy at issue unconstitutional.

———

NOTES AND QUESTIONS

1. What does the *Acton* Court mean in stating that school officials stand *in loco parentis* for "many purposes"? Is this what the Court in *T.L.O.* said? The *Acton* majority quotes *Fraser* for this proposition. Is this what the *Fraser* Court said? (Go back and review that opinion and find the sentence that the *Acton* Court uses.)

What about the language that the *Acton* and *Earls* Courts employed regarding the school official acting as "guardian and tutor" and "custodian"? *See* Anne P. Dupre, *Should Students Have Constitutional Rights? Keeping Order in the Public Schools*, 65 GEO. WASH. L. REV. 49, 92 (1996) (noting the broad powers that guardians and custodians have over minor children).

2. State constitutions may provide students with broader rights than the federal constitution. In *Theodore v. Delaware Valley Sch. Dist.*, 836 A.2d 76 (Pa. 2003), the Pennsylvania Supreme Court stated that the program in question (random drug testing for all students involved in extracurricular activities and all who wanted a school parking permit) might have passed muster under the Fourth Amendment, but Pennsylvania's constitution provides greater privacy protections than the United States Constitution. There was almost no evidence indicating a real drug problem at the school. The high court emphasized that after remand the school district might develop facts that justified its program, but it had not done so when it filed its demurrer.

3. Saliva tests, already employed by some European law enforcement agencies, are gaining acceptance in the United States. Cited for being "easily accessible, noninvasive, and not embarrassing," these tests are also harder to "beat" than urine tests. Paul Recer, *Saliva Test For Drugs May Be Coming*, ATLANTA J.-CONST., Feb. 18, 2005, at A16.

"Given the ambiguity inherent in *T.L.O.* and *Acton*, it is hardly surprising to discover that the lower court cases run the gamut from rigorous scrutiny of the objective reasonableness of school searches and seizures to permitting such intrusions if school officials merely act in good faith." Martin R. Gardner, *The Fourth Amendment and the Public School: Observations on an Unsettled State of Search and Seizure Law*, 36 CRIM. LAW BULL., 373, 386 (2000). The following two cases demonstrate this point.

[C] Dog Sniffs

B.C. v. PLUMAS UNIFIED SCHOOL DISTRICT

United States Court of Appeals for the Ninth Circuit
192 F.3d 1260 (1999)

PREGERSON, CIRCUIT JUDGE:

This case involves a dog sniff of students at Quincy High School in Plumas County, California. Plaintiff B.C., a Quincy High School student, brought this action pursuant to 42 U.S.C. § 1983 and alleged several deprivations of his Fourth Amendment right to be free from unreasonable searches and seizures and various state law claims. B.C. named as defendants the Plumas Unified School District, Superintendent Joseph Hagwood, Principal Richard Spears, Vice Principal Arturo Barrera, Assistant Sheriff Rod Decrona, Deputy Sheriff Dean Canalia, and Detective Steven Hitch. B.C. sought injunctive relief, money damages, and certification of a plaintiff class.

Plaintiff and defendants filed cross motions for summary judgment. The district court denied plaintiff's motion for a preliminary injunction, plaintiff's motion for class certification, and plaintiff's motion for summary judgment. The court granted defendants' motions for summary judgment and ruled that all defendants were entitled to immunity from money damages. Finally, the court declined to exercise supplemental jurisdiction over plaintiff's state law claims. Plaintiff appeals. We affirm.

I.

The material facts are not disputed. B.C. was a student at Quincy High School in Plumas County, California, in May 1996. On May 21, 1996, Principal Spears and Vice Principal Barrera told plaintiff and his classmates to exit their classroom. As they exited, the students passed Deputy Sheriff Canalia and "Keesha," a drug-sniffing dog, stationed outside the classroom door. Keesha alerted to a student other than plaintiff.

The students were told to wait outside the classroom while the dog sniffed backpacks, jackets, and other belongings which the students left in the room. When the students were allowed to return to their classroom, they again walked past Deputy Canalia and the dog. Keesha again alerted to the same student. That student was taken away and searched by school officials. No drugs were found that day at Quincy High School.

. . . .

IV.

Plaintiff B.C. seeks money damages against all defendants in their *official* capacities. He claims that defendants conducted an unreasonable search of his person.

A.

The district court granted summary judgment in favor of the school officials in their official capacities on B.C.'s individual claims for money damages. The district court held that B.C.'s claims for money damages against Superintendent Joseph Hagwood in his official capacity were barred by the Eleventh Amendment. The district court construed B.C.'s claims against Principal Spears and Vice Principal Barrera as claims against Quincy High School as an entity and dismissed those claims on the ground that a high school is not an entity capable of being sued under § 1983. B.C. has not appealed these rulings, and we do not address them here.

B.

The district court also granted summary judgment for the Sheriff's Department officials in their official capacities on the ground that B.C. failed to demonstrate a direct causal link between an official policy or custom of the Sheriff's Department and the alleged deprivation of B.C.'s constitutional rights. We review de novo, and we affirm.

In reviewing the district court's grant of summary judgment, we must view the evidence in the light most favorable to the nonmoving party and determine whether there are any genuine issues of material fact and whether the district court correctly applied the relevant substantive law. . . . In support of their motion for summary judgment, the Sheriff's Department defendants presented evidence that departmental policy only permits the use of drug-sniffing dogs on objects and *not* on persons. In opposing the Department's motion, B.C. presented no credible evidence to refute that this is in fact the Department's policy.

B.C. also attempted to satisfy the causation requirement by contending that the Sheriff's Department failed to train its officers in the proper use of drug-sniffing dogs, and that such failure amounts to a custom and policy of deliberate indifference toward his constitutional rights. The district court properly granted summary judgment for the Sheriff's Department officials in their official capacities after those defendants produced uncontroverted evidence that officers are trained in the use of dogs, and that they are trained to use dogs to sniff property, *not* people.

V.

B.C. also sought money damages against all defendants in their *individual* capacities. Defendants moved for summary judgment on the grounds that: (1) their actions did not constitute a "search" within the meaning of the Fourth Amendment; (2) even if they performed a search, it was reasonable; and (3) even if they performed an unreasonable search, they were entitled to qualified immunity from liability. The district court determined that the dog sniff at issue here constituted an unreasonable search.[75] But the court also

---

[75] [6] The district court considered the parties' cross motions for summary judgment and concluded that "plaintiff's expectation of bodily privacy was reasonable and that its invasion through the device of a dog's sniffing constituted a search." In support of this ruling, the district court

determined that defendants were entitled to qualified immunity because the parameters of permissible dog sniff searches were not "clearly established" at the time of the search at issue. Accordingly, the court granted summary judgment for defendants on qualified immunity grounds. We review de novo "[a] district court's decision of qualified immunity in a 42 U.S.C. § 1983 action" . . . and we affirm.

When a government official asserts a defense of qualified immunity, the court must first determine whether the plaintiff has alleged facts which, if true, would constitute a deprivation of a constitutional right at all. Only then should the court determine whether "the right allegedly implicated was clearly established at the time of the events in question." Accordingly, we analyze whether B.C. has alleged facts which, if true, would constitute a deprivation of his Fourth Amendment right to be free from unreasonable searches and seizures before we proceed to the issue whether the defendants are entitled to a qualified immunity defense.

A.

"A 'search' occurs when an expectation of privacy that society is prepared to consider reasonable is infringed." *United States v. Jacobsen,* 466 U.S. 109 (1984). The Supreme Court has held that the use of a trained canine to sniff unattended luggage is not a search within the meaning of the Fourth Amendment. *See United States v. Place,* 462 U.S. 696 (1983). But neither the Supreme Court nor the Ninth Circuit has addressed the issue whether a dog sniff of a person is a search. The Ninth Circuit has recognized, however, that the level of intrusiveness is greater when the dog is permitted to sniff a person than when a dog sniffs unattended luggage. *See United States v. Beale,* 736 F.2d 1289, 1291–92 (9th Cir. 1984) (en banc). . . .

Only the Fifth and Seventh Circuits have directly addressed the question whether a dog sniff of a student's person is a search. Those courts have taken opposite positions on the issue. In *Beale,* we cited with approval the Fifth Circuit's decision in *Horton v. Goose Creek Independent School District,* 690 F.2d 470, 479 (5th Cir. 1982).

Horton involved a school's use of trained Doberman Pinschers and German Shepherds to sniff students' lockers and automobiles. On a random and unannounced basis, the dogs were also taken into classrooms to sniff the students. In *Horton,* the Fifth Circuit noted that " 'the intensive smelling of people, even if done by dogs, [is] indecent and demeaning' " and held that the sniffing by dogs of students was a search.

The Fifth Circuit in *Horton* considered and expressly rejected the approach taken by the Seventh Circuit in *Doe v. Renfrow,* 631 F.2d 91, 92 (7th Cir. 1981) (per curiam). *Renfrow* involved facts nearly identical to those of *Horton.* But the court in *Renfrow* upheld the district court's ruling that a dog sniff of students is not a search.

---

stated that "it seems obvious that the degree of intrusion which occurs from having one's body subjected to examination by a dog is far greater than that which occurs upon the sniffing of unattended belongings," and that "having one's body examined in this manner is sufficiently 'embarrassing' that it can be distinguished from the circumstance in [*United States v. Place,* 462 U.S. 696 (1983),] where unattended luggage was sniffed."

We agree with the Fifth Circuit that "close proximity sniffing of the person is offensive whether the sniffer be canine or human." Because we believe that the dog sniff at issue in this case infringed B.C.'s reasonable expectation of privacy, we hold that it constitutes a search.

Having determined that a search occurred, we must determine whether the search was constitutional. The constitutionality of a search is measured by its reasonableness in the circumstances. School officials here admit that they had no "individualized suspicion of wrongdoing" by any student.

Despite this lack of any individualized suspicion, a suspicionless search may be reasonable "in limited circumstances, where [1] the privacy interests implicated by the search are minimal, *and* [2] where an important governmental interest furthered by the intrusion would be placed in jeopardy by a requirement of individualized suspicion." Moreover, the second part of the test requires *both* the existence of an "important governmental interest furthered by the intrusion" *and* that this interest would be "placed in jeopardy by a requirement of individualized suspicion."

Applying this test, we first evaluate the Quincy High School students' privacy interests. It is well-settled that students do not "shed their constitutional rights . . . at the schooolhouse gate." While students have "a lesser expectation of privacy than members of the population generally," they nonetheless retain an expectation of privacy when they enter the school grounds. Moreover, the district court found that the dog sniff was "highly intrusive" for the following reasons. First, "the body and its odors are highly personal." Noting that dogs "often engender irrational fear" the district court further explained that the fact "that search was sudden and unannounced added to its potentially distressing, and thus invasive, character." In addition, the "search was completely involuntary." Thus, we conclude that the Quincy High School students' privacy interests were not minimal.

Having considered the students' privacy interests, we turn to the government's interest in conducting such a search. There can be no dispute that deterring drug use by students is an important — if not a compelling — governmental interest. *See Vernonia.* But the record here does not disclose that there was any drug crisis or even a drug problem at Quincy High in May 1996. In the absence of a drug problem or crisis at Quincy High, the government's important interest in deterring student drug use would not have been " 'placed in jeopardy by a requirement of individualized suspicion.' " We, therefore, conclude that the random and suspicionless dog sniff search of B.C. was unreasonable in the circumstances.

B.

Having determined that B.C. has alleged facts which, if true, would constitute an unreasonable search in violation of his Fourth Amendment right, we proceed to determine whether defendants are entitled to a qualified immunity defense. "Government officials are given qualified immunity from civil liability under § 1983 'insofar as their conduct does not violate clearly established statutory or constitutional rights of which a reasonable person would have known.' "

A right is "clearly established" if "the contours of [that] right [are] sufficiently clear that a reasonable official would understand that what he is doing violates that right." "To show that the right in question here was clearly established, [plaintiff] need not establish that [defendants'] 'behavior had been previously declared unconstitutional, only that the unlawfulness was apparent in light of preexisting law.'" "If the only reasonable conclusion from binding authority [was] that the disputed right existed, even if no case had specifically so declared, [defendants] would be on notice of the right and [they] would not be qualifiedly immune if they acted to offend it."

When the dog sniff in this case occurred, it was not clearly established that the use of dogs to sniff students in a school setting constituted a search. As such, the unlawfulness of defendants' conduct "in light of preexisting law," was not "apparent." Therefore, each of defendants could "have believed that [his] conduct was lawful." Accordingly, we conclude that all defendants in their individual capacities are entitled to qualified immunity from B.C.'s claims for money damages.

VI.

The district court dismissed B.C.'s claim that defendants subjected him to an unreasonable *seizure* of his person while the dog sniffed the classroom.[76] The relevant facts are again undisputed. The teachers at Quincy received a note from Vice Principal Barrera informing them that a drug-sniffing dog would be on campus, and instructing them to "try and keep students in their classes." B.C. asked his teacher whether he could leave the room, and his teacher told him that she had been instructed not to allow students to leave the classroom. After exiting the classroom, students were directed to stand beneath a covered snack bar forty feet from the classroom. Vice Principal Barrera did not allow B.C. to leave the area when B.C. sought to do so.

We have said that "a student is required to be on school premises, subject to the direction of school authorities, during the course of the schoolday." In the circumstances of this case, we conclude that directing students to a covered snack bar area for five to ten minutes during an unquestionably legitimate dog sniff of the students' classroom is not a seizure within the meaning of the Fourth Amendment. "[A] degree of supervision and control that could not be exercised over free adults" is permissible in the school context. The district court properly denied B.C.'s motion for summary judgment on the issue whether he suffered a seizure of his person.

The district court also ruled that B.C. suffered no seizure of his property during the search of the classroom. We agree. B.C. admits that he left none of his belongings in the room. Accordingly, there was no seizure of his property.

VII.

We . . . affirm the district court's grant of summary judgment in favor of the school officials based on the Eleventh Amendment; affirm the district

---

[76] [12] B.C. does not contend that the dog sniff of the inside of the unoccupied classroom was a search.

court's grant of summary judgment in favor of the Sheriff's Department officials on the ground that B.C. has demonstrated no unconstitutional custom or policy; affirm the district court's grant of summary judgment in favor of all individual defendants on the search issue on the basis of qualified immunity; and affirm the district court's grant of summary judgment in favor of all individual defendants on the seizure issues on the ground that B.C. suffered no unreasonable seizure of his person or his property.

Affirmed.

BRUNETTI, CIRCUIT JUDGE, *concurring in part*:

[W]hile I agree with the result reached by the majority in Part V, I write separately because the majority's conclusion that an unreasonable search occurred in this case under the Fourth Amendment is not supported by Supreme Court or circuit court precedent.

The majority correctly states that "[a] search occurs when an expectation of privacy that society is prepared to consider reasonable is infringed," yet the majority fails to identify the reasonable expectation of privacy that was infringed when the plaintiff walked past the drug dog. The interaction between the students and the dog in this case did not implicate a legitimate expectation of privacy protected by the Fourth Amendment and did not, therefore, constitute a Fourth Amendment search because the dog could have only detected the presence or absence of contraband if the dog could have detected anything at all. The majority has failed to address the expectation of privacy issue in order to reach and resolve the constitutional issue of whether an unreasonable search occurred in this case under the Fourth Amendment when the students walked past the narcotics dog.

The majority has also failed to discuss the most relevant Supreme Court and Ninth Circuit cases that address drug dogs and the Fourth Amendment. The Supreme Court has held that subjecting luggage in a public place to a sniff test by a trained narcotics dog is not a search under the Fourth Amendment, *see United States v. Place,* and that a test which merely discloses the fact that a substance is a controlled substance does not affect a legitimate privacy interest implicating the Fourth Amendment. *See United States v. Jacobsen.* After the Supreme Court's decisions in *Place* and *Jacobsen,* this Court concluded that a dog sniff is not a search under the Fourth Amendment if: "(1) it discloses *only* the presence or absence of a contraband item, and (2) its use 'ensures that the owner of the property is not subjected to the embarrassment and inconvenience entailed in less discriminate and more intrusive investigative methods.'" *United States v. Beale* (emphasis in original) (quoting *Place*). Although the majority claims that *Beale* supports its conclusion that a search occurred in this case, the majority neither mentions the *Beale* test nor attempts to demonstrate why, under the *Beale* test, a Fourth Amendment search occurred in this case. The majority also fails to acknowledge that, in *Beale,* this Court concluded that the dog sniff at issue in that case did not constitute a Fourth Amendment search.

The majority also misreads the *Beale* opinion when it asserts that this Court cited to the Fifth Circuit's decision in *Horton v. Goose Creek Indep. Sch. Dist.,*

690 F.2d 470, 479 (5th 2 Cir. 1982), with approval and recognized that the intrusiveness of dog sniffs are greater when the dog is permitted to sniff an individual. This Court did not cite to the *Horton* opinion with approval. In *Beale*, we noted that we were "not confronted with a case in which the detection dog conducted a sniff of a person rather than an inanimate object" and cited to *Horton* only as an example of a case where dogs sniffed people rather than inanimate objects. More importantly, we never stated or implicitly recognized in *Beale* that the intrusiveness of dog sniffs are greater when a dog sniffs an individual rather than an inanimate object such as luggage.

The majority's heavy reliance on the Fifth Circuit's decision in *Horton* to support its conclusion that a search occurred in this case is misplaced because *Horton* is distinguishable. In *Horton*, the Fifth Circuit held that when a dog sniffs *around* each student, puts his nose *on* ("up against") the students, *scratches at* the students, and displays other signs of excitement, a search occurs under the Fourth Amendment. The dog in this case did not sniff around each student, touch the students in any manner, or display signs of excitement. The dog was always three to four feet from the students as they exited and re-entered the classroom. The Fifth Circuit in *Horton* even specifically declined to address "whether the use of dogs to sniff people in some other manner, *e.g.*, at some distance, is a search." A full and accurate reading of the *Horton* decision demonstrates that it does not support the majority's conclusion that the dog's presence in this case constituted a search under the Fourth Amendment. It is, therefore, inadequate for the majority to simply state: "We agree with the Fifth Circuit that 'close proximity sniffing of the person is offensive whether the sniffer be canine or human.'"

. . . .

The majority also fails to acknowledge that the one circuit court decision that is most closely related to this case concluded that a Fourth Amendment search did not occur. *See Doe v. Renfrow*, 631 F.2d 91 (7th Cir. 1980) (per curiam) (adopting the district court's opinion reported at 475 F. Supp. 1012). In *Renfrow*, a narcotics dog walked up and down the aisles of classrooms *while the students remained at their desks*. The court concluded "that the students did not have a justifiable expectation of privacy that would preclude a school administrator from sniffing the air around the desks with the aid of a trained drug detecting canine." The *Renfrow* analysis is correct and, therefore, a Fourth Amendment search did not occur in this case when the plaintiff passed in front of the drug dog at a distance of three to four feet and the dog never alerted or moved.

Finally, the majority states: "We agree with the Fifth Circuit that 'close proximity sniffing of the person is offensive whether the sniffer be canine or human.'" Whether we or the public find government conduct offensive is irrelevant to Fourth Amendment analysis because Fourth Amendment analysis is not dependent upon whether government conduct is offensive. Instead, Fourth Amendment analysis depends on whether government conduct unreasonably invades a reasonable expectation of privacy. The majority has failed to conduct proper Fourth Amendment analysis and has concluded that a Fourth Amendment search occurred simply because it finds dog sniffs offensive. This analysis and conclusion can not be supported by a record which unequivocally demonstrates that the students were not sniffed by a drug dog and can not satisfy the analytical standards Fourth Amendment jurisprudence prescribes.

I also write separately because, assuming that a Fourth Amendment search occurred in this case, the majority has also failed to conduct the proper balancing test to determine whether the search in this case was unreasonable under the Fourth Amendment. "Whether a particular search meets the reasonableness standard is judged by balancing *its intrusion on the individual's Fourth Amendment interests* against its promotion of legitimate governmental interests." *Vernonia School Dist. v. Acton*, 515 U.S. 646, 652–53 (1995) (emphasis added) (quotations omitted). "In limited circumstances, *where the privacy interests implicated by the search are minimal*, and where an important governmental interest furthered by the intrusion would be placed in jeopardy by a requirement of individualized suspicion, a search may be reasonable despite the absence of such [individualized] suspicion." *Chandler v. Miller*, 520 U.S. 305 (1997) (emphasis added). The majority concludes that the searches in this case were unreasonable because the school district's interest in deterring drug abuse would not be jeopardized by requiring individualized suspicion, basing its conclusion on the fact that the record does not disclose a "drug problem" or "crisis" at Quincy High School.

This analysis is problematic. The majority fails to explain how the school district's important — if not compelling — interest in keeping its schools and students free from drugs is not jeopardized if, as the majority concludes, the school district must wait until a known drug problem or crisis exists before the district can conduct preemptive and protective drug searches. Under the majority's reasoning, school districts must wait until they experience an actual drug epidemic before they can conduct preemptive searches for illegal drugs. The Fourth Amendment does not support such a rule.

NOTES AND QUESTIONS

1. Did the court determine that the plaintiff's Fourth Amendment rights were violated? What is the remedy for the plaintiff after that determination?

2. Does the majority in *Plumas* mean that dog sniffing is a search even if the dog stays a good distance from the students? Does the proximity of the dog affect the reasonableness inquiry? For a discussion of such issues, see Martin R. Gardner, *Sniffing for Drugs in the Classroom — Perspective on Fourth Amendment Scope*, 74 Nw.U. L. Rev. 803 (1980).

3. In *Illinois v. Caballes*, 125 S. Ct. 834 (2005), the Supreme Court — in a case dealing with an adult outside the school context — held that where a dog sniff was performed on the exterior of respondent's car while he was lawfully seized for a traffic violation, any intrusion on respondent's privacy expectations did not rise to the level of a constitutionally cognizable infringement. Conduct that does not compromise legitimate privacy interests is not a search subject to the Fourth Amendment. Any interest in possessing contraband cannot be deemed "legitimate," and thus, governmental conduct

that only reveals the possession of contraband compromises no legitimate privacy interest. The use of a well-trained narcotics-detection dog — one that does not expose noncontraband items that otherwise would have remained hidden from public view (during a lawful traffic stop) generally does not implicate legitimate privacy interests.

Does this answer the question whether lockers, book bags and cars in school parking lots may be sniffed? Or does the fact that Caballes's car was sniffed during a traffic stop distinguish it from the sniff at school? What about a sniff of a student's person? If the sniff reveals nothing but the presence or absence of contraband, does it compromise a legitimate privacy interest? Or is the degree of intrusion different from when a dog sniffs an inanimate object?

Justice Souter dissented in *Caballes* and pointed to research that undercut the reliability of the dog alert. Does this relate to whether a search occurs, as Justice Souter argued, or to whether a dog alert is enough evidence to state that there is probable cause (or reasonable suspicion) to search the person further? How might this affect the degree of intrusiveness of a search that follows a dog alert? For example, if questions and a pat-down search do not reveal the contraband after an alert, should the official search the person further? *See* Andrew J. Tuck, *Who Let the Dogs In? Canine Drug Detection in Public Schools After* Illinois v. Caballes, 1 EDUC. L. & POL'Y FORUM, *available at* www.educationlawconsortium.org.

4. What if a teacher sniffs a student's breath at a school dance to detect alcohol? Is it a search? If so, under what scenario might it be reasonable? If it is unreasonable and it occurred in the Ninth Circuit after *Plumas*, will the teacher be protected by qualified immunity? Compare the Ninth Circuit analysis in *Plumas* with that in the following Eighth Circuit case.

[D]   Exclusionary Rule

THOMPSON v. CARTHAGE SCHOOL DISTRICT

United States Court of Appeals for the Eighth Circuit
87 F.3d 979 (1996)

LOKEN, CIRCUIT JUDGE:

Ramone Lea was expelled from Carthage High School after school officials found crack cocaine in his coat pocket while looking for guns and knives reported to be on school grounds. The district court awarded $ 10,000 in § 1983 damages for "wrongful expulsion" because the search had violated Lea's Fourth Amendment rights. The Carthage School District, four members of its Board of Education, the school Superintendent, and the educators who performed the search appeal. Concluding that the Fourth Amendment exclusionary rule does not apply to school disciplinary hearings, and that the search was constitutionally reasonable, we reverse.

I.

Carthage is a small, rural school district in which all grades are housed at one location. Total enrollment is about 225; 90 to 100 students attend the

High School. On the morning of October 26, 1993, a school bus driver told Norma Bartel, the High School principal, that there were fresh cuts on seats of her bus. Concerned that a knife or other cutting weapon was on the school grounds, Bartel concluded that all male students in grades six to twelve should be searched. After the search began, students told Bartel that there was a gun at the school that morning.

Bartel and science teacher Ralph Malone conducted the search by bringing each class of students to Malone's classroom. The students were told to remove their jackets, shoes, and socks, empty their pockets, and place these items on large tables in the science room. Bartel and Malone then checked the students for concealed weapons with a metal detector. Malone would pat down a student if the metal detector sounded, as it often did because of the metal brads on the students' blue jeans. Malone and Bartel also patted the students' coats and removed any objects they could feel in the coat pockets. They completed the search before Superintendent Randy King arrived at 9:30 that morning.

Lea was a ninth grade student at the time of the search. Neither Bartel nor Malone had reason to suspect that Lea had cut the school bus seats or had brought a weapon to school that morning. Lea's class was one of the last to be searched in the science room. Malone searched Lea's coat pocket and found a used book of matches, a match box, and a cigarette package. Considering these items to be contraband, Malone showed them to Bartel, and she brought them to her office. Bartel found only cereal in the cigarette package but discovered "a white substance" in the match box. She took the match box to King, who turned it over to a deputy sheriff. A test revealed that the white substance was crack cocaine. After a hearing, Lea was expelled for the remainder of the school year.

Lea and his guardian, Cleoria Thompson, commenced this § 1983 action, alleging that the search and expulsion violated Lea's Fourth Amendment rights, and that the expulsion hearing denied him due process. The parties submitted the case on depositions and affidavits. The district court held that the expulsion proceeding comported with due process, but that Lea's expulsion was wrongful because the search had violated his Fourth Amendment rights. The school officials had no "individualized, particularized suspicion" that Lea was carrying a weapon or other contraband, and "there was no adequate basis in the evidence to justify the initial decision to search all 6–12 grade boys." In addition, the court reasoned, Bartel and Malone seized the match box after they knew that Lea did not possess a knife or gun. The court awarded Lea $ 10,000 in compensatory damages against defendants Bartel, Malone, King, and the school board members who voted for expulsion. It awarded Lea a reasonable attorney's fee, granted a declaratory judgment that his Fourth Amendment rights were violated, but declined to issue an injunction. This appeal followed.

II.

At the outset, we confront an issue ignored by the parties and the district court — whether the Fourth Amendment's exclusionary rule applies in school disciplinary proceedings. At oral argument, we invited counsel to submit supplemental briefs addressing this issue, but neither side did so. The issue is critical because the district court awarded substantial damages for wrongful expulsion, based entirely on the proposition that Lea could not be expelled for possessing crack cocaine discovered during an illegal search.

The judicially-created exclusionary rule precludes admission of unlawfully seized evidence in criminal trials. "In the complex and turbulent history of the rule, the Court never has applied it to exclude evidence from a civil proceeding, federal or state." *United States v. Janis,* 428 U.S. 433, 447 (1976). In *Janis,* the Court held that the rule does not apply in federal tax proceedings to bar evidence illegally seized by state officials. In *INS v. Lopez-Mendoza,* 468 U.S. 1032 (1984), the Court held that the rule does not apply in civil INS deportation hearings. The Court's "framework" for deciding whether the exclusionary rule applies in a particular civil proceeding is to analyze whether the likely benefit of excluding illegally obtained evidence outweighs the societal costs of exclusion.

The societal costs of applying the rule in school disciplinary proceedings are very high. For example, the exclusionary rule might bar a high school from expelling a student who confessed to killing a classmate on campus if his confession was not preceded by Miranda warnings. We doubt that any parent would compromise school safety in this fashion. To the extent the exclusionary rule prevents the disciplining of students who disrupt education or endanger other students, it frustrates the critical governmental function of educating and protecting children.

Moreover, "maintaining security and order in the schools requires a certain degree of flexibility in school disciplinary procedures." *New Jersey v. T.L.O.,* 469 U.S. 325, 340 (1985). Application of the exclusionary rule would require suppression hearing-like inquiries inconsistent with the demands of school discipline, demands that led the Court to impose very limited due process requirements in *Goss v. Lopez.*

The benefit of the exclusionary rule depends upon whether it would effectively deter Fourth Amendment violations. In that regard, this case is like *Lopez-Mendoza* in one important respect — school officials both conducted the search and imposed the student discipline. Knowing that evidence they illegally seize will be excluded at any subsequent disciplinary proceeding would likely have a strong deterrent effect.

But there are also important differences between school discipline and the deportation proceeding at issue in *Lopez-Mendoza.* The dissenters in that case argued for the exclusionary rule "because INS agents are law enforcement officials whose mission is closely analogous to that of police officers and because civil deportation proceedings are to INS agents what criminal trials are to police officers." School officials, on the other hand, are not law enforcement officers. They do not have an adversarial relationship with students. "Instead, there is a commonality of interests between teachers and their pupils. The attitude of the typical teacher is one of personal responsibility for the student's welfare as well as for his education." *T.L.O.* (Powell, J., concurring). Moreover, children's legitimate expectations of privacy are somewhat limited at school. Therefore, while the Fourth Amendment applies to searches by school officials, its reasonableness standard, when applied to school searches, "stops short of probable cause."

In these circumstances, we conclude that there is little need for the exclusionary rule's likely deterrent effect. Indeed, we see some risk that application of the rule would deter educators from undertaking disciplinary proceedings that are needed to keep the schools safe and to control student misbehavior. In any event, any deterrence benefit would not begin to outweigh the high societal costs of imposing the rule. Therefore, like most district courts that have published opinions applying *Janis* and *Lopez-Mendoza*, we conclude that the exclusionary rule may not be applied to prevent school officials from disciplining students based upon the fruits of a search conducted on school grounds. Accordingly, Lea was not wrongfully expelled, and the $ 10,000 damage award must be reversed.[77]

III.

In concluding that the search violated Lea's Fourth Amendment rights, the district court emphasized the fact that Bartel and Malone had no individualized reason to suspect Lea of carrying a weapon. In *T.L.O.*, 469 U.S. at 342 n.8, the Supreme Court had left open the issue whether individualized suspicion is always required for school searches. However, after the district court decided this case, the Supreme Court upheld random drug testing of high school athletes despite the absence of individualized suspicion in *Vernonia Sch. Dist. 47J v. Acton*, 115 S. Ct. 2386 (1995). The Court clarified that individualized suspicion is not always required for school searches. It recognized that the drug testing at issue was inherently intrusive. (Taking a urine sample and requiring disclosure of health information is more intrusive than, for example, looking in a purse, the search at issue in *T.L.O.*) But the Court concluded that this significant privacy invasion was justified by the important government interest in reducing drug abuse by student athletes.

Vernonia impacts this case in one significant way — it confirms that the doctrine of qualified immunity bars any award of damages. The individual defendants did not violate clearly established law when they decided to search all the older male students for dangerous weapons reported to be on the school grounds.

The district court rejected Lea's due process claim and denied him injunctive relief. With a damage award now foreclosed by *Vernonia* and our decision that there was no wrongful expulsion, the award of an attorney's fee must also be reversed. That ends the case, except for a difficult issue that has little remaining practical significance — whether the district court erred in declaring that the search violated Lea's Fourth Amendment rights.

The Fourth Amendment inquiry in school search cases is whether the search was reasonable in all the circumstances. The inquiry focuses on whether the search was justified at its inception, whether its scope was reasonably related

---

[77] [2] Like the Supreme Court in *T.L.O.*, we do not consider whether evidence illegally seized by school officials on school grounds is admissible at a subsequent criminal trial or delinquency proceeding.

to the circumstances justifying a search, and the extent of the privacy intrusion. In a school setting, "the relevant question is whether the search is one that a reasonable guardian and tutor might undertake." *Vernonia*. We review the reasonableness issue *de novo*.

The district court concluded that the broad search for knives and guns was not justified at its inception because the Carthage School District was not facing a "serious, on-going, problem with such dangerous instrumentalities." In our view, that analysis is inconsistent with *Vernonia*. Principal Bartel had two independent reasons to suspect that one or more weapons had been brought to school that morning. Though she had no basis for suspecting any particular student, this was a risk to student safety and school discipline that no "reasonable guardian and tutor" could ignore. Bartel's response was to issue a sweeping, but minimally intrusive command, "Children, take off your shoes and socks and empty your pockets." We conclude that Bartel's decision to undertake this generalized but minimally intrusive search for dangerous weapons was constitutionally reasonable.

The district court further concluded that the scope of the search was not reasonably related to its original purpose because Lea's pockets were searched after the metal detector had revealed that he did not possess a gun or knife. But in a school setting, Fourth Amendment reasonableness does not turn on "hairsplitting argumentation." *T.L.O.* If Lea had emptied his own coat pocket, the cigarette package and match box would have become contraband in plain view. It is not constitutionally significant that teacher Malone emptied the pocket after Lea put his jacket on the table. Moreover, once Bartel and Malone reasonably decided to quickly search many children's pockets for dangerous weapons, it is not realistic to require them to abort the search of a particular child who does not appear to be in possession of such contraband.

To summarize, while we share the district court's concern over excessive use of sweeping searches of school children's persons and belongings, even in a minimally intrusive manner, we conclude that the search undertaken in this case passes muster under *T.L.O.* and *Vernonia*. The judgment of the district court is reversed and the case is remanded for entry of judgment in favor of defendants.

———

NOTES AND QUESTIONS

1. Are the factual distinctions in *Plumas* and *Thompson* sufficient to reconcile them? Or is one court analyzing the problem differently from the other?

2. The *Thompson* court states that students told the principal that there was a gun at school. Would the search have been constitutional if this tip had been anonymous? See discussion at Note 4 after *New Jersey v. T.L.O.*

3. How does the court analyze the exclusionary rule issue? Should there be more of a deterrence for teachers and other school officials to refrain from unconstitutional searches? If the Eighth Circuit analysis of the exclusionary

rule is correct here, does the same analysis apply to the question the court left open: whether evidence illegally seized by school officials on school grounds is admissible at a subsequent criminal trial or delinquency proceeding?

4. After it determines that the damages award was foreclosed by *Vernonia* and that there was no unlawful expulsion, the court states, "That ends the case, except for a difficult issue that has little remaining practical significance — whether the district court erred in declaring that the search violated Lea's Fourth Amendment rights." What *is* the practical significance of this issue?

5. Would it be permissible to install surveillance cameras at the school? Where could the cameras be placed? Is it necessary to have individualized suspicion?

What about installing metal detectors at the door to the school? Can schools require students to submit to breathalyzer tests before they are allowed to attend school events?

Suppose you are a school board attorney who has been asked advice regarding school searches. The school board wants to know: (1) Under what circumstances can school officials search students' lockers? Does it make a difference if the school handbook tells the students that school lockers are school property and not the property of the student?

[E]   Locker Searches

STATE v. OVERTON

Court of Appeals of New York
229 N.E.2d 596 (1967)

KEATING, J.

Three detectives of the Mount Vernon Police Department having obtained a search warrant went to the Mount Vernon High School. The warrant directed a search of the persons of two students and, also, of their lockers.

The detectives presented the warrant to the vice-principal, Dr. Panitz, who sent for the two students, one of whom was the defendant, Carlos Overton. The detectives searched them and found nothing. A subsequent search of Overton's locker, however, revealed four marijuana cigarettes.

The defendant moved to invalidate that portion of the search warrant which directed a search of his locker, on the ground that the papers were defective upon which it was based. This motion was granted. The court denied the motion to suppress, however, on the grounds that the vice-principal had consented to the search and that he had a right to do so. The Appellate Term reversed and dismissed the information, holding that the consent of the vice-principal could not justify an otherwise illegal search. The People have appealed from this order of the Appellate Term.

It is axiomatic that the protection of the Fourth Amendment is not restricted to dwellings. A depository such as a locker or even a desk is safeguarded from unreasonable searches for evidence of a crime.

There are situations, however, where someone other than the defendant in possession of a depository may consent to what otherwise would have been an illegal search. . . .

Dr. Panitz, in this case, gave his consent to the search of Overton's locker. The dissenting opinion suggests, however, that Dr. Panitz' consent was not freely given, because he acted under compulsion of the invalid search warrant. If this were the case, his consent might be rendered somewhat questionable. However, Dr. Panitz testified that: "Being responsible for the order, assignment, and maintenance of the physical facilities, if *any* report were given to me by *anyone* of an article or item of the nature that does not belong there, or of an illegal nature, I would inspect the locker." (Italics supplied.)

This testimony demonstrates beyond doubt that Dr. Panitz would have consented as he did regardless of the presence of the invalid search warrant.

The power of Dr. Panitz to give his consent to this search arises out of the distinct relationship between school authorities and students. The school authorities have an obligation to maintain discipline over the students. It is recognized that, when large numbers of teenagers are gathered together in such an environment, their inexperience and lack of mature judgment can often create hazards to each other. Parents, who surrender their children to this type of environment, in order that they may continue developing both intellectually and socially, have a right to expect certain safeguards.

It is in the high school years particularly that parents are justifiably concerned that their children not become accustomed to antisocial behavior, such as the use of illegal drugs. The susceptibility to suggestion of students of high school age increases the danger. Thus, it is the affirmative obligation of the school authorities to investigate any charge that a student is using or possessing narcotics and to take appropriate steps, if the charge is substantiated.

When Overton was assigned his locker, he, like all the other students at Mount Vernon High School, gave the combination to his home room teacher who, in turn, returned it to an office where it was kept on file. The students at Mount Vernon are well aware that the school authorities possess the combinations of their lockers. It appears understood that the lock and the combination are provided in order that each student may have exclusive possession of the locker vis-à-vis other students, but the student does not have such exclusivity over the locker as against the school authorities. In fact, the school issues regulations regarding what may and may not be kept in the lockers and presumably can spot check to insure compliance. The vice-principal testified that he had, on occasion, inspected the lockers of students.

Indeed, it is doubtful if a school would be properly discharging its duty of supervision over the students, if it failed to retain control over the lockers. Not only have the school authorities a right to inspect but this right becomes a duty when suspicion arises that something of an illegal nature may be secreted there. When Dr. Panitz learned of the detectives' suspicion, he was obligated to inspect the locker. This interest, together with the nonexclusive nature of the locker, empowered him to consent to the search by the officers.

Accordingly, the order of the Appellate Term should be reversed and the matter remitted to that court for consideration of the other points raised by the defendant which were not decided on the prior appeal.

BERGAN, J., *dissenting*.

The District Attorney concedes the search warrant was bad, i.e., "We acknowledge, to take as many issues out of the case as possible, that the search warrant was properly vacated". Defendant had paid for personal use of the locker and, as far as he was concerned, the People also admit, a search of the locker by police without a warrant "would be invalid".

No doubt the principal of the school had a supervisory power to inspect the locker. But if an invalid warrant was used to compel him to exercise this power, and if it adversely affected the constitutional right of the defendant to be secure against unlawful search and seizure, this invalid compulsion under a bad search warrant was as much an invasion of defendant's rights as if the police, under the purported authority of the warrant, had broken the door of the locker or compelled the defendant himself to open it.

There can be no doubt, reading this record, that the principal opened the door, not because he was exercising a free supervisory control over the locker in the interest of the school program, but because he felt the invalid search warrant compelled him to do so. He affirmatively answered the question that in opening the door he was "honoring the search warrant".

. . . .

The order should be affirmed.

NOTES AND QUESTIONS

1. In *State v. Jones*, 666 N.W.2d 142 (Iowa 2003), the Iowa Supreme Court held that a pre-holiday-break check of lockers was constitutional. Although the student had a reasonable expectation of privacy in his locker, school officials also had a legitimate interest in maintaining a proper school environment and protecting school property.

2. Under what circumstances is it constitutionally permissible for a school official to strip search a student? Should reasonable suspicion be the standard for the more intrusive search? Must the suspicion be individualized?

3. A fifth-grade student brought $26.00 to school that he had raised in selling candy for a school trip. He put it in an envelope on his teacher's desk, and the teacher later noticed it had disappeared. When asked by the teacher, the children in the class stated that they did not know what had happened to the envelope. After searching the trash can and the students' bookbags, desks and purses, the teacher asked the students to remove their shoes to see if the money was secreted in their socks, to turn out their front pockets and to allow her to pat down their back pockets. She did not find the missing envelope. A police officer, who was at the school for a drug awareness program,

noted that it was fashionable for boys to wear two pairs of pants. He took the boys in groups of four or five to the boys' restroom where he told the boys to pull down their pants. Some of the boys dropped their pants and others dropped both pants and underwear. The teacher, who was female, took the girls to the girls' restroom in groups of two to five students. The students testified that they were made to lower their pants or raise their dresses and to lift their brassieres. Is the search constitutional under either *T.L.O.* or *Acton*? Why or why not? *See Thomas v. Roberts*, 261 F.3d 1160 (11th Cir. 2001).

4. In addition to cases about school searches, courts use the *T.L.O.* standard to analyze student claims of improper seizure. In *Bisignano v. Harrison Central School District*,113 F. Supp. 2d 591 (S.D.N.Y. 2000), the court denied a summary judgment motion by a teacher regarding a student's claims that she was shut in a closet for approximately 30 seconds until she agreed to give a teacher $20 that she had picked off the floor that the teacher had told her was his. Looking at the facts in the light most favorable to the student (the teacher disputed many of the student's claims) the court stated that a reasonable jury could find that the teacher's actions were not reasonably related in scope to the circumstances under which the incident arose. *Cf. Edwards v. Rees*, 883 F.2d 882 (10th Cir. 1989) (interrogating a student for twenty minutes regarding a bomb threat made against a junior high school was reasonably related in scope to determining if he had called in the bomb threat).

In *Samuels v. Independent Sch. Dist. 279*, 2003 U.S. Dist. LEXIS 23481 (D. Minn. Dec. 8, 2003), a student engaged in a loud, verbal (but not physical) fight with a fellow student. To teach him a lesson, the administrative assistant asked the officer to handcuff the student. The court determined that the handcuff incident, though lasting only 30-40 seconds, was a seizure, and the seizure was unreasonable because the student's fight was never physical. *See also Wofford v. Evans*, 390 F.3d 318, 328 (4th Cir. 2004) (no illegal seizure where student was twice questioned concerning reports she brought a gun to school; "weapons are a matter with which schools can take no chances," and school was right to contact law enforcement officers and hold student while the police completed their investigation); *Doe v. Hawaii Dep't of Educ.*, 334 F.3d 906 (9th Cir. 2003) (when student refused to stand still against time-out wall, vice principal used masking tape to tape the student's head to a tree; court found the taping to be a seizure, and the vice principal's behavior to be unreasonable because the student posed no danger to others and the taping was so intrusive that even a fellow student questioned its appropriateness).

Professor Kathryn Urbonya argues that, in addition to scenarios where teachers use force to control students (grabbing a student who is fighting), the Fourth Amendment reasonableness standard should be used to analyze the intentional use of force in corporal punishment. Kathryn R. Urbonya, *Public School Officials' Use of Physical Force as a Fourth Amendment Seizure: Protecting Students from the Constitutional Chasm Between the Fourth and Fourteenth Amendments*, 69 GEO. WASH. L. REV. 1 (2000). She contends that using the Fourteenth Amendment substantive due process "shocks-the-conscience" standard provides insufficient protection for the student.

5. *Fifth Amendment.* Under *T.L.O.*, students have Fourth Amendment protection against unreasonable searches by a teacher, school principal or other school officials. Do students have a Fifth Amendment right to *Miranda* warnings when being questioned by school officials? In *Miranda v. Arizona,* 384 U.S. 436 (1966), the U.S. Supreme Court held that warnings must be given to a suspect before a statement that was made during custodial interrogation will be admitted into evidence. The Supreme Court of Kansas addressed the issue whether *Miranda* warnings are required before a student is questioned by a school security officer. *In the Matter of L.A.,* 270 Kan. 879 (2001). After receiving a tip from the school Crime Stoppers organization that L.A. was in possession of marijuana hidden in the band of his baseball cap, assistant vice principal asked the school security officer to bring L.A. to her office. L.A. was not advised of his *Miranda* rights and was asked if he had anything illegal in his possession He said that he did not. The vice principal then called L.A.'s mother and received permission to search L.A. The court determined that this was not an unconstitutional search, as it passed the *T.L.O.* standard and did not address whether L.A.'s mother could effectively waive his right to be free from unconstitutional searches. If the search had not been reasonable, would the mother's consent have satisfied constitutional standards?

The search turned up pills that L.A. admitted were Valium, as well as a substance that L.A. admitted was marijuana that he intended to smoke after school. The school officials called the sheriff, who advised L.A. of his *Miranda* rights when he arrived at the school. L.A. was charged with possession of diazepam and possession of marijuana, was adjudicated a juvenile offender and placed on intensive supervision. The student claimed that the statements he made to the vice principal and to the school security officer should be suppressed because the questions were the equivalent of a custodial interrogation by a law enforcement officer, and he was not given *Miranda* warnings before they questioned him. The court determined that the statutory function of the school security officer was to protect students, teachers and school property — not law enforcement. Therefore, "[d]uring an investigation of a violation of school policy, a school security officer is not required to give *Miranda* warnings." *Id.* at 890.

In *In re V.P.,* 55 S.W.3d 25 (Tex. Ct. App. 2001), the Texas Court of Appeals determined that a minor student was not "in custody," and thus had no right to silence or to counsel, during questioning performed by an assistant principal seeking information concerning a gun the minor had reportedly brought to school. The court stated that the assistant principal was acting in furtherance of his duty to protect the safety and well-being of the students and faculty at the school, and acted in furtherance of a school investigation rather than a criminal investigation. Thus, his questioning thus did not amount to "custodial interrogation" for *Miranda* purposes. *See also J.D. v. Commonwealth,* 591 S.E.2d 721, 725 (Va. 2004) (student admitted to theft in the presence of the associate principal, principal, and school resource officer; court determined there was no violation of Fifth Amendment or *Miranda* rights since student was not officially in custody or restrained at the time he confessed — the police officer's "mere presence during [the associate principal's] questioning did not convert the questioning into a custodial interrogation by a law enforcement officer"); *In re Jorge D.,* 43 P.3d 605, 608-609 (Ariz.

2003) (student was questioned by police officer on bus duty regarding the driver being hit with a bottle; court stated the "objective test for determining whether an adult was in custody for purposes of *Miranda*, giving attention to such factors as the time and place of the interrogation, police conduct, and the content and style of the questioning, applies also to juvenile interrogations, but with additional elements that bear upon a child's perceptions and vulnerability, including the child's age, maturity and experience with law enforcement and the presence of a parent or other supportive adult." Court remanded to lower court to determine "whether a ten-year-old in [the boy's] position would have reasonably considered his freedom of action to be curtailed in a significant way, *i.e.*, to a degree associated with a formal arrest"); *State v. D.R.*, 930 P.2d 350, 353 (Wash. Ct. App. 1997) (*Miranda* violation occurred where a detective questioned the student in the assistant principal's office — with the assistant principal present — about having sexual intercourse with his sister; the court found D.R. was in custody "in light of [the detective's] failure to inform him he was free to leave, D.R.'s youth, the naturally coercive nature of the school and principal's office environment for children of his age, and the obviously accusatory nature of the interrogation. [The detective] was required to formally advise D.R. of his rights under *Miranda*, and the trial court erred in admitting D.R.'s inculpatory statements").

Is it consistent to say that teachers and other school officials are agents of the state for purposes of the Fourth Amendment, but not for the Fifth? *Miranda* warnings are required for "questioning initiated by law enforcement officers after a person has been taken into custody or otherwise deprived of his freedom of action in any significant way." *Miranda*, 384 U.S. at 444. Do students who are brought to the principal's office for questioning typically believe that they are free to leave? "The warnings protect persons who, exposed to such [inherently coercive custodial] interrogation without assistance of counsel, otherwise might be unable to make a free and informed choice to remain silent." *Roberts v. United States*, 445 U.S. 552, 560–61 (1980). Is it inherently coercive for adults in authority positions to question a child by himself in a school office?

§ 4.05 DISCRIMINATION, HARASSMENT AND BULLYING

Title IX of the Education Amendments of 1972 prohibits discrimination on the basis of sex in educational programs and activities that receive federal funds. The statute provides: "No person in the United States shall, on the basis of sex, be excluded from participation in, be denied the benefits of, or be subjected to discrimination under any education program or activity receiving Federal financial assistance . . . ." 20 U.S.C. § 1681(a) (2001).[78] The statute directs federal agencies who distribute education funding to establish requirements to effectuate this nondiscrimination mandate, and allows the agencies

---

[78] There are certain exceptions listed in Title IX. For example, with regard to admissions to educational institutions, only public institutions of undergraduate higher education are included. 20 U.S.C. § 1681(a)(1). Educational institutions controlled by a religious organization are exempt if application of Title IX provisions would not be consistent with the organization's religious tenets. 20 U.S.C. § 1681(a)(3).

to enforce those requirements through "any . . . means authorized by law," which may include the termination of federal funding. 20 U.S.C. § 1682. Title IX's implementing regulations state that students may not be given "different aid, benefits, or service" based on sex, 34 C.F.R. § 106.31(b)(2), nor can recipients of federal funds require or refuse participation in any of its educational programs based on sex, 34 C.F.R. 106.34, with listed exceptions. 34 C.F.R. 106.34(c)(e)(f).

In 1988, Congress enacted the Civil Rights Restoration Act. *See* 20 U.S.C. § 1687. The Civil Rights Restoration Act emphasized the broad scope of Title IX by rejecting the U.S. Supreme Court's view, in *Grove City College v. Bell*, 465 U.S. 555 (1984), that Title IX was program-specific. Under the Civil Rights Restoration Act, all school programs and activities must comply with Title IX if any part received federal funds. The enforcement scheme of Title IX has also undergone change since its enactment in 1972. The U.S. Supreme Court held in *Cannon v. University of Chicago*, 441 U.S. 677 (1979), that, in addition to administrative enforcement, Title IX is also enforceable through an implied private right of action. Subsequently the Court determined that monetary damages are available in the implied private action. *Franklin v. Gwinnett County Public Schools*, 503 U.S. 60 (1992).

Until recently, Title IX was perhaps best known as the statute that "precipitated a virtual revolution in girls and women in sports." *See* Deborah Brake, *The Struggle for Sex Equality in Sport and the Theory Behind Title IX*, 34 U. MICH. J.L. REFORM 13,15, (2001). The Department of Education (then called the Department of Health, Education and Welfare) promulgated regulations governing athletics in 1975. Title IX compliance was divided into three separate areas: participation, scholarships, and the treatment and benefits provided to male and female athletes, all of which must be in compliance. *Id.* at 47. In response to a request for more clarity, the Department, in 1979, issued a Policy Interpretation that set forth a three-part test — a test that has been adopted by every Circuit that has considered the issue. *See* Title IX of the Education Amendments of 1972: A Policy Interpretation: Title IX and Intercollegiate Athletics, 44 Fed. Reg. 71,413, 71,418 (Dec. 11, 1979). An institution can comply with Title IX by meeting any one of the following three standards: (1) [providing] intercollegiate level participation opportunities for male and female students . . . in numbers substantially proportionate to their respective enrollments; or (2) show[ing] a history and continuing practice of program expansion which is demonstrably responsive to the developing interest and abilities of the members of [the underrepresented] sex; or (3) demonstrat[ing] that the interests and abilities of the members of [the underrepresented] sex have been fully and effectively accommodated by the present program.[79]

Although the interpretation also applies to club, intramural, and interscholastic programs in lower education, disparities in some states have been slow to disappear. A special report in the *Atlanta Journal Constitution* at the end of 1999, 27 years after Title IX was passed, pointed out that seventy-five

---

[79] The plaintiff has the burden of proof on prongs one and three of the test; the university has the burden of proof under prong two. *See Cohen v. Brown Univ.*, 991 F.2d 888–02 (1st Cir. 1993), *aff'd in part and rev'd in part*, 101 F.3d 155 (1st Cir. 1996).

percent of local salary supplements for coaching goes to support boys' sports, while twenty-five percent goes to girls' programs. Ninety-five percent of so-called "extended pay" supplements (amounting to more than $12 million per year in additional financial support for coaches) goes to the coaches of boys sports. Girls' programs get five percent. For football, an almost exclusively male sport, the ratio of students per coach statewide is 9-to-1. For softball and volleyball, exclusively female sports, the ratio is 12-to-1. Fifty-four percent of athletes are boys; thirty-six percent are girls. The state's top school official stated that a case could be made that nearly every public high school in the state might be in violation of Title IX. Mike Fish & David A. Millon, *Georgia Treats Girl Athletes Second-Class*, ATLANTA J.-CONST., Dec. 12, 1999, at A1. The participation numbers for girls would be worse if the Georgia High School Association did not count competitive cheerleading as a sport. *See* Mike Fish and David A. Millon, *Hollow Cheers*, ATLANTA J.-CONST., Dec. 18, 1999, at D1. One reader of the week-long special news series pointed out the newspaper's own bias as evidenced by its sparse coverage of girl's high school sports. *See* Letter of Robin T. Dake, *Talking Back*, ATLANTA J.-CONST., Dec. 19, 1999, at E11.

Given school budgetary concerns, what is the likely result of providing a softball team or volleyball team for girls? Will it be necessary to cut back on boys' teams? If boys' football or basketball teams generate the most revenue, do they deserve to receive the largest percentage of the budget? What if the football booster club can contribute funds to pay for better facilities or to supplement the boys' coach more than the coaches for female sports? In *Jackson v. Birmingham Bd. of Educ.*, 125 S. Ct. 1497 (2005), a teacher served as a physical education teacher and girls' basketball coach. After he discovered that the girls' team was not receiving equal funding and equal access to athletic equipment and facilities, he complained to his supervisors but to no avail. He began to receive negative work evaluations and ultimately was removed as the girls' coach. He was still employed as a teacher, but he no longer received supplemental pay for coaching. In a opinion by Justice O'Connor, the Court reasoned that retaliation against a person because that person has complained of sex discrimination was another form of intentional sex discrimination encompassed by Title IX's private cause of action. Thus, it concluded that if the school board had retaliated against the teacher because he had complained of sex discrimination, this would have constituted intentional discrimination on the basis of sex in violation of Title IX, even though he was not the victim of the discrimination. The Court remanded the case to allow Jackson to press his claim.

Lack of interest by female students may help schools prove that they are in compliance with Title IX. *See* Kathy Kiely, *Surveys Can Be Used To Show Title IX Compliance*, USA TODAY, Mar. 22, 2005, at 5C (reporting on new federal guidelines allowing "schools to avoid adding more athletic opportunities for students if an Internet survey indicates they are not interested"; the Education Department noted that "rates of non-response may be high with the e-mail procedure" but added it "will interpret such non-response as a lack of interest" by the underrepresented gender).

[A] Sexual Harassment in School

Once it was clear that Title IX allowed for money damages in a private right of action, the statute began to take on a life of its own with regard to matters of sexual harassment in school. According to the cases set forth below, Title IX allows students to sue for money damages when federally funded schools respond with deliberate indifference to known sexual harassment by teachers or students in their educational programs. *Gebser v. Lago Vista Independent School District* addressed whether Title IX would support a suit for damages against a school district for a teacher's sexual harassment of a student. One year later, in *Davis v. Monroe County Board of Education*, the Court addressed the same issue with regard to student-on-student sexual harassment. As you read these two cases, compare and contrast the Court's analysis of the theory of liability.

[1] Teacher Harassing Student

GEBSER v. LAGO VISTA INDEPENDENT SCHOOL DISTRICT

Supreme Court of the United States
524 U.S. 274 (1998)

JUSTICE O'CONNOR *delivered the opinion of the Court.*

The question in this case is when a school district may be held liable in damages in an implied right of action under Title IX of the Education Amendments of 1972 for the sexual harassment of a student by one of the district's teachers. We conclude that damages may not be recovered in those circumstances unless an official of the school district who at a minimum has authority to institute corrective measures on the district's behalf has actual notice of, and is deliberately indifferent to, the teacher's misconduct.

I

In the spring of 1991, when petitioner Alida Star Gebser was an eighth-grade student at a middle school in respondent Lago Vista Independent School District (Lago Vista), she joined a high school book discussion group led by Frank Waldrop, a teacher at Lago Vista's high school. Lago Vista received federal funds at all pertinent times. During the book discussion sessions, Waldrop often made sexually suggestive comments to the students. Gebser entered high school in the fall and was assigned to classes taught by Waldrop in both semesters. Waldrop continued to make inappropriate remarks to the students, and he began to direct more of his suggestive comments toward Gebser, including during the substantial amount of time that the two were alone in his classroom. He initiated sexual contact with Gebser in the spring, when, while visiting her home ostensibly to give her a book, he kissed and fondled her. The two had sexual intercourse on a number of occasions during the remainder of the school year. Their relationship continued through the summer and into the following school year, and they often had intercourse during class time, although never on school property.

Gebser did not report the relationship to school officials, testifying that while she realized Waldrop's conduct was improper, she was uncertain how to react and she wanted to continue having him as a teacher. In October 1992, the parents of two other students complained to the high school principal about Waldrop's comments in class. The principal arranged a meeting, at which, according to the principal, Waldrop indicated that he did not believe he had made offensive remarks but apologized to the parents and said it would not happen again. The principal also advised Waldrop to be careful about his classroom comments and told the school guidance counselor about the meeting, but he did not report the parents' complaint to Lago Vista's superintendent, who was the district's Title IX coordinator. A couple of months later, in January 1993, a police officer discovered Waldrop and Gebser engaging in sexual intercourse and arrested Waldrop. Lago Vista terminated his employment, and subsequently, the Texas Education Agency revoked his teaching license. During this time, the district had not promulgated or distributed an official grievance procedure for lodging sexual harassment complaints; nor had it issued a formal anti-harassment policy.

Gebser and her mother filed suit against Lago Vista and Waldrop in state court in November 1993, raising claims against the school district under Title IX, 42 U.S.C. § 1983, and state negligence law, and claims against Waldrop primarily under state law. They sought compensatory and punitive damages from both defendants. After the case was removed, the United States District Court for the Western District of Texas granted summary judgment in favor of Lago Vista on all claims, and remanded the allegations against Waldrop to state court. . . .

Petitioners appealed only on the Title IX claim. The Court of Appeals for the Fifth Circuit affirmed.

II

Title IX provides in pertinent part that, "no person . . . shall, on the basis of sex, be excluded from participation in, be denied the benefits of, or be subjected to discrimination under any education program or activity receiving Federal financial assistance." 20 U.S.C. § 1681(a). The express statutory means of enforcement is administrative: The statute directs federal agencies who distribute education funding to establish requirements to effectuate the nondiscrimination mandate, and permits the agencies to enforce those requirements through "any . . . means authorized by law," including ultimately the termination of federal funding. § 1682. The Court held in *Cannon v. University of Chicago* that Title IX is also enforceable through an implied private right of action, a conclusion we do not revisit here. We subsequently established in *Franklin v. Gwinnett County Public Schools* that monetary damages are available in the implied private action. . . .

Franklin thereby establishes that a school district can be held liable in damages in cases involving a teacher's sexual harassment of a student; the decision, however, does not purport to define the contours of that liability.

We face that issue squarely in this case. Petitioners, joined by the United States as *amicus curiae*, would invoke standards used by the Courts of Appeals in Title VII cases involving a supervisor's sexual harassment of an employee in the workplace. In support of that approach, they point to a passage in *Franklin* in which we stated: "Unquestionably, Title IX placed on the Gwinnett County Public Schools the duty not to discriminate on the basis of sex, and 'when a supervisor sexually harasses a subordinate because of the subordinate's sex, that supervisor "discriminates" on the basis of sex.' *Meritor Sav. Bank, FSB v. Vinson*. We believe the same rule should apply when a teacher sexually harasses and abuses a student." *Franklin, supra*, at 75. *Meritor Savings Bank, FSB v. Vinson* directs courts to look to common-law agency principles when assessing an employer's liability under Title VII for sexual harassment of an employee by a supervisor. Petitioners and the United States submit that, in light of *Franklin*'s comparison of teacher-student harassment with supervisor-employee harassment, agency principles should likewise apply in Title IX actions.

Specifically, they advance two possible standards under which Lago Vista would be liable for Waldrop's conduct. First, relying on a 1997 "Policy Guidance" issued by the Department of Education, they would hold a school district liable in damages under Title IX where a teacher is " 'aided in carrying out the sexual harassment of students by his or her position of authority with the institution,' " irrespective of whether school district officials had any knowledge of the harassment and irrespective of their response upon becoming aware. That rule is an expression of *respondeat superior* liability, *i.e.*, vicarious or imputed liability, see Restatement § 219(2)(d), under which recovery in damages against a school district would generally follow whenever a teacher's authority over a student facilitates the harassment. Second, petitioners and the United States submit that a school district should at a minimum be liable for damages based on a theory of constructive notice, *i.e.*, where the district knew or "should have known" about harassment but failed to uncover and eliminate it. Both standards would allow a damages recovery in a broader range of situations than the rule adopted by the Court of Appeals, which hinges on actual knowledge by a school official with authority to end the harassment.

Whether educational institutions can be said to violate Title IX based solely on principles of *respondeat superior* or constructive notice was not resolved by *Franklin*'s citation of *Meritor*. That reference to *Meritor* was made with regard to the general proposition that sexual harassment can constitute discrimination on the basis of sex under Title IX, *see Oncale v. Sundowner Offshore Services, Inc.*, 523 U.S. 75 (1998), an issue not in dispute here. In fact, the school district's liability in *Franklin* did not necessarily turn on principles of imputed liability or constructive notice, as there was evidence that school officials knew about the harassment but took no action to stop it. Moreover, *Meritor*'s rationale for concluding that agency principles guide the liability inquiry under Title VII rests on an aspect of that statute not found in Title IX: Title VII, in which the prohibition against employment discrimination runs against "an employer," 42 U.S.C. § 2000e-2(a), explicitly defines "employer" to include "any agent," § 2000e(b). Title IX contains no comparable reference to an educational institution's "agents," and so does not expressly call for application of agency principles.

In this case, moreover, petitioners seek not just to establish a Title IX violation but to recover *damages* based on theories of *respondeat superior* and constructive notice. It is that aspect of their action, in our view, which is most critical to resolving the case. Unlike Title IX, Title VII contains an express cause of action, § 2000e-5(f), and specifically provides for relief in the form of monetary damages, § 1981a. Congress therefore has directly addressed the subject of damages relief under Title VII and has set out the particular situations in which damages are available as well as the maximum amounts recoverable. § 1981a(b). With respect to Title IX, however, the private right of action is judicially implied, and there is thus no legislative expression of the scope of available remedies, including when it is appropriate to award monetary damages. In addition, although the general presumption that courts can award any appropriate relief in an established cause of action, coupled with Congress' abrogation of the States' Eleventh Amendment immunity under Title IX, *see* 42 U.S.C. § 2000d-7, led us to conclude in *Franklin* that Title IX recognizes a damages remedy, we did so in response to lower court decisions holding that Title IX does not support damages relief at all. We made no effort in *Franklin* to delimit the circumstances in which a damages remedy should lie.

III

Because the private right of action under Title IX is judicially implied, we have a measure of latitude to shape a sensible remedial scheme that best comports with the statute. That endeavor inherently entails a degree of speculation, since it addresses an issue on which Congress has not specifically spoken. To guide the analysis, we generally examine the relevant statute to ensure that we do not fashion the parameters of an implied right in a manner at odds with the statutory structure and purpose.

Those considerations, we think, are pertinent not only to the scope of the implied right, but also to the scope of the available remedies. We suggested as much in *Franklin*, where we recognized "the general rule that all appropriate relief is available in an action brought to vindicate a federal right," but indicated that the rule must be reconciled with congressional purpose. The "general rule," that is, "yields where necessary to carry out the intent of Congress or to avoid frustrating the purposes of the statute involved."

Applying those principles here, we conclude that it would "frustrate the purposes" of Title IX to permit a damages recovery against a school district for a teacher's sexual harassment of a student based on principles of *respondeat superior* or constructive notice, *i.e.*, without actual notice to a school district official. Because Congress did not expressly create a private right of action under Title IX, the statutory text does not shed light on Congress' intent with respect to the scope of available remedies. Instead, "we attempt to infer how the [1972] Congress would have addressed the issue had the . . . action been included as an express provision in the" statute.

As a general matter, it does not appear that Congress contemplated unlimited recovery in damages against a funding recipient where the recipient is unaware of discrimination in its programs. When Title IX was enacted in

1972, the principal civil rights statutes containing an express right of action did not provide for recovery of monetary damages at all, instead allowing only injunctive and equitable relief. It was not until 1991 that Congress made damages available under Title VII, and even then, Congress carefully limited the amount recoverable in any individual case, calibrating the maximum recovery to the size of the employer. *See* 42 U.S.C. § 1981a(b)(3). Adopting petitioners' position would amount, then, to allowing unlimited recovery of damages under Title IX where Congress has not spoken on the subject of either the right or the remedy, and in the face of evidence that when Congress expressly considered both in Title VII it restricted the amount of damages available.

Congress enacted Title IX in 1972 with two principal objectives in mind: "to avoid the use of federal resources to support discriminatory practices" and "to provide individual citizens effective protection against those practices." The statute was modeled after Title VI of the Civil Rights Act of 1964, which is parallel to Title IX except that it prohibits race discrimination, not sex discrimination, and applies in all programs receiving federal funds, not only in education programs. The two statutes operate in the same manner, conditioning an offer of federal funding on a promise by the recipient not to discriminate, in what amounts essentially to a contract between the Government and the recipient of funds.

That contractual framework distinguishes Title IX from Title VII, which is framed in terms not of a condition but of an outright prohibition. Title VII applies to all employers without regard to federal funding and aims broadly to "eradicate discrimination throughout the economy." Title VII, moreover, seeks to "make persons whole for injuries suffered through past discrimination." Thus, whereas Title VII aims centrally to compensate victims of discrimination, Title IX focuses more on "protecting" individuals from discriminatory practices carried out by recipients of federal funds. That might explain why, when the Court first recognized the implied right under Title IX in *Cannon*, the opinion referred to injunctive or equitable relief in a private action, but not to a damages remedy.

Title IX's contractual nature has implications for our construction of the scope of available remedies. When Congress attaches conditions to the award of federal funds under its spending power, U.S. Const., art. I, § 8, cl. 1, as it has in Title IX and Title VI, we examine closely the propriety of private actions holding the recipient liable in monetary damages for noncompliance with the condition. Our central concern in that regard is with ensuring "that the receiving entity of federal funds [has] notice that it will be liable for a monetary award." . . . If a school district's liability for a teacher's sexual harassment rests on principles of constructive notice or *respondeat superior*, it will . . . be the case that the recipient of funds was unaware of the discrimination. It is sensible to assume that Congress did not envision a recipient's liability in damages in that situation.

Most significantly, Title IX contains important clues that Congress did not intend to allow recovery in damages where liability rests solely on principles of vicarious liability or constructive notice. Title IX's express means of enforcement — by administrative agencies — operates on an assumption of actual notice to officials of the funding recipient. The statute entitles agencies who disburse education funding to enforce their rules implementing the non-discrimination mandate through proceedings to suspend or terminate funding or through "other means authorized by law." Significantly, however, an agency may not initiate enforcement proceedings until it "has advised the appropriate person or persons of the failure to comply with the requirement and has determined that compliance cannot be secured by voluntary means." The administrative regulations implement that obligation, requiring resolution of compliance issues "by informal means whenever possible," 34 CFR § 100.7(d) (1997), and prohibiting commencement of enforcement proceedings until the agency has determined that voluntary compliance is unobtainable and "the recipient . . . has been notified of its failure to comply and of the action to be taken to effect compliance."

In the event of a violation, a funding recipient may be required to take "such remedial action as [is] deemed necessary to overcome the effects of [the] discrimination." While agencies have conditioned continued funding on providing equitable relief to the victim, the regulations do not appear to contemplate a condition ordering payment of monetary damages, and there is no indication that payment of damages has been demanded as a condition of finding a recipient to be in compliance with the statute. . . .

Presumably, a central purpose of requiring notice of the violation "to the appropriate person" and an opportunity for voluntary compliance before administrative enforcement proceedings can commence is to avoid diverting education funding from beneficial uses where a recipient was unaware of discrimination in its programs and is willing to institute prompt corrective measures. The scope of private damages relief proposed by petitioners is at odds with that basic objective. When a teacher's sexual harassment is imputed to a school district or when a school district is deemed to have "constructively" known of the teacher's harassment, by assumption the district had no actual knowledge of the teacher's conduct. Nor, of course, did the district have an opportunity to take action to end the harassment or to limit further harassment.

It would be unsound, we think, for a statute's *express* system of enforcement to require notice to the recipient and an opportunity to come into voluntary compliance while a judicially *implied* system of enforcement permits substantial liability without regard to the recipient's knowledge or its corrective actions upon receiving notice. Moreover, an award of damages in a particular case might well exceed a recipient's level of federal funding. See Tr. of Oral Arg. 35 (Lago Vista's federal funding for 1992-1993 was roughly $120,000). Where a statute's express enforcement scheme hinges its most severe sanction on notice and unsuccessful efforts to obtain compliance, we cannot attribute to Congress the intention to have implied an enforcement scheme that allows imposition of greater liability without comparable conditions.

IV

Because the express remedial scheme under Title IX is predicated upon notice to an "appropriate person" and an opportunity to rectify any violation,

20 U.S.C. § 1682, we conclude, in the absence of further direction from Congress, that the implied damages remedy should be fashioned along the same lines. An "appropriate person" under § 1682 is, at a minimum, an official of the recipient entity with authority to take corrective action to end the discrimination.

Consequently, in cases like this one that do not involve official policy of the recipient entity, we hold that a damages remedy will not lie under Title IX unless an official who at a minimum has authority to address the alleged discrimination and to institute corrective measures on the recipient's behalf has actual knowledge of discrimination in the recipient's programs and fails adequately to respond.

We think, moreover, that the response must amount to deliberate indifference to discrimination. The administrative enforcement scheme presupposes that an official who is advised of a Title IX violation refuses to take action to bring the recipient into compliance. The premise, in other words, is an official decision by the recipient not to remedy the violation. That framework finds a rough parallel in the standard of deliberate indifference. Under a lower standard, there would be a risk that the recipient would be liable in damages not for its own official decision but instead for its employees' independent actions. Comparable considerations led to our adoption of a deliberate indifference standard for claims under § 1983 alleging that a municipality's actions in failing to prevent a deprivation of federal rights was the cause of the violation.

Applying the framework to this case is fairly straightforward, as petitioners do not contend they can prevail under an actual notice standard. The only official alleged to have had information about Waldrop's misconduct is the high school principal. That information, however, consisted of a complaint from parents of other students charging only that Waldrop had made inappropriate comments during class, which was plainly insufficient to alert the principal to the possibility that Waldrop was involved in a sexual relationship with a student. Lago Vista, moreover, terminated Waldrop's employment upon learning of his relationship with Gebser. Justice Stevens points out in his dissenting opinion that Waldrop of course had knowledge of his own actions. Where a school district's liability rests on actual notice principles, however, the knowledge of the wrongdoer himself is not pertinent to the analysis.

Petitioners focus primarily on Lago Vista's asserted failure to promulgate and publicize an effective policy and grievance procedure for sexual harassment claims. They point to Department of Education regulations requiring each funding recipient to "adopt and publish grievance procedures providing for prompt and equitable resolution" of discrimination complaints, 34 CFR § 106.8(b) (1997), and to notify students and others "that it does not discriminate on the basis of sex in the educational programs or activities which it operates," § 106.9(a). Lago Vista's alleged failure to comply with the regulations, however, does not establish the requisite actual notice and deliberate indifference. And in any event, the failure to promulgate a grievance procedure does not itself constitute "discrimination" under Title IX. Of course, the Department of Education could enforce the requirement administratively: Agencies generally have authority to promulgate and enforce requirements that effectuate the statute's non-discrimination mandate, 20 U.S.C. § 1682, even if those requirements do not purport to represent a definition of discrimination under the statute. We have never held, however, that the implied private right of action under Title IX allows recovery in damages for violation of those sorts of administrative requirements.

V

The number of reported cases involving sexual harassment of students in schools confirms that harassment unfortunately is an all too common aspect of the educational experience. No one questions that a student suffers extraordinary harm when subjected to sexual harassment and abuse by a teacher, and that the teacher's conduct is reprehensible and undermines the basic purposes of the educational system. The issue in this case, however, is whether the independent misconduct of a teacher is attributable to the school district that employs him under a specific federal statute designed primarily to prevent recipients of federal financial assistance from using the funds in a discriminatory manner. Our decision does not affect any right of recovery that an individual may have against a school district as a matter of state law or against the teacher in his individual capacity under state law or under 42 U.S.C. § 1983. Until Congress speaks directly on the subject, however, we will not hold a school district liable in damages under Title IX for a teacher's sexual harassment of a student absent actual notice and deliberate indifference. We therefore affirm the judgment of the Court of Appeals.

It is so ordered.

JUSTICE STEVENS, with whom JUSTICE SOUTER, JUSTICE GINSBURG, and JUSTICE BREYER join, *dissenting*.

The question that the petition for certiorari asks us to address is whether the Lago Vista Independent School District (respondent) is liable in damages for a violation of Title IX of the Education Amendments of 1972, 20 U.S.C. § 1681 *et seq.* (Title IX). The Court provides us with a negative answer to that question because respondent did not have actual notice of, and was not deliberately indifferent to, the odious misconduct of one of its teachers. As a basis for its decision, the majority relies heavily on the notion that because the private cause of action under Title IX is "judicially implied," the Court has "a measure of latitude" to use its own judgment in shaping a remedial scheme. This assertion of lawmaking authority is not faithful either to our precedents or to our duty to interpret, rather than to revise, congressional commands. Moreover, the majority's policy judgment about the appropriate remedy in this case thwarts the purposes of Title IX.

I

It is important to emphasize that in *Cannon v. University of Chicago*, the Court confronted a question of statutory construction. The decision represented our considered judgment about the intent of the Congress that enacted Title IX in 1972. After noting that Title IX had been patterned after Title VI of the Civil Rights Act of 1964, which had been interpreted to include a private right of action, we concluded that Congress intended to authorize the same private enforcement of Title IX.[80] As long as the intent of Congress is clear, an implicit command has the same legal force as one that is explicit. The fact that a statute does not authorize a particular remedy "in so many words is no more significant than the fact that it does not in terms authorize execution to issue on a judgment recovered under [the statute]."

In *Franklin v. Gwinnett County Public Schools*, we unanimously concluded that Title IX authorized a high school student who had been sexually harassed by a sports coach/teacher to recover damages from the school district. That conclusion was supported by two considerations. In his opinion for the Court, Justice White first relied on the presumption that Congress intends to authorize "all appropriate remedies" unless it expressly indicates otherwise. He then noted that two amendments to Title IX enacted after the decision in *Cannon* had validated *Cannon*'s holding and supported the conclusion that "Congress did not intend to limit the remedies available in a suit brought under Title IX." Justice Scalia, concurring in the judgment, agreed that Congress' amendment of Title IX to eliminate the States' Eleventh Amendment immunity, *see* 42 U.S.C. § 2000d-7(a)(1), must be read "not only 'as a validation of *Cannon*'s holding,' but also as an implicit acknowledgment that damages are available."

Because these constructions of the statute have been accepted by Congress and are unchallenged here, they have the same legal effect as if the private cause of action seeking damages had been explicitly, rather than implicitly, authorized by Congress. We should therefore seek guidance from the text of the statute and settled legal principles rather than from our views about sound policy.

II

We have already noted that the text of Title IX should be accorded "a sweep as broad as its language." That sweep is broad indeed. "No person . . . shall, on the basis of sex, . . . be subjected to discrimination under any education program or activity receiving Federal financial assistance . . . ." 20 U.S.C. § 1681(a). As Judge Rovner has correctly observed, the use of passive verbs

---

80 [1] We explained: "In 1972 when Title IX was enacted, the critical language in Title VI had already been construed as creating a private remedy . . . . It is always appropriate to assume that our elected representatives, like other citizens, know the law; in this case, because of their repeated references to Title VI and its modes of enforcement, we are especially justified in presuming both that those representatives were aware of the prior interpretation of Title VI and that that interpretation reflects their intent with respect to Title IX." 441 U.S. at 696–698. We also observed that "during the period between the enactment of Title VI in 1964 and the enactment of Title IX in 1972, this Court had consistently found implied remedies — often in cases much less clear than this. It was *after* 1972 that this Court decided *Cort v. Ash*, [422 U.S. 66 (1975),] and the other cases cited by the Court of Appeals in support of its strict construction of the remedial aspect of the statute. We, of course, adhere to the strict approach followed in our recent cases, but our evaluation of congressional action in 1972 must take into account its contemporary legal context. In sum, it is not only appropriate but also realistic to presume that Congress was thoroughly familiar with these unusually important precedents from this and other federal courts and that it expected its enactment to be interpreted in conformity with them." 441 U.S. at 698–699 (footnotes omitted).

in Title IX, focusing on the victim of the discrimination rather than the particular wrongdoer, gives this statute broader coverage than Title VII. *See Smith v. Metropolitan School Dist. Perry Twp.,* 128 F.3d 1014, 1047 (CA7 1997) (dissenting opinion).[81] Moreover, because respondent assumed the statutory duty set out in Title IX as part of its consideration for the receipt of federal funds, that duty constitutes an affirmative undertaking that is more significant than a mere promise to obey the law.

Both of these considerations are reflected in our decision in *Franklin.* Explaining why Title IX is violated when a teacher sexually abuses a student, we wrote:

> Unquestionably, Title IX placed on the Gwinnett County Public Schools the duty not to discriminate on the basis of sex, and 'when a supervisor sexually harasses a subordinate because of the subordinate's sex, that supervisor "discriminates" on the basis of sex.' We believe the same rule should apply when a teacher sexually harasses and abuses a student. *Congress surely did not intend for federal moneys to be expended to support the intentional actions it sought by statute to proscribe.*

Franklin therefore stands for the proposition that sexual harassment of a student by her teacher violates the duty — assumed by the school district in exchange for federal funds — not to discriminate on the basis of sex, and that a student may recover damages from a school district for such a violation.

. . . .

The Court nevertheless holds that the law does not provide a damages remedy for the Title IX violation alleged in this case because no official of the school district with "authority to institute corrective measures on the district's behalf" had actual notice of Waldrop's misconduct. That holding is at odds with settled principles of agency law,[82] under which the district is responsible for Waldrop's misconduct because "he was aided in accomplishing the tort by the existence of the agency relation." Restatement (Second) of Agency,

---

[81] [5] "Unlike Title VII . . . , which focuses on the discriminator, making it unlawful for an employer to engage in certain prohibited practices (see 42 U.S.C. § 2000e-2(a)), Title IX is drafted from the perspective of the person discriminated against. That statute names no actor, but using passive verbs, focuses on the setting in which the discrimination occurred. In effect, the statute asks but a single question — whether an individual was subjected to discrimination *under* a covered program or activity . . . . And because Title IX as drafted includes no actor at all, it necessarily follows that the statute also would not reference 'agents' of that non-existent actor." *Smith v. Metropolitan School Dist. Perry Twp.,* 128 F.3d 1014, 1047 (CA7 1997) (ROVNER, J., dissenting); *see also Cannon v. University of Chicago,* 441 U.S. 677, 691–693 (1977) (recognizing that Congress drafted Title IX "with an unmistakable focus on the benefited class," and did not "write it simply as a ban on discriminatory conduct by recipients of federal funds or as a prohibition against the disbursement of public funds to educational institutions engaged in discriminatory practices").

[82] [8] The Court's holding is also questionable as a factual matter. Waldrop himself surely had ample authority to maintain order in the classes that he conducted. Indeed, that is a routine part of every teacher's responsibilities. If petitioner had been the victim of sexually harassing conduct by other students during those classes, surely the teacher would have had ample authority to take corrective measures. The fact that he did not prevent his own harassment of petitioner is the consequence of his lack of will, not his lack of authority.

§ 219(2)(d) (1957).[83] This case presents a paradigmatic example of a tort that was made possible, that was effected, and that was repeated over a prolonged period because of the powerful influence that Waldrop had over Gebser by reason of the authority that his employer, the school district, had delegated to him. As a secondary school teacher, Waldrop exercised even greater authority and control over his students than employers and supervisors exercise over their employees. His gross misuse of that authority allowed him to abuse his young student's trust.[84] . . .

The reason why the common law imposes liability on the principal in such circumstances is the same as the reason why Congress included the prohibition against discrimination on the basis of sex in Title IX: to induce school boards to adopt and enforce practices that will minimize the danger that vulnerable students will be exposed to such odious behavior. The rule that the Court has crafted creates the opposite incentive. As long as school boards can insulate themselves from knowledge about this sort of conduct, they can claim immunity from damages liability.[85] Indeed, the rule that the Court adopts would preclude a damages remedy even if every teacher at the school knew about the harassment but did not have "authority to institute corrective measures on the district's behalf." It is not my function to determine whether this newly fashioned rule is wiser than the established common-law rule. It is proper, however, to suggest that the Court bears the burden of justifying its rather dramatic departure from settled law, and to explain why its opinion fails to shoulder that burden.

III

The Court advances several reasons why it would "frustrate the purposes" of Title IX to allow recovery against a school district that does not have actual

---

[83] [9] The Court suggests that agency principles are inapplicable to this case because Title IX does not expressly refer to an "agent," as Title VII does. Title IX's focus on the protected class rather than the fund recipient fully explains the statute's failure to mention "agents" of the recipient, however. Moreover, in *Meritor Savings Bank, FSB v. Vinson*, 477 U.S. 57 (1986), we viewed Title VII's reference to an "agent" as a *limitation* on the liability of the employer: "Congress' decision to define 'employer' to include any 'agent' of an employer, 42 U.S.C. § 2000e(b), surely evinces an intent to place some limits on the acts of employees for which employers under Title VII are to be held responsible."

[84] [10] For example, Waldrop first sexually abused Gebser when he visited her house on the pretense of giving her a book that she needed for a school project. *See* App. 54a (deposition of Star Gebser). Gebser, then a high school freshman, stated that she "was terrified": "He was the main teacher at the school with whom I had discussions, and I didn't know what to do." Gebser was the only student to attend Waldrop's summer advanced placement course, and the two often had sexual intercourse during the time allotted for the class. Gebser stated that she declined to report the sexual relationship because "if I was to blow the whistle on that, then I wouldn't be able to have this person as a teacher anymore." She also stated that Waldrop "was the person in Lago administration . . . who I most trusted, and he was the one that I would have been making the complaint against."

[85] [11] The Court concludes that its holding "does not affect any right of recovery that an individual may have against a school district as a matter of state law or against the teacher in his individual capacity under state law or under 42 U.S.C. § 1983." In this case, of course, the District Court denied petitioner's § 1983 claim on summary judgment, and it is undisputed that the Texas Tort Claims Act, Tex. Civ. Prac. & Rem. Code Ann. § 101.051 (1997), immunizes school districts from tort liability in cases like this one.

notice of a teacher's sexual harassment of a student. As the Court acknowledges, however, the two principal purposes that motivated the enactment of Title IX were: (1) "to avoid the use of federal resources to support discriminatory practices"; and (2) "to provide individual citizens effective protection against those practices." It seems quite obvious that both of those purposes would be served — not frustrated — by providing a damages remedy in a case of this kind. To the extent that the Court's reasons for its policy choice have any merit, they suggest that no damages should ever be awarded in a Title IX case — in other words, that our unanimous holding in *Franklin* should be repudiated.

First, the Court observes that at the time Title IX was enacted, "the principal civil rights statutes containing an express right of action did not provide for recovery of monetary damages at all." *Franklin*, however, forecloses this reevaluation of legislative intent; in that case, we "evaluated the state of the law when the Legislature passed Title IX," and concluded that "the same contextual approach used to justify an implied right of action more than amply demonstrates the lack of any legislative intent to abandon the traditional presumption in favor of all available remedies." The Court also suggests that the fact that Congress has imposed a ceiling on the amount of damages that may be recovered in Title VII cases is somehow relevant to the question whether any damages at all may be awarded in a Title IX case. The short answer to this creative argument is that the Title VII ceiling does not have any bearing on when damages may be recovered from a defendant in a Title IX case. Moreover, this case does not present any issue concerning the amount of any possible damages award.

Second, the Court suggests that the school district did not have fair notice when it accepted federal funding that it might be held liable " 'for a monetary award' " under Title IX. The Court cannot mean, however, that respondent was not on notice that sexual harassment of a student by a teacher constitutes an "intentional" violation of Title IX for which damages are available, because we so held shortly before Waldrop began abusing Gebser. Given the fact that our holding in *Franklin* was unanimous, it is not unreasonable to assume that it could have been foreseen by counsel for the recipients of Title IX funds. Moreover, the nondiscrimination requirement set out in Title IX is clear, and this Court held that sexual harassment constitutes intentional sex discrimination long before the sexual abuse in this case began. Normally, of course, we presume that the citizen has knowledge of the law.

The majority nevertheless takes the position that a school district that accepts federal funds under Title IX should not be held liable in damages for an intentional violation of that statute if the district itself "was unaware of the discrimination." The Court reasons that because administrative proceedings to terminate funding cannot be commenced until after the grant recipient has received notice of its noncompliance and the agency determines that voluntary compliance is not possible, *see* 20 U.S.C. § 1682, there should be no damages liability unless the grant recipient has actual notice of the violation (and thus an opportunity to end the harassment).

The fact that Congress has specified a particular administrative procedure to be followed when a subsidy is to be terminated, however, does not illuminate the question of what the victim of discrimination on the basis of sex must prove in order to recover damages in an implied private right of action. Indeed, in *Franklin*, we noted that the Department of Education's Office of Civil Rights had declined to terminate federal funding of the school district at issue — despite its finding that a Title IX violation had occurred — because "the district had come into compliance with Title IX" after the harassment at issue. That fact did not affect the Court's analysis, much less persuade the Court that a damages remedy was unavailable.

The majority's inappropriate reliance on Title IX's administrative enforcement scheme to limit the availability of a damages remedy leads the Court to require not only actual knowledge on the part of "an official who at a minimum has authority to address the alleged discrimination and to institute corrective measures on the recipient's behalf," but also that official's "refusal to take action," or "deliberate indifference" toward the harassment. Presumably, few Title IX plaintiffs who have been victims of intentional discrimination will be able to recover damages under this exceedingly high standard. The Court fails to recognize that its holding will virtually "render inutile causes of action authorized by Congress through a decision that *no* remedy is available."

IV

We are not presented with any question concerning the affirmative defenses that might eliminate or mitigate the recovery of damages for a Title IX violation. It has been argued, for example, that a school district that has adopted and vigorously enforced a policy that is designed to prevent sexual harassment and redress the harms that such conduct may produce should be exonerated from damages liability. The Secretary of Education has promulgated regulations directing grant recipients to adopt such policies and disseminate them to students. A rule providing an affirmative defense for districts that adopt and publish such policies pursuant to the regulations would not likely be helpful to respondent, however, because it is not at all clear whether respondent adopted any such policy, and there is no evidence that such a policy was made available to students, as required by regulation.

A theme that seems to underlie the Court's opinion is a concern that holding a school district liable in damages might deprive it of the benefit of the federal subsidy — that the damages remedy is somehow more onerous than a possible termination of the federal grant. It is possible, of course, that in some cases the recoverable damages, in either a Title IX action or a state-law tort action, would exceed the amount of a federal grant. [86] That is surely not relevant to the question whether the school district or the injured student should bear the risk of harm — a risk against which the district, but not the student, can insure. It is not clear to me why the well-settled rules of law that impose

---

[86] [18] *Amici curiae* National School Boards Association and the New Jersey School Boards Association point to a $ 1.4 million verdict in a recent Title IX case. See Brief for National School Boards Association et al. as *Amici Curiae* 5, and n.4. Significantly, however, the District Judge in that case refused to enter a judgment on that verdict; the judge instead ordered a new trial on damages, limited to medical and mental health treatment and special education expenses. *See* 887 F. Supp. 947, 957 (WD Tex. 1995), *rev'd,* 101 F.3d 393 (CA5 1996).

responsibility on the principal for the misconduct of its agents should not apply in this case. As a matter of policy, the Court ranks protection of the school district's purse above the protection of immature high school students that those rules would provide. Because those students are members of the class for whose special benefit Congress enacted Title IX, that policy choice is not faithful to the intent of the policymaking branch of our Government.

I respectfully dissent.

JUSTICE GINSBURG, with whom JUSTICE SOUTER and JUSTICE BREYER join, *dissenting.*

. . . .

In line with the tort law doctrine of avoidable consequences, see generally C. MCCORMICK, LAW OF DAMAGES 127–159 (1935), I would recognize as an affirmative defense to a Title IX charge of sexual harassment, an effective policy for reporting and redressing such misconduct. School districts subject to Title IX's governance have been instructed by the Secretary of Education to install procedures for "prompt and equitable resolution" of complaints, 34 CFR § 106.8(b) (1997), and the Department of Education's Office of Civil Rights has detailed elements of an effective grievance process, with specific reference to sexual harassment, 62 FED. REG. 12034, 12044–12045 (1997).

The burden would be the school district's to show that its internal remedies were adequately publicized and likely would have provided redress without exposing the complainant to undue risk, effort, or expense. Under such a regime, to the extent that a plaintiff unreasonably failed to avail herself of the school district's preventive and remedial measures, and consequently suffered avoidable harm, she would not qualify for Title IX relief.

———

NOTES AND QUESTIONS

1. The arguments presented in this case — both by the majority and the dissent — are based on an interweaving of the statutory language, administrative regulations, analogies to other statutes (both Title VII and Title VI), language in previous cases, in addition to the notion that "a wrong deserves a remedy." Separate out these arguments with a critical eye to which are more persuasive. For example, with regard to the express language of the statute, compare (a) — the passive verb argument — with (b) — the argument that the statute contains no language that would hold school districts liable in money damages for discrimination of which they were unaware. Should the administrative enforcement scheme, where schools are given a chance to fix any problems before federal funding is eliminated, have a bearing on the issue in this case? Does it matter that Congress's authority for enacting this statute is under the Spending Clause? Why should principles of agency law apply in the employer context, but not in the school context? What does the majority see as the difference in purpose between Title IX and Title VII? Why does this difference matter? How does the majority distinguish the *Meritor* case? How much weight should isolated sentences in the Court's own previous opinions on a different issue have when analyzing the issue before the Court?

2. To state a claim under Title IX based on an abusive education environment, a plaintiff must allege: (1) the plaintiff is a member of a protected group; (2) the plaintiff has been subjected to unwelcome sexual harassment; (3) the harassment was based on sex; (4) the harassment was sufficiently severe so as to create an abusive education environment; (5) some basis for the educational institution's liability. *Seamons v. Snow*, 84 F.3d 1226, 1232 (10th Cir. 1996).

In *Cockerham v. Stokes County Bd. of Educ.*, 302 F. Supp. 2d 490 (M.D.N.C. 2004), a teacher forced a male student to wear a pink sign asking "will you go out with me?" The student was forced to wear the sign and was taunted and physically abused by other students. The principal witnessed the behavior but did not stop it. The student's mother complained, and a doctor sent a note stating that he believed that this was not in the student's best interest. The court determined that the student had not stated a Title IX claim. According to the court, the question put forth on the sign, though it may refer to dating, is completely gender-neutral and is therefore irrelevant to finding the harassment was based on sex. The color of the sign also failed to indicate that the harassment was based on the student's sex. While it may be true that pink is a color usually associated with females, this generality is insufficient to suggest that the student was targeted for harassment because of his gender. The student alleged no other fact to show that the teacher placed the sign on his back because he is male.

The *Cockerham* court nevertheless chastised the teacher for employing this disciplinary measure:

> The court's ruling should not be interpreted to indicate approval of the perplexing and inappropriate means of discipline selected by [the teacher]. . . . Defendants admit that "[T]he teacher requested that the minor plaintiff and two other students wear a sign as described as part of a recognized technique to modify inappropriate behavior," and that Plaintiff was made to wear the sign while in [the teacher's class and during the lunch period "as part of a the behavior modification technique." Further, "it is admitted that the defendants were aware that the minor plaintiff had learning disabilities." The court recognizes its inexperience in handling school discipline, but these admissions cause the court to ponder from what source came this so-called "recognized technique" of discipline for students.

Id. at n.3.

3. What conduct will amount to deliberate indifference? In *Doe A. v. Gree*, 298 F. Supp. 2d 1025 (D. Nev. 2004), the court reviewed cases that have addressed this issue:

> The Ninth Circuit has explained that school districts will be liable for discrimination occurring on school grounds "if the need for intervention was so obvious, or if inaction was so likely to result in discrimination, that it can be said to have been deliberately indifferent to the need." Deliberate indifference exists "only where the recipient's response to the harassment or lack thereof is clearly unreasonable in

light of the known circumstances." [Citing case omitted.] . . . None of these constructions, however, provide a bright-line by which this Court can determine whether the Defendants' response to Doe's complaint was "clearly unreasonable." . . .

Most courts have similarly not discovered such a bright-line. *See, e.g., Jones v. Wellham*, 104 F.3d 620, 627 (4th Cir. 1997) ("Actions that in hindsight are 'unfortunate' or even 'imprudent' will not suffice."); and *Farmer v. Brennan*, 511 U.S. 825, 835 (1994) ("deliberate indifference describes a state of mind more blameworthy than negligence" but "is satisfied by something less than acts or omissions for the very purpose of causing harm or with knowledge that harm will result."). The Eighth Circuit provides an exception: In *Kinman v. Omaha Pub. Sch. Dist.*, the court found that the school district "did not turn a blind eye and do nothing," and therefore was not deliberately indifferent. 171 F.3d 607, 610 (8th Cir. 1999). This suggests that in some jurisdictions, a school district will not be considered deliberately indifferent so long as it has responded in some way to a complaint. Such a standard, however, has been rejected in other circuits. *Vance v. Spencer County Public School Dist.*, 231 F.3d 253, 261 (6th Cir. 2000) (expressly rejecting the school district's contention that as long as it had done "something" in response to the harassment of a student, it had satisfied the standard). In *Vance*, it was held that "such a minimalist response is not within the contemplation of a reasonable response." *Id.* at 260. This Court agrees. Permitting a school district to avoid liability on the basis of some minimalist and ineffective response to discrimination would be inconsistent with the Supreme Court's ruling that responses which are "clearly unreasonable" constitute deliberate indifference.

Other district courts have found that he deliberate indifference or clearly unreasonable standard "does not lend itself well to a determination by the Court on summary judgment," and have permitted the claim to go to the jury if the plaintiffs advanced some evidence in support. . . . Similarly, this Court finds that, in considering the facts in the light most favorable to Plaintiffs, a reasonable jury could find the Defendants' conduct constituted deliberate indifference.

Id. at 1036.

4. If a private employer is found to be liable for money damages because of sexual harassment by one of its employees, how might it recover its financial loss? Many liability insurance policies have exclusions for sexual harassment, and coverage must be bought separately for separate premiums.

In *Goodman v. Horace Mann Ins. Co.*, 100 S.W.3d 769 (Ky. App. 2003), three students settled a lawsuit for $250,000 each against former teacher for sexual molestation. The teacher stipulated that he had touched the students, but that the touching was not intentional and not intended for sexual gratification. His insurer refused to pay. The trial court held the students' claims against the insurer were excluded by an intentional acts exclusion in the teacher's policy. The appellate court held an evaluation of the policy required an analysis of whether the teacher's acts were within the meaning of educational employment activities. The plain language of the policy required that, to be covered, any claim had to come from an occurrence in the course of the teacher's educational employment activities. The teacher was not acting within his educational employment activities when he sexually molested the students. The doctrine of reasonable expectations required that the policy be construed so as to provide the teacher the protection he reasonably had a right to expect. He could not expect that exclusively personal pursuits would be protected by the policy. An insured event had to occur while the teacher was engaged in an activity reasonably related to the goal of educating children.

In addition, private companies have the option of recouping their losses by raising prices for consumers. Are these same options open to school districts? Depending on the age of the victim, the sexual intercourse in the *Gebser* case may be considered statutory rape, and thus would not be compensable under insurance policies, which have exclusions for intentional criminal acts. (Note that the acts in the *Davis* case below were considered criminal assaults.) If a school district pays out a large damages award from the public fisc, it may be forced either to cut education programs or convince local citizens to raise taxes to make up the loss.

On the other hand, if the victim is unable to obtain compensation from the school district, what other options are open to her? The majority opinion stated that the claims against Waldrop were remanded to state court. Is it likely that the student will be able to enforce a large monetary judgment against this school teacher in his individual capacity?

[2] Student Harassing Student

Before you read the next case, think about whether the same principle that holds a school liable for teacher-on-student sexual harassment would also hold the school liable for student-on-student sexual harassment. Does the statutory language of Title IX mean that recipients of federal funding should be liable in money damages only for their own (and their employee) conduct? Is the school district's control over its students greater or less than its control over its employees?

DAVIS v. MONROE COUNTY BOARD OF EDUCAITON

Supreme Court of the United States
526 U.S. 629 (1999)

Justice O'Connor *delivered the opinion of the Court.*

Petitioner brought suit against the Monroe County Board of Education and other defendants, alleging that her fifth-grade daughter had been the victim of sexual harassment by another student in her class. Among petitioner's claims was a claim for monetary and injunctive relief under Title IX of the Education Amendments of 1972 (Title IX). The District Court dismissed petitioner's Title IX claim on the ground that "student-on-student," or peer, harassment provides no ground for a private cause of action under the statute.

The Court of Appeals for the Eleventh Circuit, sitting en banc, affirmed. We consider here whether a private damages action may lie against the school board in cases of student-on-student harassment. We conclude that it may, but only where the funding recipient acts with deliberate indifference to known acts of harassment in its programs or activities. Moreover, we conclude that such an action will lie only for harassment that is so severe, pervasive, and objectively offensive that it effectively bars the victim's access to an educational opportunity or benefit.

I

Petitioner's Title IX claim was dismissed under Federal Rule of Civil Procedure 12(b)(6) for failure to state a claim upon which relief could be granted. Accordingly, in reviewing the legal sufficiency of petitioner's cause of action, "we must assume the truth of the material facts as alleged in the complaint."

A

Petitioner's minor daughter, LaShonda, was allegedly the victim of a prolonged pattern of sexual harassment by one of her fifth-grade classmates at Hubbard Elementary School, a public school in Monroe County, Georgia. According to petitioner's complaint, the harassment began in December 1992, when the classmate, G. F., attempted to touch LaShonda's breasts and genital area and made vulgar statements such as "I want to get in bed with you" and "I want to feel your boobs." Similar conduct allegedly occurred on or about January 4 and January 20, 1993. LaShonda reported each of these incidents to her mother and to her classroom teacher, Diane Fort. Petitioner, in turn, also contacted Fort, who allegedly assured petitioner that the school principal, Bill Querry, had been informed of the incidents. Petitioner contends that, notwithstanding these reports, no disciplinary action was taken against G. F.

G. F.'s conduct allegedly continued for many months. In early February, G. F. purportedly placed a door stop in his pants and proceeded to act in a sexually suggestive manner toward LaShonda during physical education class. LaShonda reported G. F.'s behavior to her physical education teacher, Whit Maples. Approximately one week later, G. F. again allegedly engaged in harassing behavior, this time while under the supervision of another classroom teacher, Joyce Pippin. Again, LaShonda allegedly reported the incident to the teacher, and again petitioner contacted the teacher to follow up.

Petitioner alleges that G. F. once more directed sexually harassing conduct toward LaShonda in physical education class in early March, and that LaShonda reported the incident to both Maples and Pippen. In mid-April 1993, G. F. allegedly rubbed his body against LaShonda in the school hallway in what LaShonda considered a sexually suggestive manner, and LaShonda again reported the matter to Fort.

The string of incidents finally ended in mid-May, when G. F. was charged with, and pleaded guilty to, sexual battery for his misconduct. The complaint alleges that LaShonda had suffered during the months of harassment, however; specifically, her previously high grades allegedly dropped as she became unable to concentrate on her studies, and, in April 1993, her father discovered that she had written a suicide note, The complaint further alleges that, at one point, LaShonda told petitioner that she "didn't know how much longer she could keep [G. F.] off her."

Nor was LaShonda G. F.'s only victim; it is alleged that other girls in the class fell prey to G. F.'s conduct. At one point, in fact, a group composed of LaShonda and other female students tried to speak with Principal Querry about G. F.'s behavior. According to the complaint, however, a teacher denied the students' request with the statement, "If [Querry] wants you, he'll call you."

Petitioner alleges that no disciplinary action was taken in response to G. F.'s behavior toward LaShonda. In addition to her conversations with Fort and Pippen, petitioner alleges that she spoke with Principal Querry in mid-May 1993. When petitioner inquired as to what action the school intended to take against G. F., Querry simply stated, "I guess I'll have to threaten him a little bit harder." Yet, petitioner alleges, at no point during the many months of his reported misconduct was G. F. disciplined for harassment. Indeed, Querry allegedly asked petitioner why LaShonda "was the only one complaining."

Nor, according to the complaint, was any effort made to separate G. F. and LaShonda. On the contrary, notwithstanding LaShonda's frequent complaints, only after more than three months of reported harassment was she even permitted to change her classroom seat so that she was no longer seated next to G. F. Moreover, petitioner alleges that, at the time of the events in question, the Monroe County Board of Education (Board) had not instructed its personnel on how to respond to peer sexual harassment and had not established a policy on the issue.

B

On May 4, 1994, petitioner filed suit in the United States District Court for the Middle District of Georgia against the Board, Charles Dumas, the school district's superintendent, and Principal Querry. The complaint alleged that the Board is a recipient of federal funding for purposes of Title IX, that "the persistent sexual advances and harassment by the student G. F. upon [LaShonda] interfered with her ability to attend school and perform her studies and activities," and that "the deliberate indifference by Defendants to the unwelcome sexual advances of a student upon LaShonda created an intimidating, hostile, offensive and abusive school environment in violation of Title IX." The complaint sought compensatory and punitive damages, attorney's fees, and injunctive relief.

With regard to petitioner's claims under Title IX, the court dismissed the claims against individual defendants on the ground that only federally funded educational institutions are subject to liability in private causes of action under Title IX. As for the Board, the court concluded that Title IX provided no basis for liability absent an allegation "that the Board or an employee of the Board had any role in the harassment."

Petitioner appealed the District Court's decision dismissing her Title IX claim against the Board, and a panel of the Court of Appeals for the Eleventh Circuit reversed.

The Eleventh Circuit granted the Board's motion for rehearing en banc and affirmed the District Court's decision to dismiss petitioner's Title IX claim against the Board. The en banc court relied, primarily, on the theory that Title IX was passed pursuant to Congress' legislative authority under the Constitution's Spending Clause, U.S. Const., art. I, § 8, cl. 1, and that the statute therefore must provide potential recipients of federal education funding with "unambiguous notice of the conditions they are assuming when they accept" it. Title IX, the court reasoned, provides recipients with notice that they must stop their employees from engaging in discriminatory conduct, but the statute fails to provide a recipient with sufficient notice of a duty to prevent student-on-student harassment.

Writing in dissent, four judges urged that the statute, by declining to identify the perpetrator of discrimination, encompasses misconduct by third parties: "The identity of the perpetrator is simply irrelevant under the language" of the statute. The plain language, the dissenters reasoned, also provides recipients with sufficient notice that a failure to respond to student-on-student harassment could trigger liability for the district.

We granted certiorari in order to resolve a conflict in the Circuits over whether, and under what circumstances, a recipient of federal educational funds can be liable in a private damages action arising from student-on-student sexual harassment. . . . We now reverse.

II

Title IX provides, with certain exceptions not at issue here, that "no person in the United States shall, on the basis of sex, be excluded from participation in, be denied the benefits of, or be subjected to discrimination under any education program or activity receiving Federal financial assistance." 20 U.S.C. § 1681(a).

Congress authorized an administrative enforcement scheme for Title IX. Federal departments or agencies with the authority to provide financial assistance are entrusted to promulgate rules, regulations, and orders to enforce the objectives of § 1681, see § 1682, and these departments or agencies may rely on "any . . . means authorized by law," including the termination of funding, to give effect to the statute's restrictions.

There is no dispute here that the Board is a recipient of federal education funding for Title IX purposes. Nor do respondents support an argument that student-on-student harassment cannot rise to the level of "discrimination" for purposes of Title IX. Rather, at issue here is the question whether a recipient of federal education funding may be liable for damages under Title IX under any circumstances for discrimination in the form of student-on-student sexual harassment.

A

Petitioner urges that Title IX's plain language compels the conclusion that the statute is intended to bar recipients of federal funding from permitting this form of discrimination in their programs or activities. She emphasizes that the statute prohibits a student from being *"subjected to discrimination under any education program or activity receiving Federal financial assistance."* 20 U.S.C. § 1681 (emphasis supplied). It is Title IX's "unmistakable focus on the benefitted class," rather than the perpetrator, that, in petitioner's view, compels the conclusion that the statute works to protect students from the discriminatory misconduct of their peers.

Here, however, we are asked to do more than define the scope of the behavior that Title IX proscribes. We must determine whether a district's failure to respond to student-on-student harassment in its schools can support a private suit for money damages. Because we have repeatedly treated Title IX as legislation enacted pursuant . . . to Congress' authority under the Spending Clause, however, private damages actions are available only where recipients of federal funding had adequate notice that they could be liable for the conduct at issue. When Congress acts pursuant to its spending power, it generates legislation "much in the nature of a contract: in return for federal funds, the States agree to comply with federally imposed conditions." *Pennhurst State School and Hospital v. Halderman.* In interpreting language in spending legislation, we thus "insist that Congress speak with a clear voice," recognizing that "there can, of course, be no knowing acceptance [of the terms of the putative contract] if a State is unaware of the conditions [imposed by the legislation] or is unable to ascertain what is expected of it."

Invoking *Pennhurst*, respondents urge that Title IX provides no notice that recipients of federal educational funds could be liable in damages for harm arising from student-on-student harassment. Respondents contend, specifically, that the statute only proscribes misconduct by grant recipients, not third parties. Respondents argue, moreover, that it would be contrary to the very purpose of Spending Clause legislation to impose liability on a funding recipient for the misconduct of third parties, over whom recipients exercise little control.

We agree with respondents that a recipient of federal funds may be liable in damages under Title IX only for its own misconduct. The recipient itself must "exclude [persons] from participation in, . . . deny [persons] the benefits of, or . . . subject [persons] to discrimination under" its "programs or activities" in order to be liable under Title IX. The Government's enforcement power may only be exercised against the funding recipient, *see* § 1682, and we have not extended damages liability under Title IX to parties outside the scope of this power.

We disagree with respondents' assertion, however, that petitioner seeks to hold the Board liable for G. F.'s actions instead of its own. Here, petitioner attempts to hold the Board liable for its own decision to remain idle in the face of known student-on-student harassment in its schools. In *Gebser v. Lago Vista Independent Sch. Dist.* we concluded that a recipient of federal education funds may be liable in damages under Title IX where it is deliberately indifferent to known acts of sexual harassment by a teacher. . . . We recognized that the scope of liability in private damages actions under Title IX is circumscribed by *Pennhurst*'s requirement that funding recipients have notice of their potential liability. We also recognized, however, that this limitation on private damages actions is not a bar to liability where a funding recipient intentionally violates the statute. . . .

. . . [W]e concluded in *Gebser* that recipients could be liable in damages only where their own deliberate indifference effectively "caused" the discrimination. The high standard imposed in *Gebser* sought to eliminate any "risk that the recipient would be liable in damages not for its own official decision but instead for its employees' independent actions."

. . . .

We consider here whether the misconduct identified in *Gebser* — deliberate indifference to known acts of harassment — amounts to an intentional violation of Title IX, capable of supporting a private damages action, when the harasser is a student rather than a teacher. We conclude that, in certain limited circumstances, it does. As an initial matter, in *Gebser* we expressly rejected the use of agency principles in the Title IX context, noting the textual differences between Title IX and Title VII. Additionally, the regulatory scheme surrounding Title IX has long provided funding recipients with notice that they may be liable for their failure to respond to the discriminatory acts of certain non-agents. . . .

The common law, too, has put schools on notice that they may be held responsible under state law for their failure to protect students from the tortious acts of third parties *See* RESTATEMENT (SECOND) OF TORTS § 320, and Comment a (1965). In fact, state courts routinely uphold claims alleging that schools have been negligent in failing to protect their students from the torts of their peers.

This is not to say that the identity of the harasser is irrelevant. On the contrary, both the "deliberate indifference" standard and the language of Title IX narrowly circumscribe the set of parties whose known acts of sexual harassment can trigger some duty to respond on the part of funding recipients. Deliberate indifference makes sense as a theory of direct liability under Title IX only where the funding recipient has some control over the alleged harassment. A recipient cannot be directly liable for its indifference where it lacks the authority to take remedial action.

The language of Title IX itself — particularly when viewed in conjunction with the requirement that the recipient have notice of Title IX's prohibitions to be liable for damage — also cabins the range of misconduct that the statute proscribes. The statute's plain language confines the scope of prohibited conduct based on the recipient's degree of control over the harasser and the environment in which the harassment occurs. If a funding recipient does not engage in harassment directly, it may not be liable for damages unless its deliberate indifference "subjects" its students to harassment. That is, the deliberate indifference must, at a minimum, "cause [students] to undergo" harassment or "make them liable or vulnerable" to it. Random House Dictionary of the English Language 1415 (1966) (defining "subject" as "to cause to undergo the action of something specified; expose" or "to make liable or vulnerable; lay open; expose"); Webster's Third New International Dictionary of the English Language 2275 (1961) (defining "subject" as "to cause to undergo or submit to: make submit to a particular action or effect: expose"). Moreover, because the harassment must occur "under" "the operations of" a funding recipient, *see* 20 U.S.C. § 1681(a); § 1687 (defining "program or activity"), the harassment must take place in a context subject to the school district's control, Webster's Third New International Dictionary of the English Language, *supra*, at 2487 (defining "under" as "in or into a condition of subjection, regulation, or subordination"; "subject to the guidance and instruction of"); Random House Dictionary of the English Language, *supra*, at 1543 (defining "under" as "subject to the authority, direction, or supervision of").

These factors combine to limit a recipient's damages liability to circumstances wherein the recipient exercises substantial control over both the harasser and the context in which the known harassment occurs. Only then can the recipient be said to "expose" its students to harassment or "cause" them to undergo it "under" the recipient's programs. We agree with the dissent that these conditions are satisfied most easily and most obviously when the offender is an agent of the recipient. We rejected the use of agency analysis in *Gebser*, however, and we disagree that the term "under" somehow imports an agency requirement into Title IX. As noted above, the theory in *Gebser* was that the recipient was directly liable for its deliberate indifference to discrimination. Liability in that case did not arise because the "teacher's actions [were] treated" as those of the funding recipient; the district was directly liable for its own failure to act. The terms "subject" and "under" impose limits, but nothing about these terms requires the use of agency principles.

Where, as here, the misconduct occurs during school hours and on school grounds — the bulk of G. F.'s misconduct, in fact, took place in the classroom — the misconduct is taking place "under" an "operation" of the funding recipient. In these circumstances, the recipient retains substantial control over the context in which the harassment occurs. More importantly, however, in this setting the Board exercises significant control over the harasser. We have observed, for example, "that the nature of [the State's] power [over public schoolchildren] is custodial and tutelary, permitting a degree of supervision and control that could not be exercised over free adults." *Vernonia School Dist. 47J v. Acton*. On more than one occasion, this Court has recognized the importance of school officials' "comprehensive authority . . . , consistent with fundamental constitutional safeguards, to prescribe and control conduct in the schools." *Tinker v. Des Moines Independent Community School Dist.*; *see also New Jersey v. T. L. O.* ("The maintenance of discipline in the schools requires not only that students be restrained from assaulting one another, abusing drugs and alcohol, and committing other crimes, but also that students conform themselves to the standards of conduct prescribed by school authorities"); ("The ability to control and influence behavior exists to an even greater extent in the classroom than in the workplace . . ."). The common law, too, recognizes the school's disciplinary authority. *See* Restatement (Second) of Torts § 152 (1965). We thus conclude that recipients of federal funding may be liable for "subjecting" their students to discrimination where the recipient is deliberately indifferent to known acts of student-on-student sexual harassment and the harasser is under the school's disciplinary authority.

. . . .

We stress that our conclusion here — that recipients may be liable for their deliberate indifference to known acts of peer sexual harassment — does not mean that recipients can avoid liability only by purging their schools of actionable peer harassment or that administrators must engage in particular disciplinary action. We thus disagree with respondents' contention that, if Title IX provides a cause of action for student-on-student harassment, "nothing short of expulsion of every student accused of misconduct involving sexual overtones would protect school systems from liability or damages." Likewise, the dissent erroneously imagines that victims of peer harassment now have a Title IX right to make particular remedial demands. In fact, as we have previously noted, courts should refrain from second guessing the disciplinary decisions made by school administrators.

School administrators will continue to enjoy the flexibility they require so long as funding recipients are deemed "deliberately indifferent" to acts of student-on-student harassment only where the recipient's response to the harassment or lack thereof is clearly unreasonable in light of the known circumstances. The dissent consistently mischaracterizes this standard to require funding recipients to "remedy" peer harassment and to "ensure that . . . students conform their conduct to" certain rules. Title IX imposes no such requirements. On the contrary, the recipient must merely respond to known peer harassment in a manner that is not clearly unreasonable. This is not a mere "reasonableness" standard, as the dissent assumes. In an appropriate case, there is no reason why courts, on a motion to dismiss, for summary judgment, or for a directed verdict, could not identify a response as not "clearly unreasonable" as a matter of law.

Like the dissent, we acknowledge that school administrators shoulder substantial burdens as a result of legal constraints on their disciplinary authority. To the extent that these restrictions arise from federal statutes, Congress can review these burdens with attention to the difficult position in which such legislation may place our Nation's schools. We believe, however, that the standard set out here is sufficiently flexible to account both for the level of disciplinary authority available to the school and for the potential liability arising from certain forms of disciplinary action. A university might not, for example, be expected to exercise the same degree of control over its students that a grade school would enjoy, and it would be entirely reasonable for a school to refrain from a form of disciplinary action that would expose it to constitutional or statutory claims.

While it remains to be seen whether petitioner can show that the Board's response to reports of G. F.'s misconduct was clearly unreasonable in light of the known circumstances, petitioner may be able to show that the Board "subjected" LaShonda to discrimination by failing to respond in any way over a period of five months to complaints of G. F.'s in-school misconduct from LaShonda and other female students.

B

The requirement that recipients receive adequate notice of Title IX's proscriptions also bears on the proper definition of "discrimination" in the context of a private damages action. We have elsewhere concluded that sexual harassment is a form of discrimination for Title IX purposes and that Title IX proscribes harassment with sufficient clarity to satisfy *Pennhurst*'s notice requirement and serve as a basis for a damages action. Having previously determined that "sexual harassment" is "discrimination" in the school context under Title IX, we are constrained to conclude that student-on-student sexual harassment, if sufficiently severe, can likewise rise to the level of discrimination actionable under the statute. . . . The statute makes clear that, whatever else it prohibits, students must not be denied access to educational benefits and opportunities on the basis of gender. We thus conclude that funding recipients are properly held liable in damages only where they are deliberately indifferent to sexual harassment, of which they have actual knowledge, that is so severe, pervasive, and objectively offensive that it can be said to deprive the victims of access to the educational opportunities or benefits provided by the school.

The most obvious example of student-on-student sexual harassment capable of triggering a damages claim would thus involve the overt, physical deprivation of access to school resources. Consider, for example, a case in which male students physically threaten their female peers every day, successfully preventing the female students from using a particular school resource — an athletic field or a computer lab, for instance. District administrators are well aware of the daily ritual, yet they deliberately ignore requests for aid from the female students wishing to use the resource. The district's knowing refusal to take any action in response to such behavior would fly in the face of Title IX's core principles, and such deliberate indifference may appropriately be subject to claims for monetary damages. It is not necessary, however, to show physical exclusion to demonstrate that students have been deprived by the actions of another student or students of an educational opportunity on the basis of sex. Rather, a plaintiff must establish sexual harassment of students that is so severe, pervasive, and objectively offensive, and that so undermines and detracts from the victims' educational experience, that the victim-students are effectively denied equal access to an institution's resources and opportunities.

Whether gender-oriented conduct rises to the level of actionable "harassment" thus "depends on a constellation of surrounding circumstances, expectations, and relationships," *Oncale v. Sundowner Offshore Services, Inc.,* 523 U.S. 75, 82 (1998), including, but not limited to, the ages of the harasser and the victim and the number of individuals involved, *see* OCR Title IX Guidelines 12041–12042. Courts, moreover, must bear in mind that schools are unlike the adult workplace and that children may regularly interact in a manner that would be unacceptable among adults. *See, e.g.,* Brief for National School Boards Association et al. as Amici Curiae 11 (describing "dizzying array of immature . . . behaviors by students"). Indeed, at least early on, students are still learning how to interact appropriately with their peers. It is thus understandable that, in the school setting, students often engage in insults, banter, teasing, shoving, pushing, and gender-specific conduct that is upsetting to the students subjected to it. Damages are not available for simple acts of teasing and name-calling among school children, however, even where these comments target differences in gender. Rather, in the context of student-on-student harassment, damages are available only where the behavior is so severe, pervasive, and objectively offensive that it denies its victims the equal access to education that Title IX is designed to protect.

The dissent fails to appreciate these very real limitations on a funding recipient's liability under Title IX. It is not enough to show, as the dissent would read this opinion to provide, that a student has been "teased," or "called . . . offensive names." Comparisons to an "overweight child who skips gym class because the other children tease her about her size," the student "who refuses to wear glasses to avoid the taunts of 'four-eyes,' " and "the child who refuses to go to school because the school bully calls him a 'scardy-cat' at recess" are inapposite and misleading. Nor do we contemplate, much less hold, that a mere "decline in grades is enough to survive" a motion to dismiss. The drop-off in LaShonda's grades provides necessary evidence of a potential link between her education and G.F.'s misconduct, but petitioner's ability to state a cognizable claim here depends equally on the alleged persistence and severity of G.F.'s actions, not to mention the Board's alleged knowledge and deliberate indifference. We trust that the dissent's characterization of our opinion will not mislead courts to impose more sweeping liability than we read Title IX to require.

Moreover, the provision that the discrimination occur "under any education program or activity" suggests that the behavior be serious enough to have the systemic effect of denying the victim equal access to an educational program or activity. Although, in theory, a single instance of sufficiently severe one-on-one peer harassment could be said to have such an effect, we think it unlikely that Congress would have thought such behavior sufficient to rise to this level in light of the inevitability of student misconduct and the amount of litigation that would be invited by entertaining claims of official indifference to a single instance of one-on-one peer harassment. By limiting private damages actions to cases having a systemic effect on educational programs or activities, we reconcile the general principle that Title IX prohibits official indifference to known peer sexual harassment with the practical realities of responding to student behavior, realities that Congress could not have meant to be ignored. Even the dissent suggests that Title IX liability may arise when a funding recipient remains indifferent to severe, gender-based mistreatment played out on a "widespread level" among students.

The fact that it was a teacher who engaged in harassment in *Franklin* and *Gebser* is relevant. The relationship between the harasser and the victim necessarily affects the extent to which the misconduct can be said to breach Title IX's guarantee of equal access to educational benefits and to have a systemic effect on a program or activity. Peer harassment, in particular, is less likely to satisfy these requirements than is teacher-student harassment.

C

Applying this standard to the facts at issue here, we conclude that the Eleventh Circuit erred in dismissing petitioner's complaint. Petitioner alleges that her daughter was the victim of repeated acts of sexual harassment by G. F. over a 5-month period, and there are allegations in support of the conclusion that G. F.'s misconduct was severe, pervasive, and objectively offensive. The harassment was not only verbal; it included numerous acts of objectively offensive touching, and, indeed, G. F. ultimately pleaded guilty to criminal sexual misconduct. Moreover, the complaint alleges that there were multiple victims who were sufficiently disturbed by G. F.'s misconduct to seek an audience with the school principal. Further, petitioner contends that the harassment had a concrete, negative effect on her daughter's ability to receive an education. The complaint also suggests that petitioner may be able to show both actual knowledge and deliberate indifference on the part of the Board, which made no effort whatsoever either to investigate or to put an end to the harassment.

On this complaint, we cannot say "beyond doubt that [petitioner] can prove no set of facts in support of [her] claim which would entitle [her] to relief." Accordingly, the judgment of the United States Court of Appeals for the Eleventh Circuit is reversed, and the case is remanded for further proceedings consistent with this opinion.

It is so ordered.

JUSTICE KENNEDY, with whom THE CHIEF JUSTICE, JUSTICE SCALIA, and JUSTICE THOMAS *join, dissenting.*

The Court has held that Congress' power " 'to authorize expenditure of public moneys for public purposes is not limited by the direct grants of legislative power found in the Constitution.' " *South Dakota v. Dole,* 483 U.S. 203, 207 (1987) (quoting *United States v. Butler).* As a consequence, Congress can use its Spending Clause power to pursue objectives outside of "Article I's 'enumerated legislative fields' " by attaching conditions to the grant of federal funds. So understood, the Spending Clause power, if wielded without concern for the federal balance, has the potential to obliterate distinctions between national and local spheres of interest and power by permitting the federal government to set policy in the most sensitive areas of traditional state concern, areas which otherwise would lie outside its reach.

A vital safeguard for the federal balance is the requirement that, when Congress imposes a condition on the States' receipt of federal funds, it "must do so unambiguously." *Pennhurst State School and Hospital v. Halderman,* 451 U.S. 1, 17 (1981). As the majority acknowledges, "legislation enacted . . . pursuant to the spending power is much in the nature of a contract," and the legitimacy of Congress' exercise of its power to condition funding on state compliance with congressional conditions "rests on whether the State voluntarily and knowingly accepts the terms of the 'contract.' " "There can, of course, be no knowing acceptance [of the terms of the putative contract] if a State is unaware of the conditions [imposed by the legislation] or is unable to ascertain what is expected of it.' "

Our insistence that "Congress speak with a clear voice" to "enable the States to exercise their choice knowingly, cognizant of the consequences of their participation," *Pennhurst,* is not based upon some abstract notion of contractual fairness. Rather, it is a concrete safeguard in the federal system. Only if States receive clear notice of the conditions attached to federal funds can they guard against excessive federal intrusion into state affairs and be vigilant in policing the boundaries of federal power. *Cf. Dole, supra,* at 217 (O'CONNOR, J., dissenting) ("If the spending power is to be limited only by Congress' notion of the general welfare, the reality, given the vast financial resources of the

Federal Government, is that the Spending Clause gives 'power to the Congress to tear down the barriers, to invade the states' jurisdiction, and to become a parliament of the whole people, subject to no restrictions save such as are self-imposed"). While the majority purports to give effect to these principles, it eviscerates the clear-notice safeguard of our Spending Clause jurisprudence.

Title IX provides:

> "No person in the United States shall, on the basis of sex be [1] excluded from participation in, [2] be denied the benefits of, or [3] be subjected to discrimination under any education program or activity receiving Federal financial assistance." 20 U.S.C. § 1681(a).

To read the provision in full is to understand what is most striking about its application in this case: Title IX does not by its terms create any private cause of action whatsoever, much less define the circumstances in which money damages are available. The only private cause of action under Title IX is judicially implied.

The Court has encountered great difficulty in establishing standards for deciding when to imply a private cause of action under a federal statute which is silent on the subject. We try to conform the judicial judgment to the bounds of likely congressional purpose but, as we observed in *Gebser v. Lago Vista Independent School District*, defining the scope of the private cause of action in general, and the damages remedy in particular, "inherently entails a degree of speculation, since it addresses an issue on which Congress has not specifically spoken."

When the statute at issue is a Spending Clause statute, this element of speculation is particularly troubling because it is in significant tension with the requirement that Spending Clause legislation give States clear notice of the consequences of their acceptance of federal funds. Without doubt, the scope of potential damages liability is one of the most significant factors a school would consider in deciding whether to receive federal funds. Accordingly, the Court must not imply a private cause of action for damages unless it can demonstrate that the congressional purpose to create the implied cause of action is so manifest that the State, when accepting federal funds, had clear notice of the terms and conditions of its monetary liability.

Today the Court fails to heed, or even to acknowledge, these limitations on its authority. The remedial scheme the majority creates today is neither sensible nor faithful to Spending Clause principles. In order to make its case for school liability for peer sexual harassment, the majority must establish that Congress gave grant recipients clear and unambiguous notice that they would be liable in money damages for failure to remedy discriminatory acts of their students. The majority must also demonstrate that the statute gives schools clear notice that one child's harassment of another constitutes "discrimination" on the basis of sex within the meaning of Title IX, and that — as applied to individual cases — the standard for liability will enable the grant recipient to distinguish inappropriate childish behavior from actionable gender discrimination. The majority does not carry these burdens.

Instead, the majority finds statutory clarity where there is none and discovers indicia of congressional notice to the States in the most unusual of places. It treats the issue as one of routine statutory construction alone, and it errs even in this regard. In the end, the majority not only imposes on States liability that was unexpected and unknown, but the contours of which are, as yet, unknowable. The majority's opinion purports to be narrow, but the limiting principles it proposes are illusory. The fence the Court has built is made of little sticks, and it cannot contain the avalanche of liability now set in motion. The potential costs to our schools of today's decision are difficult to estimate, but they are so great that it is most unlikely Congress intended to inflict them.

The only certainty flowing from the majority's decision is that scarce resources will be diverted from educating our children and that many school districts, desperate to avoid Title IX peer harassment suits, will adopt whatever federal code of student conduct and discipline the Department of Education sees fit to impose upon them. The Nation's schoolchildren will learn their first lessons about federalism in classrooms where the federal government is the ever-present regulator. The federal government will have insinuated itself not only into one of the most traditional areas of state concern but also into one of the most sensitive areas of human affairs. This federal control of the discipline of our Nation's schoolchildren is contrary to our traditions and inconsistent with the sensible administration of our schools. Because Title IX did not give States unambiguous notice that accepting federal funds meant ceding to the federal government power over the day-to-day disciplinary decisions of schools, I dissent.

I

I turn to the first difficulty with the majority's decision. Schools cannot be held liable for peer sexual harassment because Title IX does not give them clear and unambiguous notice that they are liable in damages for failure to remedy discrimination by their students. As the majority acknowledges, Title IX prohibits only misconduct by grant recipients, not misconduct by third parties. ("The recipient itself must 'exclude [persons] from participation in, . . . deny [persons] the benefits of, or . . . subject [persons] to discrimination under' its 'programs or activities' in order to be liable under Title IX"). The majority argues, nevertheless, that a school "subjects" its students to discrimination when it knows of peer harassment and fails to respond appropriately.

The mere word "subjected" cannot bear the weight of the majority's argument. As we recognized in *Gebser*, the primary purpose of Title IX is "to prevent recipients of federal financial assistance from using the funds in a discriminatory manner." We stressed in *Gebser* that Title IX prevents discrimination by the grant recipient, whether through the acts of its principals or the acts of its agents. "Whereas Title VII aims centrally to compensate victims of discrimination, Title IX focuses more on 'protecting' individuals from discriminatory practices carried out by recipients of federal funds." The majority does not even attempt to argue that the school's failure to respond to discriminatory acts by students is discrimination by the school itself.

A

In any event, a plaintiff cannot establish a Title IX violation merely by showing that she has been "subjected to discrimination." Rather, a violation of Title IX occurs only if she is "subjected to discrimination under any education program or activity," 20 U.S.C. § 1681(a), where "program or activity" is defined as "all of the operations of" a grant recipient, § 1687.

Under the most natural reading of this provision, discrimination violates Title IX only if it is authorized by, or in accordance with, the actions, activities, or policies of the grant recipient. *See* Webster's Third New International Dictionary 2487 (1981) (defining "under" as "required by: in accordance with: bound by"); American Heritage Dictionary of the English Language 1395 (1981) (defining "under" as "with the authorization of; attested by; by virtue of"); Random House Dictionary of the English Language 2059 (2d ed. 1987) (defining "under" as "authorized, warranted, or attested by" or "in accordance with"); *see also* 43 Words and Phrases 149–152 (1969) (citing cases defining "under" as, *inter alia,* " 'in accordance with' and 'in conformity with' "; "indicating subjection, guidance or control, and meaning 'by authority of' "; " 'by,' 'by reason of,' or 'by means of' "; and " 'by virtue of,' which is defined . . . as meaning 'by or through the authority of' "). This reading reflects the common legal usage of the term "under" to mean pursuant to, in accordance with, or as authorized or provided by.

It is not enough, then, that the alleged discrimination occur in a "context subject to the school district's control." The discrimination must actually be "controlled by" — that is, be authorized by, pursuant to, or in accordance with, school policy or actions. . . .

This reading is also consistent with the fact that the discrimination must be "under" the "operations" of the grant recipient. The term "operations" connotes active and affirmative participation by the grant recipient, not merely inaction or failure to respond. *See* Black's Law Dictionary 1092 (6th ed. 1990) (defining "operation," as an "exertion of power; the process of operating or mode of action; an effect brought about in accordance with a definite plan; action; activity").

Teacher sexual harassment of students is "under" the school's program or activity in certain circumstances, but student harassment is not. Our decision in *Gebser* recognizes that a grant recipient acts through its agents and thus, under certain limited circumstances, even tortious acts by teachers may be attributable to the school. We noted in *Gebser* that, in contrast to Title VII, which defines "employer" to include "any agent" — Title IX "contains no comparable reference to an educational institution's 'agents,' and so does not expressly call for application of agency principles." As a result, we declined to incorporate principles of agency liability, such as a strict application of vicarious liability, that would conflict with the Spending Clause's notice requirement and Title IX's express administrative enforcement scheme.

Contrary to the majority's assertion, however, we did not abandon agency principles altogether. Rather, we sought in *Gebser* to identify those employee actions which could fairly be attributed to the grant recipient by superimposing additional Spending Clause notice requirements on traditional agency principles. We concluded that, because of the Spending Clause overlay, a teacher's discrimination is attributable to the school only when the school has actual notice of that harassment and is "deliberately indifferent." The agency relation between the school and the teacher is thus a necessary, but not sufficient, condition of school liability. Where the heightened requirements for attribution are met, the teacher's actions are treated as the grant recipient's actions. In those circumstances, then, the teacher sexual harassment is "under" the operations of the school.

I am aware of no basis in law or fact, however, for attributing the acts of a student to a school and, indeed, the majority does not argue that the school acts through its students. Discrimination by one student against another therefore cannot be "under" the school's program or activity as required by Title IX. The majority's imposition of liability for peer sexual harassment thus conflicts with the most natural interpretation of Title IX's "under a program or activity" limitation on school liability. At the very least, my reading undermines the majority's implicit claim that Title IX imposes an unambiguous duty on schools to remedy peer sexual harassment.

B

1

Quite aside from its disregard for the "under the program" limitation of Title IX, the majority's reading is flawed in other respects. The majority contends that a school's deliberate indifference to known student harassment "subjects" students to harassment — that is, "causes [students] to undergo" harassment. The majority recognizes, however, that there must be some limitation on the third-party conduct that the school can fairly be said to cause. In search of a principle, the majority asserts, without much elaboration, that one causes discrimination when one has some "degree of control" over the discrimination and fails to remedy it.

To state the majority's test is to understand that it is little more than an exercise in arbitrary line-drawing. The majority does not explain how we are to determine what degree of control is sufficient — or, more to the point, how the States were on clear notice that the Court would draw the line to encompass students. . . .

Given the state of gender discrimination law at the time Title IX was passed, . . . there is no basis to think that Congress contemplated liability for a school's failure to remedy discriminatory acts by students or that the States would believe the statute imposed on them a clear obligation to do so. When Title IX was enacted in 1972, the concept of "sexual harassment" as gender discrimination had not been recognized or considered by the courts. *See generally* C. MacKinnon, Sexual Harassment of Working Women: A Case of Sex Discrimination 59–72 (1979). The types of discrimination that were recognized — discriminatory admissions standards, denial of access to programs or resources, hiring, etc. — could not be engaged in by students. *See, e.g.,* 20 U.S.C. § 1681(a)(2) (referencing application of Title IX prohibitions to school admissions).

2

The majority nonetheless appears to see no need to justify drawing the "enough control" line to encompass students. In truth, however, a school's control over its students is much more complicated and limited than the majority acknowledges. A public school does not control its students in the way it controls its teachers or those with whom it contracts. Most public schools do not screen or select students, and their power to discipline students is far from unfettered.

Public schools are generally obligated by law to educate all students who live within defined geographic boundaries. Indeed, the Constitution of almost every State in the country guarantees the State's students a free primary and secondary public education. In at least some States, moreover, there is a continuing duty on schools to educate even students who are suspended or expelled. *See, e.g., Phillip Leon M. v. Board of Education*, 199 W. Va. 400, 484 S.E.2d 909 (1996) (holding that the education clause of the West Virginia Constitution confers on students a fundamental right to an education and requires that a county school board provide alternative educational programs, such as an alternative school, to students who are expelled or suspended for an extended period for bringing guns to school). Schools that remove a harasser from the classroom and then attempt to fulfill their continuing-education obligation by placing the harasser in any kind of group setting, rather than by hiring expensive tutors for each student, will find themselves at continuing risk of Title IX suits brought by the other students in the alternative education program.

In addition, federal law imposes constraints on school disciplinary actions. This Court has held, for example, that due process requires "at the very minimum," that a student facing suspension "be given some kind of notice and afforded some kind of hearing."

The Individuals with Disabilities Education Act (IDEA), 20 U.S.C. 1400 et seq., (1994 ed., Supp. III), moreover, places strict limits on the ability of schools to take disciplinary actions against students with behavior disorder disabilities, even if the disability was not diagnosed prior to the incident triggering discipline. *See, e.g.,* § 1415(f)(1) (parents entitled to hearing when school proposes to change disabled student's educational placement); § 1415(k)(1)(A) (school authorities can only "order a change in the placement of a child with a disability . . . to an appropriate interim alternative educational setting, another setting, or suspension" for up to "10 school days" unless student's offense involved a weapon or illegal drugs); § 1415(k)(8) ("[A] child who has not been determined to be eligible for special education . . . and who has engaged in behavior that violated any [school rule], may assert any of the protections" of the subchapter if the school "had knowledge . . . that the child was a child with a disability before the behavior that precipitated the disciplinary action occurred"); § 1415(k)(8)(B)(ii) (school "deemed to have knowledge that a child is a child with a disability if . . . the behavior or performance of the child demonstrates the need for such [special education and related] services"). "Disability," as defined in the Act, includes "serious emotional disturbance," § 1401(3)(A)(i), which the DOE, in turn, has defined as a "condition exhibiting . . . over a long period of time and to a marked degree that adversely affects a child's educational performance" an "inability to build or maintain satisfactory interpersonal relationships with peers and teachers" or "inappropriate types of behavior or feelings under normal circumstances." 34 CFR § 300.7(b)(9) (1998). If, as the majority would have us believe, the behavior that constitutes actionable peer sexual harassment so deviates from the normal teasing and jostling of adolescence that it puts schools on clear notice of potential liability, then a student who engages in such harassment may have at least a colorable claim of severe emotional disturbance within the meaning of IDEA. When imposing disciplinary sanction on a student harasser who might assert a colorable IDEA claim, the school must navigate a complex web of statutory provisions and DOE regulations that significantly limit its discretion.

The practical obstacles schools encounter in ensuring that thousands of immature students conform their conduct to acceptable norms may be even more significant than the legal obstacles. School districts cannot exercise the same measure of control over thousands of students that they do over a few hundred adult employees. The limited resources of our schools must be conserved for basic educational services. Some schools lack the resources even to deal with serious problems of violence and are already overwhelmed with disciplinary problems of all kinds.

Perhaps even more startling than its broad assumptions about school control over primary and secondary school students is the majority's failure to grapple in any meaningful way with the distinction between elementary and secondary schools, on the one hand, and universities on the other. The majority bolsters its argument that schools can control their students' actions by quoting our decision in *Vernonia School Dist. 47J v. Acton*, for the proposition that "the nature of [the State's] power [over public school children] is custodial and tutelary, permitting a degree of supervision and control that could not be exercised over free adults." Yet the majority's holding would appear to apply with equal force to universities, which do not exercise custodial and tutelary power over their adult students.

A university's power to discipline its students for speech that may constitute sexual harassment is also circumscribed by the First Amendment. A number of federal courts have already confronted difficult problems raised by university speech codes designed to deal with peer sexual and racial harassment. *See, e.g., Dambrot v. Central Michigan University*, 55 F.3d 1177 (CA6 1995) (striking down university discriminatory harassment policy because it was overbroad, vague, and not a valid prohibition on fighting words); *UWM Post, Inc. v. Board of Regents of University of Wisconsin System*, 774 F. Supp. 1163 (ED Wis. 1991) (striking down university speech code that prohibited, *inter alia*, " 'discriminatory comments' " directed at an individual that " 'intentionally . . . demean' " the " 'sex . . . of the individual' " and " 'create an intimidating, hostile or demeaning environment for education, university related work, or other university-authorized activity' "); *Doe v. University of Michigan*, 721 F. Supp. 852 (ED Mich. 1989) (similar); *Iota XI Chapter of Sigma Chi Fraternity v. George Mason University*, 993 F.2d 386 (CA4 1993) (overturning on First Amendment grounds university's sanctions on a fraternity for conducting an "ugly woman contest" with "racist and sexist" overtones).

The difficulties associated with speech codes simply underscore the limited nature of a university's control over student behavior that may be viewed as sexual harassment. Despite the fact that the majority relies on the assumption that schools exercise a great deal of control over their students to justify creating the private cause of action in the first instance, it does not recognize the obvious limits on a university's ability to control its students as a reason to doubt the propriety of a private cause of action for peer harassment. It simply uses them as a factor in determining whether the university's response was reasonable.

3

The majority's presentation of its control test illustrates its own discomfort with the rule it has devised. Rather than beginning with the language of Title IX itself, the majority begins with our decision in *Gebser* and appears to discover there a sweeping legal duty — divorced from agency principles — for schools to remedy third-party discrimination against students. The majority then finds that the DOE's Title IX regulations and state common law gave States the requisite notice that they would be liable in damages for failure to fulfill this duty. Only then does the majority turn to the language of Title IX itself — not, it appears, to find a duty or clear notice to the States, for that the majority assumes has already been established, but rather to suggest a limit on the breathtaking scope of the liability the majority thinks is so clear under the statute. ("These factors [("subjects" and "under")] combine to limit a recipient's damages liability to circumstances wherein the recipient exercises substantial control over both the harasser and the context in which the known harassment occurs").

Our decision in *Gebser* did not, of course, recognize some ill-defined, free-standing legal duty on schools to remedy discrimination by third parties. In particular, *Gebser* gave schools no notice whatsoever that they might be liable on the majority's novel theory that a school "subjects" a student to third-party discrimination if it exercises some measure of control over the third party. We quoted the "subjected to discrimination" language only once in *Gebser,* when we quoted the text of Title IX in full, and we did not use the word "control." Instead, we affirmed that Title IX prohibits discrimination by the grant recipient.

Neither the DOE's Title IX regulations nor state tort law, moreover, could or did provide States the notice required by our Spending Clause principles. The majority contends that the DOE's Title IX regulations have "long provided funding recipients with notice that they may be liable for their failure to respond to the discriminatory acts of certain non-agents." Even assuming that DOE regulations could give schools the requisite notice, they did not do so. Not one of the regulations the majority cites suggests that schools may be held liable in money damages for failure to respond to third-party discrimination.

In addition, as discussed above, the DOE regulations provide no support for the proposition that schools were on notice that students were among those "non-agents" whose actions the schools were bound to remedy. Most of the regulations cited by the majority merely forbid grant recipients to give affirmative aid to third parties who discriminate. . . .

Requiring a school to take affirmative steps to remedy harassment by its students imposes a much heavier burden on schools than prohibiting affirmative aid or effective delegation of school functions to an entity that discriminates. Notice of these latter responsibilities, then, can hardly be said to encompass clear notice of the former. . . .

The majority also concludes that state tort law provided States the requisite notice. It is a non sequitur to suppose, however, that a State knows it is liable under a federal statute simply because the underlying conduct might form the basis for a state tort action. In any event, it is far from clear that Georgia law gave the Monroe County Board of Education notice that it would be liable even under state law for failure to respond reasonably to known student harassment. *See, e.g., Holbrook v. Executive Conference Center, Inc.*, 219 Ga. App. 104, 106 (1996) (holding that school districts are entitled to sovereign immunity for claims based on their supervision of students unless the school displayed "wilfulness, malice, or corruption").

The majority's final observation about notice confirms just how far it has strayed from the basic Spending Clause principle that Congress must, through the clear terms of the statute, give States notice as to what the statute requires. The majority contends that schools were on notice because they "were being told" by a 1993 National School Boards Association publication that peer sexual harassment might trigger Title IX liability. By treating a publication designed to help school lawyers prevent and guard against school liability as a reliable indicium of congressional notice, the majority has transformed a litigation manual — which, like all such manuals, errs on the side of caution in describing potential liability — into a self-fulfilling prophecy. It seems schools cannot even discuss potential liabilities amongst themselves without somehow stipulating that Congress had some specified intent.

II

Our decision in *Gebser* makes clear that the Spending Clause clear-notice rule requires both that the recipients be on general notice of the kind of conduct the statute prohibits, and — at least when money damages are sought — that they be on notice that illegal conduct is occurring in a given situation.

Title IX, however, gives schools neither notice that the conduct the majority labels peer "sexual harassment" is gender discrimination within the meaning of the Act nor any guidance in distinguishing in individual cases between actionable discrimination and the immature behavior of children and adolescents. The majority thus imposes on schools potentially crushing financial liability for student conduct that is not prohibited in clear terms by Title IX and that cannot, even after today's opinion, be identified by either schools or courts with any precision.

The law recognizes that children — particularly young children — are not fully accountable for their actions because they lack the capacity to exercise mature judgment. *See, e.g.,* 1 E. FARNSWORTH, FARNSWORTH ON CONTRACTS § 4.4 (2d ed. 1998) (discussing minor's ability to disaffirm a contract into which he has entered). It should surprise no one, then, that the schools that are the primary locus of most children's social development are rife with inappropriate behavior by children who are just learning to interact with their peers. The amici on the front lines of our schools describe the situation best:

> Unlike adults in the workplace, juveniles have limited life experiences or familial influences upon which to establish an understanding of appropriate behavior. The real world of school discipline is a rough-and-tumble place where students practice newly learned vulgarities, erupt with anger, tease and embarrass each other, share offensive notes, flirt, push and shove in the halls, grab and offend. Brief for National School Boards Association et al. as *Amici Curiae* 10-11 (hereinafter school amici).

No one contests that much of this "dizzying array of immature or uncontrollable behaviors by students" is inappropriate, even "objectively offensive" at times, and that parents and schools have a moral and ethical responsibility to help students learn to interact with their peers in an appropriate manner. It is doubtless the case, moreover, that much of this inappropriate behavior is directed toward members of the opposite sex, as children in the throes of adolescence struggle to express their emerging sexual identities.

It is a far different question, however, whether it is either proper or useful to label this immature, childish behavior gender discrimination. Nothing in Title IX suggests that Congress even contemplated this question, much less answered it in the affirmative in unambiguous terms. . . .

Contrary to the majority's assertion, however, respondents have made a cogent and persuasive argument that the type of student conduct alleged by petitioner should not be considered "sexual harassment," much less gender discrimination actionable under Title IX:

> At the time Petitioner filed her complaint, no court, including this Court had recognized the concept of sexual harassment in any context other than the employment context. Nor had any Court extended the concept of sexual harassment to the misconduct of emotionally and socially immature children. . . . Brief for Respondents 12–13 (citation omitted).

> *See also* Brief for Independent Women's Forum as *Amicus Curiae* 19 (questioning whether "at the primary and secondary school level" it is proper to label "sexual misconduct by students" as "sexual harassment" because there is no power relationship between the harasser and the victim).

Likewise, the majority's assertion that *Gebser* and *Franklin* settled the question is little more than ipse dixit. *Gebser* and *Franklin* themselves did nothing more than cite *Meritor Savings Bank, FSB v. Vinson*, a Title VII case, for the proposition that "when a supervisor sexually harasses a subordinate because of the subordinate's sex, that supervisor 'discriminates' on the basis of sex." To treat that proposition as establishing that the student conduct at issue here is gender discrimination is to erase, in one stroke, all differences between children and adults, peers and teachers, schools and workplaces.

In reality, there is no established body of federal or state law on which courts may draw in defining the student conduct that qualifies as Title IX gender discrimination. Analogies to Title VII hostile environment harassment are inapposite, because schools are not workplaces and children are not adults. The norms of the adult workplace that have defined hostile environment sexual harassment are not easily translated to peer relationships in schools, where teenage romantic relationships and dating are a part of everyday life. Analogies to Title IX teacher sexual harassment of students are similarly flawed. A teacher's sexual overtures toward a student are always inappropriate; a teenager's romantic overtures to a classmate (even when persistent and unwelcome) are an inescapable part of adolescence.

The majority admits that, under its approach, "whether gender-oriented conduct rises to the level of actionable 'harassment' . . . 'depends on a constellation of surrounding circumstances, expectations, and relationships, including, but not limited to, the ages of the harasser and the victim and the number of individuals involved.'" The majority does not explain how a school is supposed to discern from this mishmash of factors what is actionable discrimination. Its multifactored balancing test is a far cry from the clarity we demand of Spending Clause legislation.

The difficulties schools will encounter in identifying peer sexual harassment are already evident in teachers' manuals designed to give guidance on the subject. For example, one teachers' manual on peer sexual harassment suggests that sexual harassment in kindergarten through third grade includes a boy being "put down" on the playground "because he wants to play house with the girls" or a girl being "put down because she shoots baskets better than the boys." MINNESOTA DEPT. OF EDUCATION, GIRLS AND BOYS GETTING ALONG: TEACHING SEXUAL HARASSMENT PREVENTION IN THE ELEMENTARY CLASSROOM 65 (1993). Yet another manual suggests that one student saying to another, "You look nice" could be sexual harassment, depending on the "tone of voice," how the student looks at the other, and "who else is around." N. STEIN & L. SJOSTROM, FLIRTING OR HURTING? A TEACHER'S GUIDE ON STUDENT-TO-STUDENT SEXUAL HARASSMENT IN SCHOOLS (GRADES 6 THROUGH 12) 14 (1994). Blowing a kiss is also suspect. This confusion will likely be compounded once the sexual-harassment label is invested with the force of federal law, backed up by private damages suits.

The only guidance the majority gives schools in distinguishing between the "simple acts of teasing and name-calling among school children," said not to be a basis for suit even when they "target differences in gender" and actionable peer sexual harassment is, in reality, no guidance at all. The majority proclaims that "in the context of student-on-student harassment, damages are available only in the situation where the behavior is so serious, pervasive, and objectively offensive that it denies its victims the equal access to education that Title IX is designed to protect." The majority does not even purport to explain, however, what constitutes an actionable denial of "equal access to education." Is equal access denied when a girl who tires of being chased by the boys at recess refuses to go outside? When she cannot concentrate during class because she is worried about the recess activities? When she pretends to be sick one day so she can stay home from school? It appears the majority is content to let juries decide.

The majority's reference to a "systemic effect" does nothing to clarify the content of its standard. The majority appears to intend that requirement to do no more than exclude the possibility that a single act of harassment perpetrated by one student on one other student can form the basis for an actionable claim. That is a small concession indeed.

The only real clue the majority gives schools about the dividing line between actionable harassment that denies a victim equal access to education and mere inappropriate teasing is a profoundly unsettling one: On the facts of this case, petitioner has stated a claim because she alleged, in the majority's words, "that the harassment had a concrete, negative effect on her daughter's ability to receive an education." In petitioner's words, the effects that might have been visible to the school were that her daughter's grades "dropped" and her "ability to concentrate on her school work [was] affected." Almost all adolescents experience these problems at one time or another as they mature.

III

The majority's inability to provide any workable definition of actionable peer harassment simply underscores the myriad ways in which an opinion that purports to be narrow is, in fact, so broad that it will support untold numbers of lawyers who will prove adept at presenting cases that will withstand the defendant school districts' pretrial motions. Each of the barriers to run-away litigation the majority offers us crumbles under the weight of even casual scrutiny.

For example, the majority establishes what sounds like a relatively high threshold for liability — "denial of equal access" to education — and, almost in the same breath, makes clear that alleging a decline in grades is enough to survive 12(b)(6) and, it follows, to state a winning claim. The majority seems oblivious to the fact that almost every child, at some point, has trouble in school because he or she is being teased by his or her peers. The girl who wants to skip recess because she is teased by the boys is no different from the overweight child who skips gym class because the other children tease her about her size in the locker room; or the child who risks flunking out because he refuses to wear glasses to avoid the taunts of "four-eyes"; or the child who refuses to go to school because the school bully calls him a "scaredy-cat" at recess. Most children respond to teasing in ways that detract from their ability to learn. The majority's test for actionable harassment will, as a result, sweep in almost all of the more innocuous conduct it acknowledges as a ubiquitous part of school life.

The string of adjectives the majority attaches to the word "harassment" — "severe, pervasive, and objectively offensive" — likewise fails to narrow the class of conduct that can trigger liability, since the touchstone for determining whether there is Title IX liability is the effect on the child's ability to get an education. Indeed, the Court's reliance on the impact on the child's educational experience suggests that the "objective offensiveness" of a comment is to be judged by reference to a reasonable child at whom the comments were aimed. Not only is that standard likely to be quite expansive, it also gives schools — and juries — little guidance, requiring them to attempt to gauge the sensitivities of, for instance, the average seven year old.

The majority assures us that its decision will not interfere with school discipline and instructs that, "as we have previously noted, courts should refrain from second guessing the disciplinary decisions made by school administrators." The obvious reason for the majority's expressed reluctance to allow courts and litigants to second-guess school disciplinary decisions is that school officials are usually in the best position to judge the seriousness of alleged harassment and to devise an appropriate response. The problem is that the majority's test, in fact, invites courts and juries to second-guess school administrators in every case, to judge in each instance whether the school's response was "clearly unreasonable." A reasonableness standard, regardless of the modifier, transforms every disciplinary decision into a jury question. *Cf. Doe v. University of Illinois,* 138 F.3d 653, 655 (CA7 1998) (holding that college student had stated a Title IX claim for peer sexual harassment even though school officials had suspended two male students for 10 days and transferred another out of her biology class).

Another professed limitation the majority relies upon is that the recipient will be liable only where the acts of student harassment are "known." The majority's enunciation of the standard begs the obvious question: known to whom? Yet the majority says not one word about the type of school employee who must know about the harassment before it is actionable.

The majority's silence is telling. The deliberate indifference liability we recognized in *Gebser* was predicated on notice to "an official of the recipient entity with authority to take corrective action to end the discrimination." The majority gives no indication that it believes the standard to be any different in this context and — given its extensive reliance on the *Gebser* standard throughout the opinion — appears to adopt the *Gebser* notice standard by implication. At least the courts adjudicating Title IX peer harassment claims are likely to so conclude.

By choosing not to adopt the standard in explicit terms, the majority avoids having to confront the bizarre implications of its decision. In the context of teacher harassment, the *Gebser* notice standard imposes some limit on school liability. Where peer harassment is the discrimination, however, it imposes no limitation at all. In most cases of student misbehavior, it is the teacher who has authority, at least in the first instance, to punish the student and take other measures to remedy the harassment. The anomalous result will be that, while a school district cannot be held liable for a teacher's sexual harassment of a student without notice to the school board (or at least to the principal), the district can be held liable for a teacher's failure to remedy peer harassment. The threshold for school liability, then, appears to be lower when the harasser is a student than when the harasser is a teacher who is an agent of the school. The absurdity of this result confirms that it was neither contemplated by Congress nor anticipated by the States.

The majority's limitations on peer sexual harassment suits cannot hope to contain the flood of liability the Court today begins. The elements of the Title IX claim created by the majority will be easy not only to allege but also to prove. A female plaintiff who pleads only that a boy called her offensive names, that she told a teacher, that the teacher's response was unreasonable, and that her school performance suffered as a result, appears to state a successful claim.

There will be no shortage of plaintiffs to bring such complaints. Our schools are charged each day with educating millions of children. Of those millions of students, a large percentage will, at some point during their school careers, experience something they consider sexual harassment. A 1993 Study by the American Association of University Women Educational Foundation, for instance, found that "fully 4 out of 5 students (81%) report that they have been the target of some form of sexual harassment during their school lives." HOSTILE HALLWAYS: THE AAUW SURVEY ON SEXUAL HARASSMENT IN AMERICA'S SCHOOLS 7 (1993). The number of potential lawsuits against our schools is staggering.

The cost of defending against peer sexual harassment suits alone could overwhelm many school districts, particularly since the majority's liability standards will allow almost any plaintiff to get to summary judgment, if not to a jury. In addition, there are no damages caps on the judicially implied private cause of action under Title IX. As a result, school liability in one peer sexual harassment suit could approach, or even exceed, the total federal funding of many school districts. Petitioner, for example, seeks damages of $ 500,000 in this case. Respondent school district received approximately $ 679,000 in federal aid in 1992-1993. The school district sued in *Gebser* received only $ 120,000 in federal funds a year. 524 U.S. 289–290. Indeed, the entire 1992-1993 budget of that district was only $ 1.6 million.

The limitless liability confronting our schools under the implied Title IX cause of action puts schools in a far worse position than businesses; when Congress established the express cause of action for money damages under Title VII, it prescribed damage caps. *See Gebser*. . . . Adopting petitioners' position would amount, then, to allowing unlimited recovery of damages under Title IX where Congress has not spoken on the subject of either the right or the remedy, and in the face of evidence that when Congress expressly considered both in Title VII it restricted the amount of damages available"). In addition, in contrast to Title VII, Title IX makes no provision for agency investigation and conciliation of complaints (prior to the filing of a case in federal court) that could weed out frivolous suits or settle meritorious ones at minimal cost.

The prospect of unlimited Title IX liability will, in all likelihood, breed a climate of fear that encourages school administrators to label even the most innocuous of childish conduct sexual harassment. It would appear to be no coincidence that, not long after the DOE issued its proposed policy guidance warning that schools could be liable for peer sexual harassment in the fall of 1996, a North Carolina school suspended a 6-year-old boy who kissed a female classmate on the cheek for sexual harassment, on the theory that "unwelcome is unwelcome at any age." LOS ANGELES TIMES, Sept. 25, 1996, p. A11. A week later, a New York school suspended a second-grader who kissed a classmate and ripped a button off her skirt. BUFFALO NEWS, Oct. 2, 1996, p. A16. The second grader said that he got the idea from his favorite book "Corduroy," about a bear with a missing button. School administrators said only, "We were given guidelines as to why we suspend children. We follow the guidelines."

At the college level, the majority's holding is sure to add fuel to the debate over campus speech codes that, in the name of preventing a hostile educational environment, may infringe students' First Amendment rights. Indeed, under the majority's control principle, schools presumably will be responsible for remedying conduct that occurs even in student dormitory rooms. As a result, schools may well be forced to apply workplace norms in the most private of domains.

Even schools that resist overzealous enforcement may find that the most careful and reasoned response to a sexual harassment complaint nonetheless provokes litigation. Speaking with the voice of experience, the school *amici* remind us, "history shows that, no matter what a school official chooses to do, someone will be unhappy. Student offenders almost always view their punishment as too strict, and student complainants almost always view an offender's punishment as too lax."

A school faced with a peer sexual harassment complaint in the wake of the majority's decision may well be beset with litigation from every side. One student's demand for a quick response to her harassment complaint will conflict with the alleged harasser's demand for due process. Another student's demand for a harassment-free classroom will conflict with the alleged harasser's claim to a mainstream placement under the Individuals with Disabilities Education Act or with his state constitutional right to a continuing, free public education. On college campuses, and even in secondary schools, a student's claim that the school should remedy a sexually hostile environment will conflict with the alleged harasser's claim that his speech, even if offensive, is protected by the First Amendment. In each of these situations, the school faces the risk of suit, and maybe even multiple suits, regardless of its response. *See Doe v. University of Illinois,* 138 F.3d at 679 (POSNER, C.J., dissenting from denial of rehearing en banc) ("Liability for failing to prevent or rectify sexual harassment of one student by another places a school on a razor's edge, since the remedial measures that it takes against the alleged harasser are as likely to expose the school to a suit by him as a failure to take those measures would be to expose the school to a suit by the victim of the alleged harassment").

The majority's holding in this case appears to be driven by the image of the school administration sitting idle every day while male students commandeer a school's athletic field or computer lab and prevent female students from using it through physical threats. Title IX might provide a remedy in such a situation, however, without resort to the majority's unprecedented theory of school liability for student harassment. If the school usually disciplines students for threatening each other and prevents them from blocking others' access to school facilities, then the school's failure to enforce its rules when the boys target the girls on a widespread level, day after day, may support an inference that the school's decision not to respond is itself based on gender. That pattern of discriminatory response could form the basis of a Title IX action. (Contrary to the majority's assertion we do not suggest that mere indifference to gender-based mistreatment — even if widespread — is enough to trigger Title IX liability. We suggest only that a clear pattern of discriminatory enforcement of school rules could raise an inference that the school itself is discriminating. Recognizing that the school itself might discriminate based on gender in the enforcement of its rules is a far cry from recognizing Title

IX liability based on the majority's expansive theory that a school "subjects" its students to third-party discrimination when it has some control over the harasser and fails to take corrective action.)

Even more important, in most egregious cases the student will have state-law remedies available to her. The student will often have recourse against the offending student (or his parents) under state tort law. In some cases, like this one, the perpetrator may also be subject to criminal sanctions. And, as the majority notes, the student may, in some circumstances, have recourse against the school under state law.

Disregarding these state-law remedies for student misbehavior and the incentives that our schools already have to provide the best possible education to all of their students, the majority seeks, in effect, to put an end to student misbehavior by transforming Title IX into a Federal Student Civility Code. I fail to see how federal courts will administer school discipline better than the principals and teachers to whom the public has entrusted that task or how the majority's holding will help the vast majority of students, whose educational opportunities will be diminished by the diversion of school funds to litigation. The private cause of action the Court creates will justify a corps of federal administrators in writing regulations on student harassment. It will also embroil schools and courts in endless litigation over what qualifies as peer sexual harassment and what constitutes a reasonable response.

In the final analysis, this case is about federalism. Yet the majority's decision today says not one word about the federal balance. Preserving our federal system is a legitimate end in itself. It is, too, the means to other ends. It ensures that essential choices can be made by a government more proximate to the people than the vast apparatus of federal power. Defining the appropriate role of schools in teaching and supervising children who are beginning to explore their own sexuality and learning how to express it to others is one of the most complex and sensitive issues our schools face. Such decisions are best made by parents and by the teachers and school administrators who can counsel with them. The delicacy and immense significance of teaching children about sexuality should cause the Court to act with great restraint before it displaces state and local governments.

Heedless of these considerations, the Court rushes onward, finding that the cause of action it creates is necessary to effect the congressional design. It is not. Nothing in Title IX suggests that Congress intended or contemplated the result the Court reaches today, much less dictated it in unambiguous terms. Today's decision cannot be laid at the feet of Congress; it is the responsibility of the Court.

The Court must always use great care when it shapes private causes of action without clear guidance from Congress, but never more so than when the federal balance is at stake. As we recognized in *Gebser*, the definition of an implied cause of action inevitably implicates some measure of discretion in the Court to shape a sensible remedial scheme. Whether the Court ever should have embarked on this endeavor under a Spending Clause statute is open to question. What should be clear beyond any doubt, however, is that the Court is duty-bound to exercise that discretion with due regard for federalism and the unique role of the States in our system. The Court today disregards that obligation. I can conceive of few interventions more intrusive upon the delicate and vital relations between teacher and student, between student and student, and between the State and its citizens than the one the Court creates today by its own hand. Trusted principles of federalism are superseded by a more contemporary imperative.

Perhaps the most grave, and surely the most lasting, disservice of today's decision is that it ensures the Court's own disregard for the federal balance soon will be imparted to our youngest citizens. The Court clears the way for the federal government to claim center stage in America's classrooms. Today's decision mandates to teachers instructing and supervising their students the dubious assistance of federal court plaintiffs and their lawyers and makes the federal courts the final arbiters of school policy and of almost every disagreement between students. Enforcement of the federal right recognized by the majority means that federal influence will permeate everything from curriculum decisions to day-to-day classroom logistics and interactions. After today, Johnny will find that the routine problems of adolescence are to be resolved by invoking a federal right to demand assignment to a desk two rows away.

As its holding makes painfully clear, the majority's watered-down version of the Spending Clause clear-statement rule is no substitute for the real protections of state and local autonomy that our constitutional system requires. If there be any doubt of the futility of the Court's attempt to hedge its holding about with words of limitation for future cases, the result in this case provides the answer. The complaint of this fifth grader survives and the school will be compelled to answer in federal court. We can be assured that like suits will follow — suits, which in cost and number, will impose serious financial burdens on local school districts, the taxpayers who support them, and the children they serve. Federalism and our struggling school systems deserve better from this Court. I dissent.

———

NOTES AND QUESTIONS

1. Which school officials must have actual notice of the misconduct? Who is the appropriate person to tell? Does it matter if the misconduct is by a teacher or by another student? If a student alleges sexual harassment by a teacher, is another teacher the appropriate official to notify? If a teacher knows of the misconduct, but lacks the power to address it by terminating her fellow teacher, is this an appropriate person under the standard set forth in *Gebser*? What about the principal of the school? Is it enough that the principal has the authority to limit a teacher's contact with students after school or to call a meeting between the teacher accused of the misconduct and the parents of the student?

In *Baynard v. Lawson*, 112 F. Supp. 2d 524, 531–34 (E.D.Va. 2000), the district court noted that under Virginia law, a school principal had the authority only to submit recommendations to the superintendent regarding assignment, promotion, transfer, and dismissal of personnel and could not make this decision herself. Thus, according to the court (which granted the school board's motion for judgment notwithstanding the verdict), the plaintiff failed to show that the principal was the person with the requisite authority to take corrective action for reported abuse, and the school board could not be held vicariously liable. Is this too narrow a reading of the term "authority to institute corrective measures" as set forth in *Gebser*? This analysis was affirmed on appeal, *see Bayard v. Malone*, 268 F.3d 228 (4th Cir. 2001). *But see id.* at 242 (Michael, J., dissenting) (criticizing majority's narrow view and noting principal's authority to confront and monitor teacher and report abuse to superintendent and police). Would the outcome be the same in a case of peer-on-peer sexual harassment? *See Murrell v. School District No. 1,* 186 F.3d 1238, 1248 (10th Cir. 1999) (in student-on-student sexual harassment case, principal had requisite authority on which to base school district liability because, among other things, she had the authority to suspend students).

2. What constitutes "actual notice"? In *Gebser* the Court stated that knowledge of sexually suggestive comments in class was not sufficient. Must the appropriate official have actual knowledge of current sexual abuse, *see Baynard v. Malone,* 268 F.3d 228 (4th Cir. 2001), or is the actual notice requirement met when an appropriate official has actual notice that there is a substantial risk of abuse? *See id.* at 242 (Michael, J., dissenting).

3. How serious must the alleged harassment be to meet the standard set forth in *Davis*?

A female high school student claimed that a male student touched her leg more than once while she was sitting in class. *See Mosley v. Beaumont Independent School Dist.,* 997 S.W.2d 934 (Tex. Ct. App. 1999) (no allegation that harassment was so severe, pervasive, and objectively offensive that it could be said to deprive the female student of access to educational opportunities or benefits). *See also Cubie v. Bryan Career College, Inc.,* 244 F. Supp. 2d 1191 (D. Kan. 2003) (four instances of touching a fellow student, three times to the shoulder/back areas and once to the thigh, each lasting a few seconds, did not rise to the level of severe and pervasive considering all the circumstances).

A second-grade female student alleged a series of incidents of misconduct by a seven-year-old male, including teasing, punching, spitting, pushing, kicking and one instance of touching the student's "private spot" over her clothing. In *Manfredi v. Mount Vernon Board of Education,* 94 F. Supp. 2d 447 (S.D.N.Y. 2000), the court determined that the hitting and pushing incidents, though hurtful, were not actionable as sexual harassment. The court stated that it would be "a reach" to find that the one instance of touching the female student on her vagina was actionable under Title IX. Moreover, there was no evidence that the female child was deprived of access to even one educational opportunity, as she missed only one day of school to file a complaint at the police station and she thrived when, after the principal learned of the possible sexual touching, she was moved into another class.

4. What kind of conduct constitutes deliberate indifference? See Notes after *Gebser, supra,* for a detailed discussion. Review the Supreme Court's language on this issue carefully. The Sixth Circuit has stated, "Although Title IX does not require certain specific responses, it does require a reasonable response, which [the school district] failed to provide." *Vance v. Spencer County Public*

School District, 231 F.3d 253 (6th Cir. 2000) (principal's action of talking to students about their alleged harassment constituted deliberate indifference, as school district was required to take further reasonable action if their response was inadequate). Is this consistent with *Davis?*

5. Are students permitted to bring a private lawsuit for damages for action by a school district that violates the agency regulations that were promulgated under Title IX? Title IX contains a provision that empowers federal agencies to effectuate the substantive right to be free from discrimination based on sex. One of the regulations under Title IX bars a recipient of federal funds from retaliating against a person who complains of gender discrimination in violation of Title IX. *See* 34 C.F.R. § 100.7(e). Although the U.S. Supreme Court has stated that Title IX carries an implied private right of action, it has not stated whether that right of action exists for regulations that are set forth by a federal agency.

The Supreme Court has, however, addressed whether there is a private right of action to enforce a disparate impact regulation promulgated under Title VI of the Civil Rights Act of 1964. *Alexander v. Sandoval,* 532 U.S. 275 (2001). "For the first time . . . the Court limited that [private] cause of action to enforcing rights actually articulated by Congress, not a federal agency." *Litman v. George Mason,* 156 F. Supp. 2d 579, 580 (E.D. Va. 2001). In *Litman,* the court addressed whether *Sandoval* barred the plaintiff's claim for Title IX retaliation. The *Litman* court determined that "[t]he implied right of action to seek redress for harm suffered because of discrimination does not extend to harm suffered because of retaliation, because . . . the anti-retaliation regulation is not merely an interpretation of Section 1681 but expands the scope of prohibited conduct." *Id.* at 586. The court quoted the *Sandoval* Court: "Language in a regulation may invoke a private right of action that Congress through statutory text created, but it may not create a right that Congress has not." *Id.* at 586 (quoting *Sandoval*). The district court distinguished the provisions and the regulatory scheme of Title VII and Title IX, and it refused to use Title VII's definition of retaliation as a form of discrimination in the Title IX context. Moreover, the court determined that the plain reading of "discrimination" "on the basis of sex" as prohibited by Title IX does not encompass retaliation. According to the court, "the harm from retaliation is not a direct result of discrimination on the basis of sex but stems from the actions one took in response to the discrimination." *Id.* at 585. Thus, Ms. Litman could not bring a private suit to enforce this regulation under Title IX. The court noted that although Ms. Litman could not bring the suit for money damages, the university could lose its federal funding for failure to comply with the directives of Title IX.

6. Title VI of the Civil Rights Act of 1964, 42 U.S.C. § 2000d, provides that "no person shall, on the grounds of race, color, or national origin be excluded from participation in, be denied the benefits of, or be subjected to discrimination under any program or activity receiving Federal financial assistance." In light of *Davis,* courts apply the deliberate indifference/actual knowledge/severe and pervasive standard to claims of racial or national origin harassment under Title VI. *Curley v. Hill,* 2000 U.S. Dist. LEXIS 16665 (S.D. Ind. 2000) (granting summary judgment on claim of harassment based on student's Navajo heritage because plaintiff unable to show deliberate indifference).

In *Yap v. Oceanside Union Free Sch. Dist.*, 303 F. Supp. 2d 284, 295 (E.D.N.Y. 2004), classmates harassed a student about his Asian-American background and his parents complained to the school principal. Despite talking to the students about their behavior and giving presentations on bullying and intolerance, the harassment continued. The parents eventually sued under 42 U.S.C. § 1983 claiming that the school had racially discriminated against the student in violation of the equal protection clause. The court determined that the school was not deliberately indifferent to the discrimination. "[D]eliberate indifference . . . requires something more than a proffer indicating the ultimate inadequacy of preventative and curative measures."

In addition to Title IX, sexual harassment may be actionable under state statutes or under the equal protection clause of the United States constitution. The next case addresses same sex peer-on-peer sexual harassment under each of these claims. Recall Justice Kennedy's concern that it will be difficult for school districts to obtain summary judgment on Title IX sexual harassment cases. Reassess his arguments after you read the next case.

[3] Same Sex Harassment

MONTGOMERY v. INDEPENDENT SCHOOL DISTRICT NO. 709

United States District Court for the District of Minnesota
109 F. Supp. 2d 1081 (2000)

JOHN R. TUNHEIM, UNITED STATES DISTRICT JUDGE.

MEMORANDUM OPINION AND ORDER

Plaintiff Jesse Montgomery brings this action against Independent School District Number 709 (the "School District") based on its failure to prevent harassment by other students that he experienced during approximately eleven years of education in defendant's schools. Plaintiff asserts that the other students harassed him both because of his gender and his perceived sexual orientation. He brings claims under the Minnesota Human Rights Act ("MHRA"), the Equal Protection and Due Process Clauses of the United States and Minnesota Constitutions, and Title IX of the Education Amendments of 1972. This matter is before the court on defendant's motion for judgment on the pleadings . . . and on defendant's motion for summary judgment against all claims and on plaintiff's motion for summary judgment in his favor on the issue of liability in connection with his MHRA, Title IX, due process and equal protection claims.

BACKGROUND

Plaintiff alleges, and defendant does not dispute, that while he was a student in defendant's schools he experienced frequent and continual teasing by other students beginning in kindergarten and recurring on an almost daily basis until the end of the tenth grade, when he transferred to another school district. While some of these taunts were more general in nature, many of them appear to have been directed at plaintiff because of his perceived sexual orientation, including, "faggott," "fag," "gay," "Jessica," "girl," "princess," "fairy," "homo," "freak," "lesbian," "femme boy," "gay boy," "bitch," "queer," "pansy," and "queen." A review of plaintiff's allegations, assuming them to be true for purposes of these motions, reveals that the verbal abuse to which his peers subjected him was severe and unrelenting throughout his entire tenure in defendant's school system.

According to plaintiff, the students' misconduct escalated to the point of physical violence beginning in the sixth grade, when several students punched him, kicked him, and knocked him down on the playground.[87] Another student later super-glued him to his seat. Plaintiff claims that as he entered middle school and progressed on to high school, the harassment became noticeably worse. While the verbal taunts continued unabated, the physical threats and assaults intensified. Students threatened to beat him up on several occasions. A group of students pushed him down in the hallway in front of his family when they were at the school to attend a choir concert. Another student unzipped his backpack, threw his books to the floor and smashed his calculator. Plaintiff also states that during a gym exercise one of the students charged him and sent him flying several feet through the air, and that during hockey drills the offending students deliberately tripped him or knocked him down on several occasions, causing bruises. Plaintiff further alleges that students frequently kicked or tripped him on the school bus, and that while he was riding the bus or in art class students would throw objects at him such as crayons, paper, popcorn, water, chunks of clay, paint brushes, pencils, pen caps, trash, and other small things.

In addition to these incidents, plaintiff claims that on some occasions the physical threats and assaults he experienced were of a more sexual nature.[88] He specifically contends that a student in his middle school choir class grabbed his legs, inner thighs, chest and crotch. He states that the same student grabbed his buttocks on at least five or six occasions. Later another student approached him and asked to see him naked after gym class. Plaintiff states that he experienced similar incidents when he was in high school. According to plaintiff, students in his ninth and tenth grade choir classes sometimes put their arms around him or grabbed his inner thighs and buttocks while calling him names targeted at his perceived sexual orientation. Plaintiff states that one of the students grabbed his own genitals while squeezing plaintiff's buttocks, and on other occasions would stand behind plaintiff and grind his penis into plaintiff's backside. The same student once threw him to the ground and pretended to rape him anally, and on another occasion sat on plaintiff's lap and bounced while pretending to have intercourse with him. Other students watched and laughed during these incidents.

Plaintiff alleges that the harassment he experienced deprived him of the ability to access significant portions of the educational environment. During his tenure in defendant's schools, plaintiff generally achieved average to above

---

87 [3] Although some of the students who subjected plaintiff to verbal insults were female, the students who allegedly harassed him physically were all male.

88 [4] The students who directed these sexual behaviors towards plaintiff were all male.

average grades. Nonetheless, plaintiff states that he stayed home from school on approximately five or six occasions while he was in middle school in order to avoid the harassment. He further states that he did not participate or try to participate in intramural sports because his harassers were participants, that he avoided going to the school cafeteria unless absolutely necessary, and that he avoided using the school bathroom except in emergency situations. When plaintiff was in high school he stopped using the school bus in order to circumvent the continuous harassment he experienced there, requiring his parents and other family members to drive him to school. [89]

Plaintiff states that he reported the students' misconduct to a variety of School District officials, including teachers, bus drivers, principals, assistant principals, playground and cafeteria monitors, locker room attendants, and school counselors. Plaintiff further states that on several occasions when he was in middle school, he and his parents reported the incidents of misconduct to the office of the School District's superintendent.

The officials to whom plaintiff reported the misconduct responded with a variety of measures. Defendant gave plaintiff access to school counselors, and he made appointments with them on a regular basis. Moreover, when plaintiff was in middle school defendant required him to attend a number of group sessions with other boys to discuss strategies for responding to harassment. According to plaintiff, defendant removed him from some of his favorite classes and required him to attend these sessions involuntarily.

Defendant also implemented several disciplinary measures against the offending students, although it appears that School District officials applied such discipline inconsistently. Plaintiff's teachers responded to many of his complaints by verbally reprimanding students or sending them to the principal's office. When students harassed plaintiff on the school bus, the driver sometimes stopped the bus and reprimanded the students. Defendant asserts that it assigned special seats to students on the bus at least temporarily in an attempt to circumvent the misconduct, although plaintiff claims that these seating assignments were not adequately enforced. On some occasions the cafeteria monitor responded to plaintiff's lunchtime complaints by requiring the offending students to stand in a designated area. On two occasions plaintiff's middle school counselor and principal required the offending students to meet with plaintiff and apologize to him. Plaintiff asserts that these sessions were unhelpful and ultimately resulted in a significant amount of retaliatory harassment.

In connection with the incidents of sexual touching he experienced, plaintiff alleges that he made multiple complaints to his choir teacher about the

---

89 [5] According to plaintiff, one of the bus drivers may have deliberately facilitated the harassment he experienced. Two busses usually followed each other on the route that plaintiff took home from school. He alleges that after the first bus driver dropped him off, the second bus driver would pull into the intersection and deliberately pause so that the students on the bus could open their windows and yell insults at him as he walked towards his house. Plaintiff states that this behavior occurred for a period of several weeks. When plaintiff's father learned about these incidents he reported them to the bus driver's supervisor, and plaintiff's parents thereafter began driving him to school. It is unclear whether plaintiff ever complained about the bus driver to the principal or other managerial School District officials, and he has not asserted any independent claims against the School District based on the bus driver's alleged conduct.

student who repeatedly grabbed his thigh, buttocks, and crotch and pretended to have intercourse with him. The teacher responded to plaintiff's complaints by verbally reprimanding the student, sending him out into the hallway, or sending him to the principal's office. There is no evidence in the record as to whether or how School District officials ultimately disciplined this student once he arrived in the principal's office.

With the exception of one occasion, defendant has not shown that any of the students whom teachers sent to the principal's office in response to plaintiff's reports ever received discipline stronger than a verbal reprimand. The disciplinary measures that defendant took on that occasion were precipitated by a formal complaint that plaintiff's mother filed with the School District in March 1995. At that time plaintiff had been experiencing almost daily harassment on the school bus and in his art class by a particular group of students who called him names, kicked him, or threw objects at him. The principal eventually referred plaintiff's complaint to Terri Kronzer ("Kronzer") with the School District's Human Resources Department. Kronzer conducted an investigation and determined that plaintiff had been sexually harassed. Based on her recommendations, defendant suspended one of the harassers for five days and another for one day. Other harassers received lectures on the School District's sexual harassment policy. Defendant also revoked the bus privileges of two of the students, who were brothers, and transferred the most egregious offender out of plaintiff's art class. Defendant further instructed the hall monitor to "keep an eye" on plaintiff.

Within one week after defendant implemented these measures, the students whose bus privileges had been revoked returned to the school bus. According to defendant, the students lived in a rural area, and their father complained to the principal that driving them to school each day would be a significant hardship. Defendant states that it permitted the students to return to the school bus on the condition that they sit directly behind the bus driver each day.

Plaintiff thereafter ceased riding the school bus altogether in order to avoid his harassers, but did not notify defendant that he had done so. Plaintiff and his parents were unhappy with defendant's decision to permit the students to ride the bus again. Plaintiff's mother thereafter filed charges against the School District with the Minnesota Department of Human Rights ("MDHR") based upon its allegedly inadequate response to plaintiff's formal harassment complaint, and this lawsuit followed from those charges. Eventually, after plaintiff finished the tenth grade, he transferred to another school district altogether for his last two years of secondary education.

ANALYSIS

I. *Motion for Judgment on the Pleadings*

[The court described the standard of review — a court must accept as true all facts alleged by the non-moving party in its pleadings and grant all reasonable inferences arising therefrom in that party's favor, and judgment on the pleadings is not appropriate unless the moving party clearly establishes that there are no material issues of fact remaining to be resolved and that it is entitled to judgment as a matter of law.]

B. MHRA claims prior to August 1, 1993

Defendant seeks dismissal of that portion of plaintiff's MHRA claims arising from incidents that occurred prior to August 1, 1993. Prior to that date, the MHRA explicitly prohibited only discrimination "because of race, color, creed, religion, national origin, sex, age, marital status, [or] status with regard to public assistance or disability." MINN. STAT. § 363.03, subd. 5(1) (1993). On August 1, 1993, however, the Minnesota legislature amended the MHRA to include "sexual orientation" as a prohibited basis for discrimination. 1993 MINN. LAWS, ch. 22 §§ 8–25; see also MINN. STAT. § 363.03, subd. 5(1) (2000). This amendment was not retroactive, defendant argues, and therefore, the MHRA did not prohibit discrimination based on sexual orientation or perceived sexual orientation until August 1993. Because the students who harassed plaintiff primarily targeted him due to his perceived sexual orientation, defendant concludes that he states no claim for relief under the MHRA based on conduct that occurred prior to the effective date of the amendment.

The Court agrees that the MHRA did not prohibit discrimination based on sexual orientation prior to August 1, 1993. Pursuant to section 645.21 of the Minnesota Statutes, "no law shall be construed to be retroactive unless clearly and manifestly so intended by the legislature." The statutory language manifests no such intent, and plaintiff points to no legislative history indicating otherwise. Thus, to the extent that plaintiff asserts claims based on discrimination due to his perceived sexual orientation prior to August 1, 1993, such claims are not cognizable under the MHRA.

Nevertheless, in asserting this argument defendant too narrowly construes the scope of plaintiff's claims against it. Not only does he assert claims based on discrimination due to his perceived sexual orientation, but also due to his gender. Although the MHRA did not prohibit sexual orientation discrimination prior to 1993, it did prohibit discrimination based on sex. The MHRA defined such discrimination to include "sexual harassment." MINN. STAT. § 363.01, subd. 14 (1993). Moreover, it expressly included within the definition of sexual harassment any "unwelcome sexual advances, requests for sexual favors, sexually motivated physical contact or other verbal or physical conduct or communication of sexual nature when . . . that conduct or communication has the purpose or effect of substantially interfering with an individual's . . . education."

In Cummings v. Koehnen, 568 N.W.2d 418 (Minn. 1997), the Minnesota Supreme Court interpreted these provisions and held that an MHRA claimant alleging same sex sexual harassment is not required to prove that the alleged harassment affected one gender differently than the other or that the harasser is homosexual. In reaching this decision, the court expressly rejected the defendant's argument that no sexual harassment had occurred because the alleged harasser, a heterosexual, was not motivated by any actual sexual interest in the claimant. Importantly, although Cummings was decided after the 1993 amendment to the MHRA was enacted, the court did not rely on the prohibition against sexual orientation discrimination as a basis for its decision. Rather, the court looked to the plain meaning of the statutory definition of "sexual harassment" and found that it contains no requirement that the prohibited conduct be motivated by sexual interest, but rather, prohibits any "verbal or physical conduct of a sexual nature" if it is otherwise sufficiently severe to constitute actionable harassment.[90] Thus, under *Cummings*, the sexual orientation and motivation of the alleged harasser are not dispositive of whether an actionable claim under the MHRA exists.

Applying *Cummings* to the case at bar, the Court finds that plaintiff has plead student misconduct occurring prior to August 1, 1993 that falls within the statutory definition of sexual harassment. Plaintiff not only asserts that the students called him derogatory sexual names such as "faggot" and "queer," but also that students approached him and asked to see him naked. Under *Cummings*, it matters not whether the students who engaged in this conduct were motivated by sexual interest in plaintiff or instead by a desire to humiliate him. Rather, the Court must consider only whether they fall within list [sic] of specific behaviors included under the MHRA's broad definition of sexual harassment. The statements directed at plaintiff might properly be categorized as requests for sexual favors or verbal conduct of a sexual nature, and therefore, support a claim of discrimination based on sex. Defendant's motion for judgment on the pleadings against the portion of plaintiff's MHRA claim arising prior to August 1, 1993 is denied for these reasons.

C. Due process and equal protection claims

Defendant argues that plaintiff's due process and equal protection claims must be dismissed on the ground that persons with a particular sexual orientation or perceived sexual orientation do not constitute a definable, constitutionally protected class. In support of this argument, defendant contends that plaintiff's equal protection and due process claims must be evaluated under the standards applicable to Title VII of the Civil Rights Act of 1964 ("Title VII"), 42 U.S.C. §§ 2000e–2000e-17. Defendant further contends that no cause of action exists under Title VII for harassment based on sexual orientation, and on that basis concludes that the United States Constitution similarly provides no protection, under any circumstances, for persons treated differently on the basis of sexual orientation.

In so arguing, defendant fundamentally misapplies the most basic principles of constitutional law. Although Title VII explicitly limits its scope to persons subjected to discrimination based on "race, color, religion, sex, or national origin," 42 U.S.C. § 2000e-2, the Fourteenth Amendment contains no such limiting language. *See* U.S. Const. amend. XIV, § 1 ("nor shall any State deprive *any person* of life, liberty, or property, without due process of law; nor deny to *any person* within its jurisdiction the equal protection of the laws") (emphasis added). Thus, the Fourteenth Amendment protects all persons, whether they can prove membership in a specially protected class or not.

The Court does not, in so holding, suggest that membership in a particular class of persons is irrelevant to a determination of whether a constitutional

---

[90] [6] The *Cummings* court expressly distinguished the MHRA from federal discrimination statutes on the ground that it contains this definition.

violation has occurred. Courts must evaluate discrimination based on membership in an identified suspect class such as race, alienage, or national origin, with the most strict scrutiny. *See City of Cleburne v. Cleburne Living Center,* 473 U.S. 432, 440 (1985) (holding that such classifications are permissible only when "suitably tailored to serve a compelling state interest"). In contrast, the Eighth Circuit has held that discrimination based on homosexuality is subject only to rational basis review. *See Richenberg v. Perry,* 97 F.3d 256, 260–61 (8th Cir. 1996) (stating that under rational basis review, a claimant has the burden to demonstrate that the challenged government conduct is "not rationally related to any legitimate government purpose"). Nevertheless, a claimant's failure to prove membership in a suspect class does not automatically deprive him of any cognizable constitutional claim as defendant suggests, but instead merely lowers the standard under which the conduct at issue must be scrutinized. *See City of Cleburne,* 473 U.S. at 446 (holding that a court's refusal to recognize a group of individuals as a suspect class "does not leave them entirely unprotected from invidious discrimination").

In *Romer v. Evans,* 517 U.S. 620 (1996), the Supreme Court applied this principle to individuals classified on the basis of sexual orientation. The legislation challenged in that case prohibited any legislative, executive, or judicial act in the State of Colorado designed to protect individuals based on their homosexual or bisexual orientation. Striking down the legislation as violating the Equal Protection Clause, the Court held that even if it did not target a suspect class it nevertheless failed even the most permissive rational basis review. The Court's findings in *Romer* foreclose defendant's argument that individuals are entitled to no constitutional protection whatsoever from discrimination based on sexual orientation.

Moreover, in a case that is strikingly similar to the case at bar, the Seventh Circuit held under rational basis review that a school district's failure to protect a student from peer harassment based on sexual orientation was constitutionally impermissible. *See Nabozny v. Podlesny,* 92 F.3d 446, 458 (7th Cir. 1996). In so holding, the court reasoned, "We are unable to garner any rational basis for permitting one student to assault another based on the victim's sexual orientation, and the defendants do not offer us one." The Court agrees with the *Nabozny* court's analysis. Assuming the allegations set forth in the pleadings to be true, defendant has responded to plaintiff's complaints differently than to those of other students because of his sexual orientation or perceived sexual orientation. The School District offers no rational basis for permitting students to assault plaintiff on the basis of his sexual orientation while protecting other students from similar forms of harassment. Moreover, the Court can conceive of no legitimate government interest for doing so. Defendant's motion for judgment on the pleadings against plaintiff's due process and equal protection claims on the ground that he is not a member of a protected class is denied accordingly.[91]

---

[91] [8] The Court raises and considers defendant's remaining arguments for dismissing these claims below in connection with its motion for summary judgment.

D. Title IX claims

Defendant also argues that plaintiff's Title IX claims must be dismissed because Title IX does not protect individuals from discrimination based on sexual orientation or perceived sexual orientation. Title IX provides in relevant part that "no person in the United States shall, *on the basis of sex,* be excluded from participation in, be denied the benefits of, or be subjected to discrimination under" federally-funded educational programs or activities. 20 U.S.C. § 1681(a) (emphasis added). Thus, unlike the Fourteenth Amendment, Title IX prohibits only discrimination based on sex and does not extend to any other form of invidious discrimination. For these reasons the Court concludes that, to the extent that plaintiff asserts Title IX claims based on discrimination due to his sexual orientation or perceived sexual orientation, these claims are not actionable and must be dismissed. *Cf. Williamson v. A.G. Edwards & Sons, Inc.,* 876 F.2d 69, 70 (8th Cir. 1989) (holding that Title VII does not protect employees from harassment based on sexual orientation).

Plaintiff nevertheless contends that he has been a victim of harassment based upon sex or gender as well as harassment based upon his sexual orientation or perceived sexual orientation. In *Davis v. Monroe County Bd. of Educ.,* the Supreme Court recognized that student-against-student sexual harassment may give rise to a cognizable claim under Title IX in appropriate circumstances. No federal court appears to have addressed, however, whether the kind of conduct to which plaintiff was subjected constitutes discrimination "on the basis of sex" within the meaning of Title IX.[92] In contrast with the claims recognized as viable in *Davis,* this case primarily involves same-sex harassment by students who, through name-calling and other forms of verbal abuse, repeatedly indicated that they perceived plaintiff to be homosexual. Thus, plaintiff's harassers do not appear to have been motivated by any sexual desire towards plaintiff, but rather, by hostility based upon his perceived sexual orientation.

Plaintiff contends that the students engaged in the offensive conduct at issue not only because they believed him to be gay, but also because he did not meet their stereotyped expectations of masculinity. The facts alleged in plaintiff's complaint support this characterization of the students' misconduct. He specifically alleges that some of the students called him "Jessica," a girl's name, indicating a belief that he exhibited feminine characteristics. Moreover, the Court finds important the fact that plaintiff's peers began harassing him as early as kindergarten. It is highly unlikely that at that tender age plaintiff would have developed any solidified sexual preference, or for that matter, that he even understood what it meant to be "homosexual" or "heterosexual."[93] The likelihood that he openly identified himself as gay or that he engaged in any homosexual conduct at that age is quite low. It is much more plausible that the students began tormenting him based on feminine personality traits that

---

[92] [9] Unlike the MHRA, Title IX contains no provision specifically defining sexual harassment in terms of the behaviors that it encompasses. Because the MHRA is in this way distinguishable from Title IX, the Court's holding that plaintiff states a cognizable sexual harassment claim under the MHRA does not govern its determination of the Title IX issue that defendant raises.

[93] [10] Indeed, as of the date of his deposition in this matter, plaintiff testified that he was still confused about his sexual orientation.

he exhibited and the perception that he did not engage in behaviors befitting a boy. Plaintiff thus appears to plead facts that would support a claim of harassment based on the perception that he did not fit his peers' stereotypes of masculinity.

Whether such harassment is actionable under federal law has been the subject of significant controversy among federal courts. Although no court has addressed this issue in the context of a Title IX claim, several courts have considered whether same-sex harassment targeting the claimant's failure to meet expected gender stereotypes is actionable under Title VII. The Court looks to these precedents in analyzing plaintiff's Title IX claim, noting that Title VII similarly requires that the discrimination resulting in the plaintiff's claims be based on his or her sex. Moreover, the Supreme Court relied upon Title VII precedents in first recognizing a private cause of action for sexual harassment under Title IX. *See Franklin v. Gwinnett County Pub. Sch.* (citing *Meritor Sav. Bank, FSB v. Vinson*). In *Davis*, the Supreme Court clearly distinguished Title IX from Title VII in connection with the use of agency principles and the requisites for institutional liability under each statute. Nevertheless, the same opinion cited Title VII precedents in connection with the issue of what constitutes gender-oriented harassment. Furthermore, no logical rationale appears to exist for distinguishing Title VII and Title IX in connection with the issue raised here regarding the circumstances under which abusive or offensive conduct amounts to harassment "based on sex." The Court accordingly applies Title VII precedents in analyzing plaintiff's Title IX claim.

In *Oncale*, the Supreme Court recognized for the first time that claims based on same-sex harassment are cognizable under Title VII. 523 U.S. at 79. The Court emphasized, however, that in order to prevail on such a claim, an employee must be able to prove that he or she was harassed "because of . . . sex." The Court further suggested that a claimant could satisfy this requirement by demonstrating that the challenged conduct was motivated by sexual desire, that he or she was harassed in such sex-specific terms as to raise an inference of hostility towards his or her sex, or that employees of one sex were treated less favorably than those of the other sex. Regardless of the kinds of proof offered, the decisive issue in any sexual harassment claim is "whether members of one sex are exposed to disadvantageous terms or conditions of employment to which members of the other sex are not exposed."

The Court in *Oncale* did not specifically reach the issue of whether employees may prove harassment "because of sex" by demonstrating that the challenged conduct was motivated by a failure to meet expected gender stereotypes. Nevertheless, a number of federal courts have suggested that they can. *See Higgins v. New Balance Athletic Shoe, Inc.,* 194 F.3d 252, 261 n.4 (1st Cir. 1999); [additional cases omitted]. In evaluating the issue, the *Higgins* court rejected the lower court's contrary suggestion, stating:

> We think it prudent to note that the precise question that the district court posed is no longer open: *Oncale* . . . confirms that the standards of liability under Title VII, as they have been refined and explained over time, apply to same-sex plaintiffs just as they do to opposite-sex plaintiffs. In other words, just [sic] a woman can ground an action on

a claim that men discriminated against her because she did not meet stereotyped expectations of femininity, . . . a man can ground a claim on evidence that other men discriminated against him because he did not meet stereotyped expectations of masculinity.

Importantly, the *Higgins* court cited *Price-Waterhouse v. Hopkins*, 490 U.S. 228 (1989), for the proposition that discrimination based on a failure to meet stereotyped gender expectations is actionable under Title VII. In *Price-Waterhouse,* the Supreme Court upheld a Title VII claim raised by an employee who asserted that sex stereotyping played a role in her employer's decision not to promote her. In so doing, the Court explicitly addressed the legal relevance of sex stereotypes, holding that "we are beyond the day when an employer could evaluate employees by assuming or insisting that they matched the stereotype associated with their group, for in forbidding employers to discriminate against individuals because of their sex, Congress intended to strike at the entire spectrum of disparate treatment of men and women resulting from sex stereotypes." Thus, the *Higgins* opinion reminds courts that the Supreme Court has already determined that discrimination based on a claimant's failure to satisfy the stereotypes associated with his or her sex constitutes discrimination "because of sex" within the meaning of Title VII. Under *Oncale* the principles established in *Price-Waterhouse* apply with equal force when the individual engaging in discriminatory conduct is of the same sex as the claimant.

A few federal courts have reached decisions that are at odds with the reasoning articulated in *Higgins*. [Cited cases omitted.] Nevertheless, in finding that Title VII offers no protection to individuals suffering discrimination based on sex stereotypes, both *Klein,* 36 F. Supp. 2d at 890, and *Bibby,* 85 F. Supp. 2d at 517, cite to the reasoning articulated by the lower court in the *Higgins* case which the First Circuit later rejected as erroneous under *Oncale. See Higgins*, 21 F. Supp. 2d 66, 75–76 (D. Maine 1998), *vacated on other grounds, Higgins*, 194 F.3d at 265. Moreover, the *Dandan* court failed to acknowledge the precedential relevance of *Price-Waterhouse* and simply held that the claimant had failed to direct the court's attention to any support for the argument that Title VII protection includes harassment based on sexual stereotyping. The Court finds the rationale articulated by the First Circuit in *Higgins* to be much more persuasive, and accordingly rejects the contrary decisions of these other federal courts. The Court for these reasons concludes that by pleading facts from which a reasonable fact-finder could infer that he suffered harassment due to his failure to meet masculine stereotypes, plaintiff has stated a cognizable claim under Title IX.

. . . .

II. THE PARTIES' MOTIONS FOR SUMMARY JUDGMENT

A. Standard of Review

[The court described the standard of review — if the pleadings, depositions, answers to interrogatories, and admissions on file, together with the affidavits, if any, show that there is no genuine issue as to any material fact, the moving party is entitled to a judgment as a matter of law.]

Applying these standards to the case at bar, the Court views the supported facts in the light most favorable to plaintiff when evaluating defendant's motion, but takes the opposite approach when evaluating plaintiff's motion.

B. MHRA Claim

Defendant argues in support of its summary judgment motion that plaintiff has failed to establish a prima facie case of discrimination under the MHRA. The MHRA prohibits discrimination in access to education based on a variety of enumerated characteristics including sex and sexual orientation. *See* MINN. STAT. § 363.03, subd. 5. Sexual harassment constitutes a form of prohibited discrimination under this provision only when it "has the purpose or effect of substantially interfering with an individual's . . . education . . . or creating an intimidating . . . educational . . . environment."

Defendant argues that plaintiff has failed to meet this standard. It points to plaintiff's numerous allegations of name-calling, teasing, pencil-throwing, and playground fights from kindergarten through the tenth grade, and contends that none of these actions are sufficiently severe to give rise to a cognizable MHRA claim. The Court agrees with that assessment, finding it highly unlikely that the Minnesota Legislature intended to create a cause of action at law for every child who is teased, pushed or taunted by other children in school. Children are, by their nature, prone to engage in immature, mischievous, and sometimes mean behavior towards each other. While this is unfortunate for those children who get bullied, courts must be cognizant of the reality that this kind of behavior occurs on a frequent basis and is part of the maturation process. A student simply cannot sue his school district on the ground that he had a disagreeable childhood.

Nevertheless, plaintiff's allegations include conduct that is much more egregious than the ordinary childish behavior among school children that, although reprehensible, might be construed to be normal. Plaintiff contends that some of his peers approached him and requested sexual favors from him, including asking to see him naked. Even more disturbing, however, are plaintiff's allegations that some of his peers grabbed his inner thighs, chest, crotch and buttocks during class, that one student on several occasions stood behind plaintiff and pressed his genitals into plaintiff's backside, and that the same student repeatedly initiated physical contact with plaintiff while pretending to have involuntary sex with him. These explicitly sexual acts directed at plaintiff constitute more than ordinary juvenile bullying, and are sufficiently severe, when viewed in totality with his allegations of extraordinarily frequent and pervasive verbal abuse, to create an "intimidating, hostile, or offensive" educational environment within the meaning of the MHRA.

Defendant nonetheless contends that the conduct plaintiff alleges does not give rise to an actionable claim because he has failed to demonstrate that the harassment plaintiff experienced had "the purpose or effect of substantially interfering with" his education. The Court disagrees. Plaintiff has alleged that throughout high school and most of his junior high school years he was afraid to use the school's restroom, and avoided eating in the cafeteria, riding the school bus, or participating in intramural sports. Ultimately he felt he could no longer tolerate the circumstances that he was in and transferred to an entirely different school district. Although plaintiff's grades remained relatively average throughout his tenure in defendant's schools, grades are not the sole benefit to be derived by a student from an educational experience. The Court finds that the activities from which plaintiff allegedly was excluded due to his fear of harassment are important benefits of the educational environment. Plaintiff therefore has alleged facts that support a finding that the peer harassment he experienced had the effect of substantially interfering with his education.

Defendant further contends that plaintiff has failed to allege sufficient culpability on its part in order to hold it accountable for the student misconduct alleged. In order to state a viable claim of sexual harassment under the MHRA in the employment context, a claimant must prove that "the employer knows or should know of the existence of the harassment and fails to take timely and appropriate action." The MHRA contains no similar provision defining the scope of liability of school districts in the education context. Plaintiff contends that the actual or constructive knowledge standard applicable under the MHRA in the employment context also should apply in the context of peer sexual harassment in schools. Defendant disagrees, arguing that the more restrictive liability standards applicable under federal Title IX law should apply to such claims. No Minnesota court appears to have addressed this issue, and therefore, the scope of school district liability for peer sexual harassment under the MHRA appears to be an open question. The Court need not resolve this issue, however, because it holds that even under the more rigorous "actual knowledge plus deliberate indifference" test, plaintiff's allegations are sufficient to create a genuine fact issue as to whether the School District should be held accountable on his MHRA claims. Defendant's actual knowledge of the harassment plaintiff allegedly experienced cannot be seriously disputed on this record. Plaintiff asserts that he made hundreds of complaints about the harassment to school teachers, cafeteria and playground monitors, bus drivers, principals, assistant principals, locker room attendants, counselors, and even the superintendent. Moreover, the record reflects that these officials did little more than verbally reprimand the offending students or send them into the hallway until plaintiff filed a formal complaint about the misconduct when he was in the tenth grade.[94] Although the School District did suspend several of the students in response to plaintiff's

---

94 [12] Defendant makes much of the fact that although plaintiff was aware of its sexual harassment policy, he did not file a formal complaint about the harassment until his last year in defendant's schools. Nevertheless, according to the express language of that policy, formal complaints are not required. The policy provides, "The School District will act to investigate all complaints, either formal or informal, verbal or written, of . . . sexual harassment or violence, and to discipline or take appropriate action against any pupil . . . who is found to have violated this policy." The policy further provides, in connection with reporting procedures, that although the School District encourages written complaints, "oral reports shall be considered complaints as well." Finally, the policy requires all School District personnel receiving reports of sexual harassment to inform the building principal, who is required to reduce any verbal report into writing within the next twenty-four hours, and then to forward it to the School District's Administrator of Certified Personnel.

formal complaint, this single response must be considered in light of plaintiff's allegations of more than ten years of constant harassment and reports to School District officials of such harassment. The Court notes that, in particular, defendant has produced no evidence of any discipline taken in response to plaintiff's complaints about the student who repeatedly grabbed his body parts, rubbed up against him, and pretended to have sex with him. Although it appears that on some occasions plaintiff's choir teacher verbally reprimanded this student or sent him to the principal's office, there is absolutely no evidence that the principal or any other School District official took concrete disciplinary action against him. The Court finds this evidence sufficient to raise a fact question as to whether the School District responded to plaintiff's complaints of harassment with deliberate indifference. Plaintiff has therefore established sufficient evidence of the School District's knowledge and failure to respond to state an MHRA claim even under the more rigorous liability standards articulated in federal Title IX cases. The Court accordingly denies defendant's motion for summary judgment against this claim.

The Court further concludes, however, that whether defendant's responses to plaintiff's complaints were appropriate and whether the alleged harassment created a hostile environment or substantially interfered with plaintiff's education cannot be determined as a matter of law on this record. Rather, these issues are best left for a jury to decide. For this reason, the Court also denies plaintiff's motion for summary judgment in its favor on this claim.

C. Due Process Claims

Defendant contends that plaintiff's due process claims against it must be dismissed on the ground that it has no constitutional duty to protect students from the acts of third parties.[95] In *DeShaney v. Winnebago County Dept. of Soc. Servs.*, 489 U.S. 189 (1989), the Supreme Court established that a state's failure to protect an individual from private actors does not give rise to a constitutional violation unless a special relationship between the state and the claimant exists that creates a constitutional duty to protect. Addressing the due process claims raised in *DeShaney*, the Court argued that the Due Process Clause is merely a limitation on government action, and that neither its text nor history imposes upon the government an affirmative duty to act. Relying on *DeShaney*, the Eighth Circuit held in *Dorothy J. v. Little Rock Sch. Dist.*, that a student's claim against a school district based on sexual assault by another student is not actionable under section 1983. The court rejected the claimant's argument that the school district's custodial relationship with him gave rise to a constitutional duty to protect him. *See id.* (holding that, "[a] constitutional duty of care arises only 'when the State by the affirmative exercise of its power so restrains an individual's liberty that it renders him unable to care for himself, and at the same time fails to provide for his basic human needs.'" (citing *DeShaney,* 489 U.S. at 200)).

---

95 [13] Neither party has attempted to distinguish plaintiff's rights under the United States Constitution from his rights under the Minnesota Constitution. For this reason, the Court assumes, without deciding, that they are the same and accordingly analyzes plaintiff's claims under the state and federal constitutions together.

Although *Dorothy J.* appears to foreclose his claims, plaintiff argues that it is not applicable to this case, because the School District enacted policies pursuant to which he was required to report sexual harassment to School District officials and rely upon their assistance. He contends that these policies chilled any independent action on his part and prevented him from protecting himself, giving rise to a duty on the part of the School District to do so. The Court finds that this argument lacks merit. Plaintiff engages in hyperbole in arguing that the School District's reporting policies so restrained his liberty as to render him "unable to care for himself." Moreover, *Dorothy J.* specifically addressed the issue that plaintiff now raises, holding that "the affirmative duty to protect arises not from the State's knowledge of the individual's predicament or from its expressions of intent to help him." Thus, the School District's representations that it would respond to students' sexual harassment reports did not give rise to a constitutional duty to protect him. *Dorothy J.* is for these reasons dispositive of plaintiff's due process claims. The Court accordingly dismisses these claims and denies plaintiff's summary judgment motion in connection with them.

D. Equal Protection Claims

In *Morlock v. West Cent. Educ. Dist.*, 46 F. Supp. 2d 892, 918 (D. Minn. 1999), this Court held that the rationale articulated in *DeShaney* and *Dorothy J.* applies with equal force to equal protection claims, and therefore, school districts do not have a constitutional duty under the Equal Protection Clause to prevent student-against-student harassment motivated by the victim's class status. Thus, to the extent that plaintiff predicates his equal protection claims on the alleged misconduct of the students, these claims are not cognizable and must be dismissed.

Nevertheless, the case at bar is distinguishable from the claims asserted in *Morlock,* because in that case the claimant offered no evidence of disparate treatment in connection with the student harassment that arose from the school district's own conduct. In contrast, plaintiff alleges in this case that the School District discriminated against him on the basis of sex and sexual orientation by responding to his complaints differently than to those made by similarly situated female students and male students harassed by female students. As the Court noted in *Morlock,* although the Equal Protection Clause does not ordinarily impose upon government entities an affirmative duty to protect, it does limit the government's authority to deny protective services on the basis of an individual's disfavored class status. Thus, to the extent that plaintiff seeks to hold the School District liable for its own discriminatory conduct, his equal protection claims are actionable.

In order to establish a viable claim against the School District under the Equal Protection Clause, as enforced through 42 U.S.C. § 1983, plaintiff must demonstrate that it either had a policy or custom of responding to sexual harassment complaints more favorably when lodged by similarly situated female students or students perceived to be heterosexual. *See Monell v. Dep't of Social Servs.*, 436 U.S. 658, 690–91 (1978) (holding that government entities are subject to suit under section 1983 when the alleged unconstitutional conduct results from an official government policy or from practices of government officials that are so well-settled as to constitute a "custom or usage" with the force of law). Defendant challenges the sufficiency of plaintiff's evidence on this issue.

Upon reviewing the parties' submissions, the Court finds that a fact issue exists as to whether School District officials had a custom or practice of treating similarly situated students differently. Plaintiff has offered into evidence a variety of formal sexual harassment complaints filed by students at Ordean Middle School, along with associated letters and other documents evidencing the School District's response to the complaints. These records show that on several occasions, when girls filed sexual harassment complaints based on name-calling or inappropriate touching, the School District responded more strongly than it did to plaintiff's complaints.[96] The School District's responses appear to range, depending on severity and the number of reported offenses against a particular student, from verbal reprimands along with mandatory group counseling to revocation of bus privileges and in-school and out-of-school suspensions. In each case, no matter how small the offense, the School District notified the alleged harasser's parents about the complaint, any disciplinary action taken, and its intent to refer any future complaints to the City of Duluth Police Department. With the exception of the School District's response to the complaint plaintiff filed when he was in the tenth grade, there is absolutely no evidence in this case that it ever responded to his complaints by notifying the offending students' parents or threatening to notify the police about any future misconduct.

. . . .

The Court finds for these reasons that a genuine fact question exists as to whether the other students whose complaints were treated more seriously were similarly situated with plaintiff. Moreover, because the great majority of these students were girls, and all of them complained about opposite-sex rather than same-sex harassment or harassment based on sexual orientation, a reasonable inference of disparate treatment because of plaintiff's sex or sexual orientation arises. Furthermore, plaintiff has testified that he complained about the alleged harassment on numerous occasions to a wide variety of different School District officials. These facts support a finding that the School District had an established custom or practice of responding to his complaints differently than it did to those of girls or of boys complaining about opposite-sex harassment. Defendant's summary judgment motion against plaintiff's equal protection claim is denied for these reasons. As noted *supra*, however, there are significant fact issues involved in determining whether plaintiff was similarly situated with the other students who lodged complaints. For this reason, plaintiff's motion for summary judgment on this claim must also be denied.

E. Title IX Claim

Defendant further challenges plaintiff's Title IX claim on grounds of insufficient evidence. Defendant argues that the conduct upon which plaintiff

---

[96] [14] Only one of the formal complaints submitted was filed by a boy, who complained about opposite-sex harassment by a girl who had already filed harassment charges against him.

bases his claim is not gender-oriented. For the reasons set forth above in connection with defendant's motion to dismiss this claim on the pleadings, the Court disagrees. Defendant further argues that the alleged harassment is not sufficiently severe and pervasive to state a claim under Title IX, that it did not result in a denial of any educational opportunity, and that there is insufficient evidence of deliberate indifference to permit plaintiff's claims to proceed. For the reasons articulated in connection with defendant's summary judgment motion against plaintiff's MHRA claim, the Court also finds these arguments unpersuasive. [97]

In challenging plaintiff's Title IX claim, defendant also contends that under the Supreme Court's decision in *Gebser v. Lago Vista Ind. Sch. Dist.*, plaintiff failed to notify the appropriate authorities about the alleged harassment. *Gebser* involved a claim of sexual misconduct against a student by a teacher. In that case, the Court held that the school district did not have actual notice of the misconduct when the only official who knew about it was the offending teacher himself. The Court further held that in order to state a claim for damages under Title IX, a student must be able to prove that an official with sufficient authority to address the alleged harassment and to take corrective measures on the student's behalf has actual knowledge of it.

Defendant argues that under these holdings, a Title IX claimant may never prevail unless a principal or higher official has actual knowledge of the alleged discrimination. Defendant contends that knowledge by a teacher is therefore insufficient. This argument fails for two reasons. First, plaintiff plainly alleges that he did inform the principals in his schools about the student misconduct, and furthermore, that on at least one occasion he informed the office of the School District's superintendent. Moreover, defendant stretches the Supreme Court's holdings in *Gebser* beyond recognition in arguing that actual knowledge by a teacher is always insufficient. In this case, unlike *Gebser,* the alleged harassers were students and not teachers. Because teachers ordinarily maintain at least some level of disciplinary control over their students, it is reasonable to infer that they had authority to take disciplinary action and to institute other corrective measures to end the harassment. Indeed, the School District's sexual harassment policy imposes upon teachers a duty to convey reports of sexual harassment to the school principals. It is therefore clear that teachers had the authority to take at least this minimal corrective measure which, if effectively carried out, would impart knowledge of the harassment to higher School District officials with even greater authority to act.

Defendant also challenges plaintiff's Title IX claim on the ground that he has failed make any showing of damages as a result of the harassment he experienced. Defendant cites *Price v. City of Charlotte,* 93 F.3d 1241, 1250 (4th Cir. 1996), and *Patterson v. PHP Health Care Corp.,* 90 F.3d 927, 939

---

97 [15] In so holding, the Court does not intend to imply that the MHRA and Title IX are identical. Nevertheless, for purposes of analyzing the parties' motions, the Court evaluated plaintiff's MHRA claim under the Title IX deliberate indifference standard. Moreover Title IX is similar to the MHRA in requiring a sexual harassment claimant to show that the alleged harassment was so severe as to have the effect of denying him access to some educational benefit or opportunity. Furthermore, while ordinary teasing is insufficiently severe to state a claim under either statute, the kind of sexually-oriented physical touching that plaintiff experienced is.

(5th Cir. 1996), for the proposition that plaintiff's claim must be dismissed on this ground. Upon reviewing these authorities the Court finds that they do not support defendant's position. Rather, these cases stand for the proposition that in section 1983 cases, a plaintiff claiming emotional distress who fails to produce actual proof of injury is entitled to no more than nominal damages. They do not hold, as plaintiff suggests, that a failure to prove actual damages at the summary judgment stage constitutes grounds for dismissal on the issue of liability.

Finally, defendant challenges plaintiff's cause of action under Title IX on the ground that, as plead in his complaint, he bases this particular claim only on sexual harassment by female students. Defendant notes that plaintiff's evidence of such harassment is quite sparse. The Court agrees with defendant's characterization of the evidence. Nevertheless, when asked about the peculiar limitation on plaintiff's Title IX claim to harassment by only female students, plaintiff's counsel acknowledged that this was a mistake and stated that the focus of plaintiff's claim has always been on harassment by both male and female students. Counsel further suggested that plaintiff would be amenable to amending his complaint in order to correct this error.

Ordinarily the Court does not permit parties to amend their pleadings at this late stage in the process. Nevertheless, it does appear that defendant had ample notice of plaintiff's intent to litigate this matter on the basis of harassment by students of both sexes. Moreover, the parties conducted extensive discovery pertaining to plaintiff's allegations of harassment by male students in conjunction with his other claims. Permitting plaintiff to amend the complaint thus would not result in a need for further discovery. Although defendant argues that it would be prejudiced by an amendment to the pleadings at this point in time, it fails to articulate how such prejudice might arise. For these reasons, the Court concludes that plaintiff should be permitted to amend his complaint for the limited purposes of broadening his Title IX claim to include harassment by male as well as female students.

For all of these reasons, the Court denies defendant's summary judgment motion against plaintiff's Title IX claim. Nevertheless, because there are genuine factual issues remaining, the Court also denies plaintiff's cross-motion for summary judgment on this claim.

NOTES AND QUESTIONS

1. One survey of lesbian, gay, bisexual, and transgendered students found that 91.5 percent reported that they had heard derogatory reports such as "faggot" or "dyke" on a regular basis. Eighty-four percent reported that they had been verbally harassed and 39.1 percent reported that they had been physically harassed. Twenty-one percent reported assaults with punches, kicks, or weapons. Sixty-four percent said that they feel unsafe at school because of their sexual orientation. Eighty-five percent reported that faculty or staff never intervened or intervened only some of the time when they heard

homophobic comments. The Gay, Lesbian, and Straight Education Network, *National School Climate Survey* (2003), *available at* www.glsen.org.

Some schools have instituted policies that prohibit name-calling. *See* David Crary, *More Schools Try "No Name-Calling,"* ATLANTA J.-CONST., Jan. 24, 2005, at A6 (while taking "aim at insults of all kinds — whether based on a child's appearance, background or behavior" the program has been criticized by conservatives for references to sexual orientation harassment and using "The Misfits" as its centerpiece).

Not surprisingly, societal arguments about gay issues have made their way into the schoolhouse. *See* Caroline Hendrie, *T-Shirts on Gay Issues Spur Lawsuits*, ED. WK., Jan. 5, 2005 (lawsuits have emerged over t-shirts for both sides; one shirt stated "I'm gay and I'm proud"; another stated "Homosexuality is shameful"). To what extent should students be a captive audience for societal arguments over homosexuality? If a school allows a Gay Pride t-shirt, must it also allow a shirt proclaiming "I hate gays"? Or would this run afoul of anti-discrimination laws?

2. In *Ray v. Antioch Unified Sch. Dist.*, 107 F. Supp. 2d 1165, 1170 (N.D. Cal. 2000), the court saw no material difference between an instance where a female student is subject to unwelcome sexual comments due to the harasser's perception that she is a sex object and the instance where a male student is abused due to the harasser's perception that he is a homosexual and thus a subject of prey. "In both instances, the conduct is a heinous response to the harasser's perception of the victim's sexuality, and is not distinguished by this court." *Id.*

3. Does a student have a claim against the school district or school authorities if he or she is bullied by another student, if the bullying is not related to sex? Consider the issues presented in the following case.

[B] Bullying

STEVENSON v. MARTIN COUNTY BOARD OF EDUCATION

Court of Appeals for the Fourth Circuit
2001 U.S. App. LEXIS 1705 (2001)

PER CURIAM:

Alex Stevenson, by his father, Elmer William Stevenson, and the senior Mr. Stevenson, on his own behalf, brought this action under 42 U.S.C. § 1983 against the Martin County Board of Education and several school officials. Alex alleged that the defendants violated his liberty interest in bodily integrity and his property interest in a public education when they allowed his classmates to physically assault him at school over a period of several weeks. Alex also alleged a violation of the Safe and Drug-Free Schools and Communities Act as well as constitutional and common law claims under North Carolina law. The district court dismissed the complaint for failure to state a claim and declined to exercise supplemental jurisdiction over the state law claims. Because Alex has not alleged sufficient facts to hold the school board or its officials liable for federal constitutional violations and because a private right of action is not available under the Safe Schools Act, we affirm the dismissal of the federal claims. We also hold that the district court did not abuse its discretion in declining to exercise supplemental jurisdiction over the state law claims.

I.

The complaint sets forth a disturbing set of facts, which we take as true. In August 1998 ten-year-old Alex Stevenson began the sixth grade at Williamston Middle School in Martin County, North Carolina. He did not finish the year there, however. In November his father had to remove him from Williamston Middle School and enroll him in a private school because of the repeated assaults Alex suffered at the hands of several of his classmates.

The abuse started as soon as the school year began. On August 7, 1998, the second day of school, Alex's sixth-grade classmates Charles McEachern and Kemadrick Terrell Sherrod robbed and assaulted Alex in the lunch yard. Several days later on August 10 Sherrod threw books at Alex, and Sherrod was subsequently suspended. On August 20 McEachern picked a fight with Alex in retaliation for Sherrod's suspension. The school suspended both McEachern and Alex because of this fight.

On August 20 Alex's father, Elmer William Stevenson ("Stevenson"), met with the principal of Williamston Middle School, Harry Respass. At this meeting Stevenson told Respass that McEachern was threatening Alex, and he (Stevenson) expressed his concern that McEachern and his friends would seek revenge on Alex. Stevenson then requested that the school remove Alex from McEachern's classes. Although Respass assured Stevenson that the boys would be placed in separate classes, this was not done.

For the next month (from mid-August to mid-September) McEachern continued to harass and intimidate Alex. As he walked past Alex's locker, McEachern would hit and kick Alex in the head, chest, and back. Alex and his father complained to Principal Respass and school counselor Babbie Mills about these assaults, but McEachern was neither disciplined nor removed from Alex's classes.

The situation reached a new low on September 18. Alex and McEachern were in Swanola Chance's first-period art class, and McEachern wrongly accused Alex of breaking his glasses. When Alex denied it, McEachern began to punch Alex in the head. Alex temporarily escaped from the attack and asked Chance for help, but she responded, "There isn't anything I can do." She added, "You probably deserved it anyway." Because he was receiving no help from Chance, Alex told her that he was going to the principal's office. McEachern and a friend, Broderick Jones, followed Alex out of the classroom and chased him down the hallway. They knocked Alex to the floor, and for about ten minutes proceeded to punch and kick him in the head, throat, chest, arms, and legs. Adele Dees, a teacher in a nearby classroom, tried to stop McEachern and Jones, but they assaulted her as well. Several students eventually restrained the two attackers.

McEachern and Jones were suspended, and for several weeks they attended a school for students with disciplinary problems. Principal Respass did not, however, report the assaults to the juvenile authorities. On September 21 Stevenson filed juvenile petitions against McEachern and Jones, alleging assault with infliction of serious bodily injury. In January 1999 McEachern and Jones admitted the charges and received sentences of twelve-months probation and community service.

While the juvenile proceedings were pending, the assaults on Alex continued. On September 22 three of McEachern's friends threatened Alex during his first-period class. Alex promptly reported the threats to Principal Respass, but that did not prevent McEachern and his friends from assaulting Alex later in the day during lunch. One of the lunchtime attackers was suspended from school. On September 25 McEachern and several of his friends harassed Alex and his father while they were at a music festival in Williamston. The police intervened and escorted McEachern from the scene. Stevenson finally decided that because of the assaults and harassment, Alex would have to transfer to private school.

Alex suffered physical and emotional problems because of the repeated assaults and harassment. After the September 18 assault a doctor treated him for contusions, lacerations, and temporary eye dysfunction. A psychologist diagnosed Alex with major depression and attention deficit/hyperactivity disorder, and Alex began taking medication. He continues to receive counseling for his psychological problems.

Alex, through his father as next friend, and his father sued the Martin County Board of Education, Superintendent Willie Peele, Principal Respass, and Chance (the teacher) under 42 U.S.C. § 1983 and state law. Alex alleged that by failing to prevent McEachern and his fellow ruffians from attacking Alex, the defendants deprived him of his liberty interest in bodily integrity and his property interest in a public education, in violation of the Due Process Clause of the Fourteenth Amendment. *See* U.S. Const. amend. XIV, § 1. Alex also alleged that the defendants violated the Safe and Drug-Free Schools and Communities Act of 1994, 20 U.S.C. § 7101–7104, 7111–7143. The state law counts asserted claims of negligence, assault, negligent infliction of emotional distress, and violations of the North Carolina Constitution and the North Carolina Safe Schools Act. The district court granted the defendants' motion to dismiss, disposing of the federal claims under FED. R. CIV. P. 12(b)(6) and the state law claims under 28 U.S.C. § 1367(c)(3). Alex and his father appeal.

II.

We review de novo a grant of a motion to dismiss under FED. R. CIV. P. 12(b)(6), "accepting as true the well-pleaded facts in the complaint and viewing them in the light most favorable to the plaintiff." Because this is a civil rights case, we are also guided by the following additional principles. In testing the sufficiency of a civil rights complaint, "we must be especially solicitous of the wrongs alleged," and we "must not dismiss the complaint unless it appears to a certainty that the plaintiff would not be entitled to relief under any legal theory which might plausibly be suggested by the facts alleged." Furthermore, "claims under the Fourteenth Amendment merge[] into [a] § 1983 claim because § 1983 merely creates a statutory basis to receive a remedy for the deprivation of a constitutional right." Finally, we must keep in mind the difference between individual-capacity and official capacity suits under § 1983. A suit against a government official in his individual capacity for deprivation of federal rights seeks to impose personal liability upon the official. In contrast, a suit against a government official in his official capacity is treated as a suit against the government entity of which the official is an agent. Local government units are liable only if an official's execution of a municipal policy, practice, or custom caused the injury.

Reading the complaint with these principles in mind, we conclude that Alex intended to make the following three § 1983 claims; first, that Peele, Respass, and Chance deprived him of his constitutional property interest in a public education because the continued attacks forced him to leave Williamston Middle School; second, that the school officials deprived him of his constitutional liberty interest in bodily integrity by failing to stop the attacks by his fellow students; and third, that the Martin County Board of Education contributed to the violence by failing to develop appropriate school safety plans and by failing to train its school personnel in how to respond to violent students.

A.

Alex's first § 1983 claim is that the defendants deprived him of his property in violation of the Due Process Clause. When school officials suspend or expel a student, it triggers the student's property interest in a public education. *See Goss v. Lopez,* 419 U.S. 565, 572–76 (1975). However, a student is not deprived of his property interest when school officials engage in conduct such as reasonable corporal punishment, even though it has "the unintended effect of temporarily removing a child from" class. *See Ingraham v. Wright,* 430 U.S. 651, 674 n.43 (1977). In this case, Williamston Middle School officials did not suspend or expel Alex. Alex's father voluntarily withdrew Alex from school.

Alex argues, however, that the school "constructively expelled" him by fostering a climate of violence. Even though Alex failed to raise this argument to the district court, "we may consider such an issue if the error is 'plain' and our refusal to consider it would result in a miscarriage of justice."

Alex's constructive expulsion argument is a novel theory that has not yet been accepted by any court. It is inspired by constructive discharge cases arising under the employment laws. These cases hold that an employer constructively discharges an employee when the employer "deliberately makes an employee's working conditions intolerable and thereby forces him to quit his job." In the school violence context, the theory would mean that a student's property interest in public education is triggered when school officials deliberately make the learning environment so dangerous or intolerable that the student is forced to transfer to another school.

The question of whether we should accept the constructive expulsion theory is purely academic, however, because Alex's complaint does not allege sufficient facts to support the theory. There is no allegation that the school officials acted deliberately to force Alex out of Williamston Middle School or that they singled him out in their failure to control the hooliganism. In fact, the school took some steps, although without success, to remedy the problem. Moreover, because of the novelty of the theory, it cannot be plain error for the district court to conclude that the school officials did not deprive Alex of a property interest in public education when he voluntarily withdrew from school.

B.

Alex's second § 1983 claim is that the defendants violated his liberty interest in bodily integrity. In this case, the perpetrators of the attacks against Alex were private individuals, not the school officials. The law is clear that "a State's failure to protect an individual against private violence simply does not constitute a violation of the Due Process Clause." *DeShaney v. Winnebago County Dep't of Soc. Servs.*, 489 U.S. 189, 197 (1989). There are, however, two exceptions to this general rule.

First, if the state has a special relationship with an individual, the state has an affirmative duty to protect the individual from harm inflicted by third parties. The Supreme Court has defined a "special relationship" in the following way:

> When the State by the affirmative exercise of its power so restrains an individual's liberty that it renders him unable to care for himself, and at the same time fails to provide for his basic human needs — e.g., food, clothing, shelter, medical care, and reasonable safety — it transgresses the substantive limits on state action set by . . . the Due Process Clause. . . . It is the State's affirmative act of restraining the individual's freedom to act on his own behalf — through incarceration, institutionalization, or other similar restraint of personal liberty — which is the "deprivation of liberty" triggering the protections of the Due Process Clause, not its failure to act to protect his liberty interests against harms inflicted by other means.

Several circuits have been faced with the issue of whether a school-student relationship is a special relationship triggering the protections of the Due Process Clause. They have held uniformly that no special relationship exists because the student is not in physical custody and, along with parental help, is able to care for his basic human needs. This circuit has also recognized that "incarceration, institutionalization, or the like" is needed to "trigger the affirmative duty" under the Due Process Clause. *Pinder v. Johnson,* 54 F.3d 1169, 1175 (4th Cir. 1995) (en banc).

Following the lead of our sister circuits, we hold that the Martin County School officials did not have a "special relationship" with Alex that triggered the protections of the Due Process Clause in this case. When a student attends public school, his liberty is not restrained to the extent contemplated in *DeShaney.* Attending school is not the equivalent of incarceration or institutionalization. Although a student must remain in school during the day and the school functions much as a parent during that time, the state has not assumed total responsibility for the student's care. The student's parents retain the ability to provide for his basic human needs, and the child remains free to seek their help and protection. Therefore, the state, simply by virtue of its maintenance of a public school system, does not become constitutionally liable for failing to prevent all student-on-student violence. Although the school officials here may have been irresponsible and ineffective in not heeding the warnings that Alex was helpless at the hands of bullies, they have not committed a constitutional violation.

The second exception to the general rule that a state is not liable for the acts of third parties occurs when the state itself creates the danger. In order to create a danger, the state has to take some affirmative steps. Liability does not arise when the state stands by and does nothing in the face of danger. Failing to provide protection from danger does not implicate the state in the harm caused by third parties.

In *Pinder* this court was faced with a case in which it had to decide the contours of *DeShaney*'s state-created danger exception. Pinder's ex-boyfriend, Pittman, broke into her home, assaulted her, and threatened to kill her and her three children. Pinder called the police, and when an officer arrived, she told him about the attack and the threats. The officer arrested Pittman and assured Pinder that she could safely leave her children at home alone while she went to work because Pittman would be in custody. However, because the police charged Pittman with misdemeanor offenses, he was released almost immediately. While Pinder was at work, Pittman set fire to her house, killing her three children who were asleep. Pinder sued the arresting officer, claiming that he had created the danger. This court dismissed her suit because it was "purely an omission claim" where all that could be said was that the officer " 'stood by and did nothing when suspicious circumstances dictated a more active role.' " The state's conduct was not on that "point on the spectrum between action and inaction" such that it was implicated in the injury.

The facts in *DeShaney* are equally disturbing. Randy DeShaney beat his four-year-old son Joshua so severely that Joshua suffered permanent brain damage. This tragic incident came after the Winnebago County Department of Social Services (DDS) in Wisconsin had been informed of child abuse. In fact, DDS had obtained a court order placing Joshua in the temporary custody of a hospital after DeShaney's beatings put Joshua there, but thereafter DDS released Joshua into his father's custody. Caseworkers had also made monthly visits to the DeShaney home, in which they observed suspicious injuries on Joshua's body. *See DeShaney*, 489 U.S. at 192–93. The Court nevertheless held that the state was not liable for a constitutional violation. The facts only amounted to a failure of the DDS to protect Joshua from private violence and the state had no constitutional duty to protect Joshua. *See id.* at 202–03.

Given the rejection of the plaintiffs' § 1983 claims in *DeShaney* and *Pinder*, we have to conclude in this case that the school officials did not create the danger that Alex faced at the hands of his classmates. In fact, the school did more than just stand by while Alex was being brutalized. The school took some measures to remedy the situation. Principal Respass met with Alex's father to discuss the problem. In addition, the school suspended McEachern twice and eventually sent him to a special disciplinary program. Two other attackers, including Jones, were also suspended. The school surely could have done more to protect Alex, given the frequent and brutal attacks by McEachern and others. But the failure to protect by itself is not sufficient to trigger constitutional liability in this situation.

Furthermore, in the school violence context, some courts have required that school officials must act with deliberate indifference before there is liability for student-on-student attacks. These courts have said that the school must engage in intentional or reckless affirmative conduct that shocks the conscience of federal judges. Alex has not alleged that the school officials intentionally or recklessly took steps to contribute to the violence. Teacher Chance's response when Alex reported being punched in the head does not amount to deliberate indifference when considered in context. Chance said, "There isn't anything I can do. You probably deserved it anyway." This statement appears to express frustration and resignation more than anything else. While Chance might have tried harder to help Alex, this does not mean that she deprived Alex of his constitutional rights.

For all of the above reasons, this case does not fall into the state-created danger exception to *DeShaney*.

C.

Alex's final § 1983 claim is against the Martin County Board of Education. He alleges that the board was responsible for his brutalization because it failed to develop adequate school safety plans and failed to train teachers and administrators in proper techniques for controlling violence in school. Local government units are subject to § 1983 liability for the unconstitutional acts of their employees when the employee acts pursuant to a municipal policy, practice, or custom. In addition, a municipal entity can be liable if its failure to train its employees leads to some unconstitutional conduct. The failure to train must amount to "deliberate indifference to the rights of persons with whom [the employees] come into contact."

We do not have to reach the question of whether the school official's conduct in this case arose from a municipal policy or custom, nor do we have to determine whether the board's failure to train the teachers and administrators amounted to deliberate indifference. An award of damages against a municipality based on the actions of its officers is not available unless the officers' conduct amounted to a constitutional injury. Because we have already determined that Alex's allegations do not amount to a § 1983 violation on the part of the school officials, it follows that the school board likewise cannot be held constitutionally liable.

III.

Alex also argues that the defendants violated the Safe and Drug-Free Schools and Communities Act of 1994 (Safe Schools Act), 20 U.S.C. §§ 7101–7104, 7111–7143, by failing to develop an appropriate school safety plan that would help control student-on-student violence. The Safe Schools Act is a federal grant program that aims to prevent violence and drug abuse in schools. These goals are accomplished through federal assistance to states so that they can make grants to local educational agencies and community organizations. Federal money also goes to fund private, non-profit organizations and colleges and universities that develop anti-violence and anti-drug initiatives. *See* 20 U.S.C. § 7103. The Act does not expressly create a private right of action. Therefore, we must determine whether Alex has an implied right to maintain a Safe Schools Act claim.

In answering this question, we must first decide if the Act grants Alex any substantive rights. For a person to bring a claim under conditional spending legislation, the statute must confer substantive rights in favor of the class to which the person belongs. Substantive rights are created only if Congress provided the recipients of federal funding clear notice that by accepting funds, they have chosen to participate in a statutory scheme under which private individuals gain enforceable rights. Because the Safe Schools Act was enacted pursuant to the Spending Clause, Alex's claim will be allowed only if the statute puts funding recipients on notice of a private right of action.

Stevenson relies on *Davis v. Monroe County Bd. of Educ.*, to argue that the Safe Schools Act puts schools receiving federal funds on notice that their students can sue them for failing to implement school safety plans. In *Davis* the plaintiff, on behalf of her minor daughter, sued a school board under Title IX of the Education Amendments Act of 1972, *see* 20 U.S.C. §§ 1681–1688, after her daughter was sexually harassed by one of her classmates when she was in fifth grade. The plaintiff alleged that the school failed to take any measures against the harasser even though her daughter repeatedly reported the incidents to teachers and to the principal, asking them for help. *See id.* at 633–35. The Court held that Title IX supported a private damages action against a school for severe student-on-student harassment because the statutory scheme put schools on notice that they could be held liable for their failure to respond to students' discriminatory acts, if the failure amounted to deliberate indifference. The Court pointed to the language of the statute itself, which makes schools liable if they subject persons to discrimination under their programs or activities or deny students educational benefits. In addition, the Court relied on the fact that the Department of Education had promulgated regulations requiring recipients of federal funds to monitor third-party discrimination. The Court added that the common law puts schools on notice because it allows "claims alleging that schools have been negligent in failing to protect their students from the torts of their peers."

Unlike Title IX, the Safe Schools Act does not put schools on notice that they can be sued for failing to implement anti-violence programs. Alex has not pointed to anything in the language or purpose of the Act that would suggest otherwise. The Department of Education has not promulgated any regulations pursuant to the Act. Furthermore, no court has held that the Safe Schools Act creates a private right of action in any situation, whereas for Title IX, it had already been established before *Davis* that Title IX creates a cause of action for damages when the school officials themselves engage in the discriminatory conduct. *See Franklin v. Gwinnett County Pub. Schs.*; *Cannon v. University of Chicago.*

The fact that the common law might allow suits against schools for student-on-student violence does not help Stevenson either. The Court in *Davis* placed little, if any, emphasis on the common law in reaching the conclusion that Title IX gave schools notice of a private right of action for student-on-student harassment. It only mentioned the common law after discussing the language, purpose, and regulations of Title IX. There is nothing in *Davis* to suggest that the common law alone could put the recipient of federal funds on notice that a Spending Clause statute creates a private right of action. We hold that because the Safe Schools Act does not put schools on notice of the creation of an enforceable substantive right, Alex cannot bring a Safe Schools Act claim.

IV.

Alex also brought several state law claims against the defendants, alleging negligence, assault, and negligent infliction of emotional distress, violations of North Carolina's constitutional right to an education, N.C. Const. art. 1, § 15, art. 9, § 2, and violations of the North Carolina Safe Schools Act, N.C. GEN. STAT. § 115C-105.45. Once the district court dismissed the federal claims, it exercised its discretion to decline supplemental jurisdiction over the state claims. *See* 28 U.S.C. § 1367(c). We review a district court's decision not to exercise supplemental jurisdiction for abuse of discretion. The district court did not abuse its discretion in this case. It made a prudent decision in light of the fact that Stevenson had not stated a claim under § 1983.

V.

To summarize, we hold that all three of Stevenson's § 1983 claims were properly dismissed under FED. R. CIV. P. 12(b)(6). The school officials did not deprive Alex of his property interest in a public education because they did not expel or suspend him. The officials likewise did not deprive him of his liberty interest in bodily integrity because they did not prevent him from taking care of himself, nor did they create the dangerous situation he found himself in. The school board cannot be held liable where there was no underlying constitutional violation. We also hold that there is no private right of action under the Safe and Drug-Free Schools and Communities Act, nor is it possible to assert the statutory claim through § 1983 because the Act does not put schools on notice that they are open to suit by private parties. Finally, the district court did not abuse its discretion in declining to exercise supplemental jurisdiction over the state law claims. The judgment is affirmed.

Affirmed.

NOTES AND QUESTIONS

1. After reading the foregoing opinion, can you draft a complaint to help Alex?

2. The *Stevenson* opinion is unpublished. What reasons would the Fourth Circuit have for making that choice? Do unpublished opinions have value?

3. More fallout from Columbine: The Colorado legislature passed a statute that requires every school district in the state to have an anti-bullying policy

in place, citing bullying as one of the contributing factors in the Columbine tragedy. Mary Ann Zehr, *Legislatures Take on Bullies With New Laws*, EDUC. WK., May 16, 2001, at 18. At least 16 states have passed anti-bullying legislation. *See* Kathleen Hart, *Sticks and Stones and Shotguns at School: The Ineffectiveness of Constitutional Antibullying Legislation as a Response to School Violence*, 39 GA. L. REV. 1109 (2005). Hart divides the anti-bullying legislation into five categories, based on how the statute defines bullying:

> Tort-based definition: In Georgia, bullying includes "any willful attempt or threat to inflict injury on another person, when accompanied by an apparent present ability to do so." O.C.G.A. § 20-2-751.4(a)(1) (2001).

> *Tinker*-based definition: In New Jersey, bullying must have "the effect of insulting or demeaning any student or group of students in such a way as to cause substantial disruption in, or substantial interference with, the orderly operation of the school." N.J. STAT. ANN. § 18A:37-14(b) (West Supp. 2004).

> Creation of a hostile educational environment-based definition: In Louisiana, "harassment," "intimidation," and "bullying" is "any intentional gesture or written, verbal, or physical act that: (a) A reasonable person under the circumstances should know will have the effect of harming a student or damaging his property or placing a student in reasonable fear of harm to his life or person or damage to his property; and (b) Is so severe, persistent, or pervasive that it creates an intimidating, threatening, or abusive educational environment for a student." LA. REV. STAT. ANN. § 17:416.13(B)(2)(b) (West Supp. 2004).

> Fighting words-based definition: In New Hampshire, "insults, taunts, or challenges, whether verbal or physical in nature, which are likely to intimidate or provoke a violent or disorderly response" are prohibited. N.H. REV. STAT. § 193-F:3(II)(a) (2004).

> Intent to ridicule-based definition: In Connecticut, bullying includes "any overt acts by a student or a group of students directed against another student with the intent to ridicule, humiliate or intimidate the other student while on school grounds or at a school-sponsored activity which acts are repeated against the same student over time." CONN. GEN. STAT. ANN. § 10-222d (West Supp. 2004).

"Although the current antibullying statutes serve to raise awareness of this pressing issue, they must be augmented by resources that will equip teachers and students to effect the change in attitude and school culture necessary to prevent further 'Columbines.'" *Id.* at 1114. Other countries, including Norway, Scotland, Australia, Israel, and Japan, have implemented anti-bullying programs. In sub-Saharan African countries, cheating sometimes motivates the bullying since exam scores dictate whether a student will continue on to higher education or remain in poverty. According to Beverly Jones, the director of the Global Learning Group at the Academy for Educational Development, with three students per desk, "heaven help the student who happens to be a good student and covers up their paper so other students can't see." Marianne D. Hurst, *When It Comes to Bullying, There Are No Boundaries*, EDUC. WK., Feb. 9, 2005, at 8.

4. One proposal for an anti-bullying statute in Washington state was derailed when members of the state's chapter of the Christian Coalition claimed that the anti-bullying policies could violate the free speech rights of students who expressed opposition to homosexuality. At the same time, schools are being urged to take a more active role in stemming the harassment of gay students. Darcia H. Bowman, *Report Says Schools Often Ignore Harassment of Gay Students*, EDUC. WK., June 6, 2001, at 5 (discussing two-year study by Human Rights Watch that stated that the education of many gay students may be in jeopardy because of constant bullying and the tendency of teachers and administrators to ignore such treatment). One high school teacher noted, "In many schools, if a student uses a racial slur or an ethnic slur, they're punished for that . . . . But for some reason 'dyke' and 'fag' and those kinds of words aren't equated with the same level of discrimination." *Id.*

5. Bullying can take many forms, and the Internet has given bullies an additional method to torment their victims. Some forms of "cyberbullying" include one student sending a threatening e-mail to another and then forwarding it on to more people; several students slamming a victim with instant messages simultaneously; and creating derogatory websites dedicated to one or more victims. Although these actions take place at home, the "fallout happens during the school day, leaving teachers and administrators to clean up the mess." Julie Blair, *New Breed of Bullies Torment Their Peers on the Internet*, EDUC. WK., Feb. 5, 2003, at 6.

6. Helping children who are bullies learn to change their behavior may have far-reaching consequences. A report by Fight Crime: Invest in Kids reports that "bullying spawns loneliness, depression and suicidal tendencies among its victims and foreshadows crime and violence by perpetrators." According to the report, nearly 60 percent of the male bullies in sixth through ninth grade were convicted of at least one crime by age 24 (40 percent had three or more convictions). *Does School Bullying Lead to Crime?*, Sept. 4, 2003, *available at* http://stacks.msnbc.com/news/961312.asp.

Although the Department of Education has promulgated regulations directing grant recipients to adopt policies to prevent sexual harassment, and some states have required anti-bullying policies, school districts that adopt such policies may be sued by students who object because the policies infringe on students' right of free expression.

[C] Sexual Harassment Policies Versus Free Expression

SAXE v. STATE COLLEGE AREA SCHOOL DISTRICT

Court of Appeals for the Third Circuit
240 F.3d 200 (2001)

ALITO, CIRCUIT JUDGE:

The plaintiffs in this case challenge the constitutionality of a public school district's "anti-harassment" policy, arguing that it violates the First Amendment's guarantee of freedom of speech.[98] The District Court, concluding that the policy prohibited no more speech than was already unlawful under federal and state anti-discrimination laws, held that the policy is constitutional and entered judgment for the school district. We reverse.

I.

A.

In August 1999, the State College Area School District ("SCASD") adopted an Anti-Harassment Policy ("the Policy"). The full text of the Policy is reproduced in the Appendix to this opinion; we will briefly review the most relevant portions here.

The Policy begins by setting forth its goal — "providing all students with a safe, secure, and nurturing school environment" — and noting that "disrespect among members of the school community is unacceptable behavior which threatens to disrupt the school environment and well being of the individual." The second paragraph contains what appears to be the Policy's operative definition of harassment:

Harassment means verbal or physical conduct based on one's actual or perceived race, religion, color, national origin, gender, sexual orientation, disability, or other personal characteristics, and which has the purpose or effect of substantially interfering with a student's educational performance or creating an intimidating, hostile or offensive environment.

The Policy continues by providing several examples of "harassment":

Harassment can include any unwelcome verbal, written or physical conduct which offends, denigrates or belittles an individual because of any of the characteristics described above. Such conduct includes, but is not limited to, unsolicited derogatory remarks, jokes, demeaning comments or behaviors, slurs, mimicking, name calling, graffiti, innuendo, gestures, physical contact, stalking, threatening, bullying, extorting or the display or circulation of written material or pictures.

---

[98] [1] Plaintiffs also assert that the Policy violates the free speech guarantee of the Pennsylvania Constitution. However, plaintiffs fail to present any authority to show that Pennsylvania's guarantees are any broader than the First Amendment's. Accordingly, we confine our discussion to the plaintiffs' federal constitutional claims.

These examples are followed by a lengthy section captioned "Definitions," which defines various types of prohibited harassment, including "Sexual harassment," "Racial and color harassment," "Harassment on the basis of religion," "Harassment based on national origin," "Disability harassment," and "Other harassment" on the basis of characteristics such as "clothing, physical appearance, social skills, peer group, intellect, educational program, hobbies or values, etc." The definitions state that harassment "can include unwelcome verbal, written or physical conduct directed at" the particular characteristic. Examples of specific types of harassment are also provided. For example, "Racial and color harassment" is said to include "nicknames emphasizing stereotypes, racial slurs, comments on manner of speaking, and negative references to racial customs." Religious harassment reaches "derogatory comments regarding surnames, religious tradition, or religious clothing, or religious slurs or graffiti." National origins harassment includes "negative comments regarding surnames, manner of speaking, customs, language, or ethnic slurs." Harassment on the basis of sexual orientation extends to "negative name calling and degrading behavior." Disability harassment encompasses "imitating manner of speech or movement."

The Policy provides that "any harassment of a student by a member of the school community is a violation of this policy." It establishes procedures for the reporting, informal mediation, and formal resolution of complaints. In addition, the Policy sets a list of punishments for harassment, "including but not limited to warning, exclusion, suspension, expulsion, transfer, termination, discharge . . . , training, education, or counseling."

B.

Plaintiff David Saxe is a member of the Pennsylvania State Board of Education and serves as an unpaid volunteer for SCASD. He is the legal guardian of both student-plaintiffs, who are enrolled in SCASD schools. After the Anti-Harassment Policy was adopted, Saxe filed suit in District Court, alleging that the Policy was facially unconstitutional under the First Amendment's free speech clause. In his Complaint, he alleged that all Plaintiffs openly and sincerely identify themselves as Christians. They believe, and their religion teaches, that homosexuality is a sin. Plaintiffs further believe that they have a right to speak out about the sinful nature and harmful effects of homosexuality. Plaintiffs also feel compelled by their religion to speak out on other topics, especially moral issues.

Plaintiffs further alleged that they feared that they were likely to be punished under the Policy for speaking out about their religious beliefs, engaging in symbolic activities reflecting those beliefs, and distributing religious literature. They sought to have the Policy declared unconstitutionally vague and overbroad and its operation permanently enjoined.

The District Court found that Saxe had standing to mount a facial challenge but granted SCASD's motion to dismiss on the pleadings, holding that the Policy was facially constitutional. The Court found that the Policy's operative definition of harassment was contained in its second paragraph, which, as the Court read it, prohibited "language or conduct which is based on specified characteristics and which has the effect of 'substantially interfering with a student's educational performance' or which creates a hostile educational atmosphere." The Court went on to observe that this standard is similar to "that used by courts and agencies to define harassment for purposes of Title VII, Title IX, the Pennsylvania Human Relations Act, etc." Consequently, the Court held that the Policy does not prohibit "anything that is not already prohibited by law" and therefore cannot be unconstitutional. Rejecting the plaintiffs' vagueness argument, the Court asserted that "a more precise definition of harassment, like Justice Stewart's famous description of 'pornography,' may be virtually impossible." Plaintiffs appealed.

II.

The District Court dismissed the plaintiffs' free speech claims based on its conclusion that "harassment," as defined by federal and state anti-discrimination statutes, is not entitled to First Amendment protection. The Court rejected the plaintiffs' characterization of the Policy as a "hate speech code," holding instead that it merely prohibits harassment that is already unlawful under state and federal law. The Court observed:

> Harassment has never been considered to be protected activity under the First Amendment. In fact, the harassment prohibited under the Policy already is unlawful. The Policy is a tool which gives SCASD the ability to take action itself against harassment which may subject it to civil liability.

We disagree with the District Court's reasoning. There is no categorical "harassment exception" to the First Amendment's free speech clause. Moreover, the SCASD Policy prohibits a substantial amount of speech that would not constitute actionable harassment under either federal or state law.

A.

Because the District Court based its holding on a determination that the Policy simply replicated existing law, we begin by briefly reviewing the scope of the applicable anti-harassment statutes. At the federal level, discriminatory harassment in the public schools is governed primarily by two statutes. Title VI of the Civil Rights Act of 1964 provides that "no person in the United States shall, on the ground of race, color, or national origin, be excluded from participation in, be denied the benefits of, or be subjected to discrimination under any program or activity receiving Federal financial assistance." 42 U.S.C. § 2000d. Title IX of the Education Amendments of 1972 further provides that "no person . . . shall, on the basis of sex, be excluded from participation in, be denied the benefits of, or be subjected to discrimination under any educational program or activity receiving federal financial assistance." 20 U.S.C. § 1681(a). Although less often involved in harassment cases, the Rehabilitation Act of 1973, 29 U.S.C. § 794, makes it unlawful for programs receiving federal assistance to discriminate on the basis of disability or age.

The federal courts have held that these statutes create a private right of action similar to that available under Title VII, which prohibits discrimination in the workplace. Most significantly for this case, the Supreme Court has recognized that a public school student may bring suit against a school under Title IX for so-called "hostile environment" harassment.

The concept of "hostile environment" harassment originated in a series of Title VII cases involving sexual harassment in the workplace. In *Meritor Savings Bank v. Vinson*, the Supreme Court held that Title VII prohibits abusive and discriminatory conduct that creates a "hostile environment" — that is, harassment so severe or pervasive as "to alter the conditions of the victim's employment and create an abusive working environment." In *Harris v. Forklift Systems, Inc.*, the Court clarified that in order for conduct to constitute harassment under a "hostile environment" theory, it must both: (1) be viewed subjectively as harassment by the victim and (2) be objectively severe or pervasive enough that a reasonable person would agree that it is harassment. The Court emphasized that the objective prong of this inquiry must be evaluated by looking at the "totality of the circumstances." "These may include," the Court observed, "the frequency of the discriminatory conduct; its severity; whether it is physically threatening or humiliating, or a mere offensive utterance; and whether it unreasonably interferes with an employee's work performance." *Id.* at 23. In defining the contours of this concept, the Court has repeatedly stated that Title VII is not violated by the "mere utterance of an . . . epithet which engenders offensive feelings in an employee" or by mere " 'discourtesy or rudeness,' unless so severe or pervasive as to constitute an objective change in the conditions of employment." *Faragher v. City of Boca Raton.*

The Supreme Court has extended an analogous cause of action to students under Title IX. Originally, such claims were limited to cases involving harassment of a student by a teacher or other agent of the school. However, in 1999, in *Davis v. Monroe County Board of Education*, the Court held that Title IX also permits a plaintiff to recover damages from a federally funded educational institution for certain cases of student-on-student sexual harassment. To recover in such a case, a plaintiff must establish sexual harassment of students that is so severe, pervasive, and objectively offensive, and that so undermines and detracts from the victims' educational experience, that the victim-students are effectively denied equal access to an institution's resources and opportunities.

This determination " 'depends on a constellation of surrounding circumstances, expectations, and relationships,' including, but not limited to, the ages of the harasser and the victim, and the number of individuals involved." The Court stressed that "damages are not available for simple acts of teasing and name-calling among school children, even where these comments target differences in gender." 526 U.S. at 652. Rather, private damages actions against the school are limited to cases is which the school "acts with deliberate indifference to known acts of harassment," and those acts have "a systemic effect on educational programs and activities."[99]

---

[99] [5] Although both *Franklin* and *Davis* dealt with sexual harassment under Title IX, we believe that their reasoning applies equally to harassment on the basis of the personal characteristics enumerated in Title VI and other relevant federal anti-discrimination statutes.

B.

With this framework in mind, we now turn to the District Court's assertion that "harassment has never been considered to be protected activity under the First Amendment." The District Court's categorical pronouncement exaggerates the current state of the case law in this area.

There is of course no question that non-expressive, physically harassing conduct is entirely outside the ambit of the free speech clause. But there is also no question that the free speech clause protects a wide variety of speech that listeners may consider deeply offensive, including statements that impugn another's race or national origin or that denigrate religious beliefs. When laws against harassment attempt to regulate oral or written expression on such topics, however detestable the views expressed may be, we cannot turn a blind eye to the First Amendment implications. "Where pure expression is involved," anti-discrimination law "steers into the territory of the First Amendment."

This is especially true because, as the Fifth Circuit has noted, when anti-discrimination laws are "applied to . . . harassment claims founded solely on verbal insults, pictorial or literary matter, the statutes impose[] content-based, viewpoint-discriminatory restrictions on speech." Indeed, a disparaging comment directed at an individual's sex, race, or some other personal characteristic has the potential to create an "hostile environment" — and thus come within the ambit of anti-discrimination laws — precisely because of its sensitive subject matter and because of the odious viewpoint it expresses. [100]

This sort of content-or viewpoint-based restriction is ordinarily subject to the most exacting First Amendment scrutiny. This point was dramatically illustrated in *R.A.V. v. City of St. Paul*, in which the Supreme Court struck down a municipal hate-speech ordinance prohibiting "fighting words" that aroused "anger, alarm or resentment on the basis of race, color, creed, religion or gender." While recognizing that fighting words generally are unprotected by the First Amendment, the Court nevertheless found that the ordinance unconstitutionally discriminated on the basis of content and viewpoint:

> Displays containing some words — odious racial epithets, for example — would be prohibited to proponents of all views. But 'fighting words' that do not themselves invoke race, color, creed, religion, or gender — aspersions upon a person's mother, for example — would seemingly be usable ad libitum in the placards of those arguing in favor of racial,

---

[100] [6] Most commentators including those who favor and oppose First Amendment protection for harassing speech, agree that federal anti-discrimination law regulates speech on the basis of content and viewpoint. *See, e.g.*, Deborah Epstein, *Can a "Dumb Ass Woman" Achieve Equality in the Workplace? Running the Gauntlet of Hostile Environment Harassing Speech*, 84 GEO. L.J. 399, 433 (1996); Eugene Volokh, *How Harassment Law Restricts Free Speech*, 47 RUTGERS L. REV. 563, 571–72 (1995); Suzanne Sangree, *Title VII Prohibitions Against Hostile Environment Sexual Harassment and the First Amendment: No Collision in Sight*, 47 RUTGERS L. REV. 461, 477 (1995); Richard H. Fallon, *Sexual Harassment, Content Neutrality, and the First Amendment Dog That Didn't Bark*, 1994 SUP. CT. L. REV. 1, 8 (1994); Kingsley R. Browne, *Title VII as Censorship: Hostile-Environment Harassment and the First Amendment*, 52 OHIO STATE L.J. 481, 481 (1991); *Marcy Strauss, Sexist Speech in the Workplace*, 25 HARV. C.R.-C.L. L. REV. 1, 32–33 (1990). *But see* Charles R. Calleros, *Title VII and the First Amendment: Content-Neutral Regulation, Disparate Impact, and the "Reasonable Person"*, 58 OHIO ST. L.J. 1217 (1997).

color, etc. tolerance and equality, but could not be used by that speaker's opponents.

Striking down the law, the Court concluded that "the point of the First Amendment is that majority preferences must be expressed in some fashion other than silencing speech on the basis of content."

Loosely worded anti-harassment laws may pose some of the same problems as the St. Paul hate speech ordinance: they may regulate deeply offensive and potentially disruptive categories of speech based, at least in part, on subject matter and viewpoint. Although the Supreme Court has written extensively on the scope of workplace harassment, it has never squarely addressed whether harassment, when it takes the form of pure speech, is exempt from First Amendment protection.

SCASD relies heavily on a passage in *R.A.V.* in which the Court suggested in dictum that at least some harassing speech does not warrant First Amendment protection:

> Since words in some circumstances violate laws directed not against speech but against conduct (a law against treason, for example, is violated by telling the enemy the nation's defense secrets) a particular content-based subcategory of a proscribable class of speech can be swept up incidentally within the reach of a statute directed at conduct rather than speech. . . . Thus, for example, sexually derogatory 'fighting words,' among other words, may produce a violation of Title VII's general prohibition against sexual discrimination in employment practices. Where the government does not target conduct on the basis of its expressive content, acts are not shielded from regulation merely because they express a discriminatory idea or philosophy.

This passage suggests that government may constitutionally prohibit speech whose non-expressive qualities promote discrimination. For example, a supervisor's statement "sleep with me or you're fired" may be proscribed not on the ground of any expressive idea that the statement communicates, but rather because it facilitates the threat of discriminatory conduct. Despite the purely verbal quality of such a threat, it surely is no more "speech" for First Amendment purposes than the robber's demand "your money or your life." *Accord NLRB v. Gissel Packing Co.* (holding that employer's "threat of retaliation" on basis of union membership was "without the protection of the First Amendment").[101] Similarly, we see no constitutional problem with using

---

101 [8] The cases cited in *R.A.V.* each upheld a restriction on expressive conduct that was based solely on secondary effects of the speech that were merely incidental to its expressive content. In none of these cases, however, did the Court imply that the government may prohibit speech based on a desire to suppress the ideas it communicates. In *Barnes*, the Court found that the state's legitimate interest in preventing public nudity permitted it to enforce a public indecency statute against a nude dancing establishment:

> We do not think that when Indiana applies its statute to the nude dancing in these nightclubs it is proscribing nudity because of the erotic message conveyed by the dancers. . . . The perceived evil that Indiana seeks to address is not erotic dancing, but public nudity. The appearance of people of all shapes, sizes and ages in the nude

an employer's offensive speech as evidence of motive or intent in a case involving an allegedly discriminatory employment action.

The previously quoted passage from *R.A.V.*, however, does not necessarily mean that anti-discrimination laws are categorically immune from First Amendment challenge when they are applied to prohibit speech solely on the basis of its expressive content. "Harassing" or discriminatory speech, although evil and offensive, may be used to communicate ideas or emotions that nevertheless implicate First Amendment protections. As the Supreme Court has emphatically declared, "if there is a bedrock principle underlying the First Amendment, it is that the government may not prohibit the expression of an idea simply because society finds the idea offensive or disagreeable." *Texas v. Johnson,* 491 U.S. 397, 414 (1989).

For this reason, we cannot accept SCASD's contention that the application of anti-harassment law to expressive speech can be justified as a regulation of the speech's "secondary effects." *R.A.V.* did acknowledge that content-discriminatory speech restrictions may be permissible when the content classification merely "happens to be associated with particular 'secondary effects' of the speech, so that the regulation is 'justified without reference to the content of the . . . speech.'" The Supreme Court has made it clear, however, that the government may not prohibit speech under a "secondary effects" rationale based solely on the emotive impact that its offensive content may have on a listener: "Listeners' reactions to speech are not the type of 'secondary effects' we referred to in *Renton.* . . . The emotive impact of speech on its audience is not a 'secondary effect.'" *Boos v. Barry,* 485 U.S. 312, 321 (1988); *see also United States v. Playboy Entertainment Group,* 529 U.S. 803 (2000) ("The overriding justification for the regulation is concern for the effect of the subject matter on [listeners] . . . . This is the essence of content-based regulation."); *Forsyth County v. Nationalist Movement,* 505 U.S. 123, 134

---

at a beach, for example, would convey little if any erotic message, yet the State still seeks to prevent it. Public nudity is the evil the State seeks to prevent, whether or not it is combined with expressive activity.

Barnes, 501 U.S. at 570. Similarly, in *Supreme Court Trial Lawyers*, the Court upheld, against First Amendment challenge, the application of the Sherman Act against boycotters based on the boycott's economic effects:

A nonviolent and totally voluntary boycott may have a disruptive effect on local economic conditions. This Court has recognized the strong governmental interest in certain forms of economic regulation, even though such regulation may have an incidental effect on rights of speech and association.

Supreme Court Trial Lawyers, 493 U.S. at 428 n.12 (quoting *NAACP v. Claiborne Hardware Co.,* 458 U.S. 886, 912 (1982)). Finally, in *O'Brien*, the Court found no First Amendment impediment to prosecuting anti-war protestors who had violated federal law by burning their draft cards:

Even on the assumption that the alleged communicative element in O'Brien's conduct is sufficient to bring into play the First Amendment, it does not necessarily follow that the destruction of a registration certificate is constitutionally protected activity. . . . The many functions performed by Selective Service certificates establish beyond doubt that Congress has a legitimate and substantial interest in preventing their wanton and unrestrained destruction and assuring their continuing availability by punishing people who knowingly and wilfully destroy or mutilate them.

O'Brien, 391 U.S. at 376, 380. *Accord Wisconsin v. Mitchell,* 508 U.S. 476, 487–88 (1993) (noting that conduct not targeted on the basis of its expressive content may be regulated under Title VII).

(1992) ("Listeners' reaction to speech is not a content-neutral basis for regulation."). Nor do we believe that the restriction of expressive speech on the basis of its content may be characterized as a mere "time, place and manner" regulation. *See Reno v. ACLU,* 521 U.S. 844, 879 (1997) ("time, place and manner" analysis not applicable when statute "regulates speech on the basis of its content"); *Pacific Gas & Elec. Co. v. Public Util. Comm'n,* 475 U.S. 1, 20 (1986) ("for a time, place, or manner regulation to be valid, it must be neutral as to the content of the speech"); *Consolidated Edison Co. v. Public Serv. Comm'n,* 447 U.S. 530, 536 (1980) ("a constitutionally permissible time, place, or manner restriction may not be based upon either the content or subject matter of speech").

In short, we see little basis for the District Court's sweeping assertion that "harassment" — at least when it consists of speech targeted solely on the basis of its expressive content — "has never been considered to be protected activity under the First Amendment." Such a categorical rule is without precedent in the decisions of the Supreme Court or this Court, and it belies the very real tension between anti-harassment laws and the Constitution's guarantee of freedom of speech.

We do not suggest, of course, that no application of anti-harassment law to expressive speech can survive First Amendment scrutiny. Certainly, preventing discrimination in the workplace — and in the schools — is not only a legitimate, but a compelling, government interest. And, as some courts and commentators have suggested, speech may be more readily subject to restrictions when a school or workplace audience is "captive" and cannot avoid the objectionable speech. We simply note that we have found no categorical rule that divests "harassing" speech, as defined by federal anti-discrimination statutes, of First Amendment protection.

C.

In any event, we need not map the precise boundary between permissible anti-discrimination legislation and impermissible restrictions on First Amendment rights today. Assuming for present purposes that the federal anti-discrimination laws are constitutional in all of their applications to pure speech, we note that the SCASD Policy's reach is considerably broader.

For one thing, the Policy prohibits harassment based on personal characteristics that are not protected under federal law. Titles VI and IX, taken together with the other relevant federal statutes, cover only harassment based on sex, race, color, national origin, age and disability. The Policy, in contrast, is much broader, reaching, at the extreme, a catch-all category of "other personal characteristics" (which, the Policy states, includes things like "clothing," "appearance," "hobbies and values," and "social skills"). Insofar as the policy attempts to prevent students from making negative comments about each others' "appearance," "clothing," and "social skills," it may be brave, futile, or merely silly. But attempting to proscribe negative comments about "values," as that term is commonly used today, is something else altogether. By prohibiting disparaging speech directed at a person's "values," the Policy strikes at the heart of moral and political discourse — the lifeblood of constitutional self government (and democratic education) and the core concern of the First Amendment. That speech about "values" may offend is not cause for its prohibition, but rather the reason for its protection: "a principal 'function of free speech under our system of government is to invite dispute. It may indeed best serve its high purpose when it induces a condition of unrest, creates dissatisfaction with conditions as they are, or even stirs people to anger.'" *Texas v. Johnson,* 491 U.S. 397, 408–09 (1989) (quoting *Terminiello v. Chicago,* 337 U.S. 1, 4 (1949)). No court or legislature has ever suggested that unwelcome speech directed at another's "values" may be prohibited under the rubric of anti-discrimination.

We do not suggest, of course, that a public school may never adopt regulations more protective than existing law; it may, provided that those regulations do not offend the Constitution. Such regulations cannot be insulated from First Amendment challenge, however, based on the argument that they do no more than prohibit conduct that is already unlawful.

Moreover, the Policy's prohibition extends beyond harassment that objectively denies a student equal access to a school's education resources. Even on a narrow reading, the Policy unequivocally prohibits any verbal or physical conduct that is based on an enumerated personal characteristic and that "has the purpose or effect of substantially interfering with a student's educational performance or creating an intimidating, hostile or offensive environment." Unlike federal anti-harassment law, which imposes liability only when harassment has "a systemic effect on educational programs and activities," the Policy extends to speech that merely has the "purpose" of harassing another. This formulation, by focusing on the speaker's motive rather than the effect of speech on the learning environment, appears to sweep in those "simple acts of teasing and name-calling" that the *Davis* Court explicitly held were insufficient for liability.

D.

The District Court justifies its ruling by a syllogism: (1) the SCASD Policy covers only speech that is already prohibited under federal and state anti-harassment laws; (2) such prohibited speech is not entitled to First Amendment protection; (3) therefore, the Policy poses no First Amendment problems. This reasoning is flawed in both its major and minor premises. First, the Policy — even narrowly interpreted — covers substantially more speech than applicable federal and state laws. Second, the courts have never embraced a categorical "harassment exception" from First Amendment protection for speech that is within the ambit of federal anti-discrimination laws.

III.

Accordingly, we must examine whether the Policy may be justified as a permissible regulation of speech within the schools.

A.

We begin by reviewing the Supreme Court's cases demarcating the scope of a student's right to freedom of expression while in school. The Court set out the framework for student free speech claims in *Tinker v. Des Moines Independent Community School District*, 393 U.S. 503 (1969). . . . In *Tinker*, a group of students was suspended for wearing black armbands to protest American involvement in the Vietnam War. Taking as its premise that "it can hardly be argued that either students or teachers shed their constitutional rights to freedom of speech or expression at the schoolhouse gate," the Court reasoned that

> the school officials banned and sought to punish petitioners for a silent, passive expression of opinion, unaccompanied by any disorder or disturbance on the part of the petitioners. There is here no evidence whatever of the petitioners' interference, actual or nascent, with the school's work or of collision with the rights of other students to be secure and left alone. Accordingly, this case does not concern speech or action that intrudes upon the work of the school or the rights of other students.

Significantly, the Court emphasized that "undifferentiated fear or apprehension of disturbance is not enough to overcome the right to freedom of expression."

Under *Tinker*, then, regulation of student speech is generally permissible only when the speech would substantially disrupt or interfere with the work of the school or the rights of other students. As subsequent federal cases have made clear, *Tinker* requires a specific and significant fear of disruption, not just some remote apprehension of disturbance. In *Chandler v. McMinnville School District*, 978 F.2d 524 (9th Cir. 1992), for example, a middle school punished students who wore "SCAB" buttons to protest replacement teachers during a strike. Because the school had failed to present any evidence that the buttons were "inherently disruptive" to school activities, the court held that students could proceed with their First Amendment claim. In *Chalifoux v. New Caney Independent School District*, 976 F. Supp. 659 (S.D. Tex. 1997), a high school student challenged his school's policy against gang-related apparel. The school applied the ban to prohibit the plaintiff, a devout Catholic, from wearing a rosary to school on the ground that some gangs had adopted the rosary as their identifying symbol. The court held that the ban failed to satisfy *Tinker's* substantial disruption test:

> Although Plaintiffs wore their rosaries outside their shirts for several months, they were never misidentified as gang members nor approached by gang members. There also was no evidence that they attracted the attention of other students because of their rosaries. . . . Accordingly, the Court finds that there was insufficient evidence of actual disruption at New Caney High School, or that there was substantial reason for NCISD to anticipate a disruption, to justify the infringement on Plaintiffs' religiously-motivated speech.

Finally, in *Clark v. Dallas Independent School District*, 806 F. Supp. 116, 120 (N.D. Tex. 1992), the court held that a high school could not prohibit its students from distributing religious tracts on school grounds. Again citing

Tinker, the court held that "Defendants have failed to establish that Plaintiffs' distribution of the religious tracts gave rise to a material or substantial disruption of the operation" of the school. Noting that the only evidence of disruption was the objection of several other students, the court observed that "if school officials were permitted to prohibit expression to which other students objected, absent any further justification, the officials would have a license to prohibit virtually every type of expression."

The Tenth Circuit's recent decision in *West v. Derby Unified School District No. 260*, 206 F.3d 1358 (10th Cir. 2000), which reached a different result, nevertheless confirms *Tinker's* requirements of specificity and concreteness. In *West*, a middle school student was suspended for drawing a Confederate flag in math class under a school policy providing that a "student shall not racially harass or intimidate another student by name calling, using racial or derogatory slurs,[or] wearing or possession of items depicting or implying racial hatred or prejudice." The Court upheld the suspension under *Tinker's* substantial disruption standard, finding that the school had demonstrated a concrete threat of substantial disruption:

> Based upon recent past events, Derby School District officials had reason to believe that a student's display of the Confederate flag might cause disruption and interfere with the rights of other students to be secure and let alone. . . . The district experienced a series of racial incidents [including "hostile confrontations" and at least one fight] in 1995, some of which were related to the Confederate flag. . . . The Racial Harassment policy enacted in response to this situation was clearly something more than a mere desire to avoid the discomfort and unpleasantness that always accompany an unpopular viewpoint. The history of racial tension in the district made administrators' and parents' concerns about future substantial disruptions from possession of Confederate flag symbols at school reasonable.

As *West* makes clear, the mere desire to avoid "discomfort" or "unpleasantness" is not enough to justify restricting student speech under *Tinker*. However, if a school can point to a well-founded expectation of disruption — especially one based on past incidents arising out of similar speech — the restriction may pass constitutional muster.

Since *Tinker*, the Supreme Court has carved out a number of narrow categories of speech that a school may restrict even without the threat of substantial disruption. In *Bethel School District No. 403 v. Fraser*, 478 U.S. 675 (1986), the Court upheld the school's suspension of a high school student who, at a school assembly, nominated a peer for class office through "an elaborate, graphic, and explicit sexual metaphor." . . . According to *Fraser,* then, there is no First Amendment protection for "lewd," "vulgar," "indecent," and "plainly offensive" speech in school. . . .

Finally, in *Hazelwood School District v. Kuhlmeier*, 484 U.S. 260 (1988), the Court upheld, against First Amendment challenge, a principal's deletion of student articles on teen pregnancy from a school-sponsored newspaper. Distinguishing *Tinker*, the Court noted the school had not opened the newspaper up as a public forum and therefore could "exercise editorial control over the style and content of student speech in school-sponsored expressive activities as long as [its] actions are reasonably related to legitimate pedagogical concerns."

In *Rosenberger v. Rector & Visitors of University of Virginia*, 515 U.S. 819 (1995), the Court made clear that *Hazelwood*'s permissive "legitimate pedagogical concern" test governs only when a student's school-sponsored speech could reasonably be viewed as speech of the school itself:

> When the State is the speaker, it may make content-based choices. When the University determines the content of the education it provides, it is the University speaking, and we have permitted the government to regulate the content of what is or is not expressed when it is the speaker or when it enlists private entities to convey its own message. . . . It does not follow, however . . . that viewpoint-based restrictions are proper when the University does not itself speak or subsidize transmittal of a message it favors but instead encourages a diversity of views from private speakers. A holding that the University may not discriminate based on the viewpoint of private persons whose speech it facilitates does not restrict the University's own speech, which is controlled by different principles.

Rosenberger, 515 U.S. at 834. Similarly, a post-*Hazelwood* case from the Seventh Circuit illustrates that school "sponsorship" of student speech is not lightly to be presumed. *See Hedges v. Wauconda Comm. Unit Sch. Dist. No. 118,* 9 F.3d 1295, 1299 (7th Cir. 1993). In striking down a blanket prohibition against distributing religious materials on school grounds, the *Hedges* Court rejected the argument that the ban was justified under *Hazelwood* because observers might "infer that the school endorses whatever it permits":

> [The School District] proposes to throw up its hands, declaring that because misconceptions are possible it may silence its pupils, that the best defense against misunderstanding is censorship. . . . Public belief that the government is partial does not permit the government to become partial. Students therefore may hand out literature even if the recipients would misunderstand its provenance. The school's proper response is to educate the audience rather than squelch the speaker.

Hedges, 9 F.3d at 1299; *see also Burch v. Barker,* 861 F.2d 1149, 1159 (9th Cir. 1998) ("under ground newspaper" distributed on school grounds could not reasonably be viewed as school-sponsored).

To summarize: Under *Fraser,* a school may categorically prohibit lewd, vulgar or profane language. Under *Hazelwood,* a school may regulate school-sponsored speech (that is, speech that a reasonable observer would view as the school's own speech) on the basis of any legitimate pedagogical concern. Speech falling outside of these categories is subject to *Tinker's* general rule: it may be regulated only if it would substantially disrupt school operations or interfere with the right of others.

IV.

We turn now to the SCASD Policy itself. Saxe levies facial challenges against the Policy on both overbreadth and vagueness grounds. Because we hold that the Policy, even narrowly read, is unconstitutionally overbroad, we do not reach the merits of Saxe's vagueness claim.

A.

A regulation is unconstitutional on its face on overbreadth grounds where there is a "a likelihood that the statute's very existence will inhibit free expression" by "inhibiting the speech of third parties who are not before the Court." To render a law unconstitutional, the overbreadth must be "not only real but substantial in relation to the statute's plainly legitimate sweep."

On first reading, the Policy on its face appears both unconstitutionally vague and overbroad. As an initial matter, the Policy contains several separate passages, each of which could be read as embodying its operative definition of banned speech. The Policy's second paragraph sets forth one definition:

> Harassment means verbal or physical conduct based on one's actual or perceived race, religion, color, national origin, gender, sexual orientation, disability, or other personal characteristics, and which has the purpose or effect of substantially interfering with a student's educational performance or creating an intimidating, hostile or offensive environment.

This, however, is immediately followed two paragraphs later by a statement that harassment under the Policy "can include any unwelcome verbal, written or physical conduct which offends, denigrates or belittles an individual because of any of the characteristics described above." In addition, in a separate section, the Policy purports to set out "definitions" for various categories of harassment that do not always coincide with the above-quoted language. Religious harassment, for example, is defined as "unwelcome verbal, written or physical conduct directed at the characteristics of a person's religion, such as derogatory comments regarding surnames, religious tradition, or religious clothing, or religious slurs, or graffiti."

Certainly, some of these purported definitions of harassment are facially overbroad. No one would suggest that a school could constitutionally ban "any unwelcome verbal . . . conduct which offends . . . an individual because of" some enumerated personal characteristics. Nor could the school constitutionally restrict, without more, any "unwelcome verbal . . . conduct directed at the characteristics of a person's religion." The Supreme Court has held time and again, both within and outside of the school context, that the mere fact that someone might take offense at the content of speech is not sufficient justification for prohibiting it.

Before declaring the Policy unconstitutional, however, we must first determine whether it is susceptible to a reasonable limiting construction: "the elementary rule is that every reasonable construction must be resorted to, in order to save a statute from unconstitutionality."

When the Policy is read as a whole, it appears that its operative definition of prohibited harassment is contained in the above-quoted second paragraph, which requires that speech either "substantially interfere with a student's educational performance or create an intimidating, hostile or offensive environment." The Policy's fourth paragraph and "Definitions" section could reasonably be read as merely listing examples of conduct that might (but would not necessarily) violate this operative definition. On this narrow reading, the second paragraph would supply the Policy's "formal" definition of prohibited harassment, but the other sections of the Policy could still be relevant in clarifying vague or ambiguous terms in that operative definition.

So narrowed, the Policy would require the following elements before speech could be deemed harassing: (1) verbal or physical conduct (2) that is based on one's actual or perceived personal characteristics and (3) that has the purpose or effect of either (3a) substantially interfering with a student's educational performance or (3b) creating an intimidating hostile, or offensive environment.

It is apparent from these elements that SCASD cannot take solace in the relatively more permissive *Fraser* or *Hazelwood* standards. First, the Policy does not confine itself merely to vulgar or lewd speech; rather, it reaches any speech that interferes or is intended to interfere with educational performance or that creates or is intended to create a hostile environment. While some *Fraser*-type speech may fall within this definition, the Policy's scope is clearly broader. Second, the Policy does not contain any geographical or contextual limitations; rather, it purports to cover "any harassment of a student by a member of the school community." Thus, its strictures presumably apply whether the harassment occurs in a school-sponsored assembly, in the classroom, in the hall between classes, or in a playground or athletic facility.[102] Obviously, the Policy covers far more than just *Hazelwood*-type school-sponsored speech; it also sweeps in private student speech that merely "happens to occur on the school premises." As a result, SCASD cannot rely on *Hazelwood*'s more lenient "legitimate pedagogical concern" test in defending the Policy from facial attack.

In short, the Policy, even narrowly read, prohibits a substantial amount of non-vulgar, non-sponsored student speech. SCASD must therefore satisfy the *Tinker* test by showing that the Policy's restrictions are necessary to prevent substantial disruption or interference with the work of the school or the rights of other students. Applying this test, we conclude that the Policy is substantially overbroad.

As an initial matter, the Policy punishes not only speech that actually causes disruption, but also speech that merely intends to do so: by its terms, it covers speech "which has the purpose or effect of" interfering with educational performance or creating a hostile environment. This ignores *Tinker*'s requirement that a school must reasonably believe that speech will cause actual, material disruption before prohibiting it.

---

102 [11] Indeed, Saxe even suggests that the Policy could even be read to cover conduct occurring outside of school premises. This reading is not implausible based on the Policy's plain language, and would raise additional constitutional questions.

In addition, even if the "purpose" component is ignored, we do not believe that prohibited "harassment," as defined by the Policy, necessarily rises to the level of a substantial disruption under *Tinker*. We agree that the Policy's first prong, which prohibits speech that would "substantially interfere with a student's educational performance," may satisfy the *Tinker* standard. The primary function of a public school is to educate its students; conduct that substantially interferes with the mission is, almost by definition, disruptive to the school environment.

The Policy's second criterion, however — which prohibits speech that "creates an intimidating, hostile or offensive environment" — poses a more difficult problem. There are several possible grounds on which SCASD could attempt to justify this prohibition. First, SCASD could argue that it has an interest in avoiding liability for harassment under *Franklin* and *Davis*. However, because the Policy prohibits substantially more conduct than would give rise to liability under these cases, this justification is unavailing.

Second, SCASD could argue that speech creating a "hostile environment" may be banned because it "intrudes upon . . . the rights of other students." The precise scope of *Tinker*'s "interference with the rights of others" language is unclear; at least one court has opined that it covers only independently tortious speech like libel, slander or intentional infliction of emotional distress. In any case, it is certainly not enough that the speech is merely offensive to some listener. Because the Policy's "hostile environment" prong does not, on its face, require any threshold showing of severity or pervasiveness, it could conceivably be applied to cover any speech about some enumerated personal characteristics the content of which offends someone. This could include much "core" political and religious speech: the Policy's "Definitions" section lists as examples of covered harassment "negative" or "derogatory" speech about such contentious issues as "racial customs," "religious tradition," "language," "sexual orientation," and "values." Such speech, when it does not pose a realistic threat of substantial disruption, is within a student's First Amendment rights.

Finally, SCASD might argue that the "hostile environment" prohibition is required to maintain an orderly and non-disruptive educational environment. However, as *Tinker* made clear, the "undifferentiated fear or apprehension of disturbance" is not enough to justify a restriction on student speech. Although SCASD correctly asserts that it has a compelling interest in promoting an educational environment that is safe and conducive to learning, it fails to provide any particularized reason as to why it anticipates substantial disruption from the broad swath of student speech prohibited under the Policy.

The Policy, then, appears to cover substantially more speech than could be prohibited under *Tinker*'s substantial disruption test. Accordingly, we hold that the Policy is unconstitutionally overbroad.

V.

For the foregoing reasons, the judgment of the District Court is reversed.

RENDELL, CIRCUIT JUDGE, *concurring*:

I write separately only to note my strong disagreement with the notion, espoused by the District Court and discussed at length in Part II.B of the majority opinion, that the judicial analysis of permissible restrictions on speech in a given setting should be affected — let alone dictated — by legislative enactments intended to proscribe activity that could be classified as "harassment." Our attempt at reasoning through this postulate should demonstrate its futility, given the numerous variables that impact on any determination regarding the limits of permissible speech and the rigorous analysis that we must follow in every First Amendment case — the analysis that our opinion does in fact follow in reaching the result in this case.

Perhaps the only way, or time, that such legislation could be a guide would be if its provisions were identical to the policy at issue, or if in a case involving an as-applied challenge to a policy, the legislative provisions addressed every aspect of the particular factual setting at issue. Even then, I submit that it would be the reasoning by a court upholding its constitutionality, rather than the legislation itself, that would provide the necessary guidance.

I view the use of harassment legislation as an especially inappropriate barometer here because this case is not a harassment case. Rather, it is framed by appellants as a First Amendment speech case. Moreover, it is a school speech case. While reliance on provisions of harassment laws or policies might be an easy way to resolve difficult cases such as this one, therein lies the rub — there are no easy ways in the complex area of First Amendment jurisprudence.

———

NOTES AND QUESTIONS

1. In *Sypniewski v. Warren Hills Reg. Bd. of Educ.*, 307 F.3d 243 (3d Cir. 2002), the school district, because of a history of racial tension at district schools, adopted a racial harassment policy that read in part:

> District employees and student(s) shall not racially harass or intimidate other student(s) or employee(s) by name calling, using racial or derogatory slurs, wearing or possession of items depicting or implying racial hatred or prejudice. District employees and students shall not at school, on school property or at school activities wear or have in their possession any written material, either printed or in their own handwriting, that is racially divisive or creates ill will or hatred. (Examples: clothing, articles, material, publications or any item that denotes Ku Klux Klan, Arayan [sic] Nation-White Supremacy, Black Power, Confederate flags or articles, Neo-Nazi or any other "hate" group. This list is not intended to be all-inclusive.)

One of the plaintiff students was suspended from school for wearing a T-shirt inscribed with "redneck" jokes. The principal claimed that the t-shirt violated the school dress code. The principal was also concerned about the word "redneck," because of the troubling history of racial tension in the school and the possibility that the term " 'redneck' would incite some form of violence and at a minimum be offensive and harassing to our minority population." The school district contended that the word "redneck" was an identifier of "the Hicks," a gang-like group that allegedly had been involved in the past racial incidents.

The Third Circuit determined that the record supported a finding that the schools — particularly the high school — were afflicted with pervasive racial disturbances throughout the school year. But the court rejected the school's argument that the shirt was potentially disruptive because the word "redneck" had come to connote racial intolerance. The court saw no basis for concluding that the Hicks were also known as "the Rednecks," thus the school district could not ban the shirt as a gang or quasi-gang symbol.

Similarly, there is little or no evidence that the word "redneck" had been used to harass or intimidate, or otherwise to offend. The harassment policy limited to racially provocative speech was an acceptable non-discriminatory response by school officials to the history of race relations, with the one exception of the policy's "ill will" provision. The court determined that the mere fact that someone might take offense to certain speech is not sufficient grounds for prohibiting it, and the application of the policy to the T-shirt went too far. The school officials had not established that the shirt might genuinely threaten disruption or, indeed, that it violated any of the provisions of the harassment policy except perhaps the "ill will" provision. Stripped of this phrase, the remaining policy was deemed constitutionally permissible in the context of the recent racial history.

Judge Rosenn wrote a separate opinion, concurring in part and dissenting in part:

> The majority's conclusion that the words ill will "expands the policy too far into the domain of protected expression" is not well founded. Even though in an adult public forum or in the public press, speech spoken with malice is unprotected, the majority gives words of enmity and wickedness at heart in a children's ambience an unjustifiable sense of propriety. It does this at a time when the Nation's public schools are struggling for survival. Such protective construction of words, I fear, to children attending elementary and public schools may only encourage them to defy their teachers, discourage school teachers, and threaten to undermine a school system already under strong attack.

Id. at 275 (Rosenn, J., concurring in part and dissenting in part).

2. Justice Ginsberg's separate opinion in *Gebser* states that she would recognize an effective policy for reporting and redressing sexual harassment as an affirmative defense to a Title IX claim. Your client, the Pegasus School Board, has asked for your help in drafting a policy similar to that in *Saxe* or *Sypniewski*, but without its problems. What items would you be able to save? Would a policy that tracked the language of *Davis* pass constitutional muster?

3. Now suppose your client is a male student, Hal, who is accused of harassing speech by another male student, Hank. The school principal investigated the incident and determined that your client has repeatedly yelled, chanted, and held up signs directed at the other student stating, "Faggots sin against God. This one will burn in hell." Hank is so miserable that he has quit the basketball team and dropped his art class to avoid being in class with Hal. If the school district suspends your client from school (or otherwise punishes him), under what circumstances would your client have a claim against the school district or the principal for violating his or her First Amendment rights? If the school district does not punish Hal because it believes to do so would violate Hal's First Amendment rights, does Hank have a cause of action under Title IX? Could the school district's failure to punish Hank lead to a determination that it was deliberately indifferent?

4. Who can be a defendant under Title IX? In *Davis*, the defendant was the school district, but some plaintiffs also include individuals like teachers in their complaint. Most courts that have addressed the issue have determined that the Supreme Court, in implying a cause of action under Title IX, considered only actions against educational institutions and that individual liability must be established under Section 1983. *See Linder v. City of New York*, 263 F. Supp. 2d 585 (E.D.N.Y. 2003). *But see Mennone v. Gordon*, 889 F. Supp. 53 (D. Conn. 1995) (Title IX claim may be asserted against an individual who operates a particular educational program or activity).

5. Does the Title IX enforcement scheme subsume claims that arise under section 1983 and the Equal Protection Clause? The Circuits are split on this issue. In *Bruneau v. South Kortright Central School District*, 163 F.3d 749 (2d Cir. 1998), a student brought a lawsuit against the school district for violation of Title IX for its treatment of her allegations of peer-on-peer sexual harassment. The student also brought a claim under section 1983, alleging violations of the Equal Protection Clause. The Second Circuit relied on the "*Sea Clammers* doctrine," which states that when "the remedial devices provided in a particular Act are sufficiently comprehensive, they may suffice to demonstrate congressional intent to preclude the remedy of suits under § 1983." *Id.* at 756 (quoting *Middlesex County Sewerage Authority v. National Sea Clammers Association*, 453 U.S. 1, 20 (1981)). The court determined that Title IX's enforcement scheme was sufficiently comprehensive "so as to foreclose the use of § 1983 to implement its provisions." (This applied, said the court, only to non-individual defendants, the school district and the school board). Other courts, however, have carved out an exception to the *Sea Clammers* doctrine when plaintiffs bring a separate § 1983 action predicated on a constitutional right, even if the same set of facts gives rise to the violation of the statutory right. *See, e.g., Crawford v. Davis*, 109 F.3d 1281, 1284 (8th Cir. 1997).

6. In addition to the harassment cases, Title IX may also be used by students who claim that a school district has discriminated against them because of pregnancy.

PROBLEM: The National Honor Society and the Pregnant Student. The NHS, which has chapters in high schools throughout the United States, is sponsored by the National Association of Secondary School Principals

("NASSP"). High schools can establish local NHS chapters if they pay a chartering fee and annual initiation fee to the NHS and adopt the NHS constitution.[103] Membership in the NHS is a coveted distinction, which is open only to students with cumulative GPA's of at least 3.0 on a 4.0 scale.[104] An outstanding academic record alone, however, does not guarantee admission to the NHS.

As the NHS Constitution provides "Membership in local chapters is an honor bestowed upon a student. Selection for membership is by a faculty council and is based on outstanding *scholarship, character, leadership*, and *service*. Once selected, members have the responsibility to continue to demonstrate these qualities." NHS CONST. art. VIII (Membership), § 1 (emphasis added). But while superior grades, the foremost criterion for eligibility, are precisely quantifiable, the latter three factors are not and, indeed, are inherently subjective. Applicants' character and records of service and leadership, moreover, are secretly evaluated by a faculty committee, which is not required to divulge the basis for its decision.[105] *See* Thomas A. Schweitzer, *"A" Students Go To Court: Is Membership in the National Honor Society A Cognizable Legal Right?*, 50 SYRACUSE L. REV. 63, 65 (2000).

Arlene Pfeiffer is a high school student with excellent grades, and she is active in extracurricular activities. Her GPA is 3.9 on a scale of 4.0. Arlene, unmarried, became pregnant during her junior year of high school, and she gave birth to a baby boy early in her senior year. She was denied admission to the NHS on character grounds, although all other students with GPAs over 3.5 were admitted to NHS. The admissions committee members denied that the decision in Arlene's case was based on her sex or her pregnancy. They stated that Arlene had failed to uphold the NHS standards of leadership and character because she had engaged in premarital sex. Moreover, they contended that someone who had engaged in premarital sex should not be held up as a role model for other students. Analyze whether Arlene has a Title IX claim. *See, e.g., Chipman v. Grant County School District*, 30 F. Supp. 2d 975 (E.D. Ky. 1998); *Cazares v. Barber*, 959 F.2d 753 (9th Cir. 1992); *Pfeiffer v. Marion Ctr. Area School Dist.*, 917 F.2d 779 (3d Cir. 1990). What if Arlene admitted to having premarital sex with numerous boys and was unable to ascertain who was the father of her child? What if Arlene admitted that she had been pregnant twice before and elected to have an abortion? When a school singles out students for recognition in an "honor" society — one in which membership is based in part on outstanding character and leadership — does it convey to other students that it tolerates or perhaps condones that student's behavior?

Does it make a difference if the admissions committee is committed to denying membership to male students who have had premarital sexual relations? What evidence would the school need to have to exclude these male students? How much harder will it be to obtain such evidence about male students, as opposed to female students? Should the NHS admissions committee ask all students about their sexual histories to alleviate the unfairness

---

[103] NATIONAL HONOR SOC'Y CONST. art. IV (Local Chapters), §§ 1-3 [hereinafter NHS CONST.].

[104] NHS CONST. art. IX (Selection of Members), § 2.

[105] NHS CONST. art. IX (Selection of Members), § 3.

to female students whose pregnancies are hard to conceal? Or should the committee pursue a "don't ask, don't tell" policy concerning the sexual history of students? What are the traits that should be considered for the "character" prong of the NHS admissions process?

§ 4.06 THE DISABLED STUDENT

The education of disabled children in the public schools historically was considered a matter of little or no importance. Some states permitted school districts to exclude disabled students from all education services if school officials determined that the child was disruptive or that the child could not benefit from public education. In the last half of the twentieth century, however, things began to change. In the early 1950s new and powerful antibiotics helped control infection after surgery, and more children with severe disabilities were able to survive early childhood. *See* CAROLE MURRAY-SEEGART, NASTY GIRLS, THUGS, AND HUMANS LIKE US 17 (1989). As the population of severely disabled children increased, so did the need for social services, including education.

Two landmark decisions, *Pennsylvania Association for Retarded Children v. Commonwealth*, 343 F. Supp. 279 (E.D. Pa. 1972) (hereinafter *PARC*) and *Mills v. Board of Education*, 348 F. Supp. 866 (D.D.C. 1972), focused attention on the issue and set the stage for Congress, which enacted Section 504 of the Rehabilitation Act of 1973 and the Education for All Handicapped Children Act, shortly thereafter. Although it was a consent decree, *PARC* is generally considered the first case establishing some right to education for the disabled children. The plaintiffs claimed that mentally retarded children had been improperly excluded from public schools or had been assigned special education programs that were either inappropriate or of questionable merit. The consent order required that Pennsylvania provide:

> a free, public program of education and training appropriate to the child's capacity, within the context of a presumption that, among the alternative programs of education and training required by statute to be available, placement in regular public school class is preferable to placement in a special public school class and placement in a special public school class is preferable to placement in any other type of program of education and training.

Pennsylvania Ass'n for Retarded Children v. Commonwealth, 334 F. Supp. 1257, 1260 (E.D. Pa. 1971).

The *Mills* case not only addressed the education of retarded children, but of all disabled children who were excluded from public education. The court determined that the due process rights of the children had been violated when they were denied a publicly supported education. *Mills*, 348 F. Supp. at 875. The court directed that no child who was eligible for public education could be excluded unless provided with "adequate alternative educational services suited to the child's needs" and with a "constitutionally adequate prior hearing."

In 1973 Congress passed the Section 504 of the Rehabilitation Act, 29 U.S.C. § 794 and in 1975 the Education for All Handicapped Children Act (EAHCA), 20 U.S.C. § 1401 et seq. EAHCA's name was changed in 1990 to the Individuals with Disabilities Education Act (IDEA). Section 504 prohibits discrimination against individuals with disabilities in all programs receiving federal financial assistance. Section 504 provides that "No otherwise qualified handicapped individual . . . shall, solely by reason of his or her handicap, be excluded from participation in, be denied the benefits of, or be subjected to discrimination under any program or activity receiving Federal financial assistance." 29 U.S.C. § 794. This broad prohibition includes discrimination in public schools, but it is not nearly as detailed as IDEA, also a funding statute, which sets forth substantive and procedural rights for disabled students. To qualify for federal special education funds, a state must demonstrate that it has in place a policy that ensures that the right "to a free appropriate public education (FAPE) is available to all children with disabilities." 20 U.S.C. § 1412. Schools must develop a written Individualized Education Plan (IEP) for each disabled child. 20 U.S.C. § 1414(d). A more detailed description of the requirements for the IEP is contained in the *Rowley* case, immediately below.

The "free appropriate public education" to which the disabled child is entitled includes special education — specially designed instruction, at no cost to parents to meet the unique needs children with disabilities, and related services, which include a myriad of developmental, corrective and other support services "as may be required to assist a child with a disability to benefit from special education." The services that a public school would be required to provide a disabled child include speech pathology and audiology services, psychological services, physical and occupational therapy, recreation, including therapeutic recreation, social work services, counseling services, including rehabilitation counseling, and medical services, except that such medical services shall be for diagnostic and evaluation purposes only. *See* 20 U.S.C. § 1401(22).

Parents must receive written notice if a school proposes (or refuses) either to initiate or to change the educational placement of the child. 20 U.S.C. § 1415(b)(3). The school must provide the parents with an opportunity to present complaints relating to any matter respecting the child's educational placement or the provision of a free appropriate public education. 20 U.S.C. § 1415(b)(6). If the parents' complaints are not resolved to their satisfaction, they are entitled to an impartial due process hearing before a hearing officer who is not employed by the school district or state education department. 20 U.S.C. § 1415(f). If, after the hearing officer renders a decision, the parents still are not satisfied, they may appeal and receive a hearing at the state educational agency, which must also conduct an impartial review of the first hearing. 20 U.S.C. § 1415(g). If the parents still are not satisfied after the state educational agency has reach a final decision, a lawsuit may be commenced in either state court or federal district court. 20 U.S.C. § 1415(i)(2)(A). If the parents prevail, the courts may award them attorneys' fees. 20 U.S.C. § 1415(i)(3).

[A] "Free Appropriate Public Education"

BOARD OF EDUCATION OF THE HENDRICK HUDSON CENTRAL SCHOOL DISTRICT v. ROWLEY

Supreme Court of the United States
458 U.S. 176 (1982)

CHIEF JUSTICE REHNQUIST *delivered the opinion of the Court.*

This case presents a question of statutory interpretation. Petitioners contend that the Court of Appeals and the District Court misconstrued the requirements imposed by Congress upon States which receive federal funds under the Education of the Handicapped Act. We agree and reverse the judgment of the Court of Appeals.

I

The Education of the Handicapped Act provides federal money to assist state and local agencies in educating handicapped children, and conditions such funding upon a State's compliance with extensive goals and procedures. The Act represents an ambitious federal effort to promote the education of handicapped children, and was passed in response to Congress' perception that a majority of handicapped children in the United States "were either totally excluded from schools or [were] sitting idly in regular classrooms awaiting the time when they were old enough to 'drop out.' " H.R. REP. No. 94-332, p. 2 (1975) (H.R. REP.). . . .

Dissatisfied with the progress being made under earlier enactments, and spurred by two District Court decisions holding that handicapped children should be given access to a public education, Congress in 1974 greatly increased federal funding for education of the handicapped and for the first time required recipient States to adopt "a goal of providing full educational opportunities to all handicapped children." PUB. L. 93-380, 88 STAT. 579, 583 (1974 statute). The 1974 statute was recognized as an interim measure only, adopted "in order to give the Congress an additional year in which to study what if any additional Federal assistance [was] required to enable the States to meet the needs of handicapped children." H. R. Rep., at 4. The ensuing year of study produced the Education for All Handicapped Children Act of 1975.

In order to qualify for federal financial assistance under the Act, a State must demonstrate that it "has in effect a policy that assures all handicapped children the right to a free appropriate public education." 20 U.S.C. § 1412(1). That policy must be reflected in a state plan submitted to and approved by the Secretary of Education, § 1413, which describes in detail the goals, programs, and timetables under which the State intends to educate handicapped children within its borders. §§ 1412, 1413. States receiving money under the Act must provide education to the handicapped by priority, first "to handicapped children who are not receiving an education" and second "to handicapped children . . . with the most severe handicaps who are receiving an inadequate education," § 1412(3), and "to the maximum extent appropriate" must educate handicapped children "with children who are not handicapped." § 1412(5).[106] The Act broadly defines "handicapped children" to include "mentally retarded, hard of hearing, deaf, speech impaired, visually handicapped, seriously emotionally disturbed, orthopedically impaired, [and] other health impaired children, [and] children with specific learning disabilities." § 1401(1).[107]

The "free appropriate public education" required by the Act is tailored to the unique needs of the handicapped child by means of an "individualized educational program" (IEP). § 1401(18). The IEP, which is prepared at a meeting between a qualified representative of the local educational agency, the child's teacher, the child's parents or guardian, and, where appropriate, the child, consists of a written document containing

> (A) a statement of the present levels of educational performance of such child, (B) a statement of annual goals, including short-term instructional objectives, (C) a statement of the specific educational services to be provided to such child, and the extent to which such child will be able to participate in regular educational programs, (D) the projected date for initiation and anticipated duration of such services, and (E) appropriate objective criteria and evaluation procedures and schedules for determining, on at least an annual basis, whether instructional objectives are being achieved.

§ 1401(19).

Local or regional educational agencies must review, and where appropriate revise, each child's IEP at least annually. § 1414(a)(5).

In addition to the state plan and the IEP already described, the Act imposes extensive procedural requirements upon States receiving federal funds under its provisions. Parents or guardians of handicapped children must be notified of any proposed change in "the identification, evaluation, or educational placement of the child or the provision of a free appropriate public education to such child," and must be permitted to bring a complaint about "any matter relating to" such evaluation and education. §§ 1415(b)(1)(D) and (E). Complaints brought by parents or guardians must be resolved at "an impartial due process hearing," and appeal to the State educational agency must be provided if the initial hearing is held at the local or regional level. §§ 1415(b)(2) and (c).[108] Thereafter, "[any] party aggrieved by the findings

---

[106] [4] Despite this preference for "mainstreaming" handicapped children — educating them with nonhandicapped children — Congress recognized that regular classrooms simply would not be a suitable setting for the education of many handicapped children. The Act expressly acknowledges that "the nature or severity of the handicap [may be] such that education in regular classes with the use of supplementary aids and services cannot be achieved satisfactorily." § 1412(5). The Act thus provides for the education of some handicapped children in separate classes or institutional settings. *See ibid.,* § 1413(a)(4).

[107] [5] In addition to covering a wide variety of handicapping conditions, the Act requires special educational services for children "regardless of the severity of their handicap." §§ 1412(2)(C), 1414(a)(1)(A).

[108] [7] "Any party" to a state or local administrative hearing must "be accorded (1) the right to be accompanied and advised by counsel and by individuals with special knowledge or training with respect to the problems of handicapped children, (2) the right to present evidence and

and decision" of the state administrative hearing has "the right to bring a civil action with respect to the complaint . . . in any State court of competent jurisdiction or in a district court of the United States without regard to the amount in controversy." § 1415(e)(2).

Thus, although the Act leaves to the States the primary responsibility for developing and executing educational programs for handicapped children, it imposes significant requirements to be followed in the discharge of that responsibility. Compliance is assured by provisions permitting the withholding of federal funds upon determination that a participating state or local agency has failed to satisfy the requirements of the Act, §§ 1414(b)(2)(A), 1416, and by the provision for judicial review. At present, all States except New Mexico receive federal funds under the portions of the Act at issue today.

II

This case arose in connection with the education of Amy Rowley, a deaf student at the Furnace Woods School in the Hendrick Hudson Central School District, Peekskill, N. Y. Amy has minimal residual hearing and is an excellent lipreader. During the year before she began attending Furnace Woods, a meeting between her parents and school administrators resulted in a decision to place her in a regular kindergarten class in order to determine what supplemental services would be necessary to her education. Several members of the school administration prepared for Amy's arrival by attending a course in sign-language interpretation, and a teletype machine was installed in the principal's office to facilitate communication with her parents who are also deaf. At the end of the trial period it was determined that Amy should remain in the kindergarten class, but that she should be provided with an FM hearing aid which would amplify words spoken into a wireless receiver by the teacher or fellow students during certain classroom activities. Amy successfully completed her kindergarten year. As required by the Act, an IEP was prepared for Amy during the fall of her first-grade year. The IEP provided that Amy should be educated in a regular classroom at Furnace Woods, should continue to use the FM hearing aid, and should receive instruction from a tutor for the deaf for one hour each day and from a speech therapist for three hours each week. The Rowleys agreed with parts of the IEP but insisted that Amy also be provided a qualified sign-language interpreter in all her academic classes in lieu of the assistance proposed in other parts of the IEP. Such an interpreter had been placed in Amy's kindergarten class for a 2-week experimental period, but the interpreter had reported that Amy did not need his services at that time. The school administrators likewise concluded that Amy did not need such an interpreter in her first-grade classroom. They reached this conclusion after consulting the school district's Committee on the Handicapped, which had received expert evidence from Amy's parents on the importance of a sign-language interpreter, received testimony from Amy's teacher and other persons familiar with her academic and social progress, and visited a class for the deaf.

---

confront, cross examine, and compel the attendance of witnesses, (3) the right to a written or electronic verbatim record of such hearing, and (4) the right to written findings of fact and decisions." § 1415(d).

When their request for an interpreter was denied, the Rowleys demanded and received a hearing before an independent examiner. After receiving evidence from both sides, the examiner agreed with the administrators' determination that an interpreter was not necessary because "Amy was achieving educationally, academically, and socially" without such assistance. The examiner's decision was affirmed on appeal by the New York Commissioner of Education on the basis of substantial evidence in the record. Pursuant to the Act's provision for judicial review, the Rowleys then brought an action in the United States District Court for the Southern District of New York, claiming that the administrators' denial of the sign-language interpreter constituted a denial of the "free appropriate public education" guaranteed by the Act.

The District Court found that Amy "is a remarkably well-adjusted child" who interacts and communicates well with her classmates and has "developed an extraordinary rapport" with her teachers. It also found that "she performs better than the average child in her class and is advancing easily from grade to grade," but "that she understands considerably less of what goes on in class than she could if she were not deaf" and thus "is not learning as much, or performing as well academically, as she would without her handicap." This disparity between Amy's achievement and her potential led the court to decide that she was not receiving a "free appropriate public education," which the court defined as "an opportunity to achieve [her] full potential commensurate with the opportunity provided to other children." According to the District Court, such a standard "requires that the potential of the handicapped child be measured and compared to his or her performance, and that the resulting differential or 'shortfall' be compared to the shortfall experienced by nonhandicapped children." The District Court's definition arose from its assumption that the responsibility for "[giving] content to the requirement of an 'appropriate education' " had "been left entirely to the [federal] courts and the hearing officers."

A divided panel of the United States Court of Appeals for the Second Circuit affirmed. . . . We granted certiorari to review the lower courts' interpretation of the Act. Such review requires us to consider two questions: What is meant by the Act's requirement of a "free appropriate public education"? And what is the role of state and federal courts in exercising the review granted by 20 U.S.C. § 1415? We consider these questions separately.

III

A

This is the first case in which this Court has been called upon to interpret any provision of the Act. As noted previously, the District Court and the Court of Appeals concluded that "[the] Act itself does not define 'appropriate education'," but leaves "to the courts and the hearing officers" the responsibility of "[giving] content to the requirement of an 'appropriate education'." Petitioners contend that the definition of the phrase "free appropriate public education" used by the courts below overlooks the definition of that phrase actually found in the Act. Respondents agree that the Act defines "free appropriate public education," but contend that the statutory definition is not "functional" and thus "offers judges no guidance in their consideration of controversies involving 'the identification, evaluation, or educational placement of the child or the provision of a free appropriate public education.'" The United States, appearing as amicus curiae on behalf of respondents, states that "[although] the Act includes definitions of a 'free appropriate public education' and other related terms, the statutory definitions do not adequately explain what is meant by 'appropriate.'"

We are loath to conclude that Congress failed to offer any assistance in defining the meaning of the principal substantive phrase used in the Act. It is beyond dispute that, contrary to the conclusions of the courts below, the Act does expressly define "free appropriate public education":

> The term "free appropriate public education" means *special education* and *related services* which (A) have been provided at public expense, under public supervision and direction, and without charge, (B) meet the standards of the State educational agency, (C) include an appropriate preschool, elementary, or secondary school education in the State involved, and (D) are provided in conformity with the individualized education program required under section 1414(a)(5) of this title.

§ 1401(18) (emphasis added).

"Special education," as referred to in this definition, means "specially designed instruction, at no cost to parents or guardians, to meet the unique needs of a handicapped child, including classroom instruction, instruction in physical education, home instruction, and instruction in hospitals and institutions." § 1401(16). "Related services" are defined as "transportation, and such developmental, corrective, and other supportive services . . . as may be required to assist a handicapped child to benefit from special education." § 1401(17).[109]

Like many statutory definitions, this one tends toward the cryptic rather than the comprehensive, but that is scarcely a reason for abandoning the quest for legislative intent. Whether or not the definition is a "functional" one, as respondents contend it is not, it is the principal tool which Congress has given us for parsing the critical phrase of the Act. We think more must be made of it than either respondents or the United States seems willing to admit.

According to the definitions contained in the Act, a "free appropriate public education" consists of educational instruction specially designed to meet the unique needs of the handicapped child, supported by such services as are necessary to permit the child "to benefit" from the instruction. Almost as a checklist for adequacy under the Act, the definition also requires that such instruction and services be provided at public expense and under public supervision, meet the State's educational standards, approximate the grade levels used in the State's regular education, and comport with the child's IEP.

---

[109] [10] Examples of "related services" identified in the Act are "speech pathology and audiology, psychological services, physical and occupational therapy, recreation, and medical and counseling services, except that such medical services shall be for diagnostic and evaluation purposes only." § 1401(17).

Thus, if personalized instruction is being provided with sufficient supportive services to permit the child to benefit from the instruction, and the other items on the definitional checklist are satisfied, the child is receiving a "free appropriate public education" as defined by the Act.

Other portions of the statute also shed light upon congressional intent. Congress found that of the roughly eight million handicapped children in the United States at the time of enactment, one million were "excluded entirely from the public school system" and more than half were receiving an inappropriate education. In addition, as mentioned in Part I, the Act requires States to extend educational services first to those children who are receiving no education and second to those children who are receiving an "inadequate education." When these express statutory findings and priorities are read together with the Act's extensive procedural requirements and its definition of "free appropriate public education," the face of the statute evinces a congressional intent to bring previously excluded handicapped children into the public education systems of the States and to require the States to adopt procedures which would result in individualized consideration of and instruction for each child.

Noticeably absent from the language of the statute is any substantive standard prescribing the level of education to be accorded handicapped children. Certainly the language of the statute contains no requirement like the one imposed by the lower courts — that States maximize the potential of handicapped children "commensurate with the opportunity provided to other children." That standard was expounded by the District Court without reference to the statutory definitions or even to the legislative history of the Act. Although we find the statutory definition of "free appropriate public education" to be helpful in our interpretation of the Act, there remains the question of whether the legislative history indicates a congressional intent that such education meet some additional substantive standard. For an answer, we turn to that history.[110]

---

110 [11] The dissent, finding that "the standard of the courts below seems . . . to reflect the congressional purpose" of the Act, concludes that our answer to this question "is not a satisfactory one." Presumably, the dissent also agrees with the District Court's conclusion that "it has been left entirely to the courts and the hearing officers to give content to the requirement of an 'appropriate education.'" It thus seems that the dissent would give the courts *carte blanche* to impose upon the States whatever burden their various judgments indicate should be imposed. Indeed, the dissent clearly characterizes the requirement of an "appropriate education" as open-ended, noting that "if there are limits not evident from the face of the statute on what may be considered an 'appropriate education,' they must be found in the purpose of the statute or its legislative history." Not only are we unable to find any suggestion from the face of the statute that the requirement of an "appropriate education" was to be limitless, but we also view the dissent's approach as contrary to the fundamental proposition that Congress, when exercising its spending power, can impose no burden upon the States unless it does so unambiguously.

No one can doubt that this would have been an easier case if Congress had seen fit to provide a more comprehensive statutory definition of the phrase "free appropriate public education." But Congress did not do so, and "our problem is to construe what Congress has written. After all, Congress expresses its purpose by words. It is for us to ascertain — neither to add nor to subtract, neither to delete nor to distort." We would be less than faithful to our obligation to construe what Congress has written if in this case we were to disregard the statutory language and legislative history of the Act by concluding that Congress had imposed upon the States a burden of unspecified proportions and weight, to be revealed only through case-by-case adjudication in the courts.

B

(i)

As suggested in Part I, federal support for education of the handicapped is a fairly recent development. Before passage of the Act some States had passed laws to improve the educational services afforded handicapped children, but many of these children were excluded completely from any form of public education or were left to fend for themselves in classrooms designed for education of their nonhandicapped peers. As previously noted, the House Report begins by emphasizing this exclusion and misplacement, noting that millions of handicapped children "were either totally excluded from schools or [were] sitting idly in regular classrooms awaiting the time when they were old enough to 'drop out.' " One of the Act's two principal sponsors in the Senate urged its passage in similar terms: "While much progress has been made in the last few years, we can take no solace in that progress until all handicapped children are, in fact, receiving an education. The most recent statistics provided by the Bureau of Education for the Handicapped estimate that . . . 1.75 million handicapped children do not receive any educational services, and 2.5 million handicapped children are not receiving an appropriate education." 121 Cong. Rec. 19486 (1975) (remarks of Sen. Williams).

This concern, stressed repeatedly throughout the legislative history, confirms the impression conveyed by the language of the statute: By passing the Act, Congress sought primarily to make public education available to handicapped children. But in seeking to provide such access to public education, Congress did not impose upon the States any greater substantive educational standard than would be necessary to make such access meaningful. Indeed, Congress expressly "[recognized] that in many instances the process of providing special education and related services to handicapped children is not guaranteed to produce any particular outcome." Thus, the intent of the Act was more to open the door of public education to handicapped children on appropriate terms than to guarantee any particular level of education once inside.

Both the House and the Senate Reports attribute the impetus for the Act and its predecessors to two federal-court judgments rendered in 1971 and 1972. As the Senate Report states, passage of the Act "followed a series of landmark court cases establishing in law the right to education for all handicapped children." The first case, *Pennsylvania Assn. for Retarded Children v. Commonwealth*, 334 F. Supp. 1257 (ED Pa. 1971) and 343 F. Supp. 279 (1972) (*PARC*), was a suit on behalf of retarded children challenging the constitutionality of a Pennsylvania statute which acted to exclude them from public education and training. The case ended in a consent decree which enjoined the State from "[denying] to any mentally retarded child *access* to a free public program of education and training." 334 F. Supp., at 1258 (emphasis added).

PARC was followed by *Mills v. Board of Education of District of Columbia*, 348 F. Supp. 866 (DC 1972), a case in which the plaintiff handicapped children had been *excluded* from the District of Columbia public schools. The court's judgment, quoted in S. Rep., at 6, provided that no [handicapped] child eligible for a publicly supported education in the District of Columbia public schools shall be excluded from a regular school assignment by a Rule, policy, or practice of the Board of Education of the District of Columbia or its agents unless such child is provided (a) *adequate* alternative educational services suited to the child's needs, which may include special education or tuition grants, and (b) a constitutionally adequate prior hearing and periodic review of the child's status, progress, and the *adequacy* of any educational alternative.

348 F. Supp. at 878 (emphasis added).

Mills and *PARC* both held that handicapped children must be given access to an adequate, publicly supported education. Neither case purports to require any particular substantive level of education. Rather, like the language of the Act, the cases set forth extensive procedures to be followed in formulating personalized educational programs for handicapped children. The fact that both *PARC* and *Mills* are discussed at length in the legislative Reports suggests that the principles which they established are the principles which, to a significant extent, guided the drafters of the Act. Indeed, immediately after discussing these cases the Senate Report describes the 1974 statute as having "incorporated the major principles of the right to education cases." Those principles in turn became the basis of the Act, which itself was designed to effectuate the purposes of the 1974 statute.

That the Act imposes no clear obligation upon recipient States beyond the requirement that handicapped children receive some form of specialized education is perhaps best demonstrated by the fact that Congress, in explaining the need for the Act, equated an "appropriate education" to the receipt of some specialized educational services. The Senate Report states: "[The] most recent statistics provided by the Bureau of Education for the Handicapped estimate that of the more than 8 million children . . . with handicapping conditions requiring special education and related services, only 3.9 million such children are receiving an appropriate education." This statement, which reveals Congress' view that 3.9 million handicapped children were "receiving an appropriate education" in 1975, is followed immediately in the Senate Report by a table showing that 3.9 million handicapped children were "served" in 1975 and a slightly larger number were "unserved." A similar statement and table appear in the House Report.

It is evident from the legislative history that the characterization of handicapped children as "served" referred to children who were receiving some form of specialized educational services from the States, and that the characterization of children as "unserved" referred to those who were receiving no specialized educational services. . . . By characterizing the 3.9 million handicapped children who were "served" as children who were "receiving an appropriate education," the Senate and House Reports unmistakably disclose Congress' perception of the type of education required by the Act: an "appropriate education" is provided when personalized educational services are provided.[111]

(ii)

Respondents contend that "the goal of the Act is to provide each handicapped child with an equal educational opportunity." Brief for Respondents 35. We think, however, that the requirement that a State provide specialized educational services to handicapped children generates no additional requirement that the services so provided be sufficient to maximize each child's potential "commensurate with the opportunity provided other children." . . .

The educational opportunities provided by our public school systems undoubtedly differ from student to student, depending upon a myriad of factors that might affect a particular student's ability to assimilate information presented in the classroom. The requirement that States provide "equal" educational opportunities would thus seem to present an entirely unworkable standard requiring impossible measurements and comparisons. Similarly, furnishing handicapped children with only such services as are available to nonhandicapped children would in all probability fall short of the statutory requirement of "free appropriate public education"; to require, on the other hand, the furnishing of every special service necessary to maximize each handicapped child's potential is, we think, further than Congress intended to go. Thus to speak in terms of "equal" services in one instance gives less than what is required by the Act and in another instance more. The theme of the Act is "free appropriate public education," a phrase which is too complex to be captured by the word "equal" whether one is speaking of opportunities or services.

The legislative conception of the requirements of equal protection was undoubtedly informed by the two District Court decisions referred to above.

---

[111] [21] In seeking to read more into the Act than its language or legislative history will permit, the United States focuses upon the word "appropriate," arguing that "the statutory definitions do not adequately explain what [it means]." Whatever Congress meant by an "appropriate" education, it is clear that it did not mean a potential-maximizing education.

The term as used in reference to educating the handicapped appears to have originated in the *PARC* decision, where the District Court required that handicapped children be provided with "education and training appropriate to [their] learning capacities." The word appears again in the *Mills* decision, the District Court at one point referring to the need for "an appropriate educational program," and at another point speaking of a "suitable publicly-supported education." Both cases also refer to the need for an "adequate" education.

The use of "appropriate" in the language of the Act, although by no means definitive, suggests that Congress used the word as much to describe the settings in which handicapped children should be educated as to prescribe the substantive content or supportive services of their education. For example, § 1412(5) requires that handicapped children be educated in classrooms with nonhandicapped children "to the maximum extent appropriate." Similarly, § 1401(19) provides that, "whenever appropriate," handicapped children should attend and participate in the meeting at which their IEP is drafted. In addition, the definition of "free appropriate public education" itself states that instruction given handicapped children should be at an "appropriate preschool, elementary, or secondary school" level. § 1401(18)(C). The Act's use of the word "appropriate" thus seems to reflect Congress' recognition that some settings simply are not suitable environments for the participation of some handicapped children. At the very least, these statutory uses of the word refute the contention that Congress used "appropriate" as a term of art which concisely expresses the standard found by the lower courts.

But cases such as *Mills* and *PARC* held simply that handicapped children may not be excluded entirely from public education. . . .

The District Court and the Court of Appeals thus erred when they held that the Act requires New York to maximize the potential of each handicapped child commensurate with the opportunity provided nonhandicapped children. Desirable though that goal might be, it is not the standard that Congress imposed upon States which receive funding under the Act. Rather, Congress sought primarily to identify and evaluate handicapped children, and to provide them with access to a free public education.

(iii)

Implicit in the congressional purpose of providing access to a "free appropriate public education" is the requirement that the education to which access is provided be sufficient to confer some educational benefit upon the handicapped child. It would do little good for Congress to spend millions of dollars in providing access to a public education only to have the handicapped child receive no benefit from that education. The statutory definition of "free appropriate public education," in addition to requiring that States provide each child with "specially designed instruction," expressly requires the provision of "such . . . supportive services . . . as may be required to assist a handicapped child to *benefit* from special education." § 1401(17) (emphasis added). We therefore conclude that the "basic floor of opportunity" provided by the Act consists of access to specialized instruction and related services which are individually designed to provide educational benefit to the handicapped child.[112]

---

[112] [23] This view is supported by the congressional intention, frequently expressed in the legislative history, that handicapped children be enabled to achieve a reasonable degree of self-sufficiency. After referring to statistics showing that many handicapped children were excluded from public education, the Senate Report states:

> "The long range implications of these statistics are that public agencies and taxpayers will spend billions of dollars over the lifetimes of these individuals to maintain such persons as dependents and in a minimally acceptable lifestyle. With proper education services, many would be able to become productive citizens, contributing to society instead of being forced to remain burdens. Others, through such services, would increase their independence, thus reducing their dependence on society." Similarly, one of the principal Senate sponsors of the Act stated that "providing appropriate educational services now means that many of these individuals will be able to become a contributing part of our society, and they will not have to depend on subsistence payments from public funds." 121 Cong. Rec. 19492 (1975) (remarks of Sen. Williams). . . .

The desire to provide handicapped children with an attainable degree of personal independence obviously anticipated that state educational programs would confer educational benefits upon such children. But at the same time, the goal of achieving some degree of self-sufficiency in most cases is a good deal more modest than the potential-maximizing goal adopted by the lower courts.

Despite its frequent mention, we cannot conclude, as did the dissent in the Court of Appeals, that self-sufficiency was itself the substantive standard which Congress imposed upon the States. Because many mildly handicapped children will achieve self-sufficiency without state assistance while personal independence for the severely handicapped may be an unreachable goal, "self-sufficiency" as a substantive standard is at once an inadequate protection and an overly demanding requirement. We thus view these references in the legislative history as evidence of Congress' intention that the services provided handicapped children be educationally beneficial, whatever the nature or severity of their handicap.

The determination of when handicapped children are receiving sufficient educational benefits to satisfy the requirements of the Act presents a more difficult problem. The Act requires participating States to educate a wide spectrum of handicapped children, from the marginally hearing-impaired to the profoundly retarded and palsied. It is clear that the benefits obtainable by children at one end of the spectrum will differ dramatically from those obtainable by children at the other end, with infinite variations in between. One child may have little difficulty competing successfully in an academic setting with nonhandicapped children while another child may encounter great difficulty in acquiring even the most basic of self-maintenance skills. We do not attempt today to establish any one test for determining the adequacy of educational benefits conferred upon all children covered by the Act. Because in this case we are presented with a handicapped child who is receiving substantial specialized instruction and related services, and who is performing above average in the regular classrooms of a public school system, we confine our analysis to that situation.

The Act requires participating States to educate handicapped children with nonhandicapped children whenever possible. When that "mainstreaming" preference of the Act has been met and a child is being educated in the regular classrooms of a public school system, the system itself monitors the educational progress of the child. Regular examinations are administered, grades are awarded, and yearly advancement to higher grade levels is permitted for those children who attain an adequate knowledge of the course material. The grading and advancement system thus constitutes an important factor in determining educational benefit. Children who graduate from our public school systems are considered by our society to have been "educated" at least to the grade level they have completed, and access to an "education" for handicapped children is precisely what Congress sought to provide in the Act.

C

When the language of the Act and its legislative history are considered together, the requirements imposed by Congress become tolerably clear. Insofar as a State is required to provide a handicapped child with a "free appropriate public education," we hold that it satisfies this requirement by providing personalized instruction with sufficient support services to permit the child to benefit educationally from that instruction. Such instruction and services must be provided at public expense, must meet the State's educational standards, must approximate the grade levels used in the State's regular education, and must comport with the child's IEP. In addition, the IEP, and therefore the personalized instruction, should be formulated in accordance with the requirements of the Act and, if the child is being educated in the regular classrooms of the public education system, should be reasonably calculated to enable the child to achieve passing marks and advance from grade to grade.

IV

A

As mentioned in Part I, the Act permits "[any] party aggrieved by the findings and decision" of the state administrative hearings "to bring a civil action" in "any State court of competent jurisdiction or in a district court of the United States without regard to the amount in controversy." The complaint, and therefore the civil action, may concern "any matter relating to the identification, evaluation, or educational placement of the child, or the provision of a free appropriate public education to such child." § 1415(b)(1)(E). In reviewing the complaint, the Act provides that a court "shall receive the record of the [state] administrative proceedings, shall hear additional evidence at the request of a party, and, basing its decision on the preponderance of the evidence, shall grant such relief as the court determines is appropriate." The parties disagree sharply over the meaning of these provisions, petitioners contending that courts are given only limited authority to review for state compliance with the Act's procedural requirements and no power to review the substance of the state program, and respondents contending that the Act requires courts to exercise de novo review over state educational decisions and policies. We find petitioners' contention unpersuasive, for Congress expressly rejected provisions that would have so severely restricted the role of reviewing courts. In substituting the current language of the statute for language that would have made state administrative findings conclusive if supported by substantial evidence, the Conference Committee explained that courts were to make "independent [decisions] based on a preponderance of the evidence."

But although we find that this grant of authority is broader than claimed by petitioners, we think the fact that it is found in § 1415, which is entitled "Procedural safeguards," is not without significance. When the elaborate and highly specific procedural safeguards embodied in § 1415 are contrasted with the general and somewhat imprecise substantive admonitions contained in the Act, we think that the importance Congress attached to these procedural safeguards cannot be gainsaid. It seems to us no exaggeration to say that Congress placed every bit as much emphasis upon compliance with procedures giving parents and guardians a large measure of participation at every stage of the administrative process, as it did upon the measurement of the resulting IEP against a substantive standard. We think that the congressional emphasis upon full participation of concerned parties throughout the development of the IEP, as well as the requirements that state and local plans be submitted to the Secretary for approval, demonstrates the legislative conviction that adequate compliance with the procedures prescribed would in most cases assure much if not all of what Congress wished in the way of substantive content in an IEP.

Thus the provision that a reviewing court base its decision on the "preponderance of the evidence" is by no means an invitation to the courts to substitute their own notions of sound educational policy for those of the school authorities which they review. The very importance which Congress has attached to compliance with certain procedures in the preparation of an IEP would be frustrated if a court were permitted simply to set state decisions at nought. The fact that § 1415(e) requires that the reviewing court "receive the records of the [state] administrative proceedings" carries with it the implied requirement that due weight shall be given to these proceedings. And we find nothing in the Act to suggest that merely because Congress was rather sketchy in establishing substantive requirements, as opposed to procedural requirements for the preparation of an IEP, it intended that reviewing courts should have a free hand to impose substantive standards of review which cannot be derived from the Act itself. In short, the statutory authorization to grant "such relief as the court determines is appropriate" cannot be read without reference to the obligations, largely procedural in nature, which are imposed upon recipient States by Congress.

Therefore, a court's inquiry in suits brought under § 1415(e)(2) is twofold. First, has the State complied with the procedures set forth in the Act?[113] And second, is the individualized educational program developed through the Act's procedures reasonably calculated to enable the child to receive educational benefits? If these requirements are met, the State has complied with the obligations imposed by Congress and the courts can require no more.

B

In assuring that the requirements of the Act have been met, courts must be careful to avoid imposing their view of preferable educational methods upon the States.[114] The primary responsibility for formulating the education to be accorded a handicapped child, and for choosing the educational method most suitable to the child's needs, was left by the Act to state and local educational agencies in cooperation with the parents or guardian of the child. The Act expressly charges States with the responsibility of "acquiring and disseminating to teachers and administrators of programs for handicapped children significant information derived from educational research, demonstration, and similar projects, and [of] adopting, where appropriate, promising educational practices and materials." § 1413(a)(3). In the face of such a clear statutory directive, it seems highly unlikely that Congress intended courts to overturn a State's choice of appropriate educational theories in a proceeding conducted pursuant to § 1415(e)(2).[115]

We previously have cautioned that courts lack the "specialized knowledge and experience" necessary to resolve "persistent and difficult questions of

---

[113] [27] This inquiry will require a court not only to satisfy itself that the State has adopted the state plan, policies, and assurances required by the Act, but also to determine that the State has created an IEP for the child in question which conforms with the requirements of § 1401(19).

[114] [29] In this case, for example, both the state hearing officer and the District Court were presented with evidence as to the best method for educating the deaf, a question long debated among scholars. *See* Large, *Special Problems of the Deaf Under the Education for All Handicapped Children Act of 1975*, 58 WASH. U. L.Q. 213, 229 (1980). The District Court accepted the testimony of respondents' experts that there was "a trend supported by studies showing the greater degree of success of students brought up in deaf households using [the method of communication used by the Rowleys]."

[115] [30] It is clear that Congress was aware of the States' traditional role in the formulation and execution of educational policy. "Historically, the States have had the primary responsibility for the education of children at the elementary and secondary level." 121 Cong. Rec. 19498 (1975) (remarks of Sen. Dole). *See also Epperson v. Arkansas*, 393 U.S. 97, 104 (1968) ("By and large, public education in our Nation is committed to the control of state and local authorities").

educational policy." *San Antonio Independent School Dist. v. Rodriguez,* 411 U.S., at 42. We think that Congress shared that view when it passed the Act. As already demonstrated, Congress' intention was not that the Act displace the primacy of States in the field of education, but that States receive funds to assist them in extending their educational systems to the handicapped. Therefore, once a court determines that the requirements of the Act have been met, questions of methodology are for resolution by the States.

V

Entrusting a child's education to state and local agencies does not leave the child without protection. Congress sought to protect individual children by providing for parental involvement in the development of state plans and policies and in the formulation of the child's individual educational program. As the Senate Report states:

> The Committee recognizes that in many instances the process of providing special education and related services to handicapped children is not guaranteed to produce any particular outcome. By changing the language [of the provision relating to individualized educational programs] to emphasize the process of parent and child involvement and to provide a written record of reasonable expectations, the Committee intends to clarify that such individualized planning conferences are a way to provide parent involvement and protection to assure that appropriate services are provided to a handicapped child.

As this very case demonstrates, parents and guardians will not lack ardor in seeking to ensure that handicapped children receive all of the benefits to which they are entitled by the Act.

VI

Applying these principles to the facts of this case, we conclude that the Court of Appeals erred in affirming the decision of the District Court. Neither the District Court nor the Court of Appeals found that petitioners had failed to comply with the procedures of the Act, and the findings of neither court would support a conclusion that Amy's educational program failed to comply with the substantive requirements of the Act. On the contrary, the District Court found that the "evidence firmly establishes that Amy is receiving an 'adequate' education, since she performs better than the average child in her class and is advancing easily from grade to grade." In light of this finding, and of the fact that Amy was receiving personalized instruction and related services calculated by the Furnace Woods school administrators to meet her educational needs, the lower courts should not have concluded that the Act requires the provision of a sign-language interpreter. Accordingly, the decision of the Court of Appeals is reversed, and the case is remanded for further proceedings consistent with this opinion.

So ordered.

[JUSTICE BLACKMUN's opinion, concurring in the judgment, is omitted.]

Justice White, with whom Justice Brennan and Justice Marshall join, *dissenting.*

In order to reach its result in this case, the majority opinion contradicts itself, the language of the statute, and the legislative history. Both the majority's standard for a "free appropriate education" and its standard for judicial review disregard congressional intent.

I

The majority first turns its attention to the meaning of a "free appropriate public education.". . . I agree that the language of the Act does not contain a substantive standard beyond requiring that the education offered must be "appropriate." However, if there are limits not evident from the face of the statute on what may be considered an "appropriate education," they must be found in the purpose of the statute or its legislative history. The Act itself announces it will provide a "full educational opportunity to all handicapped children." This goal is repeated throughout the legislative history, in statements too frequent to be " 'passing references and isolated phrases.' " These statements elucidate the meaning of "appropriate." According to the Senate Report, for example, the Act does "guarantee that handicapped children are provided equal educational opportunity." This promise appears throughout the legislative history. Indeed, at times the purpose of the Act was described as tailoring each handicapped child's educational plan to enable the child "to achieve his or her maximum potential." Senator Stafford, one of the sponsors of the Act, declared: "We can all agree that education [given a handicapped child] should be equivalent, at least, to the one those children who are not handicapped receive." The legislative history thus directly supports the conclusion that the Act intends to give handicapped children an educational opportunity commensurate with that given other children.

The majority opinion announces a different substantive standard, that "Congress did not impose upon the States any greater substantive educational standard than would be necessary to make such access meaningful." While "meaningful" is no more enlightening than "appropriate," the Court purports to clarify itself. Because Amy was provided with some specialized instruction from which she obtained some benefit and because she passed from grade to grade, she was receiving a meaningful and therefore appropriate education. . . .

The Act requires more. It defines "special education" to mean "specifically designed instruction, at no cost to parents or guardians, *to meet the unique needs* of a handicapped child . . . ." Providing a teacher with a loud voice would not meet Amy's needs and would not satisfy the Act. The basic floor of opportunity is instead, as the courts below recognized, intended to eliminate the effects of the handicap, at least to the extent that the child will be given an equal opportunity to learn if that is reasonably possible. Amy Rowley, without a sign-language interpreter, comprehends less than half of what is said in the classroom — less than half of what normal children comprehend. This is hardly an equal opportunity to learn, even if Amy makes passing grades.

. . . .

II

The Court's discussion of the standard for judicial review is as flawed as its discussion of a "free appropriate public education." According to the Court, a court can ask only whether the State has "complied with the procedures set forth in the Act" and whether the individualized education program is "reasonably calculated to enable the child to receive educational benefits." Both the language of the Act and the legislative history, however, demonstrate that Congress intended the courts to conduct a far more searching inquiry. . . .

The legislative history shows that judicial review is not limited to procedural matters and that the state educational agencies are given first, but not final, responsibility for the content of a handicapped child's education. The Conference Committee directs courts to make an "independent decision." The deliberate change in the review provision is an unusually clear indication that Congress intended courts to undertake substantive review instead of relying on the conclusions of the state agency. . . .

Parents can challenge the IEP for failing to supply the special education and related services needed by the individual handicapped child. That is what the Rowleys did. As the Government observes, "courts called upon to review the content of an IEP, in accordance with 20 U.S.C. [§] 1415(e) inevitably are required to make a judgment, on the basis of the evidence presented, concerning whether the educational methods proposed by the local school district are 'appropriate' for the handicapped child involved." Brief for United States as *Amicus Curiae* 13. The courts below, as they were required by the Act, did precisely that.

Under the judicial review provisions of the Act, neither the District Court nor the Court of Appeals was bound by the State's construction of what an "appropriate" education means in general or by what the state authorities considered to be an appropriate education for Amy Rowley. Because the standard of the courts below seems to me to reflect the congressional purpose and because their factual findings are not clearly erroneous, I respectfully dissent.

———

NOTES AND QUESTIONS

1. What is the statutory obligation of a school district with regard to the kind of services it must provide to a disabled student? What did this mean for Amy Rowley?

What if a child is both severely autistic and severely mentally retarded? Is the school district required to provide the child with residential treatment? What if the residential treatment center is in another state? What if it is in Japan? The Eleventh Circuit, in *Drew P. v. Clarke County School District*, 877 F.2d 927 (11th Cir. 1989), reviewed a determination by the district court that a severely autistic and severely mentally retarded boy needed residential treatment. *See* 676 F. Supp. 1559 (M.D. Ga. 1987). The boy had been in a special education program (with a small staff-to-student ratio) in the school district, the district provided him with an in-home trainer, and he spent one year in the Georgia Retardation Center, a residential treatment center. His parents withdrew the boy from the district's program when he became increasingly aggressive and failed to achieve the goals set by his IEP. They placed him in a private residential center for the severely mentally retarded. He was evaluated at this center, and the staff concluded that he was not "receiving the optimum educational benefits" at the center and recommended placement in a residential facility for autistic children. *Id.* at 929. No such center existed in the state of Georgia, although there was evidence in the record that group homes for autistic children were available in North Carolina. 676 F. Supp. at 1570.

The boy's parent's placed him in a residential center in Tokyo, Japan. After two years, he was transferred to the Japanese school's newly opened sister school in Boston, Massachusetts. The Eleventh Circuit affirmed the district court's order that required the school district to pay for the tuition, school fees and uniform fees for the residential facilities in Tokyo and Boston. The district court, overruling the regional hearing officer and the state administrative officer, had found that a residential treatment center for autistic children was necessary for the boy to receive educational benefit. Although the school district presented expert testimony that the boy could receive an educational benefit in the school district's program, another expert testified that residential treatment was necessary for the boy to receive any educational benefit. According to *Burlington School Comm. v. Department of Education*, 471 U.S. 359 (1985), reimbursing the parents for private schooling is proper under IDEA if the court determines that the placement is proper. "Because the district judge found that Drew's parents were justified in placing him in the residential facilities, he had the authority to order reimbursement for their costs for the facilities under consideration and for attorneys fees." *Drew P.*, 877 F.2d at 931. *See also Missouri Dept. of Elementary and Secondary Educ. v. Springfield R-12 Sch. Dist.*, 358 F.3d 992, 997 (8th Cir. 2004) (affirming the Department's responsibility for the costs of private program for $175,000 a year for a deaf-blind student).

Reimbursement when parents place their child in a private school is one of the more contentious issues — along with "inclusion" and discipline, *supra*, — that arise under IDEA. For example, in *L.M. v. Evesham Township Bd. of Educ.*, 256 F. Supp. 2d 290 (D.N.J. 2003), parents who were dissatisfied with their child's IEP, placed him in a private Quaker school and sought public reimbursement. The ALJ refused reimbursement since a New Jersey statute banned reimbursement when parents unilaterally decide to place their child in a private, sectarian school. The court rejected the school board's argument, and held that the sectarian nature of a private school did not bar reimbursement under state or federal law. Therefore, if it is determined that the public school does not provide the disabled student with a FAPE, the parents are entitled unilaterally to remove the student and receive public reimbursement of private tuition costs.

The Eleventh Circuit took a less sanguine view of private placement in *Loren F. v. Atlanta Indep. Sch. Sys.*, 349 F.3d 1309, 1318 (11th Cir. 2003). Loren had attended a private school for two years before being diagnosed with a learning disability. The parents applied to a private school for their son's ninth grade year but indicated they would have trouble paying the tuition. At the same time, the parents contacted public school officials about enrolling their son in public schools and developing an IEP. Five days after the IEP was instituted, the parents transferred their son to a private school and later rejected his IEP. They filed for reimbursement of the private school tuition. The Eleventh Circuit remanded the case to the district court to determine whether plaintiff's parents were "gaming the system to extract free tuition for private school, or simply hedging their bets when faced with a demonstrably under-resourced public school system."

The intricacies of the private placement analysis and the many complex issues surrounding special education law now comprise an entire casebook. *See* MARK C. WEBER, ET AL., SPECIAL EDUCATION LAW: CASES AND MATERIALS (2004).

Should the parents be reimbursed for the cost of visiting their child if the child is placed in a distant residential facility? *See* Sam Allis, *The Struggle to Pay for Special Ed,* TIME, Nov. 4, 1996, at 82 (discussing how annual cost to a school district in South Dakota for sending boy to private school in Connecticut — including eight trips per year for his family to visit him — reached $125,000 per year). How might a school district's budget be affected by costs like these? *See id.* (school district reported that of 80% increase in school budget and 55% rise in property taxes, one quarter of this increase was attributable to expenses for one disabled child). *See also Clevenger v. Oak Ridge Sch. Bd.,* 744 F.2d 514 (6th Cir. 1984) (determining $88,000 per year program was only program appropriate for child); *T.G. v. Board of Educ.,* 576 F. Supp. 420 (D.N.J. 1983) (requiring school district to pay for psychotherapy services for one child totaling over $25,000); *60 Minutes: Special Education — Moneys Spent on Special Education Students Funds Are Decreased* (CBS television broadcast, June 9, 1996) (recounting that severely disabled boy was sent to special private school at cost of $100,000 per year).

Should there be some sort of sliding income scale included in IDEA so that wealthier parents are required to pay some of the costs of private placement for their child, rather than requiring taxpayers of all income brackets to foot the entire bill?

2. Are there some children whose disabilities are so severe that the school district has no obligation to provide education and related services because the child will receive no educational benefit? Timothy W., born two months premature, was multiply handicapped and profoundly mentally retarded. *Timothy W. v. Rochester School District,* 875 F.2d 954 (1st Cir. 1989). He suffered from "complex developmental disabilities, spastic quadriplegia, cerebral palsy, seizure disorder, and cortical blindness." At a meeting to determine whether the boy was entitled to special education and related services, the school district heard testimony from several experts. Some of the experts recommended that the boy receive some kind of occupational therapy and a program that would increase his responses to his environment. Others

testified that hydrocephalus had destroyed part of Timothy's brain and that he had no educational potential. At another meeting, one specialist determined that the boy's educational needs include "postural drainage, motion exercises, sensory stimulation, positioning, and stimulation of head control." At various other meetings and hearings numerous specialists testified, some stating that Timothy could not benefit from an education program, while others testified that he could. (For example, one physician stated that the boy responded to sounds and recommended physical therapy and stimulation.) The district court found that Timothy was not capable of benefitting from special education. The court of appeals reviewed IDEA's legislative history. Because language in the statute and its legislative history nowhere indicated that there must be proof that a disabled child can benefit from special education, the court determined that education for disabled children is a "universal right." That right is not "predicated on any type of guarantees that the child will benefit from the special education and services . . . ."

After *Timothy W.*, is there any child with any disability who is not eligible for special education and related services?

3. What are the "related services" that a school district must provide to a disabled student? According to the statutory language in IDEA, 20 U.S.C. § 1401(22), the services that a public school is required to provide a disabled child include "speech-language pathology and audiology services, psychological services, physical and occupational therapy, recreation, including therapeutic recreation, social work services, counseling services, including rehabilitation counseling, orientation and mobility services and medical services, except that such medical services shall be for diagnostic and evaluation purposes only."

If a child is severely disabled, must a school district provided one-on-one continuous nursing care? In *Cedar Rapids Community School District v. Garret F.*, 526 U.S. 66 (1999), Garret F. was wheelchair-bound and ventilator dependent; he therefore required a responsible individual nearby to attend to certain physical needs during the school day. He needed assistance with urinary bladder catheterization once a day, the suctioning of his tracheotomy tube as needed, but at least once every six hours, with food and drink at lunchtime, in getting into a reclining position for five minutes of each hour, and ambu bagging occasionally as needed when the ventilator is checked for proper functioning. He also needed assistance from someone familiar with his ventilator in the event of a malfunction or electrical problem, and someone who can perform emergency procedures in the event he experiences autonomic hyperreflexia. (Autonomic hyperreflexia is an uncontrolled visceral reaction to anxiety or a full bladder. Blood pressure increases, heart rate increases, and flushing and sweating may occur.) The school district declined to accept financial responsibility for the services Garret needs, believing that it was not legally obligated to provide continuous one-on-one nursing care.

The Supreme Court determined that IDEA required the school district to provide Garret with the nursing services he requires during school hours. The "related services" definition broadly encompasses those supportive services that "may be required to assist a child with a disability to benefit from special education. Furthermore, the statute's general "related services" definition is illuminated by a parenthetical phrase listing examples of services that are included within the statute's coverage, including "medical services" if they are "for diagnostic and evaluation purposes." Although the IDEA itself does not define "medical services" more specifically, the Supreme Court in *Irving Indep. Sch. Dist. v. Tatro*, 468 U.S. 883 (1984), concluded that the Secretary of Education had reasonably determined that "medical services" referred to services that must be performed by a physician, and not to school health services. Thus, only certain medical services are excluded from the definition.

The school district did not contend that the services Garret required could be performed only by a physician but asked that the Court apply a test that had been used by some lower federal courts that had addressed the issue. The school district pointed out that these courts had not asked whether the requested health services must be delivered by a physician, but instead have applied a multi-factor test that considered, generally speaking, the nature and extent of the services at issue. The school district proposed a test that considered a series of factors such as (1) whether the care is continuous or intermittent, (2) whether existing school health personnel can provide the service, (3) the cost of the service, and (4) the potential consequences if the service is not properly performed. The Court acknowledged that the school district may have legitimate concerns about the financial burden of providing the services Garret needs, but decided that accepting its cost-based standard as the sole test for determining IDEA's scope would require the Court to engage in judicial lawmaking without any guidance from Congress.

Justice Thomas and Justice Kennedy in dissent focused on the statutory language which expressly states that school districts are not required to provide medical services, except for diagnostic and evaluation purposes. The dissent argued that IDEA's regulations should be interpreted so that school districts need only provide disabled children with "health-related services that school nurses can perform as part of their normal duties."

4. Disability harassment in school may be the next area to receive the attention of reformers and the courts. *See* Mark C. Weber, *Disability Harassment in the Public Schools*, 43 Wm. & Mary L. Rev. 1079 (2002).

[B] Inclusion

In *Rowley*, the U.S. Supreme Court addressed the meaning of the word "appropriate" with regard to IDEA's requirement in § 1412(1) that disabled students must receive a "free, appropriate public education." The use of the word "appropriate" in another provision in IDEA has also bewildered both the schools and the courts. Title 20 U. S. C. § 1412(5) requires that participating States establish policies to ensure that, "[T]o the maximum extent *appropriate*, children with disabilities . . . are educated with children who are not disabled, and that special classes, separate schooling, or other removal of disabled children from the regular educational environment occurs only when the nature or severity of the disability is such that education in regular classes with the use of supplementary aids and services cannot be achieved satisfactorily." (emphasis added). IDEA does not provide any guidance on how to strike the balance between its requirements that the disabled student receive an "appropriate" education and that the disabled child be educated "to the maximum extent appropriate" with nondisabled students.

The issue of the disabled student's placement began as a push for "mainstreaming." Under this model, a disabled child's primary placement may be in a separate special education class, but the child is "mainstreamed" in a regular classroom for part of the day. The mainstreaming concept has changed into what is now termed "inclusion. Under this model, a disabled child is placed in the general education classroom for the entire day. Advocates of full inclusion maintain that all disabled children — regardless of the characteristics or severity of the disability — must be placed in the general education classroom "for all of the school day in every school setting, preschool through high school." James McCleskey & Nancy Waldron, *Responses to Questions Teachers and Administrators Frequently Ask About Inclusive School Programs*, 78 PHI DELTA KAPPAN 150, 152 (1996). The courts of appeal have developed divergent tests to determine whether IDEA's statutory requirement has been met. In so doing, some courts have tacitly accepted the premises of the full inclusion advocates, suggesting that the purported social benefits of inclusion can be more important than either the academic achievement of the disabled child or the cost to the learning environment in the general education classroom. Other courts have stated that the social benefit of inclusion does not outweigh the child's failure to progress academically in the regular classroom. The following two cases are examples of the conflicting views in the courts of appeals.

OBERTI v. BOARD OF EDUCATION

Court of Appeals for the Third Circuit
995 F.2d 1204 (1993)

BECKER, CIRCUIT JUDGE.

The Individuals with Disabilities Education Act (IDEA), 20 U.S.C. §§ 1400–1485 (formerly the "Education for All Handicapped Children Act"), provides that states receiving funding under the Act must ensure that children with disabilities are educated in regular classrooms with nondisabled children "to the maximum extent appropriate." 20 U.S.C. § 1412(5)(B). Plaintiff-appellee Rafael Oberti is an eight year old child with Down's syndrome who was removed from the regular classroom by defendant-appellant Clementon School District Board of Education (the "School District") and placed in a segregated special education class. In this appeal, we are asked by the School District to review the district court's decision in favor of Rafael and his co-plaintiff parents Carlos and Jeanne Oberti concerning Rafael's right under IDEA to be educated in a regular classroom with nondisabled classmates. This court has not previously had occasion to interpret or apply the "mainstreaming" requirement of IDEA.[116]

---

[116] [1] Integrating children with disabilities in regular classrooms is commonly known as "mainstreaming." *See Daniel R.R. v. State Bd. of Educ.*, 874 F.2d 1036, 1039 (5th Cir. 1989); *Board of Educ. Sacramento City Unified School Dist. v. Holland*, 786 F. Supp. 874, 878 (E.D. Cal. 1992). The Obertis point out that some educators and public school authorities have come to disfavor

We construe IDEA's mainstreaming requirement to prohibit a school from placing a child with disabilities outside of a regular classroom if educating the child in the regular classroom, with supplementary aids and support services, can be achieved satisfactorily. In addition, if placement outside of a regular classroom is necessary for the child to receive educational benefit, the school may still be violating IDEA if it has not made sufficient efforts to include the child in school programs with nondisabled children whenever possible. We also hold that the school bears the burden of proving compliance with the mainstreaming requirement of IDEA, regardless of which party (the child and parents or the school) brought the claim under IDEA before the district court.

Although our interpretation of IDEA's mainstreaming requirement differs somewhat from that of the district court, we will affirm the decision of the district court that the School District has failed to comply with IDEA. More precisely, we will affirm the district court's order that the School District design an appropriate education plan for Rafael Oberti in accordance with IDEA, and we will remand for further proceedings consistent with this opinion.

. . . .

I. FACTUAL AND PROCEDURAL BACKGROUND

A. *Rafael Oberti's educational history*

Rafael is an eight year old child with Down's syndrome, a genetic defect that severely impairs his intellectual functioning and his ability to communicate. Now and throughout the period in question, Rafael and his parents have lived within the Clementon School District, in southern New Jersey. Prior to his entry into kindergarten, Rafael was evaluated in accordance with federal and state law by the School District's Child Study Team (the "Team").[117] Based on its evaluation, the Team recommended to Rafael's parents that he be placed in a segregated special education class located in another school district for the 1989-90 school year. The Obertis visited a number of special classes recommended by the School District and found them all unacceptable.

---

use of the term "mainstreaming" because it suggests, in their view, the shuttling of a child with disabilities in and out of a regular class without altering the classroom to accommodate the child. They prefer the term "inclusion" because of its greater emphasis on the use of supplementary aids and support services within the regular classroom to facilitate inclusion of children with disabilities. *See Winners All: A Call for Inclusive Schools*, REPORT TO THE NATIONAL ASSOCIATION OF STATE BOARDS OF EDUCATION BY STUDY GROUP ON SPECIAL EDUCATION (October 1992). While "inclusion" may be a more precise term, we will nonetheless use the term "mainstreaming" because it is currently the common parlance. Moreover, as we discuss below, "mainstreaming" as required under IDEA does not mean simply the placement of a child with disabilities in a regular classroom or school program.

117 [2] The Child Study Team is "an interdisciplinary group of appropriately certified persons," which, pursuant to New Jersey regulations, includes a school psychologist, a learning disabilities teacher-consultant and a school social worker, all of whom are employees of the School District. *See* N.J.A.C. 6:28-3.1. The Team was responsible for evaluating Rafael to determine his eligibility for special education and related services under IDEA, and continues to be responsible for developing, monitoring and evaluating the effectiveness of his individualized education program.

Thereafter the Obertis and the School District came to an agreement that Rafael would attend a "developmental" kindergarten class (for children not fully ready for kindergarten) at the Clementon Elementary School (Rafael's neighborhood school) in the mornings, and a special education class in another school district in the afternoons.

The Individualized Education Plan (IEP) developed by the School District for Rafael for the 1989-90 school year assigned all of Rafael's academic goals to the afternoon special education class. In contrast, the only goals for Rafael in the morning kindergarten class were to observe, model and socialize with nondisabled children. While Rafael's progress reports for the developmental kindergarten class show that he made academic and social progress in that class during the year, Rafael experienced a number of serious behavioral problems there, including repeated toileting accidents, temper tantrums, crawling and hiding under furniture, and touching, hitting and spitting on other children. On several occasions Rafael struck at and hit the teacher and the teacher's aide.

These problems disrupted the class and frustrated the teacher, who consulted the school psychologist and other members of the Child Study Team to discuss possible approaches to managing Rafael's behavior problems. The teacher made some attempts to modify the curriculum for Rafael, but Rafael's IEP provided no plan for addressing Rafael's behavior problems. Neither did the IEP provide for special education consultation for the kindergarten teacher, or for communication between the kindergarten teacher and the special education teacher. In March of 1990, the School District finally obtained the assistance of an additional aide, which had been requested by the parents much earlier in the school year, but the presence of the extra aide in the kindergarten class did little to resolve the behavior problems. According to Rafael's progress reports for the afternoon special education class, and as the district court found, Rafael did not experience similar behavior problems in that class.

At the end of the 1989-90 school year, the Child Study Team proposed to place Rafael for the following year in a segregated special education class for children classified as "educable mentally retarded." Since no such special education class existed within the Clementon School District, Rafael would have to travel to a different district. The Team's decision was based both on the behavioral problems Rafael experienced during the 1989-90 school year in the developmental kindergarten class and on the Team's belief that Rafael's disabilities precluded him from benefiting from education in a regular classroom at that time.

The Obertis objected to a segregated placement and requested that Rafael be placed in the regular kindergarten class in the Clementon Elementary School. The School District refused, and the Obertis sought relief by filing a request for a due process hearing. . . . Through mediation, the Obertis and the School District came to an agreement that for the 1990-91 school year Rafael would attend a special education class for students labeled "multiply handicapped" in a public elementary school in the Winslow Township School District ("Winslow"), approximately 45 minutes by bus from Rafael's home. As part of the agreement, the School District promised to explore mainstreaming possibilities at the Winslow school and to consider a future placement for Rafael in a regular classroom in the Clementon Elementary School.

The special education class in Winslow that Rafael attended during the 1990-91 school year was taught by an instructor and an instructional aide and included nine children. Although Rafael initially exhibited some of the same behavioral problems he had experienced in the Clementon kindergarten class, his behavior gradually improved: he became toilet trained and his disruptiveness abated. Rafael also made academic progress. However, by December of 1990, Rafael's parents found that the School District was making no plans to mainstream Rafael. The Obertis also learned that Rafael had no meaningful contact with nondisabled students at the Winslow school.[118]

B. *The due process hearing*

In January of 1991, the Obertis brought another due process complaint, renewing their request under IDEA that Rafael be placed in a regular class in his neighborhood elementary school. A three-day due process hearing was held in February of 1991 before an Administrative Law Judge (ALJ). On March 15, 1991, the ALJ affirmed the School District's decision that the segregated special education class in Winslow was the "least restrictive environment" for Rafael. Based on the testimony of Rafael's kindergarten teacher and other witnesses for the School District who described Rafael's disruptive behavior in the developmental kindergarten class, the ALJ found that Rafael's behavior problems in that class were extensive and that he had achieved no meaningful educational benefit in the class.[119] The ALJ concluded that Rafael was not ready for mainstreaming.

---

[118] [5] Rafael's class went to the lunchroom and assemblies with nondisabled children, but he and his classmates had no opportunity to socialize with the other children. Rafael did not participate in any classes, such as art, music, or physical education, with nondisabled children.

[119] [7] The School District presented eight witnesses before the ALJ. Melinda Reardon, the teacher of the developmental kindergarten class, testified to Rafael's behavioral problems that disrupted the class throughout the year, including repeated toileting accidents, touching and hitting other children, throwing objects, not following instructions, and running and hiding from the teacher and the aides. She also testified that throughout the year she had great difficulty communicating with Rafael, and that she had consulted with the school psychologist to come up with methods of controlling Rafael's behavior. Karen Lightman, the speech therapist at the Clementon Elementary School, testified that Rafael regularly disrupted her small-group speech therapy sessions during the 1989-90 school year. She testified that Rafael slapped her on one occasion, refused to follow instructions, threw paper, and touched other students. She stated that these behaviors disrupted the session and took away therapy time from the other students. William Sherman, the superintendent of Schools for the School District and acting principal of the Clementon Elementary School in May and June of 1990 testified that he was called to Rafael's kindergarten class several times by the teacher to help her address Rafael's disciplinary problems. Valeria Costino, an instructional aide for that class, corroborated the testimony of the teacher and the acting principal regarding Rafael's behavior problems.

Peggy McDevit, the Clementon Elementary School psychologist, a member of the Child Study Team, and a qualified expert in child placement and child psychology, testified that she had observed Rafael engaging in disruptive behavior in the kindergarten class and that, in her opinion, placement in a regular classroom would not be feasible for Rafael at that time because of his behavior problems. David Hinlicky, the principal of the Clementon Elementary School, described a visit he paid to a summer school class Rafael attended in 1991 in which he observed Rafael misbehaving and disrupting the class.

In reaching this conclusion, the ALJ discounted the testimony of the Obertis' two expert witnesses. Dr. Gail McGregor, a professor of education at Temple University and an expert in the education of children with disabilities, testified that Rafael could be educated satisfactorily in a regular class at the Clementon Elementary School with supplementary aids and services, and that Rafael would learn important skills in a regular classroom that could not be learned in a segregated setting.[120] The ALJ disregarded Dr. McGregor's testimony because, unlike the School District's witnesses, she did not have daily experience with Rafael. Likewise, the ALJ discounted the testimony of the Obertis' other expert witness, Thomas Nolan, a teacher and special education specialist who had taught a child with Down's syndrome in a regular classroom, because he too had not had day-to-day experience with Rafael.[121] The ALJ thus concluded that the Winlsow placement was in compliance with IDEA.

C. *The proceedings before the district court*

Seeking independent review of the ALJ's decision pursuant to 20 U.S.C. § 1415(e)(2), the Obertis filed this civil action in the United States District Court for the District of New Jersey. . . .

In contrast, Nancy Leetch, Rafael's speech therapist at Winslow, and Lisa Mansfield, the special education teacher at Winslow, both testified that Rafael had made significant academic and social progress in the Winslow special education class.

[120] [9] Based on her observation of Rafael in the Winslow program, observation of the Clementon Elementary School, review of Rafael's education records, and her expertise in this area, Dr. McGregor testified that there were no aspects of Rafael's disability that would preclude him from being educated in a regular classroom with supplementary aids and services. She testified that many of the educational aids and techniques that were provided for Rafael at Winslow could be transferred to a regular classroom. She described various types of special support that could be provided to enable Rafael to learn in a regular classroom, including use of a behavior modification plan to address Rafael's specific behavior problems, working in small groups with tutoring by peers, and multisensory instructional techniques that are often used in special education classes.

As to the behavioral problems Rafael experienced in the kindergarten class in 1989-90, Dr. McGregor testified that those problems could be contained through use of adequate supplementary aids and services (such as those described above), which, she explained, had not been provided for Rafael in the kindergarten class.

Dr. McGregor also testified that it is extremely important for a child like Rafael to learn to work and communicate with nondisabled peers, and that this type of learning could only be provided by including him as much as possible in a regular classroom. Finally, Dr. McGregor testified that she did not observe any opportunities for Rafael to interact with nondisabled students in the Winslow program.

[121] [10] In addition to the two experts, the Obertis presented the testimony of both of Rafael's parents, who testified that from their experience with and understanding of their son, they were convinced that Rafael would be successful in a regular classroom with adequate aids and services. Jeanne Oberti testified that she believed the segregated Winslow class had a negative emotional impact on Rafael, who would cry regularly before boarding the bus for the 45 minute trip to Winslow. She also testified that she and her husband understood that Rafael could not be expected to master the curriculum in a regular class in the same way as the nondisabled students, but that they did not believe Rafael should be excluded for that reason. Michelle Zbrozek, a neighbor of the Obertis and a parent of a nondisabled child in the Clementon kindergarten class, testified that her son played with Rafael and other neighborhood children and that she believed Rafael and the nondisabled children learned from each other by working and playing together. *See infra* n.24. The ALJ considered this testimony but was nonetheless convinced by the School District's witnesses that Rafael's behavior problems in the kindergarten class during the 1989-90 school year precluded an integrated placement at that time.

In May of 1992, the district court held a three-day bench trial, receiving new evidence from both parties to supplement the state agency record. *See* 20 U.S.C. § 1415(e)(2). The Obertis presented the testimony of two additional experts who had not testified in the administrative proceedings: Dr. Lou Brown, a professor of special education at the University of Wisconsin, and Amy Goldman, an expert in communication with children with developmental disabilities.

Dr. Brown, who over the past twenty years has been a consultant to hundreds of school districts throughout the country regarding the education of severely disabled children, interviewed and evaluated Rafael on two occasions, and reviewed Rafael's educational records, as well as a set of videotapes showing Rafael at age seven working with his mother, being taught by a language professional, and participating in a Sunday school class with nondisabled children. Dr. Brown testified that he saw no reason why Rafael could not be educated at that time in a regular classroom with appropriate supplementary aids and services. He told the court that if such aids and services were provided, he had no reason to believe that Rafael would be disruptive at that time (more than two years after the experience in the Clementon kindergarten class). He also stated that integrating Rafael in a regular class at his local school would enable Rafael to develop social relationships with nondisabled students and to learn by imitating appropriate role models, important benefits which could not be realized in a segregated, special education setting.

Dr. Brown outlined a number of commonly applied strategies which could be used, in combination, by the School District to integrate Rafael in a regular classroom, including: (1) modifying some of the curriculum to accommodate Rafael's different level of ability; (2) modifying only Rafael's program so that he would perform a similar activity or exercise to that performed by the whole class, but at a level appropriate to his ability; (3) "parallel instruction," i.e., having Rafael work separately within the classroom on an activity beneficial to him while the rest of the class worked on an activity that Rafael could not benefit from; and (4) removing Rafael from the classroom to receive some special instruction or services in a resource room, completely apart from the class. Dr. Brown explained that with proper training, a regular teacher would be able to apply these techniques and that, in spite of Rafael's severe intellectual disability, a regular teacher with proper training would be able to communicate effectively with Rafael. Dr. Brown also testified that many of the special educational techniques applied in the segregated Winslow class could be provided for Rafael within a regular classroom.

Based on her evaluation of Rafael and her expertise in developing communication skills for disabled children, Amy Goldman testified that the speech and language therapy Rafael needs could be most effectively provided within a regular classroom; otherwise, she explained, a child with Rafael's disabilities would have great difficulty importing the language skills taught in a separate speech therapy session into the regular class environment, where those skills are most needed. She testified that language and speech therapy could easily be provided by a therapist inside the regular class during ongoing instruction if the therapist were able to collaborate ahead of time with the instructor regarding the upcoming lesson plans. . . .

The Obertis also offered the videotape evidence that had been reviewed by Dr. Brown, the testimony of Jeanne Oberti,[122] and the testimony of Joanne McKeon, the mother of a nine year old child with Down's Syndrome who had been successfully mainstreamed in a regular classroom.

To counter the Obertis' experts, the School District offered Dr. Stanley Urban, a professor of special education at Glassboro State College. After observing Rafael in a special class for perceptually impaired children at the St. Luke's School (a private school that Rafael attended for two months in the fall of 1991), observing Rafael for two hours in his home, reviewing the programs available at the Clementon Elementary School, reviewing Rafael's education records, and reviewing the written evaluations of the Obertis' experts, Dr. Urban testified that in his opinion Rafael could not be educated satisfactorily in a regular classroom, and that the special education program at Winslow was appropriate for Rafael.[123]

More specifically, Dr. Urban testified that Rafael's behavior problems could not be managed in a regular class, that a regular teacher would not be able to communicate with a child of Rafael's ability level, and that it would be difficult if not impossible to adapt a first grade-level curriculum to accommodate Rafael without adversely affecting the education of the other children in the class. Dr. Urban, however, also stated that if Rafael did not have serious behavior problems, integration in a regular classroom might be feasible.

The School District presented several additional witnesses, including the teacher and teacher's aide of a non-academic summer school class for elementary school children which Rafael attended in the summer of 1991, and the teacher of the St. Luke's class, which Rafael attended for two months in the fall of 1991. These witnesses recounted examples of Rafael's disruptive behavior, including pushing and hitting other children, disobeying and running away from the instructors, and throwing books.

In August of 1992, after reviewing all of this new evidence along with the evidence that had been adduced at the administrative proceedings, the district court issued its decision, finding that the School District had failed to establish by a preponderance of the evidence that Rafael could not at that time be educated in a regular classroom with supplementary aids and services. The court therefore concluded that the School District had violated IDEA.

In particular, the court was persuaded by the Obertis' experts that many of the special education techniques used in the Winslow class could be implemented in a regular classroom. The court also found that the School District did not make reasonable efforts to include Rafael in a regular classroom with supplementary aids and services (e.g., an itinerant teacher trained in aiding students with mental retardation, a behavior management program, modification of the regular curriculum to accommodate Rafael, and

---

[122] [12] Jeanne Oberti testified before the district court that Rafael was at that time involved in a number of extra-curricular activities with nondisabled children in his neighborhood, including T-ball league, bowling league, Sunday school classes, and other church-related activities for children. She told the court that she had received no complaints about behavior problems in connection with any of these activities.

[123] [13] Dr. Urban also testified that, in his view, Dr. Brown's evaluation of Rafael was highly suspect because Dr. Brown had never observed Rafael in a classroom environment.

special education training and consultation for the regular teacher); that Rafael's behavior problems during the 1989-90 school year in the developmental kindergarten class were largely the result of the School District's failure to provide adequate supplementary aids and services; and that the record did not support the School District's contention that Rafael would present similar behavior problems at that time (more than two years after the kindergarten class) if included in a regular classroom setting with adequate aids and services. The court declined to defer to the findings of the ALJ because it found that "they were largely and improperly based upon Rafael's behavior problems in the developmental kindergarten as well as upon his intellectual limitations, without proper consideration of the inadequate level of supplementary aids and services provided by the School District." . . . This appeal followed. . . .

II. THE MAINSTREAMING REQUIREMENT OF IDEA

The Education for All Handicapped Children Act (IDEA's predecessor statute) was enacted in 1975 in response to a Congressional finding that "more than half of the children with disabilities in the United States do not receive appropriate educational services." The Act provides federal funds to participating states for the education of children with disabilities. As a condition of receiving these funds, states must have "in effect a policy that assures all children with disabilities the right to a free appropriate public education."

In *Board of Educ. v. Rowley*, 458 U.S. 176, 188–89 (1982), the Supreme Court held that a "free appropriate public education" under the Act "consists of educational instruction specially designed to meet the unique needs of the handicapped child, supported by such services as are necessary to permit the child 'to benefit' from the instruction." This court in turn interpreted *Rowley* to require the state to offer children with disabilities individualized education programs that provide more than a trivial or de minimis educational benefit.

In addition to the free appropriate education requirement, IDEA provides that states must establish

> procedures to assure that, to the maximum extent appropriate, children with disabilities . . . are educated with children who are not disabled, and that special classes, separate schooling, or other removal of children with disabilities from the regular educational environment occurs only when the nature and severity of the disability is such that education in regular classes with the use of supplementary aids and services cannot be achieved satisfactorily . . . .

20 U.S.C. § 1412(5)(B). As numerous courts have recognized, this provision sets forth a "strong congressional preference" for integrating children with disabilities in regular classrooms.

One of our principal tasks in this case is to provide standards for determining when a school's decision to remove a child with disabilities from the regular classroom and to place the child in a segregated environment violates IDEA's presumption in favor of mainstreaming. This issue is particularly difficult in light of the apparent tension within the Act between the strong preference for mainstreaming, 20 U.S.C. § 1412(5)(B), and the requirement that schools provide individualized programs tailored to the specific needs of each disabled child, 20 U.S.C. §§ 1401, 1414(a)(5). *See Daniel R.R.; Greer v. Rome City School Dist.*.

The key to resolving this tension appears to lie in the school's proper use of "supplementary aids and services," 20 U.S.C. § 1412(5)(B), which may enable the school to educate a child with disabilities for a majority of the time within a regular classroom, while at the same time addressing that child's unique educational needs. We recognize, however, that "regular classes . . . will not provide an education that accounts for each child's particular needs in every case." *Daniel R.R.*, 874 F.2d at 1044; *see also Devries*, 882 F.2d at 878–80 (holding that 17 year old autistic student could not benefit from "monitoring" regular high school academic classes and was appropriately placed at county vocational center).

We also recognize that "in assuring that the requirements of the Act have been met, courts must be careful to avoid imposing their view of preferable educational methods upon the States." We are mindful that the Act leaves questions of educational policy to state and local officials. On the other hand, as the Supreme Court recognized in *Rowley*, the Act specifically "requires participating States to educate handicapped children with nonhandicapped children whenever possible."

In *Daniel R.R.*, the Fifth Circuit derived from the language of 20 U.S.C. § 1412(5)(B) a two-part test for determining whether a school is in compliance with IDEA's mainstreaming requirement. First, the court must determine "whether education in the regular classroom, with the use of supplementary aids and services, can be achieved satisfactorily." Second, if the court finds that placement outside of a regular classroom is necessary for the child to benefit educationally, then the court must decide "whether the school has mainstreamed the child to the maximum extent appropriate," i.e., whether the school has made efforts to include the child in school programs with nondisabled children whenever possible. Id. We think this two-part test, which closely tracks the language of § 1412(5)(B), is faithful to IDEA's directive that children with disabilities be educated with nondisabled children "to the maximum extent appropriate," and to the Act's requirement that schools provide individualized programs to account for each child's specific needs, 20 U.S.C. §§ 1401, 1414(a)(5).

The district court in this case adopted the somewhat different test set forth by the Sixth Circuit in *Roncker v. Walter,* 700 F.2d 1058 (6th Cir. 1983), the first federal court of appeals case to interpret IDEA's mainstreaming requirement. In *Roncker*, the court stated:

> In a case where the segregated facility is considered superior [academically], the court should determine whether the services which make that placement superior could be feasibly provided in a non-segregated setting. If they can, the placement in the segregated school would be inappropriate under the Act.

We believe, however, that the two-part *Daniel R.R.* test is the better standard because the *Roncker* test fails to make clear that even if placement in the regular classroom cannot be achieved satisfactorily for the major portion of a particular child's education program, the school is still required to include that child in school programs with nondisabled children (specific academic classes, other classes such as music and art, lunch, recess, etc.) whenever possible. We therefore adopt the two-part *Daniel R.R.* test rather than the standard espoused in *Roncker.*

In applying the first part of the *Daniel R.R.* test, *i.e.,* whether the child can be educated satisfactorily in a regular classroom with supplementary aids and services, the court should consider several factors. First, the court should look at the steps that the school has taken to try to include the child in a regular classroom. As we have explained, the Act and its regulations require schools to provide supplementary aids and services to enable children with disabilities to learn whenever possible in a regular classroom. The regulations specifically require school districts to provide "a continuum of placements . . . to meet the needs of handicapped children." The continuum must "make provision for supplementary services (such as resource room or itinerant instruction) to be provided in conjunction with regular class placement."

Accordingly, the school "must consider the whole range of supplemental aids and services, including resource rooms and itinerant instruction," speech and language therapy, special education training for the regular teacher, behavior modification programs, or any other available aids or services appropriate to the child's particular disabilities. The school must also make efforts to modify the regular education program to accommodate a disabled child. If the school has given no serious consideration to including the child in a regular class with such supplementary aids and services and to modifying the regular curriculum to accommodate the child, then it has most likely violated the Act's mainstreaming directive. "The Act does not permit states to make mere token gestures to accommodate handicapped students; its requirement for modifying and supplementing regular education is broad."

A second factor courts should consider in determining whether a child with disabilities can be included in a regular classroom is the comparison between the educational benefits the child will receive in a regular classroom (with supplementary aids and services) and the benefits the child will receive in the segregated, special education classroom. The court will have to rely heavily in this regard on the testimony of educational experts. Nevertheless, in making this comparison the court must pay special attention to those unique benefits the child may obtain from integration in a regular classroom which cannot be achieved in a segregated environment, *i.e.,* the development of social and communication skills from interaction with nondisabled peers. As IDEA's mainstreaming directive makes clear, Congress understood that a fundamental value of the right to public education for children with disabilities is the right to associate with nondisabled peers.[124]

---

124 [24] Courts should also consider the reciprocal benefits of inclusion to the nondisabled students in the class. Teaching nondisabled children to work and communicate with children with disabilities may do much to eliminate the stigma, mistrust and hostility that have traditionally been harbored against persons with disabilities. *See* Minow, *Learning to Live with the Dilemma of Difference,* 48 LAW & CONTEMP. PROBS. at 160, 202–11; WINNERS ALL: A CALL FOR INCLUSIVE SCHOOLS, REPORT TO THE NATIONAL ASS'N OF STATE BDS. OF EDUC., at 14 (1992); *Oberti II,* 801 F. Supp. at 1404 (nondisabled children are likely to benefit and learn from children with disabilities who are included in regular classroom). . . .

Thus, a determination that a child with disabilities might make greater academic progress in a segregated, special education class may not warrant excluding that child from a regular classroom environment. We emphasize that the Act does not require states to offer the same educational experience to a child with disabilities as is generally provided for nondisabled children. *See Rowley*, 458 U.S. at 189, 202. To the contrary, states must address the unique needs of a disabled child, recognizing that that child may benefit differently from education in the regular classroom than other students. In short, the fact that a child with disabilities will learn differently from his or her education within a regular classroom does not justify exclusion from that environment.

A third factor the court should consider in determining whether a child with disabilities can be educated satisfactorily in a regular classroom is the possible negative effect the child's inclusion may have on the education of the other children in the regular classroom. While inclusion of children with disabilities in regular classrooms may benefit the class as a whole, a child with disabilities may be "so disruptive in a regular classroom that the education of other students is significantly impaired." Moreover, if a child is causing excessive disruption of the class, the child may not be benefitting educationally in that environment. Accordingly, if the child has behavioral problems, the court should consider the degree to which these problems may disrupt the class. In addition, the court should consider whether the child's disabilities will demand so much of the teacher's attention that the teacher will be required to ignore the other students.

We emphasize, however, that in considering the possible negative effect of the child's presence on the other students, the court must keep in mind the school's obligation under the Act to provide supplementary aids and services to accommodate the child's disabilities. An adequate individualized program with such aids and services may prevent disruption that would otherwise occur. With respect to the concerns of nondisabled children in the regular classroom, we note that the comment to 34 C.F.R. § 300.552 reads: "It should be stressed that, where a handicapped child is so disruptive in a regular classroom that the education of other students is significantly impaired, the needs of the handicapped child cannot be met in that environment. Therefore, regular placements would not be appropriate to his or her needs. . . ." On the other hand, "a handicapped child who merely requires more teacher attention than most other children is not likely to be so disruptive as to significantly impair the education of other children." *Greer,* 950 F.2d at 697.

In sum, in determining whether a child with disabilities can be educated satisfactorily in a regular class with supplemental aids and services (the first prong of the two-part mainstreaming test we adopt today), the court should consider several factors, including: (1) whether the school district has made reasonable efforts to accommodate the child in a regular classroom; (2) the educational benefits available to the child in a regular class, with appropriate supplementary aids and services, as compared to the benefits provided in a special education class; and (3) the possible negative effects of the inclusion of the child on the education of the other students in the class.[125]

If, after considering these factors, the court determines that the school district was justified in removing the child from the regular classroom and providing education in a segregated, special education class, the court must consider the second prong of the mainstreaming test — whether the school has included the child in school programs with nondisabled children to the maximum extent appropriate. IDEA and its regulations "do not contemplate an all-or-nothing educational system in which handicapped children attend either regular or special education." *Id.* at 1050. The regulations under IDEA require schools to provide a "continuum of alternative placements . . . to meet the needs of handicapped children." As the Fifth Circuit stated:

> the school must take intermediate steps wherever appropriate, such as placing the child in regular education for some academic classes and in special education for others, mainstreaming the child for nonacademic classes only, or providing interaction with nonhandicapped children during lunch and recess. The appropriate mix will vary from child to child and, it may be hoped, from school year to school year as the child develops.

Thus, even if a child with disabilities cannot be educated satisfactorily in a regular classroom, that child must still be included in school programs with nondisabled students wherever possible.

III. BURDEN OF PROOF UNDER IDEA'S MAINSTREAMING REQUIREMENT

Before we apply the two-part analysis discussed above to the facts in this case, we must address the School District's argument that the district court improperly placed the burden of proof under the Act on it. In the School District's view, while it may have had the initial burden at the state administrative level of justifying its educational placement, once the agency decided in its favor, the burden should have shifted to the parents who challenged the agency decision in the district court. Courts must place the burden on the party seeking to reverse the agency decision, the School District argues, in order to effectuate IDEA's requirement that "due weight shall be given to [the state administrative] proceedings." We disagree.

IDEA instructs district courts and state trial courts reviewing the decisions of state educational agencies to "receive the records of the administrative proceedings, . . . hear additional evidence at the request of a party, and, basing its decision on the preponderance of the evidence, . . . grant such relief as the court determines is appropriate." As construed by the Supreme Court in *Rowley*, § 1415(e)(2) requires courts to give "due weight" to the agency

---

[125] [25] Additional factors may be relevant depending on the circumstances of the specific case. For example, other courts have considered cost as a relevant factor in determining compliance with the Act's mainstreaming requirement. *See, e.g., Greer*, 950 F.2d at 697; *Roncker*, 700 F.2d at 1063. Since the parties have not raised cost as an issue, we do not consider it here. *See Daniel R.R.*, 874 F.2d at 1049 n.9.

proceedings. However, neither *Rowley* nor the Act itself specifically addresses which party bears the burden of proof at the district court level, an issue which we believe is quite different from the district court's obligation to afford due weight to the administrative proceedings.

The School District points to several cases that hold, either directly or implicitly, that even if the school district bears the burden of proving compliance with IDEA in the state administrative proceedings, the burden of proof shifts to the party challenging the agency decision at the district court level. We find these cases unpersuasive.

In reviewing the decision of a state agency under IDEA, the district court "must make an independent determination based on a preponderance of the evidence." Given that the district court must independently review the evidence adduced at the administrative proceedings and can receive new evidence, we see no reason to shift the ultimate burden of proof to the party who happened to have lost before the state agency, especially since the loss at the administrative level may have been due to incomplete or insufficient evidence or to an incorrect application of the Act. The purpose of the "due weight" obligation is to prevent the court from imposing its own view of preferable educational methods on the states. Accordingly, the due weight is owed to the administrative proceedings, not to the party who happened to prevail in those proceedings. Moreover, the amount of deference to be afforded the administrative proceedings "is an issue left to the discretion of the district court. . . . The district court must consider the administrative findings of fact, but is free to accept or reject them." The district court can give due weight to the agency proceedings (i.e., refrain from imposing its own notions of educational policy on the states), while the ultimate burden of proof remains on the school.

Underlying the Act is "an abiding concern for the welfare of handicapped children and their parents." Requiring parents to prove at the district court level that the school has failed to comply with the Act would undermine the Act's express purpose "to assure that the rights of children with disabilities and their parents are protected," and would diminish the effect of the provision that enables parents and guardians to obtain judicial enforcement of the Act's substantive and procedural requirements, *see* 20 U.S.C. § 1415(e). In practical terms, the school has an advantage when a dispute arises under the Act: the school has better access to the relevant information, greater control over the potentially more persuasive witnesses (those who have been directly involved with the child's education), and greater overall educational expertise than the parents.

In light of the statutory purpose of IDEA and these practical considerations, we believe that when IDEA's mainstreaming requirement is specifically at issue, it is appropriate to place the burden of proving compliance with IDEA on the school. Indeed, the Act's strong presumption in favor of mainstreaming, would be turned on its head if parents had to prove that their child was worthy of being included, rather than the school district having to justify a decision to exclude the child from the regular classroom. . . .

IV. DID THE SCHOOL DISTRICT COMPLY WITH IDEA?

We now reach the dispositive question in this case: whether the district court erred in holding that the School District failed to comply with IDEA's mainstreaming requirement. Initially, applying the first part of the two-part test set forth above, we consider whether the School District has met its burden of proving that Rafael could not be educated satisfactorily in a regular classroom with supplementary aids and services.

A. *Standard of review*

Our deferential standard of review over the district court's fact finding is essential to our decision here. We accept the district court's findings of fact unless they are clearly erroneous. A finding of fact is clearly erroneous when, after reviewing the evidence, the court of appeals is "left with a definite and firm conviction that a mistake has been committed." Thus, even if we might have come to different factual conclusions based on this record, we defer to the findings of the district court unless we are convinced that the record cannot support those findings.

We also consider, in reviewing the district court's fact findings in an IDEA case, whether the court has abused its discretion in failing to afford "due weight" to the agency proceedings. . . . The district court must give due weight to the administrative proceedings (so as not to impose the court's own view of preferable educational policy on the states), but the court is free to accept or reject the agency findings depending on whether those findings are supported by the new, expanded record and whether they are consistent with the requirements of the Act. Accordingly, we review the district court's decisions regarding whether to adopt the agency fact findings under the deferential, clearly erroneous standard.

B. *Application of the* Daniel R.R. *test*

In Part II of this opinion, we outlined three factors that should be considered by a court in determining whether a child with disabilities can be educated satisfactorily in a regular classroom (the first part of the *Daniel R.R.* test): (1) whether the school district has made reasonable efforts to accommodate the child in a regular classroom with supplementary aids and services; (2) a comparison of the educational benefits available in a regular class and the benefits provided in a special education class; and (3) the possible negative effects of inclusion on the other students in the class. We now consider each of these factors, looking to the relevant fact findings of the district court to determine whether those findings are clearly erroneous, and if not, whether they support the district court's ultimate legal conclusion that the School District violated the mainstreaming requirement of IDEA.

As to the first factor, the district court found that the School District made only negligible efforts to include Rafael in a regular classroom. Specifically, the court found that during the 1989-90 school year, the only period during which the School District mainstreamed Rafael in a regular classroom, the School District placed Rafael in the developmental kindergarten class "without a curriculum plan, without a behavior management plan, and without providing adequate special education support to the teacher." Further, the court found that the School District has since refused to include Rafael in a regular classroom largely based on the behavioral problems experienced by Rafael in the kindergarten class during the 1989-90 school year. For the 1990-91 year, the court found that Rafael was placed in a segregated class with "no meaningful mainstreaming opportunities," and that "the School District's consideration of less restrictive alternatives for the 1990-91 school year was perfunctory."

There is very little evidence in the record that conflicts with these findings. The School District produced some evidence that the kindergarten teacher and the school psychologist attempted to modify the curriculum in that class and to come up with methods of controlling Rafael's behavior problems. However, the record reflects that the School District had access to information and expertise about specific methods and services to enable children with disabilities like Rafael to be included in a regular classroom, but that the School District did not provide such supplementary aids and services for Rafael in the kindergarten class.

Rafael's IEP for the 1989-90 school year included no provisions for supplementary aids and services in the kindergarten class aside from stating that there will be "modification of regular class expectations" to reflect Rafael's disability. The only goal provided for the regular kindergarten teacher was to "facilitate Rafael's adjustment to the kindergarten classroom." After reviewing this IEP along with the rest of Rafael's education records, Dr. McGregor testified that no supplementary aids and services were provided for Rafael in the 1989-90 kindergarten class.

Moreover, there is no evidence in the record that the School District gave any serious consideration to including Rafael in a regular classroom with supplementary aids and services after the 1989-90 school year; and the School District does not appear to dispute this fact. Further, Nancy Leech, the Winslow speech therapist (and one of the School District's witnesses) admitted that Rafael had not been included in any school programs with nondisabled children at Winslow, apart from attending lunch and school assemblies.

In view of the foregoing, the district court's finding that the School District has not taken meaningful steps to try to include Rafael in a regular classroom with supplementary aids and services is not clearly erroneous.

As to the second factor — a comparison of the educational benefits of the segregated placement in Winslow with the benefits Rafael could obtain from placement in a regular classroom — the district court found that "various experts who testified on Rafael's behalf have convincingly refuted the School District's assertion that such services could not be delivered within the matrix of a regular education class without disrupting the class or converting it into a special education class." The court also found that Rafael would benefit academically and socially from inclusion in a regular classroom. Moreover, the district court found, based on expert testimony, that "nondisabled children in the class will likewise benefit" from the inclusion of Rafael in a regular classroom.

The School District points to some evidence in the record that conflicts with these findings. Specifically, Dr. Urban testified for the School District that, in his opinion, a regular teacher would not be able to communicate with Rafael and that a regular curriculum would have to be modified beyond recognition to accommodate Rafael. However, the Obertis' experts, Drs. Brown and McGregor, described various commonly applied methods that could be used to educate Rafael in a regular classroom and testified that, although Rafael has severe intellectual disabilities, a regular teacher with appropriate training would be able to communicate effectively with Rafael. They testified that many of the special education techniques used in the segregated Winslow class could be imported successfully into a regular classroom and that the regular teacher could be trained to apply these techniques. Further, the Obertis' experts testified at length that inclusion in a classroom with nondisabled students would benefit Rafael substantially. In addition, Amy Goldman testified that speech and language therapy not only could be provided in a regular class-room, but would be more effective for Rafael in an integrated setting.

In short, the parties' experts disagreed on the respective benefits of a segregated versus an integrated placement for Rafael, and the district court was in a better position than we are to evaluate their testimony. We therefore defer to that court's findings, which, at all events, are not clearly erroneous. We note also that the district court did not fail to give due weight to the agency proceedings on this factor since the court's findings were based largely on new expert testimony that was not before the ALJ. Additionally, we agree with the district court's legal conclusion that, although including Rafael in a regular classroom would require the School District to modify the curriculum, the need for such modification is "not a legitimate basis upon which to justify excluding a child" from the regular classroom unless the education of other students is significantly impaired. Thus, a comparison of the educational benefits of a segregated versus an integrated placement for Rafael supports the district court's conclusion that the School District's selection of a segregated place-ment did not comply with IDEA.

As to the third factor — the potentially disruptive effect of Rafael's presence on the other children in a regular classroom — the record again contains conflicting evidence. The School District presented numerous witnesses before both the ALJ and the district court who testified to Rafael's extremely disruptive behavior in the 1989-90 kindergarten class and in several other teaching environments. In contrast, the Obertis' experts Drs. McGregor and Brown evaluated Rafael and testified that in their opinion he would not at that point in time (nearly two years after Rafael's experience in the kindergar-ten class) cause any significant disruption in a regular classroom if provided with adequate supplementary aids and services, such as the assistance of an itinerant instructor with special education training, special education training for the regular teacher, modification of some of the academic curriculum to accommodate Rafael's disabilities, parallel instruction to allow him to learn at his academic level, and use of a resource room. . . .

Although the School District presented ample evidence of Rafael's disruptive behavior in the 1989-90 kindergarten class, the Obertis' evidence supports the district court's finding that Rafael would not have had such severe behavior problems had he been provided with adequate supplementary aids and services in that kindergarten class, and that Rafael (who at the time of the district court trial was two years older than when he attended the kindergarten class) would most likely not present such problems if he were included in a regular class at that time. We therefore conclude that the district court's findings on this issue are not clearly erroneous, and, accordingly, that consideration of the possible negative effects of Rafael's presence on the regular classroom environment does not support the School District's decision to exclude him from the regular classroom.

We also conclude that the district court did not abuse its discretion in deciding not to defer to the findings of the ALJ on the issue of whether Rafael would significantly disrupt a regular classroom. As the court noted, the ALJ's findings "were largely and improperly based upon Rafael's behavior problems in the developmental kindergarten, as well as upon his intellectual limitations, without proper consideration of the inadequate level of supplementary aids and services provided by the School District."

For all of these reasons, we agree with the district court's conclusion that the School District did not meet its burden of proving by a preponderance of the evidence that Rafael could not be educated satisfactorily in a regular classroom with supplementary aids and services. We will therefore affirm the district court's decision that the School District has violated the mainstreaming requirement of IDEA. Because we have come to this conclusion based on application of the first part of the *Daniel R.R.* two-part test, we need not apply the second part of the test (whether the child has been included in programs with nondisabled children whenever possible). We note, however, that in the event that the Child Study Team were to determine in designing an IEP for Rafael in the future that education in a regular classroom with supplementary aids and services could not be achieved satisfactorily at that time and therefore would not be required under IDEA, the Team would then have to satisfy the second part of the *Daniel R.R.* test, ensuring that Rafael is included in regular school programs with nondisabled students whenever possible.

. . . .

The order of the district court will be affirmed.

———

HARTMANN v. LOUDOUN COUNTY BOARD OF EDUCATION

Court of Appeals for the Fourth Circuit
118 F.3d 996 (1997)

WILKINSON, CHIEF JUDGE

Roxanna and Joseph Hartmann brought suit on behalf of their disabled son Mark against the Loudoun County Board of Education under the Individuals With Disabilities Education Act (IDEA), 20 U.S.C. § 1400 et seq. The Hartmanns alleged that the Board had failed to ensure that Mark was educated with non-handicapped children "to the maximum extent appropriate" as required by the IDEA's mainstreaming provision, 20 U.S.C. § 1412(5)(B). The district court agreed, rejecting the findings of both the local hearing officer and the state review officer. The Board appeals, contending that the court's decision is contrary to the law and the evidence in the record. We agree. As Supreme Court precedent makes clear, the IDEA does not grant federal courts a license to substitute their own notions of sound educational policy for those of local school authorities, or to disregard the findings developed in state administrative proceedings. Upon careful review of the record, however, we are forced to conclude that this is precisely what has occurred in this case. Accordingly, we reverse and remand with directions to dismiss.

I.

Mark Hartmann is an eleven-year-old autistic child. Autism is a developmental disorder characterized by significant deficiencies in communication skills, social interaction, and motor control. Mark is unable to speak and suffers severe problems with fine motor coordination. Mark's writing ability is extremely limited; he does not write by hand and can consistently type only a few words such as "is" and "at" by himself on a keyboard device known as a Canon communicator. The parties agree that Mark's greatest need is to develop communication skills.

Mark spent his pre-school years in various programs for disabled children. In kindergarten, he spent half his time in a self-contained program for autistic children and half in a regular education classroom at Butterfield Elementary in Lombard, Illinois. Upon entering first grade, Mark received speech and occupational therapy one-on-one, but was otherwise included in the regular classroom at Butterfield full-time with an aide to assist him.

After Mark's first-grade year, the Hartmanns moved to Loudoun County, Virginia, where they enrolled Mark at Ashburn Elementary for the 1993-1994 school year. Based on Mark's individualized education program (IEP) from Illinois, the school placed Mark in a regular education classroom. To facilitate Mark's inclusion, Loudoun officials carefully selected his teacher, hired a full-time aide to assist him, and put him in a smaller class with more indedpendent children. Mark's teacher, Diane Johnson, read extensively about autism, and both Johnson and Mark's aide, Suz Leitner, received training in facilitated communication, a special communication technique used with autistic children. Mark received five hours per week of speech and language therapy with a qualified specialist, Carolyn Clement. Halfway through the year, Virginia McCullough, a special education teacher, was assigned to provide Mark with three hours of instruction a week and to advise Mark's teacher and aide.

Mary Kearney, the Loudoun County Director of Special Education, personally worked with Mark's IEP team, which consisted of Johnson, Leitner, Clement, and Laurie McDonald, the principal of Ashburn. Kearney provided in-service training for the Ashburn staff on autism and inclusion of disabled children in the regular classroom. Johnson, Leitner, Clement, and McDonald also attended a seminar on inclusion held by the Virginia Council for Administrators of Special Education. Mark's IEP team also received assistance from educational consultants Jamie Ruppmann and Gail Mayfield, and Johnson conferred with additional specialists whose names were provided to her by the Hartmanns and the school. Mark's curriculum was continually modified to ensure that it was properly adapted to his needs and abilities.

Frank Johnson, supervisor of the county's program for autistic children, formally joined the IEP team in January, but provided assistance throughout the year in managing Mark's behavior. Mark engaged in daily episodes of loud screeching and other disruptive conduct such as hitting, pinching, kicking, biting, and removing his clothing. These outbursts not only required Diane Johnson and Leitner to calm Mark and redirect him, but also consumed the additional time necessary to get the rest of the children back on task after the distraction.

Despite these efforts, by the end of the year Mark's IEP team concluded that he was making no academic progress in the regular classroom. In Mark's May 1994 IEP, the team therefore proposed to place Mark in a class specifically structured for autistic children at Leesburg Elementary. Leesburg is a regular elementary school which houses the autism class in order to facilitate interaction between the autistic children and students who are not handicapped. The Leesburg class would have included five autistic students working with a special education teacher and at least one full-time aide. Under the May IEP, Mark would have received only academic instruction and speech in the self-contained classroom, while joining a regular class for art, music, physical education, library, and recess. The Leesburg program also would have permitted Mark to increase the portion of his instruction received in a regular education setting as he demonstrated an improved ability to handle it.

The Hartmanns refused to approve the IEP, claiming that it failed to comply with the mainstreaming provision of the IDEA, which states that "to the maximum extent appropriate," disabled children should be educated with children who are not handicapped. 20 U.S.C. § 1412(5)(B). The county initiated due process proceedings, and on December 14, 1994, the local hearing officer upheld the May 1994 IEP. She found that Mark's behavior was disruptive and that despite the "enthusiastic" efforts of the county, he had obtained no academic benefit from the regular education classroom. On May 3, 1995, the state review officer affirmed the decision, adopting both the hearing officer's findings and her legal analysis. The Hartmanns then challenged the hearing officer's decision in federal court.

While the administrative process continued, Mark entered third grade in the regular education classroom at Ashburn. In December of that year, the Hartmanns withdrew Mark from Ashburn. Mark and his mother moved to Montgomery County, Virginia, to permit the Hartmanns to enroll Mark in public school there. Mark was placed in the regular third-grade classroom for the remainder of that year as well as the next.

The district court reversed the hearing officer's decision. The court rejected the administrative findings and concluded that Mark could receive significant educational benefit in a regular classroom and that "the Board simply did not take enough appropriate steps to try to include Mark in a regular class." The court made little of the testimony of Mark's Loudoun County instructors, and instead relied heavily on its reading of Mark's experience in Illinois and Montgomery County. While the hearing officer had addressed Mark's conduct in detail, the court stated that "given the strong presumption for inclusion under the IDEA, disruptive behavior should not be a significant factor in determining the appropriate educational placement for a disabled child." Loudoun County now appeals.

II.

The IDEA embodies important principles governing the relationship between local school authorities and a reviewing district court. Although section 1415(e)(2) provides district courts with authority to grant "appropriate" relief based on a preponderance of the evidence, that section "is by no means an invitation to the courts to substitute their own notions of sound educational policy for those of the school authorities which they review." *Board of Education of Hendrick Hudson Central Sch. Dist. v. Rowley.* Absent some statutory infraction, the task of education belongs to the educators who have been charged by society with that critical task. Likewise, federal courts must accord "due weight" to state administrative proceedings. *Id.* Administrative findings in an IDEA case "are entitled to be considered prima facie correct," and "the district court, if it is not going to follow them, is required to explain why it does not." *Doyle v. Arlington County Sch. Bd.*, 953 F.2d 100, 105 (4th Cir. 1991).

These principles reflect the IDEA's recognition that federal courts cannot run local schools. Local educators deserve latitude in determining the individualized education program most appropriate for a disabled child. The IDEA does not deprive these educators of the right to apply their professional judgment. Rather it establishes a "basic floor of opportunity" for every handicapped child. States must provide specialized instruction and related services "sufficient to confer some educational benefit upon the handicapped child," *id.* at 200, but the Act does not require "the furnishing of every special service necessary to maximize each handicapped child's potential."

In this same vein, the IDEA's mainstreaming provision establishes a presumption, not an inflexible federal mandate. Under its terms, disabled children are to be educated with children who are not handicapped only "to the maximum extent appropriate." Section 1412(5)(B) explicitly states that mainstreaming is not appropriate "when the nature or severity of the disability is such that education in regular classes with the use of supplementary aids and services cannot be achieved satisfactorily."

III.

The district court's ruling strayed generally from the aforementioned principles. It diverged in particular from our decision in *DeVries v. Fairfax County Sch. Bd.*, 882 F.2d 876 (4th Cir. 1989). In *DeVries*, we held that mainstreaming is not required where (1) the disabled child would not receive an educational benefit from mainstreaming into a regular class; (2) any marginal benefit from mainstreaming would be significantly outweighed by benefits which could feasibly be obtained only in a separate instructional setting; or, (3) the disabled child is a disruptive force in a regular classroom setting. Although the district court failed to mention *DeVries*, its opinion suggests that none of these three categories describes Mark's situation. The district court found that Mark could receive substantial educational benefit in a regular classroom, that his disruptive behavior was not sufficient to justify a more segregated instructional setting, and that the Leesburg program would not have been an appropriate placement. After careful examination of the record, however, we are forced to conclude that the district court's decision fails to account for the administrative findings and is not supported by the evidence based on a correct application of the law. In effect, the court simply substituted its own judgment regarding Mark's proper educational program for that of local school officials.

A.

In finding that Mark could receive an educational benefit in a regular classroom, the district court disregarded both the hearing officer's finding and the overwhelming evidence that Mark made no academic progress in the regular second grade classroom at Ashburn. Mark's teacher testified, for example, that he was unable to retain skills: "once we thought he mastered [a math skill] and we left it alone and went onto another concept, if we went back to review, it seemed that he had forgotten." She confessed, "I felt like he lost a year in my classroom." Other Loudoun County personnel testified to the same effect. His speech therapist, for instance, stated that "the only gain that I saw him make was in the one-to-one setting." The supervisor for the county's program for autistic students likewise concluded, "I think there has been no progress academically in the inclusive settings;" "I think we're wasting his time." The hearing officer accordingly found that "Mark made no measurable academic progress attributable to his placement in the regular classroom."

Mark's situation is similar to the one we faced in *DeVries*. In upholding Fairfax County's decision not to place Michael DeVries in Annandale High School, the court observed not only that Michael would derive virtually no academic benefit from the regular classroom, but also that his work would be at a much lower level than his classmates and that he would in effect "simply be monitoring classes." Here the hearing officer made an identical finding, concluding that Mark "did not participate in the regular curriculum, but was provided his own curriculum." Mark's special education teacher in Loudoun County explained, "Mark needs a completely different program . . . . His skills have to be taught in a different way, in a different sequence, and even a different group of skills . . . from what his typical functioning peers are learning."

The district court acknowledged the testimony of Mark's second grade teacher regarding his lack of progress, but asserted that the hearing officer's conclusions were erroneous because the officer failed to give due weight to the testimony of Cathy Thornton, Mark's private tutor during second grade, and to Mark's first grade experience in Illinois. To the contrary, the administrative decisions took careful note of both. The hearing officer fully credited Thornton's testimony, finding that Mark made progress with both her and his speech therapist. The officer went further, however, and observed that both the tutoring and speech instruction occurred in a one-to-one setting outside of the regular class. In light of Mark's failure to progress in the regular classroom, the officer drew the only reasonable inference from this evidence, namely that separate instruction was precisely what Mark needed to make educational progress. As to Mark's experience in Illinois, the state review officer explained that the Illinois assessment of Mark's capabilities was flawed:

> It became clear during the course of the second grade that Mark's academic skills were not as advanced as the Illinois school system thought. Mark cannot read and cannot add, yet the Illinois teachers thought he was reading at first grade level and progressing in the first grade math workbook. . . . Mark apparently did not make the academic progress in first grade the records forwarded to Loudoun County from Illinois indicated . . . .

While the district court opinion references the hearing officer's decision, its failure to address the administrative findings noted above simply does not reflect the teachings of *Rowley* that state proceedings must command considerable deference in federal courts.

The district court also relied heavily on Mark's subsequent performance in the Montgomery County schools during fourth grade. While Montgomery County personnel did make some conclusory statements asserting that Mark made progress, the evidence is inconclusive at best. The district court pointed to math skills Mark demonstrated at the end of fourth grade, for example, but Mark was pulled out of the regular class for math instruction, just as Loudoun County had recommended. Any progress he made in math therefore simply supports the conclusion that separate, one-on-one instruction is appropriate for Mark. Mark also continued to receive speech therapy one-on-one, and his special education teacher in Montgomery County admitted that the county had no reliable method for assessing Mark's reading ability.

Finally, the district court pointed to perceived improvement in Mark's social skills due to interaction with his non-disabled peers. Any such benefits, however, cannot outweigh his failure to progress academically in the regular classroom. The mainstreaming provision represents recognition of the value of having disabled children interact with non-handicapped students. The fact that the provision only creates a presumption, however, reflects a congressional judgment that receipt of such social benefits is ultimately a goal subordinate to the requirement that disabled children receive educational benefit. Here the evidence clearly supports the judgment of the local education officials and the administrative hearing officers that Mark's educational progress required significant instruction outside of the regular classroom setting.

B.

The district court attributed Mark's lack of progress in Loudoun County to the county's alleged failure to make reasonable efforts to accommodate him in the regular classroom. We interpret this as a ruling that the county failed to provide the supplementary aids and services contemplated by the IDEA's mainstreaming provision.

The district court's conclusion is remarkable in light of the extensive measures taken on Mark's behalf. The hearing officer found that Loudoun personnel were "enthusiastic" about including Mark at Ashburn, a description fully supported by the record. The Ashburn principal deliberately reduced the size of Mark's class and ensured that it was composed of students who were more independent and had higher level skills. Mark's teacher was selected because of her excellent teaching abilities, and the county hired a full-time, one-on-one aide for Mark. Mark received a full hour of speech and language instruction daily. Frank Johnson, the supervisor of the county's program for autistic children, provided assistance in behavior management throughout the year. Halfway through the year, the school's efforts increased when Virginia McCullough began providing special education services directly to Mark as well as advising Mark's teacher and aide. Inclusion specialists Gail Mayfield and Jamie Ruppmann consulted with the school during the fall, and Mark's teacher sought advice from other experts whose names were provided to her by the school or the Hartmanns. The teacher testified that she met constantly with Mark's aide, his speech therapist, the IEP team, and others to work on Mark's program — daily at the beginning of the year and at least twice a week throughout.

The district court nonetheless found the county's efforts insufficient. The court relied primarily on its conclusion that the Loudoun educators involved with Mark had inadequate training and experience to work with an autistic child. The court found the credentials of two groups to be lacking. Neither the special education professionals nor the regular education instructors were deemed properly qualified. The conclusion that Mark had inadequately trained personnel developing and implementing his program, however, is irreconcilable with either the law or the record.

As to special education personnel, the district court concedes that the individuals working with Mark during the first half of the year, Mary Kearney and Jamie Ruppmann, were fully competent to assist him. Kearney led Mark's IEP team, while Ruppmann provided consultation services. In addition to serving as the county Director of Special Education, Kearney had participated in the Virginia Systems Change Project, a two-year state program on mainstreaming which involved selected schools from across the state. Ruppmann is an experienced, highly qualified consultant.

During the second half of the year, Frank Johnson led the IEP team, and Virginia McCullough provided Mark with special education services. The district court rejected their qualifications, asserting, for example, that Johnson's credentials were clearly inadequate because they were inferior to those of Kearney and Ruppmann. However, in addition to serving as the supervisor of Loudoun County's program for autistic children, Johnson had a special education masters degree, did graduate work with an autistic child, worked directly with approximately ten autistic children as a teacher, and had attended special education courses and seminars relating to autism throughout his professional career. Both McCullough's early childhood degree program and her work in Loudoun County focused specifically on integrating children with disabilities into the regular classroom.

To dismiss Johnson's and McCullough's qualifications is to adopt exactly the sort of potential-maximizing standard rejected by the Supreme Court in *Rowley*. We think the Court's admonition that the IDEA does not require "the furnishing of every special service necessary to maximize each handicapped child's potential" encompasses the notion that the IDEA likewise does not require special education service providers to have every conceivable credential relevant to every child's disability. Not all school systems will have the resources to hire top-notch consultants, nor will every school have the good fortune to have personnel who were involved in a major state program related to the needs of every disabled child. We note that in Virginia, there is no certification for autism. Furthermore, at the time of the trial, Loudoun County had eleven autistic children in a total school population of approximately 20,000 students. In this light, Johnson's experience teaching ten autistic children was substantial. Johnson and McCullough were clearly qualified to work with Mark as special educators, even accepting the district court's assertion that Ruppmann and Kearney had better credentials.

The suggestion that the regular education instructors, Mark's teacher and aide, were not adequately qualified also does not survive close scrutiny. Diane Johnson was an experienced professional properly certified under state law, and Virginia law does not require teaching assistants to be certified. Furthermore, Johnson and Leitner both obtained special training to work with Mark. Both received in-service instruction and attended an outside seminar on inclusion of disabled children in the regular classroom. They also were trained in facilitated communication, a special communication method used with Mark in Illinois.

To demand more than this from regular education personnel would essentially require them to become special education teachers trained in the full panoply of disabilities that their students might have. Virginia law does not require this, nor does the IDEA. First, such a requirement would fall afoul of *Rowley*'s admonition that the IDEA does not guarantee the ideal educational opportunity for every disabled child. Furthermore, when the IDEA was passed, "Congress' intention was not that the Act displace the primacy of States in the field of education, but that States receive funds to assist them in extending their educational systems to the handicapped." The IDEA "expressly incorporates State educational standards." We can think of few steps that would do more to usurp state educational standards and policy than to have federal courts re-write state teaching certification requirements in the guise of applying the IDEA.

In sum, we conclude that Loudoun County's efforts on behalf of Mark were sufficient to satisfy the IDEA's mainstreaming directive.

C.

The district court also gave little or no weight to the disruptive effects of Mark's behavior in the classroom, stating that "given the strong presumption for inclusion under the IDEA, disruptive behavior should not be a significant factor in determining the appropriate educational placement for a disabled child." This statement simply ignores *DeVries*, where we specifically held that mainstreaming is inappropriate when "the handicapped child is a disruptive force in the non-segregated setting." In this case, disruptive behavior was clearly an issue. The hearing officer summarized:

[Mark's] misbehaviors include continual vocalization, especially whining, screeching and crying when unhappy or frustrated, hitting, pinching, kicking, biting, sucking the leg of a chair, rolling on the floor, and removing his shoes and clothing. Mark is a big strong child who cannot be easily restrained when he engages in injurious behaviors such as hitting, kicking, pinching and biting. His continual vocalizations are distracting and make it difficult for other children to stay on task. When Jamie Ruppmann observed Mark in his classroom, she observed two instances of significant disruption, in which he threw himself on the floor. She noted that in each instance it took about five to eight minutes to get Mark settled down. His loud screeching outbursts, which occur daily, take the attention of the teacher and the aide to redirect him; these outbursts also take the other children off task and they then have to be redirected. Mark hits and pinches others several times a day.

While the hearing officer did not find Mark's disruptive behavior by itself to be dispositive, the attention she gave to Mark's conduct was entirely appropriate, indeed required, under *DeVries*.

D.

The district court also found that Leesburg would not have been an appropriate placement. This conclusion generally derived from the same analysis that led to the court's determination that Mark should remain in the regular classroom. To the contrary, we hold that the proposed Leesburg placement was carefully tailored to ensure that he was mainstreamed "to the maximum extent appropriate." Leesburg was a regular elementary school. Responding to Mark's lack of academic progress in the regular classroom, the May IEP would have placed Mark in the self-contained class for his academic subjects, while including him with his non-disabled peers for all other school activities such as art, music, and physical education. To promote the success of this partial mainstreaming, the hearing officer required the school to have an aide or teacher accompany Mark whenever he was in the regular classroom environment and to place Mark with the same regular education class for all his nonacademic activities.

IV.

This is not a case which either the local educational authorities or the reviewing administrative officers took lightly. We have sketched in great detail the efforts that Loudoun County made to provide Mark Hartmann with a suitable education. Furthermore, the administrative review process could not have been more thorough. The hearing officer heard testimony from eighteen witnesses over a two month period and made detailed factual findings regarding all aspects of Mark's educational experience. The officer's analysis carefully incorporated those findings and specifically addressed the evidence the Hartmanns presented in support of their position. The district court, however, set all this extensive effort and review at nought. The court failed to mention, let alone discuss, critical administrative findings inconsistent with its conclusions. While making much of the credentials and credibility of witnesses endorsing full inclusion, the court gave little or no attention to the testimony of Loudoun professionals. In some instances the court, without listening to local educators, discounted their views despite the fact that the hearing officer had found them credible. One Loudoun official was dismissed outright as "a philosophical opponent of inclusion" for daring to state that he saw no evidence that Mark had progressed in the regular classroom.

The IDEA encourages mainstreaming, but only to the extent that it does not prevent a child from receiving educational benefit. The evidence in this case demonstrates that Mark Hartmann was not making academic progress in a regular education classroom despite the provision of adequate supplementary aids and services. Loudoun County properly proposed to place Mark in a partially mainstreamed program which would have addressed the academic deficiencies of his full inclusion program while permitting him to interact with nonhandicapped students to the greatest extent possible. This professional judgment by local educators was deserving of respect. The approval of this educational approach by the local and state administrative officers likewise deserved a deference from the district court which it failed to receive. In rejecting reasonable pedagogical choices and disregarding well-supported administrative findings, the district court assumed an educational mantle which the IDEA did not confer. Accordingly, the judgment must be reversed, and the case remanded with directions to dismiss it.

Reversed and remanded.

————

NOTES AND QUESTIONS

1. How does the standard for inclusion differ in *Oberti* and *Hartmann*?

2. Do the opinions differ in their willingness to defer to the professional judgment of educators who are making decisions regarding inclusion? Note that the Fourth Circuit is willing to allow educators the right to apply their professional judgment when those educators have made a "reasonable pedagogical choice." *Hartmann*, 118 F.3d at 1005. Review Justice Harlan's dissent in *Tinker* and the majority opinion in *Hazelwood* for a similar formulation of a standard for school decisions in a different context.

According to the district court in *Hartmann*, the County Supervisor of Special Education "appear[ed] to be a philosophical opponent of inclusion." The court's based this statement on the fact that the county supervisor "testified in regards to Mark's academic progress, 'I think there has been no progress academically in the inclusive setting. I see no evidence in the records that there's been any academic progress whatsoever.'" The court of appeals chastised the district court for dismissing the testimony of this professional educator as 'a philosophical opponent of inclusion' "for daring to say that he saw no evidence that [the child] had progressed in the regular classroom." 118

F. 3d at 1005. But other courts have suggested that courts *should* second-guess educators' testimony regarding placement for that very reason. For example, in *Roncker v. Walter*, 700 F.2d 1058, 1063 (6th Cir. 1983), the Sixth Circuit considered a school's decision that a separate classroom was academically superior for a severely mentally retarded boy. Without referring to any evidence that the placement decision was something other than a reasoned professional judgment, the court called it a "perception . . . [that] may reflect no more than a basic disagreement with the mainstreaming concept."

Note how the district court and court of appeals in *Oberti* discounted the testimony of numerous educators who had day-to-day experience with the boy and deferred to the testimony of the parents' experts, even though one of those experts had evaluated the boy only twice and had *never* observed him in a classroom. In another section of the opinion, the *Oberti* court split with other circuits on the issue of which party carries the burden of proof before the district court, holding that the school district, rather than the party that lost at the administrative level, continues to have the burden of proving compliance with IDEA. In this section of its opinion, the court reasoned that because of the school's *"educational expertise,"* it is best able to meet the burden of proof. Is the court's analysis internally inconsistent? For an analysis of the level of deference that courts afford educators in institutions of lower education see Anne Proffitt Dupre, *Disability, Deference and the Integrity of the Academic Enterprise*, 32 Georgia. L. Rev. 393 (1998).

3. The Eleventh Circuit has stated that even when the disabled child "will make academic progress more quickly in a self-contained special education environment," placement in such an environment may not be justified unless the child will make "significantly more progress" there and placement in the regular classroom might cause the disabled child to fall behind his or her disabled peers in the separate classroom." *Greer v. Rome City Sch. Dist.*, 950 F.2d 688, 697 (11th Cir. 1991). Thus, a disabled child must be educated in a general education classroom even if "a special education placement may be academically superior to placement in a regular classroom" and "even if [the regular classroom] is not the best academic setting for the child." *Board of Education v. Holland*, 786 F. Supp. 874, 879 (E.D. Cal. 1992), *aff'd sub nom, Sacramento City Unified School District v. Rachel H.*, 14 F.3d 1398 (9th Cir. 1994). Do both the *Oberti* and *Hartmann* courts agree with this assessment? Which of the two — the social versus the academic benefits of inclusion — should be weighed more heavily in the placement decision? Does the statutory language help in this analysis?

What is the basis for the assertion that there are social benefits from inclusion? One court of appeals has stated that even if a disabled child can "absorb only a minimal amount of the regular education program," and "even if the child cannot flourish academically," the child "may" benefit from the language models that his nonhandicapped peers provide for him" and this benefit may "tip the balance in favor of mainstreaming" despite lack of academic progress. *Daniel R.R. v. State Board of Education*, 874 F.2d 1036, 1049 (5th Cir. 1989). The court cited to no evidence regarding how disabled children benefit from language modeling and set forth no standard for how much modeling must occur before the academic benefit is discounted to serve the modeling function of inclusion. Courts also fail to explain whether this modeling function — sometimes called observational learning — can be addressed sufficiently if a child is included in art, music, physical education, lunch and recess.

Moreover, the assumption that language and behavior modeling will help the disabled student, while accepted uncritically by many courts, is open to question. "[Children need] instruction in what to pay attention to, how to remember and rehearse modeled behavior, how to judge when and where to produce imitative responses, as well as external and explicit motivation for appropriate imitation. These instructional needs go way beyond the social curriculum offered in the typical classroom." Betty A. Hallenback & James Kauffman, *How Does Observational Learning Affect the Behavior of Students with Emotional or Behavior Disorders?*, 29 J. SPECIAL EDUC. 46–47 (1995). Disabled children do not spontaneously imitate the appropriate behavior of nondisabled students and observing a model may even result in the acceleration of the opposite behavior. *Id.* at 57–58 (describing studies).

Does the modeling rationale reinforce troubling stereotypes of disabled students? Is its underlying premise that disabled students will have a negative influence on each other and that "[s]tudents with disabilties need to be alongside those who don't have disabilities, because the normal ones will know how to behave and will be good examples?" James M. Kauffman & Patricia L. Pullen, *Eight Myths About Special Education*, FOCUS ON EXCEPTIONAL CHILDREN, Jan. 1996, at 1, 6.

Is there any positive value to be gained from the opportunity for disabled students to be models for each other as they engage in struggles "that share characteristics of ability, culture, status or environment?" Daniel P. Hallahan & James M. Kauffman, *Toward a Culture of Disability in the Aftermath of Denno and Dunn*, 27 J. SPECIAL EDUC. 496, 505 (1994). Full inclusion advocates maintain that disabled students are stigmatized if they are placed in a separate special education classroom, and that this results in a decrease in self-esteem. Greater self-esteem is presumed to lead to greater achievement. *See Holland*, 786 F. Supp. at 879. Yet the notion that there is a causal connection between self-esteem and achievement has been increasingly under fire. *See, e.g.*, Martin Covington, *Self-Esteem and Failure in School: Analysis and Policy Implications* in THE SOCIAL IMPORTANCE OF SELF-ESTEEM, 72, 79 (Andrew M. Mecca et al. eds. 1989) (describing and citing studies that show generally low magnitude of association between self-esteem and achievement, with one study showing that 97% of variation in academic performance can be explained by other than self-concept). Even if increased self-esteem is somehow desirable of disabled students, is it clear that inclusion will always have that effect or could attending a special class sometimes be less destructive of self-concept? *See* Joseph R. Jenkins & Amy Heinen, *Students' Preferences for Service Delivery: Pull-out, In-class or Integrated Models,* 55 EXCEPTIONAL CHILDREN 516, 519–20 (1989) (reporting interviews with children that suggest that many feel more stigmatized when they are given special help in the general education classroom than when they are pulled out for special help in separate classrooms); Kauffman & Pullen, *supra*, at 7–8 (explaining how disabled child lost motivation in general education classroom and regained it in special class).

Is one message stemming from the stigma/self-esteem rationale that the preferred method for disabled students to feel better about themselves is to sit in a class next to nondisabled students? Are disabled students being sent the message that there is something "wrong" with being disabled that can only be cured by being with and being more like nondisabled students? Is there any way to foster the development of pride in difference and the belief that separation is because of difference, not inferiority?

Full inclusionists argue that the inclusion movement is based on the same premise as the movement for racial equality, even referring to language in *Brown v. Board of Education*. Yet some critics of the racial integration model claim that its implied message — that going to an all-black school somehow stigmatized black students — was "just as harmful to their self-esteem as the idea of forced segregation." Wendy Brown-Scott, *Justice Thurgood Marshall and the Integrative Ideal*, 26 ARIZ. ST. L.J. 535 (1994). Professor Kevin Brown has stated, "The very remedies that were undertaken in an attempt to eliminate a belief in African-American inferiority were also — like segregation that had preceded it — standing as symbols for it." Kevin Brown, *The Legal Rhetorical Structure for the Conversion of Desegregation Lawsuits to Quality Education Lawsuits*, 42 EMORY L.J. 791, 817 (1993). To what extent is school segregation because of race similar to school segregation because of disability? Should advocates for disabled children in school follow the racial integration model despite its critics? *See* Anne Proffitt Dupre, *Disability and the Public Schools: The Case Against Inclusion*, 72 WASH. L. REV. 775 (1997).

4. How much should the disabled student's disruptive behavior affect the placement analysis? Have the courts struck the correct balance?

Is disruption the only way that a disabled student may have a negative effect on learning in the classroom? What about teacher attention? Consider the scenario where a teacher must focus a large proportion of her time and energy on the needs of a disabled student (or students) by (a) modifying the materials in the curriculum, (b) modifying the actual teaching of the curriculum, and (c) attending to the needs of the disabled student during the lesson. Will teachers need to shorten the time spent teaching other students because time is needed elsewhere to meet the needs of the disabled child who is learning at a different level with different materials? Will constant concern over the needs of a severely disabled child deplete the energy and enthusiasm levels of teachers for other endeavors?

5. Many children who have severe disabilities have overwhelming problems that will not disappear when the child is included in a general education classroom. To attempt to meet with some success, the child will need a massive infusion of additional individualized special aids and services. The *Oberti* court determined that even though the disabled student interfered with the learning of others, he merely needed additional aids and services to be educated satisfactorily in the general education classroom. What supplementary aids and services did the court suggest? Is there a cost limit on the obligation to provide the additional aids and services that may be necessary to include a disabled child in the general education classroom?

The Eleventh Circuit has employed a balancing test: "If the cost of educating a handicapped child in a regular classroom is so great that it would significantly impact upon the education of other children in the district, then education in the regular classroom is not appropriate." *Greer*, 950 F.2d at 697. The court stated that a school district need not provide a disabled student with his own individual teacher in order that he might be included in a regular classroom. *Id.*

Does the court's test take into account the full impact on a school system when it must provide the necessary aids and services to include many disabled children throughout an entire district? Indeed, one upshot of the full inclusion movement is that it leads to individual classrooms where a teacher must address the needs of several disabled students. One study by the American Federation of Teachers cited instances where teachers were responsible for as many as ten to sixteen disabled students in one classroom. Nancy Webb, *Special Education: With New Court Decisions Backing Them, Advocates See Inclusion as a Question of Values*, HARV. EDUC. LETTER (July-Aug. 1994). The cost for aids and services necessary to include one child in a general education classroom may not always have a significant impact across an entire district, but might the aggregate cost to include all the children with severe behavior problems have such an impact? Should that be part of the test for cost that is beyond "practicable?" Should a school district be forced to wait until there is a significant impact on the education of its students before it can curb the cost of inclusion?

6. Disabled students often receive academic accommodation (like more time to work on a test) as part of their IEP. In New Jersey, a student with chronic fatigue syndrome received at-home instruction during the afternoons as part of her IEP. When the student earned the highest GPA in her class, parents complained that she had an unfair advantage since she was able to earn more "weighted grades" than her general education peers because of the availability of many AP courses in her home instruction program. Moreover, they claimed that she was able to secure higher grades in her home instruction classes than students enrolled in the same courses at the high school. The school then named co-valedictorians — the disabled student and another student with a lower GPA.

In granting the student's request for a temporary restraining order enjoining the school district from naming multiple valedictorians, the court chastised the school for trying to appease school parents and in doing so, losing "sight of the fact that plaintiff, unlike her peers, suffers from a debilitating medical condition . . . her accommodations were aimed at putting her on a level playing field with her healthy classmates," not giving her an academic advantage. The school district should "revel in the success of their IDEA program and the academic star it has produced" rather than "seek to diminish the honor that she has rightly earned." *Hornstine v. Township of Moorestown*, 263 F. Supp. 2d 887, 913 (D.N.J. 2003). *But see* Craig S. Lerner, *Accommodations for the Learning Disabled: A Level Playing Field or Affirmative Action for Elites*, 57 VAND. L. REV. (2004) (questioning the assumption that the ADA in higher education entitles most learning disabled students to accommodation and arguing that the learning disabled diagnosis is mired in nondeterminacy).

7. Courts have split on the issue as to which side bears the legal burden of proof when disagreements arise over the services or placement that disabled

children require. In *Schaffer v. Weast*, 377 F.3d 449 (4th Cir. 2004), the Fourth Circuit refused to depart from the general rule that the party seeking relief in a proceeding has the burden of proof. The majority found that IDEA has enough procedural safeguards as to offset any advantage given to the school district. The dissent argued that "parents simply do not have, and cannot easily acquire, the cumulative, institutional knowledge gained by representatives of the school district from their experiences with other, similarly disabled children." The Supreme Court granted certioriari to decide the issue, 125 S. Ct. 1300 (2005), and affirmed the Fourth Circuit opinion. 126 S. Ct. 528 (2005).

[C] Discipline

School discipline and the disabled student is an issue that is steeped in controversy. IDEA changed the traditional notion that schools possessed significant discretion in their dealings with serious student misbehavior. The nation's courts, including the United States Supreme Court, began telling school officials that their discretion in dealing with serious student misconduct may be greatly limited.

Until 1997, IDEA did not expressly address the authority of school officials to discipline disabled students. *See* Mark G. Yudof et al., *Educational Policy and the Law* 734 (1992). This lacuna caused confusion and uncertainty for educators who were uncertain as to their rights and responsibilities. The issue of school discipline and the disabled student thus became a matter of "great controversy and confusion," Mitchell L. Yell, Honig v. Doe: *The Suspension and Expulsion of Handicapped Students,* 56 EXCEPTIONAL CHILDREN 60, 69 (1989), as courts have "struggl[ed] under the weight of litigation involving [disabled] students." Larry Bartlett, *Disciplining Handicapped Students: Legal Issues in Light of* Honig v. Doe, 55 EXCEPTIONAL CHILDREN 357 (1989).

In 1988 — thirteen years after IDEA was enacted — the U. S. Supreme Court addressed the issue of expelling disabled students and determined that school officials could not unilaterally expel even a dangerous disabled student from school. *See* Dori Meinert, *Schools' Power to Expel Limited: High Court Ruling Protects Emotionally Troubled Pupils,* SAN DIEGO UNION AND TRIB., Jan. 21, 1988, at A1 (stating that the *Honig* opinion, *infra*, "sharply limited public school officials' power to suspend or expel emotionally disturbed pupils for disruptive or dangerous behavior"). In *Honig v. Doe*, 484 U.S. 305, 308 (1988), the Court addressed whether the San Francisco Unified School District could expel two emotionally disturbed children indefinitely for disruptive and violent behavior. One of the students, a seventeen-year-old, assaulted another student, choking the other student with sufficient force to leave abrasions on the child's neck, — and kicked out a school window while being escorted to the principal's office afterwards. The school commenced expulsion proceedings (which included a hearing) and suspended the student until the proceedings could be completed.

At the time, a suspension in excess of ten days or an expulsion was considered a "change in the placement" of the disabled child. Thus, according to the statute, the parents had the right to notice, an opportunity to present complaints concerning the school's decision, and an opportunity for a due process hearing respecting any complaints. *See* § 20 U.S.C. 1415(b)(1)–(2) (1994); *see also Honig*, 484 U.S. at 311–12. If the parents were unsatisfied after the hearing, they could obtain further administrative review. *See* § 20 U.S.C. § 1415(c) (1994). If still unsatisfied, the parents could file a civil action in state or federal court and could appeal the result of that action. *See* § 20 U.S.C. § 1415(e)(2) (1994).

Because these numerous hearings and court proceedings often take a long time to run their course, *see Honig*, 484 U.S. at 323, the school must determine how to deal with the child during this time. IDEA states that pending the completion of any review proceedings, the disabled child "shall remain in [his or her] then current placement" unless the parents agree to the change. 20 U.S.C. § 1415(e)(3)(A) (1994). This was termed the "stay-put" provision. *See* 20 U.S.C. § 1415(e)(3)(A) (1994). The provision provides in part: "During the pendency of any proceedings conducted pursuant to this section, unless the State or local educational agency and the parents or guardian otherwise agree, the child shall remain in the then current placement of such child." A change in placement also can occur even if the school wishes to continue educational services in a more restrictive environment — if, for instance, a school wished to move a student with a severe behavioral problem from a regular classroom to a special education classroom. The educators claimed and, some courts had agreed, that the residual authority of school officials to exclude dangerous students meant that the school could keep violent or dangerous students from the classroom until the review process was complete.

The Supreme Court stated that the statute had no exception for dangerous students and that these students could be removed only with permission of the parents or with the approval of a court. *See Honig*, 484 U.S. at 323–24. "We think it is clear, however, that Congress very much meant to strip schools of the unilateral authority they had traditionally employed to exclude disabled students, particularly emotionally disturbed students, from school." Congress thereby denied school officials "their former right to 'self-help' and directed that in the future the removal of disabled students could be accomplished only with the permission of the parents or, as a last resort, the courts." After *Honig*, school officials could go to court to seek an injunction dissolving the stay-put provision if they have sufficient evidence that the disabled student is "truly dangerous." *Id.* at 326.

Honig's effect on school discipline became clearer as it was applied by lower courts. Professor Michael Heise has observed, "It's pretty clear that, by gaming the legal rules, parents can effectively hamstring school officials under IDEA." *See also* Stuart Anderson, *Why Schools Don't Dare to Discipline the Disabled*, Wkly. Stand., Feb. 19, 1996, at 29 (quoting Heise and decrying a double standard that "defies common sense and leaves children, particularly other special education students, to face dangerous peers who are above the law"). Educators began to claim that IDEA's stay-put provision as interpreted by *Honig* "can make it impossible to protect teachers and other students if a disabled student turns dangerous." Don J. DeBenedictis, *Schools See Disabled Protection as Threat to Safety*, Nat'l L.J., June 27, 1994, at A9. Advocates for the disabled claim that "[t]he stay-put provision is necessary because all too often schools make judgments solely on the basis of a child's superficial behavior, rather than by trying to figure out what's causing the behavior." DeBenedictis, *supra*, n.135, at A9 (quoting Steven Novick, Executive Director of the Oklahoma Disability Law Center).

Discipline was both the "top concern," Robert Greene, *Revised Law on Disabled Students Hard to Follow*, ATHENS DAILY NEWS, Jul. 5, 1998, at 5C, and the "most contentious issue," *How to Get Regular Education Peers Off Your Back and On Your Side*, THE SPECIAL EDUCATOR, Aug. 4, 1995, at 10, when Congress sought to reauthorize the Individuals with Disabilities Education Act — a process that began in 1995 and culminated in the IDEA amendments of 1997. *See* Joetta Sack, *Delay of Rules Leaves Schools in Doubt on IDEA*, EDUC. WK., Mar. 10, 1999, at 1.

For a discussion of the testimony before Congress on the discipline issue, see Anne P. Dupre, *A Study in Double Standards, Discipline, and the Disabled Student*, 72 WASH. L. REV. 1, 30–37 (2000). Teachers claimed they were increasingly frustrated when school districts were unable or reluctant to act in the face of severe behavioral problems and instead meted out light punishments of two or three days suspension for violent acts against teachers. *See Examining the Effect of Federal Policy on the Ability of School Systems to Discipline Students with Disabilities: Hearing Before the Subcomm. on Disability Policy of the Comm. on Labor and Human Resources*, 104th Cong. 70 (1995) [hereinafter *Federal Disability Policy Hearing*] (statement of Marcia Reback, President, Rhode Island Federation of Teachers). Because the inclusion movement has resulted in more and more students with significant emotional and behavioral problems being moved from residential settings and special education classrooms into the regular general education classrooms, teachers in the regular classrooms are now "confronted with situations and behaviors that are totally outside of their experience and preparation." *Id.* at 70.

Advocates for the disabled maintained that no changes were needed to the existing law because schools frequently try to exclude disabled students under the guise of "serious behavioral" concerns and violence. *See Federal Disability Policy Hearing, supra,* at 98. (statement of Kathleen Boundy, Co-Director, Center for Law and Education). Creating an exception for disruptive behavior was also rejected, because "school personnel should continue to work with parents to develop alternative strategies." *Federal Disability Policy Hearing, supra,* n.22, at 101 (statement of Kathleen Boundy).

Congress passed amendments to IDEA in 1997. Included in the amendments were several provisions relating to school discipline, some of which are outlined below.

1. *Continued Education Services*

The amendments provide that a free appropriate public education must be available for all students with disabilities, "including students who have been suspended or expelled from school." 20 U.S.C. § 1412(a)(1)(A) (Supp. III). This is a change for schools in those jurisdictions where courts had held that schools could cease services for students who are suspended or expelled for conduct unrelated to their disability. *See, e.g., Department of Education v. Riley,* 106 F.3d 559, 561 (4th Cir. 1997).

The school is also permitted to place the disabled student in an interim alternative educational setting for a ten-day suspension, thus avoiding the services-during-suspension issue. But the school can only do so "to the extent such alternatives would be applied to [students] without disabilities." 20 U.S.C. § 1415(k)(1)(A)(i).

2. *Weapons and Drugs*

The statute allows school officials to move a disabled student to an "appropriate interim alternative educational setting" for not more than forty-five days, but only if the student (1) carries a weapon to school or a school function or (2) possesses or uses illegal drugs or sells or solicits the sale of a controlled substance while at school or a school function. 20 U.S.C. § 1415 (k)(1)(A)(ii). A proposal that would have expanded the covered behavior to include assaults on school personnel was not enacted. Under the Gun-Free Schools Act, a nondisabled student who carries a gun to school would be expelled for one year with no provision for educational services. *See* 20 U.S.C. § 8921(b)(1) ("[E]ach state receiving Federal Funds under the chapter shall have in effect a State law requiring local education agencies to expel from school for a period of not less than one year a student who is determined to have brought a weapon to a school.").

The IDEA regulations set forth more explicit requirements for the interim setting for the disabled student: The interim setting must (1) allow the disabled student to continue to progress in the general curriculum, (2) allow the child to continue to receive the services and modifications that were set out in the student's IEP and (3) include any additional services and modifications that have been designed to prevent the misconduct from recurring. *See* 34 C.F.R. 300.522. The IDEA regulations state that the interim alternative setting must be determined by the IEP team. Because of the requirements set forth in the regulations, home schooling may not be an appropriate interim setting.

3. *Violent Students*

School officials must obtain permission from a hearing officer before removing a violent student from the classroom. The statute allows for placement, with the approval of a hearing officer, for up to forty-five days in an appropriate interim alternative educational setting. 20 U.S.C. § 1415(k)(2). There is no provision for the removal of a disruptive disabled student who is not violent. The amendments added a new "substantial evidence" requirement: Before a school can remove a violent student, the school must demonstrate by "substantial evidence" that the disabled student is "substantially likely" to injure himself or others. 20 U.S.C. § 1415(k)(2)(A). IDEA defines "substantial evidence" as "beyond a preponderance of the evidence." 20 U.S.C. § 1415(k)(10(C). The hearing officer must consider whether the school has made reasonable efforts to minimize the risk of harm in the student's current placement. The parent may file an action in district court if the parent disagrees with the hearing officer's determination.

4. *Staying Put in the Alternative Placement*

If a parent makes such a challenge, an elaborate "stay-put" mechanism kicks in while the appeal proceeds. For example, if a parent challenges an interim placement for either the weapons, drugs or violence provision, the student will remain in the alternative placement until the appeals process is complete or the forty-five days are up, whichever comes first. 20 U.S.C. § 1415(k)(7)(A). If the appeals process goes beyond forty-five days and the school wants the student to stay in the interim placement, the school must request an expedited hearing and show by substantial evidence that the student is dangerous. 20 U.S.C. § 1415(k)(7)(C)(i).

5. *The Manifestation Determination*

Misconduct that is a manifestation of the student's disability is to be treated differently from conduct that is related to the disability. After any decision to take any disciplinary action allowed by the statute or for any change in placement for over ten days for any other misconduct, the IEP team must meet within ten days. 20 U.S.C. § 1415(k)(4)(A)(ii). The statute outlines several steps that the team must take, and it requires the team to decide whether the student's disability "impair[ed]" the student's "ability . . . to understand the impact and consequences of the behavior" *and* whether "the disability impair[ed]" the student's "ability . . . to control the behavior." 20 U.S.C. § 1415(k)(4)(C)(ii). If, after review, the IEP team decides that the behavior was not a manifestation of the disability, the student may be disciplined in the same way as a student without disabilities. 20 U.S.C. § 1415(k)(4)(C)(ii) (Supp. III 1997). As noted above, another provision in the new amendments requires that a free appropriate education must be "available to all children with disabilities . . . including students who have been suspended or expelled from school." 20 U.S.C. § 1412(a)(1)(A). Thus, even if a student can be removed from the classroom because the conduct is deemed unrelated to the disability, education services must still be provided to the student.

6. *Students Who Are Not Yet Eligible for Special Education*

If a school attempts to discipline a student who has not been termed disabled, the student may claim all the protections afforded disabled students if school officials "had knowledge" that the student had a disability before the behavior occurred. School officials will be deemed to have knowledge (1) if the parent expressed concern in writing or has requested evaluation of the child, (2) if the behavior or performance of the child demonstrates that the child needs special education services, or (3) if the teacher or other school personnel expressed concern about the child to the director of special education or to other school personnel. 20 U.S.C. § 1415(k)(8)(B)(i-iv) (Supp. III)

For a more detailed analysis of the 1997 Amendments to IDEA as they relate to school discipline, see Anne P. Dupre, *A Study in Double Standards, Discipline, and the Disabled Student,* 72 WASH. L. REV. 1 (2000); Terry J. Seligmann, *Not As Simple As ABC: Disciplining Children With Disabilities Under the 1997 IDEA Amendments,* 42 ARIZ. L. REV. 77 (2000).; Theresa J. Bryant, *The Death Knell For School Expulsion: The 1997 Amendments to the Individuals With Disabilities Education Act,* 47 AM. U.L. REV. 487 (1998).

What should school officials do if a female student reports that a disabled student who has been included in her classroom is sexually harassing her? Reread Justice Kennedy's dissent in *Davis v. Monroe County.*

Congress passed the 2004 IDEA Amendments (Individuals With Disabilities Education Improvement Act of 2004) amidst much dissension. Some of the more significant changes are set forth below.

Placements:

"School personnel may consider any unique circumstances on a case-by-case basis when determining whether to order a change in placement for a child with a disability who violates a code of student conduct." 20 U.S.C. § 1415(k)(1)(A).

Removal for any code of conduct violation:

"School personnel under this subsection may remove a child with a disability who violates a code of student conduct from their current placement to an appropriate interim alternative educational setting, another setting, or suspension, for not more than 10 school days (to the extent such alternatives are applied to children without disabilities)." 20 U.S.C. § 1415(k)(1)(B).

Services:

Students may (i) continue to receive educational services, as provided in section 612(a)(1), so as to enable the child to continue to participate in the general education curriculum, although in another setting, and to progress toward meeting the goals set out in the child's IEP; and (ii) receive, as appropriate, a functional behavioral assessment, behavioral intervention services and modifications, that are designed to address the behavior violation so that it does not recur. 20 U.S.C. § 1415(k)(1)(D)(i), (ii).

Manifestation Determination:

Determination is made by the LEA, the parent and the relevant members of the IEP Team (under the 1997 Amendments, the LEA had to prove that the child's action resulting in the discipline infraction was not caused by the child's disability). According to The Guide to "Frequently Asked Questions," IDEA (written by committee members), "the new IDEA places the obligation on the parent to show that the child's action resulting in the discipline infraction was the direct result of the child's disability."

The definition of "manifestation" has tightened — the conduct in question must be "caused by, or had a direct and substantial relationship to, the child's disability." 20 U.S.C. § 1415(k)(1)(E)(i)(I). According to the FAQ, "previously any tangential or attenuated relationship between the discipline infraction and the child's disability was sufficient to determine that the infraction was a 'manifestation'." To read the FAQ, see http://edworkforce.house.gov/issues/109th/education/idea/ideafaq.pdf.

Interim Alternative Educational Settings:

Rather than 45 days, it is now 45 school days (this expands the removal from roughly six weeks to nine weeks). 20 U.S.C. § 1415(k)(1)(G).

Grounds for removing a student for not more than 45 school days expanded:

Still have "carries or possesses a weapon to or at school, on school premises, or to or at a school function under the jurisdiction of a State or local educational agency," 20 U.S.C. § 1415(k)(1)(G)(i), and "knowingly possesses or uses illegal drugs, or sells or solicits the sale of a controlled substance, while at school, on school premises, or at a school function under the jurisdiction of a State or local educational agency." 20 U.S.C. § 1415(k)(1)(G)(ii).

But adds:

"has inflicted serious bodily injury upon another person while at school, on school premises, or at a school function under the jurisdiction of a State or local educational agency." 20 U.S.C. § 1415(k)(1)(G)(iii).

"Serious bodily injury" means bodily injury involving:

(A) a substantial risk of death;

(B) extreme physical pain;

(C) protracted and obvious disfigurement; or

(D) protracted loss or impairment of the function of a bodily member, organ, or mental faculty. 20 U.S.C. § 1415(k)(7)(D).

Notification to the parents is now required after a disciplinary action is made:

"Not later than the date on which the decision to take disciplinary action is made, the local educational agency shall notify the parents of that decision, and of all procedural safeguards accorded under this section." 20 U.S.C. § 1415(k)(1)(H).

Regarding knowledge of a child's disability:

Amendments keep two of the four previous grounds for knowledge. 20 U.S.C. § 1415(k)(5)(B).

Deletes the "Behavior or performance of the child demonstrates the need for such services."

Changes the teacher reporting provision:

Rather than imposing knowledge if the teacher expresses concern to "other personnel of the agency," the provision reads "to other supervisory personnel of the agency." 20 U.S.C. § 1415(k)(5)(B)(iii).

Provides an exception for the school if the parents refused an evaluation:

"Exception. A local educational agency shall not be deemed to have knowledge that the child is a child with a disability if the parent of the child has not allowed an evaluation of the child pursuant to section 614 [20 U.S.C. § 1414] or has refused services under this part [20 U.S.C. § 1411 *et seq.*] or the child has been evaluated and it was determined that the child was not a child with a disability under this part [20 U.S.C. § 1411 *et seq.*]." 20 U.S.C. § 1415(k)(5)(C).

§ 4.07 LEAVING NO CHILD BEHIND?

Signed into law in 2002, the No Child Left Behind Act (NCLBA) affects every public school, teacher, and student in the nation. This section highlights some of the core provisions of NCLBA.

The stated purpose of the NCLBA is to "close the achievement gap with accountability, flexibility, and choice so that no child is left behind." 20 U.S.C. § 1 (short title). It requires that states develop and implement "challenging" academic standards in reading and math, set annual statewide progress objectives to ensure that all groups of students reach proficiency within 12 years and then test children annually in grades 3 through 8 in reading and math to measure their progress. *See* § 6311(a)(3).

States must select their own tests and make the results public in annual "report cards." The results must be reported with respect to at-risk students, including students who have limited English proficiency, students with disabilities, economically disadvantaged students, and students from major racial and ethnic groups. § 6311(b)(2)(C)(v)(II). At least 95 percent of the students in each of these subgroups must be assessed. § 6311(b)(2)(I)(ii). Schools are required to show "adequate yearly progress" (A.Y.P.) toward their statewide objectives, and they must be on course to reach 100 percent proficiency for all groups of students within 12 years. The states decide what is proficient and what is an adequate rate of progress for each group, but if the school or one subgroup fails, the entire school fails. Those schools that fall behind may be subject to various "school improvement," "corrective action," or "restructuring" measures. Underperforming schools may avoid such measures if they can demonstrate a 10 percent reduction in the number of students who are not meeting the annual proficiency goals. § 6311(b)(2)(I).

The U.S. Department of Education addressed one of the criticisms of IDEA in 2005 when it issued regulations that increased the one percent cap for students with severe cognitive disabilities who could be assessed under alternative assessments using modified academic achievement standards. The new guidelines allow schools to add an additional two percent of students to that number if they are students who have "persistent academic disabilities." *Raising Achievement: Alternate Assessments for Students with Disabilities*, *available at* www.ed.gov.

To ensure that states set a benchmark that is high enough, each state's test results will also be compared against an independent benchmark — the National Assessment of Educational Progress (NAEP), which will be given to a small sample of each state's 4th and 8th-grade students in reading and math every other year.

To say that the NCLBA has been criticized does not even begin to tell the story. *See, e.g.*, James E. Ryan, *The Perverse Incentives of the No Child Left Behind Act*, 79 N.Y.U. L. REV. 932 (2004); Beth Keller, *Rigor Disputed in Standards for Teachers*, EDUC. WK., July 14, 2004 (claiming states are not implementing NCLB's requirements for "highly qualified" teachers in a way that weeds out poor veteran teachers); David J. Hoff, *Debate Grows on True Cost of School Law*, EDUC. WK., Feb. 4, 2004 (some states are claiming that they are spending much more than they receive in federal funding to implement NCLBA); Lisa Goldstein, *Harvard Analysis is Critical of "No Child" Law*, EDUC. WK., Feb. 18, 2004 (reporting on study by Harvard Civil Rights Project that says that educators are confused and frustrated with the legislation); Bess Keller & Joetta Sack, *Union, States, Raise Frontal Attack on NCLB*, EDUC. WK., April 27, 2005 (reporting on lawsuit by National Education Association that charges that federal underfunding of NCLBA forces states to use their own money, contrary to a provision in the statute providing that it shall not be construed to mandate that a state must spend funds that are not paid for under the Act itself); Jeff Archer, *Connecticut Pledges First State Legal Challenge to NCLB Law*, EDUC. WK., Apr. 13, 2005 (state attorney general pledges to sue Dept. of Education over funding of testing mandates). Does the heated debate over NCLBA mean that it is bad law? Or does it mean that big changes are hard to implement without controversy?

Chapter 5

THE JUVENILE JUSTICE SYSTEM

§ 5.01 OVERVIEW

Until the late nineteenth century, juveniles who committed crimes were dealt with through the same criminal justice system that addressed the offenses of adults. While minors were afforded a defense of infancy, they received no other legally recognized special attention. However, functionaries in the criminal justice system no doubt exercised discretion from time to time in favor of lenient treatment for youthful offenders. Young people who engaged in untoward or self-destructive conduct that was non-criminal in nature were subjected to no public intervention of any sort.

This all changed with the emergence of juvenile courts at the turn of the twentieth century. Reformers saw the need for a nonpunitive *parens patriae* alternative to the criminal justice system for juvenile criminal offenders. As juvenile court statutes became ubiquitous, the bulk of juvenile criminal offenses were dealt with in juvenile court, although mechanisms existed to "waive" certain cases to adult criminal court. Juvenile court jurisdiction was not limited to criminal misbehavior, however, but also extended to so-called "status offenses," non-criminal behavior deemed harmful to the juvenile actor's healthy growth and development. In exercising either its criminal ("delinquency") or status offense jurisdiction, the juvenile courts, untrammeled by rigorous procedural rules, sought to impose dispositions beneficial to the individual young person appearing before the court.

This Chapter examines the juvenile justice system by first considering several seminal United States Supreme Court cases. While these cases speak directly only to procedural requirements in delinquency adjudications, their rulings have arguably had an impact on other aspects of the juvenile justice system. With the Supreme Court cases as an introduction, attention will be directed to characteristic features of juvenile court systems and consideration of cases treating legal questions raised therefrom.

§ 5.02 THE SUPREME COURT AND JUVENILE COURT PROCEDURE

[A] Supreme Court Cases

KENT v. UNITED STATES

Supreme Court of the United States
383 U.S. 541 (1966)

MR. JUSTICE FORTAS *delivered the opinion of the Court.*

. . . The facts and the contentions of counsel raise a number of disturbing questions concerning the administration by the police and the Juvenile Court authorities of the District of Columbia laws relating to juveniles. . . . [This] case presents important challenges to the procedure of the police and Juvenile Court officials upon apprehension of a juvenile suspected of serious offenses. Because we conclude that the Juvenile Court's order waiving jurisdiction of petitioner was entered without compliance with required procedures, we remand the case to the trial court.

Morris A. Kent, Jr., first came under the authority of the Juvenile Court of the District of Columbia in 1959. He was then aged 14. He was apprehended as a result of several housebreakings and an attempted purse snatching. He was placed on probation, in the custody of his mother. . . .

On September 2, 1961, an intruder entered the apartment of a woman in the District of Columbia. He took her wallet. He raped her. The police found in the apartment latent fingerprints. They were developed and processed. They matched the fingerprints of Morris Kent, taken when he was 14 years old and under the jurisdiction of the Juvenile Court. At about 3 p.m. on September 5, 1961, Kent was taken into custody by the police. Kent was then 16 and therefore subject to the 'exclusive jurisdiction' of the Juvenile Court. He was still on probation to that court as a result of the 1959 proceedings.

Upon being apprehended, Kent was taken to police headquarters where he was interrogated by police officers. It appears that he admitted his involvement in the offense which led to his apprehension and volunteered information as to similar offenses involving housebreaking, robbery, and rape. His interrogation proceeded from about 3 p.m. to 10 p.m. the same evening.[1] Some time after 10 p.m. petitioner was taken to the Receiving Home for Children. The next morning he was released to the police for further interrogation at police headquarters, which lasted until 5 p.m.

The record does not show when his mother became aware that the boy was in custody. . . .

---

[1] [1] There is no indication in the file that the police complied with the requirement of the District Code that a child taken into custody, unless released to his parent, guardian or custodian, "shall be placed in the custody of a probation officer or other person designated by the court, or taken immediately to the court or to a place of detention provided by the Board of Public Welfare, and the officer taking him shall immediately notify the court and shall file a petition when directed to do so by the court."

Counsel, together with petitioner's mother, promptly conferred with the Social Service Director of the Juvenile Court. In a brief interview, they discussed the possibility that the Juvenile Court might waive jurisdiction . . . and remit Kent to trial by the District Court. Counsel made known his intention to oppose waiver.

Petitioner was detained at the Receiving Home for almost a week. There was no arraignment during this time, no determination by a judicial officer of probable cause for petitioner's apprehension.

During this period of detention and interrogation, petitioner's counsel arranged for examination of petitioner by two psychiatrists and a psychologist. He thereafter filed with the Juvenile Court a motion for a hearing on the question of waiver of Juvenile Court jurisdiction, together with an affidavit of a psychiatrist certifying that petitioner "is a victim of severe psychopathology" and recommending hospitalization for psychiatric observation. Petitioner's counsel, in support of his motion to the effect that the Juvenile Court should retain jurisdiction of petitioner, offered to prove that if petitioner were given adequate treatment in a hospital under the aegis of the Juvenile Court, he would be a suitable subject for rehabilitation.

At the same time, petitioner's counsel moved that the Juvenile Court should give him access to the Social Service file relating to petitioner which had been accumulated by the staff of the Juvenile Court during petitioner's probation period, and which would be available to the Juvenile Court judge in considering the question whether it should retain or waive jurisdiction. Petitioner's counsel represented that access to this file was essential to his providing petitioner with effective assistance of counsel.

The Juvenile Court judge did not rule on these motions. He held no hearing. He did not confer with petitioner or petitioner's parents or petitioner's counsel. He entered an order reciting that after "full investigation, I do hereby waive" jurisdiction of petitioner and directing that he be "held for trial for [the alleged] offenses under the regular procedure of the [court]." He made no findings. He did not recite any reason for the waiver. He made no reference to the motions filed by petitioner's counsel. We must assume that he denied, *sub silentio*, the motions for a hearing, . . . the request for access to the Social Service file, and the offer to prove that petitioner was a fit subject for rehabilitation under the Juvenile Court's jurisdiction.

. . . .

The provision of the Juvenile Court Act governing waiver expressly provides only for "full investigation." It states the circumstances in which jurisdiction may be waived and the child held for trial under adult procedures, but it does not state standards to govern the Juvenile Court's decision as to waiver. The provision reads as follows:

> If a child sixteen years of age or older is charged with an offense which would amount to a felony in the case of an adult, or any child charged with an offense which if committed by an adult is punishable by death or life imprisonment, the judge may, after full investigation, waive jurisdiction and order such child held for trial under the regular procedure of the court which would have jurisdiction of such offense

if committed by an adult; or such other court may exercise the powers conferred upon the juvenile court in this subchapter in conducting and disposing of such cases.

. . . .

. . . [P]etitioner was indicted by a grand jury of the United States District Court for the District of Columbia. The indictment contained eight counts alleging two instances of housebreaking, robbery, and rape, and one of housebreaking and robbery. On November 16, 1961, petitioner moved the District Court to dismiss the indictment on the ground that the waiver was invalid. . . .

The District Court denied the motion to dismiss the indictment. The District Court ruled that it would not "go behind" the Juvenile Court judge's recital that his order was entered "after full investigation." It held that "The only matter before me is as to whether or not the statutory provisions were complied with and the Courts have held . . . with reference to full investigation, that that does not mean a quasi judicial or judicial hearing. No hearing is required."

. . . .

At trial, petitioner's defense was wholly directed toward proving that he was not criminally responsible because "his unlawful act was the product of mental disease or mental defect." Extensive evidence, including expert testimony, was presented to support this defense. The jury found as to the counts alleging rape that petitioner was "not guilty by reason of insanity." Under District of Columbia law, this made it mandatory that petitioner be transferred to . . . a mental institution, until his sanity is restored. On the six counts of housebreaking and robbery, the jury found that petitioner was guilty.

Kent was sentenced to serve . . . a total of 30 to 90 years in prison. The District Court ordered that the time to be spent at St. Elizabeth's on the mandatory commitment after the insanity acquittal be counted as part of the 30-to 90-year sentence. Petitioner appealed to the United States Court of Appeals for the District of Columbia Circuit. That court affirmed.

. . . [P]etitioner's counsel has urged a number of grounds for reversal. He argues that petitioner's detention and interrogation, described above, were unlawful. He contends that the police failed to follow the procedure prescribed by the Juvenile Court Act in that they failed to notify the parents of the child and the Juvenile Court itself, that petitioner was deprived of his liberty for about a week without a determination of probable cause which would have been required in the case of an adult; that he was interrogated by the police in the absence of counsel or a parent without warning of his right to remain silent or advice as to his right to counsel, in asserted violation of the Juvenile Court Act and in violation of rights that he would have if he were an adult. . . .

. . . .

It is to petitioner's arguments as to the infirmity of the proceedings by which the Juvenile Court waived its otherwise exclusive jurisdiction that we address our attention. Petitioner attacks the waiver of jurisdiction on a number of statutory and constitutional grounds. He contends that the waiver is defective because no hearing was held; because no findings were made by the Juvenile Court; because the Juvenile Court stated no reasons for waiver; and because counsel was denied access to the Social Service file which presumably was considered by the Juvenile Court in determining to waive jurisdiction.

We agree that the order of the Juvenile Court waiving its jurisdiction and transferring petitioner for trial in the United States District Court for the District of Columbia was invalid. . . . The issue is the standards to be applied upon such review.

We agree with the Court of Appeals that the statute contemplates that the Juvenile Court should have considerable latitude within which to determine whether it should retain jurisdiction over a child or — subject to the statutory delimitation — should waive jurisdiction. But this latitude is not complete. At the outset, it assumes procedural regularity sufficient in the particular circumstances to satisfy the basic requirements of due process and fairness, as well as compliance with the statutory requirement of a "full investigation." The statute gives the Juvenile Court a substantial degree of discretion as to the factual considerations to be evaluated, the weight to be given them and the conclusion to be reached. It does not confer upon the Juvenile Court a license for arbitrary procedure. The statute does not permit the Juvenile Court to determine in isolation and without the participation or any representation of the child the "critically important" question whether a child will be deprived of the special protections and provisions of the Juvenile Court Act. It does not authorize the Juvenile Court, in total disregard of a motion for hearing filed by counsel, and without any hearing or statement or reasons, to decide — as in this case — that the child will be taken from the Receiving Home for Children and transferred to jail along with adults, and that he will be exposed to the possibility of a death sentence instead of treatment for a maximum, in Kent's case, of five years, until he is 21.

We do not consider whether, on the merits, Kent should have been transferred; but there is no place in our system of law for reaching a result of such tremendous consequences without ceremony — without hearing, without effective assistance of counsel, without a statement of reasons. It is inconceivable that a court of justice dealing with adults, with respect to a similar issue, would proceed in this manner. It would be extraordinary if society's special concern for children, as reflected in the District of Columbia's Juvenile Court Act, permitted this procedure. We hold that it does not.

1. The theory of the District's Juvenile Court Act, like that of other jurisdictions, is rooted in social welfare philosophy rather than in the *corpus juris*. Its proceedings are designated as civil rather than criminal. The Juvenile Court is theoretically engaged in determining the needs of the child and of society rather than adjudicating criminal conduct. The objectives are to provide measures of guidance and rehabilitation for the child and protection for society, not to fix criminal responsibility, guilt and punishment. The State is *parens patriae* rather than prosecuting attorney and judge. But the admonition to function in a "parental" relationship is not an invitation to procedural arbitrariness.

2. Because the State is supposed to proceed in respect of the child as *parens patriae* and not as adversary, courts have relied on the premise that the proceedings are "civil" in nature and not criminal, and have asserted that the child cannot complain of the deprivation of important rights available in criminal cases. It has been asserted that he can claim only the fundamental due process right to fair treatment. For example, it has been held that he is not entitled to bail; to indictment by grand jury; to a speedy and public trial; to trial by jury; to immunity against self-incrimination; to confrontation of his accusers; and in some jurisdictions [but not in the District of Columbia] that he is not entitled to counsel.

While there can be no doubt of the original laudable purpose of juvenile courts, studies and critiques in recent years raise serious questions as to whether actual performance measures well enough against theoretical purpose to make tolerable the immunity of the process from the reach of constitutional guaranties applicable to adults. There is much evidence that some juvenile courts, including that of the District of Columbia, lack the personnel, facilities and techniques to perform adequately as representatives of the State in a *parens patriae* capacity, at least with respect to children charged with law violation. There is evidence, in fact, that there may be grounds for concern that the child receives the worst of both worlds: that he gets neither the protections accorded to adults nor the solicitous care and regenerative treatment postulated for children.

This concern, however, does not induce us in this case to accept the invitation to rule that constitutional guaranties which would be applicable to adults charged with the serious offenses for which Kent was tried must be applied in juvenile court proceedings concerned with allegations of law violation. The Juvenile Court Act and the decisions of the United States Court of Appeals for the District of Columbia Circuit provide an adequate basis for decision of this case, and we go no further.

3. It is clear beyond dispute that the waiver of jurisdiction is a "critically important" action determining vitally important statutory rights of the juvenile. The Court of Appeals for the District of Columbia Circuit has so held. The statutory scheme makes this plain. The Juvenile Court is vested with "original and exclusive jurisdiction" of the child. This jurisdiction confers special rights and immunities. He is, as specified by the statute, shielded from publicity. He may be confined, but with rare exceptions he may not be jailed along with adults. He may be detained, but only until he is 21 years of age. The court is admonished by the statute to give preference to retaining the child in the custody of his parents "unless his welfare and the safety and protection of the public can not be adequately safeguarded without . . . removal." The child is protected against consequences of adult conviction such as the loss of civil rights, the use of adjudication against him in subsequent proceedings, and disqualification for public employment.

The net, therefore, is that petitioner — then a boy of 16 — was by statute entitled to certain procedures and benefits as a consequence of his statutory right to the "exclusive" jurisdiction of the Juvenile Court. In these circumstances, considering particularly that decision as to waiver of jurisdiction and transfer of the matter to the District Court was potentially as important to petitioner as the difference between five years' confinement and a death sentence, we conclude that, as a condition to a valid waiver order, petitioner is entitled to a hearing, including access by his counsel to the social records and probation or similar reports which presumably are considered by the court, and to a statement of reasons for the Juvenile Court's decision. We believe that this result is required by the statute read in the context of constitutional principles relating to due process and the assistance of counsel.

. . . .

We are of the opinion that the Court of Appeals misconceived the basic issue and the underlying values in this case. It did note . . . that the determination of whether to transfer a child from the statutory structure of the Juvenile Court to the criminal processes of the District Court is "critically important." We hold that it is, indeed, a "critically important" proceeding. The Juvenile Court Act confers upon the child a right to avail himself of that court's "exclusive" jurisdiction. "[I]t is implicit in [the Juvenile Court] scheme that non-criminal treatment is to be the rule — and the adult criminal treatment, the exception which must be governed by the particular factors of individual cases."

Meaningful review requires that the reviewing court should review. It should not be remitted to assumptions. It must have before it a statement of the reasons motivating the waiver including, of course, a statement of the relevant facts. It may not "assume" that there are adequate reasons, nor may it merely assume that "full investigation" has been made. Accordingly, we hold that it is incumbent upon the Juvenile Court to accompany its waiver order with a statement of the reasons or considerations therefore. We do not read the statute as requiring that this statement must be formal or that it should necessarily include conventional findings of fact. But the statement should be sufficient to demonstrate that the statutory requirement of "full investigation" has been met; and that the question has received the careful consideration of the Juvenile Court; and it must set forth the basis for the order with sufficient specificity, to permit meaningful review.

Correspondingly, we conclude that an opportunity for a hearing, which may be informal, must be given the child prior to entry of a waiver order. . . . [T]he child is entitled to counsel in connection with a waiver proceeding, and . . . counsel is entitled to see the child's social records. These rights are meaningless — an illusion, a mockery — unless counsel is given an opportunity to function.

The right to representation by counsel is not a formality. It is not a grudging gesture to a ritualistic requirement. It is of the essence of justice. Appointment of counsel without affording an opportunity for hearing on a "critically important" decision is tantamount to denial of counsel. There is no justification for the failure of the Juvenile Court to rule on the motion for hearing filed by petitioner's counsel, and it was error to fail to grant a hearing.

We do not mean by this to indicate that the hearing to be held must conform with all of the requirements of a criminal trial or even of the usual administrative hearing; but we do hold that the hearing must measure up to the essentials of due process and fair treatment.

With respect to access by the child's counsel to the social records of the child, we deem it obvious that since these are to be considered by the Juvenile Court in making its decision to waive, they must be made available to the child's counsel. . . . There is no doubt as to the statutory basis for this conclusion. . . . We cannot agree with the Court of Appeals in the present case that the statute is "ambiguous." The statute expressly provides that the record shall be withheld from "indiscriminate" public inspection, "except that such records or parts thereof shall be made available by rule of court or special order of court to such persons . . . as have a legitimate interest in the protection . . . of the child. . . ." [C]ounsel must be afforded to the child in waiver proceedings. Counsel, therefore, have a "legitimate interest" in the protection of the child, and must be afforded access to these records.

We do not agree with the Court of Appeals' statement, attempting to justify denial of access to these records, that counsel's role is limited to presenting "to the court anything on behalf of the child which might help the court in arriving at a decision; it is not to denigrate the staff's submissions and recommendations." On the contrary, if the staff's submissions include materials which are susceptible to challenge or impeachment, it is precisely the role of counsel to "denigrate" such matter. There is no irrebuttable presumption of accuracy attached to staff reports. If a decision on waiver is "critically important" it is equally of "critical importance" that the material submitted to the judge — which is protected by the statute only against "indiscriminate" inspection — be subjected, within reasonable limits having regard to the theory of the Juvenile Court Act, to examination, criticism and refutation. While the Juvenile Court judge may, of course, receive ex parte analyses and recommendations from his staff, he may not, for purposes of a decision on waiver, receive and rely upon secret information, whether emanating from his staff or otherwise. The Juvenile Court is governed in this respect by the established principles which control courts and quasi-judicial agencies of the Government.

For the reasons stated, we conclude that the Court of Appeals and the District Court erred in sustaining the validity of the waiver by the Juvenile Court. . . . "[T]he waiver question was primarily and initially one for the Juvenile Court to decide and its failure to do so in a valid manner cannot be said to be harmless error. It is the Juvenile Court, not the District Court, which has the facilities, personnel and expertise for a proper determination of the waiver issue."

Ordinarily we would reverse the Court of Appeals and direct the District Court to remand the case to the Juvenile Court for a new determination of waiver. If on remand the decision were against waiver, the indictment in the District Court would be dismissed. However, petitioner has now passed the age of 21 and the Juvenile Court can no longer exercise jurisdiction over him. In view of the unavailability of a redetermination of the waiver question by the Juvenile Court, it is urged by petitioner that the conviction should be vacated and the indictment dismissed. In the circumstances of this case, . . . we do not consider it appropriate to grant this drastic relief. Accordingly, we vacate the order of the Court of Appeals and the judgment of the District Court and remand the case to the District Court for a hearing de novo on waiver, consistent with this opinion. If that court finds that waiver was inappropriate, petitioner's conviction must be vacated. If, however, it finds that the waiver order was proper when originally made, the District Court may proceed, after consideration of such motions as counsel may make and such further proceedings, if any, as may be warranted, to enter an appropriate judgment. . . .

Reversed and remanded.

APPENDIX TO OPINION OF THE COURT

Policy Memorandum No. 7, November 30, 1959.

The authority of the Judge of the Juvenile Court of the District of Columbia to waive or transfer jurisdiction to the U.S. District Court for the District of Columbia is contained in the Juvenile Court Act. This section permits the Judge to waive jurisdiction "after full investigation" in the case of any child "sixteen years of age or older [who is] charged with an offense which would amount to a felony in the case of an adult, or any child charged with an offense which if committed by an adult is punishable by death or life imprisonment."

The statute sets forth no specific standards for the exercise of this important discretionary act, but leaves the formulation of such criteria to the Judge. A knowledge of the Judge's criteria is important to the child, his parents, his attorney, to the judges of the U.S. District Court for the District of Columbia, to the United States Attorney and his assistants and to the Metropolitan Police Department, as well as to the staff of this court, especially the Juvenile Intake Section.

Therefore, the Judge has consulted with the Chief Judge and other judges of the U.S. District Court for the District of Columbia, with the United States Attorney, with representatives of the Bar, and with other groups concerned and has formulated the following criteria and principles concerning waiver of jurisdiction which are consistent with the basic aims and purpose of the Juvenile Court Act.

An offense falling within the statutory limitations [set forth above] will be waived if it has prosecutive merit and if it is heinous or of an aggravated character, or — even though less serious — if it represents a pattern of repeated offenses which indicate, that the juvenile may be beyond rehabilitation under Juvenile Court procedures, or if the public needs the protection afforded by such action.

The determinative factors which will be considered by the Judge in deciding whether the Juvenile Court's jurisdiction over such offenses will be waived are the following:

    1. The seriousness of the alleged offense to the community and whether the protection of the community requires waiver.

    2. Whether the alleged offense was committed in an aggressive, violent, premeditated or willful manner.

    3. Whether the alleged offense was against persons or against property, greater weight being given to offenses against persons especially if personal injury resulted.

4. The prosecutive merit of the complaint, i.e., whether there is evidence upon which a Grand Jury may be expected to return an indictment [to be determined by consultation with the United States Attorney].

5. The desirability of trial and disposition of the entire offense in one court when the juvenile's associates in the alleged offense are adults who will be charged with a crime in the U. S. District Court for the District of Columbia.

6. The sophistication and maturity of the juvenile as determined by consideration of his home, environmental situation, emotional attitude and pattern of living.

7. The record and previous history of the juvenile, including previous contacts with the Youth Aid Division, other law enforcement agencies, juvenile court's and other jurisdictions, prior periods of probation to this Court, or prior commitments to juvenile institutions.

8. The prospects for adequate protection of the public and the likelihood of reasonable rehabilitation of the juvenile [if he is found to have committed the alleged offense] by the use of procedures, services and facilities currently available to the Juvenile Court.

It will be the responsibility of any officer of the Court's staff assigned to make the investigation of any complaint in which waiver of jurisdiction is being considered to develop fully all available information which may bear upon the criteria and factors set forth above. Although not all such factors will be involved in an individual case, the Judge will consider the relevant factors in a specific case before reaching a conclusion to waive juvenile jurisdiction and transfer the case to the U.S. District Court for the District of Columbia for trial under the adult procedures of that Court.

NOTES AND QUESTIONS

1. Is the *Kent* decision grounded in constitutional law or is the case merely a matter of statutory interpretation? Is the opinion binding on state waiver provisions?

2. Suppose a statutory scheme allowed prosecutors to decide whether to bring a case in either juvenile or criminal court. Would the *Kent* protections be required to review a prosecutor's exercise of discretion? Consider *United States v. Bland* at § 5.03[C][1], *infra*.

3. Is the Policy Memorandum in the Appendix to the Court's opinion in *Kent* a useful device for judges making waiver decisions? Can you explain and justify each of the eight factors specified?

IN RE GAULT

Supreme Court of the United States
387 U.S. 1 (1967)

MR. JUSTICE FORTAS *delivered the opinion of the Court.*

This is an appeal from a judgment of the Supreme Court of Arizona affirming the dismissal of a petition for a writ of *habeas corpus*. The petition sought the release of Gerald Francis Gault, appellants' 15-year-old son, who had been committed as a juvenile delinquent to the State Industrial School by the Juvenile Court of Gila County, Arizona. The Supreme Court of Arizona affirmed dismissal of the writ against various arguments which included an attack upon the constitutionality of the Arizona Juvenile Code because of its alleged denial of procedural due process rights to juveniles charged with being "delinquents." The court agreed that the constitutional guarantee of due process of law is applicable in such proceedings. It held that Arizona's Juvenile Code is to be read as "impliedly" implementing the "due process concept." It then proceeded to identify and describe "the particular elements which constitute due process in a juvenile hearing." It concluded that the proceedings ending in commitment of Gerald Gault did not offend those requirements. We do not agree, and we reverse. We begin with a statement of the facts.

I

On Monday, June 8, 1964, at about 10 a.m., Gerald Francis Gault and a friend, Ronald Lewis, were taken into custody by the Sheriff of Gila County. Gerald was then still subject to a six-month's probation order which had been entered on February 25, 1964, as a result of his having been in the company of another boy who had stolen a wallet from a lady's purse. The police action on June 8 was taken as the result of a verbal complaint by a neighbor of the boys, Mrs. Cook, about a telephone call made to her in which the caller or callers made lewd or indecent remarks. It will suffice for purposes of this opinion to say that the remarks or questions put to her were of the irritatingly offensive, adolescent, sex variety.

At the time Gerald was picked up, his mother and father were both at work. No notice that Gerald was being taken into custody was left at the home. No other steps were taken to advise them that their son had, in effect, been arrested. Gerald was taken to the Children's Detention Home. When his mother arrived home at about 6 o'clock, Gerald was not there. Gerald's older brother was sent to look for him at the trailer home of the Lewis family. He apparently learned then that Gerald was in custody. He so informed his mother. The two of them went to the Detention Home. The deputy probation officer, Flagg, who was also superintendent of the Detention Home, told Mrs. Gault "why Jerry was there" and said that a hearing would be held in Juvenile Court at 3 o'clock the following day, June 9.

Officer Flagg filed a petition with the court on the hearing day, June 9, 1964. It was not served on the Gaults. Indeed, none of them saw this petition until the *habeas corpus* hearing on August 17, 1964. The petition was entirely formal. It made no reference to any factual basis for the judicial action which it initiated. It recited only that "said minor is under the age of eighteen years, and is in need of the protection of this Honorable Court; [and that] said minor is a delinquent minor." It prayed for a hearing and an order regarding "the care and custody of said minor." Officer Flagg executed a formal affidavit in support of the petition.

On June 9, Gerald, his mother, his older brother, and Probation Officers Flagg and Henderson appeared before the Juvenile Judge in chambers. Gerald's father was not there. He was at work out of the city. Mrs. Cook, the complainant, was not there. No one was sworn at this hearing. No transcript or recording was made. No memorandum or record of the substance of the proceedings was prepared. Our information about the proceedings and the subsequent hearing on June 15, derives entirely from the testimony of the Juvenile Court Judge, Mr. and Mrs. Gault and Officer Flagg at the *habeas corpus* proceeding conducted two months later. From this, it appears that at the June 9 hearing Gerald was questioned by the judge about the telephone call. There was conflict as to what he said. His mother recalled that Gerald said he only dialed Mrs. Cook's number and handed the telephone to his friend, Ronald. Officer Flagg recalled that Gerald had admitted making the lewd remarks. Judge McGhee testified that Gerald "admitted making one of these [lewd] statements." At the conclusion of the hearing, the judge said he would "think about it." Gerald was taken back to the Detention Home. He was not sent to his own home with his parents. On June 11 or 12, after having been detained since June 8, Gerald was released and driven home.[2] There is no explanation in the record as to why he was kept in the Detention Home or why he was released. At 5 p.m. on the day of Gerald's release, Mrs. Gault received a note signed by Officer Flagg. It was on plain paper, not letterhead. Its entire text was as follows:

"Mrs. Gault: "Judge McGhee has set Monday June 15, 1964 at 11:00 a.m. as the date and time for further Hearings on Gerald's delinquency

"/s/ Flagg"

At the appointed time on Monday, June 15, Gerald, his father and mother, Ronald Lewis and his father, and Officers Flagg and Henderson were present before Judge McGhee. Witnesses at the *habeas corpus* proceeding differed in their recollections of Gerald's testimony at the June 15 hearing. Mr. and Mrs. Gault recalled that Gerald again testified that he had only dialed the number and that the other boy had made the remarks. Officer Flagg agreed that at this hearing Gerald did not admit making the lewd remarks. But Judge McGhee recalled that "there was some admission again of some of the lewd statements. He — he didn't admit any of the more serious lewd statements." Again, the complainant, Mrs. Cook, was not present. Mrs. Gault asked that Mrs. Cook be present "so she could see which boy that done the talking, the dirty talking over the phone." The Juvenile Judge said "she didn't have to be

---

2 [2] There is a conflict between the recollection of Mrs. Gault and that of Officer Flagg. Mrs. Gault testified that Gerald was released on Friday, June 12, Officer Flagg that it had been on Thursday, June 11. This was from memory; he had no record, and the note hereafter referred to was undated.

present at that hearing." The judge did not speak to Mrs. Cook or communicate with her at any time. Probation Officer Flagg had talked to her once — over the telephone on June 9.

At this June 15 hearing a "referral report" made by the probation officers was filed with the court, although not disclosed to Gerald or his parents. This listed the charge as "Lewd Phone Calls." At the conclusion of the hearing, the judge committed Gerald as a juvenile delinquent to the State Industrial School "for the period of his minority [that is, until 21], unless sooner discharged by due process of law." An order to that effect was entered. It recites that "after a full hearing and due deliberation the Court finds that said minor is a delinquent child, and that said minor is of the age of 15 years."

No appeal is permitted by Arizona law in juvenile cases. On August 3, 1964, a petition for a writ of *habeas corpus* was filed with the Supreme Court of Arizona and referred by it to the Superior Court for hearing. At the *habeas corpus* hearing on August 17, Judge McGhee was vigorously cross-examined as to the basis for his actions. He testified that he had taken into account the fact that Gerald was on probation. He was asked "under what section of . . . the code you found the boy delinquent?"

His answer is set forth in the margin.[3] In substance, he concluded that Gerald came within ARS § 8-201(6)(a), which specifies that a "delinquent child" includes one "who has violated a law of the state or an ordinance or regulation of a political subdivision thereof." The law which Gerald was found to have violated is ARS § 13-377. This section of the Arizona Criminal Code provides that a person who "in the presence or hearing of any woman or child . . . uses vulgar, abusive or obscene language, is guilty of a misdemeanor. . . ." The penalty specified in the Criminal Code, which would apply to an adult, is $5 to $50, or imprisonment for not more than two months. The judge also testified that he acted under ARS § 8-201(6)(d) which includes in the definition of a "delinquent child" one who, as the judge phrased it, is "habitually involved in immoral matters."[4]

Asked about the basis for his conclusion that Gerald was "habitually involved in immoral matters," the judge testified, somewhat vaguely, that two years earlier, on July 2, 1962, a "referral" was made concerning Gerald, "where the boy had stolen a baseball glove from another boy and lied to the Police Department about it." The judge said there was "no hearing," and "no

---

[3] [5] "Q. All right. Now, Judge, would you tell me under what section of the law or tell me under what section of — of the code you found the boy delinquent?

"A. Well, there is a — I think it amounts to disturbing the peace. I can't give you the section, but I can tell you the law, that when one person uses lewd language in the presence of another person, that it can amount to — and I consider that when a person makes it over the phone, that it is considered in the presence, I might be wrong, that is one section. The other section upon which I consider the boy delinquent is § 8-201(d), habitually involved in immoral matters."

[4] [6] ARS § 8-201(6), the section of the Arizona Juvenile Code which defines a delinquent child, reads: "Delinquent child" includes:

   "(a) A child who has violated a law of the state or an ordinance or regulation of a political subdivision thereof. "(b) A child who, by reason of being incorrigible, wayward or habitually disobedient, is uncontrolled by his parent, guardian or custodian. "(c) A child who is habitually truant from school or home. "(d) A child who habitually so deports himself as to injure or endanger the morals or health of himself or others."

accusation" relating to this incident, "because of lack of material foundation." But it seems to have remained in his mind as a relevant factor. The judge also testified that Gerald had admitted making other nuisance phone calls in the past which, as the judge recalled the boy's testimony, were "silly calls, or funny calls, or something like that."

The Superior Court dismissed the writ, and appellants sought review in the Arizona Supreme Court. That court stated that it considered appellants' assignments of error as urging (1) that the Juvenile Code is unconstitutional because it does not require that parents and children be appraised of the specific charges, does not require proper notice of a hearing, and does not provide for an appeal; and (2) that the proceedings and order relating to Gerald constituted a denial of due process of law because of the absence of adequate notice of the charge and the hearing; failure to notify appellants of certain constitutional rights including the rights to counsel and to confrontation, and the privilege against self-incrimination; the use of unsworn hearsay testimony; and the failure to make a record of the proceedings. Appellants further asserted that it was error for the Juvenile Court to remove Gerald from the custody of his parents without a showing and finding of their unsuitability, and alleged a miscellany of other errors under state law.

The Supreme Court handed down an elaborate and wide-ranging opinion affirming dismissal of the writ and stating the court's conclusions as to the issues raised by appellants and other aspects of the juvenile process. In their jurisdictional statement and brief in this Court, appellants do not urge upon us all of the points passed upon by the Supreme Court of Arizona. They urge that we hold the Juvenile Code of Arizona invalid on its face or as applied in this case because, contrary to the Due Process Clause of the Fourteenth Amendment, the juvenile is taken from the custody of his parents and committed to a state institution pursuant to proceedings in which the Juvenile Court has virtually unlimited discretion, and in which the following basic rights are denied:

1. Notice of the charges;

2. Right to counsel;

3. Right to confrontation and cross-examination;

4. Privilege against self-incrimination;

5. Right to a transcript of the proceedings; and

6. Right to appellate review.

. . . .

II

The Supreme Court of Arizona held that due process of law is requisite to the constitutional validity of proceedings in which a court reaches the conclusion that a juvenile has been at fault, has engaged in conduct prohibited by law, or has other wise misbehaved with the consequence that he is committed to an institution in which his freedom is curtailed. This conclusion is in accord with the decisions of a number of courts under both federal and state constitutions.

This Court has not heretofore decided the precise question. In *Kent v. United States*, we considered the requirements for a valid waiver of the "exclusive" jurisdiction of the Juvenile Court of the District of Columbia so that a juvenile could be tried in the adult criminal court of the District. Although our decision turned upon the language of the statute, we emphasized the necessity that "the basic requirements of due process and fairness" be satisfied in such proceedings. . . . [W]hatever [the] precise impact, neither the Fourteenth Amendment nor the Bill of Rights is for adults alone.

We do not in this opinion consider the impact of these constitutional provisions upon the totality of the relationship of the juvenile and the state. We do not even consider the entire process relating to juvenile "delinquents." For example, we are not here concerned with the procedures or constitutional rights applicable to the pre-judicial stages of the juvenile process, nor do we direct our attention to the post-adjudicative or dispositional process. We consider only the problems presented to us by this case. These relate to the proceedings by which a determination is made as to whether a juvenile is a 'delinquent' as a result of alleged misconduct on his part, with the consequence that he may be committed to a state institution. As to these proceedings, there appears to be little current dissent from the proposition that the Due Process Clause has a role to play. The problem is to ascertain the precise impact of the due process requirement upon such proceedings.

From the inception of the juvenile court system, wide differences have been tolerated — indeed insisted upon — between the procedural rights accorded to adults and those of juveniles. In practically all jurisdictions, there are rights granted to adults which are withheld from juveniles. In addition to the specific problems involved in the present case, for example, it has been held that the juvenile is not entitled to bail, to indictment by grand jury, to a public trial or to trial by jury. It is frequent practice that rules governing the arrest and interrogation of adults by the police are not observed in the case of juveniles.

The history and theory underlying this development are well-known, but a recapitulation is necessary for purposes of this opinion. The Juvenile Court movement began in this county at the end of the last century. From the juvenile court statute adopted in Illinois in 1899, the system has spread to every State in the Union, the District of Columbia, and Puerto Rico.[5] The constitutionality of juvenile court laws has been sustained in over 40 jurisdictions against a variety of attacks.

---

[5] [14] *See* NATIONAL COUNCIL OF JUVENILE COURT JUDGES, DIRECTORY AND MANUAL (1964). The number of Juvenile Judges as of 1964 is listed as 2,987, of whom 213 are full-time Juvenile Court Judges. The Nat'l Crime Comm'n Report indicates that half of these judges have no undergraduate degree, a fifth have no college education at all, a fifth are not members of the bar, and three-quarters devote less than one-quarter of their time to juvenile matters. *See also* McCune, *Profile of the Nation's Juvenile Court Judges*, which is a detailed statistical study of Juvenile Court Judges, and indicates additionally that about a quarter of these judges have no law school training at all. About one-third of all judges have no probation and social work staff available to them; between eighty and ninety percent have no available psychologist or psychiatrist. It has been observed that while "good will, compassion, and similar virtues are . . . admirably prevalent throughout the system . . . expertise, the keystone of the whole venture, is lacking." In 1965, over 697,000 delinquency cases (excluding traffic) were disposed of in these courts, involving some 601,000 children, or 2% of all children between 10 and 17.

The early reformers were appalled by adult procedures and penalties, and by the fact that children could be given long prison sentences and mixed in jails with hardened criminals. They were profoundly convinced that society's duty to the child could not be confined by the concept of justice alone. They believed that society's role was not to ascertain whether the child was "guilty" or "innocent," but "What is he, how has he become what he is, and what had best be done in his interest and in the interest of the state to save him from a downward career." The child — essentially good, as they saw it — was to be made "to feel that he is the object of [the state's] care and solicitude," not that he was under arrest or on trial. The rules of criminal procedure were therefore altogether inapplicable. The apparent rigidities, technicalities, and harshness which they observed in both substantive and procedural criminal law were therefore to be discarded. The idea of crime and punishment was to be abandoned. The child was to be "treated" and "rehabilitated" and the procedures, from apprehension through institutionalization, were to be "clinical" rather than punitive.

These results were to be achieved, without coming to conceptual and constitutional grief, by insisting that the proceedings were not adversary, but that the state was proceeding as *parens patriae*.[6] The Latin phrase proved to be a great help to those who sought to rationalize the exclusion of juveniles from the constitutional scheme; but its meaning is murky and its historic credentials are of dubious relevance. The phrase was taken from chancery practice, where, however, it was used to describe the power of the state to act *in loco parentis* for the purpose of protecting the property interests and the person of the child. But there is no trace of the doctrine in the history of criminal jurisprudence. At common law, children under seven were considered incapable of possessing criminal intent. Beyond that age, they were subjected to arrest, trial, and in theory to punishment like adult offenders. In these old days, the state was not deemed to have authority to accord them fewer procedural rights than adults.

The right of the state, as *parens patriae*, to deny to the child procedural rights available to his elders was elaborated by the assertion that a child, unlike an adult, has a right "not to liberty but to custody." He can be made to attorn to his parents, to go to school, etc. If his parents default in effectively performing their custodial functions — that is, if the child is "delinquent" — the state may intervene. In doing so, it does not deprive the child of any rights, because he has none. It merely provides the "custody" to which the child is entitled. On this basis, proceedings involving juveniles were described as "civil" not "criminal" and therefore not subject to the requirements which restrict the state when it seeks to deprive a person of his liberty.

---

6 [18] There seems to have been little early constitutional objection to the special procedures of juvenile courts. *But see* Waite, *How Far Can Court Procedure Be Socialized Without Impairing Individual Rights*, 12 J.Crim. L. & Criminology 339, 340 (1922):

> The court which must direct its procedure even apparently to do something to a child because of what he has done, is parted from the court which is avowedly concerned only with doing something for a child because of what he is and needs, by a gulf too wide to be bridged by any humanity which the judge may introduce into his hearings, or by the habitual use of corrective rather than punitive methods after conviction.

Accordingly, the highest motives and most enlightened impulses led to a peculiar system for juveniles, unknown to our law in any comparable context. The constitutional and theoretical basis for this peculiar system is — to say the least — debatable. And in practice the results have not been entirely satisfactory.[7] Juvenile Court history has again demonstrated that unbridled discretion, however benevolently motivated, is frequently a poor substitute for principle and procedure. In 1937, Dean Pound wrote: "The powers of the Star Chamber were a trifle in comparison with those of our juvenile courts . . ."[8] The absence of substantive standards has not necessarily meant that children received careful, compassionate, individualized treatment. The absence of procedural rules based upon constitutional principle has not always produced fair, efficient, and effective procedures. Departures from established principles of due process have frequently resulted not in enlightened procedure, but in arbitrariness. The Chairman of the Pennsylvania Council of Juvenile Court Judges has recently observed: "Unfortunately, loose procedures, high-handed methods and crowded court calendars, either singly or in combination, all too often, have resulted in depriving some juveniles of fundamental rights that have resulted in a denial of due process."

Failure to observe the fundamental requirements of due process has resulted in instances, which might have been avoided, of unfairness to individuals and inadequate or inaccurate findings of fact and unfortunate prescriptions of remedy. Due process of law is the primary and indispensable foundation of individual freedom. It is the basic and essential term in the social compact which defines the rights of the individual and delimits the powers which the state may exercise. As Mr. Justice Frankfurter has said: "The history of American freedom is, in no small measure, the history of procedure." But, in addition, the procedural rules which have been fashioned from the generality of due process are our best instruments for the distillation and evaluation of essential facts from the conflicting welter of data that life and our adversary methods present. It is these instruments of due process which enhance the possibility that truth will emerge from the confrontation of opposing versions and conflicting data. "Procedure is to law what 'scientific method' is to science."

It is claimed that juveniles obtain benefits from the special procedures applicable to them which more than offset the disadvantages of denial of the substance of normal due process. As we shall discuss, the observance of due

---

[7] [23] There is evidence . . . that there may be grounds for concern that the child receives the worst of both worlds: that he gets neither the protections accorded to adults nor the solicitous care and regenerative treatment postulated for children." . . . On the other hand, while this opinion and much recent writing concentrate upon the failures of the Juvenile Court system to live up to the expectations of its founders, the observation of the Nat'l Crime Comm'n Report should be kept in mind: "Although its shortcomings are many and its results too often disappointing, the juvenile justice system in many cities is operated by people who are better educated and more highly skilled, can call on more and better facilities and services, and has more ancillary agencies to which to refer its clientele than its adult counterpart."

[8] [24] Foreword to Young, *Social Treatment in Probation and Delinquency* (1937), p. xxvii. The 1965 Report of the United States Commission on Civil Rights, *"Law Enforcement — A Report on Equal Protection in the South,"* pp. 80–83, documents numerous instances in which "local authorities used the broad discretion afforded them by the absence of safeguards [in the juvenile process]" to punish, intimidate, and obstruct youthful participants in civil rights demonstrations.

process standards, intelligently and not ruthlessly administered, will not compel the States to abandon or displace any of the substantive benefits of the juvenile process. But it is important, we think, that the claimed benefits of the juvenile process should be candidly appraised. Neither sentiment nor folklore should cause us to shut our eyes, for example, to such startling findings as that reported in an exceptionally reliable study of repeaters or recidivism conducted by the Standford Research Institute for the President's Commission on Crime in the District of Columbia. This Commission's Report states:

> In fiscal 1966 approximately 66 percent of the 16-and 17-year-old juveniles referred to the court by the Youth Aid Division had been before the court previously. In 1965, 56 percent of those in the Receiving Home were repeaters. The SRI study revealed that 61 percent of the sample Juvenile Court referrals in 1965 had been previously referred at least once and that 42 percent had been referred at least twice before.

Certainly, these figures and the high crime rates among juveniles to which we have referred could not lead us to conclude that the absence of constitutional protections reduces crime, or that the juvenile system, functioning free of constitutional inhibitions as it has largely done, is effective to reduce crime or rehabilitate offenders. We do not mean by this to denigrate the juvenile court process or to suggest that there are not aspects of the juvenile system relating to offenders which are valuable. But the features of the juvenile system which its proponents have asserted are of unique benefit will not be impaired by constitutional domestication. For example, the commendable principles relating to the processing and treatment of juveniles separately from adults are in no way involved or affected by the procedural issues under discussion.[9] Further, we are told that one of the important benefits of the special juvenile court procedures is that they avoid classifying the juvenile as a "criminal." The juvenile offender is now classed as a "delinquent." There is, of course, no reason why this should not continue. It is disconcerting, however, that this term has come to involve only slightly less stigma than the term "criminal" applied to adults.[10] It is also emphasized that in practically all jurisdictions, statutes provide that an adjudication of the child as a delinquent shall not operate as a civil disability or disqualify him for civil

---

[9] [30] Here again, however, there is substantial question as to whether fact and pretension, with respect to the separate handling and treatment of children, coincide. While we are concerned only with procedure before the juvenile court in this case, it should be noted that to the extent that the special procedures for juveniles are thought to be justified by the special consideration and treatment afforded them, there is reason to doubt that juveniles always receive the benefits of such a quid pro quo. . . . The high rate of juvenile recidivism casts some doubt upon the adequacy of treatment afforded juveniles. In fact, some courts have recently indicated that appropriate treatment is essential to the validity of juvenile custody, and therefore that a juvenile may challenge the validity of his custody on the ground that he is not in fact receiving any special treatment.

[10] [31] "[T]he word "delinquent" has today developed such invidious connotations that the terminology is in the process of being altered; the new descriptive phrase is "persons in need of supervision," usually shortened to "pins." The N.Y. Family Court Act § 712 distinguishes between "delinquents" and "persons in need of supervision."

service appointment. There is no reason why the application of due process requirements should interfere with such provisions.

Beyond this, it is frequently said that juveniles are protected by the process from disclosure of their deviational behavior. As the Supreme Court of Arizona phrased it in the present case, the summary procedures of Juvenile Courts are sometimes defended by a statement that it is the law's policy "to hide youthful errors from the full gaze of the public and bury them in the graveyard of the forgotten past." This claim of secrecy, however, is more rhetoric than reality. Disclosure of court records is discretionary with the judge in most jurisdictions. Statutory restrictions almost invariably apply only to the court records, and even as to those the evidence is that many courts routinely furnish information to the FBI and the military, and on request to government agencies and even to private employers. Of more importance are police records. In most States the police keep a complete file of juvenile "police contacts" and have complete discretion as to disclosure of juvenile records. Police departments receive requests for information from the FBI and other law-enforcement agencies, the Armed Forces, and social service agencies, and most of them generally comply. Private employers word their application forms to produce information concerning juvenile arrests and court proceedings, and in some jurisdictions information concerning juvenile police contacts is furnished private employers as well as government agencies.

In any event, there is no reason why, consistently with due process, a State cannot continue if it deems it appropriate, to provide and to improve provision for the confidentiality of records of police contacts and court action relating to juveniles. . . .

Further, it is urged that the juvenile benefits from informal proceedings in the court. The early conception of the Juvenile Court proceeding was one in which a fatherly judge touched the heart and conscience of the erring youth by talking over his problems, by paternal advice and admonition, and in which, in extreme situations, benevolent and wise institutions of the State provided guidance and help "to save him from downward career." Then, as now, goodwill and compassion were admirably prevalent. But recent studies have, with surprising unanimity, entered sharp dissent as to the validity of this gentle conception. They suggest that the appearance as well as the actuality of fairness, impartiality and orderliness — in short, the essentials of due process — may be a more impressive and more therapeutic attitude so far as the juvenile is concerned. . . . While due process requirements will, in some instances, introduce a degree of order and regularity to Juvenile Court proceedings to determine delinquency, and in contested cases will introduce some elements of the adversary system, nothing will require that the conception of the kindly juvenile judge be replaced by its opposite, nor do we here rule upon the question whether ordinary due process requirements must be observed with respect to hearings to determine the disposition of the delinquent child.

Ultimately, however, we confront the reality of that portion of the Juvenile Court process with which we deal in this case. A boy is charged with misconduct. The boy is committed to an institution where he may be restrained of liberty for years. It is of no constitutional consequence — and of limited practical meaning — that the institution to which he is committed is called an Industrial School. The fact of the matter is that, however euphemistic the title, a "receiving home" or an "industrial school" for juveniles is an institution of confinement in which the child is incarcerated for a greater or lesser time. His world becomes "a building with whitewashed walls, regimented routine and institutional hours. . . ." Instead of mother and father and sisters and brothers and friends and classmates, his world is peopled by guards, custodians, state employees, and "delinquents" confined with him for anything from waywardness to rape and homicide.

In view of this, it would be extraordinary if our Constitution did not require the procedural regularity and the exercise of care implied in the phrase "due process." Under our Constitution, the condition of being a boy does not justify a kangaroo court. The traditional ideas of Juvenile Court procedure, indeed, contemplated that time would be available and care would be used to establish precisely what the juvenile did and why he did it — was it a prank of adolescence or a brutal act threatening serious consequences to himself for society unless corrected? Under traditional notions, one would assume that in a case like that of Gerald Gault, where the juvenile appears to have a home, a working mother and father, and an older brother, the Juvenile Judge would have made a careful inquiry and judgment as to the possibility that the boy could be disciplined and dealt with at home, despite his previous transgressions. Indeed, so far as appears in the record before us, except for some conversation with Gerald about his school work and his "wanting to go to . . . [the] Grand Canyon with his father," the points to which the judge directed his attention were little different from those that would be involved in determining any charge of violation of a penal statute. The essential difference between Gerald's case and a normal criminal case is that safeguards available to adults were discarded in Gerald's case. The summary procedure as well as the long commitment was possible because Gerald's was 15 years of age instead of over 18.

If Gerald had been over 18, he would not have been subject to Juvenile Court proceedings. For the particular offense immediately involved, the maximum punishment would have been a fine of $5 to $50, or imprisonment in jail for not more than two months. Instead, he was committed to custody for a maximum of six years. If he had been over 18 and had committed an offense to which such a sentence might apply, he would have been entitled to substantial rights under the Constitution of the United States as well as under Arizona's laws and constitution. The United States Constitution would guarantee him rights and protections with respect to arrest, search, and seizure, and pretrial interrogation. It would assure him of specific notice of the charges and adequate time to decide his course of action and to prepare his defense. He would be entitled to clear advice that he could be represented by counsel, and, at least if a felony were involved, the State would be required to provide counsel if his parents were unable to afford it. If the court acted on the basis of his confession, careful procedures would be required to assure its voluntariness. If the case went to trial, confrontation and opportunity for cross-examination would be guaranteed. So wide a gulf between the State's treatment of the adult and of the child requires a bridge sturdier than mere verbiage, and reasons more persuasive than cliche can provide. . . .

. . . .

We now turn to the specific issues which are presented to us in the present case.

III

NOTICE OF CHARGES

. . . .

We cannot agree with the court's conclusion that adequate notice was given in this case. Notice, to comply with due process requirements, must be given sufficiently in advance of scheduled court proceedings so that reasonable opportunity to prepare will be afforded, and it must "set forth the alleged misconduct with particularity." It is obvious, as we have discussed above, that no purpose of shielding the child from the public stigma of knowledge of his having been taken into custody and scheduled for hearing is served by the procedure approved by the court below. The "initial hearing" in the present case was a hearing on the merits. Notice at that time is not timely; and even if there were a conceivable purpose served by the deferral proposed by the court below, it would have to yield to the requirements that the child and his parents or guardian be notified, in writing, of the specific charge or factual allegations to be considered at the hearing, and that such written notice be given at the earliest practicable time, and in any event sufficiently in advance of the hearing to permit preparation. Due process of law requires notice of the sort we have described — that is, notice which would be deemed constitutionally adequate in a civil or criminal proceeding. It does not allow a hearing to be held in which a youth's freedom and his parents' right to his custody are at stake without giving them timely notice, in advance of the hearing, of the specific issues that they must meet. Nor, in the circumstances of this case, can it reasonably be said that the requirement of notice was waived.

IV

RIGHT TO COUNSEL

Appellants charge that the Juvenile Court proceedings were fatally defective because the court did not advise Gerald or his parents of their right to counsel, and proceeded with the hearing, the adjudication of delinquency and the order of commitment in the absence of counsel for the child and his parents or an express waiver of the right thereto. The Supreme Court of Arizona pointed out that "[t]here is disagreement [among the various jurisdictions] as to whether the court must advise the infant that he has a right to counsel." . . . It noted its own decision . . . to the effect "that *the parents* of an infant in a juvenile proceeding cannot be denied representation by counsel of their choosing." It referred to a provision of the Juvenile Code which it characterized as requiring "that the probation officer shall look after the interests of neglected, delinquent and dependent children," including representing their interests in court. The court argued that "The parent and the probation officer

may be relied upon to protect the infant's interests." Accordingly it rejected the proposition that "due process requires that an infant have a right to counsel." It said that juvenile courts have the discretion, but not the duty, to allow such representation; it referred specifically to the situation in which the Juvenile Court discerns conflict between the child and his parents as an instance in which this discretion might be exercised. We do not agree. Probation officers, in the Arizona scheme, are also arresting officers. They initiate proceedings and file petitions which they verify, as here, alleging the delinquency of the child; and they testify, as here, against the child. And here the probation officer was also superintendent of the Detention Home. The probation officer cannot act as counsel for the child. His role in the adjudicatory hearing, by statute and in fact, is as arresting officer and witness against the child. Nor can the judge represent the child. There is no material difference in this respect between adult and juvenile proceedings of the sort here involved. In adult proceedings, this contention has been foreclosed by decisions of this Court. A proceeding where the issue is whether the child will be found to be "delinquent" and subjected to the loss of his liberty for years is comparable in seriousness to a felony prosecution. The juvenile needs the assistance of counsel to cope with problems of law, to make skilled inquiry into the facts, to insist upon regularity of the proceedings, and to ascertain whether he has a defense and to prepare and submit it. The child "requires the guiding hand of counsel at every step in the proceedings against him."
. . .

During the last decade, court decisions, experts, and legislatures have demonstrated increasing recognition of this view. In at least one-third of the States, statutes now provide for the right of representation by retained counsel in juvenile delinquency proceedings, notice of the right, or assignment of counsel, or a combination of these. In other States, court rules have similar provisions.

The President's Crime Commission has recently recommended that in order to assure "procedural justice for the child," it is necessary that "Counsel . . . be appointed as a matter of course wherever coercive action is a possibility, without requiring any affirmative choice by child or parent." . . .

. . . .

We conclude that the Due Process Clause of the Fourteenth Amendment requires that in respect of proceedings to determine delinquency which may result in commitment to an institution in which the juvenile's freedom is curtailed, the child and his parents must be notified of the child's right to be represented by counsel retained by them, or if they are unable to afford counsel, that counsel will be appointed to represent the child.

. . . .

V

CONFRONTATION, SELF-INCRIMINATION, CROSS-EXAMINATION

Appellants urge that the writ of *habeas corpus* should have been granted because of the denial of the rights of confrontation and cross-examination in the Juvenile Court hearings, and because the privilege against self-incrimination was not observed. The Juvenile Court Judge testified at the *habeas corpus* hearing that he had proceeded on the basis of Gerald's admissions at the two hearings. Appellants attack this on the ground that the admissions were obtained in disregard of the privilege against self-incrimination. If the confession is disregarded, appellants argue that the delinquency conclusion, since it was fundamentally based on a finding that Gerald had made lewd remarks during the phone call to Mrs. Cook, is fatally defective for failure to accord the rights of confrontation and cross-examination which the Due Process Clause of the Fourteenth Amendment of the Federal Constitution guarantees in state proceedings generally.

. . . .

We shall assume that Gerald made admissions of the sort described by the Juvenile Court Judge, as quoted above. Neither Gerald nor his parents were advised that he did not have to testify or make a statement, or that an incriminating statement might result in his commitment as a "delinquent."

The Arizona Supreme Court rejected appellants' contention that Gerald had a right to be advised that he need not incriminate himself. It said: "We think the necessary flexibility for individualized treatment will be enhanced by a rule which does not require the judge to advise the infant of a privilege against self-incrimination."

In reviewing this conclusion of Arizona's Supreme Court, we emphasize again that we are here concerned only with a proceeding to determine whether a minor is a "delinquent" and which may result in commitment to a state institution. Specifically, the question is whether, in such a proceeding, an admission by the juvenile may be used against him in the absence of clear and unequivocal evidence that the admission was made with knowledge that he was not obliged to speak and would not be penalized for remaining silent. In light of *Miranda v. State of Arizona*, 384 U.S. 436 (1966), we must also consider whether, if the privilege against self-incrimination is available, it can effectively be waived unless counsel is present or the right to counsel has been waived.

. . . .

The privilege against self-incrimination is, of course, related to the question of the safeguards necessary to assure that admissions or confessions are reasonably trustworthy, that they are not the mere fruits of fear or coercion, but are reliable expressions of the truth. The roots of the privilege are, however, far deeper. They tap the basic stream of religious and political principle because the privilege reflects the limits of the individuals's attornment to the state and — in a philosophical sense — insists upon the equality of the individual and the state. In other words, the privilege has a broader and deeper thrust than the rule which prevents the use of confessions which are the product of coercion because coercion is thought to carry with it the danger of unreliability. One of its purposes is to prevent the state, whether by force or by psychological domination, from overcoming the mind and will of the person under investigation and depriving him of the freedom to decide whether to assist the state in securing his conviction.

It would indeed be surprising if the privilege against self-incrimination were available to hardened criminals but not to children. The language of the Fifth Amendment, applicable to the States by operation of the Fourteenth Amendment, is unequivocal and without exception. . . .

. . . .

Against the application to juveniles of the right to silence, it is argued that juvenile proceedings are "civil" and not "criminal," and therefore the privilege should not apply. It is true that the statement of the privilege in the Fifth Amendment, which is applicable to the States by reason of the Fourteenth Amendment, is that no person "shall be compelled in any criminal case to be a witness against himself." However, it is also clear that the availability of the privilege does not turn upon the type of proceeding in which its protection is invoked, but upon the nature of the statement or admission and the exposure which it invites. The privilege may, for example, be claimed in a civil or administrative proceeding, if the statement is or may be inculpatory.

It would be entirely unrealistic to carve out of the Fifth Amendment all statements by juveniles on the ground that these cannot lead to "criminal involvement. In the first place, juvenile proceedings to determine "delinquency," which may lead to commitment to a state institution, must be regarded as "criminal" for purposes of the privilege against self-incrimination. To hold otherwise would be to disregard substance because of the feeble enticement of the "civil" label-of-convenience which has been attached to juvenile proceedings. Indeed, in over half of the States, there is not even assurance that the juvenile will be kept in separate institutions, apart from adult "criminals." In those States juveniles may be placed in or transferred to adult penal institutions after having been found "delinquent" by a juvenile court. For this purpose, at least, commitment is a deprivation of liberty. It is incarceration against one's will, whether it is called "criminal" or "civil." And our Constitution guarantees that no person shall be "compelled" to be a witness against himself when he is threatened with deprivation of his liberty — a command which this Court has broadly applied and generously implemented in accordance with the teaching of the history of the privilege and its great office in mankind's battle for freedom.

In addition, apart from the equivalence for this purpose of exposure to commitment as a juvenile delinquent and exposure to imprisonment as an adult offender, the fact of the matter is that there is little or no assurance in Arizona, as in most if not all of the States, that a juvenile apprehended and interrogated by the police or even by the Juvenile Court itself will remain outside of the reach of adult courts as a consequence of the offense for which he has been taken into custody. In Arizona, as in other States, provision is made for Juvenile courts to relinquish or waive jurisdiction to the ordinary criminal courts. In the present case, when Gerald Gault was interrogated concerning violation of a section of the Arizona Criminal Code, it could not be certain that the Juvenile Court Judge would decide to "suspend" criminal prosecution in court for adults by proceeding to an adjudication in Juvenile Court.

It is also urged, as the Supreme Court of Arizona here asserted, that the juvenile and presumably his parents should not be advised of the juvenile's right to silence because confession is good for the child as the commencement of the assumed therapy of the juvenile court process, and he should be encouraged to assume an attitude of trust and confidence toward the officials of the juvenile process. This proposition has been subjected to widespread challenge on the basis of current reappraisals of the rhetoric and realities of the handling of juvenile offenders.

In fact, evidence is accumulating that confessions by juveniles do not aid in "individualized treatment," as the court below put it, and that compelling the child to answer questions, without warning or advice as to his right to remain silent, does not serve this or any other good purpose. In light of the observations of [some], it seems probable that where children are induced to confess by "paternal" urgings on the part of officials and the confession is then followed by disciplinary action, the child's reaction is likely to be hostile and adverse — the child may well feel that he has been led or tricked into confession and that despite his confession, he is being punished.

Further, authoritative opinion has cast formidable doubt upon the reliability and trustworthiness of "confessions" by children. . . .

. . . .

The "confession" of Gerald Gault was first obtained by Officer Flagg, out of the presence of Gerald's parents, without counsel and without advising him of his right to silence, as far as appears. The judgment of the Juvenile Court was stated by the judge to be based on Gerald's admissions in court. Neither "admission" was reduced to writing, and, to say the least, the process by which the "admissions," were obtained and received must be characterized as lacking the certainty and order which are required of proceedings of such formidable consequences. Apart from the "admission" there was nothing upon which a judgment or finding might be based. There was no sworn testimony. Mrs. Cook, the complainant, was not present. The Arizona Supreme court held that "sworn testimony must be required of all witnesses including police officers, probation officers and others who are part of or officially related to the juvenile court structure." We hold that this is not enough. No reason is suggested or appears for a different rule in respect of sworn testimony in juvenile courts than in adult tribunals. Absent a valid confession adequate to support the determination of the Juvenile Court, confrontation and sworn testimony by witnesses available for cross-examination were essential for a finding of "delinquency" and an order committing Gerald to a state institution for a maximum of six years.

. . . .

As we said in *Kent* with respect to waiver proceedings, "there is no place in our system of law of reaching a result of such tremendous consequences without ceremony. . . ." We now hold that, absent a valid confession, a determination of delinquency and an order of commitment to a state institution cannot be sustained in the absence of sworn testimony subjected to the opportunity for cross-examination in accordance with our law and constitutional requirements.

VI

APPELLATE REVIEW AND TRANSCRIPT OF PROCEEDINGS

Appellants urge that the Arizona statute is unconstitutional under the Due Process Clause because, as construed by its Supreme Court, "there is no right of appeal from a juvenile court order. . . ." The court held that there is no right to a transcript because there is no right to appeal and because the proceedings are confidential and any record must be destroyed after a prescribed period of time. Whether a transcript or other recording is made, it held, is a matter for the discretion of the juvenile court.

This Court has not held that a State is required by the Federal Constitution "to provide appellate courts or a right to appellate review at all." In view of the fact that we must reverse the Supreme Court of Arizona's affirmance of the dismissal of the writ of *habeas corpus* for other reasons, we need not rule on this question in the present case or upon the failure to provide a transcript or recording of the hearings — or, indeed, the failure of the Juvenile Judge to state the grounds for his conclusion. [In] *Kent* we said, in the context of a decision of the juvenile court waiving jurisdiction to the adult court, which by local law, was permissible: ". . . it is incumbent upon the Juvenile Court to accompany its waiver order with a statement of the reasons or considerations therefor." As the present case illustrates, the consequences of failure to provide an appeal, to record the proceedings, or to make findings or state the grounds for the juvenile court's conclusion may be to throw a burden upon the machinery for *habeas corpus*, to saddle the reviewing process with the burden of attempting to reconstruct a record, and to impose upon the Juvenile Judge the unseemly duty of testifying under cross-examination as to the events that transpired in the hearings before him.

For the reasons stated, the judgment of the Supreme Court of Arizona is reversed and the cause remanded for further proceedings not inconsistent with this opinion. It is so ordered.

Judgment reversed and cause remanded with directions.

[The concurring of opinion of JUSTICE BLACK and the concurring opinion of JUSTICE WHITE have been omitted.]

MR. JUSTICE HARLAN, *concurring in part and dissenting in part.*

Each of the 50 States has created a system of juvenile or family courts, in which distinctive rules are employed and special consequences imposed. The jurisdiction of these courts commonly extends both to cases which the States have withdrawn from the ordinary processes of criminal justice, and to cases which involve acts that, if performed by an adult, would not be penalized as criminal. Such courts are denominated civil, not criminal, and are characteristically said not to administer criminal penalties. One consequence of these systems, at least as Arizona construes its own, is that certain of the rights guaranteed to criminal defendants by the Constitution are withheld from juveniles. This case brings before this Court for the first time the question of what limitations the Constitution places upon the operation of such tribunals. For reasons which follow, I have concluded that the Court has gone too far in some respects, and fallen short in others, in assessing the procedural requirements demanded by the Fourteenth Amendment.

. . . .

The central issue here, and the principal one upon which I am divided from the Court, is the method by which the procedural requirements of due process should be measured. . . .

. . . .

No more evidence of the importance of the public interests at stake here is required than that furnished by the opinion of the Court; it indicates that "some 601,000 children under 18, or 2% of all children between 10 and 17, came before juvenile courts" in 1965, and that "about one-fifth of all arrests for serious crimes" in 1965 were of juveniles. The Court adds that the rate of juvenile crime is steadily rising. All this, as the Court suggests, indicates the importance of these due process issues, but it mirrors no less vividly that state authorities are confronted by formidable and immediate problems involving the most fundamental social values. The state legislatures have determined that the most hopeful solution for these problems is to be found in specialized courts, organized under their own rules and imposing distinctive consequences. The terms and limitations of these systems are not identical, nor are the procedural arrangements which they include, but the States are uniform in their insistence that the ordinary processes of criminal justice are inappropriate, and that relatively informal proceedings, dedicated to premises and purposes only imperfectly reflected in the criminal law, are instead necessary.

It is well settled that the Court must give the widest deference to legislative judgments that concern the character and urgency of the problems with which the State is confronted. Legislatures are, as this Court has often acknowledged, the "main guardian" of the public interest, and, within their constitutional competence, their understanding of that interest must be accepted as "wellnigh" conclusive. This principle does not, however, reach all the questions essential to the resolution of this case. The legislative judgments at issue here embrace assessments of the necessity and wisdom of procedural guarantees; these are questions which the Constitution has entrusted at least in part to courts, and upon which courts have been understood to possess particular competence. The fundamental issue here is, therefore, in what measure and fashion the Court must defer to legislative determinations which encompass constitutional issues of procedural protection.

It suffices for present purposes to summarize the factors which I believe to be pertinent. It must first be emphasized that the deference given to legislators upon substantive issues must realistically extend in part to ancillary procedural questions. Procedure at once reflects and creates substantive rights, and every effort of courts since the beginnings of the common law to separate the two has proved essentially futile. The distinction between them is particularly inadequate here, where the legislature's substantive preferences directly and unavoidably require judgments about procedural issues. The procedural framework is here a principal element of the substantive legislative system; meaningful deference to the latter must include a portion of deference to the former. The substantive-procedural dichotomy is nonetheless, an indispensable tool of analysis, for it stems from fundamental limitations upon judicial authority under the Constitution. Its premise is ultimately that courts may not substitute for the judgments of legislators their own understanding of the public welfare, but must instead concern themselves with the validity under the Constitution of the methods which the legislature has selected. The Constitution has in this manner created for courts and legislators areas of primary responsibility which are essentially congruent to their areas of special competence. Courts are thus obliged both by constitutional command and by their distinctive functions to bear particular responsibility for the measurement of procedural due process. These factors in combination suggest that legislatures may properly expect only a cautious deference for their procedural judgments, but that, conversely, courts must exercise their special responsibility for procedural guarantees with care to permit ample scope for achieving the purposes of legislative programs. Plainly, courts can exercise such care only if they have in each case first studied thoroughly the objectives and implementation of the program at stake; if, upon completion of those studies, the effect of extensive procedural restrictions upon valid legislative purposes cannot be assessed with reasonable certainty, the court should necessarily proceed with restraint.

The foregoing considerations, which I believe to be fair distillations of relevant judicial history, suggest three criteria by which the procedural requirements of due process should be measured here: first, no more restrictions should be imposed than are imperative to assure the proceedings' fundamental fairness; second, the restrictions which are imposed should be those which preserve, so far as possible, the essential elements of the State's purpose; and finally, restrictions should be chosen which will later permit the orderly selection of any additional protections which may ultimately prove necessary. In this way, the Court may guarantee the fundamental fairness of the proceeding, and yet permit the State to continue development of an effective response to the problems of juvenile crime.

Measured by these criteria, only three procedural requirements should, in my opinion, now be deemed required of state juvenile courts by the Due Process Clause of the Fourteenth Amendment: first, timely notice must be provided to parents and children of the nature and terms of any juvenile court proceeding in which a determination affecting their rights or interests may be made; second, unequivocal and timely notice must be given that counsel may appear in any such proceeding in behalf of the child and its parents, and that in cases in which the child may be confined in an institution, counsel may, in circumstances of indigency, be appointed for them; and third, the court must maintain a written record, or its equivalent, adequate to permit effective review on appeal or in collateral proceedings. These requirements would guarantee to juveniles the tools with which their rights could be fully vindicated, and yet permit the States to pursue without unnecessary hindrance the purposes which they believe imperative in this field. Further, their imposition now would later permit more intelligent assessment of the necessity under the Fourteenth Amendment of additional requirements, by creating suitable records from which the character and deficiencies of juvenile proceedings could be accurately judged. . . .

[The dissenting opinion of JUSTICE STEWART has been omitted.]

––––––

NOTES AND QUESTIONS

1. Prior to *Gault*, policy makers had been free from Supreme Court oversight to fashion juvenile court systems as they saw fit. Historically, procedural informality was considered an essential virtue of juvenile court practice. As one commentator noted:

> Not only was the aim of a court for children to differ from that of the criminal court; its way of going about things was to be changed as well. Procedure had to be 'socialized.' 'The purpose of the juvenile court is to prevent the child's being tried and treated as a criminal; all means should be taken to prevent the child and his parents from forming the conception that the child is being tried for a crime.' The respondent to a petition filed in his own interest replaced the defendant to a criminal charge filed in the interest of the state. Trials by jury should be permitted 'under no circumstances,' because 'they are inconsistent with both the law and the theory upon which children's codes are founded.' Hearings were not to be 'public trials' lest youngsters be damaged by publicity. Little or no need would be found for the respondent to have a lawyer; 'the judge represents both parties and the law.' . . .

> Not to be overlooked is another aspect of the insistence on informality in court. The community has never been much concerned with the impact of criminal procedure on the feelings of an accused. If he is terrified by the courtroom scene, so much the better. A malefactor might thus be convicted never to return. The reformers, on the other hand, sought to dispel the fear that can accompany a child's day in court. They perceived the appearance before the juvenile court judge as the beginning of the treatment process, a beginning that should not make the total job of serving a child's needs more difficult. If the state is to act like a father, its representative, the judge, should act like one at the hearing. The respondent child . . . should 'be made to feel that he is the object of [the court's] care and solicitude. The ordinary trappings of the courtroom are out of place in such hearings. The judge on a bench, looking down upon the boy standing at the bar, can never evoke a proper sympathetic spirit. Seated at a desk, with the child at his side, where he can on occasion put his arm around his shoulder and draw the lad to him, the judge, while losing none of his judicial dignity, will gain immensely in the effectiveness of his work.'

Monrad G. Paulsen, Kent v. United States: *The Constitutional Context of Juvenile Cases,* 1966 SUP. CT. REV. 167, 170–72.

Professor Barry Feld has summarized the traditional rationale for, and the extent of, relaxed procedure in juvenile court:

In distinguishing children from adult offenders, the juvenile court . . . rejected the procedures of criminal prosecution. It introduced a euphemistic vocabulary and a physically separate court building to avoid the stigma of adult prosecutions, and it modified courtroom procedures to eliminate any implication of a criminal proceeding. For example, proceedings were initiated by a petition in the welfare of the child, rather than by a criminal complaint. Because the important issues involved the child's background and welfare rather than the commission of a specific crime, courts dispensed with juries, lawyers, rules of evidence, and formal procedures. To avoid stigmatization, hearings were confidential and private, access to court records was limited, and youths were found to be 'delinquent' rather than guilty of an offense. To make proceedings more personal and private, the judge was supposed to sit next to the child while court personnel presented a treatment plan to meet the child's needs as determined by a background investigation identifying the sources of the child's misconduct. Dispositions were indeterminate and nonproportional and could continue for the duration of minority. The events that brought the child before the court affected neither the degree nor the duration of intervention because each child's needs differed and no limits could be defined in advance. The dispositional process was designed to determine why the child was in court in the first instance and what could be done to change the character, attitude, and behavior of the youth to prevent a reappearance.

Barry C. Feld, *Criminalizing Juvenile Justice: Rules of Procedure for the Juvenile Court*, 69 MINN. L. REV. 141, 150–51 (1984).

To what degree did the *Gault* Court alter the traditional procedural practices of the juvenile courts? Is there merit to Justice Harlan's dissenting view that some of the requirements imposed by the *Gault* majority go too far because they frustrate the substantive mission of juvenile courts?

2. At several points the *Gault* Court mentions that its opinion speaks to "delinquency adjudications." Is such language meant to limit *Gault* to that context, or might the opinion extend to other phases of juvenile justice such as status offense adjudications or to pre or post adjudication proceedings?

3. Suppose that Gerald Gault is readjudicated, this time with all the protections required by the *Gault* Court. If he is again found to have committed the act of delinquency (making the obscene phone call), could he again be committed to the State Industrial School until he turns twenty-one years old? If so, are there serious questions about such a commitment that are left unresolved by *Gault* and its focus on procedural issues?

4. Despite *Gault's* promise of a right to counsel for juvenile offenders, there is reason to believe that the promise remains unrealized. Statistics indicate that in some jurisdictions, more than half of the juveniles appearing in juvenile court did so without counsel. Barry C. Feld, In re Gault *Revisited: A Cross-State Comparison of the Right to Counsel in Juvenile Court,* 34 CRIME & DELING. 33, 394 (1988). Moreover, juveniles with counsel are more likely to be incarcerated than juveniles without counsel, regardless of the types of

offenses with which they are charged. *Id.* at 396. Does this mean that juveniles with lawyers are actually *disadvantaged*? If so, what might account for such a situation?

5. Considering the discussion of general theories of juvenile rights in Chapter 1, does the *Gault* Court appear to embrace either the protectionist or personhood view?

IN RE WINSHIP

Supreme Court of the United States
397 U.S. 358 (1970)

Mr. Justice Brennan *delivered the opinion of the Court.*

Constitutional questions decided by this Court concerning the juvenile process have centered on the adjudicatory stage at "which a determination is made as to whether a juvenile is a 'delinquent' as a result of alleged misconduct on his part, with the consequence that he may be committed to a state institution." *Gault* decided that, although the Fourteenth Amendment does not require that the hearing at this stage conform with all the requirements of a criminal trial or even of the usual administrative proceeding, the Due Process Clause does require application during the adjudicatory hearing of "the essentials of due process and fair treatment." This case presents the single, narrow question whether proof beyond a reasonable doubt is among the "essentials of due process and fair treatment" required during the adjudicatory stage when a juvenile is charged with an act which would constitute a crime if committed by an adult.[11] Section 712 of the New York Family Court Act defines a juvenile delinquent as "a person over seven and less than sixteen years of age who does any act which, if done by an adult, would constitute a crime." During a 1967 adjudicatory hearing, a judge in New York Family Court found that appellant, then a 12-year-old boy, had entered a locker and stolen $112 from a woman's pocketbook. The petition which charged appellant with delinquency alleged that his act, "if done by an adult, would constitute . . . [l]arceny." The judge acknowledged that the proof might not establish guilt beyond a reasonable doubt, but rejected appellant's contention that such proof was required by the Fourteenth Amendment. The judge relied instead on § 744(b) of the New York Family Court Act which provides that "[a]ny determination at the conclusion of [an adjudicatory] hearing that a [juvenile] did an act or acts must be based on a preponderance of the evidence." During a subsequent dispositional hearing, appellant was ordered

---

[11] [1] . . . [W]e do not see how it can be said in dissent that this opinion "rests entirely on the assumption that all juvenile proceedings are 'criminal prosecutions,' hence subject to constitutional limitations." As in *Gault,* "we are not here concerned with . . . the pre-judicial stages of the juvenile process, nor do we direct our attention to the post-adjudicative or dispositional process." . . . In New York, the adjudicatory stage of a delinquency proceeding is clearly distinct from both the preliminary phase of the juvenile process and from its dispositional stage. . . . Similarly, we intimate no view concerning the constitutionality of the New York procedures governing children "in need of supervision." . . . Nor do we consider whether there are other "essentials of due process and fair treatment" required during the adjudicatory hearing of a delinquency proceeding. Finally, we have no occasion to consider appellant's argument that [the statute] is a violation of the Equal Protection Clause, as well as a denial of due process.

placed in a training school for an initial period of 18 months, subject to annual extensions of his commitment until his 18th birthday — six years in appellant's case. The Appellate Division of the New York Supreme Court, First Judicial Department, affirmed. . . . The New York Court of Appeals then affirmed by a four-to-three vote, expressly sustaining the constitutionality of § 744(b). . . . We reverse.

I

The requirement that guilt of a criminal charge be established by proof beyond a reasonable doubt dates at least from our early years as a Nation. . . . Expressions in many opinions of this Court indicate that it has long been assumed that proof of a criminal charge beyond a reasonable doubt is constitutionally required. Mr. Justice Frankfurter stated that "[i]t is the duty of the Government to establish . . . guilt beyond a reasonable doubt. This notion — basic in our law and rightly one of the boasts of a free society — is a requirement and a safeguard of due process of law in the historic, procedural content of "due process."" . . . These rules are historically grounded rights of our system, developed to safeguard men from dubious and unjust convictions, with resulting forfeitures of life, liberty and property. . . .

The reasonable-doubt standard plays a vital role in the American scheme of criminal procedure. It is a prime instrument for reducing the risk of convictions resting on factual error. The standard provides concrete substance for the presumption of innocence — that bedrock "axiomatic and elementary" principle whose "enforcement lies at the foundation of the administration of our criminal law." . . . "[A] person accused of a crime . . . would be at a severe disadvantage, a disadvantage amounting to a lack of fundamental fairness, if he could be adjudged guilty and imprisoned for years on the strength of the same evidence as would suffice in a civil case."

The requirement of proof beyond a reasonable doubt has this vital role in our criminal procedure for cogent reasons. The accused during a criminal prosecution has at stake interest of immense importance, both because of the possibility that he may lose his liberty upon conviction and because of the certainty that he would be stigmatized by the conviction. Accordingly, a society that values the good name and freedom of every individual should not condemn a man for commission of a crime when there is reasonable doubt about his guilt. . . . "Due process commands that no man shall lose his liberty unless the Government has borne the burden of . . . convincing the fact finder of his guilt." To this end, the reasonable-doubt standard is indispensable, for it "impresses on the trier of fact the necessity of reaching a subjective state of certitude of the facts in issue."

Moreover, use of the reasonable-doubt standard is indispensable to command the respect and confidence of the community in applications of the criminal law. It is critical that the moral force of the criminal law not be diluted by a standard of proof that leaves people in doubt whether innocent men are being condemned. It is also important in our free society that every individual going about his ordinary affairs have confidence that his government cannot adjudge him guilty of a criminal offense without convincing a proper fact finder of his guilt with utmost certainty.

Lest there remain any doubt about the constitutional statute of the reasonable-doubt standard, we explicitly hold that the Due Process Clause protects the accused against conviction except upon proof beyond a reasonable doubt of every fact necessary to constitute the crime with which he is charged.

II

We turn to the question whether juveniles, like adults, are constitutionally entitled to proof beyond a reasonable doubt when they are charged with violation of a criminal law. The same considerations that demand extreme caution in fact finding to protect the innocent adult apply as well to the innocent child. We do not find convincing the contrary arguments of the New York Court of Appeals, *Gault* rendered untenable much of the reasoning relied upon by that court to sustain the constitutionality of § 744(b). The Court of Appeals indicated that a delinquency adjudication "is not a 'conviction'; that it affects no right or privilege, including the right to hold public office or to obtain a license; and a cloak of protective confidentiality is thrown around all the proceedings." The court said further: "The delinquency status is not made a crime; and the proceedings are not criminal. There is, hence, no deprivation of due process in the statutory provision. . . ." In effect the Court of Appeals distinguished the proceedings in question here from a criminal prosecution by use of what *Gault* called the "civil label-of-convenience which has been attached to juvenile proceedings." But *Gault* expressly rejected that distinction as a reason for holding the Due Process Clause inapplicable to a juvenile proceeding. The Court of Appeals also attempted to justify the preponderance standard on the related ground that juvenile proceedings are designed "not to punish, but to save the child." Again, however, *Gault* expressly rejected this justification. We made clear in that decision that civil labels and good intentions do not themselves obviate the need for criminal due process safeguards in juvenile courts, for "[a] proceeding where the issue is whether the child will be found to be 'delinquent' and subjected to the loss of his liberty for years is comparable in seriousness to a felony prosecution."

Nor do we perceive any merit in the argument that to afford juveniles the protection of proof beyond a reasonable doubt would risk destruction of beneficial aspects of the juvenile process.[12] Use of the reasonable-doubt standard during the adjudicatory hearing will not disturb New York's policies that a finding that a child has violated a criminal law does not constitute a criminal conviction, that such a finding does not deprive the child of his civil rights, and that juvenile proceedings are confidential. Nor will there be any effect on the informality, flexibility, or speed of the hearing at which the fact finding

---

12 [4] Appellee, New York City, apparently concedes as much in its Brief . . . where it states: "A determination that the New York law unconstitutionally denies due process because it does not provide for use of the reasonable doubt standard probably would not have a serious impact if all that resulted would be a change in the quantum of proof." And Dorsen & Rezneck . . . have observed:

> [T]he reasonable doubt test is superior to all others in protecting against an unjust adjudication of guilt, and that is as much a concern of the juvenile court as of the criminal court. It is difficult to see how the distinctive objectives of the juvenile court give rise to a legitimate institutional interest in finding a juvenile to have committed a violation of the criminal law on less evidence than if he were an adult.

takes place. And the opportunity during the post-adjudicatory or dispositional hearing for a wide-ranging review of the child's social history and for his individualized treatment will remain unimpaired. Similarly, there will be no effect on the procedures distinctive to juvenile proceedings that are employed prior to the adjudicatory hearing.

The Court of Appeals observed that "a child's best interest is not necessarily, or even probably, promoted if he wins in the particular inquiry which may bring him to the juvenile court." It is true, of course, that the juvenile may be engaging in a general course of conduct inimical to his welfare that calls for judicial intervention. But that intervention cannot take the form of subjecting the child to the stigma of a finding that he violated a criminal law[13] and to the possibility of institutional confinement of proof insufficient to convict him were he an adult.

We conclude, as we concluded regarding the essential due process safeguards applied in *Gault*, that the observance of the standard of proof beyond a reasonable doubt "will not compel the States to abandon or displace any of the substantive benefits of the juvenile process."

Finally, we reject the Court of Appeals' suggestion that there is, in any event, only a "tenuous difference" between the reasonable-doubt and preponderance standards. The suggestion is singularly unpersuasive. In this very case, the trial judge's ability to distinguish between the two standards enabled him to make a finding of guilt that he conceded he might not have made under the standard of proof beyond a reasonable doubt. Indeed, the trial judge's action evidences the accuracy of the observation of commentators that "the preponderance test is susceptible to the misinterpretation that it calls on the trier of fact merely to perform an abstract weighing of the evidence in order to determine which side has produced the greater quantum, without regard to its effect in convincing his mind of the truth of the proposition asserted."

III

In sum, the constitutional safeguard of proof beyond a reasonable doubt is as much required during the adjudicatory stage of a delinquency proceeding as are those constitutional safeguards applied in *Gault* — notice of charges, right to counsel, the rights of confrontation and examination, and the privilege against self-incrimination. We therefore hold . . . "that, where a 12-year-old child is charged with an act of stealing which renders him liable to confinement for as long as six years, then, as a matter of due process . . . the case against him must be proved beyond a reasonable doubt."

Reversed.

Mr. Justice Harlan, *concurring*.

No one, I daresay, would contend that state juvenile court trials are subject to no federal constitutional limitations. . . .

---

[13] [5] The more comprehensive and effective the procedures used to prevent public disclosure of the finding, the less the danger of stigma. As we indicated in *Gault*, however, often the "claim of secrecy . . . is more rhetoric than reality."

. . . While I am in full agreement that this statutory provision offends the requirement of fundamental fairness embodied in the Due Process Clause of the Fourteenth Amendment, I [write separately] lest the true nature of the constitutional problem presented become obscured or the impact on state juvenile court systems of what the Court holds today be exaggerated.

. . . .

II

When one assesses the consequences of an erroneous factual determination in a juvenile delinquency proceeding in which a youth is accused of a crime, I think it must be concluded that, while the consequences are not identical to those in a criminal case, the differences will not support a distinction in the standard of proof. First, and of paramount importance, a factual error here, as in a criminal case, exposes the accused to a complete loss of his personal liberty through a state-imposed confinement away from his home, family, and friends. And, second, a delinquency determination, to some extent at least, stigmatizes a youth in that it is by definition bottomed on a finding that the accused committed a crime.[14] Although there are no doubt costs to society (and possibly even to the youth himself) in letting a guilty youth go free, I think here, as in a criminal case, it is far worse to declare an innocent youth a delinquent. I, therefore, agree that a juvenile court judge should be no less convinced of the factual conclusion that the accused committed the criminal act with which he is charged than would be required in a criminal trial.

III

I wish to emphasize, as I did in my separate opinion in *Gault* that there is no automatic congruence between the procedural requirements imposed by due process in a criminal case, and those imposed by due process in juvenile cases. It is of great importance, in my view, that procedural strictures not be constitutionally imposed that jeopardize "the essential elements of the State's purpose" in creating juvenile courts. In this regard, I think it worth emphasizing that the requirement of proof beyond a reasonable doubt that a juvenile committed a criminal act before he is found to be a delinquent does not (1) interfere with the worthy goal of rehabilitating the juvenile, (2) make any significant difference in the extent to which a youth is stigmatized as a

---

14 [6] The New York statute was amended to distinguish between a "juvenile delinquent," *i.e.,* a youth "who does any act which, if done by an adult, would constitute a crime" and a "[p]erson in need of supervision" [PINS] who is a person "who is an habitual truant or who is incorrigible, ungovernable or habitually disobedient and beyond the lawful control of parent or other lawful authority." The PINS category was established . . . to avoid the stigma of finding someone to be a "juvenile delinquent" unless he committed a criminal act. The Legislative Committee report stated: "juvenile delinquent" is now a term of disapproval. The judges of the Children's Court and the Domestic Relations Court of course are aware of this and also aware that government officials and private employers often learn of an adjudication of delinquency." Moreover, the powers of the police and courts differ in these two categories of cases. Thus, in a PINS type case, the consequences of an erroneous factual determination are by no means identical to those involved here.

"criminal" because he has been found to be a delinquent, or (3) burden the juvenile courts with a procedural requirement that will make juvenile adjudications significantly more time consuming, or rigid. Today's decision simply requires a juvenile court judge to be more confident in his belief that the youth did the act with which he has been charged.

With these observations, I join the Court's opinion, subject only to the constitutional reservations expressed in my opinion in *Gault*.

MR. CHIEF JUSTICE BURGER, with whom MR. JUSTICE STEWART joins, *dissenting*.

The Court's opinion today rests entirely on the assumption that all juvenile proceeds are "criminal prosecutions," hence subject to constitutional limitations. This derives from earlier holdings, which, like today's holding, were steps eroding the difference between juvenile courts and traditional criminal courts. The original concept of the juvenile court system was to provide a benevolent and less formal means than criminal courts could provide for dealing with the special and often sensitive problems of youthful offenders. Since I see no constitutional requirement of due process sufficient to overcome the legislative judgment of the States in this area, I dissent from further strait jacketing of an already overly restricted system. What the juvenile court system needs is not more but less of the trappings of legal procedure and judicial formalism; the juvenile court system requires breathing room and flexibility in order to survive, if it can survive the repeated assaults from this Court.

Much of the judicial attitude manifested by the Court's opinion today and earlier holdings in this field is really a protest against inadequate juvenile court staffs and facilities. . . . The lack of support and the distressing growth of juvenile crime have combined to make for a literal breakdown in many if not most juvenile courts. Constitutional problems were not seen while those courts functioned in an atmosphere where juvenile judges were not crushed with an avalanche of cases.

My hope is that today's decision will not spell the end of a generously conceived program of compassionate treatment intended to mitigate the rigors and trauma of exposing youthful offenders to a traditional criminal court; each step we take turns the clock back to the pre-juvenile-court era. I cannot regard it as a manifestation of progress to transform juvenile courts into criminal courts, which is what we are well on the way to accomplishing. We can only hope the legislative response will not reflect our own by having these courts abolished.

[The dissenting opinion of MR. JUSTICE BLACK is omitted.]

————

NOTES AND QUESTIONS

1. As in *Gault*, *Winship* arises in the context of a delinquency adjudication. Is there reason to believe that the Court's requirement of proof beyond a reasonable doubt might extend to status offense adjudications? This question

will be considered later in materials addressing status offense jurisdiction. *See* § 5.04[B], *infra*.

2. What is a "reasonable doubt"? What does it mean to be convinced *beyond* such a doubt? How *much* proof is "beyond a reasonable doubt?" While the answers to such questions are unclear, studies suggest that while factfinders sometimes disagree on how much proof is necessary, they do agree that "beyond a reasonable doubt" is more rigorous than the "preponderance of the evidence" standard. *See, e.g.,* JUDITH SIMON, JUDGES' TRANSLATIONS OF PROOF INTO STATEMENTS OF PROBABILITY (1969).

McKEIVER v. PENNSYLVANIA

Supreme Court of the United States
403 U.S. 528 (1971)

MR. JUSTICE BLACKMUN announced the judgments of the Court and an opinion in which THE CHIEF JUSTICE, MR. JUSTICE STEWART, and MR. JUSTICE WHITE join.

These cases present the narrow but precise issue whether the Due Process Clause of the Fourteenth Amendment assures the right to trial by jury in the adjudicative phase of a state juvenile court delinquency proceeding.

. . . .

. . . Joseph McKeiver, then age 16, in May 1968 was charged with robbery, larceny, and receiving stolen goods (felonies under Pennsylvania law . . .) as acts of juvenile delinquency. . . . McKeiver was adjudged a delinquent upon findings that he had violated a law of the Commonwealth. . . . On appeal, the Superior Court affirmed without opinion.

Edward Terry, then age 15, in January 1969 was charged with assault and battery on a police officer and conspiracy (misdemeanors under Pennsylvania law . . .) as acts of juvenile delinquency. His counsel's request for a jury trial was denied. . . . Terry was adjudged a delinquent on the charges. This followed an adjudication and commitment in the preceding week for an assault on a teacher. He was committed . . . to the Youth Development Center at Cornwells Heights. On appeal, the Superior Court affirmed without opinion.

The Supreme Court of Pennsylvania granted leave to appeal in both cases and consolidated them. The single question considered, as phrased by the court, was "whether there is a constitutional right to a jury trial in juvenile court." The answer, one justice dissenting, was in the negative. . . .

The details of the McKeiver and Terry offenses are set forth in Justice Roberts' opinion for the Pennsylvania court. . . . It suffices to say that McKeiver's offense was his participating with 20 or 30 youths who pursued three young teenagers and took 25 cents from them; that McKeiver never before had been arrested and had a record of gainful employment; that the testimony of two of the victims was described by the court as somewhat inconsistent and as "weak"; and that Terry's offense consisted of hitting a police officer with his fists and with a stick when the officer broke up a boys' fight Terry and others were watching.

. . . Barbara Burrus and approximately 45 other black children, ranging in age from 11 to 15 years, were the subjects of juvenile court summonses issued in Hyde County, North Carolina, in January 1969.

The charges arose out of a series of demonstrations in the county in late 1968 by black adults and children protesting school assignments and a school consolidation plan. Petitions were filed by North Carolina state highway patrolmen. Except for one relating to James Lambert Howard, the petitions charged the respective juveniles with wilfully impeding traffic. The charge against Howard was that he wilfully made riotous noise and was disorderly in the O. A. Peay School in Swan Quarter, interrupted and disturbed the school during its regular sessions; and defaced school furniture. The acts so charged are misdemeanors under North Carolina Law. . . .

The several cases were consolidated into groups for hearing before District Judge Hallett S. Ward, sitting as a juvenile court. The same lawyer appeared for all the juveniles. Over counsel's objection, made in all except two of the cases, the general public was excluded. A request for a jury trial in each case was denied.

The evidence as to the juveniles other than Howard consisted solely of testimony of highway patrolmen. No juvenile took the stand or offered any witness. The testimony was to the effect that on various occasions the juveniles and adults were observed walking along Highway 64 singing, shouting, clapping, and playing basketball. As a result, there was interference with traffic. The marchers were asked to leave the paved portion of the highway and they were warned that they were committing a statutory offense. They either refused or left the roadway and immediately returned. The juveniles and participating adults were taken into custody. Juvenile petitions were then filed with respect to those under the age of 16.

The evidence as to Howard was that on the morning of December 5, he was in the office of the principal of the O. A. Peay School with 15 other persons while school was in session and was moving furniture around; that the office was in disarray; that as a result the school closed before noon; and that neither he nor any of the others was a student at the school or authorized to enter the principal's office.

In each case the court found that the juvenile had committed "an act for which an adult may be punished by law." A custody order was entered declaring the juvenile a delinquent "in need of more suitable guardianship" and committing him to the custody of the County Department of Public Welfare for placement in a suitable institution "until such time as the Board of Juvenile Correction or the Superintendent of said institution may determine, not inconsistent with the laws of this State." The court, however, suspended these commitments and placed each juvenile on probation for either one or two years conditioned upon his violating none of the State's laws, upon his reporting monthly to the County Department of Welfare, upon his being home by 11 p.m. each evening, and upon his attending a school approved by the Welfare Director. None of the juveniles has been confined on these charges.

On appeal, the cases were consolidated into two groups. The North Carolina Court of Appeals affirmed. In its turn the Supreme Court of North Carolina deleted that portion of the order in each case relating to commitment, but otherwise affirmed. . . . We granted certiorari.

III

It is instructive to review, as an illustration, the substance of Justice Roberts' opinion for the Pennsylvania court. He observes . . . "[f]or over sixty-five years the Supreme Court gave no consideration at all to the constitutional problems involved in the juvenile court area"; that *Gault* "is somewhat of a paradox, being both broad and narrow at the same time"; that it "is broad in that it evidences a fundamental and far-reaching disillusionment with the anticipated benefits of the juvenile court system"; that it is narrow because the court enumerated four due process rights which it held applicable in juvenile proceedings, but declined to rule on two other claimed rights; that as a consequence the Pennsylvania court was "confronted with a sweeping rationale and a carefully tailored holding"; that the procedural safeguards "*Gault* specifically made applicable to juvenile courts have already caused a significant 'constitutional domestication' of juvenile court proceedings"; that those safeguards and other rights, including the reasonable-doubt standard established by *Winship*, "insure that the juvenile court will operate in an atmosphere which is orderly enough to impress the juvenile with the gravity of the situation and the impartiality of the tribunal and at the same time informal enough to permit the benefits of the juvenile system to operate"; that the "proper inquiry, then, is whether the right to a trial by jury is 'fundamental' . . . , in the context of a juvenile court which operates with all of the above constitutional safeguards"; and that his court's inquiry turned "upon whether there are elements in the juvenile process which render the right to a trial by jury less essential to the protection of an accused's rights in the juvenile system than in the normal criminal process."

Justice Roberts then concluded that such factors do inhere in the Pennsylvania juvenile system: (1) Although realizing that "faith in the quality of the juvenile bench is not an entirely satisfactory substitute for due process" the judges in the juvenile courts "take a different view of their role than that taken by their counterparts in the criminal courts." (2) While one regrets its inadequacies, "the juvenile system has available and utilizes much more fully various diagnostic and rehabilitative services" that are "far superior to those available in the regular criminal process." (3) Although conceding that the post-adjudication process "has in many respects fallen far short of its goals, and its reality is far harsher than its theory," the end result of a declaration of delinquency "is significantly different from and less onerous than a finding of criminal guilt" and "we are not yet convinced that the current practices do not contain the seeds from which a truly appropriate system can be brought forth." (4) Finally, "of all the possible due process rights which could be applied in the juvenile courts, the right to trial by jury is the one which would most likely be disruptive of the unique nature of the juvenile process." It is the jury trial that "would probably require substantial alteration of the traditional practices." The other procedural rights held applicable to the juvenile process "will give the juveniles sufficient protection" and the addition of the trial by jury "might well destroy the traditional character of juvenile proceedings."

The court concluded that it was confident "that a properly structured and fairly administered juvenile court system can serve our present societal needs without infringing on individual freedoms."

IV

The right to an impartial jury "(i)n all criminal prosecutions" under federal law is guaranteed by the Sixth Amendment. Through the Fourteenth Amendment that requirement has now been imposed upon the States "in all criminal cases which — were they to be tried in a federal court — would come within the Sixth Amendment's guarantee." This is because the Court has said it believes "that trial by jury in criminal cases is fundamental to the American scheme of justice."

This, of course, does not automatically provide the answer to the present jury trial issue, if for no other reason than that the juvenile court proceeding has not yet been held to be a "criminal prosecution," within the meaning and reach of the Sixth Amendment, and also has not yet been regarded as devoid of criminal aspects merely because it usually has been given the civil label.

Little, indeed, is to be gained by any attempt simplistically to call the juvenile court proceeding either "civil" or "criminal." The Court carefully has avoided this wooden approach. Before *Gault* was decided in 1967, the Fifth Amendment's guarantee against self-incrimination had been imposed upon the state criminal trial. So, too, had the Sixth Amendment's right of confrontation and cross-examination. Yet the Court did not automatically and peremptorily apply those rights to the juvenile proceeding. A reading of *Gault* reveals the opposite. And the same separate approach to the standard-of-proof issue is evident from the carefully separated application of the standard, first to the criminal trial, and then to the juvenile proceeding, displayed in *Winship*.

Thus, accepting "the proposition that the Due Process Clause has a role to play," our task here with respect to trial by jury, as it was in *Gault* with respect to other claimed rights, "is to ascertain the precise impact of the due process requirement."

V

The Pennsylvania juveniles' basic argument is that they were tried in proceedings "substantially similar to a criminal trial." They say that a delinquency proceeding in their State is initiated by a petition charging a penal code violation in the conclusory language of an indictment; that a juvenile detained prior to trial is held in a building substantially similar to an adult prison; that in Philadelphia juveniles over 16 are, in fact, held in the cells of a prison; that counsel and the prosecution engage in plea bargaining; that motions to suppress are routinely heard and decided; that the usual rules of evidence are applied; that the customary common-law defenses are available; that the press is generally admitted in the Philadelphia juvenile courtrooms; that members of the public enter the room; that arrest and prior record may be reported by the press (from police sources, however, rather than from the juvenile court records); that, once adjudged delinquent, a juvenile may be confined until his majority in what amounts to a prison and that the stigma attached upon delinquency adjudication approximates that resulting from conviction in an adult criminal proceeding.

The North Carolina juveniles particularly urge that the requirement of a jury trial would not operate to deny the supposed benefits of the juvenile court system; that the system's primary benefits are its discretionary intake procedure permitting disposition short of adjudication, and its flexible sentencing permitting emphasis on rehabilitation; that realization of these benefits does not depend upon dispensing with the jury; that adjudication of factual issues on the one hand and disposition of the case on the other are very different matters with very different purposes; that the purpose of the former is indistinguishable from that of the criminal trial; that the jury trial provides an independent protective factor; that experience has shown that jury trials in juvenile courts are manageable; that no reason exists why protection traditionally accorded in criminal proceedings should be denied young people subject to involuntary incarceration for lengthy periods; and that the juvenile courts deserve healthy public scrutiny.

VI

All the litigants here agree that the applicable due process standard in juvenile proceedings, as developed by *Gault* and *Winship*, is fundamental fairness. As that standard was applied in those two cases, we have an emphasis on fact-finding procedures. The requirements of notice, counsel, confrontation, cross-examination, and standard of proof naturally flowed from this emphasis. But one cannot say that in our legal system the jury is a necessary component of accurate fact-finding. There is much to be said for it, to be sure, but we have been content to pursue other ways for determining facts. Juries are not required, and have not been, for example, in equity cases, in workmen's compensation, in probate, or in deportation cases. Neither have they been generally used in military trials. . . .

We must recognize, as the Court has recognized before, that the fond and idealistic hopes of the juvenile court proponents and early reformers of three generations ago have not been realized. The devastating commentary upon the system's failures as a whole . . . reveals the depth of disappointment in what has been accomplished. Too often the juvenile court judge falls far short of that stalwart, protective, and communicating figure the system envisaged. The community's unwillingness to provide people and facilities and to be concerned, the insufficiency of time devoted, the scarcity of professional help, the inadequacy of dispositional alternatives, and our general lack of knowledge all contribute to dissatisfaction with the experiment.[15]

---

15 [5] "What emerges, then, is this: In theory the juvenile court was to be helpful and rehabilitative rather than punitive. In fact the distinction often disappears, not only because of the absence of facilities and personnel but also because of the limits of knowledge and technique. In theory the court's action was to affix no stigmatizing label. In fact a delinquent is generally viewed by employers, schools, the armed services — by society generally — as a criminal. In theory the court was to treat children guilty of criminal acts in noncriminal ways. In fact it labels truants and runaways as junior criminals.

"In theory the court's operations could justifiably be informal, its findings and decisions made without observing ordinary procedural safeguards, because it would act only in the best interest

The Task Force Report, however, also said: "To say that juvenile courts have failed to achieve their goals is to say no more than what is true of criminal courts in the United States. But failure is most striking when hopes are highest."

Despite all these disappointments, all these failures, and all these shortcomings, we conclude that trial by jury in the juvenile court's adjudicative stage is not a constitutional requirement. We so conclude for a number of reasons:

1. The Court has refrained, in the cases heretofore decided, from taking the easy way with a flat holding that all rights constitutionally assured for the adult accused are to be imposed upon the state juvenile proceedings. What was done in *Gault* and in *Winship* is aptly described. . . : "It is clear to us that the Supreme Court has properly attempted to strike a judicious balance by injecting procedural orderliness into the juvenile court system. It is seeking to reverse the trend (pointed out in *Kent*) whereby 'the child received the worst of both worlds'. . . ."

2. There is a possibility, at least, that the jury trial, if required as a matter of constitutional precept, will remake the juvenile proceeding into a fully adversary process and will put an effective end to what has been the idealistic prospect of an intimate, informal protective proceeding.

3. The Task Force Report, although concededly pre-*Gault*, is notable for its not making any recommendation that the jury trial be imposed upon the juvenile court system. This is so despite its vivid description of the system's deficiencies and disappointments. Had the Commission deemed this vital to the integrity of the juvenile process, or to the handling of juveniles, surely a recommendation or suggestion to this effect would have appeared. The intimations, instead, are quite the other way. . . . Further, it expressly recommends against abandonment of the system and against the return of the juvenile to the criminal courts.

. . . .

5. The imposition of the jury trial on the juvenile court system would not strengthen greatly, if at all, the fact-finding function, and would, contrarily, provide an attrition of the juvenile court's assumed ability to function in a unique manner. It would not remedy the defects of the system. . . . [A jury trial] would be regressive, would lose what has been gained, and would tend once again to place the juvenile squarely in the routine of the criminal process.

6. The juvenile concept held high promise. We are reluctant to say that, despite disappointments of grave dimensions, it still does not hold promise, and we are particularly reluctant to say . . . that the system cannot accomplish its rehabilitative goals. So much depends on the availability of resources, on the interest and commitment of the public, on willingness to learn, and

---

of the child. In fact it frequently does nothing more nor less than deprive a child of liberty without due process of law — knowing not what else to do and needing, whether admittedly or not, to act in the community's interest even more imperatively than the child's. In theory it was to exercise its protective powers to bring an errant child back into the fold. . . . [T]here is increasing reason to believe that its intervention reinforces the juvenile's unlawful impulses. In theory it was to concentrate on each case the best of current social science learning. In fact it has often become a vested interest in its turn, loathe to cooperate with innovative programs or avail itself of forward-looking methods."

on understanding as to cause and effect and cure. In this field, as in so many others, one perhaps learns best by doing. We are reluctant to disallow the States to experiment further and to seek in new and different ways the elusive answers to the problems of the young, and we feel that we would be impeding that experimentation by imposing the jury trial. The States, indeed, must go forward. If, in its wisdom, any State feels the jury trial is desirable in all cases, or in certain kinds, there appears to be no impediment to its installing a system embracing that feature. That, however, is the State's privilege and not its obligation.

7. Of course there have been abuses. . . . We refrain from saying at this point that those abuses are of constitutional dimension. They relate to the lack of resources and of dedication rather than to inherent unfairness.

8. There is, of course, nothing to prevent a juvenile court judge, in a particular case where he feels the need, or when the need is demonstrated, from using an advisory jury.

9. "The fact that a practice is followed by a large number of states is not conclusive in a decision as to whether that practice accords with due process, but it is plainly worth considering in determining whether the practice 'offends some principle of justice so rooted in the traditions and conscience of our people as to be ranked as fundamental.'" It therefore is of more than passing interest that at least 28 States and the District of Columbia by statute deny the juvenile a right to a jury trial in cases such as these. The same result is achieved in other States by judicial decision. In 10 States statutes provide for a jury trial under certain circumstances.

10. Since *Gault* . . . the great majority of States . . . that have faced the issue have concluded that the considerations that led to the result in those two cases do not compel trial by jury in the juvenile court.

. . . .

12. If the jury trial were to be injected into the juvenile court system as a matter of right, it would bring with it into that system the traditional delay, the formality, and the clamor of the adversary system and, possibly, the public trial. It is of interest that these very factors were stressed by the District Committee of the Senate when . . . it recommended, and Congress then approved, as a provision in the District of Columbia Crime Bill, the abolition of the jury trial in the juvenile court.

13. Finally, the arguments advanced by the juveniles here are, of course, the identical arguments that underlie the demand for the jury trial for criminal proceedings. The arguments necessarily equate the juvenile proceeding — or at least the adjudicative phase of it — with the criminal trial. Whether they should be so equated is our issue. Concern about the inapplicability of exclusionary and other rules of evidence, about the juvenile court judge's possible awareness of the juvenile's prior record and of the contents of the social file; about repeated appearances of the same familiar witnesses in the persons of juvenile and probation officers and social workers — all to the effect that this will create the likelihood of pre-judgment — chooses to ignore it seems to us, every aspect of fairness, of concern, of sympathy, and of paternal attention that the juvenile court system contemplates.

If the formalities of the criminal adjudicative process are to be superimposed upon the juvenile court system, there is little need for its separate existence. Perhaps that ultimate disillusionment will come one day, but for the moment we are disinclined to give impetus to it.

Affirmed.

[The concurring opinion of MR. JUSTICE WHITE has been omitted. The concurring and dissenting opinion by MR. JUSTICE BRENNAN has been omitted. The concurring and dissenting opinion of MR. JUSTICE DOUGLAS, joined by Justices BLACK and MARSHALL, has been omitted.]

———

NOTES AND QUESTIONS

1. After its decisions in *Gault* and *Winship*, is the Court's decision in *McKeiver* surprising? Do the reasons for extending the procedural rights in *Gault* and *Winship* similarly support recognition of the protection of jury trials? Are you convinced that jury trials, unlike the *Gault/Winship* protections, would frustrate the ability of juvenile courts to achieve their substantive goals?

2. One critic of *McKeiver* has argued that being deprived a jury trial hurts juveniles in several ways. Juries traditionally have been preferred because they lack access to background information about the accused that might cause judges and prosecutors to prejudge the case. Janet E. Ainsworth, *"Re-Imagining Childhood and Reconstructing the Legal Order: The Case for Abolishing the Juvenile Court,"* 69 N.C. L. REV. 1083, 1119 (1991). Morever, judges arguably convict more often than do juries, and jury trials require judges to articulate the law through instructions, which if erroneous, may be corrected on appeal, while judges conducting bench trials need not articulate instructions outlining their understanding of the law thus perhaps concealing from reviewing courts their misunderstanding or misapplication of the law. *Id.*

3. Whatever the possible negative impact of jury trials in juvenile courts, youthful offenders apparently seldom avail themselves of opportunities to jury trials in the few jurisdictions that allow such in juvenile proceedings. *See* Barry C. Feld, *Violent Youth and Public Policy: A Case Study of Juvenile Justice Law Reform,* 79 MINN. L. REV. 965, 1107 (1995).

4. *McKeiver* has not been well received by the commentators. *See, e.g.,* Barry C. Feld, *Criminalizing Juvenile Justice: Rules of Procedure for the Juvenile Court,* 69 MINN. L. REV. 141 (1984); Martin Guggenheim & Randy Hertz, *Reflections on Judges, Juries and Justice: Ensuring the Fairness of Juvenile Delinquency Trials,* 38 WAKE FOREST L. REV. 553 (1998); Irene M. Rosenberg, *The Constitutional Rights of Children Charged with Crime: Proposal for a Return to the Not So Distant Past,* 27 UCLA L. REV. 656 (1980).

BREED v. JONES

Supreme Court of the United States
421 U.S. 519 (1975)

Mr. Chief Justice Burger *delivered the opinion of the Court.*

We granted certiorari to decide whether the prosecution of respondent as an adult, after Juvenile Court proceedings which resulted in a finding that respondent had violated a criminal statute and a subsequent finding that he was unfit for treatment as a juvenile, violated the Fifth and Fourteenth Amendments to the United States Constitution.

On February 9, 1971, a petition was filed . . . [a]lleging that respondent, then 17 years of age, was a person described by Cal. Welf. & Inst'ns Code § 602 (1966), in that, on or about February 8, while armed with a deadly weapon, he had committed acts which, if committed by an adult, would constitute the crime of robbery . . . . The following day, a detention hearing was held, at the conclusion of which respondent was ordered detained pending a hearing on the petition. [At a subsequent adjudication hearing, the court found the allegations were true, and at a later disposition hearing, the court found the respondent was "not amenable to treatment." The court then ordered the respondent to be prosecuted as an adult.]

. . . .

After a preliminary hearing respondent was ordered held for trial in Superior Court, where an information was subsequently filed accusing him of having committed robbery . . . while armed with a deadly weapon . . . . Respondent entered a plea of not guilty, and he also pleaded that he had "already been placed once in jeopardy and convicted of the offense charged, by the judgment of the Superior Court of the County of Los Angeles, Juvenile Court, rendered . . . on the 1st day of March, 1971." . . . The court found respondent guilty of robbery in the first degree . . . and ordered that he be committed to the California Youth Authority. . . .

On December 10, 1971, respondent, through his mother as *guardian ad litem*, filed the instant petition for a writ of *habeas corpus* in the United States District Court for the Central District of California. In this petition he alleged that his transfer to adult court . . . and subsequent trial there "placed him in double jeopardy." . . . The District Court denied the petition, rejecting respondent's contention that jeopardy attached at his adjudicatory hearing. It concluded that the "distinctions between the preliminary procedures and hearings provided by California law for juveniles and a criminal trial are many and apparent and the effort of [respondent] to relate them is unconvincing," and that "even assuming jeopardy attached during the preliminary juvenile proceedings . . . it is clear that no new jeopardy arose by the juvenile proceeding sending the case to the criminal court."

The Court of Appeals reversed, concluding that applying double jeopardy protection to juvenile proceedings would not "impede the juvenile courts in carrying out their basic goal of rehabilitating the erring youth," and that the contrary result might "do irreparable harm to or destroy their confidence in our judicial system." The court therefore held that the Double Jeopardy Clause" is fully applicable to juvenile court proceedings."

Turning to the question whether there had been a constitutional violation in this case, the Court of Appeals pointed to the power of the Juvenile Court to "impose severe restrictions upon the juvenile's liberty," in support of its conclusion that jeopardy attached in respondent's adjudicatory hearing. It rejected petitioner's contention that no new jeopardy attached when respondent was referred to Superior Court and subsequently tried and convicted, finding "continuing jeopardy" principles advanced by petitioner inapplicable. Finally, the Court of Appeals observed that acceptance of petitioner's position would "allow the prosecution to review in advance the accused's defense and, as here, hear him testify about the crime charged," a procedure it found offensive to "our concepts of basic, even-handed fairness." The court therefore held that once jeopardy attached at the adjudicatory hearing, a minor could not be retried as an adult or a juvenile "absent some exception to the double jeopardy prohibition," and that there "was none here."

We granted certiorari because of a conflict between Courts of Appeals and the highest courts of a number of States on the issue presented in this case. . . .

. . . .

II

Jeopardy denotes risk. In the constitutional sense, jeopardy describes the risk that is traditionally associated with a criminal prosecution. Although the constitutional language, "jeopardy of life or limb," suggests proceedings in which only the most serious penalties can be imposed, the Clause has long been construed to mean something far broader than its literal language. At the same time, however, we have held that the risk to which the Clause refers is not present in proceedings that are not "essentially criminal."

Although the juvenile-court system had its genesis in the desire to provide a distinctive procedure and setting to deal with the problems of youth, including those manifested by antisocial conduct, our decisions in recent years have recognized that there is a gap between the originally benign conception of the system and its realities. With the exception of *McKeiver v. Pennsylvania*, the Court's response to that perception has been to make applicable in juvenile proceedings constitutional guarantees associated with traditional criminal prosecutions. In so doing the Court has evinced awareness of the threat which such a process represents to the efforts of the juvenile court system, functioning in a unique manner, to ameliorate the harshness of criminal justice when applied to youthful offenders. That the system has fallen short of the high expectations of its sponsors in no way detracts from the broad social benefits sought or from those benefits that can survive constitutional scrutiny.

We believe it is simply too late in the day to conclude, as did the District Court in this case, that a juvenile is not put in jeopardy at a proceeding whose object is to determine whether he has committed acts that violate a criminal law and whose potential consequences include both the stigma inherent in such a determination and the deprivation of liberty for many years.[16] For it is clear under our cases that determining the relevance of constitutional policies, like determining the applicability of constitutional rights, in juvenile proceedings, requires that courts eschew "the 'civil' label-of-convenience which as been attached to juvenile proceedings," and that "the juvenile process . . . be candidly appraised."

As we have observed, the risk to which the term jeopardy refers is that traditionally associated with "actions intended to authorize criminal punishment to vindicate public justice." Because of its purpose and potential consequences, and the nature and resources of the State, such a proceeding imposes heavy pressures and burdens — psychological, physical, and financial — on a person charged. The purpose of the Double Jeopardy Clause is to require that he be subject to the experience only once "for the same offence."

In *In re Gault*, this Court concluded that, for purposes of the right to counsel, a "proceeding where the issue is whether the child will be found to be 'delinquent' and subjected to the loss of his liberty for years is comparable in seriousness to a felony prosecution." The Court stated that the term "delinquent" had "come to involve only slightly less stigma than the term 'criminal' applied to adults," and that, for purposes of the privilege against self-incrimination, "commitment is a deprivation of liberty. It is incarceration against one's will, whether it is called criminal or civil."[17]

Thus, in terms of potential consequences, there is little to distinguish an adjudicatory hearing such as was held in this case from a traditional criminal prosecution. For that reason, it engenders elements of "anxiety and insecurity" in a juvenile, and imposes a "heavy personal strain." And we can expect that, since our decisions implementing fundamental fairness in the juvenile court system, hearings have been prolonged, and some of the burdens incident to a juvenile's defense increased, as the system has assimilated the process thereby imposed. . . .

We deal here, not with "the formalities of the criminal adjudicative process," but with an analysis of an aspect of the juvenile-court system in terms of the kind of risk to which jeopardy refers. Under our decisions we can find no persuasive distinction in that regard between the proceeding conducted in this case and a criminal prosecution, each of which is designed "to vindicate [the] very vital interest in enforcement of criminal laws." We therefore conclude that respondent was put in jeopardy at the adjudicatory hearing. Jeopardy attached when respondent was "put to trial before the trier of the facts," that is, when the Juvenile Court, as the trier of the facts, began to hear evidence.

---

16 [11] At the time of respondent's dispositional hearing, permissible dispositions included commitment to the California Youth Authority until he reached the age of 21 years. Petitioner has conceded that the "adjudicatory hearing is, in every sense, a court trial." . . .

17 [12] Nor does the fact "that the purpose of the commitment is rehabilitative and not punitive . . . change its nature. . . . Regardless of the purposes for which the incarceration is imposed, the fact remains that it is incarceration. The rehabilitive goals of the system are admirable, but they do not change the drastic nature of the action taken. Incarceration of adults is also intended to produce rehabilitation." *See* President's Commission on Law Enforcement and Administration of Justice, Task Force Report; Juvenile Delinquency and Youth Crime 8–9 (1967).

III

Petitioner argues that, even assuming jeopardy attached at respondent's adjudicatory hearing, the procedures by which he was transferred from Juvenile Court and tried on a felony information in Superior Court did not violate the Double Jeopardy Clause. The argument is supported by two distinct, but in this case overlapping, lines of analysis. First, petitioner reasons that the procedure violated none of the policies of the Double Jeopardy Clause or that, alternatively, it should be upheld by analogy to those cases which permit retrial of an accused who has obtained reversal of a conviction on appeal. Second, pointing to this Court's concern for "the juvenile court's assumed ability to function in a unique manner," petitioner urges that, should we conclude traditional principles "would otherwise bar a transfer to adult court after a delinquency adjudication," we should avoid that result here because it "would diminish the flexibility and informality of juvenile court proceedings without conferring any additional due process benefits upon juveniles charged with delinquent acts."

A

We cannot agree with petitioner that the trial of respondent in Superior Court on an information charging the same offense as that for which he had been tried in Juvenile Court violated none of the policies of the Double Jeopardy Clause. For, even accepting petitioner's premise that respondent "never faced the risk of more than one punishment," we have pointed out that "the Double Jeopardy Clause . . . is written in terms of potential or risk of *trial* and conviction, not punishment." (emphasis added.) And we have recently noted: "The policy of avoiding multiple trials has been regarded as so important that exceptions to the principle have been only grudgingly allowed." Initially, a new trial was thought to be unavailable after appeal, whether requested by the prosecution or the defendant. . . . It was not until 1896 that it was made clear that a defendant could seek a new trial after conviction, even though the Government enjoyed no similar right. . . . Following the same policy, the Court has granted the Government the right to retry a defendant after a mistrial only where "there is a manifest necessity for the act, or the ends of public justice would otherwise be defeated."

Respondent was subjected to the burden of two trials for the same offense; he is twice put to the task of marshaling his resources against those of the State, twice subjected to the "heavy personal strain" which such an experience represents. We turn, therefore, to inquire whether either traditional principles or "the juvenile court's assumed ability to function in a unique manner," supports an exception to the "constitutional policy of finality" to which respondent would otherwise be entitled.

B

In denying respondent's petitions for writs of *habeas corpus*, the California Court of Appeal first, and the United States District Court later, concluded that no new jeopardy arose as a result of his transfer from Juvenile Court and trial in Superior Court. In the view of those courts, the jeopardy that attaches at an adjudicatory hearing continues until there is a final disposition of the case under the adult charge.

. . . .

. . . [T]he fact that the proceedings against respondent had not "run their full course," within the contemplation of the California Welfare and Institutions Code, at the time of transfer, does not satisfactorily explain why respondent should be deprived of the constitutional protection against a second trial. If there is to be an exception to that protection in the context of the juvenile court system, it must be justified by interests of society, reflected in that unique institution, or of juveniles themselves, of sufficient substance to render tolerable the costs and burdens, noted earlier, which the exception will entail in individual cases.

C

The possibility of transfer from juvenile court to a court of general criminal jurisdiction is a matter of great significance to the juvenile. At the same time, there appears to be widely shared agreement that not all juveniles can benefit from the special features and programs of the juvenile court system and that a procedure for transfer to an adult court should be available. This general agreement is reflected in the fact that an overwhelming majority of jurisdictions permits transfer in certain circumstances. As might be expected, the statutory provisions differ in numerous details. Whatever their differences, however, such transfer provisions represent an attempt to impart to the juvenile court system the flexibility needed to deal with youthful offenders who cannot benefit from the specialized guidance and treatment contemplated by the system.

We do not agree with petitioner that giving respondent the constitutional protection against multiple trials in this context will diminish flexibility and informality to the extent that those qualities relate uniquely to the goals of the juvenile court system.[18] We agree that such a holding will require, in most cases, that the transfer decision be made prior to an adjudicatory hearing. To the extent that evidence concerning the alleged offense is considered relevant,[19] it may be that, in those cases where transfer is considered and

---

[18] [15] That the flexibility and informality of juvenile proceedings are diminished by the application of due process standards is not open to doubt. Due process standards inevitably produce such an effect, but that tells us no more than that the Constitution imposes burdens on the functioning of government and especially of law enforcement institutions.

[19] [16] Under CAL. WELF. & INST'NS CODE § 707 (1972), the governing criterion with respect to transfer, assuming the juvenile is 16 years of age is charged with a violation of a criminal statute or ordinance, is amenability "to the care, treatment and training program available through the facilities of the juvenile court." The section further provides that neither "the offense, in itself" nor a denial by the juvenile of the facts or conclusions set forth in the petition shall be "sufficient to support a finding that [he] is not a fit and proper subject to be dealt with under the provisions of the Juvenile Court law." The California Supreme Court has held that the only factor a juvenile court must consider is the juvenile's "behavior pattern as described in the probation officer's report," but that it may also consider, inter alia, the nature and circumstances of the alleged offense. In contrast to California, which does not require any evidentiary showing with respect to the commission of the offense, a number of jurisdictions require a finding of probable cause to believe the juvenile committed the offense before transfer is permitted. In addition, two jurisdictions appear presently to require a finding of delinquency before the transfer of a juvenile to adult court. ALA. CODE, Tit. 13, § 364 (1959); W. VA. CODE ANN. § 49-5-14 (1966).

rejected, some added burden will be imposed on the juvenile courts by reason of duplicative proceedings. Finally, the nature of the evidence considered at a transfer hearing may in some States require that, if transfer is rejected, a different judge preside at the adjudicatory hearing.

We recognize that juvenile courts, perhaps even more than most courts, suffer from the problems created by spiraling caseloads unaccompanied by enlarged resources and manpower. And courts should be reluctant to impose on the juvenile court system any additional requirements which could so strain its resources as to endanger its unique functions. However, the burdens that petitioner envisions appear to us neither qualitatively nor quantitatively sufficient to justify a departure in this context from the fundamental prohibition against double jeopardy.

A requirement that transfer hearings be held prior to adjudicatory hearings affects not at all the nature of the latter proceedings. More significantly, such a requirement need not affect the quality of decisionmaking at transfer hearings themselves. In *Kent*, the Court held that hearings under the statute there involved "must measure up to the essentials of due process and fair treatment." However, the Court has never attempted to prescribe criteria for, or the nature and quantum of evidence that must support, a decision to transfer a juvenile for trial in adult court. We require only that, whatever the relevant criteria, and whatever the evidence demanded, a State determine whether it wants to treat a juvenile within the juvenile court system before entering upon a proceeding that may result in an adjudication that he has violated a criminal law and in a substantial deprivation of liberty, rather than subject him to the expense, delay, strain, and embarrassment of two such proceedings.[20]

Moreover, we are not persuaded that the burdens petitioner envisions would pose a significant problem for the administration of the juvenile court system. The large number of jurisdictions that presently require that the transfer decision be made prior to an adjudicatory hearing, and the absence of any indication that the juvenile courts in those jurisdictions have not been able to perform their task within that framework, suggest the contrary. The likelihood that in many cases the lack of need or basis for a transfer hearing can be recognized promptly reduces the number of cases in which a commitment of resources is necessary. In addition, we have no reason to believe that the resources available to those who recommend transfer or participate in the process leading to transfer decisions are inadequate to enable them to gather the information relevant to informed decision prior to an adjudicatory hearing.[21]

---

[20] [18] We note that nothing decided today forecloses States from requiring, as a prerequisite to the transfer of a juvenile, substantial evidence that he committed the offense charged, so long as the showing required is not made in an adjudicatory proceeding. The instant case is not one in which the judicial determination was simply a finding of, *e.g.,* probable cause. Rather, it was an adjudication that respondent had violated a criminal statute.

[21] [20] We intimate no views concerning the constitutional validity of transfer following the attachment of jeopardy at an adjudicatory hearing where the information which forms the predicate for the transfer decision could not, by the exercise of due diligence, reasonably have been obtained previously.

To the extent that transfer hearings held prior to adjudication result in some duplication of evidence if transfer is rejected, the burden on juvenile courts will tend to be offset somewhat by the cases in which, because of transfer, no further proceedings in juvenile court are required. Moreover, when transfer has previously been rejected, juveniles may well be more likely to admit the commission of the offense charged, thereby obviating the need for adjudicatory hearings, than if transfer remains a possibility. Finally, we note that those States which presently require a different judge to preside at an adjudicatory hearing if transfer is rejected also permit waiver of that requirement. Where the requirement is not waived, it is difficult to see a substantial strain on judicial resources.

Quite apart from our conclusions with respect to the burdens on the juvenile court system envisioned by petitioner, we are persuaded that transfer hearings prior to adjudication will aid the objectives of that system. What concerns us here is the dilemma that the possibility of transfer after an adjudicatory hearing presents for a juvenile, a dilemma to which the Court of Appeals alluded. Because of that possibility, a juvenile, thought to be the beneficiary of special consideration, may in fact suffer substantial disadvantages. If he appears uncooperative, he runs the risk of an adverse adjudication, as well as of an unfavorable dispositional recommendation.[22] If, on the other hand, he is cooperative, he runs the risk of prejudicing his chances in adult court if transfer is ordered. We regard a procedure that results in such a dilemma as at odds with the goal that, to the extent fundamental fairness permits, adjudicatory hearings be informal and nonadversary. Knowledge of the risk of transfer after an adjudicatory hearing can only undermine the potential for informality and cooperation which was intended to be the hallmark of the juvenile court system. Rather than concerning themselves with the matter at hand, establishing innocence or seeking a disposition best suited to individual correctional needs, the juvenile and his attorney are pressed into a posture of adversary wariness that is conductive to neither.[23]

IV

We hold that the prosecution of respondent in Superior Court, after an adjudicatory proceeding in Juvenile Court, violated the Double Jeopardy Clause of the Fifth Amendment, as applied to the States through the Fourteenth Amendment. The mandate of the Court of Appeals, which was stayed by that court pending our decision, directs the District Court "to issue a writ of *habeas corpus* directing the state court, within 60 days, to vacate the adult

---

22 [22] Although denying respondent's petition for a writ of *habeas corpus*, the judge of the Juvenile Court noted: "If he doesn't open up with a probation officer there is of course the danger that the probation officer will find that he is so uncooperative that he cannot make a recommendation for the kind of treatment you think he really should have and, yet, as the attorney worrying about what might happen a[t] the disposition hearing, you have to advise him to continue to more or less stand upon his constitutional right not to incriminate himself. . . ."

23 [23] With respect to the possibility of "making the juvenile proceedings confidential and not being able to be used against the minor," the judge of the Juvenile Court observed: "I must say that doesn't impress me because if the minor admitted something in the Juvenile Court and named his companions nobody is going to eradicate from the minds of the district attorney or other people the information they obtained."

conviction of Jones and either set him free or remand him to the juvenile court for disposition." Since respondent is no longer subject to the jurisdiction of the California Juvenile Court, we vacate the judgement and remand the case to the Court of Appeals for such further proceedings consistent with this opinion as may be appropriate in the circumstances.

So ordered.

Judgment vacated and case remanded.

NOTES AND QUESTIONS

1. Is it clear from the *Breed* opinion exactly when a defendant is placed in "jeopardy" for purposes of the Fifth Amendment? The Court specifies that a juvenile is put in jeopardy "at a proceeding whose object is to determine whether he has committed acts that violate a criminal law and whose potential consequences include both the stigma inherent in such a determination and the deprivation of liberty for many years." Does this mean that if probation were the sole possible disposition for committing a given act of delinquency (an act that would be a crime if committed by an adult) the adjudication proceeding would not be one at which jeopardy attached? What if a fine (increasingly employed in juvenile systems) were the only possible disposition? What if a jurisdiction employed several whacks with a paddle to the buttocks of offending juveniles as the only sanction for a given offense? Assuming the paddling is constitutionally permissible, would (should?) the adjudication proceeding with paddling as the potential consequence be one at which jeopardy attaches?

2. In *Swisher v. Brady*, 438 U.S. 204 (1978), a case subsequent to *Breed*, the Court upheld against double jeopardy attack a state procedure permitting the state to file exceptions with the juvenile court to proposed findings and recommendations made by a master of that court even if the master proposed a finding of nondelinquency or recommended a lenient disposition. The procedure at issue in *Swisher* permitted the juvenile court judge to act only on the basis of the record made before the master unless the parties agreed to permit additional evidence. The Court found such a procedure analogous to the common and permissible procedure in criminal cases where evidence is presented and recorded in proceedings conducted by one not authorized to declare guilt.

[B] The Significance of Sanctions: Punishment Versus Therapy

Leaving *McKeiver* aside, perhaps the best way to understand *Gault, Winship,* and *Breed* is to view the Court as holding that the juvenile justice system, at least so far as delinquency jurisdiction is concerned, has become essentially punitive. Therefore, because they are applying the sanction of the criminal law, juvenile courts must afford the procedural protections of the criminal law. Yet, at the same time, *McKeiver* makes clear that the juvenile and criminal systems are not constitutional equivalents. The *McKeiver* Court holds out hope that the rehabilitative mission of juvenile courts may still be attainable.

The legacy of *Gault* is that the Court will look behind dispositional labels and examine what is actually going on in juvenile justice. To the extent that the system is in fact punitive, legal principles applicable to dispensing punishment will be applied. On the other hand, such consequences need not be visited upon the system to the extent that it operates as a rehabilitative or therapeutic model.

This suggests that in order to understand a host of legal issues, one must be clear about the difference between systems that punish and those that dispense therapy. The following excerpt examines the punishment/therapy distinction, one that will be relevant at a variety of points throughout the remainder of these materials.

Martin R. Gardner, *Punishment and Juvenile Justice: A Conceptual Framework for Assessing Constitutional Rights of Youthful Offenders*

35 VANDERBILT LAW REVIEW 791, 792–795, 815–816, 817–818 (1982)

In his dissenting opinion in *In re Gault*, Justice Stewart articulated the traditionally accepted distinction between the juvenile justice system and the criminal justice system as follows: "[A] juvenile proceeding's whole purpose and mission is the very opposite of the mission and purpose of a prosecution in a criminal court. The object of the one is correction of a condition. The object of the other is conviction and punishment for a criminal act." Juvenile justice descends from the therapeutic tradition. Thus, the interventions of the juvenile system into youthful lives supposedly represent benign *parens patriae* attempts to cure undesirable or unhealthy states of being. Unlike the criminal law, juvenile justice responds to the status of children in need, treating them for what they are rather than punishing them for what they have done.

Apart from its obvious importance in shaping decisions and actions of policymakers, Justice Stewart's punishment/therapy distinction also carries important legal consequences. Punished persons are entitled to certain rights, both procedural and substantive, which are not necessarily available to persons receiving nonpunitive dispositions.

The therapeutic model, however, probably never provided a totally accurate description of juvenile justice. In any event, by the time that *Gault* was decided, a majority of the United States Supreme Court acknowledged that juvenile law could not be conceptualized entirely in terms of rehabilitative considerations. Indeed, although Justice Stewart saw no constitutional need to criminalize the nonpunitive juvenile system by requiring the system to provide the same procedural protections to juveniles as the criminal law provides to criminal defendants, the *Gault* majority held that the actual dispositions of juvenile delinquents often have little, if anything, to do with therapy. The majority further held that these dispositions constitute such severe restrictions of liberty that many of the procedural protections required in criminal trials also are necessary in delinquency adjudications. *Gault*, however, does not stand for the proposition that juvenile justice schemes are systematically nontherapeutic. Indeed, the Court in *McKeiver v. Pennsylvania* later denied juveniles the right to jury trials in delinquency proceedings, in part on the theory that the presence of juries might interfere with the rehabilitative goal of the juvenile system. Thus, *McKeiver* specifically recognizes the therapeutic potential of juvenile court dispositions.

The Supreme Court cases suggest that juvenile justice systems are often hybrids, sometimes punitive — or so like punitive models to require procedural protections unique to the criminal law — sometimes therapeutic, and often both punitive and therapeutic. As a consequence, courts that have addressed the constitutionality of the juvenile justice system since *Gault* have done so with the understanding that the system reflects a mixture of theoretical underpinnings. Not surprisingly, the courts have had difficulty defining the constitutional rights of juveniles who are thrust into a system that is simultaneously punitive and therapeutic.

The difficult task facing the courts ultimately is assessing the extent to which the juvenile system is punitive in nature. Because the concept of punishment includes a discrete set of constitutional protections, Justice Stewart's punishment/therapy distinction, although not utilized explicitly by the *Gault* majority — and perhaps even misapplied by Justice Stewart himself — remains a useful analytical device for developing a coherent constitutional framework for juvenile law. Judicial attention to the concept of punishment and its relationship to juvenile justice will be increasingly necessary in light of recent legislative trends toward punitive sanctions for certain youthful offenders. Moreover, the Supreme Court, in dicta accompanying its . . . holding that eighth amendment considerations are inapplicable to corporal punishment of public school children, specifically left open the question whether the eighth amendment's protection against cruel and unusual punishment applies to juvenile justice dispositions. The Court, thus, invited inquiry into whether, and to what extent, these dispositions constitute punishment.

    . . . .

PUNISHMENT v. THERAPY

Therapeutic dispositions, like preventive detentions, sometimes display punitive characteristics. Involuntary therapy often entails not only a stigma to the patient and severe restriction of his liberty, but also painful and unpleasant treatment. Despite its similarity to punishment, however, therapy is a concept analytically distinct from punishment. Thus, the Supreme Court suggested in *Robinson v. California* that while the Constitution may allow the state to subject drug addicts to involuntary therapy, the state violates the eighth amendment when it punishes addicts for their addiction. Although the Court frequently has discussed the concept of punishment, it has never directed much attention to defining therapy and to distinguishing it from punishment. Fortunately, commentators have provided valuable insights into this distinction by describing therapy as purposeful behavior toward another person that is intended to alter that person's condition in a manner beneficial to him. This purportedly beneficial behavior is always subject to revision upon a showing that a different mode of behavior would produce more beneficial results, or that a change in the person's condition has eliminated the need for further therapy.

Examination of the role of offensive conduct illustrates the essential difference between coercive therapy and punishment. The distinction is similar to that between preventive detention and punishment. In cases of punishment, the state imposes restraints upon persons because they have committed offenses. Cases of therapy, however, do not involve necessarily a relation between the restraints imposed upon the person and his past conduct. Therapy — like preventive detention and unlike punishment — is a forward-looking response to a person's present undesirable status. Unlike preventive detention, which merely incapacitates, therapy seeks to alleviate the undesirable status conditions.

In summary, the surveyed cases reveal the following punishment framework:

(1) Punishment is the purposeful imposition of unpleasant restraints by one person or authority upon another person.

(2) Punishment is a sanction imposed upon a person for his offense or alleged offense against social or moral norms of conduct that also are usually, but not always, the subject of a preexisting legal rule that defines the offense and sets the amount of penalty for its commission.

(3) Punishment is imposed to exact retribution and may also operate to deter undesirable conduct.

(4) Punishment is often imposed upon offenders who, in addition to violating legal rules, are (or are believed to be) morally culpable.

Courts may discern punitive purpose from either the express words or actions of the alleged punisher or from independent inquiries into the possible functions of an allegedly punitive sanction. When the state imposes restraints that suspiciously resemble punishment, courts may infer a punitive purpose if the restraints are unreasonably harsh in relation to articulated nonpenal objectives. Punishment is a concept analytically distinct from regulation, preventive detention, and therapy. Regulation is the imposition of sanctions to control future conduct without necessarily attending to anyone's past wrongdoing. Preventive detention is the purposeful restriction of liberty of a person, who because of his present status, [is perceived to] pose a danger. Unlike punishment, which is generally determinate — that is, knowable in kind and duration at the time the triggering offense is committed — preventive detention is indeterminate — that is, unknowable in duration at the time of imposition. Therapy is the alteration of a person's undesirable physical or mental condition in a manner beneficial to the person [imposed] until the undesirable condition no longer exists. Therapy is characteristically indeterminate because its effectiveness is generally unknown in advance.

§ 5.03 JURISDICTION

[A] Overview

Originally, juvenile justice theory drew no distinction between offending and victimized children. *Parens patriae* provided the conceptual justification for court interventions aimed at helping both neglected and criminal children.

These original jurisdictional grounds are retained in many juvenile court systems where courts hear child neglect and abuse cases as well as cases alleging that a child is "in need of supervision" or has committed either a criminal or status offense. These materials addressed the issues of neglect and abuse in earlier chapters and will not revisit those matters here. Instead, attention will be limited to juvenile court jurisdiction over delinquency (acts by minors that would be criminal if committed by adults) and status offenses (offenses such as truancy and running away that are prohibited only for children and status conditions such as being "wayward" or "in need of supervision" that trigger judicial intervention).

Early in the juvenile court movement, the distinction between the concepts of delinquency and status offense carried little legal importance. Recently, however, as the United States Supreme Court has addressed delinquency adjudications, the distinction has taken on constitutional significance. Moreover, it is now common for legislatures and courts to draw a variety of distinctions between the processing of delinquency and status offense cases. In light of these considerations, it is useful to consider the delinquency and status offense categories separately. Before considering these categories, however, the relevance of age as a jurisdictional issue will be discussed.

[B] Age

[1] Maximum Age

All juvenile court systems establish a maximum age below which children are deemed subject to the ameliorative processes of the court. Generally, the age, usually eighteen, is the same for delinquency or status offense jurisdiction. Some states set the age at seventeen, while a few lower it to sixteen. As the following case illustrates, some states historically drew statutory age distinctions based on gender, setting a higher jurisdictional age for females than for males.

LAMB v. BROWN

United States Court of Appeals
456 F.2d 18 (1972)

Barrett, Circuit Judge.

Danny Ray Lamb, then 17 years of age, was tried as an adult under 10 Okl. St. Ann. § 1101 (Supp. 1969) for the crime of burglary of an automobile, a felony. . . .

Lamb contends that he should have been proceeded against as a juvenile in juvenile court. He argues that 10 OKL. ST. ANN. § 1101 (Supp. 1969) is unconstitutional in that it allows females the benefits of juvenile court proceedings under the age of 18 years while limiting those same benefits to males under the age of 16 years. The Oklahoma Supreme Court ruled on this issue [saying]: ". . . [A]s we view the section of the statutes, we do not find it to be so repugnant to the Constitution of the United States as the defendants would attempt to lead the Court to believe. As we view the situation, the statute exemplifies the legislative judgment of the Oklahoma State Legislature, premised upon the demonstrated facts of life; and we refuse to interfere with that judgment." . . .

Lamb filed a habeas corpus application in the federal district court below alleging [the statute violates] the equal protection clause of the Fourteenth Amendment of the United States Constitution. He appeals from denial of relief.

10 OKL. ST.ANN. § 1101(a) provides in pertinent part: "The term 'child' means any male person under the age of sixteen (16) years and any female person under the age of eighteen (18) years." Appellant urges that this distinction between the sexes amounts to an invidious discrimination against males violative of the equal protection clause of the Fourteenth Amendment.

. . . .

We are strongly disinclined to hold that the considered judgment of the Oklahoma Legislature in the enactment of 10 OKL. ST. ANN. § 1101(a) does not meet the measure of federal constitutional standards. The United States Supreme Court has said this with regard to the equal protection test: "The Fourteenth Amendment means 'that no person or class of persons shall be denied the same protection of the laws which is enjoyed by other persons or other classes in the same place and under like circumstances.' The general doctrine is that that amendment, in respect of the administration of criminal justice, requires that no different degree or higher punishment shall be imposed on one than is imposed on all for like offenses." . . . "Judicial inquiry under the Equal Protection Clause, therefore, does not end with a showing of equal application among the members of the class defined by the legislation. The courts must reach and determine the question whether the classifications drawn in a statute are reasonable in light of its purpose. . . ."

[Our previous precedent] is not helpful in our search for a rational justification for the disparity in treatment between 16–18 year-old males and 16–18 year-old females under the statute. "Demonstrated facts of life" could mean many things. The "demonstrated facts" which the Court relied upon are not spelled out. They are not obvious or apparent. We therefore cannot weigh them to determine if they "might suffice to characterize the classification as reasonable rather than arbitrary and invidious."

We have not been presented with a logical constitutional justification for the discrimination inherent in 10 OKL. ST. ANN. § 1101(a). The State, in its brief and oral argument has simply relied upon the unexplained "demonstrated facts of life."

Because the purpose of the disparity in the age classification between 16–18 year-old males and 16–18 year-old females has not been demonstrated, we hold that 10 OKL. ST. ANN. § 1101(a) is violative of the equal protection clause. This ruling shall not apply retroactively.

Reversed and remanded.

————

NOTES AND QUESTIONS

1. Are there any differences ("demonstrated facts of life," in the words of the Oklahoma Supreme Court) between males and females that could justify the age distinction drawn by the Oklahoma legislature? What about the fact that females risk pregnancy while males do not? For a case considering and rejecting this factor as a constitutionally adequate basis for New York's statute extending jurisdiction for "persons in need of supervision" to age eighteen for females but only to age sixteen for males, see *Patricia A. v. City of New York*, 286 N.E.2d 432 (N.Y. 1972).

The *Lamb* case was subsequently given retroactive application by the Tenth Circuit. *See Radcliff v. Anderson*, 509 F.2d 1093 (10th Cir. 1974), *cert. denied*, 421 U.S. 939 (1975).

2. The United States Supreme Court has never considered the constitutionality of rules setting different jurisdictional ages for girls than for boys. However, in *Michael M. v. Superior Court*, 450 U.S. 464, 473 (1981), a plurality of the Court suggested that statutes similar to those struck down in *Lamb* and *Patricia A.* might be constitutional as attempts to address the problem of pregnancy if the state criminally punished males, exempted from juvenile court jurisdiction, for the male-only crime of statutory rape. The plurality observed: "Because virtually all of the significant harmful and inescapably identifiable consequences of teenage pregnancy fall on the young female, a legislature acts well within its statutory authority when it elects to punish only the [male] participant who, by nature, suffers none of the consequences of his conduct." The plurality further supported this view by noting that the risk of pregnancy itself constitutes a deterrence to young females while the criminal sanction imposed solely on males arguably provides an equalizing deterrent.

3. For a discussion of sexual bias in juvenile justice generally, see Samuel M. Davis & Susan C. Chairez, *Equal Protection for Juveniles: The Present Status of Sex-Based Discrimination in Juvenile Court Law*, 7 GA. L. REV. 494 (1973), Staphanie Hoyt & David G. Scherer, *Female Juvenile Delinquency: Misunderstood by the Juvenile Justice System, Neglected by Social Science*, 22 L. & HUM. BEHAV. 81 (1998).

[2] Minimum Age

Most juvenile statutes do not specify a minimum jurisdictional age. The common law infancy defense, still available to minors tried in adult criminal court, imposed immunity from criminal court jurisdiction for children under age seven. Some states statutorily adopt the common law rule for delinquency jurisdiction, *see, e.g.*, Mass. Gen. Laws Ann. ch. 119 § 52 (West 1993) ("delinquent child" is a child between seven and seventeen who commits a criminal offense"), while others raise it, *see, e.g.*, Tex. Fam. Code Ann. § 51.02(2)(A) (1996) (age ten is minimum age). Some jurisdictions specify a minimum age for delinquency cases but impose no limit for status offense jurisdiction. *See, e.g.*, N.Y. Fam. Ct. Act §§ 301.2(1), 712(a) (McKinney 1999) (setting minimum age at seven for delinquency jurisdiction but setting no minimum for "persons in need of supervision").

Some jurisdictions have raised from seven years the minimum age for criminal liability. Assuming that a legislature does not specifically address the minimum age for juvenile court jurisdiction, what effect if any, should its limitation on criminal jurisdiction have on the state's exercise of jurisdiction in juvenile court? Consider the following case:

IN RE INTEREST OF DOW

Court of Appeals of Illinois, District 1
393 N.E.2d 1346 (1979)

Johnson, Justice:

On September 11, 1976, petitions for adjudication of wardship were filed in the Juvenile Division of the Circuit Court of Cook County, Illinois, alleging that Peter Dow, age 11, and his brother, Patrick Dow, age 9, committed the offense of aggravated battery against Paul Mueller. After an adjudicatory hearing, the respondents were found delinquent. Respondent Patrick Dow appeals that finding. We affirm the trial court.

The main issue presented for review is whether a minor under the age of 13 years may be adjudicated a delinquent in Illinois.

Paul Mueller testified at the adjudicatory hearing that on September 10, 1976 he and a friend were playing in a football field. At approximately 6 p.m., he was approached by Peter and Patrick Dow and invited to see their clubhouse. Paul rode on Peter's bicycle to a truck yard next to the football field.

Paul stated that after they arrived the respondents locked him inside the truck, climbed on top of the truck, and told him to remove his clothes. Paul would not comply until the boys opened the truck door and threatened to undress him. After he removed his clothes, the respondents began to hit him in the face. He received further injuries from a dog who was in the truck and who jumped on Paul at the direction of respondents. Peter and Patrick then threatened Paul with further beating if he did not perform the act of fellatio. Paul complied but was, nevertheless, subjected to further beating by respondents. Peter and Patrick then ordered Paul to go into the Chicago River and get a duck. Paul told them he could not swim, but they still commanded him to enter the water. Shortly thereafter, when Paul noticed they had gone, he came ashore. Paul called his father, the police were notified, and Paul was taken to the hospital where he was given shots and X-rays. He was confined to the hospital for 6 days, the first 2 of which were spent in the intensive care unit. The police brought Peter and Patrick Dow to the hospital where Paul identified them as the offenders.

Roger Mueller, Paul's father, testified that on September 10, 1976 he received a telephone call from his son and was told that someone had pushed him into the river. He met his son, saw the lacerations, and transported him to the hospital.

Three witnesses were called by the respondents. Geraldine Dow, respondents' 12-year-old sister, testified that on September 10, 1976 she saw Peter and Patrick going home at 4:45 p.m. Mrs. Dow, the respondents' mother, testified that Peter and Patrick returned home at approximately 5:25 that evening. Art Rogers, Mrs. Dow"s husband, testified that on the date in question he returned home from work at 5:30 p.m. and saw Peter and Patrick at that time, but then did not see them again until 6:30 p.m.

On December 7, 1976, the trial court found both respondents delinquent and adjudged them wards of the court. The respondents filed a motion to vacate the findings of delinquency or for a new trial. The motion was denied on January 27, 1977.

Peter Dow alleged that the judge was in error as to the burden of proof at his fitness hearing. . . . The People agreed and filed a confession of error as to appellant Peter Dow. The confession of error was allowed on June 1, 1978 and this appeal relates only to Patrick Dow.

The issue presented for determination by this court arises from the assertion by appellant that a minor under the age of 13 years may not be adjudged a delinquent. We cannot agree with appellant's contention.

Appellant contends that § 6-1 of the Criminal Code forbids conviction of a minor under thirteen years of a criminal offense, and it therefore must forbid finding him delinquent as well because a finding of delinquency is based on a violation or attempted violation of a criminal law.

We do not agree with appellant's view of the law and, instead, believe the State's position is correct.

The State contends that both the Criminal Code and the Juvenile Court Act prohibit criminal prosecution of a person under 13, but the delinquency provisions of the Juvenile Court Act were established as an alternative to criminal prosecution.

Section 6-1 reads, "No person shall be convicted of any offense unless he had attained his 13th birthday at the time the offense was committed." Under the Juvenile Court Act, a delinquent minor is defined as, "Those who are delinquent include any minor who prior to his 17th birthday has violated or attempted to violate, regardless of where the act occurred, any federal or state law or municipal ordinance; . . ."

Appellant, in his argument, alleges that § 6-1 of the Criminal Code and § 2-2 of the Juvenile Court Act must be analyzed together to arrive at the correct interpretation of a child's capacity under the age of 13 years to commit an offense. In so doing, appellant cites the Committee Comments to chapter 38, § 6-1, stating that a child 12 years of age or younger is not capable of forming the requisite capacity to commit an offense. Therefore, § 6-1 must apply to the commission of offenses which can result in a finding of delinquency under the Juvenile Court Act, and regardless of the court in which the case is tried the capacity to commit the offense is the same.

In our reading of the Committee Comments, we find that the relevant portions are: "[C]riminal capacity shall not be deemed to exist below the age of thirteen. Persons falling in this category and committing acts which would otherwise be criminal thus fall within the exclusive cognizance of the Family Court to be treated according to the provisions of the Family Court Act."

Appellant contends that since a child under the age of 13 years lacks criminal capacity he cannot therefore violate or attempt to violate any law as stated in § 2-2 of the Juvenile Court Act, which would, in essence, then preclude him from being adjudged a delinquent.

The Committee Comments state that such an individual would fall within the "exclusive cognizance" of the Juvenile Court Act, and we believe that any other result would be unsatisfactory.

. . . .

. . . [T]he legislative intention was . . . to prevent the conviction of children under the age of 13 years. The section was not intended to remove such children from the benefits of the Juvenile Court Act, but the Act's purpose was to aid children of tender years.

We . . . hold that a child under the age of 13 years can be adjudged delinquent under the provisions of the Juvenile Court Act.

Appellant further asserts that germane to the administration of criminal justice for juveniles is that the child must appreciate the wrongfulness of his act before he may be punished.

The purpose of the Juvenile Court Act is not to punish but to correct. "Society is interested for its own sake as well as for the minor's individual welfare in guiding and rehabilitating." The appellant has a misconception about the Juvenile Court Act regarding an intent to punish. It was clearly not the legislative focus to punish children of that age.

The purpose of delinquency hearings is not penal but protective and, therefore, no suggestion or taint of criminality attaches to any finding of delinquency by a juvenile court.

Appellant cites the case of *In re Robert F. Urbasek*, 232 N.E.2d 716 (Ill. 1967), to stand for the proposition that juvenile delinquency proceedings have essentially penal characteristics. This is not quite an accurate statement of the *Urbasek* case. The case makes reference to committing a juvenile to an institution and that such a confinement is not "devoid of penal characteristics" and, with this, we cannot disagree. However, this does not render a juvenile delinquency proceeding criminal in nature, and ". . . courts of Illinois have stopped short of investing juvenile proceedings with all of the technical attributes of a criminal proceeding." Given the differences between criminal and juvenile proceedings, we believe appellant's argument is unfounded and that delinquency proceedings are protective, not penal.

Appellant further contends that due process requires that minors who are adjudged delinquent must be afforded the basic safeguards of criminal defendants when they are faced with potential incarceration in the Department of Corrections.

We do not find a due process violation in the instant case. As stated earlier, minors are not found guilty of crimes and punished by incarceration.

Certain due process safeguards generally associated with criminal proceedings have been extended for the protection of juveniles to allow them fundamental fairness; *e.g.,* a finding of delinquency is valid only when the acts of delinquency are proved "beyond a reasonable doubt" to have been done by the individual charged.

But, "[I]t is not indicated that to assure the concept of fundamental fairness a juvenile proceeding should be developed into a fully adversary process or that the idealistic prospect of an intimate, informal protective proceeding be abandoned and the juveniles returned to the criminal court."

We hold that delinquency proceedings, although subject to the due process protections, are not criminal in nature and, therefore, the result is not punishment, but rehabilitative in nature.

We find a minor child under the age of 13 years may be adjudicated a delinquent but may not be found guilty of a crime.

For the foregoing reasons, the judgment of the circuit court of Cook County adjudicating appellant as a delinquent is affirmed.

Affirmed.

NOTES AND QUESTIONS

1. Is the *Dow* court's analysis sound in light of *Gault*, *Winship*, and *Breed*? Is the *Dow* court correct in concluding that "no suggestion or taint of criminality attaches to any finding of delinquency by a juvenile court"? How can the court admit the "penal characteristics" of committing a juvenile to an institution but still maintain that "delinquency proceedings are protective, not penal"?

Does it follow, as the *Dow* court maintains, that "delinquency proceedings, although subject to . . . due process protections, are not criminal in nature and, therefore, the result is not punishment"? Is the presence or absence of "punishment" determined by the nature of the proceedings or does the presence or absence of punishment define the nature of the proceedings? Consider again § 5.02[B], *supra.*

2. Does it follow from *Dow* that in Illinois there is no minimum age for delinquency jurisdiction? What if the defendants in *Dow* were ages three and five respectively?

3. In addition to granting immunity from criminal prosecution at age seven, the common law infancy defense created a presumption of incapacity and thus immunity from prosecution for minors between the ages of seven and fourteen.

Whether this presumption of incapacity is applicable in juvenile courts has become a controversial issue that will be considered later in these materials at § 5.04[A][2][c], *infra*.

[C] Delinquency

A leading commentator has noted that "[p]erhaps the most significant part of the juvenile court's jurisdiction over conduct is its jurisdiction over delinquent conduct." Samuel M. Davis, Rights of Juveniles: The Juvenile Justice System 2-15 (2000). Most modern juvenile court statutes define "delinquency" as acts that are in violation of state or federal law, local ordinance, or sometimes of an order of the juvenile court.

Some jurisdictions continue the earlier practice of including within the concept of delinquency "status offenses" such as truancy, incorrigibility, running away from home, and other types of conduct relating to the child's physical, mental, and moral well-being. *See, e.g.*, Ind. Code Ann. §§ 31-37-1-1 to 31-37-2-6 (1997). Other jurisdictions do not utilize the "delinquent" label, but rather list all conduct subject to juvenile court jurisdiction in one general category. *See, e.g.*, Neb. Rev. Stat. § 43-247 (1998) at § 5.03[C][2], *infra*.

[1] Exclusive Jurisdiction

Although juvenile justice is premised on the theory that youthful offenders should be dealt with outside the criminal system, minors committing criminal acts do not necessarily avoid criminal court. In some states, juvenile courts have exclusive jurisdiction over some crimes, generally misdemeanors, committed by minors regardless of their age. Some of these states subject juveniles accused of felony offenses, or certain specified felonies, to possible waiver to criminal court regardless of the age of the juvenile. The remainder of these states permit waivers of juvenile court jurisdiction only if the minor charged with a felony has reached a certain age. Some statutes also preclude waivers of first-time offenders.

Other states afford original jurisdiction to juvenile courts over all cases alleging criminal activity by a minor but, because of statutory provisions permitting waivers to criminal court regardless of the crime, deny exclusive juvenile court jurisdiction over any specific category of crime. In some such states, waivers are limited to juveniles who have reached a certain age, but other states permit waivers regardless of age.

In yet another group of states, statutes grant exclusive jurisdiction to criminal courts in cases where minors are charged with designated offenses, generally serious felonies. Some such statutes impose age minimums, as low as age thirteen. Some statutes limit exclusive criminal jurisdiction to minors who have a record of prior convictions. Finally, some statutes impose original jurisdiction over certain offenses in criminal court but permit transfers to juvenile court in certain circumstances.

The statute considered in the *Kent* case, § 5.02[A], *supra*, represents historically the most common model of original and exclusive jurisdiction in juvenile court with a possibility of judicial waiver to criminal court. The *Bland* case which follows represents an example of a legislature imposing exclusive jurisdiction in criminal court for certain designated offenses.

UNITED STATES v. BLAND

United States Court of Appeals, District of Columbia Circuit
472 F.2d 1329 (1972)

WILKEY, CIRCUIT JUDGE:

The United States as statutory appellant seeks review of a memorandum opinion and order of the United States District Court for the District of Columbia, holding 16 D.C. CODE § 2301(3)(A) unconstitutional as (1) an arbitrary legislative classification and (2) a negation of the presumption of innocence. Section 2301(3)(A) provides: "The term 'child' means an individual who is under 18 years of age, except that the term 'child' does not include an individual who is sixteen years of age or older and-(A) charged by the United States Attorney with (i) murder, forcible rape, burglary in the first degree, robbery while armed, or assault with intent to commit any such offense, or (ii) an offense listed in clause (i) and any other offense properly joinable with such an offense. . . .

The appellee, . . . had been indicted pursuant to § 2301(3)(A) as an adult (he was sixteen at the time of his arrest and indictment) on charges of armed robbery of a post office and related offenses. . . . Appellee moved below to dismiss the indictment for lack of jurisdiction, asserting that the statutory basis for prosecuting him as an adult was constitutionally deficient in that it failed to provide him with procedural due process. The District Court dismissed the indictment.

I. THE LEGISLATIVE BACKGROUND

Congress, pursuant to its constitutional authority to exercise exclusive jurisdiction over the District of Columbia, created the Family Division of the Superior Court of the District of Columbia. In defining the jurisdiction of the Family Division, Congress conferred on it exclusive jurisdiction of "proceedings in which a child, as defined in § 16-2301, is alleged to be delinquent, neglected, or in need of supervision." Thus, the Family Division's jurisdiction extends over a person — a child — alleged to have committed delinquent acts, a child being classified as a person not having yet reached the chronological age of 18 and not charged by the United States Attorney with certain specified crimes listed in 16 D.C. CODE § 2301. As to any other individual, either one who has reached 18 or who has reached the age of 16 and has been charged by the United States Attorney with one or more of the enumerated felonies, he is not a child and is to be prosecuted in the regular adult court system, whether it be the D.C. Superior Court or the United States District, Court.

. . . .

II. THE DUE PROCESS AND EQUAL PROTECTION OF THE LAW ISSUE

The District Court found § 2301(3)(A) invalid as violative of due process of law: The determination that a child should be tried as an adult cannot be made without the safeguard of basic due process. . . .

To the Government's objection below that the statute specifically classifies those individuals who are at least 16 years of age and charged with certain enumerated crimes by the United States Attorney as exempt from the Family Division's jurisdiction, the District Court found no standards in the statute to guide the United States Attorney in making this determination, hence it held that the statute denies due process to those individuals so charged.

A

. . . .

. . . [L]egislative exclusion of individuals charged with certain specified crimes from the jurisdiction of the juvenile justice system is not unusual. The Federal Juvenile Delinquency Act excludes offenses which are punishable by death or life imprisonment. Several states have similarly excluded certain crimes in defining the jurisdiction of their respective systems of juvenile justice, while others vest concurrent jurisdiction over enumerated crimes in both their adult and juvenile courts. . . .

B

The disagreement of our dissenting colleague arises almost solely from his fundamental unwillingness to accept Congress' power to define what is a "child." The words "child," "infant," and "minor" from early times in various legal systems have been susceptible to definition by statute; the critical "age" for specified purposes has varied, and differed between male and female. Before 1970 the District of Columbia Code . . . defined "child" as "a person under 18 years of age." Our dissenting colleague seems to consider this statute and its definition immutable, apparently because it was involved in *Kent v. United States*; we accept the fact that Congress has abolished this statutory definition and by statute substituted another, to which we simply give full effect. . . .

. . . [T]he appellee's argument on an alleged "waiver" of the jurisdiction of the Family Court is based on the now outmoded definition. The District of Columbia Code states clearly that the jurisdiction of the Family Division of the Superior Court in delinquency cases is limited to those who come within the statutory definition of "child." 11 D.C. Code § 1101 provides: The Family Division of the Superior Court shall be assigned . . . exclusive jurisdiction of (13) proceedings in which a child, as defined in 16-2301, is alleged to be a delinquent. . . . Until it is determined whether a person is a "child" within the statutory definition, there is no jurisdiction; therefore, a *fortiori* there can be no waiver of jurisdiction.

Nor is it true "a suspected juvenile remains a child until he is charged with an enumerated offense by the United States Attorney." There is just no classification of the person as a child or an adult until (1) his age is accurately ascertained, and (2) the decision on prosecution is made. Congress has incorporated more than one element in the definition of a "child." Until all the elements of the definition are ascertained, the status of the person is simply uncertain. . . .

C

The District Court's finding in the case at bar, and appellee's assertion to the same effect — that the exercise of the discretion vested by § 2301(3)(A) in the United States Attorney to charge a person 16 years of age or older with certain enumerated offenses, thereby initiating that person's prosecution as an adult, violates due process — ignores the long and widely accepted concept of prosecutorial discretion, which derives from the constitutional principle of separation of powers." . . . [I]t is as an officer of the executive department that [the prosecutor] exercises a discretion as to whether or not there shall be prosecution in a particular case. It follows, as an incident of the constitutional separation of powers, that the courts are not to interfere with the free exercise of the discretionary powers of the attorneys of the United States in their control over criminal prosecutions.

. . . .

The District Court and appellee in the case at bar point to the acknowledged significant effect of the United States Attorney's decision whether to charge an individual 16 years of age or older with certain enumerated offenses, and conclude that, in the absence of a hearing, due process is violated when such a decision is made. This, however, overlooks the significance of a variety of other common prosecutorial decisions, *e.g.*, whether to charge one person but not another possible co-defendant; whether to charge an individual with a misdemeanor or a felony, etc. Furthermore, the decision whether to charge an individual with a misdemeanor or a felony has long determined the court in which that person will be tried. We cannot accept the hitherto unaccepted argument that due process requires an adversary hearing before the prosecutor can exercise his age-old function of deciding what charge to bring against whom. Grave consequences have always flowed from this, but never has a hearing been required.

While the Supreme Court was presented with the precise question raised by this appeal on an earlier occasion, it declined to rule on the question because of "the barrenness of the record on this issue," including the failure of the Nebraska Supreme Court to pass on it. . . .[24] The Federal Juvenile Delinquency Act, however, presents an analogous situation on which courts have passed judgment. Section 5032 of the Act provides in relevant part: A juvenile alleged to have committed one or more acts in violation of a law of the United States not punishable by death or life imprisonment, and not surrendered to the authorities of a state, shall be proceeded against as a

---

[24] [28] *DeBacker v. Brainard,* 396 U.S. 28 (1969), in which the Supreme Court dismissed the grant of certiorari as "improvidently granted." In a subsequent case, the Nebraska Supreme Court considered the same question and found the exercise of such discretion did not violate due process. [*DeBacker v. Sigler,* 185 Neb. 352, 175 N.W.2d 912 (1969).]

juvenile delinquent if he consents to such procedure, unless the Attorney General, in his discretion, has expressly directed otherwise.

The discretion provided the Attorney General under this section can, of course, result in vastly different consequences for an individual subject to the Act since commitment of a juvenile adjudicated delinquent may continue under the Act, as under the comparable provision of the D.C. CODE, only for the remainder of the youth's minority. . . .

. . . [J]udicial consideration of the legitimate scope of prosecutorial discretion clearly encompasses the exercise of such discretion where it has the effect of determining whether a person will be charged as a juvenile or as an adult. In the absence of such "suspect" factors as "race, religion, or other arbitrary classification," the exercise of discretion by the United States Attorney in the case at bar involves no violation of due process or equal protection of the law.

III. THE PRESUMPTION OF INNOCENCE ISSUE

The District Court and appellee assert that the exercise of discretion by the United States Attorney under § 2301(3)(A) violates due process in that it denies the individual charged the presumption of innocence.

This, however, mistakes the nature of the United States Attorney's decision in the case at bar to charge appellee with an offense enumerated in § 2301(3)(A). While the decision does have the effect of determining whether appellee is to be tried as an adult or a juvenile, it is not a judgment of guilt or an imposition of penalty. On the contrary, it is simply the result of a determination by the United States Attorney that there is sufficient evidence to warrant prosecution of the appellee for the offense charged and that adult prosecution is appropriate. It in no manner relieves the Government of its obligation to prove appellee's guilt beyond a reasonable doubt. Nor does it remove appellee's right to a jury trial. . . .

The presumption of innocence, as the Supreme Court has long held, applies to the prosecution at trial and ". . . is a conclusion drawn by the law in favor of the citizen, by virtue whereof, when brought to trial upon a criminal charge, he must be acquitted, unless he is proven [beyond a reasonable doubt] to be guilty." . . . [T]he United States Attorney's decision in the case at bar marks only the beginning of the process of adjudication of appellee's guilt, a process marked by the presence of all the traditional protections or procedural due process, followed by the extraordinarily liberal rehabilitation provisions of the Federal Youth Corrections Act.

IV. CONCLUSION

For these reasons, the order of the District Court dismissing appellee's indictment, on the basis of its opinion holding 16 D.C. CODE § 2301(3)(A) unconstitutional as an arbitrary legislative classification and as a negation of the presumption of innocence, is accordingly reversed and the case remanded for trial.

Reversed and remanded.

J. Skelly Wright, Circuit Judge, *dissenting*:

As a matter of abstract legal analysis, the opinion of my brethren might appear to some degree persuasive. But we do not sit to decide questions in the abstract, and we are not writing on a clean slate. In 1966 the Supreme Court spoke clearly and specifically about this area. [*Kent v. United States*] held, in unmistakable terms, that before a child under 18 can be tried in adult court the Constitution requires a hearing "sufficient in the particular circumstances to satisfy the basic requirements of due process and fairness . . ." I had not supposed that it was within our power as a lower federal court to change this mandate. Nor had I imagined that Congress could "overrule" this constitutional decision by a simple statutory enactment. Yet the majority holds that whereas before passage of the Court Reform Act of 1970 the Constitution required a hearing, after its passage the Constitution requires no such thing. . . . I would therefore hold that appellee is entitled to a hearing with counsel and a statement of reasons before he can be charged and tried as an adult.

I

. . . .

As a moment's reflection makes clear, this so-called "definition" in fact establishes a second, parallel waiver procedure whereby a juvenile can be transferred from the Family Division to adult court. If the Government chooses, it may institute waiver proceedings in Family Court and attempt to convince the judge that under the standards enunciated in the Act the child could more appropriately be tried in adult court. It would be surprising if this procedure were much utilized in cases covered by 16 D.C. Code § 2301(3)(A), however, since under it the Government must observe the procedural rules mandated by *Kent*. Moreover, there is always the possibility that the Government will not carry its burden before the Family Court judge, in which case the waiver attempt would fail.

These risks and inconveniences can be avoided by following the second alternative. If the prosecutor simply charges the juvenile with one of the enumerated offenses, the juvenile ceases to be a "child" under 16 D.C. Code § 2301(3)(A) and, hence, the Family Court is automatically divested of jurisdiction. Thus if the prosecutor follows the second alternative the waiver decision becomes his alone, and he is permitted to make it without the encumbrance of a hearing, the requirement that he state reasons, the inconvenience of bearing the burden of proof, or the necessity of appointing counsel for the accused.

I think it obvious that this second procedure was written into the Act in order to countermand the Supreme Court's decision in *Kent*. . . . Indeed, the House Committee primarily responsible for drafting the provision virtually admitted as much. The Committee Report explains 16 D.C. Code § 2301(3)(A) as follows: "Because of the great increase in the number of serious felonies committed by juveniles *and because of the substantial difficulties in transferring juvenile offenders charged with serious felonies to the jurisdiction of the adult court under present law*, provisions are made in this subchapter for a better mechanism for separation of the violent youthful offender and recidivist from the rest of the juvenile community." . . . The "substantial difficulties . . . under present law" to which the Committee coyly refers are, of course, none other than the constitutional rights explicated in the *Kent* decision. And the "better mechanism" which the Committee proposes is a system for running roughshod over those rights in a manner which is unlikely to encourage those of us still committed to constitutionalism and the rule of law.

This blatant attempt to evade the force of the *Kent* decision should not be permitted to succeed. The result in *Kent* did not turn on the particular wording of the statute involved or on the particular waiver mechanism there employed. Rather, as the Court itself made clear, the rights expounded in *Kent* are fundamental and immutable. "The right to representation by counsel is not a formality. It is not a grudging gesture to a ritualistic requirement. It is of the essence of justice." I must confess, therefore, that I find myself unable to approach the majority's elaborate argumentation with an entirely open mind. As one who has long believed that our Constitution prohibits abrogations of due process "whether accomplished ingeniously or ingenuously," I react with a good deal of skepticism to an argument which supposes that "the essence of justice" can be defeated by a juggling of the definition of juvenile or a minor modification of Family Court jurisdiction. Nonetheless, I am willing to meet the majority on its own ground, since I am convinced that when its arguments are closely examined they must inevitably fall of their own weight.

II

I take it that my brethren and I begin our analysis of 16 D.C. CODE § 2301(3)(A) with a common premise: Nothing in the Constitution prevents Congress from shifting the waiver decision from the Family Court judge to the United States Attorney or from establishing a supplemental waiver proceeding before the United States Attorney to complement the Family Court proceeding. . . .

. . . The issue in this case is not whether the prosecutor should be permitted to make waiver decisions, but rather how he should go about making those decisions. Put slightly differently, the question is whether the shift in decision making responsibility from the court to the prosecutor eliminates the need for the procedural rights expounded in *Kent*. I would, of course, answer that question "no." The transfer of the waiver decision from the neutral judge to the partisan prosecutor increases rather than diminishes the need for due process protection for the child. . . .

. . . .

. . . [T]he majority seems to contend that *Kent* is inapposite because it applied to a judicial decision, whereas 16 D.C. CODE § 2301 contemplates a prosecutorial decision. Thus the majority apparently concedes, as it must, that *Kent* continues to guarantee procedural rights when the waiver is effected by a judge. But these rights do not attach when the same decision is made by a prosecutor, apparently because "the United States Attorney's decision . . . marks only the beginning of the process of adjudication of appellee's guilt, a process marked by the presence of all the traditional protections of procedural due process, followed by the extraordinarily liberal rehabilitation provisions of the Federal Youth Corrections Act." This argument will not stand analysis. The decision by a juvenile judge or by the United States Attorney to treat the child as an adult for prosecution purposes marks the beginning of precisely the same process of adjudication. And it cannot be doubted that the United States Attorney is certainly a less disinterested decision maker than the Juvenile Court judge. It would seem then that, in order to compensate for lack of neutrality, procedural niceties should be *more* rather than less carefully observed when the prosecutor is the decision maker.

. . . .

It should be clear, then, that the test for when the Constitution demands a hearing depends not on which government official makes the decision, but rather on the importance of that decision to the individual affected. . . .

All of these cases involved decision by executive, rather than judicial, officers. Yet in each case the Constitution was held to require a hearing, presumably because "the [individual's] interest in avoiding . . . loss outweigh[ed] the governmental interest in summary adjudication." In *Kent* the Supreme Court weighed the grievous consequences of a waiver decision against the Government's relatively meager interest in summary procedures. In the end the Court struck the balance in favor of fair procedures, and that balance is good enough for me.

. . . .

The majority's opinion suggests reliance on a broad appeal to prosecutorial discretion, but ultimately comes to rest on the more specialized argument that the prosecutor has unreviewable discretion as to whether or not to grant a hearing. As should be readily apparent, this formulation merely assumes the answer to the very question before us for decision. The assumption is made, moreover, on the basis of flimsy evidence and a fallacious analogy.

My brothers point to "the significance of a variety of other common prosecutorial decisions, e. g., whether to charge one person but not another possible codefendant; whether to charge an individual with a misdemeanor or a felony; etc. . . . Grave consequences have always flowed from this, but never has a hearing been required." . . . [E]ven if one assumes, arguendo, that a hearing is not necessary in these situations, it hardly follows that a child may be summarily deprived of his right to juvenile treatment without being heard. As the majority itself indicates, there are dramatically real differences between run-of-the-mill charging decisions and prosecutorial waiver of Family Court jurisdiction. A normal charging decision is "only the beginning of the process of adjudication of [defendant's] guilt, a process marked by the presence of all the traditional protections of procedural due process. . . ." A defendant has the opportunity to show that he was improperly charged — that is, that he is not guilty — at the preliminary hearing, at the trial itself, and, if necessary, on appeal.

In contrast, the waiver decision marks not only the beginning but also the end of adjudication as to the child's suitability for juvenile treatment. It is well established that, barring equal protection problems, a guilty person has no right not to be charged with a criminal offense. But a "guilty" child may, under certain circumstances, have a right to be charged as a juvenile. The question of juvenile treatment turns not on the issue of guilt, but on such factors as the maturity of the child and his susceptibility to rehabilitation. These factors, unlike the question of guilt, drop out of the case once the initial waiver decision is made. Hence it is especially vital that the procedures be fair at the one point in the criminal process where these matters are considered. The very fact that the prosecutor's decision is largely unreviewable and therefore final argues for, rather than against, making certain that he has all the facts before him when he exercises his great responsibility.

Nor is the majority on firm ground when it compares prosecutorial waiver to the decision "whether to charge an individual with a misdemeanor or a felony [which] has long determined the court in which that person will be tried." . . . It trivializes the juvenile court system to suggest that it represents merely an alternative forum for the trial of criminal offenses. The Family Court is more than just another judicial body; it is another system of justice with different procedures, a different penalty structure, and a different philosophy of rehabilitation. We play a cruel joke on our children by arguing that the juvenile system is a nonadversary, noncriminal, beneficent instrument of rehabilitation when determining whether criminal procedures are to be required at trial while at the same time maintaining that it is just another criminal court when determining the procedures which must accompany waiver.

III

It will not do to minimize or ignore the consequences of the decision reached today. The majority suggests that youths tried in adult court will still receive a measure of protection, since conviction may be "followed by the extraordinarily liberal rehabilitation provisions of the Federal Youth Corrections Act." There is, however, more than a touch of irony in this suggestion. A similar point was made by District Judge Gesell: "It should be noted that . . . in the event of convictions the extraordinarily flexible provisions of the Federal Youth Correction [sic] Act designed to create programs for limited incarceration and effective rehabilitation are completely available." Yet Judge Gesell has also found that large numbers of eligible youths are being denied Youth Corrections Act treatment precisely because there presently are no youth facilities available, and that "[t]he pressures from overcrowding [have resulted] in a complete frustration of the Youth Corrections Act program."

Thus I do not think we can escape the fact that after our decision today there will be many impressionable 16-and 17-year-olds who will be packed off to adult prisons where they will serve their time with hardened criminals. These children will be sentenced, moreover, without any meaningful inquiry into the possibility of rehabilitation through humane juvenile disposition. Sometimes I think our treatment of these hapless "criminals" is dictated by the age-old principle "out of sight-out of mind." Yet there is no denying . . . that we cannot write these children off forever. Some day they will grow up and at some point they will have to be freed from incarceration. We will inevitably hear from the Blands and Kents again, and the kind of society we have in the years to come will in no small measure depend upon our treatment of them now.

. . . Nor do I believe that a fair and constitutional waiver system would rescue from the clutches of adult punishment every juvenile capable of rehabilitation in a more beneficent environment. As Chief Judge Bazelon has pointed out, "The job of saving the boy who has compiled a long juvenile record and then committed a serious offense after his sixteenth birthday may be so costly, or so difficult even if no cost were spared, that the [waiver procedures] required by statute cannot but be a pious charade in many cases."

I must admit, then, to considerable uncertainty as to the ultimately proper disposition of a case such as Bland's, given our scarce societal resources, our limited knowledge of juvenile corrections, and the intractable nature of the root problems of poverty and social disintegration. I am certain of a few propositions, however. I am confident that a child is unlikely to succeed in the long, difficult process of rehabilitation when his teachers during his confinement are adult criminals. I am sure that playing fast and loose with fundamental rights will never buy us "law and order": Constitutional rights for children won in *Kent*, like other constitutional rights, are protected from "sophisticated as well as simple-minded" modes of revision or repeal. And I am convinced that the beginning of wisdom in this area, as in so many others, is a respect and concern for the individual — the kind of respect and concern which the due process clause guarantees. I would therefore hold that Congress may not abrogate a child's constitutional rights to a hearing, representation by counsel and a statement of reasons before he is charged and tried as an adult.

I must respectfully dissent.

———

NOTES AND QUESTIONS

1. Throughout his dissenting opinion in *Bland*, Judge Wright refers to a "fundamental and immutable . . . right to be charged as a juvenile." Does such a right exist and, if so, what is its source? Does Judge Wright suggest that offending juveniles possess a basic constitutional right to rehabilitation through the juvenile justice system rather than being subjected to punishment through the criminal justice system? Could such a right be entailed in the general theory of protectionist rights discussed in Chapter 1?

On the other hand, if one sees young people's rights as grounded in personhood rather than protectionist theory, would a right to punishment in lieu of rehabilitative treatment be entailed? *See* Martin R. Gardner, *The Right of Juvenile Offenders to be Punished: Some Implications of Treating Kids as Persons*, 68 NEB. L. REV. 182 (1989).

2. Under the statute considered in *Bland*, suppose a seventeen-year-old hits another youth over the head with a baseball bat causing the victim to fall into a coma. The prosecutor elects to bring the case in juvenile court. While the case is pending, the victim dies and the prosecutor now chooses to bring a

murder charge in criminal court. Under *Bland*, is the defendant entitled to the protections of the *Kent* case before his case can be transferred to criminal court? *See Pendergast v. United States*, 332 A.2d 919 (D.C. App. 1975).

[2] Concurrent Jurisdiction

A few states confer upon the prosecutor authority to bring cases in either juvenile or criminal court. In addition to the Nebraska provision below, see, *e.g.*, WYO. STAT. ANN. §§ 14-6-203(c)–(f), 14-6-211 (Michie 1999); ARIZ. REV. STAT. ANN § 13-501(B) (West Supp. 1999).

NEBRASKA REVISED STATUTES
§ 43-247 (1998)

Juvenile court jurisdiction. The juvenile court shall have exclusive original jurisdiction as to any juvenile defined in subdivision (1) of this section who is under the age of sixteen, as to any juvenile defined in subdivision (3) of this section, and as to the parties and proceedings provided in subdivisions (5), (6), and (8) of this section. As used in this section, all references to the juvenile's age shall be the age at the time the act which occasioned the juvenile court action occurred. The juvenile court shall have concurrent original jurisdiction with the district court as to any juvenile defined in subdivision (2) of this section. The juvenile court shall have concurrent original jurisdiction with the district court and county court as to any juvenile defined in subdivision (1) of this section who is age sixteen or seventeen, any juvenile defined in subdivision (4) of this section, and any proceeding under subdivision (7) or (10) of this section. The juvenile court shall have concurrent original jurisdiction with the county court as to any proceeding under subdivision (9) of this section. Notwithstanding any disposition entered by the juvenile court under the Nebraska Juvenile Code, the juvenile court's jurisdiction over any individual adjudged to be within the provisions of this section shall continue until the individual reaches the age of majority or the court otherwise discharges the individual from its jurisdiction.

The juvenile court in each county as herein provided shall have jurisdiction of:

(1) Any juvenile who has committed an act other than a traffic offense which would constitute a misdemeanor or an infraction under the laws of this state, or violation of a city or village ordinance;

(2) Any juvenile who has committed an act which would constitute a felony under the laws of this state;

(3) Any juvenile (a) who is homeless or destitute, or without proper support through no fault of his or her parent, guardian, or custodian; who is abandoned by his or her parent, guardian, or custodian; who lacks proper parental care by reason of the fault or habits of his or her parent, guardian, or custodian; who parent, guardian, or custodian neglects or refuses to provide proper or necessary subsistence, education, or other care necessary for the health, morals, or well-being of such juvenile; whose parent, guardian, or custodian is unable to provide or neglects or refuses to provide special care made

necessary by the mental condition of the juvenile; or who is in a situation or engages in an occupation dangerous to life or limb or injurious to the health or morals of such juvenile, (b) who, by reason of being wayward or habitually disobedient, is uncontrolled by his or her parent, guardian, or custodian; who deports himself or herself so as to injure or endanger seriously the morals or health of himself, herself, or others; or who is habitually truant from home or school, or (c) who is mentally ill and dangerous as defined in § 83-1009;

(4) Any juvenile who has committed an act which would constitute a traffic offense as defined in § 43-245;

(5) The parent, guardian, or custodian who has custody of any juvenile described in this section;

(6) The proceedings for termination of parental rights as provided in the Nebraska Juvenile Code;

(7) The proceedings for termination of parental rights as provided in § 42-364;

(8) Any juvenile who has been voluntarily relinquished, pursuant to § 43-106.01, to the Department of Health and Human Services or any child placement agency licensed by the Department of Health and Human Services;

(9) The adoption or guardianship proceedings for a child over which the juvenile court already has jurisdiction under another provision of the Nebraska Juvenile Code; and

(10) The paternity determination for a child over which the juvenile court already has jurisdiction.

Notwithstanding the provisions of the Nebraska Juvenile code, the determination of jurisdiction over any Indian child as defined in § 43-1503 shall be subject to the Nebraska Indian Child Welfare Act.

————

STATE v. MOHI

Supreme Court of Utah
901 P.2d 991 (1995)

DURHAM, JUSTICE:

This case is a consolidation of appeals of defendants Asipeli Mohi, Phillip Daniel Lundquist, and Daniel Rodrigo Chaides from interlocutory orders of the Third Judicial District and Fourth Judicial Circuit Courts. Defendants challenge the constitutionality of portions of Utah's Juvenile Courts Act (the Act).[25] In all three cases, the trial courts below denied defendants' motions

---

[25] [1] Section 78-3a-25 was amended after Mohi was charged but before Lundquist and Chaides were charged. This section was further amended during the 1995 legislative session. To clarify which version is being addressed, we will refer to the 1994 version of the statute as the amended version. However, we stress that our decision today addresses the Juvenile Courts Act in use when these defendants were arrested. We do not treat the subsequent amendments.

that the trial courts rule portions of the Act unconstitutional. Defendants ask this court to reverse the trial courts' findings and hold unconstitutional the portions of the Act that allow prosecutors discretion to file some charges against juveniles directly in adult circuit or district court while leaving other similarly accused offenders in juvenile court. *See*, UTAH CODE ANN. § 78-3a-25.

FACTS

Asipeli Mohi

The State alleges that on September 1, 1993, Asipeli Mohi (Mohi) intentionally or recklessly caused the death of Aaron Chapman with a firearm or facsimile thereof. Several witnesses have identified Mohi as the person who shot Chapman. A criminal information was filed against Mohi on September 8, 1993, pursuant to the direct-file provisions of UTAH CODE ANN. § 78-3a-25(6)(b). Mohi was born on January 3, 1976, and was thus approximately seventeen years and eight months of age at the time of the alleged crime, four months short of the age of majority.

Mohi has been represented by counsel since being charged. The direct-file statute under which Mohi was charged provided that when an information was filed in district or circuit court against a juvenile, the defendant or his or her guardian or representative could file a "recall motion" with the juvenile court within ten days of the original filing. Neither Mohi nor his counsel filed a recall motion.

Mohi was bound over to stand trial in district court. In November and December of 1993, Mohi filed amended motions and supporting memoranda asking the court to rule the direct-file provision unconstitutional pursuant to Article I, §§ 7 (due process) and 24 (uniform operation of laws) of the Utah Constitution. In January 1994, Judge Iwasaki entered findings of fact and conclusions of law upholding the constitutionality of the direct-file statutes. This court granted Mohi's petition for an interlocutory appeal from that order.

Phillip Daniel Lundquist and Daniel Rodrigo Chaides

Phillip Daniel Lundquist (Lundquist) and Daniel Rodrigo Chaides (Chaides) were jointly charged by criminal information, filed March 17, 1994, with one count each of aggravated burglary, a first degree felony; aggravated robbery, a first degree felony; and theft of a vehicle, a second degree felony. Lundquist alone was charged with a fourth count, theft of a firearm, a second degree felony. The information noted the State's intent to seek penalty enhancement on each of the aggravated burglary and aggravated robbery charges for use of a firearm or a facsimile of a firearm.

Lundquist and Chaides bring this appeal to challenge the constitutionality of the amended direct-file statute, and second the order placing them in the county jail rather than in a juvenile detention center. The direct-file provision used to charge Lundquist and Chaides differs from the earlier version of the statute used to charge Mohi in that the amended statute did not, in this instance, allow for a recall hearing regarding the propriety of adult jurisdiction. Lundquist and Chaides raise the same claims regarding the Act as Mohi does, with additional arguments that the amended statute deprives them of due process under both the state and federal constitutions by eliminating the chance for recall and that § 78-3a-25 violates the state constitutional provision requiring separation of powers. . . .

ANALYSIS

I. STANDARD OF REVIEW

All issues in this case present questions of law. We therefore review the trial courts' conclusions for correctness. While ruling on the constitutionality of a statute, we will resolve doubts in favor of constitutionality.

II. UNIFORM OPERATION OF LAWS

Defendants attack the direct-file provision of the Act under Article I, § 24 of the Utah Constitution, which states, "All laws of a general nature shall have uniform operation." Defendants contend that § 78-3a-25 of the Code violates this provision by creating a scheme that treats one class of persons charged with a particular crime differently than another class of persons charged with the same crime. Defendants define the different "classes" created by the statute as (1) those accused of serious felony offenses who remain subject to the jurisdiction of the juvenile court and (2) those accused of identical offenses against whom the prosecutor files a criminal information in circuit or district court, or against whom a prosecutor obtains a criminal indictment. This arbitrary classification scheme is not reasonably related to any state interest, defendants argue, because the legislation is devoid of any reason for permitting identically situated juveniles to receive disparate treatment, resulting in one group that is eligible for rehabilitation in the juvenile system and another that faces the very different circumstances of the adult system. Defendants argue that no state interest is served by allowing such unreasonable disparity.

The State responds to these arguments first by claiming that defendants have not proven that the statute is applied in an uneven-handed way. Because the statute does not, according to the State, on its face create unreasonable classifications, defendants should have the burden of showing that the State actually afforded specific, like-situated juveniles different, more favorable treatment than that accorded these defendants. Because no such evidence was produced, the State contends, defendants' challenge must fail. . . .

We begin by clarifying the level of scrutiny used in deciding the constitutionality of the statutes in question under the state constitution. Defendants contend that the statute touches and concerns a "liberty" interest and therefore the legislature's actions must be reasonable in relation to the state's need to enact such statutes. The State contends, however, that being tried as a juvenile is not a constitutional right and therefore the legislature's actions in adopting the ordinance must be only rationally related to the state's interest in preserving the peace.

In *State in re Clatterbuck,* 700 P.2d 1076, 1079 (Utah 1985), we held that a juvenile's interest in his or her trial forum touched and concerned a "critical" interest. "We agree that whether a juvenile is to be transferred to the adult system is a 'critically important' question and that a juvenile must be afforded appropriate procedural protections when that determination is made." . . . "In scrutinizing a legislative measure under Article I, § 24, we must determine whether the classification is *reasonable,* whether the objectives of the legislative action are legitimate, and whether there is a *reasonable relationship* between the classification and the legislative purposes." The burden of demonstrating unconstitutionality, however, remains a heavy one. Therefore, we will uphold the statute unless defendants demonstrate that the state's interest in protecting the public and addressing the needs of juveniles is not reasonably related to the state's course of action in passing the statutory provisions in question.

. . . .

We begin by addressing the contours of Article I, § 24 of the Utah Constitution. We most recently discussed this provision:

> Although this provision is sometimes thought to have the same effect and impose the same legal standards on legislative action as the equal protection guarantee found in the Fourteenth Amendment to the United States Constitution, the language and history of the two provisions are entirely different, and even though there are important areas of overlap in the concepts embodied in the two provisions, the differences can produce different legal consequences.

Utah's uniform operation of laws provision establishes different requirements than does the federal Equal Protection Clause. The most important of these requirements, for the present analysis, is the requirement that "[f]or a law to be constitutional under [the provision], it is not enough that it be uniform on its face. What is critical is that the *operation* of the law be uniform. A law does not operate uniformly if 'persons similarly situated' are not 'treated similarly'. . . ." Hence, the challenged direct-file statute will not survive constitutional challenge if it is found to treat similarly situated juveniles in an unreasonably different fashion.

Analysis under Utah's uniform operation of laws provision requires two assessments. "First, a law must apply equally to all persons within a class. Second, the statutory classifications and the different treatment given the classes must be based on differences that have a reasonable tendency to further the objectives of the statute." Therefore, we must first determine what classifications, if any, are created by the statute. Second, we must determine whether different classes or subclasses are treated disparately. Finally, if any disparate treatment exists between classes or subclasses, we must determine whether the legislature had any reasonable objective that warrants the disparity.

Defendants claim, as set out above, that § 78-3a-25 of the Utah Code establishes at least two classes of similarly situated juvenile offenders: (1) sixteen-to seventeen-year-old juveniles accused of capital or first degree felonies over whom the juvenile court retains jurisdiction for all purposes, and (2) sixteen-to seventeen-year-old juveniles accused of capital or first degree felonies against whom a criminal information is filed in district or circuit court and over whom the district or circuit court retains jurisdiction. The State responds that the classes complained of are not created until the prosecutor decides how to proceed on a particular case. Therefore, the State contends, the statute does not on its face contain a system of classification and any classes that result are created by the prosecutor, not the statute.

The State [argues] that prosecutors, not the statute, "create" the challenged classes. . . . The State argues that the statute is facially neutral because it does not "by its own terms" segregate juvenile offenders into the classes complained of. We disagree.

The amended statute plainly states that a certain class of juveniles will be treated in one way (remain in juvenile jurisdiction) while another class of like-accused juveniles will be treated in another (singled out by prosecutors to be tried as adults). Although a prosecutor's decision triggers the assignment of any given defendant to one class or another, the statutory scheme itself contemplates the two classes. . . .

We next consider whether the law in question "applies equally" to all members within each class or subclass. Defendants contend that because they are being tried as adults for the same crimes that some of their peers will be tried for as juveniles, they are treated disparately. The State counters that being tried as a juvenile is not a "right" of anyone *per se* and that by bestowing a benefit on some juveniles but choosing not to bestow that same benefit on others, the legislature is not taking any rights away but merely giving benefits to appropriate persons. We are unable to reconcile this argument with the concept of uniform operation of laws because the selection process for beneficial treatment is arbitrary and standardless.

We agree with defendants that the present Act treats a certain subclass of juveniles nonuniformly. Juveniles against whom indictments or informations are filed are statutorily indistinguishable from those who remain in juvenile jurisdiction. By the very terms of the statute, they are accused of the same offenses and fall into the same age ranges. There is absolutely nothing in the statute to identify the juveniles to be tried as adults; it describes no distinctive characteristics to set them apart from juveniles in the other statutory class who remain in juvenile jurisdiction. However, there are critically important differences in the treatment of those juveniles tried as adults compared to those left in the juvenile system. For instance, cases tried in the juvenile court are considered civil rather than criminal proceedings. This has significant ramifications for an individual's future criminal record. Moreover, any juvenile committed to a secure facility under the direction of the Division of Youth Corrections must be released at age twenty-one. Therefore, because § 78-3a-25 applies only to individuals sixteen years of age or older, a juvenile in the statutory class who is left in the juvenile system faces a maximum potential sentence of five years or less.

The foregoing scenario is a dramatic contrast to that facing another juvenile in the same statutory class who is charged as an adult. "The effect of certification is to conduct the proceedings in every way as if the juvenile were an adult." Aside from acquiring a permanent criminal record, this juvenile faces a potential life sentence or, in the case of a capital felony, death, obviously a much greater deprivation of personal liberty than that risked by his or her counterpart who is tried as a juvenile. Moreover, rather than facing detention at a juvenile facility, these offenders are eligible for housing in the state prison or other adult facilities. Therefore, the statute permits two identically situated juveniles, even co-conspirators or co-participants in the same crime, to face radically different penalties and consequences without any statutory guidelines for distinguishing between them. This amounts to unequal treatment as that term has been used in the context of Article I, § 24. However, this finding alone does not invalidate the statute. The principle of uniform operation of laws requires invalidation of the statute only if defendants can demonstrate that this disparity is unreasonable in relation to the purpose of the statute. The final step in our analysis, therefore, is to determine whether there is a "reasonable relationship" between the purpose of the Act and the means adopted by the legislature to enact that purpose.

Section 78-3a-1 of the Code states that the purpose of the Act is to:

> promote public safety and individual accountability by the imposition of appropriate sanctions on persons who have committed acts in violation of law [and]; consistent with the ends of justice, strive to act in the best interests of the children in all cases and attempt to preserve and strengthen family ties where possible.

Defendants concede that this is a legitimate purpose for enacting a juvenile courts act. The only consideration, then, is whether the scheme imposed by § 78-3a-25 is reasonable in relation to this purpose. We conclude that it is not.

The State argues that the direct-file provision of the Act is reasonably related to the statute's stated purpose because there is a legitimate need to try certain violent juveniles as adults. We agree with the State's assertion of need but observe that the legislature has failed to specify *which* violent juveniles require such treatment, instead delegating that discretion to prosecutors who have no guidelines as to how it is to be exercised. Legitimacy of a goal cannot justify an arbitrary means. The State asserts that this problem is cured by the fact that prosecutors often have legitimate reasons for wanting to leave persons eligible for adult prosecution in juvenile court. But the *statute* does not require the prosecutor to have any reason, legitimate or otherwise, to support his or her decision of who stays in juvenile jurisdiction and who does not. Legitimacy in the purpose of the statute cannot make up for a deficiency in its design. Section 78-3a-25 is wholly without standards to guide or instruct prosecutors as to when they should or should not use such influential powers.[26] The total absence of such standards makes the Utah statute unique among those of all other states employing any type of adult prosecution of juvenile offenders. It is ironic that the Act sets out in thirteen

---

[26] [6] We note that this power is appropriately vested in the courts in § 78-3a-25(1)(a)(iii), which allows district courts to impose juvenile sentences when appropriate and allows juvenile courts to certify juveniles into adult jurisdiction. Significantly, this section specifies fairly extensive guidelines for making such determinations.

full paragraphs all of the factors that a *court* must consider to certify a juvenile into the adult system, but contains *no* guidelines for a prosecutor who may choose for any reason or no reason to place that juvenile into the adult system.[27]

The parties in these cases have briefed this court at length on the use of direct-file statutes in other jurisdictions; pursuant to rule 24 of the Utah Rules of Appellate Procedure, both the State and Mohi filed supplemental briefs on this point. All parties contend that the use or nonuse of discretionary direct-file schemes in other jurisdictions should be persuasive on the question of the reasonableness of Utah's statute. Unfortunately, the parties' reports regarding the discretion given to prosecutors in other jurisdictions are in conflict.

In his opening brief, Mohi alleged that only five jurisdictions in the United States employ impure direct-file acts[28] in which prosecutors have discretion as to which juveniles to remove from juvenile to adult criminal jurisdiction.[29] In his brief and in oral argument, Mohi argued that because only one comparable statute has been challenged on constitutional grounds, there is relatively little guidance for this court from other jurisdictions. In response to this contention, the State filed a supplemental "All-states Summary" which, together with the State's oral argument, contended that thirteen statutes[30] contain impure direct-file provisions and that no court has ever ruled such a statute unconstitutional on any ground.

Having reviewed the applicable juvenile courts acts of all fifty states and the District of Columbia, together with any published opinions in which the constitutionality of such statutes has been treated, we conclude that Utah's Act is unique in the amount of uncircumscribed discretion given to prosecutors.

---

27 [7] In several places the dissent argues that the guarantees of Article I, § 24 are satisfied by Utah's direct-file scheme because members of each subgroup created by § 78-3a-25 are treated equally. That is, the dissent argues that all juveniles who are chosen to be prosecuted as adults are treated alike and, likewise, all juveniles kept in the juvenile system are treated alike. Therefore, the dissent claims, there is no disparate treatment of like-situated individuals. The dissent repeats this argument by pointing out that all juveniles within the group of potential direct-file cases are possible subjects of prosecutor discretion and, therefore, because all were exposed to the risk of prosecutor selection, those actually chosen for removal have not been treated differently from those left in the juvenile system. Such reasoning, however, would justify the numerous "separate but equal" systems that have long been rejected as impermissible. A scheme which prosecuted all Caucasians in one way and all minorities in another could not be justified on the basis that all Caucasians were treated alike and all minorities were treated alike. Therefore, the dissent's argument ignores the core protections of Article I, § 24, that persons similarly situated (such as all sixteen-year-old juveniles accused of murder) must be treated alike.

28 [8] There are at least three types of statutory schemes that allow juveniles to be prosecuted as adults: (1) "pure" direct-file schemes, which *automatically* send certain juveniles to the adult criminal system on the basis of specific and articulated indicia, (2) "impure" direct-file schemes, which allow a prosecutor at least some discretion to choose which of similarly situated juveniles to remove from juvenile jurisdiction into the adult criminal system, and (3) *Kent* hearing schemes, taken from the case of *Kent v. United States,* 383 U.S. 541 (1966), in which removal from juvenile to adult jurisdiction is preceded by a judicial hearing. Under such nomenclature, Utah's scheme would be considered impure.

29 [9] The five states cited by Mohi are Arkansas, Colorado, Louisiana, Michigan, and Utah.

30 [10] The thirteen jurisdictions cited by the State are Arkansas, Colorado, District of Columbia, Florida, Georgia, Louisiana, Michigan, Minnesota, Nebraska, New York, Utah, Vermont, and Wyoming.

Currently, only eight jurisdictions, including Utah, employ impure direct-file provisions to any degree.[31] Of these eight, three provide statutory guidelines to help the prosecutor determine whether juvenile or adult jurisdiction would be proper.[32] Therefore, there are only five states, including Utah, in which prosecutors are granted "unguided" discretion. In one of these five states, Colorado, statutory prerequisites narrow the field of juveniles who face potential prosecutor discretion. For example, one prerequisite is that only juveniles with prior records may be removed to adult jurisdiction. Therefore, in actuality, there are only three states with schemes substantially similar to Utah's.[33]

. . . .

Having considered the authorities cited by all parties, we conclude that Utah's Act, which grants prosecutors totally unguided discretion in deciding which members of the class of potential juveniles to actually try as adults, is unique among statutes currently in use in the United States. Our statutory scheme is at the extreme end of the spectrum of systems employing prosecutor

---

[31] [11] The eight jurisdictions are (1) Arkansas, *see* Ark. Code Ann. § 9-27-318 (Michie 1993); (2) Colorado, *see* Colo. Rev. Stat. § 19-2-805 (Supp. 1994); (3) Florida, *see* Fla. Stat. ch. 39.047 (1993); (4) Louisiana, *see* La. Child. Code Ann. art. 305 (Supp. 1994); (5) Michigan, *see* Mich. Comp. Laws § 600.606 (1993); (6) Nebraska, *see* Neb. Rev. Stat. §§ 43-247, -276 (1988); (7) Utah, *see* Utah Code Ann. § 78-3a-25 (Supp. 1994); and (8) Wyoming, *see* Wyo.Stat. § 14-6-203(f) (1994).

The remaining five statutes characterized by the State as discretionary, which we consider to be either pure or *Kent* certification statutes, can be quickly distinguished from the other eight statutes listed above:

(1) District of Columbia, D.C. Code Ann. § 16-2301(3) (Supp. 1989). We do not consider this an impure scheme because the code defines all persons sixteen and above as adult. *See id.* Therefore, statutorily, *all* violent offenders sixteen years old or older, rather than only those selected by the prosecutor, would be tried as adults.

(2) Georgia, Ga. Code Ann. § 15-11-5 (Supp. 1994). The Georgia statute allows prosecutors discretion only in deciding which juveniles who would otherwise be tried as adults to remove *into* the juvenile system. No discretion is allowed in determining which juveniles to prosecute as adults. Therefore, Georgia's scheme functions primarily as do New York's and Vermont's, discussed below.

(3) Minnesota, Minn. Stat. § 260.131(4) (1994). This statute gives prosecutors only the discretion to label a case "extended juvenile jurisdiction," which allows the court to consider both adult and juvenile penalties. This is not comparable to an impure statute. Ultimately, the discretion of which system to follow lies with the court, not with the prosecutor. *See* Minn. Stat. § 260.126 (1984).

(4) New York, N.Y. Crim. Proc. Law § 180.75 (McKinney 1993). This statute *requires* juveniles sixteen years old and older who are accused of certain crimes to be tried as adults unless the district attorney requests that the case be tried in juvenile court. Here, any prosecutor discretion is limited to selecting juveniles to remain in family court; there is no prosecutor discretion as to which juveniles to place into the adult scheme. Moreover, it is not clear that a court would be bound to accept a prosecutor's recommendation even in this limited instance. Therefore, this statute is also free of the discretion employed in the statutes we are considering today.

(5) Vermont, Vt. Stat. Ann. tit. 33, § 5505 (1991). Like Georgia's and New York's schemes, Vermont's statute only allows prosecutors to select certain cases which would otherwise be tried in adult court to be tried in juvenile court. This scheme, which we note is further limited by precluding prosecutors from removing violent juveniles back into the juvenile system, does not allow prosecutors the discretion of where to file charges against violent juvenile offenders and is therefore inapplicable to our discussion today.

[32] [12] Florida, Nebraska, and Wyoming.

[33] [13] Arkansas, Louisiana, and Michigan.

discretion. While not dispositive, the fact that no other state has, at present, undertaken a process as arbitrary and unbridled as Utah's contributes significantly to our conclusion that the statute goes too far. There is no rational connection between the legislature's objective of balancing the needs of children with public protection and its decision to allow prosecutors total discretion in deciding which members of a potential class of juvenile offenders to single out for adult treatment. Such unguided discretion opens the door to abuse without any criteria for review or for insuring evenhanded decision making. No checks exist in this scheme to prevent such acts as a prosecutor's singling out members of certain unpopular groups for harsher treatment in the adult system while protecting equally culpable juveniles to whom a particular prosecutor may feel some cultural loyalty or for whom there may be broader public sympathy. Furthermore, the State has offered no plausible explanation of the necessity for such open-ended discretion.

The type of discretion incorporated in the Act is unlike traditional prosecutor discretion. Selecting a charge to fit the circumstances of a defendant and his or her alleged acts is a necessary step in the chain of any prosecution. It requires a legal determination on the part of the prosecutor as to which elements of an offense can likely be proved at trial. Moreover, such discretion is also beneficial to the public; it allows prosecutors to plea-bargain with offenders in some cases, saving the public the expense of criminal prosecutions. However, none of these benefits accompany the discretion to choose which juveniles to prosecute in adult rather than in juvenile court. The elements of the offense are determined by the *charging* decision, and it is only the charging decision that is protected by traditional notions of prosecutor discretion. Choosing which court to file charges in has significant consequences for the offender, and the statute does not indicate what characteristics of the offender mandate that choice. The scope for prosecutor stereotypes, prejudices, and biases of all kinds is simply too great. If it is the legislature's determination to have all members of a certain group of violent juveniles (such as repeat offenders, those who use guns, etc.) tried as adults, it is free to do so.[34] However, the legislature may not create a scheme which permits the random and unsupervised separation of all such violent juveniles into a relatively privileged group on the one hand and a relatively burdened group on the other.

Utah's uniform operation of laws provision speaks directly to the type of discretion involved in § 78-3a-25, as opposed to the traditional discretion allotted prosecutors to determine what crime to charge. The challenged statute permits prosecutors to treat different offenders accused of the same criminal offense differently. Thus, the same law operates disparately and nonuniformly on similarly situated juveniles. In a case where the prosecutor chooses to charge like-situated suspects with different crimes, the classic "prosecutorial discretion" question is *which* law to apply to an offender rather than how to apply the *same* law to different offenders. Once an offender is charged with

---

[34] [19] Whether the legislature can try all juveniles as adults without any opportunity for review may raise federal constitutional questions. *See, e.g., Kelley v. Kaiser,* 992 F.2d 1509 (10th Cir. 1993). "Having created the juvenile court system, under *Kent,* it is the State's decision to seek to treat a juvenile as an adult that, *in and of itself triggers the need for a hearing.*"

a particular crime, that offender must be subjected to the same or substantially similar procedures and exposed to the same level of jeopardy as all other offenders so charged to satisfy the constitutional requirement of uniform operation of the laws.

We conclude that the provisions in § 78-3a-25 of the Code giving prosecutors undirected discretion to choose where to file charges against certain juvenile offenders are unconstitutional under Article I, § 24 of the Utah Constitution.[35] Therefore, Mohi, Lundquist, and Chaides are remanded to the appropriate juvenile jurisdictions for certification proceedings consistent with the requirements in § 78-3a-25.

III. STATUTORY RECALL PROVISIONS

Because we have already remanded the cases of these defendants for certification hearings in juvenile court, there may be no immediate need for a ruling on the use or the lack of an appropriate recall remedy. However, because this issue is likely to recur and because Lundquist and Chaides challenge the repeal of the recall provision in the amended statute, we nevertheless consider defendants' claims concerning the need and use of recall procedures to reclaim juvenile jurisdiction for minors tried as adults.

. . . .

Lundquist and Chaides challenge the amended Act in part on the ground that the legislature has removed the recall provision that Mohi claims was inadequate. They argue that by depriving them of a hearing to determine whether adult or juvenile court would be a proper forum for their cases, the amended statute denies them due process. This argument is also without merit. As stated above (and as conceded by all parties), juveniles have no constitutional right to be tried as juveniles. Therefore, if they were properly charged in adult court in the first place, Lundquist and Chaides would have no state due process right to a hearing to determine whether they can be retained as adults for trial. As part II of this opinion states, the state is not required to give juvenile status to anyone. However, once the legislature enacts a law classifying a certain group as juveniles, it must apply that law uniformly. If, on the other hand, it uniformly decides to remove a certain class of persons from the category of "juvenile offender," it does not need to allow those persons a hearing on the matter. Because they have no "right" to juvenile treatment, defendants cannot claim that their juvenile status was unconstitutionally removed by the legislature.

CONCLUSION

On the basis of the foregoing analysis, we hold § 78-3a-25(6)(b) and (7) to violate Article I, § 24 of the Utah Constitution. Consequently, the orders of

---

[35] [21] Defendants have also challenged the direct-file provisions under state and federal due process and separation of powers claims. Because we invalidate the challenged sections of the statute under the uniform operation of laws provision of the state constitution, we do not reach defendants' other constitutional challenges, and we express no opinion on the merits of those contentions.

. . . .

the trial courts herein are reversed, and defendants are remanded to the jurisdiction of the juvenile courts for certification proceedings.

RUSSON, JUSTICE, *dissenting*:

I strongly disagree with the majority's analysis and result in part II, "Uniform Operation of Laws." In part II, the majority addresses UTAH CODE ANN. § 78-3a-25, which grants prosecutors discretion in cases involving a juvenile offender to file either criminal charges in "adult" court [36] or a civil action in juvenile court. [37] The majority holds this section unconstitutional on the basis of an erroneous interpretation of the uniform operation of laws provision of Article I, § 24 of the Utah Constitution. Because the majority's interpretation oversteps any reasonable boundary of the rights which that provision is designed to protect, I dissent.

I. PROSECUTORIAL DISCRETION GENERALLY

To place the prosecutorial discretion granted by UTAH CODE ANN. § 78-3a-25 in its proper perspective, it is important to first examine the breadth of discretion generally given to prosecutors. It is well established that a prosecutor's decision to charge or not to charge an individual with a criminal violation is protected by traditional notions of prosecutorial discretion. *See Bordenkircher v. Hayes,* 434 U.S. 357, 364 (1978). As the Supreme Court stated therein:

> In our system, so long as the prosecutor has probable cause to believe that the accused committed an offense defined by statute, the decision whether or not to prosecute, and *what charge to file* or bring before a grand jury, *generally rests within his discretion.* Within the limits set by the legislature's constitutionally valid definition of chargeable offenses, *"the conscious exercise of some selectivity in enforcement is not in itself a federal constitutional violation"* so long as *"the selection was [not] deliberately based upon an unjustifiable standard such as race, religion, or other arbitrary classification."*

. . . .

There are numerous instances in which prosecutors are granted the same or substantially similar discretion that is at issue in the case before us. For example, the prosecutor has the discretion in regard to an alleged criminal act to file felony charges, or misdemeanor charges, or no charges whatsoever. In fact, the prosecutor can even do so in relation to a single criminal act involving more than one person. For instance, assume that three men, A, B, and C, commit an armed robbery together. A has a long history of felony arrests and convictions and is the one who actually perpetrates the offense. B has a couple of misdemeanor convictions and stands watch while A carries

---

[36] [1] For ease of reference, district and circuit courts will be referred to collectively as adult courts.

[37] [2] All proceedings before the juvenile court are civil proceedings. *See* UTAH CODE ANN. § 78-3a-44(1) (stating that "[p]roceedings in children's cases shall be regarded as civil proceedings, with the court exercising equitable powers").

out the crime. C has no criminal record, drives the getaway car, was reluctantly talked into being a part of this crime by the coercion of his comrades, and agrees to testify against them. I doubt that members of this court would proclaim "unconstitutional discretion" if the prosecutor charged A with a felony, B with a misdemeanor, and C with nothing at all.

. . . .

In the present case, there are no allegations of discrimination arising from selective prosecution. Rather, defendants attack § 78-3a-25 merely because it gives prosecutors discretion to file either criminal charges in adult court or a civil action in juvenile court, arguing that such discretion constitutes a violation of the uniform application of the laws under Article I, § 24 of the Utah Constitution. However, as this court has stated in a similar context, "[I]n the absence of some showing that the prosecutor is classifying persons improperly, the mere existence of the discretionary power to select which mechanism to use does not offend the uniform operation of the laws provision of Article I, § 24." There are no allegations in the case before us that the discretion at issue was being practiced in a discriminatory manner. Accordingly, the prosecutor's discretion to file a criminal charge in adult court or a civil petition in juvenile court is the sort of prosecutorial discretion that has traditionally been permitted.

We have no "crazy quilt" here; rather, § 78-3a-25 is a well-reasoned effort to give prosecutors the discretion necessary to bring a charge carrying appropriate sanctions against juvenile offenders. This sort of discretion has never been considered vulnerable to facial equal protection challenges. Rather, it has been recognized as an integral component of our scheme of criminal justice. As the United States Supreme Court stated in *Wayte v. United States,* 470 U.S. 598, 607 (1985):

> This broad discretion rests largely on the recognition that the decision to prosecute is particularly ill-suited to judicial review. Such factors as the strength of the case, the prosecution's general deterrence value, the Government's enforcement priorities, and the case's relationship to the Government's overall enforcement plan are not readily susceptible to the kind of analysis the courts are competent to undertake.

In summary, the majority's argument erroneously assumes that similarly situated people are being treated differently. Under § 78-3a-25, all juvenile offenders who commit the offenses enumerated therein are subject to the same initial nondiscriminatory exercise of prosecutorial discretion as to whether to file criminal charges or a civil juvenile action against a certain offender. Accordingly, the prosecutorial discretion provided for in that statute is not different from all other kinds of prosecutorial discretion.

While the majority correctly concludes that "[o]nce an offender is charged with a particular crime, that offender must be subjected to the same or substantially similar procedures . . . as all other offenders so charged," that is not at issue in this case. Because § 78-3a-25 specifically pertains to the prosecutor's charging decision, the equal protection concerns raised by the majority are not violated by this statute.

III. OTHER STATES

Additionally, the majority has chosen, in accepting defendants' argument and overturning UTAH CODE ANN. § 78-3a-25, to depart from the accepted wisdom of every other court which has ruled on the issue. In examining their own direct-filing statutes, courts in virtually every other jurisdiction have consistently held that the discretion vested in prosecutors to decide which juveniles to file criminal charges against comports with equal protection principles. *See, e.g., United States v. Bland,* 472 F.2d 1329 (D.C.Cir. 1972); *People v. Thorpe,* 641 P.2d 935 (Colo. 1982); *In re Wood,* 768 P.2d 1370 (Mont. 1989); *State ex rel. Coats v. Rakestraw,* 610 P.2d 256 (Okla. Crim. App. 1980). As this court acknowledged in the lead opinion in *State v. Bell,* 785 P.2d 390 (Utah 1989):

> This jurisdiction has long recognized the vital role of the prosecution and the importance of affording that body the discretion, within permissible limits, to exercise its function. Certainly, we are compelled, as are our sister states, to recognize this discretion as it preserves the constitutional concept of separation of powers. Also, it must be recognized that the prosecutor has at his or her disposal in making such a decision the criteria provided for elsewhere in the statute, the purpose of the Juvenile Courts Act, and the standards governing the duties of his or her office.

The fact that this discretion has been codified into the statute at issue simply underscores the legislature's determination that to achieve the multiple and sometimes cross-cutting purposes of the juvenile court system, which concern both rehabilitation of the juvenile offender and the safety of the community, a prosecutor must be granted some degree of freedom to differentiate between juvenile offenders.

Nor is the majority persuasive in its attempt to distinguish Utah's statutory scheme from that of those states which have upheld direct-filing statutes. The majority initially draws a distinction based on whether the statute in question is a "pure" direct-filing statute or an "impure" direct-filing statute and does not even address pure direct-filing systems in other states, simply stating that they are "noncomparable." In pure direct-filing statutes, the prosecutorial discretion lies in deciding what charges to file: Certain charges must be tried in an adult criminal action, while other charges must be tried in a juvenile proceeding. In essence, this system is no different from ours. As noted above, under § 78-3a-25, if the prosecutor elects to criminally charge a juvenile offender, that juvenile must be tried in adult court; conversely, if the prosecutor decides to file a civil petition against the juvenile, the matter proceeds to juvenile court.

Furthermore, other states with impure direct-filing statutes have found such statutes to be constitutional. For example, in *People v. Thorpe,* 641 P.2d 935 (Colo. 1982), the Colorado Supreme Court concluded in circumstances similar to those in the present case that although an "as-applied" challenge could be sustained if there was selective prosecution, a facial constitutional challenge to its direct-filing system fails. We should conclude that the same is true in our case.

. . . .

The majority states that Utah's scheme is "arbitrary and unbridled" and results in "uncircumscribed discretion" on the part of the prosecutor. However, among the states that allow direct filing, the Utah statute is one of the strictest in limiting the number of offenses which qualify for direct filing. The prosecutor is not given unbridled discretion; only certain specifically enumerated types of violations are eligible for direct filing. Accordingly, it is comparable to other states' systems and should likewise be held constitutional.

Lastly, the majority's claim that a "parade of horribles" would ensue if prosecutors were allowed the discretion provided by this statute is groundless. There is no evidence supporting the majority's assertion that § 78-3a-25 would lead to prosecutors' singling out members of unpopular groups for harsher treatment in the adult system. In fact, the very same argument, that prosecutors could single out certain groups for harsher treatment, could be made in reference to every criminal statute in the state code. In any event, defendants have not challenged the statute on the ground that it is being applied in a discriminatory manner; they only challenge the statute *on its face*. Since the majority's concerns go to the application of the statute, not to its facial constitutionality, those concerns are irrelevant to the case at bar.

This is not to say, of course, that the legislature has unfettered power to enact laws relating to prosecutorial discretion. Prosecutorial discretion is always, at the very least, subject to review for abuse. The standards for determining that abuse should be filtered through the judiciary's reluctance to interfere with prosecutorial decision making. Since no allegations of abuse of prosecutorial discretion have been raised in the present case, I would hold § 78-3a-25 constitutional under Article I, § 24 of the Utah Constitution. Accordingly, I dissent from the majority's holding to the contrary.

IV. CONCLUSION

Based on the foregoing, I dissent from section II.

HOWE, J., *concurs in the dissenting opinion of* RUSSON, J.

————

NOTES AND QUESTIONS

1. Is the discretion granted the prosecutor under the Utah "direct file" provision different, for example, from the discretion uniformly granted prosecutors either to file criminal charges for arson against one who starts fires or to bring civil commitment proceedings against him for pyromania?

2. In *Hughes v. State*, 653 A.2d 241 (Del. 1994), the Delaware Supreme Court held that a statutory amendment eliminating judicial investigation into the factual basis for felony charges in criminal court against offenders who reach age 18 while charges are pending in juvenile court violates due process and equal protection of law. In holding that such juveniles are entitled to a "reverse amenability" hearing where they can present evidence that they should be tried in juvenile court, the court stated:

In essence, the statutory amendment has stripped the judiciary of its independent jurisdictional role in the adjudication of children by granting the charging authority the unbridled discretion to unilaterally determine which forum has jurisdiction. . . . [T]he statute has deprived children . . . [of] the judicial counterweight which they are constitutionally entitled to receive.

Do these views of the *Hughes* court assume that juveniles have a constitutional right to juvenile court jurisdiction?

[3] Waiver

As the above materials make clear, even with the advent of juvenile courts some juveniles have always been "waived" to adult court for criminal prosecution. The last twenty years, however, have witnessed a dramatic shift in the incidence of and mechanism for waiver of juvenile court jurisdiction. As more young offenders are considered appropriate subjects for the punitive dispositions of criminal court, many jurisdictions have enacted expanded provisions for juvenile waiver to adult court. Waiver provisions take three basic forms: (1) judicial waiver, historically the most common method, whereby, as in the *Kent* case, § 5.02[A], *supra*, a juvenile court judge conducts an individual evaluation on the basis of offender and offense-based criteria; (2) prosecutorial waiver (also known as "concurrent jurisdiction" or "direct file") which permits, as in the *Mohi* case *supra*, prosecutors to decide to file charges in either juvenile or criminal court and (3) statutory exclusion (also referred to as "legislative waiver" which requires, as in the *Bland* case, *supra*, that juveniles of a minimum age accused of designated serious offenses be prosecuted in adult court. One commentator described the present situation as follows: "All fifty states and the District of Columbia have waiver provisions of some kind, with most having hybrid combinations of the three basic forms." Wayne A. Logan, *Proportionality and Punishment: Imposing Life Without Parole on Juveniles*, 33 WAKE FOREST L. REV. 681, 688 (1998). For a detailed examination of waiver statutes nationwide, see Barry C. Feld, *The Juvenile Court Meets the Principle of the Offense: Legislative Changes in Juvenile Waiver Statutes*, 78 J. CRIM. L. & CRIMINOLOGY 471 (1987).

NEVADA REVISED STATUTES
§ 62.080 (2000)

Procedure when child 14 years or older is charged with felony; certification for criminal proceedings required under certain circumstances.

1. Except as otherwise provided in subsection 2 and NRS 62.081, if:

(a) A child is charged with an offense that would be a felony if committed by an adult; and

(b) The child was 14 years of age or older at the time he allegedly committed the offense, the juvenile court, upon a motion by the district attorney and after a full investigation, may retain jurisdiction or certify the child for proper criminal proceedings to any court that would have jurisdiction to try the offense if committed by an adult.

2. If a child:

(a) Is charged with:

(1) A sexual assault involving the use or threatened use of force or violence against the victim; or

(2) An offense or attempted offense involving the use or threatened use of a firearm; and

(b) Was 14 years of age or older at the time he allegedly committed the offense, the juvenile court, upon a motion by the district attorney and after a full investigation, shall certify the child for proper criminal proceedings to any court that would have jurisdiction to try the offense if committed by an adult, unless the court specifically finds by clear and convincing evidence that the child's actions were substantially the result of his substance abuse or emotional or behavioral problems and such substance abuse or problems may be appropriately treated through the jurisdiction of the juvenile court.

3. If a child is certified for criminal proceedings as an adult pursuant to subsection 1 or 2, the court shall also certify the child for criminal proceedings as an adult for any other related offense arising out of the same facts as the offense for which the child was certified, regardless of the nature of the related offense.

4. If a child has been certified for criminal proceedings as an adult pursuant to subsection 1 or 2 and his case has been transferred out of the juvenile court, original jurisdiction of his person for that case rests with the court to which the case has been transferred, and the child may petition for transfer of his case back to the juvenile court only upon a showing of exceptional circumstances. If the child's case is transferred back to the juvenile court, the judge of that court shall determine whether the exceptional circumstances warrant accepting jurisdiction.

CALIFORNIA WELFARE & INSTITUTIONS CODE
§ 707 (WEST SUPP. 2001)

Fitness Hearing

(a)(1) In any case in which a minor is alleged to be a person described in § 602(a) by reason of the violation, when he or she was 16 years of age or older, of any criminal statute or ordinance except those listed in subdivision (b), upon motion of the petitioner made prior to the attachment of jeopardy the court shall cause the probation officer to investigate and submit a report on the behavioral patterns and social history of the minor being considered for a determination of unfitness. Following submission and consideration of the report, and of any other relevant evidence which the petitioner or the minor may wish to submit, the juvenile court may find that the minor is not a fit and proper subject to be dealt with under the juvenile court law if it concludes that the minor would not be amenable to the care, treatment, and training program available through the facilities of the juvenile court, based upon an evaluation of the following criteria:

(1) The degree of criminal sophistication exhibited by the minor.

(2) Whether the minor can be rehabilitated prior to the expiration of the juvenile court's jurisdiction.

(3) The minor's previous delinquent history.

(4) Success of previous attempts by the juvenile court to rehabilitate the minor.

(5) The circumstances and gravity of the offense alleged in the petition to have been committed by the minor.

A determination that the minor is not a fit and proper subject to be dealt with under the juvenile court law may be based on any one or a combination of the factors set forth above, which shall be recited in the order of unfitness. In any case in which a hearing has been noticed pursuant to this section, the court shall postpone the taking of a plea to the petition until the conclusion of the fitness hearing, and no plea which may already have been entered shall constitute evidence at the hearing.

(2) This paragraph shall apply to a minor alleged to be a person described in § 602 by reason of the violation, when he or she has attained the age of 16 years, of any felony offense when the minor has been declared to be a ward of the court pursuant to § 602 on one or more prior occasions if both of the following apply:

(A) The minor has previously been found to have committed two or more felony offenses.

(B) The offenses upon which the prior petition or petitions were based were committed when the minor had attained the age of 14 years.

Upon motion of the petitioner made prior to the attachment of jeopardy the court shall cause the probation officer to investigate and submit a report on the behavioral patterns and social history of the minor being considered for a determination of unfitness. Following submission and consideration of the report, and of any other relevant evidence that the petitioner or the minor may wish to submit, the minor shall be presumed to be not a fit and proper subject to be dealt with under the juvenile court law unless the juvenile court concludes, based upon evidence, which evidence may be of extenuating or mitigating circumstances that the minor would be amenable to the care, treatment, and training program available through the facilities of the juvenile court, based upon an evaluation of the following criteria:

(A) The degree of criminal sophistication exhibited by the minor.

(B) Whether the minor can be rehabilitated prior to the expiration of the juvenile court's jurisdiction.

(C) The minor's previous delinquent history.

(D) Success of previous attempts by the juvenile court to rehabilitate the minor.

(E) The circumstances and gravity of the offense alleged in the petition to have been committed by the minor.

A determination that the minor is a fit and proper subject to be dealt with under the juvenile court law shall be based on a finding of amenability after consideration of the criteria set forth above, and findings therefore recited in the order as to each of the above criteria that the minor is fit and proper under each and every one of the above criteria. In making a finding of fitness, the court may consider extenuating and mitigating circumstances in evaluating each of the above criteria. In any case in which the hearing has been noticed pursuant to this section, the court shall postpone the taking of a plea to the petition until the conclusion of the fitness hearing and no plea which may already have been entered shall constitute evidence at the hearing. If the minor is found to be a fit and proper subject to be dealt with under the juvenile court law pursuant to this subdivision, the minor shall be committed to placement in a juvenile hall, ranch camp, forestry camp, boot camp, or secure juvenile home pursuant to § 730, or in any institution operated by the Youth Authority.

(3) If, pursuant to this subdivision, the minor is found to be not a fit and proper subject for juvenile court treatment and is tried in a court of criminal jurisdiction and found guilty by the trier of fact, the judge may commit the minor to the Youth Authority in lieu of sentencing the minor to the state prison, unless the limitations specified in § 1732.6 apply.

(b) Subdivision (c) shall be applicable in any case in which a minor is alleged to be a person described in § 602 by reason of the violation, when he or she was 16 years of age or older, of one of the following offenses:

(1) Murder.

(2) Arson, as provided in subdivision (a) or (b) of § 451 of the Penal Code.

(3) Robbery.

(4) Rape with force or violence or threat of great bodily harm.

(5) Sodomy by force, violence, duress, menace, or threat of great bodily harm.

(6) Lewd or lascivious act as provided in subdivision (b) of § 288 of the Penal Code.

(7) Oral copulation by force, violence, duress, menace, or threat of great bodily harm.

(8) Any offense specified in subdivision (a) of § 289 of the Penal Code.

(9) Kidnapping for ransom.

(10) Kidnapping for purpose of robbery.

(11) Kidnapping with bodily harm.

(12) Attempted murder.

(13) Assault with a firearm or destructive device.

(14) Assault by any means of force likely to produce great bodily injury.

(15) Discharge of a firearm into an inhabited or occupied building.

(16) Any offense described in § 1203.09 of the Penal Code.

(17) Any offense described in § 12022.5 or 12022.53 of the Penal Code.

(18) Any felony offense in which the minor personally used a weapon listed in subdivision (a) of § 12020 of the Penal Code.

(19) Any felony offense described in § 136.1 or 137 of the Penal Code.

(20) Manufacturing, compounding, or selling one-half ounce or more of any salt or solution of a controlled substance specified in subdivision (e) of § 11055 of the Health and Safety Code.

(21) Any violent felony, as defined in subdivision (c) of § 667.5 of the Penal Code, which would also constitute a felony violation of subdivision (b) of § 186.22 of the Penal Code.

(22) Escape, by the use of force or violence, from any county juvenile hall, home, ranch, camp, or forestry camp in violation of subdivision (b) of § 871 where great bodily injury is intentionally inflicted upon an employee of the juvenile facility during the commission of the escape.

(23) Torture . . . as described in §§ 206 and 206.1 of the Penal Code.

(24) Aggravated mayhem, as described in § 205 of the Penal Code.

(25) Carjacking, as described in § 215 of the Penal Code, while armed with a dangerous or deadly weapon.

(26) Kidnapping, as punishable in subdivision (d) of § 208 of the Penal Code.

(27) Kidnapping, as punishable in § 209.5 of the Penal Code.

(28) The offense described in subdivision (c) of § 12034 of the Penal Code.

(29) The offense described in § 12308 of the Penal Code.

(30) Voluntary manslaughter, as described in subdivision (a) of § 192 of the Penal Code.

(c) With regard to a minor alleged to be a person described in § 602 by reason of the violation, when he or she was 14 years of age or older, of any of the offenses listed in subdivision (b), upon motion of the petitioner made prior to the attachment of jeopardy the court shall cause the probation officer to investigate and submit a report on the behavioral patterns and social history of the minor being considered for a determination of unfitness. Following submission and consideration of the report, and of any other relevant evidence which the petitioner or the minor may wish to submit the minor shall be presumed to be not a fit and proper subject to be dealt with under the juvenile court law unless the juvenile court concludes, based upon evidence, which evidence may be of extenuating or mitigating circumstances, that the minor would be amenable to the care, treatment, and training program available through the facilities of the juvenile court based upon an evaluation of each of the following criteria:

(1) The degree of criminal sophistication exhibited by the minor.

(2) Whether the minor can be rehabilitated prior to the expiration of the juvenile court's jurisdiction.

(3) The minor's previous delinquent history.

(4) Success of previous attempts by the juvenile court to rehabilitate the minor.

(5) The circumstances and gravity of the offenses alleged in the petition to have been committed by the minor.

A determination that the minor is a fit and proper subject to be dealt with under the juvenile court law shall be based on a finding of amenability after consideration of the criteria set forth above, and findings therefor recited in the order as to each of the above criteria that the minor is fit and proper under each and every one of the above criteria. In making a finding of fitness, the court may consider extenuating or mitigating circumstances in evaluating each of the above criteria. In any case in which a hearing has been noticed pursuant to this section, the court shall postpone the taking of a plea to the petition until the conclusion of the fitness hearing and no plea which may already have been entered shall constitute evidence at the hearing. If, pursuant to this subdivision, the minor is found to be not a fit and proper subject for juvenile court treatment and is tried in a court of criminal jurisdiction and found guilty by the trier of fact, the judge may commit the minor to the Youth Authority in lieu of sentencing the minor to the state prison, unless the limitations specified in § 1732.6 apply.

. . . .

(e) Any report submitted by a probation officer pursuant to this section regarding the behavioral patterns and social history of the minor being considered for a determination of unfitness shall include any written or oral statement offered by the victim's parent or guardian if the victim is a minor, or if the victim has died, the victim's next of kin, as authorized by subdivision (b) of § 656.2. Victims' statements shall be considered by the court to the extent they are relevant to the court's determination of unfitness.

Nebraska Revised Statutes
(1998)

§ 43-261 Juvenile charged in court other than juvenile court; transfer to juvenile court; procedure.

Before the plea is entered, or in case a felony is charged, at any time prior to or at the preliminary hearing, the court shall advise any person who was a juvenile at the time of the commission of the alleged act charged in any court other than a juvenile court that such juvenile may orally or in writing move the court in which the charge is pending to waive jurisdiction to the juvenile court for further proceedings under the Nebraska Juvenile Code. If a felony is charged, such motion shall be filed in the county or district court, and the hearing shall be held before a county or district judge. Such motion may be entered at any time prior to commencement of trial or acceptance of a plea of guilty or no contest by the court. The court shall schedule a hearing on the motion within fifteen days. The customary rules of evidence shall not be followed at such hearing. The county attorney shall present the evidence and reasons why the case should be retained, and the defendant shall present evidence and reasons why the case should be transferred, and both sides shall consider the criteria set forth in § 43-276. In deciding the motion the court shall, after considering the evidence and the reasons presented by the parties and the matters required to be considered by the county attorney pursuant to § 43-276, transfer the case unless a sound basis exists for retaining jurisdiction.

Nothing in this section shall prohibit the county attorney from waiving any objection to such a transfer even when a complaint is filed. In such cases it shall be sufficient for the court to sustain the motion of the juvenile without entering a finding.

The court shall set forth findings for the reason for its decision, which shall not be a final order for the purpose of enabling an appeal. If the court determines that the juvenile should be transferred to the juvenile court, the complete file in the court shall be transferred to the juvenile court and the complaint may be filed in place of a petition therein. The court making such transfer shall order the juvenile to be taken forthwith to the juvenile court and designate where the juvenile shall be kept pending determination by the juvenile court. The juvenile court shall then proceed as provided in the Nebraska Juvenile Code.

Nothing in this section shall be construed to require more than one transfer proceeding.

§ 276 County attorney; criminal charge, juvenile court petition, or mediation referral; determination; considerations.

In cases coming within subdivision (1) of § 43-247, when there is concurrent jurisdiction, or subdivision (2) or (4) of § 43-247, when the juvenile is under the age of sixteen years, the county attorney shall, in making the determination whether to file a criminal charge, juvenile court petition, or mediation referral, consider: (1) The type of treatment such juvenile would most likely be amenable to; (2) whether there is evidence that the alleged offense included violence or was committed in an aggressive and premeditated manner; (3) the motivation for the commission of the offense; (4) the age of the juvenile and the ages and circumstances of any others involved in the offense; (5) the previous history of the juvenile, including whether he or she had been convicted of any previous offenses or adjudicated in juvenile court, and, if so, whether such offenses were crimes against the person or relating to property, and other previous history of antisocial behavior, if any, including any patterns of physical violence; (6) the sophistication and maturity of the juvenile as determined by consideration of his or her home, school activities, emotional attitude and desire to be treated as an adult, pattern of living, and whether he or she has had previous contact with law enforcement agencies and courts and the nature thereof; (7) whether there are facilities particularly available to the juvenile court for treatment and rehabilitation of the juvenile; (8) whether the best interests of the juvenile and the security of the public may require that the juvenile continue in custody or under supervision for a period extending beyond his or her minority and, if so, the available alternatives best suited to this purpose; (9) whether the victim agrees to participate in mediation; and (10) such other matters as the county attorney deems relevant to his or her decision.

NOTES AND QUESTIONS

1. The statutory excerpts above represent three of the variety of approaches utilized in juvenile codes. The Nevada statute is an example of perhaps the most common model which vests original and exclusive jurisdiction in the juvenile court with provisions to waive certain cases to criminal court. The Nevada statute is a bit unique, however, in its absence of a list of statutory criteria along the lines of those articulated in the Appendix to the *Kent* case, *see* § 5.02[A], *supra*, and those spelled out in the California and Nebraska statutes, respectively. The Nevada statute permits waiver so long as the court conducts a "full investigation." The Nevada Supreme Court has upheld the "full investigation" standard against attack for unconstitutional vagueness. In *Lewis v. State*, 478 P.2d 168 (Nev. 1970), the court supplied criteria to assist judges in applying the "full investigation" standard. After initially adopting the *Kent* criteria as the guiding principles, the court eventually determined that the sole criterion for waiving jurisdiction is "whether the public interest requires that the youth be placed within the jurisdiction of the adult courts." In making that determination, the court identified three factors to be taken into account: 1) the nature and seriousness of the crime; 2) the presence or absence of past offenses; and 3) the juvenile's age, maturity, character, personality, and family situation.

2. The California statute above elaborately illustrates another model. Sections (a)–(c) vest exclusive original jurisdiction in the juvenile courts but with a presumption that articulated serious offenses will be waived to criminal court. As noted above, some jurisdictions have opted for "legislative waiver" provisions that place exclusive jurisdiction for certain serious offenses under certain circumstances in criminal court. *See, e.g.*, CONN. GEN. STAT. § 46b-127 (West Supp. 2001) (criminal court with exclusive jurisdiction in cases of juveniles over age 14 who commit capital and other serious felonies).

3. As is evident from NEB. REV. STAT. § 43-247, § 5.03[C][2], *supra*, and the provisions immediately above, the Nebraska system is a concurrent jurisdiction system with "reverse waiver" from criminal to juvenile court. The Nebraska statute spells out waiver criteria with the final criterion on the list being any "matter [that] the county attorney deems relevant to his or her [waiver] decision." What is the effect of this criterion?

MATTER OF JOHNSON

Court of Special Appeals of Maryland
304 A.2d 859 (1973)

GILBERT, JUSTICE.

. . . .

The Legislature has mandated that five factors are to be considered by the juvenile judge in any waiver proceeding. . . . Those factors are:

"(1) Age of child.

(2) Mental and physical condition of child.

(3) The child's amenability to treatment in any institution, facility, or programs available to delinquents.

(4) The nature of the offense.

(5) The safety of the public."

Not all of the five factors need be resolved against the juvenile . . . for the waiver to be justifiable.

". . . [T]he purpose of a juvenile waiver hearing is to determine whether or not the juvenile is a fit subject for juvenile rehabilitative measures."

. . . [A] waiver hearing is a determination of whether a juvenile will receive non-punitive rehabilitation as a juvenile from the State's social agencies, or whether he, if found guilty, will be sentenced as if the juvenile were an adult. . . .

In the instant case, the appellant, Diane Connie Johnson, was charged . . . with being a delinquent child, "For the reason that on May 21, 1972, Hrs. 5:30 p.m. . . . [she] unlawfully in a grossly negligent manner did kill and slay Lawrence Brittingham, [age 2 years]." Miss Johnson was 16 years of age at the time of the occurrence.

On September 14, 1972, the State's Attorney for Baltimore City sought a waiver of jurisdiction. The waiver hearing was held on November 1, 1972, at which time the appellant was 17 years of age. At the hearing, the judge stated that the "ground rules" were to be "an examination of the five criteria set forth in the statute to determine whether or not to waive jurisdiction." The Assistant State's Attorney then told the juvenile court judge: ". . . [T]he basis for the State's request for waiver is that this charge is too serious to be tried in juvenile court." The State then stated to the judge that: "[Miss Johnson], who is an unlicensed driver, asked the boy friend, who was twenty-one years old and is a licensed driver, if she could drive the car. He gave her permission. A short while later as she was turning the corner, she made a wide turn . . . and instead of putting her foot on the brake she put her foot on the accelerator and she went up on the sidewalk and struck three children. One of them was pronounced dead upon arrival at the hospital."

After the incident, Miss Johnson was sent home by her boy friend, and he told the police upon their arrival at the scene that he was the driver of the car at the time of the accident. Information supplied to the police by witnesses led the investigating officers to conclude that the "boy friend" had not told them the truth. When confronted with the statements of witnesses, the boy friend recanted and implicated Miss Johnson.

The Assistant State's Attorney concluded his presentation of facts with the remark that, "We also feel . . . that the safety of the public would dictate that this case be tried in criminal court rather than [in] juvenile court."

A "Waiver Summary" . . . was prepared by the Department of Juvenile Services and submitted to the judge. The "Summary" stated that Miss Johnson was in the eleventh grade at Dunbar High School and was an above average student. She was described by her tenth grade counselor as "very responsible and reliable and has presented no conduct problem." According to the "Summary" the appellant has been an active participant in "extra-curricular activities," and in the opinion of the counselor had the "potential to be a productive citizen." Mss Johnson attends church on a regular basis and is a member of her church choir.

The appellant offered the testimony of Rev. Leroy Gill, Sr. who informed the court that Miss Johnson was active in civic affairs, and that from his association with her it was apparent to him that she was "very concerned about what has happened," and that there were times when "she has been crying because of the death of the two-year-old." Rev. Gill expressed the opinion that if Miss Johnson were tried in the juvenile court "it would be [a] greater help [to her] rather than being tried in a criminal court type environment." The hearing judge opined:

> Well, I am going to grant the State's request and waive jurisdiction in this petition. It is a very difficult step for me to take because we have a young lady who has had a very credible record for herself. She has not been in any difficulty and she has done well in school and has been active in school activities, has been active in community activities, but I base my decision on her age, almost seventeen when this occurred, *but essentially on the very grievous nature of the offense*; the fact that there was this very tragic killing, the fact that the respondent used subterfuge, the responsibility for it, all of this is a tragedy of immense proportions as we all recognize. It is essentially because of this that I feel that this is not the appropriate tribunal for this matter. (Emphasis supplied).

When asked whether the State had any recommendation to make relative to bail for Miss Johnson, the Assistant State's Attorney, who had professed the belief that waiver should be granted because of the involvement of the "safety to the public," stated: ". . . [T]he State would recommend that [Miss Johnson] be released on her own recognizance. . . ."

On appeal to this Court, Miss Johnson avers that the judge abused his discretion by granting waiver. The State's answer is somewhat unique. They urge upon us that the juvenile court "had before it testimony relating to all of the five factors. . . . While the court made its decision primarily on Appellant's age, the nature of the offense and her subterfuge in attempting to avoid responsibility . . . such was proper. . . . All that is necessary is that the court consider all five factors. That the court so considered is evident from the record." After conceding on oral argument before this Court that this was not "the strongest case" for waiver of jurisdiction, the State suggested that Miss Johnson was not in need of the rehabilitative measures afforded by the Department of Juvenile Services and that because she did not need rehabilitation she should be tried in the Criminal Court.

We think it apparent that the hearing judge was unduly influenced by the "nature of the offense" to the extent that the amenability of the appellant to rehabilitation was cast aside and not considered, or, if considered, was not afforded its proper weight. The mere statement that the five legislative factors were considered by the hearing judge does not divest this Court of its right to determine whether *vel non* those factors were actually considered and properly weighed in relation to each other and relative to the legislative purpose embodied in § 70.

It is specious to argue that because Miss Johnson is not in need of rehabilitative measures that she should be charged as an adult. Such an argument is the inverse of the legislative will, § 70, and injects into waiver hearings the anomalistic proposition that waiver should be granted because the juvenile is too good for rehabilitation, and, as such, should be subjected to the regular criminal procedures. It creates a penalty for good conduct.

We think it apparent from the "Waiver Summary" and the testimony of Rev. Gill that the juvenile appellant is, if adjudged a delinquent child, an ideal subject for the rehabilitative measures available from the Department of Juvenile Services.

. . . "We are not unmindful that, 'disposition in a juvenile case is committed to the sound discretion of the juvenile judge, to be disturbed on appeal only upon a finding that such discretion has been abused.' "

. . . [This] is equally applicable to waiver hearings. . . . [W]e find an abuse of discretion in the juvenile court judge's failure to consider sufficiently the appellant's "amenability to treatment in any institution, facility, or programs available. . . ."

On the record before us, there exists no justification for a waiver jurisdiction. Waiver of jurisdiction reversed and case remanded for further proceedings in the juvenile court.

———

QUESTIONS

1. Do you agree with the court in *Johnson* that the trial court abused its discretion in waiving the case to criminal court? Specifically do you agree with the following statement of the *Johnson* court?

> It is specious to argue that because Miss Johnson is not in need of rehabilitative measures that she should be charged as an adult. Such an argument is the inverse of the legislative will, and injects into waiver hearings the anomalistic proposition that waiver should be granted because the juvenile is too good for rehabilitation, and, as such, should be subjected to the regular criminal procedures. It creates a penalty for good conduct.

2. How should the trial court in *Johnson* have weighed the different criteria: "age of child, mental . . . condition of child, child's amenability to treatment in programs available to delinquents, the nature of the offense, and the safety of the public"?

ROPER v. SIMMONS

Supreme Court of the United States
125 S. Ct. 1183 (2005)

Justice KENNEDY *delivered the opinion of the Court.*

This case requires us to address, for the second time in a decade and a half, whether it is permissible under the Eighth and Fourteenth Amendments to the Constitution of the United States to execute a juvenile offender who was older than 15 but younger than 18 when he committed a capital crime. In *Stanford v. Kentucky*, 492 U.S. 361 (1989), a divided Court rejected the proposition that the Constitution bars capital punishment for juvenile offenders in this age group. We reconsider the question.

I

At the age of 17, when he was still a junior in high school, Christopher Simmons, the respondent here, committed murder. About nine months later, after he had turned 18, he was tried and sentenced to death. There is little doubt that Simmons was the instigator of the crime. Before its commission Simmons said he wanted to murder someone. In chilling, callous terms he talked about his plan, discussing it for the most part with two friends, Charles Benjamin and John Tessmer, then aged 15 and 16 respectively. Simmons proposed to commit burglary and murder by breaking and entering, tying up a victim, and throwing the victim off a bridge. Simmons assured his friends they could "get away with it" because they were minors.

The three met at about 2 a.m. on the night of the murder, but Tessmer left before the other two set out. (The State later charged Tessmer with conspiracy, but dropped the charge in exchange for his testimony against Simmons.) Simmons and Benjamin entered the home of the victim, Shirley Crook, after reaching through an open window and unlocking the back door. Simmons turned on a hallway light. Awakened, Mrs. Crook called out, "Who's there?" In response Simmons entered Mrs. Crook's bedroom, where he recognized her from a previous car accident involving them both. Simmons later admitted this confirmed his resolve to murder her.

Using duct tape to cover her eyes and mouth and bind her hands, the two perpetrators put Mrs. Crook in her minivan and drove to a state park. They reinforced the bindings, covered her head with a towel, and walked her to a railroad trestle spanning the Meramec River. There they tied her hands and feet together with electrical wire, wrapped her whole face in duct tape and threw her from the bridge, drowning her in the waters below.

By the afternoon of September 9, Steven Crook had returned home from an overnight trip, found his bedroom in disarray, and reported his wife missing. On the same afternoon fishermen recovered the victim's body from the river. Simmons, meanwhile, was bragging about the killing, telling friends he had killed a woman "because the bitch seen my face."

The next day, after receiving information of Simmons' involvement, police arrested him at his high school and took him to the police station in Fenton,

Missouri. They read him his *Miranda* rights. Simmons waived his right to an attorney and agreed to answer questions. After less than two hours of interrogation, Simmons confessed to the murder and agreed to perform a videotaped reenactment at the crime scene.

The State charged Simmons with burglary, kidnaping, stealing, and murder in the first degree. As Simmons was 17 at the time of the crime, he was outside the criminal jurisdiction of Missouri's juvenile court system. He was tried as an adult. At trial the State introduced Simmons' confession and the videotaped reenactment of the crime, along with testimony that Simmons discussed the crime in advance and bragged about it later. The defense called no witnesses in the guilt phase. The jury having returned a verdict of murder, the trial proceeded to the penalty phase.

The State sought the death penalty. As aggravating factors, the State submitted that the murder was committed for the purpose of receiving money; was committed for the purpose of avoiding, interfering with, or preventing lawful arrest of the defendant; and involved depravity of mind and was outrageously and wantonly vile, horrible, and inhuman. The State called Shirley Crook's husband, daughter, and two sisters, who presented moving evidence of the devastation her death had brought to their lives.

In mitigation Simmons' attorneys first called an officer of the Missouri juvenile justice system, who testified that Simmons had no prior convictions and that no previous charges had been filed against him. Simmons' mother, father, two younger half brothers, a neighbor, and a friend took the stand to tell the jurors of the close relationships they had formed with Simmons and to plead for mercy on his behalf. Simmons' mother, in particular, testified to the responsibility Simmons demonstrated in taking care of his two younger half brothers and of his grandmother and to his capacity to show love for them.

During closing arguments, both the prosecutor and defense counsel addressed Simmons' age, which the trial judge had instructed the jurors they could consider as a mitigating factor. Defense counsel reminded the jurors that juveniles of Simmons' age cannot drink, serve on juries, or even see certain movies, because "the legislatures have wisely decided that individuals of a certain age aren't responsible enough." Defense counsel argued that Simmons' age should make "a huge difference to [the jurors] in deciding just exactly what sort of punishment to make." In rebuttal, the prosecutor gave the following response: "Age, he says. Think about age. Seventeen years old. Isn't that scary? Doesn't that scare you? Mitigating? Quite the contrary I submit. Quite the contrary."

The jury recommended the death penalty after finding the State had proved each of the three aggravating factors submitted to it. Accepting the jury's recommendation, the trial judge imposed the death penalty.

Simmons obtained new counsel, who moved in the trial court to set aside the conviction and sentence. One argument was that Simmons had received ineffective assistance at trial. To support this contention, the new counsel called as witnesses Simmons' trial attorney, Simmons' friends and neighbors, and clinical psychologists who had evaluated him.

Part of the submission was that Simmons was "very immature," "very impulsive," and "very susceptible to being manipulated or influenced." The experts testified about Simmons' background including a difficult home environment and dramatic changes in behavior, accompanied by poor school performance in adolescence. Simmons was absent from home for long periods, spending time using alcohol and drugs with other teenagers or young adults. The contention by Simmons' postconviction counsel was that these matters should have been established in the sentencing proceeding.

The trial court found no constitutional violation by reason of ineffective assistance of counsel and denied the motion for postconviction relief. In a consolidated appeal from Simmons' conviction and sentence, and from the denial of postconviction relief, the Missouri Supreme Court affirmed.

After these proceedings in Simmons' case had run their course, this Court held that the Eighth and Fourteenth Amendments prohibit the execution of a mentally retarded person. *Atkins v. Virginia*, 536 U.S. 304 (2002). Simmons filed a new petition for state postconviction relief, arguing that the reasoning of *Atkins* established that the Constitution prohibits the execution of a juvenile who was under 18 when the crime was committed.

The Missouri Supreme Court agreed [and] set aside Simmons' death sentence and resentenced him to "life imprisonment without eligibility for probation, parole, or release except by act of the Governor."

We granted certiorari and now affirm.

II

The Eighth Amendment provides: "Excessive bail shall not be required, nor excessive fines imposed, nor cruel and unusual punishments inflicted." The provision is applicable to the States through the Fourteenth Amendment. As the Court explained in *Atkins*, the Eighth Amendment guarantees individuals the right not to be subjected to excessive sanctions. The right flows from the basic " 'precept of justice that punishment for crime should be graduated and proportioned to [the] offense.' " By protecting even those convicted of heinous crimes, the Eighth Amendment reaffirms the duty of the government to respect the dignity of all persons.

The prohibition against "cruel and unusual punishments," like other expansive language in the Constitution, must be interpreted according to its text, by considering history, tradition, and precedent, and with due regard for its purpose and function in the constitutional design. To implement this framework we have established the propriety and affirmed the necessity of referring to "the evolving standards of decency that mark the progress of a maturing society" to determine which punishments are so disproportionate as to be cruel and unusual.

In *Thompson v. Oklahoma*, 487 U.S. 815 (1988), a plurality of the Court determined that our standards of decency do not permit the execution of any offender under the age of 16 at the time of the crime. The plurality opinion explained that no death penalty State that had given express consideration to a minimum age for the death penalty had set the age lower than 16. The plurality also observed that "[t]he conclusion that it would offend civilized standards of decency to execute a person who was less than 16 years old at the time of his or her offense is consistent with the views that have been expressed by respected professional organizations, by other nations that share our Anglo-American heritage, and by the leading members of the Western European community." The opinion further noted that juries imposed the death penalty on offenders under 16 with exceeding rarity; the last execution of an offender for a crime committed under the age of 16 had been carried out in 1948, 40 years prior.

Bringing its independent judgment to bear on the permissibility of the death penalty for a 15-year-old offender, the *Thompson* plurality stressed that "[t]he reasons why juveniles are not trusted with the privileges and responsibilities of an adult also explain why their irresponsible conduct is not as morally reprehensible as that of an adult." According to the plurality, the lesser culpability of offenders under 16 made the death penalty inappropriate as a form of retribution, while the low likelihood that offenders under 16 engaged in "the kind of cost-benefit analysis that attaches any weight to the possibility of execution" made the death penalty ineffective as a means of deterrence. With Justice O'Connor concurring in the judgment on narrower grounds, the Court set aside the death sentence that had been imposed on the 15-year-old offender.

The next year, in *Stanford v. Kentucky*, 492 U.S. 361 (1989), the Court, over a dissenting opinion joined by four Justices, referred to contemporary standards of decency in this country and concluded the Eighth and Fourteenth Amendments did not proscribe the execution of juvenile offenders over 15 but under 18. The Court noted that 22 of the 37 death penalty States permitted the death penalty for 16-year-old offenders, and, among these 37 States, 25 permitted it for 17-year-old offenders. These numbers, in the Court's view, indicated there was no national consensus "sufficient to label a particular punishment cruel and unusual." A plurality of the Court also "emphatically reject[ed]" the suggestion that the Court should bring its own judgment to bear on the acceptability of the juvenile death penalty.

The same day the Court decided *Stanford*, it held that the Eighth Amendment did not mandate a categorical exemption from the death penalty for the mentally retarded. *Penry v. Lynaugh*, 492 U.S. 302 (1989). In reaching this conclusion it stressed that only two States had enacted laws banning the imposition of the death penalty on a mentally retarded person convicted of a capital offense. According to the Court, "the two state statutes prohibiting execution of the mentally retarded, even when added to the 14 States that have rejected capital punishment completely, [did] not provide sufficient evidence at present of a national consensus."

Three Terms ago the subject was reconsidered in *Atkins*. We held that standards of decency have evolved since *Penry* and now demonstrate that the execution of the mentally retarded is cruel and unusual punishment. The Court noted objective indicia of society's standards, as expressed in legislative enactments and state practice with respect to executions of the mentally retarded. When *Atkins* was decided only a minority of States permitted the practice, and even in those States it was rare. On the basis of these indicia the Court determined that executing mentally retarded offenders "has become truly unusual, and it is fair to say that a national consensus has developed against it."

The inquiry into our society's evolving standards of decency did not end there. The *Atkins* Court neither repeated nor relied upon the statement in *Stanford* that the Court's independent judgment has no bearing on the acceptability of a particular punishment under the Eighth Amendment. Instead we returned to the rule, established in decisions predating *Stanford*, that " 'the Constitution contemplates that in the end our own judgment will be brought to bear on the question of the acceptability of the death penalty under the Eighth Amendment.' " Mental retardation, the Court said, diminishes personal culpability even if the offender can distinguish right from wrong. The impairments of mentally retarded offenders make it less defensible to impose the death penalty as retribution for past crimes and less likely that the death penalty will have a real deterrent effect. Based on these considerations and on the finding of national consensus against executing the mentally retarded, the Court ruled that the death penalty constitutes an excessive sanction for the entire category of mentally retarded offenders, and that the Eighth Amendment " 'places a substantive restriction on the State's power to take the life' of a mentally retarded offender."

Just as the *Atkins* Court reconsidered the issue decided in *Penry*, we now reconsider the issue decided in *Stanford*. The beginning point is a review of objective indicia of consensus, as expressed in particular by the enactments of legislatures that have addressed the question. This data gives us essential instruction. We then must determine, in the exercise of our own independent judgment, whether the death penalty is a disproportionate punishment for juveniles.

III

A

The evidence of national consensus against the death penalty for juveniles is similar, and in some respects parallel, to the evidence *Atkins* held sufficient to demonstrate a national consensus against the death penalty for the mentally retarded. When *Atkins* was decided, 30 States prohibited the death penalty for the mentally retarded. This number comprised 12 that had abandoned the death penalty altogether, and 18 that maintained it but excluded the mentally retarded from its reach. By a similar calculation in this case, 30 States prohibit the juvenile death penalty, comprising 12 that have rejected the death penalty altogether and 18 that maintain it but, by express provision or judicial interpretation, exclude juveniles from its reach. *Atkins* emphasized that even in the 20 States without formal prohibition, the practice of executing the mentally retarded was infrequent. Since *Penry*, only five States had executed offenders known to have an IQ under 70. In the present case, too, even in the 20 States without a formal prohibition on executing juveniles, the practice is infrequent. Since *Stanford*, six States have executed prisoners for crimes committed as juveniles. In the past 10 years, only three have done so: Oklahoma, Texas, and Virginia. In December 2003 the Governor of Kentucky decided to spare the life of Kevin Stanford, and commuted his sentence to one of life imprisonment without parole, with the declaration that " '[w]e ought not be executing people who, legally, were children.' " By this act the Governor ensured Kentucky would not add itself to the list of States that have executed juveniles within the last 10 years even by the execution of the very defendant whose death sentence the Court had upheld in *Stanford v. Kentucky.*

There is, to be sure, at least one difference between the evidence of consensus in *Atkins* and in this case. Impressive in *Atkins* was the rate of abolition of the death penalty for the mentally retarded. Sixteen States that permitted the execution of the mentally retarded at the time of *Penry* had prohibited the practice by the time we heard *Atkins*. By contrast, the rate of change in reducing the incidence of the juvenile death penalty, or in taking specific steps to abolish it, has been slower. Five States that allowed the juvenile death penalty at the time of *Stanford* have abandoned it in the intervening 15 years — four through legislative enactments and one through judicial decision.

Though less dramatic than the change from *Penry* to *Atkins* . . . we still consider the change from *Stanford* to this case to be significant. As noted in *Atkins*, with respect to the States that had abandoned the death penalty for the mentally retarded since *Penry*, "[i]t is not so much the number of these States that is significant, but the consistency of the direction of change." In particular we found it significant that, in the wake of *Penry*, no State that had already prohibited the execution of the mentally retarded had passed legislation to reinstate the penalty. The number of States that have abandoned capital punishment for juvenile offenders since *Stanford* is smaller than the number of States that abandoned capital punishment for the mentally retarded after *Penry*; yet we think the same consistency of direction of change has been demonstrated. Since *Stanford*, no State that previously prohibited capital punishment for juveniles has reinstated it. This fact, coupled with the trend toward abolition of the juvenile death penalty, carries special force in light of the general popularity of anticrime legislation, and in light of the particular trend in recent years toward cracking down on juvenile crime in other respects. Any difference between this case and *Atkins* with respect to the pace of abolition is thus counterbalanced by the consistent direction of the change.

The slower pace of abolition of the juvenile death penalty over the past 15 years, moreover, may have a simple explanation. When we heard *Penry*, only two death penalty States had already prohibited the execution of the mentally retarded. When we heard *Stanford*, by contrast, 12 death penalty States had already prohibited the execution of any juvenile under 18, and 15 had prohibited the execution of any juvenile under 17. If anything, this shows that the impropriety of executing juveniles between 16 and 18 years of age gained wide recognition earlier than the impropriety of executing the mentally retarded. In the words of the Missouri Supreme Court: "It would be the ultimate in irony if the very fact that the inappropriateness of the death penalty for juveniles was broadly recognized sooner than it was recognized for the mentally retarded were to become a reason to continue the execution of juveniles now that the execution of the mentally retarded has been barred."

Petitioner cannot show national consensus in favor of capital punishment for juveniles but still resists the conclusion that any consensus exists against it. Petitioner supports this position with, in particular, the observation that when the Senate ratified the International Covenant on Civil and Political Rights (ICCPR), it did so subject to the President's proposed reservation regarding Article 6(5) of that treaty, which prohibits capital punishment for juveniles. This reservation at best provides only faint support for petitioner's argument. First, the reservation was passed in 1992; since then, five States have abandoned capital punishment for juveniles. Second, Congress considered the issue when enacting the Federal Death Penalty Act in 1994, and determined that the death penalty should not extend to juveniles. The reservation to Article 6(5) of the ICCPR provides minimal evidence that there is not now a national consensus against juvenile executions.

As in *Atkins*, the objective indicia of consensus in this case — the rejection of the juvenile death penalty in the majority of States; the infrequency of its use even where it remains on the books; and the consistency in the trend toward abolition of the practice — provide sufficient evidence that today our society views juveniles, in the words *Atkins* used respecting the mentally retarded, as "categorically less culpable than the average criminal."

B

A majority of States have rejected the imposition of the death penalty on juvenile offenders under 18, and we now hold this is required by the Eighth Amendment.

Because the death penalty is the most severe punishment, the Eighth Amendment applies to it with special force. Capital punishment must be limited to those offenders who commit "a narrow category of the most serious crimes" and whose extreme culpability makes them "the most deserving of execution." This principle is implemented throughout the capital sentencing process. . . .

Three general differences between juveniles under 18 and adults demonstrate that juvenile offenders cannot with reliability be classified among the worst offenders. First, as any parent knows and as the scientific and sociological studies respondent and his *amici* cite tend to confirm, "[a] lack of maturity and an underdeveloped sense of responsibility are found in youth more often than in adults and are more understandable among the young. These qualities often result in impetuous and ill-considered actions and decisions." It has been noted that "adolescents are overrepresented statistically in virtually every category of reckless behavior." In recognition of the comparative immaturity and irresponsibility of juveniles, almost every State prohibits those under 18 years of age from voting, serving on juries, or marrying without parental consent.

The second area of difference is that juveniles are more vulnerable or susceptible to negative influences and outside pressures, including peer pressure. . . . This is explained in part by the prevailing circumstance that juveniles have less control, or less experience with control, over their own environment. See Steinberg & Scott, Less Guilty by Reason of Adolescence: Developmental Immaturity, Diminished Responsibility, and the Juvenile Death Penalty, 58 Am. Psychologist 1009, 1014 (2003) (hereinafter Steinberg

& Scott) ("[A]s legal minors, [juveniles] lack the freedom that adults have to extricate themselves from a criminogenic setting").

The third broad difference is that the character of a juvenile is not as well formed as that of an adult. The personality traits of juveniles are more transitory, less fixed.

These differences render suspect any conclusion that a juvenile falls among the worst offenders. The susceptibility of juveniles to immature and irresponsible behavior means "their irresponsible conduct is not as morally reprehensible as that of an adult." Their own vulnerability and comparative lack of control over their immediate surroundings mean juveniles have a greater claim than adults to be forgiven for failing to escape negative influences in their whole environment. The reality that juveniles still struggle to define their identity means it is less supportable to conclude that even a heinous crime committed by a juvenile is evidence of irretrievably depraved character. From a moral standpoint it would be misguided to equate the failings of a minor with those of an adult, for a greater possibility exists that a minor's character deficiencies will be reformed. Indeed, "[t]he relevance of youth as a mitigating factor derives from the fact that the signature qualities of youth are transient; as individuals mature, the impetuousness and recklessness that may dominate in younger years can subside." Steinberg & Scott 1014 ("For most teens, [risky or antisocial] behaviors are fleeting; they cease with maturity as individual identity becomes settled. Only a relatively small proportion of adolescents who experiment in risky or illegal activities develop entrenched patterns of problem behavior that persist into adulthood").

In *Thompson*, a plurality of the Court recognized the import of these characteristics with respect to juveniles under 16, and relied on them to hold that the Eighth Amendment prohibited the imposition of the death penalty on juveniles below that age. We conclude the same reasoning applies to all juvenile offenders under 18.

Once the diminished culpability of juveniles is recognized, it is evident that the penological justifications for the death penalty apply to them with lesser force than to adults. We have held there are two distinct social purposes served by the death penalty: " 'retribution and deterrence of capital crimes by prospective offenders.' " As for retribution, we remarked in *Atkins* that "[i]f the culpability of the average murderer is insufficient to justify the most extreme sanction available to the State, the lesser culpability of the mentally retarded offender surely does not merit that form of retribution." The same conclusions follow from the lesser culpability of the juvenile offender. Whether viewed as an attempt to express the community's moral outrage or as an attempt to right the balance for the wrong to the victim, the case for retribution is not as strong with a minor as with an adult. Retribution is not proportional if the law's most severe penalty is imposed on one whose culpability or blameworthiness is diminished, to a substantial degree, by reason of youth and immaturity.

As for deterrence, it is unclear whether the death penalty has a significant or even measurable deterrent effect on juveniles, as counsel for the petitioner acknowledged at oral argument. In general we leave to legislatures the assessment of the efficacy of various criminal penalty schemes. Here, however, the absence of evidence of deterrent effect is of special concern because the same characteristics that render juveniles less culpable than adults suggest as well that juveniles will be less susceptible to deterrence. In particular, as the plurality observed in *Thompson*, "[t]he likelihood that the teenage offender has made the kind of cost-benefit analysis that attaches any weight to the possibility of execution is so remote as to be virtually nonexistent." To the extent the juvenile death penalty might have residual deterrent effect, it is worth noting that the punishment of life imprisonment without the possibility of parole is itself a severe sanction, in particular for a young person.

In concluding that neither retribution nor deterrence provides adequate justification for imposing the death penalty on juvenile offenders, we cannot deny or overlook the brutal crimes too many juvenile offenders have committed. Certainly it can be argued, although we by no means concede the point, that a rare case might arise in which a juvenile offender has sufficient psychological maturity, and at the same time demonstrates sufficient depravity, to merit a sentence of death. Indeed, this possibility is the linchpin of one contention pressed by petitioner and his *amici*. They assert that even assuming the truth of the observations we have made about juveniles' diminished culpability in general, jurors nonetheless should be allowed to consider mitigating arguments related to youth on a case-by-case basis, and in some cases to impose the death penalty if justified. A central feature of death penalty sentencing is a particular assessment of the circumstances of the crime and the characteristics of the offender. The system is designed to consider both aggravating and mitigating circumstances, including youth, in every case. Given this Court's own insistence on individualized consideration, petitioner maintains that it is both arbitrary and unnecessary to adopt a categorical rule barring imposition of the death penalty on any offender under 18 years of age.

We disagree. The differences between juvenile and adult offenders are too marked and well understood to risk allowing a youthful person to receive the death penalty despite insufficient culpability. An unacceptable likelihood exists that the brutality or cold-blooded nature of any particular crime would overpower mitigating arguments based on youth as a matter of course, even where the juvenile offender's objective immaturity, vulnerability, and lack of true depravity should require a sentence less severe than death. In some cases a defendant's youth may even be counted against him. In this very case, as we noted above, the prosecutor argued Simmons' youth was aggravating rather than mitigating. While this sort of overreaching could be corrected by a particular rule to ensure that the mitigating force of youth is not overlooked, that would not address our larger concerns.

It is difficult even for expert psychologists to differentiate between the juvenile offender whose crime reflects unfortunate yet transient immaturity, and the rare juvenile offender whose crime reflects irreparable corruption. As we understand it, this difficulty underlies the rule forbidding psychiatrists from diagnosing any patient under 18 as having antisocial personality disorder, a disorder also referred to as psychopathy or sociopathy, and which is characterized by callousness, cynicism, and contempt for the feelings, rights, and suffering of others. If trained psychiatrists with the advantage of clinical testing and observation refrain, despite diagnostic expertise, from assessing any juvenile under 18 as having antisocial personality disorder, we conclude that States should refrain from asking jurors to issue a far graver condemnation — that a juvenile offender merits the death penalty. When a juvenile offender commits a heinous crime, the State can exact forfeiture of some of the most basic liberties, but the State cannot extinguish his life and his potential to attain a mature understanding of his own humanity.

Drawing the line at 18 years of age is subject, of course, to the objections always raised against categorical rules. The qualities that distinguish juveniles from adults do not disappear when an individual turns 18. By the same token, some under 18 have already attained a level of maturity some adults will never reach. For the reasons we have discussed, however, a line must be drawn. The plurality opinion in *Thompson* drew the line at 16. In the intervening years the *Thompson* plurality's conclusion that offenders under 16 may not be executed has not been challenged. The logic of *Thompson* extends to those who are under 18. The age of 18 is the point where society draws the line for many purposes between childhood and adulthood. It is, we conclude, the age at which the line for death eligibility ought to rest.

These considerations mean *Stanford v. Kentucky* should be deemed no longer controlling on this issue. To the extent *Stanford* was based on review of the objective indicia of consensus that obtained in 1989, it suffices to note that those indicia have changed. It should be observed, furthermore, that the *Stanford* Court should have considered those States that had abandoned the death penalty altogether as part of the consensus against the juvenile death penalty; a State's decision to bar the death penalty altogether of necessity demonstrates a judgment that the death penalty is inappropriate for all offenders, including juveniles. Last, to the extent *Stanford* was based on a rejection of the idea that this Court is required to bring its independent judgment to bear on the proportionality of the death penalty for a particular class of crimes or offenders, it suffices to note that this rejection was inconsistent with prior Eighth Amendment decisions. It is also inconsistent with the premises of our recent decision in *Atkins*.

In holding that the death penalty cannot be imposed upon juvenile offenders, we take into account the circumstance that some States have relied on *Stanford* in seeking the death penalty against juvenile offenders. This consideration, however, does not outweigh our conclusion that *Stanford* should no longer control in those few pending cases or in those yet to arise.

IV

Our determination that the death penalty is disproportionate punishment for offenders under 18 finds confirmation in the stark reality that the United States is the only country in the world that continues to give official sanction to the juvenile death penalty. This reality does not become controlling, for the task of interpreting the Eighth Amendment remains our responsibility. Yet, . . . the Court has referred to the laws of other countries and to international authorities as instructive for its interpretation of the Eighth Amendment's prohibition of "cruel and unusual punishments." . . .

As respondent and a number of *amici* emphasize, Article 37 of the United Nations Convention on the Rights of the Child, which every country in the world has ratified save for the United States and Somalia, contains an express prohibition on capital punishment for crimes committed by juveniles under 18. No ratifying country has entered a reservation to the provision prohibiting the execution of juvenile offenders. Parallel prohibitions are contained in other significant international covenants.

Respondent and his *amici* have submitted, and petitioner does not contest, that only seven countries other than the United States have executed juvenile offenders since 1990: Iran, Pakistan, Saudi Arabia, Yemen, Nigeria, the Democratic Republic of Congo, and China. Since then each of these countries has either abolished capital punishment for juveniles or made public disavowal of the practice. In sum, it is fair to say that the United States now stands alone in a world that has turned its face against the juvenile death penalty.

Though the international covenants prohibiting the juvenile death penalty are of more recent date, it is instructive to note that the United Kingdom abolished the juvenile death penalty before these covenants came into being. The United Kingdom's experience bears particular relevance here in light of the historic ties between our countries and in light of the Eighth Amendment's own origins. The Amendment was modeled on a parallel provision in the English Declaration of Rights of 1689, which provided: "[E]xcessive Bail ought not to be required nor excessive Fines imposed; nor cruel and unusual Punishments inflicted." As of now, the United Kingdom has abolished the death penalty in its entirety; but, decades before it took this step, it recognized the disproportionate nature of the juvenile death penalty; and it abolished that penalty as a separate matter. . . . In the 56 years that have passed since the United Kingdom abolished the juvenile death penalty, the weight of authority against it there, and in the international community, has become well established.

It is proper that we acknowledge the overwhelming weight of international opinion against the juvenile death penalty, resting in large part on the understanding that the instability and emotional imbalance of young people may often be a factor in the crime. The opinion of the world community, while not controlling our outcome, does provide respected and significant confirmation for our own conclusions.

Over time, from one generation to the next, the Constitution has come to earn the high respect and even, as Madison dared to hope, the veneration of the American people. The document sets forth, and rests upon, innovative principles original to the American experience, such as federalism; a proven balance in political mechanisms through separation of powers; specific guarantees for the accused in criminal cases; and broad provisions to secure individual freedom and preserve human dignity. These doctrines and guarantees are central to the American experience and remain essential to our present-day self-definition and national identity. Not the least of the reasons we honor the Constitution, then, is because we know it to be our own. It does not lessen our fidelity to the Constitution or our pride in its origins to acknowledge that the express affirmation of certain fundamental rights by other nations and peoples simply underscores the centrality of those same rights within our own heritage of freedom.

The Eighth and Fourteenth Amendments forbid imposition of the death penalty on offenders who were under the age of 18 when their crimes were committed. The judgment of the Missouri Supreme Court setting aside the sentence of death imposed upon Christopher Simmons is affirmed.

It is so ordered.

[The Appendixes to the Court's opinion are omitted.]

JUSTICE STEVENS, with whom JUSTICE GINSBURG joins, *concurring*.

Perhaps even more important than our specific holding today is our reaffirmation of the basic principle that informs the Court's interpretation of the Eighth Amendment. If the meaning of that Amendment had been frozen when it was originally drafted, it would impose no impediment to the execution of 7-year-old children today. The evolving standards of decency that have driven our construction of this critically important part of the Bill of Rights foreclose any such reading of the Amendment. In the best tradition of the common law, the pace of that evolution is a matter for continuing debate; but that our understanding of the Constitution does change from time to time has been settled since John Marshall breathed life into its text. If great lawyers of his day — Alexander Hamilton, for example — were sitting with us today, I would expect them to join Justice Kennedy's opinion for the Court. In all events, I do so without hesitation.

JUSTICE O'CONNOR, *dissenting*.

The Court's decision today establishes a categorical rule forbidding the execution of any offender for any crime committed before his 18th birthday, no matter how deliberate, wanton, or cruel the offense. Neither the objective evidence of contemporary societal values, nor the Court's moral proportionality analysis, nor the two in tandem suffice to justify this ruling.

Although the Court finds support for its decision in the fact that a majority of the States now disallow capital punishment of 17-year-old offenders, it refrains from asserting that its holding is compelled by a genuine national consensus. Indeed, the evidence before us fails to demonstrate conclusively that any such consensus has emerged in the brief period since we upheld the constitutionality of this practice in *Stanford v. Kentucky*, 492 U.S. 361 (1989).

Instead, the rule decreed by the Court rests, ultimately, on its independent moral judgment that death is a disproportionately severe punishment for any 17-year-old offender. I do not subscribe to this judgment. Adolescents as a class are undoubtedly less mature, and therefore less culpable for their misconduct, than adults. But the Court has adduced no evidence impeaching the seemingly reasonable conclusion reached by many state legislatures: that at least some 17-year-old murderers are sufficiently mature to deserve the death penalty in an appropriate case. Nor has it been shown that capital sentencing juries are incapable of accurately assessing a youthful defendant's maturity or of giving due weight to the mitigating characteristics associated with youth.

On this record — and especially in light of the fact that so little has changed since our recent decision in *Stanford* — I would not substitute our judgment about the moral propriety of capital punishment for 17-year-old murderers for the judgments of the Nation's legislatures. Rather, I would demand a clearer showing that our society truly has set its face against this practice before reading the Eighth Amendment categorically to forbid it.

. . . .

[JUSTICE O'CONNOR reviews the Court's prior case law, disagreeing with the Majority's application of the cases to the instant case.]

C

Seventeen-year-old murderers must be categorically exempted from capital punishment, the Court says, because they "cannot with reliability be classified among the worst offenders." That conclusion is premised on three perceived differences between "adults," who have already reached their 18th birthdays, and "juveniles," who have not. First, juveniles lack maturity and responsibility and are more reckless than adults. Second, juveniles are more vulnerable to outside influences because they have less control over their surroundings. And third, a juvenile's character is not as fully formed as that of an adult. Based on these characteristics, the Court determines that 17-year-old capital murderers are not as blameworthy as adults guilty of similar crimes; that 17-year-olds are less likely than adults to be deterred by the prospect of a death sentence; and that it is difficult to conclude that a 17-year-old who commits even the most heinous of crimes is "irretrievably depraved." The Court suggests that "a rare case might arise in which a juvenile offender has sufficient psychological maturity, and at the same time demonstrates sufficient depravity, to merit a sentence of death." However, the Court argues that a categorical age-based prohibition is justified as a prophylactic rule because "[t]he differences between juvenile and adult offenders are too marked and well understood to risk allowing a youthful person to receive the death penalty despite insufficient culpability."

It is beyond cavil that juveniles as a class are generally less mature, less responsible, and less fully formed than adults, and that these differences bear on juveniles' comparative moral culpability. But even accepting this premise, the Court's proportionality argument fails to support its categorical rule.

First, the Court adduces no evidence whatsoever in support of its sweeping conclusion, that it is only in "rare" cases, if ever, that 17-year-old murderers are sufficiently mature and act with sufficient depravity to warrant the death penalty. The fact that juveniles are generally less culpable for their misconduct than adults does not necessarily mean that a 17-year-old murderer cannot be sufficiently culpable to merit the death penalty. At most, the Court's argument suggests that the average 17-year-old murderer is not as culpable as the average adult murderer. But an especially depraved juvenile offender may nevertheless be just as culpable as many adult offenders considered bad enough to deserve the death penalty. Similarly, the fact that the availability of the death penalty may be less likely to deter a juvenile from committing a capital crime does not imply that this threat cannot effectively deter some

17-year-olds from such an act. Surely there is an age below which no offender, no matter what his crime, can be deemed to have the cognitive or emotional maturity necessary to warrant the death penalty. But at least at the margins between adolescence and adulthood — and especially for 17-year-olds such as respondent — the relevant differences between "adults" and "juveniles" appear to be a matter of degree, rather than of kind. It follows that a legislature may reasonably conclude that at least some 17-year-olds can act with sufficient moral culpability, and can be sufficiently deterred by the threat of execution, that capital punishment may be warranted in an appropriate case.

Indeed, this appears to be just such a case. Christopher Simmons' murder of Shirley Crook was premeditated, wanton, and cruel in the extreme. Well before he committed this crime, Simmons declared that he wanted to kill someone. On several occasions, he discussed with two friends (ages 15 and 16) his plan to burglarize a house and to murder the victim by tying the victim up and pushing him from a bridge. Simmons said they could " 'get away with it' " because they were minors. In accord with this plan, Simmons and his 15-year-old accomplice broke into Mrs. Crook's home in the middle of the night, forced her from her bed, bound her, and drove her to a state park. There, they walked her to a railroad trestle spanning a river, "hog-tied" her with electrical cable, bound her face completely with duct tape, and pushed her, still alive, from the trestle. She drowned in the water below. One can scarcely imagine the terror that this woman must have suffered throughout the ordeal leading to her death. Whatever can be said about the comparative moral culpability of 17-year-olds as a general matter, Simmons' actions unquestionably reflect " 'a consciousness materially more "depraved" than that of' . . . the average murderer." And Simmons' prediction that he could murder with impunity because he had not yet turned 18 — though inaccurate — suggests that he did take into account the perceived risk of punishment in deciding whether to commit the crime. Based on this evidence, the sentencing jury certainly had reasonable grounds for concluding that, despite Simmons' youth, he "ha[d] sufficient psychological maturity" when he committed this horrific murder, and "at the same time demonstrate[d] sufficient depravity, to merit a sentence of death."

The Court's proportionality argument suffers from a second and closely related defect: It fails to establish that the differences in maturity between 17-year-olds and young "adults" are both universal enough and significant enough to justify a bright-line prophylactic rule against capital punishment of the former. The Court's analysis is premised on differences in the aggregate between juveniles and adults, which frequently do not hold true when comparing individuals. Although it may be that many 17-year-old murderers lack sufficient maturity to deserve the death penalty, some juvenile murderers may be quite mature. Chronological age is not an unfailing measure of psychological development, and common experience suggests that many 17-year-olds are more mature than the average young "adult." In short, the class of offenders exempted from capital punishment by today's decision is too broad and too diverse to warrant a categorical prohibition. Indeed, the age-based line drawn by the Court is indefensibly arbitrary — it quite likely will protect a number of offenders who are mature enough to deserve the death penalty and may well leave vulnerable many who are not.

For purposes of proportionality analysis, 17-year-olds as a class are qualitatively and materially different from the mentally retarded. "Mentally retarded" offenders, as we understood that category in *Atkins*, are defined by precisely the characteristics which render death an excessive punishment. A mentally retarded person is, "by definition," one whose cognitive and behavioral capacities have been proven to fall below a certain minimum. Accordingly, for purposes of our decision in *Atkins*, the mentally retarded are not merely less blameworthy for their misconduct or less likely to be deterred by the death penalty than others. Rather, a mentally retarded offender is one whose demonstrated impairments make it so highly unlikely that he is culpable enough to deserve the death penalty or that he could have been deterred by the threat of death, that execution is not a defensible punishment. There is no such inherent or accurate fit between an offender's chronological age and the personal limitations which the Court believes make capital punishment excessive for 17-year-old murderers. Moreover, it defies common sense to suggest that 17-year-olds as a class are somehow equivalent to mentally retarded persons with regard to culpability or susceptibility to deterrence. Seventeen-year-olds may, on average, be less mature than adults, but that lesser maturity simply cannot be equated with the major, lifelong impairments suffered by the mentally retarded.

The proportionality issues raised by the Court clearly implicate Eighth Amendment concerns. But these concerns may properly be addressed not by means of an arbitrary, categorical age-based rule, but rather through individualized sentencing in which juries are required to give appropriate mitigating weight to the defendant's immaturity, his susceptibility to outside pressures, his cognizance of the consequences of his actions, and so forth. In that way the constitutional response can be tailored to the specific problem it is meant to remedy. The Eighth Amendment guards against the execution of those who are "insufficiently culpable," by requiring sentencing that "reflect[s] a reasoned moral response to the defendant's background, character, and crime." Accordingly, the sentencer in a capital case must be permitted to give full effect to all constitutionally relevant mitigating evidence. A defendant's youth or immaturity is, of course, a paradigmatic example of such evidence.

Although the prosecutor's apparent attempt to use respondent's youth as an aggravating circumstance in this case is troubling, that conduct was never challenged with specificity in the lower courts and is not directly at issue here. As the Court itself suggests, such "overreaching" would best be addressed, if at all, through a more narrowly tailored remedy. The Court argues that sentencing juries cannot accurately evaluate a youthful offender's maturity or give appropriate weight to the mitigating characteristics related to youth. But, again, the Court presents no real evidence — and the record appears to contain none — supporting this claim. Perhaps more importantly, the Court fails to explain why this duty should be so different from, or so much more difficult than, that of assessing and giving proper effect to any other qualitative capital sentencing factor. I would not be so quick to conclude that the constitutional safeguards, the sentencing juries, and the trial judges upon which we place so much reliance in all capital cases are inadequate in this narrow context.

D

I turn, finally, to the Court's discussion of foreign and international law. Without question, there has been a global trend in recent years towards abolishing capital punishment for under-18 offenders. Very few, if any, countries other than the United States now permit this practice in law or in fact. While acknowledging that the actions and views of other countries do not dictate the outcome of our Eighth Amendment inquiry, the Court asserts that "the overwhelming weight of international opinion against the juvenile death penalty . . . does provide respected and significant confirmation for [its] own conclusions." Because I do not believe that a genuine national consensus against the juvenile death penalty has yet developed, and because I do not believe the Court's moral proportionality argument justifies a categorical, age-based constitutional rule, I can assign no such confirmatory role to the international consensus described by the Court. In short, the evidence of an international consensus does not alter my determination that the Eighth Amendment does not, at this time, forbid capital punishment of 17-year-old murderers in all cases.

. . . .

Reasonable minds can differ as to the minimum age at which commission of a serious crime should expose the defendant to the death penalty, if at all. Many jurisdictions have abolished capital punishment altogether, while many others have determined that even the most heinous crime, if committed before the age of 18, should not be punishable by death. Indeed, were my office that of a legislator, rather than a judge, then I, too, would be inclined to support legislation setting a minimum age of 18 in this context. But a significant number of States, including Missouri, have decided to make the death penalty potentially available for 17-year-old capital murderers such as respondent. Without a clearer showing that a genuine national consensus forbids the execution of such offenders, this Court should not substitute its own "inevitably subjective judgment" on how best to resolve this difficult moral question for the judgments of the Nation's democratically elected legislatures. I respectfully dissent.

JUSTICE SCALIA, with whom THE CHIEF JUSTICE and JUSTICE THOMAS join, *dissenting*.

. . . .

Today's opinion provides a perfect example of why judges are ill equipped to make the type of legislative judgments the Court insists on making here. To support its opinion that States should be prohibited from imposing the death penalty on anyone who committed murder before age 18, the Court looks to scientific and sociological studies, picking and choosing those that support its position. It never explains why those particular studies are methodologically sound; none was ever entered into evidence or tested in an adversarial proceeding. . . .

We need not look far to find studies contradicting the Court's conclusions. As petitioner points out, the American Psychological Association (APA), which claims in this case that scientific evidence shows persons under 18 lack the ability to take moral responsibility for their decisions, has previously taken precisely the opposite position before this very Court. In its brief in *Hodgson v. Minnesota*, 497 U.S. 417 (1990), the APA found a "rich body of research" showing that juveniles are mature enough to decide whether to obtain an abortion without parental involvement. The APA brief, citing psychology treatises and studies too numerous to list here, asserted: "[B]y middle adolescence (age 14-15) young people develop abilities similar to adults in reasoning about moral dilemmas, understanding social rules and laws, [and] reasoning about interpersonal relationships and interpersonal problems." Given the nuances of scientific methodology and conflicting views, courts — which can only consider the limited evidence on the record before them — are ill equipped to determine which view of science is the right one. Legislatures "are better qualified to weigh and 'evaluate the results of statistical studies in terms of their own local conditions and with a flexibility of approach that is not available to the courts.'"

Even putting aside questions of methodology, the studies cited by the Court offer scant support for a categorical prohibition of the death penalty for murderers under 18. At most, these studies conclude that, on average, or in most cases, persons under 18 are unable to take moral responsibility for their actions. Not one of the cited studies opines that all individuals under 18 are unable to appreciate the nature of their crimes.

Moreover, the cited studies describe only adolescents who engage in risky or antisocial behavior, as many young people do. Murder, however, is more than just risky or antisocial behavior. It is entirely consistent to believe that young people often act impetuously and lack judgment, but, at the same time, to believe that those who commit premeditated murder are — at least sometimes — just as culpable as adults. Christopher Simmons, who was only seven months shy of his 18th birthday when he murdered Shirley Crook, described to his friends beforehand — "[i]n chilling, callous terms," as the Court puts it, — the murder he planned to commit. He then broke into the home of an innocent woman, bound her with duct tape and electrical wire, and threw her off a bridge alive and conscious. In their *amici* brief, the States of Alabama, Delaware, Oklahoma, Texas, Utah, and Virginia offer additional examples of murders committed by individuals under 18 that involve truly monstrous acts. In Alabama, two 17-year-olds, one 16-year-old, and one 19-year-old picked up a female hitchhiker, threw bottles at her, and kicked and stomped her for approximately 30 minutes until she died. They then sexually assaulted her lifeless body and, when they were finished, threw her body off a cliff. They later returned to the crime scene to mutilate her corpse. Other examples in the brief are equally shocking. Though these cases are assuredly the exception rather than the rule, the studies the Court cites in no way justify a constitutional imperative that prevents legislatures and juries from treating exceptional cases in an exceptional way — by determining that some murders are not just the acts of happy-go-lucky teenagers, but heinous crimes deserving of death.

That "almost every State prohibits those under 18 years of age from voting, serving on juries, or marrying without parental consent," is patently irrelevant — and is yet another resurrection of an argument that this Court gave a decent burial in *Stanford*. As we explained in *Stanford*, it is "absurd to think that one must be mature enough to drive carefully, to drink responsibly, or to vote intelligently, in order to be mature enough to understand that murdering another human being is profoundly wrong, and to conform one's conduct to that most minimal of all civilized standards." Serving on a jury or entering into marriage also involve decisions far more sophisticated than the simple decision not to take another's life.

Moreover, the age statutes the Court lists "set the appropriate ages for the operation of a system that makes its determinations in gross, and that does not conduct individualized maturity tests." The criminal justice system, by contrast, provides for individualized consideration of each defendant. In capital cases, this Court requires the sentencer to make an individualized determination, which includes weighing aggravating factors and mitigating factors, such as youth. In other contexts where individualized consideration is provided, we have recognized that at least some minors will be mature enough to make difficult decisions that involve moral considerations. For instance, we have struck down abortion statutes that do not allow minors deemed mature by courts to bypass parental notification provisions. It is hard to see why this context should be any different. Whether to obtain an abortion is surely a much more complex decision for a young person than whether to kill an innocent person in cold blood.

The Court concludes, however, that juries cannot be trusted with the delicate task of weighing a defendant's youth along with the other mitigating and aggravating factors of his crime. This startling conclusion undermines the very foundations of our capital sentencing system, which entrusts juries with "mak[ing] the difficult and uniquely human judgments that defy codification and that 'buil[d] discretion, equity, and flexibility into a legal system.' " The Court says, that juries will be unable to appreciate the significance of a defendant's youth when faced with details of a brutal crime. This assertion is based on no evidence; to the contrary, the Court itself acknowledges that the execution of under-18 offenders is "infrequent" even in the States "without a formal prohibition on executing juveniles," suggesting that juries take seriously their responsibility to weigh youth as a mitigating factor.

Nor does the Court suggest a stopping point for its reasoning. If juries cannot make appropriate determinations in cases involving murderers under 18, in what other kinds of cases will the Court find jurors deficient? We have already held that no jury may consider whether a mentally deficient defendant can receive the death penalty, irrespective of his crime. Why not take other mitigating factors, such as considerations of childhood abuse or poverty, away from juries as well? Surely jurors "overpower[ed]" by "the brutality or cold-blooded nature" of a crime, could not adequately weigh these mitigating factors either.

The Court's contention that the goals of retribution and deterrence are not served by executing murderers under 18 is also transparently false. The argument that "[r]etribution is not proportional if the law's most severe penalty is imposed on one whose culpability or blameworthiness is diminished," is simply an extension of the earlier, false generalization that youth always defeats culpability. The Court claims that "juveniles will be less susceptible to deterrence," because " '[t]he likelihood that the teenage offender has made the kind of cost-benefit analysis that attaches any weight to the possibility of execution is so remote as to be virtually nonexistent.'" The Court unsurprisingly finds no support for this astounding proposition, save its own case law. The facts of this very case show the proposition to be false. Before committing the crime, Simmons encouraged his friends to join him by assuring them that they could "get away with it" because they were minors. This fact may have influenced the jury's decision to impose capital punishment despite Simmons' age. Because the Court refuses to entertain the possibility that its own unsubstantiated generalization about juveniles could be wrong, it ignores this evidence entirely.

. . . .

. . . In a system based upon constitutional and statutory text democratically adopted, the concept of "law" ordinarily signifies that particular words have a fixed meaning. Such law does not change, and this Court's pronouncement of it therefore remains authoritative until (confessing our prior error) we overrule. The Court has purported to make of the Eighth Amendment, however, a mirror of the passing and changing sentiment of American society regarding penology. The lower courts can look into that mirror as well as we can; and what we saw 15 years ago bears no necessary relationship to what they see today. Since they are not looking at the same text, but at a different scene, why should our earlier decision control their judgment?

However sound philosophically, this is no way to run a legal system. We must disregard the new reality that, to the extent our Eighth Amendment decisions constitute something more than a show of hands on the current Justices' current personal views about penology, they purport to be nothing more than a snapshot of American public opinion at a particular point in time (with the timeframes now shortened to a mere 15 years). We must treat these decisions just as though they represented real law, real prescriptions democratically adopted by the American people, as conclusively (rather than sequentially) construed by this Court. Allowing lower courts to reinterpret the Eighth Amendment whenever they decide enough time has passed for a new snapshot leaves this Court's decisions without any force — especially since the "evolution" of our Eighth Amendment is no longer determined by objective criteria. To allow lower courts to behave as we do, "updating" the Eighth Amendment as needed, destroys stability and makes our case law an unreliable basis for the designing of laws by citizens and their representatives, and for action by public officials. The result will be to crown arbitrariness with chaos.

———

NOTES AND QUESTIONS

1. The *Simmons* Court notes three "general differences" characteristic of juveniles as compared to adults: (a) tendencies to act impetuously; (b) susceptibility to the influence of peers; and (c) incomplete character development. Has the Court systematically appreciated these differences in its other cases? For example, do these differences in juveniles and adults cast doubt

about the Court's decisions in the area of abortion and birth control? *See* § 3.03, *supra*.

2. From the facts given in *Simmons*, do the "general differences" between juveniles and adults appear to apply to the particular juvenile charged in the case? If not, is the persuasiveness of the Court's opinion called into question?

[D] Status Offenses

In addition to delinquency jurisdiction, the juvenile courts have authority to deal with children who do not commit criminal offenses. Statutes defining so-called "status offense" jurisdiction characteristically proscribe certain actions or omissions, such as running away from home or failing to attend school, that are wrongful for children because of their "status" as children. Georgia, for example, provides the following definition of "status offender":

> "Status offender" means a juvenile who is charged with or adjudicated of an offense which would not be a crime if it were committed by an adult, in other words, an act which is only an offense because of the perpetrator's status as a child. Such offenses shall include, but are not limited to, truancy, running away from home, incorrigibility, and unruly behavior.

GA. CODE ANN. § 15-11-2(11) (Harrison 2001).

Some state statutes proscribe violating curfews, *see, e.g.*, CAL. WELF. & INST. CODE § 601 (West Supp. 1998) (juvenile court jurisdiction extends to persons under 18 years who violate a "curfew based solely on age"). Curfew statutes have been attacked on a variety of constitutional grounds, sometimes successfully. See the *Schleifer* case, *infra*, and the note following it.

Statutes routinely prohibit minors from possessing alcohol and sometimes from using tobacco, *see, e.g.*, NEB. REV. STAT. §§ 28-1418, 43-247 (Reissue 1995, Reissue 1998) (misdemeanor for minors under age 18 to smoke or use tobacco; juvenile court jurisdiction over minors under age 16 who commit misdemeanors). Some jurisdictions employ catch-all statutes to subject all misconduct by youth to the jurisdiction of the juvenile court. For example, a California statute provides: "Any person who is under the age of 18 years when he violates any law of this state or of the United States or any ordinance of any city or county of this state defining crime . . . based solely on age, is within the jurisdiction of the juvenile court." CAL. WELF. & INST. CODE § 602 (West 1998).

Status offense jurisdiction extends beyond the kinds of misconduct just described. Virtually all juvenile codes also include provisions permitting juvenile court intervention if a minor's situation fits within a statutorily designated category of undesirable status conditions. Such categories include being an "undisciplined," "wayward," or "unruly" child. Ohio, for example, defines an "unruly child" as:

> Any child who does not subject himself or herself to the reasonable control of his or her parents, teachers, guardian, or custodian, by reason of being wayward or habitually disobedient; any child who so

deports himself or herself as to injure or endanger his or her health or morals or the health or morals of others; . . . . Any child who is found in a disreputable place, visits or patronizes a place prohibited by law, or associates with vagrant, vicious, criminal, notorious, or immoral persons. . . .

OHIO REV. CODE ANN. § 2151.022 (Anderson Supp. 1995). Thus, typical statutes lump doing certain things (running away from home, for example) with being a certain kind of child (one "in need of supervision," for example) as predicates for juvenile court jurisdiction. Several states utilize the classifications "person in need of supervision" or "child in need of supervision" to describe troubled children under juvenile court jurisdiction. *See, e.g.,* N.Y. FAM. CT. ACT § 712(a) (McKinney 1983) ("person in need of supervision" includes children who are "incorrigible, ungovernable or habitually disobedient and beyond the lawful control of parent"); WYO. STAT. ANN. § 14-6-201(a)(iv) (Supp. 1996) ("child in need of supervision" includes children who are "ungovernable and beyond control").

S.S. v. STATE

Supreme Judicial Court of Maine
299 A.2d 560 (1973)

POMEROY, JUSTICE.

These consolidated cases are before us on report pursuant to Rule 72(b), Maine Rules of Civil Procedure.

The Agreed Statement describes the issues presented as follows:

"1. Whether the offense for which S.S. and L. B. were adjudged juvenile offenders is unconstitutionally vague, and thus, their commitments are in violation of the Due Process Clause of the Fourteenth Amendment of the United States Constitution and Article 1, § 6-A of the Maine Constitution.

"2. Whether S.S. and L. B. were adjudged juvenile offenders in violation of the Due Process Clause of the Fourteenth Amendment to the United States Constitution and Article 1, § 6-A of the Maine Constitution, insofar as the conduct upon which the judgment of the Juvenile Court rested would not have been a criminal offense of committed by an adult.

"3. Whether S.S. and L. B. were adjudged juvenile offenders in violation of the Equal Protection Clause of the Fourteenth Amendment to the United States Constitution and Article I, § 6-A of the Maine Constitution insofar as the conduct upon which the judgment of the Juvenile Court rested would not have been a criminal offense if committed by an adult."

This Court is charged by the rule with rendering such decision as the rights of the party require.

Both cases originated by the filing of a petition for a writ of *habeas corpus* (postconviction).

We note from the pleadings that both petitioners were adjudged juvenile offenders in the Juvenile Court on the basis of a petition which alleged in each case the petitioners were juveniles within the meaning of 15 M.R.S.A. 2502-(4).

The petition alleged in each case the juvenile was "living in circumstances of manifest danger of falling into habits of vice or immorality." No other material circumstances of the cases are presented in the record before us. We are not informed by the record exactly what conduct of the juveniles was alleged in the petitions as supporting the conclusory allegation. Suffice it to say the cases as presented to this Court raise no issue as to the legal sufficiency of the petitions.

We are confronted then with a facial attack on the constitutionality of 15 M.R.S.A. 2552 insofar as it purports to give jurisdiction to juvenile courts to treat as a juvenile offender, a juvenile whose conduct is described therein as "living in circumstances of manifest danger of falling into habits of vice or immorality."

The petitioners argue the reference section of the statute is unconstitutionally vague. The petitioners here clearly equate due process requirements in juvenile proceedings with the well established due process requirements of criminal proceedings. With this contention we do not agree.

The petitioners further argue that because a juvenile proceeding can result in restrictions upon a juvenile's liberty or even his loss of liberty, the conclusion is compelled that the due process requirements of criminal prosecution must apply. We answer this by saying it is not every loss of liberty which gives rise to an application of the standards of due process required in criminal proceedings. Just as the natural parent may constitutionally place limitation on the child's freedom of locomotion and may substitute the will and judgment of the parent for that of the child and thus constrain the child's will for his own protection, so also may the State in the exercise of its *parens patriae* guardianship. The juvenile proceeding is not a criminal proceeding. Its purpose is not punishment. "The basic and primary idea of the legislature is salvation, not punishment."

It, therefore, follows that the due process requirements of the Constitution must be equated to this *sui generis* proceeding and not to a criminal proceeding.

The statute with which we are here concerned calls for the protective facilities of the State to come into play whenever a juvenile, as defined by the Act, commits an offense and whenever the conduct of the juvenile is such that he or she is living in circumstances of manifest danger of falling into habits of vice or immorality. The statute does not relate to a status. By its express terms it relates to conduct of the juvenile. It treats with a class of persons, *i.e.,* a person under the age of 17 in whom the State has asserted a special protective interest with constitutional validity.

The statute is unconstitutionally vague on its face even if the strictest standard applicable to criminal proceedings were to be followed only if when considering this limited class of persons, i. e., persons under the age of 17, men and women of common intelligence can only guess as to its meaning. The due process clause of the Constitution does not permit legislation which purports to regulate human conduct with sanctions imposed for violation to stand as valid if "men of common intelligence must necessarily guess at its meaning."

If no standard of conduct is specified at all, legislation is unconstitutionally vague. It is valid legislation, however, if it requires a person to conform his conduct to an imprecise but comprehensible normative standard. We conclude that when applied to this class, the language of the statute is sufficiently definite to withstand constitutional attack on grounds of vagueness.

The meaning of the reference phrase becomes clear when one considers the history and purpose of our juvenile laws. The basic purpose of affording juveniles special treatment is that the State as *parens patriae* has a duty to avoid giving children criminal records and, insofar as possible, prepare the child to cope with life and not become a criminal in his adult years.

The Legislature accords special treatment to those juveniles whose conduct would be criminal if done by an adult, and based on the predictive concept, offers its preventive and corrective facilities to those juveniles whose conduct, if unchanged, is likely to become criminal when the child becomes an adult. Thus, the conduct of a juvenile which constitutes living in circumstances of manifest danger of falling into habits of vice or immorality means conduct of the juvenile while living in circumstances which make it clear that if such conduct is continued, there is manifest danger of falling into habits of criminal conduct — such conduct being considered vice and immorality.

The terms vice or immorality mean those vices and those immoral acts which are defined by statute as criminal and the constituent elements of which are clearly described in the statute and in the case law interpreting the statute or by common law definition.[38]

Stated simply, the judgment which must be made by the juvenile judge is: On the basis of the allegations of the petition and the facts presented in support thereof, has the juvenile demonstrated a pattern of conduct which manifests or makes clear to all reasonable men that if persisted in and not changed, there is real danger that the conduct will, when the child becomes an adult, bring about violation of the criminal statutes?

The proceedings must be initiated by the filing of a verified petition which must contain a "plain statement of the facts which bring the juvenile complained against within chapters 401 to 409."

Thus, it may be said the petition must state facts demonstrating that the juvenile's conduct constitutes "living in circumstances of manifest danger of

---

[38] [4] We recognize a statute couched in these terms presents dangers of overbroad application. Even though as we have pointed out the core meaning describes a comprehensive normative standard, though imprecise at the periphery, there is danger that the complainant or the juvenile judge might attempt to apply his own particular moral standards or to force life-style or physical appearance into a mold he considers acceptable. In short, statutes framed as imprecisely as this appears to be, do create possibilities of attempted overbroad application. We are here faced, however, with a facial attack on the statute not an 'as applied' attack. . . .

falling into habits of vice or immorality." Appeal procedure is provided by the statute: The sufficiency of the allegations of the petition to establish that the conduct is, in fact, "living in circumstances of manifest danger of falling into habits of vice or immorality" is easily tested by reference to the facts alleged in the petition.

The petitioners' complaint that there is denial of equal protection of the law because the conduct sufficient to bring the juvenile within the ambit of the juvenile statute would not have been a criminal offense, if committed by an adult, is answered by pointing out that the child is not charged with criminal conduct. The statute merely provides that the protective custody of the State shall come into play whenever there is conduct manifesting a danger that if persisted in, it will become criminal when the child becomes an adult.

Much of the petitioners' brief is dedicated to an attempt to demonstrate that the predictive system has failed and as Mr. Justice Fortas said in *Gault*, the child winds up with the worst of two worlds. We concede that the statistics cited in *Gault* make a powerful case for the conclusion that the juvenile offender system has been neither well funded nor well administered. Despite this impressive documentation, our faith in the soundness of the predictive system is not shaken. We think no reasonable man would shoot a sound horse because his saddle stirrup needs repairs. The only alternative it seems to us would be to take what Mr. Justice Blackmun described as the easy way and to flatly hold the full scope of rights constitutionally assured for the adult accused in criminal proceedings are to be imposed on this State's juvenile proceedings. This would be overlooking the difference in substance as well as procedure in the two. In fact, the criteria for determining due process requirements of non-criminal proceedings by the State are the same for children as for adults.

We fear, should deviant children be diverted to the criminal processes, great social harm would result.

By the Act of 1854 (Act and Resolves of Maine 1853) and by the Act of 1931 (Laws of Maine 1931, chap. 241) Maine embarked upon a humanitarian program designed to save deviant children from a life of adult lawlessness. To make the program feasible it required children to give up some rights they had formerly enjoyed when they were treated through the criminal process. Thus, the State by law committed itself to:

> . . . carry out a modern method of dealing with youthful offenders, so that there may be no criminal record against immature youth to cause detrimental local gossip and future handicaps because of childhood errors and indiscretions, and also that the child who is not inclined to follow legal or moral patterns, may be guided or reformed to become, in his mature years, a useful citizen.

To divert children back into the stream of criminal process would surely result in restoration of all the constitutional safeguards accorded adult criminals, but we fear it would have the effect of diverting public attitudes from the humanitarian goal of providing a helping hand to the deviant young.[39]

We are confident that a properly structured and fairly administered juvenile court system can serve our needs without infringing on individual freedoms. The time may come when we are disabused of our belief that the potential for growth inherent in the juvenile system cannot be ignored.

That time has not yet come.

This facial attack on this statute must fail.

The entry must be,

Writ of *Habeas Corpus* denied in both cases.

DUFRESNE, CHIEF JUSTICE (*dissenting*).

. . . .

The reported issue is, whether 15 M.R.S.A. § 2552 prohibiting the following conduct of juveniles — "living in circumstances of manifest danger of falling into habits of vice or immorality" — is facially unconstitutional on the ground of vagueness. The Maine Juvenile Act is no different from most of the statutes on the subject in the various states. In certain aspects, the Act is very specific in that it makes it an offense for a juvenile to commit any of the offenses made criminal when committed by adults, plus habitual truancy and repetitive desertion of one's home without just cause, but, then, in an effort to vest a broad discretion in the Juvenile Court, the Legislature extends the definition of a juvenile offense to include an open-ended general concept of offensive conduct such as "behaving in an incorrigible or indecent and lascivious manner," "knowingly and willfully associating with vicious, criminal or grossly immoral people" and "living in circumstances of manifest danger of falling into habits of vice or immorality." We are only concerned with the last portion of the statute.

The "void for vagueness" doctrine, applicable to test the constitutionality of any statutory provision, requires that a statute be sufficiently certain and definite in meaning to afford a reasonable degree of guidance as to just what constitutes the conduct required or prohibited to all involved in its application, to the persons whose activity the statute attempts to regulate, to the courts who must decide rights or obligations under it, and, in the criminal and juvenile sectors, to the police who are charged with its enforcement. Stated otherwise, the rule is that "a statute which either forbids or requires the doing of an act in terms so vague that men of common intelligence must necessarily

---

[39] [6] A theme of paternalism and benign motivation permeates the history and present posture of the juvenile system. This requires special comment of a cautionary nature. It is not the motivation of the State in this area which justifies the application of non-criminal standards of due process, but it is, rather, recognition of the Legislature's right to establish a separate and non-criminal system for juveniles. The Court is not and must not be beguiled by the commendable intentions of the State, but must, because of them, all the more diligently scrutinize the separate system established to insure that it contains the safeguards necessary to protect the rights of the individual juvenile from abuse. As Justice Brandeis said, "Experience should teach us to be most on our guard to protect liberty when the government's purposes are beneficent. . . . The greatest dangers to liberty lurk in insidious encroachment by men of zeal, well-meaning but without understanding. . . ." These words of caution must be considered in evaluating the holding in the instant case and in dealing with future problems which arise out of the juvenile system.

guess at its meaning and differ as to its application violates the first essential of due process . . . ."

This Court has equated, at least in criminal jurisprudence, the requirement of reasonable certainty in statutory enactments with due process of law.

Reasonable precision in the definition of proscribed conduct for juveniles should occupy a position of the highest order in the scheme of constitutional values, equally so with similar reasonable particularity in the definition of prohibited adult criminal activity. A juvenile's forfeiture of his liberty for committing a juvenile offense is just as weighty on the scales of justice in terms of due process of law as an adult's loss of liberty for conviction of crime. Statutory vagueness in legislation regulating juvenile conduct under penalty of State wardship is equally abhorrent under considerations of fair play, if not more so, as uncertainty in criminal statutes may be to the adult world. Definitional uncertainty in a juvenile offense statute is an open invitation to virtually unfettered administration by the police and arbitrary judicial adjudication by the courts. It lends itself to an unconstitutional delegation of legislative power to the juvenile judge by permitting him to decide without reasonable legislative standards what the law is in each case. It makes for unequal dispensation of justice. All persons are entitled to be informed as to what the State commands or forbids.

The "void for vagueness" doctrine applies in any area, including the sphere of juvenile-conduct regulatory legislation. Vague laws in any context suffer a constitutional infirmity. The power of the State to act as *parens patriae* for the benefit of children and adolescents does not override the constitutional privilege of substantive due process to while minor children are entitled equally as much as adults.

It is contended that the Maine Juvenile Act, in defining juvenile offenses in terms of "living in circumstances of manifest danger of falling into habits of vice or immorality" is unconstitutionally vague and violative of due process, because it imposes a loss of liberty upon the status or mode of life of the juvenile. It is true that, according to Webster's definitions of "living," the term may refer to the "state" of a person, to the "fact of being" in circumstances of manifest danger of falling into habits of vice or immorality. On the other hand, it could refer to the concept of "producing . . . action" which brings about such circumstances. Construing the statute in the light of the benevolent purposes of the juvenile legislation, I do ascribe to the Legislature an intent to proscribe active conduct and not to penalize a juvenile's status as such acquired by the pursuit of a certain pattern of living. Thus, the Act in this area would pass constitutional requirements, provided the definition of the juvenile offense in its totality furnishes the necessary intelligible standards to guide the child, his parents, the police and the courts.

. . . .

It is within the legislative domain to prohibit juvenile conduct conducive to future criminality. The Legislature may pass laws designed to protect minor children against a life of delinquency and determine in its wisdom what activities involve danger that a child will become a hazard either to himself or to society. The State may, to protect its interest in the proper operation, control and discipline of the family unit, pass legislation tending to insure the existence of harmonious relations between family members, and between the family unit and the rest of the public society, to the extent of making it a crime or a juvenile offense for juveniles persistently to disobey reasonable and lawful parental commands. But, all such laws, designed to suppress crime in the future through preventive conviction and incarceration in the case of adults or preventive adjudication of delinquency and wardship when juveniles are involved, as desirable as they may be to combat crime or juvenile delinquency, cannot be achieved through techniques that trample on constitutional rights. The rule of law implies equality and justice in application which cannot exist when legislation provides no reasonable standard to determine prohibited conduct.

Some courts have said that in a sphere so vital to the community as the welfare of its youth, the use of words of general meaning in a statute designed to enable the Legislature to come to grips effectively with the problem of juvenile delinquency should be upheld where their frequent use in penal statutes gives assurance that they are understood by men of ordinary intelligence, or that terms such as general welfare, health, peace, morals and safety of the people, and sense of decency have a well-accepted and understood meaning. Such assumptions, contrary to factual reality, are non-persuasive.

I believe that the Due Process Clause of the Fourteenth Amendment establishes a sphere of personal liberty for every individual, and this includes juveniles, subject to reasonable intrusions by the State in furtherance of legitimate state interests. A juvenile has a constitutional right to freedom from being state institutionalized except for justifiable state action in furtherance of a legitimate public interest but, even then, the State's exercise of power must be energized, and deployed within proper constitutional strictures, one of which is that the statute defining the State's right to interfere must provide reasonable standards to guarantee against arbitrary and unequal application of the law.

The concept of juveniles found "living in circumstances of manifest danger of falling into habits of vice or immorality" is not of recent vintage. The Legislature made it the basis for civil commitment of young girls to the Maine Industrial School for Girls under Public Laws, 1873, chapter 141. The Legislature then also permitted State wardship for young girls "leading an idle, vagrant or vicious life." We must, therefore, approach the construction of the reference statute having in mind that the Legislature was thinking in terms of modes of life in juveniles mostly characterized by idleness and vagrancy which were then philosophically considered fertile soil of future criminality. Far from the minds of our Legislators was the modern precision of constitutional due process espoused by the *Gault*, *Winship* and *McKeiver* decisions.

The reference section of the Juvenile Act is so vague that it affords an almost boundless area for individual subjective assessment of a child's behavior as the test for determination of prohibited juvenile conduct. In the instant case, where the offensive conduct is not before us, First Amendment rights may be involved and the statute as written is subject to unconstitutional overbreadth. To a great portion of the people of this State, juveniles participating in demonstrations are living in circumstances of manifest danger of falling into habits of vice or immorality. By reason of its constitutional overbreadth in the area of First Amendment rights, this Court should outlaw this offensive section of the statute. When a legislative act is so clearly, manifestly and irreconcilably conflicting with the constitution by any reasonable construction, this Court has no alternative then to declare it invalid in fulfillment of its own imperative and unceasing obligation to support the constitution. A statute which may sweep within its broad scope activities constitutionally protected by the First Amendment must be stricken down as unconstitutional.

For this Court to narrow the meaning of the Act beyond any reasonable belief of factual legislative intent smacks of judicial legislation rather than judicial construction. I am satisfied that the Legislature is fully capable of delineating with reasonable precision the type of activity which it considers likely to develop habits of undesired social misconduct in juveniles. The youth of this State are entitled to know what conduct will jeopardize their right to live at home and force them into a State institution. The application of due process requirements to the statute defining juvenile offenses will in no way affect the informality, flexibility, or speed of the juvenile hearing, except that it will protect the child against the uncontrolled subjective discretion of well-meaning officials. Instead of being disruptive of the juvenile process, compliance with fair notice requirements will advance the basic philosophy, idealism and purposes of the system.

It is conceded that the language of the statute "habits of vice or immorality" when used in their unbridled connotation, fails to meet that degree of specificity which due process enjoins on legislative enactments purporting to regulate conduct the violation of which subjects the individual to the loss of his liberties. Indeed, "vice," according to Webster's Dictionary, is defined as a moral fault or failing, especially immoral conduct or habit, as in the indulgence of degrading appetites, such as the vice of gluttony; other meanings include the state of being given up to evil conduct or habit, depravity, wickedness and corruption. "Immorality," on the other hand, is stated to be vice, wickedness, especially unchastity or an immoral act or practice. The concept of morality, and the same would be true of its near-synonym "vice," has occupied men of extraordinary intelligence for centuries, without notable progress (among even philosophers and theologians) toward a common understanding. Certainly, the present generation has a much different conception of the term from that entertained by past generations. A legislative directive addressed to children couched in terms so broad that men of extraordinary intelligence cannot agree as to meaning must perforce be constitutionally deficient for vagueness.

On the merits, I would declare the section of the statue at issue unconstitutional and would set aside the original adjudication of a juvenile offense in each case and order the respective petitioners released from their commitment and detention under it, since I conclude it gives insufficient notice to youth as to the reach of the law, provides law enforcement officers with no clear guide for evaluation of prohibited juvenile conduct, and offers the judge inadequate standards for inclusion and exclusion in the dispensation of even justice. It is impermissibly vague.

NOTES AND QUESTIONS

1. The *S.S.* court notes that the statute under consideration "does not relate to a status" but relates to "conduct of the juvenile." Why might this distinction be significant? *See Gesicki v. Oswald*, 336 F. Supp. 371 (S.D.N.Y. 1971) (holding punishment of "wayward minors" unconstitutional pursuant to *Robinson v. California*, 370 U.S. 660 (1962) (punishment of "status" conditions cruel and unusual punishment under the Eighth Amendment)).

2. The *S.S.* court interprets the statute to apply only where a juvenile is "living in circumstances of manifest danger of falling into habits of vice or immorality" which makes it clear that if the juvenile's conduct continues "there is a manifest danger of falling into habits of criminal conduct." Does such a limitation on the statute's applicability preclude the state from intervening in cases where young people engage in sexual promiscuity, assuming that consensual sexual activity is not "criminal"? Is it not possible (likely?) that sexual promiscuity, particularly female, was within the legislative concept of "immorality"?

Commentators have documented that the exercise of discretion in regulating noncriminal misconduct engaged in by young people often has had a disproportionate impact on female juveniles, often in order to enforce a double standard of protecting female sexual morality. *See, e.g.*, Meda Chisney-Lind, *Judicial Paternalism and the Female Status Offender: Training Women to Know Their Place*, 23 CRIME & DELINQ. 121 (1977); Alan Conway & Carol Bogdan, *Sexual Delinquency: The Persistence of a Double Standard*, 23 CRIME & DELINQ. 131 (1977); P. Hale Andrews, Jr. & Andrew H. Cohn, *Ungovernability: The Unjustifiable Jurisdiction*, 83 YALE L.J. 1383, 1386–87 (1974) (the youths alleged to be "ungovernable" in New York State are predominantly girls).

3. In his dissenting opinion, Chief Justice Dufresne assesses the constitutionality of the Maine statute in light of *Gault*, *Winship*, and *McKeiver*. Are those decisions, all of which address delinquency adjudications, relevant in the context of status offenses? Would it be helpful to know the consequences for the juvenile of being adjudicated a status offender under the Maine statute before concluding whether or not the *Gault* line of cases is relevant?

4. Chief Justice Dufresne states that "the youth of this State are entitled to know what conduct will jeopardize their right to live at home and force them into a State institution." Could it be argued that the "rule of law," or "the principle of legality" as it is often referred to in substantive criminal law theory, is inapposite in the context of *parens patriae* status offense legislation? Specifically, could it be maintained that the point of status offense provisions is not to notify juveniles but to inform juvenile justice functionaries how and when to intervene in order to help troubled youth?

Consider the following possible analogy to the law of civil commitment: Is a civil commitment statute that authorizes the state to hospitalize against their will persons "mentally ill and dangerous to themselves or others" unconstitutionally vague because it fails to notify those at risk of civil commitment what conduct will trigger state intervention? Or is the statute constitutionally adequate because its goal is not to notify the subjects of state intervention but rather to define the authority of governmental decision makers? In considering these questions, see Meir Dan-Cohen, *Decision Rules and Conduct Rules: An Acoustic Separation in Criminal Law*, 97 HARV. L. REV. 625 (1984).

5. Considering the discussion of theories of rights in Chapter 1, are juveniles less "entitled" to notice under status offense provisions if a protectionist theory of rights is embraced? On the other hand, are strict notice requirements demanded if personhood rights are applicable?

6. The *S.S.* case represents the approach of the majority of courts in upholding status offense statutes when attacked as unconstitutionally vague. *See, e.g., E.S.G. v. State,* 447 S.W.2d 225 (Tex. Ct. Civ. App. 1969) (upholding a statute extending juvenile court jurisdiction to a child who "habitually so deports himself as to injure or endanger the morals or health of himself or others"); *District of Columbia v. B.J.R.,* 332 A.2d 58 (D.C. 1975) (upholding statute defining "children in need of supervision" as children who are "habitually disobedient of reasonable . . . commands of parents and are ungovernable"). Some courts however, have struck down status offense provisions as unconstitutionally vague. *See, e.g., State v. Schriver,* 542 A.2d 686 (Conn. 1988) (striking down as unconstitutionally vague a statute prohibiting "any act likely to impair the health or morals of any . . . child").

For a general discussion of the vagueness issue in connection with status offense statutes, see Al Katz & Lee E. Teitelbaum, *PINS Jurisdiction, the Vagueness Doctrine, and the Rule of Law*, 53 IND. L.J. 1 (1977).

SCHLEIFER v. CHARLOTTESVILLE

United States Court of Appeals for the Fourth Circuit
159 F.3d 843 (1998)

WILKINSON, CHIEF JUDGE:

This appeal involves a challenge to the constitutionality of a juvenile nocturnal curfew ordinance enacted by the City of Charlottesville. The district court held that the ordinance did not violate the constitutional rights of minors, their parents, or other affected parties and declined to enjoin its enforcement. We agree that the ordinance is constitutional and affirm the judgment of the district court.

I

On December 16, 1996, the Charlottesville City Council, after several months of study and deliberation, amended Section 17-7 of the City Code to enact a new juvenile nocturnal curfew ordinance. The City Council designed the curfew ordinance to:

(i) promote the general welfare and protect the general public through the reduction of juvenile violence and crime within the City;

(ii) promote the safety and well-being of the City's youngest citizens, persons under the age of seventeen (17), whose inexperience renders them particularly vulnerable to becoming participants in unlawful activities, particularly unlawful drug activities, and to being victimized by older perpetrators of crime; and

(iii) foster and strengthen parental responsibility for children.

Effective March 1, 1997, the ordinance generally prohibits minors, defined as unemancipated persons under seventeen, from remaining in any public place, motor vehicle, or establishment within city limits during curfew hours. The curfew takes effect at 12:01 a.m. on Monday through Friday, at 1:00 a.m. on Saturday and Sunday, and lifts at 5:00 a.m. each morning.

The ordinance does not restrict minors' activities that fall under one of its eight enumerated exceptions. Minors may participate in any activity during curfew hours if they are accompanied by a parent; they may run errands at a parent's direction provided that they possess a signed note. The ordinance allows minors to undertake employment, or attend supervised activities sponsored by school, civic, religious, or other public organizations. The ordinance exempts minors who are engaged in interstate travel, are on the sidewalk abutting their parents' residence, or are involved in an emergency. Finally, the ordinance does not affect minors who are "exercising First Amendment rights protected by the United States Constitution, such as the free exercise of religion, freedom of speech and the right of assembly."

The ordinance sets forth a scheme of warnings and penalties for minors who violate it. For a first violation, a minor receives a verbal warning, followed by a written warning to the minor and the minor's parents. For subsequent violations, the minor is charged with a Class 4 misdemeanor. The ordinance also makes it unlawful for certain other individuals, including parents, knowingly to encourage a minor to violate the ordinance. . . .

Plaintiffs are five minors under age seventeen who are subject to the ordinance, one eighteen-year-old, and two parents of minor children. The minors allege that, with their parents' permission, they occasionally wish to engage in lawful activities which the curfew will not permit. These activities include attending late movies; getting a "bite to eat"; playing in a band; socializing with older siblings; and attending concerts in Richmond, which would bring them back through Charlottesville during curfew hours. The eighteen-year-old plaintiff alleges that he has been deprived of opportunities to associate with his younger friends by the ordinance. The parent plaintiffs allege that the ordinance interferes with their decisions on which activities, at what times, are appropriate for their children.

Plaintiffs brought this action for declaratory and injunctive relief, alleging that the ordinance violates their rights under the First, Fourth, Fifth and Fourteenth Amendments. At trial, plaintiffs dismissed their Fourth Amendment claims. Following trial, by order dated May 20, 1997, the district court rejected plaintiffs' remaining claims and denied their motion for a permanent injunction. Plaintiffs now appeal.

II

Initially we must consider the level of scrutiny appropriate to this case. Plaintiffs contend that the ordinance infringes minors' constitutional liberties and therefore should be subject to strict scrutiny. It is true that "[a] child, merely on account of his minority, is not beyond the protection of the Constitution." Minors enjoy some rights under the First and Fourteenth Amendments before they attain adulthood. *Tinker v. Des Moines Indep. Community Sch. Dist.*, 393 U.S. 503 (1969). At the same time, the Supreme Court has made abundantly clear that children's rights are not coextensive with those of adults. *See, e.g., Bethel Sch. Dist. No. 403 v. Fraser*, 478 U.S. 675 (1986); *Ginsberg v. New York*, 390 U.S. 629 (1968); *Prince v. Massachusetts*, 321 U.S. 158 (1944). "Traditionally at common law, and still today, unemancipated minors lack some of the most fundamental rights of self-determination — including even the right of liberty in its narrow sense, *i.e.*, the right to come and go at will." *Vernonia Sch. Dist. 47J v. Acton*, 515 U.S. 646, 654 (1995).

In recognition of these customary limitations, "[t]he state's authority over children's activities is broader than over like actions of adults." State laws do not permit children to drive a car before they reach a certain age. Compulsory attendance laws require children to attend school. Labor laws limit the opportunities of children to engage in gainful employment. These types of laws reflect the state's "general interest in youth's well being."

In light of the case law, two things seem clear. First, children do possess at least qualified rights, so an ordinance which restricts their liberty to the extent that this one does should be subject to more than rational basis review. Second, because children do not possess the same rights as adults, the ordinance should be subject to less than the strictest level of scrutiny. We thus believe intermediate scrutiny to be the most appropriate level of review and must determine whether the ordinance is "substantially related" to "important" governmental interests. We also conclude, however, that the ordinance survives constitutional attack under either a substantial or a compelling state interest standard. The narrow means chosen by the City in the ordinance serve strong and indeed compelling public needs.

III

A

The text of the Charlottesville curfew ordinance identifies three legislative purposes: (1) to reduce juvenile violence and crime within the city; (2) to protect juveniles themselves from being swept up in unlawful drug activities and from becoming prey to older perpetrators of crime; and (3) to strengthen parental responsibility for children. These enumerated purposes represent important and compelling governmental interests.

. . . .

The City contends that its curfew ordinance was passed to combat the marked growth in the rate of juvenile crime both nationwide and within

Virginia. During the preliminary injunction hearing Dr. William Ruefle, a criminologist expert in juvenile curfews, testified that these state and national growth trends were reflected in Charlottesville. . . .

. . . .

Likewise, the City's strong interest in fostering the welfare of children and protecting the youngest members of society from harm is well-established. Courts have recognized "the peculiar vulnerability of children," and the Supreme Court long ago observed that "streets afford dangers for [children] not affecting adults." Those dangers have not disappeared; they simply have assumed a different and more insidious form today. Each unsuspecting child risks becoming another victim of the assaults, violent crimes, and drug wars that plague America's cities. Given the realities of urban life, it is not surprising that courts have acknowledged the special vulnerability of children to the dangers of the streets.

Charlottesville's third purpose — strengthening parental responsibility for children — is also a significant interest. The City shares with parents and guardians a responsibility to protect children. State authority complements parental supervision, and "the guiding role of parents in the upbringing of their children justifies limitations on the freedoms of minors." The Supreme Court has acknowledged "the special interest of the State" in encouraging minors to seek parental advice in making important decisions. And the Court has confirmed that the state is appropriately concerned with the integrity of the family unit. Therefore, like the City's two preceding interests in reducing the incidence of juvenile crime and juvenile victimization, the City's third aim constitutes an important governmental purpose.

B

. . . .

Charlottesville was constitutionally justified in believing that its curfew would materially assist its first stated interest — that of reducing juvenile violence and crime. The City Council acted on the basis of information from many sources, including records from Charlottesville's police department, a survey of public opinion, news reports, data from the United States Department of Justice, national crime reports, and police reports from other localities. On the basis of such evidence, elected bodies are entitled to conclude that keeping unsupervised juveniles off the streets late at night will make for a safer community. The same streets may have a more volatile and less wholesome character at night than during the day. Alone on the streets at night children face a series of dangerous and potentially life-shaping decisions. Drug dealers may lure them to use narcotics or aid in their sale. Gangs may pressure them into membership or participation in violence. "[D]uring the formative years of childhood and adolescence, minors often lack the experience, perspective, and judgment to recognize and avoid choices that could be detrimental to them." Those who succumb to these criminal influences at an early age may persist in their criminal conduct as adults. Whether we as judges subscribe to these theories is beside the point. Those elected officials with their finger on the pulse of their home community clearly did. In attempting to reduce through its curfew the opportunities for children to come into contact with criminal influences, the City was directly advancing its first objective of reducing juvenile violence and crime.

. . . .

C

The Charlottesville curfew is not only "substantially related" to its stated purposes. The limited scope of the curfew and its numerous exceptions would satisfy even the strict scrutiny requirement of narrow tailoring. Plaintiffs urge, however, that we follow the lead of the Ninth Circuit, which held that San Diego's curfew ordinance failed strict scrutiny review because the exceptions to the ordinance were not sufficiently detailed and comprehensive to make the curfew the least restrictive means of serving San Diego's compelling ends. *Nunez* [*v. San Diego*], 114 F.3d 935, 948-49 (9th Cir. 1997).

The San Diego curfew applied to all minors under the age of eighteen, began at 10:00 p.m., and extended until "daylight immediately following." It contained four exceptions: (1) when a minor is accompanied by a parent or other qualified adult; (2) when a minor is on an emergency errand for his parent; (3) when a minor is returning from a school-sponsored activity; and (4) when a minor is engaged in employment.

By contrast, Charlottesville's curfew applies only to minors less than seventeen years of age, does not begin until midnight on weekdays and 1:00 a.m. on weekends, lifts at 5:00 a.m. each morning, and contains no fewer than eight detailed exceptions. Under Charlottesville's curfew, minors are allowed, *inter alia*, to remain on the sidewalk directly abutting their residences; to attend supervised activities sponsored by school, religious, public, civic or other similar organizations; to run errands for their parents; to undertake interstate travel; and to engage freely in any activity protected by the First Amendment.

The Charlottesville ordinance carefully mirrors the Dallas curfew ordinance that the Fifth Circuit found to satisfy strict scrutiny in *Qutb* [*v. Strauss*, 11 F.3d 488 (5th Cir. 1993)]. . . . This curfew, with its narrow scope and comprehensive list of exceptions, represents the least restrictive means to advance Charlottesville's compelling interests. Thus, it would survive even strict scrutiny if that were the appropriate standard of review.

IV

[The court discussed and dismissed arguments that the Charlottesville ordinance violates constitutional rights of parents.]

V

Finally, we consider plaintiffs' claims that various exceptions to the ordinance are unconstitutionally vague. A law is not void for vagueness so long as it "(1) establishes 'minimal guidelines to govern law enforcement,' and (2) gives reasonable notice of the proscribed conduct." . . .

. . . .

The Charlottesville ordinance provides an exception for those minors who are "exercising First Amendment rights protected by the United States Constitution, such as the free exercise of religion, freedom of speech and the right of assembly." Plaintiffs insist that this exception accords standardless discretion to law enforcement officers to decide whether or not the exception applies. According to plaintiffs, it also forces citizens to learn a complex body of constitutional law in order to comprehend its scope.

We decline to punish the City for its laudable effort to respect the First Amendment. A broad exception from the curfew for such activities fortifies, rather than weakens, First Amendment values. Plaintiffs basically attempt to place city councils between a rock and a hard place. If councils draft an ordinance with exceptions, those exceptions are subject to a vagueness challenge. If they neglect to provide exceptions, then the ordinance is attacked for not adequately protecting First Amendment freedoms. It hardly seems fitting, however, for courts to chastise elected bodies for protecting expressive activity. The Charlottesville ordinance is constitutionally stronger with that protection than without.

The First Amendment exception also does not accord unfettered discretion to law enforcement officials. Every criminal law, of course, reposes some discretion in those who must enforce it. The mere possibility that such discretion might be abused hardly entitles courts to strike a law down. . . .

The First Amendment exception provides adequate notice to citizens. It is perfectly clear that core First Amendment activities such as political protest and religious worship after midnight would be protected. It is equally clear that rollerblading would not. Between these poles may lie marginal cases, which can be taken as they come.

. . . .

The ordinance also creates an exception in cases where a minor is involved in an emergency. Without citation to authority, plaintiffs pose a variety of hypothetical situations in which this exception may or may not apply. For example, they wonder whether the exception would include the need to go to a store to purchase cough medicine or a thermometer. Once again, the existence of questions at the margins does not justify striking down the exception altogether. A brief review of the exception illuminates many situations to which it plainly applies. The ordinance specifically defines emergency as "refer[ring] to unforeseen circumstances, or the status or condition resulting therefrom, requiring immediate action to safeguard life, limb or property." . . .

Plaintiffs' vagueness claims threaten to make the drafting of a curfew ordinance an impossible task. The practical exceptions to the City's curfew shall not provide the cause of its demise.

VI

Our dissenting colleague insists that the Charlottesville ordinance must satisfy strict scrutiny, that it is not narrowly tailored, and that it is void for vagueness. Under the dissent's stringent application of these standards, however, no curfew ever would pass constitutional muster. . . . Any locality in the nation that chose to enact a curfew would ultimately see it picked to death in the courts. A brief look at the dissent's analysis indicates why this is so.

To begin with, the dissent downplays the interests of the community, namely Charlottesville's goals of promoting the well-being of its youngest citizens and of fostering parental responsibility. The dissent's suggestion that these interests are compelling only when the state proceeds in a manner "supportive of the parental role," is not consistent with the prevalence of legislative measures (such as age limitations on drinking and on driving) that may, on occasion, frustrate the desires of individual parents. Moreover, by granting a citizen's veto to every parent in the community, the dissent would convert the compelling interest requirement into a rule of unanimity. This high a constitutional bar is antithetical to the values of democratic innovation.

The same disablement of democratic authority is evident in the dissent's strict reading of means. The dissent does agree that Charlottesville's interest in reducing juvenile crime is compelling, but then subjects the curfew to an impossibly narrow tailoring standard. Tellingly, the dissent fails to point to less restrictive means that the City might have employed. Forbidding preventive measures such as curfews propels localities to the harshest of alternatives — waiting for juveniles actually to commit criminal offenses and then apprehending, prosecuting, and punishing them. Neither minors nor the City would gain from this result.

Finally, no ordinance could ever meet the precision envisioned by the dissent's "strict vagueness standard." The dissent argues that the labyrinthine nature of First Amendment doctrine requires a curfew exception drawn in labyrinthine detail. Forcing city councils to pursue such an elusive goal would prevent them from ever passing an ordinance. The vagueness doctrine's basic notice principle does not impose such an impediment.

The Charlottesville curfew serves not only to head off crimes before they occur, but also to protect a particularly vulnerable population from being lured into participating in such activity. Contrary to the dissent's protestation, we do not hold that every such curfew ordinance would pass constitutional muster. The means adopted by a municipality must bear a substantial relationship to significant governmental interests; the restrictiveness of those means remains the subject of judicial review. . . . Charlottesville's curfew, compared to those in other cities, is indeed a mild regulation: it covers a limited age group during only a few hours of the night. Its various exceptions enable minors to participate in necessary or worthwhile activities during this time. We hold that Charlottesville's juvenile curfew ordinance comfortably satisfies constitutional standards.

Accordingly, we affirm the judgment of the district court. We do so in the belief that communities possess constitutional latitude in devising solutions to the persistent problem of juvenile crime.

Affirmed.

MICHAEL, CIRCUIT JUDGE, *dissenting*:

Today, the majority relegates kids to second-class citizenship by upholding Charlottesville's nighttime curfew for minors. Forbidding children to go out at night affects their fundamental rights, and such a restriction can be valid only if it withstands strict scrutiny. The Charlottesville curfew ordinance fails the test because it sweeps too broadly and usurps rather than supports parental authority over child rearing. The ordinance has another constitutional defect as well. Although it is a crime to violate the ordinance, the crime is only vaguely defined. The curfew does not apply when minors are "exercising First Amendment rights." This exception is unconstitutionally vague, leaving children, their parents, and the police to guess whether particular conduct is punishable as a crime. I respectfully dissent.

The majority attempts to brush this dissent aside by claiming that under my approach "no curfew ever would pass constitutional muster." I can as easily say that under the majority's approach no curfew would ever fail constitutional muster. I'm afraid that my claim will be proven true. As long as the majority's standard is the law, a city council can pass a juvenile curfew as a routine measure because the justification is so easy to articulate. This should not stand under the Constitution. Children make up a quarter of our population, and their rights must not be ignored. A city council cannot order such a large segment of the community to stay at home for thirty-three hours of every week unless its curfew satisfies strict scrutiny. Subjecting Charlottesville's ordinance to this test does not subvert the "democratic authority" of the City Council. On the contrary, the Council's authority must be exercised within constitutional bounds. The Council cannot, in the name of majority rule, take away constitutional rights of a minority, in this case all children under seventeen.

. . . .

II

Because the curfew criminalizes conduct of persons under the age of seventeen, the City's use of this age-based classification is subject to the limitations of the Fourteenth Amendment's Equal Protection Clause. Generally, laws making age-based classifications are subject to rational basis review, and thus are upheld if there is a rational relationship that ties the use of the classification to a legitimate governmental purpose. However, when an age-based classification affects fundamental rights, a court must review the classification with "the most exacting scrutiny."

The Charlottesville curfew ordinance does implicate fundamental rights. *Cf. Kolender v. Lawson*, 461 U.S. 352, 358 (1983) (loitering statute implicates First Amendment liberties and "constitutional right to freedom of movement"); *Nunez v. City of San Diego*, 114 F.3d 935, 944-45 (9th Cir. 1997) (holding that curfew infringed minors' fundamental rights). Normally, this would require the City to demonstrate that the ordinance satisfies strict scrutiny. However, because this case involves the fundamental rights of minors, and not those of adults, the majority concludes that equal protection requires only intermediate scrutiny. I disagree. Like the Fifth and Ninth Circuits, I would hold that the Equal Protection Clause subjects to strict scrutiny all governmental classifications that impact fundamental constitutional rights. *See Nunez*, 114 F.3d at 945-46; *Qutb v. Strauss*, 11 F.3d 488, 492 & n. 6 (5th Cir. 1993). Under this standard the Charlottesville curfew is unconstitutional.

A

Some mention of the unique status of children in our society is necessary to set the stage for the explanation of why strict scrutiny is necessary. The Supreme Court has long recognized that " '[c]hildren have a very special place in life which the law should reflect.' " . . .

The Supreme Court has consistently reflected the traditional Western concept of the family as a "unit with broad parental authority over minor children." Indeed, the Court's " 'constitutional interpretation has consistently recognized [that] parents' claim to authority in their own household to direct the rearing of their children is basic in the structure of our society.' " This authority is undoubtedly broad. When parental control comes into play, "unemancipated minors lack some of the most fundamental rights of self-determination — including even the right of liberty in its narrow sense, i.e., the right to come and go at will."

However, a parent's broad authority does not generally carry over to the state. . . . The Court has repeatedly said that it is " 'cardinal with us that the custody, care and nurture of the child reside first in the parents, whose primary function and freedom include preparation for obligations the state can neither supply nor hinder.' " This broad recognition of the parents' right to control the upbringing of their children and of constitutional deference to parental authority is linked to the parents' duty to raise and protect their children. This deference to parents rests on the strong presumptions that "natural bonds of affection lead parents to act in the best interests of their children" and that "parents possess what a child lacks in maturity, experience, and capacity for judgment required for making life's difficult decisions."

Only in limited instances is the state able to assert a parent's broad power to control the activities of minors. For example, when the state acts as the legal guardian for a child, it will assume much, if not all, of a parent's traditional prerogatives. Similarly, the teachers and administrators of a public school will act *"in loco parentis"* while children are in their physical custody because parents " 'delegate part of [their] authority' " to the school by placing their children under its instruction.

In a similar way, the state (as parens patriae) may occasionally displace the parents' primary role in child rearing in order to protect a child's welfare. Thus, the state may trump parental discretion in delinquency proceedings (because parental control has already faltered), or in situations where a child's "physical or mental health is jeopardized." In these circumstances, the strong presumption that parents are able and willing to act in the best interests of their children may be rebutted. The state's power to displace parental discretion is limited, however, and must be justified on a case-by-case basis. . . . Indeed, "[s]imply because the decision of a parent is not agreeable to a child or because it involves risks does not automatically transfer the power to make that decision from the parents to some agency or officer of the state." Thus, except in special circumstances, the state normally must defer to the exercise of a broad degree of parental discretion.

It is also clear that while the state does have an independent interest in the welfare of children, this interest may be superseded by the parents' right to exercise broad discretion in raising their children. Consequently, the rights of minors in relation to the state must be analyzed to consider not only the interests of the minor and the state but also the interests of parents. Thus, the analysis of a minor's rights is complicated by the addition of this third party (a parent) who can bolster either the state's claim of authority or the minor's assertion of rights.

. . . .

This discussion underscores the Supreme Court's recognition of the special status of children and the predominance of the family unit. In particular, it underscores the Court's deference to the traditional authority of parents over the activities of their children. With this background, I now turn to the proper standard of scrutiny that must be applied in this case.

B

The minors' equal protection challenge in this case must be analyzed under strict scrutiny. This conclusion flows from the basic question the majority ignores. Why are the federal constitutional rights of persons who are defined as minors under state law different from those of adults? The answer is that a minor's constitutional rights are basically the same as those of adults, but in certain situations there may be "significant state interest[s] . . . that [are] not present in the case of an adult" that will support a broader authority to regulate minors. When these interests justify regulation, they do so not because a minor's constitutional rights are always inferior to those of an adult but rather because the government's specific interests as regards minors are sometimes sufficient to allow a regulation to survive strict scrutiny. Accordingly, I would hold that the "fundamental rights" of minors are no less fundamental than those of adults and, thus, must be protected with the same vigor under a strict scrutiny analysis.

1

This conclusion is drawn from the Supreme Court's general approach to analyzing the rights of minors. The Court makes it clear that "[m]inors, as well as adults, are protected by the Constitution and possess constitutional rights." . . . [The dissent reviewed the Supreme Court's cases addressing reproductive rights in support of its conclusion that strict scrutiny is the proper standard to be applied in the instant case.]

2

. . . .

It is clear from the discussion above that the majority's categorical approach is wrong. The majority would apply intermediate scrutiny in all cases involving minors, even those in which the government has no justification specific to minors for infringing upon their fundamental rights. In the latter situation the governmental interest in regulating minors under the majority's approach is identical to its interest in regulating adults. Yet the rights of minors could still be treated differently because their "fundamental" rights are not protected with strict scrutiny review. This has far ranging implications. Legislative bodies can pass many laws regulating conduct that would pass intermediate scrutiny but fail strict scrutiny. Under the majority's approach, such laws could be applied to all minors but could not be applied to any adults (whose fundamental rights are protected by strict scrutiny), even though the government had no reason to regulate minors any more than it did adults. The majority's holding, therefore, allows a minor to be deprived of constitutional rights when a similar deprivation would be constitutionally intolerable for adults, even though the state lacks any reason for different treatment. This result cannot be justified and essentially creates a second-class citizenship for all persons under the age of majority.

. . . .

I would avoid these difficulties by applying strict scrutiny to all equal protection challenges involving fundamental rights, regardless of whether minors or adults are involved. Under this approach, minors must be treated the same as adults whenever the government lacks interests specific to minors to support more restrictive regulatory authority over them. However, when circumstances trigger governmental interests that are particular to minors, these interests, when coupled with the government's other interests, can make the government's claim for greater restrictions on minors much stronger. If these interests taken as a whole are compelling, the government's regulation (if narrowly tailored) will survive strict scrutiny with respect to minors, even though it would fail the test in the case of adults. This approach therefore provides a principled approach for deciding when children may be treated differently from adults for constitutional purposes.

. . . .

C

The Charlottesville curfew ordinance cannot withstand strict scrutiny and should be struck down. . . . The Charlottesville ordinance fails the strict scrutiny test, notwithstanding its stated (and worthy) objectives of (1) reducing juvenile crime, (2) promoting the safety and wellbeing of juveniles, and (3) fostering and strengthening parental responsibility.

1

I quite agree with the majority that protecting the community from serious crime is a compelling governmental interest. The problem is that the Charlottesville curfew is not narrowly tailored to forward this goal. . . .

By restricting the freedom of minors during curfew hours, the ordinance treats all minors under the age of seventeen as a threat to society in order to protect the community from juvenile crime. This broad restriction is not narrowly tailored to meet its objective of crime prevention. The ordinance treats all minors the same even though an exceedingly small percentage commit crimes. The Equal Protection Clause forbids such a crude grouping when fundamental rights are at stake, and limiting the curfew's hours and providing exceptions does not diminish this shortcoming.

. . . .

2

The City's second objective of promoting the safety and well-being of juveniles also falls short under strict scrutiny. This interest is not compelling in this case because the curfew displaces parental authority. Indeed, the majority says only that the City has a "strong" interest in protecting the youngest members of society from harm. "Strong" interests are not sufficient to satisfy strict scrutiny. Only compelling interests suffice.

The City's stated interest in protecting minors under the age of seventeen is not compelling here because the curfew was not designed to be supportive of the parental role. . . . This authority can be present when the governmental interest in regulation complements the traditional authority of the parent. By supporting the exercise of parental discretion, the state aligns its regulatory power with the interests of parents who have broad discretion to control the activities of their children. The combined interests of parents and the state therefore strengthen the justification for governmental regulation. . . .

The Charlottesville ordinance, however, paternalistically displaces the exercise of parental discretion by making it illegal for parents to allow their children to move about independently at night. Yet parents are better able to assess their children's maturity and capacity for judgment than a city council. Parents may legitimately decide that the best way to raise their children is to permit them to be out on their own after midnight on occasion. In other words, parents may legitimately conclude that the risk of granting children some independence is small compared to the benefits resulting from the gradual development of maturity and judgment that is needed in preparation for a responsible adult life. This exercise of parental discretion is impossible under the ordinance.

Indeed, the ordinance was purposefully designed to displace parental discretion with the will of the City Council. On the day the curfew was enacted, the Council's agenda said the following about the curfew's purpose: "parental responsibility for the whereabouts of their children is the norm and where that does not exist, then the legal sanction should enforce such responsibility. Further, well communicated curfew ordinances . . . impose a community-wide standard on parents who are unable or unwilling to set such limits." Rather than supporting the parental role, this curfew supersedes it. It reflects the "statist notion that governmental power should supersede parental authority in all cases because some parents" fail to exercise control over their children. This governmental paternalism is "repugnant to American tradition." Consequently, because the curfew attempts to achieve its stated purpose of promoting the safety and well-being of minors by displacing parental authority over the upbringing of children, the curfew does not serve a compelling governmental interest.

3

It follows that the ordinance's third stated purpose of fostering and strengthening parental responsibility also falls short. When laws displace the primacy of parental discretion by imposing community-wide norms, the traditional authority of parents over child rearing is no longer available to support any limitation on the rights of minors. The curfew's attempt to foster and strengthen parental responsibility by displacing parental authority does not support a compelling state interest.

For these reasons, I would hold that the Charlottesville curfew fails to satisfy strict scrutiny and thus violates the Equal Protection Clause.

III

Even if I could conclude that Charlottesville's curfew passed strict scrutiny, I would hold that the ordinance as adopted is void for vagueness under the Due Process Clause. More specifically, I would hold that the ordinance's First Amendment "exception" is impermissibly vague.

. . . .

The vagueness of the First Amendment exception is intuitively plain. Indeed, its language is anything but clear. What are "First Amendment rights"? What is considered to be "speech"? Does it include written communication? What of expressive conduct that does not involve oral or written communication? What types of speech are "protected" by "freedom of speech"? Is commercial speech protected? If so, to what extent? What is the "free exercise" of religion? And what of the "right of assembly"? Do two friends have the "right" to "assemble" or meet at a coffeehouse? This says nothing of the general First Amendment rights (*e.g.*, association, press, petition) that the City's exception leaves unmentioned. The questions above are difficult enough for courts, Congress, and constitutional scholars, let alone for someone with no legal training. And when answers are given, they are often imprecise and turn on the specifics of a case and a balancing of many factors. Furthermore, First Amendment jurisprudence is a vast and complicated body of law that grows with each passing day. As a result, criminal conduct cannot be defined by simply referring to the title (First Amendment) or subtitle (speech or assembly) of a particular right.

. . . .

The testimony of Charlottesville's Chief of Police proves the statute's ambiguity. When asked whether two fifteen-year-olds violate the ordinance by discussing politics in a coffee shop during the curfew, the Chief said, "You're indoors, it's a public location, I . . . think technically under the ordinance it may be a violation. I doubt whether we would deal with it." Similarly, when asked if a fifteen-year-old who plays in a band in a local restaurant after curfew hours violates the curfew when he is not paid for the performance, the Chief answered, "I think that technically [the minor] is possibl[y] in violation of the ordinance." However, "the officer would obviously have to make a decision about whether they're in violation or not. And I believe there's some discretion allowed." It is this discretion combined with the failure to define with specificity what conduct is illegal that makes the statute unconstitutional. The danger of chilling the exercise of constitutionally protected activity arises because of the uncertainty associated with the First Amendment exception.

The majority errs in supporting its reasoning with the fact that city councils appear to be placed "between a rock and a hard place." While it is true that curfews without exceptions will almost always impermissibly infringe upon substantive constitutional rights and that curfews with exceptions may be subject to vagueness challenges, invalidation of this ordinance is still mandated by our Constitution. . . .

Taken to its logical conclusion, the majority's reasoning would immunize all statutes regulating conduct involving the exercise of First Amendment rights whenever they contain a First Amendment "exception." Because such provisions would not be impermissibly vague under the majority's analysis, the statutes would be immune from both substantive and vagueness challenges. Substantively the statute cannot, according to its own terms, violate the constitution. In fact, it incorporates the Constitution's protections. The upshot is that facial attacks could never be brought and that statutes containing these exceptions could be challenged only as they are applied. This squarely conflicts with the Supreme Court's long-standing concern with the potential chill of constitutionally protected activity created by the mere existence of vague criminal statutes and the potential for their arbitrary enforcement.

For these reasons, I would hold that the curfew's First Amendment "exception" renders the ordinance impermissibly vague on its face. Until the ordinance is amended by the City Council or given a construction by state courts that sufficiently reduces its unconstitutional vagueness, its enforcement conflicts with the constitutional guarantee of due process of law.

IV

In sum, I would hold that equal protection challenges by minors to laws that regulate in the area of fundamental rights must be subject to strict scrutiny. In my opinion the Charlottesville ordinance fails this standard. Even if the ordinance survived the equal protection challenge, however, it would be unconstitutional in its present form. The curfew's First Amendment exception is impermissibly vague in violation of the Due Process Clause. For these reasons, I respectfully dissent.

NOTES AND QUESTIONS

1. As *Schleifer* makes clear, the federal courts are divided on the constitutionality of curfew measures and on the level of scrutiny to be applied in assessing their constitutionality. *Schleifer* is not alone in subjecting curfew provisions to intermediate scrutiny. *See, e.g., Hutchins v. District of Columbia*, 188 F.3d 531 (D.C. Cir. 1999) (en banc). Should courts follow *Schleifer* in

applying intermediate scrutiny or strictly scrutinize curfew regulations as argued by Judge Michael in his *Schleifer* dissent? For a comprehensive treatment of the matter, see Danny R. Veilleux, *Annotation, Validity, Construction, and Effect of Juvenile Curfew Regulations*, 83 A.L.R. 4th 1056 (1991).

2. The Charlottsville ordinance considered in *Schleifer* sets forth a scheme that requires that offending minors be warned upon initial violation of the ordinance and punished as a misdemeanant upon subsequent violations. Is punishment appropriate or should a non-punitive sanction be applied?

NOTE ON PROPOSALS TO ABOLISH
STATUS OFFENSES JURISDICTION

As the above cases suggest, status statutes raise serious questions of constitutional law. Moreover, status offense jurisdiction is controversial from a policy standpoint. The following excerpts highlight some of the controversy.

Orman W. Ketcham, *Why Jurisdiction Over Status Offenders Should be Eliminated From Juvenile Courts*

57 BOSTON UNIVERSITY LAW REVIEW 645, 645–655, 661 (1977)

In 1971, having recently completed the long task of developing Standards of Criminal Justice for the American Bar Association, the Institute of Judicial Administration turned its considerable talents to the preparation of Juvenile Justice Standards. The American Bar Association became a co-sponsor in February 1973, and the IJA/ABA Joint Commission of the Juvenile Justice Standards Project was established. . . .

. . . .

. . . Parents who bring complaints against their children are not always reasonable; independent and unruly youths are not necessarily antisocial and headed for criminal careers; and juvenile court intervention rarely remedies the interpersonal family conflicts that are at the root of such adolescent deviance. In fact, the Joint Commission concluded that far more harm than benefit occurs by lumping youthful miscreants with juvenile criminal offenders. It also found that persistent statutory efforts in the last decade to separate these two categories within the juvenile justice system have been largely ineffective. Thus, the Standards propose the elimination of coercive official intervention in unruly child cases because the cure is worse than the illness. . . .

. . . .

. . . For me, the issue seems less complicated. Under our American constitutional principles, coercive judicial action is not justifiable unless a vital state purpose is concerned and then only if judicial intervention equitably applied will carry out the defined purpose of the state. By such measurements, juvenile court intervention into status offenses is neither justifiable nor effective. Hence, I believe we should admit having strayed (for whatever noble motives) from the guiding principles of our limited and balanced governmental system and should concede that status offense jurisdiction should cease and desist henceforth. The half measure of retaining juvenile court jurisdiction over status offenses but prohibiting the commitment of status offenders to secure institutions may be politically appealing as a step in the right direction. But, in my opinion, it is not a permanent solution to the violation of legal principle involved in coercive intervention into the lives of status offenders.

. . . .

. . . Juvenile court jurisdiction over status offenses seeks to assure juveniles the care and custody that should have been given them by good parents. Such jurisdiction asserts that morality will be restored, that juveniles will honor their father and mother and obey their reasonable commands, and that children will not grow up in idleness and vice nor associate with depraved or criminal companions. In short, its assertions are pretentious and overly ambitious. The inevitable failure of juvenile courts to produce such exaggerated results has brought disrepute upon the entire judicial system and should be discontinued.

. . . Most juvenile courts give undue credence to parental accusations that the child refuses to obey, is sexually promiscuous, or has undesirable friends. The impact of this judicial deference to parental authority is serious as seventy-two percent of all status offenders are turned in by adults, usually a relative. Most of these are parents who are motivated by feelings of vindictiveness or hostility toward their children. By seeking the aid of judicial control, they are implicitly admitting inadequacy in coping with their children and hoping to escape their parental obligations. Although some juvenile court judges may privately question the wisdom of certain parents, the rule is "the parents right or wrong."

Once the parent is successful in bringing the miscreant child before the juvenile court, the judicial sanctions of coercive intervention or treatment are universally applied against the juvenile. Thus, should the pressures of home life become so unbearable as to force the child to run away and escape them, the parent can use the juvenile court to affect the child's punishment by refusing to allow the child to return home. Consequently, the child may be detained in protective custody despite evidence that much of the underlying problem is attributable to one of the parents. Unwavering and unqualified support for parental authority, regardless of where the fault lies, is unreasonable and constitutes an improper delegation of judicial authority. This practice should be stopped by the termination of coercive juvenile court jurisdiction over disputes between parent and child.

. . . .

The due process requirement of fundamental fairness in court intervention for adult or juvenile criminal offenses requires that judicial sanctions be usual and logically coupled to a reasonable punishment or correction for the offense. But juvenile court dispositions in status offense cases frequently are not calculated to produce the goal sought. For example, truants incarcerated for failing to attend school are committed to institutions and thus permanently prevented from obtaining an academic education; youths who run away from home are incarcerated and thus permanently denied a home; girls who are promiscuous and lacking in self-control are committed to institutions where there is no individual choice and thus no capacity to learn self-control. Without a more logical correlation to the misbehavior, such sanctions in status offenses are not rehabilitative and often are counterproductive. It is unprincipled for juvenile courts to continue to impose coercive sanctions upon status offenders without convincing proof that such action is justified and likely to produce the intended results.

. . . If, in fact, juvenile court intervention into status offenses is truly in the best interests of the juvenile, it need not be coercive. Rehabilitative benefits should be available as a matter of right that is exercised or rejected voluntarily by the juvenile or by someone such as a guardian *ad litem* acting solely on his or her behalf.

. . . .

. . . [T]he evidence indicates that community interests and safety are substantially diminished because the juvenile court exercises status offense jurisdiction. The public is directly affected by the increasing incidence of violent crimes committed by juveniles. Because the juvenile court is forced to direct between one third and one half of its attention to status offenses at public expense, valuable resources are being improperly allocated. If there were no status offense cases, juvenile courts could devote most of their time and attention to the most pressing problem of the decade — juvenile crime.

. . . .

There are substantial indications that those juveniles who are adjudicated status offenders are more likely to become criminal offenders than youths who are not so labeled. Many observers attribute this to the self-fulfilling prophecy theory; a juvenile who is officially designated a nonconforming offender is thus alienated and tends to justify such classification by more serious antisocial acts. Others believe that the underlying problems causing a youth to engage in noncriminal misbehavior eventually will escalate into more serious antisocial behavior constituting criminal offenses. Whatever the theory, there is not certainty that treatment of such youths by the juvenile court prevents or deters subsequent criminal acts. . . .

. . . So long as the public continues to provide and fund a statutory procedure for problems of noncriminal misbehavior, there is little incentive for the development of private, nonprofit agencies designed to aid the concerned parent and youth in voluntary, cooperative ways most likely to assure successful rehabilitation. Because the type of private agencies that are impeded by present public policies are voluntary, any parent or child who feels that their legal rights are not respected by such an agency can discontinue the association. No court-ordered referral would be involved. Hence, the fears expressed by spokesmen for the existing juvenile court system that such agencies might not observe the requirements of legal due process are not relevant.

. . . The more fortunate status offenders are those not referred to a juvenile court or those adjudicated and returned home for probation and counseling. But each year a large number of children are removed from their families and committed to juvenile institutions that provide little more than containment and punishment. Such coercive intervention may be responsible for the many suicides, mental breakdowns and psychotic episodes among institutionalized juveniles. The incidence of such traumatic events is markedly greater among incarcerated status offenders than among juvenile criminal offenders, who are more accepting of their incarceration. Thus, unless there is a clear and present danger to the community's safety, failure of the juvenile justice system to intervene will be more beneficial to both the juvenile and the community than current forms of coercive intervention.

. . . The Juvenile Justice and Delinquency Prevention Act of 1974 denies federal funds to juvenile justice systems that fail to remove all status offenders from secure institutions within two years. Many efforts have also been made to establish community-based facilities and treatment centers for status offenders in lieu of secure institutions.

In the past fifteen years, there have been repeated efforts to separate status offenders from juveniles who have violated the criminal laws when they are placed in detention centers, training schools and juvenile institutions. Statutory definitions and legal rules have been developed. But only the semantics and the definitions are distinct. The juveniles are inevitably commingled. In reality, the dispositional treatment afforded a status offender hardly differs from that given a juvenile criminal offender. Despite statutory prohibitions, status offenders like juvenile delinquents are repeatedly detained in adult jails in great numbers. And, because of the greater difficulty in finding an acceptable solution to their problems, status offenders are customarily detained in juvenile institutions for longer periods of time than their criminal counterparts.

. . . .

. . . My conclusion is that status offense jurisdiction is so inherently discretionary in principle that it is subject to manipulation by police, parents and social workers. Consequently, I believe that further efforts to restore status offense jurisdiction to its intended purpose as a socially beneficial and rehabilitative process are doomed to fail. Better to cut the losses now and seek a more effective solution through noncoercive, voluntary social service methods than to attempt renovation of the badly flawed, though well-intended, status offense concept.

———

John DeWitt Gregory, *Juvenile Court Jurisdiction Over Noncriminal Misbehavior: The Argument Against Abolition*

39 OHIO STATE LAW JOURNAL 242, 267–272 (1978)

Perhaps the most troubling aspect of proposals for abolition of PINS jurisdiction is the failure of the proponents to devise, or even to suggest, realistic alternatives for resolving the problems that the courts in exercising the jurisdiction have sought to address. To the extent that an alternative is offered at all, it is to insist that the "community," or more specifically the schools and private social agencies, meet their responsibilities to troubled children. This option would seem necessarily to be based on a number of highly questionable assumptions. First, it rests on the assumption voluntary agencies, in those communities where they exist, either have resources to take on the task or the necessary resources will in some way be made available to them. It should, however, be apparent that the facts are to the contrary. The New York State Judicial Conference study notes, for example, that after the New York legislature failed to allocate funds to establish new specialized facilities for the newly created PINS provisions, it became clear that adequate services for PINS children who required placement would not be furnished by private, voluntary agencies. Further, community services were least available where they were most needed. Thus, experience suggests that the view that elimination of PINS jurisdiction would "stimulate the creation and extension of a wider range of voluntary services than is presently available" or require the community to devise solutions is at best speculative and at worst quixotic.

A second questionable assumption underlying the proposed reliance on voluntary agencies is that where such agencies exist, they would be willing to offer a full range of services to children who would otherwise be subject to the PINS jurisdiction of the courts. Again, experience provides no reason to be optimistic on this score. Both empirical evidence and the observation of knowledgeable commentators support the conclusion that the children most needing services would be least likely to receive them. Furthermore, even if the willingness of voluntary agencies to meet the challenge of providing noncoercive services to the PINS population were not in doubt, there would still be questions about their ability to do so. There is no significant evidence that voluntary agencies are any more competent than governmentally supported institutions. Accordingly, the authors of the New York Judicial Conference study have cautioned that "[t]hese children cannot be left dependent on a social services system or on schools and voluntary programs that have failed and continue to fail to meet their needs."

Finally, it is fair to ask what reason there is to believe that PINS children will be willing to make use of the services of voluntary agencies. It seems unlikely that children who have refused voluntarily to go to school or to respond to the parents who are charged with responsibility for their tutelage will be any more willing to look to and respond to the guidance of strangers. It is not suggested here that voluntary agencies do not play or should not play a critical role in the function of juvenile courts. It is doubtful, however, that the child requiring services, or his parents, will seek out the agency furnishing services in the absence of the coercive power of the court to make alternative dispositions. Rather, in the absence of PINS jurisdiction, there is reason to believe that significant numbers of children will be abandoned to their own devices.

Even if the critics of PINS jurisdiction are correct in their judgment that it has failed to achieve any significant benefits, abolition might nevertheless be a mixed blessing at best. For at least some children, the cure may be worse than the disease. As a number of observers have pointed out, in any number of cases the conduct which brings a child within the PINS jurisdiction of the juvenile court includes behavior which could also subject the child to the court's juvenile delinquency jurisdiction because it involves acts which would be criminal if committed by an adult. One view of this phenomenon is that it is an example of the misuse or abuse of PINS jurisdiction. It has been seen as particularly inappropriate in view of the fact that a proper adjudication of juvenile delinquency requires that constitutional due process protections be afforded to the respondent child, including the stringent requirement of proof beyond a reasonable doubt. In PINS cases, this protection is not required in many jurisdictions and has not been held uniformly to be a constitutional requisite.

There is, however, another side to the coin. It is at least arguable that in some cases in which a juvenile delinquency charge is, as a technical matter, properly sustainable, a reduction to PINS would be appropriate and, at least from the child's point of view, desirable. Whether a PINS petition replaces a juvenile delinquency charge as a result of a kind of juvenile court "plea bargaining" or by reason of the exercise of discretion by the court, there may be, again from the viewpoint of the child, an important advantage. Despite the not infrequent claim that juvenile delinquents and children adjudicated as PINS are treated identically, this is clearly not always the case. It promises to be less so in the future if we may judge by recent legislative developments.

Pursuant to the provisions of the federal Juvenile Justice and Delinquency Prevention Act of 1974, financial assistance to states in developing and implementing delinquency prevention programs is conditioned upon the submission of plans that bar the placement of PINS children in juvenile detention or correctional facilities and mandates that such placements be in shelter facilities. The legislative response of the State of New York to the federal enactment may prove to be prototypal, for New York has eliminated the placement of PINS children in training schools and secure detention facilities operated by the State Division for Youth.

Even if this legislation is regarded as beneficial to children adjudicated as PINS offenders, it does not come without a price. At the same time that the New York legislature was "deinstitutionalizing" PINS offenses in order to ensure that the state would continue to receive federal financial assistance for its delinquency prevention programs, it was also accelerating the trend toward more severe dispositions for certain adjudicated juvenile delinquents. The state's Juvenile Reform Act of 1976, which enacted a number of definitional and procedural changes with respect to juvenile delinquency jurisdiction, most importantly provides not only for significantly increased periods of confinement, but also mandates specific periods of secure confinement for fourteen-and fifteen-year olds who have been adjudicated juvenile delinquents by reason of having committed certain "designated felony acts." Although the severe dispositions authorized by the Act are limited to serious or violent juvenile offenses, it would be incautious to rule out the possibility that an increasingly harsh view will be taken of delinquency in general.

If this speculation is correct, it may very well be that even deinstitutionalization of PINS, apart from the radical step of eliminating it from the jurisdiction of juvenile courts altogether, is not, from the standpoint of the misbehaving or offending child, entirely a benefit. It is not difficult to imagine, for example, one possible response when the police encounter a child wandering the streets at all hours of the night, or are summoned by a parent to deal with a child who is violently out of control.

A policeman facing a situation where even temporary detention is not authorized may choose the obvious alternative of lodging a form of cover charge such as harassment, resisting arrest or the like, available under the court's juvenile delinquency jurisdiction, as a basis for detaining the child, and thereby at least resolving the immediate problem. In summary, the removal of PINS from the jurisdiction of the juvenile court, rather than eliminating old problems, may create new ones.

———

As the above experts point out, federal legislation encourages states to discontinue the practice of placing status offenders in secure detention and correctional facilities. However, amendments to the Federal Juvenile Justice and Delinquency Prevention Act of 1980, 42 U.S.C. § 5633(a)(12)(A) (1994) permit incarceration of status offenders who run away from non-secure placements or violate court orders. *See* Jan Costello & Nancy Worthington, *Incarcerating Status Offenders: Attempts to Circumvent the Juvenile Justice and Delinquency Act*, 16 HARV. C.R.-C.L. L. REV. 41 (1981) (pointing out that states participating in the federal legislation circumvent its goals by using contempt power to "bootstrap" a status offender into a delinquent, committing status offenders to secure mental health facilities, alleging delinquency where facts support only a status offense and developing "semi-secure" facilities for status offenders).

§ 5.04 THE PRE-ADJUDICATION PROCESS

[A] Police Investigation

Police involvement in the juvenile justice system is manifested in a variety of ways. Law enforcement officers routinely encounter juveniles suspected as delinquents or status offenders. Such encounters often trigger more extensive investigations which raise Fourth Amendment issues when the police search for and seize evidence and take suspects into custody. Furthermore, when police interrogate juveniles, Fifth and Sixth Amendment issues are commonly raised. As will be evident from the following materials, police investigation of young people sometimes raises unique legal issues.

[1] Search and Seizure

As made clear in Chapter 4, the Supreme Court has recognized the applicability of Fourth Amendment rights to school children, albeit with accommodations to school authorities. While students enjoy diminished protection against searches and seizures at the hands of educators, the courts have generally recognized the same Fourth Amendment protections for juveniles against police intrusions occurring outside of school as are enjoyed by adults under similar circumstances.

LANES v. STATE

Court of Criminal Appeals of Texas (en banc)
767 S.W.2d 789 (1989)

WHITE, JUDGE.

Appellant, a juvenile certified for trial as an adult under § 54.02 [of the] Family Code, was, convicted of burglary of a habitation. Punishment was assessed at twenty years imprisonment.

The Ninth Court of Appeals affirmed the conviction holding *inter alia*, that a fingerprint order, issued pursuant to § 51.15 [of the] Family Code, provided sufficient probable cause to arrest and fingerprint a juvenile. . . . Appellant petitioned this Court for discretionary review arguing that, independent of the § 51.15 . . . probable cause requirement to fingerprint a child, Article I, § 9 of the Texas Constitution and the Fourth and Fourteenth Amendments of the United States Constitution require probable cause to arrest a child . . . to obtain his fingerprints. Because this raises a question of first impression, *i.e.,* whether the probable cause requirement of Art. I, Sec. 9 and the Fourth Amendment applies in full force to a juvenile arrest,[40] we granted appellant's petition. . . . After having carefully considered the issues, we now hold that it does.

The facts of the case can be simply stated. Pursuant to a consent order from the juvenile court authorizing the taking of appellant's fingerprints, a police officer arrested appellant at his high school, transported him to the police station and took his fingerprints. The trial court as well as the Court of Appeals found that this order provided sufficient authority for an arrest. We disagree.

The issue presented is whether the probable cause requisite of Art. I, Sec. 9 of the Texas Constitution and the Fourth Amendment of the U.S. Constitution, applicable to the states through the Fourteenth, applies to the arrest of a child.[41] . . . It has . . . long been settled that the Fourth Amendment

---

[40] [3] We use the term "arrest" advisedly. The arrest of a child is often labeled as merely "detainment" or "protective custody." In the instant context, however, we find it appropriate to dispense with such euphemistic nomenclature. [The Family Code states] "[t]he taking of a child into custody is not an arrest except for the purpose of determining the validity of taking him into custody . . . under the laws of and constitution of this state or of the United States."

[41] [5] While in many instances Texas law is merely coextensive with Federal law, . . . the Texas Legislature has made evident its intent to give greater protections to its juveniles through enactment of the Texas Family Code. . . . Texas has statutorily enacted greater protections under state law than currently received under the Federal Constitution. For example, *McKeiver v. Pennsylvania*, 403 U.S. 528 (1971), denies juveniles the Federal Due Process guarantee of a jury trial whereas V.T.C.A., FAMILY CODE SEC. 54.03(c) requires a jury trial in delinquency proceedings. The Texas Family Code also extends to juveniles guarantees on which the U.S. Supreme Court has not yet ruled. For example, V.T.C.A., FAMILY CODE SEC. 54.03(e), excludes illegally seized evidence from trial and also prohibits an adjudication of delinquency founded only upon either uncorroborated accomplice testimony or the child's out-of-court statement. Therefore,

is, to some undetermined extent, applicable to juvenile proceedings. This rule was best expressed in the seminal opinion on juvenile rights — *In re Gault*, 387 U.S. 1 (1967). The *Gault* Court stated, "[n]either the Fourteenth Amendment nor the Bill of Rights is for adults alone.". . .

In order to best understand the unique framework from which this question is to be decided, a terse historical explanation of the juvenile system is necessary. From its inception in Cook County, Illinois, in 1899, the juvenile justice system has been protectively maintained as a civil, socio-legal entity distinct and separate from the criminal justice system. The philosophical basis of this separation was to create a system wherein juveniles were rehabilitated rather than incarcerated, protected rather than punished — the very antithesis of the adult criminal system.

The creators of the juvenile system rejected the adult example as punitive, cruel and nonrehabilitative. This rejection was so extreme that even the vocabulary of the criminal system was discarded and replaced by more palatable terminology. Instead of being "arrested," "jailed" and "indicted," juveniles were to be "taken into custody," "detained" and a "petition" was to be filed for further "protection." Terms such as "trial," "criminal," and "imprisonment" were replaced with the softer terms of "hearing," "juvenile delinquent" or "a child in need of supervision," and "commitment." Medical metaphors such as diagnosis, rehabilitation, and counseling accented the new juvenile vocabulary in order to better characterize the type of treatment intended.

. . . .

The entire juvenile system was engineered to create a setting of informality and openness in order to facilitate prompt, personalized and professional responses to the child's individual needs. A relaxed atmosphere was considered integral to engendering a rehabilitative sense of trust and dispelling fear and anxiety. The rigid, punitive and nonforgiving adult model was completely discarded and envisioned in its place was a system of sociological jurisprudence which dispensed a higher form of justice. Thus, our juvenile system was wrought from the most enlightened and humanitarian motives.

These noble ideals, however, had the practical, paradoxical effect of denying juveniles many fundamental constitutional and procedural rights. . . . Because the system was designed to help rather than punish and all were charged with acting in the child's best interests, the procedural and constitutional rights inherent in the adult system were deemed unnecessary, and, in fact, counter to the juvenile system's goals. Procedural requisites were considered detrimental to flexibility, swiftness, openness, honesty and simplicity. Throughout all proceedings discretion was maximized in order to provide optimal flexibility in diagnosis and treatment with the constant focus being the child's lifestyle and character rather than whether he committed the crime.

---

although the protections offered by Art. I, sec. 9 and the Fourth Amendment are identical, our extension of the probable cause requirement inherent in both is based upon the particular and more protective purposes and policies of the Texas juvenile system. Consequently, although we rule on both Federal and State questions, we find it more appropriate to base our holding primarily on State constitutional grounds. . . . We do, however, heavily rely on Fourth Amendment precedent since Texas has adopted such as authoritative of Art. I sec. 9 protections.

Ideally, information collected from and about the child would be used for the child rather than against him; thus, any limitations on the collection of information would only serve to subvert such aid. Because the system's aims were to be benevolent, solicitude individualized and intervention scientifically founded, there was no perceived need for the State's power to be narrowly circumscribed. Thus, as ironical as it may seem, one can logically deduce how the initial protective purposes of the system validly subrogated procedural and constitutional requisites. . . .

Especially at the genesis of the system, juveniles were denied virtually all rights. The adult adversarial construct was discarded along with the rights of confrontation, a record, a jury, a right to appeal, notice, proof beyond a reasonable doubt, and even counsel. . . . Juvenile proceedings were defined as civil rather than criminal, rendering inapplicable the rules of criminal evidence and their appropriate safeguards against admittance of prejudicial and inflammatory evidence. . . .

Thus, the juvenile system's protective rejection of the adult system came at the cost of the procedural and constitutional protections attendant thereto; a dubious tradeoff — to say the least — and, as was recognized early on, the results have been less than satisfactory

As the system grew, it soon became overwhelmed. Crowded dockets and overburdened placement facilities doused and embittered rehabilitative spirits. The lack of procedural safeguards allowed the overwrought juvenile courts to operate in an atmosphere conducive to discretionary abuse, arbitrariness, and discrimination. . . . As early as 1937, Dean Pound likened the juvenile system to the Star Chamber stating, "[t]he powers of the Star Chamber were a trifle in comparison with those of our juvenile courts." . . . Likewise in 1967 the Supreme Court recognized, "Juvenile Court history has again demonstrated that unbridled discretion, however benevolently motivated, is frequently a poor substitute for principle and procedure." Thus, as practical reality brought into focus the injustices being wrought by the lack of procedural safeguards, Justice Frankfurter's famous words, "[t]he history of American Freedom is, in no small measure, the history of procedure" began to ring as true to the juvenile system as it had to its adult counterpart . . . .

In response to this procedural injustice and as early as 1948, the Supreme Court began a case-by-case determination of the applicability of fundamental constitutional protections to the juvenile system. *In re Gault* was the grandfather case that activated a constitutional revolution wherein the juvenile system became subject to due process domestication.

Through time, eight central cases have been decided by the Supreme Court, each delineating which specific rights were applicable to juvenile proceedings. . . . From these eight foundation cases can be distilled a test to determine the extent to which constitutional protections are to be afforded juveniles. In order to determine whether and to what degree each protection extended to juvenile proceedings, the Supreme Court seemed to utilize a comparative analysis wherein the purposes and goals of the juvenile system were compared to the particular right being asserted. The Court balanced the function that a constitutional or procedural right served against its impact or degree of impairment on the unique processes of the juvenile court and then factored in consideration of the degree of realistic success the juvenile system had obtained. Because this balancing test constitutes a neutral, pragmatic analysis of all protective intentions involved, we find it valid and now adopt it as our own.

Application of such an analysis to the instant facts initially requires an exploration of the specific purposes of both the juvenile system and the constitutional right being asserted. The purposes of the Texas juvenile system have remained basically the same as they were at its inception. Conveniently, the specific intent of the Texas juvenile scheme is set out in § 51.01, V.T.C.A., Family Code, which states,

> This title shall be construed to effectuate the following public purposes:
>
> (1) to provide for the care, the protection, and the wholesome moral, mental, and physical development of children coming within its provisions;
>
> (2) to protect the welfare of the community and to control the commission of unlawful acts by children;
>
> (3) consistent with the protection of the public interest, to remove from children committing unlawful acts the taint of criminality and the consequences of criminal behavior and to substitute a program of treatment, training, and rehabilitation;
>
> (4) to achieve the foregoing purposes in a family environment whenever possible, separating the child from his parents only when necessary for his welfare or in the interest of public safety and when a child is removed from his family, to give him the care that should be provided by parents; and
>
> (5) to provide a simple judicial procedure through which the provisions of this title are executed and enforced and in which the parties are assured a fair hearing and their constitutional and other legal rights recognized and enforced.

Additionally, § 54.04(c), V.T.C.A., FAMILY CODE, requires that even after a finding of guilt, a child cannot be sentenced or detained unless the court further finds that he is in need of rehabilitation or that the protection of the public or the child requires such. If the court does not so find, it must immediately release the child. . . . Thus, as statutorily evidenced, rehabilitation and child protection remain as the pervasive and uniform themes of the Texas juvenile system. . . .

Article I, sec. 9 and the Fourth Amendment are also protection attentive entities. Art. I, sec. 9 requires that the "people be secure in their persons . . . from all unreasonable seizures and searches" and the Fourth Amendment requires: "[t]he right of the people to be secure in their persons . . . against unreasonable searches and seizures, shall not be violated." The purpose of these two provisions is the same — to safeguard the privacy and security of individuals against arbitrary governmental invasions. The requirement of probable cause has historically been the stalwart enforcer of these privacy protections. . . . Probable Cause is defined as that evidence which is sufficient to warrant a reasonable and prudent person in believing that a particular person has committed or is committing an offense. . . . This requisite for a warrant-less arrest protects individuals from being at the complete mercy of an officer's arbitrary caprice and prevents oppressive or prejudicial use of the power to arrest, while, at the same time, providing for community protection through valid law enforcement. . . . Thus, the probable cause requisite safeguards citizens from rash and unreasonable interferences of privacy and from unfounded charges of crime.

With these basic purposes of the juvenile system and the probable cause requirement in mind, we now turn to compare the ramifications involved in enforcement of the two. One of the fundamental goals of the juvenile system is rehabilitation. . . . Essential to a rehabilitative environment is the proper attitudinal setting. Children have the strongest sense of justice — a product of youth, energy, and innocence. Such an inherent sense of justice, however, is fragile and can easily be turned to cynicism, helplessness, disillusionment and disrespect. Not only would such an attitude be contra-rehabilitative, but it could breed dissention and reactionary criminal behavior. . . .

A child arrested without valid reason by a seemingly all-powerful and challengeless exercise of police power would instantly intuit the injustice and react accordingly. Even a juvenile who has violated the law but is unfairly arrested will feel deceived and thus resist any rehabilitative efforts. Inherent in youth is a malleable nature, and example can be the most formidable teacher. We must institutionalize justice in order to engender it among our youth. Affording a child the essentials of basic human dignity and announcing a respect for their autonomy through the extension of constitutional privacy protections can only further these efforts.

Other important goals of the Texas juvenile scheme include protection of the community and the child. We as a society have decided that evidence less than that which would convince a reasonable man that an offense is being or has been committed does not constitute a sufficient showing of guilt to validate the deprivation of personal freedom attendant to an arrest. . . . Thus, implicit in the probable cause requirement is the presumption of innocence. The community need not be protected from a child who has presumptively not committed an offense. Nor does a child need to be protected from himself when he is not in trouble. . . . Thus, requiring probable cause can only help to prevent such erroneous and unnecessary arrests.

The Texas juvenile system also seeks to avoid the taint of criminality in order to prevent recidivism and promote rehabilitation. The best method of avoiding attachment of a criminal taint is keeping the child completely out of the system. Studies are legion which conclude that once a child is arrested and becomes involved in the juvenile system the chances are almost non-existent that he can later withdraw himself or be cleansed of the criminal taint. . . . Even a single arrest can brand a child as a delinquent to outsiders. He could be stigmatized as criminal by teachers, parents, employers, and law enforcement officers and could be labeled as "cool" among his peers. Both reputations would be injurious. Discrimination by parents, teachers, employ-ers, and police would severely limit the child's educational or employment goals or subject him to unwarranted arrests or police purview. Peer pressure could result in the child striving to live up to his "cool" reputation by committing other crimes. Requiring probable cause to arrest a child can only serve to reduce the risk that innocent youths will be so erroneously stigmatized.

An almost unavoidable consequence of arrest is detention. Pre-trial detention can be extremely destructive to a child's life and act as the determinative factor toward recidivism. The impressionability of juveniles can make even the most minimal experience of incarceration extremely injurious, and such injury is compounded where confinement is unfounded. All too quickly juveniles subjected to detention come to view society at large as "oppressive" and "hostile" and to "regard themselves as irremediably 'delinquent.'" . . . One court noted:

> It is difficult for an adult who has not been through the experience to realize the terror that engulfs a youngster the first time he loses his liberty and has to spend the night or several days or weekends in a cold, impersonal cell or room away from home or family. . . . The experience tells the youngster that he is no good and that society has rejected him. So he responds to society's expectation, sees himself as a delinquent, and acts like one.

. . . Such negative self-labeling is clearly counter-rehabilitative and can easily lead to self-fulfilling prophecy. It seems appropriate to require some probable cause evidence of wrongdoing before subjecting a child to the possibility of such detriment.

A further purpose of the juvenile system is preservation of the family environment either at home or, when detention is a necessity, to perpetuate a family-type atmosphere in the detention facility. Obviously, the optimal method of family preservation is keeping the family intact. By requiring some evidence of wrongdoing before disrupting the family and removing the child can only further this goal.

The old adage that a child, by virtue of his age, has no right to freedom but only a right to custody since he is presumably under constant parental control, does not withstand scrutiny or application in the instant context. Assuredly, a child is or should be under constant parental authority, but this comprises an entirely different form of custody than that of State detention. No one seriously argues anymore that State custody in any way approximates the family environment. . . .

. . . Surely we are beyond equating this institutional reality with parental supervision. To require probable cause prior to placement of a juvenile in such an institutional setting can only serve to prevent erroneous disruption and destruction of the family environment.

The foregoing discussion renders the conclusion that the purposes of the Texas juvenile system and the probable cause requirement of Art. I, sec. 9 are in harmony. The limitations imposed by these two protective entities do not conflict or undermine one another, but rather accommodate and enhance the goals sought by both. Probable cause protects the sanctity of personal freedom through the prevention of unnecessary arrests. The juvenile system was designed to protect and rehabilitate children. We in no way see how imposing a probable cause requirement will deter juvenile courts from pursuing its ameliorative goals.

The final consideration to be factored in is the realistic fact that, even at the expense of procedural protections, the exalted ideals of the juvenile system have failed in achievement. . . . Many of the foundation cases, each with growing concern, the disappointing results of the juvenile ideal. Reading these cases elicits a growing sense of frustration in that the Court over a span of forty years constantly criticized yet patiently abided and awaited the success of a system that was failing.

In *McKeiver*, . . . the Court, after an extensive discussion of the failings of the juvenile system and whether it should be abandoned, noted, "[p]erhaps that ultimate disillusionment will come one day, but for the moment we are disinclined to give impetus to it." . . . The juvenile justice system will soon be 100 years old. At this point in time this Court is prepared to realistically face and, to some extent, rebuff the system's failings.

Research and program analysis evaluations have shown that the efficacy of the juvenile system's rehabilitative institutions is challengeable. Patience and the passage of time have failed to vindicate the system. Quite to the contrary, there is ample historical as well as current data to demonstrate that juvenile justice has been a consistently retrogressive social enterprise. Although there are examples of quality probation and other treatment services, the truth is that these are few and far between. The majority of our youths are falling through rehabilitative cracks. Juveniles are often either exposed to experimental therapeutic techniques that are demeaning or violate fairness, or they are banished to institutions that fail to offer any treatment or accord with even minimal constitutional requisites. . . . The system is clearly far more punitive than rehabilitative. . . .

Further, reality fails to reflect the protective and professional intentions expected of all participants in the system. In this area in particular the gap between rhetoric and reality is phenomenal. The success of the system is completely dependent upon the availability of resources and on the interest, expertise, commitment and concern of the system's participants. . . . Too often juvenile court personnel fall "far short" of being the "stalwart," sympathetic, paternalistic, and "communicating" professionals envisaged by the system. . . . The "community's unwillingness" to provide funding for staff and facilities, the "insufficiency of time devoted," the "scarcity" of truly professional resources, the "inadequacy of dispositional alternatives," and the "general lack" of diagnostic expertise all contribute to the system's failing. . . . Once again, time has served to exacerbate rather than absolve these problems. Our juveniles are being thrust into a precarious system where all personnel are presumed to consider the child's best interests, yet none has the time, training, resources or sometimes even the inclination to do so. . . .

Nor does the palatable terminology of the juvenile system alter this reality. The adoption of a soft vocabulary in an attempt to dispel labeling and promote professionalism has been ineffective. Words such as "detention," "juvenile delinquent," and "commitment" have proven no less severe or to carry no less of a criminal taint. Further, utilization of medical terminology has not rendered treatment which is medically founded. Reality reflects that the juvenile court's unique terminology consists of nothing more than euphemisms unable to alter the punitive consequences inherent in any kind of judicial intervention.

Although the denial of certain procedural protections could be countenanced by the founders goals, when these goals fail in achievement, then the time has come for change. It is now poignantly evident that good intentions alone cannot replace constitutional safeguards. Reincarnated is . . . *Gault*'s announcement that the "condition of being a boy does not justify a kangaroo court." . . . In the face of the unpredictable and arbitrary dispositional and rehabilitative atmosphere of the system, procedure must become the unifying stalwart of fairness, uniformity and predictability.

This is not to say that the rehabilitative intent of the juvenile processes should be completely overridden; nor do we mean to denigrate the admirable aspirations and ideals of the founders. Even in the face of the system's failures, we are not convinced that current practice does not contain the philosophical progeny from which a truly rehabilitative, treatment-oriented system can be created. We do, however, intend to eschew the protective "label-of-convenience" and extinguish the heretofore blinding aspects of tradition, sentiment, naive faith, and habit in order to set the stage for candid judicial confrontation of the realities of the system. . . .

The failure of the juvenile system is not merely a legalistic problem or a singular problem of the individual involved. It is a problem shared by all. Society as a whole shares not only the blame for the system's failures but also will undoubtedly carry the economic and emotional burden of its repeat offenders. . . . We are now attempting to evolve a new methodology to truly provide a child with the best of both the juvenile and criminal worlds — the treatment model of the juvenile system and the procedural protections of the adult. Thus, while we dispel the antiquated and unrealistic resistance to procedural safeguards, we continue to embrace a rehabilitative and treatment oriented spirit.

Based on the foregoing analysis, we now extend the probable cause requirement of Art. I, sec. 9 and the Fourth Amendment to juvenile proceedings.[42] Our holding today represents an accommodation between the aspirations of the juvenile court and the grim realities of the system. . . . Although we are adopting another requisite of the criminal system, we find that requiring probable cause for arrest will not compel abandonment or displacement of the juvenile system's commendable rehabilitative intentions. Such a requisite places minimal fetters on police discretion in making decisions that concern fundamental rights of personal privacy and freedom and have the potential for particularly detrimental effects on a child's life. This holding is also in line with Texas statutory guidelines for a juvenile arrest. Section 52.01 states,

---

[42] [13] We include in our holding all juveniles covered by Title 3, children having engaged in delinquent conduct and children having engaged in conduct indicating a need for supervision. However, we expressly preclude children encompassed by Title 2 of the Family Code (abused and neglected children).

"(a) A child may be taken into custody:

. . . .

(3) by a law-enforcement officer if there are reasonable grounds to believe that the child has engaged in delinquent conduct or conduct indicating a need for supervision. . . ."

The Draftsman comments to this statute states

"Prior law . . . authorized "any peace officer or probation officer . . . to take into custody any child who is found violating any law or ordinance, or who is reasonably believed to be a fugitive from his parents or from justice, or whose surroundings are such as to endanger his health, welfare or morals.

"Subsection (a), based upon § 13 of the Uniform Juvenile Court Act, substantially narrows this grant of authority. A child may now be taken into custody only where there is reasonable grounds or probable cause exists to indicate that the child committed delinquent acts, engaged in conduct indicating a need for supervision, or violated the conditions of his probation. Thus, the broad authority to take a child into custody when his "surroundings are such as to endanger his health, welfare, or morals," is eliminated." . . .

Thus, the intent in drafting this section was to require probable cause to arrest a child.

Further, in light of the most recent caselaw in this area, there is great need for application of this probable cause protection. Most recently . . . this Court held that the Article 14.04, V.A.C.C.P., warrant requirement is not applicable to juveniles. We determined that to require a warrant would unnecessarily restrict the flexibility of protective police action. This holding was predicated upon the expectation that the officer would himself have probable cause to arrest. . . . Thus, juveniles can freely be arrested without a warrant. Since there is no unbiased judicial probable cause determination prior to arrest, at the very least, law enforcement officers can be expected to personally have probable cause for a juvenile arrest and also be held responsible for a reasonable articulation of such at a later hearing. The hope is that through this requirement dubious or unjust arrests will be generally deterred and prevented from the outset.

Also relatively recently, the U.S. Supreme Court held that juveniles can properly be subject to pre-trial detention without a judicial determination of probable cause for up to six days. . . . The Court further announced that juveniles can properly be denied any opportunity to pre-trial release. . . . Thus, once a juvenile is arrested he can be subjected to continual incarceration for a disruptively lengthy period of time without an unbiased judicial determination that such incarceration is at all warranted. . . . This is especially true in Texas, where there is no statutory requirement of a judicial probable cause determination for pretrial detention. . . . Although caselaw mandates a finding of probable cause for valid extended detention, . . . it is not clear that such a determination is routinely made. As discussed ante, detention can be extremely detrimental and contra to the goals of the juvenile court, especially when it is unjustified; thus, a minimal probable cause restriction at the time of arrest can only serve to help prevent such detriment.

Finally, imposition of a probable cause requirement will not severely limit or disrupt proper law enforcement since it is not an ultra-restrictive requirement. Rather, it was purposely designed as a realistic, practical, and workable determination to be based upon the "totality of the circumstances" presented. . . . Because the probable cause standard is a commonsense test, its application is sufficiently flexible to ensure reasonable law enforcement as well as juvenile protection. . . .

The probable cause requirement rests on the principal that a true balance between an individual — whether youth or adult — and the government depends on the recognition and respect of "the right to be let alone — the most comprehensive of rights and the right most valued by civilized men.". . . Today we are proudly able to afford such a right to juveniles.

Application of this law to the instant facts requires reversal. . . .

. . . .

It is agreed that the officers had authority to fingerprint appellant pursuant to the § 51.15 consent order; however, this order in no way conferred authority to arrest. At a suppression hearing, the State carries the burden of either producing a warrant and supporting affidavit or establishing evidentiary facts sufficient to show probable cause. . . . In the instant case the State did not come forward with a warrant, but only introduced the fingerprint consent form. The State and the Court of Appeals seem to argue that this form takes the place of an arrest warrant, thus shifting the burden of proof back to appellant. This argument does not withstand scrutiny. The bare-bones fingerprint consent order neither facially confers authority to arrest nor evinces any factual probable cause basis. Further, there is nothing on the face of the order which exhibits any judicial intent to authorize an arrest. Having none of the protective characteristics or purposes of a warrant, this order simply cannot take the place of such.

Without a warrant, the State carried the burden of establishing the validity of the arrest. This burden the State wholly failed to carry. At the suppression hearing, the judge who issued the order did not testify and no facts were elicited concerning probable cause. Thus we find that appellant's fingerprints were taken during an illegal juvenile arrest which was not founded on probable cause. Because the only direct evidence linking appellant to the scene of the crime was his fingerprints, we cannot say beyond a reasonable doubt that their introduction made no contribution to the verdict. . . . Consequently, we reverse the holding of the Court of Appeals and remand this cause to the trial court.

QUESTIONS

1. The *Lanes* court holds that "the Fourth Amendment applies in full force to a juvenile arrest." Is this the correct conclusion? If the consequences of

suppressing the fingerprint evidence in *Lanes* is that an obviously guilty juvenile is set free, is that a result consistent with the underlying protectionist theory of juvenile justice? Considering the protectionist views expressed in Chapter 1, is *Lanes* correctly decided?

2. Does the *Lanes* court articulate a consistent theory of juvenile rights to support its opinion? Does the court vacillate back and forth between protectionist and personhood theory? If so, does this lack of a coherent theory of juvenile rights undermine the persuasiveness of the *Lanes* opinion?

STATE IN INTEREST OF J.B.

Juvenile and Domestic Relations Court of New Jersey, Union County
328 A.2d 46 (1974)

BRODY, J.J.D.R.C.

The juvenile, charged with delinquency for possessing more than 25 grams of marijuana, moves to suppress the fruits of a warrantless search of his person.

Plainfield police officers Peter Cochin and Robert Robinson were on radio car patrol early December 9, 1973 when at approximately 1:30 a.m. they received a dispatch from headquarters followed shortly by a dispatch from an officer at the scene of an accident. The substance of these dispatches was that a car had struck a parked car, that witnesses had observed a white male with long hair alight from the errant vehicle and flee on foot toward nearby railroad tracks, and that the ignition key was missing from the vehicle which caused the accident.

As the officers drove toward where the fleeing driver was reported heading, they saw a 15-year-old white boy with long hair walking on the sidewalk in a black neighborhood several blocks from the accident site. His lip was bleeding, his right arm appeared to be hurt and his clothes were wet. At the time, bushes along the railroad tracks were wet from an earlier rain.

The officers stopped the boy, the juvenile in this case, and asked him to account for himself. He offered a succession of three inconsistent stories. Initially he claimed to have been beaten by a "black dude" but could not give details. He then claimed he got hurt in a tavern fight but was unable to give any corroborating detail. Finally, after being advised where he was, he described being beaten up somewhere on Richmond Street in Plainfield but was unable to give details.

Officer Cochin then conducted a full search of the juvenile. He testified that he was looking for the ignition key to the car involved in the accident. In a right jacket pocket he uncovered two plastic bags allegedly containing marijuana, whereupon he told the juvenile that he was under arrest. The officers took the boy to a hospital where they conducted a more extensive search, uncovering in one of his socks a third bag allegedly containing marijuana.

After the searches the officers learned that the vehicle causing the accident had been reported stolen. They both testified that at the time of the searches they believed the juvenile guilty only of "hit and run." It did not then occur to them that the car he was driving might have been stolen.

On the State's motion before hearing, the judge dismissed for lack of evidence all complaints against the juvenile predicated on his use of the car at the time of the accident.

In a juvenile case the court will suppress evidence unlawfully obtained by an unreasonable search. Where the search was warrantless, the State has the burden of establishing its legality. It offers to do so in this case by showing that before the search the police had probable cause to believe that the juvenile had committed any one of several offenses and that the circumstances were exigent. The juvenile contends that the only offense for which there might have been probable cause was "leaving the scene of an accident," a motor vehicle offense which must be — but was not — committed in the presence of the officers for their search to have been lawful.

I

While the term "arrest" is not to be used to describe taking a juvenile into custody, it will be so used in this opinion for the purpose of evaluating the lawfulness of the search.

New Jersey adheres to the common-law rule that a warrantless arrest for a felony is lawful if the arresting officer has probable cause, but unlawful for a misdemeanor unless the offense was committed in the presence of the officer. . . . An exception to the rule occurs where the person arrested first admits to the officer that he committed a misdemeanor, in which event the arrest is lawful even though the offense was not committed in the officer's presence.

. . . .

A lawful custodial arrest itself justifies a full search of the person arrested. When facts known to the officer meet the criteria for a lawful custodial arrest, he may legally conduct a full search of the person even though, as here, the formal arrest comes after. However, when facts known to the officer fall short of meeting the criteria for a lawful arrest, he may not legally conduct such a search because a full search of the person is a sufficient intrusion on privacy to require being tested by the same criteria applied to a custodial arrest.

The criteria for the lawful arrest of a juvenile are those applicable to arrest for an adult offense . . . supplemented by criteria contained in rules of court pertaining to juvenile offenses.

II

A preliminary question is whether an officer may lawfully make a warrantless arrest for a motor vehicle offense. . . .

The state describes the offense which prompted the search as "leaving the scene of an accident." Conceding that the in-presence requirement applies to this motor vehicle offense, the state contends that it occurred in the presence of the arresting officers in that they had probable cause to believe that the juvenile was literally leaving the scene of an accident when he was stopped and searched.

. . . .

. . . There are two elements to the offense under consideration: (a) driving a vehicle involved in an accident and (b) failing to leave behind proper notice of identification. Unless all elements of an offense occur in the presence of the arresting officers it cannot be said that the in-presence requirement has been satisfied. Because the purpose of the in-presence requirement is to prevent a mistaken arrest, the arresting officers would have to sense something more than what would appear to them to be nonoffensive behavior. . . . Since the arresting officers did not observe the juvenile when the accident occurred, the offense did not occur in their presence.

The arresting officers did not believe before the search that the juvenile had committed the equivalent common-law felony of stealing the motor vehicle he was driving. Nonetheless, the State next contends that the in-presence requirement is inapplicable because they had probable cause for such a belief. Probable cause exists if the facts and circumstances known to the officer warrant a prudent man's believing that an offense has been committed by the person to be arrested or searched. The test is an objective one determined by the reviewing judge; whether the officer believed he had probable cause is not dispositive.

. . . .

. . . I find that the police did not have probable cause to believe that the juvenile stole the vehicle. To be sure, the juvenile's apparent abandonment of the car suggests that he had not been using it lawfully. But theft requires intent to deprive the rightful owner of the car's use indefinitely. . . . [T]he boy's youth, apparent to the officers, militates against larcenous intent. He could hardly expect to keep the car for long without being caught and it is not likely that a professional ring of car thieves would employ an unlicenced 15-year-old [w]hose inability to drive was amply demonstrated by the accident. Lacking larcenous intent, the juvenile would be guilty of joy-riding, a disorderly persons offense.

In addition, while the officers' view of the matter is not a bar to considering whether there was probable cause, their expertise may be taken into account. . . . The gist of both officers' testimony is that even in retrospect they did not believe the juvenile had stolen the car until they learned it had been reported stolen.

The State has not met its burden of proving that before the search the officers had probable cause to believe the juvenile stole the car that caused the accident.

The State next contends that in the presence of the arresting officers the juvenile committed the disorderly persons offense of failing to give a good account of himself. When the officers stopped him, the juvenile was indeed unable to give a good account of himself. . . . [T]he failure to give a good account may not be the basis or even evidence of a basis for an offense. . . . The statute gives police the authority to head off an offense about to be committed. The officers had no probable cause to believe that the juvenile, when stopped, was about to commit any offense.

Finally, the State contends that in attempting to account for himself the juvenile admitted to the disorderly persons offense of fighting. While this admission may satisfy the in-presence requirement, it is and was then perceived by the officers to be incredible and therefore cannot form the basis of probable cause.

III

The Juvenile Act and implementing rules of court, both effective March 1, 1974, address themselves to searches and arrests of juveniles. N.J.S.A. 2A: 4-60 guarantees juveniles "the right to be secure from unreasonable searches and seizures." N.J.S.A. 2A:4-54(a)(2) delegates to the Supreme Court the authority to establish appropriate standards for making a warrantless arrest for delinquency.

R. 5:8-2, implementing the new statute, provides in part: A law enforcement officer may take into custody without process any juvenile who he has probable cause to believe is delinquent or in need of supervision. Since delinquency is now a violation of any penal statute, had the events in this case occurred on or after March 1, 1974, the search would have been lawful because the officers had probable cause to believe that the juvenile violated N.J.S.A. 39:4-129 by failing to attach notice of his identity to the parked car. N.J.S.A. 2A:4-44(d). Lacking an in-presence requirement, the new rule thus renders admissible against a juvenile evidence which would be excluded from the trial of an adult.

This disparity is not constitutionally offensive. . . . Because the applicability of the requirement depends upon the severity of the punishment attached to an offense, the requirement is alien to juvenile cases, where there is no punishment. This is not just a matter of semantics. Juvenile offenses are not classified in terms of the severity of possible judicial dispositions. Under the new act, juveniles coming within the jurisdiction of the court are classified either as delinquent or in need of supervision. The disposition of a case turns less on what the juvenile has done or failed to do, than on what needs to be done for the juvenile. The absence of the in-presence requirement does not, therefore, deny juveniles due process, the constitutional standard established for juvenile cases in *In re Gault*.

The search and arrest in the present case, however, occurred before the effective date of the Juvenile Act and its implementing rules of court. Because the purpose of the exclusionary rule is to curb police excesses, the standards of a lawful arrest and search are those in effect at the time of the police action.

R. 5:8-2 then in effect provided in part: A law enforcement officer may take into custody without process any juvenile who in his opinion is engaging in conduct defined by law as juvenile delinquency (emphasis added).

Unlike the new rule which has no in-presence requirement, the former rule required it in all cases. The Supreme Court avoided this aspect of the former rule in a juvenile homicide case by holding that the arrest criteria for adult offenses are also applicable to juveniles. As discussed . . . above, however, the search in this case cannot be sustained under those criteria.

The conduct which the arresting officer must have witnessed under the former rule is "juvenile delinquency" as then defined by law. That definition, found in the former Juvenile Act, includes "idly roaming the streets at night" and any "deportment endangering the morals, health or general welfare of (a child under 18 years of age)." The constitutionality of these definitions has been sustained [in previous case law].

The words of the former rule, "in his opinion," do not permit the officer to arrest at whim. He must be held to the constitutional standard of probable cause which is implicit in the language of the rule.

I have no difficulty finding that the arresting officers had probable cause to believe that the juvenile was at the time of the search engaging in conduct then defined by law as juvenile delinquency. Indeed, if "idly roaming" the streets at night is inaccurate, it is so only because there was probable cause to believe that the juvenile was purposefully escaping from the scene of an accident he had just caused which together with his apparent injuries was deportment endangering his morals, health and general welfare.

The initial search was lawful. The later search was also lawful either as a continuation of the first search or as an incident to the former lawful arrest.

The juvenile's motion to suppress is denied.

NOTES AND QUESTIONS

1. The *J.B.* court holds that the marijuana is admissible against the juvenile. Would the evidence have been admissible if *J.B.* were an adult?

Does *J.B.* suggest that police may sometimes rely on status offense statutes ("idly roaming the streets," being a "person in need of supervision" etc.) to take into custody juveniles they suspect of criminal activities in circumstances where they could not otherwise make arrests for a criminal offense for want of probable cause or a warrant?

If the police rely on protective jurisdiction, for example, a belief that a minor appears in danger of "leading a dissolute life," *see In re Daniel R.*, 79 Cal. Rptr. 247, 250 (Cal. Ct. App. 1969), should they be permitted to use evidence obtained therefrom in either delinquency or criminal actions against the minor?

2. The validity of the searches in *J.B.*, especially the search at the hospital, has been called into question by subsequent New Jersey case law. In *State ex rel. J.M.*, 771 A.2d 651 (N.J. Super. Ct. App. Div. 2001), the court invalidated a search at the police station of a minor who had been taken into custody for suspected trespass. The court found that the search could not be justified as a warrantless search "incident to arrest" because it was "remote in both time and place from the location of the arrest."

The *J.M.* court discussed *J.B.* and made the following observation: "If [*J.B.*] can be read to sustain a full search incident to arrest for juvenile delinquency based on a motor vehicle violation, we overrule it." Does such a view leave intact the initial search in *J.B.* immediately incident to the arrest for "idly roaming the streets"?

3. Under traditional Fourth Amendment principles, arresting officers are permitted to conduct warrantless searches of persons "incident to their arrest" and to utilize as evidence the fruits of such warrantless searches. *See United States v. Robinson*, 414 U.S. 218 (1973). Some courts have not applied this doctrine in the context of police interventions for "pure" status offenses. See, *e.g.*, *State v. Kinzy*, 5 P.3d 668 (Wash. 2000), where the police stopped a juvenile when they observed her in a dangerous area known for narcotics, on a school night, with adults whom the officers remembered from an earlier drug operation. The juvenile appeared to the officers to be between 11 and 13 years of age. The officers patted the juvenile down and felt a hard object. After ordering the juvenile to open her coat, the officers noticed a white powdery substance on her clothes. The police conducted a field test which revealed that the substance was cocaine. The juvenile then admitted that she possessed more cocaine in her bra. The Washington Supreme Court eventually held the cocaine inadmissible, rejecting the officers' argument that their stop of the juvenile as a "child at risk" justified their subsequent warrantless pat down and seizure of the cocaine from the juvenile's clothing. The court found that the state's interest in "[m]aintaining the safety of children did not outweigh the [juvenile's] constitutional interests in freedom of association, expression, and movement."

On the other hand, courts apparently routinely uphold warrantless searches incident to "arrests" for status offenses such as "minors in possession of illegal substances" or truancy. *See, e.g.*, *State v. Michael M.*, 772 A.2d 1179 (Me. 2001) (knife found admissible after police officer seized it from the pocket of a minor whom the officer was searching for cigarettes subsequent to the officer's warrantless arrest of the minor for cigarette smoking); *In re Humberto O.*, 95 Cal. Rptr. 2d 248 (Cal. Ct. App. 2000) (dagger held admissible after police seized the dagger from a backpack of a juvenile incident to a warrantless "arrest" of the juvenile for truancy).

4. For discussion of search and seizure issues, see Lourdes M. Rosado, *Minors and the Fourth Amendment: How Juvenile Status Should Invoke Different Standards for Searches and Seizures on the Street*, 71 N.Y.U. L. Rev. 762 (1996)

[B] Interrogation

FARE v. MICHAEL C.

Supreme Court of the United States
442 U.S. 707 (1979)

Mr. Justice Blackmun *delivered the opinion of the Court.*

In *Miranda v. Arizona*, 384 U.S. 436 (1966), this Court established certain procedural safeguards designed to protect the rights of an accused, under the

Fifth and Fourteenth Amendments, to be free from compelled self-incrimination during custodial interrogation. The Court specified, among other things, that if the accused indicates in any manner that he wishes to remain silent or to consult an attorney, interrogation must cease, and any statement obtained from him during interrogation thereafter may not be admitted against him at his trial.

In this case, the State of California, in the person of its acting chief probation officer, attacks the conclusion of the Supreme Court of California that a juvenile's request, made while undergoing custodial interrogation, to see his probation officer is *per se* an invocation of the juvenile's Fifth Amendment rights as pronounced in *Miranda*.

I

Respondent Michael C. was implicated in the murder of Robert Yeager. The murder occurred during a robbery of the victim's home on January 19, 1976. A small truck registered in the name of respondent's mother was identified as having been near the Yeager home at the time of the killing, and a young man answering respondent's description was seen by witnesses near the truck and near the home shortly before Yeager was murdered.

On the basis of this information, Van Nuys, Cal., police took respondent into custody at approximately 6:30 p.m. on February 4. Respondent then was 16½ years old and on probation to the Juvenile Court. He had been on probation since the age of 12. Approximately one year earlier he had served a term in a youth corrections camp under the supervision of the Juvenile Court. He had a record of several previous offenses, including burglary of guns and purse snatching, stretching back over several years.

Upon respondent's arrival at the Van Nuys station house two police officers began to interrogate him. The officers and respondent were the only persons in the room during the interrogation. The conversation was tape-recorded. One of the officers initiated the interview by informing respondent that he had been brought in for questioning in relation to a murder. The officer fully advised respondent of his *Miranda* rights. The following exchange then occurred:

"Q. . . . Do you understand all of these rights as I have explained them to you?

"A. Yeah.

"Q. Okay, do you wish to give up your right to remain silent and talk to us about this murder?

"A. What murder? I don't know about no murder.

"Q. I'll explain to you which one it is if you want to talk to us about it.

"A. Yeah, I might talk to you.

"Q. Do you want to give up your right to have an attorney present here while we talk about it?

"A. Can I have my probation officer here?

"Q. Well I can't get a hold of your probation officer right now. You have the right to an attorney.

"A. How I know you guys won't pull no police officer in and tell me he's an attorney?

"Q. Huh?

"A. [How I know you guys won't pull no police officer in and tell me he's an attorney?]

"Q. Your probation officer is Mr. Christiansen.

"A. Yeah.

"Q. Well I'm not going to call Mr. Christiansen tonight. There's a good chance we can talk to him later, but I'm not going to call him right now. If you want to talk to us without an attorney present, you can. If you don't want to, you don't have to. But if you want to say something, you can, and if you don't want to say something you don't have to. That's your right. You understand that right?

"A. Yeah.

"Q. Okay, will you talk to us without an attorney present?

"A. Yeah I want to talk to you."

Respondent thereupon proceeded to answer questions put to him by the officers. He made statements and drew sketches that incriminated him in the Yeager murder.

Largely on the basis of respondent's incriminating statements, probation authorities filed a petition in Juvenile Court alleging that respondent had murdered Robert Yeager . . . and that respondent therefore should be adjudged a ward of the Juvenile Court. Respondent thereupon moved to suppress the statements and sketches he gave the police during the interrogation. He alleged that the statements had been obtained in violation of *Miranda* in that his request to see his probation officer at the outset of the questioning constituted an invocation of his Fifth Amendment right to remain silent, just as if he had requested the assistance of an attorney. Accordingly, respondent argued that since the interrogation did not cease until he had a chance to confer with his probation officer, the statements and sketches could not be admitted against him in the Juvenile Court proceedings. . . .

In support of his suppression motion, respondent called his probation officer, Charles P. Christiansen, as a witness. Christiansen testified that he had instructed respondent that if at any time he had "a concern with his family," or ever had "a police contact" he should get in touch with his probation officer immediately. The witness stated that, on a previous occasion, when respondent had had a police contact and had failed to communicate with Christiansen, the probation officer had reprimanded him. This testimony, respondent argued, indicated that when he asked for his probation officer, he was in fact asserting his right to remain silent in the face of further questioning.

In a ruling from the bench, the court denied the motion to suppress. . . .

On appeal, the Supreme Court of California . . . held that respondent's "request to see his probation officer at the commencement of interrogation negated any possible willingness on his part to discuss his case with the police [and] thereby invoked his Fifth Amendment privilege." The court based this conclusion on its view that, because of the juvenile court system's emphasis on the relationship between a probation officer and the probationer, the officer was "a trusted guardian figure who exercises the authority of the state as *parens patriae* and whose duty it is to implement the protective and rehabilitative powers of the juvenile court." As a consequence, the court found that a minor's request for his probation officer was the same as a request to see his parents during interrogation, and thus under the rule of *Burton* constituted an invocation of the minor's Fifth Amendment rights.

. . . .

The court accordingly held that the probation officer would act to protect the minor's Fifth Amendment rights in precisely the way an attorney would act if called for by the accused. In so holding, the court found the request for a probation officer to be a *per se* invocation of Fifth Amendment rights in the same way the request for an attorney was found in *Miranda* to be, regardless of what the interrogation otherwise might reveal. . . .

The State of California petitioned this Court for a writ of certiorari . . . [and] we thereafter issued the writ.

II

. . . We . . . must examine the California court's decision to determine whether that court's conclusion so to extend *Miranda* is in harmony with *Miranda*'s underlying principles. For it is clear that "a State may not impose . . . greater restrictions as a matter of federal constitutional law when this Court specifically refrains from imposing them."[43] . . .

The rule the Court established in *Miranda* is clear. . . . [T]o be able to use statements obtained during custodial interrogation of the accused, the State must warn the accused prior to such questioning of his right to remain silent and of his right to have counsel, retained or appointed, present during interrogation. "Once [such] warnings have been given, the subsequent procedure is clear." "If the individual indicates in any manner, at any time prior to or during questioning, that he wishes to remain silent, the interrogation must cease. At this point he has shown that he intends to exercise his Fifth Amendment privilege; any statement taken after the person invokes his privilege cannot be other than the product of compulsion, subtle or otherwise. . . . If the individual states that he wants an attorney, the interrogation must cease until an attorney is present. At that time, the individual must have an opportunity to confer with the attorney and to have him present during

---

43 [4] Indeed, this Court has not yet held that *Miranda* applies with full force to exclude evidence obtained in violation of its proscriptions from consideration in juvenile proceedings, which for certain purposes have been distinguished from formal criminal prosecutions. *See McKeiver v. Pennsylvania*, 403 U.S. 528 (1971). We do not decide that issue today. In view of our disposition of this case, we assume without deciding that the *Miranda* principles were fully applicable to the present proceedings.

any subsequent questioning. If the individual cannot obtain an attorney and he indicates that he wants one before speaking to police, they must respect his decision to remain silent." . . . Any statements obtained during custodial interrogation conducted in violation of these rules may not be admitted against the accused, at least during the State's case in chief.

. . . .

The California court in this case, however, significantly has extended this rule by providing that a request by a juvenile for his probation officer has the same effect as a request for an attorney. Based on the court's belief that the probation officer occupies a position as a trusted guardian figure in the minor's life that would make it normal for the minor to turn to the officer when apprehended by the police, and based as well on the state-law requirement that the officer represent the interest of the juvenile, the California decision found that consultation with a probation officer fulfilled the role for the juvenile that consultation with an attorney does in general, acting as a " 'protective [device] . . . to dispel the compulsion inherent in custodial surroundings.' "

The rule in *Miranda*, however, was based on this Court's perception that the lawyer occupies a critical position in our legal system because of his unique ability to protect the Fifth Amendment rights of a client undergoing custodial interrogation. . . . Moreover, the lawyer's presence helps guard against overreaching by the police and ensures that any statements actually obtained are accurately transcribed for presentation into evidence.

. . . Whether it is a minor or an adult who stands accused, the lawyer is the one person to whom society as a whole looks as the protector of the legal rights of that person in his dealings with the police and the courts. . . .

A probation officer is not in the same posture with regard to either the accused or the system of justice as a whole. Often he is not trained in the law, and so is not in a position to advise the accused as to his legal rights. Neither is he a trained advocate, skilled in the representation of the interests of his client before both police and courts. He does not assume the power to act on behalf of his client by virtue of his status as adviser, nor are the communications of the accused to the probation officer shielded by the lawyer-client privilege.

Moreover, the probation officer is the employee of the State which seeks to prosecute the alleged offender. He is a peace officer, and as such is allied, to a greater or lesser extent, with his fellow peace officers. He owes an obligation to the State, notwithstanding the obligation he may also owe the juvenile under his supervision. In most cases, the probation officer is duty bound to report wrongdoing by the juvenile when it comes to his attention, even if by communication from the juvenile himself. Indeed, when this case arose, the probation officer had the responsibility for filing the petition alleging wrongdoing by the juvenile and seeking to have him taken into the custody of the Juvenile Court. It was respondent's probation officer who filed the petition against him, and it is the acting chief of probation for the State of California, a probation officer, who is petitioner in this Court today.

In these circumstances, it cannot be said that the probation officer is able to offer the type of independent advice that an accused would expect from a lawyer retained or assigned to assist him during questioning. Indeed, the probation officer's duty to his employer in many, if not most, cases would conflict sharply with the interests of the juvenile. . . .

By the same token, a lawyer is able to protect his client's rights by learning the extent, if any, of the client's involvement in the crime under investigation, and advising his client accordingly. To facilitate this, the law rightly protects the communications between client and attorney from discovery. We doubt, however, that similar protection will be afforded the communications between the probation officer and the minor. Indeed, we doubt that a probation officer, consistent with his responsibilities to the public and his profession, could withhold from the police or the courts facts made known to him by the juvenile implicating the juvenile in the crime under investigation.

We thus believe it clear that the probation officer is not in a position to offer the type of legal assistance necessary to protect the Fifth Amendment rights of an accused undergoing custodial interrogation that a lawyer can offer. The Court in *Miranda* recognized that "the attorney plays a vital role in the administration of criminal justice under our Constitution." It is this pivotal role of legal counsel that justifies the *per se* rule established in *Miranda*, and that distinguishes the request for counsel from the request for a probation officer, a clergyman, or a close friend. A probation officer simply is not necessary, in the way an attorney is, for the protection of the legal rights of the accused, juvenile or adult. He is significantly handicapped by the position he occupies in the juvenile system from serving as an effective protector of the rights of a juvenile suspected of a crime.

The California Supreme Court, however, found that the close relationship between juveniles and their probation officers compelled the conclusion that a probation officer, for purposes of *Miranda*, was sufficiently like a lawyer to justify extension of the *per se* rule. . . . [A] relationship of trust and cooperation between a probation officer and a juvenile [that] might exist, however, does not indicate that the probation officer is capable of rendering effective legal advice sufficient to protect the juvenile's rights during interrogation by the police, or of providing the other services rendered by a lawyer. To find otherwise would be "an extension of the *Miranda* requirements [that] would cut this Court's holding in that case completely loose from its own explicitly stated rationale." Such an extension would impose the burdens associated with the rule of *Miranda* on the juvenile justice system and the police without serving the interests that rule was designed simultaneously to protect. If it were otherwise, a juvenile's request for almost anyone he considered trustworthy enough to give him reliable advice would trigger the rigid rule of *Miranda*.

Similarly, the fact that the State has created a statutory duty on the part of the probation officer to protect the interests of the juvenile does not render the probation officer any more capable of rendering legal assistance to the juvenile or of protecting his legal rights, especially in light of the fact that the State has also legislated a duty on the part of the officer to report wrongdoing by the juvenile and serve the ends of the juvenile court system. The State cannot transmute the relationship between probation officer and juvenile offender into the type of relationship between attorney and client that was essential to the holding of *Miranda* simply by legislating an amorphous "duty to advise and care for the juvenile defendant." Though such a statutory duty might serve to distinguish to some degree the probation officer from the coach and the clergyman, it does not justify the extension of *Miranda* to requests to see probation officers. If it did, the State could expand the class of persons covered by the *Miranda per se* rule simply by creating a duty to care for the juvenile on the part of other persons, regardless of whether the logic of *Miranda* would justify that extension.

Nor do we believe that a request by a juvenile to speak with his probation officer constitutes a *per se* request to remain silent. As indicated, since a probation officer does not fulfill the important role in protecting the rights of the accused juvenile that an attorney plays, we decline to find that the request for the probation officer is tantamount to the request for an attorney. And there is nothing inherent in the request for a probation officer that requires us to find that a juvenile's request to see one necessarily constitutes an expression of the juvenile's right to remain silent. As discussed below, courts may take into account such a request in evaluating whether a juvenile in fact had waived his Fifth Amendment rights before confessing. But in other circumstances such a request might well be consistent with a desire to speak with the police. In the absence of further evidence that the minor intended in the circumstances to invoke his Fifth Amendment rights by such a request, we decline to attach such overwhelming significance to this request.

We hold, therefore, that it was error to find that the request by respondent to speak with his probation officer *per se* constituted an invocation of respondent's Fifth Amendment right to be free from compelled self-incrimination. It,therefore, was also error to hold that because the police did not then cease interrogating respondent the statements he made during interrogation should have been suppressed.

III

Miranda further recognized that after the required warnings are given the accused, "[i]f the interrogation continues without the presence of an attorney and a statement is taken, a heavy burden rests on the government to demonstrate that the defendant knowingly and intelligently waived his privilege against self-incrimination and his right to retained or appointed counsel." . . . [T]he question whether the accused waived his rights "is not one of form, but rather whether the defendant in fact knowingly and voluntarily waived the rights delineated in the *Miranda* case." Thus, the determination whether statements obtained during custodial interrogation are admissible against the accused is to be made upon an inquiry into the totality of the circumstances surrounding the interrogation, to ascertain whether the accused in fact knowingly and voluntarily decided to forgo his rights to remain silent and to have the assistance of counsel.

This totality-of-the-circumstances approach is adequate to determine whether there has been a waiver even where interrogation of juveniles is involved. We discern no persuasive reasons why any other approach is required where the question is whether a juvenile has waived his rights, as opposed to whether an adult has done so. The totality approach permits — indeed, it mandates — inquiry into all the circumstances surrounding the interrogation. This includes evaluation of the juvenile's age, experience, education, background, and intelligence, and into whether he has the capacity to understand the warnings given him, the nature of his Fifth Amendment rights, and the consequences of waiving those rights.

Courts repeatedly must deal with these issues of waiver with regard to a broad variety of constitutional rights. There is no reason to assume that such courts — especially juvenile courts, with their special expertise in this area — will be unable to apply the totality-of-the-circumstances analysis so as to take into account those special concerns that are present when young persons, often with limited experience and education and with immature judgment, are involved. Where the age and experience of a juvenile indicate that his request for his probation officer or his parents is, in fact, an invocation of his right to remain silent, the totality approach will allow the court the necessary flexibility to take this into account in making a waiver determination. At the same time, that approach refrains from imposing rigid restraints on police and courts in dealing with an experienced older juvenile with an extensive prior record who knowingly and intelligently waives his Fifth Amendment rights and voluntarily consents to interrogation.

In this case, we conclude that the California Supreme Court should have determined the issue of waiver on the basis of all the circumstances surrounding the interrogation of respondent. The Juvenile Court found that under this approach, respondent in fact had waived his Fifth Amendment rights and consented to interrogation by the police after his request to see his probation officer was denied. Given its view of the case, of course, the California Supreme Court did not consider this issue, though it did hold that the State had failed to prove that, notwithstanding respondent's request to see his probation officer, respondent had not intended to invoke his Fifth Amendment rights.

We feel that the conclusion of the Juvenile Court was correct. The transcript of the interrogation reveals that the police officers conducting the interrogation took care to ensure that respondent understood his rights. They fully explained to respondent that he was being questioned in connection with a murder. They then informed him of all the rights delineated in *Miranda*, and ascertained that respondent understood those rights. There is no indication in the record that respondent failed to understand what the officers told him. Moreover, after his request to see his probation officer had been denied, and after the police officer once more had explained his rights to him, respondent clearly expressed his willingness to waive his rights and continue the interrogation.

Further, no special factors indicate that respondent was unable to understand the nature of his actions. He was a 16½-year-old juvenile with considerable experience with the police. He had a record of several arrests. He had served time in a youth camp, and he had been on probation for several years. He was under the full-time supervision of probation authorities. There is no indication that he was of insufficient intelligence to understand the rights he was waiving, or what the consequences of that waiver would be. He was not worn down by improper interrogation tactics or lengthy questioning or by trickery or deceit.

On these facts, we think it clear that respondent voluntarily and knowingly waived his Fifth Amendment rights. . . .

. . . As noted, the police took care to inform respondent of his rights and to ensure that he understood them. The officers did not intimidate or threaten respondent in any way. Their questioning was restrained and free from the abuses that so concerned the Court in *Miranda*. The police did indeed indicate that a cooperative attitude would be to respondent's benefit, but their remarks in this regard were far from threatening or coercive. . . .

IV

We hold, in short, that the California Supreme Court erred in finding that a juvenile's request for his probation officer was a *per se* invocation of that juvenile's Fifth Amendment rights under *Miranda*. We conclude, rather, that whether the statements obtained during subsequent interrogation of a juvenile who has asked to see his probation officer, but who has not asked to consult an attorney or expressly asserted his right to remain silent, are admissible on the basis of waiver remains a question to be resolved on the totality of the circumstances surrounding the interrogation. On the basis of the record in this case, we hold that the Juvenile Court's findings that respondent voluntarily and knowingly waived his rights and consented to continued interrogation, and that the statements obtained from him were voluntary, were proper, and that the admission of those statements in the proceeding against respondent in Juvenile Court was correct.

The judgment of the Supreme Court of California is reversed, and the case is remanded for further proceedings not inconsistent with this opinion.

It is so ordered.

MR. JUSTICE MARSHALL, with whom MR. JUSTICE BRENNAN and MR. JUSTICE STEVENS join, *dissenting*.

. . . .

As this Court has consistently recognized, the coerciveness of the custodial setting is of heightened concern where, as here, a juvenile is under investigation. . . .

It is therefore critical in the present context that we construe *Miranda*'s prophylactic requirements broadly to accomplish their intended purpose — "dispel[ling] the compulsion inherent in custodial surroundings." To effectuate this purpose, the Court must ensure that the "protective device" of legal counsel be readily available, and that any intimation of a desire to preclude questioning be scrupulously honored. Thus, I believe *Miranda* requires that interrogation cease whenever a juvenile requests an adult who is obligated to represent his interests. Such a request, in my judgment, constitutes both an attempt to obtain advice and a general invocation of the right to silence. For, as the California Supreme Court recognized, " '[i]t is fatuous to assume that a minor in custody will be in a position to call an attorney for assistance,' " or that he will trust the police to obtain a lawyer for him.[44] A juvenile in these circumstances will likely turn to his parents, or another adult responsible for his welfare, as the only means of securing legal counsel. Moreover, a request for such adult assistance is surely inconsistent with a present desire to speak freely. Requiring a strict verbal formula to invoke the protections of *Miranda* would "protect the knowledgeable accused from station house coercion while abandoning the young person who knows no more than to ask for the . . . person he trusts."

On my reading of *Miranda*, a California juvenile's request for his probation officer should be treated as a *per se* assertion of Fifth Amendment rights. The California Supreme Court determined that probation officers have a statutory duty to represent minors' interests and, indeed, are "trusted guardian figure-[s]" to whom a juvenile would likely turn for assistance. In addition, the court found, probation officers are particularly well suited to assist a juvenile. . . . Hence, a juvenile's request for a probation officer may frequently be an attempt to secure protection from the coercive aspects of custodial questioning.

This Court concludes, however, that because a probation officer has law enforcement duties, juveniles generally would not call upon him to represent their interests, and if they did, would not be well served. But that conclusion ignores the California Supreme Court's express determination that the officer's responsibility to initiate juvenile proceedings did not negate his function as personal adviser to his wards. I decline to second-guess that court's assessment of state law. Further, although the majority here speculates that probation officers have a duty to advise cooperation with the police . . . respondent's probation officer instructed all his charges "not to go and admit openly to an offense, [but rather] to get some type of advice from . . . parents or a lawyer." Absent an explicit statutory provision or judicial holding, the officer's assessment of the obligations imposed by state law is entitled to deference by this Court.

Thus, given the role of probation officers under California law, a juvenile's request to see his officer may reflect a desire for precisely the kind of assistance *Miranda* guarantees an accused. . . . At the very least, such a request signals a desire to remain silent until contact with the officer is made. Because the Court's contrary determination withdraws the safeguards of *Miranda* from those most in need of protection, I respectfully dissent.

[The opinion of JUSTICE POWELL dissenting in a separate opinion has been omitted.]

NOTES AND QUESTIONS

1. What if the juvenile in *Fare* had requested to consult with his parent rather than his probation officer? Some lower courts hold that a minor's request to speak to a parent during custodial interrogation is tantamount to

---

[44] [1] The facts of the instant case are illustrative. When the police offered to obtain an attorney for respondent, he replied: "How I know you guys won't pull no police officer in and tell me he's an attorney?" Significantly, the police made no attempt to allay that concern.

a request to speak to an attorney. *See, e.g., People v. Rivera*, 710 P.2d 362 (1985) (request for parent as *per se* invocation of self-incrimination rights may not be compelled by the *federal* self-incrimination clause but is established as part of California state law). Other courts following perceived implications of *Fare* hold to the contrary. *See, e.g., State v. Witaker*, 578 A.2d 1031 (Conn. 1990).

Would the presence of a parent during interrogation afford the juvenile similar protection to that afforded by counsel? Is there reason to believe that a parent might routinely urge their children to confess their wrongdoing to interrogating police officers? *See In the Matter of C.P.*, 411 A.2d 643, 650 (D.C. Ct. App. 1980) (mother urged son to "tell the truth" to police interrogator); *Anglin v. State,* 259 So. 2d 752 (Fla. Dist. Ct. App. 1972) (mother repeatedly urged son to "tell the truth" or "she would clobber him"); *see also* Thomas Grisso & Melissa Ring, *Parents Attitudes Toward Juveniles Rights in Interrogation*, 6 CRIM. JUST. & BEHAV. 211, 224 (1979) (describing data suggesting "that parental guidance . . . often is not an adequate substitute for the advice of trained legal counsel").

2. Empirical studies suggest that young people under age 15 generally misunderstand and fail to comprehend *Miranda* warnings significantly more often than adults. Thomas Grisso, *Juveniles' Capacities to Waive* Miranda *Rights: An Empirical Analysis*, 68 CALIF. L. REV. 1134, 1160 (1980); Barry C. Feld, *Criminalizing Juvenile Justice: Rules of Procedure for the Juvenile Court*, 69 MINN. L. REV. 141, 169–90 (1984); Larry E. Holtz, Miranda *in a Juvenile Setting: A Child's Right to Silence*, 78 J. CRIM. L. & CRIMINOLOGY 534 (1987).

YARBOROUGH v. ALVORADO

Supreme Court of the United States
541 U.S. 652 (2004)

MR. JUSTICE KENNEDY *delivered the opinion of the Court.*

Under the Antiterrorism and Effective Death Penalty Act of 1996 (AEDPA), 110 Stat. 1214, a federal court can grant an application for a writ of habeas corpus on behalf of a person held pursuant to a state-court judgment if the state-court adjudication "resulted in a decision that was contrary to, or involved an unreasonable application of, clearly established Federal law, as determined by the Supreme Court of the United States." The United States Court of Appeals for the Ninth Circuit ruled that a state court unreasonably applied clearly established law when it held that the respondent was not in custody for *Miranda* purposes. We disagree and reverse.

I

Paul Soto and respondent Michael Alvarado attempted to steal a truck in the parking lot of a shopping mall in Santa Fe Springs, California. Soto and Alvarado were part of a larger group of teenagers at the mall that night. Soto decided to steal the truck, and Alvarado agreed to help. Soto pulled out a . 357 Magnum and approached the driver, Francisco Castaneda, who was standing near the truck emptying trash into a dumpster. Soto demanded money and the ignition keys from Castaneda. Alvarado, then five months short of his 18th birthday, approached the passenger side door of the truck and crouched down. When Castaneda refused to comply with Soto's demands, Soto shot Castaneda, killing him. Alvarado then helped hide Soto's gun.

Los Angeles County Sheriff's detective Cheryl Comstock led the investigation into the circumstances of Castaneda's death. About a month after the shooting, Comstock left word at Alvarado's house and also contacted Alvarado's mother at work with the message that she wished to speak with Alvarado. Alvarado's parents brought him to the Pico Rivera Sheriff's Station to be interviewed around lunchtime. They waited in the lobby while Alvarado went with Comstock to be interviewed. Alvarado contends that his parents asked to be present during the interview but were rebuffed.

Comstock brought Alvarado to a small interview room and began interviewing him at about 12:30 p.m. The interview lasted about two hours, and was recorded by Comstock with Alvarado's knowledge. Only Comstock and Alvarado were present. Alvarado was not given a warning under *Miranda v. Arizona*, 384 U.S. 436 (1966). Comstock began the interview by asking Alvarado to recount the events on the night of the shooting. On that night, Alvarado explained, he had been drinking alcohol at a friend's house with some other friends and acquaintances. After a few hours, part of the group went home and the rest walked to a nearby mall to use its public telephones. In Alvarado's initial telling, that was the end of it. The group went back to the friend's home and "just went to bed."

Unpersuaded, Comstock pressed on:

"Q. Okay. We did real good up until this point and everything you've said it's pretty accurate till this point, except for you left out the shooting.

"A. The shooting?

"Q. Uh huh, the shooting.

"A. Well I had never seen no shooting.

"Q. Well I'm afraid you did.

"A. I had never seen no shooting.

"Q. Well I beg to differ with you. I've been told quite the opposite and we have witnesses that are saying quite the opposite.

"A. That I had seen the shooting?

"Q. So why don't you take a deep breath, like I told you before, the very best thing is to be honest. You can't have that many people get involved in a murder and expect that some of them aren't going to tell the truth, okay? Now granted if it was maybe one person, you might be able to keep your fingers crossed and say, god I hope he doesn't tell the truth, but the problem is is that they have to tell the truth, okay? Now all I'm simply doing is giving you the opportunity to tell the truth and when we got that many people telling a story and all of a sudden you tell something way far fetched different."

At this point, Alvarado slowly began to change his story. First he acknowledged being present when the carjacking occurred but claimed that he did not know what happened or who had a gun. When he hesitated to say more, Comstock tried to encourage Alvarado to discuss what happened by appealing to his sense of honesty and the need to bring the man who shot Castaneda to justice. ("[W]hat I'm looking for is to see if you'll tell the truth"); ("I know it's very difficult when it comes time to 'drop the dime' on somebody[,] [but] if that had been your parent, your mother, or your brother, or your sister, you would darn well want [the killer] to go to jail 'cause no one has the right to take someone's life like that."). Alvarado then admitted he had helped the other man try to steal the truck by standing near the passenger side door. Next he admitted that the other man was Paul Soto, that he knew Soto was armed, and that he had helped hide the gun after the murder. Alvarado explained that he had expected Soto to scare the driver with the gun, but that he did not expect Soto to kill anyone. Toward the end of the interview, Comstock twice asked Alvarado if he needed to take a break. Alvarado declined. When the interview was over, Comstock returned with Alvarado to the lobby of the sheriff's station where his parents were waiting. Alvarado's father drove him home.

A few months later, the State of California charged Soto and Alvarado with first-degree murder and attempted robbery. Citing *Miranda*, Alvarado moved to suppress his statements from the Comstock interview. The trial court denied the motion on the ground that the interview was noncustodial. Alvarado and Soto were tried together, and Alvarado testified in his own defense. He offered an innocent explanation for his conduct, testifying that he happened to be standing in the parking lot of the mall when a gun went off nearby. The government's cross-examination relied on Alvarado's statement to Comstock. Alvarado admitted having made some of the statements but denied others. When Alvarado denied particular statements, the prosecution countered by playing excerpts from the audio recording of the interview.

During cross-examination, Alvarado agreed that the interview with Comstock "was a pretty friendly conversation," that there was "sort of a free flow between [Alvarado] and Detective Comstock," and that Alvarado did not "feel coerced or threatened in any way" during the interview. The jury convicted Soto and Alvarado of first-degree murder and attempted robbery. The trial judge later reduced Alvarado's conviction to second-degree murder for his comparatively minor role in the offense. The judge sentenced Soto to life in prison and Alvarado to 15-years-to-life.

On direct appeal, the Second Appellate District Court of Appeal (hereinafter state court) affirmed. The state court rejected Alvarado's contention that his statements to Comstock should have been excluded at trial because no Miranda warnings were given. The court ruled Alvarado had not been in custody during the interview, so no warning was required. The state court relied upon the custody test articulated in *Thompson v. Keohane*, 516 U.S. 99 (1995), which requires a court to consider the circumstances surrounding the interrogation and then determine whether a reasonable person would have felt at liberty to leave. The state court reviewed the facts of the Comstock interview and concluded Alvarado was not in custody. The court emphasized the absence of any intense or aggressive tactics and noted that Comstock had not told Alvarado that he could not leave. The California Supreme Court denied discretionary review.

Alvarado filed a petition for a writ of habeas corpus in the United States District Court for the Central District of California. The District Court agreed with the state court that Alvarado was not in custody for *Miranda* purposes during the interview.

The Court of Appeals for the Ninth Circuit reversed. First, the Court of Appeals held that the state court erred in failing to account for Alvarado's youth and inexperience when evaluating whether a reasonable person in his position would have felt free to leave. It noted that this Court has considered a suspect's juvenile status when evaluating the voluntariness of confessions and the waiver of the privilege against self-incrimination. The Court of Appeals held that in light of these authorities, Alvarado's age and experience must be a factor in the *Miranda* custody inquiry. A minor with no criminal record would be more likely to feel coerced by police tactics and conclude he is under arrest than would an experienced adult, the Court of Appeals reasoned. This required extra "safeguards commensurate with the age and circumstances of a juvenile defendant." According to the Court of Appeals, the effect of Alvarado's age and inexperience was so substantial that it turned the interview into a custodial interrogation.

. . . .

We granted certiorari.

II

We begin by determining the relevant clearly established law. . . .

Miranda itself held that preinterrogation warnings are required in the context of custodial interrogations given "the compulsion inherent in custodial surroundings." The Court explained that "custodial interrogation" meant "questioning initiated by law enforcement officers after a person has been taken into custody or otherwise deprived of his freedom of action in any significant way." The *Miranda* decision did not provide the Court with an opportunity to apply that test to a set of facts.

. . . .

Our more recent cases instruct that custody must be determined based on a how a reasonable person in the suspect's situation would perceive his circumstances. . . .

Finally, in *Thompson v. Keohane*, 516 U.S. 99 (1995), the Court offered the following description of the *Miranda* custody test:

> Two discrete inquiries are essential to the determination: first, what were the circumstances surrounding the interrogation; and second, given those circumstances, would a reasonable person have felt he or she was not at liberty to terminate the interrogation and leave. Once the scene is set and the players' lines and actions are reconstructed, the court must apply an objective test to resolve the ultimate inquiry:

was there a formal arrest or restraint on freedom of movement of the degree associated with a formal arrest.

We turn now to the case before us and ask if the state-court adjudication of the claim "involved an unreasonable application" of clearly established law when it concluded that Alvarado was not in custody. ("Under the 'unreasonable application' clause, a federal habeas court may grant the writ if the state court identifies the correct governing principle from this Court's decisions but unreasonably applies that principle to the facts of the prisoner's case"). The term "unreasonable" is "a common term in the legal world and, accordingly, federal judges are familiar with its meaning." At the same time, the range of reasonable judgment can depend in part on the nature of the relevant rule. If a legal rule is specific, the range may be narrow. Applications of the rule may be plainly correct or incorrect. Other rules are more general, and their meaning must emerge in application over the course of time. Applying a general standard to a specific case can demand a substantial element of judgment. As a result, evaluating whether a rule application was unreasonable requires considering the rule's specificity. The more general the rule, the more leeway courts have in reaching outcomes in case by case determinations.

. . . [W]e conclude that the state court's application of our clearly established law was reasonable. [I]t can be said that fair-minded jurists could disagree over whether Alvarado was in custody. On one hand, certain facts weigh against a finding that Alvarado was in custody. The police did not transport Alvarado to the station or require him to appear at a particular time. They did not threaten him or suggest he would be placed under arrest. Alvarado's parents remained in the lobby during the interview, suggesting that the interview would be brief. In fact, according to trial counsel for Alvarado, he and his parents were told that the interview was " 'not going to be long.' " During the interview, Comstock focused on Soto's crimes rather than Alvarado's. Instead of pressuring Alvarado with the threat of arrest and prosecution, she appealed to his interest in telling the truth and being helpful to a police officer. In addition, Comstock twice asked Alvarado if he wanted to take a break. At the end of the interview, Alvarado went home. All of these objective facts are consistent with an interrogation environment in which a reasonable person would have felt free to terminate the interview and leave. . . .

Other facts point in the opposite direction. Comstock interviewed Alvarado at the police station. The interview lasted two hours. Comstock did not tell Alvarado that he was free to leave. Alvarado was brought to the police station by his legal guardians rather than arriving on his own accord, making the extent of his control over his presence unclear. Counsel for Alvarado alleges that Alvarado's parents asked to be present at the interview but were rebuffed, a fact that — if known to Alvarado — might reasonably have led someone in Alvarado's position to feel more restricted than otherwise. These facts weigh in favor of the view that Alvarado was in custody.

These differing indications lead us to hold that the state court's application of our custody standard was reasonable. The Court of Appeals was nowhere close to the mark when it concluded otherwise. Although the question of what an "unreasonable application" of law might be difficult in some cases, it is not difficult here. The custody test is general, and the state court's application of our law fits within the matrix of our prior decisions. . . .

III

The Court of Appeals reached the opposite result by placing considerable reliance on Alvarado's age and inexperience with law enforcement. Our Court has not stated that a suspect's age or experience is relevant to the *Miranda* custody analysis, and counsel for Alvarado did not press the importance of either factor on direct appeal or in habeas proceedings. According to the Court of Appeals, however, our Court's emphasis on juvenile status in other contexts demanded consideration of Alvarado's age and inexperience here. The Court of Appeals viewed the state court's failure to "extend a clearly established legal principle [of the relevance of juvenile status] to a new context" as objectively unreasonable in this case, requiring issuance of the writ.

. . . .

. . . Our opinions applying the *Miranda* custody test have not mentioned the suspect's age, much less mandated its consideration. The only indications in the Court's opinions relevant to a suspect's experience with law enforcement have rejected reliance on such factors.

There is an important conceptual difference between the *Miranda* custody test and the line of cases from other contexts considering age and experience. The *Miranda* custody inquiry is an objective test. As we stated in *Keohane*, "[o]nce the scene is set and the players' lines and actions are reconstructed, the court must apply an objective test to resolve the ultimate inquiry." The objective test furthers "the clarity of [*Miranda*'s] rule. . . ." To be sure, the line between permissible objective facts and impermissible subjective experiences can be indistinct in some cases. It is possible to subsume a subjective factor into an objective test by making the latter more specific in its formulation. Thus the Court of Appeals styled its inquiry as an objective test by considering what a "reasonable 17-year-old, with no prior history of arrest or police interviews" would perceive.

At the same time, the objective *Miranda* custody inquiry could reasonably be viewed as different from doctrinal tests that depend on the actual mindset of a particular suspect, where we do consider a suspect's age and experience. For example, the voluntariness of a statement is often said to depend on whether "the defendant's will was overborne," a question that logically can depend on "the characteristics of the accused." The characteristics of the accused can include the suspect's age, education, and intelligence, as well as a suspect's prior experience with law enforcement. In concluding that there was "no principled reason" why such factors should not also apply to the *Miranda* custody inquiry, the Court of Appeals ignored the argument that the custody inquiry states an objective rule designed to give clear guidance to the police, while consideration of a suspect's individual characteristics — including his age — could be viewed as creating a subjective inquiry. For these reasons, the state court's failure to consider Alvarado's age does not provide a proper basis for finding that the state court's decision was an unreasonable application of clearly established law.

Indeed, reliance on Alvarado's prior history with law enforcement was improper. . . . In most cases, police officers will not know a suspect's interrogation history. Even if they do, the relationship between a suspect's past experiences and the likelihood a reasonable person with that experience would feel free to leave often will be speculative. True, suspects with prior law enforcement experience may understand police procedures and reasonably feel free to leave unless told otherwise. On the other hand, they may view past as prologue and expect another in a string of arrests. We do not ask police officers to consider these contingent psychological factors when deciding when suspects should be advised of their *Miranda* rights. The inquiry turns too much on the suspect's subjective state of mind and not enough on the "objective circumstances of the interrogation."

The state court considered the proper factors and reached a reasonable conclusion. The judgment of the Court of Appeals is

Reversed.

JUSTICE O'CONNOR *concurring.*

I join the opinion of the Court, but write separately to express an additional reason for reversal. There may be cases in which a suspect's age will be relevant to the *Miranda* "custody" inquiry. In this case, however, Alvarado was almost 18 years old at the time of his interview. It is difficult to expect police to recognize that a suspect is a juvenile when he is so close to the age of majority. Even when police do know a suspect's age, it may be difficult for them to ascertain what bearing it has on the likelihood that the suspect would feel free to leave. That is especially true here; 17½-year-olds vary widely in their reactions to police questioning, and many can be expected to behave as adults. Given these difficulties, I agree that the state court's decision in this case cannot be called an unreasonable application of federal law simply because it failed explicitly to mention Alvarado's age.

JUSTICE BREYER, with whom JUSTICE STEVENS, JUSTICE SOUTER, and JUSTICE GINSBURG, join, *dissenting.*

In my view, Michael Alvarado clearly was "in custody" when the police questioned him (without *Miranda* warnings) about the murder of Francisco Castaneda. To put the question in terms of federal law's well-established legal standards: Would a "reasonable person" in Alvarado's "position" have felt he was "at liberty to terminate the interrogation and leave"? A court must answer this question in light of "all of the circumstances surrounding the interrogation." And the obvious answer here is "no."

. . . .

C

What about Alvarado's youth? The fact that Alvarado was 17 helps to show that he was unlikely to have felt free to ignore his parents' request to come to the station. *See Schall v. Martin*, 467 U.S. 253, 265 (1984) (juveniles assumed "to be subject to the control of their parents"). And a 17-year-old is more likely than, say, a 35-year-old, to take a police officer's assertion of authority to keep parents outside the room as an assertion of authority to keep their child inside as well.

The majority suggests that the law might prevent a judge from taking account of the fact that Alvarado was 17. I can find nothing in the law that supports that conclusion. Our cases do instruct lower courts to apply a "reasonable person" standard. But the "reasonable person" standard does not require a court to pretend that Alvarado was a 35-year-old with aging parents whose middle-aged children do what their parents ask only out of respect. Nor does it say that a court should pretend that Alvarado was the statistically determined "average person" — a working, married, 35-year-old white female with a high school degree.

Rather, the precise legal definition of "reasonable person" may, depending on legal context, appropriately account for certain personal characteristics. In negligence suits, for example, the question is what would a "reasonable person" do " 'under the same or similar circumstances.' " In answering that question, courts enjoy "latitude" and may make "allowance not only for external facts, but sometimes for certain characteristics of the actor himself," including physical disability, youth, or advanced age. This allowance makes sense in light of the tort standard's recognized purpose: deterrence. Given that purpose, why pretend that a child is an adult or that a blind man can see?

In the present context, that of *Miranda*'s "in custody" inquiry, the law has introduced the concept of a "reasonable person" to avoid judicial inquiry into subjective states of mind, and to focus the inquiry instead upon objective circumstances that are known to both the officer and the suspect and that are likely relevant to the way a person would understand his situation. This focus helps to keep *Miranda* a workable rule.

In this case, Alvarado's youth is an objective circumstance that was known to the police. It is not a special quality, but rather a widely shared characteristic that generates commonsense conclusions about behavior and perception. To focus on the circumstance of age in a case like this does not complicate the "in custody" inquiry. And to say that courts should ignore widely shared, objective characteristics, like age, on the ground that only a (large) minority of the population possesses them would produce absurd results, the present instance being a case in point. I am not surprised that the majority points to no case suggesting any such limitation.

Nor am I surprised that the majority makes no real argument at all explaining why any court would believe that the objective fact of a suspect's age could never be relevant. *But see ante* (O'CONNOR, J., concurring) ("There may be cases in which a suspect's age will be relevant to the *Miranda* 'custody' inquiry"). The majority does discuss a suspect's "history with law enforcement," — a bright red herring in the present context where Alvarado's youth (an objective fact) simply helps to show (with the help of a legal presumption) that his appearance at the police station was not voluntary.

II

As I have said, the law in this case is clear. This Court's cases establish that, even if the police do not tell a suspect he is under arrest, do not handcuff him, do not lock him in a cell, and do not threaten him, he may nonetheless reasonably believe he is not free to leave the place of questioning — and thus be in custody for *Miranda* purposes. Our cases also make clear that to determine how a suspect would have "gaug[ed]" his "freedom of movement," a court must carefully examine "all of the circumstances surrounding the interrogation," how the suspect came to be questioned (voluntarily or against his will?), where the questioning took place (at a police station or in public?), and what the officer communicated to the individual during the interrogation (that he was a suspect? that he was under arrest? that he was free to leave at will?). In the present case, every one of these factors argues — and argues strongly — that Alvarado was in custody for *Miranda* purposes when the police questioned him.

Common sense, and an understanding of the law's basic purpose in this area, are enough to make clear that Alvarado's age — an objective, widely shared characteristic about which the police plainly knew — is also relevant to the inquiry. Unless one is prepared to pretend that Alvarado is someone he is not, a middle-aged gentleman, well-versed in police practices, it seems to me clear that the California courts made a serious mistake. I agree with the Ninth Circuit's similar conclusions.

Consequently, I dissent.

————

NOTES AND QUESTIONS

1. Does the refusal of the *Alvarado* Court to take age into account in assessing "custody" under *Miranda* mean that the Court is beginning to discount age as a basis for distinguishing adolescents from adults, at least where criminal offenses are at stake? Is *Alvarado* consistent with *Roper v. Simmons*, § 5.03[C], *supra*, where the Court held it unconstitutional to execute offenders under eighteen years of age?

2. Consider note 2 following the *Fare* case immediately prior to *Alvarado*. If young people are less able than adults to comprehend *Miranda* warnings, might they also have different perceptions than adults regarding whether or not they are in police custody?

COMMONWEALTH v. WILLIAMS

Supreme Court of Pennsylvania
475 A.2d 1283 (1984)

LARSEN, JUSTICE.

In the dark early evening of January 24, 1980, James Duggan, manager of a local Philadelphia meat market, drove to the Continental Bank at 19th and Walnut Streets to make an after-hours deposit. He parked his car at the corner, left it, and proceeded to walk toward the night depository. He was carrying a bank bag containing cash, checks and food stamps all totaling approximately $4,000.00. As he approached the deposit box he was confronted by at least two persons, one of whom positioned himself between Duggan and Duggan's automobile. The victim noticed several people standing nearby at a bus stop and he cried out for help. None of the bystanders responded to his plea and the victim started to run. On his heels was one of the attackers. As he raced into the street he slipped and fell to the ground. His pursuer snatched the money bag Duggan was carrying and fled in the darkness. The victim immediately notified the authorities of the robbery.

During the investigation of the crime a witness identified the appellant, Eric Williams, as one of the robbers. . . . On February 6, 1980, at approximately 7:00 P.M., the appellant was arrested by detectives Walsh and Russell. At the time of his arrest, appellant was 17½-years-old. He was taken to the station house where he was met by Detectives Kuhlmeier and Romano. He was informed of the circumstances of the crime and the reason for his arrest. Appellant was asked as to the whereabouts of his parents. He stated that his father could be reached at his home. Detectives Kuhlmeier and Romano left the station and drove to the Williams' residence. There they met Mr. Ollie Williams, the appellant's father. Detective Kuhlmeier informed Mr. Williams that his son had been arrested, and the reasons for the arrest. Mr. Williams accompanied the detectives back to where the appellant was being held.

Upon arriving at the station, Mr. Williams was taken to his son and the two of them were permitted to briefly consult in private. Following the father-son consultation, the appellant and his father were advised of the appellant's *Miranda* rights and they were jointly asked seven comprehension questions.[45] During the time that appellant and his father were given the *Miranda* warnings and asked the comprehension questions, they were together and had a continuing opportunity to confer.

---

[45] [6] The questions asked by the detective and the answers given by the appellant are as follows:

Q. "Do you understand that you have a right to keep quiet and do not have to say anything at all?"

The appellant answered in the affirmative.

Q. "Do you understand that anything you say can and will be used against you?"

Appellant gave an affirmative reply.

Q. "Do you understand that anything you say can and will be used against you?"

Appellant gave an affirmative reply.

Q. "Do you want to remain silent?"

The appellant's answer was in the negative.

Q. "Do you understand that you have a right to talk with a lawyer before we ask you any questions?"

Appellant replied in the affirmative.

Q. "Do you understand that if you cannot afford to hire a lawyer and you want one we will not ask you any questions until a lawyer is appointed for you free of charge?"

The appellant applied affirmatively.

Q. "Do you want either to talk with a lawyer at this time or to have a lawyer with you while we ask you questions?"

The appellant responded in the negative.

Q. "Are you willing to answer questions of your own free will, without force or fear, and without any threats or promises having been made to you.

The appellant answered affirmatively.

In the presence of his father, the appellant waived his *Miranda* rights and made an inculpatory statement. Detective Kuhlmeier, sitting in front of a typewriter, took appellant's statement, typing each question as asked and each answer as given. Shortly after 9:00 P.M. the completed formal confession was signed by both the appellant and his father.

Preliminarily, the appellant filed an omnibus pre-trial motion seeking, *inter alia*, the suppression of his confession along with all physical evidence and all in-court and out-of-court identification. Following a hearing on the motion, the lower court ordered appellant's statement suppressed. The court's ruling was based upon the testimony that appellant's father was not informed of appellant's constitutional rights prior to their private conference; and that after the *Miranda* warnings were given, the appellant was not provided an opportunity to consult with his father out of the presence of the police. The Commonwealth appealed and the Superior Court reversed holding that since his father was present when the appellant waived his rights and confessed, the waiver was knowing and the confession voluntary. We granted appellant's petition for allowance of appeal.

The principal issue raised in this appeal is whether the confession of a 17½-year-old juvenile suspect must be suppressed on the basis that he did not have an opportunity to privately consult with his father after both were given the *Miranda* warnings and asked the comprehension questions. The appellant argues that the police must give a juvenile suspect an opportunity to consult with an interested adult prior to interrogation. Further, the interested adult must be informed of the juvenile's constitutional rights before the juvenile and the adult confer in private. The appellant insists that since neither he nor his father was advised of appellant's *Miranda* rights prior to their brief consultation out of the presence of the officers, his confession should be suppressed notwithstanding that both were informed of his rights and they had an opportunity to confer in the presence of the authorities immediately before and during the time he gave his confession.

Appellant's argument is grounded upon the *per se* "interested adult" rule which evolved out of this Court's decisions in: *Commonwealth v. Roane,* 329 A.2d 286 (Pa. 1974); *Commonwealth v. Starkes,* 335 A.2d 698 (Pa. 1975); and *Commonwealth v. McCutchen,* 343 A.2d 669 (Pa. 1975).

In *Roane,* a 16-year-old juvenile defendant was arrested at his home. His mother followed him and the police officers to the station. After being made to wait more than two hours while the police questioned her son alone, the juvenile's mother found her way into the interrogation room. She then was permitted to speak with her son in that room, in the presence of the police officers. While his mother was present, the juvenile was advised of his constitutional rights. The suspect's mother told the police that she did not want her son making a statement and she wanted an attorney for him. The police ignored her comments, accepted the juvenile's waiver of rights, and took his formal statement. In a plurality opinion ruling that the statement must be suppressed, then Justice O'Brien (later Chief Justice) said:

> An important factor in establishing that a juvenile's waiver of his constitutional rights was a knowing and intelligent one would be evidence that, before he made his decision to waive those rights, he

had access to the advice of a parent, attorney, or other adult who was primarily interested in his welfare.

Since the record indicates that the Commonwealth first attempted to exclude appellant's mother from the interrogation and then, when she finally gained access, did not afford her an opportunity to advise her son privately about his constitutional rights, although she indicated that she wished him to be afforded the right of counsel, we hold that the Commonwealth failed to establish that appellant's waiver of his rights was a knowing and intelligent one.

Next, this Court considered *Commonwealth v. Starkes,* 335 A.2d 698 (Pa. 1975). In *Starkes,* the juvenile defendant was questioned alone by the police for more than an hour. During that time he denied any knowledge of the crime being investigated. He then was allowed to consult privately with his mother. She urged him to tell the truth. Following the consultation with his mother, the juvenile was questioned again. This time he gave an inculpatory statement. Later, in the presence of his mother, the juvenile was advised of his *Miranda* rights, he waived them and made a formal confession. Again in a plurality opinion, . . . the juvenile's confession was suppressed.

Where an informed adult is present the inequality of the position of the accused and police is to some extent neutralized and due process satisfied. However, where the adult is ignorant of the constitutional rights that surround a suspect in a criminal case and exerts his or her influence upon the minor in reaching the decision, it is clear that due process is offended.

Where a parent is present we must at least require that parent to be advised of the rights possessed by the minor suspect before the parent may be permitted to influence the decision which the minor must make.

Approximately four months later, this Court decided the case of *Commonwealth v. McCutchen, supra.* In a majority opinion written by then Justice O"Brien, the rationale of *Roane* and *Starkes* was approved of and applied. The *McCutchen* court held that since the juvenile defendant was not afforded an opportunity to consult with his mother before he waived his rights, his confession must be suppressed.[46]

The *per se* rule which emerged from this line of cases came to be known as the "interested adult" rule or the *McCutchen* Rule. This rule provided that no person under the age of eighteen years could waive his right to remain silent and his right to the assistance of counsel without being provided an opportunity to consult with an interested adult, who is informed of the juvenile's rights and is interested in the welfare of the juvenile.

---

[46] [11] Briefly, the facts in *McCutchen* were: At the request of two police officers, the defendant McCutchen went to the station to answer some questions about a death. He arrived at the station house at approximately 7:00 P.M. He was informed of his rights and questioned for more than two hours. He was left alone for an hour, and then with his consent, he underwent a polygraph examination. He was told that the test showed he was lying. He then gave an incriminating statement which was written in longhand and which he signed at 1:10 A.M. At this point the police brought the defendant's mother to the station. After she was told of her son's confession, she was given the opportunity to see the defendant. Later, a second formal typewritten confession was made.

Prior to the adoption of the *per se* "interested adult" rule, the standard for determining whether a juvenile knowingly waived his rights and made a voluntary confession was a traditional totality of circumstances analysis.

[I]n determining whether incriminating statements of an accused were voluntarily given and whether or not he intelligently waived his constitutional rights, all of the attending circumstances must be considered, including the age, maturity and intelligence of the individual involved.

The *per se McCutchen* rule, in discarding the totality of circumstances test, negated the relevance of all those factors which should be and must be considered in deciding whether a confession was knowingly and voluntarily given. Instead, a prophylactic principle was adopted and applied which shunned the real issue of the voluntariness of a confession.

Recently, in *Commonwealth v. Christmas,* 465 A.2d 989 (Pa. 1983),[47] this Court recognized that adherence to the inflexible *per se* rule of *McCutchen* resulted in "the exclusion from evidence of juvenile confessions that were in fact knowingly and voluntarily given."

Indeed, upon re-examination of the *per se* rule promulgated by *McCutchen,* we believe that protection of juveniles against the innate disadvantages associated with the immaturity of most youth may well be achieved in a manner that affords more adequate weight to the interests of society, and of justice, while avoiding *per se* applications of the interested and informed adult rule that serve, in an overly protective and unreasonably paternalistic fashion, to provide means for juvenile offenders to secure suppression of confessions in fact given in a knowing, intelligent and voluntary manner.

In overruling *McCutchen,* we recognized the lack of wisdom in a rule which is overly paternalistic, unnecessarily protective and sacrifices too much of the interests of justice. In its place, however, the court announced that:

[T]here shall exist *a presumption* that a statement derived in the absence of . . . an opportunity for consultation [with an interested and informed adult] is inadmissible, but that presumption shall be regarded as rebutted where the evidence *clearly demonstrates* that the statement obtained from the juvenile was in fact knowingly, intelligently, and voluntarily given.

We now reject the application of a rebuttable presumption that a juvenile is incompetent to waive his constitutional rights without first having an opportunity to consult with an interested and informed adult. The presumption adopted in *Christmas* serves no useful analytical purpose. *The so-called presumption is not a presumption at all since it merely verifies the Commonwealth's established burden of proving a knowing, intelligent and voluntary waiver on the part of a juvenile.*

---

47 [12] The facts in *Christmas* are analogous to the facts in the present case in the following respects: (a) After the juvenile was arrested, he was held without being questioned while the police summoned the suspect's father, (b) When the father arrived at the station, the juvenile and father were permitted to confer in private, (c) The father was not advised of the juvenile's constitutional rights prior to the private consultations, (d) immediately after the private conference, the juvenile was informed of his rights, he waived them and made a confession in the presence of the father.

The requirements of due process are satisfied, and the protection against the use of involuntary confessions which law and reason demand is met by application of the totality of circumstances analysis to all questions involving the waiver of rights and the voluntariness of confessions made by juveniles. All of the attending facts and circumstances must be considered and weighed in determining whether a juvenile's confession was knowingly and freely given. Among those factors are the juvenile's youth, experience, comprehension, and the presence or absence of an interested adult.

In the instant case, the appellant, at the time of his arrest, was six months away from his eighteenth birthday. He had considerable experience with the criminal justice system starting when he was placed on a consent decree probation at age 13½. Between 1978 and 1980, the appellant was adjudicated delinquent at least four times. He served a probation and later an intensive probation. On three occasions he was committed to a youth detention facility. (At least twice the appellant ran away from the facility where he was committed and he had to be returned.)

Further, the record shows that when appellant was arrested and detained, his physical condition was normal. At no time was he subjected to physical or psychological abuse. He was of normal intelligence and responsive to the questions asked of him. He was not under the influence of drugs or alcohol and there was nothing unusual about his manner of speech. He was not threatened, nor were any promises made to him. He was in custody for less than two hours and actually questioned for a little more than an hour before he made his confession. Finally, he had an opportunity to talk with his father, and his father was present during interrogation, when he waived his rights and gave his statement.

Based upon all of the relevant facts and circumstances appearing of record, it is clear from the totality of the circumstances that the appellant's confession was knowingly, intelligently, freely and voluntarily made.

The Order of the Superior Court is affirmed and this case is remanded for proceedings consistent with this opinion.

NIX, CHIEF JUSTICE, *dissenting*.

I am compelled to dissent because I continue to believe that the application of the totality of the circumstances analysis cannot truly gauge the voluntariness of a juvenile's waiver of his right to assistance of counsel and his right against self-incrimination. As we have recognized,

> [b]ecause of the unique disadvantage in the custodial interrogation process of the youthful accused due to his immaturity, . . . merely a consideration of the fact of youth in the totality of the circumstances formulation [is] inadequate to insure that a juvenile's waiver was indeed a knowing one.

In a series of our decisions beginning with *Commonwealth v. Roane*, we announced that the administering of *Miranda* warnings to a juvenile, without providing an opportunity to that juvenile to consult with a mature, informed individual concerned primarily with the interest of the juvenile, was inadequate to offset the disadvantage occasioned by his youth. The new rule ["the"

McCutchen rule] appreciates that the inexperience of the minor affects not only his or her ability to understand the full implication and consequences of the predicament but also renders the judgment inadequate to assess the spectrum of considerations encompassed in the waiver decision. It was therefore reasoned that the impediment of immaturity can only be overcome where the record establishes that the youth had access to the advice of an attorney, parent, or other interested adult and that the consulted adult was informed as to the constitutional rights available to the minor and aware of the consequences that might follow the election to be made.

I am not confident that the totality of the circumstances approach adequately considers the fact of youth or the impact of the defendant's immaturity on his ability to effectively waive his rights. Moreover, I believe that the use of the totality formulation, in practice, places upon the defendant the burden of proving that due to his immaturity he did not knowingly and intelligently waive his constitutional rights.[48] The use of the prophylactic approach of *Commonwealth v. McCutchen*, however, would assure that where the opportunity for consultation is not provided the waiver will not be effective.

The attack upon *McCutchen* has in large measure been inspired by the heinous nature of the crimes the juvenile is capable of committing. This capability on the part of some juveniles, however, does not warrant a relaxing of our vigil in determining whether the custodial statements are voluntarily made. It is legitimate to punish the juvenile offender for the crime he commits, and that punishment should be commensurate with the crime committed. However, regardless of the nature of the crime, the procedure by which we adjudicate his guilt should not ignore the impediment of immaturity. . . .

[The dissenting opinion of ZAPPALA, JUSTICE is omitted].

NOTES AND QUESTIONS

1. Does the rejection of the "interested adult" rule entail a rejection of protectionist theory as the basis for juvenile rights? *See* Chapter 1.

2. A few jurisdictions statutorily provide that statements obtained from a juvenile are inadmissible unless a parent or guardian is present during interrogation and warned of the juvenile's *Miranda* rights. *See, e.g.,* COLO. REV. STAT. § 19-2-511(1) (1999); OKLA. STAT. ANN. TIT. 10, § 7303-3.1 (A) (West 1998).

Moreover, a small number of state courts have adopted positions similar to the Pennsylvania approach prior to *Williams* by requiring the presence of an interested and informed adult as a precondition for valid wavers by juveniles. *See, e.g., In re* E.T.C., 449 A.2d 937 (Vt. 1982) (state constitution requires interested adult rule).

----

[48] [*] Under the law, the Commonwealth has the burden of proving and knowing and intelligent waiver of the rights in question. However, since the immaturity of the youthful defendant is only one factor among many considered under the totality formulation, in effect, the real significance of the defendant's immaturity on his waiver decision must be carried by the defense.

[C] Detention and Bail

State statutes routinely specify procedures dictating how juveniles taken into custody are to be handled. As the statutory examples below illustrate, parental notification requirements are common, as are provisions requiring release of the child to parental custody once parents agree to produce the child to the court at the designated time. Continued detention of the child is generally justified only if necessary to protect the minor, assure his appearance at subsequent proceedings, or prevent his commission of additional offenses.

ALABAMA CODE
§ 12-15-59 (1995)

Authority and Criteria for Continuation of Detention or Shelter Care of Children Taken into Custody.

(a) Unless otherwise ordered by the court pursuant to the provisions of this chapter, a child lawfully taken into custody as an allegedly dependent or delinquent child or a child in need of supervision shall immediately be released, upon the ascertainment of the necessary facts, to the care, custody and control of such child's parent, guardian, custodian or other suitable person able and willing to provide supervision and care for such child, except in situations where:

(1) The child has no parent, guardian, custodian or other suitable person able and willing to provide supervision and care for such child;

(2) The release of the child would present a clear and substantial threat of a serious nature to the person or property of others where the child is alleged to be delinquent;

(3) The release of such child would present a serious threat of substantial harm to such child; or

(4) The child has a history of failing to appear for hearings before the court.

(b) The criteria for continuing the child in detention or shelter or other care as set forth in subsection (a) of this section shall govern the decisions of all persons involved in determining whether the continued detention or shelter care is warranted pending court disposition and such criteria shall be supported by clear and convincing evidence in support of the decision not to release the child.

MINNESOTA STATUTES ANNOTATED
§ 260.171 (West 1998)

Release or Detention

Subdivision 1. If a child is taken into custody as provided in § 260.165, the parent, guardian, or custodian of the child shall be notified as soon as possible. Unless there is reason to believe that the child would endanger self or others, not return for a court hearing, run away from the child's parent, guardian, or custodian or otherwise not remain in the care or control of the person to whose lawful custody the child is released, or that the child's health or welfare would be immediately endangered, the child shall be released to the custody of a parent, guardian, custodian, or other suitable person. When a child is taken into custody by a peace officer under § 260.165, subdivision 1, clause (c)(2), release from detention may be authorized by the detaining officer, the detaining officer's supervisor, or the county attorney. If the social service agency has determined that the child's health or welfare will not be endangered and the provision of appropriate and available services will eliminate the need for placement, the agency shall request authorization for the child's release from detention. The person to whom the child is released shall promise to bring the child to the court, if necessary, at the time the court may direct. If the person taking the child into custody believes it desirable, that person may request the parent, guardian, custodian, or other person designated by the court to sign a written promise to bring the child to court as provided above. The intentional violation of such a promise, whether given orally or in writing, shall be punishable as contempt of court.

The court may require the parent, guardian, custodian, or other person to whom the child is released, to post any reasonable bail or bond required by the court which shall be forfeited to the court if the child does not appear as directed. The court may also release the child on the child's own promise to appear in juvenile court.

Subd. 2. (a) If the child is not released as provided in subdivision 1, the person taking the child into custody shall notify the court as soon as possible of the detention of the child and the reasons for detention.

(b) No child may be detained in a juvenile secure detention facility or shelter care facility longer than 36 hours, excluding Saturdays, Sundays, and holidays, after being taken into custody for a delinquent act as defined in § 260.015, subdivision 5, unless a petition has been filed and the judge or referee determines pursuant to § 260.172 that the child shall remain in detention.

(c) No child may be detained in an adult jail or municipal lockup longer than 24 hours, excluding Saturdays, Sundays, and holidays, or longer than six hours in an adult jail or municipal lockup in a standard metropolitan statistical area, after being taken into custody for a delinquent act as defined in § 260.015, subdivision 5, unless:

(1) a petition has been filed under § 260.131; and

(2) a judge or referee has determined under § 260.172 that the child shall remain in detention.

. . . .

Subd. 4. If the person who has taken the child into custody determines that the child should be placed in a secure detention facility or a shelter care facility, that person shall advise the child and as soon as is possible, the child's parent, guardian, or custodian:

(a) of the reasons why the child has been taken into custody and why the child is being placed in a juvenile secure detention facility or a shelter care facility; and

(b) of the location of the juvenile secure detention facility or shelter care facility. If there is reason to believe that disclosure of the location of the shelter care facility would place the child's health and welfare in immediate endangerment, disclosure of the location of the shelter care facility shall not be made; and

(c) that the child's parent, guardian, or custodian and attorney or guardian *ad litem* may make an initial visit to the juvenile secure detention facility or shelter care facility at any time. Subsequent visits by a parent, guardian, or custodian may be made on a reasonable basis during visiting hours and by the child's attorney or guardian *ad litem* at reasonable hours; and

(d) that the child may telephone parents and an attorney or guardian *ad litem* from the juvenile secure detention facility or shelter care facility immediately after being admitted to the facility and thereafter on a reasonable basis to be determined by the director of the facility; and

(e) that the child may not be detained for acts as defined in § 260.015, subdivision 5, at a juvenile secure detention facility or shelter care facility longer than 36 hours, excluding Saturdays, Sundays, and holidays, unless a petition has been filed within that time and the court orders the child's continued detention, pursuant to § 260.172; and

(f) that the child may not be detained for acts defined in § 260.015, subdivision 5, at an adult jail or municipal lockup longer than 24 hours, excluding Saturdays, Sundays, and holidays, or longer than six hours if the adult jail or municipal lockup is in a standard metropolitan statistical area, unless a petition has been filed and the court orders the child's continued detention under § 260.172; and

(g) that the child may not be detained pursuant to § 260.165, subdivision 1, clause (a) or (c)(2), at a shelter care facility longer than 72 hours, excluding Saturdays, Sundays, and holidays, unless a petition has been filed within that time and the court orders the child's continued detention, pursuant to § 260.172; and

(h) of the date, time, and place of the detention hearing, if this information is available to the person who has taken the child into custody; and

(i) that the child and the child's parent, guardian, or custodian have the right to be present and to be represented by counsel at the detention hearing, and that if they cannot afford counsel, counsel will be appointed at public expense for the child, if it is a delinquency matter, or for any party, if it is a child in need of protection or services, neglected and in foster care, or termination of parental rights matter.

. . . .

Subd. 5. If a child is to be detained in a secure detention facility or shelter care facility, the child shall be promptly transported to the facility in a manner approved by the facility or by securing a written transportation order from the court authorizing transportation by the sheriff or other qualified person. The person who has determined that the child should be detained shall deliver to the court and the supervisor of the secure detention facility or shelter care facility where the child is placed, a signed report, setting forth:

(a) the time the child was taken into custody; and

(b) the time the child was delivered for transportation to the secure detention facility or shelter care facility; and

(c) the reasons why the child was taken into custody; and

(d) the reasons why the child has been placed in detention; and

(e) a statement that the child and the child's parent have received the notification required by subdivision 4 or the reasons why they have not been so notified; . . . .

NEBRASKA REVISED STATUTES
§ 43-253 (1998)

Temporary custody; investigation; release; when

(1) Upon delivery to the juvenile court or probation officer of a juvenile who has been taken into temporary custody under §§ 43-248 and 43-250, the court or probation officer shall immediately investigate the situation of the juvenile and the nature and circumstances of the events surrounding his or her being taken into custody. Such investigation may be by hearing on the record before the court or by informal means when appropriate.

(2) No juvenile who has been taken into temporary custody under subdivision (3) of § 43-250 shall be detained in any locked facility for longer than twenty-four hours, excluding nonjudicial days, after having been taken into custody unless such juvenile has appeared personally before a court of competent jurisdiction for a hearing to determine if continued detention is necessary. If continued detention in a locked facility is ordered, such detention shall be in a juvenile detention facility, except that a juvenile charged with a felony as an adult in county or district court may be held in an adult jail as set forth in subdivision (3)(e) of § 43-250.

(3) When the court or probation officer deems it to be in the best interests of the juvenile, the court or probation officer shall immediately release such juvenile to the custody of his or her parent. If the juvenile has both a custodial and a noncustodial parent and the court or probation officer deems that release of the juvenile to the custodial parent is not in the best interests of the juvenile, the court or probation officer shall, if it is deemed to be in the best interests of the juvenile, attempt to contact the noncustodial parent, if any, of the juvenile and to release the juvenile to such noncustodial parent. If such release is not possible or not deemed to be in the best interests of the juvenile, the court or probation officer may release the juvenile to the custody of a legal guardian, a responsible relative, or another responsible person. The court may admit such juvenile to bail by bond in such amount and on such conditions and security as the court, in its sole discretion, shall determine, or the court may proceed as provided in § 43-254. In no case shall the court or probation officer release such juvenile if it appears that further detention or placement of such juvenile is a matter of immediate and urgent necessity for the protection of such juvenile or the person or property of another or if it appears that such juvenile is likely to flee the jurisdiction of the court.

HAWAII REVISED STATUTES
§ 571-32 (1993)

Detention; shelter; release; notice

(a) If a child who is believed to come within § 571-11(1) or (2) is not released as provided in § 571-31 and is not deemed suitable for diversion, the child shall be taken without unnecessary delay to the court or to the place of detention or shelter designated by the court. If the court determines that the child requires care away from the child's own home but does not require secure physical restriction, the child shall be given temporary care in any available nonsecure child caring institution, foster family home, or other shelter facility.

. . . .

(h) Provisions regarding bail shall not be applicable to children detained in accordance with this chapter, except that bail may be allowed after a child has been transferred for criminal prosecution pursuant to waiver of family court jurisdiction.

———

NOTES AND QUESTIONS

1. Note that the Nebraska statute specifically allows for juveniles to post bail while the Hawaii provision denies bail, in juvenile court cases. Unless legislatively provided, the courts have found that juveniles do not have a right to bail under either federal or state constitutional provisions extending the right to persons accused of crimes. The cases generally find adequate alternatives to bail in the release provisions of juvenile codes. For example, in *Doe v. State*, 487 P.2d 47 (Alaska 1971), the Supreme Court of Alaska found sufficient alternatives to bail release in statutory provisions requiring timely release unless detention is necessary "to protect the juvenile from others," from "caus[ing] harm to himself or others," or from being "[un]available for subsequent court proceedings." Moreover, the court noted that "blanket application of the right to bail" raises "certain problems" peculiar to juvenile proceedings:

> In some cases, a parent whose child had become involved in delinquency proceedings may be unwilling to take the child back into the home pending an adjudication hearing. In other cases, a child may not wish to return to his home, or facts adduced at a detention inquiry may show that he should not return home, because the child fears he will be in danger of abuse at the hands of his parents. But the existence of these problems does not mean that the right to remain free pending an adjudication proceeding should be denied to children. Other courts have found that the children's rules can be construed and applied so that children are provided with an adequate substitute for bail.
>
> . . . We believe . . . because of the peculiarities of children's proceedings, that the present adult bail system would be practically

unsuitable as a device for securing the child's future appearance before the court, and would not necessarily result in the child's release. Because contracts entered into by minors have been held to be voidable, a bail bondsman surely would be unwilling to deal directly with a child in providing a bail bond. Unless the child's parents are willing and financially able to secure the bond, the child's right to bail will not result in release. Where the child's parents are not able to assure the bail bondsman of their financial security, the often criticized injustices of the adult bail system as applied to indigents would be visited upon the child.

Id. at 52.

2. As the statutory excerpts illustrate, states are routinely given authority to detain youthful suspects if they are perceived to pose a danger of committing further offenses if released. As the following case makes clear, preventive detention raises constitutionally controversial questions.

SCHALL v. MARTIN

Supreme Court of the United States
467 U.S. 253 (1984)

JUSTICE REHNQUIST *delivered the opinion of the Court.*

Section 320.5(3)(b) of the New York Family Court Act authorizes pretrial detention of an accused juvenile delinquent based on a finding that there is a "serious risk" that the child "may before the return date commit an act which if committed by an adult would constitute a crime."[49] . . . The District Court struck down § 320.5(3)(b) as permitting detention without due process of law and ordered the immediate release of all class members. . . . The Court of Appeals for the Second Circuit affirmed, holding the provision "unconstitutional as to all juveniles" because the statute is administered in such a way that "the detention period serves as punishment imposed without proof of guilt established according to the requisite constitutional standard." . . . We noted probable jurisdiction . . . and now reverse. We conclude that preventive detention under the FCA serves a legitimate state objective, and that the

---

[49] [2] NEW YORK JUD. LAW § 320.5 (McKinney 1983) (Family Court Act (hereinafter FCA)) provides, in relevant part:

1. At the initial appearance, the court in its discretion may release the respondent or direct his detention.

. . .

3. The court shall not direct detention unless it finds and states the facts and reasons for so finding that unless the respondent is detained;

(a) there is a substantial probability that he will not appear in court on the return date; or

(b) there is a serious risk that he may before the return date commit an act which if committed by an adult would constitute a crime.

Appellees have only challenged pretrial detention under § 320.5(3)(b). Thus, the propriety of detention to ensure that a juvenile appears in court on the return date, pursuant to § 320.5(3)(a), is not before the Court.

procedural protections afforded pretrial detainees by the New York statute satisfy the requirements of the Due Process Clause of the Fourteenth Amendment to the United States Constitution.

I

Appellee Gregory Martin was arrested on December 13, 1977, and charged with first-degree robbery, second-degree assault, and criminal possession of a weapon based on an incident in which he, with two others, allegedly hit a youth on the head with a loaded gun and stole his jacket and sneakers. . . . Martin had possession of the gun when he was arrested. He was 14-years-old at the time and, therefore, came within the jurisdiction of New York's Family Court.[50] The incident occurred at 11:30 [P.M.], and Martin lied to the police about where and with whom he lived. He was consequently detained overnight.[51]

A petition of delinquency was filed, and Martin made his "initial appearance" in Family Court on December 14th, accompanied by his grandmother. The Family Court Judge, citing the possession of the loaded weapon, the false address given to the police, and the lateness of the hour, as evidencing a lack of supervision, ordered Martin detained. . . . A probable cause hearing was held five days later, on December 19th, and probable cause was found to exist for all the crimes charged. At the fact-finding hearing held December 27–29, Martin was found guilty on the robbery and criminal possession charges. He was adjudicated a delinquent and placed on two years' probation.[52] He had

---

[50] [4] In New York, a child over the age of 7 but less than 16 is not considered criminally responsible for his conduct. If he commits an act that would constitute a crime if committed by an adult, he comes under the exclusive jurisdiction of the Family Court. That court is charged not with finding guilt and affixing punishment, . . . but rather with determining . . . the needs and best interests of the child insofar as those are consistent with the need for the protection of the community. Juvenile proceedings are . . . civil [not] criminal, although because of the restrictions that may be placed on a juvenile adjudged delinquent, some of the same protections afforded accused adult criminals are also applicable. &helllip;

[51] [5] When a juvenile is arrested, the arresting officer must immediately notify the parent or other person legally responsible for the child's care. Ordinarily, the child will be released into the custody of his parent or guardian after being issued an "appearance ticket" requiring him to meet with the probation service on a specified day. If, however, he is charged with a serious crime, one of several designated felonies, or if his parent or guardian cannot be reached, the juvenile may be taken directly before the Family Court . . . judge [who] will make a preliminary determination as to the jurisdiction of the court, appoint a law guardian for the child, and advise the child of his or her rights, including the right to counsel and the right to remain silent. Only if, as in Martin's case, the Family Court is not in session and special circumstances exist, such as an inability to notify the parents, will the child be taken directly by the arresting officer to a juvenile detention facility. . . . If the juvenile is detained, he must be brought before the Family Court within 72 hours or the next day the court is in session, whichever is sooner. . . .

[52] [8] The "factfinding" is the juvenile's analogue of a trial. As in the earlier proceedings, the juvenile has a right to counsel at this hearing. Evidence may be suppressed on the same grounds as in criminal cases, and proof of guilt, based on the record evidence, must be beyond a reasonable doubt. If guilt is established, the court enters an appropriate order and schedules a dispositional hearing. The dispositional hearing is the final and most important proceeding in the Family Court. If the juvenile has committed a designated felony, the court must order a probation investigation and a diagnostic assessment. Any other material and relevant evidence may be offered by the probation agency or the juvenile. Both sides may call and cross-examine witnesses and recommend specific dispositional alternatives. The court must find, based on a preponderance of the evidence,

been detained pursuant to § 320.5(3)(b), between the initial appearance and the completion of the fact-finding hearing, for a total of 15 days.

Appellees Luis Rosario and Kenneth Morgan, both age 14, were also ordered detained pending their fact-finding hearings. Rosario was charged with attempted first-degree robbery and second-degree assault for an incident in which he, with four others, allegedly tried to rob two men, putting a gun to the head of one of them and beating both about the head with sticks. . . . At the time of his initial appearance, on March 15, 1978, Rosario had another delinquency petition pending for knifing a student. . . . Probable cause was found on March 21. On April 11, Rosario was released to his father, and the case was terminated. . . .[53]

Kenneth Morgan was charged with attempted robbery and attempted grand larceny for an incident in which he and another boy allegedly tried to steal money from a 14-year-old girl and her brother by threatening to blow their heads off and grabbing them to search their pockets. Morgan, like Rosario, was on release status on another petition (for robbery and criminal possession of stolen property) at the time of his initial appearance on March 27, 1978. He had been arrested four previous times, and his mother refused to come to court because he had been in trouble so often she did not want him home. A probable-cause hearing was . . . continued until April 4, when it was combined with a fact-finding hearing. Morgan was found guilty of harassment and petty larceny and was ordered placed with the Department of Social Services for eighteen months. He was detained a total of eight days between his initial appearance and the fact-finding hearing.

At trial, appellees offered in evidence the case histories of thirty-four members of the class, including the three named petitioners. Both parties presented some general statistics on the relation between pretrial detention and ultimate disposition. In addition, there was testimony concerning juvenile proceedings from a number of witnesses, including a legal aid attorney specializing in juvenile cases, a probation supervisor, a child psychologist, and a Family Court Judge. On the basis of this evidence, the District Court . . .

---

that the juvenile is delinquent and requires supervision, treatment, or confinement. Otherwise, the petition is dismissed. If the juvenile is found to be delinquent, then the court enters an order of disposition. Possible alternatives include a conditional discharge, probation for up to two years; nonsecure placement with, perhaps, a relative or the Division for Youth; transfer to the Commissioner of Mental Health; or secure placement. Unless the juvenile committed one of the designated felonies, the court must order the least restrictive available alternative consistent with the needs and best interests of the juvenile and the need for protection of the community.

[53] [9] Every accused juvenile is interviewed by a member of the staff of the Probation Department. This process is known as "probation intake." . . . In the course of the interview, which lasts an average of 45 minutes, the probation officer will gather what information he can about the nature of the case, the attitudes of the parties involved, and the child's past history and current family circumstances. . . . His sources of information are the child, his parent or guardian, the arresting officer, and any records of past contacts between the child and the Family Court. On the basis of this interview, the probation officer may attempt to "adjust," or informally resolve, the case. . . . Adjustment is a purely voluntary process in which the complaining witness agrees not to press the case further, while the juvenile is given a warning or agrees to counseling sessions or, perhaps, referral to a community agency. . . . In cases involving designated felonies or other serious crimes, adjustment is, not permitted without written approval of the Family Court. . . . If a case is not informally adjusted, it is referred to the "presentment agency." . . .

agreed with appellees that pretrial detention under the FCA violates due process [and released the appellees].[54]

The Court of Appeals affirmed. After reviewing the trial record, the court opined that "the vast majority of juveniles detained under [§ 320.5(3)(b)] either have their petitions dismissed before an adjudication of delinquency or are released after adjudication." . . . The court concluded . . . that § 320.5(3)(b) "is utilized principally, not for preventive purposes, but to impose punishment for unadjudicated criminal acts." . . . The early release of so many of those detained contradicts any asserted need for pretrial confinement to protect the community. The court therefore concluded that § 320.5(3)(b) must be declared unconstitutional as to all juveniles. Individual litigation would be a practical impossibility because the periods of detention are so short that the litigation is mooted before the merits are determined.

II

There is no doubt that the Due Process Clause is applicable in juvenile proceedings. "The problem," we have stressed, "is to ascertain the precise impact of the due process requirement upon such proceedings." We have held that certain basic constitutional protections enjoyed by adults accused of crimes also apply to juveniles. But the Constitution does not mandate elimination of all differences in the treatment of juveniles. The State has "a *parens patriae* interest in preserving and promoting the welfare of the child," . . . which makes a juvenile proceeding fundamentally different from an adult criminal trial. We have tried, therefore, to strike a balance — to respect the "informality" and "flexibility" that characterize juvenile proceedings . . . and yet to ensure that such proceedings comport with the "fundamental fairness" demanded by the Due Process Clause. . . .

The statutory provision at issue in these cases, § 320.5(3)(b), permits a brief pretrial detention based on a finding of a "serious risk" that an arrested juvenile may commit a crime before his return date. The question before us is whether preventive detention of juveniles pursuant to § 320.5(3)(b) is compatible with the "fundamental fairness" required by due process.

Two separate inquiries are necessary to answer this question. First, does preventive detention under the New York statute serve a legitimate state

---

54 [12] The District Court gave three reasons for this conclusion. First, under the FCA, a juvenile may be held in pretrial detention for up to five days without any judicial determination of probable cause. . . . The District Court concluded that pretrial detention without a prior adjudication of probable cause is, itself, a *per se* violation of due process. . . . Second, after a review of the pertinent scholarly literature, the court noted that "no diagnostic tools have as yet been devised which enable even the most highly trained criminologists to predict reliably which juveniles will engage in violent crime." . . . [T]he court concluded, a Family Court judge cannot make a reliable prediction based on the limited information available to him at the initial appearance. . . . Moreover, the court felt that the trial record was "replete" with examples of arbitrary and capricious detentions. . . . Finally, the court concluded that preventive detention is merely a euphemism for punishment imposed without an adjudication of guilt. The alleged purpose of the detention — to protect society from the juvenile's criminal conduct — is indistinguishable from the purpose of post-trial detention. And given "the inability of trial judges to predict which juveniles will commit crimes," there is no rational connection between the decision to detain and the alleged purpose, even if that purpose were legitimate. . . .

objective? . . . And, second, are the procedural safeguards contained in the FCA adequate to authorize the pretrial detention of at least some juveniles charged with crimes?

A

Preventive detention under the FCA is purportedly designed to protect the child and society from the potential consequences of his criminal acts. . . . When making any detention decision, the Family Court judge is specifically directed to consider the needs and best interests of the juvenile as well as the need for the protection of the community. FCA § 301.1. . . . As an initial matter . . . we must decide whether, in the context of the juvenile system, the combined interest in protecting both the community and the juvenile himself from the consequences of future criminal conduct is sufficient to justify such detention.

The "legitimate and compelling state interest" in protecting the community from crime cannot be doubted. . . . We have stressed before that crime prevention is "a weighty social objective," . . . and this interest persists undiluted in the juvenile context. The harm suffered by the victim of a crime is not dependent upon the age of the perpetrator. [55] And the harm to society generally may even be greater in this context given the high rate of recidivism among juveniles.

The juvenile's countervailing interest in freedom from institutional restraints, even for the brief time involved here, is undoubtedly substantial as well. . . . But that interest must be qualified by the recognition that juveniles, unlike adults, are always in some form of custody. . . . Children, by definition, are not assumed to have the capacity to take care of themselves. They are assumed to be subject to the control of their parents, and if parental control falters, the State must play its part as *parens patriae*. . . . In this respect, the juvenile's liberty interest may, in appropriate circumstances, be subordinated to the State's "*parens patriae* interest in preserving and promoting the welfare of the child." . . .

The New York Court of Appeals, in upholding the statute at issue here, stressed at some length "the desirability of protecting the juvenile from his own folly." [56]

---

[55] [14] In 1982, juveniles under 16 accounted for 7.5 percent of all arrests for violent crimes, 19.9 percent of all arrests for serious property crime, and 173 percent of all arrests for violent and serious property crimes combined. . . .

[56] [15] "Our society recognizes that juveniles in general are in the earlier stages of their emotional growth, that their intellectual development is incomplete, that they have had only limited practical experience, and that their value systems have not yet been clearly identified or firmly adopted. . . . "For the same reasons that our society does not hold juveniles to an adult standard of responsibility for their conduct, our society may also conclude that there is a greater likelihood that a juvenile charged with delinquency, if released, will commit another criminal act than that an adult charged with crime will do so. To the extent that self-restraint may be expected to constrain adults, it may not be expected to operate with equal force as to juveniles. Because of the possibility of juvenile delinquency treatment and the absence of second-offender sentencing, there will not be the deterrent for the juvenile which confronts the adult. Perhaps more significant is the fact that in consequence of lack of experience and comprehension the juvenile does not view the commission of what are criminal acts in the same perspective as an adult. . . . There is the

Society has a legitimate interest in protecting a juvenile from the consequences of his criminal activity — both from potential physical injury which may be suffered when a victim fights back or a policeman attempts to make an arrest and from the downward spiral of criminal activity into which peer pressure may lead the child. . . .

The substantiality and legitimacy of the state interests underlying this statute are confirmed by the widespread use and judicial acceptance of preventive detention for juveniles. Every State . . . permits preventive detention of juveniles accused of crime. A number of model juvenile justice Acts also contain provisions permitting preventive detention. And the courts of eight States, including the New York Court of Appeals, have upheld their statutes with specific reference to protecting the juvenile and the community from harmful pretrial conduct, including pretrial crime. . . .

"The fact that a practice is followed by a large number of states is not conclusive in a decision as to whether that practice accords with due process, but it is plainly worth considering in determining whether the practice 'offends some principle of justice so rooted in the traditions and conscience of our people as to be ranked as fundamental.'" . . . In light of the uniform legislative judgment that pretrial detention of juveniles properly promotes the interests both of society and the juvenile, we conclude that the practice serves a legitimate regulatory purpose compatible with the "fundamental fairness" demanded by the Due Process Clause in juvenile proceedings. . . .

Of course, the mere invocation of a legitimate purpose will not justify particular restrictions and conditions of confinement amounting to punishment. It is axiomatic that "[d]ue process requires that a pretrial detainee not be punished." *Bell v. Wolfish*, 441 U.S., at 535, n. 16. Even given, therefore, that pretrial detention may serve legitimate regulatory purposes, it is still necessary to determine whether the terms and conditions of confinement under § 320.5(3)(b) are in fact compatible with those purposes. . . . "A court must decide whether the disability is imposed for the purpose of punishment or whether it is but an incident of some other legitimate governmental purpose." . . . Absent a showing of an express intent to punish on the part of the State, that determination generally will turn on "whether an alternative purpose to which [the restriction] may rationally be connected is assignable for it, and whether it appears excessive in relation to the alternative purpose assigned [to it]." . . .

There is no indication in the statute itself that preventive detention is used or intended as a punishment. First of all, the detention is strictly limited in time. If a juvenile is detained at his initial appearance and has denied the charges against him, he is entitled to a probable-cause hearing to be held not more than three days after the conclusion of the initial appearance or four days after the filing of the petition, whichever is sooner. If the Family Court judge finds probable cause, he must also determine whether continued detention is necessary pursuant to § 320.5(3)(b). . . .

---

element of gamesmanship and the excitement of 'getting away' with something and the powerful inducement of peer pressures. All of these commonly acknowledged factors make the commission of criminal conduct on the part of juveniles in general more likely than in the case of adults."
. . .

Detained juveniles are also entitled to an expedited fact-finding hearing. If the juvenile is charged with one of a limited number of designated felonies, the fact-finding hearing must be scheduled to commence not more than fourteen days after the conclusion of the initial appearance. § 340.1. If the juvenile is charged with a lesser offense, then the fact-finding hearing must be held not more than three days after the initial appearance. In the latter case, since the times for the probable-cause hearing and the fact-finding hearing coincide, the two hearings are merged.

Thus, the maximum possible detention under § 320.5(3)(b) of a youth accused of a serious crime, assuming a three-day extension of the fact-finding hearing for good cause shown, is seventeen days. The maximum detention for less serious crimes, again assuming a three-day extension for good cause shown, is six days. These time frames seem suited to the limited purpose of providing the youth with a controlled environment and separating him from improper influences pending the speedy disposition of his case.

The conditions of confinement also appear to reflect the regulatory purposes relied upon by the State. When a juvenile is remanded after his initial appearance, he cannot, absent exceptional circumstances, be sent to a prison or lockup where he would be exposed to adult criminals. Instead, the child is screened by an "assessment unit" of the Department of Juvenile Justice. . . . The assessment unit places the child in either nonsecure or secure detention. Nonsecure detention involves an open facility in the community, a sort of "halfway house," without locks, bars, or security officers where the child receives schooling and counseling and has access to recreational facilities. . . .

Secure detention is more restrictive, but it is still consistent with the regulatory and *parens patriae* objectives relied upon by the State. Children are assigned to separate dorms based on age, size, and behavior. They wear street clothes provided by the institution and partake in educational and recreational programs and counseling sessions run by trained social workers. Misbehavior is punished by confinement to one's room . . . . We cannot conclude from this record that the controlled environment briefly imposed by the State on juveniles in secure pretrial detention "is imposed for the purpose of punishment" rather than as "an incident of some other legitimate governmental purpose." . . .

The Court of Appeals . . . invalidated a significant aspect of New York's juvenile justice system based solely on some case histories and a statistical study which appeared to show that "the vast majority of juveniles detained under [§ 320.5(3)(b)] either have their petitions dismissed before an adjudication of delinquency or are released after adjudication." . . . The court assumed that dismissal of a petition or failure to confine a juvenile at the dispositional hearing belied the need to detain him prior to fact-finding and that, therefore, the pretrial detention constituted punishment. . . . Since punishment imposed without a prior adjudication of guilt is *per se* illegitimate, the Court of Appeals concluded that no juveniles could be held pursuant to § 320.5(3)(b).

There are some obvious flaws in the statistics and case histories relied upon by the lower court.[57] But even assuming it to be the case that "by far the greater number of juveniles incarcerated under [§ 320.5(3)(b)] will never be confined as a consequence of a disposition imposed after an adjudication of delinquency," . . . we find that to be an insufficient ground for upsetting the widely shared legislative judgment that preventive detention serves an important and legitimate function in the juvenile justice system. We are unpersuaded by the Court of Appeals' rather cavalier equation of detentions that do not lead to continued confinement after an adjudication of guilt and "wrongful" or "punitive" pretrial detentions.

Pretrial detention need not be considered punitive merely because a juvenile is subsequently discharged subject to conditions or put on probation. In fact, such actions reinforce the original finding that close supervision of the juvenile is required. Lenient but supervised disposition is in keeping with the Act's purpose to promote the welfare and development of the child. As the New York Court of Appeals noted:

> It should surprise no one that caution and concern for both the juvenile and society may indicate the more conservative decision to detain at the very outset, whereas the later development, of very much more relevant information may prove that while a finding of delinquency was warranted, placement may not be indicated. . . .

Even when a case is terminated prior to fact finding, it does not follow that the decision to detain the juvenile pursuant to § 320.5(3)(b) amounted to a due process violation. A delinquency petition may be dismissed for any number of reasons collateral to its merits, such as the failure of a witness to testify. The Family Court judge cannot be expected to anticipate such developments at the initial hearing. He makes his decision based on the information available to him at that time, and the propriety of the decision must be judged in that light. Consequently, the final disposition of a case is "largely irrelevant" to the legality of a pretrial detention. . . .

It may be, of course, that in some circumstances detention of a juvenile would not pass constitutional muster. But the validity of those detentions must be determined on a case-by-case basis. Section 320.5(3)(b) is not invalid "on its face" by reason of the ambiguous statistics and case histories relied upon by the court below. We find no justification for the conclusion that, contrary to the express language of the statute and the judgment of the highest state court, § 320.5(3)(b) is a punitive rather than a regulatory measure. Preventive detention under the FCA serves the legitimate state objective, held in common with every State in the country, of protecting both the juvenile, and society from the hazards of pretrial crime.

---

[57] [21] For example, as the Court of Appeals itself admits . . . the statistical study on which it relied mingles indiscriminately detentions under § 320.5(3)(b) with detentions under § 320.5(3)(a). The latter provision applies only to juveniles who are likely not to appear on the return date if not detained, and appellees concede that such juveniles may be lawfully detained. . . . Furthermore, the 34 case histories on which the court relied were handpicked by appellees' counsel from over a three-year period. . . .

B

Given the legitimacy of the State's interest in preventive detention, and the nonpunitive nature of that detention, the remaining question is whether the procedures afforded juveniles detained prior to fact-finding provide sufficient protection against erroneous and unnecessary deprivations of liberty.

. . . In many respects, the FCA provides far more pre-detention protection for juveniles. . . . The initial appearance is informal, but the accused juvenile is given full notice of the charges against him and a complete stenographic record is kept of the hearing. . . . The juvenile appears accompanied by his parent or guardian. He is first informed of his rights, including the right to remain silent and the right to be represented by counsel chosen by him or by a law guardian assigned by the court. . . . The initial appearance may be adjourned for no longer than seventy-two hours or until the next court day, whichever is sooner, to enable an appointed law guardian or other counsel to appear before the court. . . . When his counsel is present, the juvenile is informed of the charges against him and furnished with a copy of the delinquency petition. . . . A representative from the presentment agency appears in support of the petition.

. . . .

In sum, notice, a hearing, and a statement of facts and reasons are given prior to any detention under § 320.5(3)(b). A formal probable-cause hearing is then held within a short while thereafter, if the fact-finding hearing is not itself scheduled within three days. These flexible procedures have been found constitutionally adequate under the Fourth Amendment and under the Due Process Clause. Appellees have failed to note any additional procedures that would significantly improve the accuracy of the determination without unduly impinging on the achievement of legitimate state purposes.

Appellees argue, however, that the risk of erroneous and unnecessary detentions is too high despite these procedures because the standard for detention is fatally vague. Detention under § 320.5(3)(b) is based on a finding that there is a "serious risk" that the juvenile, if released, would commit a crime prior to his next court appearance. We have already seen that detention of juveniles on that ground serves legitimate regulatory purposes. But appellees claim, and the District Court agreed, that it is virtually impossible to predict future criminal conduct with any degree of accuracy. Moreover, they say, the statutory standard fails to channel the discretion of the Family Court judge by specifying the factors on which he should rely in making that prediction. The procedural protections noted above are thus, in their view, unavailing because the ultimate decision is intrinsically arbitrary and uncontrolled.

. . . [F]rom a legal point of view there is nothing inherently unattainable about a prediction of future criminal conduct. Such a judgment forms an important element in many decisions, and we have specifically rejected the contention, based on the same sort of sociological data relied upon by appellees and the District Court, "that it is impossible to predict future behavior and that the question is so vague as to be meaningless." . . .

We have also recognized that a prediction of future criminal conduct is "an experienced prediction based on a host of variables" which cannot be readily codified. . . . Judge Quinones of the Family Court testified at trial that he and his colleagues make a determination under § 320.5(3)(b) based on numerous factors including the nature and seriousness of the charges; whether the charges are likely to be proved at trial; the juvenile's prior record; the adequacy and effectiveness of his home supervision; his school situation, if known; the time of day of the alleged crime as evidence of its seriousness and a possible lack of parental control; and any special circumstances that might be brought to his attention by the probation officer, the child's attorney, or any parents, relatives, or other responsible persons accompanying the child. . . . The decision is based on as much information as can reasonably be obtained at the initial appearance.

Given the right to a hearing, to counsel, and to a statement of reasons, there is no reason that the specific factors upon which the Family Court judge might rely must be specified in the statute. . . .

. . . .

The judgment of the Court of Appeals is Reversed.

JUSTICE MARSHALL, with whom JUSTICE BRENNAN and JUSTICE STEVENS join, *dissenting.*

There are few limitations on § 320.5(3)(b). Detention need not be predicated on a finding that there is probable cause to believe the child committed the offense for which he was arrested. The provision applies to all juveniles, regardless of their prior records or the severity of the offenses of which they are accused. The provision is not limited to the prevention of dangerous crimes; a prediction that a juvenile if released may commit a minor misdemeanor is sufficient to justify his detention. Aside from the reference to "serious risk," the requisite likelihood that the juvenile will misbehave before his trial is not specified by the statute.

The Court today holds that preventive detention of a juvenile pursuant to § 320.5(3)(b) does not violate the Due Process Clause. Two rulings are essential to the Court's decision: that the provision promotes legitimate government objectives important enough to justify the abridgment of the detained juveniles' liberty interests and that the provision incorporates procedural safeguards sufficient to prevent unnecessary or arbitrary impairment of constitutionally protected rights. Because I disagree with both of those rulings, I dissent.

I

. . . .

The first step in the process that leads to detention under § 320.5(3)(b) is known as "probation intake." . . . The heart of the intake procedure is a 10-to-40-minute interview of the juvenile, the arresting officer, and sometimes the juvenile's parent or guardian. The objectives of the probation officer conducting the interview are to determine the nature of the offense the child may have committed and to obtain some background information on him.

On the basis of the information derived from the interview and from an examination of the juvenile's record, the probation officer decides whether the case should be disposed of informally ("adjusted") or whether it should be referred to the Family Court. If the latter, the officer makes an additional recommendation regarding whether the juvenile should be detained. "There do not appear to be any governing criteria which must be followed by the probation officer in choosing between proposing detention and parole. . . ."

The actual decision whether to detain a juvenile under § 320.5(3)(b) is made by a Family Court judge at what is called an "initial appearance" — a brief hearing resembling an arraignment. The information on which the judge makes his determination is very limited. He has before him a "petition for delinquency" prepared by a state agency, charging the juvenile with an offense, accompanied with one or more affidavits attesting to the juvenile's involvement. Ordinarily the judge has in addition the written report and recommendation of the probation officer. However, the probation officer who prepared the report rarely attends the hearing. Nor is the complainant likely to appear. Consequently, "[o]ften there is no one present with personal knowledge of what happened."

In the typical case, the judge appoints counsel for the juvenile at the time his case is called. Thus, the lawyer has no opportunity to make an independent inquiry into the juvenile's background or character, and has only a few minutes to prepare arguments on the child's behalf. The judge ordinarily does not interview the juvenile, makes no inquiry into the truth of allegations in the petition, and does not determine whether there is probable cause to believe the juvenile committed the offense. The typical hearing lasts between five and fifteen minutes, and the judge renders his decision immediately afterward.

Neither the statute nor any other body of rules guides the efforts of the judge to determine whether a given juvenile is likely to commit a crime before his trial. In making detention decisions, "each judge must rely on his own subjective judgment, based on the limited information available to him at court intake and whatever personal standards he himself has developed in exercising his discretionary authority under the statute." Family Court judges are not provided information regarding the behavior of juveniles over whose cases they have presided, so a judge has no way of refining the standards he employs in making detention decisions.

After examining a study of a sample of thirty-four cases in which juveniles were detained under § 320.5(3)(b) along with various statistical studies of pretrial detention of juveniles in New York, the District Court made findings regarding the circumstances in which the provision habitually is invoked. Three of those findings are especially germane to appellees' challenge to the statute. First, a substantial number of "first offenders" are detained pursuant to § 320.5(3)(b). For example, at least five of the thirty-four juveniles in the sample had no prior contact with the Family Court before being detained and at least sixteen had no prior adjudications of delinquency. Second, many juveniles are released — for periods ranging from five days to several weeks — after their arrests and are then detained . . . despite the absence of any evidence of misconduct during the time between their arrests and "initial appearances." . . . Third, "the overwhelming majority" of the juveniles detained . . . are released either before or immediately after their trials, either unconditionally or on parole. . . .

Finally, the District Court made a few significant findings concerning the conditions associated with "secure detention". . . . In a "secure facility," "[t]he juveniles are subjected to strip-searches, wear institutional clothing and follow institutional regimen. At [one secured detention center] . . . some juveniles who have had dispositional determinations and were awaiting placement (long-term care) co-mingle with those in pretrial detention (short term care)."
. . .

It is against the backdrop of these findings that the contentions of the parties must be examined.

II

A

. . . Examination of the provision must of course be informed by a recognition that juveniles have different needs and capacities than adults, but the provision still "must measure up to the essentials of due process and fair treatment." To comport with "fundamental fairness," § 320.5(3)(b) must satisfy two requirements. First, it must advance goals commensurate with the burdens it imposes on constitutionally protected interests. Second, it must not punish the juveniles to whom it applies.

. . . It is manifest that § 320.5(3)(b) impinges upon fundamental rights. If the "liberty" protected by the Due Process Clause means anything, it means freedom from physical restraint. Only a very important government interest can justify deprivation of liberty in this basic sense.

The majority seeks to evade the force of this principle by discounting the impact on a child of incarceration pursuant to § 320.5(3)(b). The curtailment of liberty consequent upon detention of a juvenile, the majority contends, is mitigated by the fact that "juveniles, unlike adults, are always in some form of custody." In any event, the majority argues, the conditions of confinement associated with "secure detention" . . . are not unduly burdensome. These contentions enable the majority to suggest that § 320.5(3)(b) need only advance a "legitimate state objective" to satisfy the strictures of the Due Process Clause. The majority's arguments do not survive scrutiny. Its characterization of preventive detention as merely a transfer of custody from a parent or guardian to the State is difficult to take seriously. Surely there is a qualitative difference between imprisonment and the condition of being subject to the supervision and control of an adult who has one's best interests at heart. And the majority's depiction of the nature of confinement . . . is insupportable on this record. As noted above, the District Court found that secure detention entails incarceration in a facility closely resembling a jail and that pretrial detainees are sometimes mixed with juveniles who have been found to be delinquent. Evidence adduced at trial reinforces these findings.

For example, Judge Quinones, a Family Court Judge with eight years of experience, described the conditions of detention as follows:

"Then again, Juvenile Center, as much as we might try, is not the most pleasant place in the world. If you put them in detention, you are liable to be exposing these youngsters to all sorts of things. They are liable to be exposed to assault, they are liable to be exposed to sexual assaults. You are taking the risk of putting them together with a youngster that might be much worse than they, possibly might be, and it might have a bad effect in that respect." . . . Many other observers of the circumstances of juvenile detention in New York have come to similar conclusions.[58]

In short, fairly viewed, pretrial detention of a juvenile pursuant to § 320.5(3)(b) gives rise to injuries comparable to those associated with imprisonment of an adult. In both situations, the detainee suffers stigmatization and severe limitation of his freedom of movement. Indeed, the impressionability of juveniles may make the experience of incarceration more injurious to them than to adults; all too quickly juveniles subjected to preventive detention come to see society at large as hostile and oppressive and to regard themselves as irremediably "delinquent." Such serious injuries to presumptively innocent persons — encompassing the curtailment of their constitutional rights to liberty — can be justified only by a weighty public interest that is substantially advanced by the statute.[59]

. . . Alternatively, it might be argued that the comparatively brief period of incarceration permissible under the provision warrants a slight lowering of the constitutional bar. Applying the principle that the strength of the state interest needed to legitimate a statute depends upon the degree to which the statute encroaches upon fundamental rights, . . . it might be held that an important — but not quite "compelling" — objective is necessary to sustain § 320.5(3)(b). In the present context, there is no need to choose between these doctrinal options, because § 320.5(3)(b) would fail either test.

The applicability of the second of the two tests is admitted even by the majority. . . . [A]n adult may not be punished prior to determination that he is guilty of a crime. The majority concedes, as it must, that this principle applies to juveniles. Thus, if the only purpose substantially advanced by § 320.5(3)(b) is punishment, the provision must be struck down.

For related reasons, § 320.5(3)(b) cannot satisfy either of the requirements discussed above that together define "fundamental fairness" in the context of pretrial detention.

---

58 [13] All of the 34 juveniles in the sample were detained in Spofford Juvenile Center, the detention facility for New York City. Numerous studies of that facility have attested to its unsavory characteristics. . . . Conditions in Spofford have been successfully challenged on constitutional grounds (by a group of inmates of a different type), . . . but nevertheless remain grim. . . . Not surprisingly, a former New York City Deputy Mayor for Criminal Justice has averred that "Spofford is, in many ways, indistinguishable from a prison." . . .

59 [15] This standard might be refined in one of two ways. First, it might be argued that, because § 320.5(3)(b) impinges upon "[l]iberty from bodily restraint," which has long been "recognized as the core of the liberty protected by the Due Process Clause, . . . the provision can pass constitutional muster only if it promotes a 'compelling' government interest."

B

Appellants and the majority contend that § 320.5(3)(b) advances a pair of intertwined government objectives: "protecting the community from crime," and "protecting a juvenile from the consequences of his criminal activity." More specifically, the majority argues that detaining a juvenile for a period of up to seventeen days prior to his trial has two desirable effects: it protects society at large from the crimes he might have committed during that period if released; and it protects the juvenile himself "both from potential physical injury which may be suffered when a victim fights back or a policeman attempts to make an arrest and from the downward spiral of criminal activity into which peer pressure may lead the child."

Appellees . . . argue that public purposes of this sort can never justify incarceration of a person who has not been adjudicated guilty of a crime, at least in the absence of a determination that there exists probable cause to believe he committed a criminal offense. We need not reach that categorical argument in these cases because, even if the purposes identified by the majority are conceded to be compelling, they are not sufficiently promoted by detention pursuant to § 320.5(3)(b) to justify the concomitant impairment of the juveniles' liberty interests. To state the case more precisely, two circumstances in combination render § 320.5(3)(b) invalid in toto: in the large majority of cases in which the provision is invoked, its asserted objectives are either not advanced at all or are only minimally promoted; and, as the provision is written and administered by the state courts, the cases in which its asserted ends are significantly advanced cannot practicably be distinguished from the cases in which they are not.

I

Both of the courts below concluded that only occasionally and accidentally does pretrial detention of a juvenile under § 320.5(3)(b) prevent the commission of a crime. Three subsidiary findings undergird that conclusion. First, Family Court judges are incapable of determining which of the juveniles who appear before them would commit offenses before their trials if left at large and which would not. In part, this incapacity derives from the limitations of current knowledge concerning the dynamics of human behavior. On the basis of evidence adduced at trial, supplemented by a thorough review of the secondary literature, . . . the District Court found that "no diagnostic tools have as yet been devised which enable even the most highly trained criminologists to predict reliably which juveniles will engage in violent crime." . . . The evidence supportive of this finding is overwhelming. An independent impediment to identification of the defendants who would misbehave if released is the paucity of data available at an initial appearance. The judge must make his decision whether to detain a juvenile on the basis of a set of allegations regarding the child's alleged offense, a cursory review of his background and criminal record, and the recommendation of a probation officer who, in the typical case, has seen the child only once. In view of this scarcity of relevant information, the District Court credited the testimony of appellees' expert witness, who "stated that he would be surprised if recommendations based on intake interviews were better than chance and assessed the judge's subjective prognosis about the probability of future crime as only 4 percent better than chance — virtually wholly unpredictable." . . .

Second, § 320.5(3)(b) is not limited to . . . juveniles whose past conduct suggests that they are substantially more likely than average juveniles to misbehave in the immediate future. The provision authorizes the detention of persons arrested for trivial offenses [60] and persons without any prior contacts with juvenile court. Even a finding of . . . probable cause to believe a juvenile committed the offense with which he was charged is not a prerequisite to his detention.

Third, the courts below concluded that circumstances surrounding most of the cases in which § 320.5(3)(b) has been invoked strongly suggest that the detainee would not have committed a crime during the period before his trial if he had been released. In a significant proportion of the cases, the juvenile had been released after his arrest and had not committed any reported crimes while at large. . . ; it is not apparent why a juvenile would be more likely to misbehave between his initial appearance and his trial than between his arrest and initial appearance. . . . "[T]he vast majority" of persons detained under § 320.5(3)(b) are released either before or immediately after their trials. . . . The inference is powerful that most detainees, when examined more carefully than at their initial appearances, are deemed insufficiently dangerous to warrant further incarceration.

The rarity with which invocation of § 320.5(3)(b) results in detention of a juvenile who otherwise would have committed a crime fatally undercuts the two public purposes assigned to the statute by the State and the majority. The argument that § 320.5(3)(b) serves "the State's *parens patriae* interest in preserving and promoting the welfare of the child," now appears particularly hollow. Most juveniles detained pursuant to the provision are not benefitted thereby, because they would not have committed crimes if left to their own devices (and thus would not have been exposed to the risk of physical injury or the perils of the cycle of recidivism). On the contrary, these juveniles suffer several serious harms: deprivation of liberty and stigmatization as "delinquent" or "dangerous," as well as impairment of their ability to prepare their legal defenses. The benefits even to those few juveniles who would have committed crimes if released are not unalloyed; the gains to them are partially offset by the aforementioned injuries. . . .

The argument that § 320.5(3)(b) protects the welfare of the community fares little better. Certainly the public reaps no benefit from incarceration of the majority of the detainees who would not have committed any crimes had they been released. Prevention of the minor offenses that would have been committed by a small proportion of the persons detained confers only a slight benefit on the community. Only in occasional cases does incarceration of a juvenile pending his trial serve to prevent a crime of violence and thereby significantly

---

[60] [21] For example, Tyrone Parson, aged 15, one of the members of the sample, was arrested for enticing others to play three-card monte. After being detained for five days under § 320.5(3)(b), the petition against him was dismissed on the ground that "the offense alleged did not come within the provisions of the penal law." . . . Prediction whether a given person will commit a crime in the future is especially difficult when he has committed only minor crimes in the past. . . .

promote the public interest. Such an infrequent and haphazard gain is insufficient to justify curtailment of the liberty interests of all the presumptively innocent juveniles who would have obeyed the law pending their trials had they been given the chance.

. . . .

C

The findings reviewed in the preceding section lend credence to the conclusion reached by the courts below: § 320.5(3)(b) "is utilized principally, not for preventive purposes, but to impose punishment for unadjudicated criminal acts." . . .

The majority contends that, of the many factors we have considered in trying to determine whether a particular sanction constitutes "punishment," . . . the most useful are "whether an alternative purpose to which [the sanction] may rationally be connected is assignable for it, and whether it appears excessive in relation to the alternative purpose assigned." Assuming, arguendo, that this test is appropriate, it requires affirmance in these cases. The alternative purpose assigned by the State to § 320.5(3)(b) is the prevention of crime by the detained juveniles. But, as has been shown, that objective is advanced at best sporadically by the provision. Moreover, § 320.5(3)(b) frequently is invoked under circumstances in which it is extremely unlikely that the juvenile in question would commit a crime while awaiting trial. The most striking of these cases involve juveniles who have been at large without mishap for a substantial period of time prior to their initial appearances and detainees who are adjudged delinquent and are nevertheless released into the community. In short, § 320.5(3)(b) as administered by the New York courts surely "appears excessive in relation to" the putatively legitimate objectives assigned to it.

The inference that § 320.5(3)(b) is punitive in nature is supported by additional materials in the record. For example, Judge Quinones and even appellants' counsel acknowledged that one of the reasons juveniles detained . . . usually are released after the determination of their guilt is that the judge decides that their pretrial detention constitutes sufficient punishment. . . . Another Family Court Judge admitted using "preventive detention" to punish one of the juveniles in the sample.[61]

In summary, application of the litmus test the Court recently has used to identify punitive sanctions supports the finding of the lower courts that preventive detention under § 320.5(3)(b) constitutes punishment. Because punishment of juveniles before adjudication of their guilt violates the Due Process Clause, the provision cannot stand.

---

[61] [29] See transcript of the initial appearance of Ramon Ramos, . . . Judge Heller presiding. . . : "This business now of being able to get guns, is now completely out of proportion. We are living in a jungle. We are living in a jungle, and it is time that these youths that are brought before the Court, know that they are in a Court, and that if these allegations are true, that they are going to pay the penalty. "As for the reasons I just state[d] on the record, . . . I am remand[ing] the respondent to the Commissioner of Juvenile Justice, secure detention."

III

If the record did not establish the impossibility, on the basis of the evidence available to a Family Court judge at a § 320.5(3)(b) hearing, of reliably predicting whether a given juvenile would commit a crime before his trial, and if the purposes relied upon by the State were promoted sufficiently to justify the deprivations of liberty effected by the provision, I would nevertheless still strike down § 320.5(3)(b) because of the absence of procedural safeguards in the provision. As Judge Newman, concurring in the Court of Appeals observed, "New York's statute is unconstitutional because it permits liberty to be denied, prior to adjudication of guilt, in the exercise of unfettered discretion as to an issue of considerable uncertainty — likelihood of future criminal behavior." . . .

Appellees point out that § 320.5(3)(b) lacks two crucial procedural constraints. First, a New York Family Court judge is given no guidance regarding what kinds of evidence he should consider or what weight he should accord different sorts of material in deciding whether to detain a juvenile. For example, there is no requirement in the statute that the judge take into account the juvenile's background or current living situation. Nor is a judge obliged to attach significance to the nature of a juvenile's criminal record or the severity of the crime for which he was arrested. Second, § 320.5(3)(b) does not specify how likely it must be that a juvenile will commit a crime before his trial to warrant his detention. The provision indicates only that there must be a "serious risk" that he will commit an offense and does not prescribe the standard of proof that should govern the judge's determination of that issue.

Not surprisingly; in view of the lack of directions provided by the statute, different judges have adopted different ways of estimating the chances whether a juvenile will misbehave in the near future. "Each judge follows his own individual approach to [the detention] determination." . . . This discretion exercised by Family Court judges in making detention decisions gives rise to two related constitutional problems. First, it creates an excessive risk that juveniles will be detained "erroneously" — i.e., under circumstances in which no public interest would be served by their incarceration. Second, it fosters arbitrariness and inequality in a decision-making process that impinges upon fundamental rights.

A

One of the purposes of imposing procedural constraints on decisions affecting life, liberty, or property is to reduce the incidence of error. . . .

As Judge Newman recognized . . . a review of [the] factors in the context of New York's preventive-detention scheme compels the conclusion that the Due Process Clause is violated by § 320.5(3)(b) in its present form. First, the private interest affected by a decision to detain a juvenile is personal liberty. Unnecessary abridgment of such a fundamental right should be avoided if at all possible. Second, there can be no dispute that there is a serious risk under the present statute that a juvenile will be detained erroneously — i.e., despite the fact that he would not commit a crime if released. The findings of fact reviewed in the preceding sections make it apparent that the vast majority of detentions pursuant to § 320.5(3)(b) advance no state interest; only rarely does the statute operate to prevent crime. This high incidence of demonstrated error should induce a reviewing court to exercise utmost care in ensuring that no procedures could be devised that would improve the accuracy of the decision-making process.

The majority purports to see no value in such additional safeguards, contending that activity of estimating the likelihood that a given juvenile will commit a crime in the near future involves subtle assessment of a host of variables, the precise weight of which cannot be determined in advance. A review of the hearings that resulted in the detention of the juveniles included in the sample of thirty-four cases reveals the majority's depiction of the decision-making process to be hopelessly idealized. For example, the operative portion of the initial appearance of Tyrone Parson, the three-card monte player, [*see* note 21, *supra,*] consisted of the following:

. . . .

[Q]: Niiss Brown, [counsel for Tyrone] how many times has Tyrone been known to the COURT?

[A]: Seven times.

[Q]: Remand the respondent.

This kind of parody of reasoned decision-making would be less likely to occur if judges were given more specific and mandatory instructions regarding the information they should consider and the manner in which they should assess it.

Third and finally, the imposition of such constraints on the deliberations of the Family Court judges would have no adverse effect on the State's interest in detaining dangerous juveniles and would give rise to insubstantial administrative burdens. For example, a simple directive to Family Court judges to state on the record the significance they give to the seriousness of the offense of which a juvenile is accused and to the nature of the juvenile's background would contribute materially to the quality of the decision-making process without significantly increasing the duration of initial appearances.

. . . Especially in view of the impracticability of correcting erroneous decisions through judicial review, the absence of meaningful procedural safeguards in the provision renders it invalid. . . .

. . . .

IV

The majority acknowledges — indeed, founds much of its argument upon — the principle that a State has both the power and the responsibility to protect the interests of the children within its jurisdiction. . . . Yet the majority today upholds a statute whose net impact on the juveniles who come within its purview is overwhelmingly detrimental. Most persons detained under the provision reap no benefit and suffer serious injuries thereby. The welfare of only a minority of the detainees is even arguably enhanced. The inequity of this regime, combined with the arbitrariness with which it is administered, is bound to disillusion its victims regarding the virtues of our system of criminal justice. I can see — and the majority has pointed to — no public purpose advanced by the statute sufficient to justify the harm it works.

I respectfully dissent.

———

NOTES AND QUESTIONS

1. In upholding the New York preventive detention measure, the Supreme Court cited, with approval, the New York Court of Appeals's observation that the state has a substantial interest in "protecting the juvenile from his own folly." In footnote 15 of *Schall*, the New York Court justifies preventive detention, *inter alia*, because juveniles are less deterable than adults, see crime as "gamesmanship" induced by peer pressure and are less responsible for their conduct because they lack mature development. Do you agree with these assessments? For support for the view that youthful offenders are less deterable than adults, see Christopher Slobegin et al., *A Prevention Model of Juvenile Justice: The Promise of* Kansas v. Hendricks *for Children*, 1999 WISC. L. REV. 185, 196–200.

2. The *Schall* Court concluded that pre-adjudication detention under the New York statute was not "punishment" for purposes of the Due Process Clause. Do you agree? Consider § 5.01[B], *supra*.

§ 5.05 ADJUDICATION

Adjudication proceedings are fact-finding hearings to determine the existence or nonexistence of the allegations specified in the petition. Where the petition alleges an act of delinquency, the court must determine whether the child committed the act. In such cases, the adjudication phase of juvenile justice is in many ways synonymous with the trial stage of the criminal system.

For these reasons, this section treats adjudication issues in the context of delinquency separate from those in status offense cases.

[A] Delinquency

[1] Procedure

Gault and its progeny articulated procedural protections in "delinquency adjudications" where "loss of liberty" is a possible consequence. While it is theoretically possible that the *Gault* line of cases may be inapplicable if the disposition for an act of delinquency does not entail a loss of liberty, the courts and legislatures have generally applied at least the *Gault* right to counsel to all delinquency adjudications, regardless of the possible disposition. In any event, the issue whether the procedural protections identified by the Supreme Court apply is moot in most jurisdictions, given that incarcerative commitments are authorized as possible dispositions for acts of delinquency.

In addition to the rights identified by the United States Supreme Court (right to notice, counsel, confrontation, protection against self-incrimination and double jeopardy, and proof of charges beyond a reasonable doubt), all jurisdictions recognize a variety of other protections associated with the criminal system as equally applicable to delinquency adjudications.

For example, courts commonly limit pre-adjudication discovery to the extent it is allowed in criminal cases, *see, e.g., Joe Z. v. Superior Court,* 478 P.2d 26 (Cal. 1970). *But see People ex rel. Hanrahan v. Felt,* 269 N.E.2d 1 (Ill. 1971) (authorizing civil discovery rules in delinquency context). Some courts hold that limited discovery rules are required even where statutory provisions explicitly provide that civil discovery rules apply to juvenile court. *See, e.g., T.P.S. v. State,* 590 S.W.2d 946, 954 (Tex. Civ. App. 1979).

Although jurisdictions typically applied no formal rules of evidence to juvenile proceedings prior to *Gault,* today the rules of evidence, including the rule against hearsay, apply in delinquency adjudications. Some states specifically apply the rules applicable in criminal trials while others apply the rules utilized in civil proceedings with, of course, the *Winship* requirement that the offense be proved beyond a reasonable doubt. *See* Samuel M. Davis, Rights of Juveniles: The Juvenile Justice System § 5.5 (2d ed. 2001).

While delinquency adjudications reflect many aspects of criminal trials, some clear differences exist. The following materials reflect two such differences.

[a] Jury Determinations

Under the *McKeiver* case, the Constitution does not require jury determinations in delinquency adjudications. While a majority of jurisdictions conduct delinquency adjudications without juries, some states statutorily provide for jury trials in delinquency cases. *See, e.g.,* Tex. Fam. Code Ann. § 54.03(c) (West Supp. 2002). As the following case illustrates, constitutional claims of a right to jury trials in delinquency cases sometimes are raised notwithstanding *McKeiver.*

IN RE FELDER

Family Court of New York, Onondaga County
402 N.Y.S.2d 528 (1978)

Edward J. McLaughlin, Judge.

This juvenile delinquency proceeding involves . . . Respondent, a boy of fifteen, [who] allegedly committed a robbery in the first degree, a designated felony. When the case came before the Court, the Respondent moved for a jury trial, asserting that under *Baldwin v. New York,* 399 U.S. 66 (1970), an individual charged with a crime where the penalty could exceed six months imprisonment is entitled to a jury trial. The respondent alleged that since he can be confined in a secure facility for a period of time up to twelve months, . . . the *Baldwin* doctrine applied, and he is entitled to a trial by jury.

On the other hand, the petitioner alleged that the United States Supreme Court decision in *McKeiver v. Pennsylvania*, 403 U.S. 528, (1971), is controlling. *McKeiver* holds that a juvenile charged with a delinquency, which precludes, by definition, criminal consequences and tried in a civil court, does not have a due process right to a jury trial. Petitioner further alleged that while New York is not constitutionally precluded from granting a jury trial under *McKeiver*, it has determined not to do so. . . .

The issue before the court, then, is whether the instant proceeding is controlled by *McKeiver* or by *Baldwin*. Specifically, the question turns on whether this is a juvenile proceeding within the meaning of *McKeiver*, or, whether so many of the attributes of a juvenile proceeding have been discarded that the proceeding is in effect "criminal" in nature and thus within the ambit of *Baldwin*.

A. IS A DESIGNATED FELONY PROCEEDING A JUVENILE PROCEEDING?

. . . .

The Legislature has chosen to label this new "designated felony concept" as a "juvenile" proceeding. It is axiomatic that this court is not bound by that designation if, in fact, the new proceeding is indeed a criminal proceeding. . . .[62]

. . . .

B. BACKGROUND OF THE JUVENILE JUSTICE SYSTEM

The fundamental substantive distinction between a juvenile proceeding and a criminal proceeding is that a juvenile disposition is limited to treatment, while a criminal proceeding may impose punishment regardless of whether the punishment results in retribution and, or, deterrence. The view that the difference between criminal and juvenile proceedings is the difference between

---

[62] [2] In holding that the Fifth Amendment protection from double jeopardy applied to juvenile proceedings, a constitutional guarantee traditionally associated with criminal prosecutions, the U.S. Supreme Court in *Breed v. Jones*, 421 U.S. 519 (1974), noted:

> "We believe it is simply too late in the day to conclude . . . that a juvenile is not put in jeopardy at a proceeding whose object is to determine whether he had committed acts that violate a criminal law and whose potential consequences include both the stigma inherent in such determination and deprivation of liberty for many years. For it is clear under our cases that determining the relevance of constitutional policies, like determining the applicability of constitutional rights, in juvenile proceedings, requires that courts eschew 'the civil labels-of-convenience which have been attached to juvenile proceedings,' *In re Gault*, 387 U.S. 1, and that 'the juvenile process . . . be candidly appraised.'"

Doubtless even a clear legislative classification of a statute as "non-penal" would not alter the fundamental nature of a plainly penal statute.

retribution and deterrence, on the one hand, and treatment, on the other, is confirmed by an examination of the history of the juvenile court system. This examination will also show that a denial of a juvenile's full exercise of his constitutional rights can only be predicated upon the presence of the treatment principle of the juvenile justice system.

At common law there were no juvenile courts or juvenile proceedings. If a child, over the age of seven, committed a criminal act, he was tried in a criminal court, and afforded all of the privileges of an adult charged with the same conduct. Thus, he was arrested, indicted by a grand jury, tried by a petit jury, and, if convicted, sent to prison. . . .

The reformers of the nineteenth century were appalled by the fact that juveniles could be given long prison sentences to be served with hardened criminals. . . . To alleviate this situation, special juvenile centers were established which were authorized to admit children convicted of petty criminal offenses. The premise of these juvenile centers was that children were not criminal offenders, and, if properly treated, could be saved from a life of crime. The juvenile reform movement later became concerned not only with the disposition received by the juveniles but with the adjudication of juveniles as well. Thus, separate court proceedings were established.

The juvenile statutes were early challenged on the basis that the statutes were criminal in nature and the procedures employed were, therefore, violative of the constitutional protection applicable to criminal proceedings. In most cases the challenges were rejected on the ground that the disposition was rehabilitative and not grounded on motivations of punishment and deterrence. . . . Where the challenge succeeded was in those situations where the proceeding was, in effect, criminal in nature. . . .

This historical examination of the origins of the juvenile justice system shows that the informality, flexibility, and, concomitantly, the absence of constitutional safeguards at juvenile proceedings was justified on the ground that the juvenile was to be treated and rehabilitated. Conversely, when the juvenile proceeding was primarily for retributive and deterrent purposes, it was considered criminal in nature, and hence subject to all of the limitations of a regular criminal proceeding. . . .

It is against this background that *McKeiver v. Pennsylvania* must be viewed. It is true that *McKeiver* stated that in a juvenile proceeding trial by jury is not a constitutional requirement. The Court specifically refused to abandon the salutary goals of the juvenile system and rejected the jury trial because it could "tend to place the juvenile squarely in the routine of the criminal process." . . . In effect, the Court deferred until a more appropriate occasion the determination of when a juvenile disposition fails to meet the rehabilitative premise of the juvenile system. The determination in *McKeiver* that in a juvenile proceeding a jury trial is not required, is, therefore, necessarily limited to those proceedings that are juvenile in nature. Thus, there is no requirement of a jury trial in family court where the disposition is rehabilitative and non-penal. When, however, the protections provided to the juvenile criminal offender have been so eroded away that what is actually a punishment is characterized as a treatment, an abuse of constitutional dimension has occurred, and, a jury trial is required before punishment, although appropriate, may be inflicted.

. . . .

D. AN ANALYSIS OF THE 1976 ACT

A significant change made by the Juvenile Justice Reform Act is the requirement that restrictive placement may be ordered for a juvenile found to have committed a designated felony, when the court determines that a juvenile requires such restrictive placement. . . . Once restrictive placement is ordered by the court, the delinquent must remain in the placement for twelve months, if the placement results from an adjudication on a Class A designated felony, or for six months, if the placement results from the adjudication of any designated felony. . . . Further, during the period of restrictive placement, the right to petition the court to stay the execution, to set aside, modify, or vacate the disposition is suspended. It is this suspension of the provisions of part six, Article 7, of the Family Court Act which distinguishes a restrictive placement disposition from all other dispositions under Article 7. Thus, the Legislature has created a definite sentence of placement nearly indistinguishable from definite sentences imposed upon adults under § 70.20(2) of the Penal Law.

Further, in mandating the minimum period of restrictive placement, when restrictive placement has been found to be needed at all, the Legislature has introduced two other concepts of the criminal justice process previously unknown in the juvenile system. First, the length of the commitment is determined by the act committed rather than by the needs of the child, and second, the sentence is mandatory. In effect, the Legislature has determined that a child who at the time of his dispositional hearing requires restrictive placement will continue to require restrictive placement for the entire period of the minimum sentence. Prior to the enactment of this statute, the court was only required to determine that at the time of the dispositional hearing the needs of the child were for placement in an institution and that at any time during that initial period, if the child was successfully rehabilitated, he was entitled to release. Consistent with this philosophy of treatment was the provision that if at the end of the initial placement the child was not successfully rehabilitated, then, the period of placement could be extended. In effect, once the court makes a finding that restrictive placement is needed at the time of the disposition, the act then mandates a minimum sentence, a result which is more harsh on the juvenile than is the criminal procedure for the adult who is entitled to an indeterminate sentence in nearly all cases. . . .

The distinction between indeterminate and determinate sentencing is not semantic, but indicates fundamentally different public policies. Indeterminate sentencing is based upon notions of rehabilitation, while determinate sentencing is based upon a desire for retribution or punishment.

In his vigorous dissent *In re Gault*, 387 U.S. 1 (1967), Mr. Justice Stewart succinctly distinguished the purpose and mission of the juvenile system of justice from the purpose and mission of the criminal system. "The object of the one [juvenile] is correcting a condition. The object of the other [criminal] is conviction and punishment for a criminal act." . . . By mandating restrictive placement in a secure facility for a minimum of six months, the Legislature has created a disposition that more nearly resembles a punishment than a treatment and, thereby, has blurred the clearly distinct objectives of the juvenile justice system with those of the criminal justice system.

The thinly disguised intent of the Legislature to punish an adjudicated designated felon, based upon the criminal act and upon the characteristics of the victim of the criminal act, as opposed to rehabilitating and treating a juvenile offender is revealed by the 1977 amendment to § 753-a of the Family Court Act which states: ". . . the court shall order a restrictive placement in any case where the respondent is found to have committed a designated felony act in which the respondent inflicted serious physical injury . . . upon another person who is sixty-two years of age or more." . . . This court does not deny that punishment may be appropriate for certain designated felons. This court does insist, however, that deprivation of liberty for purposes of punishment based on the nature of criminal acts committed must be surrounded by constitutional protections not now available in family court proceedings.

The very heart of the rehabilitative nature of the juvenile justice system in New York is the array of remedies provided in part six of Article 7 of the Family Court Act, for it is these remedies that have protected the right of a juvenile to an indeterminate sentence. . . . It is the indeterminate quality of a juvenile disposition that makes the disposition rehabilitative. To refuse to allow a part six motion to modify or to terminate a placement gives the disposition clearly criminal characteristics.

E. TREATMENT

The Juvenile Justice Reform Act requires that treatment be available at restrictive placement facilities. The availability and quality of treatment available to the respondent is not at issue here. What is at issue is the mandatory time period required for treatment.

Analogies may be made between the treatment of persons confined because of mental illness and juveniles confined because of delinquency. Serious consideration has been given recently to the constitutional rights of persons involuntarily committed to mental hospitals following non-criminal dispositions. In identifying treatment as a right for the mentally ill, for instance, a court concluded that at the least an institution must make a bona fide effort to cure, since the purpose of the involuntary hospitalization is treatment, not punishment. . . .

Juveniles also have a right to treatment. . . . Moreover, one court has found that "the right to treatment" includes "the right to individualized care and treatment." The reasoning of the court is helpful in analyzing time limited restrictive placement: "Because children differ in their need for rehabilitation, individual need for treatment will differ. . . . Without a program of individual treatment the result may be that the juveniles will not be rehabilitated, but warehoused, and that at the termination of detention they will likely be incapable of taking their proper places in free society; their interests and those of the state thereby being defeated." . . .

Clearly, treatment may result in a cure in six days, or in six weeks, or in six months, or in one year, or never! By setting a mandatory minimum time period for restrictive placement, treatment becomes indistinguishable from punishment.

F. INTAKE A CRITICAL STAGE IN DESIGNATED FELONY ACT PROCEEDINGS

Intake proceedings are a unique feature of the juvenile justice system in this state. The intake conference provides for a screening out of cases not suited to court intervention. . . . It is designed to return the juvenile to the community prior to the formulation of a petition. . . . The intake procedure of the family court, as it applies to juvenile delinquency, confers authority on the probation service to offer informal, voluntary conferences to settle the differences between the petitioner and the respondent. In fact, in his concurring opinion in *McKeiver*, Mr. Justice White said that "the distinctive intake policies and procedures of the juvenile court system to a great extent obviate [the] important function of the jury." . . .

Under the 1976 amendments to the Family Court Act, a juvenile accused of a designated felony must obtain the "prior written approval of a judge of the court" before an adjustment may take place. . . . It had been the rule in New York that "no statement made during a preliminary conference may be admitted into evidence at a fact finding hearing. . . ." This rule had been interpreted as a protection for the respondent against self incrimination, and, thus, the intake conference had not been considered a "critical" stage of adjudication and, therefore, the child was not entitled to counsel at the conference. . . .

It now appears that the kind of information previously protected during intake proceedings and not admitted as evidence in fact finding hearings must be made available to the court before the court can determine whether the case is, or is not, suitable for adjustment. Thus, the informality, responsiveness, and flexibility of the intake proceeding, a unique tool of the juvenile justice process, is vitiated, and intake becomes a critical stage of the proceedings and the protection of the constitutional rights of the respondent becomes essential. Whether a respondent is entitled to counsel at a designated felony intake conference is now certainly a consideration. . . .

. . . .

H. THE NEED FOR A JURY TRIAL

The revision of the Family Court Act by the Juvenile Justice Reform Act of 1976 transformed a purely rehabilitative juvenile statute into a statute that mirrors a retributive criminal statute, but fails to reflect the constitutional protections presumed to apply to such statutes. This transformation is most particularly evidenced by the requirement of restrictive placement in a secure facility for a definite period of time for a person found to have committed a designated felony and to be in need of restrictive placement with no provision for changing the placement if rehabilitation of the juvenile offender is found to have occurred. Other aspects of the revision also indicate that the designated felony proceeding is in its very essence a criminal proceeding, although labeled a juvenile proceeding. Since it is essentially a criminal proceeding, it is required that all the safeguards mandated by the United States Constitution be afforded the accused.

The particular constitutional safeguard now before the court is the Sixth Amendment right to a trial by jury. Since it is the conclusion of this court that the designated felony portions of the Juvenile Justice Reform Act of 1976 are fundamentally criminal in nature, the respondent is entitled to a trial by jury for a criminal prosecution.

Were it possible to extend this right to the respondent, no serious problem would arise. Unfortunately, it is not possible for this court to have the facts determined by a jury, since the law in this state is clear that no court may conduct a trial by jury unless such proceeding is authorized by statute. . . .

The quandary thus created for the court is, may it proceed in this case given its inability to extend a right to a trial by jury? And further, if it may so proceed; how does it protect the rights of the respondent and the rights of society?

It is the determination of this court that it is entitled to proceed to the fact finding hearing on this alleged act of delinquency without a jury, provided that prior to the taking of any testimony the court advises the respondent that regardless of the outcome, this court will not order restrictive placement, and this it now does. . . .

If the alleged facts are proven, thereby giving this court jurisdiction to make a disposition, and if at that dispositional hearing it is determined that placement is necessary, such disposition will be ordered and the respondent may be placed for an initial period of eighteen months. If the treatment is not completed at the end of such time, placement will be extended within the provisions of the law and, accordingly, the right of society to be protected from further depredations will be as effectively insured as if a restrictive placement were ordered, and at the same time the right of the respondent to modification of that disposition as soon as he responds to treatment will be preserved.

Accordingly, motion for trial by jury is denied.

———

NOTES AND QUESTIONS

1. Do you agree that the "designated felony" provisions of the New York system manifest punitive juvenile justice? Consider again § 5.02 [B], *supra*. For a discussion of the movement towards punishment within juvenile court systems, see Martin R. Gardner, *Punitive Juvenile Justice: Some Observations on a Recent Trend*, 10 INT'L. J.L. & PSYCHIATRY 129 (1987); Andrew Walkover, *The Infancy Defense in the New Juvenile Court*, 31 UCLA L. REV. 503, 523–24 n. 82 (1980) (detailing list of jurisdictions adopting punitive or partially punitive models of juvenile justice). *See also* § 5.06[B][2], *infra*.

2. Other New York courts disagree with *Felder* and hold that juveniles do not enjoy a right to jury trial when subjected to the sanctions imposed in designated felony proceedings. *People v. Young,* 99 Misc. 2d 328, 416 N.Y.S.2d. 171 (Fam. Ct., Monroe County 1979); *In re William M.,* 90 Misc. 2d 173, 393 N.Y.S.2d 535 (Fam. Ct., Kings County 1977).

Along similar lines, in *State v. Lawley,* 591 P.2d 772, 773 (Wash. 1979), the Washington Supreme Court recognized that recent legislative revisions had imposed a system of "punishment commensurate with the age, crime, and criminal history of the juvenile offender." Nevertheless, the court denied the applicability of the Sixth Amendment right to trial by jury, in part because the legislature might have concluded that "punishment [may do] as much to rehabilitate, correct and direct an errant youth as does the prior philosophy of focusing upon the particular characteristics of the individual juvenile." *Id.* Do you agree with the court's analysis? Consider § 5.02[B], *supra.*

[b] Closed Proceedings

Historically, juvenile proceedings were not open to the public. Indeed, statutes in most states currently exclude the general public from hearings in juvenile court, although the courts are often allowed discretion to admit persons with significant interests in the proceedings. On the other hand, the Sixth Amendment guarantees a right to a public trial in all criminal prosecutions. The underlying rationale of the public trial right has been explained as follows:

> Essentially, the public-trial guarantee embodies a view of human nature, true as a general rule, that judges, lawyers, witnesses, and jurors will perform their respective functions more responsibly in an open court than in secret proceedings. . . . A fair trial is the objective, and "public trial" is an institutional safeguard for attaining it. Thus the right of "public trial" is not one belonging to the public, but one belonging to the accused, and inhering in the institutional process by which justice is administered.

Estes v. Texas, 381 U.S. 532, 588 (1965) (Harlan, J., concurring).

Although the Supreme Court has suggested that juveniles might be entitled to the presence of their friends and relatives at delinquency adjudications, the Court has not addressed the issue of whether the public trial provision applies to juvenile courts. The *McKeiver* plurality's rejection of jury trials as the possible harbingers of "public trials" that would frustrate the traditional "intimacy" of juvenile proceedings suggests that the Court might deny juveniles the right to a public trial.

The cases that follow question the legality of closed juvenile proceedings. The *R.L.R.* case considers whether public trials are mandated as a matter of state constitutional law, while *In re J.S.* addresses arguments for public proceedings made by the press.

R.L.R v. STATE

Supreme Court of Alaska
487 P.2d 27 (1971)

RABINOWITZ, JUSTICE.

This appeal raises significant issues regarding the constitutional rights of a child to a public jury trial. . . .

A probation officer for the Division of Corrections, Department of Health and Welfare, filed a petition alleging that RLR, a person under eighteen-years-old, had unlawfully sold lysergic acid diethylamide (LSD) to Joseph Want on or about December 11, 1968, and praying that RLR be adjudicated a delinquent. RLR denied the allegations. Initially, a hearing was held to perpetuate the testimony of one William J. Gowans, a chemist employed by the United States Department of Justice. RLR was not present at this proceeding, although his attorney was present. Gowans testified that a substance he had received from the Fairbanks police department was, in his opinion, LSD. At a full adjudicative hearing with RLR present, Joseph W. Want, apparently a part-time secret informer for the Fairbanks police department, testified that he had purchased "a hit" from RLR at a pool hall on December 11 or 12, 1968, and had given the tablet to a police officer. Paul W. Tannenbaum, a Fairbanks police officer, testified that he had given Want money to buy drugs and several hours later Want had given him the tablet Gowans identified as LSD. RLR testified that he had been in school at the time the alleged sale was made, and did not sell LSD to Want. The court found that the allegations of the petition had been proved and adjudicated RLR a delinquent. At the disposition hearing, which was presided over by a judge other than the one who presided at the adjudicative hearing, the court decided to continue custody in the Division of Corrections, Department of Health and Welfare, for an indefinite time up to RLR's 21st birthday, on the understanding that he was to be boarded at a ranch south of Fairbanks on a trial basis. One week later a formal disposition order was entered in which it was ordered that the Department of Health and Welfare have custody of RLR and authority to place him in a foster home, detention home, or other facility without further application to the court. This appeal followed.

. . . .

PUBLIC TRIAL

The Federal and Alaska's Constitutions provide that "[i]n all criminal prosecutions, the accused shall enjoy ['have' in Alaska's Constitution] the right to a . . . public trial. . . ." The sentence guaranteeing the right also guarantees the rights to speedy trial and an impartial jury. The leading case on public trial, *Re Oliver*, [333 U.S. 257 (1948),] holds that the Due Process Clause of the Fourteenth Amendment prohibits secret trials in criminal proceedings. *Oliver* says that the traditional Anglo-American distrust for secret trials has been attributed to the despotism of the Spanish Inquisition, the English Court of Star Chamber, and the French lettre de cachet, and quotes Bentham's charge that secret proceedings produce "indolent and arbitrary" judges, unchecked no matter how "corrupt" by recordation and appeal. The court cites as values of a public trial that it safeguards against attempts to employ the courts as instruments of persecution, restrains abuse of judicial power, brings the proceedings to the attention of key witnesses not known to the parties, and teaches the spectators about their government and gives them confidence in their judicial remedies.

. . . .

Appellant argues that he was denied his constitutional right to a public trial by AS 47.10.070. That statute provides in relevant part that:

> [t]he public shall be excluded from the hearing, but the court, in its discretion, may permit individuals to attend a hearing, if their attendance is compatible with the best interest of the minor.

Rules of Children's Procedure 12(d)(2) provides that:

> [c]hild hearings shall not be open to the general public. The court may, however, in its discretion after due consideration for the welfare of the child and of the public interest, admit particular individuals to the hearing.

The federal constitutional guarantee has not been construed to mean that all judicial proceedings must be open to any interested member of the public at any time. Some authorities hold that the right to public trial belongs to the public as well as the defendant so public trial is not subject to defendant's waiver, while others hold that the guarantee is for the benefit of the accused, and may be asserted or waived only by him. In both the federal and Alaska's constitutions, the right to public trial is part of a list of rights explicitly stated to be rights of the accused. Some jurisdictions hold that the general public may be excluded consistently with the public trial guarantee so long as the defendant has an opportunity to designate those whom he desires to have present. Others take the view that the general public cannot be excluded in this way. Where the right has been denied, no prejudice need be shown, since such a showing would be almost impossible to make. The right may be waived. We [have] held that unintentional brief exclusion of a newspaper reporter from part of the reading back to the jury of a section of testimony previously given, when at least one other spectator was present, did not deny the right to public trial.

[At least one case] holds that despite *Gault*, juveniles are not constitutionally entitled to public trial. It is weak authority, however, since it so concludes merely by labeling delinquency proceedings non-criminal, rather than by analyzing the purposes of the public trial requirement to see whether they would be served by applying the right to delinquency proceedings. Many authorities favor a policy in delinquency proceedings of avoiding total secrecy by admitting persons with a special interest in the case or the work of the court, including perhaps the press, but prohibiting disclosure of juveniles' names and excluding the general public. Various reasons are given for this policy. It is said that permitting an audience to attend the hearing would interfere with the "case work relationship" between the judge and the child. Publicity is condemned on the grounds that it is an additional and excessive punishment to that prescribed by the court, or in the alternative that it encourages delinquency by permitting a youngster to "flaunt his unregeneracy." Publication of names of juvenile delinquents is condemned on the ground that it confirms the child in his delinquent identity and impedes his integration into law-abiding society by reducing his ability to obtain legitimate employment, qualify for licenses and bonds, and join the armed services. . . .

Just as alleged bad motives of the legislature cannot be considered in determining constitutionality and construction of statutes, so we cannot withhold application of federal and state constitutional provisions on the grounds that those who created various systems of governmental activity such as the juvenile court acted from benevolent motives. Nor will constitutional problems be ignored in deference to untested empirical propositions about what sorts of judicial proceedings succeed in rehabilitating persons charged with misconduct; as between these sorts of prescriptions for what is good for society and constitutional prescriptions, the latter are authoritative. The reasons for the constitutional guarantees of public trial apply as much to juvenile delinquency proceedings as to adult criminal proceedings.[63] Delinquency proceedings as much as adult criminal prosecutions can be used as instruments of persecution, and may be subject to judicial abuse. The appellate process is not a sufficient check on juvenile courts, for problems of mootness and the cost of prosecuting an appeal screen most of what goes on from appellate court scrutiny. We cannot help but notice that the children's cases appealed to this court have often shown much more extensive and fundamental error than is generally found in adult criminal cases, and wonder whether secrecy is not fostering a judicial attitude of casualness toward the law in children's proceedings. In any event, "civil labels and good intentions do not themselves obviate the need for criminal due process safeguards in juvenile courts," for "[a] proceeding where the issue is whether the child will be found to be 'delinquent' and subjected to the loss of his liberty for years is comparable in seriousness to a felony prosecution."

Therefore, we hold that children are guaranteed the right to a public trial by the Alaska Constitution.

One additional facet of the child's right to a public trial remains to be considered. AS 47.10.070,[64] and the similar Children's Rule 12(d)(2), provide

---

[63] [71] Some of these reasons parallel those underlying the constitutional guarantees of jury trial. In one commentator's view, the jury provides the citizenry, in their capacity as jurors, with a vehicle to directly participate in government, that the jury system induces public confidence in the administration of justice; and that the jury system helps to insure the independence and the quality of the judges.

[64] [74] AS 47.10.070 provides in part that:

> "The public shall be excluded from the hearing, but the court, in its discretion, may permit individuals to attend a hearing, if their attendance is compatible with the best interests of the minor."

The statute providing for exclusion of the public from juvenile hearings is procedural, so is outside the scope of legislative authority unless two-thirds of each house of the legislature votes to change the rule promulgated by the supreme court in this matter. Children's proceedings are among the "civil and criminal cases in all courts" over which this constitutional provision gives this court

for the exclusion of the public from children's hearings. Rules of Children's Procedure 12(d)(2), which governs, provides that:

> Child hearings shall not be open to the general public. The court may, however, in its discretion after due consideration for the welfare of the child and of the public interest, admit particular individuals to the hearing.

This flexible rule must be interpreted and applied in a manner consistent with the child's constitutional right to public trial. The evils of secrecy may be avoided by permitting the child to open the adjudicative and dispositive hearings to any individuals. Where the child's choice may be adverse to his own interests, a guardian *ad litem* may be appointed under the principles discussed in the preceding section dealing with the right to trial by jury. It is an abuse of discretion for the court to refuse admittance to individuals whose presence is favored by the child, except in special circumstances such as the unavailability of a courtroom sufficiently large to hold all the individuals whose presence is sought. If the child or his guardian *ad litem* wants the press, friends, or others to be free to attend, then the hearing must be open to them: The area of discretion in the rule, where the court may refuse to open the hearing, involves persons whose presence is not desired by the child. Since we have determined that the case must be reversed on other grounds, we find it unnecessary to decide whether the denial of a public trial in the adjudicative stage in the case at bar was plain error.

. . . .

The superior court's adjudicative and dispositive orders are vacated and reversed, and the matter remanded for appropriate proceedings.

IN RE J. S.

Supreme Court of Vermont
438 A.2d 1125 (1981)

UNDERWOOD, JUSTICE.

A juvenile, J. S., appeals from an order of the juvenile court allowing the public to attend proceedings to adjudge him a delinquent child for his alleged participation in the murder of one girl and the sexual assault of another.

In an attempt to comply with the confidentiality provisions of our juvenile shield law, 33 V.S.A. § 651, one trial judge issued an order of closure which barred the public from the proceedings. The Burlington Free Press was granted permission to intervene for the sole purpose of being heard on its petition for access to any and all of the proceedings involving J. S. A second trial judge granted the petition, holding that 33 V.S.A. § 651(c) violated the

---

rule-making authority which is intended to be plenary and not capable of reduction by re-labeling of proceedings.

The statute making criminal the publication by newspapers, radio stations, and television stations of juvenile delinquents' names, [is] not challenged in this appeal.

First Amendment. He ordered that J. S.'s juvenile proceedings be held in open court and that the public and the news media be permitted to attend.

J. S. sought relief from this order . . . seeking to vacate the order and to exclude the public.

. . . .

The principal question before us is whether the limited holding of *Richmond Newspapers, Inc. v. Virginia*, 448 U.S. 555 (1980), that the First Amendment contains a right of access to criminal trials extends to a juvenile proceeding to determine delinquency and treatment. We must also consider additional arguments put forward by the Free Press in support of public proceedings.

Only a brief recital of the facts is necessary to enable us to grapple with the legal issues raised in this appeal. Two 12-year-old Essex Junction girls were brutally assaulted by two persons in or near an area park. One was killed. The other, left for dead, managed to survive. J. S. and a 16-year-old are the alleged assailants. J. S., who is 15, has been charged as a juvenile delinquent and will have his proceedings heard in juvenile court. The 16-year-old is awaiting trial as an adult in superior court on charges of first-degree murder and sexual assault.

Our juvenile shield law requires that juvenile court proceedings be confidential. The relevant portions of that law provide:

> (c) Except in hearings to declare a person in contempt of court, the general public shall be excluded from hearings under this chapter and only the parties, their counsel, witnesses and other persons accompanying a party for his assistance and such other persons as the court finds to have a proper interest in the case or in the work of the court, may be admitted by the court. If the court finds that it is to the best interest and welfare of the child, his presence may be temporarily excluded, except while a charge of his delinquency is being heard at the hearing on the petition.

> (d) There shall be no publicity given by any person to any proceedings under the authority of this chapter except with the consent of the child and his parent or guardian. 33 V.S.A § 651.

On appeal, J. S. contends that 33 V.S.A § 651 (c) mandates that the juvenile proceedings be closed to the public and the news media, and that closed proceedings are perfectly consistent with the United States and Vermont Constitutions. The State, in effect, concurs. Both J. S. and the State ask us to reverse the court below and close the proceedings.

The Free Press makes three arguments in support of public proceedings: (1) The court below was correct in holding that 33 V.S.A § 651(c) was unconstitutional. (2) Even if the statute is constitutional, the proceedings should be public because the court below erroneously found itself without discretion under § 651(c) to admit reporters, and in the proper exercise of that discretion, they should be admitted. (3) Even if we disagree with the first two arguments, the publicity involving J. S. has been and will be so pervasive that the reasons for confidentiality no longer exist, so a special exception from the general requirement of confidentiality should be made in this case to allow public access. We disagree with all three arguments and therefore reverse.

I

The Free Press claims that *Richmond Newspapers* dictates that the general public and the news media have a First Amendment right to attend juvenile delinquency proceedings and to publicly report what they see and hear in the juvenile court during those proceedings.

The question facing the Supreme Court in the *Richmond Newspapers* case, however, was whether the public and press possess a constitutional right of access to criminal trials. The Supreme Court concluded that such a right existed. The plurality held that the combination of the unbroken tradition of open criminal trials at common law and the fact that openness of criminal trials serves important First Amendment goals requires public access, absent overriding interests. That limited holding, however, does not extend to the case at hand.

Far from a tradition of openness, juvenile proceedings are almost invariably closed. All 50 states, in fact, have some sort of juvenile shield law to limit public access. Further, juvenile proceedings are not criminal prosecutions, a fact which makes at least some of the First Amendment purposes served by open criminal trials inapplicable. Finally, inherent in the very nature of juvenile proceedings are compelling interests in confidentiality which the Supreme Court itself has endorsed in cases cited below, and which we hold override any remaining First Amendment goals which access might serve.

A

The holding in *Richmond Newspapers* applies only to criminal trials. Our juvenile law expressly provides that juvenile proceedings are not criminal. The very purpose of the juvenile delinquency law is to provide an alternative to criminal prosecutions of children. Thus, the Legislature has stated: (a) The purposes of this chapter are:

. . . .

(2) to remove from children committing delinquent acts the taint of criminality and the consequences of criminal behavior. . . .

. . . .

(b) The provisions of this chapter shall be construed as superseding the provisions of the criminal law of this state to the extent the same are inconsistent herewith. 33 V.S.A § 631. An order of the juvenile court in proceedings under this chapter shall not be deemed a conviction of crime. . . .

33 V.S.A. § 662(a).

We underscore the fundamental characteristic of a juvenile proceeding:

It is a protective proceeding entirely concerned with the welfare of the child, and is not punitive. The procedures supersede the provisions of the criminal law and laws affecting minors in conflict with the authorizations of the juvenile court statutes. The inquiry relates to proper custody for the child, not his guilt or innocence as a criminal offender. The only issue in a juvenile proceeding is the care, needs and protection of the minor and his rehabilitation and restoration to useful citizenship.

B

The court below compared the similarities and differences of juvenile proceedings and criminal trials, cited the United States Supreme Court decisions in *Breed v. Jones*, 421 U.S. 519 (1975); *In re Winship*, 397 U.S. 358 (1970); and *In re Gault*, 387 U.S. 1 (1967), and concluded that a juvenile proceeding was a criminal prosecution for the purposes of the First Amendment. The differences and similarities it discussed were irrelevant in light of the fundamental distinction between the punitive purpose of a criminal prosecution and the rehabilitative purpose of a juvenile proceeding.

The cases cited by the court below do not support the proposition for which they were cited. Each merely extended certain procedural protections to the juvenile. Nothing in any one of them suggests that the Legislature may not further protect the juvenile by closing the proceedings. If anything, the great concern for the welfare of the child that they demonstrate suggests that the child's interests should prevail when in conflict with public access. To the extent that they are relevant at all, the precedents cited by the court below indicate that confidentiality is appropriate.

Thus it appears to us that a juvenile proceeding is so unlike a criminal prosecution that the limited right of access described in *Richmond Newspapers* does not govern. Certainly, neither the United States nor Vermont Constitutions expressly mandate a right of access. Nor do our opinions or those of the United States Supreme Court hint that such a right exists. The court below was in error when it held otherwise.

C

Even if there were some constitutional right of access which presumptively reached juvenile proceedings, public access would not automatically follow. Rather, the First Amendment interests would first have to be weighed against the countervailing interests in confidentiality.

The punitive purpose of criminal proceedings raises First Amendment issues which are not present here. There, public access serves as a check against unjust conviction, excessive punishment and the undeserved taint of criminality. The juvenile proceeding, by contrast, involves no criminal conviction, no punishment, and, when confidential, no taint of criminality. Thus fewer First Amendment interests are at stake here than was the case in *Richmond Newspapers*.

The other side of the balance, however, is more heavily weighted here than in *Richmond Newspapers*. The compelling interests in confidential juvenile proceedings have been recognized and implicitly endorsed by the United States Supreme Court.

Justice Rehnquist has reiterated the Supreme Court's concern for maintaining the confidentiality of juvenile proceedings:

> It is a hallmark of our juvenile justice system in the United States that virtually from its inception at the end of the last century its proceedings have been conducted outside of the public's full gaze and the youths brought before our juvenile courts have been shielded from publicity. This insistence on confidentiality is born of a tender concern for the welfare of the child, to hide his youthful errors and 'bury them in the graveyard of the forgotten past.' The prohibition of publication of a juvenile's name is designed to protect the young person from the stigma of his misconduct and is rooted in the principle that a court concerned with juvenile affairs serves as a rehabilitative and protective agency of the State.

Smith v. Daily Mail Publishing Co., 443 U.S. at 107 (Rehnquist, J., concurring) (citations omitted).

Even *Davis v. Alaska*, [415 U.S. 308 (1974)], cited by the Free Press for the proposition that the State's interest in keeping juvenile matters confidential must yield to an overwhelming First Amendment right, supports the opposite conclusion. The Court there assumed the propriety of confidentiality in juvenile proceedings when it said, "We do not and need not challenge the State's interest as a matter of its own policy in the administration of criminal justice to seek to preserve the anonymity of a juvenile offender." If a right of access existed, there certainly could be no anonymity.

The holding in the *Davis* case only went so far as to protect the defendant's Sixth Amendment right to cross-examination in the context of the factual situation confronting that court. The Court concluded that the State's witness, a juvenile called to identify the defendant, must submit to cross-examination about his juvenile delinquency record, because the defendant's right outweighed the state interest.

Any right of the Free Press to report what takes place in juvenile court is hardly equivalent to the defendant's right to cross-examine the witness who fingered him as the prime suspect in a breaking and entering case, especially where a possible motive of the juvenile for turning State's witness was to take the heat off himself as a suspect in the same crime.

There are, however, many reasons why the State's compelling interests in the confidential juvenile proceedings prescribed by 33 V.S.A. § 651(c) and 33 V.S.A. § 651(d) override the countervailing interests of the public and the news media in access to those proceedings and the news media's interest in publicly disseminating what its reporters learn while attending.

Publication of the youth's name could impair the rehabilitative goals of the juvenile justice system. Confidential proceedings protect the delinquent from the stigma of conduct which may be outgrown and avoids the possibility that the adult is penalized for what he used to be, or worse yet, the possibility that the stigma becomes self-perpetuating, thereby making change and growth impossible. Publication of a delinquent's name may handicap his prospects for adjustment into society, for acceptance by the public, or it may cause him to lose employment opportunities. Public proceedings could so embarrass the youth's family members that they withhold their support in rehabilitative efforts.

The argument of the Free Press that its pervasive newspaper publicity has already compromised these goals and so it ought to be allowed to attend and publicize the proceedings concerning J. S., ignores still another purpose served by confidentiality. Publicity sometimes serves as a reward for the hardcore juvenile delinquent, thereby encouraging him to commit further antisocial acts to attract attention. Further, the legislative goals of expunging the juvenile's delinquency record are vitiated if the same information could at any subsequent time be obtained freely from newspaper morgues.

Neither the Vermont nor the United States Constitution, as interpreted by the United States Supreme Court or our Court, provides a right of public access which overrides the compelling interests served by our juvenile confidentiality shield statutes. The trial court erred in holding otherwise and must be reversed.

II

The Free Press insists, however, that its reporters are among those persons contemplated by the Legislature as having "a proper interest in the case or in the work of the court," and that the second judge erred when he intimated in his order that the statute gave him no discretion to grant news reporters access to juvenile proceedings.

This argument collides with 33 V.S.A. § 651(d), which specifically prohibits any of those persons admitted under § 651(c) from publicly disseminating information gained from a juvenile hearing "except with the consent of the child and his parent or guardian." No provision is made in either § 651(c) or § 651(d) to give the judge discretion to permit public dissemination of these proceedings.

The Free Press, however, would have us hold that § 651 (c) gives the judge discretion to admit their reporters and that § 651(d) forbids them from publishing what they learn once admitted. So construed, they say, § 651(d) is unenforceable as an unconstitutional prior restraint of the press in violation of the First Amendment.

This statutory interpretation runs afoul of common sense and the canons of construction which we observe to keep ourselves within the bounds of judicial authority. Our function is not to pass upon the validity of a legislative concern or the wisdom of the means the Legislature chooses to address that concern, but merely to make sure that no constitutional bounds are exceeded.

When faced with a choice, we assume that the Legislature intended a constitutional result and construe statutes accordingly. . . . Further, we avoid a construction which leads to absurd or irrational results. Reading § 651(c) and § 651(d) together, to give effect to each, leads to the inescapable result that a desire to publicly disseminate the facts of a juvenile proceeding is not "a proper interest in the case or in the work of the court."

These two sections of the juvenile shield law are clear and unambiguous. The Legislature did not intend that either the news media or the general public should attend juvenile hearings or report what transpired there. We do not base this conclusion on a single sentence or word or phrase in a sentence, but we have looked at the provisions of the whole juvenile law, and to its objects and its policy.

III

The Free Press and other members of the news media apparently obtained the name of J. S. and his involvement in the murder and sexual assault of the two young girls in Essex Junction after examining the affidavits of probable cause in the two cases pending against the 16-year-old adult in superior court. Information about the juvenile will inevitably be disclosed at the adult's trial. Because this legally obtained information has been flagrantly publicized by the news media, and because more is to come, the Free Press next argues there is no longer any reason for the confidentiality imposed by 33 V.S.A. § 651(c) and § 651(d) and the Court should drop the barriers for this case as a special exception.

This argument also has several flaws. First, as we have already noted, publicity sometimes serves as a reward for incorrigible delinquents, encouraging the very behavior sought to be deterred. Secondly, this approach calls for a case by case analysis to determine if, when, and to what extent access to juvenile proceedings should be limited. Third, such a case by case analysis lets the news media determine which juvenile proceedings will be open to the public simply by turning up the volume of publicity concerning any case that strikes their fancy. Fourth, decisions to open proceedings will then be based, not on the child's needs, but on chance circumstances. Finally, it is not just the name of delinquents which are protected by the juvenile shield law. Other matters which surface in a juvenile proceeding are just as worthy of anonymity as the juvenile's name. They include the very fact of the adjudication of delinquency and the taint of criminality emanating therefrom; the specific program of treatment, training and rehabilitation ordered and the locale in which it takes place; the name of the individual or organization to whom custody of the juvenile may be entrusted; the fact and conditions of probation; disposition reports and recommendations made by the commissioner of social and rehabilitation services or the commissioner of corrections to the juvenile court; the disposition order of the juvenile court; law enforcement reports and files concerning the minor, as well as fingerprints and photographs, and the files and records of the juvenile court itself, including dismissal of the petition. These are all part and parcel of the record of a young person's life which the Legislature shielded from public access.

IV

To summarize, the Free Press has failed to establish that any right of access to J. S.'s juvenile proceeding is contained in the United States or Vermont Constitutions. The juvenile shield law does not give the court below discretion to make the proceedings public. The fact that J. S.'s name is already a household word in Essex Junction, and that the nature of the offense and his alleged participation with a named adult defendant in certain crimes will be disclosed in the trial of the adult, is no reason to dismantle our juvenile court system. Confidential proceedings continue to serve overriding interests.

Any limitations in the juvenile justice system will not be cured by a public trial of J. S. If the Free Press feels that the underlying purposes of our juvenile laws are outmoded and no longer valid, it should not look to this Court, but to the Legislature to change the law. Only the Legislature has the power to relax the limitations imposed by 33 V.S.A. § 651(c) and § 651(d) upon the general public and the news media if it believes that would be more desirable than the present law. As of the commencement of these juvenile proceedings against J. S., however, the legislative intent is clear. Juveniles, as a class, are shielded from public exposure of any proceedings conducted in juvenile court to determine delinquency.

The order of the District Court of Vermont, Unit No. 2, Chittenden Circuit, granting the public and the press the right to attend any and all proceedings in juvenile court concerning J. S. is reversed.

————

NOTES AND QUESTIONS

1. Do you agree with the *R.L.S.* court that "the reasons for the constitutional guarantees of public trial apply as much to juvenile delinquency proceedings as to adult criminal proceedings"?

Do you suppose that the court's view that juvenile court cases tend to show "much more extensive and fundamental error than is generally found in adult criminal cases" is unique to Alaska? If not, should courts and legislatures of other jurisdictions require public adjudications as a remedy? Do the advantages of public proceedings outweigh the disadvantages?

2. Are you convinced by the reasoning of the *J. S.* court for denying press access to juvenile proceedings? How compelling is the court's argument that "[f]ar from a tradition of openness, juvenile proceedings are almost invariably closed?" Were not similar arguments from tradition rejected in *Gault, Winship,* and *Breed*? Do you agree with the court's conclusion that, unlike criminal cases, juvenile proceedings involve "no punishment"? Does such a conclusion square with *Gault, Winship,* and *Breed*?

3. In *Smith v. Daily Mail Publishing Co.*, 443 U.S. 97 (1979), cited by the *J. S.* court, the Supreme Court held that states cannot impose criminal penalties on newspapers that publish the lawfully obtained names of juvenile offenders. The Court found that a statute that prohibited publishing the names of juveniles charged with criminal offenses without approval of the court violated newspapers' First Amendment rights. The Court explained its decision as follows:

> The sole interest advanced by the State to justify its criminal statute is to protect the anonymity of the juvenile offender. It is asserted that confidentiality will further his rehabilitation because publication of the name may encourage further antisocial conduct and also may

cause the juvenile to lose future employment or suffer other consequences for this single offense. . . .

The magnitude of the State's interest in this statute is not sufficient to justify application of a criminal penalty to respondents. Moreover, the statute's approach does not satisfy constitutional requirements. The statute does not restrict the electronic media or any form of publication, except "newspapers," from printing the names of youths charged in a juvenile proceeding. In this very case, three radio stations announced the alleged assailant's name before the Daily Mail decided to publish it. Thus, even assuming the statute served a state interest of the highest order, it does not accomplish its stated purpose.

In addition, there is no evidence to demonstrate that the imposition of criminal penalties is necessary to protect the confidentiality of juvenile proceedings. As the Brief for Respondents points out, all 50 states have statutes that provide in some way for confidentiality, but only 5, including West Virginia, impose criminal penalties on nonparties for publication of the identity of the juvenile. Although every state has asserted a similar interest, all but a handful have found other ways of accomplishing the objective.

Id. at 104–5.

[2] Affirmative Defenses

Historically, the juvenile system was reluctant to afford juveniles all the defenses available to criminal defendants. For courts and legislatures convinced that young people benefit from the juvenile system, it was deemed undesirable to permit youngsters in need of help to avoid rehabilitative benefits by utilizing affirmative defenses to the charges to obtain acquittals. *See* Francis Barry McCathy, *The Role of Responsibility in Juvenile Delinquency Proceedings*, 10 U. MICH. J. L. REFORM 181, 208–09 (1977). Thus all jurisdictions denied the defense of infancy, *see* Sanford J. Fox, *Responsibility in the Juvenile Court*, 11 WM. & MARY L. REV. 659, 667 (1970), many denied the defense of insanity, and some avoided rigorous application of other defenses including self-defense. McCarthy, *supra*.

As the following cases illustrate, the advent of *Gault* and *Winship* signaled a trend in most jurisdictions to recognize affirmative defenses in delinquency adjudications. Indeed, juveniles in many jurisdictions are now permitted to invoke the same array of defenses available in criminal cases with the exception of infancy, and to a lesser degree insanity, so long as adequate evidence supports raising the defense issue. As these materials point out, the unavailability of the infancy defense in a majority of jurisdictions has become controversial as juvenile court dispositions become more punitive. Moreover, as will be shown, arguments have recently been raised for expanding self-defense to cover cases of battered children who kill their abusers under circumstances where the traditional doctrine precludes the defense.

[a] Competency To Be Adjudicated

MATTER OF WELFARE OF D.D.N.

Minnesota Court of Appeals
582 N.W.2d 278 (1998)

CRIPPEN, JUDGE.

Following adjudication and disposition on a delinquency petition accusing appellant D.D.N. of a burglary offense, he challenges a pretrial determination that he is competent to proceed in the case, contending that his mental handicap prevents necessary assistance to his attorney and involves some superficiality in his understanding of the proceedings. The prosecutor's response includes the argument that delinquency proceedings may proceed against a child "when an adult with the same abilities would be considered incompetent to stand trial." Although the prosecutor's plea to relax the governing standard for juvenile cases is precluded by a supreme court decision and its subsequent juvenile court rule, we affirm the competency determination.

FACTS

In June 1997, appellant D.D.N., then 15-years-old, was charged by petition with first-degree attempted burglary. Because of competency concerns, the juvenile court ordered that appellant undergo a 35-day evaluation at a residential treatment center.

A representative from the treatment center and experts for both appellant and the prosecution testified at the competency hearing. Following the hearing, the juvenile court concluded that appellant was competent to proceed to trial. The court subsequently adjudicated appellant a delinquent and placed him in a juvenile treatment facility. Appellant now appeals the court's pretrial competency ruling.

. . . .

ANALYSIS

1. *Juvenile Competency Standard*

The briefs of the parties allude to an expanding body of research and reporting on the diminished capacity of adolescents to assist their own interests at various stages in the prosecution of their alleged offenses.[65] The

---

[65] [1] *See, e.g.,* Thomas Grisso, *Juvenile Competency to Stand Trial,* CRIM. JUST., Fall 1997, at 5; *see also* Thomas Grisso, *The Competence of Adolescents As Trial Defendants,* 3 PSYCHOL. PUB. POL'Y & L. 3 (1997); Elizabeth S. Scott et. al., *Evaluating Adolescent Decision Making in Legal Contexts,* 19 LAW & HUM. BEHAV. 221 (1995); Elizabeth S. Scott, *Judgment and Reasoning in Adolescent Decisionmaking,* 37 VILL.L.REV. 1607 (1992); Laurence Steinberg & Elizabeth Cauffman, *Maturity of Judgment in Adolscence: Psychosocial Factors in Adolescent Decision Making,* 20 LAW & HUM. BEHAV. 249 (1996).

prosecuting attorney points to the scholarly opinion in this literature that, notwithstanding evidence of the diminished capacity of adolescent offenders to participate in court proceedings, a relaxed standard of competency might be justified in proceedings where the court will make a rehabilitative disposition. But in Minnesota, a lower standard for juvenile competency is precluded both by the supreme court's juvenile justice rules and by that court's earlier decision.

Minnesota rules of court relating to juvenile and adult competency hold children and adults to the same competency standard. MINN. R. JUV. P. 20.01, subd. 1(B), which sets the standard for juvenile competency, states:

> A child shall not be permitted to enter a plea or be tried or sentenced for any offense if the child lacks sufficient ability to:
>
> (1) consult with a reasonable degree of rational understanding with defense counsel; or
>
> (2) understand the proceedings or participate in the defense due to mental illness or mental deficiency.

The adult competency standard similarly defines competency as the ability to consult with counsel and to understand the nature of the proceeding.

Here, the prosecuting attorney argues that the availability of shorter-term sanctions and the rehabilitative nature of those dispositions may justify a lower level of competency. But this argument overlooks the reality that rehabilitative sanctions can and do involve a major loss of a child's liberties.

. . . .

The prosecutor's argument also overlooks the fact that, although rehabilitation eliminates retribution and deterrence of others, it does not always eliminate punishment. The juvenile court's dispositions must be rehabilitative and tied to the needs of and opportunities for the child, but these laws do not prohibit "a rational, punitive disposition, one where the record shows that correction or rehabilitation of the child reasonably cannot be achieved without a penalty."

A determination of competency, even in the context of juvenile adjudicatory proceedings, is a fundamental right. Because of this and because dispositions in juvenile proceedings, including rehabilitative dispositions, may involve both punishment and a substantial loss of liberty, the level of competence required to permit a child's participation in juvenile court proceedings can be no less than the competence demanded for trial or sentencing of an adult. Children, like adults, must be able "to understand the nature of the proceedings against [them] and to participate in [their] own defense."[66]

---

[66] [3] We also note appellant's observation that, when making a competency determination, the court should consider not only the child's ability to consult with counsel and understand the judicial proceeding but also the child's age as measure of his capacity. Researchers confirm the characteristics of youth that bear on a person's competency. *See* Thomas Grisso, *The Competence of Adolescents as Trial Defendants*, 3 PSYCHOL. PUB. POL. & L. 3, 24 (1997). But these factors, immaturity, developmental delays, and emotional disorders unique to age, are measured in the assessment of competency, without attempting to give weight to age alone as a measure of the condition.

. . . .

3. *Competency of D.D.N.*

The competency of appellant was assessed by a residential treatment center staff person; by Dr. Harry Hoberman, a licensed psychologist named by the court; and by Dr. R. Owen Nelson, a clinical psychologist whose evaluation was requested by the defense.

Testing at the treatment center indicated that appellant's performance IQ was "Low Average," but his verbal IQ fell within the "Intellectually Deficient" range.[67] Testing also showed that appellant had "very limited verbal memory, poor verbal abstraction abilities, minimal verbal reasoning and a marginal vocabulary." Each of the experts who examined appellant found him to be limited in his communication and slow to respond to questions.

At the competency hearing, Dr. Hoberman testified that appellant was competent to stand trial. Hoberman felt that, despite the low verbal IQ score, appellant was able to respond to questions and understood what was asked of him. Dr. Hoberman testified that when appellant was asked questions about the roles of various persons involved in the judicial process, about his relationship with his attorney, about whether he understood what his attorney was telling him, and about the nature of the trial process, he was able to respond "to almost all of the questions." Hoberman also testified that he believed appellant understood the charges against him and the possible outcomes. Further, appellant recalled the reading of his *Miranda* rights and his decision not to speak to police without counsel. Dr. Hoberman further testified that appellant discussed a previous court experience and that "he had been part of making the decision" to plea bargain in that case. But the witness cautioned that, due to appellant's deficiencies in processing verbal information, appellant's understanding of the events at trial should be continually scrutinized.

Eric Beuning, the treatment center case manager, testified that appellant seemed to understand fully what was going on while at the center. He also testified that appellant was "very outgoing, very friendly" with his peers and had no apparent difficulty expressing himself. On one occasion, Beuning reported that appellant said he would "call his lawyer" when told that food spilled on the table would not be replaced.

Dr. Nelson testified that appellant "has some very significant cognitive limitations that accordingly limit to a great degree his ability to understand the proceedings and to participate in his defense." He also testified that he did not believe that appellant understood the judicial process. But Nelson admitted that appellant had "a basic awareness of what's right and wrong," a "limited" understanding of who did what in the criminal justice system, and the cognitive capability of participating in his defense.[68]

---

67 [4] Appellant's verbal IQ was in the 0.4th percentile (or in the lowest 4/10th of 1%) when compared with others his own age. To put this into context, for every 2,500 15-year-olds, only 10 would have the same score or lower.

68 [5] We are troubled by Dr. Nelson's testimony that "in terms of that part of the [trial] process that is fluid and ongoing, I can't think of anything that would in my opinion render [appellant]

To be competent to proceed to trial or sentencing, the accused person must be able to consult with counsel and understand the nature of the proceedings in which he or she is involved. Our review of the record indicates that, notwithstanding appellant's limited intellectual abilities, the trial court properly inferred from the evidence presented that appellant was competent to proceed. In our collective view, the evidence identifies narrow areas of difficulty, principally in communicating with counsel during interrogation of witnesses. These difficulties do not compel reversal of the juvenile court's finding that appellant had the ability to understand and participate in proceedings and to consult with counsel.

Affirmed.

NOTES AND QUESTIONS

1. In rejecting the prosecutor's argument that the rehabilitative nature of juvenile court dispositions justifies a lower level of competency for juveniles than that imposed in criminal courts, the *D.D.N.* court noted the "reality that rehabilitative sanctions can and do involve a major loss of a child's liberties." Does this "reality" adequately address the prosecutor's argument? Would the prosecutor's argument be addressed only by a showing that juvenile dispositions are thoroughly punitive?

2. Unlike the Minnesota situation as reflected in *D.D.N.*, most states do not statutorily address the issue of competency to be adjudicated. Some courts, however, have held that in the absence of statutory provision, juveniles are entitled to raise the incompetency issue as a matter of due process of law. *See, e.g., In re Williams,* 687 N.E.2d 507, *appeal denied* 684 N.E.2d 706 (Ohio 1997). In *Golden v. State,* 21 S.W.3d 801, 802 (Ark. 2000), the court linked the competency issue to *Gault*'s recognition of a right to counsel:

> Although this issue is one of first impression in Arkansas, the United States Supreme Court held, in the case of *In re Gault*, that while proceedings in a juvenile court need not conform with *all* the requirements of a criminal trial, primarily because of the special nature of the proceedings, essential requirements of due process and fair treatment must be met. The Court, in *Gault*, specifically acknowledged a juvenile's right to constitutionally adequate notice, the right against self-incrimination, and the right to cross-examine witnesses; further, the Court explicitly held that a juvenile must be afforded the right to counsel during these proceedings. Logically, this right to counsel means little if the juvenile is unaware of the proceedings or unable to communicate with counsel due to a psychological or developmental disability. Therefore, applying *Gault*, we hold that a juvenile

---

competent." But in light of appellant's previous experience with the juvenile court process, his understanding about the work of an attorney, his recollection of the reading of the *Miranda* rights, and his decision not to speak to police without counsel, we believe that appellant has a less sweeping kind of disability than what appears to be indicated by Dr. Nelson's generalized opinion.

must be allowed to assert incompetency and have his competency determined prior to adjudication.

The majority's position in *Golden* did not go unchallenged, however. In his dissenting opinion, Justice Smith observed:

. . . I would affirm the trial court's denial of a competency hearing. I do so because the distinctions that exist between juvenile court proceedings and adult criminal proceedings are substantial and are rationally based upon the differences between adults and children. Although according a juvenile the right to a competency hearing appears equitable, it is, I submit, unwise. It reflects the continued erosion of all distinction between juvenile court and adult criminal courts. This erosion could ultimately lead to the irrelevance of juvenile codes in general.

Juveniles do not have a fundamental due process right to not be deprived of their liberty as a result of a hearing during which they were incompetent. The State's *parens patriae* interest, under proper circumstances subordinates the child's liberty interest. A juvenile has a liberty interest, which the U.S. Supreme Court describes as "substantial," but of which they also state that "that interest must be qualified by the recognition that juveniles, unlike adults, are always in some form of custody." The U.S. Supreme Court in this same opinion also states, "Children by definition are not assumed to have the capacity to take care of themselves. They are assumed to be subject to the control of their parents, and if parental control falters, the State must play its role as *parens patriae*."

The distinctions existing between juveniles and adults are recognized by the legislature in ARK. CODE ANN. § 9-27-102, which states, 'The General Assembly recognizes that children are defenseless and that there is no greater moral obligation upon the General Assembly than to provide for the protection of our children and that our child welfare system needs to be strengthened by establishing a clear policy of the state that the best interests of the children must be paramount and shall have precedence at every stage of juvenile court proceedings. . . .' This is consistent with the *parens patriae* interest as discussed in the U.S. Supreme Court cases. Implicit in the General Assembly's statement is the recognition that juveniles will not be competent in the sense adults would be, because they are assumed not to have the capacity to take care of themselves. In fact, the juvenile proceedings are designed to accomplish its ends without regard to the juvenile's competence because its absence is presumed.

21 S.W.3d at 805 (Smith, J., dissenting).

3. For a discussion of the incompetency issue in juvenile justice, see Vance L. Cowden & Geoffrey R. McKee, *Competency to Stand Trial in Juvenile Delinquency Proceedings — Cognitive Maturity and the Attorney-Client Relationship*, 38 U. LOUISVILLE J. FAM. L. 829 (1995).

[b] The Insanity Defense

IN THE INTEREST OF CAUSEY

Supreme Court of Louisiana
363 So. 2d 472 (1978)

TATE, JUSTICE.

At the instance of a juvenile made defendant in juvenile proceedings, we granted certiorari to determine whether a juvenile has a right to plead not guilty by reason of insanity and a right to a hearing to determine his mental capacity to assist in his defense.

FACTS

Pate Causey, age 16, was petitioned into the Orleans Parish juvenile court, charged with armed robbery. His attorney filed a motion, the substance of which was that defendant be allowed to plead not guilty and not guilty by reason of insanity, and that the judge appoint a panel of psychiatrists to perform comprehensive tests to determine whether defendant was legally insane at the time the act was committed. . . . The court denied the motion.

THE RIGHT OF A JUVENILE TO PLEAD INSANITY

There is no statutory right to plead not guilty by reason of insanity in a Louisiana juvenile proceeding, since such proceedings are conducted as civil proceedings, with certain enumerated differences. We hold, however, that the due process guaranties of the Fourteenth Amendment to the United States Constitution, and of Article I, Section 2 of the Louisiana Constitution, require that a juvenile be granted this right.

The only courts ever squarely confronted with the issue have held that, at least in adult proceedings, the denial of the right to plead insanity, with no alternative means of exculpation or special treatment for an insane person unable to understand the nature of his act, violates the concept of fundamental fairness implicit in the due process guaranties. *Sinclair v. State*, 161 Miss. 142, 132 So. 581 (1931); *State v. Strasburg*, 60 Wash. 106, 110 P. 1020 (1910).

The insanity defense, and the underlying notion that an accused must understand the nature of his acts in order to be criminally responsible (the Mens rea concept), are deeply rooted in our legal tradition and philosophy, as the cited decisions note. We deem it clear, as held by the Mississippi and Washington supreme courts in *Sinclair* and *Strasburg* above cited, that the due process-fundamental fairness concepts of our state and federal constitutions would be violated, at least in adult prosecutions for crimes requiring intent, if an accused were denied the right to plead the insanity defense.

However, not every constitutional right guaranteed to adults by the concept of fundamental fairness is automatically guaranteed to juveniles. The United States Supreme Court has undertaken a case-by-case analysis of juvenile proceedings, making not only the historical inquiry into whether the rights asserted were part of fundamental fairness, but also a functional analysis of whether giving the particular right in question to the juvenile defendant would interfere with any of the beneficial aspects of a juvenile proceeding. Only those rights that are both "fundamental" and "essential," in that they perform a function too important to sacrifice in favor of the benefits theoretically afforded by a civil-style juvenile proceeding, have been held to be required in such proceedings. *McKeiver v. Pennsylvania*, 403 U.S. 528 (1970); *In re Winship*, 397 U.S. 358 (1970); *In re Gault*, 387 U.S. 1 (1967).

The same approach was adopted by a majority of this court in determining which due process rights are guaranteed to juveniles by the Louisiana Constitution, in *State in Interest of Dino*, 359 So.2d 586 (La. 1978).

McKeiver, *Winship*, and *Gault* imposed on juvenile proceedings a host of traditional criminal trial safeguards the right to appropriate notice, to counsel, to confrontation and cross-examination, and the privilege against self-incrimination and declined to impose only one safeguard, the right to a jury trial.

While the due process right to a jury trial has been held to be an element of "fundamental fairness," at least in non-petty adult proceedings, the court's emphasis in *McKeiver* was not on the degree of "fundamentality," but on the Function served by the jury trial. The plurality saw the jury as a component in the factfinding process, and as such, not "a necessary component of accurate factfinding." Only after finding that the jury trial although "fundamental" for adults was not really "essential" to a fair trial proceeding, *i.e.*, did not perform a function that could not be adequately performed by some other procedure, did the court examine the impact of a jury trial upon the beneficial effects of the juvenile system, and conclude that it would "bring with it into that system the traditional delay, the formality, and the clamor of the adversary system and, possibly, the public trial."

In *Winship*, the court held that a juvenile could not be adjudged to have violated a criminal statute by a mere preponderance of the evidence. The standard of proof "beyond a reasonable doubt" was held to play "a vital role in the American scheme of criminal procedure. It is a prime instrument for reducing the risk of convictions resting on factual error. . . . [A] person accused of a crime . . . would be at a severe disadvantage . . . if he could be adjudged guilty and imprisoned for years on the strength of the same evidence as would suffice in a civil case."

Underlying the functional analysis of the two procedures examined in *McKeiver* and *Winship*, was not only the consideration of whether equally effective safeguards existed to the rights sought to be imported into juvenile proceedings, but also a consideration of the realistic role played by these two rights in safeguarding juvenile rights at actual trials: the "beyond a reasonable doubt standard" actually kept the juvenile in *Winship* out of jail, whereas there was no evidence that a jury trial in *McKeiver* would have done so.

The availability of some procedure for differentiating between those who are culpably responsible for their act and those who are merely ill is, as we have seen, a part of "fundamental fairness." Moreover, it is hard to see that any important aim of the juvenile system is thwarted by affording such a distinction to the mentally ill juvenile.

The function of the insanity plea is much more akin to that of the burden of proof imposed on juvenile proceedings in *Winship*, than of the jury trial involved in *McKeiver*. An insanity defense, like a high burden of proof, will generically spell the difference between conviction and acquittal. That there is perhaps a lesser stigma associated with an adjudication of juvenile delinquency than with an adult criminal conviction, and that juvenile incarceration is theoretically calculated to rehabilitate rather than to punish, were deemed constitutionally insignificant in *Winship*. . . .

     . . . .

CONCLUSION

. . . The right to plead insanity, absent some other effective means of distinguishing mental illness from moral culpability, is fundamental. . . . A defendant in a juvenile proceeding has the right to plead not guilty and not guilty by reason of insanity.

Reversed and Remanded.

SANDERS, CHIEF JUSTICE (*dissenting*).

     . . . .

The holding that a plea of not guilty by reason of insanity is constitutionally required in Louisiana juvenile law is based upon the premise that the present statute is constitutionally deficient in not providing procedures for exploring insanity at the time of the offense.

In my opinion, the basic premise is untenable. The Juvenile Court Law contains ample procedures to deal with the issue.

[The court reviewed statutory provisions authorizing commitment of mentally ill juveniles.]

Thus, there is built into the juvenile court law procedures for pre-hearing mental and psychiatric examinations. Further examinations may be made in connection with the hearing. In the event a mental defect or insanity is found, the court is authorized to commit the child to a mental institution at any stage of the proceeding.

Juvenile proceedings are non-criminal. Hence, there is no provision for formal criminal-court pleas. The essential inquiry is whether the child admits or denies the factual allegations of the petition. Whether he admits or denies the allegations, however, his . . . sanity [is always a pertinent issue] under juvenile procedures. There is no room in these procedures for a plea of not guilty by reason of insanity, because the . . . sanity of the child [is] before the court at all stages.

The majority holding imports into the juvenile law formal criminal-court pleading and procedure by means of constitutional analysis based upon what I believe to be an erroneous premise. I greatly fear that the constitutional holding will disrupt juvenile procedures, so recently codified.

For the reasons assigned, I respectfully dissent.

NOTES AND QUESTIONS

1. A number of states have found the right to assert an insanity defense to be an essential part of "due process and fair treatment" that must be provided to a juvenile at the adjudicatory stage of the proceeding. *See, e.g., In re M.G.S.*, 267 Cal. App. 2d 329, 72 Cal. Rptr. 808, 811 (1968); *Matter of Two Minor Children*, 592 P.2d 166, 169 (Nev. 1979); *Winburn*, 145 N.W.2d at 184; *see also Matter of Stapelkemper*, 562 P.2d 815, 816 (Mont. 1977) (agreeing that due process includes allowing juveniles the right to assert insanity defense at adjudication of delinquency, but not in a pre-adjudicatory transfer proceeding). *Cf. K.M. v. State*, 983 S.W.2d 93 (Ark. 1998) (concluding that because the juvenile code did not expressly provide for an insanity defense, a juvenile could not asset such defense at a delinquency adjudication).

2. The District of Columbia code allows evidence of mental abnormality to be admitted into evidence at a "factfinding hearing to aid the Division in determining a material allegation of [a] petition relating to the child's mental or physical condition" but denies such evidence "for the purpose of establishing a defense of insanity." D.C. CODE ANN. § 16-2315(d) (Supp. 2001). While effectively denying the insanity defense in delinquency adjudications, the statute was nevertheless upheld, in *In re C.W.M.*, 407 A.2d 617 (D.C. 1979), against claims that it violated due process and equal protection. The Court of Appeals of the District of Columbia explained:

By this argument, appellant demonstrates a misconception of the nature and purpose of the insanity defense.

Moreover, it is well settled in this jurisdiction that proof of insanity at the time of the commission of an offense does not negate intent nor, without more, does it require an outright acquittal, since the trier of fact may not even consider the issue of insanity until after the government has established the essential elements of the offense, including intent.

Consequently, even if the defense of insanity had been permitted and appellant had been successful in obtaining an acquittal by reason of insanity, it would not have established his innocence of the charged offense because "[a]n acquittal by reason of insanity, which . . . includes mental defects, is a determination of guilt beyond a reasonable doubt of the acts charged."

Thus, the function of the insanity defense is not to establish the innocence of the accused, but rather to absolve him of the moral and penal consequences of his criminal act.

Insisting, however, that D.C. CODE (1973, § 16-2315(d)) violates the Fifth Amendment guarantees of due process and equal protection, appellant urges that because the statute precludes a child from raising the insanity defense at the factfinding hearing, he or she is afforded less protection than that afforded an adult offender who is found to have been insane at the time of the commission of the offense. Put another way, appellant says that an adult acquitted by reason of insanity is by law, committed to a mental institution, but only until such time as he is able to establish his sanity. In contrast, urges appellant, under existing law a child who was insane at the time of the commission of an offense but not at the time of the disposition hearing could nevertheless be incarcerated in a setting where psychiatric care is not available. We will presently dispose of each of these claims.

At the outset, we notice that the Supreme Court has sanctioned great flexibility in juvenile delinquency proceedings to the end that the unique rehabilitative function of the juvenile system may be preserved. . . . The Court's analysis in *McKeiver* is particularly instructive in this case. The Court there began with the proposition that fundamental fairness is the applicable due process standard in juvenile proceedings. . . . [I]n the case before us, we find that the central question is whether the insanity defense serves some function essential to fundamental fairness that cannot otherwise be performed adequately by other procedures in the juvenile system.

With this question in mind, we proceed to examine appellant's constitutional arguments, mindful in the process that the very purpose of D.C. CODE 1973, §§ 16-2301 *et seq.*, is "to avoid treatment of juveniles as adult criminal defendants to the extent practicable." Mindful also, we must be, that it is implicit in the statutory scheme that noncriminal treatment is to be the rule, and adult treatment the exception.

That there are substantial differences between the criminal and juvenile justice systems is of course apparent from an examination of the controlling statutes. However, the relevant differences come into focus only after completion of the first phase of the bifurcated proceedings conducted in this jurisdiction when a criminal defendant interposes the defense of insanity.

In a criminal case, the trier of fact may not even consider the issue of insanity until the government has established the essential elements of the offense, including intent in the first phase of that proceeding. The second phase is held only if the government is successful in proving guilt beyond a reasonable doubt and, only then, may the trier of fact reach the question of insanity. At this point, a criminal defendant may raise an insanity defense, which serves to permit the jury to decide whether the criminal defendant should be absolved of the criminal responsibility and penal consequences of his acts.

The first phase of a bifurcated criminal proceeding is analogous to the factfinding proceeding of the juvenile process during which the Division if permitted to determine only whether the juvenile committed the act charged. Accordingly, contrary to appellant's argument, precluding a juvenile from raising an insanity defense at a factfinding hearing denies him no right that is other wise accorded an adult.

A juvenile delinquency proceeding concededly does not incorporate the second step. Nevertheless, it is well settled now that unlike a criminal trial a juvenile factfinding hearing does not result in a determination of criminal responsibility. Nor is the succeeding dispositional hearing intended to result in the imposition of any penal sanction on the child. Rather, the purpose is to determine the treatment required to rehabilitate him. Accordingly, the insanity defense would be superfluous in a juvenile delinquency proceeding.

This conclusion, however, does not end our analysis. Appellant contends that the insanity defense in a criminal proceeding serves the secondary, but equally important purpose of providing a criminal defendant with procedural safeguards not otherwise available to a child. He concedes however that an adult offender found not guilty by reason of insanity must be committed to a hospital for the mentally ill until such time as he is able to establish his eligibility for release as provided in D.C. CODE 1973, § 24-301(d). In contrast, appellant maintains that D.C. CODE 1973, § 16-2315(d) does not require the Family Division to consider the result of any mental examination or make specific findings respecting a child's mental illness. Because of the broad discretion vested in the Division for dispositional purposes, appellant contends, as a possibility, that a child who was mentally ill at the time of the offense, but not at the time of disposition, could be "incarcerated for a lengthy period as an adjudicated delinquent," and that a child who was still mentally ill at the time of disposition could be institutionalized in a setting where psychiatric care is not available. We have found no support in the statute for these contentions.

We recognize that although the juvenile justice system is not intended to impose penal sanctions, the Family Division frequently orders forms of rehabilitation that a child might regard as punishment. We also recognized that an insanity acquittee, because morally blameless, may not be subject to any form of punishment. Of course, as pointed out above, an adjudication of delinquency does not result in the imposition of any penal sanction. Consequently it cannot be said with rationality that a disposition of a child offender deemed, by the Division, to serve his best interests, is punishment. Nevertheless we deem it to be an indispensable element of fundamental fairness that a mentally ill child offender be accorded the same opportunity for psychiatric treatment and ultimate release as a similarly situated adult. For these reasons, we have examined closely the statutory scheme, governing the treatment of mentally ill child offenders in order to determine whether they are being denied any required procedural protections to ensure fundamental fairness. We conclude that the statutes and rules regulating juvenile delinquency proceedings in the District of Columbia presently provide adequate means of ensuring that any mentally ill child offender receives care and treatment similar to that provided for mentally ill criminal defendants.

. . . .

It seems clear from what we have said above that if the Division finds that the child offender was mentally ill at the time of the offense, and is mentally ill at the time of disposition and therefore in need of care and treatment, certainly it would be a clear abuse of discretion to then confine the child to an institution where appropriate care and treatment was not available. Any other result would be wholly inconsistent with the primary goal of the juvenile justice system, i.e., to order the disposition that would serve the best interest of the child in effecting his rehabilitation.

On the other hand, if the Division finds that the child was mentally ill at the time of the offense, but at the time of disposition was fully restored to mental health, the Division would then be required to determine whether in view of all the facts and circumstances the child is or is not in need of care and treatment. Of particular significance, however, is § 16-2317(d) which provides that: "If the Division finds that the child is not in need of care or rehabilitation it shall terminate the proceedings and discharge the child from detention, shelter care, or other restriction previously ordered."

In summary, we conclude, after our careful analysis of the statute and the rules governing the juvenile justice system in the District of Columbia, that the child here involved was accorded treatment that was substantially similar and in some respects more beneficial than that accorded a similarly situated criminal defendant.

407 A.2d at 619–23.

[c] The Infancy Defense

IN RE TYVONNE

Supreme Court of Connecticut
558 A.2d 661 (1989)

GLASS, ASSOCIATE JUSTICE:

In this case we decide whether the common law defense of infancy applies to juvenile delinquency proceedings. The respondent appealed to the Appellate Court from an adjudication of delinquency, claiming that the trial court erred in denying his motion for judgment of acquittal. Pursuant to Practice Book § 4023, we transferred the case to ourselves. We find no error.

The relevant facts are not in dispute. The respondent was born on July 28, 1978. He lived with his mother, grandmother and two younger siblings in Hartford and attended the Clark Street School. On March 1, 1987, the respondent, who was eight-years-old, found a small pistol while he was playing in the school yard. He took the pistol and hid it under some papers in a hallway in building 38 of Bellevue Square. The following day he took the pistol to school and put it by a fence. He then went into the school and told another child about the pistol. Other children, including the victim, heard about the pistol.

The victim told Tyvonne that she thought the pistol was a fake. After school, the respondent and the victim began arguing over whether the pistol was real. Several children examined the pistol and decided that it was a toy. The victim challenged the respondent again by saying, "Shoot me, shoot me." The respondent exclaimed, "I'll show you it's real." He then pointed the pistol at the victim, pulled the trigger, and fired one shot, which struck and injured her. The respondent then swore at the victim, shouted that he had been telling the truth, and ran from the scene. Shortly thereafter he was apprehended and taken into police custody.

On March 3, 1987, the state filed a petition alleging five counts of delinquent behavior arising from the shooting. On that date, the trial court appointed a public defender to represent the respondent, conducted a detention release hearing, and released the respondent to the care of his maternal grandmother. The trial court also ordered a psychological evaluation of the respondent. The hearing on the delinquency petition commenced on June 3, 1987. After the state completed its case on the first day, the respondent made an oral motion for judgment of acquittal, claiming that the state had introduced no evidence to rebut the common law presumption that children between the ages of seven and fourteen are incapable of committing a crime. The trial court reserved decision on the motion. On June 10, 1987, the respondent filed a written motion for judgment of acquittal including the claim asserted in the oral motion. On June 22, 1987, the trial court granted the respondent's motion for an examination to determine his competency.

When the hearing resumed on July 29, 1987, the report evaluating the respondent's competency was filed and proof of his competency was waived. The trial court then denied the respondent's motion for judgment of acquittal. At the completion of the hearing, the trial court made an adjudication that the respondent was a delinquent based on a finding that he had committed assault in the second degree in violation of General Statutes § 53a-60(a)(2). The trial court dismissed the other counts. The trial court also ordered a preliminary investigation and a psychological evaluation of the respondent's mother and grandmother. At the disposition hearing on October 26, 1987, the trial court committed the respondent to the department of children and youth services (DCYS) for a period not to exceed four years.

On appeal, the respondent assigns as error the trial court's denial of his motion for judgment of acquittal. He asserts that Connecticut's juvenile justice legislation does not expressly or implicitly eliminate the common law infancy defense from delinquency proceedings. He further argues that because the original goals of rehabilitation and remediation in the juvenile justice system have not been attained, there is no justification for excluding the infancy defense from juvenile delinquency proceedings. Consequently, he claims, the trial court erred in not requiring the state to rebut the presumption that he was incapable of committing the offense underlying the delinquency adjudication. We are not persuaded.

I

The respondent argues that, even though the legislature may abolish common law rules; statutes in derogation of the common law must be strictly construed. He asserts that because the juvenile justice legislation is silent with respect to the common law infancy defense, the common law presumptions must apply to delinquency proceedings. The state argues, however, that Connecticut's juvenile justice legislation implicitly abolishes the defense and, further, that application of the defense in delinquency proceedings would frustrate the legislation's remedial objectives.

. . . .

"By the seventeenth century, the Roman classification of criminal responsibility became the basis of the English common-law approach, so that children under seven were incapable of committing a crime while those between seven and fourteen were presumed incapable. Such presumption however was rebuttable by strong and clear evidence. Those [fourteen and over] were subject to the same criminal laws as were adults."

The common law defense of infancy, like the defense of insanity, differs from the criminal law's requirement of "*mens rea*" or criminal intent. The law recognized that while a child may have actually intended to perform a criminal act, children in general could not reasonably be presumed capable of differentiating right from wrong. The presumptions of incapacity were created to avoid punishing those who, because of age, could not appreciate the moral dimensions of their behavior, and for whom the threat of punishment would not act as a deterrent. W. LaFave & A. Scott, *supra.* Although a number of states have codified the common law rule by statute; *see, e.g.,* ARIZ. REV. STAT. ANN. § 13-501; MINN. STAT. § 609.055; or. REV. STAT. ANN. 161.290; WASH. REV. CODE ANN. § 9A.04.050; there is no statutory infancy defense in Connecticut.

The concept of juvenile delinquency did not exist at common law. In most states, including Connecticut, legislation was enacted that rendered children under a certain age liable as "delinquents" for committing acts that, if committed by an adult, would be criminal. Even though the Superior Court is Connecticut's trial court of general jurisdiction, and juvenile matters are heard in the Superior Court, juvenile proceedings are conducted separately from all other business of the Superior Court. Delinquency is defined as follows: "[A] child may be found 'delinquent' (1) who has violated any federal or state law or municipal or local ordinance . . . or (2) who has violated any order of the superior court. . . ." An important feature of the legislation . . . provides: "No child shall be prosecuted for an offense before the superior court, nor shall the adjudication of such court that a child is delinquent in any case be deemed a conviction of crime except as provided in §§ 46b-126 and 46b-127."[69]

Shortly after the creation of the juvenile justice system, we addressed the issue whether a delinquency proceeding is tantamount to a criminal prosecution. [W]e stated that "the Act [creating the juvenile justice system] . . . is not of a criminal nature. . . ." "The Act is but an exercise by the State of its . . . power over the welfare of its children," and a juvenile subjected to delinquency proceedings "[is] tried for no offense," but "[comes] under the

---

[69] [6] The exceptions refer to juvenile cases subject to transfer to the regular criminal docket. See General Statutes §§ 46b-126 and 46b-127 (providing, inter alia, that juvenile subject to transfer must have been fourteen years of age at the time underlying offense was committed).

operation of the law in order that he might not be tried for any offense." [W]e have on several occasions recognized that juvenile proceedings are fundamentally different from criminal proceedings.

The rehabilitative nature of our juvenile justice system is most saliently evidenced by the statutory provisions pertaining to the disposition of delinquent juveniles. Under General Statutes § 46b-134, the trial court may not render a disposition of the case of any delinquent child until the trial court receives from the probation officer assigned to the case a comprehensive background report on the child's characteristics, history and home life. The disposition of a child found delinquent for a serious juvenile offense may be made only after the court receives a complete evaluation of the child's physical and psychological health. General Statutes § 46b-140(a) provides in part that upon an adjudication of delinquency, the trial court may place the juvenile "in the care of any institution or agency which is permitted by law to care for children, order the child to remain in his own home or in the custody of a relative or any other fit person subject to the supervision of the probation officer or withhold or suspend execution of any judgment." The court may also order the juvenile to perform public service or to make restitution when appropriate, provided that the child and his parent or guardian consent to such an order.

Significantly, commitment of the child to DCYS may be made only if the court finds that "its probation services or other services available to the court are not adequate for such child. . . ." Prior to any such commitment, however, the court must "consult with [DCYS] to determine the placement which will be in the best interest of such child." When the trial court determines that a commitment must be made, it may commit the child to DCYS for an indeterminate period not to exceed two years, or in the case of a child found delinquent for committing a serious juvenile offense, for an indeterminate period not to exceed four years. DCYS may petition for an extension of the commitment of a child originally committed for two years. An extension may not exceed an additional two years, and may only be ordered when, after a hearing, it is found to be in the best interests of the child.

Several other provisions of the General Statutes and the Practice Book delineate fundamental distinctions between delinquency and criminal proceedings. For example, Practice Book § 1034(1) provides that a juvenile delinquency hearing "shall not be conducted as a criminal trial; the proceedings shall be at all times as informal as the requirements of due process and fairness permit." Further, unlike the records of convicted criminals, the records of juvenile delinquency proceedings generally are confidential.

. . . .

It is clear from our analysis that the purpose of the comprehensive statutory treatment of "juvenile delinquents" is clinical and rehabilitative, rather than retributive or punitive. As we recently observed "[t]he objective of juvenile court proceedings is to 'determin[e] the needs of the child and of society rather than adjudicat[e] criminal conduct. The objectives are to provide measures of guidance and rehabilitation . . . not to fix criminal responsibility, guilt and punishment.' Thus the child found delinquent is not perceived as a criminal guilty of one or more offenses, but rather as a child in need of guidance and rehabilitative services." In effect, the statutes regulating juvenile misconduct represent a system-wide displacement of the common law.

With the enactment of juvenile justice legislation nationwide, several courts have addressed the issue whether the infancy defense applies to delinquency proceedings. Most have held that, in the absence of legislation codifying or adopting the defense, incapacity is not a defense in delinquency proceedings. *See, e.g., Jennings v. State,* 384 So. 2d 104, 106 (Ala. 1980); *Gammons v. Berlat,* 696 P.2d 700 (Ariz. 1985); *State v. D.H.,* 340 So. 2d 1163, 1165 (Fla. 1976); *In the Matter of Robert M.,* 441 N.Y.S.2d 860 (1981); *In re Michael,* 423 A.2d 1180, 1182 (R.I. 1981); *In the Matter of Skinner,* 249 S.E.2d 746 (S.C. 1978); *W. LaFave &A. Scott, supra,* § 4.11(c). These courts observe that because a delinquency adjudication is not a criminal conviction, it is unnecessary to determine whether the juvenile understood the moral implications of his or her behavior. In addition, some decisions recognize that the defense would frustrate the remedial purposes of juvenile justice legislation.

Because Connecticut's juvenile justice system is designed to provide delinquent minors with guidance and rehabilitation; we agree with the courts that hold that the common law infancy defense, created to protect children from being punished as criminals, has no place in delinquency proceedings. We also agree that the legislature could decide that the infancy defense would unnecessarily interfere with the state's legitimate efforts to provide structured forms of guidance for children who have committed acts of delinquency. It could conclude that the defense inevitably would exclude those children most in need of guidance from a system designed to instill socially responsible behavior.[70] To construe the legislature's silence as indicating an intent to preserve the infancy defense in delinquency proceedings is unwarranted in light of the legislation's obvious and singular remedial objectives. We are not persuaded that recognition of the defense would advance the interests of either the child or society.[71]

II

Relying on a number of decisions in other states, however, the respondent argues that the rehabilitative objectives of juvenile justice have become defunct, and cannot justify excluding the infancy defense from delinquency proceedings. Most of the decisions holding the infancy defense applicable to juvenile proceedings have been based on specific legislation adopting the

---

[70] [8] The respondent argues that the rehabilitative purposes of the statutory scheme would be served in the present case without an adjudication of delinquency because the trial court also adjudicated the respondent an "uncared for" child, and made an appropriate disposition thereon. We disagree with the respondent, however, that an adjudication of "uncared for" status presents the trial court with "an almost identical range of dispositional options." Further, it is obvious that the two adjudications do not necessarily overlap. The statutory scheme does not require the trial court to dismiss a delinquency petition, or to suspend a disposition on an adjudication of delinquency, whenever the court renders a concurrent adjudication of "uncared for" status. We decline to create such a requirement by judicial ukase.

[71] [9] Nothing in this opinion should be construed to deter the legislature from considering the desirability of a floor for such juvenile proceedings in recognition of the fact that the clinical and rehabilitative needs of a four or eight year old are different from those of a fourteen or fifteen year old.

defense, and therefore are irrelevant to the present case. *See, e.g., In re Gladys R.*, 464 P.2d 127 (Cal. 1970); *K.M.S. v. State,* 200 S.E.2d 916 (Ga. 1973); *State v. Q.D.,* 685 P.2d 557 (Wash. 1984); *State v. S.P.,* 746 P.2d 813 (Wash. 1987).

Some courts, however, have held that even absent pertinent legislation, the common law infancy defense applies to delinquency proceedings. *In re William A.,* 548 A.2d 130 (Md. 1988); *In the Matter of Andrew M.,* 91 Misc.2d 813, 815–16, 398 N.Y.S.2d 824 (1977); *Commonwealth v. Durham,* 389 A.2d 108 (Pa. 1978). These courts advance the notion that the United States Supreme Court decisions in *Kent, Gault,* and *Winship* reflect the evolving reality that the true objectives of juvenile justice legislation are not rehabilitation and treatment, but accountability and punishment. *Kent, Gault* and *Winship* establish that the state may not suspend fundamental protections of due process in juvenile proceedings. A particular procedure must be followed if it is required as a matter of "fundamental fairness." The precise principle emerging from *Kent* and *Gault* is that states may not rely on superficial exhortations of "rehabilitation" to justify *procedural* arbitrariness in delinquency proceedings. As the court observed in *Gault,* "[j]uvenile Court history has again demonstrated that unbridled discretion, however benevolently motivated, is frequently a poor substitute for principle and procedure."

The respondent does not argue that the United States Supreme Court's juvenile decisions require the common law incapacity defense in delinquency proceedings as a matter of fundamental constitutional fairness. Nor does he suggest that the exclusion of the incapacity defense introduces procedural arbitrariness. Instead, the respondent gleans from those cases the proposition that since the juvenile justice system punishes rather than rehabilitates, there is no good reason not to recognize incapacity as a defense. We are not persuaded, however, that *Kent* and *Gault* warrant the proposition that the respondent discerns.

We acknowledge that the United States Supreme Court has opined that the rehabilitative goals of the various state juvenile courts have often not been attained. The court has made it quite clear that states may not deny juveniles fundamental due process rights simply by labeling delinquency proceedings "civil," or by asserting that the purpose of delinquency proceedings is rehabilitative. Thus, the *parens patriae* doctrine does not support inroads on basic constitutional guarantees simply because a state claims that its juvenile justice system is "rehabilitative" rather than "punitive." The United States Supreme Court, however, has expressly refused to hold that the rehabilitative goals of the various systems of juvenile justice may under no circumstances justify appropriate differential treatment of a child adjudicated a delinquent. *McKeiver v. Pennsylvania,* further, the court has never suggested that such differential treatment, based on the juvenile justice systems' fundamentally nonpunitive objectives, is intrinsically illegitimate. "We are reluctant to say that, despite disappointments of grave dimensions, [the juvenile justice system] does not hold promise, and we are particularly reluctant to say . . . that the system cannot accomplish its rehabilitative goals. So much depends on the availability of resources, on the interest and commitment of the public, on willingness to learn, and on understanding. . . . We are reluctant to disallow the States to experiment further and to seek in new and different ways the elusive answers to the problems of the young. . . ." *McKeiver.*

We do not discern in *Kent* and its progeny an abandonment of the rehabilitative focus of juvenile justice. The respondent has not presented us with any grounds for concluding that the rehabilitative objectives of Connecticut's juvenile justice system are contradicted in practice. We therefore decline to adopt the somewhat cynical view expressed by some writers that the ideals of the juvenile justice system are now bankrupt, and have necessarily succumbed to the corrosive effects of institutionalization.

Further, we are not persuaded by the respondent's argument that the statutory treatment of juveniles who commit "serious juvenile offenses" requires a conclusion that there is no genuine difference between juvenile and criminal proceedings. The four year maximum commitment term for serious juvenile offenders certainly contemplates the possibility of a serious restriction on the juvenile's liberty. But as we have already observed, any commitment order must be predicated on a determination that other options not involving commitment are inadequate to address the child's needs. In addition, placement of the child in a program or facility must be based on the child's best interests. We cannot infer from these provisions a legislative intent to inflict retribution on the serious juvenile offender.

Finally, we reject the respondent's argument that the common law presumption should apply in this case because the offense charged was a serious juvenile offense. We acknowledge that the commission of a serious juvenile offense is a prerequisite to the transfer of a juvenile case to the Superior Court criminal docket. Another prerequisite to such a transfer, however, is that the child must have committed the offense after attaining the age of fourteen. In the present case, the respondent was eight years of age at the time of the predicate offense.

There is no error.

NOTES AND QUESTIONS

1. Does the court in *In re Tyvonne* convincingly dismiss the supposed "evolving reality that the true objectives of juvenile justice legislation are not rehabilitation and treatment but accountability and punishment"? Was the disposition imposed upon Tyvonne, commitment to DCYS for up to four years, possibly punitive? Should the court have explored this possibility more thoroughly? Would the considerations described in § 5.02[B], *supra*, be helpful? Would a finding that the disposition was punitive require recognition of the infancy defense?

2. Would the court's logic *In re Tyvonne* lead to the conclusion that Connecticut does not allow the *insanity* defense in delinquency adjudications assuming no legislative recognition of that defense? In discussing the applicability of the defenses of insanity and infancy, respectively, Professor Sanford Fox suggests that the courts have perhaps been more receptive to the applicability of insanity than they have to infancy. *See* Sanford J. Fox,

Responsibility in the Juvenile Court, 11 WM. & MARY L. REV. 659, 667 (1970) (unanimous rejection of infancy defense until 1970, judges increasingly coming to accept insanity as a defense in delinquency adjudications). For an argument in favor of recognizing the infancy defense in the "new," punitive, juvenile courts, see Andrew Walkover, *The Infancy Defense in the New Juvenile Court*, 31 UCLA L. REV. 503 (1984).

3. In thinking about the relevance of an infancy defense, consider the following views:

Steven J. Morse, *Immaturity and Irresponsibility*

88 JOURNAL OF CRIMINAL LAW & CRIMINOLOGY 15, 23, 49, 52–57, 59–60 (1997)

. . . To be at fault, an agent must actually breach an expectation and must have general normative competence and the general ability at the time to be guided by it. Moral and legal responsibility and blaming practices track this account.

For example, children lack normative competence because they are generally unable to grasp the good reasons not to breach an expectation. . . .

. . . .

The question of juvenile responsibility is not simply whether juveniles are generally different from adults. Surely they are in many ways. The real issue is whether they are morally different, and the resolution of that issue depends on whether a moral theory we accept dictates that the variables that behaviorally distinguish juveniles should also diminish their responsibility. Difference is not necessarily diminution, after all, and to assume otherwise is to beg the question.

. . . .

Many able scholars have reviewed the literature concerning potential legally relevant differences between adolescents and adults. I shall make the simplifying assumption that the near consensus of their findings represents the most accurate current assessment of those differences. In brief, the literature indicates that the formal reasoning ability and the level of cognitive moral development of mid-adolescents differs little from adults. Further, on narrowly conceived cognitive tasks performed under laboratory conditions that concern decisions about medical treatment, there is little difference in outcome between mid-adolescents and adults. As a class, however, adolescents: (1) have a stronger preference for risk and novelty; (2) subjectively assess the potentially negative consequences of risky conduct less unfavorably; (3) tend to be impulsive and more concerned with short-term than long-term consequences; (4) subjectively experience and assess the passage of time and time periods as longer; and (5) are more susceptible to peer pressure. All five differences diminish with maturation throughout adolescence, with most disappearing by mid- to late-adolescence, but they do appear robust for adolescents as a class. It is crucial to remember, however, that a finding of a statistically significant difference between groups does not mean that there is no overlap between them. In fact, the adolescent and adult distributions on these variables overlap considerably; large numbers of adolescents and adults are indistinguishable on measure of these variables.

Mid-adolescent and adult formal reasoning, including instrumental reasoning, are indistinguishable, but these other differences allegedly affect adolescent judgment and self-control. Adolescents make serious mistakes as a result of developmental immaturity that they would not make under similar circumstances after they mature. Consequently, many argue, adolescents should be protected from the full consequences of their immature mistakes, lest their lives be ruined by developmental factors they would outgrow in the normal course of life. It is important to remember, however, that all these characteristics are matters of degree and by mid-adolescence most juveniles are probably able to control them to a substantial degree, although it may be harder for them than for adults.

Before continuing, we must consider the relevance of the research concerning adolescence to juvenile *criminal* responsibility. Most of the research summarized above investigated adolescent decision-making and behavior in general and risk-taking in particular; it does not examine adolescent criminal behavior. Adolescent criminal conduct for the most part involves the intentional infliction of harm: the offender intentionally killed, inflicted grievous bodily harm, raped, stole, destroyed, or burned. That is, it is the adolescent's conscious objective to cause in the immediate future precisely the harm the law prohibits. Unless serious adolescent offenders are specially unlucky or unskillful, they are practically certain to produce the harm that is their conscious objective, and they know it. The intentional harmdoer knows that the conduct invades the interests of others; those interests may be given little value or otherwise ignored or rationalized away, but they must be present to the adolescent agent's mind. Adolescents can surely commit crimes of risk creation, such as reckless homicide, but primarily serious crimes of intention raise the issues that concern us. And for crimes of serious risk creation, the risk is immediate and, once again, the risked result will at least be present to the adolescent's mind.

Risky conduct in general is different in important ways from conduct intended to cause immediate harm: risky conduct often is not criminal or seriously so; it often affects primarily the risk taker; often the probability of the harm risked may not be high; and finally, often the risked result is a long-term, rather than an immediate, consequence. For example, an adolescent may intentionally drive too fast and engage in other forms of bravado, but much conduct of this sort is not criminal. Much of the risk is to themselves, and the probability of a serious harm, such as death, is not high. Adolescents may also intentionally experiment with drugs, but they face only the longer term and low probability risks of endangering their ultimate social success and health. Similarly, adolescents may intentionally engage in unprotected sex, but such behavior is not criminal and creates again the longer term, low probability risk of disease and pregnancy, and so on. The harms risked are serious, but the risky conduct does not demonstrate substantial antisocial potential, and in none of these cases is the result practically certain. When an adolescent (or anyone else) decides whether to engage in risky conduct, the potential harm does not weigh as heavily as the adolescent's gratification. The latter is certain; the former is not. Moreover, driven by a desire for gratification, it is easier to fail to weigh sufficiently the interests of others that one does not desire to harm and to underestimate the longer term risk one's conduct produces.

If risky conduct is statistically normal for adolescents, treating adolescents as criminals or proto-criminals may appear to be criminalizing "normality," but this is not the case. Again the law does not criminalize or seriously criminalize much risk-creating conduct. More important, no matter how much adolescents may prefer risk, it can scarcely be claimed that serious crime is the statistically normal mode that adolescents use to express their preference for risk. To treat an adolescent murderer, rapist, arsonist, and the like as simply a kid in search of risk and to suggest that we should consider decriminalizing such conduct among kids is neither justified by the data nor morally warranted.

In sum, the relevance of the research on adolescent immaturity and poor judgment to intentional criminal behavior is unclear. The desire for immediate gratification is likely to exert more influence when the potential harm is uncertain (and not criminal) than when it is intended (and criminal). What is more, the moral reason not to engage in conduct is in general vastly stronger and more immediate when the harm is intended rather than risked, which explains why we consider intentional harmdoing more culpable than risky harmdoing. Although poor judgment may be characteristic of adolescent risk-taking, there is no evidence that such judgement also infects intentional criminal behavior. Adolescents have stronger reason to avoid poor judgment when intentional criminal behavior is contemplated. If the primary variable adolescent offenders underestimate is the risk of getting caught for their wrongdoing, this is hardly reason to think that they are less responsible. Moreover, recent research suggests that adolescents respond to the incentive structure of the juvenile and criminal law much like adults.

. . . .

It appears, however, that the variables distinguishing adolescents from adults are not components of moral rationality. An impulsive agent or one especially subject to peer pressure, for example, may have the general capacity for normative competence. In this respect, these variables may be like other characteristics, such as hot-temper or greed, that are also not components of the general capacity for normative competence, but that may make it harder to exercise this capacity. If so, these variables would excuse only if they disabled the agent's capacity for rationality to a sufficient degree to warrant exculpation. Thus, we need to know the effect of these variables on the capacity for rationality and we need some sense of how much disability is sufficient to excuse.

. . . .

My analysis of the distinguishing variables implies that they do not undermine the general moral responsibility of an agent because they are not inconsistent with possessing the general capacity for normative competence concerning the gross, obviously wrong conduct constituting serious criminal offenses. At most, they make it harder for the agent to exercise the general capacity for normative competence. For example, consider again adolescent vulnerability to peer pressure. Adolescents are more likely to commit violent crime in groups, such as in juvenile gangs. There can be no doubt that youths defining their fluid adolescent identities in terms of their peers will find it harder to consider the interests of those their peers wish to harm. Indeed, there will be often be reasons and rituals to help the potential adolescent wrongdoer devalue and demonize victims or otherwise rationalize her conduct. But most such adolescents surely retain the general normative competence to understand and be guided by the reasons that killing, raping, burning, stealing, and so on are wrong, even when the pressure of peers motivates them to ignore or to underweight these reasons.

Although I conclude that the distinguishing characteristics canvassed so far are not themselves part of normative competence and that they probably do not undermine the general capacity for normative competence, the research has not addressed a potentially critical distinguishing variable — the capacity for empathy, which I claim is a component of normative competence. Although adolescents have adequate formal reasoning powers and understanding of the content of the moral rules, and sufficient life experience to understand the facts, including the consequences of the serious crimes that concern us, they may fully lack the general capacity for empathy that is a component of full moral agency. Put another way, although adolescents may be highly subject to peer pressure, they are also developmentally self-centered, a quality that will usually diminish with normal maturation. The research literature is not altogether clear on this question, but it seems to be a plausible assumption. If this is correct, then adolescents as a class may be less responsible moral agents in general and might deserve mitigation, if not full exoneration.

Elizabeth S. Scott & Laurence Steinberg, *Blaming Youth*

81 TEXAS LAW REVIEW 799, 801-802, 825 (2003)

Using the tools of developmental psychology, we examine two important dimensions of adolescence that distinguish this group from adults in ways that are important to criminal culpability. First, the scientific evidence indicates that teens are simply less competent decisionmakers than adults, largely because typical features of adolescent psycho-social development contribute to immature judgment. Adolescent capacities for autonomous choice, self-management, risk perception and calculation of future consequences are deficient as compared to those of adults, and these traits influence decision-making in ways that can lead to risky conduct. Second, adolescence is a developmental period in which personal identity and character are in flux, and begin to take shape through a process of exploration and experimentation. Youthful involvement in crime is often a part of this process, and, as such, it reflects the values and preferences of a transitory stage, rather than those of an individual with a settled identity. Most young law violators do not become adult criminals, because their youthful choices are shaped by factors and processes that are peculiar to (and characteristic of) adolescence.

Because these developmental factors influence their criminal choices, young wrongdoers are less blameworthy than adults under conventional criminal law conceptions of mitigation. Contemporary theorists debate whether the ultimate source of criminal responsibility is the actor's choice or his character. Choice theorists measure criminal blameworthiness by focusing on the actor's capacity for rational choice and opportunity to conform to the law. Character theorists argue instead that culpability is reduced when the actor can negate the inference that his act derived from bad character. Although neither character nor choice theorists focus seriously on how immaturity affects blameworthiness, our analysis demonstrates that a model of juvenile justice that acknowledges the immature judgment and unformed character of young actors fits comfortably within both of these frameworks.

The mitigation-based model that we advance is also consistent with criminal law doctrine and practice. Excuse and mitigation are available to two kinds of wrongdoers: those who are very different from ordinary people (because of endogenous incapacity such as mental disorder), and those who are ordinary people whose acts were responses to extraordinary circumstances or were aberrant in light of their past reputations and conduct. Young offenders in a real sense belong in both groups. Adolescent decisionmaking capacity is diminished as compared to adults due to psycho-social immaturity. At the same time, the scientific evidence suggests that most young lawbreakers are "ordinary" persons (and quite different from typical adult criminals) in that normal developmental forces drive their criminal conduct. This is important in two ways. First, ordinary adolescents are more vulnerable than are adults to exogenous pressures that can lead to criminal conduct. Further, an important source of mitigation in criminal law — evidence that the criminal act did not derive from bad moral character — is as applicable to youths as to upstanding adults who act aberrantly.

. . . .

. . . The important point for our purposes is that an analysis of adolescent culpability within either of these theoretical frameworks points to the conclusion that young actors are less culpable than are typical adults. In a framework that focuses only on choice, young law violators are poorer decisionmakers with more restricted opportunities to avoid criminal choices than are adults. Under an approach in which bad moral character is the ultimate source of culpability, ordinary adolescents, whose identity is in flux and character unformed, are less culpable than typical adult criminals.

[d] The Battered Child Defense

APPEAL IN MARICOPA COUNTY

Court of Appeals of Arizona
893 P.2d 60 (1994)

EHRLICH, PRESIDING JUDGE:

K.T., a juvenile, appeals from her adjudications of delinquency for manslaughter and theft. She [argues] that the juvenile court erred in considering manslaughter as a lesser-included offense of first-degree murder. . . . Because we find that the evidence supports a manslaughter determination . . . , we affirm the adjudications and dispositions.

FACTS AND PROCEDURAL HISTORY

On February 5, 1993, L.T., the juvenile's mother, was found dead in her home from a single gunshot to the back of her head. K.T., age twelve, was charged with theft, conspiracy to commit first-degree murder, first-degree murder and armed robbery. She admitted having killed her mother, but she claimed self-defense to the charge of first-degree murder predicated upon Battered Child Syndrome. After a delinquency proceeding, K.T. was found guilty of manslaughter and theft.

. . . .

DISCUSSION

A. *Lesser-included Offense of Manslaughter*

K.T. contends that the evidence was insufficient to support a determination of manslaughter. She specifically argues that she was either guilty of first-degree murder or not guilty and, therefore, that the juvenile court should not have considered the lesser-included offense of manslaughter. We do not agree.

When supported by the evidence, a consideration of the offense of manslaughter is required in a trial for first-degree murder. It is fundamental error not to do so. Conversely, "when the record is such that the defendant is either guilty of the crime charged or not guilty," for example, when the defendant has denied responsibility for the death, the trial court need not contemplate a lesser-included offense. Thus the central inquiry is whether there is sufficient evidence to support the lesser offense.

The pertinent portion of the manslaughter statute, ARIZ. REV. STAT. ANN. ("A.R.S.") § 13-1103, provides:

A. A person commits manslaughter by:

. . . .

2. Committing second degree murder as defined in § 13-1104, subsection A upon a sudden quarrel or heat of passion resulting from adequate provocation by the victim.

Second-degree murder is defined in relevant part in A.R.S. § 13-1104 as follows:

A. A person commits second degree murder if without premeditation:

1. Such person intentionallycauses the death of another person; . . . .

Given that K.T. admitted to having intentionally killed her mother, the issue became one of premeditation or, if that element of murder was lacking, whether there existed the requisite "heat of passion resulting from adequate provocation by the victim." The juvenile court made the following findings of fact after an exhaustive hearing:

> 1. [K.T.] intentionally killed her mother [L.T.] during the evening of February 5, 1993 by shooting her in the back of the head while the mother was asleep on the living room couch. [K.T.] knew at the time she shot and killed her mother that it was wrong.
>
> 2. [K.T.] did not act in self-defense and was not legally justified in using deadly physical force to kill [L.T.] during the evening of February 5, 1993.
>
> 3. [K.T.] acted in a heat of passion caused by years of severe physical and emotional abuse and neglect inflicted on [K.T.] and [her sister] by the victim, [L.T.].
>
> 4. The severe abuse and neglect inflicted by [L.T.] on [K.T.] and [her sister] was adequate provocation to deprive a reasonable child who was the victim of such abuse and neglect of self control.
>
>   . . . .
>
> 3. First Degree Murder in violation of A.R.S. § 13-1105 as alleged in Count III has not been proven true beyond a reasonable doubt. However, the Court finds that the lesser included offense of Manslaughter in violation of A.R.S. § 13-1103(A)(2) has been proven true beyond a reasonable doubt.

The juvenile relies on *State v. Reid,* 747 P.2d 560, 562 (Ariz. 1987), a case involving the shooting death of a father by his adult daughter in which the Arizona Supreme Court said that the evidence was insufficient to support a finding of reckless manslaughter when the victim was shot while he was asleep and 2.5 hours after a fight with his daughter. The daughter and her fiance lived with the father; the fiance's sister also was there that night. The significance of *Reid* for this case, which is not one of reckless manslaughter, is in the court's analysis that the lapse of time between the fight and the homicide negated a finding of "heat of passion" sufficient to find the daughter guilty of the lesser crime of manslaughter. However, the similar delay in this case calls into analysis the Battered Child Syndrome.

A "heat of passion must be such a passion as would naturally be aroused in the mind of an ordinarily reasonable person under the same facts and circumstances." "Adequate provocation" is "conduct or circumstances sufficient to deprive a reasonable person of self-control." These determinations are questions for the finder of fact, and thus are reviewed on appeal only for clear error.

The recognition and admission of evidence regarding the Battered Child Syndrome in Arizona is established. The Syndrome initially was described in medical terms, but since has been expanded to include psychological components.[72] The testimony by the experts on each side in this case was that

---

[72] [5] Experts from both sides in this case certified that Battered Child Syndrome is a corollary of Post-traumatic Stress Disorder and that K.T. suffered from that disorder. The condition is described in the American Psychiatric Association, *Diagnostic and Statistical Manual of Mental Disorders* (4th ed., 1994), 309.81.

victims of Battered Child Syndrome live in a state of constant fear of unpredictable violence and abuse. Frank Miller, M.D., the defense expert, described these children as "youngsters who have been subjected to horrific abuse, more than episodic or occasional, sustained repetitive terrorizing abuse over long periods of time. . . ." The record in this case is replete with examples of the terrible and degrading physical and emotional abuse suffered by the juvenile and her younger sister. Perhaps the most compelling evidence was the testimony of the defense expert, Dr. Miller:

> I have only seen a few cases in my career that approach the heinous treatment seen here. The only ones that have exceeded that that I've seen are always postmortem of the child.

Dr. Miller elaborated on K.T.'s constant fear of imminent irrational punishment. The punishment was worsening in intensity and severity to the point of possible death, punctuated by the presence of a casket in the house in which, it was threatened by L.T., K.T. and her sister could find themselves. This was underscored by the fact that both K.T. and her sister had been choked to the point of unconsciousness by L.T., whom Dr. Miller characterized as "sadistic." Indeed, he compared K.T.'s mental state to that of a concentration camp victim "[l]iving in a state of terror." He observed that such a mental state would cause someone to do an act otherwise violative of her own moral standards and that K.T. believed that, particularly given the lack of response from adult authorities from whom she repeatedly had sought help,[73] shooting her mother was her only option to protect herself and her younger sister from further peril and death. K.T. felt especially helpless with regard to protecting her younger sister, whom she believed to be suicidal; immediately before K.T. shot her mother, K.T.'s sister had told K.T. once more that she wanted to kill herself. When this obviously traumatic development is combined with the chronic emotional and physical abuse that characterizes and prompts the medical determination that Battered Child Syndrome exists, K.T.'s mental state fairly could be described as a sustained "heat of passion . . . as would naturally be aroused in the mind of an ordinarily reasonable person under the same facts and circumstances," "sufficient to deprive a reasonable person of self-control."[74] It was not error for the juvenile court to conclude that the 12-year-old girl acted in such a state and as a "result of adequate provocation," and find K.T. guilty of manslaughter.

. . . .

---

[73] [6] K.T., and persons on her behalf, had, without success, sought help numerous times from state, police, and school officials. Within a week of the killing alone, there was one more contact with the police and three with the Arizona Department of Economic Security Child Protective Services.

[74] [7] In a somewhat analogous situation, there exists A.R.S. § 13-415, to which the juvenile court alluded, which provides in the context of a battered spouse that "[i]f there have been past acts of domestic violence . . . against the defendant by the victim, the state of mind of a reasonable person . . . shall be determined from the perspective of a reasonable person who has been a victim of those past acts of domestic violence."

CONCLUSION

Because we find that the evidence before the juvenile court supports a finding of manslaughter, we affirm.

VOSS, JUDGE, . . . *dissenting.* . . .

. . . I respectfully dissent from the majority's holding that the evidence supports a manslaughter conviction.

As revealed at trial, the victim fell asleep on the living room couch. At that time, K.T. and her sister retrieved a gun, loaded it, and then walked out in the backyard. Upon returning to the living room, K.T. told her sister where to stand when the shooting took place and then pulled the trigger. Afterward, the girls took money and the keys to the van from the victim's purse and drove off to the store to make some purchases.

Arizona Revised Statutes Annotated § 13-1103 provides that "[a] person commits manslaughter by: Committing second degree murder . . . upon a sudden quarrel or heat of passion resulting from adequate provocation by the victim." The majority concedes that a sudden quarrel was not involved in the shooting, but contends that there was sufficient evidence that the shooting resulted from a heat of passion due to adequate provocation from the victim. An analogous argument was presented and rejected in *Reid*. In *Reid,* a daughter that was subjected to over twelve years of sexual, psychological, and physical abuse, shot her father in the head as he slept. The daughter's defense centered around his abuse and violent psychotic acts that caused her to fear for her life. An expert witness testified that the daughter's personality disorder compelled her to stay with her father and to believe that the only way out was to kill him. On appeal, the supreme court rejected the defendant's argument that the manslaughter instruction should have been given. The court found the evidence insufficient to support a finding that the killing occurred "upon a sudden quarrel or heat of passion resulting from adequate provocation by the victim." The court found:

> Whatever might have occurred before the victim retired for the evening is immaterial because the defendant waited two and a half hours before shooting him. The evidence presented no sudden quarrel between the victim and the accused. Neither was there any evidence that the victim provoked the accused. From testimony at trial, evidence was insufficient to indicate that the killing occurred in the heat of passion or immediately after a quarrel.

The court focused on the two and one-half hours lapse of time between the fight with his daughter and the subsequent shooting.

Here, the majority concedes that there was a similar lapse of time between the fight and the ultimate shooting; however they contend that because K.T. was a victim of battered child syndrome, she was in a constant heat of passion. The majority argues that K.T. lived in a constant state of fear, believing that shooting her mother was her only option to protect herself and her sister.

As in *Reid,* there was no evidence presented at trial that the shooting occurred upon a sudden quarrel or heat of passion. K.T. shot her mother as her mother slept after a lapse of time or "cooling off period" which would negate any heat of passion or sudden quarrel. To adopt the majority's position commissions the manslaughter instruction to any defendant claiming abuse.

Because the evidence does not support the finding that K.T. shot her mother in a heat of passion, the court erred in convicting K.T. of manslaughter.

————

NOTES AND QUESTIONS

1. Why would the juvenile in the *Maricopa County* case resist the juvenile court's consideration of manslaughter? Would such a consideration not make it less likely that she would be found guilty of murder? On the other hand, given the philosophy of juvenile courts, would it really matter whether she was convicted of manslaughter or murder?

2. The court in the *Maricopa County* cases refers in footnote 7 to the "somewhat analogous" case of a battered spouse who is justified in killing if a "reasonable person who has been a victim of . . . past acts of domestic violence would believe that physical force is immediately necessary to protect [herself] against [her abuser's] use or attempted use of unlawful physical force." ARIZ. REV. STAT. §§ 13-415, 404 (2001). Why are the battered spouse and battered child contexts only "somewhat analogous" in the eyes of the court? If a "reasonable" battered spouse feels her only alternative is to kill her abuser, even if he is not in the process of abusing her at the time she acts, would she be "justified" and thus acquitted? If so, why not a total justification defense in *Maricopa County*, rather than a partial defense mitigating the crime from murder to manslaughter?

3. The Arizona court in *Maricopa County* is not alone in suggesting less protection to battered children who kill their abusers than battered women who kill theirs. Under traditional self-defense doctrine, persons are entitled to resort to deadly force if necessary to repel another who unlawfully threatens the defender with immediate deadly force. Some courts have relaxed the requirement that the threatened attack be imminent in cases where women kill men who abuse them but where no immediate threat of abuse exists. The battered woman may be psychologically conditioned to believe that her abuser will eventually kill her and that she has no alternative short of self-help. Under such circumstances, the battered woman resorts to deadly force to avoid being killed. *See* JOSHUA DRESSLER, UNDERSTANDING CRIMINAL LAW, 215–21 (2d ed. 1995). Thus, with the aid of the testimony of mental health experts explaining the "battered woman syndrome," women who kill their abusers in nonconfrontational circumstances are sometimes allowed to present self-defense claims which would otherwise be precluded because no "immediate threat of deadly force" existed at the time of the killing. *Id.*

As noted by the *Maricopa County* court, mental health professionals have also identified a "battered child syndrome," which, like the battered woman syndrome, provides a psychological profile of abused children. Similar to battered women, battered children typically feel powerless against their abusers and experience acute feelings of fear towards them. Moreover, because battered children live in situations of pervasive abuse which may occur at any moment, they become "hypervigilant" in perceiving subtle cues from the abuser that not only create fear of impending abuse but also sometimes cause flashbacks to past abuse. *See* Michelle Ann Scott, *Self-Defense and the Child Parricide Defendant: Should Courts Make a Distinction Between Battered Woman and the Battered Child?* 44 DRAKE L. REV. 351, 361–65 (1996).

Children who kill their abusers, usually parents, in nonconfrontational circumstances have fared less well than their battered women counterparts in maintaining self-defense claims. Most of the cases have arisen in criminal court. Some courts refuse to admit expert testimony on battered child syndrome and refuse to instruct the jury on self-defense. For example, in a Wyoming case, *Jahnke v. State*, 682 P.2d 991 (Wyo. 1984), a sixteen-year-old killed his father who had physically and psychologically abused his son for much of the son's life. On the night of his death, the father had engaged in a violent altercation with the son. The father then took the boy's mother out to dinner, but before leaving warned the son not to be home when the father and mother returned. While his parents were out to dinner, the son made preparations to kill his father, placing weapons in various parts of the family home as "backups" should his initial plan fail. The son then waited in the darkened garage with a shotgun and shot and killed his father when he returned home. The son was tried for murder and the trial court refused a proffer of evidence by a mental health expert that the defendant suffered from the battered child syndrome. The trial court also refused to instruct the jury on self-defense.

On appeal, the court in *Jahnke* upheld the trial court's actions, finding insufficient evidence to support a claim of self-defense and expressing skepticism about the scientific validity of the battered child syndrome. In any event, the court saw little relevance of the syndrome to a self-defense claim given the absence of any unlawful or deadly threat by the father at the time of the attack by the son. While the court noted the battered women cases, it rejected the notion that either abused women or children should have a "special defense" which justifies killing the abuser. Finally, the court noted that the sole relevance of evidence of family abuse is to assist the jury in determining whether a defendant's belief that he was in danger of his life or serious bodily injury was reasonable under the circumstances. Finding insufficient evidence to support a claim of self-defense in the instant case, the court concluded that the proffered evidence of child abuse was properly excluded as irrelevant.

On the other hand, in *State v. Janes*, 850 P.2d 495 (Wash. 1993), the court recognized an expanded self-defense for battered children similar to that allowed battered women. The case involved seventeen-year-old Andrew, who killed his abusive stepfather after the stepfather had engaged in a prolonged and heated argument with Andrew's mother and then criticized Andrew "in a low voice" which the mother claimed was usually reserved for threats. The next day, after the stepfather had gone to work, Andrew awoke. His mother warned him that the stepfather was still angry. While his stepfather was at work, Andrew made preparations to kill him. After drinking whiskey, smoking marijuana, and loading a gun, Andrew pondered how miserable his stepfather had made him and his mother. When the stepfather arrived home that afternoon, Andrew shot and killed him as he entered the front door.

At the murder trial, a mental health professional testified that Andrew, the defendant, suffered from "post-traumatic stress disorder" as a consequence of years of the stepfather's abuse. This caused the defendant, in the opinion of the expert, to be in a constant state of fear of attack by his stepfather. Notwithstanding this evidence, the trial court denied the defendant's request for a self-defense instruction, finding insufficient evidence of imminent danger.

Upon conviction of second degree murder, the defendant appealed, contesting the denial of a self-defense instruction. The Washington Supreme Court, drawing an analogy to its cases permitting battered woman syndrome evidence, held that the evidence of battered child syndrome was properly admitted in order to assist the jury to understand the "reasonableness of the defendant's perceptions." Moreover, the court held that the trial court paid inadequate attention to Andrew's subjective fears in denying the self-defense instruction. In remanding the case to consider this issue, the court implied that if Andrew had actually feared an imminent attack by the stepfather at the time of the killing, a jury might conclude he killed in self-defense.

4. For commentary on the battered child syndrome defense, see Beth Bjerregaard & Anita Neuberger Blowers, *Chartering a New Frontier for Self-Defense Claims: The Applicability of the Battered Person Syndrome as a Defense for Parricide Offenders*, 33 U. LOUISVILLE J. FAM. L. 843 (1995); Joelle Anne Moreno, *Killing Daddy: Developing a Self-Defense Strategy for the Abused Child*, 137 U. PA. L. REV. 1281 (1989); Susan M. Kole, *Admissibility of Evidence of Battered Child Syndrome on Issue of Self-Defense*, 22 A.L.R. 5th 787 (1994).

[e] The Defense of Duress and Gang Activity

The common law defense of duress excuses a person who commits any offense except murder if: 1) the offender, or a person near to the offender, was threatened with death or serious bodily injury by another unless the offender committed the offense; 2) the offender reasonably believed the threat was impending and credible; 3) the offender had no reasonable escape from the threat except to comply with the demands of the person posing the threat; and 4) the offender was not at fault in exposing himself to the threat. JOSHUA DRESSLER, UNDERSTANDING CRIMINAL LAW 273–76 (2d ed. 1995).

While the traditional duress defense may be available in appropriate cases, some members of criminal gangs have unsuccessfully argued for an expanded defense, claiming that even though they may have been at fault in initially joining the gang, they should nevertheless be acquitted when the gang subsequently pressures them to commit a crime. *See, e.g., Meador v. State,* 664 S.W.2d 878 (Ark. Ct. App. 1984) (trial court properly rejected defendant's argument that duress defense could apply, even if he had recklessly placed himself in a situation where it was reasonably foreseeable that he would be subjected to threatened force to commit a crime). Others have been similarly unsuccessful in arguing that they were coerced into initially joining the gang and thus should enjoy a duress defense when gang pressures subsequently influence their criminal acts. *See, e.g., Williams v. State,* 646 A.2d 1101 (Md. Ct. Spec. App. 1994), *cert. denied,* 651 A.2d 855 (Md. 1995).

While the courts have rejected a new gang-duress defense, some commentators support its recognition. Citing evidence that some street gangs threaten physical injury as a means of initially recruiting members and subsequently induce criminal conduct, proponents argue that the underlying policies of the duress defense apply as readily to gang-induced crime as to traditional contexts where the defense is applicable. *See, e.g.,* David S. Rutkowski, *A Coercion Defense for the Street Gang Criminal: Plugging the Moral Gap in Existing Law*, 10 NOTRE DAME J.L. ETHICS & PUB. POL'Y 137, 155–83, 206–26 (1996).

[B] Status Offenses

[1] Procedures

[a] Constitutional Protections

The *Gault* Court specifically applied its procedural protections to delinquency adjudications, thus leaving open the question whether the protections apply in status offense cases. Indeed, as the following materials indicate, the lower court cases disagree on whether *Gault* and its progeny govern status offense adjudications, especially where "loss of liberty" in the form of an incarcerative commitment is not available as a direct disposition for status offenders.

IN THE MATTER OF SPALDING

Court of Appeals of Maryland
332 A.2d 246 (1975)

Argued before MURPHY, C. J., and SINGLEY, SMITH, DIGGES, LEVINE, ELDRIDGE and O'DONNELL, JJ.

LEVINE, JUDGE.

In the landmark decision of *In re Gault*, the Supreme Court held, for the first time, that various of the federal constitutional guarantees accompanying ordinary criminal proceedings are applicable, in certain instances, to state juvenile delinquency cases. Those safeguards, all embraced within fundamental procedural due process, are: Notice of charges; the right to counsel; confrontation and cross-examination; and the privilege against self-incrimination. Appellant seeks to extend that holding — with specific reference to self-incrimination — to another area of juvenile court jurisdiction in Maryland, known as "Children in Need of Supervision" (CINS).

The Court of Special Appeals upheld the decision of the Circuit Court for Baltimore County sitting as a Juvenile Court rejecting appellant's claim. We granted certiorari to consider whether statements made to the police by appellant — then thirteen years of age — should have been suppressed; whether she was denied her constitutional right to refuse to testify; and whether she should have been permitted to cross-examine a police officer with regard to both voluntariness of the statements made to him and the warnings mandated by *Miranda*.

In the early morning hours of January 31, 1973, Officer Joseph W. Price, a member of the Baltimore County Police Department assigned to the Dundalk station, responded on instructions from his headquarters to a call from City Hospital to investigate a possible rape and overdose of narcotics. There, he was met by a Mr. Carter, who advised him that his daughter, age eleven, had taken a white tablet which had impaired her speech, had caused a loss of equilibrium and had dilated her pupils. She had also admitted to her parents that she had engaged in sexual intercourse with an adult male on January 29 in an apartment immediately below that occupied by her family. She contrived this visit by climbing down from her bedroom window. When questioned by the police officer, the child acknowledged the episode of the 29th, and added that on the same occasion she had engaged in sexual acts with others who were present including two women. The Carters had brought their daughter to the hospital because they wanted her examined for possible sexual intercourse and treated for the drug.

Later that morning, at approximately 6:30 A.M., Officer Price again met with the Carter family at the Dundalk police station. Also there is response to a phone call from the officer were appellant and her mother. The minister of the church attended by both families was also present. Officer Price and one of his superiors then proceeded to interrogate both girls under somewhat disorganized conditions. Much of this appears to have resulted from interference by both the minister, who exercised considerable influence over the girls, and the parents. Ultimately, with permission of the latter, Officer Price obtained written statements from both girls. The officer later testified that the parents had ". . . insisted on the girls giving the information. They were at sometime, they were [sic] some yelling at the girls and the girls being upset, crying, they were trying to calm them down. They were trying to help and assist getting all the information they could."

In her oral and written statements to the police that morning, as in her statements subsequently given to Juvenile Bureau detectives, appellant admitted her participation in the same events of the 29th as had been described by the Carter youngster. In doing so, she supplied the names of all those who had been in attendance on that occasion. She also recounted additional episodes of similar sexual activity in the basement of her home with male boarders residing there; and at a number of other "parties" in the apartment below that occupied by the Carters. She was able to attend these early-morning functions amounting to nothing less than orgies at which adults and juveniles were in heavy attendance, by placing a sleeping pill in her mother's coffee. She was furnished the pills, and was driven to those bizarre parties by one Sheldon B. Coon, who apparently was the impresario of the "sex ring." He gave a pill to the girls on each occasion immediately before they departed from their residences, and again before they engaged in sexual intercourse. This seems to have had a narcotic-like influence on them.

After the police had struggled through their various interrogation procedures on the 31st, they took the girls to the Parkville police station, with the approval of the Department of Juvenile Services, where they were detained overnight. This step was taken because the statements furnished by the girls disclosed assaults upon them by Coon, who threatened to kill them if they ever revealed information to anyone concerning the parties. The official report filed by the police specified "protective custody" as the reason for the detention. Once the police had completed the interviews, they immediately sought arrest warrants for the large number of adults identified by the girls. The men in this group were charged with "statutory rape" and the women with "unnatural and perverted sexual practices." In both instances, the two girls were listed as victims.

On the following morning, February 1, 1973, both girls were brought before Juvenile Master Kahl pursuant to petitions of the Department of Juvenile Services, which charged each with being a "delinquent child" and "in need of supervision;[75] within the meaning and intent of § 70-2 of Article 26 of the Annotated Code of Maryland." The Master found both girls to be in need of care and treatment, but, significantly, did not find them to be "delinquent."[76] His memorandum, dated February 1, 1973, is quoted here:

> Police investigation indicates that these young girls have been *victimized* by a group of adults in the Dundalk area and elsewhere, for purposes of sexual abuse and drug experimentation. It is not known at this point just how much damage has already been done, physically and psychologically, to these girls. The situation is one of the most serious that I have encountered in my four years with the Juvenile Court.
>
> Both girls are in need of medical treatment immediately, and notwithstanding whatever wishes the parents of the girls may have at this time, *I find them to be Children In Need Of Supervision* and am committing them to the Department of Juvenile Services for placement, with the intention that they shall be immediately admitted to the University Hospital for *medical evaluation and treatment.*
>
> On February 7, 1973, they are to be transported to the Maryland Children's Center for evaluation and return to Court one month thereafter. (emphasis added).

During the ensuing month, extensive psychiatric and family studies were conducted at the Maryland Children's Center.

On March 7, 1973, immediately upon their return from the Children's Center, the girls attended a hearing before Juvenile Master Peach. Armed

---

[75] [2] The reasons assigned for these allegations are:

. . . investigation by the Baltimore County Police Department revealed that the respondent had consumed controlled and prohibitive [sic] narcotics and engaged in acts of sexual intercourse and sexual perversion with an unknown number of male and female adults for a period of more than one year. The respondent is ungovernable and beyond the control of her parent, deports herself in such a manner as to be a danger to herself and others and is in need of care and treatment.

[76] [4] In fact, the petition previously referred to above appears to contain the only official suggestion of delinquency in the record. Ironically, the "complaint" form of the Department of Juvenile Services, apparently completed on either the 31st or 1st, lists "child in need of supervision" as the sole "offense description."

with the thorough reports and comprehensive recommendation of the Children's Center, he adjudicated each girl to be "a child in need of supervision" and "in need of care and treatment." He therefore "committed both of them to the Department of Juvenile Services for placement and planning so that they can receive some therapy to help them cope with the problems which I am sure lie ahead for both of them." Exceptions to the findings and recommendations of the Master were duly noted on behalf of each juvenile, accompanied by a request for a de novo hearing before the court.

Pursuant to the exceptions and requests, the cases came on for trial on May 3, 1973, before the Circuit Court for Baltimore County sitting as a Juvenile Court, . . . where extensive testimony and argument ensued in accordance with Maryland Rule 908. Shortly before the trial commenced, a written motion was filed on behalf of appellant aimed at suppressing the statements made by her to the police, to the Juvenile Service workers and to the staff of the Children's Center. At the outset of the trial, the court announced that it would reserve its ruling on that motion.

During the course of the trial, objections to the admissibility of those statements were renewed on the grounds that the fourfold *Miranda* warnings had not been given by any of the interrogating officers prior to or during any questioning.[77] Officer Price, however, had announced to all those assembled at the police station that "anything they said could be used against them in a court of law if they were charged." This colloquy also appears in the testimony:

> MR. MEOLA: Your Honor, I would like to question the officer about what warning he did give these children.
>
> THE COURT: I don't think he has to give any warning. *They were not in custody for the commission of a crime or for a delinquency petition at this time.* They were volunteered statements given with the consent at the insistence of the parents. The *Miranda* warning doesn't apply to these statements, gentlemen. (emphasis added).

It is this refusal that laid the groundwork for one of the three questions framed by the Writ of Certiorari.

Later in the trial, when asked by the court to describe how he elicited the statements from the girls, Officer Price stated "They volunteered all of this information to begin with, and it was too bizarre I started asking questions to try to pinpoint dates and time and individuals." The confusion which reigned at the police station and the abbreviated warning announced by Officer Price are demonstrated in this excerpt from his testimony:

> Q: Okay, you stated earlier the parents were shouting at the girls?
>
> A: Everybody was yelling at each other trying to get information, specifically from Elaine (Carter), because she was still under the influence of drugs, trying to get through to her. The parents were upset.

---

[77] [5] Only the statements made to the police are included within the ambit of our review pursuant to the Writ of Certiorari.

Q: You stated earlier the girls were crying?

A: Yes, I did, from the yelling of the parents.

Q: Whom did you make the statement to the statement they made would be used against them, to whom did you make that statement?

A: I made it to everyone in the room there, anything they said could be used against them in a court of law.

THE COURT: Did you go any further?

A: Yes, sir, if they were charged with a crime, named offense.

Q: Was this while they were quiet or were they still yelling?

A: Everybody was milling around. I had a little bit of trouble with Reverend Gatling there. I had to threaten to arrest him just to keep him quiet.

Q: Do you know for certain that the parents heard that statement?

A: I cannot be certain anybody heard anything.

In the course of their testimony, Officer Price and the detectives from the Juvenile Bureau were permitted, over objection, to state what the girls had said during the various interviews. Then, an announcement by the prosecuting attorney that he proposed to call appellant to the stand as a witness drew a vigorous objection from counsel on the ground of self-incrimination. Prior to any definitive ruling by the court, however, she was shown her written statement given to Officer Price on January 31, and confirmed the truth of its contents. She also acknowledged on her direct testimony that she knew Coon and certain of the other persons for whom adult warrants had been issued. When asked by her own counsel whether anyone at the police station had informed her that she was not required to make any statements, she replied:

A: Well, we more or less made it on our own. We figured we could save some more kids, but they gave us no rights or anything.

THE COURT: Give you what?

A: Any kind of rights, we thought we were doing the State a favor.

THE COURT: Well, as I understand that you said you made the statement on your own?

A: Yes.

At the conclusion of the trial, the court rendered its decision orally, finding that the evidence overwhelmingly had established the girls to be in need of supervision because they had "deported themselves so as to injure or endanger themselves or others" and therefore required "guidance, treatment, or rehabilitation." These findings were incorporated into written orders, which also committed the girls to the jurisdiction of the Department of Juvenile Services for placement in foster homes with prescribed visitation rights granted to their parents. It is from those orders that the appeal was taken to the Court of Special Appeals.

The contentions that the statements made to the police should have been suppressed at the court hearing and that cross-examination of the police officer should have been permitted regarding the voluntariness of those statements and the *Miranda* warnings were rejected by the Court of Special Appeals on the basis that the questioning of the police at the hospital and at the police station was not custodial interrogation within the meaning of *Miranda*.

In holding that appellant's compelled testimony did not violate her privilege against self-incrimination, the court of Special Appeals carefully traced the enactment of the jurisdictional category, "Child in Need of Supervision." As Judge Moore noted for the court, such a child refers to one who is:

(1) Subject to compulsory school attendance who is habitually and without justification truant from school;

(2) Without substantial fault on the part of his parents, guardian, or other custodian, who is habitually disobedient, *ungovernable*, and — beyond their control;

(3) *Who so deports himself as to injure or endanger himself or others;* or

(4) Who has committed an offense applicable only to children; and

(5) Requires guidance, treatment or rehabilitation. (emphasis added).

This classification, therefore, stands in marked contrast to a "Delinquent child," defined as one " 'who commits a delinquent act and who requires supervision, treatment or rehabilitation.' [Subject to the provisions of Art. 26, § 70-2(d)] a 'Delinquent act' was defined in § 70-1(g) as 'an act which is in violation of Article 66 ½ of this Code, any other traffic violation, or an act *which would be a crime if done by a person who is not a child.*' " (Emphasis in original.)

Essentially, then, the Court of Special Appeals stressed the basic statutory distinctions between the delinquency and CINS categories, taking particular care to emphasize the differences in disposition which are prescribed for each. For example, [state statute] provided:

(a) If a child is found to be neglected, delinquent, in need of supervision, mentally handicapped, or dependent, the court may make disposition as most suited to the physical, mental, and moral welfare of the child; but *no child (except a delinquent child)* may be confined in an institution or other facility designed or operated for the benefit of delinquent children, provided that this prohibition shall not apply to facilities designated by the State Department of Juvenile Services of the Department of Health and Mental Hygiene.

(b) If an adequate facility required by this section has not been established, the court may approve a facility under the supervision and control of the State departments of juvenile services, social services, mental hygiene and other appropriate child-care agencies, for temporary use as such facility, but the use of a facility which does not meet the requirement of this section may not continue beyond January 1, 1975. (emphasis added).

And § 70-21 also provided, in relevant part, that "No child shall be committed or transferred to a penal institution or other facility used primarily for the execution of sentences of persons convicted of a crime."[78]

The Court of Special Appeals summed it all up in stating:

> It is evident, we think, that an important purpose of the legislative revision of the juvenile code was to insulate certain forms of juvenile misconduct from the consequences of an adjudication of delinquency as described in *Gault*. The creation of the category of CINS reflects a studied design of the legislature to insure that treatment of children guilty of misconduct peculiarly reflecting the propensities and suscep-tibilities of youth, will acquire none of the institutional, quasi-penal features of treatment that in *Gault*'s view had been the main differ-ence between the theory and the practice of the juvenile court system. . . .

Thus, it "decline[d] to go further and hold that in a proceeding upon a CINS petition due process requires that the child be permitted, on Fifth Amendment grounds, to have relevant evidence excluded and to refuse to testify."

We shall affirm, finding it necessary, however, to decide only that the Fifth Amendment privilege against self-incrimination is inapplicable to this pro-ceeding. Because we so hold, the related questions of *Miranda* warnings and voluntariness are subsumed within that holding. "The privilege against self-incrimination is, of course, related to the question of the safeguards necessary to assure that admissions or confessions are reasonably trustworthy, that they are not the mere fruits of fear or coercion, but are reliable expressions of the truth."

Since this case derives its impetus from *Gault*, we pause for a careful exami-nation of the relevant facts on which that decision is bottomed. . . .

. . . .

In *Gault*, the Court did not deal with the totality of the relationship between the juvenile and the state; indeed, it did not even consider the entire process applicable to juvenile "delinquents."

> . . . We consider only the problems presented to us by this case. These relate to the proceedings by which a determination is made as to whether a juvenile is a 'delinquent' as a result of alleged misconduct on his part, with the consequence that he may be committed to a state institution. As to these proceedings, there appears to be little current dissent from the proposition that the Due Process Clause has a role to play. . . .

Turning to the issue of self-incrimination, the Court again emphasized that it was ". . . concerned only with a proceeding to determine whether a minor is a 'delinquent' and which may result in commitment to a state institution."

---

[78] [8] Both appellee and the Court of Special Appeals have noted that in the 1974 recodification, § 3-832 added a prohibition against confinement "in a juvenile training school or any similar institution" for all categories except delinquency. This was not effective, however, in May 1973.

This same emphasis was repeated in even stronger terms when the Court said that ". . . juvenile proceedings to determine 'delinquency,' which may lead to commitment to a state institution, must be regarded as 'criminal' for purposes of the privilege against self-incrimination." Thus, the scope of *Gault* is clear. When the Supreme Court ". . . conclude[d] that the constitutional privilege against self-incrimination is applicable in the case of juveniles as it is with respect to adults," it was referring to a proceeding to determine "delinquency," viz., ". . . an act which would be a crime if done by a person who is not a child," which is the statutory definition in Maryland. The test enunciated in *Gault*, however, is two-pronged. In addition, the "delinquency" must be such that it may result in commitment to a state institution.

. . . .

Whatever else is established by *Gault*, it is clear that labels are not controlling in determining the applicability of the Due Process Clause to juvenile proceedings. In regard to the first "prong" of the test, for example, it is doubtful that the *Gault* result would have been different had merely the title of the proceedings been changed from "delinquency" to "CINS," and all else had remained the same. The essential element is that the juvenile be charged with an act which would be a crime if committed by an adult. In *In re Winship*, the Court relied on *Gault* in answering affirmatively the question "whether proof beyond a reasonable doubt is among the 'essentials of due process and fair treatment' required during the adjudicatory stage *when a juvenile is charged with an act which would constitute a crime if committed by an adult.*" (emphasis added). The Court later added that ". . . intervention [by a juvenile court] cannot take the form of subjecting the child to the stigma of a finding that he violated a criminal law and to the possibility of institutional confinement on proof insufficient to convict him were he an adult."

Labels are equally unimportant in terms of the second "prong," confinement in a state institution. As the Court said:

> . . . A boy is charged with misconduct. The boy is committed to an institution where he may be restrained of liberty for years. It is of no constitutional consequence — and of limited practical meaning — that the institution to which he is committed is called an Industrial School. The fact of the matter is that, however euphemistic the title, a 'receiving home' or an 'industrial school' for juveniles is an institution of confinement in which the child is incarcerated for a greater or lesser time. His world becomes 'a building with whitewashed walls, regimented routine and institutional hours . . . .' Instead of mother and father and sisters and brothers and friends and classmates, his world is peopled by guards, custodians, state employees, and 'delinquents' confined with him for anything from waywardness to rape and homicide.

"A proceeding where the issue is whether the child will be found to be 'delinquent' and subjected to the loss of his liberty for years is comparable in seriousness to a felony prosecution." Finally, the Court added: "For this purpose, at least, commitment is a deprivation of liberty. It is incarceration against one's will, whether it be called 'criminal' or 'civil.'"

In sum, then, Due Process requires that various of the federal constitutional guarantees accompanying ordinary criminal proceedings, specifically including the privilege against self-incrimination, be made applicable at the adjudicatory stage of those juvenile proceedings in which the act charged would constitute a crime if committed by an adult and which may result in confinement of the child to a state institution.

Other state courts that have considered the question of which proceedings should invoke an application of the *Gault* rights have reached similar conclusions. For example, California's statutory scheme is quite similar to Maryland's, an apparent difference, however, being that delinquent and CINS children may be sent to the same institutions under the California Code. In that state, "[j]uveniles are entitled to the fundamental protection of the Bill of Rights in proceedings that may result in confinement or other sanctions, whether the state labels these proceedings 'criminal' or 'civil.'"

The California courts have consistently held that CINS children are entitled to the same guarantees as delinquent children when they are charged with an act which would be a crime if committed by an adult. . . . Illustrative of the label fallacy is *In re H.*, 85 Cal. Rptr. 359 (1970). In that case, a juvenile was charged under § 602 [delinquency] with assault with a deadly weapon and manslaughter. The sole evidence against him was his confession that he struck the child for whom he was babysitting. The confession was suppressed, as having been illegally obtained, and the petition was dismissed. The trial judge, on his own motion, however, promptly amended the petition to charge the juvenile with being "in danger of leading an idle, dissolute, lewd, or immoral life" under § 601 [CINS]; and then admitted the confession and sustained the petition, since the defendant was no longer charged with "delinquent." The Court of Appeal reversed, holding:

> Even though the amended petition was filed under § 601 [CINS], the minor rightly may demand that proof of the allegation of the *commission of felonies* must meet the same standards as if the petition was brought under § 602 [delinquency], namely, a preponderance of evidence legally admissible in the trial of *criminal* cases. . . . "Thus, a confession illegally obtained cannot be relied upon to support a finding that a minor committed a crime" (emphasis in original).

. . . .

We turn then to Cindy Ann Spalding. The state contends that the *Gault* rights do not apply to CINS because of the significant differences between those proceedings and delinquency cases. It cites these dissimilarities: CINS children may not be confined in institutions designed or operated for the benefit of delinquent children; CINS children may not be placed in detention;[79] and CINS children may not be waived to adult criminal courts. Also,

---

[79] [13] Code (1974), § 3-823 of the Courts and Judicial Proceedings Article, effective January 1, 1974, so provides, but as we have already observed, it is the statutory scheme applicable in May 1973 that governs this case. At that time, Art. 26, § 70-12 permitted detention of CINS children, but not in a jail or other facility used for detention of adults charged with a criminal offense and children adjudicated or alleged to be delinquent. Moreover, even this statutory prohibition was riddled with exceptions.

in the teeth of the *Gault* teaching that labels are of little consequence, the State nevertheless argues that the label "CINS" bears significantly less stigma than "delinquent." Finally, the State claims that, having been placed in a foster home, appellant was not committed to a "state institution" because shelter care and foster homes are not in that category.

Understandably enough, appellant maintains that "CINS" children, though treated differently in certain respects, are the same as "delinquent" children for the purpose of applying *Gault* rights. She emphasizes that at the time of her hearing, she conceivably could have been confined with delinquent children; that she could have been committed to a "state institution," and thus compelled to leave her home with a resulting curtailment of her freedom; that she is now one step closer to incarceration; and that she was charged with violating a criminal statute. Although there is much to commend these arguments, we need not decide whether the second prong of the *Gault* test, *i. e.,* potential confinement of the child to a state institution, mandated an application of the privilege against self-incrimination in this case. We reach this conclusion because, in any event, we think that appellant was not charged in this proceeding with an act which would constitute a crime if committed by an adult.

As we noted earlier, the petition filed on February 1, 1973, did allege that appellant was both a "delinquent child" and a "child in need of supervision." The reasons assigned for these allegations were the consumption of narcotics, the acts of sexual intercourse and perversion practiced upon her, and her ungovernability. But, in the context of all the material events, which ensued during the critical period, since she was, in fact, a victim, the charge of "delinquency" in the petition must be regarded as simply an unexplained anomaly.

The testimony describing the circumstances at the hospital and the police station clearly depicts the girls as victims of "sex" crimes committed by the adults. That this was the position of the police is borne out not merely by their subsequent testimony, but also by their immediate application for adult arrest warrants listing the girls as victims; the overnight detention for the purpose of "protective custody"; and the total absence of suggested criminality on the part of the girls in any police records.

Even within the Department of Juvenile Services, the "delinquency" charge is out-of-step with every other official record or entry pertaining to the girls. Its own complaint form, completed on the same day as the petition, lists "child in need of supervision" as the single "offense description." Again, on that same day, February 1, the Master referred to the girls as having "been victimized by a group of adults," found them to be "in Need of Supervision" and omitted any mention of "delinquency." Nothing in their four-week commitment to Maryland Children's Center for psychiatric evaluation was inconsistent with this official attitude. Nor do the reports and recommendations of that institution reflect a contrary view.

In sum, with the elimination of the delinquency "charge" by the Master on February 1, the claims of alleged "criminal" conduct, on which it was premised, vanished with it. What remained was the single allegation that appellant ". . . is ungovernable and beyond the control of her parent, deports herself in such a manner as to be a danger to herself and others and is in need of care and treatment." From that time forward, at least, appellant was not charged in this proceeding with any acts which would constitute a crime if committed by an adult.

As we have said, we do not find it necessary to rest our decision on the second prong of the test laid down by *Gault*, pertaining to possible confinement in a "state institution." It is sufficient to hold that since appellant was not charged with an act which, in the circumstances of this case, would constitute a crime if committed by an adult, the privilege against self-incrimination is not applicable to these proceedings.

Judgment affirmed; appellant to pay costs.

ELDRIDGE, JUDGE (*dissenting*):

The majority's decision in this case cannot be reconciled with *In re Gault*, and later Supreme Court cases dealing with the constitutional rights to be accorded accused children in juvenile proceedings.

The majority opinion, in my view, correctly construes *Gault*, and the subsequent Supreme Court cases, as setting forth a two-pronged test for determining whether the Fifth Amendment privilege against self-incrimination is applicable to a juvenile proceeding. The test is: (1) whether the juvenile "is charged with an act that would constitute a crime if committed by an adult," and (2) whether the child may be "subjected to the loss of his liberty," or whether the proceedings "may result in commitment to a state institution."

Moreover, as the majority opinion in this case seems initially to acknowledge, labels are not controlling as to either aspect of the test. It does not matter whether the name of the proceedings is "delinquency" or "child in need of supervision" ("CINS"), or whether the loss of liberty may be commitment to an "industrial school" or a "receiving home." The child's entitlement to the protection of the privilege against self-incrimination depends upon the substance of the matter, namely whether he or she is charged with an act that would be a crime if committed by an adult and whether the proceedings could result in a deprivation of liberty.

Despite an apparent recognition of these principles by the majority in this case, and specifically a recognition that labels are not controlling, the majority opinion goes on to make the labels "victim" and "CINS" determinative. Although the acts by petitioner Cindy Ann Spalding which caused these proceedings, and her subsequent deprivation of liberty, would have been criminal acts if committed by an adult, the majority labels her the "victim" of "sex crimes." Based upon this label, and the fact that the charge and title of the proceedings were later limited to a "child in need of supervision," the majority denies petitioner the constitutional right not to incriminate herself and upholds the action of the trial court in compelling her to take the witness stand and testify against herself.

There can be no question in this case about the fact that the original basis for the charges against petitioner, and one of the grounds for the ultimate adjudication of a "child in need of supervision," was her commission of acts which would have constituted crimes if committed by an adult. In the petition to the juvenile court, filed February 1, 1973, Cindy Ann Spalding was charged with being a delinquent child and a child in need of supervision. The only specific facts alleged in the petition as a basis for the charges were that "respondent has consumed controlled and prohibited narcotics and engaged in acts of sexual intercourse and sexual perversion with an unknown number of male and female adults for a period of more than one year." It was also alleged, without any additional supporting facts being set forth, that Cindy Ann Spalding was "ungovernable and beyond the control of her parent" and was "a danger to herself and others."

The juvenile court master, Mr. Kahl, on February 1, 1973, signed a "Commitment Order," which recited that Cindy Ann Spalding has been adjudged a child in need of supervision and which committed her to the custody of the Department of Juvenile Services. The Memorandum of Master Kahl which accompanied that order stated, "Police investigation indicates that these young girls have been victimized by a group of adults in the Dundalk area and elsewhere, for purposes of sexual abuse and drug experimentation." Other than a reference to the fact that the girls needed medical treatment, the sexual conduct and drug abuse constituted the only facts or basis set forth in the memorandum for the commitment order.

On March 7, 1973, petitioner was returned from the Maryland Children's Center and was committed to the custody of the Department of Juvenile Services by Juvenile Court Master Peach. In Master Peach's memorandum accompanying the order committing petitioner, he referred to her "participation in unbelievable sex orgies" and the use of drugs. While the master also referred to the fact that petitioner had not been attending school and had been in the habit of sleeping until two or three o'clock in the afternoon, there is no doubt that the behavior which furnished in large part the basis for the commitment order was engaging in "sex orgies" and drug abuse.

At the juvenile court trial itself, testimony offered by the prosecution to sustain the charge of "child in need of supervision" largely related to the girls' use of narcotics, to petitioner's having "drugged" her mother, and to the "sex orgies." The trial judge, in his opinion delivered at the end of the trial adjudicating petitioner and her co-defendant to be "children in need of supervision," found as a fact that the girls "have been associated in immoral sexual activities" and have "indulged" in the taking of "drugs of a narcotic nature." While the trial judge also placed some weight upon petitioner's failure to attend school, there is no question but that the sexual and drug abuse activities furnished the principal factual basis for the judge's adjudication and commitment order.

Of course, using "controlled and prohibited narcotics" and engaging in "acts of . . . sexual perversion," to use the language of the petition against Cindy Ann Spalding, are serious crimes in Maryland. . . . Petitioner was clearly "charged with . . . act[s] which would constitute . . . crime[s] if committed by an adult;" and these acts furnished a large part of the basis for the ultimate "CINS" adjudication and commitment.

The majority opinion states that there is a "marked contrast" between the "delinquent" classification and the "CINS" or "child in need of supervision" classification.[80] However, as this case illustrates, criminal conduct may furnish the factual basis for the "CINS" adjudication. For example, "CINS" includes children who are "habitually disobedient, ungovernable, and beyond [their parents] control." The evidence of such characteristics, as in this case, may be criminal acts. "CINS" also includes a child who "[d]eports himself so as to injure or endanger himself or others." Of course, a child who commits criminal acts such as using narcotic drugs or "drugging" someone else, is deporting herself "so as to injure or endanger" herself or others. This is why "labels" should not be, and under the Supreme Court's decisions are not, controlling.

While not dealt with in the majority opinion, the other "prong" or requirement of the *Gault* test was also met in this case. While petitioner was in fact committed to a "foster home" instead of an "institution," forced living for a period of years in a "foster home and away from one's own home and family is a loss of his liberty," Moreover, even if commitment to a foster home, and against the will of the child and her parents, would not be deemed to meet the second requirement of the *Gault* test, petitioner was subjected to the possibility of commitment to an institution. Code (1972 Repl. Vol., 1974 Cum. Supp.) Art. 52A, § 5(c), specifically authorizes a juvenile court judge to commit a "CINS" child "to any public or private institution . . . ." As to limitations upon this authority, the pertinent statute in effect at the time of petitioner's trial, authorized confinement of a "CINS" child in an institution provided that the institution were not designed or operated for the benefit of delinquent children. There were exceptions even to that proviso. The present statute, adds the further limitation to the authority to commit "CINS" children to institutions, requiring that such institutions may not be juvenile training schools or something similar to juvenile training schools. Limitations upon the nature of the institutions to which "CINS" children may be committed do not change the fact that under Maryland law, a child adjudicated to be in need of supervision may be committed to "an institution of confinement in which the child is incarcerated for a greater or lesser time."

The two-pronged test of *Gault* was therefore met in this case. Petitioner was charged with acts that would be crimes if committed by adults, and petitioner was subjected to the prospect of a loss of liberty or confinement in an institution. Consequently, under *Gault*, the Fifth Amendment privilege against self-incrimination was fully applicable to this proceeding.

There can be no doubt in this case that the petitioner's Fifth Amendment rights were violated. At no time were the warnings required by *Miranda* given. Both the trial court and the Court of Special Appeals stated that petitioner was not yet in custody when her incriminating statements were first made to the police on January 31, 1973, and therefore under *Miranda* warnings were not required. This view of what constitutes "custody" is a dubious one. The Supreme Court in *Miranda* defined custodial interrogation as "questioning initiated by law enforcement officers after a person has been taken into custody or otherwise deprived of his freedom of action in any significant way."

---

[80] [1] Actually, as the opinion of the Court of Special Appeals in this case points out, much of what is now contained in the "CINS" definition was formerly included in the definition of a "delinquent" child.

Here, petitioner was brought to the police station by her mother at 6:30 a. m. on January 31, 1973, following a phone call from the investigating police officer and a request from the officer that she be brought to the station. As far as the record shows, she has never been at liberty to return home since that time. She was interrogated during the day at the station, gave a written statement, and was then taken to another police station where, with the approval of the Department of Juvenile Services, she was "detained" over-night. On the following morning, February 1, 1973, petitioner was formally charged and committed to the custody of the Department of Juvenile Services. To say that petitioner was not in custody from and after the morning of January 31, 1973, is to be unrealistic. Moreover, even if it be assumed arguendo that petitioner was not yet in custody on January 31st, the record shows that after the first hearing before the juvenile master and the commit-ment order on February 1st, petitioner was interrogated further by the police and the juvenile authorities, gave information to them, and no *Miranda* warnings were given at those times either.

Finally, wholly apart from the matter of *Miranda* warnings, petitioner's Fifth Amendment rights were violated when at the trial she was compelled, over her attorney's objection, to take the witness stand and testify against herself. At the trial, after several prosecution witnesses testified, the following took place:

> MR. NEWELL [prosecuting attorney]: I call Cindy Ann Spalding to the stand.
>
> MR MEOLA [petitioner's attorney]: Objection.
>
> THE COURT: Well —
>
> MR. MEOLA: I instruct my witness not to testify at all. She may be —
>
> THE COURT: All right, take the stand, Cindy, step up to the stand. All right, you'll be sworn first.

Petitioner was then examined extensively by the trial judge and the prosecuting attorney. Objections made by her attorney to incriminating questions were ignored or overruled. The language of the Fifth Amendment is that "No person . . . shall be compelled in any criminal case to be a witness against himself . . . ." No more clear-cut violation of that provision could be imagined than what occurred at petitioner's trial.

The majority opinion in this case could have significant consequences. Because Cindy Ann Spalding is labeled a "victim," and because the proceed-ings are called "CINS" instead of "delinquent," she is deemed not entitled to those constitutional rights which the Supreme Court has held are applicable in juvenile proceedings. However, if petitioner was a "victim," anytime a juvenile is engaged in criminal activity with adults, the juvenile could be said to be a "victim." A teenager might be enticed by an adult into engaging in a series of armed robberies with the adult, and could be viewed as a "victim." Turning to the name of the proceeding, since criminal acts may be the basis for "CINS" proceedings, and since an adjudication that a child is in need of supervision may lead to confinement in an institution for as long a period as an adjudication that he is delinquent, virtually all juvenile proceedings could be labeled "CINS" by the authorities without significant consequences. Thus by using the right labels, *i.e.,* "victim" and "CINS," the police and juvenile authorities will be able to bypass the requirements laid down by the Supreme Court in *Gault.*

NOTES AND QUESTIONS

1. Is there a meaningful distinction for *Gault* purposes between "delinquency" and "CINS" cases? If so, is the *Spaulding* court correct in seeing the distinction grounded, at least in part, by the different connotations of the "delinquency" and "CINS" labels?

2. Some courts define the applicability of *Gault* merely in terms of whether or not a status offense adjudication carries the possibility of "commitment to an institution in which the juvenile's freedom is curtailed." *See, e.g., In re K,* 554 P.2d 180 (Or. Ct. App. 1976) (*Gault* not applicable in status offense proceedings where institutional confinement was not a possible disposition); *State ex rel. Wilson v. Bambrick,* 195 S.E.2d 721 (W. Va. 1973) (*Gault* protections must be afforded to "runaway children" who risk incarceration in state industrial school upon adjudication).

The question whether a status offense adjudication carries the possibility of incarceration has proven to be controversial. For example, in *In re Walker,* 191 S.E.2d 702 (N.C. 1972), juvenile authorities initiated proceedings to determine whether a young woman was an "undisciplined child" for failing to obey her parents. The applicable statutory provisions made incarcerative commitments available dispositional alternatives only for "delinquents" (statutorily defined to include children who violate conditions of probation) and not for undisciplined children.

The trial court found the juvenile to be an undisciplined child and placed her on probation in a proceeding in which she was not represented by counsel. In a subsequent proceeding in which the juvenile was represented by counsel, the juvenile was charged with being a delinquent for violating her earlier probation. The juvenile's lawyer moved to vacate the earlier status offense adjudication and probation disposition because the minor was not represented by counsel in those proceedings. The trial court rejected the motion, finding *Gault* inapplicable because incarcerative dispositions were not a possible consequence of the status offense proceeding, and therefore no right to counsel existed. The court then adjudicated the young woman a delinquent for violating her probation and committed her to the custody of the state correctional officials. On appeal, the North Carolina Supreme Court affirmed the trial court's actions, rejecting the argument that the *Gault* protections were triggered at the status offense proceeding because it subjected the child to the risk of probation, a violation of which in turn subjected her to the risk of being adjudicated a delinquent with attendant confinement in a state institution.

Other courts, however, take a different view. Thus, in *In re Hutchins*, 345 So. 2d 703 (Fla. 1977), the court held that a juvenile could not be incarcerated pursuant to a statutory provision permitting incarceration for juveniles upon their second status offense adjudication when counsel was not available at the original status offense proceeding. Nevertheless, the court held that juveniles charged with status offenses do not enjoy a right to counsel in initial status offense proceedings where no direct risk of incarceration exists.

[b] Statutory Provisions and Judicial Interpretation

While some courts hold that the procedural protections recognized by the United States Supreme Court's juvenile justice cases are inapplicable in status offense cases, some state statutes extend at least some of the protections to all status offense proceedings. *See, e.g.*, GA. CODE ANN. §§ 15-11-6, 65 (2001) (right to counsel, proof beyond reasonable doubt); NEV. REV. STAT. § 62.085 (2000) (right to counsel). On the other hand, other legislatures provide *Gault* rights without specifying whether or not they apply to status offense as well as delinquency cases. *See, e.g.*, NEB. REV. STAT. § 43-272(1) (Reissue 1998). Moreover, many statutes limit *Winship* to delinquency cases by specifying that proof beyond a reasonable doubt is not required in status offense proceedings. *See, e.g.*, CAL. WELF. & INST. CODE § 701 (West 1998) ("preponderance of evidence" sufficient in cases adjudicating status offenses); N.M. STAT. ANN. § 32A-3B-14(B) (Michie 1999) ("clear and convincing evidence" required to find child "in need of court-ordered services" including truancy and runaways); TENN. CODE ANN. § 37-1-129(c) (2001) ("clear and convincing evidence" required to find child "unruly").

Apart from the issue of burden of proof, where many states permit status offense adjudications on standards less demanding than the delinquency standard of proof beyond a reasonable doubt, many jurisdictions apply the same evidentiary rules in status offense and delinquency adjudications. Thus, most jurisdictions apply rules forbidding hearsay evidence. For example, in *In re J.L.M.*, 430 A.2d 448 (Vt. 1981), the court found prejudicial error where the trial court adjudicated a juvenile an "unmanageable child" based on the testimony of two social workers as to the contents of a social report drawn from interviews with third persons. The court focused on the risk of possible confinement in a facility used for the treatment of delinquent children as a crucial factor in its rejection of hearsay in unmanageable child adjudications.

Some jurisdictions, on the other hand, permit hearsay evidence in status offense proceedings. In *In re R.*, 357 N.Y.S.2d 1001 (N.Y. Fam. Ct. 1974), a New York court, for example, found no error when a trial court adjudicated a juvenile a truant and thus a "person in need of supervision" (PINS) solely on the basis of hearsay evidence composed of certified transcripts of school attendance records prepared by teachers from their roll books pursuant to state statutes that permitted truancy to be established in this manner. Even though the teachers who prepared the roll books did not testify at the adjudication proceedings, the court found that the transcripts were inherently reliable and thus satisfied the "competent evidence" standard required in PINS cases. Furthermore, the court concluded that cross-examination of the teachers keeping the attendance records would add nothing to the reliability of the evidence.

Another New York court held, in *In re Keith H.*, 594 N.Y.S.2d 268, 273 (N.Y. App. Div. 1993), that PINS petitions may be based on hearsay allegations even though such allegations would not support a delinquency petition. The court gave the following explanation for the acceptability of hearsay in status offense adjudications:

> The basis for a PINS adjudication is somewhat imprecise, requiring, for example, findings such as that the respondent is 'incorrigible' or 'habitually disobedient.' On the other hand, since a JD [juvenile delinquency] adjudication requires a finding that the respondent committed an act which, if committed by an adult, would have constituted a crime, the elements to be proved are precise and defined by the penal statues. A PINS adjudication requires a finding that the respondent needs supervision or treatment while a JD adjudication requires a finding that the respondent needs supervision, treatment or confinement and secure detention is a dispositional alternative only in a JD proceeding. In view of the different nature of these proceedings, we find that the hearsay form of a PINS petition is consistent with the objective of providing a more informal procedure for those respondents whose conduct does not rise to the level of criminal conduct at issue in a JD proceeding.

For courts finding *Gault* inapplicable in status offense proceedings, the Confrontation Clause poses no barrier to the admissibility of hearsay. Indeed, some courts see virtue in permitting hearsay evidence in status offense cases. The court, in *In re Farms*, 268 A.2d 170 (Pa. Super. Ct. 1970), explained:

> In juvenile cases, where the judge sits alone as the trier of fact and where it is his duty to become as knowledgeable and inquisitive as reasonably possible, it is better for him to admit hearsay 'for what it's worth.' He can make the determination whether responsible people would rely upon it in serious affairs when he makes his findings. He, by his experience in dealing with thousands of juveniles, being exposed to their statements, both forthright and delusive, will not be swayed, as a jury would, by hearsay which is not to be relied upon.

> Of course, we would not allow an adjudication of delinquency based on hearsay. Such a result would be in violation of a juvenile's right of confrontation.

Id. at 175.

Similarly, for courts finding *Gault* inapplicable to status offense adjudications, the privilege against self-incrimination is sometimes held inapplicable. An Iowa case, *In re Henderson,* 199 N.W.2d 111 (Iowa 1972), for a example found that the privilege did not apply in a case alleging that a child was "wayward and habitually disobedient" and thus in need of special care which his mother could not provide. The alleged violation of the privilege occurred when the child gave statements in response to questioning from a probation officer and from mental health professionals without being informed of his right to remain silent. The trial court found the child to be "uncontrolled," evidenced in part on the basis of his contested statements, and ordered the child to be placed in a juvenile institution. The child appealed and the Iowa Supreme Court found no violation of the privilege against self-incrimination. A four-member plurality of the court distinguished juvenile proceedings involving "pubic offenses," where the privilege is available, and the instant case where it was not. The plurality explained:

> [T]he purpose of juvenile proceedings is to help and assist the child, not to punish. The constitutional safeguard of 'fundamental fairness' must be preserved in that setting. However, where there is no public offense charged we believe the requirement of advising the juvenile and his parents of his right to remain silent would frustrate the very purposes of the juvenile proceeding. Admittedly, upon the findings of the trial court the child may have to spend some time away from his home but such time will not be spent in a completely institutionalized setting. The record establishes visitation rights are lenient, and that the average stay for a child at the Home is about one year.

> We conclude, therefore, that in a juvenile proceeding where no public offense is charged, the question of self-incrimination is not presented.

Id. at 119.

[2] Affirmative Defenses

As mentioned above, young people were traditionally denied a broad arsenal of defenses in juvenile court proceedings. While that situation has changed in the context of delinquency, some jurisdictions continue to favor a narrow scope of available defense theories for defendants in status offense cases.

To understand the role of defenses in status offense cases, it is useful to distinguish cases where noncriminal misconduct is charged from those where jurisdiction is premised on an allegation that a juvenile manifests an undesirable status condition. In the latter category of cases, as made clear by the *Gesicki* case, § 5.03[D], *supra*, punitive dispositions cannot constitutionally be imposed and thus culpability defenses such as insanity, infancy, and duress are theoretically inapposite. Indeed, all of the criminal law defenses relating to *mens rea* or *actus reus* may be considered irrelevant, given that the action is not premised on the claim that the juvenile intentionally or negligently engaged in statutorily proscribed acts of misconduct. These ideas are reflected sporadically in the cases, some of which hold, for example, that the infancy defense is applicable in delinquency cases, where issues of punishment and *mens rea* are at stake, but not in cases addressing status issues such as whether a juvenile is a "person in need of supervision." *See, e.g., In re William A.*, 548 A.2d 130 (Md. 1988) (holding infancy defense available in delinquency context, suggesting in *dicta* that the defense is not available in PINS cases).

In cases where a juvenile is alleged to have committed specific acts of noncriminal misconduct, such as running away from home or absenting himself from school, the *actus reus* and *mens rea* defenses available in delinquency actions are more clearly relevant. *See, In re L.Z.*, 396 N.W.2d 214 (Minn. 1986) (child permitted to introduce evidence that he did not "absent himself" from school through "volitional conduct"). Indeed, if punitive dispositions are imposed for such misconduct, denying the juvenile the full array of defenses available in criminal court is difficult to justify.

§ 5.06   DISPOSITIONS

Although historically juvenile courts often considered the dispositional issue in the same proceeding that determined whether the child had committed a status offense or an act of delinquency, the common practice today is to conduct adjudication and disposition in separate proceedings. Through bifurcating the adjudication and disposition stages, jurisdictions routinely apply different procedures at disposition than those mandated by *Gault* and *Winship* or otherwise applied at the adjudication stage.

Whether or not dispositional orders occur in a separate proceeding, they are among the most important matters decided by juvenile court judges. Traditionally, judges and legislatures drew no distinctions between delinquents and status offenders in evoking the goal of rehabilitation as the theoretical premise for all juvenile court dispositions. In the post-*Gault* era, however, several jurisdictions have questioned the continuance of the rehabilitative ideal as the sole dispositional predicate, at least in delinquency cases. *See generally* Barry C. Feld, *Criminalizing the American Juvenile Court*, 17 CR. & JUST. 197 (1993). Indeed, a variety of juvenile justice systems now adopt punitive sanctions for certain acts of delinquency as additions to, or alternatives for, traditional rehabilitative dispositions. Some jurisdictions expressly appeal to theories of deterrence and retribution in systematically employing punitive dispositions, while other jurisdictions impose pockets of punishment within systems that nominally disavow punitive dispositions as inconsistent with the traditional rehabilitative ideal. As of the late 1980's, one commentator summarized the situation as follows: "[A]bout one-third of the states use at least some explicitly punitive sentencing strategies." *Id.* at 219.

The emergence of punitive juvenile justice constitutes not only an important redirection of policy, but also entails a host of new legal issues not traditionally associated with the rehabilitative model of juvenile justice. Because punitive dispositions occur predominantly in the area of delinquency, and because many jurisdictions explicitly provide different dispositional alternatives for delinquents and status offenders, it is useful to distinguish between those two contexts in order to understand the law governing juvenile court dispositions. Therefore, after considering procedural matters, this Chapter will separately examine delinquency and status offense dispositions.

[A]   Hearing Procedure

In *Gault*, the Court included a footnote suggesting that the holding of that case might have no application to the disposition phase of juvenile proceedings. The Court observed that "the problems of . . . postadjudication are unique to the juvenile process; hence, what we hold in this opinion with regard to the procedural requirements at the adjudication stage has no necessary applicability to other steps of the juvenile process."

Because the United States Supreme Court has not addressed constitutional issues at disposition, arguably the states are free to structure the process however they reasonably see fit. A state might, for example, merge the adjudication and disposition phases into a single proceeding so long as the *Gault* and *Winship* requirements are met. The clear trend, however, is towards a bifurcated process with fewer procedural formalities observed at the dispositional stage. *See* SAMUEL M. DAVIS, RIGHTS OF JUVENILES 6-1–6-3 (2d ed. 2001).

In jurisdictions requiring separate proceedings for adjudications and dispositions, the courts have held that adjudicated juveniles have a right to a dispositional hearing, *see, e.g., J.L.P.*, 100 Cal. Rptr. 601 (Cal. Ct. App. 1972), except perhaps where disposition decisions are based entirely on the gravity of the offense committed. *See id.* at 603 (suggesting in *dicta* that hearing might not be required if disposition decision were based solely on the gravity of the "crime"). In fact, however, disposition decisions are generally based on a variety of considerations in addition to judgments assessing the gravity of the offense. Indeed, the disposition decision routinely involves determinations of how best to promote the child's welfare in a way consistent with the public interest. Such judgments require courts to assess the child's background, environment, health, family, and educational situation. Thus, where disposition decisions consider such factors, the juvenile is entitled to be notified of the proceedings, *see, e.g., In re D.L.W.*, 543 N.E.2d 542 (Ill. App. Ct. 1989), afforded the opportunity to be heard and allowed to present any evidence relevant to the dispositional decision. *See, J.L.P., supra.*

Notwithstanding *Gault*'s language suggesting the applicability of the case only to the adjudication phase, several courts have held that juveniles possess a due process right to counsel at disposition, *see, e.g., A.A. v. State*, 538 P.2d 1004 (Alaska 1975), sometimes even in status offense cases, *see, e.g., In re Cecelia R.*, 327 N.E.2d 812 (N.Y. 1975). However, in jurisdictions that deny counsel rights at status offense adjudications, a denial of counsel at disposition would also arguably be permitted, although there apparently are no reported cases addressing the issue. In a number of states, the child possesses a statutory right to counsel at adjudication, often entailed in statutory language granting counsel rights at "all stages of the proceedings." *See, e.g.,* GA. CODE ANN. § 15-11-6(b) (2001); N.M. STAT. ANN. § 32A-2-14(H) (Michie 1999) (delinquency petitions).

Dispositional decisions are generally aimed at promoting the welfare of the child. That inquiry requires judicial access to as much information as possible regarding the child's background. As a consequence, any and all evidence relevant to the child's general situation is generally admissible at dispositional proceedings. Thus, usual rules of evidence are not applicable. *See, e.g.,* NEB. REV. STAT. § 43-283 (Reissue 1998) ("strict rules of evidence shall not be applied at any dispositional hearing"). Hearsay, often in the form of a social report, is routinely considered by the court in making its dispositional decision. Moreover, the exclusionary rule is generally inapplicable, *see, e.g., In re Michael V.*, 223 Cal. Rptr. 503 (Cal. Ct. App. 1986) (illegally seized evidence suppressed at earlier hearing held admissible at disposition), and some cases suggest that the juvenile may be interrogated by the court without observing the formalities otherwise necessary for effectuating waivers of the privilege against self-incrimination. *See, e.g., In re Smith*, 337 N.E.2d 209 (Ill. App. Ct. 1975) (no error where trial judge informed juvenile that juvenile need not tell the judge anything but then admonished the juvenile to divulge the whereabouts of a weapon, suggesting that such information may influence a disposition beneficial to the juvenile and thus arguably causing the juvenile to admit to selling the weapon).

[B] Delinquency Cases

[1] The Traditional Theory: Promoting the Juvenile's Best Interests

Barry C. Feld, *The Juvenile Court Meets the Principle of Offense: Punishment, Treatment, and the Difference it Makes*

68 Boston University Law Review 821, 822–25 (1988)

The social history of the juvenile court is an oft-told tale. Economic modernization brought with it changes in family structure, the function of the family in society, and a new cultural perception of childhood. Rapid industrialization and urbanization fostered the Progressive movement, many of whose programs shared a unifying child-centered theme.

The Progressives introduced a variety of criminal justice reforms at the turn of the century — probation, parole, indeterminate sentences, and the highly flexible policies to rehabilitate the deviant. Discretionary decisionmaking precluded uniform treatment or standardized criteria.

The Progressive criminal justice reforms reflected basic changes in the ideological assumptions about the sources of crime and deviance. Positivism — the effort to identify the antecedent variables that cause crime and deviance — challenged the classic formulations of crime as the product of conscious free-will choices. Positivist criminology regarded deviance as determined rather than chosen, and sought to identify the causes of crime and delinquency. By attributing criminal behavior to external forces, the Progressive movement reduced an actor's moral responsibility for crime and thus focused on efforts to reform rather than punish the offender. Criminology borrowed both methodology and vocabulary from the medical profession; pathology, infection, diagnosis, and treatment provided popular analogues for criminal justice professionals. The conjunction of positivistic criminology, the use of medical models in the treatment of criminals, and the emergence of social science professionals gave rise to the "Rehabilitative Ideal."

The juvenile court movement attempted to remove children from the adult criminal justice and corrections systems and provide them with individualized treatment in a separate system. The Progressives envisioned juvenile court professionals using indeterminate procedures, substituting a scientific and preventative approach for the traditional punitive scheme of the criminal law, to achieve benevolent goals and better society. Under the guise of *parens patriae*, juvenile courts emphasized treatment, supervision, and control rather than punishment and allowed the State ever wider discretion to intervene in the lives of young offenders. As a result, the juvenile court's jurisdiction over "status" offenders encompassed situations that might previously have been ignored.

In separating the child from adult offenders, the juvenile court system also rejected the jurisprudence and procedure of adult criminal prosecutions. Courtroom procedures were modified to eliminate any implication of a criminal proceeding; a euphemistic vocabulary and a physically separate court building were introduced to avoid the stigma of adult prosecutions. To avoid stigmatizing a youth, hearings were confidential, access to court records limited, and children were found to be delinquent rather than guilty of committing a crime. Juvenile court proceedings concentrated on the child's background and welfare rather than the details surrounding the commission of a specific crime. Consequently, juries and lawyers were excluded from juvenile court proceedings, as were the rules of evidence and formal procedures.

The system proffered by the Progressives left judges, assisted by social workers, to investigate the problematic child's background, identify the sources of the misconduct at issue, and develop a treatment plan to meet the child's needs. Juvenile court personnel enjoyed enormous discretion to make dispositions in the "best interest of the child." Principles of psychology and social work, rather than formal rules, guided decisionmakers. The court collected as much information as possible about the child — his life history, character, social environment, and individual circumstances — on the assumption that a scientific analysis of the child's past would reveal the proper diagnosis and cure. The overall inquiry accorded minor significance to the offense committed by the child, as it indicated little about the child's "real needs." At hearings and dispositions, the court directed its attention first and foremost to the child's character and lifestyle.

Dispositions continued for the duration of minority, and were indeterminate and nonproportional. The courts were given maximum discretion to allow for flexibility in diagnosis and treatment. The offense that brought the child before the court affected neither the intensity nor the duration of intervention because each child's "real needs" differed.

SOUTH DAKOTA CODIFIED LAWS
§ 26-8C-7 (1999)

Dispositional decree — Alternatives. If a child has been adjudicated as a delinquent child, the court shall enter a decree of disposition according to the least restrictive alternative available in keeping with the best interests of the child. The decree shall contain one or more of the following alternatives:

(1) The court may make any one or more of the dispositions in § 26-8B-6,

[which provides:

(1) the court may place the child on probation or under protective supervision in the custody of one or both parents, guardian, custodian, relative, or another suitable person under conditions imposed by the court;

. . . .

(3) If the court finds that the child has violated a valid court order, the court may place the child in a detention facility, for purposes of disposition if:

(a) The child is not deprived of the schooling that is appropriate for the child's age, needs, and specific rehabilitative goals;

(b) The child had a due process hearing before the order was issued;

(c) Before the issuance of such order, a local interagency team, authorized pursuant to § 27A-15-56 shall review the behavior of the child and the circumstances under which such child was brought before the court and made subject to such order; determine the reasons for the behavior that caused such child to be brought before the court and made subject to such order; determine that all dispositions, including treatment, other than placement in a detention facility or the Department of Corrections, have been exhausted or are clearly inappropriate; and submit to the court a written report stating the results of the review and determinations made;

(4) The court may require the child to pay for any damage done to property or for medical expenses under conditions set by the court if payment can be enforced without serious hardship or injustice to the child;

(5) The court may commit the child to the Department of Corrections for placement in a juvenile correctional facility, foster home, group home, group care center, or residential treatment center pursuant to chapter 26-11A;

(6) The court may place a child in an alternative education program;

(7) The court may order the child to be examined and treated at the Human Services Center;]

except that a delinquent child may be incarcerated in a detention facility established pursuant to provisions of chapter 26-7A for not more than ninety days, which may be in addition to any period of temporary custody;

(2) The court may impose a fine not to exceed one thousand dollars;

(3) The court may place the child on probation under the supervision of a court services officer or another designated individual. The child may be required as a condition of probation to report for assignment to a supervised work program, provided the child is not deprived of the schooling that is appropriate for the child's age, needs and specific rehabilitative goals. The supervised work program shall be of a constructive nature designed to promote

rehabilitation, appropriate to the age level and physical ability of the child, and shall be combined with counseling by the court services officer or other guidance personnel. The supervised work program assignment shall be made for a period of time consistent with the child's best interest, but for not more than ninety days;

(4) The court may place the child at the Human Services Center for examination and treatment;

(5) The court may commit the child to the Department of Corrections;

(6) The court may place the child in a detention facility for not more than ninety days, which may be in addition to any period of temporary custody;

. . . .

(8) The court may order the suspension or revocation of the child's driving privilege or restrict the privilege in such manner as it sees fit.

NEBRASKA REVISED STATUTES
§ 43-286 (Reissue 1988)

Juvenile violator or juvenile in need of special supervision; disposition; violation of probation; procedure.

(1) When any juvenile is adjudicated to be a juvenile described in subdivision (1), (2), or (4) of § 43-247:

(a) The court may continue the dispositional portion of the hearing, from time to time upon such terms and conditions as the court may prescribe, including an order of restitution of any property stolen or damaged or an order requiring the juvenile to participate in community service programs, if such order is in the interest of the juvenile's reformation or rehabilitation, and, subject to the further order of the court, may:

(i) Place the juvenile on probation subject to the supervision of a probation officer;

(ii) Permit the juvenile to remain in his or her own home, subject to the supervision of the probation officer; or

(iii) Cause the juvenile to be placed in a suitable family home or institution, subject to the supervision of the probation officer. If the court has committed the juvenile to the care and custody of the Department of Health and Human Services, the department shall pay the costs of the suitable family home or institution which are not otherwise paid by the juvenile's parents.

Under subdivision (1)(a) of this section, upon a determination by the court that there are no parental, private, or other public funds available for the care, custody, and maintenance of a juvenile, the court may order a reasonable sum for the care, custody, and maintenance of the juvenile to be paid out of a fund which shall be appropriated annually by the county where the petition is filed until a suitable provision may be made for the juvenile without such payment; or

(b) The court may commit such juvenile to the Office of Juvenile Services, but a juvenile under the age of twelve years shall not be placed at the Youth

Rehabilitation and Treatment Center-Geneva or the Youth Rehabilitation and Treatment Center-Kearney unless he or she has violated the terms of probation or has committed an additional offense and the court finds that the interests of the juvenile and the welfare of the community demand his or her commitment. This minimum age provision shall not apply if the act in question is murder or manslaughter.

(2) When any juvenile is found by the court to be a juvenile described in subdivision (3)(b) of § 43-247, the court may enter such order as it is empowered to enter under subdivision (1)(a) of this section or enter an order committing or placing the juvenile to the care and custody of the Department of Health and Human Services.

(3) Beginning July 15, 1998, when any juvenile is adjudicated to be a juvenile described in subdivision (1), (2), (3)(b), or (4) of § 43-247 because of a nonviolent act or acts and the juvenile has not previously been adjudicated to be such a juvenile because of a violent act or acts, the court may, with the agreement of the victim, order the juvenile to attend juvenile offender and victim mediation with a mediator or at an approved center selected from the roster made available pursuant to § 25-2908.

(4)(a) When a juvenile is placed on probation or under the supervision of the court and it is alleged that the juvenile is again a juvenile described in subdivision (1), (2), (3)(b), or (4) of § 43-247, a petition may be filed and the same procedure followed and rights given at a hearing on the original petition. If an adjudication is made that the allegations of the petition are true, the court may make any disposition authorized by this section for such adjudications.

(b) When a juvenile is placed on probation or under the supervision of the court for conduct under subdivision (1), (2), (3)(b), or (4) of § 43-247 and it is alleged that the juvenile has violated a term of probation or supervision or that the juvenile has violated an order of the court, a motion to revoke probation or supervision or to change the disposition may be filed and proceedings held as follows:

(i) The motion shall set forth specific factual allegations of the alleged violations and a copy of such motion shall be served on all persons required to be served by §§ 43-262 to 43-267;

(ii) The juvenile shall be entitled to a hearing before the court to determine the validity of the allegations. At such hearing the juvenile shall be entitled to those rights relating to counsel provided by § 43-272 and those rights relating to detention provided by §§ 43-254 to 43-256. The juvenile shall also be entitled to speak and present documents, witnesses, or other evidence on his or her own behalf. He or she may confront persons who have given adverse information concerning the alleged violations, may cross-examine such persons, and may show that he or she did not violate the conditions of his or her probation or, if he or she did, that mitigating circumstances suggest that the violation does not warrant revocation. The revocation hearing shall be held within a reasonable time after the juvenile is taken into custody;

(iii) The hearing shall be conducted in an informal manner and shall be flexible enough to consider evidence, including letters, affidavits, and other material, that would not be admissible in an adversarial criminal trial.

———

IN RE INTEREST OF J.A.

Supreme Court of Nebraska
510 N.W.2d 68 (1994)

WHITE, JUSTICE.

J.A., a minor female, appeals an order of the juvenile court committing her to the Youth Development Center in Geneva, Nebraska. We affirm.

On June 25, 1992, the Sarpy County Attorney filed a petition in the juvenile court alleging that appellant had committed two misdemeanors: obstructing a police officer (count I) and disturbing the peace (count II). At the arraignment, appellant denied the allegations of the petition.

One month later, the county attorney filed an amended petition, adding a second allegation of disturbing the peace (count III). At the hearing, the court dismissed counts I and II on the motion of the county attorney. Appellant then admitted the allegations of count III, and the court accepted the admission. The court found that appellant was a juvenile as described in NEB.REV.STAT. § 43-247(1) (Reissue 1988) and ordered her to attend a 30-day evaluation at the Youth Development Center-Geneva (Geneva). Finally, the court continued the matter for a disposition hearing following the 30-day evaluation.

From September 1992 through January 1993, the court held disposition hearings approximately once per month. After each hearing, the court issued an order continuing the matter for further disposition. After the October hearing, the court order not only continued the matter for further disposition, but also imposed certain terms and conditions upon appellant. Two such conditions are relevant here. First, appellant was ordered not to violate any laws or municipal ordinances, and second, appellant was ordered to abstain from consuming alcohol and from using controlled substances.

On January 19, 1993, the county attorney filed a motion to review appellant's disposition. The motion alleged that appellant had been arrested after fighting with her mother, that she had been drinking alcohol and sniffing paint, and that she had been found with a blood alcohol content of .05.

On January 21, at the hearing to review appellant's disposition, appellant admitted the allegations in the motion. After hearing testimony regarding possible placements for appellant, the court took the matter under advisement. Four days later, the court issued an order committing appellant to Geneva. Appellant appeals from that order.

. . . .

Appellant claims that the juvenile court erred in committing her to Geneva without explicitly providing reasons for her commitment. Appellant asserts that the court was required to articulate such reasons. Appellant derives this requirement from the language of Neb.Rev.Stat. § 43-286(4)(f) (Cum. Supp. 1992). . . .

We first address appellant's claim as it relates to § 43-286(4)(f). Appellant contends that the juvenile court violated § 43-286(4)(f) by committing her to Geneva without articulating any reason why she should be so committed. We disagree.

In essence, appellant contends that § 43-286(4)(f) applies to the facts of her case. Statutory interpretation is a matter of law in connection with which an appellate court has an obligation to reach an independent, correct conclusion irrespective of the determination made by the court below. An appellate court reviews juvenile proceedings:

> de novo on the record and is thus required to reach a conclusion independent of the juvenile court's findings; provided, however, that where the evidence conflicts, [an appellate] court considers and may give weight to the juvenile court's observation of the witnesses and acceptance of one version of facts over another.

Section 43-286 applies when a child is adjudicated to be a juvenile as described in § 43-247(1), (2), (3)(b), or (4). The juvenile court found that appellant was a juvenile as described in § 43-247(1): a juvenile who has committed a misdemeanor or violated a city ordinance other than a traffic offense. This finding was based on appellant's admission that she had committed the misdemeanor offense of disturbing the peace.

Under § 43-286, a juvenile court has broad discretion as to the disposition of a delinquent juvenile. Specifically, § 43-286 provides that a juvenile court may continue the dispositional portion of the juvenile's hearing from time to time under such terms and conditions as the court may prescribe, may place the juvenile on probation, or may place the juvenile in a family home or institution. A juvenile court may also commit a juvenile to Geneva. § 43-286(2).

Under § 43-286(4), a juvenile court also has the power to change the juvenile's disposition. Section 43-286(4) provides, in relevant part:

> When a juvenile is placed on probation or under the supervision of the court . . . and it is alleged that the juvenile has violated a term of probation or supervision or that the juvenile has violated an order of the court, a motion to revoke probation or supervision or to change the disposition may be filed and proceedings held as follows:
>
>   . . . .
>
> (f) *In cases when the court revokes probation,* it shall enter a written statement as to the evidence relied on and the reasons for revocation.

(Emphasis Supplied.) In other words, subsection (4) outlines the procedures which must be followed when a court revokes probation, revokes supervision, or otherwise changes the juvenile's disposition. Subsection (4)(f) describes more particularly the procedures which must be followed when a court revokes probation.

In the instant case, the juvenile court continued the dispositional portion of appellant's hearing several times. At one point, as described above, the court imposed terms and conditions upon appellant. When appellant violated one of the terms set forth by the court, the court ordered her committed to Geneva. The court indisputably possessed the statutory authority, under § 43-286, to take each of these actions.

Appellant contends that although the court had the power to act as it did, the court was required, by virtue of § 43-286(4)(f), to give a reason why she should be committed to Geneva. This contention is without merit. Section 43-286(4)(f), by its terms, applies only when a juvenile court revokes probation. The court never placed appellant on probation. The court therefore had no obligation, under § 43-286(4)(f), to provide reasons on the record for committing her to Geneva.

. . . .

In committing appellant to Geneva without specifically articulating the reasons for the commitment, the juvenile court did not violate § 43-286(4)(f). . . .

Affirmed.

IN RE APPEAL NO. 179

Court of Special Appeals of Maryland
327 A.2d 793 (1974)

GILBERT, JUDGE.

The appellant, age fifteen, was adjudged to be a juvenile delinquent. The finding resulted from his participation in three housebreakings and malicious destruction of properties which occurred during the afternoon hours. Appellant readily admitted his culpability. He said that the reason he and two other juveniles broke into the three residences was that they were hungry. One hundred twenty-two dollars was stolen from one house, and in the other two homes the destruction committed by the juveniles took the form of slashed portraits, torn pictures, a mutilated diary and splattered eggs in and about the house.[81] Appellant did not explain, nor was he asked, how the mutilation and the hurling of eggs throughout the houses sated his hunger. Approximately one and one-half months following the adjudicatory hearing, a disposition hearing was held. At that time the court possessed a report of a clinical psychologist. Testimony was taken from the school principal in which it was indicated that the appellant, sometime after the adjudicatory hearing, had been suspended from school because a fire had occurred in his locker. Although the appellant denied that he set fire to his own locker, the principal was of

---

[81] [1] The record reveals that restitution has been made.

the impression that the juvenile had done so. The principal stated that the young man was a "B-C student who could be A," and that "the youngster has the potential to do even better." The psychologist's report, after indicating most strongly that there was a conflict between the juvenile and his father which emotionally "terrorized" the juvenile, stated:

> It is this examiner's opinion that this child should not be removed from his parents' home but should remain on probation. Counseling will be made available to the parents if possible through the court to help especially the father to deal more appropriately with his attitude towards the child. The father seems to be more interested and most eager to help his children and that he might have been over zealous in his efforts to make them the kind of men he wants them to be.

The hearing judge stated:

> We have had an epidemic of housebreakings, and we are not going to countenance it. We are not going to have people's homes broken into, their property vandalized and stolen, and the message should go out loud and clear that we are not going to have it. . . .
>
> I have a job to do. There are a lot of things that I do that are difficult, but I have to do it. I have to do what I think is right and in the long run is going to best protect and help you boys and at the same time protect the community. . . .
>
> I'm very much impressed with your behavior since January 17th when you had a hearing. There was a finding, and you knew that a disposition hearing was coming up and that this case would be disposed of following an investigation. I am not deciding the truth or falsity of any charges for which you were suspended, that has already been determined by the school authorities, but it is important to me because it is indicative of your attitude. It is indicative of the fact that notwithstanding a finding of delinquency in these serious cases you will not comply with the regulations and will not behave as you know you should behave in society. . . .
>
> . . . I will sign an order committing these boys [82] to the appropriate institution. . . .

An appeal was entered on March 4, 1974 to this Court. Three days later appellant applied to us for a stay of the juvenile court's order pending a determination of his appeal. We conducted a hearing on March 12, 1974, and on March 13, issued our Order staying the effect of the commitment by the juvenile court. Following the receipt of our Order, the juvenile court judge directed that the juvenile be released from the custody of the Secretary of Health and Mental Hygiene, and he placed the child under parental control. [83]

---

[82] [2] The cases of all three juveniles were heard at the same time by the juvenile court judge. Two of them did not appeal.

[83] [3] The order placing the child under parental control provided:

> While on probation the probationer shall refrain from further delinquent behavior;

The case is now before us on its merits. Courts Art. § 3-802 provides:

(a) The purposes of this subtitle are:

(1) To provide for the care, protection, and wholesome mental and physical development of children coming within the provisions of this subtitle;

(2) To remove from children committing delinquent acts the taint of criminality and the consequences of criminal behavior;

(3) To provide for a program of treatment, training, and rehabilitation consistent with the protection of the public interest;

(4) To place a child in a wholesome family environment whenever possible;

(5) To separate a child from his parents only when necessary for his welfare or in the interest of public safety;

(6) To provide judicial procedures for carrying out the provisions of this subtitle.

(b) This subtitle shall be liberally construed to effectuate these purposes.

Although we are cognizant of the general rule that the disposition in a juvenile case rests within the sound discretion of the juvenile judge and will only be disturbed on appeal upon a finding of an abuse of that discretion, we think that the record in this case demonstrates such an abuse because it does not show that the separation of the child from his parents is in "his welfare or in the interest of public safety." We repeat:

. . . [I]t is clear that the Legislature intended no departure in philosophy from that underlying previous juvenile court enactments in Maryland, as interpreted by the Court of Appeals, viz., that juvenile proceedings are of a special nature designed to meet the problems peculiar to the adolescent; that the proceedings of a juvenile court are not criminal in nature and its dispositions are not punishment for crime; that the juvenile law has as it underlying concept the protection of the juvenile, so that judges, in making dispositions in juvenile cases, think not in terms of guilt, but of the child's need for protection or

---

shall avoid persons and places of disreputable or harmful character; shall report as directed and obey the instructions of his Probation Officer; shall not leave the jurisdiction without permission and shall comply with other conditions as specified below or may at any time be imposed by the Court.

1. Attend school every day and every period.

2. Achieve academically to the best of your ability.

3. Not to associate with those who are involved, in any way, with any form of drugs or narcotics.

4. Not to leave school grounds at anytime during school day without specified written permission.

5. To report to the Probation Officer every Tuesday after school.

6. Not to leave Dorchester County unless accompanied by and under the supervision of your parents.

> rehabilitation; that the juvenile act does not contemplate the punishment of children where they are found to be delinquent, but rather an attempt to correct and rehabilitate them in 'a wholesome family environment whenever possible,' although rehabilitation may have to be sought in some instances in an institution.

The record in the instant case does not justify uprooting the child from his parents' home and placing him in a training center or other juvenile institution. We, therefore, vacate the judgment of the juvenile court and remand the matter with instructions that the court conduct a new disposition hearing. At that hearing the court should reconsider its disposition in the light of the legislative purpose, our decisions in as well as the conduct of this youthful offender since his placement on probation following our Order of March 13, 1974.

Judgment vacated. Case remanded without affirmance or reversal for further proceedings not inconsistent with this opinion. Costs to be paid by the County Commissioners of Dorchester County.

IN RE ALINE D.

Supreme Court of California (en banc)
536 P.2d 65 (1975)

RICHARDSON, JUSTICE.

We consider the question whether a minor who has previously been adjudicated a ward of the juvenile court and then placed, with unsuccessful results, in various local treatment facilities, may thereafter be committed to the California Youth Authority ("CYA") despite the expressed doubt of the court, acting through its referee, that she would benefit from such a commitment. The record before us reflects that the referee ordered the CYA commitment solely because there appeared to be no other available placement facility. We have concluded that, under the existing statutory scheme, and particularly Welfare and Institutions Code § 734, the commitment was improper and, accordingly, that the cause should be remanded to the juvenile court for reconsideration.

We recite pertinent portion of the troubled history of the minor, Aline D. At the time of her commitment to CYA, she was 16, her father was absent from the family home and her mother had rejected her. She had an I. Q. of 67 and a behavioral history of assaultive conduct and association with juvenile gangs. She was originally placed in a family treatment program at juvenile hall, for reasons not specified in the record. This placement continued from February 23, 1972, to May 1, 1972, and, according to a probation report, was "singularly unsuccessful." Thereafter, she was released to the care of her mother but, one week later, ran away from home. An attempt was made to place her in a probation department community daycare program, but her limited intellectual potential disqualified her. On September 25, 1972, Aline was placed at the McKinnon Girls Home in Los Angeles, but soon thereafter the Home reported that she was having "problems with stealing, shoplifting, . . . refusal to attend school," and was participating in a juvenile gang. Her placement with the Home terminated a few weeks later when she was arrested following an incident at a high school campus. Aline was returned to juvenile court on allegations that she had violated Education Code § 13560 (wilful insult and abuse of teacher) and Penal Code § 6538 (unlawful loitering about a school). Following a hearing, the first charge was sustained and, on November 10, 1972, Aline's wardship was continued and "suitable placement" ordered for her.

Thereafter, on November 20, 1972, Aline was placed at the Penny Lane residential school in Los Angeles where she remained for ten days after which time her placement was terminated for various reasons, including her use of marijuana, bullying of associates, and membership in a juvenile gang.

On December 14, 1972, Aline was placed at the Detroit Arms Home, where she remained until January 10, 1973. Her placement there was terminated as a result of her "active association" with the gang. A probation report, describing the circumstances of her association with the gang, reported that Aline let in eight or nine boy members of the gang who thereafter took three of four girls and left for two days, causing considerable difficulties.

Aline was returned to juvenile hall, pending further efforts to place her. A report of the foregoing placement efforts summarizes as follows: "Since this current detention on January 10, 1973 all efforts to place minor have met with defeat. Placements are not willing to handle the kinds of behavior minor has displayed in former placements." The responsible placement coordinator indicated that Los Angeles County has had no facilities capable of coping with the minor other than the Los Palmas Girls School.

On February 13, 1973, Las Palmas rejected Aline as unsuitable, because of her record of "assaultive behavior." The Las Palmas officials by letter recommended a commitment to CYA "where she would have the structure she obviously needs and also vocational training." On March 1, 1973, the probation officer filed a supplemental petition in juvenile court, alleging that Aline is not acceptable for placement in Los Angeles County institutions or facilities.

On May 21, 1973, a hearing was held before a juvenile court referee. The referee heard testimony from Mrs. Holt, a probation officer, and considered the contents of her placement report as well as letters and evaluations from psychiatrists regarding Aline's situation. The officer described her investigation of all conceivable placements available to Aline, including her mother and potential foster parents. The investigation included seven different facilities. Each placement was found unsuitable for Aline, although Mrs. Holt learned that Penny Lane eventually planned to establish a "closed setting for girls." According to Mrs. Holt, Aline, as a "severely delinquent young girl," requires a "closed facility" (by which is meant one with locked doors and limited visitation privileges), similar to county camps available for the placement of delinquent boys. If Aline were male, rather than female, Mrs. Holt would have recommended a camp community placement rather than CYA.

The reports of two psychiatrists and a clinical psychologist were before the court but have not been filed with us. The record does, however, contain their recommendations that Aline not be committed to CYA. One psychiatrist stated his opinion that Aline is not truly delinquent and that involvement with more delinquent and criminally oriented youths may adversely influence her. Near the conclusion of the hearing, the referee noted his lack of options. He observed that Aline could not simply be left in juvenile hall, as that facility serves only as a temporary detention facility. He explained his reluctance to order the proceedings dismissed, for Aline's mother had refused to accept her, and Aline would be back "on the streets." He agreed with Aline's counsel that it would be "very unwise to commit this minor to the California Youth Authority for the sole reason that it does not seem that there is anything else." Moreover, the referee acknowledged that "The fact remains, nevertheless, that all agree, including two psychiatrists, a clinical psychologist, Mrs. Holt, *all agree that she's not an appropriate subject for commitment to the youth authority, but that it is being done only because that seems to be the only recourse.*" (Italics added.)

After suspending the hearing temporarily to determine whether Aline might be eligible for placement by the Department of Public Social Services, and after learning that such placement, would be refused, the referee concluded that he must order Alice committed to CYA, since ". . . the only other alternative that seems available to me now would be to dismiss this case and turn this lady out in the street, and I'm not going to do that". . . . Aline appeals.

Although the referee, following the hearing, signed a written form which contained a printed "finding" to the effect that the ward probably would benefit from the CYA commitment, our review of the record, summarized above, leads us to conclude that the referee ordered Aline committed to CYA solely because there appeared to be no other suitable placement for her. The motivation of the referee appears in his conclusion that "it seems that we are powerless" to avoid a CYA commitment. . . . [T]he provisions of the Juvenile Court Law do not permit a CYA commitment under such circumstances.

Preliminarily, we note the provisions of Welfare and Institutions Code § 502, which express in broad terms the general purposes of the Juvenile Court Law. These are to "secure for each minor . . . such care and guidance, preferably in his own home, as will serve the . . . welfare of the minor and the best interests of the State; . . . and, when the minor is removed from his own family, to secure for him custody, care, and discipline as nearly as possible equivalent to that which should have been given by his parents." . . .

In specific amplification of the foregoing purposes and with particular reference to the matter before us, [the statute] provides that "No ward of the juvenile court shall be committed to the Youth Authority unless the judge of the court is *fully satisfied* that the mental and physical condition and qualifications of the ward are such as to render it *probable that he will be benefitted* by the reformatory educational discipline or other treatment provided by the Youth Authority." (Italics added.)

The foregoing language makes it clear that a CYA commitment may not be made for the sole reason that suitable alternatives do not exist. Instead, the court must be "fully satisfied" that a CYA commitment probably will benefit the minor. In the instant case, the referee's in-court statements, far from indicating that he was "fully satisfied," disclosed instead a substantial dissatisfaction with a CYA commitment. The requirements of § 734 not having been met, the commitment order must be reversed.

. . . .

. . . "The statutory scheme . . . contemplates a progressively restrictive and punitive series of disposition orders in cases such as that now before us — namely, home placement under supervision, foster home placement, placement in a local treatment facility and, as a last resort, Youth Authority placement."

As is evident from the applicable statutes, "Commitments to the California Youth Authority are made only in the most serious cases and only after all else has failed." This concept is well established and has been expressed by the CYA itself. In light of the general purposes of juvenile commitments expressed in Welfare and Institutions Code ". . . commitment to the Youth Authority is generally viewed as *the final treatment resource* available to the juvenile court and which least meets the description in the [statute]. Within the Youth Authority system, there is gathered from throughout the State the most severely delinquent youths which have exhausted local programs." (Italics added).

. . . .

Furthermore, statistics compiled by CYA indicate that at Ventura School for Girls (the only suitable CYA institution for Aline), Aline would be placed in the company of girls who had committed serious criminal offenses, including 16 homicides, 31 robberies and 38 assaults. . . . According to the CYA's 1973 annual report, 85 percent of all youths committed to CYA had three or more delinquency "contacts," and 35 percent had eight or more such contacts.

In sum, the record before the juvenile court discloses that CYA may not be a suitable placement facility for Aline, and that the referee himself, acting for the juvenile court, entertained very substantial doubt in the matter. The record does not disclose that the court was, in the language of the statute, "fully satisfied that the . . . condition and qualifications of the ward are such as to render it probable that he will be benefitted" by the discipline or treatment available at CYA.

. . . [T]o assist the juvenile court in its reconsideration of the cause, we note a few possible alternative dispositions. Our suggestions should not be considered exhaustive of the possibilities, and the court should explore, of course, any other placement opportunities which the parties or the probation officer may suggest.

If the report indicates that Aline would not benefit from the treatment she would receive at CYA, and if no appropriate alternative placement exists at that time, then the proceedings should be dismissed. Section 888 of the Welfare and Institutions Code provides in pertinent part that, "Any county establishing such juvenile home, ranch, or camp under the provisions of this article may, by mutual agreement, accept children committed to such home, ranch, or camp by the juvenile court of another county in the State and the State shall reimburse the county maintaining the home, ranch, or camp to the amount of one-half the administrative cost of maintaining each child so committed. . . ."

Second, reference was made at the May 1973 hearing to the anticipated establishment of closed facilities at the Penny Lane school where Aline had once been placed. Mrs. Holt seemed to believe that such closed facilities might be a suitable placement for Aline.

Third, testimony at Aline's hearing described facilities in Los Angeles County for Boys of the type appropriate for minors such as Aline. Although appearing to be the least promising alternative, conceivably some arrangement could be made to provide care and treatment for Aline at these facilities under some segregated arrangement.

Fourth, the record indicates that Aline may be a "borderline" mentally retarded child. [The statute allows] for the commitment to state hospital of juvenile court wards found (following evaluation and report) to be mentally retarded or mentally disordered.

Finally, if on reconsideration the court determines that no appropriate alternative placement exists, but also finds that Aline probably would benefit from a CYA commitment under present circumstances, the court could consider the possibility of a temporary 90-day CYA commitment for purposes of observation and diagnosis, with provision for a report by the director of CYA concerning Aline's amenability to treatment. If the report indicates that Aline is not benefitting from the treatment she is receiving at CYA, and if no appropriate alternative placement exists at the time, then the proceedings should be dismissed.

Juvenile commitment proceedings are designed for the purposes of rehabilitation and treatment, not punishment. We fully recognize that in some cases, as in that before us, the question of appropriate placement poses to the appropriate officials seemingly insurmountable difficulties. Budgetary limitations, varying from county to county, may well preclude the maintenance of those specialized facilities otherwise necessary to provide the minor with optimum care and treatment. Even if such facilities exist, the minor's past conduct may itself require his or her exclusion therefrom. Nevertheless, under the present statutory scheme, supported by sound policy considerations, a commitment to CYA must be supported by a determination, based upon substantial evidence in the record, of probable benefit to the minor. The unavailability of suitable alternatives, standing alone, does not justify the commitment of a nondelinquent or marginally delinquent child to an institution primarily designed for the incarceration and discipline of serious offenders.

The order of commitment is reversed and the cause remanded for further proceedings consistent with this opinion.

CLARK, JUSTICE (*dissenting*).

Welfare and Institutions Code § 734 . . . only requires that the juvenile court find CYA commitment to be the most beneficial disposition available. The record reveals this statutory requirement has been more than satisfied.

Aline's history of delinquency includes shoplifting, theft, smoking marijuana and assaulting a grandmother. Her behavior has frequently been characterized as "assaultive," leading her probation officer to describe her as "a severely delinquent young girl . . . in terms of being a public menace."

Exhaustive efforts — all unsuccessful — were made to place Aline within the community. The first placement, in a family treatment program, was regarded as "singularly unsuccessful" and terminated after two months. Admission in a community day care program was then denied the ward due to her low intelligence. McKinnon Girls Home released Aline in two weeks because of "problems with stealing, shoplifting, bed wetting, refusal to attend school" and the claim she was a leader of a local street gang, the Cripts.

Aline's fourth placement, at Penny Lane School, lasted only 10 days because she "[s]moked grass at a concert — is muscle of the resistive kids — threatens weaker girls — girls are terrified as she leans on being a member of the Cript gang. About five Cript boys came to Penny Lane to see her — 'freaked out' staff as one got into the house." Her fifth disposition, at the Detroit Arms, was terminated when Aline "let in eight or nine Cripts in the placement who took three or four girls and split for two days."

At this point the Los Angeles County placement coordinator concluded the county had no facility capable of coping with Aline, "other than possibly Las Palmas Girls School." However, Las Palmas declined to enroll the ward, concluding her assaultive behavior, low intelligent level and nonacceptance of responsibility revealed Aline "could not benefit from either our school or group therapy, the two main aspects of our program." Las Palmas recommended she be committed to the CYA "where she could have the structure she obviously needs and also vocational training."

Before Aline's commitment to the Youth Authority seven additional placement alternatives were investigated, all proving unsatisfactory. . . .

The record clearly reveals that all parties at the hearing — including Aline's counsel — agreed that every conceivable placement alternative had been exhausted, the only remaining disposition being to either completely dismiss Aline's wardship or to commit her to the CYA. Since Aline's mother has refused to accept her back into the home, dismissal would place this child in the streets and under the influence of her gang. In these circumstances, release would provide Aline nothing but the opportunity to qualify more fully for CYA commitment — hardly a course of action to be recommended to the juvenile court system.

In contrast, CYA commitment offers Aline foreseeable benefit through treatment and training. . . . Far from being a single "placement facility," the CYA is an administration comprised of many facilities, capable of providing individualized treatment where necessary.

The propriety of a CYA commitment under these circumstances cannot be negated by a juvenile court judge's expression of concern and regret. Such expression is not uncommon and should be commended — not masked by judicial indifference. . . .

. . . .

Finally, the majority's holding will stifle communication between judge and ward, replacing it with the formalism characteristic of the adult criminal trial. This is unfortunate. The closer a juvenile hearing moves toward becoming an adversarial proceeding, the more a child tends to view the law as either his oppressor or his fool — depending on who "wins the contest."

In conclusion, Aline must be characterized as an aggressive, assaultive delinquent who may benefit from CYA training and discipline. Disposition of her case should not rest on a judge's expression of sorrow or dismay. If it does, we fail both Aline and the juvenile justice system.

I would affirm the judgment of the juvenile court.

NOTES AND QUESTIONS

1. The above cases represent different approaches taken by appellate courts in reviewing juvenile court dispositions. The *J.A.* case is an example of deferring to the discretion of the trial court to fashion appropriate dispositions suited to the needs of particular juvenile offenders. The *Appeal No. 179* and *Aline D.* cases, on the other hand, reflect more aggressive review by appellate courts.

(a) By refusing to require the trial court to provide reasons for committing the juvenile to the Youth Development Center, in Geneva, does *J.A.* essentially leave the disposition decision entirely to the trial court? Does the Nebraska statute, provided immediately prior to *J.A.*, require such a result?

(b) Do you agree that the trial judge in *Appeal No. 179* abused his discretion in "sending a loud and clear" message that "we are not going to countenance housebreakings"? Is the trial court's approach essentially punitive? If so, is that approach at odds with the statutorily articulated purposes of dispositions in Maryland?

(c) The California court in *Aline D.* finds that the "statutory scheme . . .contemplates a progressively restrictive and punitive series of disposition orders in cases such as that now before us — namely, home placement under supervision, placement in a local treatment facility and, as a last resort, Youth Authority placement." Given the court's requirement that the lower court consider alternatives to CYA placement, does *Aline D.* stand for the proposition that juvenile offenders are entitled to the least restrictive dispositional alternative sufficient to serve the "welfare of the minor and the best interests of the State"?

Could the court in *J.A.* have interpreted the Nebraska statute as requiring the least drastic alternative suited to achieve the purposes of juvenile dispositions?

2. Other California cases, subsequent to *Aline D.*, more specifically embrace the least restrictive alternative approach. For example, in *In re Jose P.*, 161 Cal. Rptr. 400 (Cal. Ct. App. 1980), a fifteen-year-old Mexican nonresident alien was adjudicated a delinquent for the offense of unlawful use of a motor vehicle. The youth had earlier admitted to a charge of attempted auto theft and had been turned over to immigration officials who returned him to Mexico. At the disposition hearing, probation officials recommended placement with

the California Youth Authority (CYA), the most restrictive placement available in the state. In the opinion of the probation officers the two auto offenses revealed that the youth was probably making a living by stealing cars in California and selling them in Mexico. The court adopted the probation office recommendation after concluding that the youth was probably unamenable to treatment as evidenced by the fact that he reentered the United States and committed a criminal act after the immigration authorities had sent him back to Mexico.

The youth appealed the order committing him to CYA and the appellate court reversed, finding that the juvenile court abused its discretion by not considering less drastic alternatives. The court emphasized that juvenile dispositions are meant to be rehabilitative, not punitive, and that confinement in CYA thrusts the detainee into custody with some offenders having lengthy involvement in violent activity. The court noted that the statute imposing juvenile court dispositions listed the alternatives in ascending order of severity, ranging from probation to commitment to CYA. This list suggested to the court a legislative plan of imposing progressively restrictive dispositions and requiring that CYA placements be deferred until "lesser remedies of probation or other placements have failed or are clearly inappropriate." The court saw the sole reason for the trial judge's CYA order as an attempt to deter the juvenile from reentering the state. Moreover, the court found no evidence to support a conclusion that the juvenile could not benefit from a less severe disposition. Because "the record [did] not reveal the unavailability of suitable alternative dispositions," the CYA commitment could not stand and the court remanded the case directing the juvenile court to consider the viability of less restrictive alternative placements.

3. Other jurisdictions also recognize the least drastic alternative approach. *See, e.g., In re J.S.S.,* 610 N.W.2d 364 (Minn. Ct. App. 2000); *In re Michael "QQ,"* 638 N.Y.S.2d 851 (N.Y. App. Div. 1996).

Some state courts recognize a constitutional right to the least drastic alternative. For example, in *State ex rel. R.S. v. Trent,* 289 S.E.2d 166 (W. Va. 1982), the West Virginia Supreme Court noted that juveniles are "constitutionally entitled to the least restrictive treatment that is consistent with the purpose of their custody," statutorily defined as "the best interests and welfare of the public and the child." The court explained how this principle applies to decisions to commit juveniles to the State Industrial School:

> [T]he court's decision to commit the juvenile to an industrial school or correctional facility must be grounded on a number of factors indicating that incarceration is the appropriate disposition.
>
> In this regard the court should specifically address the following: (1) the danger which the child poses to society; (2) all other less restrictive alternatives which have been tried either by the court or by other agencies to whom the child was previously directed to avoid formal juvenile proceedings; (3) the child's background with particular regard to whether there are pre-determining factors such as acute poverty, parental abuse, learning disabilities, physical impairments, or any other discrete, causative factors which can be corrected by the State or other social service agencies in an environment less restrictive

than an industrial school; (4) whether the child is amenable to rehabilitation outside an industrial school, and if not, why not; (5) whether the dual goals of deterrence and juvenile responsibility can be achieved in some setting less restrictive than an industrial school and if not, why not; (6) whether the child is suffering from no recognizable, treatable determining force and therefore is entitled to punishment; (7) whether the child appears willing to cooperate with the suggested program of rehabilitation; and, (8) whether the child is so uncooperative or so ungovernable that no program or rehabilitation will be successful without the coercion inherent in a secure facility.

Before ordering the incarceration of the child, the juvenile court is required to set forth upon the record the facts which lead to the conclusion that no less restrictive alternative is appropriate.

Id. at 170.

In an earlier case, the West Virginia Supreme Court discussed the relevance of the offense committed in determining a proper disposition:

Whether the rehabilitation of a child adjudged delinquent can be accomplished by any less restrictive means than incarceration is a determination which requires an inquiry into the individual needs and circumstances of the child. . . .

This is only in keeping with the purpose of our juvenile law which is to promote the rehabilitation of troubled children rather than to punish them. This purpose is expressed with regard to dispositions in the requirement that the juvenile court arrive at a disposition which will affect the rehabilitation of the child in the least restrictive manner concomitant with the best interests of the child and of the public. . . .

. . . .

Respondent . . . found that relator had previously been on "unofficial" probation in another county prior to the commission of the offense and that that attempt at rehabilitation had proved "singularly unsuccessful." Respondent maintains that this fact, coupled with the serious nature of the offense of armed robbery, justified the incarceration of the child in a correctional facility. We disagree.

This Court has already stated that the gravity of the offense and previous acts of delinquency, their frequency, seriousness and relationship to the present charge are relevant considerations in determining the rehabilitative prospects of the juvenile. We have also held that the nature of the offense is not alone sufficient to warrant transfer of juvenile proceedings to the criminal jurisdiction of the circuit court. As we stated there,

All persons who commit violent crimes are not alike in their prospects for rehabilitation. Some violent offenders can be rehabilitated, others cannot be. Placing undue weight on the nature of the crime and excluding other factors assures that no distinction is made between these groups.

This reasoning appears equally applicable to the determination of which of the statutorily enumerated dispositions will accomplish the rehabilitation of the child.

State ex rel. S.J.C. v. Fox, 268 S.E.2d 56, 59–60 (W. Va. 1980).

4. Some states statutorily require the least drastic alternative approach. *See, e.g.*, ARK. CODE ANN. § 9-27-329(d) (Michie 1998); IOWA CODE ANN. § 232.52(1) (West 2000).

[a] Disposition Alternatives

[i] Probation

Probation, the most common disposition in delinquency cases, allows the juvenile to continue life within a familiar environment without being subjected to institutionalized confinement. Judges who order probation specify conditions, tailored to the needs of the specific child, that must be observed in an attempt to provide structure to the child's "normal" life. Probation orders are generally monitored by probation officers who are expected to maintain regular contact with the child. Should the child fail to follow the imposed conditions, probation may be revoked and a more severe disposition imposed.

Traditionally, courts have had discretion to impose probation regardless of the severity of the offense committed by the juvenile. Although probation is generally considered to be the least restrictive of the various dispositional alternatives, some juveniles have argued that it is unduly harsh in some circumstances. For example, in *In re Wayne T.*, 159 Cal. Rptr. 106 (Cal. Ct. App. 1979), a juvenile argued that the court violated his equal protection rights when it imposed an order of home probation after finding that the minor had committed a misdemeanor offense punishable by a $100 fine in criminal court. The minor argued that probation was a more onerous disposition than the sanction that would have been imposed on an adult in similar circumstances, thus violating equal protection. The court rejected this argument, finding that juvenile court probation, unlike the fine imposed in criminal court, is non-punitive and therefore places delinquents in a situation dissimilar to that of adult offenders. The court elaborated:

> One of the purposes of the Juvenile Court Law is to secure for each minor under the jurisdiction of the juvenile court such care and guidance, preferably in his own home, as will best serve his welfare and "preserve and strengthen the minor's family ties." Thus with this in mind, a comprehensive statutory scheme was devised to best provide for the placement and treatment of juveniles. It is apparent . . . that probation in a juvenile proceeding is not an act of leniency which a minor can refuse but the preferred disposition if warranted by the circumstances. . . .
>
> . . . Appellant's position ignores the nature and purposes of the Juvenile Court law, the options available to the court in dealing with the youthful offender, and the involvement of the probation officer in virtually every phase of the juvenile court process, in particular, his

role in representing the interest of the minor and supplying the need for supervision and assistance of a trained counselor. The difference in treatment seems justified by the differing characteristics and needs of adult and juvenile offenders.

. . . [W]hatever test is used to analyze the distinction between placement in the parents' home under the supervision of the probation officer, and imposition of a fine and/or summary probation on the adult who violates the same statute, we find the distinction reasonable, and necessary to facilitate the purposes of the Juvenile Court Law and the rehabilitation of the minor. . . .

. . . The conditions of probation required the minor to do little more than that appropriate to any minor who resides at home (with the exception of obeying all orders of and reporting to the probation officer). The benefit of probation to the minor under the circumstances is that he is able to remain at home and is given needed guidance and discipline which his parents should, but in many cases cannot or will not give him, and he and his parents are afforded the assistance of a professional counselor in the person of the probation officer. The great advantage of this kind of counseling in such a case as this is the lasting effect it may have on molding the minor's attitudes for the better.

Id. at 108–110.

Juvenile court judges enjoy broad discretion not only in choosing probation over other dispositional alternatives, but also in tailoring probation orders with obligatory conditions deemed beneficial to the particular juvenile. Statutes routinely allow juvenile courts to impose "reasonable conditions" of probation, thus allowing judges virtually complete discretion to follow their personal judgement.

The courts have upheld orders of probation, potentially extending for the entire period of the delinquent's minority, even though the underlying offense is a relatively minor misdemeanor. *See, e.g., In re Westbrooks,* 288 S.E.2d 395 (S.C. 1982) (shoplifting). Juvenile court judges routinely order regular school attendance as a probation condition, *see, e.g., In re Gerald B.,* 164 Cal. Rtpr. 193 (Cal. Ct. App. 1980), and sometimes add an additional requirement that the student receive passing grades, *see, e.g., In re Angel J.,* 11 Cal. Rptr. 2d 776 (Cal. Ct. App. 1992). Other permissible and commonly imposed conditions include obedience to all laws, periodic reports to probation officers, remaining within the jurisdiction, and obeying a curfew. In addition, the courts have upheld conditions restricting juveniles' association only to persons approved by parents or probation officers, *see, e.g., In re Frank V.,* 285 Cal. Rptr. 16 (Cal. Ct. App. 1991). The courts have also upheld conditions prohibiting the probationer's presence at known gathering areas of gang activity and wearing of gang clothing and insignia. *In re Laylah K.,* 281 Cal. Rpt. 6 (Cal. Ct. App. 1991).

On the other hand, some courts have invalidated orders requiring church attendance on the theory that such orders violate First Amendment doctrines of separation of church and state, *see, e.g., L.M. v. State,* 587 So. 2d 648 (Fla. Dist. Ct. App. 1991) *(per curiam). But see L.M. v. State,* 610 So. 2d 1314 (Fla. Dist. Ct. App. 1992) (upholding probation condition that juvenile obey all lawful and reasonable demands of his mother including participation in the mother's church's youth program). In rare circumstances, courts have ordered youthful offenders not to attend religious activities, *see, e.g., In re A.H.,* 459 A.2d 1045 (D.C. 1983) (upholding a probation condition ordering the child to stay away from the Islamic Center, the place where he had been arrested in connection with incidents of violence occurring on those premises).

On occasion, courts strike down other probation conditions. In *In re L.L.W.,* 626 S.W.2d 261 (Mo. Ct. App. 1981), for example, the court reversed an order of "shock probation" consisting of confinement in the county jail for a period of seven days. The court found the order illegal "for whatever time or reason."

PROBATION REVOCATION

Alleged violations of probation conditions may result in revocation of probation. Often such actions are initiated by the probation officers who are authorized to take their probationers into custody when there is probable cause to believe a probationer has violated probation.

Basic due process protections apply to revocation proceedings. Summary revocations are thus impermissible and the juvenile is entitled to a hearing, *see, e.g., In re Gerald B.,* 164 Cal. Rptr. 193 (Cal. Ct. App. 1980) (no summary detention permitted where child violates legitimate probation condition requiring regular school attendance). The probationer is entitled to advance notice of the alleged violation, *see, e.g., In re Litdell,* 232 So. 2d 733 (Miss. 1970). Probationers enjoy rights to present evidence, confront opposing witnesses and have counsel appointed where, under the facts of the particular case, counsel is needed to assure the effectiveness of the due process rights available at the hearing. *See* SANFORD J. FOX, JUVENILE COURTS 230 (3d ed. 1984).

Jurisdictions split on the burden of proof required in probation revocation proceedings. Some states require "proof beyond a reasonable doubt," *see, e.g., In the Interest of C.B.,* 585 P.2d 281 (Colo. 1978), while others permit proof by "clear and convincing evidence," MINN R. JUV. PROC 15.07 Subd. 4 (D) (2002), and still others require only a "preponderance" of the evidence, *see, e.g., People v. Belcher,* 371 N.W.2d 474 (Mich. Ct. App. 1985).

[ii] Restitution

STATE IN INTEREST OF D.G.W.

Supreme Court of New Jersey
361 A.2d 513 (1976)

HUGHES, C.J.

D.G.W., a juvenile, was charged with participating in 1973 and 1974 with three others in four instances of breaking and entering certain residences and school buildings and with theft and destruction of property therein worth thousands of dollars. If found guilty of these offenses, D.G.W. could be adjudicated a juvenile delinquent and incur statutory sanctions. . . .

Pleas of guilty to three of the charges were entered by agreement and one charge was dismissed.

The Juvenile and Domestic Relations Court judge placed the appellant on probation for one year, which he had authority to do under the statute. . . . He determined, over the objection of defense counsel, to apply as a condition to such grant of probation the making of restitution to a victim of the offense.

The court ordered that the specific amount of restitution (as related to the damages caused by the juvenile misdeeds) be "worked out" with the probation department of the county. . . .

. . . [T]he probation department assembled a list of specific items of damage at one of the school buildings totaling $626. Since four individuals had taken part in the depredations, D.G.W. was ordered to be responsible for one-fourth of the total damage or $156.50. . . . The estimated values of the damaged items of property were "based on the cost of repairing damaged machines plus the cost of materials and overtime estimated by their maintenance supervisor for damages to the building." . . .

. . . .

The omission by the Legislature of the sanction of a fine against a juvenile offender seems clearly responsive to the general legislative purpose. Fines are essentially punitive in nature . . . whereas the statutory policy with respect to juveniles is to correct and rehabilitate rather than punish. . . . "Centuries of history indicate that the pathway lies not in unrelenting and vengeful punishment, but in persistently seeking and uprooting the causes of juvenile delinquency and in widening and strengthening the reformative process through socially enlightened movements." . . . "Child delinquency is largely due to broken homes and parental irresponsibility and default, and unfavorable environmental and associated factors, involving pressures that are oft times beyond the child's control; and the State, as *parens patriae*, undertakes . . . to provide for the wayward victims protective custody, care, discipline, and correctional treatment to fit them, psychologically and physically, for a useful social life. . . . The policy is both preventive and reformative. . . . Wayward children are a community problem; adult behavior oft times has its roots in childhood experiences. The redemptive process concerns diagnostic techniques and child therapy, by psychologic, psychiatric and other modes and methods which are not of immediate interest. There are those who would question the wisdom and efficacy of sociological techniques. But, once the legislative field of action is conceded, the legislative policy is not a justiciable issue." . . .

It is against this background that we must determine the threshold question; — whether restitution in its broad sense, including the concept of reparation, may be a valid condition of probation imposed upon a juvenile offender; — or whether it, in essence, would . . . [be] discordant with the legislative purpose. Beyond the validity of the restitution condition itself and the procedural due process necessary for the determination of the extent and terms of restitution to be made, are subsumed other questions raised by appellant. Where several participants are involved in a joint act of theft or vandalism, and all are required to make restitution, is a *pro rata* distribution of its burden appropriate? What is the relationship between indigency or ability to make restitution and the enforceability of the remedy of compelling restitution? What is the status of such remedy in the face of actual or potential claim for such damages in a civil action?

I

As to the disposition of juvenile delinquency cases, the statute provides:

. . . Disposition of delinquency cases.

If a juvenile is adjudged delinquent the juvenile and domestic relations court may order any of the following dispositions:

c. Place the juvenile on probation to the chief probation officer of the county or to any other suitable person who agrees to accept the duty of probation supervision for a period not to exceed three years upon such written conditions as the court deems will aid rehabilitation of the juvenile; or

i. Such other disposition not inconsistent with this act as the court may determine. (emphasis added).

The general statute dealing with the power of courts to suspend sentence and place offenders on probation provides:

Power of courts to suspend sentence and place on probation; period of probation. The courts having jurisdiction over juvenile or domestic relations cases, when it shall appear that the best interests of the public as well as of the person adjudged guilty of any offense . . . before such court will be subserved thereby, shall have power to place the defendant on probation for a period of not less than one year nor more than five years. Such courts shall also have the power to place on probation under the same conditions children who shall come within the jurisdiction of the court. . . .

The statute authorizing the fixing of conditions of probation provides:

Conditions of probation.

The court shall determine and may, at any time, modify the conditions of probation, and may, among others, include any of the following: That the probationer shall avoid injurious, immoral or vicious habits; shall avoid places or persons of disreputable or harmful character, shall report to the probation officer as directed by the court or probation officer, shall permit the probation officer to visit him at his place of abode or elsewhere; shall answer all reasonable inquiries on the part of the probation officer; shall work faithfully at suitable employment; shall not change his residence without the consent of the court or probation officer, shall pay a fine or the costs of the prosecution, or both, in one or several sums, *shall make reparation or restitution to the aggrieved parties for the damage or loss caused by his offense*; shall support his dependents. (emphasis added).

The court rule emphasizes . . . the rehabilitative purpose of probation:

Manner of Disposition. The court may make the following disposition of juvenile matters: (2) Make an adjudication and (C) Place the juvenile on probation to the chief probation officer of the county or to any other suitable person who agrees to accept the duty of probation supervision upon such written conditions as the court deems will aid rehabilitation of the juvenile; (emphasis added).

It is thus apparent that the legislative purpose would accommodate reparation or restitution . . . as a probation condition. . . .

We are bound to think, then, that unless restitution has to be considered primarily as punishment and little or nothing else, and thus discordant with the legislative plan . . . , its use as a condition of probation would not [be proper].

The dichotomy of punitive and rehabilitative purpose and effect implicit in probation was recognized by Chief Justice Weintraub in *In re Buehrer*, 236 A.2d 592, 596 (1967):

The argument assumes that punishment and rehabilitation are somehow incompatible. Of course they are not. . . . Punishment and rehabilitation are not antagonists. Probation assumes the offender can be rehabilitated without serving the suspended jail sentence. But this is not to say that probation is meant to be painless. Probation has an inherent sting, and restrictions upon the freedom of the probationer are realistically punitive in quality. . . . Probation is meant to serve the overall public interest as well as the good of the immediate offender. Thus N.J. S.A. 2A:168–1 authorizes the use of probation "(w)hen it shall appear that the best interests of the public as well as of the defendant will be subserved thereby."

It is significant that the same test is expressed by the Legislature with regard to probation for the juvenile offender, — "when it shall appear that the best interests of the public as well as of the person adjudged guilty . . . will be subserved thereby . . . ." And if probation is to be granted for the accomplishment of the rehabilitative goals outlined by the statute, we think it follows, unless otherwise interdicted, that restitution as a condition thereof must be weighed in the same balance. Restitution manifestly serves the interest of the public for it is not right that either victim or the public should bear the whole burden, let us say, of loss from extensive juvenile vandalism. Quaere: does an order for restitution so clearly disserve the "best interests" of the juvenile offender that it must be abandoned as a rehabilitative tool? We think not.

. . . "[T]he object of the juvenile process is to make men out of errant boys."[84]

---

[84] [2] The "best interest" of society is primarily subserved by the rehabilitative aspect of restitution, — for the chastening effect of making amends holds a possibility at least that one day there will be emerging into the law-abiding mainstream, a decent citizen rather than an "errant boy" grown into a predatory criminal.

We hold that a just and fair order as to restitution is a valid and may indeed be a salutary condition of a term of probation. In the case here reviewed the imposition of that condition was proper, but its effectuation, as we shall point out, was procedurally deficient.

[The court held that because appellant was denied a hearing to challenge the amount of restitution owed, the appellant's due process rights were violated.]

. . . .

The juvenile has an obvious "property" interest in his earnings or other income to be paid over in satisfaction of the restitutionary amount. Additionally he has an obvious "liberty" interest in his continued probationary "freedom" which is subject to termination upon his unjustified failure or refusal to meet the restitutionary condition.

We are satisfied that deprivation of these interests triggers the juvenile's entitlement to due process. . . .

. . . To protect his interest in his earnings and income and his interest in continued liberty the juvenile, minimally, is concerned about (1) the amount of damage he will be held responsible for, (2) the method of determining the value, (3) his *pro rata* share where several defendants are involved and (4) a reasonable method of repayment which realistically assesses his ability to pay.

. . . .

[The court discussed the precise requirements necessary to ensure the appellant's due process rights are satisfied.]

Also pertinent is the amount of money which the offender can or will be able to pay.

. . . .

. . . [T]he statutory power to impose restitution as a condition of probation must be exercised reasonably. Therefore, . . . the offender's present and probable future ability to repay the damages caused, [is necessary] for [the court] to properly fix the amount to be imposed.[85]

. . . .

The appellant raises . . . an objection to the pro rata assessment of damages against him as one of the four persons involved on the basis that there was no express finding that he was personally responsible for one-quarter of the damages. . . . As indicated, the record here discloses that four persons participated in the vandalism of certain high school facilities and that D.G.W. admitted his role therein. . . .

Bearing in mind the rehabilitative purpose of probation restitution he may distinguish between culprit "A," let us say, existing in the most meager

---

[85] [4] In fixing the terms of restitution, the court will be aware that, in case of law default; in no event may the juvenile offender be institutionalized, or probation be terminated, solely because of inability to pay. Consequently a restitution order against a school boy, for instance, without any prospect of even part-time employment (particularly under present economic conditions) might be a meaningless gesture. The judge however, being mindful of the rehabilitation factor, might suggest a search for part-time employment as bearing on good faith amends.

poverty, whose restitution, if any, will be rehabilitative because earned by the sweat of his brow; whereas as to culprit "B," perhaps the scion of a wealthy and supportive family, the same restitution requirement would be meaningless as a rehabilitative tool. In the latter case reparation in kind might be deemed more effective.

. . . .

We remand to the Juvenile and Domestic Relations Court for re-establishment of the restitution amount upon which appellant's probation was conditioned, and for the completion of proceedings not inconsistent with this opinion.

So ordered.

———

NOTES AND QUESTIONS

1. The *D.G.W.* court finds that "restitution" is a permissible juvenile disposition but that "fines" are not. How would you distinguish a permissible restitution award of $626 and an impermissible fine of $626? What is it about a fine that makes it "punitive"? For another case which, like *D.G.W.*, draws the restitution/fines distinction, see *In re Gardini*, 365 A.2d 1252 (Pa. Super. Ct. 1976) (invalidating an order that a juvenile pay $200 as an impermissible fine).

2. Some jurisdictions permit courts to require the parents of juvenile offenders to make restitution for damage caused by their children. *See, e.g.,* ARK. CODE ANN. § 9-27-330(a)(7) (Michie Supp. 2001); MISS. CODE ANN. § 43-21-619(2) (1999).

3. Statutes in some states forbid restitution in cases where the juvenile does not have, and could not reasonably acquire, the means to pay restitution. *See, e.g.,* N.C. GEN. STAT. § 7B-2506(4) (1999). Where no such statutory provisions exist, courts sometimes impose similar limitations on the power of juvenile courts to order restitution. *See, e.g., In re Damien C.,* 35 Cal. Rptr. 2d 766 (Cal. Ct. App. 1994).

[iii] Community Service

M.J.W. v. STATE

Court of Appeals of Georgia
210 S.E.2d 842 (1974)

CLARK, JUDGE.

Does the imposition of a requirement that a juvenile delinquent contribute free labor to the Parks and Recreation Department amount to involuntary servitude in violation of his constitutional rights? Is the imposition of such requirement similar to a monetary fine which is prohibited? These interesting questions are presented for determination.

. . . As a condition to the offender being placed on probation for one year, he was required to "contribute 100 hours to Parks and Recreation Department of DeKalb County." Appellant's able attorney argues this condition to be invalid for two reasons. These are: (1) the court in effect was placing a fine upon the offender contrary to the ruling of *E.P. v. State of Ga.*, 203 S.E.2d 757 (1973), that no statutory authority exists for imposing a monetary fine on a minor adjudged to be delinquent; and (2) this would constitute involuntary servitude in violation of the juvenile's constitutional rights.

We hold that [the] attack has [no] merit in the light of the provisions of our Juvenile Court Code and the nature of probation. The permeating premise of our statute is that juvenile offenders can be rehabilitated and transformed into productive citizens by a system specially designed to achieve those ends. One of the methods provided in that statute is probation. In *P.R. v. State of Ga.*, 210 S.E.2d 839 (1974), we made an exhaustive examination into this subject of probation conditions and concluded that a requirement of restitution was permissible because it was not in the nature of a fine. The reasoning in that case applies here in two respects. The first is that designation of work of a public purpose for destruction of public property is akin to restitution and does not resemble a monetary penalty. Secondly, useful services for the public good are in the pattern of probation, which is a specialized judicial tool and is helpful towards achieving the statute's pervading purpose of producing a good adult citizen. As the trial judge stated: "This is specific action designed to foster in him an understanding that he's got some responsibilities and what it takes to create something as opposed to going around destroying things." It is constructive rather than punitive. It comes within the statutory mandate that juvenile court judges are to make such disposition of a delinquent child as is "best suited to his treatment, rehabilitation, and welfare."

Nor does this condition amount to prohibited involuntary servitude. . . . Even though juvenile court proceedings are not criminal proceedings, we must recognize "the quasi-criminal aspects of juvenile law." Additionally, the courts frequently apply criminal law procedural safeguards to juveniles. The Juvenile Court Code defines a delinquent act as one "designated a crime by the laws of Georgia." Accordingly, a juvenile court order of this type would come within the constitutional exception as it is "punishment for crime," even though it is rehabilitative rather than punitive. . . .

We reiterate that the requirement of performing public service is in accord with the theme of probation. In considering the State Wide Probation Act we pointed out that our statute was not exclusive in its provisions and that 'the court has authority to impose restrictions not specifically listed therein. This reasoning is most apropos to the letter and spirit of our enlightened Juvenile Court Code with its broad probation provisions and its curative goal or rehabilitation. The instant public-work condition conforms to today's approach which courts make in seeking alternatives to jail. . . . This innovative and imaginative approach seeks to avoid a trauma lift on the victim or the community while aiming to give the offender a chance "for a sense of satisfaction and accomplishment that prison rarely offers." In short, to make the punishment fit the offender rather than follow The Mikado's musical mandate: "Let the punishment fit the crime."

Judgment affirmed.

――――

NOTES AND QUESTIONS

1. In light of the materials in § 5.02[B], *supra*, does the *M.J.W.* court's statement that community service is "punishment for crime even though it is rehabilitative rather than punitive" make sense? Can a sanction be "punishment" for purposes of the constitutional exception prohibiting involuntary servitude, but not "punishment" for other purposes? What if the juvenile in *M.J.W.* had argued that his 100 hours of community service constituted cruel and unusual punishment and was thus unconstitutional?

2. For other cases upholding community service orders, see, *e.g.*, *In re P.E.K.*, 558 N.E.2d 763 (Ill. App. Ct. 1990) (work in rural cemeteries); *In re Shannon A.*, 483 A.2d 363 (Md. Ct. Spec. App. 1984) (1,000 hours of working with a brain-damaged child under the supervision of juvenile services). Some cases, however, hold that the amount of time imposed for community service may not exceed the period of imprisonment set in the criminal code for the underlying crime. *See, e.g., M.G. v. State,* 556 So. 2d 820 (Fla. Dist. Ct. App. 1990) (interpreting state statute to limit juvenile community service to amount of imprisonment set for underlying crime, here 60 days for the second degree misdemeanor of simple assault). Does the limitation on community service imposed by the *M.G.* court make sense as a rehabilitative disposition?

3. Some states statutorily authorize community service as a possible disposition. *See, e.g.*, CONN. GEN. STAT. ANN. § 46(b)-14(b), (e) (West Supp. 2001); S.C. CODE ANN. § 20-7-7805(A)(3) (Supp. 2001) (community mentor program). For a discussion of community service as a juvenile court disposition, see H. Ted Rubin, *Community Service Restitution by Juveniles: Also in Need of Guidance*, 37 JUV. & FAM. CT. J. 1 (1986).

[iv] Confinement

NELSON v. HEYNE

United States Court of Appeals for the Seventh Circuit
491 F.2d 352 (1973)

KILEY, SENIOR CIRCUIT JUDGE.

The district court in this class civil rights action enjoined defendants from implementing alleged unconstitutional practices and policies in conducting the Indiana Boys School under their administration; and declared the practices and policies unconstitutional. [On appeal], defendants challenge the validity of the judgment granting the injunction, and . . . challenge the declaratory judgment. We affirm.

The School, located in Plainfield, Indiana, is a medium security state correctional institution for boys twelve to eighteen years of age, an estimated one-third of whom are non-criminal offenders. The boys reside in about sixteen cottages. The School also has academic and vocational school buildings, a gymnasium and an administrative building. The average length of a juvenile's stay at the School is about six and one-half months. Although the School's maximum capacity is less than 300 juveniles, its population is generally maintained at 400. The counseling staff of twenty individuals includes three psychologists with undergraduate academic degrees, and one part-time psychiatrist who spends four hours a week at the institution. The medical staff includes one part-time physician, one registered nurse, and one licensed practical nurse.

The complaint alleged that defendants' practices and policies violated the 8th and 14th Amendments rights of the juveniles under their care. Plaintiffs moved for a temporary restraining order to protect them from, *inter alia*, defendants' corporal punishment and use of control-tranquilizing drugs. After hearing, the district court denied the motion. . . .

The court found that . . . the corporal punishment and the method of administering tranquilizing drugs by defendants constituted cruel and unusual punishment in violation of plaintiffs' 8th and 14th Amendment rights. The judgment restraining the challenged practices followed. The court thereafter, in a separate judgment, declared plaintiffs had the right to adequate rehabilitative treatment.

I

CRUEL AND UNUSUAL PUNISHMENT

A

It is not disputed that the juveniles who were returned from escapes or who were accused of assaults on other students or staff members were beaten routinely by guards under defendants' supervision. There is no proof of formal procedures that governed the beatings which were administered after decision by two or more staff members. Two staff members were required to observe the beatings.

In beating the juveniles, a "fraternity paddle" between ½-inch and 2-inches thick, 12-inches long, with a narrow handle, was used. There is testimony that juveniles weighing about 160 pounds were struck five blows on the clothed buttocks, often by a staff member weighing 285 pounds. The beatings caused painful injuries.[86] The district court found that this disciplinary practice

---

[86] [3] The trial record indicates that one juvenile was struck with such force that it caused him to sleep on his face for three days, with black, blue and numb buttocks. One juvenile testified that he bled after receiving five blows on his buttocks. Another . . . testified that once he pleaded, to no avail, with staff personnel not to be beaten until after certain blisters on his buttocks ceased to cause him pain.

violated the plaintiffs' 8th and 14th Amendment rights, and ordered it stopped immediately. We recognize that the School is a correctional, as well as an academic, institution.[87] No case precisely in point has been cited or found which decided whether supervised beatings in a juvenile reformatory violated the "cruel and unusual" clause of the 8th Amendment. However, the test of "cruel and unusual" punishment has been outlined. In his concurring opinion in *Furman v. Georgia,* 408 U.S. 238, 279, 92 S.Ct. 2726, 2747, 33 L.Ed.2d 346 (1971), Justice Brennan stated that:

> The final principle inherent in the (Cruel and Unusual Punishment) Clause is that a severe punishment must not be excessive. A punishment is excessive under this principle if it is unnecessary: The infliction of a severe punishment by the State cannot comport with human dignity when it is nothing more than the pointless infliction of suffering. If there is a significantly less severe punishment adequate to achieve the purposes for which the punishment is inflicted, the punishment inflicted is unnecessary and therefore excessive.

Expert evidence adduced at the trial unanimously condemned the beatings. The uncontradicted authoritative evidence indicates that the practice does not serve as useful punishment or as treatment, and it actually breeds counter-hostility resulting in greater aggression by a child. For these reasons we find the beatings presently administered are unnecessary and therefore excessive. We think, under the test of *Furman,* that the district court did not err in deciding that the disciplinary beatings shown by this record constituted cruel and unusual punishment.[88]

. . . .

There is nothing in the record to show that a less severe punishment would not have accomplished the disciplinary aim. And it is likely that the beatings have aroused animosity toward the School and substantially frustrated its

---

[87] [4] (a) The law appears to be well settled in both state and federal jurisdictions that school officials do not violate 8th Amendment proscriptions against cruel and unusual punishment where the punishment is reasonable and moderate. *Ware v. Estes,* 328 F. Supp. 657 (ND.Tex. 1971); *Sims v. Board of Education,* 329 F. Supp. 678 (D.C.N.M. 1971); . . . In *Ware* there was evidence of beatings usually administered by hitting the student on his buttocks with a paddle. The paddle was wooden, 12 inches long, 1/4-inch to 1/2-inch thick, 6 inches wide, used under a written rule which proscribed corporal punishment without parents' permission. The district court found that "some of the seven thousand" teachers in the public school district abused the policy, but that that fact, and nothing more, would not make the policy itself unconstitutional. In *Sims,* the court found that beatings by school officials did not constitute cruel and unusual punishment where the plaintiff student received three blows with a paddle on the buttocks and experienced slight physical harm. In our case, there is ample evidence that the beatings caused severe injury. . . . The courts in recent years have frowned upon the use of corporal punishment in penal and correctional institutions. . . . Corporal punishment has not been used for years in federal prisons. . . . Courts have enjoined prison personnel from inflicting corporal punishment including the use of a strap for whipping. *Talley v. Stephens,* 247 F. Supp. 683 (E. D-Ark. 1965). . . . In *Talley* the court did not hold prison whippings are per se unconstitutional, but stated that they will be enjoined if excessive, and not applied under recognizable standards. In *Jackson* the 8th Circuit held that use of a strap in Arkansas penitentiaries was cruel and unusual punishment. . . .

[88] [6] We do not hold that all corporal punishment in juvenile institutions or reformatories is *per se* cruel and unusual.

rehabilitative purpose. We find in the record before us, to support our holding, general considerations similar to those, the court in Jackson found relevant: (1) corporal punishment is easily subject to abuse in the hands of the sadistic and unscrupulous, and control of the punishment is inadequate; (2) formalized School procedures governing the infliction of the corporal punishment are at a minimum; (3) the infliction of such severe punishment frustrates correctional and rehabilitative goals; and (4) the current sociological trend is toward the elimination of all corporal punishment in all correctional institutions.

. . . .

B

Witnesses for both the School and the juveniles testified at trial that tranquilizing drugs, specifically Sparine and Thorazine, were occasionally administered to the juveniles, not as part of an ongoing psychotherapeutic program, but for the purpose of controlling excited behavior.[89] The registered nurse and licensed practical nurse prescribed intramuscular dosages of the drugs upon recommendation of the custodial staff under standing orders by the physician. Neither before nor after injections were the juveniles examined by medically competent staff members to determine their tolerances.

The district court also found this practice to be cruel and unusual punishment. Accordingly the court ordered the practice stopped immediately, and further ordered that no drug could be administered intramuscularly unless specifically authorized or directed by a physician in each case, and unless oral medication was first tried, except where the staff was directed otherwise by a physician in each case.

We agree with defendants that a judge lacking expertise in medicine should be cautious when considering what are "minimal medical standards" in particular situations. However, practices and policies in the field of medicine, among other professional fields, are within judicial competence when measured against requirements of the Constitution. We find no error in the competent district court's determination here that the use of tranquilizing drugs as practiced by defendants was cruel and unusual punishment.

We are not persuaded by defendants' argument that the use of tranquilizing drugs is not "punishment." Experts testified that the tranquilizing drugs administered to the juveniles can cause: the collapse of the cardiovascular system, the closing of a patient's throat with consequent asphyxiation, a depressant effect on the production of bone marrow, jaundice from an affected

---

[89] [8] Plaintiff Steven Hegg testified that on one occasion while he was recuperating from a blow to the nose inflicted upon him by another student, his nose began to bleed profusely and he began to vomit and "holler for help." The nurse told him there was nothing seriously wrong with him; but when Steven continued to request help, she became infuriated and injected him with a tranquilizing drug. Eric Nelson testified to the effect that he was given shots of tranquilizing drugs on several occasions for the purpose of preventing him from running away from the School.

liver, and drowsiness, hemotological disorders, sore throat and ocular changes. [90]

The interest of the juveniles, the School, and the state must be considered in determining the validity of the use of the School's tranquilizing drugs policy. The interest of the state appears to be identical more or less with the interest of the maladjusted juveniles committed to the School's care, i.e., reformation so that upon release from their confinement juveniles may enter free society as well adjusted members. The School's interest is in the attainment and maintenance of reasonable order so that the state's purpose may be pursued in a suitable environment. The School's interest, however, does not justify exposing its juveniles to the potential dangers noted above. Nor can Indiana's interest in reforming its delinquent or maladjusted juveniles be so compelling that it can use "cruel and unusual" means to accomplish its benevolent end of reformation.

We hold today only that the use of disciplinary beatings and tranquilizing drugs in the circumstances shown by this record violates plaintiffs' 14th Amendment right protecting them from cruel and unusual punishment. We do not intend that penal and reform institutional physicians cannot prescribe necessary tranquilizing drugs in appropriate cases. Our concern is with actual and potential abuses under policies where juveniles are beaten with an instrument causing serious injuries, and drugs are administered to juveniles intramuscularly by staff, without trying medication short of drugs and without adequate medical guidance and prescription. [91]

---

[90] [10] Dr. James W. Worth, psychologist with the Mental Health Center of St. Joseph County, Indiana, also testified as follows:

> I think the use of major tranquilizing drugs without intelligent and informed medical observation have no place . . . in the institution. These are serious drugs. They have serious effect on the individual. . . . If this is not done with a full medical understanding of this individual with a physician present, harm could occur and furthermore, I think it tends to be degrading to an individual.

[91] [11] Experts testified that the following minimum medical safeguards should be followed in the use of tranquilizing drugs:

> (1) The individual administered the drug should be observed, during the duration of the drug's effect, by trained medical personnel, familiar with the possible adverse and harmful side effects of the drug used.

> (2) The person receiving an IM (intramuscular) injection of a major tranquilizing drug should first receive a diagnosis or prescription authorizing the use of said drug by a qualified medical doctor, child psychiatrist, psychologist or physician.

> (3) IM injections should only be administered by a physician or intern and only after all attempts have failed to get the individual to take the drug orally.

> (4) Major tranquilizing drugs, such as Thorazine and Sparine, should not be administered IM, unless given in a hospital where there is an intensive care unit and emergency facilities which could deal with possible adverse effects from the use of said drugs.

> (5) Major tranquilizing drugs should only be used to control psychotic or pre-psychotic breakdowns or as a followup in assisting a schizophrenic patient from having a recurrence of a psychotic breakdown.

> (6) Major tranquilizing drugs should not be used merely to induce sleep or unconsciousness for a period of time, but only as a part of a psychotherapeutic program of treatment.

———

NOTES AND QUESTIONS

1. In light of its opinion in *Ingrahm v. Wright*, § 4.03[B][1], *supra*, how do you think the United States Supreme Court would decide the corporal punishment issues raised in *Nelson*? Is it clear that the use of the tranquilizing drugs was "punishment" as concluded by the *Nelson* court? For discussion of this issue, see Martin R. Gardner, *Punishment and Juvenile Justice: A Conceptual Framework for Assessing Constitutional Rights of Youthful Offenders*, 35 VAND. L. REV. 791, 843–46 (1982).

2. Regarding the punitive paddling, is the issue in *Nelson* that the paddling was excessive (too many blows) or that the paddling itself was an unconstitutional kind of punishment? Is the *Nelson* court clear on this point?

[b] The Right to Rehabilitative Treatment

NELSON v. HEYNE

United States Court of Appeals for the Seventh Circuit
491 F.2d 352 (1973)

[For other aspects of this case, see page 1137, *supra*.]

II

THE RIGHT TO REHABILITATIVE TREATMENT

The School staff-to-juvenile ratio for purposes of treatment is approximately one to thirty. The sixteen counselors are responsible for developing and implementing individualized treatment programs at the institution, but the counselors need have no specialized training or experience. Administrative tasks ("paper work") occupy more than half of the counselors' time. The duties of the staff psychiatrist are limited to crises. He has no opportunity to develop and manage individual psychotherapy programs. The three staff psychologists do not hold graduate degrees and are not certified by Indiana. They render, principally, diagnostic services, mostly directed toward supervising in-take behavior classifications.

In June, 1971, the School adopted what was described as a differential treatment program, bottomed mainly on the Quay Classification System. Under the Quay System, upon their admission to the School, juveniles are classified with respect to four personality and behavior types on the basis of standardized tests: the inadequate, the neurotic, the aggressive, and the subcultural. Each of the sixteen cottages at the School houses twenty to thirty juveniles, with common personality and behavior patterns. Each cottage is served by a staff comprising a house manager, a counselor, an educator, and a consulting psychologist. The cottage staff meets weekly for evaluation of the rehabilitation program of each inmate. Upon admission to a cottage, each juvenile agrees to improve his behavior in four areas of institutional life: "cottage," "recreation," "school," and "treatment." Correspondingly, each has responsibility for physical maintenance of the residential area, social and athletic activities, specified levels of academic or vocational skills, and improved personality goals. With success in each of the four areas, the juvenile earns additional privileges, ultimately culminating in a parole date.

The district court decided that both Indiana law and the federal Constitution secure for juvenile offenders a "right to treatment," and that the School failed to provide minimal rehabilitative treatment. Defendants contend that there exists no right to treatment under the Constitution or Indiana law, and that if there is the right, the Quay Classification System used at the School did not violate the right. We hold, with the district court, that juveniles have a right to rehabilitative treatment.

The right to rehabilitative treatment for juvenile offenders has roots in the general social reform of the late nineteenth century, was nurtured by court decisions throughout the first half of this century, and has been established in state and federal courts in recent years. In *In re Gault*, 387 U.S. 1 (1967), the Court stated:

> The early reformers were appalled by adult procedures and penalties, and by the fact that children could be given long prison sentences and mixed in jails with hardened criminals . . . .

> The child was to be 'treated' and 'rehabilitated' and the procedures, from apprehension through institutionalization, were to be 'clinical' rather than punitive.

Since the beginning, state courts have emphasized the need for "treatment" in their Juvenile Court Acts.

The United States Supreme Court has never definitively decided that a youth confined under the jurisdiction of a juvenile court has a constitutionally guaranteed right to treatment. But the Court has assumed, in passing on the validity of juvenile proceedings, that a state must provide treatment for juveniles.

"There is evidence, in fact, that there may be grounds for concern that the child receives the worst of both worlds: that he gets neither the protections accorded to adults nor the solicitous care and regenerative treatment postulated for children. . . ."

[S]everal recent state and federal cases, out of concern-based upon the *parens patriae* doctrine underlying the juvenile justice system — that . . . juvenile inmates have a constitutional right to that treatment. . . . *Martarella v. Kelley,* 349 F.Supp. 575 (S.D.N.Y. 1972).

In *Martarella* the court found a clear constitutional right to treatment for juveniles based on the 8th and 14th Amendments: "What we have said, although the record would justify more, is sufficient to establish that, however benign the purposes for which members of the plaintiff class are held in custody, and whatever the sad necessities which prompt their detention, they are held in penal condition. Where the State, as *parens patriae*, imposes such detention, it can meet the Constitution's requirement of due process and prohibition of cruel and unusual punishment if, and only if, it furnishes adequate treatment to the detainee. . . ."

. . . .

We hold that on the record before us the district court did not err in deciding that the plaintiff juveniles have the right under the 14th Amendment due process clause to rehabilitative treatment.[92]

III

ADEQUACY OF TREATMENT

Experts testified at the trial, and the defendants admit, that the Quay System of behavior classification is not treatment. And case histories of maladjusted juveniles show that use of the System falls far short of its improved personality goals. . . . The record shows very little individual treatment programmed, much less implemented, at the School; and it is unclear exactly how much time is spent in individual counseling. We conclude that the district court could properly infer that the Quay System as used in the School failed to provide adequate rehabilitative treatment.

We leave to the competent district court the decision: what is the minimal treatment required to provide constitutional due process, having in mind that the juvenile process has elements of both the criminal and mental health processes.

In our view the "right to treatment" includes the right to minimum acceptable standards of care and treatment for juveniles and the right to individualized care and treatment. Because children differ in their need for rehabilitation, individual need for treatment will differ. When a state assumes the place of a juvenile's parents, it assumes as well the parental duties, and its treatment of its juveniles should, so far as can be reasonably required, be what proper parental care would provide. Without a program of individual treatment the result may be that the juveniles will not be rehabilitated, but warehoused, and that at the termination of detention they will likely be incapable of taking their proper places in free society; their interests and those of the state and the school thereby being defeated.

We therefore affirm the judgment of the district court in each appeal, and remand only for the limited purpose of further proceedings . . . with respect to the right to rehabilitative treatment.

---

[92] [12] We note that the district court additionally determined that a right to treatment in this case has a statutory basis in view of the "custody, care, and discipline" language of the Indiana Juvenile Court Act. . . . We agree with this conclusion. . . .

NOTES AND QUESTIONS

1. Assuming that juveniles in Indiana enjoy a "right to rehabilitative treatment," does the *Nelson* court explain what such a right entails or what remedy should be applied for its violation? For discussion of this and other questions, see Nicholas N. Kittrie, *Can the Right to Treatment Remedy the Ills of the Juvenile Process?*, 57 GEO. L.J. 848 (1969); Patricia Wald & Larry Schwartz, *Trying a Juvenile Right to Treatment Suit: Pointers and Pitfalls for Plaintiffs*, 12 AM. CRIM. L. REV. 125 (1974); Bill Britt, *Judicial Recognition and Implementation of a Right to Treatment for Institutionalized Juveniles*, 49 NOTRE DAME L. REV. 1051 (1974); Michael Frisch, *Constitutional Right to Treatment for Juveniles Adjudicated to be Delinquent:* Nelson v. Heyne, 12 AM. CRIM. L. REV. 209 (1974); Recent Developments, *Limits on Punishment and Entitlement to Rehabilitative Treatment of Institutionalized Juveniles:* Nelson v. Heyne, 60 VA. L. REV. 864 (1974).

For a case more recent than *Nelson* recognizing the right of incarcerated juveniles to rehabilitative treatment, see *Alexander v. Boyd*, 876 F. Supp. 773 (D.S.C. 1995).

2. Not all courts agree with the *Nelson* court that juveniles committed to detention facilities possess a right to treatment, even under traditional rehabilitative models of juvenile justice. For example, in *Santana v. Collazo*, 714 F.2d 1172 (1st Cir. 1983), the court said:

> Plaintiffs challenge, as violative of their right to rehabilitative treatment, the inadequate intake assessment of each juvenile's psychiatric, medical, academic, vocational and social strengths, weaknesses and needs, coupled with the inadequate classification system (based on age and physical characteristics); the absence of adequate individualized treatment plans covering all aspects of each juvenile's care, education, growth and development; the absence of adequate educational, vocational and recreational programs; the deficient qualifications and training of the staff; and over reliance on the custodial staff. Basically, they claim that the juveniles are just being incarcerated, not rehabilitated, and that in light of the state's professed purpose in institutionalizing the juveniles — to treat them — the state has an obligation to provide the promised treatment.

> A number of courts have found that juveniles involuntarily incarcerated have a right to rehabilitative treatment. The reasoning of these courts is two-fold. First, relying on the Supreme Court's insistence, that 'the nature and duration of commitment must bear some reasonable relation to the purpose for which the individual is committed', courts have reasoned that because the state's authority over delinquent juveniles derives from its *parens patriae* interest in their welfare, due process requires that juveniles confined under that authority be given treatment consistent with the beneficent purpose of their confinement. Second, courts have relied on the fact that the

juvenile justice system denies certain due process safeguards, which denials have been found constitutionally acceptable because the purpose of incarceration is rehabilitation, not punishment. Thus, the '*quid pro quo*' for the denied safeguards is the promised rehabilitation.

As the district court in this case recognized, both of the theoretical bases for the claimed right to rehabilitative treatment are questionable. Although states have asserted their *parens patriae* authority in exercising control over problem juveniles, they may legitimately confine individuals solely to protect society from them. In addition, even without treatment, simply removing a juvenile from a dangerous or unhealthy environment may be a legitimate exercise of the state's *parens patriae* authority. In short, since rehabilitative treatment is not the only legitimate purpose of juvenile confinement, the Supreme Court's insistence that the nature of confinement must bear a reasonable relationship to the purpose of that confinement gains plaintiffs little ground in their effort to establish a right to rehabilitative treatment.

The second aspect of the *quid pro quo* theory has even less merit. The procedural protections accorded juvenile offenders may differ from those accorded criminal defendants, because the demands of due process differ according to the interests of the individual and of society in the given situation. The Supreme Court has found certain distinctions between the protections accorded juveniles and those accorded criminal defendants constitutionally acceptable. Were that not the case, no amount of treatment would make up for the denial of due process along the way.

In short, there is no legally cognizable *quo* to trigger a compensatory *quid*. We therefore agree with the district court that although rehabilitative training is no doubt desirable and sound as a matter of policy and, perhaps, of state law, plaintiffs have no constitutional right to that rehabilitative training. With that in mind, we turn to plaintiffs' challenge to the practice of confining juveniles to the isolation unit at Mayaguez as punishment for disciplinary infractions.

. . . .

. . . [J]uvenile plaintiffs, who have not been convicted of crimes, have a due process interest in freedom from unnecessary bodily restraint which entitles them to closer scrutiny of their conditions of confinement than that accorded convicted criminals. . . .

The Supreme Court has recognized that the deprivation of liberty and conditions of confinement of both juvenile detention and involuntary confinement of the mentally ill may be sufficiently analogous to criminal punishment to warrant the protection of the Eighth Amendment. *See Ingraham v. Wright,* 430 U.S. at 669 n. 37, 97 S.Ct. at 1411 n. 37. The possibility of Eighth Amendment protection, however, does not mean that the state may assert punishment as a legitimate goal of incarceration. Thus, because the state has no legitimate interest in punishment, the conditions of juvenile confinement, like those of confinement of the mentally ill, are subject to more exacting scrutiny than conditions imposed on convicted criminals.

The distinction between conditions imposed for the legitimate purpose of maintaining institutional order and safety and those that amount to retribution is a fine one. Certainly, administrators of a juvenile home must be free to discipline the home's residents. And, in doing so, the state of course inflicts punishment for offending behavior. The distinction, however, is not an entirely meaningless one. In a case such as this, it may simply be a matter of the closeness with which courts should be willing to scrutinize the state's asserted interest in imposing burdensome conditions of confinement. When the conditions are imposed on convicted criminals, the Supreme Court has deferred to the judgment of prison administrators unless the conditions are cruel and unusual, because '[t]o the extent that such conditions are restrictive and even harsh, they are part of the penalty that criminal offenders pay for their offenses against society.' For an individual not convicted of a crime, however, restrictions on his liberty beyond his initial incarceration must be reasonably related to some legitimate government objective — of rehabilitation, safety or internal order and security.

The district court made no findings regarding the legitimacy and weight of the state's interest in confining the juveniles in isolation. Were there nothing of concern in the record, we might be inclined to assume that the state's interest, presumably in protecting the juveniles from harm, in discouraging offending behavior and in preventing escapes, was sufficient to justify the deprivations imposed. A number of experts testified, however, that isolation for longer than a few hours serves no legitimate therapeutic or disciplinary purpose and is unnecessary to prevent harm unless a juvenile is severely emotionally disturbed. In addition, the experts testified, extended isolation can be psychologically damaging and, under the conditions of Mayaguez, may be physically harmful. The district court recognized that '[i]solation as a disciplinary measure, under the circumstances present in this case, entails a substantial curtailment of a juvenile's freedom.' We agree and are satisfied that the curtailment is substantial enough to warrant further examination of the necessity for and conditions of this confinement.

. . . .

. . . [R]emanded for further proceedings consistent with this opinion.

Id. at 1176–1183.

[2] Punitive Juvenile Justice

Andrew Walkover, *The Infancy Defense in the New Juvenile Court*

31 UCLA Law Review 503, 503–05, 523–25, 527–31 (1984)

During the past twenty years two successive waves of reform have struck the juvenile justice system, radically revamping both its conceptual basis and its constituent elements. Led by the Supreme Court, the judiciary has substantially eviscerated the *parens patriae* doctrine by imposing basic requirements of procedural due process on the juvenile court. In response, many legislatures have reformulated the substantive law of the juvenile justice court by limiting its jurisdiction to youths committing acts that would be crimes if committed by adults and by substituting principles of personal accountability and punishment for treatment as the animating forces in allocating dispositions.

This rejection of *parens patriae* theory, the constitutionalization of juvenile process, and the shift toward more traditional principles of criminal law raises practical and conceptual problems for the juvenile justice court that can no longer be wished away by reference to its "benign" purposes. . . .

. . . .

Four key characteristics delineate the new juvenile law. First, in many jurisdictions accountability and punishment have emerged among the express purposes of juvenile justice statutes. Second, much of the law comports with the dictates of due process. Third, delinquency jurisdiction in general is limited to children committing offenses that would be crimes if committed by adults. Fourth, there is a movement toward weighing issues of culpability and accountability more heavily in the waiver and dispositional decisions.

The roots of the new juvenile law are complex and interdependent. Fear of rising juvenile crime, a perceived shift in the kinds of crime committed (and race of the individual committing the crime), and shifting public perceptions of the nature of childhood and adolescence led to the movement toward accountability. Much of the conceptual framework of the new juvenile law was triggered by *Gault* and its progeny. Both the impetus for the *Gault* decision and its acceptance in the legal, political, and academic worlds were enhanced in large measure by a growing criticism of the rehabilitative ideal in general, and the effectiveness of the treatment modality in particular.

Two threads of particular importance in giving intellectual justification to the new juvenile court may be drawn out of this fabric, one sociological and the other philosophical. In the 1960's and 1970's, students of juvenile delinquency largely abandoned the interventionist model of dealing with the problem of delinquency that had dominated sociological studies of the juvenile court and had provided its theoretical basis since its inception.

. . . .

[A] major intellectual force shaping the new juvenile court grew from the post-World War II emphasis on retribution theory in defining the limits of the criminal sanction. Retribution theory presupposes that the criminal sanction is justifiably imposed only where blameworthy behavior exists. Reacting in part to the social engineering program of the legal realists, retribution theory drew strength both from concerns about the appropriate reach of the criminal sanction in a liberal democratic society and from philosophical and ethical imperatives. The impact of retribution theory, embodied in part in the Model Penal Code's culpability requirements, did not remain exclusively within the adult criminal justice system. Its concern with individual autonomy provided a powerful intellectual force against the claims of treatment-oriented juvenile courts.

That retribution theory has spread its influence from the adult to the juvenile system is reflected in the adoption of the institute of Judicial Administration/American Bar Association's Juvenile Justice Standards of the Model Penal Code requirement that culpability precede imposition of criminal liability. The Standards, the definitive professional statement on the new juvenile justice, reject the rehabilitative rationale. It is instead the concept of culpability that animates its purposes section, that justifies its limitation on juvenile justice jurisdiction to the blameworthy, and that informs its determinate sentencing scheme.

Basic criminal procedural protections and substantive juvenile law rooted in the logic of non-interventionism and retribution theory are reflected increasingly in state juvenile codes. Washington's revised juvenile justice code, discussed in the next section, may be seen as a paradigmatic expression of the new juvenile justice. . . .

VI

THE WASHINGTON MODEL

In Washington's new Juvenile Justice Act classical principles of justice have largely replaced diagnosis and therapy in the law's treatment of juveniles. As revised, the Act's purposes include a litany of traditional criminal justice concerns. Focus on the needs of the offender is tempered by a systematic commitment to making juveniles accountable for their criminal behavior, providing punishment commensurate with their age, crime, and criminal history.

Consistent with its new theoretical underpinnings, the Act restricts juvenile justice jurisdiction to those juveniles who commit offenses that would be crimes or violations if committed by adults. . . .

     . . . .

On a symbolic level the criminalization of Washington juvenile justice is revealed most clearly in the opening of juvenile proceedings to the public. The new juvenile justice is no longer a closed, informal, and private forum for the resolution of family problems, with the state acting as parent. Now the system, like its adult model, is open to public scrutiny.

A presumptive sentencing scheme plays a key role in ensuring juvenile accountability for offenses committed. Presumptive dispositions are tied to the youth's age, the offense committed, and the history and seriousness of previous offenses. The statute provides both upper and lower limits on the standard dispositional range and sets out aggravating and mitigating factors for sentencing within the range. Dispositions can be made outside the standard range only where to do otherwise would create a manifest injustice. The import of this shift should not be underestimated. Juvenile sentencing practice may be said to no longer focus on the "needs" of the offender. Rather, dispositions are carefully tailored to hold juveniles accountable in proportion to the culpability of their acts and their criminal history.

Provisions of the Act dealing with the maturity of juveniles are consistent with its overall concern with accountability and process. For example, factoring age into dispositional ranges reflects a frank recognition that the capacity to be culpable, and thus to be held accountable, increases with age. Provisions for diversion programs and community service do not undercut the Act's punishment-oriented rationale. Their use is clearly suggested only where less blameworthy offenses are committed and a less blameworthy criminal history is presented.

NORTH CAROLINA GENERAL STATUTES (1999)

§ 7B-2500. Purpose.

The purpose of dispositions in juvenile actions is to design an appropriate plan to meet the needs of the juvenile and to achieve the objectives of the State in exercising jurisdiction, including the protection of the public. The court should develop a disposition in each case that:

(1) Promotes public safety;

(2) Emphasizes accountability and responsibility of both the parent, guardian, or custodian and the juvenile for the juvenile's conduct; and

(3) Provides the appropriate consequences, treatment, training, and rehabilitation to assist the juvenile toward becoming a nonoffending, responsible, and productive member of the community.

. . . .

§ 7B-2506. Dispositional Alternatives for Delinquent Juveniles.

The court exercising jurisdiction over a juvenile who has been adjudicated delinquent may use the following alternatives in accordance with the dispositional structure set forth in G.S. 7B-2508.

(1) In the case of any juvenile who needs more adequate care or supervision or who needs placement, the judge may:

a. Require that a juvenile be supervised in the juvenile's own home by the department of social services in the juvenile's county, a court counselor, or other personnel as may be available to the court, subject to conditions applicable to the parent, guardian, or custodian or the juvenile as the judge may specify; or

b. Place the juvenile in the custody of a parent, guardian, custodian, relative, private agency offering placement services, or some other suitable person; or

c. Place the juvenile in the custody of the department of social services in the county of his residence, or in the case of a juvenile who has legal residence outside the State, in the physical custody of a department of social services in the county where the juvenile is found so that agency may return the juvenile to the responsible authorities in the juvenile's home state. The director may, unless otherwise ordered by the judge, arrange for, provide, or consent to, needed routine or emergency medical or surgical care or treatment. In the case where the parent is unknown, unavailable, or unable to act on behalf of the juvenile or juveniles, the director may, unless otherwise ordered by the judge, arrange for, provide, or consent to any psychiatric, psychological, educational, or other remedial evaluations or treatment for the juvenile placed by a judge or his designee in the custody or physical custody of a county department of social services under the authority of this or any other Chapter of the General Statutes. Prior to exercising this authority, the director shall make reasonable efforts to obtain consent from a parent, guardian, or custodian of the affected juvenile. If the director cannot obtain consent, the director shall promptly notify the parent, guardian, or custodian that care or treatment has been provided and shall give the parent, guardian, or custodian frequent status reports on the circumstances of the juvenile. Upon request of a parent, guardian, or custodian of the affected juvenile, the results or records of the aforementioned evaluations, findings, or treatment shall be made available to the parent, guardian, or custodian by the director unless prohibited by G.S. 122C-53(d).

(2) Excuse the juvenile from compliance with the compulsory school attendance law when the court finds that suitable alternative plans can be arranged by the family through other community resources for one of the following:

a. An education related to the needs or abilities of the juvenile including vocational education or special education;

b. A suitable plan of supervision or placement; or

c. Some other plan that the court finds to be in the best interests of the juvenile.

(3) Order the juvenile to cooperate with a community-based program, an intensive substance abuse treatment program, or a residential or nonresidential treatment program. Participation in the programs shall not exceed 12 months.

(4) Require restitution, full or partial, up to five hundred dollars ($500.00), payable within a 12-month period to any person who has suffered loss or damage as a result of the offense committed by the juvenile. The court may determine the amount, terms, and conditions of the restitution. If the juvenile participated with another person or persons, all participants should be jointly and severally responsible for the payment of restitution; however, the court shall not require the juvenile to make restitution if the juvenile

satisfies the court that the juvenile does not have, and could not reasonably acquire, the means to make restitution.

(5) Impose a fine related to the seriousness of the juvenile's offense. If the juvenile has the ability to pay the fine, it shall not exceed the maximum fine for the offense if committed by an adult.

(6) Order the juvenile to perform up to 100 hours supervised community service consistent with the juvenile's age, skill, and ability, specifying the nature of the work and the number of hours required. The work shall be related to the seriousness of the juvenile's offense and in no event may the obligation to work exceed 12 months.

(7) Order the juvenile to participate in the victim-offender reconciliation program.

(8) Place the juvenile on probation under the supervision of a court counselor, as specified in G.S. 7B-2510.

(9) Order that the juvenile shall not be licensed to operate a motor vehicle in the State of North Carolina for as long as the court retains jurisdiction over the juvenile or for any shorter period of time. The clerk of court shall notify the Division of Motor Vehicles of that order.

(10) Impose a curfew upon the juvenile.

(11) Order that the juvenile not associate with specified persons or be in specified places.

(12) Impose confinement on an intermittent basis in an approved detention facility. Confinement shall be limited to not more than five 24-hour periods, the timing of which is determined by the court in its discretion.

(13) Order the juvenile to cooperate with placement in a wilderness program.

(14) Order the juvenile to cooperate with placement in a residential treatment facility, an intensive nonresidential treatment program, an intensive substance abuse program, or in a group home other than a multipurpose group home operated by a State agency.

(15) Place the juvenile on intensive probation under the supervision of a court counselor.

(16) Order the juvenile to cooperate with a supervised day program requiring the juvenile to be present at a specified place for all or part of every day or of certain days. The court also may require the juvenile to comply with any other reasonable conditions specified in the dispositional order that are designed to facilitate supervision.

(17) Order the juvenile to participate in a regimented training program.

(18) Order the juvenile to submit to house arrest.

(19) Suspend imposition of a more severe, statutorily permissible disposition with the provision that the juvenile meet certain conditions agreed to by the juvenile and specified in the dispositional order. The conditions shall not exceed the allowable dispositions for the level under which disposition is being imposed.

(20) Order that the juvenile be confined in an approved juvenile detention facility for a term of up to 14 24-hour periods, which confinement shall not be imposed consecutively with intermittent confinement pursuant to subdivision (12) of this section at the same dispositional hearing. The timing of this confinement shall be determined by the court in its discretion.

(21) Order the residential placement of a juvenile in a multipurpose group home operated by a State agency.

(22) Require restitution of more than five hundred dollars ($500.00), full or partial, payable within a 12-month period to any person who has suffered loss or damage as a result of an offense committed by the juvenile. The court may determine the amount, terms, and conditions of restitution. If the juvenile participated with another person or persons, all participants should be jointly and severally responsible for the payment of the restitution; however, the court shall not require the juvenile to make restitution if the juvenile satisfies the court that the juvenile does not have, and could not reasonably acquire, the means to make restitution.

(23) Order the juvenile to perform up to 200 hours supervised community service consistent with the juvenile's age, skill, and ability, specifying the nature of work and the number of hours required. The work shall be related to the seriousness of the juvenile's offense.

(24) Commit the juvenile to the Office for placement in a training school in accordance with G.S. 7B-2513 for a period of not less than six months. . . .

§ 7B-2507. Delinquency History Levels.

(a) Generally. — The delinquency history level for a delinquent juvenile is determined by calculating the sum of the points assigned to each of the juvenile's prior adjudications and to the juvenile's probation status, if any, that the court finds to have been proved in accordance with this section.

(b) Points. — Points are assigned as follows:

(1) For each prior adjudication of a Class A through E felony offense, 4 points.

(2) For each prior adjudication of a Class F through I felony offense or Class A1 misdemeanor offense, 2 points.

(3) For each prior adjudication of a Class 1, 2, or 3 misdemeanor offense, 1 point.

(4) If the juvenile was on probation at the time of offense, 2 points.

(c) Delinquency History Levels. — The delinquency history levels are:

(1) Low — No more than 1 point.

(2) Medium — At least 2, but not more than 3 points.

(3) High — At least 4 points.

In determining the delinquency history level, the classification of a prior offense is the classification assigned to that offense at the time the juvenile committed the offense for which disposition is being ordered.

(d) Multiple Prior Adjudications Obtained in One Court Session. — For purposes of determining the delinquency history level, if a juvenile is adjudicated delinquent for more than one offense in a single session of district court, only the adjudication for the offense with the highest point total is used.

(e) Classification of Prior Adjudications From Other Jurisdictions. — Except as otherwise provided in this subsection, and adjudication occurring in a jurisdiction other than North Carolina is classified as a Class I felony if the jurisdiction in which the offense occurred classifies the offense as a felony, or is classified as a Class 3 misdemeanor if the jurisdiction in which the offense occurred classifies the offense as a misdemeanor. If the juvenile proves by the preponderance of the evidence that an offense classified as a felony in the other jurisdiction is substantially similar to an offense that is a misdemeanor in North Carolina, the conviction is treated as that class of misdemeanor for assigning delinquency history level points. If the State proves by the preponderance of the evidence than an offense classified as either a misdemeanor or a felony in the other jurisdiction is substantially similar to an offense in North Carolina that is classified as a Class I felony or higher, the conviction is treated as that class of felony for assigning delinquency history level points. If the State proves by the preponderance of the evidence that an offense classified as a misdemeanor in the other jurisdiction is substantially similar to an offense classified as a Class A1 misdemeanor in North Carolina, the adjudication is treated as a Class A1 misdemeanor for assigning delinquency history level points.

(f) Proof of Prior Adjudications. — A prior adjudication shall be proved by any of the following methods:

    (1) Stipulation of the parties.

    (2) An original or copy of the court record of the prior adjudication.

    (3) A copy of records maintained by the Division of Criminal Information or by the Office.

    (4) Any other method found by the court to be reliable.

The State bears the burden of proving, by a preponderance of the evidence, that a prior adjudication exists and that the juvenile before the court is the same person as the juvenile named in the prior adjudication. The original or a copy of the court records or a copy of the records maintained by the Division of Criminal Information or of the Office, bearing the same name as that by which the juvenile is charged, is *prima facie* evidence that the juvenile named is the same person as the juvenile before the court, and that the facts set out in the record are true. For purposes of this subsection, "a copy" includes a paper writing containing a reproduction of a record maintained electronically on a computer or other data processing equipment, and a document produced by a facsimile machine. The prosecutor shall make all feasible efforts to obtain and present to the court the juvenile's full record. Evidence presented by either party at trial may be utilized to prove prior adjudications. If asked by the juvenile, the prosecutor shall furnish the juvenile's prior adjudications to the juvenile within a reasonable time sufficient to allow the juvenile to determine if the record available to the prosecutor is accurate. (1998-202, § 6.)

§ 7B-2508. Dispositional Limits for Each Class of Offense and Delinquency History Level.

(a) Offense Classification. — The offense classifications are as follows:

(1) Violent — Adjudication of a Class A through E felony offense;

(2) Serious — Adjudication of a Class F through I felony offense or a Class A1 misdemeanor;

(3) Minor — Adjudication of a Class 1, 2, or 3 misdemeanor.

(b) Delinquency History Levels. — A delinquency history level shall be determined for each delinquent juvenile as provided in G.S. 7B-2507.

(c) Level 1 — Community Disposition. — A court exercising jurisdiction over a juvenile who has been adjudicated delinquent and for whom the dispositional chart in subsequent (f) of this section prescribes a Level 1 disposition may provide for evaluation and treatment under G.S. 7B-2502 and for any of the dispositional alternatives contained in subdivisions (1) through (13) of G.S. 7B-2506. In determining which dispositional alternative is appropriate, the court shall consider the needs of the juvenile as indicated by the risk and needs assessment contained in the predisposition report, the appropriate community resources available to meet those needs, and the protection of the public.

(d) Level 2 — Intermediate Disposition. — A court exercising jurisdiction over a juvenile who has been adjudicated delinquent and for whom the dispositional chart in subsection (f) of this section prescribes a Level 2 disposition may provide for evaluation and treatment under G.S. 7B-2502 and for any of the dispositional alternatives contained in subdivisions (1) through (23) of G.S. 7B-2506, but shall provide for at least one of the intermediate dispositions authorized in subdivisions (13) through (23) of G.S. 7B-2506. However, notwithstanding any other provision of this section, a court may impose a Level 3 disposition if the juvenile has previously received a Level 3 disposition in a prior juvenile action. In determining which dispositional alternative is appropriate, the court shall consider the needs of the juvenile as indicated by the risk and needs assessment contained in the predisposition report, the appropriate community resources available to meet those needs, and the protection of the public.

(e) Level 3 — Commitment. — A court exercising jurisdiction over a juvenile who has been adjudicated delinquent and for whom the dispositional chart in subsection (f) of this section prescribes a Level 3 disposition shall commit the juvenile to the Office for placement in a training school in accordance with G.S. 7B-2506(24). However, a court may impose a Level 2 disposition rather than a Level 3 disposition if the court submits written findings on the record that substantiate extraordinary needs on the part of the offending juvenile.

(f) Dispositions for Each Class of Offense and Delinquency History Level; Disposition Chart Described. — The authorized disposition for each class of offense and delinquency history level is as specified in the chart below. Delinquency history levels are indicated horizontally on the top of the chart. Classes of offense are indicated vertically on the left side of the chart. Each cell on the chart indicates which of the dispositional levels described in subsections (c) through (e) of this section are prescribed for that combination of offense classification and delinquency history level:

DELINQUENCY HISTORY

OFFENSE	LOW	MEDIUM	HIGH
VIOLENT	Level 2 or 3	Level 3	Level 3
SERIOUS	Level 1 or 2	Level 2	Level 2 or 3
MINOR	Level 1	Level 1 or 2	Level 2

(g) Notwithstanding subsection (f) of this section, a juvenile who has been adjudicated for a minor offense may be committed to a Level 3 disposition if the juvenile has been adjudicated of four or more prior offenses. For purposes of determining the number of prior offenses under this subsection, each successive offense is one that was committed after adjudication of the preceding offense.

(h) If a juvenile is a adjudicated of more than one offense during a session juvenile court, the court shall consolidate the offenses for disposition and impose a single disposition for the consolidated offenses. The disposition shall be specified for the class of offense and delinquency history level of the most serious offense.

. . . .

§ 7B-2513. Commitment of Delinquent Juvenile to Office.

(a) Pursuant to G.S. 7B-2506 and G.S. 7B-2508, the court may commit a delinquent juvenile who is at least 10 years of age to the Office for placement in a training school. Commitment shall be for an indefinite term of at least six months. In no event shall the term exceed:

(1) The twenty-first birthday of the juvenile if the juvenile has been committed to the Office for an offense that would be first-degree murder pursuant to G.S. 14-17, first-degree rape pursuant to G.S. 14-27.2, or first-degree sexual offense pursuant to G.S. 14-27.4 if committed by an adult;

(2) The nineteenth birthday of the juvenile if the juvenile has been committed to the Office for an offense that would be a Class B1, B2, C, D, or E felony if committed by an adult, other than an offense set forth in subdivision (1) of this subsection; or

(3) The eighteenth birthday of the juvenile if the juvenile has been committed to the Office for an offense other than an offense that would be a Class A, B1, B2, C, D, or E felony if committed by an adult.

No juvenile shall be committed to a training school beyond the minimum six-month commitment for a period of time in excess of the maximum term of imprisonment for which an adult in prior record level VI for felonies or in prior conviction level III for misdemeanors could be sentenced for the same offense, except when the Office pursuant to G.S. 7B-2515 determines that the juvenile's commitment needs to be continued for an additional period of time to continue care or treatment under the plan of care or treatment developed under subsection (f) of this section. At the time of commitment to a training school, the court shall determine the maximum period of time the juvenile may remain committed before a determination must be made by the Office pursuant to G.S. 7B-2515 and shall notify the juvenile of that determination.

(b) The court may commit a juvenile to a definite term of not less than six months and not more than two years if the court finds that the juvenile is 14 years of age or older, has been previously adjudicated delinquent for two or more felony offenses, and has been previously committed to a training school.

. . . .

(j) When a juvenile is committed to the Office for placement in a training school for an offense that would have been a Class A or B1 felony if committed by an adult, the chief court counselor shall notify the victim and members of the victim's immediate family that the victim, or the victim's immediate family members may request in writing to be notified in advance of the juvenile's scheduled release date. . . .

CALIFORNIA WELFARE & INSTITUTIONS CODE
§ 202 (Supp. 2002)

Purpose; protective services; reunification with family; guidance for delinquents; accountability for objectives and results; punishment defined.

(a) The purpose of this chapter is to provide for the protection and safety of the public and each minor under the jurisdiction of the juvenile court and to preserve and strengthen the minor's family ties whenever possible, removing the minor from the custody of his or her parents only when necessary for his or her welfare or for the safety and protection of the public. When removal of a minor is determined by the juvenile court to be necessary, reunification of the minor with his or her family shall be a primary objective. When the minor is removed from his or her own family, it is the purpose of this chapter to secure for the minor custody, care, and discipline as nearly as possible equivalent to that which should have been given by his or her parents. This chapter shall be liberally construed to carry out these purposes.

(b) Minors under the jurisdiction of the juvenile court who are in need of protective services shall receive care, treatment and guidance consistent with their best interest and the best interest of the public. Minors under the jurisdiction of the juvenile court as a consequence of delinquent conduct shall, in conformity with the interests of public safety and protection, receive care, treatment, and guidance that is consistent with their best interest, that holds them accountable for their behavior, and that is appropriate for their circumstances. This guidance may include punishment that is consistent with the rehabilitative objectives of this chapter. If a minor has been removed from the custody of his or her parents, family preservation and family reunification are appropriate goals for the juvenile court to consider when determining the disposition of a minor under the jurisdiction of the juvenile court as a consequence of delinquent conduct when those goals are consistent with his or her best interests and the best interests of the public. When the minor is no longer a ward of the juvenile court, the guidance he or she received should enable him or her to be a law-abiding and productive member of his or her family and the community.

. . . .

(d) Juvenile courts and other public agencies charged with enforcing, interpreting, and administering the juvenile court law shall consider the safety and protection of the public, the importance of redressing injuries to victims, and the best interests of the minor in all deliberations pursuant to this chapter. Participants in the juvenile justice system shall hold themselves accountable for its results. They shall act in conformity with a comprehensive set of objectives established to improve system performance in a vigorous and ongoing manner. . . .

(e) As used in this chapter, "punishment" means the imposition of sanctions. It shall not include a court order to place a child in foster care as defined by § 727.3. Permissible sanctions may include the following:

(1) Payment of a fine by the minor.

(2) Rendering of compulsory service without compensation performed for the benefit of the community by the minor.

(3) Limitations on the minor's liberty imposed as a condition of probation or parole.

(4) Commitment of the minor to a local detention or treatment facility, such as a juvenile hall, camp, or ranch.

(5) Commitment of the minor to the Department of the Youth Authority.

"Punishment," for the purposes of this chapter, does not include retribution.

(f) In addition to the actions authorized by subdivision (e), the juvenile court may, as appropriate, direct the offender to complete a victim impact class, participate in victim offender conferencing subject to the victim's consent, pay restitution to the victim or victims, and make a contribution to the victim restitution fund after all victim restitution orders and fines have been satisfied, in order to hold the offender accountable or restore the victim or community.

———

IN RE ERIC J.

Supreme Court of California
601 P.2d 549 (1979)

CLARK, JUSTICE.

Eric J., a minor, appeals from an order continuing his juvenile court wardship and committing him to the Youth Authority after findings he committed burglary and was in contempt of court for violating conditions of an earlier order granting probation. The maximum term for [confinement was] three and one-half years-three years for the burglary and six months for the misdemeanor contempt.

FACTS

A month after 10 pairs of roller skates were taken in a burglary of the Sweetwater Roller Rink, Midge Rhoda, a professional skating instructor, informed the owner that appellant was at the Palisades Gardens Skating Rink attempting to sell roller skates which might be the ones stolen. In response to a call from the owner, Officer Merrell Davis went to the Sweetwater rink and was advised by the manager, Buddy Morris, of appellant's identity and his employment at the rink. Officer Davis had a copy of the burglary report.

The uniformed officer drove Morris to the Palisades Gardens where they met Rhoda. She suggested they talk to appellant in her office and summoned him. During questioning by Morris for 45 minutes to an hour, appellant confessed to the burglary, implicated his brother as his accomplice, and stated that he had sold some of the skates to individuals still at the Palisades Gardens, and that the remaining skates were at his house. . . .

. . . .

EQUAL PROTECTION

. . . [A]ppellant contends Welfare and Institutions Code § 726 denies him equal protection of the laws by providing that the maximum term of confinement for a juvenile is the longest term imposable upon an adult for the same offense, without the necessity of finding circumstances in aggravation of the crime justifying imposition of the upper term as, is required in adult criminal procedure by Penal Code § 1170, subdivision (b).

Section 726, subdivision (c), of the Welfare and Institutions Code provides in relevant part:

> In any case in which the minor is removed from the physical custody of his parent or guardian as the result of an order of wardship made pursuant to § 602, the order shall specify that the minor may not be held in physical confinement for a period in excess of the maximum term of imprisonment which could be imposed upon an adult convicted of the offense or offenses which brought or continued the minor under the jurisdiction of the juvenile court. As used in this section and in § 731, 'maximum term of imprisonment' means the longest of the three time periods set forth in paragraph (2) of subdivision (a) of § 1170 of the Penal Code, but without the need to follow the provisions of subdivision (b) of § 1170 of the Penal Code or to consider time for good behavior or participation pursuant to §§ 2930, 2931, and 2932 of the Penal Code, plus enhancements which must be proven if pled.

Section 1170, subdivision (b), of the Penal Code provides:

> When a judgment of imprisonment is to be imposed and the statute specifies three possible terms, the court shall order imposition of the

middle term, unless there are circumstances in aggravation or mitigation of the crime. At least four days prior to the time set for imposition
of judgment either party may submit a statement in aggravation or
mitigation to dispute facts in the record or the probation officer's report, or to present additional facts. . . . The court shall set forth on
the record the facts and reasons for imposing the upper or lower
term. . . .

Appellant was found to have committed burglary. . . . Because the court
failed to find the degree of the offense, it is deemed to be of the second
degree. . . . Second degree burglary is punishable "by imprisonment in the
county jail not exceeding one year or in the state prison." . . . Where it is not
otherwise specified, the term for an offense punishable by imprisonment in
a state prison is "16 months, or two or three years." . . . Pursuant to Welfare
and Institutions Code § 726, subdivision (c), the maximum term for which
appellant might be confined for the burglary was determined to be three years.
He contends that, in the absence of any finding of aggravation, it is a denial
of equal protection of the law not to set the maximum at two years.

In *People v. Olivas*, 551 P.2d 375 (1975), this court held that § 1770 of the
Welfare and Institutions Code violated the equal protection clauses of the
California and United States Constitutions insofar as it permitted misdemeanants between the ages of 16 and 21 to be committed to the Youth
Authority . . . for a term potentially longer than the maximum jail term which
might have been imposed for the same offense if committed by a person over
the age of 21 years. We emphasized that youthful misdemeanants committed
pursuant to § 1731.5 "have been prosecuted *as adults*, adjudged by the same
standards which apply to *any competent adult*, and convicted as adults *in
adult courts*." . . . "We are not confronted," we stressed, "by a situation in
which a juvenile adjudged under *the Juvenile Court Law as a juvenile* contends
that his term of involuntary confinement may exceed that which might have
been imposed on an adult or juvenile who committed the identical unlawful
act and was thereafter convicted in the criminal courts." Since that situation
is not before us, we reserve consideration of the issue should it arise in some
future case and we express no opinion on the merits of such a contention."
. . .

The situation not before us in *Olivas* is presented here. Appellant was
adjudged under Juvenile Court Law as a juvenile. Pursuant to Welfare and
Institutions Code § 726, subdivision (c), the maximum term for which he
might be confined for the burglary was automatically set at three years. An
adult or juvenile convicted in the criminal courts of committing the identical
unlawful act could not, without a finding of aggravating circumstances, be
imprisoned more than two years.

Despite this disparity, appellant has not been denied equal protection of
the laws. The first prerequisite to a meritorious claim under the equal
protection clause is a showing that the state has adopted a classification that
affects two or more similarly situated groups in an unequal manner. Adults
convicted in the criminal courts and sentenced to prison and youths adjudged
wards of the juvenile courts and committed to the Youth Authority are not
"similarly situated."

For purposes of this discussion, the most significant difference between minors and adults is that "[t]he liberty interest of a minor is qualitatively different than that of an adult, being subject both to reasonable regulation by the state to an extent not permissible with adults . . . , and to an even greater extent to the control of the minor's parents unless 'it appears that the parental decisions will jeopardize the health or safety of the child or have a potential for significant social burdens.'" . . . When the minor must be removed from the custody of his parents for his own welfare or for the safety and protection of the public . . . , the state assuming the parents' role, the state also assumes the parents' authority to limit the minor's freedom of action.

" 'The concept of the equal protection of the laws compels recognition of the proposition that persons similarly situated with respect to the legitimate purpose of the law receive like treatment.'" . . . The state does not have the same purpose in sentencing adults to prison that it has in committing minors to the Youth Authority. Adults convicted in the criminal courts are sentenced to prison as punishment . . . while minors adjudged wards of the juvenile courts are committed to the Youth Authority for the purposes of treatment and rehabilitation. . . .

This distinction has been significantly sharpened recently. Under the Indeterminate Sentence Law, which was the system under review in *Olivas*, the purposes of imprisonment were deterrence, isolation and rehabilitation. . . . Not the least of these was rehabilitation. "It is generally recognized by the courts and by modern penologists that the purpose of the indeterminate sentence law, like other modern laws in relation to the administration of the criminal law, is to mitigate the punishment which would otherwise be imposed upon the offender. These laws place emphasis upon the reformation of the offender. They seek to make the punishment fit the criminal rather than the crime." . . .

The enactment of the Uniform Determinate Sentencing Act marked a significant change in the penal philosophy of this state regarding adult offenders. "The Legislature finds and declares that the purpose of imprisonment for crime is punishment. This purpose is best served by terms proportionate to the seriousness of the offense with provision for uniformity in the sentences of offenders committing the same offense under similar circumstances. The Legislature further finds and declares that the elimination of disparity and the provision of uniformity of sentences can best be achieved by determinate sentences fixed by statute in proportion to the seriousness of the offense as determined by the Legislature to be imposed by the court with specified discretion." . . .

There has been no like revolution in society's attitude toward juvenile offenders. It is still true that "[j]uvenile commitment proceedings are designed for the purposes of rehabilitation and treatment, not punishment." . . . Therefore, Juvenile Court Law continues to provide for indeterminate terms, with provision for parole as soon as appropriate. . . .

In *Olivas* this court objected that "[t]here has been no showing made that youthful offenders necessarily require longer periods of confinement for rehabilitative purposes than older adults." . . . No such objection is appropriate here since under the Determinate Sentencing Act rehabilitation is no longer the standard for term fixing.

. . . .

In conclusion, because minors and adults are not "similarly situated" with respect to their interest in liberty, and because minors adjudged wards of the juvenile courts and committed to the Youth Authority and adults convicted in the criminal courts and sentenced to prison are not confined for the same purposes, Welfare and Institutions Code § 726 does not deny minors equal protection of the laws.

[T]he judgment is affirmed.

NEWMAN, JUSTICE, *dissenting*:

I dissent . . . .

There are those who will undoubtedly say the juvenile has the best of both worlds. He obtains the benefits of the Indeterminate Sentencing Law within the juvenile system with the opportunity of being released earlier than the outer limits of his commitment and the benefits of the limitation of a maximum term determined in accordance with the adult penal system. We do not view this as a dramatic result. It is only consistent with the purpose of the juvenile justice system which will still permit the juvenile to be released at any time before the service of the maximum term if deemed rehabilitated or retained for the maximum term if efforts at rehabilitation are unsuccessful. . . . As a practical matter, we suspect our decision will have little or no impact on the operation of the Youth Authority. There should be a direct correlation between the length of term imposed and successful rehabilitation of youthful offenders, *i.e.*, those who are more likely to be rehabilitated will be given lesser terms; those less likely, longer terms. We anticipate the same class of offenders upon whom are imposed the upper term because of circumstances in aggravation will be identical to the class that would have otherwise remained incarcerated for the upper term.

We recognize our decision creates an additional facet to the dispositional hearing . . . causing additional work for the presently overburdened personnel within the juvenile court system. We cannot allow this administrative consideration, important as it is, to outweigh the guarantees afforded to minors.

NOTES AND QUESTIONS

1. In light of § 5.02[B], *supra*, is *Eric J.* correctly decided? Although the current language of CAL. WELF. & INST. CODE § 202 was not applicable at the time of the *Eric J.* decision, the then-applicable language of § 202, in addition to promoting "the welfare of the minor," also expressed interests in "protect[ing] the public from criminal conduct by minors [and] impos[ing] on the minor a sense of responsibility for his own acts" (1977 amendment to

§ 202). Should the *Eric J.* court have taken this amendment into account? If so, how would it bear on the outcome of the case?

2. The Washington statutory scheme summarized in the Walkover excerpt, *supra*, is probably the most systematically punitive model adopted in any jurisdiction. The original system, enacted in 1977 and later revised, has withstood a variety of attacks in the courts. *See, e.g., State v. Rhodes,* 600 P.2d 1264 (Wash. 1979) (upholding against a vagueness attack the "manifest injustice" provision that allows courts to deviate from defined sentencing standards); *State v. Bryan,* 606 P.2d 1228 (Wash. 1980) (upholding the constitutionality of sentencing standards set by the statute and sentencing guidelines promulgated pursuant to the statute); *State v. Rice,* 655 P.2d 1145 (Wash. 1983) (holding, *inter alia,* that imposing longer terms of confinement on juveniles than on adults not violative of equal protection).

3. For a sampling of scholarly commentary discussing the movement towards punitive juvenile justice, see, *e.g.,* Barry C. Feld, *Juvenile Court Legislative Reform and the Serious Young Offender: Dismantling the "Rehabilitiave Ideal,"* 65 MINN. L. REV. 167 (1980); Martin R. Gardner, *The Right of Juvenile Offenders to be Punished: Some Implications of Treating Kids as Persons,* 68 NEB. L. REV. 146 (1989); Julianne P. Sheffer, *Serious and Habitual Juvenile Offender Statutes: Reconciling Punishment and Rehabilitation within the Juvenile Justice System,* 48 VAND. L. REV. 479 (1995).

[3] "Blended Sentencing"

IN THE MATTER OF S.L.M.

Supreme Court of Montana
951 P.2d 1365 (1997)

LEAPHART, JUSTICE.

The appellants in these five appeals challenge the Extended Jurisdiction Prosecution Act, §§ 41-5-1601 through -1607, MCA, (EJPA) as being unconstitutional under the equal protection, due process and double jeopardy clauses of the United States and Montana constitutions, as well as under Article II, § 15 of the Montana Constitution. Although there are some factual differences in how each prosecution evolved as well as differences in the conclusions reached by the various District Courts, the constitutional issues presented encompass each of the appeals. Accordingly, we consolidate these appeals for purposes of an opinion. Since we determine that the EJPA violates Article II, § 4 (equal protection) of the Montana Constitution and Article II, § 15 (rights of minors) of the Montana Constitution, we need not address the double jeopardy and due process challenges.

PROCEDURAL BACKGROUND OF EACH APPEAL

The Youth S.L.M. was charged with perjury and the criminal sale of dangerous drugs, both punishable as felonies if committed by an adult. The State alleged that S.M. sold $150 worth of marijuana to an undercover agent.

At the time of the offense, S.M. was under the age of 18 years. The State requested extended jurisdiction under the EJPA. The District Court held a hearing and granted extended jurisdiction over the charge of criminal sale of dangerous drugs, but did not extend jurisdiction over the charge of perjury, an offense which is not enumerated for extended jurisdiction under the EJPA. At the disposition hearing, the Youth argued that the EJPA violates the equal protection, double jeopardy, and due process guarantees of the Montana and United States constitutions. The District Court rejected the Youth's contentions and committed him to the Department of Corrections until he reaches the age of 19. The District Court then entered and stayed a Sentence and Judgment of 10 years on the charge of criminal sale of dangerous drugs. The Youth filed a motion for correction of sentence or reconsideration. That motion was denied, and the Youth appealed to this Court.

ISSUES PRESENTED

1. Does the EJPA violate the equal protection clauses of the United States Constitution and/or the Montana Constitution?

2. Does the EJPA violate the provisions of Article II, § 15 of the Montana Constitution?

3. Does the EJPA violate the double jeopardy clauses of the United States Constitution and/or the Montana Constitution?

4. Does the EJPA violate the due process clauses of the United States Constitution and/or the Montana Constitution?

DISCUSSION

I. *Overview of the Extended Jurisdiction Prosecution Act*

In 1995, the legislature substantially revised the Montana Youth Court Act, including amending the Declaration of Purpose to effectuate the following purpose:

> to prevent and reduce youth delinquency through immediate, consistent, enforceable, and avoidable consequences of youths' actions and to establish a program of supervision, care, rehabilitation, detention, competency development, community protection, and, in appropriate cases, restitution as ordered by the youth court[.]

Section 41-5-102(2), MCA (1995).

As part of the broad 1995 revision of the Youth Court Act, the EJPA was enacted. The EJPA is now codified at Title 41, Chapter 5, Part 16, MCA. Although the youths herein were all sentenced under the EJPA as it was enacted in 1995, the 1997 legislature amended the EJPA to provide for more procedural due process in revocation of stay proceedings. If the State were to initiate revocation of stay proceedings against any of the appellants, the 1997 amendments would inure to their benefit. However, for purposes of our equal protection analysis, the sentencing provisions of the Act remain the same in that they still provide for imposition of an adult sentence in addition to a juvenile disposition. Accordingly, we will refer to the Act as amended and codified at Title 45, Chapter 5, Part 16, MCA.

A youth court case may be designated an "extended jurisdiction juvenile prosecution" when the offender is at least 14 years of age, the county attorney requests that the case be designated an extended jurisdiction juvenile prosecution, a hearing is held, and the youth court designates the case as such. If, after a hearing, the county attorney has shown by clear and convincing evidence that designating the case an extended jurisdiction prosecution serves the public safety, the youth court may so designate.

A case may also fall under the EJPA if the youth is alleged to have committed one or more of the offenses listed under § 41-5-206, MCA, and the county attorney designates the case as an extended jurisdiction prosecution. The case may also fall under the EJPA if the youth was at least 12 years of age, allegedly committed an offense which, if committed by an adult, would be punishable as a felony, and allegedly used a firearm in the commission of the offense. Additionally, the case may be designated an extended jurisdiction prosecution if, after a hearing on the motion to transfer the case for prosecution in district court, the youth court designates the case an extended jurisdiction prosecution.

After the case is designated an extended jurisdiction prosecution, the case proceeds to an adjudicatory hearing. If the youth admits to committing, or is adjudicated to have committed, an offense which would be a felony if committed by an adult, the youth court must impose one or more of the juvenile dispositions under § 41-5-1512, MCA, and any sentence which could be imposed on an adult offender of the same offense. The statute expressly provides that execution of the sentence imposed "must be stayed on the condition that the youth not violate the provisions of the disposition order and not commit a new offense."

If the court is subsequently informed that any condition of the disposition has been violated, or if it is alleged that the youth has committed a new offense, the court may, without notice, order the youth be taken into custody. The district court must then notify the youth, in writing, of the reasons alleged for revocation of the stay.

If the youth challenges the reasons for the revocation, the court must hold a hearing at which the youth is entitled to notice, an opportunity to be heard, right to counsel, and the right to cross-examine witnesses. If, after the hearing, the court finds by a preponderance of the evidence that the conditions of the stay have been violated or that the youth has committed a new offense, the court shall provide a written statement of the reasons for the revocation and shall: 1) continue the stay and place the youth on probation; 2) impose one or more dispositions under §§ 41-5-1512 or — 1513, MCA, if the youth is under age 18; or 3) order execution of the sentence imposed.

Upon revocation and disposition, the youth court shall transfer the case to the district court. Upon transfer, the offender's extended jurisdiction juvenile status is terminated, and the youth court jurisdiction is terminated. Ongoing supervision of the offender is with the Department of Corrections rather than with the youth court's juvenile probation services.

II. *Standing*

The State contends that certain of the youths lack standing to challenge the constitutionality of the EJPA. The youths contend that the EJPA violates equal protection by subjecting them to a longer period of incarceration than that permitted for an adult offender. The State points out, however, that the adult portion of the sentence is only triggered if the youth violates the terms of his juvenile disposition and the stay of the adult sentence is revoked. Those youths who have not had the stay revoked have not been adversely affected by imposition of an adult sentence and thus, the State contends, lack standing.

We conclude that the youths, each of whom have been sentenced under the EJPA, have standing to challenge its provisions.

. . . .

The threat of injury to the youths herein is apparent. . . . Although the adult sentences of some of the youths may be presently stayed on the condition that they comply with their juvenile dispositions, they suffer a "legitimate and realistic" fear that the adult sentence will be imposed should they violate the disposition. We conclude that the youths, regardless of whether their stays have been lifted, have standing to challenge the constitutionality of the EJPA on equal protection grounds.

III. *Does the EJPA violate the equal protection clauses of the United States Constitution and/or the Montana Constitution and the rights of minors under Article II, § 15 of the Montana Constitution?*

. . . .

In addressing an equal protection challenge, we first identify the classes involved and determine whether they are similarly situated. The two classes involved in the present appeals are: 1) juveniles who are sentenced as adults under the EJPA; and 2) adults who are sentenced for committing the same offense as the juveniles. Since both classes are composed of persons who have committed the same act and who are sentenced "as adults," the classes are similarly situated for equal protection purposes.

In the present appeals, the EJPA's imposition of an adult sentence in addition to a juvenile disposition infringes on the juvenile's physical liberty, which is a fundamental right. We must therefore apply a strict scrutiny analysis and determine whether there is a compelling state interest sufficient to justify such an infringement and whether such an infringement is consistent with the mandates of Article II, § 15 of the Montana Constitution.

Article II, § 15 provides:

> Rights of persons not adults. The rights of persons under 18 years of age shall include, but not be limited to, all the fundamental rights of this Article unless specifically precluded by laws which enhance the protections of such persons.

. . . .

As compared to the pre-1995 Declaration of Purpose, the Act now espouses much more preventative, if not punitive, goals; that is, the Act now seeks to prevent delinquency through imposition of enforceable and immediate consequences and to establish programs of detention and community protection. The State asserts that the EJPA was designed by the legislature to address the rising tide of juvenile criminal conduct in Montana and dispel the notion held by some juveniles that their criminal conduct holds no consequences for them. The EJPA, as noted by the State, gives the courts "a bigger stick to help keep kids in line — to let them know their crimes are serious and this is their last chance to cooperate." Obviously, it is no longer accurate to reason, that Youth Court Act infringements upon a juvenile's physical liberty are legitimate means of enhancing their protection. Indeed, in requiring the court to impose an adult sentence in addition to the juvenile disposition, the EJPA goes beyond mere rehabilitation and injects the specter of retribution.

All juveniles subject to the EJA are at risk of serving an adult sentence in addition to their juvenile disposition. Thus, the EJPA, on its face, violates the equal protection clause of Article II, § 10 by treating EJPA offenders more harshly than their adult counterparts. The EJPA also violates Article II, § 15 by reducing, rather than enhancing, a juvenile's rights as compared to an adult's. While the State has a clear interest in deterring serious juvenile crime and while it can, within the limits of equal protection, further this interest by increasing the sanctions imposed upon juveniles, it has no compelling state interest in treating them as adults and restricting their physical liberty beyond the restrictions which are imposed upon an adult for the same offense.

Where the offender is sanctioned with an "adult" sentence, as under the EJPA, we cannot rely on the doctrine of *parens patriae* to distinguish between the treatment of juveniles and adults. *Parens patriae* traditionally refers to the role of the State as sovereign or guardian of persons who are under a legal disability, such as juveniles — "the principle that the state must care for those who cannot take care of themselves, such as minors who lack proper care and custody from their parents." Where, as under the EJPA, the offender is no longer sentenced solely as a juvenile, but as an adult as well, the doctrine's paternalistic rationale no longer applies.

CONCLUSION

Under the framework of the EJPA, a juvenile receives a juvenile disposition plus an adult sentence. If the juvenile violates the terms of the juvenile disposition, it is possible for the youth to serve a longer term of detention or imprisonment than an adult who has committed the same offense. The State has not shown a compelling interest to be advanced by this unequal treatment of similarly situated persons, nor has it shown that the EJPA provides juveniles with increased, rather than decreased, protection under the law. Therefore, we hold that the EJPA violates Article II, § 4 (equal protection) and Article II, § 15 (rights of minors).

NOTES AND QUESTIONS

1. Subsequent to *S.L.M.*, the Montana legislature attempted to remedy the constitutional defects identified by the *S.L.M.* by amending the EJPA as follows:

> The combined period of time of a juvenile disposition under subsection (1)(a)(i) plus an adult sentence under subsection (1)(a)(ii) may not exceed the maximum period of imprisonment that could be imposed on an adult convicted of the offense or offenses that brought the youth under the jurisdiction of the youth court. This subsection does not limit the power of the department to enter into a parole agreement with the youth pursuant to 52-5-126.

MONT. CODE ANN. § 41-5-1604(1)(b) (2001).

2. Is the analysis of the *S.L.M.* court convincing? Contrary to the court's view, could it not be the case that the juvenile court disposition, while a restriction on liberty, is actually rehabilitative and therefore a *benefit* to the juvenile, thus belying the conclusion that the minor risks "serving a longer term of detention or imprisonment than an adult who has committed the same offense"? Is the issue whether the juvenile may be *detained* longer than a similarly situated adult or whether the juvenile may be *punished* longer? Does it follow that the juvenile disposition is necessarily punitive simply because the juvenile risks punishment if she subsequently misbehaves?

3. The concept of "blended sentencing" or "extended jurisdiction" is an attempt to balance the interests of the juvenile offender with the interest in making juveniles accountable for the crimes they commit. This form of sentencing had its genesis in the state of Minnesota, which as part of the 1992 Omnibus Crime Control Act created a task force whose primary purpose was to examine the structure of the state's current juvenile justice system and to recommend policies, including juvenile courts' sentencing practices.

At the conclusion of its studies, the task force proposed the creation of a new category of juvenile offenders, and a host of other dispositional options to juvenile judges faced with youths committing serious offenses. As a result of this proposal, in 1995, the Minnesota Legislature adopted MINN. STAT. ANN. § 260.126 (1995) (now codified at MINN. STAT. ANN. § 260B.130 (2001)), the first statute invoking the concept of "blended jurisdiction."

As described by one commentator:

> The Minnesota prototype, indeed the pioneer of blended sentencing statutes, purports to try youths in juvenile court, while affording them all of the procedural safeguards defendants receive in adult criminal court. Upon conviction, the judge would then impose on the juvenile both a juvenile court disposition and a stayed adult criminal sentence. If the juvenile showed signs of rehabilitation upon completion of his

sentence, the judge could grant the juvenile probation after his twenty-first birthday. If, however, the juvenile violated the conditions set forth in the juvenile sentence, or committed a new offense before completion of the juvenile sentence, the stayed adult criminal sanction could then be executed. In essence, . . . the new sentencing provisions would give juvenile offenders 'one last chance at success in the juvenile system, with the threat of adult sanctions as an incentive not to reoffend.'

Randi-Lynn Smallheer, *Sentence Blending and the Promise of Rehabilitation: Bringing the Juvenile Justice System Full Circle*, 28 HOFSTRA L. REV. 259, 278-79 (1999).

With the adoption of Minnesota's extended jurisdiction provision, several states have followed suit and begun to fashion similar statutory schemes. As evidenced by *S.L.M.*, such statutes may not be immune to constitutional attack. MINN. STAT. ANN. § 260B.130 (2001) specifically provides that "no credit shall be given for time served in juvenile facility custody," but to date the statute has withstood constitutional challenge. *See In the Matter of L.J.S.*, 539 N.W.2d 408 (Minn. 1996) (upholding Minnesota's extended jurisdiction statute against separation of powers, equal protection and due process challenges).

On the other hand, *S.L.M.* appears to have influence outside the State of Montana. For example, the Kansas Legislature, in recently adopting its extended jurisdiction statute, may have taken *S.L.M.* into consideration by providing that a juvenile "offender shall be credited for time served in a juvenile correctional or detention facility on the juvenile sentence as service on any authorized adult sanction". KAN. STAT. ANN. § 36, 126(b) (2000). For another example of an extended jurisdiction statute patterned after that adopted in Minnesota, see ARK. CODE ANN. § 9-27-501-510 (2000).

4. In addition to those states that have chosen to adopt blended jurisdiction legislation modeled after the Minnesota prototype, numerous variants have begun to emerge in various jurisdictions. New Mexico and Texas provide examples of the two most common alternatives.

New Mexico classifies juvenile defendants into three categories: (1) "delinquent offender;" (2) "youthful offender;" and (3) "serious youthful offender." N.M. STAT. ANN. § 32A-2-3(C),(H),(1) (1993). The decision to place a juvenile into a category is made by the prosecutor, and is based primarily on age and seriousness of the offense. The most serious category of offender is the "serious youthful offender," and it is reserved for those youths fifteen to eighteen years of age who are charged or bound over for trial for first degree murder. *See* N.M. STAT. ANN. § 32A-2-3(H) (1993). The court is required to sentence a "serious youthful offender" as an adult. A "youthful offender" is a juvenile fourteen to eighteen years of age who is adjudicated for one of several enumerated offenses, including second degree murder and criminal sexual penetration. All other offenders not fitting within the categories of "serious youthful offender" or "youthful offender" are categorized as a "delinquent offender."

The New Mexico scheme gets its extended jurisdiction flavor in its treatment of those classified as "youthful offenders." In essence, these youths are tried in juvenile court with adult criminal procedural safeguards, including a right to a jury trial. Upon conviction, the judge will then undergo an assessment of the offender's amenability to treatment in a sentencing hearing to decide whether to impose an adult sentence or juvenile disposition. N.M. STAT. ANN. § 32A-2-20 (1998). Depending upon the judge's assessment of the youth's amenability to treatment, the judge is given the sole discretion to decide whether the offender will receive an adult criminal sentence, or a juvenile disposition with jurisdiction extended until the age of twenty-one. *See* N.M. STAT. ANN. § 32A-2-20(E) (1998).

Another statutory scheme has been labeled the "Juvenile Contiguous Blend Model." Under this model, the juvenile court retains jurisdiction and responsibility for adjudication of the case and has the authority to impose a sanction that would be in force beyond the age of the court's extended jurisdiction, usually twenty-one. The juvenile court is then given the authority to determine whether the remainder of the sanction should be completed in an adult correctional facility. In particular, a juvenile court judge in Texas is given the authority to impose a one-to-forty year sentence for the commission of one of twelve named violent offenses. The sentence is begun in the juvenile correctional system until the age of eighteen, at which time transfer to an adult facility is authorized if deemed necessary after a court review. Transfer to an adult facility is mandatory at age twenty-one. *See* TEX. ANN. FAMILY CODE § 54.04 (Supp. 2002).

Although the varying statutory schemes relating to the practice of "blended jurisdiction" differ in many respects, a common theme runs through these statutes. By providing youthful offenders with the procedural safeguards guaranteed adults in criminal court, the state retains the option to punish these juveniles to the fullest extent possible (as an adult convicted of a similar crime). Such statutes can be viewed as serving a variety of functions, from setting forth a get-tough-on-juvenile-crime mentality to providing a viable alternative to mandatory waiver to adult criminal court for those youths deemed to be amenable to treatment in the juvenile system. With a carrot and stick approach, the youthful offender is given one last chance to rehabilitate while at the same time possessing the knowledge that an adult sentence has been imposed and may be enforced at the state's discretion.

5. For commentary on the issue of "blended jurisdiction", see Connie Hickman Tanner, *Arkansas's Extended Juvenile Jurisdiction Act: The Balance of Offender Rehabilitation and Accountability*, 22 U. ARK. LITTLE ROCK L. REV. 647 (2000); Randi-Lynn Smallheer, *Sentence Blending and the Promise of Rehabilitation: Bringing the Juvenile Justice System Full Circle*, 28 HOFSTRA L. REV. 259 (1999); Mary E. Spring, *Extended Jurisdiction Juvenile Prosecution: A New Approach to the Problem of Juvenile Delinquency in Illinois*, 31 J. MARSHALL L. REV. 1351 (1998); Robert E. Henderson, *Blended Sentencing in Montana: A New Way to Look at an Old Problem*, 61 MONT. L. REV. 337 (2000) (discussing the decision in *S.L.M.* as well as the subsequent statutory amendment).

[C] Status Offense Cases

Although some jurisdictions make no distinctions between delinquents and status offenders for dispositional purposes, *see* SAMUEL M. DAVIS, RIGHTS OF

JUVENILES 6-26 (2d ed. 2001), many others attempt to lessen the dispositional severity for status offenders. Some states permit secure confinement of status offenders but require their segregation from confined delinquents. *See, e.g., In re Levette M.*, 316 N.E.2d 314 (N.Y. 1974). Other courts have taken the view that secure confinement, even where segregated from delinquents, should be a last resort that is employed only after all less drastic alternatives have been exhausted. One court expressed the matter as follows:

> We are . . . concerned with incarceration of children for status offenses. Particularly . . . we are concerned with a child who is incorrigible, ungovernable, habitually disobedient and beyond the control of his parents, truant, repeatedly deserts his home or place of abode, engages in an occupation which is in violation of law, or frequents a place the existence of which is in violation of law. The Legislature has vested the juvenile court with jurisdiction over children who commit these status offenses so that the court may enforce order, safety, morality, and family discipline within the community. The intention of the law is laudable; however, the means employed to accomplish these ends are unconstitutional insofar as they result in the commitment of status offenders to secure, prison-like facilities which also house children guilty of criminal conduct, or needlessly subject status offenders to the degradation and physical abuse of incarceration.

> At the outset the Court should make clear that we are not impressed with euphemistic titles used to disguise what are in fact secure, prison-like facilities. We define a secure, prison-like facility, regardless of whether it be called a "home for girls," "industrial school," "forestry camp," "children's shelter," "orphanage," or other imaginative name, as a place which relies for control of children upon locked rooms, locked buildings, guards, physical restraint, regimentation, and corporal punishment. Somehow, it appears to us that if the State's purpose is to develop a society characterized by peace and love, that our institutions for children should reflect those qualities and not their opposite.

> . . . .

> [B]efore [a status offender] may be committed to a penal institution . . . [there] must be evidence on the record which clearly supports the conclusion, and the juvenile court must specifically find as a matter of fact, that no other reasonable alternative either is available or could with due diligence and financial commitment on the part of the State be made available to help the child, and that the child is so totally unmanageable, ungovernable, and anti-social that he or she is amenable to no treatment or restraint short of incarceration in a secure, prison-like facility.

State ex rel. Harris v. Calendine, 233 S.E.2d 318, 324-25, 331 (W. Va. 1977).

Some courts go even further by altogether precluding institutional confinement of status offenders under statutes that do not expressly state such a preclusion. In *In re E.M.D.*, 490 P.2d 658 (Alaska 1971), for example, the Alaska Supreme Court invalidated the institutional commitment of a fourteen-year-old runaway girl, finding that the statutory distinction between "delinquents" and "child[ren] in need of supervision" permitted institutionalized confinement for delinquents only, even though the statutory language literally authorized both classes of juveniles to be committed to the Department of Health and Welfare for disposition. The court noted provisions of the statutes specifying that in delinquency cases the courts have the option of placing minors under the care of the Department or ordering commitment to "a [juvenile] correctional school, detention home, or detention facility designated by the [D]epartment." The court concluded:

> Thus the only instance under children's laws authorizing institutionalization or incarceration is when the child has violated the laws of the state, or any of its political subdivisions, and in turn has been adjudged a delinquent minor. Since the runaway child in the case at bar was found to be a child in need of supervision, not a delinquent minor, no legal basis existed for her incarceration.

Id. at 660.

Many states statutorily distinguish delinquency and status offense dispositions. *See, e.g.,* NEB. REV. STAT. § 43-286, § 5.06[B][1], *supra.* MISS. CODE ANN. § 43-21-607 (2001 Supp.) provides:

Authorized dispositions, children in need of supervision

(1) In children in need of supervision cases, the disposition order may include any of the following alternatives or combination of the following alternatives, giving precedence in the following sequence:

(a) Release the child without further action;

(b) Place the child in the custody of the parent, a relative or other person subject to any conditions and limitations as the youth court may prescribe;

(c) Place the child under youth court supervision subject to any conditions and limitations the youth court may prescribe;

(d) Order terms of treatment calculated to assist the child and the child's parent, guardian or custodian which are within the ability of the parent, guardian or custodian to perform;

(e) Order terms of supervision which may include participation in a constructive program of service or education or restitution not in excess of actual damages caused by the child to be paid out of his own assets or by performance of services acceptable to the parties and reasonably capable of performance within one (1) year;

(f) Give legal custody of the child to any of the following but in no event to any state training school;

(i) The Department of Human Services for appropriate placement which may include a wilderness training program; or

(ii) Any private or public organization, preferably community-based, able to assume the education, care and maintenance of the child, which has been found suitable by the court. Prior to assigning the custody of any child to any private institution or agency, the youth court through its designee shall first inspect the physical facilities to determine that they provide a reasonable standard of health and safety for the child; or

(g) Order the child to participate in a youth court work program as provided in § 32-21-627.

———

INCARCERATION AS A SECONDARY DISPOSITION

As discussed above in the context of counsel rights for status offenders at adjudication, § 5.05[B][1][a], *supra*, even in states forbidding incarceration as an initial disposition, status offenders may be subjected to institutional confinement if they violate conditions of probation or run away from community-based dispositions. In some jurisdictions, the minor becomes a "delinquent" by virtue of violating probation conditions, thus justifying secure confinement as a delinquent. *See, e.g., In re C.H.*, 683 P.2d 931 (Mont. 1984); *see also* NEB. REV. STAT. §§ 43-247, 286, § 5.06[B][1], *supra*.

Moreover, some courts find that juvenile court judges possess inherent authority to institutionalize status offenders for contempt without finding the juvenile a "delinquent" under statutory law, even though the legislature has mandated that status offenders not be placed in secure confinement facilities. For example, in *In re Darlene C.*, 301 S.E.2d 136 (S.C. 1983), the South Carolina Supreme Court recognized the "inherent judicial power [of juvenile courts] to punish contemnors" in a case where the juvenile court had ordered the institutionalization of a young woman for contempt after she had initially been found to be a "runaway child" and subsequently absconded from a court ordered community-based commitment. The court noted that the minor had a previous history of truancy and running away. Moreover, the court observed that in its original disposition, the juvenile court had informed the minor that she would be held in contempt if she ran away again. The court explained the rationale for upholding the lower court's action as follows:

> The issue is whether a juvenile who commits criminal contempt by running away in violation of a court order may be given a disposition reserved for delinquents who have committed offenses which would be crimes if committed by an adult. We conclude that, under the most egregious circumstances as we have here, family courts may exercise their contempt power in such a manner that a status offender will be incarcerated in a secure facility.

> Although we have held that juvenile offenders may be punished only as prescribed by the South Carolina Children's Code, the Code specifically provides that it shall be interpreted in conjunction with all relevant laws and regulations. Therefore, when dealing with juveniles, family courts may look to their inherent powers as well as to the Children's Code. All courts possess the inherent power to punish contemnors. That power is essential to the preservation of order in

judicial proceedings, and to the enforcement of the courts' judgments, orders and writs and consequently to the due administration of justice.

Nevertheless, we hold that *only* under the most egregious circumstances should family courts exercise their contempt power in such a manner that a status offender will be incarcerated in a secure facility. Before a chronic status offender is placed in a secure facility, the record must show that all less restrictive alternatives have failed in the past. Additionally the following elements should exist: (1) the existence of a valid order directing the alleged contemnor to do or refrain from doing something and the court's jurisdiction to enter that order; (2) the contemnor's notice of the order with sufficient time to comply with it; and in most cases, (3) the contemnor's ability to comply with the order; and (4) the contemnor's willful failure to comply with the order. Furthermore, the record must reflect the juvenile understood that disobedience would result in incarceration in a secure facility.

Id. at 137–38.

Other courts are more lenient in permitting incarceration of status offenders for contempt. For example, in upholding the power of a juvenile court judge to incarcerate a status offender for fifteen days for contempt when she failed to abide by conditions of her original disposition, an Illinois court said:

The minor's final argument is that the court did not have the power to sentence the minor to fifteen days detention in a secured facility. The minor argues that she was adjudicated a minor in need of supervision and not a delinquent. Since the Juvenile Act does not permit a minor to be detained in a secured facility unless the minor is a delinquent, she argues that the court could not so order in a contempt hearing. We disagree.

In re R.R., 417 N.E.2d 237, 239 (Ill. App. Ct. 1981), *rev'd,* 442 N.E.2d 252 (Ill. 1982) (failure of lower court to specify a term for the original disposition on which the contempt charge was based rendered the contempt order void). *See also In re Walker,* 191 S.E.2d 702 (N.C. 1972).

On the other hand, some jurisdictions hold that where statutes clearly prohibit placing status offenders in secure confinement, courts may not employ contempt power to incarcerate contemptuous status offenders. In *In re Tasseing,* 422 A.2d 530 (Pa. Super Ct. 1980), for example, a juvenile court judge held several juveniles in contempt for running away from an unrestricted facility to which they had been committed after being adjudicated status offenders. The juvenile court ordered the juveniles to be detained in secure facilities and they appealed, arguing, among other things, that the court lacked authority to hold them in contempt. The appellate court agreed and vacated the lower court's actions. The court explained its position as follows:

We sympathize with the well-intentioned efforts of the juvenile court judge to cope with the problems resulting from the revisions of the

Juvenile Act removing status offenders from the ambit of a delinquency adjudication providing for their separate treatment. However inconsistent it may seem to place a runaway in a nonphysically restrained setting, the legislature has ordained that this is the manner of treatment to be employed, and we must abide by their judgment. The responsibility for action to cure the problem of devising an effective method of treating chronic runaways from shelter care lies with the legislature and not with this court.

Id. at 537–38. *See also W.M. v. State,* 437 N.E.2d 1028 (Ind. Ct. App. 1982) (under then-current statute, juvenile courts lack contempt power to incarcerate child who repeatedly ran away from facility to which he had been committed for running away from home).

RIGHT TO REHABILITATIVE TREATMENT

Finally, like some decisions in the delinquency context, some courts recognize a right to rehabilitative treatment for status offenders. If anything, courts have been more receptive to such claims by status offenders than by delinquents, given the tendency to see status offense dispositions as more centrally grounded in *parens patriae* principles than those visited upon at least some categories of delinquents. As discussed earlier, in many jurisdictions *parens patriae* considerations no longer provide the sole rationale for delinquency dispositions. Thus, social protection might afford the basis for confining some delinquents, but that theory provides little justification for incarcerating youngsters who have not been shown to have committed a criminal offense. Moreover, while punishment theories might reasonably explain the basis for incarcerating some status offenders (for example, habitual runaways, truants, or minors acting in contempt of court orders), punitive incarceration generally appears more theoretically at home as a disposition for juveniles who have committed criminal acts than for status offenders. Thus, to the extent that rehabilitation of the offender provides the essential rationale for secure confinement of status offenders, the courts have scrutinized confinement devoid of rehabilitation. One court put the matter this way: "Juveniles . . . who have not been convicted of crimes[ ] have a due process interest in freedom from unnecessary bodily restraint which entitles them to closer scrutiny of their conditions of confinement than accorded convicted criminals." *Santana v. Collazo,* 714 F.2d 1172, 1179 (1st Cir. 1983), *cert. denied,* 466 U.S. 974 (1984).

State ex. rel. Calendine, 233 S.E.2d 318 (W. Va. 1977), illustrates the heightened judicial concern for the interests of status offenders subjected to secure confinement. The case involved a sixteen-year-old who had been committed to a forestry camp pursuant to a juvenile court order based on the court's finding that the boy was a habitual truant. At the time of the disposition, the juvenile had nearly reached the age after which school attendance was no longer required. Nevertheless, the court ordered the juvenile to be held for a period extending beyond the age compelling mandatory school attendance. The juvenile appealed the disposition to the state supreme court which found, among other things, that the order of the juvenile court violated the due process rights of the juvenile, because it bore no rational relationship to the statutory dispositional goal of protecting the welfare of the child. The court explained its conclusion as follows:

> [T]he Court finds no rational connection between the legitimate legislative purposes of enforcing family discipline, protecting children, and protecting society from uncontrolled children, and the means by which the State is permitted to accomplish these purposes, namely incarceration of children in secure, prison-like facilities.

> It is generally recognized that the greatest colleges for crime are prisons and reform schools. The most egregious punishment inflicted upon a child incarcerated in a West Virginia penal institution is not the deprivation of his liberty but rather his forced association with reprehensible persons. Prisons, by whatsoever name they may be known, are inherently dangerous places. Sexual assaults, physical violence, psychological abuse and total degradation are the likely consequences of incarceration. If one hopes to find rehabilitation in a penal institution, his hopes will be confounded . . . . [W]hen the State is proceeding under color of its *parens patriae* authority, it must actually have fair prospects of achieving a beneficent purpose, otherwise the reason for the authority fails.

> . . . We find with regard to status offenders . . . that the State means, namely incarceration in secure, prison-like facilities, except in a limited class of cases, bears no reasonable relationship to legitimate State purposes, namely rehabilitation, protection of the children, and protection of society.

Id. at 326–29.

§ 5.07   THE FUTURE OF JUVENILE JUSTICE

As is clear from the materials throughout this Chapter, the juvenile justice system has become a controversial institution. Earlier, attention was drawn to whether status offense jurisdiction should be abolished, *see* § 5.03[D], *supra*. Similar questions have been raised about the continued viability of juvenile courts as a vehicle for dealing with criminal conduct engaged in by young people. A host of commentators have voiced views addressing the future of the juvenile justice system. As the following excerpts make clear, opinions vary.

Barry C. Feld, *The Transformation of the Juvenile Court*

75 MINNESOTA LAW REVIEW 691, 722–25 (1991)

The recent changes in juvenile court jurisdiction, sentencing, and procedures reflect ambivalence about the role of juvenile courts and the control of children. As juvenile courts converge procedurally and substantively with criminal courts, is there any reason to maintain a separate court whose only distinctions are procedures under which no adult would agree to be tried?

The juvenile court is at a philosophical crossroads that cannot be resolved by simplistic formulations, such as treatment versus punishment. In reality, there are no practical or operational differences between the two. Acknowledging that juvenile courts punish, imposes an obligation to provide all criminal procedural safeguards because, in the words of *Gault*, "the condition of being a boy does not justify a kangaroo court." While procedural parity with adults may sound the death-knell of the juvenile court, to fail to do so perpetuates injustice. To treat similarly situated juveniles differently, to punish them in the name of treatment, and to deny them basic safeguards fosters a sense of injustice that thwarts any efforts to rehabilitate.

Abolishing juvenile courts is desirable both for youths and society. After more than two decades of constitutional and legislative reform, juvenile courts continue to deflect, co-opt, ignore, or absorb ameliorative tinkering with minimal institutional change. Despite its transformation from a welfare agency to a criminal court, the juvenile court remains essentially unreformed. The quality of justice youths receive would be intolerable if it were adults facing incarceration. Public and political concerns about drugs and youth crime foster a "get tough" mentality to repress rather than rehabilitate young offenders. With fiscal constraints, budget deficits, and competition from other interest groups, there is little likelihood that treatment services for delinquents will expand. Coupling the emergence of punitive policies with our societal unwillingness to provide for the welfare of children in general, much less to those who commit crimes, there is simply no reason to believe that the juvenile court can be rehabilitated.

Without a juvenile court, an adult criminal court that administers justice for young offenders could provide children with all the procedural guarantees already available to adult defendants and additional enhanced protections because of the children's vulnerability and immaturity. The only virtue of the contemporary juvenile court is that juveniles convicted of serious crimes receive shorter sentences than do adults. Youthfulness, however, long has been recognized as a mitigating, even if not an excusing, condition at sentencing. The common law's infancy defense presumed that children below age fourteen lacked criminal capacity, emphasized their lack of fault, and made youthful irresponsibility explicit. Youths older than fourteen are mature enough to be responsible for their behavior, but immature enough as to not deserve punishment commensurate with adults. If shorter sentences for diminished responsibility is the rationale for punitive juvenile courts, then providing an explicit "youth discount" to reduce adult sentences can ensure an intermediate level of just punishment. Reduced adult sentences do not require young people to be incarcerated with adults; existing juvenile prisons allow the segregation of offenders by age.

Full procedural parity in criminal courts coupled with mechanisms to expunge records, restore civil rights, and the like can more adequately protect young people than does the current juvenile court. Abolishing juvenile courts, however, should not gloss over the many deficiencies of criminal courts such as excessive case loads, insufficient sentencing options, ineffective representation, and over-reliance on plea bargains. These are characteristics of juvenile courts as well.

Ideological changes in strategies of social control and the conception of children produced the juvenile court. One of these ideas, strategies of social control, no longer distinguishes juvenile from criminal courts. Despite their inability to prevent or reduce youth crime, juvenile courts survive and even prosper. Despite statutory and judicial reforms, official discretion arguably has increased rather than decreased. Why, even without empirical support, does the ideology of therapeutic justice persist so tenaciously?

The answer is that the social control is directed at children. Despite humanitarian claims of being a child-centered nation, our cultural conception of children supports institutional arrangements that deny the personhood of young people. In legal doctrine, children are not entitled to liberty, but to custody. We care less about other people's children than we do our own, especially when those children are of other colors or cultures.

Children, especially by adolescence, are more competent than the law acknowledges. We can recognize young people's competence as a basis for greater autonomy without equating it with full criminal responsibility. Many social institutions — families, schools, the economy, and the law — systematically disable adolescents, deny them opportunities to be responsible and autonomous, and then use the resulting immaturity to justify imposing further disabilities. Rejecting the juvenile court's premise that young people are inherently irresponsible can begin a process of reexamining childhood that extends to every institution that touches their lives.

Barry C. Feld, *Abolish the Juvenile Court: Youthfulness, Criminal Responsibility, and Sentencing Policy*

88 JOURNAL OF CRIMINAL LAW & CRIMINOLOGY 68, 131–36 (1997)

Law reforms that tinker with the boundaries of childhood or modify judicial procedures do not appear to reduce appreciably offenders' probabilities of recidivism or increase public safety. Even far-reaching justice system changes can have only a marginal impact on social problems as complex as crime and violence. Rather, a proposal to abolish the juvenile court and to try all young offenders in an integrated justice system makes no utilitarian claims, but represents a commitment to honesty about state coercion. States bring young offenders who commit crimes to juvenile court for social control and to punish them. Juvenile courts' rehabilitative claims fly in the face of their penal reality, undermine their legitimacy, and impair their ability to function as judicial agencies. Because punishment is an unpleasant topic, juvenile courts attempt to evade those disagreeable qualities by obscuring their reality with rehabilitative euphemisms, psycho-babble, and judicial "double-speak" like "sometimes punishment is treatment."

The shortcomings of the "rehabilitative" juvenile court run far deeper than inadequate resources and rudimentary and unproven treatment techniques. Rather, the flaw lies in the very *idea* that the juvenile court can combine successfully criminal social control and social welfare in one system. Similarly, a separate "criminal" juvenile court cannot succeed or long survive because it lacks a coherent rationale to distinguish it from a "real" criminal court. A scaled-down separate criminal court for youths simply represents a temporary way-station on the road to substantive and procedural convergence with the criminal court. Only an integrated criminal justice that formally recognizes adolescence as a developmental continuum may effectively address many of the problems created by our binary conceptions of youth and social control.

Enhanced procedural protections, a "youth discount" of sentences, and age-segregated dispositional facilities recognize and respond to the "real" developmental differences between young people and adult offenders in the justice system. . . .

I propose to abolish the juvenile court with trepidation. On the one hand, combining enhanced procedural safeguards with a "youth discount" in an integrated criminal court can provide young offenders with greater protections and justice than they currently receive in the juvenile system, and more proportional and humane consequences than judges presently inflict on them in the criminal justice system. Integration may foster a more consistent crime control response than the present dual systems permit to violent and chronic young offenders at various stages of the developmental and criminal career continuum. . . .

. . . .

The idea of the juvenile court is fundamentally flawed because it attempts to combine criminal social control and social welfare goals. My proposal to abolish the juvenile court does not entail an abandonment of its welfare ideal. Rather, uncoupling policies of social welfare from penal social control enables us to expand a societal commitment to the welfare of all children regardless of their criminality. If we frame child welfare policy reforms in terms of child welfare rather than crime control, then we may expand the possibilities for positive intervention for all young people. For example, a public health approach to youth crime that identified the social, environmental, community structural, and ecological correlates or youth violence, such as poverty, the proliferation of handguns, and the commercialization of violence, would suggest wholly different intervention strategies than simply incarcerating minority youths. Youth violence occurs as part of a social ecological structure; high rates of violent youth crime arise in areas of concentrated poverty, high teenage pregnancy, and AFDC dependency. Such social indicators could identify census tracts or even zip-codes for community organizing, economic development, and preventive and remedial intervention.

Three aspects of youth crime and violence suggest future social welfare policy directions regardless of their immediate impact on recidivism. First, it is imperative to provide a *hopeful future for all young people.* As a result of structural and economic changes since the 1980s, the ability of families to raise children, to prepare them for the transition to adulthood, and to provide them with a more promising future has declined. Many social indicators of the status of young people — poverty, homelessness, violent victimization, and crime — are negative and some of those adverse trends are accelerating. Without realistic hope for their future, young people fall into despair, nihilism, and violence. Second, the disproportionate over-representation of minority youths in the juvenile justice system makes imperative the pursuit of *racial and social justice.* . . . Today, we reap the bitter harvest of racial segregation, concentrated poverty, urban social disintegration, and youth violence sown by social policies and public neglect a generation ago. Third, youth violence has become increasingly lethal as the proliferation of handguns transforms adolescent altercations into homicidal encounters. Only public policies that reduce and reverse the proliferation of guns in the youth population will stem the carnage.

While politicians may be unwilling to invest scarce social resources in young "criminals," particularly those of other colors or cultures, a demographic shift and an aging population give all of us a stake in young people and encourage us to invest in their human capital for their and our own future well-being and to maintain an inter-generational compact. Social welfare and legal policies to provide all young people with a hopeful future, to reduce racial and social inequality, and to reduce access to and use of firearms require a public and political commitment to the welfare of children that extends far beyond the resources or competencies of any juvenile justice system.

Katherine Hunt Federle, *The Abolition of the Juvenile Court: A Proposal for the Preservation of Children's Rights*

16 JOURNAL OF CONTEMPORARY LAW 23, 24, 49–51 (1990)

The call to eliminate the juvenile court is not new. Since the 1970s, both conservative and liberal commentators have criticized the continued existence of a separate legal system for children, albeit for different reasons. At the heart of those differences lie some fundamental assumptions about juveniles' legal rights and their capacity to exercise them. The failure of the juvenile system is the result of a dualistic juvenile law that is attributable to our schizophrenic attitude about children and their powerlessness. The challenge lies in the development of a coherent jurisprudence framed within the rights-based tradition of western legal thought.

A rights-based juvenile law, coupled with recent political, social, and legal changes compel the abolition of the juvenile court. Statistics indicate that violent juvenile crime is increasing while sociological studies reveal that young offenders continue to recidivate. In response to the public's growing disillusionment with the system of justice, state governments have enacted sweeping legislation that reaffirms community safety. The juvenile court now routinely considers the punishment of the young offender in its sentencing and waiver decisions. . . .

. . . .

Although the juvenile system has become increasingly legalistic, the courts have not extended the full panoply of rights to children. The United States Supreme Court, in several of its earlier decisions, recognized that children do have certain constitutional rights. . . .

. . . .

The true stumbling block to a juvenile jurisprudence is the concept of power and capacity. Once overcome, the development and implementation of a jurisprudence sensitive to children's rights requires little restructuring of our present legal system. Rights are recognized and enforced by the courts which act as restraints on unfettered state power. No longer may we justify discriminatory treatment of children based on childhood. The abolition of the juvenile court is essential to the preservation of children's legal rights.

The abolition of the juvenile court will insure the adoption of a rights-based jurisprudence for children. The separate juvenile system, which as meaning only as long as a viable justification for treating children differently exists, no longer bears a relationship to the present reality of childhood. The elimination of the juvenile system will guarantee that those charged with violating the law will receive the full panoply of protections both constitutional and statutory. The criminal court will have jurisdiction over all those accused of criminal offenses. No longer will the courts resort to legal gymnastics in attempting to exonerate legal doctrine discriminating against children. The accused, whether an adult or a child, will receive the same guarantees and protections consistent with the Anglo-American legal system of individual rights.

Those who participate in such a court will reinforce the child's rights model. The attorney, who previously saw her role as guardian, will advance the interests of her client regardless of the client's age. The judge will no longer be a parental figure but will be a neutral and impartial arbiter of justice. Charging decisions by the prosecuting attorney will no longer reflect a highly interventionist *parens patriae* model but one consistent with concerns for community safety. Police behavior will conform to constitutional requisites in the revised system because of its adversarial nature. Finally, sentencing will be proportional to the seriousness of the crime rather than to the attitude of the child.

The abolition of the juvenile court proffers a more coherent legal model for the treatment of law violators. Criminalizing the juvenile court creates legal inconsistencies in the way children are treated. Automatic waiver provisions inherently contradict the concept of child incompetence and eliminate the very justification for a separate juvenile court. These provisions permit children to be tried as adults simply because they have been accused of an enumerated crime. Waiver, however, is no longer needed in the revised system because criminal courts traditionally are responsive to community concerns about crime and safety.

. . . .

The abolition of the juvenile court need not preclude an emphasis on rehabilitation and treatment of the young offender. Many criminal codes provide for alternatives to incarceration, and rehabilitation and treatment are not inconsistent with the exercise of the criminal court's jurisdiction. An alternative sentencing model for child offenders provides such an option and is not without precedent. In the federal system, for example, special sentencing provisions existed for adult offenders under the age of twenty-two. While alternative sentencing options and facilities for child offenders are consistent with the child's rights model, they may also have an ameliorative effect on sentencing schemes for adults. Thus, children's participation in the criminal system may force a revision of the proportionality doctrine.

. . . .

Recent statutory trends evince an intent to punish juveniles and to protect the community from delinquent behavior. Legislators explain this apparent departure from the juvenile court's traditional role as *parens patriae* with statistical evidence of an increase in juvenile crime. The juvenile court's rehabilitative function, however, is a primary justification for according juveniles fewer constitutional protections. Although the distinction between delinquency and crime has blurred, there has been no concomitant expansion of constitutional protections nor a willingness to enforce existing legal rights. Despite findings confirming children's competence to make decisions, the courts continue to emphasize a paternalistic approach to juvenile law.

Conceptually, there appears to be no reason for denying children legal rights. But recent legal and sociological changes indicate a contrary reality. A jurisprudence based on power remains the primary obstacle to the creation of a rights-based model of juvenile law. Once placed in its proper perspective, a coherent jurisprudence may easily be developed. Such a jurisprudence requires the abolition of the juvenile court for the preservation of children's legal rights.

Irene Merker Rosenberg, *Leaving Bad Enough Alone: A Response to the Juvenile Court Abolitionists*

1993 WISCONSIN LAW REVIEW 163, 166, 169–71, 173

Throughout my legal career, I have been an unabashed reformer and a fervent advocate of children's rights, decrying the diminished constitutional protection and inadequate treatment afforded minors accused of crime in juvenile court. Now, however, I find myself in the awkward and uncomfortable position of arguing to preserve the status quo — albeit with improvements — in the world of juvenile court injustice. Although this gives me considerable pause, it does not change my mind: I do not believe that it would be wise to abolish the delinquency jurisdiction and try children as criminals in the adult court. . . .

. . . .

Before deciding whether to abandon the juvenile courts, two basic questions must be addressed: (1) is the disparity in procedural and constitutional protection between the adult and juvenile courts significant enough to justify opting out of the juvenile justice system; and (2) if children are tried in the criminal courts, will their immaturity and vulnerability be taken into account adequately in assessing culpability and determining sentences? In my view, the answers to these questions are no and no.

First, the abolitionists claim that there is a significant disparity between the constitutional and procedural rights afforded adults charged with crime and children charged with delinquency. In my opinion, these differences are not as substantial as they appear to be, or at least not substantial enough to be a basis for giving up on the juvenile justice system. The conceded inequality in safeguards should not blind us to the incremental changes over the years that have benefitted children. The *Gault* line of cases does give alleged delinquents significant constitutional protection. . . .

The major setback for juveniles was denial of the right to a jury trial in *McKeiver v. Pennsylvania.* [I]n the insular world of the juvenile courts, a jury is necessary to protect children from oppression by the government and to assure more accurate and impartial fact-finding. I do not, however, view the loss of even this right as catastrophic. After all, there are relatively few jury trials in the adult criminal court. Instead, the right to trial by jury is primarily a chip to be used in the poker game of plea bargaining — a game of far greater seriousness in the adult courts, where the sentencing stakes, at least for serious offenses, are much higher. Nonetheless, denial of the jury trial to juveniles as a matter of federal constitutional law is significant. One way of dealing with the problem is state law reform. In fact, a number of states already grant juveniles such a right as a matter of state law, and the "New Federalism" is an opportunity for advocates to push for jury trials in juvenile courts.

More broadly, I think we have not sufficiently appreciated that in a substantial number of jurisdictions state law gives children many of the same rights as adult defendants, and sometimes more. . . .

It seems to me that underlying the views of the abolitionists, at least unconsciously, is a somewhat idealized or romanticized vision of adult courts in which the criminal guarantees of the Bill of Rights are meaningfully enforced. Yes, there is a right to trial by jury that is missing in the juvenile court unless supplied by state law. Yes, there is a right to counsel that . . . is too often denied in practice in juvenile court. And I surely would not denigrate either of these important safeguards. At the same time, however, the reality of adult criminal proceedings is crowded courtrooms in which justice is dispensed through waivers and pleas negotiated by defense attorneys who are often less than zealous and well-prepared advocates, and in which racism is at least as much a fact of life as in juvenile court. For the most part, the typical criminal court in urban areas is a harsh, tough, mean institution cranking out pleas, with few pauses for individualized attention. It is no place for an adult defendant to be, much less a child. Given such an environment in the criminal courts, will children really perceive the criminal justice process as fairer than the juvenile courts . . . ?

Initially, perhaps there would be a burst of concern for the kiddie defendants. But once the glow wore off, and that would not take long, it would be back to business as usual: treadmill processing for adults both over and under the age of eighteen. Let us face it: As bad as the juvenile courts are, the adult criminal courts are worse. Adding a new class of defendants to an already overburdened system can only exacerbate the situation, all to the detriment of children.

That brings me to the second question. [Some] abolitionists believe that if children are tried in criminal court, rationales will be developed to give them special protection in ascertaining guilt and punishment. While I agree that is what children should get, I am not so sure that is what they will get. . . .

If states are unwilling to give minors enhanced constitutional and procedural protection when they are within the supposedly benevolent confines of the juvenile court, why would they do so in the criminal court? Bringing children within the criminal jurisdiction is an assertion by the state that minors do not deserve specialized treatment. While it is true that the state will no longer have the bogus rehabilitation argument as a basis for diminishing constitutional protection, the state may argue that because it has elected to treat children and adults the same, there is no reason to give youngsters enhanced safeguards.

. . . .

[Professor Rosenberg suggests that abolitionist's reliance on the ameliorative powers of the infancy defense may place too high a reliance on the availability of the defense.]

Even assuming, however, that the infancy defense were either constitutionally mandated or afforded as a matter of state law, it might still be insufficiently protective of children tried in adult criminal courts. The irrebuttable presumption for children under seven would be invoked in very few cases because there are few crimes committed by children so young, and when they are, the state generally chooses not to prosecute them even in the juvenile courts. At the other end of the spectrum, children over fourteen are presumed to be criminally responsible, and many of the juveniles accused of serious crimes fall within that age bracket, making the infancy defense irrelevant in such cases. Thus, the defense generally would be applicable only to children between seven and fourteen, who are entitled to the rebuttable presumption of incapacity, and a large number of juveniles accused of crime do fall within that age bracket. Many of those within this intermediate category are approaching fourteen, however, and unfortunately the rebuttable presumption decreases in strength as the child gets older. Therefore, the closer a child is to fourteen, the less evidence the state needs to prove capacity. Moreover, the prosecutor can establish capacity simply by showing consciousness of wrongdoing, not an onerous burden, especially since many jurisdictions allow that burden to be met by inferences from the very circumstances of the crime. Finally, since it is based on chronological rather than mental age, and is concerned with cognitive rather than volitional capacity, the infancy defense would not, in my view, give children parity in the criminal courts.

Infancy, of course, would be constitutionally relevant insofar as it relates to *mens rea* in the specific sense, that is, the mental state required by definition of the crime. If the offense with which a child is charged has such a *mens rea* element, then [Supreme Court case law would] require that it be proved beyond a reasonable doubt. Evidence relating to that *mens rea* requirement would be admissible, and, presumably, that would include evidence that the child was too immature to form the requisite intent. For example, in a larceny case, testimony that the minor defendant was too young to form the intent to deprive the owner of his or her property permanently would be relevant. As with the general *mens rea* infancy defense, however, it is unlikely to affect children over the age of ten, most of whom have a good sense of mine and thine. . . .

. . . .

If children are tried as adults, and convicted, they presumably will be subject to the jurisdiction of adult correctional authorities rather than youth services agencies, which are at least to some extent child oriented. Sometimes

I think we forget how terrible the prison facilities for adult criminals in this country are. . . .

Abandoning the juvenile court is an admission that its humane purposes were misguided or unattainable. I do not believe that. We should stay and fight — for a reordering of societal resources, one that will protect and nourish children. . . .

Despite all their failings, of which there are many, the juvenile courts do afford benefits that are unlikely to be replicated in the criminal courts, such as the institutionalized intake diversionary system, anonymity, diminished stigma, shorter sentences, and recognition of rehabilitation as a viable goal. We should build on these strengths rather than abandon ship.

It is important to take into account both the chimerical quality of enhanced constitutional safeguards in the criminal courts and the significant benefits afforded to minors even by the existing juvenile justice system, before relegating children to criminal courts and prisons with no guarantee that their immaturity will be adequately considered or their vulnerability meaningfully protected.

Elizabeth S. Scott & Laurence Steinberg, *Blaming Youth*

81 TEXAS LAW REVIEW 799, 829, 832, 835-39 (2003)

. . . A fair system of juvenile justice will respond to youth crime by imposing punishment that is proportionate to the blameworthiness of young offenders. And, under standard criminal law measures, the criminal acts of typical adolescents are less culpable than those of their adult counterparts. A justice policy grounded in a mitigation model coherently harmonizes the treatment of young offenders with the response to mitigating conditions generally under the criminal law.

. . . .

. . . Adolescent offenders indeed are different from the rest of us, but they (or most of them) are also ordinary persons — although not ordinary adults. This is not to say, of course, that all adolescents will commit crimes, or that those who do are without blame. It is to say, however, that those whom psychologists call normative adolescents may well succumb to the extraordinary pressures of a criminogenic social context. Beyond this, the typical adolescent can be distinguished from most criminals and aligned with ordinary persons whose crimes deserve less than full punishment, because his wrongful act does not derive from attitudes and values that are part of his continuing identity as a person; in other words, his crime is not an expression of bad character. Here again, immature youths are not like ordinary adults — fully realized selves who have internalized the law's values. Instead, adolescent crime is a costly manifestation of influences and processes that are characteristic of a discrete stage in human development.

. . . .

If, in fact adolescent offenders are generally less culpable than their adult counterparts, how should the legal system recognize their diminished responsibility? At a structural level, the first important policy choice is whether immaturity should be considered on an individualized basis, as is typical of most other mitigating conditions, or as the basis for a separate category of young offenders. Traditional juvenile justice policy employed a categorical approach that continues in a diluted form in the contemporary juvenile court and correctional system. As the boundary between the juvenile and adult system breaks down, however, evaluation of immaturity as a mitigator increasingly takes place (if at all) on an individualized basis in a transfer hearing or at sentencing.

The uniqueness of immaturity as a mitigating condition argues for the adoption of (or renewed commitment to) a categorical approach in this context. Other mitigators — emotional disturbance and coercive external circumstances, for example — affect criminal choices with endless variety and idiosyncratic impact on behavior. Thus, individualized consideration of mitigation is appropriate when these phenomena are involved. In contrast, the capacities and processes associated with adolescence are characteristic of individuals in a relatively defined group, whose development follows a roughly prescribed course to maturity, and whose criminal choices are predictably affected in ways that mitigate culpability. Although individual variations exist within the age cohort of adolescence, coherent boundaries can delineate a minimum age for adult adjudication, as well as a period of years beyond this minimum when a strong presumption of reduced culpability operates to keep most youths in a separate system. The age boundary is justified if the presumption of immaturity can be applied confidently to most individuals in the group. This approach offers substantial efficiencies over one in which immaturity is assessed on a case-by-case basis, particularly since mitigation claims likely would be a part of every criminal adjudication involving a juvenile.

Adopting a mitigation framework does not mean that all youths are less mature than adults in their decisionmaking capacity or that all juveniles are unformed in their identity development. Some individuals exhibit mature judgment at an early age — although most of these youths are not offenders. For others, antisocial tendencies that begin in childhood continue in a stable pattern of criminal conduct that defines their adult characters. Adult punishment of mature youths might be fair if these individuals could be identified with some degree of certainty. But we currently lack the diagnostic tools to evaluate psycho-social maturity reliably on an individualized basis or to distinguish young career criminals from ordinary adolescents who, as adults, will repudiate their reckless experimentation. Litigating maturity on a case-by-case basis is likely to be an error-prone undertaking, with the outcomes determined by factors other than immaturity.

A developmentally-informed boundary constraining decisionmakers represents a collective pre-commitment to recognizing the mitigating character of youth in assigning blame. Otherwise, immaturity often may be ignored when the exigencies of a particular case engender a punitive response; indeed, it is likely to count as mitigating only when the youth otherwise presents a sympathetic case. This concern is critical, given the evidence that illegitimate racial and ethnic biases influence attitudes about the punishment of young offenders and that decisionmakers appear to discount the mitigating impact of immaturity in minority youths. The integrity and legitimacy of any individualized decisionmaking process is vulnerable to contamination from racist attitudes or from unconscious racial stereotyping that operates even among individuals who may lack overt prejudice. . . .

Categorical recognition of the mitigating impact of immaturity provides the conceptual framework for a separate justice system for juveniles but does not itself dictate a particular set of institutional arrangements. A variety of arrangements, including a systematic sentencing discount for young offenders in adult court, might satisfy the demands of proportionality. Ultimately, the case for a separate system rests on utilitarian considerations as well as on proportionality concerns. Because most young lawbreakers are "adolescent-limited" offenders, the social cost of youth crime will be minimized by policies that attend to the impact of punishment on the future lives and prospects of young offenders. The research suggests that a separate juvenile court and correctional system are more likely than the adult justice system to offer an environment in which youths can successfully "mature out" of their antisocial tendencies and to provide educational and job training programs to prepare young offenders for conventional adult roles. Thus, to a considerable extent, social welfare and fairness converge to support a separate juvenile justice system grounded in mitigation.

Sometimes, however, youths should be subject to adult punishment. A policy that treats immaturity as a mitigating condition is viable only to the extent that public protection is not seriously compromised. Immature offenders can be a threat to public safety, and public tolerance of youthful misconduct, as we have seen, is tenuous at best. Moreover, both proportionate punishment and public protection are important purposes of the criminal law. At some point, public safety concerns dictate that young recidivists who inflict large amounts of social harm must be incapacitated as adults. This response may undermine proportionality to some extent, but, in practice, the sacrifice is likely to be modest. This is so because the small group of youths who are recidivist violent offenders are generally older teens, and they are more likely than other adolescent lawbreakers to be young career criminals of settled dispositions. That is not to say that we should "throw away the key" when we incapacitate these youths. Given the uncertainty of predicting adult character during adolescence, efforts should be made to protect against iatrogenic prison effects and to invest in the future post-incarceration lives of even serious chronic offenders. Nonetheless, a mechanism to protect society from harms caused by dangerous youths is a critically important safety valve for a well-functioning juvenile justice system based on mitigation.

Implementing a mitigation-based model of juvenile justice will require significant shifts in crime policy, but it will not require a radical overhaul of the juvenile justice system itself. Probably because of the scathing criticisms of its inadequacies, the juvenile system has undergone substantial change in the past generation, evolving toward one that increasingly emphasizes accountability and public protection. Although the public image of the modern juvenile court continues to be distorted by lingering echoes of the traditional rhetoric, delinquents under its jurisdiction are increasingly subject to proportionate punishment for their offenses.

Nonetheless, a large gap separates contemporary youth crime policy from one that is optimally grounded in mitigation, in part because the purposes and rationale of the contemporary juvenile system lack a coherent theory. First, rather than systematically seeking to reform the system pursuant to a goal of tailoring dispositions to the culpability of young offenders, lawmakers have incorporated accountability and public protection in a piecemeal fashion, mostly in response to political pressures. More importantly, in response to those same forces, the boundary between the juvenile and adult systems has become very porous under recent reforms. Youths can be subject to adult adjudication and punishment today for a broad range of crimes, including many, such as car theft and drug transactions, that appear to be quintessential adolescent behavior. Young criminals can also be tried as adults for first offenses which may well be experimental behavior that would not be repeated. Neither fairness nor utility are well served by these responses.

Martin R. Gardner, *Punitive Juvenile Justice: Some Observations on a Recent Trend*

10 INTERNATIONAL JOURNAL OF LAW & PSYCHIATRY 129, 148–51
(1987)

For many, the justification for a separate system of juvenile justice evaporates once the punitive model, complete with the protections of the criminal process, is embraced. If juvenile justice is to be no more than a system of "kiddie crime and punishment" why not, in the name of efficiency, employ Occam's Razor to the whole enterprise and return to a single system of criminal law for adults and children alike? The infancy defense could perform its historic task of deflecting punishment from non-culpable youngsters. A single criminal system could even adopt a "juvenile division" in which minors would receive scaled-down punishments. Separate confinement facilities for adults and minors could be retained and, if avoiding the collateral civil disabilities often attending criminal convictions is desirable for youthful offenders, statutes could be passed exempting persons convicted of crimes under a certain age from such disabilities. The traditional intake and diversion mechanisms of the juvenile system could, if deemed worthy of preservation, either be adopted as components of the criminal systm for all offenders or provided solely for youngsters.

. . . .

Perhaps the strongest reason for retaining a separate punishment system for juveniles is the possibility that youngsters might, thereby, be spared some of the stigmatic effect flowing from the "criminal" label. Assuming that youthful offenders are less culpable than their adult counterparts, they should no more be saddled with the same stigma imposed upon adult offenders than with the same punishment. While being branded "delinquent" by a punitive juvenile system is surely stigmatic, it may well carry fewer negative connotations, both in the minds of offenders and to the community at large, than flow from being convicted a "criminal" by the adult court.

Labeling theory presumes that those who confront negative reactions from others, such as being found guilty of a criminal offense by a court, come to think of themselves from the vantage point of those others. Moreover, the community tends to perceive stigmatized persons in terms of the stigmatic labels attached by official evaluators.

While empirical support for the contentions of labeling theorists is inconclusive, the plausibility of the theory cannot be ruled out. If negative labels stigmatize, some negative labels may be more stigmatic than others. Many have assumed that the labels "criminal" and "delinquent" are equally stigmatic, but it is at least arguable that the latter is less stigmatic.

"Delinquency" jurisdiction is, by definition, an intervention by juvenile courts in the lives of youthful offenders who have been judged inappropriate subjects for disposition by the criminal system. Assertions of criminal jurisdiction, even in misdemeanor cases, result in dispositions within the same system which treats the most culpable offenders and serious offenses and are, therefore, especially stigmatic. For the same reasons that many call for removing minor offenses from the stigmatic reach of the criminal courts, the offenses of juveniles should not automatically be brought under the umbrella of the criminal system.

Carving out a separate "juvenile division within the criminal system" would likely result in a significant blurring of the distinction between "delinquents" and "criminals." Convictions within the "juvenile division" would still be convictions by "criminal" courts. The distinction between criminal convictions for "misdemeanors" versus "felonies" likely carries little significance for purposes of labeling theory. Similarly, a disposition by the "juvenile division" of the criminal court likely would not be perceived as significantly less stigmatic than a regular criminal disposition, assuming that the distinction between "juvenile division" and "regular criminal courts" is even taken into account in the first place.

It must be noted that virtually no empirical research has been conducted testing the relative stigmatization of the labels "delinquent" attached by juvenile courts and "criminal" imposed by the adult system. Until substantial evidence establishes that the distinction is insignificant, separate juvenile courts should continue to adjudicate, and punish if appropriate, "delinquents" while criminal courts deal with adult offenders and those juveniles deemed proper subjects of criminal jurisdiction.

A variety of practical considerations argue against merging juvenile and criminal courts. In the first place, the claimed efficiency of the merger is not clear. Removing delinquency jurisdiction to the criminal courts would increase the workload of an already overburdened system. Merger would likely not result in a savings of court time on the "waiver" issue because, unless a system of "legislative waiver" were adopted, judges would still be required to distinguish cases to be tried in the "juvenile division" and those handled in regular criminal courts.

While efficiency might be promoted by abolishing the juvenile court system entirely and merging it into a new, "streamlined," criminal system, complete dismantling of juvenile courts is unlikely given that system's continued need to exercise jurisdiction over neglected children and, more controversially, status offenders. If a separate system of juvenile courts will survive the removal of delinquency jurisdiction to the criminal courts, it is difficult to see how such removal will necessarily result in a more streamlined, efficient system.

Moreover, because of its historic interest in protecting the welfare of youngsters, the juvenile system now in place, while far from perfect, might, in some localities at least, provide sensitive attention to the unique problems of juvenile offenders. Where this is already the case or where it might yet occur within the juvenile model, merger into the criminal system may risk loss of valuable expertise acquired by conscientious juvenile court functionaries in return for the cold indifference towards offenders which often characterizes the criminal courts.

Given these considerations, the burden of persuasion rests on those favoring merger into the criminal system. Until they produce solid evidence establishing their case, the wiser course is to continue to deal with youthful offenders through a system separate from the criminal model, even if punishment is the system's earmark.

TABLE OF CASES

[References are to page numbers. Principal cases appear in capital letters.]

A

A.A. v. State 1051
Abeyta v. Chama Valley Independent School
   District 572
Abington School District v. Schempp .. 525
ACCENT SERVICE COMPANY, INC. v. EB-
   SEN 192; *196*
ACLU v. Reno 385; 517
Addington v. Texas 149; 374; 406
Adler v. Duval County 529
Adoption of (see name of party)
Agostini v. Felton 520
A.H., In re 1073
A.J.M. v. State 615
Akron v. Akron Center for Reproductive
   Health, Inc. 394; 401; 408
Akron Center for Reproductive Health v. Slaby
   394
Alabama v. White 616
Alexander v. Boyd 1088
Alexander v. Sandoval 698
Alfonso v. Fernandez 524
ALINE D., IN RE *1119*
Alleged Contempt of (see name of party)
Altman v. Bedford Central Sch. Dist .. 531
Ambach v. Norwick ... 439; 456; 488; 492;
   493
American Amusement Machine Assoc. v. Ken-
   drick 384
American College of Obstetricians and
   Gynecologists v. Thornburgh 404
American Library Ass'n; United States v. ..
   516
American Library Ass'n, Inc. v. U.S. .. 516
ANDERSON v. STREAM 176; *180*
Andrew M., In the Matter of 1019
Angel J., In re 1072
Angelia D.B.; State v. 615
Anglin v. State 953
Appeal of (see name of party)
Appeal of Estate of (see name of party)
Application of (see name of applicant)
Archey v. Hyche 571
Arkansas Dept. of Human Services (DHS) v.
   Collier 229
Aschroft v. ACLU 385; 517
Ashcroft v. Free Speech Coalition 387
Ashford v. State 233
Atkins v. Virginia 898

B

Baby Boy Doe, In re 332

Baby Girl, L.J., Adoption of, Matter of ....
   92n14
BABY M., IN RE *81*
BAILEY v. C.S. 417; *430*
Bailey v. Richardson 544
Baker v. Owen 552n40; 566
Balch v. Anders 576
Baldwin v. New York 984
Baltimore City Dept. of Social Services v. Bouk-
   night 407n10
Barber v. Dearborn Public Schools ... 436
Bartels v. Iowa 427
Bartels; State v. 33
Bayard v. Malone 697
Baynard v. Lawson 697
Baynard v. Malone 697
B.C. v. PLUMAS UNIFIED SCHOOL DIS-
   TRICT 634; *652*
Bd. of Regents v. Roth 544
Beal v. Doe 409
Beale; United States v. 636
Beckley; People v. 264
Beidler v. North Thurston Sch. Dist. .. 481
Belcher; People v. 1073
Bell; State v. 884
Bell v. Wolfish 970
Bellotti v. Baird 390; 394; 401
Bernstein v. Menard 547
BETHEL SCHOOL DISTRICT v. FRASER
   ... 437; 447; 450; *451*; 457; 468;
   524; 545; 617; 735; 911
Beussink v. Woodland R-IV School Dist. ...
   479
Bisignano v. Harrison Central School District
   650
Bivens v. Albuquerque Public Schls. .. 474
B.K., Matter of 145
Blackwell v. Issaquena County Board of Educa-
   tion 426n1
BLAND; UNITED STATES v. ... 808; 862;
   884; *890*
Blau v. Fort Thomas Pub. Sch. Dist. .. 475
Blew v. Verta 105
Bludsworth v. State, Nev. 233
Board of Curators v. Horowitz 547
Board of Educ. Sacramento City Unified School
   Dist. v. Holland 765n116; 791
BOARD OF EDUCATION, ISLAND TREES
   UNION FREE SCHOOL DISTRICT v. PICO
   .... 440; 462; 484; *502*; 514
BOARD OF EDUCATION OF HENDRICK
   HUDSON CENTRAL SCH. DIST. v. ROW-
   LEY 767; 771; 783

[References are to page numbers. Principal cases appear in capital letters.]

BOARD OF EDUCATION OF INDEPEN-
DENT SCHOOL DISTRICT NO. 92 OF v.
EARLS 617; *637*

Board of Regents v. Roth 162

Bookcase, Inc. v. Broderick 376

Boos v. Barry 732

Bordenkircher v. Hayes 882

BOROFF v. VAN WERT CITY BOARD OF
EDUCATION 467; *480*

Boucher v. School Board of the School District
of Greenfield 466

Bown v. Gwinnett County Sch. Dist. . . 524

BREED v. JONES . . 370; 843; *871*; 985n62;
998

Briseno v. State 615

Brooks v. School Board of Richmond . . 570

Brown v. Board of Education . . . 454; 456;
493; 536; 603; 792

Brown v. Gilmore 524

Brown v. Hot, Sexy, and Safer Products, Inc.
. . . . 522

Brown v. Johnson 571

Brown; People v. 265n67

BROWN v. RAMSEY 567; *585*

Bruker v. New York, City of 165

Bruneau v. South Kortright Central School
District 741

Bryan; State v. 1105

B.S., In re 410

Buehrer, In re 1076

Burch v. Barker 465; 736

Burlington School Comm. v. Department of
Education 761

BURNETTE v. WAHL 182; *185*

Burnside v. Byars 426

Bush v. Holmes 521

Butler; United States v. 680

C

Caban v. Mohammed 116

CABRERA, IN THE MATTER OF . . . *346*

Camlin v. Beecher Community Sch. Dist. . .
546

Canady v. Bossier Parish School Bd. . . 475

Cannon v. University of Chicago 652;
655; 662; 663n81; 723

Cardwell v. Bechtol 351

Carey v. Population Servs. Int'l 94

Carney, In re Marriage of 71

Carter v. Jays Motors 413

Carter; State v. 222

Case v. Unified Sch. Dist. No. 233 . . . 515

Cass; Commonwealth v. 223

Castle Rock, Town of v. Gonzales 321

Castorina v. Madison County Sch. Bd. . . . .
476

CAUSEY, IN THE INTEREST OF . . . *1064*

Cazares v. Barber 742

C.B. v. Driscoll 546

Cecelia R., In re 1051

Cedar Rapids Community School District v.
Garret F. 763

Central Hudson Gas and Electric Corp. v. Public Service Commission of N.Y. 384

Central Missouri v. Danforth 361

CENTRAL SCHOOL DISTRICT v. ROWLEY
. . . . 745

C.H. v. Oliva 529; 530

C.H., In re 1116

Chalifoux v. New Caney Independent School
District 532; 734

Chandler v. McMinnville Sch. Dist. . . . 477;
734

Chandler v. Miller 641

Cheryl H., Matter of 265n67

Chesebrough v. State 386

Chipman v. Grant County School District . .
742

Christmas; Commonwealth v. 957n47

Church of the Lukumi Babalu Aye, Inc. v.
Hialeah, City of 523

City v. (see name of defendant)

City and County of (see name of city and
county)

Clark v. Dallas Independent School District
. . . . 735

Clatterbuck, In re 875

Cleburne, City of v. Cleburne Living Center
. . . . 173; 704

Cleveland Board of Education v. LaFleur . .
163; 225

Clevenger v. Oak Ridge Sch. Bd. 762

Coats, State ex rel. v. Rakestraw 884

Cockerham v. Stokes County Bd. of Educ. . .
669

Codispoti v. Pennsylvania 560n45

Cohen v. Brown Univ. 652n79

Cohen v. California 439

Colautti v. Franklin 405

Colin B., In re 260

Commission v. (see name of opposing party)

Commissioner v. (see name of opposing party)

Commissioner of Internal Revenue (see name of
defendant)

Committee for Public Education v. Nyquist
. . . . 521

Commonwealth v. (see name of defendant)

Commonwealth ex rel. (see name of relator)

Condel v. Savo 423n17

Conservatorship of (see name of party)

Consolidated Edison Co. v. Public Serv. Comm'n
. . . . 732

Cort v. Ash 662n80

Counts v. Cedarville Sch. Dist. . . . 514; 515

[References are to page numbers. Principal cases appear in capital letters.]

County v. (see name of defendant)
County of (see name of county)
Cox v. Louisiana 432
Coy v. Iowa 276; 298
C.P., In the Matter of 953
Crawford v. Davis 741
Crawford v. Washington 299
Crowley v. McKinney 79
Cubie v. Bryan Career College, Inc. . . . 697
Cummings v. Koehnen 703
Curley v. Hill 698
Custody of (see name of party)
C.W.M., In re 1012

D

Dambrot v. Central Michigan University . .
                                        686
Damien C., In re 1078
Dangler v. Yorktown Central Sch. 548
Daniel R., In re 942
Daniel R.R. v. State Bd. of Educ. . . . . . .
                                 765n116; 791
Darden v. Watkins 571
Darlene C., In re 1116
Daubert v. Merrell Dow Pharmaceuticals, Inc.
    261
Davis v. Alaska 999
DAVIS v. MONROE COUNTY BOARD OF
    EDUCAITON . . 653; 670; 689; 706; 722;
                              728; 798
D.D.N., MATTER OF WELFARE OF . . . . .
                                   1059
DeBacker v. Brainard 865n24
DeBacker v. Sigler 865n24
DeJesus; People v. 233
Demers v. Leominster School Dep't . . . 477
Denno v. Sch. Bd. of Volusia County . . 476
Department of Education v. Riley 796
DESHANEY v. WINNEBAGO COUNTY DE-
    PARTMENT OF SOCIAL SERVICES . . .
          313; 322; 407n10; 617; 711; 719
Desilets v. Clearview Regional Board of Educa-
    tion 462
DeVries v. Fairfax County Sch. Bd. . . . 784
DEWEES v. STEVENSON 171; 174
D.F.D., In re Marriage of 70
D.G. v. Independent Sch. Dist 477
D.G.W., STATE IN INTEREST OF . . 1130
D.H.; State v. 1018
Dickens v. Johnson County School Board of
    Educ. 547
Dilworth; People v. 615
District of Columbia v. B.J.R. 911
D.K., IN RE INTEREST OF 125
D.L.E., IN THE INTEREST OF 355
D.L.W., In re 1051
DODSON v. SHRADER 412; 425

Doe v. Bolton 409
Doe v. Clark 223; 224; 227
Doe v. Hawaii Dept. of Educ. 576; 650
Doe v. Lafayette, City of 272
Doe v. Pennsylvania 547
Doe v. Pulaski County Special School District
    478
Doe v. Renfrow 636; 640
Doe v. School District of Norfolk 529
Doe v. State 964
Doe v. Sundquist 176
Doe v. University of Illinois 692; 694
Doe v. University of Michigan 686
Doe A. v. Gree 669
Doe, In re 617
Donovan v. Ritchie 546
Dorothy J. v. Little Rock Sch. Dist. . . . 711
DOW, IN RE INTEREST OF 885
Doyle v. Arlington County Sch. Bd. . . . 783
D.R.; State v. 651
Drew P. v. Clarke County School District . .
                                        761
Dunkle; Commonwealth v. 261
Durham; Commonwealth v. 1019

E

Edward C.L.; State v. 265n67
Edwards v. Aguillard 522
Edwards v. Rees 650
E.G., IN RE 357
Egelkamp v. Egelkamp 71
Eisenstadt v. Baird 390
Elk Grove Unified School Dist. v. Newdow
    . . . . 70; 425
E.M.D., In re 1114
Emmett v. Kent Sch. Dist. 480
Employment Division v. Smith 61
Engel v. Vitale 525
Engerud; State v. 595n60
E.P. v. Ga., State of 1079
Epperson v. Arkansas . . 487; 488; 496; 521;
                         537; 541; 757n115
ERIC J., IN RE 1158
Erznoznik v. Jacksonville 383
E.S.G. v. State 911
Est. of (see name of party)
Estate of (see name of party)
Estelle v. Gamble 553; 563n48; 564
Estes v. Texas 991
Euclid, Village of v. Ambler Realty Co. . . . .
                                        513

Ex parte (see name of applicant)
Ex rel. (see name of relator)

F

Faragher v. Boca Raton, City of 728

[References are to page numbers. Principal cases appear in capital letters.]

FARE v. MICHAEL C. 944; *990*
Farmer v. Brennan 669
Farms, In re 1048
F.C.C. v. Pacifica Foundation . . 384; 442n4;
           445; 472; 483; 524
Fee v. Herndon 568n51
FELDER, IN RE *1039*
Feldman v. Feldman 70
Ferguson v. Charleston, City of 230
FETUS BROWN, IN RE *339*
First National Bank of Boston v. Bellotti . .
           489
Fischer v. Metcalf 320
Flaherty v. Keystone Oaks Sch. Dist. . . 480
Fletcher v. Fletcher 74
Florida v. J.L. 616
The Florida Star v. B. J. F. 404
Forsyth County v. Nationalist Movement . . .
           732
Fortune v. Detroit Public Schools, City of . .
           546
Fowler v. Woodward 220
Frank V., In re 1072
Franklin v. Gwinnett County Public Schools
         . . . . 652; 655; 662; 723
Freedom From Religion Foundation v. Bugher
         519
Furman v. Georgia 553; 1082

G

Gammons v. Berlat 1018
Garcia v. Miera 569
Gardini, In re 1078
GAULT, IN RE . . 59; 117n17; 358n87; 370;
        828; *837*; 845; 851; 929; 930; 941;
        985n62; 987; 998; 1007; 1009;
        14032; 1042; 1086
GEBSER v. LAGO VISTA INDEPENDENT
    SCHOOL DISTRICT 653; 654; *673*;
        681; 714
Gerald B., In re 1072; 1073
Gesicki v. Oswald 910
Gethers; State v. 222
Geyman; State v. 265n67
Gibson v. Gibson 178
GINSBERG v. NEW YORK 375; *385*;
        431; 440; 442n4; 483; 911
Gladys R., In re 1019
Glendening v. State 265n67
Golden v. State 1007
Goller v. White 178
Gonzales v. Passino 576
Goodman v. Horace Mann Ins. Co. . . . 669
GOSS v. LOPEZ . . 370; 444; 447; 533; *550*;
        557n42; 558; 559, n44; 564; 584;
        590; 597; 601; 602n66; 603; 644;
        719

Gray; State v. 222
Green, In re 341; 345
Greer v. Rome City School Dist. . . 772; 791
Gregg v. Georgia 553
Griswold v. Connecticut 94; 386; 489
Grove City College v. Bell 652
Guardianship of (see name of party)

H

H., In re 1040
H. L. v. Matheson . . . 394; 401; 405; 407n9
Halbman v. Lemke 413
Hale v. Pringle 571
Hall v. Butterfield 413
Hall v. Murphy 220
Hall v. Tawney 568
Hanhart v. Hanhart 70
Hanrahan, People ex rel. v. Felt 984
Hardy; People v. 222
Harris v. Forklift Systems, Inc. 728
Harris, State ex rel. v. Calendine . . . 1114
HARTMANN v. LOUDOUN COUNTY BOARD
    OF EDUCATION 781; *803*
Harvey v. State 244
Havercamp v. Unified School District . . 547
Haydocy Pontiac Inc. v. Lee 414
HAZELWOOD SCHOOL DISTRICT v. KUHL-
    MEIER . . . 448; *462*; 468; 483; 526; 736
Hedges v. Wauconda Comm. Unit Sch. Dist.
    No. 118 736
Heirtzler; State v. 615
Henderson, In re 1048
Henson; People v. 235
Henson v. State 271
Hernandez v. Commissioner 532
Hester v. Commonwealth 264n66
Hester; State v. 265n67
Hicks v. Halifax County Bd. of Educ. . . 476
Higgins v. New Balance Athletic Shoe, Inc.
    707
Hill; State v. 211
H.J., In the Matter of v. Indiana, State of . .
        483
Hobbs v. Germany 435
Hodgson v. Minnesota 391; 394; 898
Holbrook v. Executive Conference Center, Inc.
    688
Holodook v. Spencer 192
Honig v. Doe 794
Horne; State v. 220
Hornstine v. Township of Moorestown . . . .
        793
Horton v. Goose Creek Independent School
    District 636; 640
Howard v. Fleming 554
Hughes v. State 886
Humberto O., In re 943

[References are to page numbers. Principal cases appear in capital letters.]

Hutchins v. District of Columbia 911
Hutchins, In re 1047

I

IDAHO v. WRIGHT 287; *295*; 298n73
Illinois v. Caballes 641
I.M.L. v. State 482
In re (see name of party)
INGRAHAM v. WRIGHT . . . 549; *567*; 595;
601; 719; 1085; 1089
INS v. Lopez-Mendoza 644
Interactive Digital Software Assoc. v. St. Louis
County 384
Iota XI Chapter of Sigma Chi Fraternity v.
George Mason University 686
IRELAND v. SMITH *73*
Irving Indep. Sch. Dist. v. Tatro 763
Isaacs v. Board of Educ. 474

J

J.A., IN RE INTEREST OF *1114*
Jackson v. Birmingham Bd. of Educ. . . 653
Jackson v. Bishop 561n47; 563n48
Jackson; People v. 232; 259
Jacobsen; United States v. 636; 639
Jahnke v. State 1030
Janes; State v. 1030
Janis; United States v. 644
J.B., STATE IN INTEREST OF *985*
J.D. v. Commonwealth 651
Jeglin v. San Jacinto Unified Sch. Dist . . . .
474
Jennings; People v. 209
Jennings v. State 1018
Jimmy Swaggart Ministries v. Board of Equal-
ization 532
J.L.M., In re 1047
Joe Z. v. Superior Court 984
JOHNSON, MATTER OF *921*
Johnson v. Glick 573
Johnson v. State 222; 229
Jonathan G., In re 165
Jones v. Haraway 104
Jones; State v. 649
Jones v. Wellham 669
Jones v. Witinski 571
Jorge D., In re 651
Jose P., In re 1068
J.S. v. Bethlehem Area School Dist. . . 477;
479; 480
J.S., IN RE 991; *1050*
J.S.S., In re 1069

K

K, In re 1046

K. S., In re 151n26
Kadrmas v. Dickinson Public Schools . . 548
Karnstein v. Pewaukee Sch. Bd. 548
Kathleen R. v. Livermore, City of 517
K.C.B., In re 617
Keith H., In re 1048
Kelley v. Kaiser 880n34
Kemmler, In re 554
Kemp; Commonwealth v. 222
KENNEDY v. KENNEDY *63*
Kenny A. v. Perdue 165
KENT v. UNITED STATES 800; 813;
828; 863; 866; 878n28
Keyishian v. Board of Regents . . . 430; 489;
493
Killion v. Franklin Regional Sch. Dist. . . . .
479
Kincaid v. Gibson 463
Kinman v. Omaha Pub. Sch. Dist. 669
Kinzy; State v. 943
Kirby; State v. 211; 212
Kirkland v. Greene Co. Bd. of Educ. . . 576
Kleindienst v. Mandel 489
K.M. v. State 1011
K.M.S. v. State 1019
Knox Cty. Educ. Ass'n v. Knox Cty. Bd. of Educ.
586
Kolender v. Lawson 911
Kristine H. v. Lisa R. 104
Kuhlmeier v. Hazelwood 465
KUHNS v. BRUGGER 418; *432*
Kurilla v. Callahan 572
Kyees v. County Department of Public Welfare
. . . . 165

L

L.A., In the Matter of 650
Lacks v. Ferguson School Dist. 466
Lacy v. Laird 354
LAMB v. BROWN 855; *882*
Lamb's Chapel v. Center Moriches Union Free
School Dist. 519
Lamont v. Postmaster General 489
LANDEROS v. FLOOD 309; *318*
LANES v. STATE 928; *975*
Lassiter v. Department of Social Services . .
148; 159; 160
Lassonde v. Pleasanton Unified School District
. . . . 529
Lawley; State v. 991
Lawrence; Commonwealth v. 223
Lawrence v. Texas 176
Laylah K., In re 1072
Lee v. Weisman 525, n31
Leeb v. DeLong 465
Leebaert v. Harrington 524
Lehr v. Robertson 94; 116; 121; 167

[References are to page numbers. Principal cases appear in capital letters.]

Lemon v. Kurtzman 519
Levette M., In re 1113
Lewis v. State 895
License of (see name of party)
Lillard v. Shelby County Board of Education
. 572
Linder v. New York, City of 741
Litdell, In re 1073
Litman v. George Mason 698
Littlefield v. Forney Indep. Sch. Dist. . . 476
L.J.S., In the Matter of 1112
L.L. v. COLORADO 139
L.L.W., In re 1073
L.M. v. Evesham Township Bd. of Educ. . . .
761
L.M. v. State 1073
Locke v. Davey 521
Loebach v. State 249
Loebach; State v. 248
Lofton v. Secretary of the Dept. of Children and
Family Services 176
Loren F. v. Atlanta Indep. Sch. Sys. . . 761
Lorillard Tobacco Co. v. Reilly 384
Louisiana ex rel. Francis v. Resweber . . . .
553
Loving v. Virginia 174
Luster; State v. 222
L.Z., In re 1050

M

M.A.B. v. R.B. 70
Maher v. Roe 402; 408
Mainstream Loudoun v. Bd. of Trustees of
Loudoun 517
Manfredi v. Mount Vernon Board of Education
. . . . 697
MARICOPA COUNTY, APPEAL IN . . 1081
Marriage of (see name of party)
Martarella v. Kelley 1086
Martin v. Struthers 489
Mary L., In re v. New York Dept. Soc. Serv.
. 329
MARYLAND v. CRAIG 274; 281
Mathews v. Eldridge . . 148; 151; 327; 545;
557
Matter of (see name of party)
MATTHEW S., IN RE 131
McCutchen; Commonwealth v. . . 955; 956;
959
MCKEIVER v. PENNSYLVANIA 835;
844; 852; 863; 928n41; 946n43;
985; 986; 1009; 1020; 1126
McMichael v. State 236n57
Meador v. State 1032
MEINERT; STATE v. 210; 214
Mellegrini; Commonwealth v. 222
Memoirs v. Massachusetts 376

Mennone v. Gordon 741
Meritor Sav. Bank, FSB v. Vinson . . . 656;
664n83; 689; 707; 728
Metzger v. Osbeck 570
MEYER v. NEBRASKA . . 29; 33; 35; 40; 54;
94; 108; 118; 360; 368; 377; 379;
427; 433; 487; 493; 496; 556
M.G. v. State 1080
M.G.S., In re 1011
Miami Univ.; U.S. v. 514
Michael H. v. Gerald D. 116; 121
Michael, In re 1018; 1069
Michael M.; State v. 943
Michael M. v. Superior Court 856
Michael V., In re 1052
Middlesex County Sewerage Authority v. Na-
tional Sea Clammers Association . . . 741
Miller v. California 385; 387; 446; 517
Mills v. Board of Education of District of Co-
lumbia 743; 751
Minersville School District v. Gobitis . . 425
Miranda v. Arizona . . . 650; 821; 953; 1045
Missouri Dept. of Elementary and Secondary
Educ. v. Springfield R-12 Sch. Dist. . . . .
761
Mitchell v. Commonwealth 264n66
Mitchell v. Helms 520
Mitchell v. Mitchell 192
M.J.W. v. STATE 1079; 1135
M.L.B. v. S.L.J. 160
MOHI; STATE v. 873; 900
Monteiro v. Tempe Union High Sch. Dist. . .
515
MONTGOMERY v. INDEPENDENT SCHOOL
DISTRICT NO. 709 . . . . 699; 718
Moore v. East Cleveland 163
Morlock v. West Cent. Educ. Dist. 712
Morrison v. State 348n85
Morrissey v. Brewer 157
Mosley v. Beaumont Independent School Dist.
. . . . 697
Mozert v. Hawkins County Bd. of Educ. . . .
522
Mulder; State v. 241
Mullane v. Central Hanover Trust Co. . . . .
537
Muniz v. Hoffman 560n45
Murphy v. Fort Worth Indep. Sch. Dist. . . .
546
Murrell v. School District No. 1 697

N

NAACP v. Claiborne Hardware Co. . . . . . .
731n101
Nabozny v. Podlesny 705
Nancy S. v. Michele G. 104

[References are to page numbers. Principal cases appear in capital letters.]

NELSON v. HEYNE . . . 1081; 1085; 1088; 1137; 1142
NEW JERSEY v. T.L.O. . . . 439; 441; 586; 591; 610; 615; 617; 644; 646
New State Ice Co. v. Liebmann 157
New York v. Ferber 387; 388
Newdow v. United States Congress . . . 425
Newkirk v. Commonwealth 272
Newmark v. Williams 354
N.G.B.; State v. 615
Nichols v. DeStefano 546
Nims v. Harrison 481; 482
NO. 179, IN RE APPEAL OF 1116
Nuessle v. Nuessle 177
Nunez v. San Diego, City of 911

O

OBERTI v. BOARD OF EDUCATION 765; 785
O'Brien; United States v. 475
OHIO v. AKRON CENTER FOR REPRODUC-TIVE HEALTH 392; 404
Ohio v. Roberts 290; 299
Olesen v. Bd. of Educ. 475
Olivas; People v. 1103
Olmstead v. United States 610
Oncale v. Sundowner Offshore Services, Inc. 656; 678
Overton; People v. 595n60
OVERTON; STATE v. 647; 665
Owens v. Colorado Congress of Parents, Teachers and Students 521

P

Pacific Gas & Elec. Co. v. Public Util. Comm'n 732
Palmore v. Sidoti 175
Pangle v. Bend-Lapine School Dist. . . . 466
Papish v. Board of Curators 465
Parentage of MJ, In re 104
PARHAM v. J. R. . . 116; 117n17; 355; 364
Pater v. Pater 71
Patricia A. v. New York, City of 856
Patterson v. PHP Health Care Corp. . . . 715
Paul v. Davis 536; 548
Payne v. North Carolina Dept. of Human Resources 436
P.E.K., In re 1080
Pellegrini; Commonwealth v. 222
Pendergast v. United States 871
Pennhurst State School and Hospital v. Halderman 673; 680
Pennsylvania Ass'n for Retarded Children v. Commonwealth 743; 751
Penry v. Lynaugh 898

People v. (see name of defendant)
People ex (see name of defendant)
People ex rel. (see name of defendant)
Perry Education Assn. v. Perry Local Educators' Assn. 451; 526
Pervear v. Commonwealth 554
Petition of (see name of party)
Pfeiffer v. Marion Ctr. Area School Dist. . . . 742
Phillip Leon M. v. Board of Education 685
PHILLIPS; PEOPLE v. 250; 255
PIERCE v. SOCIETY OF SISTERS . . . 33; 40; 41; 54; 108; 114; 115n16; 360; 377; 389; 427
Pinder v. Johnson 720
Place; United States v. . . 635n75; 636; 639
Planned Parenthood v. Casey . . . 223; 226
Planned Parenthood v. Danforth 388
Planned Parenthood Assn. of Kansas City, Mo., Inc. v. Ashcroft 394; 403
Planned Parenthood Assn. of the Atlanta Area, Inc. v. Harris 404
Planned Parenthood League of Massachusetts v. Bellotti 403; 404
Planned Parenthood of Central Mo. v. Danforth 117n17; 370; 394; 401
Playboy Entertainment Group; United States v. 474; 732
Plyler v. Doe 37; 501; 548
Pohl v. State 33
Poling v. Murphy 463
Porter v. Ascension Parish Sch. Bd. . . . 478
Powell v. Texas 553
P.R. v. Ga., State of 1079
Price v. Charlotte, City of 715
Price v. Young 548
Price-Waterhouse v. Hopkins 708
PRINCE v. MASSACHUSETTS . . . 37; 53; 58n4; 59; 108; 159; 163; 340; 360; 371; 377, n2; 378; 431; 483; 911
Pyle v. South Hadley School Committee . . . 472

Q

Q.D.; State v. 1019
Quilloin v. Walcott 94; 121; 166
Qutb v. Strauss 911

R

R., In re 1047
Radcliff v. Anderson 856
Rainey v. Lange 123
Ratner v. Loudoun Cty. Pub. Sch. 591
R.A.V. v. St. Paul, City of 729
Ray v. Antioch Unified Sch. Dist. 715

[References are to page numbers. Principal cases appear in capital letters.]

R.C. v. State 615
Regents of the Univ. of Mich. v. Ewing . . .
547
Reid; State v. 1026
Reid v. Texas 260
Reno v. ACLU 385; 516; 518; 732
Reno; United States v. 516
Reyes v. Superior Court 222
Rhodes; State v. 1105
Rice; State v. 1106
Richenberg v. Perry 704
Richmond Newspapers, Inc. v. Virginia . . .
996
Rivera; People v. 953
R.L.R v. STATE 992; 1047
Roane; Commonwealth v. 955; 958
Robert F. Urbasek, In re 860
Robert M., In the Matter of 1018
Roberts v. Roberts 105
Roberts v. United States 651
Robinson v. California 553; 852; 910
Robinson; Commonwealth v. 259
Robinson; United States v. 943
Roe v. Conn 145
Roe v. Roe 70
Roe v. Wade . . 94; 223; 226; 225; 388; 389;
390; 402; 405
Romanik v. Toro Co. 177
Romer v. Evans 705
Roncker v. Walter 773; 790
ROPER v. SIMMONS 898; 925; 953
Rosenberger v. Rector and Visitors of Univ. of
Va. 472; 525; 736
Ross; United States v. 595
Rossignol v. Voorhaar 514
Roth v. United States 376; 383
R.R., In re 1117
R.S., State ex rel. v. Trent 1069
Ruiz v. Hull 514
Rutherford v. Cypress-Fairbanks Ind. Sch.
Dist. 477

S

Sacramento City Unified School District v. Ra-
chel H. 791
Sampson, In re 345
Samuels v. Independent Sch. Dist. 279 . . . .
650
San Antonio Independent School Dist. v. Rodri-
guez 37; 540; 757
Sanders v. State 248
SANTA FE INDEPENDENT SCHOOL
DISTRICT v. DOE 519; 525; 542
Santana v. Collazo 1088; 1118
Santmier v. Santmier 70
SANTOSKY v. KRAMER . . . 94; 141; 146;
147; 397; 406

SAXE v. STATE COLLEGE AREA SCHOOL
DISTRICT 725; 746
Saylor v. Board of Education 571
Schaffer v. Weast 793
SCHALL v. MARTIN 953; 965; 1020
SCHLEIFER v. CHARLOTTESVILLE . . . .
911; 954
Schneider v. Board of Sch. Trustees . . 546
Schriver; State v. 911
Schuloff v. Fields 514
Schultz v. Schultz 68
Scott v. School Board of Alachua County . .
477
SEAL v. MORGAN 576; 594
Seamons v. Snow 669
Sees v. Baber 88
Selman v. Cobb County Sch. Dist. 522
SHANE T., IN THE MATTER OF . . . 218
Shannon A., In re 1080
Sherpell v. Humnoke Sch. Dist. . . 546; 547
Shoemaker v. State 477
Silesky v. Kelman 176
Simmons-Harris v. Zelman 520
Sims v. Board of Education 1082n87
Sinclair v. State 1009
SINICA; STATE v. 207; 211
S.J.C., State ex rel. v. Fox 1071
Skinner v. Oklahoma 94
Skinner, In the Matter of 1018
S.L.M., IN THE MATTER OF 1163
Smith v. Daily Mail Publishing Co. . . . 999;
1002
Smith v. Metropolitan School Dist. Perry Twp.
. . . . 663, n81
Smith v. O.F.F.E.R. 161; 165
Smith, In re 1052
SNYDER, IN RE 200
South Dakota v. Dole 680
S.P.; State v. 1019
SPALDING, IN THE MATTER OF . . 1089
S.S. v. STATE 902; 945
Stanford v. Kentucky 898
Stanley v. Georgia 489; 497
Stanley v. Illinois 94; 141; 154; 166
Stapelkemper, Matter of 1011
Starkes; Commonwealth v. 955; 956
State v. (see name of defendant)
State ex (see name of state)
State ex rel. (see name of state)
State of (see name of state)
Stephenson v. Davenport Community Sch.
Dist. 474; 546
STEVENSON v. MARTIN COUNTY BOARD
OF EDUCATION 716; 735
STEWARD v. STATE 260; 265
Strasburg; State v. 1009
Student Members of SAME v. Rumsfeld . . .
514

[References are to page numbers. Principal cases appear in capital letters.]

Student Press Law Center v. Alexander . . . 514

Surrogate Parenting Assocs. v. Commonwealth 92n14

SWALBERG v. HANNEGAN 410; *424*

Swisher v. Brady 850

Sypniewski v. Warren Hills Board of Educ. 477; 740

T

Talley v. Stephens 1082n87

Tannenbaum; People v. 376n1

TANNER; STATE v. 231; *236*

Tarasoff v. Regents of Univ. of Cal. . . . 309

Tasseing, In re 1117

Taylor v. Hayes 560n45

Taylor v. Taylor 77

Terminiello v. Chicago 733

Terry v. Ohio 595; 616

Terry, Ex parte 560n45

Texas v. Johnson 474; 475; 731; 733

T.G. v. Board of Educ. 762

Theodore v. Delaware Valley Sch. Dist. . . . 632

Thomas v. Board of Education, Granville Central School Dist. 440

Thomas v. Roberts 650

THOMPSON v. CARTHAGE SCHOOL DISTRICT 615; 642; *660*

Thompson v. Keohane 953

Thompson v. Oklahoma 898

Thornburgh v. American College of Obstetricians and Gynecologists 401

Thorpe; People v. 884; 885

Timothy W. v. Rochester School District . . . 762

Timperio; State v. 265n67

TINKER v. DES MOINES INDEPENDENT COMMUNITY SCHOOL DISTRICT 117n17; 370; 389; 426; 438; *440*; 447; 452n8; 488; 493; 533; 535; 541; 545n38; 560; 595; 676; 734; 911

Townsend v. State 265n67

T.P.S. v. State 984

Trop v. Dulles 553

TROXEL v. GRANVILLE . . . 105; *108*; 141

Trust Estate of (see name of party)

Tucker; State v. 235

Turner v. Gaither 415

Two Minor Children, Matter of 1011

TYVONNE, IN RE 1021; *1070*

U

United States v. (see name of defendant)

U.S. v. (see name of defendant)

U.S. Gypsum Co.; United States v. . . . 590

UWM Post, Inc. v. Board of Regents of University of Wisconsin System 686

V

VALMONTE v. BANE 321; *330*

Vance v. Spencer County Public School Dist. 669; 698

Vernonia School District 47J v. Acton 617; 641; 645; 676; 686; 911

Video Software Dealers Assoc. v. Maleng . . 384

V.P., In re 651

W

Wagner-Garay v. Fort Wayne Cmty. Sch. . . . 546

Walker, In re 1046; 1117

WALKEY; PEOPLE v. 244; *249*

Wallace v. Jaffree 524

Wallace, People ex rel. v. Labrenz 333

Walz v. Egg Harbor Township Bd. of Educ. 531

Ward v. Rock Against Racism 518

Ware v. Estes 1082n87

Warren v. National Ass'n of Secondary School Principals 548

Watkins v. Millennium School 615

Watts v. United States 477

Wayne T, In re 1071

Wayte v. United States 883

Webb v. McCullough 569

Webster v. Reproductive Health Services . . 223; 396; 400; 409

Weems v. United States 553

Weimerslage v. Maine Township High School 546

Welch; Commonwealth v. 222

West v. Derby Unified School District No. 260 . . . . 476; 735

West Virginia State Bd. of Educ. v. Barnette . . . 40; 377; 425; 427; 462; 472; 491; 493; 526; 535; 594; 617

Westbrooks, In re 1072

Westfield High Sch. L.I.F.E. Club v. Westfield, City of 531

Whalen v. Roe 390; 403

Wheat v. State 264

Wheaton v. East 413

WHITE v. ILLINOIS 295; 299; *303*

White v. Rochford 318

WHITNER v. STATE 218; *222*

Wilkerson; State v. 243

Wilkerson v. Utah 554

William A., In re 1019

William, In re 1050

William M., In re 991

[References are to page numbers. Principal cases appear in capital letters.]

WILLIAMS; COMMONWEALTH v. . . 953; *1008*
Williams v. Lavender 418
Williams v. State 1032
Williams, In re 1007
Williamson v. A.G. Edwards & Sons, Inc. . . 706
Wilson v. Hinsdale Elementary Sch. Dist. 181 481
Wilson; State v. 214
Wilson, State ex rel. v. Bambrick . . . 1046
WINSHIP, IN RE 59; 406; *857*; 998; 1009; 1039
Wisconsin v. Mitchell 731n101
WISCONSIN v. YODER . . *46*; 71; 360; 523; 524; 532
Wise v. Pea Ridge School District 571
Witaker; State v. 953
W.M. v. State 1117
Wofford v. Evans 650
Wood v. Strickland 565n49
Wood, In re 884

Wooten v. Pleasant Hope R-VI School District. 547

X

Y

Yap v. Oceanside Union Free Sch. Dist. . . . 699
YARBOROUGH v. ALVORADO 953; *1000*
Yates v. Keane 92n14
Young; People v. 990
Young v. Young 72
Younts v. St. Francis Hosp. & School of Nursing, Inc. 354

Z

Zablocki v. Redhail 94
Zamora v. Pomeroy 595n60
Zelman v. Simmons-Harris 521
Zykan v. Warsaw Community School Corp. 508

INDEX

[References are to pages.]

A

ABORTION
Privacy rights of minors . . . 400

ABUSE OF CHILDREN (See CHILD ABUSE)

ADOLESCENCE
Generally . . . 3
Decision making, evaluation of . . . 5

ADOPTION
Generally . . . 169
Reproductive technology and . . . 81

B

BATTERED CHILD SYNDROME (BCS)
Adjudicating . . . 236
Affirmative defense, as . . . 1081

BATTERING PARENT SYNDROME (BPS)
Child abuse . . . 249

BCS (See BATTERED CHILD SYNDROME (BCS))

BIRTH CONTROL
Privacy rights of minors . . . 400

BPS (See BATTERING PARENT SYNDROME (BPS))

BULLYING
Generally . . . 735

C

CHILD ABUSE
Generally . . . 204
"Abuse" defined . . . 218
Adjudicating
    Generally . . . 235
    Battered child syndrome (BCS) . . 236
    Battering parent syndrome (BPS) 249
    Child sexual abuse accommodation syndrome (CSAAS) . . . 265
    Child witness in sexual abuse cases . . . 280
    Munchausen syndrome by proxy (MSP) . . . 255
Central registries . . . 329
"Child" defined . . . 222
Constitutional issues . . . 211
Defining child abuse . . . 205
Reporting statutes . . . 309

CHILD ABUSE—Cont.
Scope issues . . . 218
Statutory provisions . . . 206

CHILD SEXUAL ABUSE ACCOMMODATION SYNDROME (CSAAS)
Adjudicating . . . 265

CONFRONTATION CLAUSE
Child sexual abuse cases . . . 280

CONSTITUTIONAL ISSUES
Child abuse . . . 211
Status offense procedures . . . 1089
Students (See SCHOOLS)

CRIMES AGAINST CHILDREN
Child abuse (See CHILD ABUSE)
Obscenity and pornography . . . 385

CSAAS (See CHILD SEXUAL ABUSE ACCOMMODATION SYNDROME (CSAAS))

CUSTODY
Generally . . . 61
Best interest of child, factors in
    Generally . . . 62
    Child care issues . . . 73
    Child's preference . . . 71
    Domestic violence . . . 73
    Physical and mental disability . . . 72
    Primary caretaker . . . 63
    Religion . . . 72
    Sexual conduct and sexual orientation of parent . . . 71
Joint custody . . . 78
Reproductive technology and . . . 81

D

DELINQUENCY (See JUVENILE JUSTICE SYSTEM)

DISABLED PARENTS
Best interest of child analysis, as factor in . . . 72

DISABLED STUDENTS (See SCHOOLS)

DISCRIMINATION
Generally . . . 670

DOMESTIC VIOLENCE
Best interest of child analysis, as factor in . . . 73

[References are to pages.]

E

EDUCATION
Compulsory . . . 46
Schools (See SCHOOLS)

EMANCIPATION OF MINOR
Generally . . . 196

F

FAMILY
Intrafamily tort actions . . . 180
Visitation . . . 107

FOSTER CARE
Generally . . . 162

G

GANG ACTIVITY
Duress and . . . 1088

H

HEALTH OF CHILD
Mental health . . . 364
Physical health . . . 339
Protection of . . . 339
Religious practice . . . 339

HEARSAY
Child sexual abuse cases . . . 280

I

INFANCY DEFENSE
Affirmative defenses . . . 1070

INSANITY DEFENSE
Affirmative defenses . . . 1064

INTERNET
First Amendment rights of students . . 496

J

JOINT CUSTODY
Generally . . . 78

JURISDICTION
Generally . . . 882
Delinquency
    Generally . . . 889
    Concurrent jurisdiction . . . 899
    Exclusive jurisdiction . . . 889
    Waiver . . . 914
Maximum age . . . 882
Minimum age . . . 884
Status offenses . . . 944

JUVENILE JUSTICE SYSTEM
Generally . . . 827
Adjudication . . . 1038
Affirmative defenses
    Delinquency adjudications (See subhead:
        Delinquency)
    Status offenses . . . 1106
Age, jurisdiction based on . . . 882
Delinquency
    Generally . . . 1038
    Affirmative defenses
        Generally . . . 1058
        Battered child defense . . . 1081
        Competency to be adjudicated . . .
            1059
        Defense of duress and gang activity
            . . . 1088
        Infancy defense . . . 1070
        Insanity defense . . . 1064
    Dispositions
        Generally . . . 1109
        Alternatives . . . 1128
        "Blended sentencing" . . . 1163
        Community service . . . 1135
        Confinement . . . 1137
        Juvenile's best interests . . . 1109
        Probation . . . 1128
        Punitive juvenile justice . . . 1148
        Rehabilitative treatment . . . 1142
        Restitution . . . 1130
    Jurisdiction (See JURISDICTION)
Dispositions
    Generally . . . 1107
    Delinquency cases (See subhead: Delin-
        quency)
    Hearing procedure . . . 1107
    Status offense cases . . . 1170
Future of juvenile justice . . . 1176
Jurisdiction (See JURISDICTION)
Pre-adjudication process
    Generally . . . 974
    Detention and bail . . . 1015
    Interrogation . . . 990
    Police investigation . . . 974
    Search and seizure . . . 974
Procedure
    Generally . . . 1038
    Closed proceedings . . . 1046
    Jury determinations . . . 1039
    Status offenses . . . 1089
Punishment *vs.* therapy . . . 878
Status offenses
    Generally . . . 1089
    Abolition of . . . 968
    Affirmative defenses . . . 1106
    Dispositions . . . 1170
    Jurisdiction . . . 944

[References are to pages.]

JUVENILE JUSTICE SYSTEM—Cont.
Status offenses—Cont.
    Procedures
        Constitutional protections . . 1089
        Judicial interpretation . . . 1104
        Statutory provisions . . . 1104
Supreme Court cases . . . 828
Therapy *vs.* punishment . . . 878

JUVENILE RIGHTS
First Amendment rights of students (See SCHOOLS)
Legal status (See LEGAL STATUS, MINORITY AS)
Privacy rights . . . 400

L

LEGAL STATUS, MINORITY AS
Generally . . . 1
Adolescence
    Generally . . . 3
    Decision making, evaluation of . . . 5
Chronological age rules . . . 1
Common law . . . 1
Individualized standards for assessing maturity . . . 2
Modern statutes . . . 1
Privacy rights . . . 400
Rights of juveniles
    Generally . . . 10
    Contrasting theories . . . 10
    Mixed theories . . . 26
    Personhood theory . . . 18
    Privacy rights . . . 400
    Protectionist theory . . . 11

LIABILITY
Contract liability . . . 423
Tort liability . . . 430

M

MENTAL HEALTH
Generally . . . 364
Best interest of child analysis, as factor in . . . 72

MINORITY AS LEGAL STATUS (See LEGAL STATUS, MINORITY AS)

MSP (See MUNCHAUSEN SYNDROME BY PROXY (MSP))

MUNCHAUSEN SYNDROME BY PROXY (MSP)
Child abuse . . . 255

N

NCLBA (See NO CHILD LEFT BEHIND ACT (NCLBA))

NEGLECT
Abuse (See CHILD ABUSE)
Endangerment and . . . 124

NO CHILD LEFT BEHIND ACT (NCLBA)
Generally . . . 823

O

OBSCENITY
Generally . . . 385

P

PARENTAL AUTHORITY
Generally . . . 29
Abortion and birth control . . . 400
Adoption . . . 169
Child abuse (See CHILD ABUSE)
Compulsory education . . . 46
Custody (See CUSTODY)
Emancipation of minor . . . 196
Family visitation . . . 107
Foster care . . . 162
Health of child, protection of . . . 339
Intrafamily tort actions . . . 180
Mental health of minor . . . 364
Neglect and endangerment . . . 124
Religious practice and health of child 339
Reproductive technology and . . . 81
Termination of parental rights . . . 147

PARENTAL RIGHTS
Termination of . . . 81; 147

PORNOGRAPHY
Generally . . . 385

PRIVACY RIGHTS OF MINORS
Abortion and birth control . . . 400

R

RELIGION
Best interest of child analysis, as factor in . . . 72
Physical health of child and religious practice . . . 339
Schools, in (See SCHOOLS)

REPRODUCTIVE TECHNOLOGY
Generally . . . 81

[References are to pages.]

S

SCHOOLS
Generally . . . 439
Disabled student
    Generally . . . 765
    Discipline . . . 817
    "Free appropriate public education" . . 767
    Inclusion . . . 786
Discipline and the Constitution
    Generally . . . 550
    Corporal punishment
        Eighth Amendment and procedural due process . . . 567
        Substantive due process . . . 585
    Suspension . . . 550
    "Zero tolerance" policies . . . 594
Discrimination, harassment and bullying
    Generally . . . 670
    Bullying . . . 735
    Sexual harassment (See subhead: Sexual harassment in school)
First Amendment rights of students
    Generally . . . 439
    Disrespect and threats . . . 493
    Dress codes . . . 480
    Information and ideas, right to receive . . . 501
    Internet speech . . . 496
    Political speech . . . 491
    School uniforms . . . 490
    Societal consequences . . . 498
    Speech and expression . . . 440
    Student publications . . . 462
Fourth Amendment (See subhead: School searches and the Fourth Amendment)
No Child Left Behind Act (NCLBA) . . 823
Religion in school
    Generally . . . 535
    Establishment clause
        Generally . . . 535
        Curriculum controversy . . . 538
        Evolution vs. creation . . . 538
        Financial aid to religious institutions . . . 535
        Prayer and religious expression . . . 541
        Sex education . . . 539
    Free exercise clause . . . 548
School searches and the Fourth Amendment
    Generally . . . 610
    Dog sniffs . . . 652
    Exclusionary rule . . . 660
    Individualized suspicion . . . 610

SCHOOLS—Cont.
School searches and the Fourth Amendment—Cont.
    Locker searches . . . 665
    Urinalysis drug testing . . . 636
Sexual harassment in school
    Generally . . . 673
    Free expression . . . 746
    Same sex harassment . . . 718
    Student harassing student . . . 689
    Teacher harassing student . . . 673
Speech
    Expression and . . . 440
    Internet speech . . . 496
    Political speech . . . 491

SEXUAL ABUSE
Child sexual abuse accommodation syndrome (CSAAS) . . . 265
Hearsay doctrine in child sexual abuse cases . . . 280

SEXUAL CONDUCT OF PARENT
Best interest of child analysis, as factor in . . . 71

SEXUAL HARASSMENT
School, in (See SCHOOLS)

SUPREME COURT
Juvenile justice system . . . 828

T

TERMINATION OF PARENTAL RIGHTS
Generally . . . 147
Reproductive technology and . . . 81

THERAPY
Punishment vs. . . . 878

TORT ACTIONS
Intrafamily tort actions . . . 180
Liability . . . 430

U

UNIFORM MARRIAGE AND DIVORCE ACT
Visitation . . . 107

V

VISITATION RIGHTS
Generally . . . 107
Reproductive technology and . . . 81